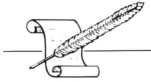

HISTORIC
DOCUMENTS
OF
1977

Cumulative Index 1973-77

Congressional Quarterly, Inc.

Historic Documents of 1977

Major Contributor: W. Allan Wilbur

Other Contributors: Martha V. Gottron, James R. Ingram,
Barbara L. Risk, Margaret C. Thompson, Laura B. Weiss
Cumulative Index: Diane Huffman
Production Manager: I. D. Fuller
Assistant Production Manager: Maceo Mayo

Copyright 1978 by Congressional Quarterly Inc.
1414 22nd Street, N.W., Washington, D.C. 20037

Library of Congress Cataloging in Publication Data

Historic documents. 1972—
Washington. Congressional Quarterly Inc.

1. United States—Politics and government—1945—   —Yearbooks.
2. World politics—1945—   —Yearbooks.   I. Congressional Quarterly Inc.

E839.5.H57   917.3′03′9205   72-97888
ISBN 0-87187-126-2

FOREWORD

Publication of *Historic Documents of 1977* carries through a sixth year the project launched by Congressional Quarterly with *Historic Documents 1972*. The purpose of this continuing series of volumes is to give students, scholars, librarians, journalists and citizens convenient access to documents of basic importance in the broad range of public affairs.

To place the documents in perspective, each entry is preceded by a brief introduction containing background materials, in some cases a short summary of the document itself and, where necessary, relevant subsequent developments. We believe these introductions will prove increasingly useful in future years when the events and questions now covered are less fresh in one's memory and the documents may be hard to find or unobtainable.

The year 1977 saw a spectacular journey to Jerusalem by Egyptian President Anwar el-Sadat. Sadat's dramatic peace initiative did not resolve the deep-rooted disagreements between Israel and the Arab states, but it did set in motion forces that brightened somewhat the outlook for an overall settlement in the Middle East.

Many of the top news stories of the year reported on the first months in office of the new President, Jimmy Carter. Hoping to redeem the promises of his campaign, Carter sent Congress a large package of far-reaching proposals. An assertive legislative branch, however, was not easily persuaded. Even the President's plan for energy conservation, which he made the centerpiece of all his domestic programs, was not enacted in his first year in office.

Carter faced a difficult challenge in the wake of disclosures of the freewheeling banking practices of Bert Lance before Lance had become director of the Office of Management and Budget. The President stood loyally by his friend as Lance, during Senate hearings, denied all allegations of wrongdoing. The controversy subsided when Lance resigned. As the year ended, Carter left Washington on the first leg of a trip that would take him to three continents and seven countries in nine days.

These developments added substantially to the usual outpouring of presidential statements, court decisions, commission reports, special studies and speeches of national or international importance. We have selected for inclusion in this book as many as possible of the documents that in our judgment will be of more than transitory interest. Where space limitations prevented reproduction of the full texts, the excerpts used were chosen to set forth the essentials and, at the same time, preserve the flavor of the materials.

Patricia Ann O'Connor
Editor

Washington, D.C.
January 1978

How to Use This Book

The documents are arranged in chronological order. If you know the approximate date of the report, speech, statement, court decision or other document you are looking for, glance through the titles for that month in the Table of Contents below.

If the Table of Contents does not lead you directly to the document you want, make a double check by turning to the subject Index at the end of the book. There you may find references not only to the particular document you seek but also to other entries on the same or a related subject. The Index in this volume is a **five-year cumulative index** of Historic Documents covering the years 1973-77.

The introduction to each document is printed in italic type. The document itself, printed in roman type, follows the spelling, capitalization and punctuation of the original or official copy. Where the full text is not given, omissions of material are indicated by the customary series of dots.

TABLE OF CONTENTS

February

March

April

May

June

October

November

December

HISTORIC
DOCUMENTS
OF
1977

January

STATE DEPARTMENT REPORTS ON HUMAN RIGHTS

January 1, 1977

The House International Relations Committee Jan. 1 released State Department reports on human rights violations in six countries receiving U.S. military aid. The reports recommended that military assistance to Argentina, Haiti, Indonesia, Iran, Peru and the Philippines be continued for strategic and diplomatic reasons, despite violations of human rights by the governments of those six countries.

The State Department, reluctant to produce reports on human rights violations because the revelations could prove embarrassing to allies and injure negotiations with adversaries, initially classified the reports secret. The documents were made available to the public at the insistence of the House International Relations Committee. The reports recounted alleged violations of human rights through the use of torture, arbitrary arrest, prolonged detention without charges or trial and other infringements of human life, liberty and security. The reports frequently quoted from Amnesty International, a private organization that publicized violations of the human rights of political prisoners.

Reasons offered by the State Department for continuing aid included: U.S. interest in maintaining contact with the leadership in Argentina and security interests in that country's 1,000-mile coastline along the South Atlantic; the strategic importance of friendly relations with Indonesia, the largest and most populous of the 10 Southeast Asian countries; the maintenance of constructive relations with the government of Peru through the aid program; U.S. interest in the continuing stability of the government of Iran and that nation's importance as an oil supplier to the

United States and Japan; the U.S. desire to keep important military bases in the Philippines which, the State Department report said, would be jeopardized by the withdrawal of U.S. military aid; and the humanitarian interest served by the improved air-sea rescue capability U.S. aid to Haiti provided for U.S. mariners.

Background

Congress intended the request for reports on the six countries as an initial test of the executive branch's compliance with the 1976 Foreign Military Assistance Act (HR 13680—PL 94-329). That law stated that no security aid should be granted to governments that engaged in a "consistent pattern of gross violations" of human rights by torture, cruel punishment and political repression. The law provided that under "extraordinary circumstances," however, aid could be continued. Under the terms of the law, the State Department was required, upon the request of a member of Congress, to evaluate and report on the condition of human rights in nations designated each year to receive military aid. Based on the State Department reports, the Congress could attempt to cut off or reduce funds by passing a joint resolution. (A joint resolution requires the approval of both houses and the signature of the President, just as a bill does, and has the force of law if approved.)

President Gerald R. Ford May 7, 1976, had vetoed an earlier version of the foreign military aid and arms sales bill because some of its provisions, Ford said, represented "congressional encroachment" on the President's authority to conduct foreign policy. One of those provisions would have permitted Congress by concurrent resolution to curtail military aid or arms sales to countries violating human rights. (A concurrent resolution must be passed by both houses but does not require the signature of the President and does not have the force of law.) In a major concession to the White House, the new version of the bill passed by Congress and signed by Ford June 30, 1976, provided that Congress—by joint resolution rather than a concurrent resolution—could limit military aid and arms sales to nations failing to observe human rights standards.

The Ford administration opposed aid cuts aimed at promoting human rights, preferring instead quiet diplomatic talks, which it viewed as a way to avoid antagonizing foreign governments or giving the impression of U.S. interference in the internal affairs of other countries. During the 1976 presidential election campaign Jimmy Carter criticized the Ford administration for not paying enough attention to human rights abroad and pledged his administration would do more to "support the humanitarian aspirations of the world's peoples...." (Carter on human rights, p. 189)

Following are excerpts from the State Department reports on human rights violations in Argentina, Haiti, Indonesia, Iran, Peru and the Philippines, released Jan. 1, 1977, by the House International Relations Committee:

ARGENTINA

Human Rights Information

Argentina is a federal republic headed by President Jorge Rafael Videla, who came to power on March 24, 1976, after a coup overthrew the administration of President Isabel de Peron.

The March 1976 coup was precipitated by serious political and economic instability which fed upon each other. In March the Consumer Price Index was increasing at a 566-percent annual rate (on an accelerating curve). There was deepening recession and an external payments crisis threatened default on foreign debts. Violence was rampant. In the 3 years of the Peronist administration (1973-76), over 2,000 Argentines died as a result of left- and right-wing terrorism. Since March political violence has claimed at least 1,000 lives.

The current cycle of violence in Argentina began in the late sixties with the formation of the People's Revolutionary Army (ERP) and the Montoneros, both terrorist organizations dedicated to violent revolution and working closely with guerrilla groups in Uruguay, Chile, and Bolivia. When guerrilla organizations were defeated or ousted in these three countries, many of their members fled to Argentina, beginning in the early 1970's with the defeat of the Tupamaros in Uruguay. Significant rightist counterterror commenced under the Peron regime and with the sponsorship of his confidant Lopez Rega....

Observance of Internationally Recognized Human Rights

Integrity of the Person

The rights of life, liberty, and security of person are violated regularly by terrorists at both ends of the political spectrum. Both the current and predecessor administrations have reportedly acquiesced in violations attributable to persons associated with the government; the legal security forces have reportedly killed detainees suspected of terrorism. Right-wing terrorism or counterterrorism has been carried out by vigilante squads operating with apparent impunity. Active duty and retired military and police personnel are reportedly members of such squads. Their victims have included a wide variety of individuals, suspected terrorists, other leftists, priests and foreign political exiles. There are no reliable statistics on the number of victims of these groups, but a reasonable estimate would be in the hundreds. The most notorious episode took place on August 30 when 30 leftist prisoners were allegedly executed in Pilar, in part as retaliation for the murder of a retired general, and in part apparently as a warning to leftist extremists. (The Amnesty International Report 1975-76 attributes 2,000 political assassinations since 1973 to the AAA, Argentine-Anti-Communist Alliance, a vigilante organization initially associated with the Peron government.) It should be noted that reported instances of rightist

5

violence have declined in recent weeks, but it is too early to draw any conclusions at this time.

Leftist terrorism continues and has been responsible for hundreds of political assassinations and kidnapings. Many policemen, military personnel, and businessmen have been murdered at random. Argentine executives of American business firms have been frequent victims in 1976. American and foreign executives in considerable numbers have left Argentina to escape kidnaping and/or murder. In 1975 the American Consular Agent in Cordoba, John Patrick Egan, was murdered by the Montoneros, while a USIA officer, Alfred Laun, was kidnaped and narrowly escaped death in the same city.

While torture, cruel, inhuman and degrading treatment or punishment have not been a general practice in Argentina, such methods are reportedly used by the security forces to extract information from some prisoners, particularly suspected or proven terrorists. After initial questioning prisoners of this type apparently receive more or less normal treatment. Olga Talamante, an American released shortly after the March coup, has alleged that she was tortured....

Legal redress for governmental abuse of basic rights is normally available in Argentina but may well be denied in cases involving charges of subversion.

The security forces have detained numerous persons for investigation and questioning under the provisions of the State of Siege or other laws, e.g., arms controls laws. Some are held indefinitely, others are freed after a short time, and still others are passed on to the regular courts or to military courts as prescribed by law. An accurate estimate of persons detained under the State of Siege is impossible to calculate. At the time of the March coup, The Amnesty International Report 1975-76 estimated that over 4,000 people were under detention without trial for unlimited periods. The figure is currently lower in all probability. In October 1976 during a visit to the United States, the Argentine Foreign Minister told the press there were 1,000 prisoners as of that date. He reportedly said that 300 persons had been released a few days earlier. We have no independent information to corroborate any of the above statistics....

...Argentine courts function normally in most cases, insuring the right to a fair trial. The exception applies to individuals held under the State of Siege. In such cases the Argentine Supreme Court has ruled that the jurisdiction of the military justice system over subversion and arms control cases applies only when it is clear that the offense is actually linked to the security of the nation. Right- and left-wing intimidation of lawyers and judges has made it difficult to insure fair trials in cases of alleged subversion and/or terrorism....

Other Freedoms

Argentines are treated equally before the law regardless of race or religion. Freedom to leave the country and return is the general rule. Freedom of thought and religion are generally respected in Argentina. The

Jehovah's Witnesses, however, are encountering problems, as they have elsewhere in Latin America, because of their refusal to serve in the armed forces or salute the flag. In August 1976 the Argentine Government banned the Witnesses. This ban is being appealed in Argentine courts by the Witnesses.

Anti-Semitism has been a recurrent phenomenon in Argentina's modern history. In mid-1976 there were a series of bombings of synagogues and machinegun attacks against store fronts....

Freedom of expression and opinion in Argentina has been somewhat restricted by the banning of some rightwing and leftwing publications. The Argentine press is required to exercise self-censorship, and is specifically prohibited from mentioning terrorist and antiterrorist operations unless officially authorized by the Government. There is, nevertheless, criticism of human rights abuses in the Argentine press. Few journalists have suffered arrest and only for short periods. Foreign correspondents file stories freely....

Upon taking power in March, the military junta dissolved the parliament and banned political labor activity. Some labor unions were taken over temporarily by the Government and, on September 8, a law was passed providing for up to 10 years in prison for strike organizers.

U.S. Government Action in Human Rights Area

The subject of human rights has been raised repeatedly with representatives of the Government of Argentina during 1976 by the Department of State and our Embassy in Buenos Aires. Aware of our interest in this matter, Argentina officials have themselves broached the subject with us on a number of occasions. In fact, no other substantive subject has been discussed more often with the incumbent Argentine Government than human rights.... In these discussions the following topics have been raised repeatedly by American officers:

- —Access to and the treatment of American prisoners held on political charges;
- —Deep concern over reports of mass murders, and the indiscriminate killings of political refugees and priests;
- —The urgent need to control vigilante groups and punish terrorism of both the left and the right;
- —The safety of political refugees;
- —Anti-Semitism;
- —The need to bring to trial or release alleged subversives; and
- —The need to publish the names of prisoners.

The Government of Argentina has stated that the current situation is temporary and that normal conditions will be restored within a short time....

U.S. Security Assistance Program

The amount of U.S. security assistance to Argentina proposed for fiscal year 1977 is $48.4-million in foreign military sales credits and less than

$700,000 in grant military training. These sums were justified to Congress and approved soon after the Videla government came to power.

The United States does not extend aid to the Argentine police, except to control and interdict the flow of narcotics.

U.S. military credits are used almost exclusively for major investment items, such as ships and aircraft. They have little or no bearing on the counterterrorist capability of the armed forces.

Security assistance demonstrates our desire to cooperate militarily with a country which has 1,000 miles of coastline on the south Atlantic reaching to Cape Horn. Our assistance orients the Argentine military professionally toward the United States, exposing them to our technology and methods. In return, it offers the United States the possibility of improved communication with the Argentine military who have always influenced events in their country and are now the dominant sector. This helps promote and protect our various interests and helps insure that we will get a hearing on matters of concern to the United States....

...In order to preserve a professional relationship with the Argentine Armed Forces and demonstrate our interest in constructive overall relations with Argentina, thereby promoting the U.S. policy objectives outlined above, the Department of State is of the opinion at this time that it is in the national interest of the United States to provide continued security assistance to Argentina. The Department is monitoring the situation closely.

HAITI

Human Rights Information

Haiti, the poorest country in the Western Hemisphere, has never enjoyed a democratic tradition. Since it became independent in 1804, the political history of the country has been one of authoritarian leadership, punctuated by continual attempts by those out of power to remove the regime in power by force. Human rights, due process, and political freedoms as known in Western Europe and the United States have not been part of Haiti's political traditions.

In the 1960's, attention focused on the human rights situation in Haiti because of a number of particularly serious abuses under the late President. Due to Duvalier's authoritarian style of rule and in reaction to a series of coup attempts mounted from abroad, an atmosphere of suspicion and insecurity prevailed in Haiti. All opposition to the regime was suppressed.

Since 1971, there has been an improvement of the political atmosphere; this slow trend continues, with occasional setbacks. President Jean-Claude Duvalier has declared policies of domestic détente and national reconciliation; and political repression has eased. Over 500 prisoners, including a number of political prisoners, have been released in 6 separate amnesties. The President has publicly assured Haitian exiles they could return without reprisals, and hundreds have done so.

Nonetheless, the government in Haiti remains basically authoritarian. Opposition political activity is not permitted....

Observance of Internationally Recognized Human Rights

Integrity of the Person

...Under the Francois Duvalier regime in Haiti, there was widespread danger to life and personal security, including the risk of prolonged incarceration due to false denunciations. This situation has improved under the Presidency of Jean-Claude Duvalier. Detention for extended periods without regard to due process still occurs, but it now appears limited largely to those considered to be serious security risks or violators....

Conditions in Haitian prisons are generally poor.

The Amnesty International Report, 1975-76, states that arbitrary executions, starvation, appalling hygienic conditions, disease, and torture account for one of the highest mortality rates among prisoners in any country. However, AI and other international reports do not describe any specific accusations of cases of torture in Haiti in recent years.

Two prisoners released from the national penitentiary in 1975 and 1976 have reported that political prisoners today receive plain but basically adequate food and live in tolerable conditions in the three blocks reserved for them at the penitentiary....

...Persons considered a threat to security are still subject to arrest and detention without civil trial. The Amnesty International Report, 1975-76, states that it is difficult to assess accurately the present number of political prisoners in Haiti, a statement with which we concur....

...A fair hearing is available in most ordinary trials in Haiti. Fair hearings are less likely in the countryside, where few trials take place, or for persons detailed on security grounds and tried in the military courts....

Other Freedoms

Haitians can generally move freely within the country. They require a passport and exit visa to travel abroad. Haitians abroad for an extended period require a re-entry visa to return. Documents are refused persons considered subversive or against whom charges are pending, but these are understood to be a small minority of the total number of applicants. According to the airlines serving Haiti, hundreds of Haitians depart and enter the country every week....

...Catholicism is the state religion in Haiti, but other religious groups exist freely. Communism and anarchism are outlawed.

There are limitations on the public expression of opinions. The press exercises self-censorship, although it is gradually acquiring a greater margin for constructive criticism of the Government's administrative shortcomings....

...The exercise of the right of assembly is restricted. Political gatherings, however peaceful, are not permitted.

U.S. Government Action in Human Rights Area

Over the past 2 years, U.S. officials have pursued our concern for human rights with a wide range of Haitian Government officials, from the President on down.... We make the following points in dealing with Haitian leaders:

(a) We follow closely all developments in the field of human rights in Haiti and carefully evaluate all available information bearing on this topic. This reflects the principal U.S. policy goal of promoting increased observance of internationally recognized human rights by all countries.

(b) We have noted the pattern of evolution in the observance of human rights in Haiti, particularly over the past 4 years, and believe that liberalization is a wise policy that well serves the national interests of Haiti.

(c) In the case of Haitians deported from the United States for illegal entry, we consider it extremely important that we have full information as to their treatment upon arrival in Haiti. This permits us to establish clearly that their treatment is in accordance with international human rights standards.

(d) It is highly desirable that the Haitian Government make further clarification on the status of political prisoners and that the Government liberalize regulations on visits to and correspondence with these and other prisoners. None should be held without proper charges; and convictions and sentences—past or current—should be made public....

...The Haitian Government is well aware of the general connections we made between our assistance programs and the extent of human rights observance. A major underlying reason for the withdrawal in 1963 of our Haiti military training mission, as well as of our AID [Agency for International Development] mission, was the abuse of human rights at that time. Conversely, the Haitian Government understands that only by virtue of substantially improved performance in the field of human rights could the U.S. Government have considered resuming assistance programs, as we have done.

The present military training program, begun late in fiscal year 1975, is extremely modest in scale, has little or no public profile in Haiti, and was carefully and deliberately designed to concentrate upon sea and air rescue and the strengthening of associated logistic and communication capabilities. Nothing in the present limited military training program has any application to the internal security capability of the Government. Our security assistance has been effectively disassociated from any potential violation of human rights and, conversely, its reintroduction has been associated with the gradual improvement in the Government's performance in this field.

U.S. Interests Justifying a Security Assistance Program

The very small U.S. security assistance program for Haiti is designed specifically to assist the Haitians to build up a capability for sea and air rescue and the maintenance of navigational aids, an important humanitarian capability for any government and one which will in fact also assist in protection to U.S. mariners now totally dependent on the U.S. Coast Guard.

The Department of State is of the opinion that the current U.S. security program for Haiti should be continued. Elimination of the modest U.S. security assistance program would have no impact on Government of Haiti human rights practices. To the contrary, it would lessen our ability to influence the Haitian Government on a range of U.S. interests in Haiti, including promotion of human rights.

INDONESIA

Human Rights Information

...An important factor in contemporary Indonesian political life is the continuing impact of the unsuccessful 1965 coup attempt supported by the large Indonesian Communist Party (PKI) which at that time claimed 3.5 million members and additional millions in its front groups....

Most of those detained in connection with the 1965 coup attempt have since been released, and the Government has recently announced an accelerated program of releases for the remainder. By 1975, according to the Indonesian Government, fewer than 35,000 remained in detention, of whom about 11,000 were on Buru Island. The Indonesian Government announced in the fall of 1975 that an additional 1,300 of those detainees were being released and that 2,500 more would be released in 1976. Senior Indonesian officials who visited the United States in October 1975 and discussed the problem with Members of Congress indicated that many additional releases were planned for the future and that the Government hoped to resolve the issue entirely after the 1977 general election....

Observance of Internationally Recognized Human Rights

...[T]here continues to be some disagreement among foreign observers about the number and treatment of prisoners in Indonesia. The Amnesty International's 1974-75 annual report, for example, referred to the "desperate" position of more than "55,000 political prisoners...now in their 10th year of prison." Amnesty International has also made allegations about mistreatment of individual prisoners. In its recent statements, Amnesty International appears to have relied heavily on information provided by a former Communist who is the wife of one of the Communist detainees and was herself an official of the displaced Sukarno regime.

Integrity of the Person

The right of life, liberty, and security of persons is conditioned by the 1966 emergency powers. However, the Indonesian Government does not practice unlawful killings, and liberty and security of the person are generally observed.

11

Torture, cruel, inhuman, or degrading treatment or punishment are not used by the Government as an instrument of policy nor officially tolerated by the Government.

Access to legal remedies can be difficult because of the 1966 State of Emergency Act and the complexity of several coexisting systems of law and understaffed and overcrowded courts.

Arbitrary arrests and detentions occur in Indonesia in cases involving national security. The Indonesian Government states that continued detention of about 31,000 persons results from the fear that if the Communists are allowed to regroup, Indonesia will again be plunged into disorder and the apprehension that feelings still exist against those detained which would cause disturbances if they returned to their homes.

Procedural guarantees during the hearing process are still evolving.

Appropriate safeguards appear to be followed in criminal trials. Such procedures also appear to be followed in political trials. Under the 1966 emergency powers detainees need not be brought to trial.

Other Important Freedoms

The rigorous suppression of the Indonesian press during the latter part of the Sukarno era was reversed by the present government. Between 1966 and 1974 the Indonesian press reportedly enjoyed a greater degree of freedom than existed almost anywhere in East Asia outside of Japan. Following the outbreak of severe riots in Jakarta in January 1974, however, a number of publications were closed by the Government. Since that time, the press has been less free to criticize the Government or its senior leadership, although criticism of specific actions and policies of the Government is accepted and there has been a general easing over time. In early 1976 a Christian Science Monitor correspondent found the press once again more free than in most of East Asia. There is no formal censorship....

...Except for the outlawing of the Communist party, there are no unusual limitations on freedom of association which apply to the general public.... Freedom of assembly is limited, to the extent that large-scale demonstrations are prohibited, and students and other groups must obtain permission to hold large meetings. This latter requirement is, in most cases, flexibly enforced.

U.S. Government Action in Human Rights Area

United States officials have had frequent discussions with Indonesian Government officials about our concern over the human rights situation in Indonesia. The Indonesians recognize that the detention of large number of Indonesian citizens without trial constitutes a human rights problem and they have been willing to discuss this problem with U.S. officials. At the same time, they feel they must weigh human rights considerations against the background of the 1965 attempted pro-Communist coup, as a serious internal security problem.

United States officials have made Indonesian leaders aware of those sections of U.S. legislation relevant to human rights and of the overall concern of the Congress and the administration in this regard....

...The Embassy has made the Indonesian Government clearly aware of the provisions of security assistance legislation dealing with human rights and of the overall interest of the U.S. Government in this regard. In addition, our security assistance program is focused principally on providing Indonesia with a self-defense capability against a possible external threat. The emphasis of the program is on equipment designed to help protect the integrity of Indonesia and to prevent infiltration and subversion from outside. Priority is given to providing communications, marine surveillance, and transportation equipment, although we have also helped to reequip certain units of the strategic reserve. U.S. security programs are focused on providing basic skills, such as language and equipment maintenance training. There is no longer any assistance to the national police except for a small antinarcotics program.

U.S. Interest Justifying a Security Assistance Program

The U.S. security assistance program is based primarily on a recognition of the strategic importance of Indonesia in Southeast Asia and the interest of the United States in the maintenance of an independent and friendly Indonesia. Indonesia is the largest and most populous of the 10 Southeast Asian countries and an important Western trading partner. It is a potential leader in the region and throughout the Third World....

The Department of State believes that it is in the interest of regional security and continued good United States-Indonesian relations to try to be responsive to Indonesia, particularly at this time when it feels increasingly concerned about its national security. Specifically, the Department is of the opinion that continuation of our security assistance program to Indonesia is in the U.S. national interest....

IRAN

Human Rights Information

...[Reform programs], along with Iran's economic development programs, form the core of the government's domestic activities. In the past 15 years, they have resulted in major progress in fields related to landownership, education, the local court system, rural development, health, and the rights of women. In sum, they amount to a significant improvement in the quality of life and rights of most Iranians.

Beginning in the late 1960s, Iran has also been confronted with a small number of terrorist organizations operating within the country. These terrorist groups have not delineated fully their economic and social programs, but they appear to be motivated by either the extreme conservative desire to oppose the social-economic changes in the society brought about by the Shah or to advocate even more sweeping, radical leftist changes. There is evidence that they have received substantial foreign support and training. While those groups pose no serious political threat to the Government, terrorists have been responsible for the murders of Iranian Government officials and Americans, including three colonels and three civilian defense contractor personnel over the past 34 months....

...Iranian constitutional law provides a comprehensive system of guarantee of basic human rights, combining traditional Moslem legal principles with codification largely patterned after the French system. Civil and criminal cases are handled with full guarantees of civil rights. The civilian court system which handles the large majority of civil and criminal cases has been recognized by outsiders as giving fair and balanced treatment to those brought before it. Most recently a team from the International Commission of Jurists praised certain aspects of this regular Iranian judicial system.

On the other hand, the same team recommended reforms in the handling of civilians charged with crimes involving state security. These recommendations stemmed from the fact that the security police (SAVAK) are empowered, without supervision of the regular courts, to function as military magistrates with regard to persons they may detain while protecting state security and carrying out other functions described in the Establishment of Security Organization Act of 1957. The great majority of those so detained are released within a few hours. Others are held for varying periods pending military trial or release....

...[T]here are currently in prison about 2,800-3,500 persons. They are sometimes referred to as "political prisoners." These figures are based on a definition of "political prisoners" which includes those convicted of crimes related to terrorism and other forms of violence. If instead the definition used is "persons who have been detained, arrested or punished for their beliefs or opinions but who have neither used nor advocated violence" the total of political prisoners in Iran is much smaller, probably about 100-150. Most persons in this latter group have been convicted for what the Iranian Government considers to be communist activities which are in violation of Iranian law.

In 1975, Iran agreed to a request by the International Commission of Jurists to send two observers into the country. Iranian authorities cooperated fully with the visitors. Also in 1975, the UN Human Rights Commission reviewed accusations of violations of human rights by Iran, based on material presented by Iranian students studying abroad and decided, on the basis of information before it, that no action was called for in the case of Iran.

Observance of Internationally Recognized Human Rights

Integrity of the Person

...The Iranian penal code specifically prohibits torture and provides severe penalties for anyone who tortures a prisoner or orders the use of torture. While we have no verifiable evidence of the use of torture, one cannot discount the reports, particularly with regard to persons alleged to be involved in terrorist violence, that such methods have been used by the Iranian police and security services. We also have no information that any official has ever been prosecuted for the use of torture. Fewer allegations of torture have been brought to our attention in recent years than in the past....

...[A]n American human rights legal expert stated: "In the opinion of the writer there can be no doubt that torture has been systematically practiced over a number of years against recalcitrant suspects under interrogation by the SAVAK. The number of detailed allegations which have been made, the absence of any impartial investigation, and the fact that the SAVAK is, and knows itself to be, a law unto itself, point inevitably to this conclusion."

The Shah has stated on several occasions that torture was probably used in the past, but has added that it is no longer used; he has said that "intelligent ways of questioning" prisoners are used.

In most cases, Iranians can obtain an effective remedy for violations of their rights with[in] the judicial system. However, the persons who allege that their rights were violated during the prosecution of their cases by SAVAK and the military courts have more limited possibilities of obtaining redress. Decisions by military courts can be and are appealed to a military appelate court, but are not subject to review by the Supreme Court. The Shah has final review of these decisions and has on occasion lessened sentences.

In cases involving state security, terrorism or similar crimes of violence, detention without initial charges does occur and pretrial confinement has been lengthy. Internal exile is permitted by law but has been used in recent years only with respect to price fixing and corruption cases after full and fair, usually public trials.

Iranian law provides for equal treatment before the law. Persons suspected of violating civil and most criminal laws are normally charged shortly after arrest and many are able to gain release by posting bond.

Except in state security cases trials in Iran are generally public and fair and afford guarantees necessary for defense. Security cases are tried in military courts, often in camera, and without the possibility of appeal to the civil judiciary. A military officer is assigned to act as defense counsel.

Other Freedoms

While there are some manifestations of discrimination in Iranian society, largely related to traditional religious practice, equal rights before the law are guaranteed. Freedom of movement, both within the country and abroad, the right to property, and freedom of thought and religion are observed in Iran, which has a long tradition of religious freedom....

The observers from the International Commission of Jurists noted that "in practice" freedom of the press did not exist....

Special rules govern the behavior of the Iranian military. There are restrictions on the peaceful assembly of groups which the Government considers political or subversive.

15

U.S. Government Action in Human Rights Area

Over the past 2 years, U.S. Government officials have discussed privately with Iranian officials our views about human rights in general and the human rights situation in Iran specifically. These contacts have been guided by our belief that handling this subject privately would be most effective in the Iranian context. To do otherwise would certainly become widely known and would put the matter of human rights in confrontational and self-defeating terms....

...The U.S. security assistance program in Iran is devoted to developing a militarily strong Iran. This goal, because of Iran's strategic geopolitical location, its long border with the Soviet Union, and the broad similarity of our political-strategic perceptions and security policies in the Middle East and Asia, is a major national interest for both Iran and the United States. It has always been clear to Iranian officials that the military strength of Iran is the overriding purpose of our security assistance program.

There is in Iran no U.S. public safety or other assistance program having to do with the Iranian police or penal authorities. There have been some sales of U.S. equipment to the Iranian gendarmerie, but we are not aware of any case in which that equipment has been used in connection with a possible violation of human rights.

Iranian officials are well aware of the provisions in the current law linking possible violations of human rights to the entire U.S. security assistance program.

U.S. Interests Justifying a Security Assistance Program

The U.S. security assistance program for Iran is composed only of cash sales of military equipment to Iran. In fiscal year 1976, including the transitional quarter, Iran received deliveries from the United States valued at $1.6-billion. That same figure for fiscal year 1977 will probably be about $1.2-billion.

These Iranian purchases are the heart of a program designed to develop a strong Iran. Iran's strength is important to us because of the parallel in Iranian and U.S. national interests found in (1) Iran's defense of its long border with the Soviet Union; (2) the transportation and communications bridge between Europe and Asian countries to the east; (3) Iran's interest in assuming major Persian Gulf security responsibilities previously carried out by the British; (4) Iran's willingness to serve as a reliable source of critical amounts of oil for the United States, Israel, our European allies and Japan; and (5) Iran's activities as a politically stabilizing force throughout that important region from Turkey into the Indian subcontinent.

For these reasons, the Department of State is of the opinion that continuation of our security assistance program with Iran is in the U.S. national interest.

PERU

Human Rights Information

...Although the general character of the regime has remained authoritarian, [the current President] Morales Bermudez' style of governing has been more moderate than that of his predecessor. One of his first measures on assuming the presidency was to promise an amnesty for the politicians and journalists who had been jailed or exiled under [former President Gen. Juan] Velasco. By early 1976 he had largely fulfilled that promise and had begun to develop policies designed to strengthen individual initiative and consolidate the reform programs.

An increasingly difficult economic situation created by the world recession and by the dislocations and uncertainties caused by previous internal reform policies led the Government of Peru to enact needed but unpopular economic austerity measures in June-July 1976. Following disturbances, the government decreed a national state of emergency and imposed a curfew in the capital. Some opposition activists have again been arrested or deported and several weekly magazines have been closed. However, the appointment of civilian ministers for the first time in 8 years, and intensified government discussion of popular participation in the political process at lower administration levels have led traditional political parties to hope for a renewed "opening toward democracy."

The basic Peruvian law is the constitution of 1933, as amended, which guarantees universally recognized human rights. However, the military government considers the revolutionary statute of 1968 to supercede the constitution wherever the two conflict. The Congress has been disbanded and elections suspended. Laws are enacted by decree, although some are submitted to an involved process of consultation and quasi-referendum before being promulgated.

The constitution permits the suspension of its legal protections when the security of the state requires. The current state of emergency was enacted in July 1976 in accordance with the constitution. Since then, the number of arrests and detentions has increased and there have been unsubstantiated reports of missing persons. Those detained, however, are generally released following interrogation.

Although Peruvian courts are nominally independent of the executive, the government has occasionally overruled them on policy matters. Civilian courts have no jurisdiction in security cases.

Observance of Internationally Recognized Human Rights

Integrity of the Person

...The rights of life, liberty, and security of person are generally respected. The government does not execute political prisoners, nor does it condone flagrant denials of personal security.

17

The Peruvian Government insists it does not condone torture and other inhuman and degrading treatment of detainees. However, law enforcement techniques and prison conditions in Peru have given rise to occasional reports of police brutality.

The 1974 "Report on Torture" of Amnesty International (AI) stated that "police brutality during interrogation of common and political prisoners has allegedly been common practice in Peru for many years." It noted, however, that "very few allegations had been received" and "there was no reason to believe that torture is carried out beyond the interrogation stage." In September 1974, following a series of denunciations of torture in the domestic Peruvian press, then-President Velasco publicly condemned police torture and announced an investigation into its practice.

Peruvian citizens can seek legal redress for government acts violating fundamental rights granted by the constitution. However, because some of those rights have been suspended by decree under the state of emergency, they cannot be sure of obtaining a remedy in court.

Persons suspected of hostile political or security activities are occasionally subjected to arbitrary arrest and detention without charges. During the Velasco regime, particularly its last years, an estimated 100 to 150 persons were expelled from Peru or chose voluntary exile. These included students, union activists, and peasant leaders. President Morales Bermudez granted amnesty to many thus affected. Under the state of emergency, however, his government has resorted to similar measures to prevent a deterioration of the internal security situation in the face of economic difficulties and to forestall labor agitation. The GOP insists such measures are directed exclusively against those who advocate violent overthrow of the government. The AI annual report for 1975-76 cites 14 political prisoners as either under AI adoption or being investigated by AI toward adoption; no further details are given.

Some persons arrested for suspected political and security violations have not had an open court hearing to determine rights and charges. Detention incommunicado is also resorted to. The AI annual report for 1975-76 refers to such detention suffered by a number of trade unionists and legal advisers to unions; they have since been released in an amnesty declared by President Morales Bermudez in April 1976.

The right to a fair trial is generally observed in Peru, within the traditional constraints of Latin American jurisprudence. In a small number of cases, political or security factors are given priority, and trial is by special courts martial.

Other Freedoms

The Peruvian Government does not condone racial discrimination of any kind, and that which is evident results from traditional attitudes of the society. The revolutionary government has taken active steps to improve access to legal resources and provide improved economic and educational opportunities to its large Indian population, which has been exploited since the Spanish conquest.

Peruvians are free to travel within the country, within the context of the restraints of the present state of emergency. No significant political limitations are placed on travel abroad.

In the process of attempting to achieve broader state and popular participation in Peru's economic processes, the military government has expropriated property. Compensation has been paid to U.S. investors in these cases under the aegis of agreements negotiated with the good offices of the U.S. Government. Personal property, as differentiated from income-producing property, is respected.

National circulation newspapers were expropriated in 1974, and were to be assigned within a specified time period to various organized sectors of society (peasants, labor organizations, intellectuals, et cetera) under a variety of government controls. However, government relinquishment of direct editorial control of newspapers has been postponed twice since 1974, and a new high-level commission has been appointed to study the situation of the press and make recommendations. Radio, television, and wire service reportings are monitored by a national information office. The Morales Bermudez government permitted privately owned weekly journals closed by Velasco to reopen. Following the July 1, 1976 disturbances, however, political periodicals of both right and left were closed.

Although political parties continue to exist legally in Peru, they are permitted no direct role in shaping government policies. Under the present state of emergency, they do not enjoy the rights of public assembly. In normal times the parties hold outdoor assemblies only with express government permission.

U.S. Government Action in Human Rights Area

We have not formally raised with the GOP [Government of Peru] any specific cases of imputed violation of human rights involving Peruvians. Both in Washington and Lima, however, we have emphasized to the GOP our basic commitment to human rights and called attention to recent human rights legislation affecting assistance to Peru.

Recent U.S. cultural exchange programs in Peru have made clear our concern for the full and proper observance of human rights. Under U.S. Government auspices, George Reedy, dean of Marquette University's Journalism School, spoke clearly to the Peruvian press of the U.S. commitment to human rights, and feminist leader Joan Goodin of the U.S. Railworkers Union elucidated worldwide developments in women's rights. Labor leader exchanges have also demonstrated U.S. support for human rights and the development of free and independent institutions.

U.S. Government concern over human rights has been demonstrated as well in U.S. citizen protection cases. In July 1976, the Ambassador called upon the Foreign Minister to request that U.S. citizens caught up in the drug traffic receive speedier trials. In August our Chargé d'Affaires also called upon the acting head of the National Council of Justice (overseer of the court system) to drive home the need for speedy trials. The Embassy is in regular contact with the GOP attorney general on principles of human rights protection in regard to specific cases involving U.S. citizens.

Peru has cooperated in the international protection of human rights through the U.N. and the OAS. The Peruvian immigration office has cooperated closely with the U.S. Embassy and the U.N. Human Rights Commission to facilitate the immigration to the United States of Chilean refugees.

No U.S. aid is extended to the Peruvian police, except in the field of drug control and interdiction. Assistance to the Peruvian military has been modest and has not contributed directly to any capability to engage in repression.

U.S. Security Assistance Program

The U.S. security assistance program for Peru consists of: grants limited to foreign military training, at a cost of about $900,000 a year; $20-million in FMS credit sales in fiscal year 1976; and clearance for commercial military procurement from the United States—up to $18-million maximum.

These programs are carefully monitored to avoid any U.S. Government contribution to regional tensions or to any direct or indirect violations of human rights.

The U.S. interests served by security assistance lie primarily in the maintenance of constructive relations with Peru. The training component fosters greater understanding of the United States and its policies among an important leadership group.

Elimination of the U.S. security assistance program in Peru would deprive the United States of an important instrument of communication and cooperation with that country. It cannot be argued that U.S. security assistance can insure the observance of human rights. But to the extent that the observance of these rights is enhanced by an atmosphere of confidence and cooperation, the elimination of U.S. security assistance might contribute in the end to the exact opposite of our present concerns—the degradation of the respect for human rights in Peru, not to their widening observance.

On the basis of the purposes served by the security assistance program as described above, it is the Department of State's view that it is in the United States national interest that the security assistance program in Peru be continued along present lines.

PHILIPPINES

Human Rights Information

Martial law has been in effect in the Philippines since September 1972, and legislative bodies ceased functioning at that time. President [Ferdinand Edralin] Marcos governs by decree, assisted by his civilian cabinet and the military. In September 1976, President Marcos created a legislative advisory council preparatory to organizing an interim legislative body in 1977. All of the members of the legislative advisory council are appointed by the President. Amendments to the 1973 constitution, revising the form of the interim legislative body provided for by that document, were approved in a referendum/plebiscite on October 16, 1976. The revised interim legislative body is to include elected representatives from the various geographic regions of the country, as well as appointed members and members selected to represent specific sectors of the society, but the method of election has not yet been prescribed and no date for the election has yet been established. Under the new amendments, the interim legislative body is to be convened within 30 days of the election and selection of its members.

The civilian bureaucracy and the judicial system function normally in most cases, although military tribunals exercise criminal jurisdiction in some cases previously handled by regular civilian courts. All members of the judiciary, however, submitted letters of resignation at the outset of martial law. The President may accept these resignations at any time. The supreme court has upheld President Marcos' position in all cases challenging his martial law powers since its declaration. The armed forces of the Philippines are subordinate to Presidential control, but in the last 4 years have played a constantly increasing role in national life.

There is little formal political activity in a traditional sense under the martial law administration in the absence of either legislative bodies or political elections. While political parties, except for the Communist Party, have not been outlawed, they have been inactive....

Observance of Internationally Recognized Human Rights

Integrity of the Person

...Most Filipinos enjoy the right to life, liberty, and the security of person, but the nature of the martial law administration is such that any of these rights can be abridged. Duly constituted civil courts are functioning in the Philippines and the great majority of nonpolitical cases, both civil and criminal, are processed in accordance with normal due process of law. However, the writ of habeas corpus was suspended for certain categories of people as a result of the declaration of martial law.

Since the imposition of martial law, there have been reports of torture as well as of cruel, inhuman, and degrading punishment in the cases of some political detainees in the Philippines. The incidence of such reports was most frequent in the immediate aftermath of the declaration of martial law. In recent years, although the incidence appears to have decreased, the reports themselves have been more fully documented. When torture has been alleged, it is said to have taken place usually in the first stages of interrogation as a result of activities by lower ranking military personnel prior to the assignment of detainees to regular detention centers. Evidence indicates that instances of torture and maltreatment represent aberrations and are not the result of explicit Government policy at the political level.

The conditions and atmosphere of martial law, however, may help to nurture the practice of torture.

The "Report of an Amnesty International Mission to the Republic of the Philippines," November 22-December 5, 1975, released in September 1976, states that of 107 prisoners interviewed, 71 reported to the Amnesty International representatives that they had been tortured. With few exceptions, the reported incidents of torture on which specific data was given occurred in 1974 or earlier, and nearly all were limited to incidents taking place during initial periods of interrogation. Information published by religious organizations in the Philippines concerned with human rights matters indicates that incidents of torture have continued to occur since the visit of the Amnesty International mission, but suggests that, during 1976, the proportion of persons subjected to torture or maltreatment during initial interrogation may have been significantly lower than that reported by Amnesty International among those it interviewed, who had been arrested and detained during an earlier period.

In September 1976, the Government announced the creation of a military committee to investigate torture charges against members of the armed forces. The Government also initiated court-martial proceedings against several officers and enlisted men for maltreatment of detainees. On a number of occasions, the Philippine Government has facilitated and cooperated with visiting missions from private or international organizations interested in the status of human rights in the Philippines. In addition to the visit of the Amnesty International mission, teams from the International Commission of the Red Cross (ICRC) have inspected Philippine detention centers in March 1973, November and December 1974, and July 1976. Representatives of the International Commission of Jurists (ICJ) visited the Philippines in 1975.

Since the institution of martial law, there have been numerous arrests and detentions of prisoners without charge or trial, in some cases for as long as 4 years. At the outset of martial law, the great majority of persons detained who would fall into the category of "political prisoner" were released within a few months. Firm figures for numbers of political prisoners still in detention are not available, but most estimates range between about 500 and 6,000, depending on which categories of individuals are included within varying definitions of "political prisoners." Generally, the number of detainees held who are nonviolent opponents of the martial law regime is believed to fall in the lower part of this range.

Both military and civilian courts are in existence to try persons detained under martial law, but few cases have actually been brought to trial. Those hearings and trials which have been held have been open to the public. Most political prisoners have had access to their families from early in the period of their detention. Access to lawyers has been considerably more restricted. However, once such prisoners are charged to be tried by a military commission, they are to be provided a judge advocate as defense counsel unless they employ their own attorney. In July 1976, President Marcos directed that all cases pending before military tribunals, which would include cases of political prisoners, be tried prior to August 1976. The only case which has come to trial since July, however, is that of former Senator Benigno Aquino, and that trial has not yet been completed. The cases of two other prominent detainees, Eugenio Lopez Jr., and Sergio Osmena III, remain in abeyance, as does that of American citizen August Lehman who, like Lopez and Osmena, has been held for 4 years without bail and without his case coming to actual trial.

Other Freedoms

Discrimination, legal or otherwise, on the basis of religion, race, or color is remarkably lacking in the multiracial Philippine society. Personal property is protected under law. There are some travel restrictions within the country pertaining to travel to insurgent areas in Mindanao and the Sulu Archipelago, and travel restrictions are sometimes placed on former political prisoners released on parole. Filipinos wishing to travel abroad must obtain exit permits. Travel abroad for tourism is theoretically not allowed but as a practical matter is permitted, although applicants usually must fall within certain specified categories: scholars, government officials, delegates to conferences, businessmen, et cetera.

There is limited freedom of expression in the Philippines. During the Information campaign prior to the 1975 and 1976 referendums, opponents of the Government spoke to civic groups and on university campuses although little of this criticism was carried in the press. The media exercise self-censorship, which in effect means they carry nothing critical of the Government and are essentially controlled.

The Government has not actively abridged freedom of association even for many of its outspoken critics, and it has allowed some small opposition rallies and peaceful assemblies to take place. However, it monitors these events carefully and insures that they receive little or no media coverage. Political parties have been inactive since the inception of martial law, but only the Communist Party is officially banned.

U.S. Government Action in Human Rights Area

During the past several years U.S. Government officials have had wide-ranging and numerous discussion[s] with key Philippine Government officials about our concern over the human rights situation in the Philippines and worldwide. The Philippine Government, up to and including the President, is fully aware of our concern and interest in human rights. It has demonstrated sensitivity to the impact which reported violations of human rights in the Philippines have had on opinion within the United States. During the discussions, U.S. officials have made Philippine officials aware of those sections of U.S. legislation relevant to human rights, have made specific representations concerning, or have attempted to facilitate the resolution of, certain specific cases, and have impressed on the Philippine Government the overall moral and ethical concern of the Congress and the Administration....

...[T]he Embassy has continued to make other efforts to promote understanding of an adherence to internationally recognized standards of human rights. Educational and cultural exchange programs, for example, have significant potential for making a positive impact on the human rights situation. Full account of this potential is taken by the Embassy in its planning. Other opportunities for promoting human rights are found by the Embassy in its many unofficial, informal contacts with a broad cross section of Philippine leadership.

Although there are no current aid programs specifically aimed at the promotion of human rights in the Philippines, many aid projects dealing with such fields as rural electrification, irrigation and population programs support and promote opportunities for the poor to improve their economic and social conditions and thereby are broadly supportive of human rights.

The Philippine Government has been well aware of the provisions of the International Security Assistance and Arms Export Control Act dealing with human rights and of the overall interest of the U.S. Government in this regard. Our security assistance program in the Philippines dates from the early days of Philippine independence in 1946 and is a long-established component of our larger security relationship with the Philippines, which since its independence has been a close and valued ally.

The U.S. security assistance program for the Philippines long predates the present Muslim and Communist insurgencies. We are aware that military equipment originally provided by the United States is being used to counter the Muslim insurgency in the southern Philippines as well as the smaller threat posed by Communist guerrillas in the north and central Philippines. It has, however, been firm U.S. policy and practice not to become involved with Philippine efforts to suppress either of these domestic insurgencies. We keep American military personnel strictly out of the Muslim areas. Our small U.S. military advisory group is not involved in combat operations of any kind and is assigned a military assistance role only at the national level. U.S. military personnel do not perform direct advisory functions below the level of the Department of National Defense, the Armed Forces of the Philippines General Headquarters or Service Headquarters, all of which are located in the Manila area. These advisory efforts do not directly support operations of the Philippine Armed Forces but are limited to military procurement, distribution, utilization, maintenance and the like.

U.S. Interest Justifying a Security Assistance Program

The Philippines has traditionally been one of our closest and most important treaty allies in East Asia. The defense commitments and mutual security interests of both countries are formally embodied in longstanding agreements. We have major military bases in the Philippines, the maintenance of which is important both for the defense of the Philippines and for the broader security interests of the United States. Continued security assistance to the Philippines is a critical factor in assuring continued U.S. access to the important facilities at Clark Air Base and the naval base at Subic Bay. U.S. security assistance has been viewed by the Philippine Government as an implicit quid pro quo for our use of these facilities, and our continued access to these facilities is related to the maintenance of U.S. global security and the implementation of a forward strategy in the Pacific. Suspension of security assistance could motivate the Philippine Government to abrogate the military bases agreement between the two countries, which is currently under renegotiation, and invite the United States to withdraw. Beyond the unfortunate bilateral implications of such a development, ejection of the United States from the Philippine bases could seriously affect regional stability and erode confidence in U.S. security commitments in other important nations, both in the East Asian region and elsewhere.

The Department of State is of the opinion that the U.S. security assistance program for the Philippines should be continued. Elimination of the U.S. security assistance program could lessen the ability of the United States to influence the Philippine Government on a range of U.S. interests in the Philippines, including the promotion of human rights, adversely affect our security position in the East Asian region and elsewhere, and decrease confidence in U.S. security commitments to many important nations.

▼▼▼

CARTER'S ETHICS GUIDELINES

January 4, 1977

*President-elect Jimmy Carter issued guidelines Jan. 4 to prohibit con-
flicts of interest by members of his administration. Policymakers in the
Carter administration, including the President himself, will play by a
tougher set of rules than their predecessors when it comes to heading off
prospective conflicts of interest, Carter said.*

*Carter at the same time announced his intention to place most of his own
business holdings and personal wealth in a blind trust.*

*Carter's guidelines covered three basic areas: public disclosure of finan-
cial assets, divestiture of assets that could involve appointees in possible
conflicts of interest, and restrictions on the employment of the policymakers after they have left the government.*

*The guidelines would apply not only to Cabinet officers and Carter's
White House staff, but to nearly 2,000 political appointees and to the tens
of thousands of career federal employees in policymaking posts. The persons Carter named to his Cabinet already had signed letters of intent to
abide by the guidelines, and the others were expected to follow suit.*

*The Carter code required full financial disclosure, updated annually and
continued for two years after an individual left government service. Other
guidelines for policymakers in the Carter administration required:*

*● Divesting themselves of interests and investments that could involve
conflicts of interest. Exemptions were made for real estate, savings certificates, governmental securities and diversified holdings such as mutual
funds.*

• *Tightening restrictions on benefits from previous private employers on items such as severance, pensions and stock options.*

• *Extending to two years the existing one-year restriction on private handling, after they have left government, of matters in which policy-makers had been personally involved while they were members of the administration.*

• *Imposing a one-year restriction on contracts by departed officials with the agency in which they served.*

The code recommended new regulations, subject to congressional approval, to close what Carter spokesmen called the "revolving door" between federal agencies and businesses affected by agency rulings. A former government official would be barred for a period of two years from handling any paid private business with his former agency if it concerned matters the official had dealt with during his last year in government. An individual would be required to refrain for a period of one year from doing business with his former agency on any matter, whether he had worked on the issue in the last year of service or not.

The existing public financial disclosure law which Carter wished to tighten required full public disclosure for Cabinet officers, but reports on other top officials were kept confidential and contained only the name of companies in which a financial interest was held, not the value of the interest.

In his statement Carter noted that to require an individual to exist only on his salary during the period of public service seriously limited the ability of the government to recruit top talent. He expressed hope that divestiture causing severe tax burdens would, except in rare circumstances, be unnecessary.

For Carter himself, the plan required:

• *Placing most of his financial holdings in trust.*

• *Establishing a charitable foundation to finance a future Carter library in his hometown of Plains, Ga. Royalties from Carter's autobiography and a forthcoming book of his speeches would go to the foundation.*

• *Leasing for four years, for a fixed amount established in 1977, the 3,400 acres of farmland he and his family owned.*

• *Leasing for four years under conditions similar to those applying to the land, or selling at the discretion of the trustee, the family's peanut business and warehouse.*

Jody Powell, Carter's press spokesman, said the guidelines fulfilled a campaign pledge to restore confidence in the leaders of government and to insure that Carter's appointees were worthy of trust.

Much of the work of drafting the guidelines was done by John L. Moore, an Atlanta lawyer and a member of the Carter transition team. At a brief-

ing on release of the text of the code, Moore said that violations could be reported to the Justice Department. Injunctions could be sought, he said, to prevent top federal employees from taking government-related jobs barred by the guidelines or otherwise violating their "contract" with Carter.

Much of the guidelines' content followed recommendations of Common Cause, the self-described citizens' lobby. John W. Gardner, chairman of Common Cause, called the guidelines "a major breakthrough in the fight to eliminate conflicts of interest in the executive branch."

Following are the texts of the statements on ethics and conflicts of interest that were released Jan. 4, 1977, in Plains, Ga. (Boldface headings in brackets have been added by Congressional Quarterly to highlight the organization of the text.):

The Transition Group has studied existing laws and regulations bearing on conflicts of interest and the regulation of ethics of officials in the Executive Branch of Government. The existing law is extremely strong in prohibiting outside earned income. Governor Carter heavily approves of that law and its policy.

The existing law and regulations do not go as far as Governor Carter felt appropriate as to the public disclosure of sources of income and statements of assets and liabilities. The President-elect, the Vice President-elect and all those appointed to Cabinet and White House posts will voluntarily make such statements available to the public shortly after the Inauguration. Under powers delegated to the President by Congress, an Executive Order will be issued requiring such disclosure by all policy-making officials of the Executive Branch.

It appears that for those positions requiring confirmation by the Senate, a careful job is done by Senate Committees of screening assets and liabilities of nominees for potential conflicts of interests and, in most cases, appropriate divestitures have been made. However, there appears to be a need for more uniform policies and more thorough screening of assets and liabilities of policy-making officials in posts not requiring Senate confirmation. Therefore, we are releasing today guidelines designed to make more uniform the policies relating to divestiture, including policies on the characteristics of trusts. The new Administration will give special emphasis to better enforcement of screening procedures for officials in policy-making posts not requiring confirmation by the Senate.

The transition study does not regard present law on employment subsequent to government service as adequate. Studies by Congressional committees and citizen groups show that further steps are needed to insure that former government officials cannot use their personal contacts gained in public service for private benefit. Governor Carter has asked all persons nominated to positions in the Executive Branch and to independent agencies to make voluntary commitments in this regard. Those commitments are contained in an attachment to the guidelines released today.

It appears that additional legislative action will be needed to satisfactorily close the "revolving door." Such action will need to give separate attention to each agency or department. The Carter Administration will work, beginning immediately after the Inauguration, with interested citizens groups and the Congress to develop such legislation.

[Policy Guidelines]

It will be the policy of the Carter-Mondale Administration to appoint and nominate for appointment, only persons of high ability who will carry out their official duties without fear or favor and with an equal hand, unfettered by any actual or apparent conflicts of interests. To decree that no persons can have any financial interests other than a salary from the Government would seriously limit the ability to recruit the most qualified persons. The Carter-Mondale Administration will require full disclosure of all continuing affiliations and of assets and liabilities of nominees and their immediate families. It is hoped that except in rare circumstances divestiture causing severe tax burdens will be unnecessary if the present laws and regulatory framework are diligently and fairly administered.

The following guidelines pertain to the assets and liabilities of a nominee, the spouse of the nominee, and the nominee's minor child or children, partner, or any organization in which the nominee continues to serve as an officer, director, trustee, partner, or employee while in the government service or any private organization with which the nominee has negotiated or has any arrangement concerning prospective employment.

All nominees will be expected to comply with all relevant statutes (particularly 18 U.S.C. Section 208) and the rules and practices of the particular Department or Agency served.

If the person is nominated to a Level I or II position divestiture should occur if compliance with the provisions of 18 U.S.C. Section 208 indicates a conflict requiring disqualification from action for the Government more than rarely. Nominees for positions at Level III and other positions in the Government should require divestiture because of conflicts arising under 18 U.S.C. Section 208 only if use of disqualification will seriously impair the capability of the officer to perform the duties of the office to which nominated.

Beyond the requirements of 18 U.S.C. Section 208, persons nominated to positions at Level I or II should divest holdings and liabilities where the nature of the holding or liability is such that it will be broadly affected by governmental monetary and budgetary policies. Generally excepted from requirements of divestiture (unless the particular position indicates continuing conflicts arising in government service with respect to a particular interest) will be made for:

a. real estate interests whether in the form of ownership of land or participations in partnerships.

b. savings certificates and accounts and U.S. and other governmental securities.

c. other holdings which are diversified; e.g. less than a 1% holding of a well-diversified mutual fund or a total of not more than approximately $500,000 invested in diversified assets.

Blind trusts will be recognized as appropriate methods of divestiture where divestiture is required provided:

a. the trustee is truly independent.

b. the assets transferred in trust are either cash or diversified assets;

c. the trustee is given entire discretion and express direction to sell or buy without discussion with the government officer or anyone close to such officer and the only reports given to the government officer are the schedules necessary to file with income tax returns (which schedules do not list anything more than totals of taxable items from the trust).

The attention of nominees will be directed to the provisions of 18 U.S.C. Section 209 prohibiting receipt of any compensation for government service from any party other than the United States. While the matter of payments for services prior to entry into government service is properly addressed by legal counsel to the appointee and the organization making the payment, the following general guidelines seem appropriate:

a. If there is a pre-existing established plan of the particular organization to reward past service, obviously such plan can be recognized and followed.

b. If there is no pre-existing established plan of the particular organization it is suggested that a payment in excess of 6 months of salary or in excess of a range of $50,000 to $75,000 would need careful examination.

In all events, it is expected that payment of any severance benefits will be completed prior to the nominee's taking office in the Government or within a reasonable time thereafter and that a copy of a favorable opinion of counsel to the nominee and the organization making the payment that it is lawful will be furnished.

While 18 U.S.C. Section 209(b) allows continuing participation in a bona fide pension, retirement, group life, health or accident insurance, profit sharing, stock bonus, or other employee welfare benefit plan maintained by a former employer, nominees will be asked generally to exercise any stock options prior to commencement of government service (unless, because of the requirements of the Securities Exchange Act, such exercise should occur within a reasonable period after beginning government service in which case the government officer may exercise within such limited period, providing other guidelines are followed concerning conflicts of interests as above stated). Nominees will also be asked not to have contributions made to profit sharing plans by former employers based on earnings of the former employer after the government officer takes office.

Deviations from the foregoing guidelines will only be made with the express consent of the President-Elect with respect to Level I and II appointments and by heads of departments or agencies with reference to other appointments. The reasons for the deviations will be made public.

It is proposed to ask appointees to enter into a letter of commitment, a copy of which...[follows], which, in several respects calls for the disclosure of financial information beyond the requirements of existing law and regulations. It is contemplated that the financial disclosure requirements will be made subject to an Executive Order shortly after the new Administration takes office. The attached letter of commitment also describes certain restrictions requested of nominees following government service. Shortly after the new Administration takes office Congress will be requested to take action along the lines spelled out in the attached letter of commitment.

It will be the policy of the new Administration to encourage every Department and Agency of the Government to advise every new employee of existing laws and regulations relating to conflicts of interests and to have a prior screening of such conflicts at the time of appointment. It will be a further policy to encourage Departments and Agencies to institute procedures for continuing policing of conflicts.

It is the objective of the new Administration to avoid any conflict which could in any way influence any government officer except in the even interest of all the people.

[Letter of Agreement]

Date:

Honorable Jimmy Carter
President-Elect of the United States

Dear Sir:

Sharing your determination to assure the American people of the integrity of your Administration and appreciating the confidence you have shown in me by proposing to nominate me to be

In addition to complying with applicable federal laws and regulations relating to conflicts of interest, if I am nominated, confirmed, and take office, I agree that:

(1) I have already filed, or will file within 30 days of taking office with those persons you specify, the following information which may be made available to the public as you may direct:

(a) a complete current net worth statement itemizing all assets and liabilities of myself, my spouse, my minor children, and other members of my immediate household; and

(b) a source of income statement for the year 1975 and for the period of time ending no earlier than 60 days before the above date listing all sources and amounts of all items of value received by me, my spouse, my minor children, and other members of my immediate household including, but not limited to, salaries, wages, fees, honoraria or other compensation, dividends, interest, rents, royalties, proceeds from the sale or exchange of property, and gifts.

(2) While in office, in addition to complying with 18 U.S.C. § 208, I will similarly refrain from participating in any particular matter, as that term is used in § 208, in which any party as hereinafter specified has a direct and substantial interest:

(a) any party with which I am associated for financial gain within the year prior to taking office as officer, employee, director, trustee, partner, or owner of more than 1% of value of the outstanding equity ownership; or

(b) with which I am negotiating or have an arrangement whether as a consultant, employee, partner, or any other position to be held for financial gain;

(3) In addition to complying with the restrictions which will be imposed on me by federal law after termination of my government service, including those contained in 18 U.S.C. § 207, I will not for two years following such termination, engage in any activity from which § 207(b) will bar me during the first year after such termination. Also for two years following termination of government service I will not, for compensation or financial gain, on behalf of any party other than the United States, make any formal or informal appearance before, or contact with, any officer or employee of the Executive Branch with respect to any particular matter as defined in § 207 which was within my official responsibility as defined in 18 U.S.C. § 202(b) during the twelve months preceding termination of my government service.

(4) For one year following termination of my government service I will not, for compensation or financial gain, on behalf of any party other than the United States, make any formal or informal appearance before, or contact with, any officer or employee of the (insert appropriate name of department or agency).

(5) I will, while in government service and for two years after leaving government service, file periodically in accordance with regulations to be promulgated by you statements of sources of income more particularly described in subparagraph (1)(b) above.

(6) In accepting the position for which you propose to nominate me, it is my intention to serve for the entire term for which you appoint me and, if my term is indefinite, it is my intention to serve as long as you wish me to serve.

Very truly yours,

[Statement on Carter's Assets]

In order to prevent possible financial conflicts of interest while President, Governor Jimmy Carter is taking the following actions:

1. All common stock is being sold, consisting of 100 shares of Rich's, Inc., and 956 shares of Advance Investors. A small net loss on this stock is likely.

2. Jimmy Carter's interest in (a) Carter's Warehouse and Carter Farms, Inc., and any funds related to them, (b) all property except the private home and personal items, and (c) his father's estate will be transferred to a trust. Income or principal from the trust will be available to Jimmy Carter but only as distributions of cash.

3. No reports will be made to Jimmy Carter from the trustee or any investment advisers other than minimum tax information and an annual statement of the net asset value of the trust. Such information, when received, will be made available to the public.

4. All salaries, profits and direct or indirect benefits from the farms or warehouse will be terminated as of January 20, 1977, except as described above.

5. The trust agreement will require that investment decisions be delegated to an independent institution if investment assets, other than land, exceed $200,000.

6. Carter Farms, Inc., comprised of all farm land owned by members of the immediate family (Jimmy Carter, his wife and children) will be retained by the trust but will be rented for an annual fixed amount. Annual after tax income to Jimmy Carter will not exceed the amount established during the first year (Calendar Year 1977). Thus, the Carter family will not be affected financially from profits or losses of any of the farm operations. Jimmy and Rosalynn Carter are resigning as officers and directors of this corporation.

7. Carter's Warehouse, a partnership consisting of Jimmy Carter, his brother Billy and his mother Lillian, will be either leased for four years for a fixed amount, or sold, at the discretion of the trustee. Again, neither Jimmy Carter, his wife nor children will be affected financially from profits or losses of any of the warehouse operations.

8. An independent charitable foundation will receive contributions, outright ownership of a book of speeches soon to be published and royalties from "Why Not the Best." The primary purpose of this foundation will be to establish a future library to house presidential papers, documents and memorabilia.

▼▼▼

SUPREME COURT ON ZONING REGULATIONS

January 11, 1977

The Supreme Court Jan. 11, by a 5-3 vote, upheld a Chicago suburb's zoning regulations. The court ruled that the regulations which, in effect, barred housing for low-income minorities were not inherently uncon-stitutional. (Village of Arlington Heights *v.* Metropolitan Housing Development Corporation)

Justice Lewis F. Powell Jr., writing for the majority, concluded that there was no evidence of discriminatory intent and said that the fact that the refusal to rezone had a racially discriminatory effect did not raise a constitutional issue. The justices reversed the United States' 7th Circuit Court of Appeals' finding that the village zoning regulations of Arlington Heights, Ill., were discriminatory because the effect of the ordinances was to deny black families the opportunity to move into the community. Arlington Heights, an almost all-white Chicago suburb, had refused to change its zoning laws to allow the construction of a 190-unit housing project for low- and moderate-income families.

The Supreme Court referred back to its 1976 ruling in Washington *v.* Davis *in which the court rejected the contention that a Washington, D.C., police department qualifying examination was discriminatory because of the high rate of failure among black examinees. There, said Powell, the court made clear "that official action will not be held unconstitutional solely because it results in a racially disproportionate impact.... Proof of racially discriminatory intent or purpose is required to show a violation of the Equal Protection Clause."*

Powell went on to discuss factors that might be examined to determine whether a regulation had been motivated by racial discrimination. "The impact of the official action...may provide an important starting point" for such an inquiry, Powell noted. The examination might include the historical background of a regulation, departures from normal procedures and the legislative or administrative history, he said. The Arlington Heights regulation would appear in a different light if the village had not consistently applied its zoning policy, Powell argued, or if unusual procedures had been followed in handling this particular request for rezoning, or if the zoning for the particular parcel had been recently changed from multi-family to single-family use.

Dissenting Views

Justices William J. Brennan Jr. and Thurgood Marshall concurred with the majority's analysis of discriminatory intent but dissented from the finding regarding Arlington Heights on the grounds that the case should have been sent back to the circuit court for reconsideration because the circuit court had rendered its opinion prior to the Supreme Court's decision in Washington v. Davis.

Justice Byron R. White, who wrote the majority opinion in the Washington v. Davis *case, dissented, saying that the majority opinion articulated "a legal standard nowhere mentioned in* Davis." *White agreed with Marshall and Brennan that the ruling in* Washington v. Davis *should not have been applied to the* Arlington Heights *case before giving the court of appeals the chance to do so. White called Powell's discussion of the standard for providing a racially discriminatory intent "wholly unnecessary."*

The court remanded the case to the 7th Circuit Court of Appeals but solely to determine whether or not the Arlington Heights action violated the Federal Fair Housing Act of 1968 prohibiting racial discrimination in the rental and sale of housing.

The ruling followed several decisions in which the justices upheld the use of zoning powers to keep out communes and to prevent the concentration of places of "adult" entertainment within one neighborhood of a city. The ruling limited a 1976 decision which upheld the power of a federal judge to order a metropolitan area-wide remedy for segregated public housing in Chicago. (Historic Documents of 1976, p. 223)

Impact of Decision

The court's opinion in Arlington Heights *pointed up the continuing tensions between the inner-city and the suburbs over the question of whether suburbs should be required to aid in the solution of inner-city problems such as housing, education and high unemployment. The Suburban Action Institute, an organization involved in an effort to open up New York City's suburbs to low-cost housing, stated, when the* Arlington Heights *decision was handed down, that the group's efforts at that time were based on state laws and constitutional provisions, and that the legal battles were being waged in the state rather than federal courts.*

Following are excerpts from the Supreme Court's opinion, decided Jan. 11, 1977, permitting restrictive zoning in instances where racial exclusion was an unintended result of the zoning code:

No. 75—616

Village of Arlington Heights et al., Petitioners, *v.* Metropolitan Housing Development Corporation et al.	On Writ of Certiorari to the United States Court of Appeals for the Seventh Circuit.

[January 11, 1977]

MR. JUSTICE POWELL delivered the opinion of the Court. [MR. JUSTICE STEVENS took no part in the consideration or decision of this case.]

In 1971 respondent Metropolitan Housing Development Corporation (MHDC) applied to petitioner, the Village of Arlington Heights, Ill., for the rezoning of a 15-acre parcel from single-family to multiple-family classification. Using federal financial assistance, MHDC planned to build 190 clustered townhouse units for low and moderate income tenants. The Village denied the rezoning request. MHDC, joined by other plaintiffs who are also respondents here, brought suit in the United States District Court for the Northern District of Illinois. They alleged that the denial was racially discriminatory and that it violated, *inter alia,* the Fourteenth Amendment and the Fair Housing Act of 1968, 42 U.S.C. § 3601 *et seq.* Following a bench trial, the District Court entered judgment for the Village, ...and respondents appealed. The Court of Appeals for the Seventh Circuit reversed, finding that the "ultimate effect" of the denial was racially discriminatory, and that the refusal to rezone therefore violated the Fourteenth Amendment.... We granted the Village's petition for certiorari, ...and now reverse.

I

...[T]he District Court held that the petitioners were not motivated by racial discrimination or intent to discriminate against low-income groups when they denied rezoning, but rather by a desire "to protect property values and the integrity of the Village's zoning plan." ...The District Court concluded also that the denial would not have a racially discriminatory effect.

A divided Court of Appeals reversed. It first approved the District Court's finding that the defendants were motivated by a concern for the integrity of the zoning plan, rather than by racial discrimination. Deciding whether their refusal to rezone would have discriminatory effects was more complex. The court observed that the refusal would have a disproportionate impact on blacks. Based upon family income, blacks constituted 40% of those Chicago area residents who were eligible to become tenants of Lincoln Green [the name of the MHDC project], although they comprised a far lower percentage of total area population. The court reasoned, however, that under our decision in *James* v. *Valtierra*... (1971), such a disparity in racial impact alone does not call for strict scrutiny of a municipality's decision that prevents the construction of the low-cost housing.

There was another level to the court's analysis of allegedly discriminatory results. Invoking language from *Kennedy Park Homes Association* v. *City of Lackawanna*...(1970), the Court of Appeals ruled that the denial of rezoning must be examined in light of its "historical context and ultimate effect." Northwest Cook County was enjoying rapid growth in employment opportunities and population, but it continued to exhibit a high degree of residential segregation. The court held that Arlington Heights could not simply ignore this problem. Indeed, it found that the Village had been "exploiting" the situation by allowing itself to become a nearly all-white community. ...The Village had no other current plans for building low and moderate income housing, and no other R-5 parcels in the Village were available to MHDC at an economically feasible price.

Against this background, the Court of Appeals ruled that the denial of the Lincoln Green proposal had racially discriminatory effects and could be tolerated only if it served compelling interests. Neither the buffer policy nor the desire to protect property values met this exacting standard. The court therefore concluded that the denial violated the Equal Protection Clause of the Fourteenth Amendment.

II

A

...[T]here can be little doubt that MHDC meets the constitutional standing requirements. The challenged action of the petitioners stands as an absolute barrier to constructing the housing MHDC had contracted to place on the Victorian site. [The Clerics of St. Viator, a religious order, owned the property.] If MHDC secures the injunctive relief it seeks, that barrier will be removed. An injunction would not, of course, guarantee that Lincoln Green will be built. MHDC would still have to secure financing, qualify for federal subsidies, and carry through with construction. But all housing developments are subject to some extent to similar uncertainties. When a project is as detailed and specific as Lincoln Green, a court is not required to engage in undue speculation as a predicate for finding that the plaintiff has the requisite personal stake in the controversy. MHDC has shown an injury to itself that is "likely to be redressed by a favorable decision." *Simon* v. *Eastern Kentucky Welfare Rights Org....*[1976].

Petitioners nonetheless appear to argue that MHDC lacks standing because it has suffered no economic injury. MHDC, they point out, is not the owner of the property in question. Its contract of purchase is contingent upon securing rezoning. MHDC owes the owners nothing if rezoning is denied.

We cannot accept petitioners' argument. In the first place, it is inaccurate to say that MHDC suffers no economic injury from a refusal to rezone, despite the contingency provisions in its contract. MHDC has expended thousands of dollars on the plans for Lincoln Green and on the studies submitted to the Village in support of the petition for rezoning. Unless rezoning is granted, many of these plans and studies will be worthless even if MHDC finds another site at an equally attractive price.

Petitioners' argument also misconceives our standing requirements. It has long been clear that economic injury is not the only kind of injury that can support a plaintiffs standing. *United States* v. *SCRAP...*(1973); *Sierra Club* v. *Morton...*(1972); *Data Processing Service* v. *Camp...*(1970). MHDC is a nonprofit corporation. Its interest in building Lincoln Green stems not from a desire for economic gain, but rather from an interest in making suitable low-cost housing available in areas where such housing is scarce. This is not mere abstract concern about a problem of general interest.... The specific project MHDC intends to build, whether or not it will generate profits, provides that "essential dimension of specificity" that informs judicial decisionmaking. *Schlesinger* v. *Reservists Committee to Stop the War...*(1974).

B

Clearly MHDC has met the constitutional requirements and it therefore has standing to assert its own rights. Foremost among them is MHDC's right to be free of arbitrary or irrational zoning actions.... *Euclid* v. *Ambler Realty Co....*(1926); *Nectow* v. *Cambridge...*(1928); *Village of Belle Terre* v. *Boraas...*(1974). But the heart of this litigation has never been the claim that the Village's decision fails the generous *Euclid* test, recently reaffirmed in *Belle Terre.* Instead it has been the claim that the Village's refusal to rezone discriminates against racial minorities in violation of the Fourteenth Amendment. As a corporation, MHDC has no racial identity and cannot be the direct target of the petitioners' alleged discrimination. In the ordinary case, a party is denied standing to assert the rights of third persons. *Warth* v. *Seldin...*(1975). But we need not decide whether the circumstances of this case would justify departure from that prudential limitation and permit MHDC to assert the constitutional rights of its prospective minority tenants.... For we have at least one individual plaintiff who has demonstrated standing to assert these rights as his own.

Respondent Ransom, a Negro, works at the Honeywell factory in Arlington Heights and lives approximately 20 miles away from Evanston in a 5-room house with his mother and his son. The complaint alleged that he seeks and would qualify for the housing MHDC wants to build in Arlington Heights. Ransom testified at trial that if Lincoln Green were built he would probably move there, since it is closer to his job.

The injury Ransom asserts is that his quest for housing nearer his employment has been thwarted by official action that is racially discriminatory. If a court grants the relief he seeks, there is at least a "substantial probability," *Warth* v. *Seldin*...that the Lincoln Green project will materialize, affording Ransom the housing opportunity he desires in Arlington Heights.... Unlike the individual plaintiffs in *Warth,* Ransom has adequately averred an "actionable causal relationship" between Arlington Heights' zoning practices and his asserted injury.... We therefore proceed to the merits.

III

Our decision last Term in *Washington* v. *Davis*...(1976), made it clear that official action will not be held unconstitutional solely because it results in a racially disproportionate impact. "Disproportionate impact is not irrelevant, but it is not the sole touchstone of an invidious racial discrimination." ...Proof of racially discriminatory intent or purpose is required to show a violation of the Equal Protection Clause. Although some contrary indications may be drawn from some of our cases, the holding in *Davis* reaffirmed a principle well established in a variety of contexts. *E. g., Keys* v. *School District No. 1*...(1973) (schools); *Wright* v. *Rockefeller*...(1964) (election districting); *Akins* v. *Texas*...(1945) (jury selection).

Davis does not require a plaintiff to prove that the challenged action rested solely on racially discriminatory purposes. Rarely can it be said that a legislature or administrative body operating under a broad mandate made a decision motivated solely by a single concern, or even that a particular purpose was the "dominant" or "primary" one. In fact, it is because legislators and administrators are properly concerned with balancing numerous competing considerations that courts refrain from reviewing the merits of their decisions, absent a showing of arbitrariness or irrationality. But racial discrimination is not just another competing consideration. When there is a proof that a discriminatory purpose has been a motivating factor in the decision, this judicial deference is no longer justified.

Determining whether invidious discriminatory purpose was a motivating factor demands a sensitive inquiry into such circumstantial and direct evidence of intent as may be available. The impact of the official action—whether it "bears more heavily on one race than another," *Washington* v. *Davis*...may provide an important starting point. Sometimes a clear pattern, unexplainable on grounds other than race, emerges from the effect of the state action even when the governing legislation appears neutral on its face.... The evidentiary inquiry is then relatively easy. But such cases are rare. Absent a pattern as stark as that in

Gomillion [v. *Lightfoot* (1960)] or *Yick Wo* [v. *Hopkins* (1886)], impact alone is not determinative, and the Court must look to other evidence.

The historical background of the decision is one evidentiary source, particularly if it reveals a series of official actions taken for invidious purposes.... The specific sequence of events leading up to the challenged decision also may shed some light on the decisionmaker's purposes.... For example, if the property involved here always had been zoned R-5 but suddenly was changed to R-3 when the town learned of MHDC's plans to erect integrated housing, we would have a far different case. Departures from the normal procedural sequence also might afford evidence that improper purposes are playing a role. Substantive departures too may be relevant, particularly if the factors usually considered important by the decision-maker strongly favor a decision contrary to the one reached.

The legislative or administrative history may be highly relevant, especially where there are contemporary statements by members of the decisionmaking body, minutes of its meetings, or reports. In some extraordinary instances the members might be called to the stand at trial to testify concerning the purpose of the official action, although even then such testimony frequently will be barred by privilege....

The foregoing summary identifies, without purporting to be exhaustive, subjects of proper inquiry in determining whether racially discriminatory intent existed. With these in mind, we now address the case before us.

IV

This case was tried in the District Court and reviewed in the Court of Appeals before our decision in *Washington* v. *Davis*.... The respondents proceeded on the erroneous theory that the Village's refusal to rezone carried a racially discriminatory effect and was, without more, unconstitutional. But both courts below understood that at least part of their function was to examine the purpose underlying the decision. In making its findings on this issue, the District Court noted that some of the opponents of Lincoln Green who spoke at the various hearings might have been motivated by opposition to minority groups. The court held, however, that the evidence "does not warrant the conclusion that this motivated the defendants."...

On appeal the Court of Appeals focused primarily on respondents' claim that the Village's buffer policy had not been consistently applied and was being invoked with a strictness here that could only demonstrate some other underlying motive. The court concluded that the buffer policy, though not always applied with perfect consistency, had on several occasions formed the basis for the Board's decision to deny other rezoning proposals. "The evidence does not necessitate a finding that Arlington Heights administered this policy in a discriminatory manner." ...The Court of Appeals therefore approved the District Court's findings concerning the Village's purposes in denying rezoning to MHDC.

We have reviewed the evidence. The impact of the Village's decision does arguably bear more heavily on racial minorities. Minorities comprise 18% of the Chicago area population, and 40% of the income groups said to be eligible for Lincoln Green. But there is little about the sequence of events leading up to the decision that would spark suspicion. The area around the Viatorian property has been zoned R-3 since 1959, the year when Arlington Heights first adopted a zoning map. Single-family homes surround the 80-acre site, and the Village is undeniably committed to single-family homes as its dominant residential land use. The rezoning request progressed according to the usual procedures. The Plan Commission even scheduled two additional hearings, at least in part to accommodate MHDC and permit it to supplement its presentation with answers to questions generated at the first hearing.

The statements by the Plan Commission and the Village Board members, as reflected in the official minutes, focused almost exclusively on the zoning aspects of the MHDC petition, and the zoning factors on which they relied are not novel criteria in the Village's rezoning decisions. There is no reason to doubt that there has been reliance by some neighboring property owners on the maintenance of single-family zoning in the vicinity. The Village originally adopted its buffer policy long before MHDC entered the picture and has applied the policy too consistently for us to infer discriminatory purpose from its application in this case. Finally, MHDC called one member of the Village Board to the stand at trial. Nothing in her testimony supports an inference of invidious purpose.

In sum, the evidence does not warrant overturning the concurrent findings of both courts below. Respondents simply failed to carry their burden of proving that discriminatory purpose was a motivating factor in the Village's decision.* This conclusion ends the constitutional inquiry. The Court of Appeals' further finding that the Village's decision carried a discriminatory "ultimate effect" is without independent constitutional significance.

V

Respondents' complaint also alleged that the refusal to rezone violated the Fair Housing Act…. They continue to urge here that a zoning decision made by a public body may, and that petitioners' action did, violate § 3604 or § 3617. The Court of Appeals, however, proceeding in a somewhat un-

---

* Proof that the decision by the Village was motivated in part by a racially discriminatory purpose would not necessarily have required invalidation of the challenged decision. Such proof would, however, have shifted to the Village the burden of establishing that the same decision would have resulted even had the impermissible purpose not been considered. If this were established, the complaining party in a case of this kind no longer fairly could attribute the injury complained of to improper consideration of a discriminatory purpose. In such circumstances, there would be no justification for judicial interference with the challenged decision. But in this case respondents failed to make the required threshold showing….

orthodox fashion, did not decide the statutory question. We remand the case for further consideration of respondents' statutory claims.

Reversed and remanded.

MR. JUSTICE MARSHALL, with whom MR. JUSTICE BRENNAN joins, concurring in part and dissenting in part.

I concur in Parts I-III of the Court's opinion. However, I believe the proper result would be to remand this entire case to the Court of Appeals for further proceedings consistent with *Washington* v. *Davis*...(1976), and today's opinion. The Court of Appeals is better situated than this Court both to reassess the significance of the evidence developed below in light of the standards we have set forth and to determine whether the interests of justice require further District Court proceedings directed towards those standards.

MR. JUSTICE WHITE, dissenting.

The Court reverses the judgment of the Court of Appeals because it finds, after re-examination of the evidence supporting the concurrent findings below, that "respondents failed to carry their burden of proving that discriminatory purpose was a motivating factor in the Village's decision." ...The court reaches this result by interpreting our decision in *Washington* v. *Davis*...(1976), and applying it to this case, notwithstanding that the Court of Appeals rendered its decision in this case before *Washington* v. *Davis* was handed down, and thus did not have the benefit of our decision when it found a Fourteenth Amendment violation.

The Court gives no reason for its failure to follow our usual practice in this situation of vacating the judgment below and remanding in order to permit the lower court to reconsider its ruling in light of our intervening decision. The Court's articulation of a legal standard nowhere mentioned in *Davis* indicates that it feels that the application of *Davis* to these facts calls for substantial analysis. If this is true, we would do better to allow the Court of Appeals to attempt that analysis in the first instance. Given that the Court deems it necessary to re-examine the evidence in the case in light of the legal standard it adopts, a remand is especially appropriate. As the cases relied upon by the Court indicate, the primary function of this Court is not to review the evidence supporting findings of the lower courts.... A further justification for remanding on the constitutional issue is that a remand is required in any event on respondents' Fair Housing Act claim...not yet addressed by the Court of Appeals. While conceding that a remand is necessary because of the Court of Appeals' "unorthodox" approach of deciding the constitutional issue without reaching the statutory claim...the Court refuses to allow the Court of Appeals to reconsider its constitutional holding in light of *Davis* should it become necessary to reach that issue.

Even if I were convinced that it was proper for the Court to reverse the judgment below on the basis of an intervening decision of this Court and after a re-examination of concurrent findings of fact below, I believe it is wholly unnecessary for the Court to embark on a lengthy discussion of the standard for proving the racially discriminatory purpose required by *Davis* for a Fourteenth Amendment violation. The District Court found that the Village was motivated "by a legitimate desire to protect property values and the integrity of the Village's zoning plan." The Court of Appeals accepted this finding as not clearly erroneous, and the Court quite properly refuses to overturn it on review here. There is thus no need for this Court to list various "evidentiary sources" or "subjects of proper inquiry" in determining whether a racially discriminatory purpose existed.

I would vacate the judgment of the Court of Appeals and remand the case for consideration of the statutory issue and, if necessary, for consideration of the constitutional issue in light of *Washington* v. *Davis*.

STATE OF THE
UNION MESSAGE
January 12, 1977

Gerald R. Ford, 38th President of the United States, went before an evening joint session of Congress Jan. 12 to deliver his third and final State of the Union message. Ford reported that the state of the union was "good" and that "today we have a more perfect union than when my stewardship began."

Ford received a warm and enthusiastic reception on Capitol Hill and drew laughter when he told Congress in a teasing way: "This report will be my last—maybe." The President used the occasion of his final official appearance before Congress to highlight what he felt was a solid record of re-establishing peace, stability and economic health to a nation that had none of those things when he entered office Aug. 9, 1974, following the resignation of Richard M. Nixon. Ford contrasted the condition of the nation with that prevailing when he gave Congress his first message Jan. 13, 1975. (Historic Documents of 1975, p. 15; 1976, p. 13). The President voiced particular pride for the part he played in "rebuilding confidence in the Presidency, confidence in our free system and confidence in our future. Once again Americans believe in themselves, in their leaders, and in the promise that tomorrow holds for their children."

Throughout the message Ford praised the advantages of the American social and political system. He had no main theme to develop in his speech and his message contained no surprises. The President had no program to recommend to Congress and preferred, as he said, not to "infringe" on President-elect Jimmy Carter's responsibility for legislative recommendations.

Ford dwelled at length on issues of national defense and strategic competition with the Soviet Union. He implicitly criticized his predecessors for a 15-year period when domestic spending "soared" while "our national security needs were steadily shortchanged." The President added that America's first priority was "peace with honor." America must remain first in keeping peace in the world, Ford continued, and "we can remain first in peace only if we are never second in defense." Saying that the United States "can never tolerate a shift in the strategic balance against us," Ford reiterated his support of weapons systems including the Trident submarine, the B-1 bomber, and an advanced intercontinental ballistic missile (ICBM) that could survive nuclear attack. The President urged Congress to re-examine its role in international affairs, and reminded Congress to respect the presidential war-waging powers: "There can be only one commander-in-chief."

The message expressed optimism on the domestic front. The President said he was encouraged by the continued recovery from recession. The nation, Ford said, was on a path "to sound economic growth." His greatest regret as he left office, Ford observed, was that there were still "too many Americans unemployed." He urged his successor to follow "prudent policies that encourage productive investment and discourage destructive inflation" and "we will come out on top." He wished his successor "the very best."

In addition to high unemployment, other disappointments noted by the President included the absence of "satisfactory progress" toward energy independence. He urged Congress and the new administration to move quickly on energy issues. Ford also expressed disappointment in his inability to complete organizational reforms for the federal government and said that Congress had "sidetracked" most of his requests for authority to carry out his various proposals.

Ford's memories of his 25 years as a member of the House of Representatives brought tears to his eyes at the conclusion of his speech as he recalled "many a lively battle" he fought with friends in the House chamber. Ford thanked his former colleagues for "all those memories and the many, many kindnesses." The outgoing President concluded with the hope that the nation's third century would "be illuminated by liberty and blessed with brotherhood...."

Following is the text of Gerald R. Ford's third State of the Union address, delivered Jan. 12, 1977. (Boldface headings in brackets have been added by Congressional Quarterly to highlight the organization of the text.):

To the Congress of the United States:
    In accordance with the Constitution, I come before you once again to report on the State of the Union.
    This report will be my last, maybe.

But for the Union, it is only the first of such reports in our Third Century of Independence, the close of which none of us will ever see. We can be confident, however, that 100 years from now a freely elected President will come before a freely elected Congress chosen to renew our great Republic's pledge to Government of the people, by the people, and for the people.

For my part, I pray the Third Century we are beginning will bring to all Americans, our children and their children's children, a greater measure of individual equality, opportunity and justice, a greater abundance of spiritual and material blessings, and a higher quality of life, liberty and the pursuit of happiness.

The State of the Union is a measurement of the many elements of which it is composed—a political union of diverse states, an economic union of varying interests, an intellectual union of common convictions and a moral union of immutable ideals.

Taken in sum, I can report that the State of the Union is good. There is room for improvement as always, but today we have a more perfect union than when my stewardship began.

As a people, we discovered that our Bicentennial was much more than a celebration of the past; it became a joyous reaffirmation of all that it means to be Americans, a confirmation before all the world of the vitality and durability of our free institutions.

I am proud to have been privileged to preside over the affairs of our Federal Government during these eventful years when we proved, as I said in my first words upon assuming office, that "our Constitution works; our Great Republic is a Government of laws and not of men; here, the people rule."

The people have spoken; they have chosen a new President and a new Congress to work their will; I congratulate you—particularly the new members—as sincerely as I did President-elect Carter. In a few days, it will be his duty to outline for you his priorities and legislative recommendations. Tonight, I will not infringe on that responsibility, but rather wish him the very best in all that is good for our country.

During the period of my own service in this Capitol and in the White House I can recall many orderly transitions of governmental responsibility—of problems as well as of position, of burdens as well as of power. The genius of the American system is that we do this so naturally and so normally; there are no soldiers marching in the streets except in the Inaugural Parade; no public demonstrations except for some of the dancers at the Inaugural Ball; the opposition party doesn't go underground but goes on functioning vigorously in the Congress and the country; and our vigilant press goes right on probing and publishing our faults and our follies, confirming the wisdom of the framers of the First Amendment.

Because the transfer of authority in our form of government affects the state of the union, and of the world, I am happy to report to you that the current transition is proceeding very well. I was determined that it should; I wanted the new President to get off to an easier start than I had.

When I became President on August 9, 1974, our Nation was deeply divided and tormented. In rapid succession, the Vice President and the President had resigned in disgrace. We were still struggling with the after-effects of a long, unpopular and bloody war in Southeast Asia. The economy was unstable and racing toward the worst recession in 40 years. People were losing jobs. The cost of living was soaring. The Congress and the Chief Executive were at loggerheads. The integrity of our Constitutional process and of other institutions was being questioned.

For more than 15 years, domestic spending had soared as Federal programs multiplied and the expense escalated annually. During the same period, our national security needs were steadily shortchanged.

In the grave situation which prevailed in August 1974, our will to maintain our international leadership was in doubt.

I asked for your prayers, and went to work.

In January 1975, I reported to the Congress that the state of the union was not good. I proposed urgent action to improve the economy and to achieve energy independence in ten years. I reassured America's allies and sought to reduce the danger of confrontation with potential adversaries. I pledged a new direction for America.

Nineteen seventy-five was a year of difficult decisions, but Americans responded with realism, common sense and self-discipline.

By January 1976, we were headed in a new direction, which I hold to be the right direction for a free society. I was guided by the belief that successful problem-solving requires more than Federal action alone; that it involves a full partnership among all branches and levels of government, and public policies which nurture and promote the creative energies of private enterprises, institutions and individual citizens.

A year ago, I reported that the state of the union was better—in many ways a lot better—but still not good enough.

Common sense told me to stick to the steady course we were on, to continue to restrain the inflationary growth of government, to reduce taxes as well as spending, to return local decisions to local officials, to provide for long-range sufficiency in energy and national security needs. I resisted the immense pressures of an election year to open the floodgates of Federal money and the temptation to promise more than I could deliver. I told it as it was to the American people and demonstrated to the world that, in our spirited political competition, as in this chamber, Americans can disagree without being disagreeable.

[Signs of Progress]

Now, after 30 months as your President I can say that while we still have a way to go, I am proud of the long way we have come together.

I am proud of the part I have had in rebuilding confidence in the Presidency, confidence in our free system and confidence in our future. Once again, Americans believe in themselves, in their leaders, and in the promise that tomorrow holds for their children.

I am proud that today America is at peace. None of our sons are fighting and dying in battle anywhere in the world. And the chance for peace among all nations is improved by our determination to honor our vital commitments in the defense of peace and freedom.

I am proud that the United States has strong defenses, strong alliances and a sound and courageous foreign policy.

—Our alliances with our major partners, the great industrial democracies of Western Europe, Japan, and Canada, have never been more solid. Consultations on mutual security, defense and East-West relations have grown closer. Collaboration has branched out into new fields, such as energy, economic policy and relations with the Third World.

We have used many avenues for cooperation, including summit meetings held among major allied countries. The friendship of the democracies is deeper, warmer and more effective than at any time in 30 years.

—We are maintaining stability in the strategic nuclear balance, and pushing back the spectre of nuclear war. A decisive step forward was taken in the Vladivostok Accord which I negotiated with General Secretary Brezhnev—joint recognition that an equal ceiling should be placed on the number of strategic weapons on each side.

With resolve and wisdom on the part of both nations, a good agreement is well within reach this year.

—The framework for peace in the Middle East has been built. Hopes for future progress in the Middle East were stirred by the historic agreements we reached and the trust and confidence we formed.

—Thanks to American leadership, the prospects for peace in the Middle East are brighter than they have been in three decades. The Arab states and Israel continue to look to us to lead them from confrontation and war to a new era of accommodation and peace. We have no alternative but to persevere and I'm sure we will. The opportunities for a final settlement are great, and the price of failure is a return to the bloodshed and hatred that for too long have brought tragedy to all the peoples of this area, and repeatedly edged the world to the brink of war.

—Our relationship with the People's Republic of China is proving its importance and its durability. We are finding more and more common ground between our two countries on basic questions of international affairs.

In my two trips to Asia as President, we have reaffirmed America's continuing vital interest in the peace and security of Asia and the Pacific Basin, established a new partnership with Japan, confirmed our dedication to the security of Korea, and reinforced our ties with the free nations of Southeast Asia.

—An historic dialogue has begun between industrial nations and the developing nations. Most proposals on the table are the initiatives of the United States, including those on food, energy, technology, trade, investment and commodities. We are well launched on this process of shaping positive and reliable economic relations between rich nations and poor nations over the long-term.

—We have made progress in trade negotiations and avoided protectionism during recession. We strengthened the international monetary system. During the past two years the free world's most important economic powers have already brought about important changes that serve both developed and developing economies. The momentum already achieved must be nurtured and strengthened, for the prosperity of rich and poor depends upon it.

—In Latin America, our relations have taken on a new maturity and a sense of common enterprise.

—In Africa, the quest for peace, racial justice and economic progress is at a crucial point. The United States, in close cooperation with the United Kingdom, is actively engaged in that historic process. Will change come about by warfare and chaos and foreign intervention? Or will it come about by negotiated and fair solutions, ensuring majority rule, minority rights and economic advance? America is committed to the side of peace and justice, and to the principle that Africa should shape its own future free of outside intervention.

—American leadership has helped to stimulate new international efforts to stem the proliferation of nuclear weapons and to shape a comprehensive treaty governing the use of the oceans.

I am gratified by these accomplishments. They constitute a record of broad success for America, and for the peace and prosperity of all mankind. This Administration leaves to its successor a world in better condition than we found. We leave, as well, a solid foundation for progress on a range of issues that are vital to the well being of America.

What has been achieved in the field of foreign affairs, and what can be accomplished by the new administration, demonstrate the genius of Americans working together for the common good. It is this, our remarkable ability to work together, that has made us a unique nation. It is Congress, the President, and the people striving for a better world.

I know all patriotic Americans want this Nation's foreign policy to succeed.

I urge members of my party in this Congress to give the new President loyal support in this area.

I express the hope that this new Congress will re-examine its constitutional role in international affairs.

The exclusive right to declare war, the duty to advise and consent on the part of the Senate, and the power of the purse on the part of the House, are ample authority for the legislative branch and should be jealously guarded.

But because we may have been too careless of these powers in the past does not justify congressional intrusion into, or obstruction of, the proper exercise of Presidential responsibilities now or in the future. There can be only one Commander-in-Chief. In these times crises cannot be managed and wars cannot be waged by committee. Nor can peace be pursued solely by parliamentary debate. To the ears of the world, the President speaks for the Nation. While he is, of course, ultimately accountable to the Congress, the courts and the people, he and his emissaries must not be handicapped in advance in their relations with foreign governments as has sometimes happened in the past.

[Economic Recovery]

At home, I am encouraged by the Nation's recovery from the recession and our steady return to sound economic growth. It is now continuing after the recent period of uncertainty, which is part of the price we pay for free elections.

Our most pressing need today and in the future is more jobs—productive and permanent jobs created by a thriving economy.

We must revise our tax system both to ease the burden of heavy taxation and to encourage the investment necessary for the creation of productive jobs for all Americans who want to work. Earlier this month I proposed a permanent income tax reduction of ten billion dollars below current levels including raising the personal exemption from $750 to $1,000. I also recommended a series of measures to stimulate investment, such as accelerated depreciation for new plants and equipment in areas of high unemployment, a reduction in the corporate tax rate from 48 to 46 per cent, and eliminating the present double taxation of dividends. I strongly urge the Congress to pass these measures to help create the productive, permanent jobs in the private economy that are essential to our future. All of the basic trends are good; we are not on the brink of another recession or economic disaster. If we follow prudent policies that encourage productive investment and discourage destructive inflation, we will come out on top, and I'm sure we will.

We have successfully cut inflation by more than half: when I took office, the Consumer Price Index was rising at 12.2 per cent a year. During 1976, the rate of inflation was five per cent.

We have created more jobs. Over four million more people have jobs today than in the spring of 1975. Throughout this nation today we have over 88 million people in useful, productive jobs—more than at any other time in our nation's history. But, there are still too many Americans unemployed. This is the greatest regret that I have as I leave office.

We brought about with the Congress, after much delay, the renewal of general revenue sharing. We expanded community development and federal manpower programs. We began a significant urban mass transit program. Federal programs today provide more funds for our states and local governments than ever before—$70-billion for the current fiscal year.

Through these programs and others that provide aid directly to individuals we have kept faith with our tradition of compassionate help for those who need it. As we begin our third century we can be proud of the progress we have made in meeting human needs for all of our citizens.

We have cut the growth of crime by nearly 90 per cent. Two years ago, crime was increasing at a rate of 18 per cent annually. In the first three quarters of 1976, that growth rate had been cut to two per cent. But crime, and the fear of crime, remains one of the most serious problems facing our citizens.

We have had some successes. And there have been some disappointments.

Bluntly, I must remind you that we have not made satisfactory progress toward achieving energy independence.

[Energy]

Energy is absolutely vital to the defense of our country, to the strength of our economy, and to the quality of our lives. Two years ago I proposed to the Congress the first comprehensive national energy program:

A specific and coordinated set of measures that would end our vulnerability to embargo, blockade, or arbitrary price increases, and would mobilize U.S. technology and resources to supply a significant share of the free world's energy needs after 1985.

Of the major energy proposals I submitted two years ago, only half belatedly became law. In 1973, we were dependent upon foreign oil imports for 36 per cent of our needs. Today we are 40 per cent dependent, and we'll pay out 34 billion U.S. dollars for foreign oil this year. Such vulnerability at present or in the future is intolerable and must be ended.

The answer to where we stand on our national energy effort today reminds me of the old argument over whether the tank is half full or half empty. The pessimist will say we have half failed to achieve our ten-year energy goals, the optimist will say that we have half succeeded. I am always an optimist, but we must make up for lost time.

We have laid a solid foundation for completing the enormous task which confronts us. I have signed into law five major energy bills which contain significant measures for conservation, resource development, stockpiling and standby authorities.

We have moved forward to develop the Naval Petroleum Reserves; to build a five hundred-million barrel strategic petroleum stockpile; to phase-out unnecessary government allocation and price controls; to develop a lasting relationship with other oil consuming nations; to improve the efficiency of energy use through conservation in automobiles, buildings and industry; and to expand research on new technology and renewable resources, such as wind power, geothermal and solar energy.

All these actions, significant as they are for the long term, are only the beginning. I recently submitted to the Congress my proposals to reorganize the federal energy structure, and the hard choices which remain if we are serious about reducing our dependence upon foreign energy.

These include programs to reverse our declining production of natural gas and increase incentives for domestic crude oil production. I propose to minimize environmental uncertainties affecting coal development, expand nuclear power generation and create an energy independence authority to provide government financial assistance for vital energy programs where private capital is not available.

We must explore every reasonable prospect for meeting our energy needs when our current domestic reserves of oil and natural gas begin to dwindle in the next decade.

I urgently ask Congress and the new Administration to move quickly on these issues. This Nation has the resources and capability to achieve our energy goals if its government has the will to proceed and I think we do.

[Reorganization]

I have been disappointed by inability to complete many of the meaningful organizational reforms which I contemplated for the Federal Government, although a start has been made.

For example, the Federal Judicial System has long served as a model for other courts. But today it is threatened by a shortage of qualified Federal judges and an explosion of litigation claiming Federal jurisdiction.

I commend to the new Administration and the Congress the recent report and recommendations of the Department of Justice, undertaken at my request, on "the needs of the Federal Courts." I especially endorse its proposals for a new commission on the judicial appointment process.

While the Judicial Branch of our Government may require reinforcement, the budgets and payrolls of the other branches remain staggering. I cannot help but observe that while the White House Staff and the Executive Office of the President have been reduced and the total number of civilians in the Executive Branch contained during the 1970s, the Legislative Branch has increased substantially, although the membership of the Congress remains at 535. Congress now costs the taxpayers more than a million dollars a year per member; the whole Legislative budget has passed the billion dollar mark.

I set out to reduce the growth in the size and spending of the Federal Government, but no President can accomplish this alone. The Congress sidetracked most of my requests for authority to consolidate overlapping programs and agencies, to return more decision-making and responsibility to State and local governments through block grants instead of rigid categorical programs and to eliminate unnecessary red tape and outrageously complex regulations.

We have made some progress in cutting back the expansion of Government and its intrusion into individual lives—but believe me, there is much more to be done and you and I know it. It can only be done by tough and temporarily painful surgery by a Congress as prepared as the President to face up to this very real political problem.

Again, I wish my successor, working with a substantial majority of his own party, the best of success in reforming the costly and cumbersome machinery of the Federal Government.

The task of self-government is never finished. The problems are great; the opportunities are greater.

[Defense]

America's first goal is and always will be peace with honor. America must remain first in keeping peace in the world. We can remain first in peace only if we are never second in defense.

In presenting the State of the Union to the Congress and to the American people, I have a special obligation as Commander-in-Chief to report on our national defense. Our survival as a free and independent people requires, above all, strong military forces that are well-equipped and highly trained to perform their assigned mission.

I am particularly gratified to report that over the past two and a half years we have been able to reverse the dangerous decline of the previous decade in the real resources this country was devoting to national defense. This was an immediate problem I faced in 1974. The evidence was unmistakable that the Soviet Union had been steadily increasing the resources it applied to building its military strength.

During this same period the United States' real defense spending declined. In my three budgets, we not only arrested that dangerous decline, but we have established the positive trend which is essential to our ability to contribute to peace and stability in the world.

The Vietnam War both materially and psychologically affected our overall defense posture. The dangerous antimilitary sentiment discouraged defense spending and unfairly disparaged the men and women who served in our armed forces.

The challenge that now confronts this country is whether we have the national will and determination to continue this essential defense effort over the long term, as it must be continued. We can no longer afford to oscillate from year to year in so vital a matter. Indeed, we have a duty to look beyond the immediate question of budgets, and to examine the nature of the problem we will face over the next generation.

I am the first recent President able to address long-term basic issues without the burden of Vietnam. The war in Indochina consumed enormous resources, at the very time that the overwhelming strategic superiority we once enjoyed was disappearing. In past years, as a result of decisions by the United States, our strategic forces levelled off. Yet, the Soviet Union continued a steady, constant build-up of its own forces, committing a high percentage of its national economic effort to defense.

The United States can never tolerate a shift in the strategic balance against us, or even a situation where the American people or our allies believe the balance is shifting against us. The United States would risk the most serious political consequences if the world came to believe that our adversaries have a decisive margin of superiority. To maintain a strategic balance we must look ahead to the 1980s and beyond. The sophistication of modern weapons requires that we make decisions now if we are to ensure our security ten years from now.

Therefore I have consistently advocated and strongly urged that we pursue three critical strategic programs: the Trident missile launching submarine; the B-1 bomber, with its superior capability to penetrate modern air defenses; and a more advanced intercontinental ballistic missile that will be better able to survive nuclear attack and deliver a devastating retaliatory strike.

In an era where the strategic nuclear forces are in rough equilibrium, the risks of conflict below the nuclear threshold may grow more perilous. A major long-term objective, therefore, is to maintain capabilities to deal with, and thereby deter, conventional challenges and crises, particularly in Europe.

We cannot rely solely on strategic forces to guarantee our security or to deter all types of aggression. We must have superior Naval and Marine forces to maintain freedom of the seas, strong multi-purpose tactical Air Forces, and mobile, modern ground forces.

Accordingly: I have directed a long-term effort to improve our worldwide capabilities to deal with regional crises.

—I have submitted a five year Naval building program indispensable to the Nation's maritime strategy.

—Because the security of Europe and the integrity of NATO remain the cornerstone of American defense policy, I have initiated a special, long-term program to ensure the capacity of the alliance to deter or defeat aggression in Europe.

As I leave office, I can report that our national defense is effectively deterring conflict today. Our Armed Forces are capable of carrying out the variety of missions assigned to them. Programs are underway which will assure we can deter war in the years ahead.

But I also must warn that it will require a sustained effort over a period of years to maintain these capabilities. We must have the wisdom, the stamina and the courage to prepare today for the perils of tomorrow, and I believe we will.

As I look to the future—and I assure you I intend to go on doing that for a good many years—I can say with confidence that the State of the Union is good, but we must go on making it better and better.

This gathering symbolizes the Constitutional foundation which makes continued progress possible, synchronizing the skills of three independent branches of government, reserving fundamental sovereignty to the people of this great land.

It is only as the temporary representatives and servants of the people that we meet here—we bring no hereditary status or gift of infallibility and none follows us from this place. Like President Washington, like the more fortunate of his successors, I look forward to the status of private citizen with gladness and gratitude. To me, being a citizen of the United States of America is the greatest honor and privilege in this world.

From the opportunities which fate and my fellow citizens have given me, as a member of the House, as Vice President and President of the Senate, and as President of all the people, I have come to understand and to place the highest value on the checks and balances which our founders imposed on government through the separation of powers, among co-equal Legislative, Executive and Judicial Branches.

This often results in difficulty and delay, as I well know, but it also places supreme authority under God, beyond any one person, any one branch, any majority great or small, or any one party. The Constitution is the bedrock of all our freedoms; guard and cherish it; keep honor and order in your own house; and the Republic will endure.

It is not easy to end these remarks; in this chamber, along with some of you, I have experienced many, many of the highlights of my life. It was here that I stood 28 years ago with my freshman colleagues as Speaker Sam Rayburn administered the oath—I see some of you now, Charlie Bennett, Dick Bolling, Carl Perkins, Pete Rodino, Harley Staggers, Tom Steed, Sid Yates and Clem Zablocki, and I remember those who have gone to their rest.

It was here we waged many, many a lively battle, won some, lost some, but always remaining friends. It was here surrounded by such friends, that the distinguished Chief Justice swore me in as Vice President on December 6, 1973. It was here I returned eight months later as your President to ask you not for a honeymoon, but for a good marriage.

I will always treasure those memories and the many, many kindnesses. I thank you for them.

My fellow Americans, I once asked for your prayers, and now I give you mine: May God guide this wonderful country, its people, and those they have chosen to lead them. May our third century be illuminated by liberty and blessed with brotherhood, so that we and all who come after us may be the humble servants of thy peace. Amen.

Good night and God bless you.

GERALD R. FORD

THE WHITE HOUSE,
January 12, 1977.

FORD'S BUDGET MESSAGE

January 17, 1977

On Jan. 17—three days before the end of his term—President Ford sent Congress a proposed budget for fiscal 1978. The budget document was an outline of Ford's philosophy of government priorities, which had often differed dramatically from the priorities of the Democratic Congress over the 30 months of his administration. It contained many familiar proposals which Ford had offered in the past and Congress had either ignored or voted down. The budget also reflected Ford's priorities by focusing attention on the five-year impact of spending decisions, on the dimensions of spending by agencies not included in the regular budget and on the steady increases in individual income taxes that resulted from inflation. (Carter budget revisions, p. 125; Historic Documents of 1976, p. 37)

In looking beyond the fiscal year beginning Oct. 1, 1977, Ford was unable to fulfill one campaign promise. He had pledged that if re-elected, he would submit a balanced budget for fiscal 1979, which would begin Oct. 1, 1978. In his budget message, Ford said he was unable to propose that without making deeper program cuts than he felt were justified and without dropping proposals for individual income tax relief. Instead, his estimates showed the budget "fairly close to balance" in fiscal 1979 with an $11.6-billion deficit, followed by a surplus of $13.4-billion in fiscal 1980 and increasing surpluses after that. The surpluses could have been larger under current law, the budget pointed out, but Ford coupled with his spending projections a plan to cut individual taxes in fiscal years 1980-82 to offset the automatic increases brought about by inflation and by economic growth.

Ford proposed outlays of $440-billion in fiscal 1978 and estimated receipts at $393-billion for a deficit of $47-billion. The growth in spending was 7 per cent over the estimate of $411.2-billion for fiscal 1977 and was, Ford said in his budget message, "a marked slowdown" in the rate of growth which had averaged 10 per cent per year over the past decade. The proposed level of spending was $5.4-billion below the estimated "current services" level of spending—that is, the cost of continuing current programs and government activities without policy changes. Ford's estimate of receipts of $393-billion was $14.6-billion below the amount that could be expected to be generated by current law, because of the income tax cuts he had proposed earlier and reiterated in the budget.

The budget called for budget authority in fiscal 1978 of $480.4-billion. About 65 per cent of that, according to the budget, would require action by Congress to become available. The other 35 per cent was available through previous legislative action. Budget authority exceeds outlays because it covers the full cost of such things as construction and procurement programs, subsidy contracts and long-term financing costs, in which payments actually are made over a period of at least several years.

The budget document also gave updated estimates for fiscal 1977, which ended Sept. 30, 1977. It estimated receipts of $354-billion and outlays of $411.2-billion, resulting in a deficit of $57.2-billion. Those figures differed considerably from the July 15, 1976, estimates by the Office of Management and Budget (OMB) of receipts of $352.5-billion, outlays of $400-billion and a deficit of $47.5-billion.

Program Increases and Reductions

In arriving at outlays $5.4-billion less than a straight extension of current policy, Ford proposed program increases totaling $7-billion and cuts totaling $12.4-billion. While the increases were spread throughout the budget, the most costly were in the areas of defense modernization and procurement, research and development; changes in Medicare benefits; expansion of park lands; energy research and development; mass transit grants and airport development; and education assistance grants. Nearly one-third of the proposed increases fell into the national defense category. If the proposals were put into effect, the total program expansions would grow from $7-billion in fiscal 1978 to $15.7-billion in fiscal 1979.

In proposing program reductions, Ford said in his budget message: "Members of the Congress must begin to share the burden of the President in saying no to special interest groups—even those in their own districts or states." The heaviest cuts predictably fell into the domestic assistance categories and were similar to proposals Ford had made earlier in his administration. The proposals included limited rises in Medicare hospital reimbursement and charging beneficiaries for some of their costs, consolidating 15 child nutrition programs into a single block grant, revising food stamp eligibility and administration, eliminating the earned income *tax credit for low-income families, phasing out temporary employment assistance, and focusing on direct student assistance. Other large cuts included limiting GI bill eligibility, eliminating certain retroactive Social Security benefits, limiting federal impact aid for school districts and disposing of excess defense stockpile materials. If all the cutbacks were implemented, the budget estimated that total savings would rise to $22.4-billion in fiscal 1979.*

Congressional Reaction

Reaction in Congress showed that members remained as opposed to many of Ford's proposals as when they were initially offered. Rep. Robert N. Giaimo (D Conn.), chairman of the House Budget Committee, said of the proposed budget Jan. 17: "Unfortunately, it simply does not deal adequately with either the nation's severe economic problems, or with the needs of millions of our citizens. In short, it continues the President's basically conservative approach which was rejected by the nation two months ago." Giaimo pointed out that Congress had restored to current service levels many programs that Ford had proposed cutting the previous year. "I think Congress will retain its commitment to those programs," he said. "I think Mr. Ford knew that when he sent his proposals up here."

Senate Budget Committee Chairman Edmund S. Muskie (D Maine) said that the proposals reflected the administration's posture of the past two years. "His consolidation proposals remain as unworkable, his savings assumptions as unrealistic and his regressive tax proposals as unacceptable as when he introduced them before."

An analysis by the Senate Budget Committee said Ford's budget essentially would have no stimulative effect on the economy compared to current policy, and that its estimate of 5 per cent real growth in the economy resulted from optimism about the strength of the private sector rather than from any fiscal prescriptions. The budget also would do less than current policy to reduce unemployment, the analysis said. The Congressional Budget Office estimated that 250,000 fewer persons would be employed under Ford's proposals than under an extension of current policies.

Following is the text of President Ford's fiscal 1978 budget message, sent to Congress on Jan. 17, 1977. (Boldface headings in brackets have been added by Congressional Quarterly to highlight the organization of the text.):

To the Congress of the United States:

The budget is the President's blueprint for the operation of the Government in the year ahead. It records his views on priorities and directions for the future—balancing the American desire to solve every perceived problem at once with the practical reality of limited resources and competing needs.

The thirty budgets I have either shaped or helped to shape are a chronicle of our lives and times. They tell us what we have aspired to be and what we have been in fact. They tell us about the growing complexity of our society, about the changing and growing role of our Government, and about new problems we have identified and our attempts to solve them.

In shaping my budgets as President, I have sought to renew the basic questions about the composition and direction of the Government and its programs. In my reviews of existing and proposed programs and activities I have asked:

—Is this activity important to our national security or sense of social equity?

—Is this activity sufficiently important to require that we tax our people or borrow funds to pay for it?

—Must the federal government raise the taxes or borrow the funds or should state or local government do so?

—Should the federal government direct and manage the activity or should it limit its role to the provision of financing?

—How has the program performed in the past? Have the benefits outweighed the costs in dollars or other burdens imposed?

—Have the benefits gone to the intended beneficiary?

—Does this activity conflict with or overlap another?

As a result of these reviews I have proposed to reverse some trends and to accelerate others.

[Government Spending Slowdown]

I have proposed, and repropose this year, a marked slowdown in the rate of growth in government spending. Over the last three decades, federal, state, and local government spending has grown from 18 per cent of GNP to 34 per cent of GNP. Federal spending growth alone has averaged 10 per cent per year over the last decade. And even these percentages do not tell the whole story. As the budget documents illustrate, there has been a trend over the last few years toward so-called "off-budget" spending. This is an undesirable practice because it obscures the real impact of the federal government and makes it more difficult for any but the most technically knowledgeable citizens to understand what their government is doing. Therefore, I am calling for legislation to halt this practice so that our budget system will fully reflect the financial activities of the government.

In a related attempt to gain greater control over the rate of growth of government spending I have given special attention this year to spending plans for fiscal year 1979, the year after the budget year. For the first time, the federal budget shows detailed planning amounts for the year beyond the budget year. This innovation grows out of my conviction that our only real hope of curbing the growth of federal spending is to plan further in advance and to discipline ourselves to stick to those plans.

From the standpoint of deficits of most recent years the 1978 budget I present shows us fairly close to balance in 1979 and shows balanced budgets thereafter. The effects on 1978 and 1979 spending of congressional action in the last session rejecting many of the restraints I proposed for the current fiscal year, 1977, made total balance in 1979 impossible unless I was willing to abandon, at least in part, the further immediate tax relief I have advocated since October of 1975 and, for no reason other than being able to show such a 1979 balance, cut back from program levels I feel are justified. These alternatives were unacceptable, but given the greatly reduced deficit for 1979 this budget implies, congressional cooperation on the restraints I propose and a slightly better economic performance in the months ahead than we have used in preparing this 1978 budget, it is entirely possible that when the 1979 budget is due to be submitted, a year from now, it could be in total balance as I have strived to achieve.

[Permanent Tax Cuts Sought]

With restraint on the growth of federal spending, we can begin to provide for permanent tax reductions to ease the burden on middle-income taxpayers and businesses. For too long government has presumed that it is "entitled" to the additional tax revenues generated as inflation and increases in real income push taxpayers into higher brackets. We need to reverse this presumption. We need to put the burden of proof on the government to demonstrate the reasons why individuals and businesses should not keep the income and wealth they produce. Accordingly, my long-term budget projections assume further tax relief will be provided, rather than presuming, as has been the practice in the past, that positive margins of receipts over expenditures that show up in projections are "surpluses" or "fiscal dividends" that must be used primarily for more federal spending, on existing or new programs or both.

One trend has been reversed in the past two years. After several years of decline in real spending for national security purposes the Congress has agreed in substantial part to my recommendations for increases in defense spending. The budget I propose this year and the planning levels for the succeeding four years assume a continuation of this real growth trend. My recommendations are the result of a careful assessment of our own defense posture and that of our potential adversaries. In this area as in all others, I am recommending spending I consider essential while at the same time proposing savings in outmoded or unwarranted activities. For the longer term, my recommendations recognize the simple fact that we must plan now for the defense systems we will need 10 years from now.

[Higher R&D Spending Urged]

This same approach was reflected last year in my recommendations for the federal government's basic research and development programs. In spite of the financial pressures on the federal budget, I recommended real growth. I am again proposing real growth for basic research and development programs this year because I am convinced that we must maintain our world leadership in science and technology in order to increase our national productivity and attain the better life we want for our people and the rest of the world.

I am also calling again for an end to the proliferation of new federal programs and for consolidation of many of the programs we now have. At last count there are 1,044 programs identified in the Catalog of Federal Domestic Assistance. While our nation has many needs, there is no rational justification for the maze that has been created.

Overlap and duplication are not the only defects of these programs; nor are they the most serious. More importantly the current programs too often fail to aid the intended beneficiaries, rewarding instead those who have learned how to work the Washington system. Some of these programs fail to pinpoint responsibility and accountability for performance and too many of them impose a managerial and operating burden on the federal government, diverting attention from the functions that must be performed at the federal level and at the same time usurping the proper roles of state and local governments and the private sector.

[Program Reforms Needed]

If we could ever afford the "luxury" of this inefficiency and ineptitude, we can no longer. Federal programs for health services, elementary and secondary education, child nutrition and welfare, for example, are areas that desperately need reform. I called for action last year and prepared detailed legislative proposals. Those who truly care about the needs of our people will not let another year go by without reform. There is no excuse, for example, for the federal government to have 15 different child nutrition programs spending over $3-billion per year and still have 700,000 children from families below the poverty line who receive no aid. Nor is there any reason to take the money out of the general taxpayers' pocket to subsidize their own children's school lunch.

It will take real courage to correct these problems and the others I have identified for congressional action without following the all too familiar pattern of the past—simply adding more programs. But, increasingly, courage is not a choice; it is an absolute requirement if we are to avoid ever larger, less responsive government.

The task ahead will not be easy because it will require some fundamental changes in our expectations for government. As a start, we need to understand that income and wealth are not produced in Washington, they are only redistributed there. As a corollary, we need to overcome the idea that members of the Congress are elected to bring home federal projects for their district or state. Until this idea is totally rejected, higher funding levels for old programs and more new programs will be enacted each year as members of the Congress seek to insure their re-election. We also need to overcome the prevalent attitude that only new programs with multibillion dollar price tags are worthy of media attention and public discussion and worthy of being judged bold and innovative. The multitude of programs already in a budget of more than $400-billion and initiatives to do something about them are worthy of intense public scrutiny, discussion and judgment in their own right.

These changes in attitude will require leadership not only by the executive branch, but, at least equally important, on the part of each member of the Congress. Members of the Congress must begin to share the burden of the President in saying no to special interest groups—even those in their own districts or states.

The changes that have occurred in the congressional budget-making process in recent years provide some basis for optimism for the future. The new budget committees have begun to provide a counterbalance to the spending and taxing committees, offering hope that the total effect of the splintered actions of the other committees will be given equal weight in the congressional process.

[Special Task Forces Urged]

But more progress is needed. Just as the budget process cannot do the whole job in the executive branch, it cannot in the Congress either. No matter how streamlined and properly organized the departments and agencies of the executive branch or the committees and subcommittees of the Congress become—and there is surely room for substantial improvement in this respect at both ends of Pennsylvania Avenue—the executive branch must continue to refine and the Congress must adopt processes whereby recommendations to the President or to the House or Senate, as the case may be, on major issues are developed by task force groups representing the competing priorities of various departments and agencies and the various congressional committees and subcommittees. The reason is simply that most major issues cut across jurisdictional lines, no matter how well drawn—energy, international affairs, and welfare reform, to name but a few examples. I urge the new Administration to build on what has been accomplished in this regard in the executive branch. I urge the Congress promptly to put into place the necessary counterpart mechanisms. Such improvements in process, coupled with further progress in the development of the budget process, will help substantially in addressing and meeting our problems and attaining the goals we have set for our Nation.

The last thirty budgets record a turbulent period in our history: wars, domestic strife, and serious economic problems. In the last two years, we have laid the foundation for a positive future. We have stabilized international relationships and created the framework for global progress. At home, we have restored confidence in government while reversing the trends of inflation and unemployment. Building on this solid base, the policies and programs contained in this budget can help us to fulfill the promise of America.

GERALD R. FORD

January 17, 1977.

PRESIDENT'S ECONOMIC REPORT, ECONOMIC ADVISERS' REPORT

January 18, 1977

In his annual economic report to Congress Jan. 18, President Gerald R. Ford said that the key to continuing recovery was more business investment in new plants and equipment and that economic policy must be directed toward stimulating such investment. "A stronger spur to investment in productive plant and equipment is necessary for the further improvement in production and employment in 1977 and beyond," Ford told Congress two days before he left office.

Ford's report called 1976 a year of "sound economic achievement." The gross national product rose by more than 6 per cent in 1976, the President noted, and "substantial headway" had been made during the year in reducing the rate of inflation. The consumer price index showed that the inflation rate had dropped to a 5 per cent level—a full percentage point below the government economic forecast—and down sharply from the double-digit inflation levels of 1973-1974.

Surveying the economic state of the nation, the President reiterated his view that stimulation of investment was the key to economic recovery. He urged the Congress to adopt his tax program which called for a permanent tax reduction in the corporate income tax from 48 to 46 per cent, an accelerated depreciation allowance for investment in new plants and equipment in areas where unemployment remained at or above the 7 per cent figure, and an increase in the individual income tax exemption to $1,000 from $750.

Ford's report expressed the hope that Congress would develop, as rapidly as feasible, a strategic oil reserve to reduce the increasing rate of U.S.

dependence on imported oil. Ford called upon Congress to deregulate the price of domestic oil and natural gas to allow those fuels to rise to the higher world market price in order to discourage consumption and encourage production.

The outgoing President recommended that Congress adopt his legislative proposals to reduce the government's role in the economy. The President stated: "Although all Americans are aware of the substantial benefits which regulations produce in their everyday lives, we frequently lose sight of the effects of such programs in restricting the growth of productivity."

The report implicitly criticized President-elect Carter's plans for additional federal spending to create more jobs. The report advised Congress to resist the "self-deception" that a little larger federal deficit or monetary inflation would bring "costless benefits" to the American people. President Ford repeated his hope that federal expenditures would be restrained and that the government would pursue a "prudent fiscal policy" to continue economic expansion and bring about full employment.

Report of the Council of Economic Advisers

Ford's message to Congress on the state of the economy was based on the Annual Report of the Council of Economic Advisers (CEA). The CEA report analyzed the economic posture of the nation and forecast moderate gains for 1977. Ford's economic advisers asserted: "The main elements of continued economic growth in the United States are well established, despite the slowdown which occurred in the second half of 1976."

The council expected the gross national product to be 5-5½ per cent higher in 1977 than in 1976 and to average a 5½ to 6 per cent rate of growth for 1977 in "real" terms, after accounting for inflation. The rate of growth, the report stated, should mean a "modest" reduction in unemployment to nearly 7 per cent by the end of 1977, while inflation should not go above 5 to 6 per cent. In contrast, the unemployment rate for December 1976 was 7.8 per cent. "In any event," the report stated, "unemployment will still be unacceptably high during the year."

The council's study of economic trends concluded that the nation's capacity to produce had been growing at a slower pace than previously projected. Economic productivity since 1966 had been rising by only 2.1 per cent a year—a figure much lower than the 3.3 per cent annual growth rate during the period 1948-1966. Factors cited as contributing to the slowdown in growth included the recent recession, higher energy costs, slower technical progress, slower growth in capital per worker and a larger proportion of less experienced workers in the labor force. "However, the reasons for the slowdown are not fully understood at this time because the decline in productivity growth appears to be larger than the sum of the estimated effects of these factors," the analysis said.

The gross national product rose 6.2 per cent in 1976, the council report stated, with an increase in employment by three million people. The council expressed concern over the pattern of "erratic" economic growth during 1976, with a very strong increase in the first quarter of the year and much slower growth in succeeding quarters.

The report listed four principles that it said should guide the formulation of economic policy over the next several years and which were reflected in Ford's proposed budget for fiscal 1978. They included using tax cuts instead of increased government spending to stimulate the economy, permanent rather than temporary tax cuts, more emphasis on measures to encourage business investment and continued efforts to hold down inflation.

In an indirect slap at Congress, the CEA report was critical of the various employment programs which members of Congress had favored over tax cuts as a way of lowering unemployment and improving the economy.

The report differed with the view that public service jobs and job training programs increased opportunities for persons who had been unemployed for a long time. "Thus far...these spending programs have had little net impact on employment compared to tax reductions that increase the deficit by the same magnitude," the report said. "The long run job-creating impact of federally financed PSE (public service employment) programs appears to be quite limited."

The report contended that federal funds were used to fill jobs that would be opening up anyway, that it was difficult to target the jobs to persons who had been out of work for a long time and that the relatively high wages attracted persons who would be employable in the private sector. For these reasons, the report recommended limiting public service jobs to the long-term unemployed (for example, those persons who had used up all their unemployment compensation) and keeping wages low in comparison to wages paid by private business.

Training programs also had been disappointing, according to the CEA. The "effects of the training programs on real wages and employment appear to be small," it said, explaining that persons with good training characteristics and prospects were likely to obtain training either on their own or on the job.

CEA also examined the impact of government regulation. "Unfortunately, it often turns out that regulatory processes are not capable of achieving their intended goals or have generated greater costs than would result from their original problem." the report concluded.

Following are excerpts from the Economic Report of the President and the Annual Report of the Council of Economic Advisers issued Jan. 18, 1977. (Boldface

headings in brackets have been added by Congressional
Quarterly to highlight the organization of the text.):

ECONOMIC REPORT OF THE PRESIDENT

To the Congress of the United States:

The past year was a year of sound economic achievement. A year ago I
said that my key economic goal was "to create an economic environment in
which sustainable noninflationary growth can be achieved." While much
remains to be done, we have built a very solid foundation for further
economic gains in 1977 and beyond. The recovery has continued to produce
substantial gains in output and employment. Unemployment remains
much too high, but the marked reduction that we see in inflation as well as
in inflationary expectations represents significant progress toward regain-
ing the stable noninflationary prosperity that has been our goal.

The gross national product, adjusted for inflation, rose by slightly more
than 6 percent last year. The rise in production was extremely rapid at the
beginning of 1976. The advance moderated during the spring, but at the
close of the year the recovery showed signs of reacceleration. In December
more than 88 million Americans were employed, an increase of about 3
million from last December and more than 4 million above the 1975 recession low. Economic gains were widespread. Real incomes continued their
rise, consumer expenditures also moved upward, business investment
began to recover, and housing construction improved significantly.
Unemployment dropped sharply in the early months of last year, although
it rose again as the extraordinarily rapid expansion in the labor force out-
paced the creation of new jobs.

Substantial headway was also made on the inflation front. Since late
1975 the consumer price index has risen only 5 percent, a full percentage
point less than was anticipated and a noteworthy improvement over the 12
percent inflation rate of 1974. Wage settlements continued to moderate.
Record crops and more ample supplies of farm products halted the sharp
increases in food prices. As fears of inflation ebbed, interest rates declined,
contrary to most expectations at the beginning of the year; and the stock
market, reflecting this heightened confidence, was close to the highs of the
year when trading ended in 1976. The lower rate of inflation and the improved state of financial markets attest to the significant progress we have
made during the past year toward reestablishing a stable, noninflationary,
full-employment economy.

If this goal is to be fully realized, the present policy of moderation in
fiscal and monetary affairs and of relying on a restored vitality in the
private sector must continue. We need tax reductions to support a lasting
economic recovery and to provide relief from the increases in real tax
burdens induced by inflation. In the long run, inflation and real economic
growth will constantly push taxpayers into higher and higher tax brackets
unless tax laws are changed. Some believe that these additional tax
receipts should be spent on new Government programs. I do not. Instead I

believe that the Congress should counteract the growing burden imposed by the tax system—and the reduction of private incentives that it implies—by periodically providing offsetting tax cuts while continuing to restrain the rate of growth of Government spending.

The creation of permanent, meaningful, and productive jobs for our growing labor force requires a higher level of private investment. Tax reductions must be so designed that measures to stimulate consumption are balanced by those which will increase investment. Investment has for some time been falling short of the levels required if we are to provide enough productive jobs for our people at rising real wage rates, and if we hope to renew and improve our capital stock so that we can meet our requirements for energy and make headway toward environmental, job safety, and other goals. Investment has grown more slowly than would normally be true at this stage of a recovery. A stronger spur to investment in productive plant and equipment is necessary for the further improvement in production and employment in 1977 and beyond.

Tax Reductions

In October 1975, I presented to the Congress a program of tax cuts and spending restraints that would have reduced the burden of government for all taxpayers. It would have given the American people more freedom to spend their incomes as they choose rather than as Washington chooses for them, and it would have increased incentives to expand investment. However, the Congress decided otherwise—to increase spending far more than I wanted and to cut taxes far less than I wanted.

Earlier this month I again sent to Congress my recommendations to cut taxes. I have once more urged a permanent increase in the personal exemption from $750 to $1,000 to replace the system of temporary tax credits that has so greatly complicated the individual income tax return. I am also recommending a higher income allowance and a series of permanent tax rate reductions. My proposals provide income tax relief for individuals that will total $10-billion in 1977.

To encourage the investment that will mean good steady jobs for our expanding labor force, I am recommending once again a permanent reduction in the corporate income tax from 48 to 46 percent. I urge as well the enactment of legislation to make permanent the extension of the 10 percent investment tax credit and the increased corporate surtax exemption provided by the Tax Reform Act of 1976. In the longer run we must eliminate the double taxation of dividend payments. I am therefore renewing my proposal to integrate corporate and personal income taxes gradually over a period of years beginning in 1978.

I am also renewing my recommendation of accelerated depreciation for investment in new plants and equipment undertaken in areas where unemployment is 7 percent or higher. I am firmly convinced that this is a far better way to raise employment where the economy has not caught up with the recovery than adding layer upon layer of new spending programs.

Although such tax cuts for individuals and businesses are desirable at this time to support stronger consumer and capital goods markets, we must be mindful of the need to bring down our large Federal budget deficit as quickly as possible. As the economy improves and the demand for private credit becomes greater, Federal borrowing requirements to finance the deficit must be lowered to avoid preempting funds needed for private investment and to ensure steady progress in the battle against inflation. Accordingly, in my Budget Message I am again recommending responsible restraint in the growth of Federal budget outlays. These policies will also bring us closer to our goals of stable noninflationary prosperity.

International Developments

Much progress was evident in the rest of the world last year, and international economic cooperation continued to improve. Restoration of a stable growth path, however, has proved difficult. Throughout the world, countries are still grappling with the complicated and painful aftermath of inflation, recession, and the sharp increases in the relative price of energy. Serious social and political problems have made these adjustments more difficult.

When I met with the leaders of the major industrial nations in the summer of 1976, the restoration of full employment in our several economies was the most important item on our agenda. Stable full employment and continued improvement in the well-being of our own peoples and the world population at large, we agreed, will take a number of years. Although the course of faster expansion seems attractive, it is clearly risky. Impatience which leads to a reacceleration of inflation could jeopardize the significant progress we have achieved so far.

The costly lessons of the past decade are inescapable. High and variable inflation rates are incompatible with sustainable growth. Overly expansionary policies contributed to the very high inflation rate and, in turn, to the deepest worldwide recession since the 1930s. Policy changes and adjustments will doubtless be needed in 1977 and thereafter. But policies must hold to a reasonably steady and predictable course. In particular, the measures we select to further our economic expansion must not raise the risk of future inflation.

The growing recognition among nations of their interdependence has helped to create the cooperation that is now apparent among members of the industrial community. The mutuality of the policy goals of the developed and developing countries needs to be better understood on each side. For this reason the discussions between developed and developing countries during 1976 have attempted to foster a climate in which our joint interests and our diverse concerns can be freely expressed. Although the progress so far achieved has disappointed some, it has helped us avoid the sometimes easier but mutually destructive course of trade restrictions.

Energy Policy

Energy matters retain their troublesome hold among the problems threatening the Nation's long-run prosperity. The sharp increases in oil prices in 1973-75 imposed major costs upon our economy. We have done much to accommodate the new higher prices for energy, but some aspects of energy policy have hampered the adjustment. The Congress has continued to hold prices for domestically produced oil and natural gas well below world market levels. These lower energy prices have encouraged the inefficient use of energy and discouraged efforts to expand domestic supplies and improve the energy efficiency of the overall capital stock.

The recovery has heightened the demand for energy and thus resulted in greater imports of oil. In consequence the United States now depends even more heavily upon imported petroleum and is even more vulnerable than a year ago to future price manipulation and interruptions in supply. Now that the problems of recession and inflation are receding, we can more vigorously address this difficulty. The energy program that I have presented before is designed to answer the longer need.

First steps are under way toward creating a strategic oil reserve which will help shield us from disruptions in supply. The OPEC pricing decisions of December were a forceful reminder of the Nation's growing need for protection against foreign moves that affect the price and can alter the availability of imported oil. Strategic storage will provide a first line of defense against the threat of disrupted supplies. This vital program must be implemented, and we must also take positive steps to lessen our economic dependence upon foreign oil.

Measures that will make us less dependent on foreign energy supplies have been proposed by this Administration; but unfortunately many of the most important proposals have not yet been accepted by the Congress. Some of the measures involve present costs which will yield...future benefits. Others, which would lead to more efficient use of our energy resources, would benefit the Nation immediately as well as in the future.

It is critically important—for energy security, environmental quality, and long-term economic productivity—that prices of domestic petroleum and natural gas be allowed to match more closely the full cost of these fuels. In the immediate future oil prices should be allowed to rise as they were intended to do under the Energy Policy and Conservation Act. Steps should also be taken which would help close the gap more rapidly between domestic and world market prices for petroleum, allow a free-market price for North Slope Alaskan oil, and deregulate the wellhead price of new natural gas.

Although a number of inconsistencies remain, the relation between the Nation's goals for energy and for the environment has become clearer and the effects of existing policies more fully known. The time is ripe for reexamining environmental policy and determining whether the ends we all seek can be achieved at a lower cost to the economy and to the security of our energy supplies.

Taken together, all of the actions recommended here would help the economy to adjust to the new energy situation and do much to ensure more reliable supplies of energy for the future. They would also signal to the world that this Nation is serious about developing secure supplies of energy. Most important, these efforts would encourage conservation and give industry the confidence that will spur the production of both conventional fuels and substitutes.

Regulatory Reform

As economic problems have arisen and been dealt with by new policy initiatives, the Government's role in the economy has grown ever larger. The number of commissions, agencies, administrations, bureaus, and offices set up to conduct programs increases constantly. Each appears important when it is first established. The trouble is that they are seldom, if ever, terminated when they have accomplished their original mission. By one recent count there were 1,200 Federal Government organizations alone having significant powers to regulate a wide and growing range of economic activities.

The direct Federal outlay to control practices in the private sector is substantial. Even more important are the losses that these activities impose on the production and distribution of goods and services throughout the economy. No accurate measure of the total costs and benefits of actions by the regulatory agencies is possible at this time or perhaps ever. Although all Americans are aware of the substantial benefits which regulations produce in their everyday lives, we frequently lose sight of the efforts of such programs in restricting the growth of productivity.

The use of newly developed technology, the development of new companies and products, and the opening up of new occupations have all been impeded by the need for licenses, certification, review, and legal judgments introduced by one agency or another. When innovative activities are discouraged progress is curbed throughout the economy, even in those areas where some regulation is justified. Regulations must therefore be reexamined to ensure the removal of costly and counterproductive regulations and to identify those whose need has passed. Where benefits seem large we should make sure that the benefits are realized at the least possible cost.

To reduce the regulatory burden, I asked the Congress in the last year to eliminate unnecessary and anticompetitive regulation in the airline and trucking industries. This action was to follow the path of regulatory reform that the railroad industry achieved in the Railroad Revitalization and Regulatory Reform Act of 1976. I also urged the Congress to eliminate the Federal Power Commission's controls on new gas prices, which have held back exploration and sales to the interstate pipelines serving northern and western cities. Earlier this month I once again submitted to the Congress a plan to eliminate controls on gasoline refining and marketing.

Among agencies under my jurisdiction I have set out new regulatory procedures which will make controls more effective and less costly to all concerned, but such steps are only a beginning. The Congress and the executive branch must undertake a comprehensive review to ascertain the effects of present controls, and then offer to the American people a corrective program that will cut across administrative boundaries. Only a sweeping reform will remove the regulatory burden where it is no longer justified and place the initiative for production and distribution back in the more efficient hands of private enterprise.

Role of the Government in Society

I firmly believe that if we dedicate our efforts to the major problems I have outlined here we can successfully resolve them. As a people we have an extraordinary capacity to marshal our resources against even the gravest difficulties.

Unfortunately many of our problems are self-made. One which has concerned me particularly over the years is a tendency, born of goodwill and a desire to improve the state of American life, which makes us think we can create costless benefits for our people. We are unwilling to confront some of our hardest choices. We persist in the belief that we can always tolerate a little larger Federal deficit, or the creation of a little more money, especially for the sake of programs which seem to promise clear and readily definable benefits. This is a kind of self-deception that we must learn to resist.

Certainly we must adopt measures that promise to keep the economic expansion going and reduce the high unemployment. But overly expansive policies with their inevitable risk of renewed inflation are realities which are easily overlooked in the understandable desire for the immediately tangible benefits foreseen from specific programs. What we seek is a sustainable expansion and the restoration of full employment without inflation, and we must settle for no less.

The discipline implicit in a prudent fiscal policy is not easy but it offers very considerable and lasting rewards. I am hopeful that the recent creation of the budget committees to serve the Congress will help to provide this necessary discipline. Prudent budget policies are essential if we are to restore stable full-employment conditions and provide the productive jobs which our people need and want. Some part of our present deficit is the result of the recession and will accordingly disappear as full employment is restored. Beyond this, however, we must restrain the growth of Federal expenditures. If we do not, we shall have to resign ourselves to higher taxes or to high employment deficits with their inflationary consequences.

Nowhere are these tradeoffs so evident as in our social security program and our efforts to provide medical insurance for our people. I have emphasized the need to maintain a fiscally sound social security system and repeatedly rejected proposals to fund increased benefits out of what are called general revenues. The purpose of linking social security benefits to specially designated taxes is to balance the benefits to one segment of society with the costs to another segment. Our democratic processes of government work better when the costs of programs are open and visible to those who pay them. Funding our social security benefits through specifically designed payroll taxes strengthens the discipline that should govern these decisions. Benefits are not costless, and we should not allow this fact to be submerged in any general revenue funding of the social security system.

[Medical Care]

Similar pressures are building up with respect to medical care. We have become concerned, and rightly so, over sharp increases in the cost of medical care which emphasize the need to improve the efficiency and effectiveness in the delivery of health care services. These have arisen in part because the large expansion in health insurance coverage under both private and public programs has reduced the sensitivity of consumers to costs and weakened the incentives to achieve efficiencies. Individuals, businesses, and unions, confronted with the higher costs of private health insurance have begun to exert curbs on the systems for delivering health and medical service, and their influence should be salutary. I hope we will not choose to fund these costs through a comprehensive national health insurance system, since this will only weaken the incentives for improvement and efficiency that are now emerging.

These are but two examples of the pressures which threaten to erode our fiscal processes. We must recognize that making governmental expenditure policy the principal arm of demand management has undesirable consequences. Expenditure programs once in place are extremely difficult to cut back. The result is a permanent rise in Federal outlays and the risk of ever-increasing growth in the government relative to the private sector. As the experience of other countries forcibly illustrates, this is a dangerous path. It weakens incentives, reduces efficiency, leads to lagging standards of living, and carries inevitable risks of inflation. It is much better to provide fiscal adjustments through tax reductions than through Federal spending programs.

The solid improvement of this year means continued progress toward a better life for all Americans. Problems will always remain, but the future is bright with opportunities to continue strengthening our economy. Improvement is part of the American way of life, but we must recognize that few problems, when viewed realistically, lend themselves to quick and easy solution. Our policies must take into account the full costs and lasting implications of the changes we make today for whatever worthwhile reason. If they attack symptoms rather than causes, policies will be ineffective and may even preclude the very goals which we seek. Enduring improvement in the economic welfare of the American people requires that the courses we embark on to meet today's problems will also bring us closer to our more distant goals and aspirations.

THE ANNUAL REPORT OF THE
COUNCIL OF ECONOMIC ADVISERS

Chapter 1
Economic Policy and Outlook

The U.S. economic recovery is now almost 2 years old. In 1976 real gross national product (GNP) rose by 6.2 percent, and employment increased by almost 3 million persons. Although the pattern of real GNP growth during 1976 was more erratic than had been anticipated, showing rapid growth in the first quarter followed by more moderate gains in subsequent quarters, the rise in real GNP for the year as a whole was about what had been projected a year ago. The growth of production and employment for 1976 was accompanied by a further significant moderation of the inflation rate. The average annual rate of change in the GNP deflator was 5 percent over the 4 quarters of 1976 compared with a 7 percent average in 1975.

The unemployment rate declined by almost 1 percentage point from 1975 to 1976, but it is still much too high and must be reduced further. The 3.2 percent increase in employment in 1976 indicates that progress is being made in alleviating the economic and social hardships remaining from the recession. Owing to the combination of secular and cyclical increases in labor force participation rates and in the growth of the working-age population, the labor force grew by 2.3 percent in 1976. This rapid growth of the labor force means that jobs must be created at a fast pace in order to reduce the rate of unemployment.

A continuation of rapid employment and real income gains will require a strong growth in private investment demand in the years ahead. Little extra impetus to the economic expansion will be forthcoming from inventory investment and personal consumption, because inventories already have risen and saving rates have dropped closer to normal levels. Although business fixed investment has begun to recover from the low levels of the recession, its growth has been slower than in past recoveries. Without a sharper upturn in investment the expansionary momentum, already slower in the second half of last year, cannot easily be maintained. Even if final sales growth could be bolstered without a strong recovery of business fixed investment, the implied lesser growth of productive capital would not be sufficient to provide new jobs at a faster rate in the future without a slower growth of productivity and real wages.

In our 1976 *Report* we indicated that business fixed investment would have to account for approximately 12 percent of GNP during the last half of the 1970s if the Nation is to achieve full employment by 1980, meet specified productivity and environmental objectives, and attain greater independence in regard to energy. While it was not suggested that economic equilibrium cannot be attained under many other sets of conditions, the social and economic strains of adjusting to a slower and less widely shared improvement in living standards seem likely to become severe if we continue to fall very far short of this ratio. Business fixed investment in 1976 was less than 10 percent of GNP, and even with the improvement anticipated this year the share is likely to remain below 10 percent in 1977. The momentum of the recovery must be maintained in the near term through measures which foster growing business confidence and which support stable economic growth and decelerating inflation. If not, a slow growth of capital formation may create capacity limitations which could stall the expansion before acceptably low levels of unemployment are reached.

To provide support for an economic expansion strong enough to effect a substantial reduction in unemployment without at the same time jeopardizing the progress achieved so far in containing inflation, the President has recommended a permanent reduction in personal and business taxes beginning this year. The purpose of these measures is to further the growth of disposable income, which has been eroded in part by inflation-induced increases in taxes, and to provide more incentives to investment spending. The continuing diminution of inflation during the past year indicates that such tax reductions to promote the growth of demand are consistent with the goal of sustainable noninflationary growth—if they are accompanied by steps to restrain the growth of Federal expenditures in future years. To help consolidate our progress in curbing inflation, the President has proposed a budget which provides for a slowing of the growth in Federal outlays in 1978 and beyond. Unless surpluses can eventually be achieved in the Federal budget at high levels of employment, it may be difficult to increase the share of investment in GNP and maintain the growth of the Nation's productive capacity.

With the help of these policies the economic recovery is expected to continue in 1977. Real GNP is expected to be 5 to 5½ percent higher than in 1976, and its rate of growth should average between 5 and 6 percent during the 4 quarters of 1977. Such growth will produce further gains in employment. But unless labor force growth decelerates significantly from the current high rates, the decline in the unemployment rate is likely to be modest. In any event, unemployment will still be unacceptably high during the year. If we are to eliminate the economic loss and hardship associated with idle resources, economic growth in 1978 and beyond must continue to proceed at a more rapid pace than the longer-run rate of growth of potential output. We do not anticipate that these policies will lead to an increase in the underlying rate of inflation. Indeed, if wage settlements continue to moderate, further progress in reducing inflation could be possible in this year and in future years.

GENERAL POLICY PRINCIPLES

To assure a sustained expansion, four general principles should guide the formulation of economic policies over the next several years. Economic stimulus, where needed, should be provided by tax reduction rather than by increases in government spending. Tax reduction should be permanent rather than in the form of a temporary rebate. Policy initiatives should be balanced between measures directed toward consumption and those aimed at increasing business fixed investment. Economic policy should aim for a steady economic expansion in which the components of aggregate demand are in balance.

[Federal Spending a Dangerous Stimulus]

1. *Stimulus should be provided by tax reduction rather than by increases in government spending.* Rising government purchases of goods and services first increase income and employment in the areas that produce the increased output demanded by government. The visibility and strength of these first-round effects account for much of the political support for increased spending. A number of serious difficulties arise, however, when government expenditures are used as a tool of stabilization policy.

Our experience has been that under existing institutional arrangements the startup time for many spending programs can be quite long; this is particularly true of the large construction projects which are considered by many to be useful instruments of countercyclical fiscal policy. The danger is that the economic impact of new spending programs will not be felt when it is most needed and will then outlast the need for stimulus. In addition, when restraint rather than continued stimulus becomes desirable, it may be politically difficult to cut these programs. As a result, a fiscal policy which stimulates expansion primarily through increases in government purchases may risk overstimulating the expansion at a later stage. Another difficulty is that frictional inefficiencies arise from manipulating the level of government expenditures for stabilization purposes. Each time a government program is changed, costs are incurred as the private sector is forced to adjust and reallocate the necessary resources. And in some cases the rules and regulations associated with the enactment of these programs may necessitate widening government interference in the private sector.

Similar dangers exist with income maintenance and support programs. These programs are essential to relieve the economic hardships associated with unemployment. But we must be careful that changes in programs designed to deal with cyclical contingencies do not end by permanently increasing Federal payments, the number of beneficiaries, and the size of the individual benefits. Such a result would reduce the growth of resources available to the private sector; and the higher marginal tax rates eventually required to finance these expenditures may lower incentives to work and invest, thereby hindering the growth of our aggregate supply capabilities and heightening inflationary pressures....

[Permanent Tax Reduction]

2. *Tax reduction should be permanent rather than in the form of a temporary rebate.* The primary objectives of tax reduction in the current situation should be to provide relief from the inflation-induced increases in real tax burdens and to support a lasting economic expansion. Because con-

sumers normally adjust expenditures to their "permanent" or long-run income, a lasting reduction in personal taxes which raises both current and future after-tax income should yield a sustained rise in consumer spending, as happened following the permanent tax reduction in 1964. Sustained growth in consumer spending is required to promote a durable economic expansion.

On the other hand, any stimulative effect that a temporary tax rebate may have on consumer spending will diminish quickly. For example, a substantial increase in expenditures for durables did occur after the payment of the 1975 rebate. Part of the effect of such a one-time windfall, however, may have been to shift some expenditures to the present that had been planned for a later time, with the result that spending would be correspondingly lower in subsequent periods. This phenomenon may be the reason for the very low rates of increase in purchases of consumer durables in the last 3 quarters of 1976. Such fluctuations in the movements of demand contribute to uncertainty about fiscal policy and damage the prospects for steady growth. Thus temporary tax rebates are not consistent with the objective of sustaining an economic expansion. While they may be useful in helping to bring about a reversal of generally declining demands during a recession, they are not consistent with the maintenance of an expansion of demand that is already under way.

Moreover transitory increases in consumer spending associated with temporary tax cuts are not likely to stimulate investment as much as more permanent increases in demand would do. Business firms may realize that an expansion in sales will not last if the increase is apparently due to a temporary reduction in taxes and will have less incentive to expand capacity than if they expect a more sustained rise in sales. A permanent reduction in income taxes has a more lasting impact on household consumption demand and consequently on business firms' willingness to invest in productive capital.

It is sometimes argued that tax cuts should be temporary in order to maintain a permanent revenue base for future spending programs. A strong and more certain growth in 1977 and beyond, however, is ultimately the key to whether resources will become available to support these expenditures. Moreover taxes automatically increase faster than income over time because of the combined effects exerted by inflation, real growth, and our graduated tax rate structure. Unless permanent reductions are made from time to time, taxes will account for an ever larger share of taxable income. Thus there is little danger that a permanent tax reduction will destroy the revenue base for the Federal Government. Indeed, another fear may be more realistic: if taxes are not reduced periodically we run the risk of allowing the tax burden to rise over time and thus inhibit the growth of demand in the private sector.

[Business Investment Incentives]

3. *Economic initiatives should be balanced between measures to stimulate consumption and those designed to increase business in-*

vestment. We noted above that investment must grow somewhat faster than GNP for some years to achieve long-run goals of employment and income growth. It is therefore essential that economic policy create an environment which will encourage business investment. Clearly, investment spending will be stimulated by substantial increases in final sales, which tend to reduce excess capacity and increase expected profitability. A cut in personal income taxes which sustains real consumption growth will thus encourage investment. However, in the current economic environment we believe this consumption-induced investment growth can usefully be augmented by direct stimulus to private investment. Consumption-oriented growth in demand will not necessarily bring aggregate investment to the levels needed to offset the inadequate investment of the past few years. On the contrary, direct stimulus may be necessary to counteract forces which have deterred investment.

...[B]usiness fixed investment currently accounts for a relatively low proportion of GNP, approximating the percentage of the early 1960s. Even with substantial increases in business fixed investment next year this ratio will remain under 10 percent and far below the ratios we believe are desirable. Furthermore the slow growth of labor productivity...does not suggest that productive capital has become relatively more abundant over the last decade. The policy response to comparable problems in the early 1960s was to stimulate investment directly with such measures as a reduction in corporate tax rates.

A number of factors may have prevented the restoration of business confidence and hence restrained investment growth. Wage and price controls are still a recent memory, and fears of a reacceleration of inflation have not been completely dispelled. Recollections of the severe 1974-75 recession may also restrain business confidence. Because fears of a renewed inflation-recession cycle may encourage businesses to increase liquidity rather than invest in plant and equipment, confidence must be rebuilt before sales growth will be translated into higher capital outlays.

Laws and regulations to provide necessary protection for the environment also create costs and uncertainties. Not only does the spread of regulations raise productions costs, but long-run cost and profit calculations are made less certain because of the possibility of future changes in regulations. For instance, if a change in environmental laws may affect the operations of a new plant, then the risk associated with building this plant is correspondingly increased. The impact is more severe on longer-lived investments which require longer commitments with less flexibility once they are made.

It is of course very difficult to prove that a decline in business confidence or an increase in risk premiums is responsible for the failure of investment to rise as much as might have been expected during the current recovery. This difficulty results partly from our inability to directly measure the uncertainty or accurately assess the expectational factors and the environment within which long-term investment decisions are made. Most evidence for the view that business confidence remains poor is qualitative and involves a degree of casual empiricism. One quantitative indicator of the expectations affecting business investment is the market value of a corporation's stocks and of net interest-bearing debt relative to the replacement cost of its assets. If, for example, assets are valued in the market significantly above their replacement cost, corporations will be encouraged to invest in new equipment and thereby create capital gains for the owners of their securities. On the other hand, if assets are valued below their replacement cost, corporations which sell new securities to buy new capital goods may be creating capital losses for their security holders. In the latter case we can infer that the cost of capital has risen relative to the average profitability of past investment projects and that new investment will be discouraged. Of course, at the margin the expected rate of return on a significant number of potential new investments will remain above the cost of capital, even though existing assets on average are valued below their replacement cost. Thus even if the market value of a firm fell below the replacement cost of its assets this would not mean the end of investment incentives. It would be especially inappropriate to draw such conclusions from estimated aggregates composed of heterogeneous corporations.

Nevertheless it is probably safe to infer that the most continuous decline in the ratio of the market value of nonfinancial corporations to the replacement cost of their assets during the last few years...is an indication that investment incentives are much lower currently than in the second half of the 1960s. Even allowing for the possibility that the high values of the ratio in the 1960s reflected some temporary overconfidence in the evaluation of future returns, the significant downward trend is an indicator that a lack of confidence may be a factor holding back long-term investment commitments now. One inference from this evidence is that a direct stimulus to investment, such as a corporate tax reduction would provide, could hasten the restoration of business confidence and be useful to supplement the normal accelerator mechanism. Another is that measures which would help reduce the risks of substantial changes in the regulatory climate over the normal life of fixed assets would also raise investment. Such measures would help to offset the uncertainties which are still restraining investment and would make up for the slow growth of productive capital in the past few years.

[Expansion With Balance]

4. *Policy should aim at a steady expansion with balance among the components of aggregate demand.* An important policy decision in the years ahead concerns the appropriate amount of fiscal and monetary stimulus to sustain the recovery. In the effort to achieve continued progress toward full employment we must not create inherently unstable and ultimately counterproductive conditions along the way. With a high inflation rate and many uncertainties still remaining to hamper the economy, stimulus which aims for a balanced composition of demand and a steady pace will provide the safest and surest path of advance. A steady recovery allows aggregate production to expand gradually toward full capacity,

thereby avoiding such imbalances as overaccumulation of inventories, shortages of strategic commodities, or insufficient accumulation of fixed capital. Moreover, if unexpected shortages or demand deficiencies begin to rise, policy can react before either inflationary or deflationary pressures become too severe. In this way the possibility of renewed instabilities is minimized. In turn the improved outlook should help restore confidence, encourage investment, and assure that increases in demand raise employment rather than inflation rates.

[Inflation]

Evidence showing the impact of inflation and expectations of inflation on business decisions is very limited. Nevertheless an overly rapid expansion could generate a rise in inflationary expectations which might restrain capital accumulation and threaten to cut off the expansion before full employment is reached. In the short run, increases in inflation may appear to stimulate investment because of delays in the upward adjustment of market interest rates and the estimates of the risk associated with inflation. However, high rates of inflation may be associated with high variability in individual prices. If this is so, the expected variance of future returns on investment would increase with inflation, thereby adding a risk premium to the rate of return required to undertake new investment projects. Thus the cost-price uncertainties which could be associated with high inflation because of larger, more frequent, and less predictable changes in relative prices may eventually discourage business spending. In the long run, the effect of inflation may be negative as market interest rates adjust to offset the inflation stimulus and only the negative effect of greater uncertainty remains.

Another factor which will call for moderation at a later stage if the expansion is to be sustainable is the current uncertainty about the level of potential output in the U.S. economy and the likelihood that the potential has been growing at a lower rate in the 1970s than during most of the 1960s. There is also some uncertainty about the unemployment rate that should be used to represent a constant degree of tightness in the labor market at full employment either now or in the future. These uncertainties suggest the wisdom of proceeding with a greater degree of caution in our return to full employment than was previously thought necessary....

International considerations provide a further reason for maintaining a steady recovery. If a too rapid expansion at home is accompanied by rapid expansions followed by bottlenecks in other major industrial countries, inflationary forces can be intensified by worldwide excess demand for strategic commodities. On the other hand, in a situation where the world's economic development is lagging, it is important that U.S. growth should not be so slow as to contribute to sluggishness in world trade. This would reinforce rather than alleviate demand deficiencies and increase the risk of another recession.

ECONOMIC POLICY FOR 1977

Fiscal Policy

With these general principles in mind, the President has proposed a permanent tax cut for individuals and corporations which will reduce tax liabilities by about $12.5-billion in calendar 1977. The largest part of the tax cut, $10-billion, would go to individuals in the form of higher personal exemptions, an increase in the low-income allowance, and lower tax rates. The rest would go to corporations in the form of a 2 percentage point reduction in the corporate income tax rate. Federal expenditures on a national income and product accounts (NIPA) basis are expected to be $429-billion in 1977. This will yield an actual deficit of $57-billion for the year and a decline in the full-employment surplus of $13-billion in 1977. As private sector spending continues to expand, it is expected that the Federal deficit will gradually diminish to make room for the necessary private savings flows to finance new capital formation.

The proposed $10-billion permanent reduction in personal income taxes would be implemented by an increase in the individual exemption from $750 to $1,000, an increase in the low-income allowance to $1,800 for single persons and $2,500 for joint returns, and a reduction in rates in the lower- and middle-income brackets. Furthermore, the temporary tax credits first enacted in 1975 would be repealed. These changes would offset the increase in the real tax burden of middle-income families resulting from the high inflation rates of recent years. The reduction in personal taxes would lead to a permanent increase in after-tax income and a more confident outlook in the household sector, both of which should significantly boost consumer spending in the year ahead. By creating stronger markets and raising the rate of capacity utilization, the personal tax cut would also indirectly stimulate additional investment.

The proposed reduction in the corporate income tax rate from 48 percent to 46 percent would reduce corporate tax liabilities by about $2.5-billion in 1977. It would thus improve the net return on all capital assets and enlarge the flow of internal funds to finance new projects. The supply of savings has been adequate since the recovery began in 1975; but as the expansion proceeds and pressure on capacity builds, the increased cash flow would be an important source of finance for new investment. The tax cut would also have a beneficial effect on expectations in the business community, possibly yielding further gains in investment spending. The President is also renewing several previous recommendations to improve business profitability: a program of accelerated depreciation for newly installed plant and equipment in areas of high unemployment; the partial integration of corporate and personal income taxes over a period years, beginning in 1978, to offset the double tax on corporate earnings; and permanent extensions of the 10 percent investment tax credit, the 20 percent tax on the first $25,000 of corporate income, and the $50,000 corporate surtax exemption.

As noted in the 1963 *Economic Report of the President,* at a time when there was a similar concern that stagnating investment could damage the prospects for long-term growth:

...it is essential to our employment and growth objectives...that we stimulate more rapid expansion and modernization of America's productive facilities.... Investment in private plant and equipment is a principal source of long-term gains in productivity.... A high rate of investment is needed to equip our growing labor force with better and more modern equipment.... The investment needed to gain our growth objectives will be achieved only if we eliminate economic slack—only if we strengthen demand and broaden incentives to take risks.

The tax program outlined in this *Report* is designed to achieve these same objectives in 1977 and beyond. If business confidence does not improve and if investment does not begin to grow rapidly, additional stimulative measures for investment should be considered in the future.

[Monetary Policy]

The Federal Reserve Board has projected growth ranges for the three major money supply measures through the third quarter of 1977. Barring unforeseen changes in financial conditions, monetary growth within these ranges should be sufficient to finance continued economic expansion without risking a resurgence of inflation. However, the unusual uncertainties which have recently clouded the relationship between monetary growth—especially M_1 growth—and nominal GNP will require special caution and adaptability in setting, and revising if necessary, the growth ranges in the near future.

The specific ranges which have been set for the year ending in the third quarter of 1977 are 4½ to 6½ percent for M_1, 7½ to 10 percent for M_2, and 9 to 11½ percent for M_3. The projected ranges for M_1 reflect a projected structural shift in the growth of demand for this aggregate. The Federal Reserve has estimated that a number of regulatory and technological changes encouraging the use of alternatives to demand deposits for transactions will reduce the demand for M_1 in 1977. Quantitatively the most significant of these changes appear to be regulations permitting the use of savings deposits by businesses and State and local governments, the growing use of negotiable orders of withdrawal (NOW) savings accounts, which can provide the equivalent of checking services, and the use of telephonic transfers of funds from savings to checking accounts.

To the extent that these developments will continue to reduce the growth of demand for M_1 in 1977 the announced ranges for M_1 growth are consistent with a monetary policy that will encourage a stable economic recovery. If the effects of these changes are forecast correctly, then a sustained growth of M_1 beyond the new upper boundary would be more than is needed to finance the recovery, and hence it might overstimulate the economy and carry a risk of renewed inflation. However, if these structural changes cease to have this expected negative effect on M_1 demand, then a reconsideration of the ranges would be necessary to ensure that the growth in M_1 is consistent with a continuation of the recovery. In interpreting the impact of these structural changes it is important to recognize that a further slowdown in the economic recovery could be a direct cause of slower M_1 growth. If so, it would be inappropriate to adjust the growth range downward. A sustained rather than a reduced M_1 growth would be an important stabilizing influence, offsetting the weakness in aggregate demand. Because the current forecast of the structural change in M_1 demand is necessarily imprecise, financial developments must be closely monitored to determine the underlying causes of observed monetary growth trends.

This is not to say that the current uncertainties in the demand for M_1 suggest an abandonment of monetary growth ranges in favor of market interest rates or other money market indicators. The ranges directly act to dampen inflationary expectations by indicating a commitment to a monetary policy consistent with long-run price stability. Moreover interest rates alone cannot serve as a guide to monetary policy, especially during periods of high and variable inflation rates. A monetary policy which attempts to hold market interest rates steady for too long would be destabilizing. In the face of an unanticipated and excessive economic boom, such a policy would result in a rapid monetary expansion which would reinforce the boom and prevent the moderating effect of a rise in interest rates. On the other hand, if an unnoticed fall in inflationary expectations developed, a policy which stabilizes market interest rates would effectively raise real rates and be contractionary. Properly interpreted, however, interest rates as well as other economic variables, such as business investment, should be useful in projecting and revising the monetary growth ranges. Because a strong growth in the capital stock is crucial both for the near-term economic expansion and for the long-run sustainability of income growth, policy must be flexible enough to minimize the risk of not providing sufficient credit for long-term productive investment.

The upper boundary for M_2 and M_3 growth has been increased by one-half of 1 percentage point since the previous Federal Reserve growth projection...and this may provide some additional flexibility. One of the serious problems facing the monetary authorities is the choice of an appropriate measure of the money supply. Theoretical or empirical evidence does not indicate the clear superiority of any one of the measures, and at times they give conflicting indications. Throughout much of 1976, M_1 growth was near the lower boundary of its range and M_2 growth near the upper boundary. Until there is a reversal of these diverse patterns, the increase in the upper boundary for M_2 may permit a slightly faster growth of both aggregates if this is necessary to finance the recovery.

Our forecast for nominal GNP growth for the year ending in the third quarter of 1977 is about 11 percent. Along with these projected monetary growth ranges it implies that the velocity of M_1—the ratio of GNP to M_1—will increase by 4½ to 6½ percent. For the 4 quarters of 1976, M_1 velocity growth was 4.5 percent. Thus even if M_1 grows near the upper boundary of its range, velocity growth in 1977 will be about the same as in 1976. Some reduction in velocity growth normally occurs in the advanced stages of economic recoveries, especially during periods of slower economic growth like the latter part of 1976. The 4½ percent velocity growth of M_1 is unusually large and presupposes a continued structural shift in M_1 demand. The projections also imply that the velocity of M_2 will increase by 1 to 3½ percent over the year ending in the third quarter of 1977. This compares with a decline in M_2 velocity over the 4 quarters of 1976. Given our GNP forecasts, velocity gains closer to the larger of the above estimates—6½ and 3½ percent for M_1 and M_2 velocity respectively—would be unusual under any circumstances, and could generate a substantial increase in interest rates, unless the shift in money demand is even larger than last year.

For the longer run, fiscal policy will have to absorb proportionately more of the burden of restraint than monetary policy, if we are to meet our capital growth needs. In 1975 the Federal deficit absorbed 40 percent of the net funds raised in U.S. credit markets, and although the proportion was reduced to 30 percent in the first 3 quarters of 1976 it is not expected to be reduced further in 1977. This has not yet constrained private finance because overall credit needs have been low. As the borrowing requirements for private investment grow in the years ahead, however, fiscal stimulus will have to be lessened in order to release funds to meet these needs. Smaller Federal deficits, and eventually surpluses, will permit a less restrictive monetary policy with easier conditions in the credit market. In the years ahead aggregate demand management must rely less on consumption-oriented fiscal policy for stimulus, in order that monetary policy, which generally has a disproportionate effect on investment, is not forced to take all the burden of restraining inflationary forces.

Energy Policy

Assurance of sufficient supplies of energy resources will be required to sustain a steady economic expansion. To promote this end the President has recommended an energy program which stresses expanded domestic energy production and increased utilization of our most abundant resources, particularly coal. The key feature of this program is the phased elimination of controls on prices of natural gas and oil. While such a change would entail higher prices for these products in the near term, it would help to ensure that the U.S. economy is less vulnerable to sudden changes in the availability and cost of imported resources in coming years. Moreover, the most efficient production and allocation of the economy's resources, which would be encouraged by decontrol, would increase our aggregate supply capabilities and reduce inflationary pressures in the longer run.

Higher prices for oil and natural gas in the short run would reduce the relative share of imported oil and gas in total energy consumption. The higher price would also tend to shift fuel use away from oil and natural gas in favor of coal, and this would further moderate the economic impact of price increases by the Organization of Petroleum Exporting Countries (OPEC). The phased elimination of price controls on natural gas would help remove the risk that a period of severe cold weather could disrupt the economic recovery by forcing a random, unscheduled closing of factories owing to curtailment of supplies. Such forced closing did not cause significant disruptions in 1974 and 1975, when there was excess capacity; but as utilization rates increase during the next 2 years the risk of shortages in manufacturing capacity could become more serious with resulting inflationary pressures.

The President has also proposed measures to encourage the use of nuclear power. If they succeed, they will further reduce our dependence on imported oil and natural gas. Increased funds for general energy development have also been proposed. While these may contribute little in the near future, in the longer run the benefits to our energy supply capabilities could be substantial.

These actions would ease and hasten the adjustment of the economy to the new energy situation, and they would help to ensure more stable and reliable energy supplies for the future. The OPEC pricing decisions of December were a forceful reminder of the Nation's growing need for protection against foreign moves that affect the price and availability of imported oil. The proposed measures mean somewhat larger increases in domestic energy prices in the near term, and they would combine with the upward adjustments of U.S. petroleum prices under the Energy Policy and Conservation Act and the long overdue upward adjustments in natural gas prices under the Federal Power Commission (FPC) decisions of 1976. Taken together, however, these energy price increases would not be great enough to exert a significant restraining influence upon the expansion.

THE OUTLOOK

The main elements of continued economic growth in the United States are well established, despite the slowdown which occurred in the second half of 1976. With the assistance of the monetary and fiscal policies discussed above, and with continued strength in the private sector, real GNP is expected to rise by 5 to 5½ percent from 1976 to 1977, and its annual growth rate is expected to average between 5½ and 6 percent over the 4 quarters of 1977. This will permit a further expansion of employment and bring the rate of unemployment down to nearly 7 percent by year's end. At the same time, because the recovery over the past 2 years has avoided the excesses in public and private demand which characterized the previous upturn, the rate of inflation is not expected to rise above the 5 to 6 percent range.

With a much smaller expected rise in inventory investment compared to earlier stages of this recovery, the expansion in 1977 will require a strong growth in final demand. The expected recovery of business fixed investment will be an essential component of this demand. The proposed reduction in personal income taxes, which will stimulate a higher rate of real consumption growth, as well as the reduced corporate tax rate will help to encourage such an investment recovery. A continued strengthening of residential investment is also expected to boost the rate of growth in final sales in 1977....

Policy Implications

Neither potential GNP nor the full-employment unemployment rate will be reached in 1977. However, both may set limits to growth in coming years which cannot be exceeded without risking accelerating inflation and renewed instability. For example, the uncertainty that surrounds the estimates of potential output implies that caution must be observed as potential GNP is approached. If the 1974-75 reduction in the level of productivity proves to be permanent, physical capacity constraints similar to those encountered in 1973 may appeal well before an unemployment rate of 4.9 percent is reached. If so, they will seriously interfere with our full-employment goals.

As discussed previously, there are reasons to believe that the full-employment rate may be above the 4.9 percent benchmark we have used to estimate potential output. In any case, policy makers should realize that a 4 percent goal is not likely to be sustainable in the current economic environment; and because of the tentative nature of the full-employment rate estimates they should watch closely for signs of accelerating wage inflation when the overall rate of unemployment falls to about 5½ percent. The analysis suggests, for example, that the 4.9 percent unemployment rate in 1973 may have been partly responsible for the accelerating inflation in 1973-74, although this interpretation is clouded by other events such as the wage and price controls and the extraordinary increases in the prices of food and fuel. It also suggests that economic programs which aim to reduce unemployment in particularly depressed areas or among disadvantaged groups can be a useful supplement to policies which focus on the economy as a whole. Moreover it must be remembered that even with our revised estimates, the current output is far below potential, and unemployment is much above full-employment levels. Thus aggregate demand policies, such as the tax program proposed by the President, are still necessary to reduce unemployment and close the existing gap between potential and actual output.

The uncertainty about the lowest rate of unemployment that will not result in accelerating inflation also has important policy implications. Not too long ago economic policy makers were able to illustrate the difficulties of achieving both a stable price level and a full-employment economy by referring to the fairly close negative association between the unemployment rate and the inflation rate during the 1950s and early 1960s. While it was never thought to be exact, the relationship indicated the inevitable upward pressure of high utilization of labor and capital on prices and wages, and it was used to calculate the tradeoff between inflation and unemployment.

According/ to this relationship, the cost of an excessively low unemployment rate was a higher, though not necessarily increasing, rate of inflation.

During the last 10 years, however, this relationship has shifted dramatically and the concept of a stable tradeoff has become untenable. Nevertheless it is difficult to deny the essential fact that excessive expansion and extremely low unemployment rates ultimately produce higher and perhaps accelerating inflation. Nor can one deny that a slack economy with low utilization of capital and labor resources is usually a moderating influence on prices and wages. However, because of an economy-wide persistence in price and wage inflation, these excess demand and excess supply effects sometimes seem to work very slowly, with their influence spread over a long period.

In the long run the lower estimated growth rate of potential output, if projected into the future, implies a decrease in the "fiscal dividend" to be gained from full employment. Projection of the new potential GNP estimates through 1980 gives an output that is 4.8 percent lower than the previous estimate, a difference amounting to about $130-billion in current dollars. The estimate of Federal tax receipts in 1980 is thus more than $30-billion lower if output is assumed to be the new potential GNP rather than the old estimate. Lower total output implies lower tax revenues available for further tax cuts or for new or expanded Federal Government programs.

The challenge for the future will be to devise new policies to cope with the problems of economic growth and productivity. Increased productivity growth is necessary if the economy is to provide jobs without incurring declines in the growth of real income for the many new workers in the labor force....

CARTER'S INAUGURAL ADDRESS
January 20, 1977

Jimmy Carter was sworn in as the 39th President of the United States Jan. 20. At his inauguration he called for a "new national spirit of unity and trust" and a government "both competent and compassionate."

Chief Justice Warren E. Burger administered the oath of office to the 52-year-old Georgian at two minutes after noon. A crowd estimated at 150,000 cheered as Carter repeated the 35-word pledge with his hand resting on a family bible.

Carter began his 14-minute inaugural speech, one of the shortest in history, by thanking outgoing Republican President Gerald R. Ford "for all he has done to heal our land." In the low-key speech which followed, Carter reiterated his campaign themes of "a new beginning, a new dedication within our government and a new spirit among us all." He admitted, as the first Chief Executive of the nation's third century, that "I have no new dream to set forth today, but rather urge a fresh faith in the old dream."

The newly inaugurated President spent little time or words on domestic issues, saying simply that the government must be "absolute" in the commitment to human rights, "our laws fair, our natural beauty preserved; the powerful must not persecute the weak, and human dignity must be enhanced."

America's strength should be based, Carter said, "not merely on the size of an arsenal, but on the nobility of ideas." The enemies to be fought, he continued, were poverty, ignorance and injustice. Carter cited a rising "passion for freedom" around the world. He said that "there can be no nobler nor more ambitious task for America to undertake on this day of a new beginning than to help shape a just and peaceful world that is truly humane."

The President received applause seven times during the speech. Some of the most enthusiastic applause followed his comments on the arms race: "We pledge perseverance and wisdom in our efforts to limit the world's armaments to those necessary for each nation's own domestic safety. And we will move this year toward our ultimate goal—the elimination of all nuclear weapons from this earth."

In a brief but carefully worded sentence, Carter cautioned the nation's potential adversaries: "We are a proudly idealistic nation, but let no one confuse our idealism with weakness."

Carter drew his inaugural address from a variety of sources—a letter from one of his school teachers, Thomas Jefferson's first inaugural address, the Old Testament prophet Micah and themes from his 1,400 campaign speeches. The speech was spiritual in tone, with frequent references to religious and moral values. Five times during the speech Carter used the term "a new spirit."

Throughout the inaugural observances, Carter stressed that it was a celebration of the people. One such touch was in the way he dressed. For the swearing-in ceremony at the Capitol, he wore a dark blue suit instead of the traditional formal morning coat. He was hatless, as were the other men beside him on the platform: Ford, Vice President Walter F. Mondale and former Vice President Nelson A. Rockefeller. Ford wore a black suit.

Carter broke another precedent after the inauguration ceremony. Instead of riding at the head of the inaugural parade to the White House, he and his family walked the mile and a half down Pennsylvania Avenue from Capitol Hill.

> *Following is the full text of President Jimmy Carter's inaugural address, as it was delivered on Jan. 20, 1977. (Boldface headings in brackets have been added by Congressional Quarterly to highlight the organization of the text.):*

For myself and for our nation, I want to thank my predecessor for all he has done to heal our land.

In this outward and physical ceremony we attest once again to the inner and spiritual strength of our nation.

As my high school teacher, Miss Julia Coleman, used to say, "We must adjust to changing times and still hold to unchanging principles."

Here before me is the Bible used in the inauguration of our first President in 1789, and I have just taken the oath of office on the Bible my mother gave me just a few years ago, opened to a timeless admonition from the ancient prophet Micah:

"He hath showed thee, o man, what is good; and what does the Lord require of thee, but to do justly, and to love mercy, and to walk humbly with thy God." (Micah 6:8)

[New Spirit]

This inauguration ceremony marks a new beginning, a new dedication within our government, and a new spirit among us all. A President may sense and proclaim that new spirit, but only a people can provide it.

Two centuries ago our nation's birth was a milestone in the long quest for freedom, but the bold and brilliant dream which excited the founders of this nation still awaits its consummation. I have no new dream to set forth today, but rather urge a fresh faith in the old dream.

Ours was the first society openly to define itself in terms of both spirituality and human liberty. It is that unique self-definition which has given us an exceptional appeal—but it also imposes on us a special obligation—to take on those moral duties which, when assumed, seem invariably to be in our own best interests.

You have given me a great responsibility—to stay close to you, to be worthy of you, and to exemplify what you are. Let us create together a new national spirit of unity and trust. Your strength can compensate for my weakness, and your wisdom can help to minimize my mistakes.

Let us learn together and laugh together and work together and pray together, confident that in the end we will triumph together in the right.

The American dream endures. We must once again have full faith in our country—and in one another. I believe America can be better. We can be even stronger than before.

Let our recent mistakes bring a resurgent commitment to the basic principles of our nation, for we know that if we despise our own government we have no future. We recall in special times when we have stood briefly, but magnificently, united; in those times no prize was beyond our grasp.

But we cannot dwell upon remembered glory. We cannot afford to drift. We reject the prospect of failure or mediocrity or an inferior quality of life for any person.

Our government must at the same time be both competent and compassionate.

We have already found a high degree of personal liberty, and we are now struggling to enhance equality of opportunity. Our commitment to human rights must be absolute, our laws fair, our natural beauty preserved; the powerful must not persecute the weak, and human dignity must be enhanced.

We have learned that "more" is not necessarily "better," that even our great nation has its recognized limits, and that we can neither answer all questions nor solve all problems. We cannot afford to do everything, nor can we afford to lack boldness as we meet the future. So together, in a spirit of individual sacrifice for the common good, we must simply do our best.

[Example to Others]

Our nation can be strong abroad only if it is strong at home, and we know that the best way to enhance freedom in other lands is to demonstrate here that our democratic system is worthy of emulation.

To be true to ourselves, we must be true to others. We will not behave in foreign places so as to violate our rules and standards here at home, for we know that the trust which our nation earns is essential to our strength.

The world itself is now dominated by a new spirit. Peoples more numerous and more politically aware are craving and now demanding their place in the sun—not just for the benefit of their own physical condition, but for basic human rights.

The passion for freedom is on the rise. Tapping this new spirit, there can be no nobler nor more ambitious task for America to undertake on this day of a new beginning than to help shape a just and peaceful world that is truly humane.

We are a strong nation and we will maintain strength so sufficient that it need not be proven in combat—a quiet strength based not merely on the size of an arsenal, but on the nobility of ideas.

We will be ever vigilant and never vulnerable, and we will fight our wars against poverty, ignorance and injustice, for those are the enemies against which our forces can be honorably marshalled.

We are a proudly idealistic nation, but let no one confuse our idealism with weakness.

Because we are free we can never be indifferent to the fate of freedom elsewhere. Our moral sense dictates a clearcut preference for those societies which share with us an abiding respect for individual human rights. We do not seek to intimidate, but it is clear that a world which others can dominate with impunity would be inhospitable to decency and a threat to the well-being of all people.

[Arms Race]

The world is still engaged in a massive armaments race designed to insure continuing equivalent strength among potential adversaries. We pledge perseverance and wisdom in our efforts to limit the world's armaments to those necessary for each nation's own domestic safety. And we will move this year a step toward our ultimate goal—the elimination of all nuclear weapons from this earth.

We urge all other people to join us, for success can mean life instead of death.

Within us, the people of the United States, there is evident a serious and purposeful rekindling of confidence, and I join in the hope that when my time as your President has ended, people might say this about our nation:

That we had remembered the words of Micah and renewed our search for humility, mercy and justice;

That we had torn down the barriers that separated those of different race and region and religion, and where there had been mistrust, built unity, with a respect for diversity;

That we had found productive work for those able to perform it;

That we had strengthened the American family, which is the basis of our society;

That we had ensured respect for the law, and equal treatment under the law, for the weak and the powerful, for the rich and the poor;

And that we had enabled our people to be proud of their own government once again.

I would hope that the nations of the world might say that we had built a lasting peace, based not on weapons of war but on international policies which reflect our own most precious values.

These are not just my goals. And they will not be my accomplishments, but the affirmation of our nation's continuing moral strength and our belief in an undiminished, ever-expanding American dream.

CARTER'S DRAFT EVADER PARDON
January 21, 1977

Fulfilling a campaign promise in his first executive order as President, Jimmy Carter Jan. 21 granted a blanket pardon to all Vietnam-era draft evaders who had not been involved in a violent act.

Military deserters were not included in the pardon, but Carter ordered a study of their cases. He also ordered a study of the possible upgrading of bad conduct discharges and undesirable discharges.

The provisions in the President's proclamation and executive order granted "full, complete and unconditional pardon" to all persons convicted of violating the draft laws during the Vietnam era (Aug. 4, 1964-March 28, 1973) and to all those who might have violated the draft laws but had not been convicted.

Other provisions of the executive order permitted Americans who had become citizens of another country, after fleeing the United States to avoid the draft, to visit the United States freely and reapply for citizenship; and granted relief afforded by the Carter pardon to persons who had participated in President Ford's clemency program, which had required alternative service for draft evaders. (Historic Documents of 1974, p. 819).

Excluded from the pardon were: persons who violated the draft laws through force or violence; employees of the Selective Service System who violated the draft laws; and military deserters.

The pardon would apply to a group of 10,000 young men who had fled the country or had refused to enter military service. Nearly 100,000 men who entered and then deserted the armed forces during the Vietnam conflict were not included in Carter's pardon.

Reaction to the Pardon

Reaction to the pardon was both sharp and mixed. Edward M. Kennedy (D Mass.) said the President's action was "a major, impressive and compassionate step toward healing the wounds of Vietnam." Barry Goldwater (R Ariz.) called the pardon "the most disgraceful thing that a President has ever done." George McGovern (D S.D.), the Democratic presidential candidate in 1972, observed that Carter's move was "a compassionate and courageous first step." Robert Dole (R Kan.), Ford's running mate in the 1976 presidential campaign, commented, "It's distressing to see conscious disobedience condoned on a blanket basis."

Outside Congress, Carter's pardon drew sharp denunciations from major veterans' organizations and qualified praise from pro-amnesty groups. "We deeply regret and strongly protest the President's action," said William J. Rogers, the national commander of the American Legion. Cooper Holt, the executive director of the Washington office of the Veterans of Foreign Wars called the action "...a sad day in the history of our nation," because the President, he said, had "shown a lack of concern for the 30 million living veterans who have served our nation in time of war."

Aryeh Neier, executive director of the American Civil Liberties Union, said he was delighted by the President's action but noted that there were only 4,000 draft evasion cases that remained open. Neier stated that "99 per cent of the people who could have benefited from full amnesty still needed to be dealt with." The Safe Return Amnesty Committee in New York issued a statement that called Carter's plan for a Pentagon review of deserter and qualified discharge cases "totally unacceptable." "It's like asking the prosecutor to be the jury," said Tod Ensign, an attorney for the group. A spokesman for the National Council for Universal and Unconditional Amnesty said that "since draft resisters are essentially white, middle-class and well educated, and the military resisters [deserters] are primarily disproportionately from the poor and minority groups, we feel that this is a very discriminatory pardon."

Senate Opposition to the Pardon

The Senate Jan. 25 narrowly defeated an attempt to put itself on record in opposition to President Carter's pardon of Vietnam-era draft resisters. Killed by a two-vote margin (48-46) was a resolution (S Res 18), introduced by James B. Allen (D Ala.), expressing the sense of the Senate that Carter should not have issued his unconditional pardon to persons who violated the draft laws in the 1960s and early 1970s.

Supporters of the resolution conceded that they could not legally restrict the President's pardon power, which is granted by the Constitution. According to Allen, the purpose of the resolution was to express what he termed the "overwhelming public opinion" against the pardon as well as to discourage Carter from pardoning military deserters.

Opponents charged that the resolution was moot, an empty gesture, because the pardon had already been issued. Russell B. Long (D La.), who supported the Allen resolution in earlier procedural votes, argued that it was time for the Senate to drop the matter in order to move on to more important business.

Rejection of the resolution came on a motion by Robert C. Byrd (D W.Va.) to table, and thus kill, S Res 18. The vote split along conservative-liberal lines, resulting in a conservative coalition vote in which a majority of voting Republicans and southern Democrats opposed the position taken by a majority of voting northern Democrats.

Background: Ford Clemency Program

President Ford in 1974 announced a conditional clemency program for Vietnam-era military deserters and draft evaders.

The program offered deserters and draft evaders a chance to clear their records by swearing allegiance to the United States and performing up to 24 months of low-paid alternative service in schools, hospitals and other public institutions.

Ford first disclosed his plans in an Aug. 19, 1974, speech before the Veterans of Foreign Wars. The program was formally unveiled Sept. 16, when the President proclaimed his "earned re-entry" clemency offer. Because of initial poor response and confusion over the program, the original Jan. 31, 1975, reporting deadline to request clemency was extended to March 31, 1975.

Before closing its doors Sept. 15, 1975, the Presidential Clemency Board, headed by former Sen. Charles E. Goodell (R N.Y. 1968-71), processed some 21,500 applications for presidential pardons and clemency discharges from convicted deserters and draft dodgers.

Under a second component of the clemency program, the Justice Department reviewed the applications of unconvicted draft evaders, but only 680 out of 4,000 persons who were eligible applied for alternate service. Only 5,300 of the 12,500 unconvicted military deserters applied to the Defense Department for either an undesirable or a clemency discharge.

Of the 21,500 applications received by the board, 5,950 were found ineligible for the program, principally because their period of service in the military fell before Aug. 4, 1964, the cutoff date for participation.

Disposition of the remaining 15,500 cases, which were reviewed on an individual basis and then forwarded to the President for approval, indicated that 43 per cent of the cases were pardoned without a requirement for service, and 51 per cent were pardoned with a service requirement of 12 *months or less. Six per cent were denied pardons and less than one per cent of the cases required more than 12 months service.*

Following are the texts of President Carter's Jan. 21, 1977, proclamation and executive order granting pardons to draft evaders from the Vietnam War era:

PROCLAMATION
Granting Pardon for Violations of the Selective Service Act, August 4, 1964, to March 28, 1973

Acting pursuant to the grant of authority in Article II, Section 2, of the Constitution of the United States, I, Jimmy Carter, President of the United States, do hereby grant a full, complete and unconditional pardon to: (1) all persons who may have committed any offense between August 4, 1964 and March 28, 1973 in violation of the Military Selective Service Act or any rule or regulation promulgated thereunder; and (2) all persons heretofore convicted, irrespective of the date of conviction, of any offense committed between August 4, 1964 and March 28, 1973 in violation of the Military Selective Service Act, or any rule or regulation promulgated thereunder, restoring to them full political, civil and other rights.

This pardon does not apply to the following who are specifically excluded therefrom:

(1) All persons convicted of or who may have committed any offense in violation of the Military Selective Service Act, or any rule or regulation promulgated thereunder, involving force or violence; and

(2) All persons convicted of or who may have committed any offense in violation of the Military Selective Service Act, or any rule or regulation promulgated thereunder, in connection with duties or responsibilities arising out of employment as agents, officers or employees of the Military Selective Service system.

IN WITNESS WHEREOF, I have hereunto set my hand this 21st day of January, in the year of our Lord nineteen hundred and seventy-seven, and of the Independence of the United States of America the two hundred and first.

EXECUTIVE ORDER

Relating to Violations of the Selective Service Act, August 4, 1964, to March 28, 1973

The following actions shall be taken to facilitate Presidential Proclamation of Pardon of January 21, 1977:

1. The Attorney General shall cause to be dismissed with prejudice to the government all pending indictments for violations of the Military Selective Service Act alleged to have occurred between August 4, 1964 and March 28, 1973 with the exception of the following:

(a) Those cases alleging acts of force or violence deemed to be so serious by the Attorney General as to warrant continued prosecution; and

(b) Those cases alleging acts in violation of the Military Selective Service Act by agents, employees or officers of the Selective Service System arising out of such employment.

2. The Attorney General shall terminate all investigations now pending and shall not initiate further investigations alleging violations of the Military Selective Service Act between August 4, 1964 and March 28, 1973, with the exception of the following:

(a) Those cases involving allegations of force or violence deemed to be so serious by the Attorney General as to warrant continued investigation, or possible prosecution; and

(b) Those cases alleging acts in violation of the Military Selective Service Act by agents, employees or officers of the Selective Service System arising out of such employment.

3. Any person who is or may be precluded from reentering the United States under 8 U.S.C. 1182(a)(22) or under any other law, by reason of having committed or apparently committed any violation of the Military Selective Service Act shall be permitted as any other alien to reenter the United States.

The Attorney General is directed to exercise his discretion under 8 U.S.C. 1182(d)(5) or other applicable law to permit the reentry of such persons under the same terms and conditions as any other alien.

This shall not include anyone who falls into the exceptions of paragraphs 1(a) and (b) and 2(a) and (b) above.

4. Any individual offered conditional clemency or granted a pardon or other clemency under Executive Order 11803 or Presidential Proclamation 4313, dated September 16, 1974, shall receive the full measure of relief afforded by this program if they are otherwise qualified under the terms of this Executive Order.

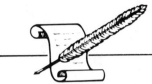

February

CARTER'S "FIRESIDE CHAT"
February 2, 1977

President Carter asked the American people Feb. 2 to rekindle the World War II spirit of dedication and sacrifice necessary to achieve national goals. In an informal 25-minute talk, Carter—wearing a cardigan sweater and sitting in a chair near a fireplace in the White House library—discussed his administration's plans. Carter's talk, reminiscent of President Franklin D. Roosevelt's occasional "fireside chats" on the radio, ranged over such topics as the energy crisis, the state of the economy, plans for government reorganization and foreign policy.

Energy policy was uppermost in the President's mind. "We must face the fact that the energy shortage is permanent," Carter said. "There is no way we can solve it quickly." The United States, he said, as he had during his campaign, "is the only major industrial country without a comprehensive, long-range energy policy." Rather than promise energy independence, as two previous Presidents had done, Carter shifted the emphasis to conservation by pointing out that the nation wasted more energy each year than it had imported. A comprehensive energy plan would be presented April 20, Carter said, that would demand an equitable distribution of the required sacrifices so that the "burden [would] be borne fairly among all our people." Its emphasis would be on conservation, the development of coal resources, research on solar energy and other renewable energy sources, and strict safeguards on atomic energy. (Energy plan, p. 277)

Carter seemed to go out of his way to find praise for Congress. He spoke of the cooperation of Congress with his administration's advisers in developing economic stimulus legislation. (Carter budget revisions, p.

125). *Some of President Carter's advisers had expressed concern, before the "fireside chat" was given, about congressional sensitivity to Carter's going to the public with his programs before he outlined them to senators and representatives. The President mentioned the need for "careful study and close cooperation with Congress" to achieve, among other program goals, tax reform and welfare reform.*

Carter touched several bases in his discussion of economic problems. Finding jobs for the unemployed was his primary concern and particularly jobs for Vietnam veterans "as one more step toward binding up the wounds of the war years." The President talked about permanent tax changes as well as the economic perils of high inflation. He said that increasing the standard income tax deduction would not only save many taxpayers money, but also would allow 75 per cent of all taxpayers to file a simplified return.

Returning to his campaign themes of competence and compassion in government, the President called for elimination of waste by his administration. "Whenever the government must perform a function, it should do it efficiently," he said. "Wherever free competition would do a better job of serving the public, the government should stay out." Among the steps Carter has taken to increase efficiency are:

●Development of a reorganization plan to include zero-based budgeting, removal of unnecessary regulations, "sunset" laws to cancel outdated programs, and streamlining of overlapping or duplicative services.

●Development of a new welfare system to replace the old one. (Carter's welfare plan, p. 551)

●Review of the 1,250 federal advisory committees and commissions, with an eye toward abolishing the unnecessary ones.

Most of the talk was a restatement of policies that Carter had expressed earlier. He did, however, make a few new commitments. Carter said that the White House staff, numbering about 500 under President Ford, would be reduced by one-third, as would the top staffs of Cabinet officers. A ceiling would be put on employment in government agencies "so we can bring the growth of government under control," Carter said. Government regulations would be reduced in number, would carry their author's name and would be "written in plain English, for a change," according to the President.

The strict rules he had imposed on his appointees for financial disclosure and avoidance of conflicts of interest would be made permanent, Carter said. And he pledged to choose his appointees in a way that "will close the revolving door between government regulatory agencies, on the one hand, and the businesses they regulate, on the other." (Carter's ethics statement, p. 27)

Carter spelled out in greater detail than he had in previous public statements, his attitude toward frugality at high levels and his plans for reaching out toward ordinary people." Government officials can't be sensitive to your problems if we are living like royalty here in Washington," he said.

While most of Carter's talk focused on domestic problems, Carter pledged to maintain a "strong, lean, efficient fighting force" coupled with an effort to reduce armaments. "Our policy should be based on close cooperation with our allies and worldwide respect for human rights, and it must always reflect our own moral values," he stated. Carter said he would work toward improving U.S. relations with the Soviet Union and China. But he said, too, that the United States "would continue to express... concern about violations of human rights...without upsetting...efforts toward friendly relations with other countries." (Carter on human rights, p. 189)

> *Following is the text of President Carter's address to the nation, televised from the White House Feb. 2, 1977* (Boldface headings in brackets have been added by Congressional Quarterly to highlight the organization of the text.):

Good evening.

Tomorrow it will be two weeks since I became President.

I've spent a lot of time deciding how I can be a good President. This talk, which the broadcast networks have agreed to bring to you, is one of several steps that I will take to keep in close touch with the people of our country, and to let you know informally about our plans for the coming months.

When I was running for President, I made a number of commitments.

I take them very seriously. I believe that they were the reason that I was elected.

And I want you to know that I intend to carry them out.

As you've probably noticed already, I have acted on several of my promises.

I will report to you from time to time about our government—both our problems and our achievements, but tonight I want to tell you how I plan to carry out some of my other commitments.

Some of our obvious goals can be achieved very quickly—for example, through executive orders and decisions made directly by me. But in many other areas we must move carefully, with full involvement by the Congress, allowing time for citizens to participate in careful study, in order to develop predictable, long-range programs that we can be sure are affordable and that we know will work.

Some of these efforts will also require dedication—perhaps even some sacrifice—from you. But I don't believe that any of us are afraid to learn that our national goals require cooperation and mutual effort.

[Energy]

One of our most urgent projects is to develop a national energy policy.

As I pointed out during the campaign, the United States is the only major industrial country without a comprehensive long-range energy policy.

The extremely cold weather this winter has dangerously depleted our supplies of natural gas and fuel oil and forced hundreds of thousands of workers off the job. I congratulate the Congress for its quick action on the Emergency Natural Gas Act which was passed today and signed just a few minutes ago.

But the real problem—our failure to plan for the future or to take energy conservation seriously—started long before this winter, and it will take much longer to solve. I realize that many of you have not believed that we really have an energy problem. But this winter has made all of us realize that we have to act.

Now the Congress has already made many of the preparations for energy legislation. Presidential assistant Dr. James Schlesinger is beginning to direct an effort to develop a national energy policy. Many groups of Americans will be involved. On April 20, we will have completed the planning for our energy program and will immediately then ask the Congress for its help in enacting comprehensive legislation.

Our program will emphasize conservation. The amount of energy being wasted which could be saved is greater than the total energy that we are importing from foreign countries. We will also stress development of our rich coal reserves in an environmentally sound way; we'll emphasize research on solar energy and other renewable energy sources; and we'll maintain strict safeguards on necessary atomic energy production.

The responsibility for setting energy policy is now split among more than 50 different agencies, departments and bureaus in the federal government. Later this month, I will ask the Congress for its help in combining many of these agencies in a new Energy Department to bring order out of chaos. Congressional leaders have already been working on this for quite awhile.

We must face the fact that the energy shortage is permanent. There is no way we can solve it quickly.

But if we all cooperate and make modest sacrifices, if we learn to live thriftily and remember the importance of helping our neighbors, then we can find ways to adjust, and to make our society more efficient and our own lives more enjoyable and productive. Utility companies must promote conservation and not consumption. Oil and natural gas companies must be honest with all of us about their reserves and profits. We will find out the difference between real shortages and artificial ones. We will ask private companies to sacrifice, just as private citizens must do.

All of us must learn to waste less energy. Simply by keeping our thermostats, for instance, at 65 degrees in the daytime and 55 degrees at night we could save half the current shortage of natural gas.

There is no way that I, or anyone else in the government, can solve our energy problems if you are not willing to help.

I know that we can meet this energy challenge if the burden is borne fairly among all our people—and if we realize that in order to solve our energy problems we need not sacrifice the quality of our lives.

The Congress has made great progress toward responsible strip-mining legislation, so that we can produce more energy without unnecessary destruction of our beautiful lands. My administration will support these efforts this year. We will also ask Congress for its help with legislation which will reduce the risk of future oil-tanker spills and help deal with those that do occur.

[Economy]

I also stated during my campaign that our administration would do everything possible to restore a healthy American economy.

Our nation was built on the principle of work and not welfare—productivity and not stagnation.

But I took office a couple of weeks ago in the middle of the worst economic slowdown of the last 40 years.

More than seven and a half million people who want to work cannot find it, according to the latest statistics. Because of high unemployment and idle factories, the average American family, like yours, has been losing $1,800 a year in income, and many billions of dollars have been added to the federal deficit.

Also, inflation hurts us all. In every part of the country, whether we have a job or whether we are looking for a job, we must race just to keep up with the constant rise in prices.

Inflation has hit us hardest not in luxuries, but in the essentials—food, energy, health, housing. You see it every time you go shopping. I understand that unemployment and inflation are very real, and have done great harm to many American families.

Nothing makes it harder to provide decent health, housing, and education for our people, protect our environment, or to realize our goal of a balanced budget, than a stagnant economy.

As soon as I was elected, the leaders of the Congress and my own advisers began to work with me to develop a proposal for economic recovery. We were guided by the principle that everyone who is able to work ought to work; that our economic strength is based on a healthy, productive private business sector; that we must provide the greatest help to those with the greatest need; and that there must be a predictable and a steady growth in our economy.

Two days ago I presented this plan to the Congress. It is a balanced plan, with many elements, to meet the many causes of our economic problems.

One element that I'm sure you'll like is reducing taxes. This year, the one-time tax benefits to the average family of four with $10,000 in income will be $200—a 30 per cent reduction in income taxes.

But my primary concern is still jobs, and these one-time tax rebates are the only quick, effective way to get money into the economy and create those jobs.

But at the same time, we are reducing taxes permanently by increasing the standard deduction, which most taxpayers claim. Again, this family of four earning $10,000 will save $133 on a permanent basis—about 20 per cent—on future income taxes. This will also be a major step toward tax simplification, allowing 75 per cent of all taxpayers to take the standard deduction and to file a very simple tax return—quite different from the one that you will file this year.

We will also provide tax incentives to business firms, to encourage them to fight inflation by expanding output and to hire more of our people who are eager for work. I think it makes more sense for the government to help workers stay on the payroll than to force them onto unemployment benefits or welfare payments.

We have several proposals, too, in this legislation, to help our cities, which have been especially hard-hit by nationwide economic problems. Communities where unemployment is worst will be eligible for additional money through the revenue-sharing program. A special program of public service employment will enable those who are now unemployed to contribute to their communities in hospitals, nursing homes, park and recreation programs and other related activities. A strong public works program will permit the construction of selected projects which are needed most.

These will not be make-work projects. They will be especially valuable in communities where budget cutbacks have reduced municipal services, and they will also help to prevent local tax increases.

Now because unemployment is the most severe among special groups of our people—the young, the disabled, minority groups—we will focus our training programs on them.

The top priority in our job-training programs will go to young veterans of the Vietnam War. Unemployment is much higher among veterans than among others of the same age who did not serve in the military. I hope that putting many thousands of veterans back to work will be one more step toward binding up the wounds of the war years and toward helping those who have helped our country in the past.

I realize that very few people will think that this total economic plan is perfect. Many groups would like to see more of one kind of aid and less of another.

But I am confident that this is the best-balanced plan that we can produce for the overall economic health of the nation.

It will produce steady, balanced, sustainable growth. It does not ignore inflation to solve unemployment—or vice versa.

It does not ask one group of people to sacrifice solely for the benefit of another group. It asks all of us to contribute, participate and share to get the country on the road back to work again.

It is an excellent investment in the future.

[Reorganization]

I also said many times during the campaign that we must reform and reorganize the federal government.

I have often used the phrase "competent and compassionate" to describe what our government should be. When the government must perform a function, it should do it efficiently. Wherever free competition would do a better job of serving the public, the government should stay out. Ordinary people should be able to understand how our own government works, and to get satisfactory answers to questions.

Our confused and wasteful system that took so long to grow will take a long time to change. The place to start is at the top—in the White House.

I am reducing the size of the White House staff by nearly one-third, and I have asked the members of the Cabinet to do the same at the top staff level. Soon I will put a ceiling on the number of people employed by federal government agencies, so we can bring the growth of government under control.

We are now reviewing the government's 1,250 advisory committees and commissions, to see how many could be abolished without harm to the public.

We have eliminated expensive and unnecessary luxuries, such as door-to-door limousine service for many top officials, including all members of the White House staff. Government officials can't be sensitive to your problems if we are living like royalty here in Washington. While I am deeply grateful for the good wishes that lie behind them, I would like to ask that people not send gifts to me or to my family, or to anyone else who serves in my administration.

We will cut down also on government regulations, and we will make sure that those that are written are in plain English for a change. Whenever a regulation is issued, it will carry its author's name. And I will request the Cabinet members to read all regulations personally before they are released.

This week I will ask the Congress for enabling legislation to let me reorganize the government. The passage of this legislation, which will give me the same authority extended to every President from Franklin Roosevelt through Richard Nixon and used by many governors across the country, is absolutely crucial to a successful reorganization effort. So far, news from the Congress, because of their support, is very encouraging.

The Office of Management and Budget is now working on this plan, which will include zero-based budgeting, removal of unnecessary government regulations, sunset laws to cancel programs that have outlived their purpose and elimination of overlap and duplication among government services.

We will not propose changes until we have done our best to be sure they are right. But we will be eager to learn from experience. If a program does not work, we will end it, instead of just starting another to conceal our first mistakes.

We will also move quickly to reform our tax system and welfare system.

I said in the campaign that our income tax system was a disgrace, because it is so arbitrary, complicated and unfair. I made a commitment to a total overhaul of the income tax laws.

The economic program that I have already mentioned earlier will, by enabling more taxpayers to use the standard deduction, be just a first step toward a much better tax system.

My advisers have already started working with Congress on a study of a more complete tax reform, which will give us a fairer, simpler system. We will outline the study procedures very soon, and, after consultation with many American citizens and with the Congress, we will present a comprehensive tax reform package before the end of this year.

[Welfare]

The welfare system also needs a complete overhaul. Welfare waste robs both the taxpayers of our country and those who genuinely need help. It often forces families to split. It discourages people from seeking work.

The Secretary of Labor and the Secretary of Health, Education and Welfare, and others, have already begun a review of the entire welfare system. They will of course work with the Congress to develop proposals for a new system which will minimize abuse, strengthen the family—and emphasize adequate support for those who cannot work and training and jobs for those who can work. We expect their first report to be ready within 90 days.

In the meantime, I will support the Congress in its efforts to deal with the widespread fraud and waste and abuse of our Medicaid system.

Reforming the government also means making the government as open and honest as it can be. Congress is moving strongly on ethics legislation.

I have asked the people appointed by me to high positions in government to abide by strict rules of financial disclosure and to avoid all conflicts of interest. I intend to make those rules permanent, and I will select my appointees in such a way which will close the revolving door between government regulatory agencies on the one hand and the businesses they regulate on the other.

My Cabinet members and I will conduct an open administration, with frequent press conferences and reports to the people and with "town hall" meetings all across the nation, where you can criticize, make suggestions and ask questions.

We are also planning with some of the radio networks live call-in sessions in the Oval Office during which I can accept your phone calls and answer the questions that are on your mind. I have asked the members of the Cabinet to travel regularly around the country to stay in close touch with you out in your communities, where government services are delivered.

There are many other areas of domestic policy—housing, health, crime, education, agriculture and others—that will concern me as President but which I do not have time to discuss tonight.

All of these projects will take careful study and close cooperation with the Congress. Many will take longer than I would like. But we are determined to work on all of them. Later, through other reports, I will explain how, with your help and the help of Congress, we can carry them out.

[Foreign Policy]

I have also made commitments about our nation's foreign policy. As commander in chief of the armed forces, I am determined to have a strong, lean, efficient fighting force. Our policy should be based on close cooperation with our allies and worldwide respect for human rights, a reduction in world armaments—and it must always reflect our own moral values. I want our nation's actions to make you proud.

Yesterday, Vice President Mondale returned from his 10-day visit with leaders of Western Europe and Japan. I asked him to make this trip to demonstrate our intention to consult our traditional allies and friends on all important questions. I have been pleased with his report. Vice President Mondale will be a constant and close adviser for me.

In a spirit of international friendship, we will soon welcome here in the United States the leaders of several nations, beginning with our neighbors, Canada and Mexico.

This month the Secretary of State, Cyrus Vance, will go to the Middle East, seeking ways to achieve a genuine peace between Israel and its Arab neighbors.

Our ambassador to the United Nations, Andrew Young, left last night on a visit to Africa to demonstrate our friendship for its peoples and our commitment to peaceful change towards majority rule in southern Africa.

I will also strive to improve our relations with the Soviet Union and the Peoples' Republic of China, ensuring our security while seeking to reduce the risk of conflict.

We will continue to express our concern about violations of human rights, as we have during this past week, without upsetting our efforts toward friendly relationships with other countries. Later, on another program, I will make a much more complete report to you on foreign policy matters.

[Public Cooperation]

I would like to tell you now about one of the things I have already learned in my brief time in office. I have learned that there are many things that a President cannot do.

There is no energy policy that we can develop that would do more good than voluntary conservation.

There is no economic policy that would do as much as shared faith in hard work, efficiency and in the future of our system.

I know that both the Congress and the administration, as partners in leadership, have limited powers. That's the way it ought to be.

But in the months in which I have campaigned, prepared to take office, and now begun to serve as your President, I have found a reason for optimism.

With the help of my predecessor, we have come through a very difficult period in our nation's history. But for almost 10 years we have not had a sense of common national interest.

We have lost faith in joint efforts and mutual sacrifices. Because of the divisions in our country, many of us cannot remember a time when we really felt united.

But I remember another difficult time in our nation's history when we felt a different spirit.

During World War II, we faced a terrible crisis—but the challenge of fighting Nazism drew us together.

Those of us old enough to remember know that they were dark and frightening times—but many of our memories are of people ready to help each other for the common good.

I believe that we are ready for that same spirit again—to plan ahead, to work together and to use common sense. Not because of war, but because we realize that we must act together to solve our problems, and because we are ready to trust one another.

As President, I will not be able to provide everything that every one of you might like. I am sure to make many mistakes.

But I can promise you that your needs will never be ignored, nor will we forget who put us in office.

We will always be a nation of differences—business and labor, blacks and whites, men and women, people of different regions and religions and different ethnic backgrounds—but with faith and confidence in each other, our differences can be a source of personal fullness and national strength rather than a cause of weakness and division.

If we are a united nation, then I can be a good President. But I will need your help to do it. I will do my best. I know you will do yours.

Thank you very much, and good night.

REVIEW OF MARTIN LUTHER KING INVESTIGATION

February 18, 1977

A Justice Department task force concluded, after an eight-month study, that the Federal Bureau of Investigation's inquiry into the murder of civil rights leader Martin Luther King Jr. was "thoroughly, honestly and successfully" conducted and that James Earl Ray, King's convicted murderer, had acted alone. The findings of the special task force were released by the Justice Department Feb. 18.

The task force also reviewed the FBI's security investigation of King. It found that the investigation initially may have been justifiable, but that its continuation for six years had been "unwarranted." The task force branded the FBI methods and attempts to discredit King as "very probably...felonious."

The review of the FBI investigations had been ordered April 26, 1976, by then Attorney General Edward H. Levi. Levi's order came after the Senate Select Committee to Study Governmental Operations with Respect to Intelligence had disclosed Dec. 3-4, 1975, that both the Central Intelligence Agency (CIA) and the FBI had committed numerous abuses in their pursuit of intelligence. (Historic Documents of 1975, p. 873). The Senate committee revealed that the FBI had engaged in a six-year surveillance of King, involving wiretaps, electronic bugs and paid informants. (Historic Documents of 1976, pp. 115, 235, 321).

Levi directed the task force to review all of the FBI files pertaining to King with four objectives in mind: "First, whether the FBI investigation of...King's assassination was thorough and honest; second, whether there was any evidence that the FBI was involved in the assassination of Dr.

King; third, in light of the first two questions, whether there is any new evidence which has come to the attention of the Department concerning the assassination...which should be dealt with by the appropriate authorities; fourth, whether the nature of the relationship between the Bureau and Dr. King calls for criminal prosecution." The Attorney General directed the Justice Department's Office of Professional Responsibility to carry out the investigation.

The report on the King probe had gone to Levi shortly before he left office Jan. 20. Public release had been delayed to give incoming Attorney General Griffin B. Bell time to review the report and to avoid creating the appearance that the Justice Department was trying to influence the House of Representatives in its deliberations on reviving the Select Committee on Assassinations, created by the 94th Congress to investigate the deaths of King and President John F. Kennedy.

Investigation of King Murder

The task force report agreed with the FBI's conclusion that James Earl Ray acted alone in King's murder in Memphis, Tennessee, on April 4, 1968. The report noted, however, that the notion of a conspiracy had lingered on in the public mind because of Ray's "self-serving tales" about an alleged gun runner named "Raoul." Ray had stated that Raoul was the mysterious killer who shot King and then set Ray up to be arrested for King's murder. The task force study, noting that several versions of Ray's story were contradictory, concluded that Ray had lied and that Raoul never existed. No evidence was found by either the FBI or the task force to substantiate the existence of a conspiracy to murder Dr. King.

The failure of the FBI or the task force to explain how Ray supported himself between the time he escaped from Missouri State Prison April 23, 1967, and his apprehension for the murder of King June 8, 1968, at the London airport, remained a source of controversy and speculation. During the 13½ months Ray was a fugitive he spent more than $5,000 and had a traceable income of $664. The task force report explained the discrepancy by suggesting that Ray had committed several robberies or burglaries to get money; but the report admitted that "the sources of Ray's funds still remain a mystery today."

Security Investigation

The task force report reviewed the FBI's security investigation of King and its extensive effort to discredit King and his influence in the civil rights movement. The task force concluded that the inquiry began with a legitimate investigation by the FBI of one of King's advisers who had been tabbed by the FBI as a member of the Communist Party. Apart from the fact that the adviser (unnamed in the task force report) wrote speeches for King and advised King on matters of strategy, the FBI never obtained any evidence to suggest that King was affiliated with the Communist Party or ever varied from his belief in non-violent protest. The task force study said that when it became clear to FBI Director J. Edgar Hoover that King was not influenced by the adviser's leftist ideology, the FBI's use of its counterintelligence program (COINTELPRO) against King should have been terminated. According to the task force, the FBI operation against King included the bugging of hotel rooms, telephone wiretaps and the leaking of derogatory information about King's personal life.

Recommendations

On the basis of its review of the FBI murder investigation, the task force recommended the following steps:

• *The appropriate division chief within the Justice Department should determine what progress reports he wants from the FBI during sensitive investigations. To exercise tighter control over the FBI, the Bureau's public relations activities should be controlled by the Attorney General's Office of Public Information.*

• *The FBI should not be permitted to take criminal action in sensitive investigations without the closest coordination and consultation with the Justice Department.*

The task force observed that because there were no black special agents in the Bureau in the 1960s, and none in the hierarchy, the investigation into King's death was hindered by the inability of investigators to communicate fully with members of the black community.

The task force made the following recommendations and findings based on its review of the FBI security investigation of King:

• *No criminal action could be taken against FBI personnel, past or present, because the five-year statute of limitations had run out. Those who ordered the extensive investigation were either dead or retired.*

• *The tapes and the transcripts obtained by the FBI during its surveillance of King should be sealed and sent to the National Archives with the recommendation that Congress pass legislation denying the public access to the material, and that Congress authorize the destruction of all tapes and transcripts, and material derived from them.*

• *The Senate Select Committee on Intelligence should serve as the oversight committee of the FBI.*

• *A felony penalty, rather than a misdemeanor, should be levied for the malicious dissemination of investigative data from FBI files.*

• *The FBI should have no further authority to engage in COINTELPRO type activities which involved affirmative punitive action.*

Ray Prison Escape

Four months after the Justice Department task force issued its report, James Earl Ray, serving a 99-year sentence in Brushy Mountain Prison in Petros, Tenn., escaped from the maximum security prison with a group of six other convicts. He was captured three days later, on June 13, unharmed.

The escape rekindled public interest in the King murder and doubts in the minds of many over the role Ray played in the assassination, despite the task force's conclusion that Ray had acted alone and that there had been no conspiracy.

> *Following are excerpts from the Justice Department Task Force to Review the FBI Martin Luther King Jr. Security and Assassination Investigations, dated Jan. 11, 1977, and released to the public Feb. 18, 1977. (Boldface headings in brackets have been added by Congressional Quarterly to highlight the organization of the text.):*

...Based on our review of the files, the task force is satisfied that the FBI did a credible and thorough job in attempting to identify any possible conspiracy or persons who could have been involved in the murder [of Dr. Martin Luther King Jr.]. In each of the allegations received, the Bureau immediately interviewed the person who was the source of the allegation where this was possible (i.e. where the source was not anonymous). In situations where the complaint was not an obvious hoax the Bureau then attempted immediately to identify the alleged participants and interview them. Where there was not a satisfactory explanation to dispel the allegation concerning such matters as whereabouts or associations, the Bureau then would check further. This does not mean that every allegation was pursued to the ultimate degree. Judgment based on experience dictated many of the decisions.

These judgments were also tempered by a critical factor. Within fifteen days after the murder, the FBI was convinced that Galt [Eric Starvo Galt, an alias used by James Earl Ray] and Ray were the same person, that this individual purchased the rifle, rented the room across from the Lorraine Motel, and fired the shot that killed Dr. King. While there were many other people who were antagonistic toward Dr. King and many who had apparently discussed killing him, any successful conspiracy would have to have involved Ray based on the evidence at hand. In all the years following the assassination, the investigation has failed to reveal any connection between any alleged conspirator(s) and James Earl Ray including those alleged by Ray himself. Indeed, the overwhelming evidence indicates that Ray was almost totally alone during the year after his escape from the Missouri State Prison....

...Absent a statement to us from Ray, four existing Ray explanations were compared and are here briefly noted.

First, no one, other than his attorneys talked with Ray before the plea bargaining resulted in his conviction of the First Degree murder of Martin Luther King Jr., and sentencing in open court on March 10, 1969, before Judge W. Preston Battle, Criminal Court of Shelby County, Tennessee.... At that time, ...Judge Battle asked Ray: "Are you pleading guilty to Murder in the First Degree under such circumstances that would make you legally guilty of Murder in the First Degree under the law as explained to you by your lawyers?"

Ray answered: "Yes."

Ray then acknowledged that he was pleading guilty freely, voluntarily and understandingly. He and his attorney, Percy Foreman, initialed the copy of these questions and answers. Ray also signed a detailed stipulation confessing that he fired the fatal shot....

...Second, Ray...acknowledged that he bought the murder weapon, made his way to Memphis, rented the room there at 422 South Main on April 4, 1968, using the alias "John Willard," waited in the white Mustang, and drove "Raoul" away from the crime scene after the murder wholly unaware of the killing of Dr. King. In this version "Raoul," or "Roual," is the mysterious killer whom Ray thought to be an international gun-runner; Ray bought the murder weapon for "Raoul" thinking it was to be displayed to prospective Mexican buyers in Room 5-B of the "flop house" on South Main Street....

Third, in a statement read on a program of Station KMOX-TV St. Louis, Missouri, in August of 1969 by his brother Jerry, James Earl Ray was quoted as alleging that he was the innocent victim, "the fall guy" of a scheme by the FBI.... This description of the crime contains no reference to Raoul.

Fourth, the most recent story available to the task force is reported as the result of a four hour interview by Wayne Chastain, Jr., for the Pacific News Service, October 20, 1974. It is to the effect that Ray was "set up as a patsy" for "Raoul." ...Ray was instructed by Raoul to have the white Mustang at the curb for "Raoul's" use that evening. Ray, however, drove away from the area at about 6:00 p.m. to get air in a low tire and found police swarming all over the place when he tried to return at 7:05 p.m. He could not park, was turned back by police and learned only after driving 100 miles into Mississippi that he had been associated with the men who killed Dr. King....

The task force views the exculpatory content of these varying and patently self-serving tales to be unbelievable. The varying details are materially self-refuting. Ray first admits full guilt. He then says he waited innocently at the curb and took off after the shot with "Raoul" as a passenger. He next says he was the catspaw of the FBI. And finally, he and the Mustang were not in the area when the shot was fired and he never saw "Raoul" after the event.

The eye witnesses to the "get away" saw only one man who resembled Ray. The man left in a hurry in a white Mustang as Ray admitted doing in version...two. We concluded Ray was lying about the existence of a "Raoul."

Ray's stipulated judicial confession comports in detail with the facts disclosed by the investigation and the failure of the self-serving stories persuasively undermines the likelihood of any conspiracy....

[Ray's Motive]

...Ray openly displayed a strong racist attitude towards blacks. While in prison, Ray stated he would kill Dr. King if given the opportunity and Ray was prepared to threaten or attack black persons in Puerto Vallarta, Mexico, with a weapon for apparently a racial reason. These events and occurrences leading to the assassination of Dr. King and the assassination itself certainly do not illustrate a single, conclusive motive. Yet, Ray's apparent hatred for the civil rights movement, his possible yearning for recognition, and a desire for a potential quick profit may have, as a whole, provided sufficient impetus for him to act, and to act alone.

Sources Of [Ray's] Funds

Shortly after the search for Ray began, it was recognized that he had traveled extensively following his escape from the Missouri Penitentiary. Moreover, in addition to normal living expenses, Ray had made several substantial purchases, e.g., cars, photo equipment, dance lessons.... These expenditures suggested that he had financial assistance and hence possible co-conspirators. Therefore, the Bureau was particularly interested in determining his sources of income....

...It is the Bureau's opinion that Ray most likely committed on a periodic basis several robberies or burglaries during this period in order to support himself. Ray's criminal background does lend credence to this theory.

The task force interviewed Ray's brother, Jerry Ray.... He stated that to his knowledge family members did not provide James with any funds. Jerry admitted he met with his brother two or three times during his employment at the Winnetka restaurant and advised that he, not James, paid for their eating and drinking expenses. However, when Jerry again saw his brother on his return from Canada in August, 1967, James did have some money because it was he who paid for their expenses which included a motel room. Jerry added that James also gave him his car commenting that he would purchase a more expensive car in Alabama. Jerry stated he was unaware of where his brother had obtained his money as well as the amount of money he had at this time.

Accordingly, the sources for Ray's funds still remain a mystery today....

Critical Evaluation Of The Assassination Investigation

...First, the task force has concluded that the investigation by the FBI to ascertain and capture the murderer of Dr. Martin Luther King, Jr., was thoroughly, honestly and successfully conducted. We submit that the minute details compacted in this report amply support this conclusion.

At the very outset of the investigation telegrams went to all field offices of the Bureau instructing the Special Agents in Charge to take personal supervision of the investigation, to check out all leads in 24 hours, and noting that they would be held personally responsible.... The files we reviewed show that this directive was conscientiously followed. The Bureau sought first to identify and locate the murderer using the obvious leads. They checked out aliases, tracked the traces left under the Galt alias, and used the known fingerprints from the murder weapon and the contents of the blue zipper bag left on South Main Street to eliminate suspects. This backtracking ended in Atlanta. At this point the Bureau initiated a check of the crime site fingerprints against the white male "wanted fugitive" print file. This produced the almost "instant" discovery that the wanted man, Galt, was James Earl Ray, an escapee from Missouri State Prison. In fact the "instant" discovery was a tedious hand search started in a file of some 20,000 prints. That it took only two hours to make a match is said by the Bureau experts to be largely sheer luck; it could have taken days. We accept the explanation that the fingerprint search was a normal next resort after normal lead procedures were exhausted.

Second, the task force views the evidence pointing to the guilt of James Earl Ray as the man who purchased the murder gun and who fired the fatal shot to be conclusive....

...We saw no credible evidence probative of the possibility that Ray and any co-conspirator were together at the scene of the assassination. Ray's assertions that someone else pulled the trigger are so patently self-serving and so varied as to be wholly unbelievable. They become, in fact, a part of the evidence of his guilt by self-refutation.

Third, we found that conspiracy leads...had been conscientiously run down by the FBI even though they had no possible relation to Ray's stories or to the known facts. The results were negative.

We found no evidence of any complicity on the part of the Memphis Police Department or of the FBI.

We acknowledge that proof of the negative, i.e., proof that others were not involved, is here as elusive and difficult as it has universally been in criminal law. But the sum of all of the evidence of Ray's guilt points to him so exclusively that it most effectively makes the point that no one else was involved. Of course, someone could conceivably have provided him with logistics, or even paid him to commit the crime. However, we have found no competent evidence upon which to base such a theory.

Fourth, it is true that the task force unearthed some new data—data which answers some persistent questions and which the FBI did not seek. But the Bureau concentrated on the principal in the case and much was not considered important to his discovery and apprehension. We find no dishonesty in this. A lead suggesting that one or both of James Earl Ray's brothers were in contact with him after, and in aid of, his escape in 1967 from the Missouri State Prison, and before the murder of Dr. King, was not followed. It was not unearthed until after Ray's capture in England on

June 8, 1968; it was then apparently deemed a lead made sterile by supervening events. By hindsight the task force believes Jerry and John Ray could have been effectively interrogated further to learn their knowledge, if any, of James Earl Ray's plans, his finances and whether they helped him after King's death.

Finally, the task force observed instances of FBI headquarter's reluctance to provide the Civil Rights Division and the Attorney General with timely reports on the course of the murder investigation....

The Bureau files reflect a significant degree of disdain for the supervisory responsibilities of the Attorney General and the operating Divisions of the Department. For example, the Attorney General authorized the institution of prosecutive action against the suspect "Galt."...But then, apparently without further consulting with the Attorney General or the Civil Rights Division, the Bureau prepared and filed a criminal complaint. The Bureau selected Birmingham as the venue in which to file the complaint in preference to Memphis because the Bureau "could not rely on the U.S. Attorney at Memphis" and "would lose control of the situation." ...The Bureau scenario called for then advising the Attorney General "that circumstances have required the action taken."...

We submit that in this sensitive case the Departmental officials in Washington should have been consulted....

...The task force views this lack of coordination and cooperation as highly improper. The Attorney General and the Division of the Department having prosecutorial responsibility for an offense being investigated should be kept fully abreast of developments. The responsible Division, moreover, should have sufficient control of the Bureau's investigations to insure that the legal necessities of pleading and proof are met.

In fairness to the Bureau it has to be observed that it is the obligation of the Department to insist on these prerogatives. We do not think it effectively did so in the King murder case.

[FBI Investigation of King]

...Given...the history of the sometimes overpowering influence of the views of the late Director J. Edgar Hoover on his subordinates and on successive Attorneys General, it was understandable that a security investigation should be initiated into the possible influence of the Communist Party, U.S.A., on Dr. Martin Luther King, Jr. Two of King's close advisors, at the outset of the security matter, were reported to be Communist Party members by sources relied upon by the Bureau.

The security investigation continued for almost six years until Dr. King's death. It verified, in our view, that one alleged Communist was a very influential advisor to Dr. King (and hence the Southern Christian Leadership Conference) on the strategy and tactics of King's leadership of the black civil rights movement of the early and mid-sixties. Another had no such weight although he seemed to be of use to King. But this very lengthy investigative concentration on King and on the principal advisor established, in our opinion, that he did not "sell" Dr. King any course of conduct or of advocacy which can be identified as communist or "Party line." King, himself, never varied publicly or privately from his commitment to non-violence and did not advocate the overthrow of the government of the United States by violence or subversion. To the contrary, he advocated an end to the discrimination and disenfranchisement of minority groups which the Constitution and the courts denounced in terms as strong as his. We concluded that Dr. King was no threat to domestic security.

And the Bureau's continued intense surveillance and investigation of the advisor clearly developed that he had disassociated himself from the Communist Party in 1963 because he felt it failed adequately to serve the civil rights movement. Thus the linch-pin of the security investigation of Dr. King had pulled himself out.

We think the security investigation which included both physical and technical surveillance, should have been terminated on the basis of what was learned in 1963. That it was intensified and augmented by a COINTELPRO [counterintelligence program] type campaign against Dr. King was unwarranted; the COINTELPRO type campaign, moreover, was...very probably...felonious.

The continuing security investigation reflects also that the Attorney General and the Division charged with responsibility for internal security matters failed badly in what should have been firm supervision of the FBI's internal security activities.

Recommendations

The task force does not fault the technical competence of the investigation conducted into the death of Dr. King. We found no new evidence which calls for action by State or Federal Authorities. Our concern has developed over administrative concomitants of the crime detection tactics....

...As a corollary of our espousal of tighter Department authority over the FBI, we recommend that the Bureau's public relations activities and press relations be controlled by the Attorney General's Office of Public Information. Clear directives to prevent the development of personality cults around particular Bureau Directors and officials should be drawn. Bureau press releases should be cleared through the Office of Public Information.

The task force recommends that in sensitive cases no criminal action be instituted by the Bureau without the closest coordination and consultation with the supervising Division of the Department. This supervision by the Department should be as tight as the control and consultation the Bureau had with its Field Offices as exhibited in our review of the assassination investigation.

It was observed that almost no blacks were in the FBI special agent's corps in the 1960's and none in the Bureau's hierarchy. This undoubtedly had the effect of limiting not only the outlook and understanding of the problems of race relations, but also must have hindered the ability of investigators to communicate fully with blacks during the murder investigation. By way of illustration had there been black agents in the Memphis Field Office participating fully in the investigation of Dr. King's murder, it is unlikely that the interviews with at least three black members of the Memphis Police and Fire Department would have been overlooked. It is also very probable that black citizen "lead" input would have been greater.

The task force was charged to address itself particularly to the question of whether the nature of the relationship between the Bureau and Dr. King called for criminal prosecution, disciplinary proceedings, or other appropriate action. Our responses follow.

Because the five year statute of limitations has long since run [out] we cannot recommend criminal prosecution of any Bureau personnel, past or present, responsible for the possible criminal harrassment of Dr. King.... No evidence of a continuing conspiracy was found.

The responsibility for initiating and prolonging the security investigation rested on the deceased Director of the Bureau and his immediate lieutenants, some of whom are also deceased and the remainder of whom are retired. They are beyond the reach of disciplinary action. The few Bureau personnel who had anything to do with the King security investigation and who are still in active service, did not make command decisions and merely followed orders. We do not think they are the proper subjects of any disciplinary action. Some of the activities conducted, such as the technical electronic surveillance, had the approval of the then Attorney General. The Courts had not adequately dealt with what authority rested in the executive branch to initiate such surveillance in the interest of "national security." We do not think the "leg men" in the Bureau should be held to an undefined standard of behavior, much less a standard not observed by the highest legal officer of the government.

The Bureau's COINTELPRO type activities, the illicit dissemination of raw investigative data to discredit Dr. King, the efforts to intimidate him, to break up his marriage, and the explicit and implicit efforts to blackmail him, were not fully known to the Department, but were none-the-less ordered and directed by Director Hoover, Assistant to the Director DeLoach, Assistant Director Sullivan and the Section Chief under him.

In our view their subordinates were far removed from decision responsibility. Moreover, we think the subordinates clearly felt that, by reason of Director Hoover's overpowering and intimidating domination of the Bureau, they had no choice but to implement the Bureau's directions. Punitive action against the very few remaining subordinate agents would seem to the task force to be inappropriate in these circumstances and at this very late date.

The Bureau's illicit surveillance produced tapes and transcripts concerning King and many others. These may be sought by King's heirs and representatives. Worse still, they may be sought by members of the public at large under the Freedom of Information Act. We recommend that these tapes and transcripts be sealed and sent to the National Archives and that the Congress be asked to pass legislation denying any access to them whatever and authorizing and directing their total destruction along with the destruction of material in reports and memoranda derived from them.

The potential for abuse by the individual occupying the office of Director of the FBI has been amply demonstrated by our investigation. We think it is a responsibility of the Department in the first instance and, secondarily, of the Congress to oversee the conduct of the FBI (and the other police agencies of the government). We endorse the establishment by the Attorney General of the Office of Professional Responsibility on December 9, 1975, as an effective means for intra-departmental policing of the Bureau. We also think the permanent Senate Select Committee on Intelligence is an appropriate agency of the legislative arm to oversee the performance of the Bureau. Both the Office of Professional Responsibility and the Senate Select Committee should be expressly designated in their respective enabling regulations and resolutions to be a place to which Bureau subordinates may complain, confidentially and with impunity, of orders which they believe to threaten a violation of the civil rights and liberties of citizens and inhabitants of the United States.

It seems to us that the unauthorized malicious dissemination of investigative data from FBI files should be more than the presently prescribed misdemeanor.... A felony penalty should be added.

Parenthetically, it should be noted here that it should be made clear that it is improper (but not criminal) for the Bureau to by-pass the Attorney General and deal directly with the White House.

The task force recommends that the FBI have no authority to engage in COINTELPRO type activities which involve affirmative punitive action following Star Chamber decisions with respect to citizens or inhabitants.... We believe that the guidelines which the present Attorney General has established to govern the FBI's domestic security investigations effectively preclude these activities. Those guidelines moreover, appear to us to permit only strictly legal investigative techniques to be employed in full scale domestic security investigations. This too we endorse....

CARTER BUDGET REVISIONS

February 22, 1977

President Carter Feb. 22 sent his version of the fiscal 1978 budget to Congress. Revisions by the Carter administration called for a spending level $19.4-billion higher than recommended by former President Gerald R. Ford in his Jan. 17 budget message and a deficit almost $11-billion higher. (Ford budget message, p. 57).

"The 1978 budget is essentially still President Ford's budget," Carter said, "with only such limited revisions as my administration has had time to make.... But these revisions...are important first steps toward a federal government that is more effective and responsive to our people's needs." Office of Management and Budget Director Bert Lance noted that in the month since the Carter administration took office there simply had not been time to go through a line-by-line revision of the Ford budget. The President observed that the zero-based budgeting concept, which requires annual justification for every spending program, would be incorporated in the budget planning for fiscal 1979.

The revised budget totals proposed outlays of $459.4-billion and estimated receipts at $401.6-billion. The growth in spending was 10 per cent more than the latest estimate of fiscal 1977 outlays of $417.4-billion, and the deficit was $57.7-billion.

Major Revisions

Lance and other administration officials stressed that while they believed the new budget "corrected the major defects" of the Ford budget, it also did not make all the changes they would have liked.

Almost all the revisions, apart from the economic stimulus package, involved the restoration of Ford's proposed cuts that the Carter administration considered unwarranted, said the budget document. The new figures, it continued, "are on the whole closer to those needed to maintain current programs at their present levels" than were the Ford proposals.

Of a total $12.4-billion in cuts in outlays below current services levels in fiscal 1978 proposed by Ford, the Carter administration recommended restoring $7.8-billion, with the fiscal stimulus accounting for $2.8-billion of that. Ford also had recommended program cuts in fiscal 1977 outlays below current services totaling $1.2-billion. The Carter budget restored all but $40-million of the Ford cuts and increased outlays over current services in some areas.

Ford also had included a number of program initiatives, "very few" of which were continued in the Carter document, according to an OMB official.

Carter's proposals for increases over the Ford budget covered the spectrum of government activity, with all functional areas except defense showing gains. But they were concentrated in the areas of employment, health, education, income security and housing.

Controversial Cuts

While Carter restored many of the cuts proposed by Ford which Congress had either ignored or opposed, he also showed no reluctance to risk congressional ire with some of his own proposals.

The only functional area to show a decline in budget authority and outlays was defense, in which Carter proposed to reduce budget authority by $2.7-billion. The revisions, said the budget document, were designed to begin an improvement in the efficiency of military programs. The results of a major review of U.S. defense policy and programs would be reflected in the fiscal 1979 budget, it added. Most of the revisions, explained the document, resulted from slowing down or postponing various procurement and operations and maintenance programs, along with some production cancellations.

Proposed fiscal 1978 outlays for national defense were down slightly, $300-million. The budget authority figure was more important because it reflected future commitments.

During his campaign Carter had pledged much larger defense reductions, and at the press briefing Lance defended the fiscal 1978 cuts, saying that "significant progress" had been made toward the larger goal.

Carter also proposed to save nearly $300-million in budget authority by eliminating fiscal 1978 appropriations for 19 water resources development projects, a proposal that raised immediate controversy in Congress and some of the states affected.

Another controversy was certain over one of the few Ford recommendations that Carter sustained—reforms in the impact aid program that would limit federal aid to school districts where federal activities placed a heavy economic burden on them, at an estimated savings of $447-million.

Other major reductions included cuts in nuclear research and development, and proposed legislation to limit increases in reimbursements to hospitals paid by Medicare, Medicaid, state and local governments, insurance companies and private individuals.

The prospect of a $68-billion deficit in fiscal 1977 and nearly $58-billion in fiscal 1978 raised some concern among private economists and the business community about a new round of rising inflation in the country.

One warning was voiced by the influential chairman of the Federal Reserve Board, Arthur F. Burns, in hearings Feb. 23 before the Joint Economic Committee.

"I don't want to criticize anyone," said Burns, "...but the increase in the federal budget is stirring up new fears, new expectations of inflation that to some degree may be a self-fulfilling prophecy."

Revisions in Stimulus

The budget document also presented revised figures for the total size of the administration's economic stimulus package. The total cost came to $15.7-billion in fiscal 1977 rather than the original estimate of $15.5-billion, and $15.9-billion in fiscal 1978 rather than $15.7-billion, for a total two-year package of $31.6-billion.

The changes resulted from new levels for the personal standard deduction and from increases in countercyclical assistance to state and local governments.

The stimulative effect of the countercyclical aid program was revised upward to $700-million each in fiscal 1977 and 1978, from $500-million and $600-million respectively.

The Ford administration had not sought the continuation of the $1.25-billion program designed to prevent cutbacks in employment and public services at the state and local levels beyond its Sept. 30 expiration date. The program was expected to run out of funds before then because of high unemployment rates—a factor in the program's funding formula.

The Carter administration requested fiscal 1978 outlays of $1.55-billion for the extension and expansion of the program as proposed in its stimulus package. It also requested an additional $925-million in fiscal 1977 outlays over the Ford levels to continue the program to Sept. 30 and to put into effect April 1 a new funding formula that would more closely reflect fluctuations in the unemployment rate.

The Carter budget restored funds which Ford had proposed to cut in the food stamp and child nutrition programs and in Medicare and Medicaid.

Other Carter revisions reflected greater emphasis on energy conservation and the development of nonnuclear power sources and expansion of the petroleum storage program.

The Ford budget had proposed the phasing out of three major jobs programs on the grounds that improvement in the private sector of the economy would take up the unemployment slack. Carter's budget sought to expand these programs as a central part of his economic stimulus program.

The administration proposed a total increase of $25-billion in fiscal 1977 and in 1978 for subsidized housing programs, and recommended that $400-million be set aside in the fiscal year that begins Oct. 1 for aid to "distressed cities."

The Democratic President turned away from the Ford-Nixon emphasis on block grants of federal funds to state and local government which permitted these local authorities to spend federal money in their own way. Carter noted that Washington was more aware of national needs and should monitor federal spending.

> *Following is the text of President Carter's Feb. 22, 1977, message to Congress on revisions of the fiscal 1978 budget submitted earlier by President Gerald R. Ford:*

To the Congress of the United States:

I am presenting today proposed changes in the 1978 budget.

Although I have not been able to analyze this budget in depth, these proposals do differ significantly from those of the previous administration.

Proposals have been rejected that would have needlessly added to the burden on the elderly and those who depend upon medicare, medicaid, and food programs.

I have withdrawn proposals that would have placed further financial strain on State and local governments.

Changes are included that will help us move more quickly to meet our commitments in such vital areas as the environment, education, and housing; and I am introducing measures that will help us control unacceptable inflation in medical costs.

The planned increase in defense spending, has been reduced while our real military strength is enhanced.

Revisions have been made that reflect new priorities for water resources development and also for energy, placing greater emphasis on conservation, development of non-nuclear power sources, and expanding our petroleum storage program. Later in the spring, work with the Congress will be completed on a comprehensive, long-range national energy policy.

This budget includes the economic stimulus package, which will reduce unemployment and promote steady, balanced economic growth. The package, which has been slightly changed since it was first presented to the Congress last month, provides for $15.7-billion in tax reductions and increased outlays in 1977 and $15.9-billion in 1978. It includes a $50 per capita rebate on personal income taxes; an increase in the standard deduction; reduction in business taxes to stimulate employment and provide incentives for investment; expansion in training and employment programs; increases in public works funding; and additional money for counter-cyclical revenue sharing grants to State and local governments.

I am also asking the Congress to extend the supplemental payments program, which is now expiring, so that unemployed workers will be able to qualify through the end of this year for up to 52 weeks of unemployment benefits.

There are several important goals which these revisions do not reflect, because my administration has not yet had time to review all current tax and spending programs or fully prepare our own proposals. The 1978 budget is essentially still President Ford's budget, with only such limited revisions as my administration has had time to make. But these revisions do reflect our careful choices among many possible options; they are important first steps toward a Federal Government that is more effective and responsive to our people's needs.

Last year, spending estimates were too high, and economic policymaking was adversely affected. Because time did not permit detailed review of the current estimates, I have instructed the Office of Management and Budget to make a thorough review of these estimates. The Congress will be informed of any resulting revisions.

The revised budget outlined in this document continues to reflect the current overlapping and unwieldy structure of the Federal Government—a structure I intend, with the help of the Congress, to simplify and improve.

Although it has not been possible in these revisions to the 1978 budget, future budgets will reflect detailed, zero-based reviews of Federal spending programs, comprehensive reform of the tax system, and fundamental reorganization of the Government.

JIMMY CARTER

February 22, 1977

COURT ON WATER POLLUTION
February 23, 1977

The Supreme Court Feb. 23 unanimously upheld the federal government's authority to impose uniform industry-wide regulations controlling the amount of pollutants that factories may dump into the nation's waterways. The ruling confirmed the Environmental Protection Agency's broad authority, under the Federal Water Pollution Control Act Amendments of 1972, to control the dumping of industrial wastes into rivers and streams.

Under authority granted by the 1972 amendments, the EPA had promulgated industry-wide regulations imposing three sets of limitations on the discharge of inorganic chemical pollutants into the waterways. The first two regulations imposed higher pollutant control levels on existing discharge point sources, the first to be achieved by July 1, 1977, and the second to be reached by July 1, 1983. The third regulation imposed limitations on new sources—such as new industrial plants—of effluent discharge that might be constructed in the future.

EPA argued that it could set out these limits in regulations which would apply to all plants within a certain category. Eight chemical manufacturers challenged this view, arguing that Congress intended for EPA to apply these limits on a case-by-case basis.

The court rejected the manufacturers' argument, citing the language and legislative history of the 1972 law and considerations of feasibility and practicality. Congress intended EPA to set these limits as regulations governing categories of polluting plants and other sources, the court held, not just as guidelines to be applied as individual plants requested operating permits under the clean water program.

If the chemical companies' argument was accepted, wrote Justice Stevens for the court, it "would place an impossible burden on EPA. It would require EPA to give individual consideration to the circumstances of each of the more than 42,000 dischargers who have applied for permits...and to issue or approve all these permits well in advance of the 1977 deadline in order to give industry time to install the necessary pollution control equipment. We do not believe Congress would have failed so conspicuously to provide EPA with the authority needed to achieve the statutory goals."

On two subsidiary issues, the court held that Congress did not authorize EPA to grant any exceptions—or variances—from the standards set out to govern effluents from new plants, and that all of these standards were reviewable only in federal courts of appeals, not in federal district courts.

The court held that some allowance for variances in individual plants must be made, except in the case of new plants, where Congress intended to impose "absolute prohibitions" on pollution. A variance is a license to do something contrary to the usual rule—in this instance extant industrial plants seeking to be excused from compliance with the pollution regulations set forth under the Federal Water Pollution Control Act Amendments of 1972 as administered by the Environmental Protection Agency.

Chemical companies involved in the suit were E.I. duPont de Nemours & Co., Olin Corp., FMC Corp., American Cyanimid Co., Monsanto Co., Dow Chemical Corp. and Hercules Inc.

> *Following are excerpts from the Supreme Court's unanimous opinion upholding the authority of the Environmental Protection Agency to impose industry-wide regulations controlling the dumping of industrial wastes into rivers and streams, delivered Feb. 23, 1977. (Boldface headings in brackets have been added by Congressional Quarterly to highlight the organization of the text.):*

Nos. 75-978, 75-1473 and 75-1705

E. I. duPont de Nemours and
  Company et al., Petitioners,
75-978   v.
Russell E. Train, Administrator,
  Environmental Protection
      Agency, et al.

On Writs of Certiorari to the United States Court of Appeals for the Fourth Circuit.

E. I. duPont de Nemours and
  Company, et al., Petitioners,
75-1473   v.

Russell E. Train, Administrator,
  Environmental Protection
      Agency.

Russell E. Train, Administrator,
  Environmental Protection
      Agency, Petitioner,

75-1705   *v.*

E. I. duPont de Nemours and
  Company, et al.

[February 23, 1977]

MR. JUSTICE STEVENS delivered the opinion of the Court. [MR. JUSTICE POWELL took no part in the consideration or decision of these cases.]

Inorganic chemical manufacturing plants operated by the eight petitioners discharge various pollutants into the Nation's waters and therefore are "point sources" within the meaning of the Federal Water Pollution Control Act Amendments of 1972, 86 Stat. 816, 33 U.S.C. § 1251 *et seq.* (Supp. IV) ("The Act"). The Environmental Protection Agency has promulgated industry-wide regulations imposing three sets of precise limitations on petitioners' discharges. The first two impose progressively higher levels of pollutant control on existing point sources after July 1, 1977, and after July 1, 1983, respectively. The third set imposes limits on "new sources" that may be constructed in the future.

These cases present three important questions of statutory construction: (1) whether EPA has the authority under § 301 of the Act to issue industry-wide regulations limiting discharges by existing plants; (2) whether the Court of Appeals, which admittedly is authorized to review the standards for new sources, also has jurisdiction under § 509 to review the regulations concerning existing plants; and (3) whether the new source standards issued under § 306 must allow variances for individual plants.

As a preface to our discussion of these three questions, we summarize relevant portions of the statute and then describe the procedure which EPA followed in promulgating the challenged regulations.

[The Statute]

The statute, enacted on October 18, 1972, authorized a series of steps to be taken to achieve the goal of eliminating all discharges of pollutants into the nation's waters by 1985. § 101 (a)(1).

The first steps required by the Act are described in § 304, which directs the [EPA] Administrator to develop and publish various kinds of technical data to provide guidance in discharging responsibilities imposed by other sections of the Act. Thus, within 60 days, 120 days, and 180 days after the date of enactment, the Administrator was to promulgate a series of guidelines to assist the States in developing and carrying out permit programs pursuant to § 402. § § 304 (h), (f), (g). Within 270 days, he was to develop the information to be used in formulating standards for new plants pursuant to § 306, § 304 (c). And within one year he was to publish regulations providing guidance for effluent limitations on existing point sources. Section 304 (b) goes into great detail concerning the contents of these regulations. They must identify the degree of effluent reduction attainable through use of the best practicable or best available technology for a class of plants. The guidelines must also "specify factors to be taken into account" in determining the control measures applicable to point sources within these classes. A list of factors to be considered then follows. The Administrator was also directed to develop and publish, within one year, elaborate criteria for water quality accurately reflecting the most current scientific knowledge, and also technical information on factors necessary to restore and maintain water quality. § 304 (a). The title of § 304 describes it as the "information and guidelines" portion of the statute.

Section 301 is captioned "effluent limitations." Section 301 (a) makes the discharge of any pollutant unlawful unless the discharge is in compliance with certain enumerated sections of the Act. The enumerated sections which are relevant to this case are § 301 itself, § 306, and § 402. A brief word about each of these sections is necessary.

Section 402 authorizes the Administrator to issue permits for individual point sources, and also authorizes him to review and approve the plan of any State desiring to administer its own permit program. These permits serve "to transform generally applicable effluent limitations...into the obligations (including a timetable for compliance) of the individual discharger[s.]..." *EPA* v. *State Water Resources Control Board....* Petitioner chemical companies' position in this litigation is that § 402 provides the only statutory authority for the issuance of enforceable limitations on the discharge of pollutants by existing plants. It is noteworthy, however, that although this section authorizes the imposition of limitations in individual permits, the section itself does not mandate either the Administrator or the States to use permits as the method of prescribing effluent limitations.

Section 306 directs the Administrator to publish within 90 days a list of categories of sources discharging pollutants and, within one year thereafter, to publish regulations establishing national standards of performance for new sources within each category. Section 306 contains no provision for exceptions from the standards for individual plants; on the contrary, subsection (e) expressly makes it unlawful to operate a new source in violation of the applicable standard of performance after its effective date. The statute provides that the new source standards shall reflect the greatest degree of effluent reduction achievable through application of the best available demonstrated control technology.

Section 301 (b) defines the effluent limitations that shall be achieved by existing point sources in two stages. By July 1, 1977, the effluent limitations shall require the application of the best *practicable* control technology currently available; by July 1, 1983, the limitations shall require application of the best *available* technology economically achievable.

The statute expressly provides that the limitations which are to become effective in 1983 are applicable to "categories and classes of point sources"; this phrase is omitted from the description of the 1977 limitations. While § 301 states that these limitations "shall be achieved," it fails to state who will establish the limitations.

Section 301 (c) authorizes the Administrator to grant variances from the 1983 limitations. Section 301 (e) states that effluent limitations established pursuant to § 301 shall be applied to all point sources.

To summarize, § 301 (b) requires the achievement of effluent limitations requiring use of the "best practicable" or "best available" technology. It refers to § 304 for a definition of these terms. Section 304 requires the publication of "regulations, providing guidelines for effluent limitations." Finally, permits issued under § 402 must require compliance with § 301 effluent limitations. Nowhere are we told who sets the § 301 effluent limitations, or precisely how they relate to § 304 guidelines and § 402 permits.

[The Regulations]

The various deadlines imposed on the Administrator were too ambitious for him to meet. For that reason, the procedure which he followed in adopting the regulations applicable to the inorganic chemical industry and to other classes of point sources, is somewhat different from that apparently contemplated by the statute. Specifically, as will appear, he did not adopt guidelines pursuant to § 304 before defining the effluent limitations for existing sources described in § 301 (b) or the national standards for new sources described in § 306. This case illustrates the approach the Administrator followed in implementing the Act.

EPA began by engaging a private contractor to prepare a Development Document. This document provided a detailed technical study of pollution control in the industry. The study first divided the industry into categories. For each category, present levels of pollution were measured and plants with exemplary pollution control were investigated. Based on this information, other technical data, and economic studies, a determination was made of the degree of pollution control which could be achieved by the various levels of technology mandated by the statute. The study was made available to the public and circulated to interested persons. It formed the basis of "effluent limitation guideline" regulations issued by EPA after receiving public comment on proposed regulations. These regulations divide the industry into 22 subcategories. Within each subcategory, precise numerical limits are set for various pollutants. The regulations for each subcategory contain a variance clause, applicable only to the 1977 limitations.

Eight chemical companies filed petitions in the United States Court of Appeals for the Fourth Circuit for review of these regulations. The Court of Appeals rejected their challenge to EPA's authority to issue precise, single-number limitations for discharges of pollutants from existing sources. It held, however, that these limitations and the new plant standards were only "presumptively applicable" to individual plants. We granted the chemical companies' petitions for certiorari in order to consider the scope of EPA's authority to issue existing-source regulations. We also granted the Government's cross-petition for review of the ruling that new source standards are only presumptively applicable.... For convenience, we will refer to the chemical companies as the "petitioners."

[The Issues]

The broad outlines of the parties' respective theories may be stated briefly. EPA contends that § 301 (b) authorizes it to issue regulations establishing effluent limitations for classes of plants. The permits granted under § 402, in EPA's view, simply incorporate these across-the-board limitations, except for the limited variances allowed by the regulations themselves and by § 301 (c). The § 304 (b) guidelines, according to EPA, were intended to guide it in later establishing § 301 effluent limitation regulations. Because the process proved more time consuming than Congress assumed when it established this two-stage process, EPA condensed the two stages into a single regulation.

In contrast, petitioners contend that § 301 is not an independent source of authority for setting effluent limitations by regulation. Instead, § 301 is seen as merely a description of the effluent limitations which are set for each plant on an individual basis during the permit-issuance process. Under the industry view, the § 304 guidelines serve the function of guiding the permit issuer in setting the effluent limitations.

The jurisdictional issue is subsidiary to the critical question whether EPA has the power to issue effluent limitations by regulation. Section 509 (b) (1) provides that "[r]eview of the Administrator's action...(E) in approving or promulgating any effluent limitation under section 301" may be had in the courts of appeals. On the other hand, the Act does not provide for judicial review of § 304 guidelines. If EPA is correct that its regulations are "effluent limitations under section 301," the regulations are directly reviewable in the Court of Appeals. If industry is correct that the regulations can only be considered § 304 guidelines, suit to review the regulations could probably be brought only in the District Court, if anywhere. Thus, the issue of jurisdiction to review the regulations is intertwined with the issue of EPA's power to issue the regulations.

I

We think § 301 itself is the key to the problem. The statutory language concerning the 1983 limitation, in particular, leaves no doubt that these limitations are to be set by regulation. Subsection (b) (2) (A) of § 301 states that by 1983 "effluent limitations *for categories and classes* of point sources" are to be achieved which will require "application of the best available technology economically achievable *for such category or class.*"

(Emphasis added.) These effluent limitations are to require elimination of all discharges if "such elimination is technologically and economically achievable for a *category or class* of point sources." (Emphasis added.) This is "language difficult to reconcile with the view that individual effluent limitations are to be set when each permit is issued." *American Meat Institute* v. *EPA*...(CA7 1975). The statute thus focuses expressly on the characteristics of the "category or class" rather than the characteristics of individual point sources. Normally, such class-wide determinations would be made by regulation, not in the course of issuing a permit to one member of the class.

Thus, we find that § 301 unambiguously provides for the use of regulations to establish the 1983 effluent limitations. Different language is used in § 301 with respect to the 1977 limitations. Here, the statute speaks of "effluent limitations for point sources," rather than "effluent limitations for categories and classes of point sources." Nothing elsewhere in the Act, however, suggests any radical difference in the mechanism used to impose limitations for the 1977 and 1983 deadlines.... For instance, there is no indication in either § 301 or § 304 that the § 304 guidelines play a different role in setting 1977 limitations. Moreover, it would be highly anomalous if the 1983 regulations and the new source standards were directly reviewable in the Court or Appeals, while the 1977 regulations based on the same administrative record were reviewable only in the District Court. The magnitude and highly technical character of the administrative record involved with these regulations makes it almost inconceivable that Congress would have required duplicate review in the first instance by different courts. We conclude that the statute authorizes the 1977 limitations as well as the 1983 limitations to be set by regulation, so long as some allowance is made for variations in individual plants, as EPA has done by including a variance clause in its 1977 limitations.

The question of the form of § 301 limitations is tied to the question whether the Act requires the Administrator or the permit issuer to establish the limitations. ...[T]he language of the statute supports the view that § 301 limitations are to be adopted by the Administrator, that they are to be based primarily on classes and categories, and that they are to take the form of regulations.

The legislative history supports this reading of § 301. The Senate Report states that "pursuant to subsection 301 (b) (1) (A), and Section 304 (b)" the Administrator is to set a base level for all plants in a given category, and "[i]n no case...should any plant be allowed to discharge more pollutants per unit of production than is defined by that base level."...The Conference Report on § 301 states that "the determination of the economic impact of an effluent limitation [will be made] on the basis of classes and categories of point sources, as distinguished from a plant by plant determination."... In presenting the Conference Report to the Senate, Senator Muskie, perhaps the Act's primary author, emphasized the importance of uniformity in setting § 301 limitations. He explained that this goal of uniformity required that EPA focus on classes or categories of sources in formulating effluent limitations. Regarding the requirement contained in § 301 that plants use the "best practicable control technology" by 1977, he stated:

> "The modification of subsection 304 (b) (1) is intended to clarify what is meant by the term 'practicable.' The balancing test between total cost and effluent reduction benefits is intended to limit the application of technology only where the additional degree of effluent reduction is wholly out of proportion to the costs of achieving such marginal level of reduction for *any class or category* of sources.
>
> "The Conferees agreed upon this limited cost-benefit analysis in order to maintain *uniformity within a class and category* of point sources subject to effluent limitations, and to avoid imposing on the Administrator any requirement to consider the location of sources within a category or to ascertain water quality impact or effluent controls, or to determine the economic impact of controls on any individual plant in a single community." ...(emphasis added).

He added that:

> "The Conferees intend that the factors described in section 304 (b) be considered only within classes or categories of point sources and that such factors not be considered at the time of the application of an effluent limitation to an individual point source within such a category or class."

This legislative history supports our reading of § 301 and makes it clear that the § 304 guidelines are not merely aimed at guiding the discretion of permit issuers in setting limitations for individual plants.

What, then, is the function of the § 304 (b) guidelines? As we noted earlier, § 304 (b) requires EPA to identify the amount of effluent reduction attainable through use of the best practicable or available technology and to "specify factors to be taken into account" in determining the pollution control methods "to be applicable to point sources...within such categories or classes." These guidelines are to be issued "[f]or the purpose of adopting or revising effluent limitations under this Act." As we read it, § 304 requires that the guidelines survey the practicable or available pollution control technology for an industry and assess its effectiveness. The guidelines are then to describe the methodology EPA intends to use in the § 301 regulations to determine the effluent limitations for particular plants. If the technical complexity of the task had not prevented EPA from issuing the guidelines within the statutory deadline, they could have provided valuable guidance to permit issuers, industry, and the public, prior to the issuance of the § 301 regulations.

Our construction of the Act is supported by § 501 (a), which gives EPA the power to make "such regulations as are necessary to carry out" its functions, and by § 101 (d), which charges the agency with the duty of administering the Act. In construing this grant of authority, as Justice Harlan wrote in connection with a somewhat similar problem:

" '[C]onsiderations of feasibility and practicality are certainly germane' to the issues before us.... We cannot, in these circumstances, conclude that Congress has given authority inadequate to achieve with reasonable effectiveness the purposes for which it has acted.''...

The petitioners' view of the Act would place an impossible burden on EPA. It would require EPA to give individual consideration to the circumstances of each of the more than 42,000 dischargers who have applied for permits...and to issue or approve all these permits well in advance of the 1977 deadline in order to give industry time to install the necessary pollution control equipment. We do not believe that Congress would have failed so conspicuously to provide EPA with the authority needed to achieve the statutory goals.

Both EPA and petitioners refer to numerous other provisions of the Act and fragments of legislative history in support of their positions. We do not find these conclusive, and little point would be served by discussing them in detail. We are satisfied that our reading of § 301 is consistent with the rest of the legislative scheme.

...When as in this case, the Agency's interpretation is also supported by thorough, scholarly opinions written by some of our finest judges, and has received the overwhelming support of the courts of appeals, we would be reluctant indeed to upset the Agency's judgment. In this case, on the contrary, our independent examination confirms the correctness of the Agency's construction of the statute.

Consequently, we hold that EPA has the authority to issue regulations setting forth uniform effluent limitations for categories of plants.

II

Our holding that § 301 does authorize the Administrator to promulgate effluent limitations for classes and categories of existing point sources necessarily resolves the jurisdictional issue as well. For, as we have already pointed out, § 509 (b) (1) provides that "[r]eview of the Administrator's action...in approving or promulgating any effluent limitation or other limitation under sections 301, 302, or 306, ...may be had by any interested person in the Circuit Court of Appeals of the United States for the Federal judicial district in which such person resides or transacts such business...."

Petitioners have argued that the reference to § 301 was intended only to provide for review of the grant or denial of an individual variance pursuant to § 301 (c). We find this argument unpersuasive for two reasons in addition to those discussed in Part I of this opinion. First, in other portions of § 509, Congress referred to specific subsections of the Act and presumably would have specifically mentioned § 301 (c) if only action pursuant to that subsection were intended to be reviewable in the Court of Appeals. More importantly, petitioners' construction would produce the truly perverse situation in which the Court of Appeals would review numerous individual actions issuing or denying permits pursuant to § 402 but would have no power of direct review of the basic regulations governing those individual actions....

We regard § 509 (b) (1) (E) as unambiguously authorizing Court of Appeals review of EPA action promulgating an effluent limitation for existing point sources under § 301. Since those limitations are typically promulgated in the same proceeding as the new source standards under § 306, we have no doubt that Congress intended review of the two sets of regulations to be had in the same forum.

III

The remaining issue in this case concerns new plants. Under § 306, EPA is to promulgate "regulations establishing Federal standards of performance for new sources...." § 306 (b) (1) (B). A "standard of performance" is a "standard for the control of the discharge of pollutants which reflects the greatest degree of effluent reduction which the Administrator determines to be achievable through application of the best available demonstrated control technology...including, where practicable, a standard permitting no discharge of pollutants." § 306 (a) (1). In setting the standard, "[t]he Administrator may distinguish among classes, types, and sizes within categories of new sources...and shall consider the type of process employed (including whether batch or continuous)." § 306 (b) (2). As the House Report states, the standard must reflect the best technology for "that category of sources, and for class, types and sizes within categories."...

The Court of Appeals held that:

"Neither the Act nor the regulations contain any variance provision for new sources. The rule of presumptive applicability applies to new sources as well as existing sources. On remand EPA should come forward with some limited escape mechanism for new sources."...

The Court's rationale was that "[p]rovisions for variances, modifications, and exceptions are appropriate to the regulatory process."

[Intent of Congress]

The question, however, is not what a court thinks is generally appropriate to the regulatory process; it is what Congress intended for *these* regulations. It is clear that Congress intended these regulations to be absolute prohibitions. The use of the word "standards" implies as much. So does the description of the preferred standard as one "permitting *no* discharge of pollutants." (Emphasis added.) It is "unlawful for *any* owner or operator of *any* new source to operate such source in violation of any standard of performance applicable to such source." § 306 (e) (emphasis added). In striking contrast to § 301 (c), there is no statutory provision for variances, and a variance provision would be inappropriate in a standard that was intended to insure national uniformity and "maximum feasible control of new sources."...

That portion of the judgment of the Court of Appeals requiring EPA to provide a variance procedure for new sources is reversed. In all other aspects, the judgment of the Court of Appeals is affirmed.

It is so ordered.

AMIN'S MESSAGE TO CARTER
February 25, 1977

Ugandan President Idi Amin Feb. 25 warned President Carter against U.S. interference in his government's affairs and temporarily barred all U.S. nationals from leaving Uganda. In a broadcast message over Kampala radio, Amin accused Carter of being under the influence of "Zionist Israel" and the CIA.

Amin's strongly worded criticism also accused the CIA of plotting to overthrow him and charged the United States with crimes against humanity "which are worse than the violation of human rights." The Ugandan president also on Feb. 25 ordered all Americans in Uganda to meet with him at the international conference center in Kampala that same day.

Amin apparently was reacting to President Carter's Feb. 23 press conference remarks in which he said that Amin's actions, particularly the alleged murder Feb. 16 of the Anglican Archbishop of Uganda, Janani Luwum, had "disgusted the entire civilized world." Carter also said that he supported a British proposal at the United Nations calling for the U.N. Human Rights Commission to "go into Uganda to assess the horrible murders that apparently are taking place in that country." Reports of the Ugandan government's systematic assaults and repression of certain Ugandan tribes had been attracting world-wide attention.

U.S. Warns Amin

Amin's threat to the safety of about 200 Americans, mostly missionaries living in Uganda, caused the U.S. State Department to issue a stern warn-

ing to Amin saying that the United States would not tolerate using Americans as hostages. The crisis abated when Amin twice postponed the scheduled meeting with American nationals and offered assurances to President Carter Feb. 26 that U.S. citizens in Uganda had no cause for alarm.

Amin March 1 dropped the ban on American departures and put off indefinitely the meeting with U.S. nationals after speaking to a small group of U.S. airline workers at Entebbe Feb. 28. The Ugandan president praised the airline workers, saying that Ugandans were their "brothers and sisters." U.S. Secretary of State Cyrus R. Vance called Amin's decision to allow the Americans to leave Uganda "a very positive step."

Amin's Earlier Threats to U.S.

This was not the first time Amin had detained foreign nationals. In July 1973, a plane carrying 112 Peace Corps volunteers to Zaire was forced to remain at Entebbe for two days after stopping to refuel. The volunteers were questioned because of the allegation that some of them were U.S. intelligence agents.

Four months later Amin ordered the expulsion of the Marine guard at the American embassy, and the U.S. government closed the embassy. Uganda, however, was permitted to keep its embassy in Washington open.

> *Following is the text of President Idi Amin's Feb. 25 broadcast message to President Carter over Kampala radio as monitored by the United States government.* (Boldface headings in brackets have been added by Congressional Quarterly to highlight organization of the text.):

Your excellency, I would like to comment on and reply to your recent reaction to the present situation in Uganda concerning the alleged violation of human rights. There is documentary evidence which is contained in the report of the Commission of Inquiry set up by me to look into the disappearance of people since 1971. The conclusion of the inquiry, which was headed by the Chief Justice, utterly refuted the allegations on this particular matter.

[Archbishop Luwum's Death]

Concerning the death of the Archbishop and the two Cabinet ministers, this has been published with the title "Obote's War Call to Langos and Acholis." I will send you a copy of this book. In it you will be able to understand that the Archbishop and the two Cabinet ministers were killed in a car accident.

Photographs of the cars are shown and also the post-mortem of the three is also reproduced. The doctor who carried out the post-mortem is not my relative. He is a Christian and belongs to the same tribe as the late Oboth-

Ofumbi, former Minister of Internal Affairs. [The question of the death] of the Archbishop and the two ministers is a purely police case.

However, on the question of the plot to cause chaos and murder people in Uganda, you will see in the book photographs of [the] most modern weapons which were displayed before a cross section of people of Uganda, the armed forces and the members of the diplomatic corps. This included the late Archbishop and the two ministers.

We cannot isolate this plan from the invasion of the Entebbe airport by the Israelis on 3 July 1976, where 20 Ugandans and seven Palestinians were killed. A lot of Ugandan property, including modern planes and sophisticated weapons, was destroyed.

In spite of these inhuman acts by Zionist Israel, the Western imperialist press did not show any sympathy to Uganda. In the same way, the Western world does not show any sympathy to the Palestinians who were butchered and booted out of Palestine in 1946 and 1947, and they had to live in caves and gutters.

Now the Palestinians do not have a home. Again the Western world did not show sympathy when Zionists took the West Bank of Jordan, Sinai and the Golan Heights, including the city of Quneitra. The city of Quneitra had been a live city but was blown up by explosives which even excavated the dead that had been buried many years before. Is this not a violation of human rights?

[American-Israeli Relations]

The pressure you referred to from the American people is artificial. It is a pressure from Zionists. I know that the black Americans, as well as many white Americans, cannot be against Uganda. But some Zionist Jews who control the news media are the ones exerting pressure.

The U.S. government and the American people should not be used as exhaust pipes of the Zionist Israel lorries. It seems that any American President who does not support Zionist Israel is gunned down. It is not surprising, therefore, that even you, Mr. President, you are getting a lot of pressure from the Zionists.

I know that although I supported you and your policies from the beginning and in spite of being a new President, it is very hard to remain in that office unless the Zionists put you in their pockets.

[CIA Plot]

As to the involvement of the United States in the plan to invade Uganda, this information was provided by the 16 people who were actively involved in this plot and were arrested in Uganda. They are the ones who revealed that the U.S. C.I.A., the British and the Israelis were involved.

However, it is not surprising that your government denies the knowledge of the U.S. involvement because it appears that the C.I.A. has many faces. Only yesterday it was reported by two columnists, Roland Evans [sic] and Robert Novak of *The Washington Post,* which is an American paper, that the U.S. C.I.A. secretly paid tens of millions of dollars to the Israeli intelligence service for operations in black Africa. The money, which is especially controlled by the Israeli Prime Minister, was designed to help the Israeli intelligence agency to penetrate the newly independent black Africa.

It is also reported that these payments were approved by your present Secretary of State, Mr. Cyrus Vance, when he was the Deputy Secretary of Defense. It appears, therefore, that we should ask the American C.I.A. to give you the full information about the involvement in the plot against Uganda. Zionist Israel and the C.I.A. should give you a true picture and correct information as the new President so that you can take sound decisions based on factual information.

Zionist Israel and the C.I.A. should not chain and [pull] the American Government and people like slaves. It should be the U.S. government and people who control Israel and the C.I.A., rather than the other way round. Therefore Israel should follow America, and America should not follow Israel with its false propaganda, which it propagates through American news media which is under Zionist control. The Zionists can embarrass you and put you in a big mess. You have the power to tell Israel what to do.

You should therefore be like Field Marshal Amin, who is a black superpower in Africa. Therefore, no country can force Uganda to be in its pocket.

According to reports from Nairobi, 5,000 American Marines near the eastern coast are supposed to come and rescue 250 American missionaries in Uganda. This is impossible, as the Americans in Uganda are happy and are scattered all over the country. In any case, Uganda has the strength to crush any invaders.

[Arms Sales]

Regarding your appeal to other countries to stop selling arms to Uganda, this again is impossible. The U.S. Government cannot stop friendly countries to Uganda to sell her all the arms she requires.

Uganda can even buy the most sophisticated American-made arms without the knowledge of the U.S. Government. If a government has money it can buy any arms anywhere. The U.S. Government should know that all governments cannot follow its decisions like a slave following his or her master. The United States should know that it is only puppet regimes which follow blindly and even read statements which are written for them by the U.S. C.I.A.

Uganda will continue to act as an independent country and will not follow the United States blindly. Any leader should study the situation very carefully and assess with maturity and without emotion correct information so he can reach a rational decision.

However, it appears that all you have said about Uganda is false and those who are feeding you with information have not set a foot in Uganda. They base their reports on hearsay and rumors from Uganda exiles and Zionist newspapers.

[U.S. Human Rights Violations]

It is a pity that when we invited you to send a delegation last month to the 25 [January] anniversary celebrations you failed to do so. If you had done so your delegation would have given you the true picture of Uganda. You would have been informed that Uganda is more peaceful than certain parts of the United States and Northern Ireland, where a lot of murders are taking place.

Regarding the U.S. Government's instruction to its Ambassador to the United Nations to investigate the violation of human rights in Uganda, the U.S. Government should instead instruct its Ambassador to ask the United Nations to investigate the crimes which the United States has committed in the name of democracy in the various parts of the world, crimes which are worse than the violation of human rights. To mention a few:

A. The United States has the highest record of assassination, including those of her Presidents and religious leaders;

B. Racial discrimination, [word indistinct] and murders;

C. Millions of indiscriminate killings with B-52 bombers and napalm bombs in Vietnam, Cambodia and Korea;

D. Up to date, there are huge U.S. forces in Southeast Asia which are committing crimes there;

E. The invasion of Cuba in 1960 [date as heard] at the so-called Bay of Pigs;

F. The mass murders of Japanese at Hiroshima and Nagasaki, when the United States for the first and only time in human history used the atomic bomb.

The C.I.A. is also responsible for murdering leaders in Africa and other parts of the world, including Patrice Lumumba, and overthrowing different governments from other parts of the world.

Why does not the United Nations investigate them now when they are being revealed? The United Nations should investigate the crimes and violation of human rights in Palestine and Northern Ireland.

If the U.S. government were to accept the U.N. investigations in its global mountain of crimes, then the world will judge the sincerity of the American government.

I have gone at this length, Mr. President, in order to point out that each nation should study itself carefully before pointing out an accusing finger to another nation.

As you have just taken over the office of the Presidency of the United States, you should not be blinded by those who may want to take your place even before you have seen all the rooms of the White House. You should not be blinded by those who want to overthrow you, like the C.I.A., which is feeding you with false information and rumors.

Out of over 140 members of the United Nations, it is only the United States, Britain and Israel which are involved in this dirty campaign against Uganda.

Can you allow a religious leader, such as a bishop or a sheik or anybody, to bring arms to your country in order to overthrow your government and to cause confusion and chaos?

Mr. President, I would ask you to pass my greetings to all the Americans, both white and black. I hope to visit you at the White House in the near future.

Accept, your excellency, the assurances of my highest consideration.

March

COURT ON USE OF RACE
IN LEGISLATIVE REDISTRICTING
March 1, 1977

In a decision handed down March 1, the Supreme Court ruled 7-1 that states may properly use racial criteria and racial quotas in drawing districts for electing members of their state legislatures.

The court upheld the redistricting of the New York legislature in 1974 which redrew certain districts in Kings County in such a way as to assure that in each there was a non-white majority of at least 65 per cent. Kings County was one of three New York counties brought under the coverage of the Voting Rights Act as it was amended in 1970.

The redistricting was challenged as unconstitutional by the Hasidic Jews of the Williamsburgh community, which was divided into two legislative districts in order to reduce the original district's white population. They charged that criteria for redistricting diluted their votes and denied them equal protection under the law.

*Chief Justice Warren E. Burger dissented, arguing that approval of such racial gerrymandering of districts moved the country "one step farther away from a truly homogenous society." (*United Jewish Organizations of Williamsburgh v. Carey) *Justice Thurgood Marshall did not participate.*

Majority Opinion

The reasons for which the seven justices decided to uphold the redistricting varied. Justice Byron R. White, joined by Justice John Paul Stevens, held this use of racial criteria proper under the Voting Rights Act and under the Constitution itself.

White and Stevens were joined on the first point by Justice William J. Brennan Jr. and Harry A. Blackmun. Those four justices agreed that "the Constitution does not prevent a state subject to the Voting Rights Act from deliberately creating or preserving black majorities in order to ensure that its reapportionment plan complies" with the act. They reaffirmed earlier rulings that that law and "its authorization for racial redistricting where appropriate, to avoid abridging the right to vote on account of race or color, are constitutional." They also held that the particular criteria used in this case were constitutionally proper.

Justice White and Stevens, joined by Justice William H. Rehnquist, viewed this redistricting along racial lines as justified and constitutional even without the authority of the Voting Rights Act, a position not espoused by Justices Brennan and Blackmun. The plan, wrote White on this point, "represented no racial slur or stigma with respect to whites or any other race, and we discern no discrimination violative of the Fourteenth Amendment nor any abridgement of the right to vote on account of race within the meaning of the Fifteenth Amendment."

White wrote that the deliberate decision to increase the non-white majority in certain districts did not result in the underrepresentation of the white voters in the area. White continued: "There is no authority for the proposition that the candidates who are found racially unacceptable by the majority, and the minority voters supporting those candidates, have had their Fourteenth or Fifteenth Amendment rights infringed by this process. Their position is similar to that of the Democratic or Republican minority that is submerged year after year by the adherents to the majority party who tend to vote a straight party line."

In a concurring opinion, Justices Potter Stewart and Lewis F. Powell Jr. simply said that the redistricting was proper because it had not been shown to have either the purpose or the effect of discriminating against white voters because of their race.

Justice Brennan added a concurring opinion expressing his concern about the questions of fairness raised by the use of "race-centered remedial devices"—reverse discrimination. "I am wholly content to leave this thorny question until another day," he wrote, "for I am convinced that the existence of the Voting Rights Act makes such a decision unnecessary" in this case.

Burger Dissent

"If districts have been drawn in a racially biased manner in the past (which the record does not show to have been the case here), the proper remedy is to reapportion along neutral lines," wrote Chief Justice Burger in dissent. "Manipulating the racial composition of electoral districts to assure one minority or another its 'deserved' representation will not promote the goal of a racially neutral legislature."

In its first modern case (Gomillion v. Lightfoot) *involving such "racial gerrymandering," the court in 1960 ruled that "drawing of political boundary lines with the sole, explicit objective of reaching a predetermined racial result cannot ordinarily be squared with the Constitution," he argued. In this case, the Voting Rights Act did not justify such racially motivated decisions either, Burger added.*

"The use of a mathematical formula tends to sustain the existence of ghettos by promoting the notion that political clout is to be gained or maintained by marshalling particular racial, ethnic or religious groups in enclaves. It suggests to the voter that only a candidate of the same race, religion or ethnic origins can properly represent the voter's interests and that such candidate can be elected only from a district with a sufficient minority concentration.... The notion that Americans vote in firm blocs has been repudiated in the election of minority members as mayors and legislators in numerous American cities and districts overwhelmingly white."

Following are excerpts from the Supreme Court's decision on racial redistricting delivered March 1, 1977. (Boldface headings in brackets have been added by Congressional Quarterly to highlight the organization of the text.):

No. 75-104

United Jewish Organizations of Williamsburgh, Inc., et al., Petitioners, *v.* Hugh L. Carey et al.	On Writ of Certiorari to the United States Court of Appeals for the Second Circuit.

[March 1, 1977]

MR. JUSTICE WHITE announced the judgment of the Court and filed an opinion, all of which is joined by MR. JUSTICE STEVENS, Parts I, II, and III of which are joined by MR. JUSTICE BRENNAN and MR. JUSTICE BLACKMUN, and Parts I and IV of which is joined by MR. JUSTICE REHNQUIST. [MR. JUSTICE MARSHALL took no part in the consideration or decision of this case.]

Section 5 of the Voting Rights Act prohibits a state or political subdivision subject to § 4 of the Act from implementing a legislative reapportionment unless it has obtained a declaratory judgment from the District Court for the District of Columbia, or a ruling from the Attorney General of the United States, that the reapportionment "does not have the purpose and will not have the effect of denying or abridging the right to vote on account of race or color...." The question presented is whether, in the circumstances of this case, the use of racial criteria by the State of New York in its attempt to comply with § 5 of the Voting Rights Act and to secure the approval of the Attorney General violated the Fourteenth or Fifteenth Amendment....

II

...Petitioners argue that the New York Legislature, although seeking to comply with the Voting Rights Act as construed by the Attorney General, has violated the Fourteenth and Fifteenth Amendments by deliberately revising its reapportionment plan along racial lines. In rejecting petitioners' claims, we address four propositions: first, that whatever might be true in other contexts, the use of racial criteria in districting and apportionment is never permissible; second, that even if racial considerations may be used to redraw district lines in order to remedy the residual effects of past unconstitutional reapportionments, there are no findings here of prior discriminations that would require or justify as a remedy that white voters be reassigned in order to increase the size of black majorities in certain districts; third, that the use of a "racial quota" in redistricting is never acceptable; and fourth, that even if the foregoing general propositions are infirm, what New York actually did in this case was unconstitutional, particularly its use of 65% nonwhite racial quota for certain districts. The first three arguments, as we now explain, are foreclosed by our cases construing and sustaining the constitutionality of the Voting Rights Act; the fourth we address in Parts III and IV.

It is apparent from the face of the Act, from its legislative history, and from our cases that the Act was itself broadly remedial in the sense that it was "designed by Congress to banish the blight of racial discrimination in voting...." *South Carolina* v. *Katzenbach*...(1966). It is also plain, however, that after "repeatedly try[ing] to cope with the problem by facilitating case-by-case litigation against voting discrimination,"... Congress became dissatisfied with this approach, which required judicial findings of unconstitutional discrimination in specific situations and judicially approved remedies to cure that discrimination. Instead, Congress devised more stringent measures, one of which, § 5, required the covered States to seek the approval of either the Attorney General or of a three-judge court in the District of Columbia whenever they sought to implement new voting procedures. Under § 4, a State became subject to § 5 whenever it was administratively determined that certain conditions which experience had proved were indicative of racial discrimination in voting had existed in the area—in the case of New York, as already indicated, ...that a literacy test was in use in certain counties in 1968 and that fewer than 50% of the voting age residents in these counties voted in the presidential election that year. At that point, New York could have escaped coverage by undertaking to demonstrate to the appropriate court that the test had not been used to discriminate within the past 10 years, an effort New York unsuccessfully made.

Given this coverage of the counties involved, it is evident that the Act's prohibition against instituting new voting procedures without the approval of the Attorney General or the three-judge District Court is not dependent upon proving past unconstitutional apportionments and that in operation the Act is aimed at preventing the use of new procedures until their capacity for discrimination has been examined by the Attorney General or by a court. Although recognizing that the "stringent new remedies," including § 5, were "an uncommon exercise of congressional power," we nevertheless sustained the Act as a "permissibly decisive" response to "the extraordinary stratagem of contriving new rules of various kinds for the sole purpose of perpetrating voting discrimination in the face of adverse federal court decrees." *South Carolina* v. *Katzenbach*....

It is also clear that under § 5, new or revised reapportionment plans are among those voting procedures, standards or practices that may not be adopted by a covered State without the Attorney General or a three-judge court ruling that the plan "does not have the purpose and will not have the effect of denying or abridging the right to vote on account of race or color." In *Allen* v. *State Board of Elections*...(1969), on which the Court of Appeals relied below, we held that a change from district to at-large voting for county supervisors had to be submitted for federal approval under § 5, because of the potential for a "dilution" of minority voting power which could "nullify [its] ability to elect the candidate of [its] choice...." When it renewed the Voting Rights Act in 1970 and again in 1975, Congress was well aware of the application of § 5 to redistricting. In its 1970 extension, Congress relied on findings by the United States Commission on Civil Rights that the newly gained voting strength of minorities was in danger of being diluted by redistricting plans that divided minority communities among predominantly white districts. In 1975, Congress was unmistakenly cognizant of this new phase in the effort to eliminate voting discrimination. Former Attorney General Katzenbach testified that § 5 "has had its broadest impact...in the areas of redistricting and reapportionment," and the Senate and House reports recommending the extension of the Act referred specifically to the Attorney General's role in screening redistricting plans to protect the opportunities for nonwhites to be elected to public office.

As the Court of Appeals understood the Act and our decision in *Allen*, compliance with the Act in reapportionment cases would often necessitate the use of racial considerations in drawing district lines. That the Court of Appeals correctly read the Act has become clearer from later cases.

In *Beer* v. *United States*...(1976), the Court considered the question of what criteria a legislature reapportionment must satisfy under § 5 of the Voting Rights Act to demonstrate that it does not have the "effect" of denying or abridging the right to vote on account of race. *Beer* established that the Voting Rights Act does not permit the implementation of a reapportionment that "would lead to a retrogression in the position of racial minorities with respect to their effective exercise of the electoral franchise."... This test was satisfied where the reapportionment increased the percentage of districts where members of racial minorities protected by the Act were in the majority.... But if this test were not met, clearance by the Attorney General or the District Court for the District of Columbia could not be given, and the reapportionment could not be implemented.

The reapportionment at issue in *Beer* was approved by this Court, because New Orleans had created one councilmanic district with a majority of black voters where none existed before. But had there been districts with black majorities under the previous law and had New Orleans in fact decreased the number of majority black districts, it would have had to modify its plan in order to implement its reapportionment by carving out a large enough black majority in however many additional districts would be necessary to satisfy the *Beer* test. There was division on the Court as to what a State must show to satisfy § 5; but all eight Justices who participated in the decision implicitly accepted the proposition that a State may revise its reapportionment plan to comply with § 5 by increasing the percentage of black voters in a particular district until it has produced a clear majority....

The Court has taken a similar approach in applying § 5 to the extension of city boundaries through annexation. Where the annexation has the effect of reducing the percentage of blacks in the city, the proscribed "effect" on voting rights can be avoided by a post-annexation districting plan which "fairly reflects the strength of the Negro community as it exists after the annexation" and which "would afford [it] representation reasonably equivalent to [its] political strength in the enlarged community." *City of Richmond* v. *United States*...(1975). Accord, *City of Petersburg* v. *United States*...(1973)....

Implicit in *Beer* and *City of Richmond*, then, is the proposition that the Constitution does not prevent a State subject to the Voting Rights Act from deliberately creating or preserving black majorities in particular districts in order to ensure that its reapportionment plan complies with § 5. That proposition must be rejected and § 5 held unconstitutional to that extent if we are to accept petitioners' view that racial criteria may never be used in redistricting or that they may be used, if at all, only as a specific remedy for past unconstitutional apportionments. We are unwilling to overturn our prior cases, however. Section 5, and its authorization for racial redistricting where appropriate to avoid abridging the right to vote on account of race or color, are constitutional. Contrary to petitioners' first argument, neither the Fourteenth nor the Fifteenth Amendment mandates any...rule against using racial factors in districting and apportionment. Nor is petitioners' second argument valid. The permissible use of racial criteria is not confined to eliminating the effects of past discriminatory districting on apportionment.

Moreover, in the process of drawing black majority districts in order to comply with § 5, the State must decide how substantial those majorities must be in order to satisfy the Voting Rights Act. The figure used in drawing the *Beer* plan, for example, was 54% of registered voters. At a minimum and by definition, a "black majority district" must be more than 50%

black. But whatever the specific percentage, the State will inevitably arrive at it as a necessary means to ensure the opportunity for the election of a black representative and to obtain approval of its reapportionment plan. Unless we adopted an unconstitutional construction of § 5 in *Beer* and *City of Richmond*, a reapportionment cannot violate the Fourteenth or Fifteenth Amendment merely because a State uses specific numerical quotas in establishing a certain number of black majority districts. Our cases under § 5 stand for at least this much.

III

Having rejected these three broad objections to the use of racial criteria in redistricting under the Voting Rights Act, we turn to the fourth question, which is whether the racial criteria New York used in this case—the revision of the 1972 plan to create 65% nonwhite majorities in two additional senate and two additional assembly districts—were constitutionally infirm. We hold they are not, on two separate grounds. The first is addressed in this Part III, the second in Part IV.

The first ground is that petitioners have not shown, or offered to prove, that New York did more than the Attorney General was authorized to require it to do under the nonretrogression principle of *Beer*, a principle that as we have already indicated this Court has accepted as constitutionally valid....

Petitioners have not shown that New York did more than accede to a position taken by the Attorney General that was authorized by our constitutionally permissible construction of § 5. New York adopted the 1974 plan because it sought to comply with the Voting Rights Act. This has been its primary defense of the plan, which was sustained on that basis by the Court of Appeals. Because the Court of Appeals was essentially correct, its judgment may be affirmed without addressing the additional argument by New York and by the United States that, wholly aside from New York's obligation under the Voting Rights Act to preserve minority voting strength in Kings County, the Constitution permits it to draw district lines deliberately in such a way that the percentage of districts with a nonwhite majority roughly approximates the percentage of nonwhites in the county.

IV

This additional argument, however, affords a second, and independent, ground for sustaining the particulars of the 1974 plans for Kings County. Whether or not the plan was authorized by or was in compliance with § 5 of the Voting Rights Act, New York was free to do what it did as long as it did not violate the Constitution, particularly the Fourteenth and Fifteenth Amendments; and we are convinced that neither Amendment was infringed.

There is no doubt that in preparing the 1974 legislation, the State deliberately used race in a purposeful manner. But its plan represented no racial slur or stigma with respect to whites or any other race, and we discern no discrimination violative of the Fourteenth Amendment nor any abridgment of the right to vote on account of race within the meaning of the Fifteenth Amendment.

It is true that New York deliberately increased the nonwhite majorities in certain districts in order to enhance the opportunity for election of nonwhite representatives from those districts. Nevertheless, there was no fencing out of the white population from participation in the political processes of the county, and the plan did not minimize or unfairly cancel out white voting strength.... Petitioners have not objected to the impact of the 1974 plan on the representation of white voters in the county or in the State as a whole. As the Court of Appeals observed, the plan left white majorities in approximately 70% of the assembly and senate districts in Kings County, which had a countywide population that was 65% white. Thus, even if voting in the county occurred strictly according to race, whites would not be underrepresented relative to their share of the population.

In individual districts where nonwhite majorities were increased to approximately 65%, it became more likely, given racial bloc voting, that black candidates would be elected instead of their white opponents, and it became less likely that white voters would be represented by a member of their own race; but as long as whites in Kings County, as a group, were provided with fair representation, we cannot conclude that there was a cognizable discrimination against whites or an abridgement of their right to vote on the grounds of race. Furthermore, the individual voter in the district with a nonwhite majority has no constitutional complaint merely because his candidate has lost out at the polls and his district is represented by a person for whom he did not vote. Some candidate, along with his supporters, always loses....

Where it occurs, voting for or against a candidate because of his race is an unfortunate practice. But it is not rare; and in any district where it regularly happens, it is unlikely that any candidate will be elected who is a member of the race that is in the minority in that district. However disagreeable this result may be, there is no authority for the proposition that the candidates who are found racially unacceptable by the majority, and the minority voters supporting those candidates, have had their Fourteenth or Fifteenth Amendment rights infringed by this process. Their position is similar to that of the Democratic or Republican minority that is submerged year after year by the adherents to the majority party who tend to vote a straight party line.

It does not follow, however, that the State is powerless to minimize the consequences of racial discrimination by voters when it is regularly practiced at the polls. In *Gaffney v. Cummings*...(1973), the Court upheld a districting plan "drawn with the conscious intent to...achieve a rough approximation of the statewide political strengths of the Democratic and Republican Parties."... We there recognized that districting plans would be vulnerable under our cases if *"racial or political groups* have been fenced out of the political process and their voting strength invidiously minimized"...; but that was not the case there, and no such purpose or effect may be ascribed to New York's 1974 plan. Rather, that plan can be viewed as seeking to alleviate the consequences of racial voting at the polls and to achieve a fair allocation of political power between white and non-white voters in Kings County.

In this respect New York's revision of certain district lines is little different in kind from the decision by a State in which a racial minority is unable to elect representatives from multimember districts to change to single-member districting for the purpose of increasing minority representation. This change might substantially increase minority representation at the expense of white voters, who previously elected all of the legislators but with single-member districts could elect no more than their proportional share. If this intentional reduction of white voting power would be constitutionally permissible, as we think it would be, we think it also permissible for a State, employing sound districting principles such as compactness and population equality, to attempt to prevent racial minorities from being repeatedly outvoted by creating districts that will afford fair representation to the members of those racial groups who are sufficiently numerous and whose residential patterns afford the opportunity of creating districts in which they will be in the majority.

As the Court said in *Gaffney,*

"[C]ourts have [no] constitutional warrant to invalidate a state plan, otherwise within tolerable population limits, because it undertakes, not to minimize or eliminate the political strength of any group or party, but to recognize it and, through districting, provide a rough sort of proportional representation in the legislative halls of the State."

New York was well within this rule when, under the circumstances present in Kings County, it amended its 1972 plan.

The judgment is

Affirmed.

MR. JUSTICE BRENNAN, concurring.

I join Parts I, II, and III of MR. JUSTICE WHITE's opinion. Part II effectively demonstrates that prior cases firmly establish the Attorney General's expansive authority to oversee legislative redistricting under § 5 of the Voting Rights Act.... Part III establishes to my satisfaction that as a method of securing compliance with the Voting Rights Act, the 65% rule applied to Brooklyn in this instance was not arbitrarily or casually selected. Yet, because this case carries us further down the road of race-centered remedial devices than we have heretofore traveled—with the serious questions of fairness that attend such matters—I offer this further explanation of my position.

The one starkly clear fact of this case is that an overt racial number was employed to effect petitioners' assignment to voting districts. In brief, following the Attorney General's refusal to certify the 1972 reapportionment under his § 5 powers, unnamed Justice Department officials made known that satisfaction of the Voting Rights Act in Brooklyn would necessitate creation by the state legislature of 10 state Assembly and Senate districts with threshold nonwhite populations of 65%. Prompted by the necessity of preventing interference with the upcoming 1974 election, state officials complied. Thus, the Justice Department's unofficial instruction to state officials effectively resulted in an explicit process of assignment to voting districts pursuant to race. The result of this process was a county-wide pattern of districting closely approximating proportional representation. While it is true that this demographic outcome did not "underrepresent the white population" throughout the county...—indeed, the very definition of proportional representation precludes either under- or over-representation—these particular petitioners filed suit to complain that *they* have been subjected to a process of classification on the basis of race that adversely altered *their* status.

If we were presented here with a classification of voters motivated by racial animus...or with a classification that effectively downgraded minority participation in the franchise, ...we promptly would characterize the resort to race as "suspect" and prohibit its use. Under such circumstances, the tainted apportionment process would not necessarily be saved by its proportional outcome, for the segregation of voters into "separate but equal" blocs still might well have the intent or effect of diluting the voting power of minority voters.... It follows, therefore, that if the racial redistricting involved here, imposed with the avowed intention of clustering together 10 viable nonwhite majorities at the expense of pre-existing white groupings, is not similarly to be prohibited, the distinctiveness that avoids this prohibition must arise from either or both of two considerations: the permissibility of affording preferential treatment to disadvantaged nonwhites generally, or the particularized application of the Voting Rights Act in this instance.

The first and broader of the two plausible distinctions rests upon the general propriety of so-called benign discrimination: the challenged race assignment may be permissible because it is cast in a remedial context with respect to a disadvantaged class rather than in a setting that aims to demean or insult any racial group. Even in the absence of the Voting Rights Act, this preferential policy plausibly could find expression in a state decision to overcome nonwhite disadvantages in voter registration or turnout through the application of a numerical rule—in order to achieve a proportional distribution of voting power. Such a decision, in my view, raises particularly sensitive issues of doctrine and policy. Unlike Part IV of MR. JUSTICE WHITE's opinion, I am wholly content to leave this thorny question until another day, for I am convinced that the existence of the Voting Rights Act makes such a decision unnecessary and alone suffices to support an affirmance of the judgment before us.

I begin with the settled principle that not every remedial use of race is forbidden. For example, we have authorized and even required race-conscious remedies in a variety of corrective settings.... Once it is established that circumstances exist where race may be taken into account in fashioning affirmative policies, we must identify those circumstances, and, further, determine how substantial a reliance may be placed upon race.... [I]t is instructive to consider some of the objections frequently raised to the use of overt preferential race assignment practices.

First, a purportedly preferential race assignment may in fact disguise a policy that perpetuates disadvantageous treatment of the plan's supposed beneficiaries. Accordingly, courts might face considerable difficulty in ascertaining whether a given race classification truly furthers benign rather than illicit objectives. An effort to achieve proportional representation, for example, might be aimed at aiding a group's participation in the political processes by guaranteeing safe political offices, or, on the other hand, might be a "contrivance to segregate" the group, *Wright* v. *Rockefeller...* (1964), thereby frustrating its potentially successful efforts at coalition building across racial lines.... Indeed, even the present case is not entirely free of complaints that the remedial redistricting in Brooklyn is not truly benign. Puerto Rican groups, for example, who have been joined with black groups to establish the "nonwhite" category, protested to the Attorney General that their political strength under the 1974 reapportionment actually is weaker than under the invalidated 1972 districting. ...[T]hey illustrate the risk that what is presented as an instance of benign race assignment in fact may prove to be otherwise. This concern, of course, does not undercut the theoretical legitimacy or usefulness of preferential policies. At the minimum, however, it does suggest the need for careful consideration of the operation of any racial device, even one cloaked in preferential garb. And if judicial detection of truly benign policies proves impossible or excessively crude, that alone might warrant invalidating any race-drawn line.

Second, even in the pursuit of remedial objectives, an explicit policy of assignment by race may serve to stimulate our society's latent race consciousness, suggesting the utility and propriety of basing decisions on a factor that ideally bears no relationship to an individual's worth or needs.... Furthermore, even preferential treatment may act to stigmatize its recipient groups, for although intended to correct systemic or institutional inequities, such a policy may imply to some the recipients' inferiority and especial need for protection. Again, these matters would not necessarily speak against the wisdom or permissibility of selective, benign racial classifications. But they demonstrate that the considerations that historically led us to treat race as a constitutionally "suspect" method of classifying individuals are not entirely vitiated in a preferential context.

Third, especially when interpreting the broad principles embraced by the Equal Protection Clause, we cannot well ignore the social reality that even a benign policy of assignment by race is viewed as unjust by many in our society, especially by those individuals who are adversely affected by a given classification. This impression of injustice may be heightened by the natural consequence of our governing processes that the most "discrete and insular" of whites often will be called upon to bear the immediate, direct costs of benign discrimination....[T]he impression of unfairness is magnified when a coherent group like the Hasidim disproportionately bears the adverse consequences of a race assignment policy.

In my view, if and when a decisionmaker embarks on a policy of benign racial sorting, he must weigh the concerns that I have discussed against the need for effective social policies promoting racial justice in a society beset by deep-rooted racial inequities. But I believe that Congress here adequately struck that balance in enacting the carefully conceived remedial scheme embodied in the Voting Rights Act. However the Court ultimately decides the constitutional legitimacy of "reverse discrimination" pure and simple, I am convinced that the application of the Voting Rights Act substantially minimizes the objections to preferential treatment, and legitimates the use of even overt, numerical racial devices in electoral redistricting.

The participation of the Attorney General, for example, largely relieves the judiciary of the need to grapple with the difficulties of distinguishing benign from malign discrimination. Under § 5 of the Act, the Attorney General in effect is constituted champion of the interests of minority voters, and accompanying implementing regulations ensure the availability of materials and submissions necessary to discern the true effect of a proposed reapportionment plan.... This initial right of review, coupled with the fact-finding competence of the Justice Department, substantially reduces the likelihood that a complicated reapportionment plan that silently furthers malign racial policies would escape detection by appropriate officials. As a practical matter, therefore, I am prepared to accord considerable deference to the judgment of the Attorney General that a particular districting scheme complies with the remedial objectives furthered by the Voting Rights Act.

Similarly, the history of the Voting Rights Act provides reassurance that, in the face of the potential for reinvigorating racial partisanship, the congressional decision to authorize the use of race-oriented remedies in this context was the product of substantial and careful deliberations.... Insofar as the drawing of district lines is a process that intrinsically involves numerical calculations, and insofar as state officials charged with the task of defining electoral constituencies are unlikely simply to close their eyes to considerations such as race and national origin, the resort to a numerical racial criterion as a method of achieving compliance with the aims of the Voting Rights Act is, in my view, consistent with...[congressional] consensus....

This leaves, of course, the objection expressed by a variety of participants in this litigation: that this reapportionment worked the injustice of localizing the direct burdens of racial assignment upon a morally undifferentiated group of whites, and, indeed, a group that plausibly is peculiarly vulnerable to such injustice. This argument has both normative and emotional appeal, but for a variety of reasons I am convinced that the Voting Rights Act drains it of vitality.

First, it is important to recall that the Attorney General's oversight focuses upon jurisdictions whose prior practices exhibited the purpose or effect of infringing the right to vote on account of race.... This direct nexus to localities with a history of discriminatory practices or effects enhances the legitimacy of the Attorney General's remedial authority over individuals within those communities who benefited (as whites) from those earlier discriminatory voting patterns. Moreover, the obvious remedial nature of the Act and its enactment by an elected Congress that hardly can be viewed as dominated by nonwhite representatives belie the possibility that the decisionmaker intended a racial insult or injury to those whites who are adversely affected by the operation of the Act's provisions. Finally, petitioners have not been deprived of their right to vote, a consideration that minimizes the detrimental impact of the remedial racial policies governing the § 5 reapportionment. True, petitioners are denied the opportunity to vote as a group in accordance with the earlier districting configuration, but they do not press any legal claim to a group voice as Hasidim.... In terms of their voting interests, then, the burden that they claim to suffer must be attributable solely to their relegation to increased nonwhite-dominated districts. Yet, to the extent that white and nonwhite interests and sentiments are polarized in Brooklyn, the petitioners still are indirectly "protected" by the remaining white Assembly and Senate districts within the country, carefully preserved in accordance with the white proportion of the total county population. While these considerations obviously do not satisfy petitioners, I am persuaded that they reinforce the legitimacy of this remedy.

Since I find nothing in the first three parts of MR. JUSTICE WHITE's opinion that is inconsistent with the views expressed herein, I join those parts.

MR. JUSTICE STEWART, with whom MR. JUSTICE POWELL joins, concurring in the judgment.

The question presented for decision in this case is whether New York's use of racial criteria in redistricting Kings County violated the Fourteenth or Fifteenth Amendments. The petitioners' contention is essentially that racial awareness in legislative reapportionment is unconstitutional *per se.* Acceptance of their position would mark an egregious departure from the way this Court has in the past analyzed the constitutionality of claimed discrimination in dealing with the elective franchise on the basis of race.

The petitioners have made no showing that a racial criterion was used as a basis for denying them their right to vote, in contravention of the Fifteenth Amendment.... They have made no showing that the redistricting scheme was employed as part of a "contrivance to segregate"; to minimize or cancel out the voting strength of a minority class or interest; or otherwise to impair or burden the opportunity of affected persons to participate in the political process....

Under the Fourteenth Amendment the question is whether the reapportionment plan represents purposeful discrimination against white voters....

Disproportionate impact may afford some evidence that an invidious
purpose was present....

But the record here does not support a finding that the redistricting plan
undervalued the political power of white voters relative to their numbers in
Kings County.... That the legislature was aware of race when it drew the
district lines might also suggest a discriminatory purpose. Such awareness
is not, however, the equivalent of discriminatory intent. The clear purpose
with which the New York Legislature acted—in response to the position of
the United States Department of Justice under the Voting Rights
Act—forecloses any finding that it acted with the invidious purpose of discriminating against white voters.

Having failed to show that the legislative reapportionment plan had
either the purpose or the effect of discriminating against them on the basis
of their race, the petitioners have offered no basis for affording them the
constitutional relief they seek. Accordingly, I join the judgment of the
Court.

MR. CHIEF JUSTICE BURGER, dissenting.

The question presented in this difficult case is whether New York
violated the rights of the petitioners under the Fourteenth and Fifteenth
Amendments by direct reliance on fixed racial percentages in its 1974
redistricting of Kings County. For purposes of analysis I will treat this in
two steps: (1) Is the state legislative action constitutionally permissible absent any special considerations raised by the federal Voting Rights Act;
and (2) does New York's obligation to comply with the Voting Rights Act
permit it to use these means to achieve a federal statutory objective?

(1)

I begin with this Court's holding in *Gomillion* v. *Lightfoot*...(1960), the
first case to strike down a state attempt at racial gerrymandering. If
Gomillion teaches anything, I had thought it was that drawing of political
boundary lines with the sole, explicit objective of reaching a predetermined
racial result cannot ordinarily be squared with the Constitution. The
record before us reveals—and it is not disputed—that this is precisely what
took place here. In drawing up the 1974 reapportionment scheme, the New
York Legislature did not consider racial composition as merely *one* of
several political characteristics; on the contrary, race appears to have been
the one and only criterion applied.

The principal opinion notes that after the 1972 apportionment plan was
rejected, New York officials conferred with the Justice Department as to
what plan could obtain the Attorney General's approval. One New York official testified that he "got the feeling [from a Justice Department
spokesman]...that 65 percent would be probably an approved figure."...
Further testimony by that same official is revealing:

"Q: So that your reason for dividing the Hassidic community was to effect compliance with the Department of Justice determination, and the minimum standards they impose—they appear to impose?

"A: *That was the sole reason.* We spent over a full day right around the clock, attempting to come up with some other type of districting plan that would maintain the Hassidic community as one entity, *and I think that is evidenced clearly by the fact that the district is exactly 65 percent, and it's because we went block by block, and didn't go higher or lower than that,* in order to maintain as much of the community as possible."

This official also testified that apportionment solutions which would have kept the Hassidic community within a single district, but would have resulted in a 63.4% nonwhite concentration, were rejected for fear that, falling short of "exactly 65 percent," they "would not be acceptable" to the Justice Department....

The words "racial quota" are emotionally loaded and must be used with caution. Yet this undisputed testimony shows that the 65% figure was viewed by the legislative reapportionment committee as so firm a criterion that even a fractional deviation was deemed impermissible. I cannot see how this can be characterized otherwise than a strict quota approach and I must therefore view today's holding as casting doubt on the clear-cut principles established in *Gomillion.*

(2)

My second inquiry is whether the action of the State of New York becomes constitutionally permissible because it was taken to comply with the remedial provisions of the federal Voting Rights Act.

In *South Carolina* v. *Katzenbach*...(1966) the Court, while recognizing that the "stringent new remedies" were "an uncommon exercise of Congressional power"...upheld the Act as a "permissibly decisive" response to "the extraordinary strategem of perpetrating voting discrimination in the face of adverse federal decrees."... In *Allen* v. *State Board of Elections*...(1969) the Court sustained an application of § 5 to a change from a district to an at-large election of county supervisors because of a potential for "dilution" of minority voting power which could "nullify the ability to elect the candidate of one's choice." In *Allen* and *Katzenbach* the Court acknowledged that the Voting Rights Act contemplated that the Attorney General and the affected state legislatures would be obliged to think in racial terms. In *Perkins* v. *Matthews*...(1971), and again in *Georgia* v. *United States*...(1973), I expressed doubt as to the correctness of *Allen* but acquiesced in the judgments on the basis of *stare decisis.*

The present case, however, presents a quite different situation. Faced with the straightforward obligation to redistrict so as to avoid "a retrogression in the position of racial minorities with respect to their effective exercise of the electoral franchise," *Beer* v. *United States*...(1976), the state legislature mechanically adhered to a plan designed to maintain—without tolerance for even a 1.6% deviation—a "nonwhite" population of 65% within several of the new districts. There is no indication whatever that use of this rigid figure was in any way related—much less necessary—to fulfilling the State's obligation under the Voting Rights Act as defined in *Beer*.

The principal opinion acknowledges our recent *Beer* holding by noting that "there is no evidence in the record to show whether the 1972 plan increased or decreased the number of senate or assembly districts with substantial nonwhite majorities of 65%," and by speculating that "the 1974 revisions may have accomplished nothing more than the restoration of nonwhite voting strength to 1966 levels." It then proceeds to assume that the 1974 reapportionment was undertaken in compliance with *Beer*. The lack of evidence on this subject is, of course, not surprising, since petitioners' case was dismissed at the pleading stage.... On the present sparse record, however, I cannot find support in the Voting Rights Act for the arbitrary process followed by the New York Legislature.

The record is devoid of any evidence that the 65% figure was a reasoned response to the problem of past discrimination. It is, rather, clear that under the time pressure of upcoming elections, and "in an atmosphere of hasty dickering" (Frankel, J., dissenting), the New York Legislature simply accepted the standard formula from the Department of Justice and treated it as a mandatory. Moreover, the formula appears to be based upon factually unsupportable assumptions. For example, it would make no sense to assure nonwhites a majority of 65% in a voting district unless it were assumed that nonwhites and whites vote in racial blocs, and that the blocs vote adversely to, or independent of, one another. Not only is the record in this case devoid of any evidence that such bloc voting has taken or will take place in Kings County, but such evidence as there is points in the opposite direction: We are informed that four out of the five "safe" (65%+) nonwhite districts established by the 1974 plan have since elected white representatives....

The assumption that "whites" and "non-whites" in the County form homogeneous entities for voting purposes is entirely without foundation. The "whites" category consists of a veritable galaxy of national origins, ethnic backgrounds, and religious denominations. It simply cannot be assumed that the legislative interests of all "whites" are even substantially identical. In similar fashion, those described as "non-whites" include, in addition to Negroes, a substantial portion of Puerto Ricans.... The Puerto Rican population, for whose protection the Voting Rights Act was "triggered" in Kings County...has expressly disavowed any identity of interest with the Negroes, and, in fact, objected to the 1974 redistricting scheme because it did not establish a Puerto Rican controlled district within the county.

(3)

Although reference to racial composition of a political unit may, under certain circumstances, serve as "a starting point in the process of shaping a remedy," *Swann* v. *Charlotte-Mecklenburg Board of Education*...(1971), rigid adherence to quotas, especially in a case like this, deprives citizens such as petitioners of the opportunity to have the legislature make a determination free from unnecessary bias for or against any racial, ethnic or religious group. I do not quarrel with the proposition that the New York Legislature may choose to take ethnic or community union into consideration in drawing its district lines. Indeed, petitioners are members of an ethnic community which, without deliberate purpose so far as shown on this record, has long been within a single Assembly and Senate District. While petitioners certainly have no constitutional right to remain unified within a single political district, they do have, in my view, the constitutional right not to be carved up so as to create a voting bloc composed of some other ethnic or racial group through the kind of racial gerrymandering the Court condemned in *Gomillion* v. *Lightfoot*.

If districts have been drawn in a racially biased manner in the past (which the record does not show to have been the case here) the proper remedy is to reapportion along neutral lines. Manipulating the racial composition of electoral districts to assure one minority or another its "deserved" representation will not promote the goal of a racially neutral legislature. On the contrary, such racial gerrymandering puts the imprimatur of the State on the concept that race is a proper consideration in the electoral process. "The vice lies in...placing...the power of the State behind a racial classification that induces racial prejudice at the polls." *Anderson* v. *Martin*...(1964).

The result reached by the Court today in the name of the Voting Rights Act is ironic. The use of a mathematical formula tends to sustain the existence of ghettos by promoting the notion that political clout is to be gained or maintained by marshalling particular racial, ethnic or religious groups in enclaves. It suggests to the voter that only a candidate of the same race, religion or ethnic origins can properly represent that voter's interests, and that such candidate can be elected only from a district with a sufficient minority concentration. The device employed by the State of New York, and endorsed by the Court today, moves us one step farther away from a truly homogenous society. This retreat from the ideal of the American "melting pot" is curiously out of step with recent political history—and indeed with what the Court has said and done for more than a decade. The notion that Americans vote in firm blocs has been repudiated in the election of minority members as mayors and legislators in numerous American cities and districts overwhelmingly white. Since I cannot square the mechanical racial gerrymandering in this case with the mandate of the Constitution, I respectfully dissent from the affirmance of the judgment of the Court of Appeals.

COURT ON SEX BIAS
IN SOCIAL SECURITY
March 2, 1977

The Supreme Court March 2 held unconstitutional the Social Security system's requirement that forced widowers, but not widows, to prove their financial dependence on their deceased spouses in order to receive survivors' benefits. (Califano v. Goldfarb) In a 5-4 vote, Justice William J. Brennan Jr., joined by Justices Byron R. White, Thurgood Marshall and Lewis F. Powell Jr., found that the requirement discriminated against women wage earners—who received less protection for their families than men workers although they paid in the same amount to the Social Security system.

Brennan stated that the Social Security statute discriminated against female workers because widowers had to prove that their spouses provided at least one-half of their income to receive survivors' benefits. Widows received the same benefits without the test for dependent status.

Majority, Concurring Opinions

The gender-based distinction in this payment of survivors' benefits, wrote Brennan, resulted in "the efforts of female workers required to pay Social Security taxes producing less protection for their spouses than is produced by the efforts of men." This is unconstitutional, because it is based on nothing more than "archaic and overbroad generalizations" and "old notions" of women's dependence, he concluded.

Justice John Paul Stevens concurred with the majority but concluded that the relevant discrimination was against surviving male spouses.

169

Discrimination against females was an "accidental byproduct of a traditional way of thinking about females," Stevens noted, and something more than accident was required to justify the disparate treatment of persons who have as strong a claim to equal treatment.

The reasoning applied by the majority was the same as in earlier cases when the court invalidated a regulation providing payment of mother's benefits to a young widow with children but not similar benefits to a young widower with children (Weinberger v. Wiesenfeld), and a regulation that assumed wives of military men were all dependents and should receive benefits, while requiring the husbands of military women to prove their dependence to receive the same benefits (Frontiero v. Richardson). (Historic Documents of 1975, p. 177)

Dissenting Opinion

Chief Justice Warren E. Burger and Justices Harry A. Blackmun and Potter Stewart joined with William H. Rehnquist in a dissenting opinion. Rehnquist argued that Congress had the right to create various categories of benefits based on need and administrative convenience. When 90 per cent of the claimants were likely to be millions of widows, Rehnquist observed, it was a logical step to create a dependency test for widowers who constituted only 10 per cent of the claimants. The dissenters shared Justice Stevens' view of the distinction as between surviving spouses, not wage earners, but they found it a justifiable distinction despite its basis in sex.

If the dependency proof requirement for widowers were dropped, the Social Security Administration estimated that as many as 220,000 additional widowers might become eligible for survivors' benefits, receiving more than $200-million in payments in the first full year of eligibility. And the cost could rise if the ruling was interpreted to invalidate a similar dependence proof requirement imposed upon husbands of women wage earners who applied for old age benefits. If this requirement were dropped, up to 300,000 additional men would be eligible for these benefits at a cost of around $300-million in the first year.

Following are excerpts from the Supreme Court's opinion, delivered March 2, 1977, banning dependent status tests for widowers, but not widows, in the Social Security System:

No. 75-699

Joseph A. Califano Jr., Secretary of Health, Education, and Welfare, Appellant, *v.* Leon Goldfarb.	On Appeal from the United States District Court for the Eastern District of New York.

[March 2, 1977]

MR. JUSTICE BRENNAN announced the judgment of the Court and delivered an opinion in which MR. JUSTICE WHITE, MR. JUSTICE MARSHALL, and MR. JUSTICE POWELL joined.

Under the Federal Old-Age, Survivors, and Disability Insurance Benefits program (OASDI)...survivors' benefits based on the earnings of a deceased husband covered by the Act are payable to his widow. Such benefits on the basis of the earnings of a deceased wife covered by the Act are payable to the widower, however, only if he "was receiving at least one-half of his support" from his deceased wife. The question in this case is whether this gender-based distinction violates the Due Process Clause of the Fifth Amendment.

A three-judge District Court for the Eastern District of New York held that the different treatment of men and women...constituted invidious discrimination against female wage earners by affording them less protection for their surviving spouses than is provided to male employees.... We noted probable jurisdiction.... We affirm.

I

Mrs. Hannah Goldfarb worked as a secretary in the New York City public school system for almost 25 years until her death in 1968. During that entire time she paid in full all social security taxes required by the Federal Insurance Contributions Act.... She was survived by her husband, Leon Goldfarb, now age 72, a retired federal employee. Leon duly applied for widower's benefits. The application was denied with the explanation that

> "You do not qualify for a widower's benefit because you do not meet one of the requirements for such entitlement. This requirement is that you must have been receiving at least one-half support from your wife when she died."

The District Court declared...[the requirement] unconstitutional primarily on the authority of *Weinberger* v. *Wiesenfeld*...(1975)....

II

The gender-based distinction...burdening a widower but not a widow with the task of proving dependency upon the deceased spouse—presents an equal protection question indistinguishable from that decided in *Weinberger* v. *Wiesenfeld*.... That decision and the decision in *Frontiero* v. *Richardson*...plainly require affirmance of the judgment of the District Court.

The statutes held unconstitutional in *Frontiero* provided increased quarters allowance and medical and dental benefits to a married male member of the uniformed armed services whether or not his wife in fact depended on him, while a married female service member could only receive the increased benefits if she in fact provided over one-half of her husband's support. To justify the classification, the Government argued that "as an empirical matter, wives in our society frequently are dependent on their husbands, while husbands are rarely dependent on their wives. Thus,...Congress might reasonably have concluded that it would be both cheaper and easier simply conclusively to presume that wives of male members are financially dependent on their husbands, while burdening female members with the task of establishing dependency in fact."... But *Frontiero* concluded that, by according such differential treatment to male and female members of the uniformed services for the sole purpose of achieving administrative convenience, the challenged statute violated the Fifth Amendment....

Weinberger v. *Wiesenfeld,* like the instant case, presented the question in the context of the OASDI program. There the Court held unconstitutional a provision that denied father's insurance benefits to surviving widowers with children in their care, while authorizing similar mother's benefits to similarly situated widows. Paula Wiesenfeld, the principal source of her family's support, and covered by the Act, died in childbirth, survived by the baby and her husband Stephen. Stephen applied for survivors' benefits for himself and his infant son. Benefits were allowed the baby...but denied the father on the grounds that "mother's benefits"...were available only to women. The Court reversed, holding that the gender-based distinction...was "indistinguishable from that invalidated in *Frontiero,*"...and therefore, while

> "...the notion that men are more likely than women to be the primary supporters of their spouses and children is not entirely without empirical support,...such a gender-based generalization cannot suffice to justify the denigration of the efforts of women who do work and whose earnings contribute significantly to their families' support.

...Precisely the same reasoning condemns the gender-based distinction made...in this case. For that distinction too operates "to deprive women of protection for their families which men receive as a result of their employment": social security taxes were deducted from Hannah Goldfarb's salary during the quarter-century she worked as a secretary, yet...she also "not only failed to receive for her [spouse] the same protection which a similarly situated male worker would have received [for his spouse] but she also was deprived of a portion of her earnings in order to contribute to the fund out of which benefits would be paid to others." *Wiesenfeld* thus inescapably compels the conclusion reached by the District Court that the gender-based differentiation...—that results in the efforts of female workers required to pay social security taxes producing less protection for their spouses than is produced by the efforts of men—is forbidden by the Constitution, at least when supported by no more substantial justification than "archaic and overbroad" generalizations....

III

Appellant, however, would focus equal protection analysis not upon the discrimination against the covered wage earning female, but rather upon whether her surviving widower was unconstitutionally discriminated against by burdening him but not a surviving widow with proof of dependency. The gist of the argument is that, analyzed from the perspective of the widower, "...the denial of benefits reflected the congressional judgment that aged widowers as a class were sufficiently likely not to be dependent upon their wives, that it was appropriate to deny them benefits unless they were in fact dependent."...

But *Weinberger* v. *Wiesenfeld* rejected the virtually identical argument when appellant's predecessor argued that the statutory classification there attacked should be regarded from the perspective of the prospective beneficiary and not from that of the covered wage earner. The Secretary's Brief in that case...argued that "...the pattern of legislation reflects the considered judgment of Congress that the 'probable need' for financial assistance is greater in the case of a widow, with young children to maintain, than in the case of similarly situated males." The Court, however, analyzed the classification from the perspective of the wage earner and concluded that the classification was unconstitutional because "benefits must be distributed according to classifications which do not without sufficient justification differentiate among covered employees solely on the basis of sex."... Thus, contrary to appellant's insistence...*Wiesenfeld* is "dispositive here."

From its inception, the social security system has been a program of social insurance. Covered employees and their employers pay taxes into a fund administered distinct from the general federal revenues to purchase protection against the economic consequences of old age, disability and death. But...female insureds received less protection for their spouses solely because of their sex. Mrs. Goldfarb worked and paid social security taxes for 25 years at the same rate as her male colleagues, but...the insurance protection received by the males was broader than hers. Plainly then...[the law] disadvantages women contributors to the social security system as compared to similarly situated men." The section then "impermissibly discriminates against a female wage earner because it provides her family less protection than it provides that of a male wage earner, even though the family needs may be identical."... In a sense of course both the female wage earner and her surviving spouse are disadvantaged by operation of the statute, but this is because "Social Security is designed...for the protection of the *family*,"...and the section discriminates against one particular category of family—that in which the female spouse is a wage earner covered by social security. Therefore decision of the equal protection challenge in this case cannot focus solely on the distinction drawn between widowers and widows but, as *Wiesenfeld* held, upon the gender-based discrimination against covered female wage earners as well.

173

IV

Appellant's emphasis upon the sex based distinction between widow and widower as recipients of benefits rather than that between covered female and covered male employees also emerges in his other arguments. These arguments have no merit.

A

We accept as settled the proposition argued by appellant that Congress has wide latitude to create classifications that allocate noncontractual benefits under a social welfare program....

...Therefore, *Wiesenfeld*...expressly rejected the argument of appellant's predecessor, relying on *Flemming* v. *Nestor*, that the "non-contractual" interest of a covered employee in future social security benefits precluded any claim of denial of equal protection. Rather, *Wiesenfeld* held that the fact that the interest is "non-contractual" does not mean that "a covered employee has no right whatever to be treated equally with other employees as regards the benefits which flow from his or her employment." nor does it "sanction differential protection for covered employees which is solely gender-based."... On the contrary, benefits "directly related to years worked and amount earned by a covered employee, and not to the needs of the beneficiaries directly," like the employment-related benefits in *Frontiero*, "must be distributed according to classifications which do not without sufficient justification differentiate among covered employees solely on the basis of sex."...

B

...We conclude, therefore, that the differential treatment of nondependent widows and widowers results not, as appellant asserts, from a deliberate congressional intention to remedy the arguably greater needs of the former, but rather from an intention to aid the dependent spouses of deceased wage earners, coupled with a presumption that wives are usually dependent. This presents precisely the situation faced in *Frontiero* and *Wiesenfeld*. The only conceivable justification for writing the presumption of wives' dependency into the statute is the assumption, not verified by the Government in *Frontiero*...or here, but based simply on "archaic and overbroad" generalizations, *Schlesinger* v. *Ballard*,...that it would save the Government time, money and effort simply to pay benefits to all widows, rather than to require proof of dependency of both sexes. We held in *Frontiero*, and again in *Wiesenfeld*, and therefore hold again here, that such assumptions do not suffice to justify a gender-based discrimination in the distribution of employment-related benefits.

Affirmed.

MR. JUSTICE STEVENS, concurring in the judgment.
Although my conclusion is the same, my appraisal of the relevant dis-

crimination and my reasons for concluding that it is unjustified, are somewhat different from those expressed by MR. JUSTICE BRENNAN.

First, I agree with MR. JUSTICE REHNQUIST that the constitutional question raised by this plaintiff requires us to focus on his claim for benefits rather than his deceased wife's tax obligation. She had no contractual right to receive benefits or to control their payment; moreover, the payments are not a form of compensation for her services. At the same salary level, all workers must pay the same tax, whether they are male or female, married or single, old or young, the head of a large family or a small one. The benefits which may ultimately become payable to them or to a wide variety of beneficiaries—including their families, their spouses, future spouses, and even their ex-wives—vary enormously, but such variations do not convert a uniform tax obligation into an unequal one. The discrimination against this plaintiff would be the same if the benefits were funded from general revenues. In short, I am persuaded that the relevant discrimination in this case is against surviving male spouses, rather than against deceased female wage earners.

Second, I also agree with MR. JUSTICE REHNQUIST that a classification which treats certain aged widows more favorably than their male counterparts is not "invidious." Such a classification does not imply that males are inferior to females,...does not condemn a large class on the basis of the misconduct of an unrepresentative few,...and does not add to the burdens of an already disadvantaged discrete minority.... It does, however, treat similarly situated persons differently solely because they are not of the same sex.

The administrative convenience rationale rests on the assumption that the cost of providing benefits to nondependent widows is justified by eliminating the burden of requiring those who are dependent to establish that fact. MR. JUSTICE REHNQUIST's careful analysis of the relevant data...demonstrates that at present only about 10% of the married women in the relevant age bracket are nondependent. Omitting any requirement that widows establish dependency therefore expedites the processing of about 90% of the applications. This convenience must be regarded as significant even though procedures could certainly be developed to minimize the burden.

But what is the offsetting cost that Congress imposed on the Nation in order to achieve this administrative convenience? Assuming that Congress intended only to benefit dependent spouses, and that it has authorized payments to nondependent widows to save the cost of administering a dependency requirement for widows, it has paid a truly staggering price for a relatively modest administrative gain: the cost of payments to the hundreds of thousands of widows who are not within the described purpose of the statute is perhaps 750 million dollars a year. The figures for earlier years were presumably smaller, but must still have been large in relation to the possible administrative savings. It is inconceivable that Congress would have authorized such large expenditures for an administrative purpose without the benefit of any cost analysis, or indeed, without even discussing the problem. I am therefore convinced that administrative convenience was not the actual reason for the discrimination.

It is also clear that the disparate treatment of widows and widowers is not the product of a conscious purpose to redress the "legacy of economic discrimination" against females.... The widows who benefit from the disparate treatment are those who were sufficiently successful in the job market to become nondependent on their husbands. Such a widow is the least likely to need special benefits. The widow most in need is the one who is "suddenly forced into a job market with which she is unfamiliar, and in which, because of her former economic dependency, she will have fewer skills to offer." *Kahn* v. *Shevin*...[1974].... To accept the *Kahn* justification we must presume that Congress deliberately gave a special benefit to those females least likely to have been victims of the historic discrimination discussed in *Kahn*. Respect for the legislative process precludes the assumption that the statutory discrimination is the product of such irrational lawmaking.

The step-by-step evolution of this statutory scheme included a legislative decision to provide benefits for all widows and a separate decision to provide benefits for dependent widowers. Admittedly, each of these separate judgments has a rational and benign purpose. But I consider it clear that Congress never focused its attention on the question whether to divide nondependent surviving spouses into two classes on the basis of sex. The history of the statute is entirely consistent with the view that Congress simply assumed that all widows should be regarded as "dependents" in some general sense, even though they could not satisfy the statutory support test later imposed on men. It is fair to infer that habit, rather than analysis or actual reflection, made it seem acceptable to equate the terms "widow" and "dependent surviving spouse." That kind of automatic reflex is far different from either a legislative decision to favor females in order to compensate for past wrongs, or a legislative decision that the administrative savings exceed the cost of extending benefits to nondependent widows.

I am therefore persuaded that this discrimination against a group of males is merely the accidental byproduct of a traditional way of thinking about females. I am also persuaded that a rule which effects an unequal distribution of economic benefits solely on the basis of sex is sufficiently questionable that "due process requires that there be a legitimate basis for presuming that the rule was actually intended to serve [the] interest" put forward by the government as its justification.... In my judgment, something more than accident is necessary to justify the disparate treatment of persons who have as strong a claim to equal treatment as do similarly situated surviving spouses.

But if my judgment is correct, what is to be said about *Kahn* v. *Shevin?* For that case involved a discrimination between surviving spouses which originated in 1885; a discrimination of that vintage cannot reasonably be supposed to have been motivated by a decision to repudiate the 19th Century presumption that females are inferior to males. It seems clear, therefore, that the Court upheld the Florida statute on the basis of a hypothetical justification for the discrimination which had nothing to do with the legislature's actual motivation. On this premise, I would be required to regard *Kahn* as controlling in this case, were it not for the fact that I believe precisely the same analysis applies to *Weinberger* v. *Wiesenfeld*....

In *Wiesenfeld*, the Court rejected an atempt to use "mere recitation of a benign, compensatory purpose" as "an automaticshield"...for a statute which was actually based on " 'archaic and overbroad' generalization[s]."... In *Wiesenfeld*, as in this case, the victims of the statutory discrimination were widowers. They were totally excluded from eligibility for benefits available to similarly situated widows, just as in this case nondependent widowers are totally excluded from eligibility for benefits payable to nondependent widows. The exclusion in *Wiesenfeld* was apparently the accidental byproduct of the same kind of legislative process that gave rise to *Kahn* and to this case. If there is inconsistency between *Kahn* and *Wiesenfeld*, as I believe there is, it is appropriate to follow the later unanimous holding rather than the earlier, sharply divided decision. And if the cases are distinguishable, *Wiesenfeld* is closer on its facts to this case than is *Kahn*.

For these reasons, and on the authority of the *holding* in *Wiesenfeld*, I concur in the Court's judgment.

MR. JUSTICE REHNQUIST, with whom THE CHIEF JUSTICE, MR. JUSTICE STEWART, and MR. JUSTICE BLACKMUN join, dissenting.

In the light of this Court's recent decisions beginning with *Reed* v. *Reed*...(1971), one cannot say that there is no support in our cases for the result reached by the Court. One can, however, believe as I do that careful consideration of these cases affords more support for the opposite result than it does for that reached by the Court. Indeed, it seems to me that there are two largely separate principles which may be deduced from these cases which indicate that the Court has reached the wrong result.

The first of these principles is that cases requiring heightened levels of scrutiny for particular classifications under the Equal Protection Clause, which have originated in areas of the law outside of the field of social insurance legislation, will not be uncritically carried over into that field. This does not mean that the word "social insurance" is some sort of magic phrase which automatically mutes the requirements of the Equal Protection component of Fifth Amendment. But it does suggest that in a legislative system which distributes benefit payments among literally millions of people there are at least two characteristics which are not found in many other types of statutes. The first is that the statutory scheme will typically have been expanded by amendment over a period of years so that it is virtually impossible to say that a particular amendment fits with mathematical nicety into a carefully conceived overall plan for payment of benefits. The second is that what in many other areas of the law will be relatively low-level considerations of "administrative convenience" will in this area of the law bear a much more vital relation to the overall

legislative plan because of congressional concern for certainty in determination of entitlement and promptness in payment of benefits.

The second principle upon which I believe this legislative classification
should be sustained is that set forth in our opinion in *Kahn* v.
Shevin...(1974). The effect of the statutory scheme is to make it easier for
widows to obtain benefits than it is for widowers, since the former qualify
automatically while the latter must show proof of need. Such a requirement in no way perpetuates or exacerbates the economic disadvantage
which has led the Court to conclude that gender-based discrimination must
meet a different test than other types of classifications. It is, like the
property tax exemption to widows in *Kahn*...a differing treatment which
" 'rest[s] upon some ground of difference having a fair and substantial
relation to the object of the legislation.' "...

Both *Weinberger* v. *Wiesenfeld*...(1975) and *Frontiero* v. *Richardson*...(1973) are undoubtedly relevant to the decision of this case, but the
plurality overstates that relevance when it says that these two cases
"plainly require affirmance of the judgment of the District Court."... The
disparate treatment of widows and widowers by this Act is undoubtedly a
gender-based classification, but this is the beginning and not the end of the
inquiry. In the case of classifications based on legitimacy, and in the case
of irrebuttable presumptions, constitutional doctrine which would have
invalidated the same distinctions in other contexts has been held not to
require that result when they were used within comprehensive schemes for
social insurance. The same result should obtain in the case of constitutional principles dealing with gender-based distinctions....

...Two observations about *Wiesenfeld* are pertinent. First, the provision of
the Social Security Act held unconstitutional there flatly denied surviving
widowers the possibility of obtaining benefits no matter what showing of
need might be made. The section under attack in the instant case does not
totally foreclose widowers, but simply requires from them a proof of
dependence which is not required from similarly situated widows. Second,
Wiesenfeld was decided before either *Weinberger* v. *Salfi*,...or *Mathews* v.
Lucas.... Each of those decisions refused uncritically to extend into the
field of social security law constitutional proscriptions against distinctions
based on illegitimacy and irrebuttable presumptions which had originated
in other areas of the law. While the holding of *Wiesenfeld* is not inconsistent with *Salfi* or *Lucas,* its reasoning is not in complete harmony with the
recognition in those cases of the special characteristics of social insurance
plans....

...Whatever his actual needs, Goldfarb would, of course, have no complaint if Congress had chosen to require proof of dependence by widows as
well as widowers, or if it had simply refrained from making any provision
whatever for benefits to surviving spouses. "A legislature may address a
problem 'one step at a time,' or even 'select one phase of one field and apply a remedy there, neglecting others.'... Any claim which he has must
therefore turn upon the alleged impropriety of giving benefits to widows
without requiring them to make the same proof of dependence required of

widowers. Yet, in the context of the legislative purpose, this amounts not to exclusion but to overinclusiveness for reasons of administrative convenience which, if reasonably supported by the underlying facts, is not offensive to the Equal Protection Clause in social welfare cases.

A close analogue to this case is presented by our decision last Term in *Mathews* v. *Lucas....* The plaintiffs there challenged the OASDI provisions for children's benefits, which require no proof of dependence by legitimate children or certain categories of illegitimates, but which demand that other illegitimates show dependence by proof that their father lived with them or contributed to their support prior to his death. After first stating that this classification based on legitimacy does not demand "our most exacting scrutiny," the Court concluded that a general requirement of dependency "at the time of death is not impermissibly discriminatory in providing only for those children for whom the loss of the parent is an immediate source of the need." It then upheld the waiver of dependence proof requirement for legitimates and certain others....

...The same reasoning should control in the case before us. As in *Lucas,* Congress has here adopted a test of dependence as a reasonable surrogate for proof of actual need. In *Lucas,* legitimates and certain others were not required to satisfy that test because, in the legislative view, there was a sufficiently high rate of dependence among those groups to make the requirement of actual proof administratively counter-productive. Here the dependence test was not imposed upon widows, apparently on a similar belief that the actual rate of dependence was sufficiently high that a requirement of proof would create more administrative expense than it would save in the award of benefits.

Perhaps because the reasons asserted for "heightened scrutiny" of gender-based distinctions are rooted in the fact that *women* have in the past been victims of unfair treatment,...the plurality says that the difference in treatment here is not only between a widow and a widower, but between the respective deceased spouses of the two. It concludes that wage earning wives are deprived "of protection for their families which men receive as a result of their employment."...

But this is a questionable tool of analysis which can be used to prove virtually anything. It might just as well have been urged in *Kahn* v. *Shevin,...*where we upheld a Florida property tax exemption redounding to the benefit of widows but not widowers, that the real discrimination was between the deceased spouses of the respective widow and widower, who had doubtless by their contributions to the family or marital community helped make possible the acquisition of the property which was now being disparately taxed.

Since the claim to Social Security is noncontractual in nature,...the contributions of the deceased spouse cannot be regarded as creating any sort of contractual entitlement on the part of either the deceased wife or the surviving husband. Here the female wage earner has gotten the degree of protection for her family which Congress was concerned to extend to all. Neither she nor her surviving husband has any constitutional claim to more, simply because Congress has chosen, for administrative reasons, to give benefits to widows without requiring proof of dependence.

Viewed from the perspective of the recipient of benefits, the sections involved here are entirely distinguishable from those which this Court has previously struck down....

In *Weinberger* v. *Wiesenfeld*...the Court again invalidated OASDI provisions which denied one group any opportunity to show themselves proper beneficiaries given the apparent statutory purpose. A widow not qualifying for widow's benefits was entitled to a mother's benefit if she had in her care a minor child qualifying for a child's benefit, and if she did not receive more than a certain amount of primary benefits in her own right. No such provision was made, however, for a widower in a parallel position. The Court found a purpose in the statute to allow a single parent to stay home and care for the minor child...and struck down the denial of benefits to fathers similarly situated. The defect of that statute was its conclusive exception of widowers from the benefited class, solely on the basis of their sex, and in contravention of the legislative purpose to allow parents with deceased spouses to provide personal parental care. There is no plausible claim to be made here that a statutory objective is being thwarted by under-inclusiveness of the classes of beneficiaries.

This case is also distinguishable from *Frontiero* v. *Richardson*...in the sense that social insurance differs from compensation for work done. While there is no basis for assessing the propriety of a given allocation of funds within a social insurance program apart from an identifiable legislative purpose, a compensatory scheme may be evaluated under the principle of equal pay for equal work done. This case is therefore unlike *Frontiero*...where the Court invalidated a sex discrimination among military personnel in their entitlement to increased quarters allowances on account of marriage, and in the eligibility of their spouses for dental and medical care. These compensatory fringe benefits were available to male employees as a matter of course, but were unavailable to females except on proof that their husbands depended on them for over one-half of their support. Since males got such compensatory benefits even though their wives were not so dependent, females with nondependent husbands were effectively denied equal compensation for equal efforts. The same is not true here, where the benefit payments to survivors are neither contractual nor compensatory for work done, and where there is thus no comparative basis for evaluating the propriety of a given benefit apart from the legislative purpose.

The very most that can be squeezed out of the facts of this case in the way of cognizable "discrimination" is a classification which favors aged widows. Quite apart from any considerations of legislative purpose and "administrative convenience" which may be advanced to support the classification, this is scarcely an invidious discrimination. Two of our recent cases have rejected efforts by men to challenge similar classifications. We have held that it is not improper for the military to formulate "up-or-out" rules taking into account sex-based differences in employment opportunities in a way working to the benefit of women, *Schlesinger* v.

Ballard...(1975), or to grant solely to widows a property tax exemption in recognition of their depressed plight, *Kahn* v. *Shevin*.... A waiver of the dependency prerequisite for benefits, in the case of this same class of aged widows, under a program explicitly aimed at the assistance of needy groups, appears to be well within the holding of the *Kahn* case, which upheld a flat $500 exemption to widows, without any consideration of need.

The classification challenged here is "overinclusive" only in the sense that widows over 62 may obtain benefits without a showing of need, whereas widowers must demonstrate need. Because this overinclusion is rationally justifiable, given available empirical data, on the basis of "administrative convenience," *Mathews* v. *Lucas*...is authority for upholding it. The differentiation in no way perpetuates the economic discrimination which has been the basis for heightened scrutiny of gender-based classifications, and is, in fact, explainable as a measure to ameliorate the characteristically depressed condition of aged widows. *Kahn* v. *Shevin*...is therefore also authority for upholding it. For both of these reasons, I would reverse the judgment of the District Court.

CARTER RADIO CALL-IN PROGRAM
March 5, 1977

President Carter's carefully conceived plans for reaching the people went into full swing March 5 when he answered questions from 42 citizens in 26 states during a two-hour telephone call-in radio broadcast from the Oval Office at the White House.

The program, "Ask President Carter," was carried on the CBS radio network. CBS news anchorman Walter Cronkite served as moderator for the session. Cronkite, in introductory remarks, called the program an "experiment" in communications, the first such attempt to permit citizens to question the President by telephone.

The calls began with a man from Sterling Heights, Mich., who asked a question about killings in Uganda, and they ended with an 11-year-old girl from North Benton, Ohio, who called the President "Jimmy" and asked why he sent his 9-year-old daughter, Amy, to a public school in Washington. Carter, addressing many of the callers by their first names, answered most of the questions with ease. With the help of an aide, he looked up information and supplied some answers later in the program. He promised to call four persons back, and either he or another administration official did.

Major Issues Discussed

The President dealt with a few substantive issues during the course of the broadcast. He said he supported the federal pay raises proposed by Ford which went into effect Feb. 20 because neither house of Congress vetoed the raise. The increases raised the salaries for members of Congress, federal judges and top officials in the executive branch. Carter also noted that he had been encouraged by the North Vietnamese response to suggestions that normal diplomatic ties be established. And the President said he intended "to see discussions initiated quite early" with Cuba on the renegotiation of the anti-hijacking treaty and the removal of the ban on travel to Cuba. When asked about U.S. retention of sovereignty over the Panama Canal, President Carter said he did not have any "hang-up" about the sovereignty issue. The United States would have an "assured capacity or capability" guaranteeing U.S. use of the waterway, he said. (Panama Canal treaty, p. 591)

Callers asked questions about matters that related to their personal concerns. When Mrs. Esther Thomas of Villanova, Pa., asked about tax law reform, Carter said the "income tax system of this country [is] a disgrace...we will propose...basic reforms in the income tax structure." Other callers wanted to know about Medicare benefits, a public works jobs bill, welfare reform, American Indian land claims and Carter's farm policy.

Criticism of Carter

A few citizen-callers criticized the President. A man from Maryland wanted to know why the President's son, Chip, and his family, lived at the White House "on taxpayers' money," and why Chip was not "out in his own house earning a living." Carter responded by saying that his son acted as his personal representative from time to time when Carter was unable to attend to the matter in person. Carter reassured the caller that his family members were "not mooching off the American taxpayers. All of our family's expenses are paid for out of my own pocket," the President said.

A caller from Carter's home state—Georgia—asked the President if he intended to pardon all of the draft evaders and "junkies" from the Vietnam War, and what Carter planned to do "for veterans like me who served with loyalty." The President responded that he did not intend to pardon "any more people from the Vietnam era." The deserters and others, Carter said, "will not be pardoned by me on any sort of blanket basis. My preference is to let the Defense Department handle those cases by categories or by individual cases." The appointment of Max Cleland to head the Veterans Administration, Carter stated, represented "a new generation of leadership" in that agency "more sensitive" to the needs of veterans of the Vietnam War. But, the President told his listeners, "I don't have any apology to make for what I have done...." (Carter pardon, p. 95)

A woman caller from Texas accused the President of interfering with states' rights because Carter had called individual state legislators in Texas urging them to vote for ratification of the Equal Rights Amendment. Carter said that he had always supported the ERA and that he had made calls to prominent public officials in Texas expressing his support for the amendment. But, Carter said, "I haven't tried to interfere or put pressure on them."

Carter scored obvious points with some callers such as the Pennsylvania woman who told the President, "as a registered Republican, I am behind you 100 per cent."

Mr. Cronkite interjected a question or comment on occasion during the broadcast, but Carter resisted Cronkite's attempts to cut off questioners when the questions seemed unclear or unimportant. An army sergeant, for example, asked Carter if he approved of karate training for the military services. The President gently overrode Cronkite's impatience with the line of inquiry and answered that he approved of the training as long as it was not so severe as to injure anyone.

Overtures to the Public

The President said at the conclusion of the broadcast that he liked the call-in and would be inclined to "do this again in the future," because the questions came from all over the country and are "the kind you would never get in a press conference." A spokesman for CBS said roughly nine million calls had been placed during the telephone call-in and that the network spent $55,000 to provide phone links to the White House.

In addition to the call-in program, Carter used other steps in the early months of his administration to keep in touch with the public. His first domestic trip—not counting a weekend at his home in Plains, Ga.—was to Clinton, Mass., and Charleston, W.Va., March 16-17. In Clinton Carter participated in a 90-minute "town meeting" and spent the night with a local family. In Charleston March 17 Carter participated in a panel discussion on energy policy.

As another "people" gesture, the administration mailed letters and questionnaires to 450,000 Americans, soliciting their opinions on energy conservation. The letters were signed by James R. Schlesinger, Carter's energy adviser and later Secretary of the newly created Cabinet-level Department of Energy.

> Following are excerpts from the White House transcript of President Carter's call-in radio broadcast March 5, 1977, moderated by Walker Cronkite. (Boldface headings in brackets have been added by Congressional Quarterly to highlight the organization of the text.):

[Gasoline Tax Increase]

[In response to a question about reports of plans to raise federal taxes on gasoline by 25 cents]: ...I have never proposed any such thing and don't know where the story originated.... I don't believe the story was attributed to me in any way, because I have never commented on that at all and have never even insinuated to anyone I was going to raise the gasoline tax by 25 cents.

[Relations with Cuba]

...I would like to do what I can to ease tensions with Cuba.... I don't know yet what we will do. Before any full normalization of relationships can take place, though, Cuba would have to make some fairly substantial changes in their attitude. I would like to insist, for instance, that they not interfere in the internal affairs of countries in this hemisphere, and that they decrease their military involvement in Africa and that they reinforce a commitment to human rights by releasing political prisoners that have been in jail now in Cuba for 17 or 18 years....

But I think before we can reach that point we will have to have discussions with them, and I do intend to see discussions initiated with Cuba quite early on re-establishing the anti-hijacking agreement, arriving at a fishing agreement between us and Cuba, since our 200-mile limits do overlap between Florida and Cuba, and I would not be averse in the future to seeing our visitation rights permitted as well.

[Pardon of Draft Evaders]

...I don't intend to pardon any more people from the Vietnam era. I promised the American people when I was running for office that I would pardon the ones who violated the Selective Service laws. I don't have any apology to make about it and think I made the right decision, but the deserters and others who have committed crimes against military law or civilian law will not be pardoned by me on any sort of blanket basis. My preference is to let the Defense Department handle those cases by categories or by individual cases....

[Health Care]

...I hope that over a period of years—it is not going to come easily—that we can have a comprehensive health care plan in our country. It will be very expensive, but the first step has got to be to bring some order out of chaos in the administration of the health problems we have already got, and to help poorer people like perhaps yourself—I don't know what your income is—and to be able to prevent rapidly increasing costs of programs like Medicare....

[Vertical Integration of Oil Companies]

...I think that, as a general proposition, vertical integration of major industries is not contrary to the best interests of the American people, provided you have a continued and adequate competition.

I am concerned on two ends of the vertical integration process. One is that there be an insured competition for leasing rights. I think it would be a mistake for us to require a different company to drill for oil, to extract the oil from the ground, to pump the oil to a refinery, to do the refining, and then to distribute it and then to wholesale it and then to retail it.

[Consumer Rights]

If I don't do that [do more to protect consumers]...before I go out of office, I will consider my administration to be a failure....

...I am in favor of establishment of the consumer protection agency itself to focus the consumer's interest in one agency as much as possible. This agency would be quite small. I think the budget would be in the neighborhood of $11-million a year....

...I favor, in certain instances, the right, the increased right of consumers to file class action suits; lawsuits, where a thousand consumers who have been cheated can get together and get some relief from unfair trade practices and also, on occasion, the consumers ought to have an increased right to have legal standing in court....

[Foreign Aid]

...I am going to take a position that is not very popular, politically speaking. We only spend about three-tenths of 1 per cent of our gross national product on foreign aid, which is about half of the proportion that is allotted to this purpose by other countries like France, Germany and so forth.

I don't particularly want to increase this greatly, but I would like for it to be predictable. Also, in the past, we have not had foreign aid used in an effective way. As one of my friends has said quite often, I am not in favor of taxing the poor people in our rich country and sending the money to the rich people in poor countries. Quite often that has been done in the past....

[Draft System]

...[I]f I see it is necessary in the future to initiate a draft, then I would certainly recommend to the Congress that this be done.

I would like to combine it with a much more comprehensive public service opportunity where people might go into jobs like the Peace Corps or Vista, teachers' aides or mental institutions and so forth, along with military training as well.

I would make it much more all-inclusive than it has been in the past. I would not, for instance, exclude college students. And if it becomes necessary for national security, the likelihood is that women would be included as well. But I would like to draw a distinction between military service and other service that would benefit our country just as much in a time of need or crisis....

[Congressional Pay]

...I think that the salary increases were justified.... I do think the law ought to be changed...to make sure that in the future, if any sort of salary increase goes into effect, that it not go into effect until after the following general election....

...I have seen, from my own experience, that it costs a member of Congress an enormous amount of extra money to maintain close contacts with the people back home.... Also, the Congress members...have to run for office every two years. There are also members of Congress who have no trouble raising money for a political campaign. Others have to spend a lot of their own money in a political campaign....

[Congressional War Powers]

...I have no hesitancy about communicating with Congress, consulting with them and also letting the American people know what we do before we start any combat operation. I think with that process we can minimize greatly the chances that we will get involved in combat anywhere in the world.

[Panama Canal]

As far as sovereignty is concerned, I don't have any hang-up about that. I would hope that after, and expect that after the year 2000 that we would have an assured capacity or capability of our country with Panama guaranteeing that the Panama Canal would be open and of use to our own nation and to other countries....

CARTER'S U.N. SPEECH
March 17, 1977

In an address to the United Nations General Assembly March 17, President Carter said that the organization had allowed its human rights machinery "to be ignored and sometimes politicized." Carter urged the United Nations' Commission on Human Rights to meet more often and to transfer the offices of the commission from Geneva to New York where its activities would be "in the forefront of our attention." Carter said that the U.N. charter gave member nations the right and the duty to speak out about the state of human rights in other countries.

Human Rights Theme

Carter's emphasis on human rights reiterated a theme stated in his campaign and in his inaugural address, in which the President urged an "absolute commitment" to human rights. In his nationally televised "fireside chat" Feb. 2, and in press conferences Feb. 8 and 23, he continued to speak out on the matter of violations of human rights, noting particularly the treatment of dissidents in the Soviet Union and expressing concern over the status of human rights in South Korea and Cuba. (State Department human rights reports, p. 3; inaugural address, p. 89; fireside chat, p. 103)

Not only had Carter spoken out repeatedly on human rights, but also on Feb. 17, Andrei Sakharov, the Nobel prize-winning scientist and one of the Soviet Union's leading dissidents, received a letter from Carter expressing support for Sakharov's stand on human rights. The letter, dated Feb. 5, was in response to a letter Carter had received from Sakharov Jan. 28. In his letter, Sakharov had urged Carter to intervene on behalf of 15 Soviet dissidents imprisoned in the U.S.S.R.

In his reply, Carter said "the American people and our government will continue our firm commitment to promote respect for human rights not only in our own country but also abroad." On Feb. 18, the Carter administration appealed to the U.N. Commission on Human Rights to ask Moscow for information on dissidents who had been arrested.

Carter's March 17 U.N. address—his first major speech on foreign policy since taking office—came as a response to objections by various countries, including the Soviet Union, that his earlier statements on human rights had represented interference in the internal affairs of other nations.

In a March 21 speech in Moscow, Soviet Communist Party General Secretary Leonid Brezhnev strongly criticized Carter's statements of support for Soviet dissidents.

However, on March 25, a group of 58 senators presented to Carter a letter supporting his human rights stand and praising the President's "efforts to tell the nations of the world that U.S. foreign policy will continue to be dedicated to the cause of freedom."

Other Topics in U.N. Speech

Human rights was only one of the subjects Carter addressed at the U.N. He also spoke about arms control, efforts to bring international peace, and the world economy. Following the tradition of every American President since Harry S Truman, Carter pledged his administration's support for the world organization. The President's speech, while it did not unveil any new departures in foreign policy, outlined an "agenda" of problems facing the United States and the rest of the world in 1977.

Carter emphasized the need to maintain peace and to reduce the arms race with the Soviet Union through constructive negotiations in the strategic arms limitations talks (SALT). The President noted that he had already asked the new Congress for $7.5-billion in foreign assistance programs to build a more cooperative international economic system to meet the basic needs of the developing world and help those nations improve their productive capacity. (SALT talks, p. 243)

The United States, Carter said, sought a just and permanent peace in the Middle East, supported the peaceful attainment of majority rule in southern Africa and sought to place relations with Latin America on a more constructive footing.

However, the President warned: "...I realize that the United States cannot solve the problems of the world. We can sometimes help others resolve their differences, but we cannot do so by imposing our own particular solutions."

Following is the full text of President Carter's address to the United Nations General Assembly, March 17, 1977. (Boldface headings in brackets have been added by Congressional Quarterly to highlight the organization of the text.):

Thank you, Mr. Secretary General.

Last night I was in Clinton, Massachusetts, at a Town Hall meeting where people of that small town decided their political and economic future.

Tonight I speak to a similar meeting where people representing nations all over the world come here to decide their political and economic future.

I am proud to be with you tonight in this House where the shared hopes of the world can find a voice. I have come here to express my own support, and the continuing support of my country, for the ideals of the United Nations.

We are proud that, for the 32 years since its creation, the United Nations has met on American soil. And we share with you the commitments of freedom, self-government, human dignity, mutual toleration, and peaceful resolution of disputes—which the founding principles of the United Nations and also Secretary General Curt Waldheim so well represent.

No one nation by itself can build a world which reflects all of these fine values. But the United States, my own country, has a reservoir of strength—economic strength, which we are willing to share; military strength, which we hope never to use again; and the strength of ideals, which are determined fully to maintain the backbone of our own foreign policy.

It is now eight weeks since I became President. I have brought to office a firm commitment to a more open foreign policy. And I believe that the American people expect me to speak frankly about the policies that we intend to pursue, and it is in that spirit that I speak to you tonight about our own hopes for the future.

I see a hopeful world, a world dominated by increasing demands for basic freedoms, for fundamental rights, for higher standards of human existence. We are eager to take part in the shaping of that world.

But in seeking such a better world, we are not blind to the reality of disagreement, nor to the persisting dangers that confront us all. Every headline reminds us of bitter divisions, of national hostilities, of territorial conflicts, of ideological competition.

In the Middle East, peace is a quarter of a century overdue. A gathering racial conflict threatens Southern Africa; new tensions are rising in the Horn of Africa; disputes in the Eastern Mediterranean remain to be resolved.

Perhaps even more ominous is the staggering arms race. The Soviet Union and the United States have accumulated thousands of nuclear weapons. Our two nations now have five times more missile warheads today than we had just eight years ago. But we are not five times more secure. On the contrary, the arms race has only increased the risk of conflict.

We can only improve this world if we are realistic about its complexities. The disagreements that we face are deeply rooted, and they often raise difficult philosophical as well as territorial issues. They will not be solved easily. They will not be solved quickly. The arms race is now embedded in the fabric of international affairs and can only be contained with the greatest of difficulty. Poverty and inequality, are of such monumental scope that it will take decades of deliberate and determined effort even to improve the situation substantially.

I stress these dangers and these difficulties because I want all of us to dedicate ourselves to a prolonged and persistent effort designed first to maintain peace and to reduce the arms race; second, to build a better and more cooperative international economic system; and third, to work with potential adversaries as well as our friends to advance the cause of human rights.

In seeking these goals, I realize that the United States cannot solve the problems of the world. We can sometimes help others resolve their differences, but we cannot do so by imposing our own particular solutions.

[Work to Be Done]

In the coming months, there is important work for all of us in advancing international cooperation and economic progress in the cause of peace.

Later this spring, the leaders of several industrial nations of Europe, North America, and Japan, will confer at a summit meeting in London on a broad range of issues. We must promote the health of our industrial economies. We must seek to restrain inflation and bring ways of managing our own domestic economies for the benefit of the global economy.

We must move forward with the Multilateral Trade Negotiations in Geneva.

The United States will support the efforts of our friends to strengthen the Democratic institutions in Europe, and particularly in Portugal and Spain.

We will work closely with our European friends on the forthcoming Review Conference on Security and Cooperation in Europe. We want to make certain that the provisions of the Helsinki Agreement are fully implemented and that progress is made to further East-West cooperation.

In the Middle East we are doing our best to clarify areas of disagreement, to surface underlying consensus and to help to develop mutually acceptable principles that can form a flexible framework for a just and permanent settlement.

In Southern Africa, we will work to help attain majority rule through peaceful means. We believe that such fundamental transformation can be achieved, to the advantage of both the blacks and whites who live in that region of the world. Anything less than that may bring a protracted race war, with devastating consequences to all.

This week the Government of the United States took action to bring our country into full compliance with United Nations sanctions against the illegal regime in Rhodesia. And I will sign that bill Friday in Washington.

We will put our relations with Latin America on a more constructive footing, recognizing the global character of the region's problems.

We are also working to resolve in amicable negotiations the future of the Panama Canal.

We will continue our efforts to develop further our relationships with the People's Republic of China. We recognize our parallel strategic interests in maintaining stability in Asia and we will act in the spirit of the Shanghai Communiqué.

In Southeast Asia and in the Pacific, we will strengthen our association with our traditional friends and we will seek to improve relations with our former adversaries.

We have a mission now in Vietnam seeking peaceful resolution of the differences that have separated us for so long.

Throughout the world, we are ready to normalize our relationships and to seek reconciliation with all states which are ready to work with us in promoting global progress and global peace.

[The Arms Race]

Above all, the search for peace requires a much more deliberate effort to contain the global arms race. Let me speak in this context first of the U.S.-Soviet Union relationship, and then of the wider need to contain the proliferation of arms throughout the global community.

I intend to pursue the strategic arms limitation talks between the United States and the Soviet Union with determination and with energy.

Our Secretary of State will visit Moscow in just a few days.

SALT is extraordinarily complicated. But the basic fact is that while the negotiations remain deadlocked the arms race goes on; the security of both countries and the entire world is threatened.

My preference would be for strict controls or even a freeze on new types and new generations of weaponry and with a deep reduction in the strategic arms of both sides. Such a major step towards not only arms limitations but arms reductions would be welcomed by mankind as a giant step towards peace.

Alternatively, and perhaps much more easily, we could conclude a limited agreement based on those elements of the Vladivostok Accord on which we can find complete consensus, and set aside for prompt consideration and subsequent negotiations the more contentious issues and also the deeper reductions in nuclear weapons which I favor.

We will also explore the possibility of a total cessation of nuclear testing. While our ultimate goal is for all nuclear powers to end testing, we do not regard this as a prerequisite for the suspension of tests by the two principal nuclear powers, the Soviet Union and the United States.

We should, however, also pursue a broad and permanent multilateral agreement on this issue.

We will also seek to establish Soviet willingness to reach agreement with us on mutual military restraint in the Indian Ocean, as well as on such matters as arms exports to the troubled areas of the world.

In proposing such accommodations I remain fully aware that American-Soviet relations will continue to be highly competitive—but I believe that our competition must be balanced by cooperation in preserving peace, and thus our mutual survival.

I will seek such cooperation with the Soviet Union—earnestly, constantly and sincerely.

However, the effort to contain the arms race is not a matter just for the United States and Soviet Union alone. There must be a wider effort to reduce the flow of weapons to all the troubled spots of this globe.

Accordingly, we will try to reach broader agreements among producer and consumer nations to limit the export of conventional arms, and we, ourselves, will take the initiative on our own because the United States has become one of the major arms suppliers of the world.

We are deeply committed to halting the proliferation of nuclear weapons. And we will undertake a new effort to reach multilateral agreements designed to provide legitimate supplies of nuclear fuels for the production of energy while controlling the poisonous and dangerous atomic wastes.

Working with other nations represented here, we hope to advance the cause of peace. We will make a strong and a positive contribution at the upcoming Special Session on Disarmament which I understand will commence next year.

[Economic Justice]

But the search for peace also means the search for justice. One of the greatest challenges before us as a nation, and therefore one of our greatest opportunities, is to participate in molding a global economic system which will bring greater prosperity to all the people of all countries.

I come from a part of the United States which is largely agrarian and which for many years did not have the advantages of adequate transportation, or capital, or management skills, or education—which were available in the industrial states of our country.

So I can sympathize with the leaders of the developing nations, and I want them to know that we will do our part.

To this end, the United States will be advancing proposals aimed at meeting the basic human needs of the developing world and helping them to increase their productive capacity. I have asked Congress to provide $7½-billion of foreign assistance in the coming year, and I will work to ensure sustained American assistance as the process of global economic development continues. I am also urging the Congress of our country to increase our contributions to the United Nations Development Program and meet in full our pledges to multilateral lending institutions—especially the International Development Association of the World Bank.

We remain committed to an open international trading system, one which does not ignore domestic concerns in the United States. We have extended duty-free treatment to many products from the developing countries. In the Multilateral Trade Negotiations in Geneva we have offered substantial trade concessions on the goods of primary interest to developing countries. And in accordance with the Tokyo Declaration, we are also examining ways to provide additional consideration for the special needs of developing countries.

The United States is willing to consider, with a positive and open attitude, the negotiation of agreements to stabilize commodity prices, including the establishment of a common funding arrangement for financing buffer stocks where they are a part of individual negotiated agreements.

I also believe that the developing countries must acquire fuller participation in the global economic decision-making process. Some progress has been already made in this regard by expanding participation of developing countries in the International Monetary Fund.

We must use our collective natural resources wisely and constructively. We have not always done so. Today our oceans are being plundered and defiled. With a renewed spirit of cooperation and hope we join in the conference of the Law of the Sea in order to correct the mistakes of past generations and to insure that all nations can share the bounties of the eternal seas in the future.

We must also recognize that the world is facing serious shortages of energy. This is truly a global problem. For our part, we are determined to reduce waste and to work with others towards a fair and proper sharing of the benefits and costs of energy resources.

[Commitment to Human Rights]

The search for peace and justice means also respect for human dignity. All the signatories of the UN Charter have pledged themselves to observe and to respect basic human rights. Thus, no member of the United Nations can claim that mistreatment of its citizens is solely its own business. Equally, no member can avoid its responsibilities to review and to speak when torture or unwarranted deprivation occurs in any part of the world.

The basic thrust of human affairs points toward a more universal demand for fundamental human rights. The United States has a historical birthright to be associated with this process.

We in the United States accept this responsibility in the fullest and the most constructive sense. Ours is a commitment, and not just a political posture. I know perhaps as well as anyone that our own ideals in the area of human rights have not always been attained in the United States, but the

American people have an abiding commitment to the full realization of these ideals. And we are determined, therefore, to deal with our deficiencies quickly and openly. We have nothing to conceal.

To demonstrate this commitment, I will seek Congressional approval and sign the UN covenants on economic, social and cultural rights, and the covenant on civil and political rights. And I will work closely with our own Congress in seeking to support the ratification not only of these two instruments, but the United Nations Genocide Convention, and the Treaty for the Elimination of All Forms of Racial Discrimination, as well. I have just removed all restrictions on American travel abroad, and we are moving now to liberalize almost completely travel opportunities to America.

The United Nations is the global forum dedicated to the peace and well-being of every individual—no matter how weak, no matter how poor. But we have allowed its human rights machinery to be ignored and sometimes politicized. There is much that can be done to strengthen it.

The Human Rights Commission should be prepared to meet more often. And all nations should be prepared to offer their fullest cooperation—to the Human Rights Commission—to welcome its investigations, to work with its officials, and to act on its reports.

I would like to see the entire United Nations Human Rights Division moved back here to the central headquarters where its activities will be in the forefront of our attention, and where the attention of the press corps can stimulate us to deal honestly with this sensitive issue. The proposal made 12 years ago by the Government of Costa Rica—to establish a UN High Commission for Human Rights—also deserves our renewed attention and our support.

Strengthened international machinery will help us to close the gap between promise and performance in protecting human rights. When gross or widespread violation takes place—contrary to international commitments—it is of concern to all. The solemn commitments of the United Nations Charter, of the United Nations Universal Declaration for Human Rights, of the Helsinki Accords, and of many other international instruments must be taken just as seriously as commercial or security agreements.

This issue is important in itself. It should not block progress on other important matters affecting the security and well-being of our people and of world peace. It is obvious that the reduction of tensions, the control of nuclear arms, the achievement of harmony in the troubled areas of the world and the provision of food, good health, and education will independently contribute to advancing the human condition.

In our relationships with other countries, these mutual concerns will be reflected in our political, our cultural and our economic attitudes.

These then are our basic priorities as we work with other members to strengthen and to improve the United Nations.

First, we will strive for peace in the troubled areas of the world; second, we will aggressively seek to control the weaponry of war; third, we will promote a new system of international economic progress and cooperation; and fourth, we will be steadfast in our dedication to the dignity and well-being of people throughout the world.

I believe that this is a foreign policy that is consistent with my own Nation's historic values and commitments. And I believe that it is a foreign policy that is consonant with the ideals of the United Nations.

Thank you very much.

CARTER ELECTION
REFORM PROPOSALS
March 22, 1977

With considerable fanfare and high hopes for speedy passage, President Carter sent to Congress March 22 a wide-ranging election reform package. However, at the end of 1977 Carter's proposals remained bogged down in both houses of Congress.

The cornerstone of Carter's five-part packet of reform proposals was the Universal Voter Registration Act that would permit election day voter registration. The four other measures which received administration endorsement already were under consideration in Congress. They were:

• A constitutional amendment to abolish the electoral college.

• A revision of the Hatch Act to permit federal employees to participate in partisan politics.

• Public financing of congressional elections.

• Revision of the 1974 law governing public financing of presidential campaigns.

Voter Registration

The most innovative part of his recommendations was the voter registration bill that would simplify registration and add millions of voters in federal elections. The proposal fulfilled one of the commitments made by Carter during his campaign. The same day the reform package was announced, the registration bill was introduced with bipartisan sponsorship in the House and the Senate. Vice President Walter F. Mondale, under whose auspices the review of the election laws was conducted, did the unveiling.

At a press briefing, Mondale was flanked by a dozen senators and representatives, including two Republicans. He emphasized in his opening statement that the universal registration bill "has bipartisan support" and "was developed in close cooperation with the Congress." The states, under the voter-registration proposal, would be required to sign up voters when they went to the polls for a federal election. Proof of identity and residence, such as a driver's license, would be required. Grants from the federal Treasury would help each state pay for the registration. Further money would be available to states that used election-day registration for state and local elections and to states using approved "outreach" programs to increase voter registration before election day. The administration estimated the cost of the program nationwide at some $48-million every two years.

In his message to Congress, Carter noted that "millions of Americans are prevented or discouraged from voting in every election by antiquated or overly restrictive voter registration laws." Registration on election day would remove one unnecessary obstacle, he said.

At the press briefing, several cosponsors of the voter registration legislation called attention to the failure of nearly 70 million eligible voters to cast ballots in the 1976 presidential election. The nationwide percentage was only 53.3 per cent. One estimate was that the new law would add 45 million voters to the rolls.

Questions were raised about the possible unfair advantage Democrats would be given over Republicans under the administration proposal. Mondale and others debunked that suggestion, saying that it had not been borne out in the states with election-day registration. Another concern was fraud. This had not been a problem in states using election-day registration, said Mondale. As a deterrent, the legislation contained stiff penalties.

Other Proposals

Carter went further than ever before in recommending elimination of the electoral college and election of Presidents by popular vote. "I do not recommend a constitutional amendment lightly," he said. "I think the amendment process must be reserved for an issue of overriding governmental significance. But the method by which we elect our President is such an issue."

On campaign financing, Carter said: "Public financing of candidates not only minimizes even the appearance of obligation to special-interest contributors, but also provides an opportunity for qualified persons who lack funds to seek public office." He urged Congress to act soon on public financing both for primaries and general elections for the House and Senate, so that the new law could be in effect before 1978. Carter also proposed modifications in the public financing of presidential elections.

Carter proposed removing existing political restrictions on more than 2.8 million federal Civil Service employees. "Unlike other Americans," he said in his message, "they cannot run as a partisan candidate for any public office, and cannot do even volunteer work in a partisan political campaign."

An exception to the new freedom, Carter said, would be employees, to be determined by the Civil Service Commission, "who must retain both the appearance and the substance of impartiality." Carter also said he favored "strong penalties for any federal employee who attempts to influence or coerce another federal employee into political activity, or who engages in political activity while on the job."

Election Reform Outlook

The Carter-backed election reform package met with opposition, delay and postponement during 1977. Election day registration was held off the floor in both chambers even though it had been watered down and made optional. Revision of the Hatch Act to permit most federal employees to participate actively in partisan politics passed the House June 7 but Senate floor action was postponed until 1978.

Public financing of congressional elections fell victim to a Senate filibuster, and an attempt by the House leadership to revive it also failed. A Carter-backed constitutional amendment to abolish the electoral college only barely cleared a Senate committee. Senate floor action on that amendment, which faced a potential filibuster, was also delayed until 1978. The Senate approved a bill incorporating several relatively non-controversial, administration-supported changes in the 1974 campaign financing law. But the House had not acted on the measure by the end of 1977.

Following is President Carter's March 22, 1977, message to Congress proposing major changes in election laws:

To the Congress of the United States:

I hereby transmit to the Congress my recommendations for reforms in our Nation's election system.

The Vice President and I have developed these proposals in order to meet our commitment to the American people to work toward an electoral process which is open to the participation of all our citizens, which meets high ethical standards, and which operates in an efficient and responsive manner. I know that you in the Congress share these goals, and I applaud your efforts which are already underway to achieve them.

Voter Registration

My first proposal, and the one on which I am proposing a specific bill to the Congress, is designed to open up our system of voter registration.

The basis of our democratic system is the right of every eligible citizen to vote. In the 20 years of its history, this Nation has greatly expanded the opportunity to vote to wider and wider groups of citizens.

Despite this progress, we have in recent years witnessed a disturbing trend toward lower and lower levels of voting by our citizens. I am deeply concerned that our country ranks behind at least twenty other democracies in its level of voter participation.

Our country's disappointing record cannot be remedied by any one solution or any single piece of legislation. But, millions of Americans are prevented or discouraged from voting in every election by antiquated and overly restrictive voter registration laws. We can take one immediate step toward solving this serious problem by removing antiquated and unnecessary obstacles which prevent voters from participating in the electoral process.

I am proposing to remove the unnecessary and unfair barriers by creating a method of universal voter registration. Under the legislation I will propose to the Congress, citizens qualified to vote under state laws could go to their polling places on the day of a Federal election and register there after proving their eligibility. The states would be encouraged to adopt a similar system of registration for state and local elections.

Under this plan, state and local officials will continue to administer voter registration and elections, and will still register as many voters as possible prior to election day in the usual manner, in order to avoid congestion at the polls.

We would offer financial assistance to the states to employ additional registrars and to help pay the cost of registration by mail, traveling registrars, or any other pre-election day registration efforts the state might choose.

State and local officials would also have the option of using the money they receive under the plan to modernize what are often outmoded and poorly equipped systems of election administration. A new office within the Federal Election Commission would distribute the Federal funds and oversee the program.

I also propose that we enact very strong safeguards to protect the integrity of the election process. Willful fraud in registering to vote should bear the strong criminal penalties of five years imprisonment and a $10,000 fine already found in the Voting Rights Act. Any person who takes part in a scheme to falsely identify or register voters should be similarly punished, and multiple convictions should lead to even stiffer penalties. The government should seek injunctive relief in Federal court to stop any patterns of fraudulent activity which might arise.

States should be allowed to require all persons registering at the polls to prove their identity and place of residence by approved forms of identification. All registrants should be informed of the state's qualifications for voting and be required to sign a statement, under oath and criminal penalty, that they meet those qualifications.

While these safeguards are important and necessary, I am optimistic that they will rarely be tested and the record suggests that they will rarely be needed.

This system of election-day registration is already employed in a number of states, and the record shows that it has usually increased voter participation without increasing voter fraud. Four out of five states with the highest voter turnout rates in the 1976 election permitted citizens to register and vote on election day.

Campaign Financing

My second recommendation deals with the way in which we pay the costs of Congressional campaigns.

In 1974, Congress took the historic step of establishing a system of public financing for Presidential primary and general elections. I urge the Congress to extend this important reform to campaigns for both the House and the Senate.

The record of the first publicly financed Presidential campaign has demonstrated that public financing is workable and widely accepted by the American people. Public financing of candidates not only minimizes even the appearance of obligation to special interest contributors, but also provides an opportunity for qualified persons who lack funds to seek public office. It would be a tragic irony if the 1974 law, which reduced the pressure special interests could place on Presidential candidates, increased the pressures on candidates for Congress as the large contributors look for new means of gaining influence with their political funds.

The method we select should allow each American the option of deciding whether to participate in public funding. The check-off provision on the income tax form accomplishes this goal for Presidential campaign financing. The check-off method should also be used to raise the funds necessary to support Congressional candidates.

Congress is best suited to decide on an exact formula for financing campaigns. However, I believe there are several features which should be part of any plan:

● First, the plan should require that candidates demonstrate substantial public support before they get public funds to help finance their campaigns. This would guard against frivolous candidates depleting the limited public funds available. The matching formula in the Presidential primaries provided a successful link between total support through small private donations.

● Second, the limit on overall expenditures should not be excessively low so as to prevent an adequate presentation of candidates and their platforms to the people.

● Third, we should ensure that candidates who accept public financing are not placed at a serious disadvantage in competing with opponents who have extraordinarily abundant private funds. Under the recent Supreme Court ruling, if a candidate refuses to accept public financing, then no limitation can be imposed on the amount of personal or other private funds which may be spent on the campaign. But if a less wealthy opponent does accept public financing, stricter spending limits would be imposed on him than on his opponent. I hope Congress will address this problem.

• Fourth, I favor the broadest possible application of public financing. It should apply to primaries as well as general elections. I hope the Congress will act soon to pass legislation so that public financing can be available for the 1978 Congressional campaigns. It is important to begin now with public financing for general elections, even if a plan for primaries cannot be adopted this year.

Strengthening the Federal Election Campaign Act

While public financing of the last Presidential election was highly successful, my third suggestion is for certain modifications which our experience has shown could make the system work even better.

We noticed, for example, that there was less activity than in the past at the state and local level during the general election campaign. Opportunities should be available for more grass-roots participation in Presidential races. This could be accomplished by allowing Presidential candidates to designate one committee in each state to raise and spend a limited amount of money for campaign activities within the state. A reasonable limit for this activity might be 2¢ per eligible voter. Such committees could be allowed to delegate spending authority to local committees, but they should still be responsible for reporting contributions and expenditures. Also, when Congressional candidates mention in their advertising the Presidential nominee of their party, the expenditure should not have to be reported by the Presidential candidate.

Another useful change would be to grant Presidential candidates an additional amount to cover the great costs of complying with election laws—for example, filing the many necessary financial reports. We should prohibit the private raising of funds for this purpose.

We could also simplify the reporting of contributions and expenditures by directing the Federal Election Commission to establish common reporting and accounting systems to be used by all candidates.

Finally, we must clarify the law as it applies to the financial aspects of the delegate selection process. Contributions to delegates, or candidates for delegate, should be charged against a Presidential candidate only when such delegates are pledged to the specific candidate. Also, a delegate's expenses for attending a convention should not be considered as contributions or expenditures for the candidate he or she supports.

Direct Popular Election of the President

My fourth recommendation is that the Congress adopt a Constitutional amendment to provide for direct popular election of the President.

Such an amendment, which would abolish the Electoral College, will ensure that the candidate chosen by the voters actually becomes

President. Under the Electoral College, it is always possible that the winner of the popular vote will not be elected. This has already happened in three elections, 1824, 1876, and 1888. In the last election, the result could have been changed by a small shift of votes in Ohio and Hawaii, despite a popular vote difference of 1.7 million.

I do not recommend a Constitutional amendment lightly. I think the amendment process must be reserved for an issue of overriding governmental significance. But the method by which we elect our President is such an issue.

I will not be proposing a specific direct election amendment. I prefer to allow the Congress to proceed with its work without the interruption of a new proposal.

Political Rights of Federal Employees

My fifth and final recommendation concerns the political rights of federal employees.

Over 2.8 million federal employees, including postal workers and workers for the District of Columbia, are now denied a full opportunity to participate in the electoral process. Unlike other Americans, they cannot run as a partisan candidate for any public office, cannot hold party office, and cannot even do volunteer work in a partisan political, campaign.

I favor revising the Hatch Act to free those federal employees not in sensitive positions from these restrictions. There should be exceptions for those employees who must retain both the appearance and the substance of impartiality. For employees in such sensitive positions who are not subject to Senate confirmation, restrictions on political activity are necessary. Acting on standards prescribed by Congress, the Civil Service Commission should determine which positions should be treated as sensitive in all relevant government agencies.

Under such a Hatch Act revision, the vast majority of federal employees would be able to participate in federal, state and local elections and other political functions. But, federal employees have a special obligation not to abuse their public service responsibility. I favor strong penalties for any federal employee who attempts to influence or coerce another federal employee into political activity, or who engages in political activity while on the job. I also favor maximum reliance on a strong Civil Service Commission to vigorously prosecute employees who violate regulations against this kind of behavior.

JIMMY CARTER

The White House,
March 22, 1977

MISSING IN ACTION IN INDOCHINA
March 23, 1977

A presidential commission, sent to Southeast Asia March 16-20 to negotiate the release of Americans missing in action during the Vietnam War, issued its report March 23 at the White House. The report stated that the commission's visit created a "new and favorable climate for improved relations with both Vietnam and Laos." Contrary to previous statements from Hanoi, the report pointed out, the Vietnamese had not insisted on U.S. aid in the reconstruction of Vietnam as a precondition to negotiation on the missing in action (MIA) issue. The two questions were "closely related to each other," but they were not inextricably intertwined, the report said.

On the basis of the commission's report and an exchange of personal letters with Premier Pham Van Dong of the Socialist Republic of Vietnam, President Carter March 23 announced a new round of negotiations in Paris aimed at normal relations with the governments of Laos and Vietnam.

During the 1976 presidential election campaign, candidate Carter called President Ford's efforts to obtain an accounting of American personnel missing in action in Indochina an embarrassing failure. Carter promised to send a presidential commission to Southeast Asia and to authorize it to "try to trade for the release of information" about the MIAs. (Historic Documents of 1976, p. 756).

The State Department announced Feb. 25 the creation of the presidential commission. Headed by Leonard Woodcock, president of the United Auto Workers, the five-member commission included former Sen. Mike Mansfield (D Mont.), former United Nations Ambassador Charles W.

Yost, U.S. Rep. G. V. (Sonny) Montgomery (D Miss.) and Marian Wright
Edelman, director of the Children's Defense Fund, a nonprofit children's
advocacy group.

Background

The Paris peace accords signed Jan. 27, 1973, contained a provision that
pledged the signatories to help each other secure information about personnel missing in action in the Vietnam War. (Historic Documents of 1973,
p. 135) When the Communists established control in South Vietnam (April-
May 1975), the new Provisional Revolutionary Government (PRG) refused
to permit the search for MIAs to continue unless the United States
provided postwar economic aid to Vietnam as agreed to in Article 21 of the
accords. (Historic Documents of 1973, p. 143) The Nixon administration
had maintained that North Vietnam's violations of the 1973 agreements
nullified the accord and any U.S. responsibility for honoring the aid
provision.

The Ford administration made little headway in resolving the MIA issue
in the year and one-half that separated the fall of Saigon and the election
of Jimmy Carter. As the presidential election campaign shifted into high
gear, Ford July 24, 1976, told the families of the MIAs, "I will not rest until
the fullest possible accounting of your loved ones has been made."
(Historic Documents of 1976, p. 655)

Ford emphasized Hanoi's failure to account for the MIAs Sept. 13, 1976,
when he directed United Nations Ambassador William Scranton to cast a
veto in the Security Council and thereby reject Vietnam's bid for
membership in the General Assembly. Although Ford authorized a new
round of negotiations with Vietnam Nov. 12, the Paris meetings proved
fruitless. Neither the outgoing Republican administration nor the Vietnamese government had changed its view, the latter still demanding
economic aid as the price for information on the MIAs.

A somber note was added to the issue when the House Select Committee
on Missing Persons in Southeast Asia concluded its Dec. 15, 1976, report
with the statement that there was no evidence to suggest that any MIAs
were still alive. (Historic Documents of 1976, p. 925) The Carter administration did not dispute the findings of that report; but the new
presidential commission hoped to learn what the Hanoi government knew
of the 2,550 Americans still listed as missing from forces that had been
engaged in the Vietnam conflict.

At a March 24 news conference Carter said: "We are never going to rest
until we have pursued information about those who are missing in action to
the final conclusion. I will do the best I can but I don't want to mislead
anybody by giving hope about discovery of some additional information
when I don't believe that the hope is justified."

At that same news conference Carter said he would respond favorably to the possibility of economic aid for Vietnam once normal diplomatic relations had been established. However, the President said he did not feel the United States had a moral obligation to provide aid. "I don't feel that we...owe a debt nor that we should be forced to pay reparations," Carter observed.

> *Following are excerpts from the Report on Trip to Vietnam and Laos, March 16-20, 1977, of the Presidential Commission on Americans Missing and Unaccounted for in Southeast Asia. The report was presented to the President March 23, 1977:*

...On Saturday, March 12th, the Commission met with President Carter and Secretary of State Cyrus Vance. The President expressed his deep concern about obtaining a satisfactory MIA accounting and his hope for eventual normalization of relations with Vietnam and Laos. The Commission was directed not to apologize for past relations, but to emphasize the President's desire for a new beginning with these governments on the basis of equality and mutual respect. It was instructed to seek all MIA information and to obtain all recoverable remains from the Vietnamese and Lao and to listen carefully to the concerns of these governments on other matters of mutual interest. The President asked Mr. Woodcock to deliver personal letters from him to Vietnamese Prime Minister Pham Van Dong and to Lao President Souphanouvong....

Visit to Vietnam

Atmosphere in Hanoi

...A significant aspect of the Commission's visit to Vietnam was the cordial atmosphere which prevailed throughout its stay. The Vietnamese Government appeared to have made a major effort to ensure that the Commission's stay was both pleasant and productive and that the Commission was treated with respect and dignity. This point is of importance because in Asia the form of a visit and the level of attention given to a delegation often conveys an essential political message. Using this standard, the Commission concludes that the Vietnamese leadership was indicating by this treatment the importance it attached to the Commission's visit, and its genuine desire for a new and improved relationship with the United States. This did not, of course, mean that the Vietnamese were ready to concede on substantive issues, but it was—and is—an encouraging beginning to serious discussions on them.

The spirit of cordiality carried over into meetings as well. Phan Hien [Deputy Foreign Minister] spoke in a spirit of conciliation during both of the formal meetings. There was a conspicuous absence of polemics of harsh rhetoric on either side.

Prime Minister Pham Van Dong also received the Commission for a special meeting at which the President's personal letter was delivered to him. The talks with him were candid; he expressed his government's policy firmly but without rancor or harshness despite the recent bitter past. He expressed particular appreciation for the President's message and later asked the Commission to convey back to the President a letter from him in reply.

There were sporadic attempts to restrict individual movement around Hanoi, but in general Commission members and staff were permitted to go where they wished. This was usually—but not always—under escort. Protocol officers explained that this was for security reasons, citing possible hostile acts by the populace which still remembers the "destruction caused by U.S. bombing." These restrictions eased as the visit progressed. This point is important because it reminded the Commission that, despite all the good will and cordiality which marked the visit, there will for quite a while be an element of reserve toward us because of the long period when we and the Vietnamese were adversaries.

Missing in Action

The highlight of the Commission's talks in Hanoi was the SRV's [Socialist Republic of Vietnam] formal undertaking to give the U.S. all available information on our missing men as it is found and to return remains as they are recovered and exhumed. This new commitment was contained in statements by top SRV officials and was further refined in the Technical Sub-Commission meeting with officials of the Vietnamese agency responsible for seeking information on the missing and recovering remains.

The key elements in the Vietnamese statements were as follows:

a) The remains of the 12 U.S. airmen announced last September as killed in action would be returned to the U.S. and could be taken back by the Commission if desired.

b) All living U.S. military POW's have been returned.

c) All U.S. civilians remaining in South Vietnam after April 30, 1975 who registered with the Vietnamese authorities have left the country.

d) The SRV has established a specialized office to seek information on missing Americans and to recover remains. Although terrain and the tropical conditions of Vietnam have hindered search efforts, this office is actively seeking information and the remains of missing Americans.

e) The SRV will give the U.S. "as soon as possible" all available information and remains as they are discovered.

f) The Vietnamese would welcome U.S. assistance for this work in the form of information and documents, as well as material means helpful to the search efforts.

Although the MIA undertaking was stated in unqualified terms, the Vietnamese made clear that they still considered this subject and other aspects of U.S.-SRV relations to be "inter-related." They stated that their actions on MIA's were in conformance with Article 8b of the Paris Accord, for example, and cited the need for comparable U.S. fulfillment of its alleged obligation under Article 21 to "heal the wounds of war" and provide reconstruction aid. They also raised the issue of normalization of relations in this context. They were careful to say that none of these three points (i.e., MIA's, normalization, and aid) should be considered as preconditions to the other two and it was not the SRV's intention to raise the question this way. But they did note that they were closely related to each other and that both sides should take them in an overall context and apply their position in a flexible way. This appeared to go farther than previous SRV statements in reducing the specific linkage between Vietnamese action on MIA's and U.S. agreement to provide aid. But it still suggests that actual Vietnamese performance on MIA's will probably be subject to our willingness to move concretely to implement the spirit of good will displayed by the Commission's visit....

Normalization of Relations

Vietnamese officials expressed a strong desire to move toward normal relations with the U.S. and stated that the Socialist Republic of Vietnam is prepared to establish diplomatic relations with us. At the same time they noted that obstacles still exist on the road to normalizing relations, although expressing hope that with goodwill they could all be removed. They said Vietnam is prepared to normalize on the basis of sovereignty, mutual respect, non-interference in each other's affairs and peaceful co-existence. Regarding diplomatic relations, they indicated Vietnam is prepared to establish them, but then added that this will depend on the attitude of the United States and "whether it will give up its erroneous policy of the past." They stated that the Vietnamese view is that actions such as the U.S. economic blockade and the veto of Vietnam's entry into the UN stem from this erroneous policy. Finally, they said that there are three key areas of discussion between us, the MIA's, normalization, and aid. They stated we should not consider any one as a pre-condition to the other two, but noted that they clearly are inter-related.

The Vietnamese proposed negotiations between diplomatic representatives of the U.S. and SRV to discuss the elements and process of normalization. They suggested talks in Paris. The Commission said it would convey this proposal to the President for his consideration.

Vietnamese leaders expressed clearly to the Commission their Government's foreign policy, in particular regarding their neighbors in Southeast Asia. They presented to the Commission Foreign Minister Trinh's "Four Points" as the basis for their policy:

"1. Respect for each other's independence, sovereignty and territorial integrity, non-aggression, non-interference in each other's internal affairs, equality, mutual benefit and peaceful co-existence.

2. Not to allow any foreign country to use one's territory as a base for direct or indirect aggression and intervention against the other country and other countries in the region.

3. Establishment of friendly and good-neighborly relations, economic cooperation and cultural exchanges on the basis of equality and mutual benefit. Settlement of disputes among the countries in the region through negotiations in a spirit of equality, mutual understanding and respect.

4. Development of cooperation among the countries in the region for the building of prosperity in keeping with each country's specific conditions, and for the sake of genuine independence, peace and neutrality in Southeast Asia, thereby contributing to peace in the world."

The Vietnamese complained about the negative attitude of the new Thai authorities toward Vietnam and advised the U.S., as friends of Thailand, to urge the Thais to better their relations with the SRV by living up to the Thai-Vietnamese joint communique of last August 6. The Commission expressed the new U.S. Administration's desire for a stable, peaceful, and prosperous Southeast Asia....

...Aside from the legal basis for our providing assistance, the Vietnamese discussed a humanitarian basis for aid. Suggesting they were performing a humanitarian act in working to alleviate the suffering of the MIA families, they stated that in fairness we should be willing to act humanely to repair some of the destruction caused during the war. They indicated that Vietnam has a pressing immediate need for food aid, fertilizer, farm machinery, building materials for schools and hospitals, raw materials for its factories, and medicines.

...[T]he Vietnamese made the point that actions cannot come from just one side. Obliquely referring to their accounting for the MIA's and providing aid, they indicated that each side must take steps which address the concerns of the other. As noted earlier, they did not specifically link the two issues, although they noted that aid, an MIA accounting, and normalization are "inter-related".

At other times, the Vietnamese referred to our providing aid to them as a matter of conscience or as a moral obligation. They said aid is an "obligation we should fulfill—an obligation to be fulfilled with all your conscience and all your sense of responsibility." They added that, "In brief, we have obligations which are related to each other. So we should start from this position."

The Vietnamese also indicated their government's willingness to be flexible regarding the form aid might take. While not specifically stating which they might prefer, they referred to discussion with previous U.S. administrations in which various forms of aid were mentioned, including concessional, bilateral and multilateral....

Visit to Laos

Some 550 Americans are listed as missing or dead in Laos. The President therefore asked the Commission to visit that country as well to seek the cooperation of the Lao authorities in resolving these cases. Secretary of State Vance addressed a letter to Phoune Sipaseuth, Deputy Prime Minister and Foreign Minister of the Lao People's Democratic Republic (LPDR) on February 24, 1977 asking that the Commission be received in Laos. Minister Phoune replied on March 12 accepting the Secretary's proposal.

Program in Vientiane

The Commission went from Hanoi to Vientiane, capital of Laos, early March 19 by U.S. military aircraft and remained until late afternoon March 20. The Commission met for two hours in formal talks with the LPDR delegation headed by Nouphan Sitphasay, Secretary of State (Deputy Foreign Minister) on March 19. The next day the Commission was received in separate meetings by Foreign Minister Phoune and by LPDR President Souphanouvong, to whom Chairman Woodcock delivered a personal letter from President Carter. The Commission was honored at a dinner given by the Lao Government March 19 and returned the hospitality with a luncheon March 20 attended by Minister Phoune and other high-level Lao officials....

...As in Vietnam, the tone and atmosphere of the Commission's visit to Laos was important. Chairman Woodcock made the point that the Commission had come not to replace the work of our Embassy but to underscore the President's desire to improve relations with Laos on the basis of mutual respect and benefit. He relayed the President's desire to help remove the obstacles to improved relations, such as the MIA question. This new spirit was apparently understood and accepted by the Lao, whose leaders responded in a similar vein.

Substance of Talks in Vientiane

The Commission made clear to the Lao authorities the great importance the President and the American people attach to obtaining the best accounting possible for the Americans listed as missing or dead in Laos. The Chairman stated that the Commission would welcome any definite information or remains the Lao may have on these men, and indicated U.S. willingness to cooperate fully with the Lao in casualty resolution. He expressed the hope that the two parties could agree, during the Commission's visit, on an orderly procedure to resolve the issue. He noted to all the Lao leaders that progress on this issue would be a significant step toward improvement of U.S.-Lao relations.

The Lao expressed to the Commission their sympathy with the MIA families and their wish to relieve the latter's suffering. They noted the great difficulty of finding MIA information and remains in the rugged terrain of Laos, particularly given the country's small population and lack of material means. The Lao did assure the Commission that there are no Americans who have been captured and are alive in Laos, and that all Americans captured during the war had been returned to the U.S. They stated that the Lao Government had ordered before, and will now order again, the people of Laos to seek information and remains. But they regretted that they had no such information or remains now to provide the Commission.

In both formal and informal meetings, responsible Lao officials agreed to receive further MIA case files, as well as other material that we could provide to assist their search. Commission members stressed that we understood the difficulties involved in Laos and were realistic in our expectations of what information could be developed. The Commission nevertheless emphasized the importance of all information, such as aircraft tail numbers, ID cards, dog tags, and even partial remains, as being helpful to the United States.

The Lao made clear to the Commission that they connected the MIA problem with that of U.S. assistance to "heal the wounds of war" and rebuild their country. They expressed the belief that the two problems should be resolved together, since both resulted from the war. They noted that if one speaks of humanitarian concern for the MIA's, one must also think of the damage Laos suffered at U.S. hands during the war. They said the Lao people could be expected to search for MIA information only when they see that the U.S. Government is interested in healing this damage and helping reconstruct the country. In more general terms, they indicated that the MIA problem can be resolved when there is a new relationship between the two countries and when U.S. policy has changed from hostility to friendship.

The Commission was informed during its visit of the problem of unexploded ordnance in Laos. One observer in Vientiane, who recently visited the Plain of Jars, reported that 15 persons had been killed during the past year in one village of 3,400 people by such unexploded war material. The Commission believes the U.S. could provide advice and technical assistance on how to defuse such ordnance, and that the American people would understand and support such an effort....

...The Commission concludes from its visit to Laos that the Lao probably have considerably less information on MIA's than the Vietnamese, and are less able to develop additional information or locate remains. They probably could produce some, however, and could gather more if they so desired. For example, there are a very few MIA's who were known to be in Lao hands in the 1960's and there are recent reports of scattered aircraft parts in the countryside which may resolve a few more cases....

Cambodia

Due to the current lack of communication between the U.S. and the Cambodian government and the apparent unsettled situation in Phnom Penh, the Commission decided it was best not to try to go to the Cambodian capital. Instead, it was decided to attempt to arrange a contact with an Ambassador of Democratic Cambodia at a location in Southeast Asia.

It was hoped that should such a meeting be possible, it would be a significant first step toward opening a dialogue with this new government, thus possibly improving our chances of obtaining information on those missing or killed in Cambodia, including the 25 journalists of various nationalities (four of whom are Americans). A representative of our Liaison Office in Peking delivered a formal request for such a meeting to the Democratic Cambodia Embassy in Peking.

On March 19 Radio Phnom Penh carried the text of a press communique issued by the Cambodian Foreign Ministry refusing our request and hurling harsh invective at the U.S.... The Commission therefore was unable to meet with any representatives in the Cambodian government and was unable to provide any information about our people missing or killed there.

Press

American media viewed the Commission's trip as a major news event. The MIA issue was still generating widespread interest, the prospects for normalization reflected a significant foreign affairs initiative, and a visit to Hanoi, the first by American newsmen in five years, offered obvious human interest angles....

...Because the Vietnamese insisted that our press accompany the Commission, the trip proved unusual. Aboard the plane throughout the 24,000 mile journey, the press, the Commission and the staff mixed freely. Both in Hanoi and Vientiane, the press was considered part of the delegation, was housed and ate with the Commission and staff, and attended all events except the talks themselves. The accessibility and frankness of the Commission with the press comported with the American public's great interest in the mission, and reflected the openness which characterizes the Administration's approach to public affairs....

...In their meeting with the latter, the newsmen requested approval to remain in Vietnam to cover developments in greater detail. They were told that adequate facilities were not available at this time, but the Deputy Foreign Minister also pointed out that while over the years there had been about a dozen American newsmen in Hanoi, no Vietnamese journalists had ever been to the United States. The American newsmen offered to initiate an invitation. Should the Vietnamese seek visas as a result of this invitation, it will present the Administration with an opportunity to make a meaningful positive gesture by permitting them entry into the U.S. Although the Vietnamese media obviously reflect the constraints of a communist society, reciprocal visits would be in the interests of the normalization process generally....

Commission's Conclusions

Missing in Action

Although the Commission was able to obtain only the 12 remains as well as information on Tucker Gougelmann [U.S. citizen who died in Saigon in

June 1976] and a promise to deliver another set of remains during its brief stay, the Commission's visit did appear to create a new and favorable climate for improved relations with both Vietnam and Laos. In the Commission's view, the best hope for obtaining a proper accounting for our MIAs lies in the context of such improved relations. The Commission believes that the creation of this new spirit is the most significant contribution to the accomplishment of the mission assigned it by the President.

The Commission also believes it impressed upon the Vietnamese and Lao our realistic attitude on the MIA issue and our intention to resolve it on a reasonable basis in order to remove it as an obstacle to normalization. The Commission believes this approach is more likely to elicit further information and remains than continuing past policies of confronting the Vietnamese and Lao on the issue.

On the basis of its talks with Vietnamese and Laos officials at the highest level, and on other information available to it, the Commission specifically concludes:

1. There is no evidence to indicate that any American POW's from the Indochina conflict remain alive.

2. Americans who stayed in Vietnam after April 30, 1975, who registered with the Foreign Ministry and wished to leave have probably all been allowed to depart the country.

3. Although there continue to be occasional rumors of deserters or defectors still living in Indochina, the Commission found no evidence to support this conjecture.

4. The Vietnamese have not given us all the information they probably have, in part because of their concentration on the return of remains. The Commission believes it succeeded in making clear to the Vietnamese the importance we attach to receiving all kinds of information, however slight or fragmentary it may be.

5. The Vietnamese gave a clear formal assurance that they would look for MIA information and remains and that they would provide such information and remains to the U.S. They did not make this specifically contingent on our provision of aid, but they do see action on MIA's as related to resolution of other issues of concern to them.

6. For reasons of terrain, climate, circumstances of loss, and passage of time, it is probable that no accounting will ever be possible for most of the Americans lost in Indochina. Even where information may once have been available, it may no longer be recoverable due to the ravages of time and physical changes.

7. A new procedure has been established for the continuing exchange of MIA information between the U.S. and the SRV. The U.S. will use this mechanism to furnish additional information and materials to assist MIA searches.

8. The Lao authorities called attention to the difficulty of MIA search efforts in view of the difficult terrain in their country, but undertook to provide information and remains as they were found.

9. The Commission was unable to meet with representatives of the Cambodian Government. That government has repeatedly denied that it holds any foreign prisoners, and the Commission considers it unlikely that additional MIA information will be forthcoming from that country.

Normalization of Relations

1. Both the Vietnamese and Lao leaders are clearly interested in establishing a new and friendlier relationship with the United States.

2. They indicate that they are willing to look to the future rather than the past in such a relationship, although they consider that the U.S. has remaining obligation to repair the damage caused by the war in their countries. This is likely to continue to be an important factor in working out new or improved relations with these two countries.

3. Both Vietnam and Laos have a clear interest in such a new relationship. Vietnam in particular apparently looks forward to benefits in such matters as trade and other long-term economic arrangements.

4. The Vietnamese are willing to enter into immediate high-level diplomatic discussions with the U.S. on normalization. They made clear their interest in establishing formal diplomatic relations as quickly as possible. They indicated their desire to see past "erroneous" U.S. policies on such matters as UN membership and the trade embargo changed.

5. Both the Vietnamese and Lao leaders appear to view the present U.S. intentions toward them as more positive than in the past. They have a positive attitude themselves toward the new U.S. administration. They were pleased to understand that the U.S. is prepared to deal with them on the basis of equality and mutual respect, and that the U.S. has an interest in the stability and prosperity of Southeast Asia.

6. The Lao appreciated the Commission's assurances that the U.S. government has no hostile intentions toward their regime and is not supporting elements trying to overthrow it, but they are likely to remain sensitive and suspicious as long as indigenous insurgent activity continues to give them significant problems.

Economic and Humanitarian Assistance

1. The Vietnamese clearly expect a significant U.S. contribution to their postwar economic reconstruction.

2. At the same time they indicated flexibility about the form this aid might take and the basis on which it could be given. They listed concessional aid, bilateral aid, multilateral aid and long term loans as forms of aid which have been discussed in the past, although they did not specify which of these they preferred or whether any one form alone would be acceptable.

3. The Vietnamese seem prepared to deemphasize references to this aid as coming from U.S. obligations under the Paris Agreement. This remains clearly their own position, but they appear willing to discuss aid instead in

humanitarian and moral terms. They indicated that they understand our domestic political constraints on this issue.

4. While not specifically linking provisions of U.S. aid to either an MIA accounting or normalization, the Vietnamese stated that these three issues are "inter-related" and indicated that they would expect both sides to take actions regarding the other's concerns. They did state that none of these three issues was a precondition to the other two. Nonetheless, it remains to be seen how forthcoming the Vietnamese may be in accounting for the MIA's if the U.S. does not take some steps on aid.

Recommendations

1. The Commission believes that resumption of talks in Paris between representatives of the U.S. and Vietnamese governments would be a most useful way of continuing the dialogue begun during its mission to Hanoi.

2. The Commission believes that normalization of relations affords the best prospect for obtaining a fuller accounting for our missing personnel and recommends that the normalization process be pursued vigorously for this as well as other reasons.

3. The Commission believes it most important to continue the technical exchanges with the Vietnamese Agency on Accounting for MIA's which were initiated in Hanoi.

4. In addition to talks in Paris, consideration should be given to proposing that a U.S. representative personally bring such information to Hanoi, and to inviting Vietnamese representatives to visit the U.S. Central Identification Laboratory in Honolulu.

5. In view of the Vietnamese statements that they could be glad to receive material assistance to aid their search for U.S. remains, the Commission recommends that this subject be considered promptly within the U.S. Government with a view to quickly providing whatever assistance is appropriate.

6. Consideration should also be given to offering technical advice and assistance on defusing unexploded ordnance, which the Commission understands continues to be a serious problem in some areas. An international agency such as UNHCR [United Nations Office of the High Commissioner for Refugees] could be helpful in arrangements for providing such information.

7. Another possible action would be to encourage private American groups to increase humanitarian aid programs for Indochina, in such areas as food and medical supplies, including prosthetic equipment.

COURT ON CRIMINAL PROCEDURES
March 23, 1977

The Supreme Court by a 5-4 vote March 23 rejected an opportunity offered by 22 states to overturn the controversial criminal law decision of the Warren Court, the Miranda v. Arizona *ruling of 1966.*

In the 1977 decision, the court ordered a new trial for Robert Anthony Williams, convicted of the Christmas Eve 1968 rape and murder of a 10-year-old girl in Des Moines, Iowa. (Brewer v. Williams) The court held that Williams should be retried because police violated his Sixth Amendment right to aid of legal counsel when they induced him, in the absence of his lawyer, to lead them to the body of the victim.

Chief Justice Warren E. Burger, dissenting, called the result of this decision "intolerable in any society which purports to call itself an organized society." He said that Williams' guilt was not in question and the court was "punishing the public for the mistakes and misdeeds of law enforcement officers." Burger was joined in dissent by Justices Byron R. White, Harry A. Blackmun and William H. Rehnquist.

The Case

Williams surrendered to police in Davenport, Iowa, after talking to his lawyer. He was given the warnings required by the Miranda *decision, advising him of his constitutional rights to remain silent and to legal assistance.*

Williams was transported by car from Davenport to Des Moines. Police refused the request of his attorney that he accompany Williams on the ride and Williams made the trip with two police officers. His attorney made clear to the officers that Williams should not be questioned during the trip. On the way to Des Moines, Williams told the police that once he reached Des Moines and talked to his lawyer, he would tell them "the whole story."

As they rode toward Des Moines, one of the officers pointed out that it was snowing, that it would be difficult to find a body after a heavy snow, and that the little girl's parents at least deserved to be able to give the child a "Christian burial." He did not directly ask Williams where the body was, but later on the trip Williams directed them to it. This evidence was used at Williams' trial over his lawyer's protest that it had been obtained in violation of Williams' right to counsel.

A federal district court granted Williams' petition for a new trial based on his claim that this exchange on the trip from Davenport to Des Moines had violated his constitutional rights. The U.S. Eighth Circuit Court of Appeals agreed, finding that both Williams' Miranda rights and his right to counsel had been violated.

The state appealed and was joined by 21 other states in asking the justices to overrule—or at least relax—the procedural requirements that Miranda imposed on police.

The Opinion

Finding it unnecessary to address the Miranda issues, the majority based its order for a new trial on its finding that the "Christian burial" speech was tantamount to an interrogation and so violated Williams' right to counsel.

"Whatever else it may mean, the right to counsel...means at least that a person is entitled to the help of a lawyer at or after that time that judicial proceedings have been initiated against him," wrote Justice Potter Stewart for the majority. "Once adversary proceedings have commenced against an individual, he has a right to legal representation when the government interrogates him."

Joining Stewart in the majority were Justices William J. Brennan Jr., Thurgood Marshall, Lewis F. Powell Jr. and John Paul Stevens.

They rejected the state's contention that Williams had waived his right to counsel by deciding to respond to the "Christian burial" comments; the state had not proved that Williams intentionally relinquished that right, wrote Stewart.

"The crime of which Williams was convicted was senseless and brutal, calling for swift and energetic action by the police to apprehend the perpetrator and gather evidence with which he could be convicted," concluded Stewart. "No mission of law enforcement officials is more important." Yet the court could not condone so clear a violation of the right to counsel. "The pressures on state...officers charged with the administration of the criminal law are great, especially when the crime is murder and the

victim a small child. But it is precisely the predictability of those pressures that makes imperative a resolute loyalty to the guarantees that the Constitution extends to us all."

Burger Dissent

"Williams is guilty of the savage murder of a small child; no Member of the Court contends he is not," argued Chief Justice Burger in his dissenting opinion. He criticized the majority for a decision that "mechanically and blindly keeps reliable evidence from juries."

Williams clearly intended to waive his right to remain silent until he saw his lawyer, in Burger's view. He had been fully informed of his rights and "since the Court does not question Williams' mental competence, it boggles the mind to suggest that he could not understand that leading police to the child's body would have other than the most serious consequence," wrote the Chief Justice.

The Miranda Case

In the 1966 Miranda decision, the Supreme Court ruled that statements made by an accused person during police interrogation were inadmissible at trial unless certain procedural safeguards were observed in obtaining them. A ruling had been long awaited by law enforcement officials, who sought more definitive rules for the interrogations of suspects accused of a crime.

The Miranda ruling created an explicit set of guidelines to be followed in the interrogation and investigation of a suspect. Although there had been continuous criticism that Miranda had hindered police work and coddled criminals, subsequent decisions merely further defined or modified the 1966 decision. The procedural safeguards remained, despite changes in court members and philosophy.

Following are excerpts from the Supreme Court ruling in Brewer v. Williams, delivered March 23, 1977, in which the court refused to overturn the procedural safeguards outlined in the 1966 Miranda decision:

No. 74-1263

Lou V. Brewer, Warden, Petitioner, *v.* Robert Anthony Williams, aka Anthony Erthel Williams.	On Writ of Certiorari to the United States Court of Appeals for the Eighth Circuit.

[March 23, 1977]

MR. JUSTICE STEWART delivered the opinion of the Court.

An Iowa trial jury found the respondent, Robert Williams, guilty of murder. The judgment of conviction was affirmed in the Iowa Supreme Court by a closely divided vote. In a subsequent habeas corpus proceeding a federal district court ruled that under the United States Constitution Williams is entitled to a new trial, and a divided Court of Appeals for the Eighth Circuit agreed. The question before us is whether the District Court and the Court of Appeals were wrong.

I

On the afternoon of December 24, 1968, a 10-year-old girl named Pamela Powers went with her family to the YMCA in Des Moines, Iowa, to watch a wrestling tournament in which her brother was participating. When she failed to return from a trip to the washroom, a search for her began. The search was unsuccessful.

Robert Williams, who had recently escaped from a mental hospital, was a resident of the YMCA. Soon after the girl's disappearance Williams was seen in the YMCA lobby carrying some clothing and a large bundle wrapped in a blanket. He obtained help from a 14-year old boy in opening the street door of the YMCA and the door to his automobile parked outside. When Williams placed the bundle in the front seat of his car the boy "saw two legs in it and they were skinny and white." Before anyone could see what was in the bundle Williams drove away. His abandoned car was found the following day in Davenport, Iowa, roughly 160 miles east of Des Moines. A warrant was then issued in Des Moines for his arrest on a charge of abduction.

On the morning of December 26, a Des Moines lawyer named Henry McKnight went to the Des Moines police station and informed the officers present that he had just received a long distance call from Williams, and that he had advised Williams to turn himself in to the Davenport police. Williams did surrender that morning to the police in Davenport, and they booked him on the charge specified in the arrest warrant and gave him the warnings required by *Miranda* v. *Arizona*...[1966]. The Davenport police then telephoned their counterparts in Des Moines to inform them that Williams had surrendered. McKnight, the lawyer, was still at the Des Moines police headquarters, and Williams conversed with McKnight on the telephone. In the presence of the Des Moines Chief of Police and a Police Detective named Leaming, McKnight advised Williams that Des Moines police officers would be driving to Davenport to pick him up, that the officers would not interrogate him or mistreat him, and that Williams was not to talk to the officers about Pamela Powers until after consulting with McKnight upon his return to Des Moines. As a result of these conversations, it was agreed between McKnight and the Des Moines police officials that Detective Leaming and a fellow officer would drive to Davenport to pick up Williams, that they would bring him directly back to Des Moines, and that they would not question him during the trip.

In the meantime Williams was arraigned before a judge in Davenport on the outstanding arrest warrant. The judge advised him of his *Miranda* rights and committed him to jail. Before leaving the courtroom, Williams conferred with a lawyer named Kelly, who advised him not to make any statements until consulting with McKnight back in Des Moines.

Detective Leaming and his fellow officer arrived in Davenport about noon to pick up Williams and return him to Des Moines. Soon after their arrival they met with Williams and Kelly, who, they understood, was acting as Williams' lawyer. Detective Leaming repeated the *Miranda* warnings, and told Williams:

> "...we both know that you're being represented here by Mr. Kelly and you're being represented by Mr. McKnight in Des Moines, and...I want you to remember this because we'll be visiting between here and Des Moines."

Williams then conferred again with Kelly alone, and after this conference Kelly reiterated to Detective Leaming that Williams was not to be questioned about the disappearance of Pamela Powers until after he had consulted with McKnight back in Des Moines. When Leaming expressed some reservations, Kelly firmly stated that the agreement with McKnight was to be carried out—that there was to be no interrogation of Williams during the automobile journey to Des Moines. Kelly was denied permission to ride in the police car back to Des Moines with Williams and the two officers.

The two Detectives with Williams in their charge, then set out on the 160-mile drive. At no time during the trip did Williams express a willingness to be interrogated in the absence of an attorney. Instead, he stated several times that "[w]hen I get to Des Moines and see Mr. McKnight, I am going to tell you the whole story." Detective Leaming knew that Williams was a former mental patient, and knew also that he was deeply religious.

The Detective and his prisoner soon embarked on a wide-ranging conversation covering a variety of topics, including the subject of religion. Then, not long after leaving Davenport and reaching the interstate highway, Detective Leaming delivered what has been referred to in the briefs and oral arguments as the "Christian burial speech." Addressing Williams as "Reverend," the Detective said:

> "I want to give you something to think about while we're traveling down the road.... Number one, I want you to observe the weather conditions, it's raining, it's sleeting, it's freezing, driving is very treacherous, visibility is poor, it's going to be dark early this evening. They are predicting several inches of snow for tonight, and I feel that you yourself are the only person that

knows where this little girl's body is, that you yourself have only been there once, and if you get a snow on top of it you yourself may be unable to find it. And, since we will be going right past the area on the way into Des Moines, I feel that we could stop and locate the body, that the parents of this little girl should be entitled to a Christian burial for the little girl who was snatched away from them on Christmas Eve and murdered. And I feel we should stop and locate it on the way in rather than waiting until morning and trying to come back out after a snow storm and possibly not being able to find it at all."

Williams asked Detective Leaming why he thought their route to Des Moines would be taking them past the girl's body, and Leaming responded that he knew the body was in the area of Mitchellville—a town they would be passing on the way to Des Moines. Leaming then stated: "I do not want you to answer me. I don't want to discuss it further. Just think about it as we're riding down the road."

As the car approached Grinnell, a town approximately 100 miles west of Davenport, Williams asked whether the police had found the victim's shoes. When Detective Leaming replied that he was unsure, Williams directed the officers to a service station where he said he had left the shoes; a search for them proved unsuccessful. As they continued towards Des Moines, Williams asked whether the police had found the blanket, and directed the officers to a rest area where he said he had disposed of the blanket. Nothing was found. The car continued towards Des Moines, and as it approached Mitchellville, Williams said that he would show the officers where the body was. He then directed the police to the body of Pamela Powers.

Williams was indicted for first-degree murder. Before trial, his counsel moved to suppress all evidence relating to or resulting from any statements Williams had made during the automobile ride from Davenport to Des Moines. After an evidentiary hearing the trial judge denied the motion. He found that "an agreement was made between defense counsel and the police officials to the effect that the Defendant was not to be questioned on the return trip to Des Moines," and that the evidence in question had been elicited from Williams during "a critical stage in the proceedings requiring the presence of counsel on his request." The judge ruled, however, that Williams had "waived his right to have an attorney present during the giving of such information."

The evidence in question was introduced over counsel's continuing objection at the subsequent trial. The jury found Williams guilty of murder, and the judgment of conviction was affirmed by the Iowa Supreme Court, a bare majority of whose members agreed with the trial court that Williams had "waived his right to the presence of his counsel" on the automobile ride from Davenport to Des Moines.... The four dissenting justices expressed the view that "when counsel and police have agreed defendant is not to be questioned until counsel is present and defendant has been advised not to talk and repeatedly has stated he will tell the whole story after he talks with counsel, the state should be required to make a stronger showing of intentional voluntary waiver than was made here."...

Williams then petitioned for a writ of habeas corpus in the United States District Court for the Southern District of Iowa. Counsel for the State and for Williams stipulated "that the case would be submitted on the record of facts and proceedings in the trial court, without taking of further testimony." The District Court made findings of fact as summarized above, and concluded as a matter of law that the evidence in question had been wrongly admitted at Williams' trial. This conclusion was based on three alternative and independent grounds: (1) that Williams had been denied his constitutional right to the assistance of counsel; (2) that he had been denied the constitutional protections defined by this Court's decisions in *Escobedo* v. *Illinois*...[1966], and *Miranda* v. *Arizona*...[1966] and (3) that in any event, his self-incriminatory statements on the automobile trip from Davenport to Des Moines had been involuntarily made. Further, the District Court ruled that there had been no waiver by Williams of the constitutional protections in question....

The Court of Appeals for the Eighth Circuit, with one judge dissenting, affirmed this judgment, ...and denied a petition for rehearing en banc. We granted certiorari to consider the constitutional issues presented....

II

...[T]he District Court based its judgment in this case on three independent grounds. The Court of Appeals appears to have affirmed the judgment on two of those grounds. We have concluded that only one of them need be considered here.

Specifically, there is no need to review in this case the doctrine of *Miranda* v. *Arizona*..., a doctrine designed to secure the constitutional privilege against compulsory self-incrimination.... It is equally unnecessary to evaluate the ruling of the District Court that Williams' self-incriminating statements were, indeed, involuntarily made.... For it is clear that the judgment before us must in any event be affirmed upon the ground that Williams was deprived of a different constitutional right—the right to the assistance of counsel.

This right, guaranteed by the Sixth and Fourteenth Amendments, is indispensable to the fair administration of our adversary system of criminal justice....

There has occasionally been a difference of opinion within the Court as to the peripheral scope of this constitutional right.... But its basic contours, which are identical in state and federal contexts...are too well established to require extensive elaboration here. Whatever else it may mean, the right to counsel granted by the Sixth and Fourteenth Amendments means at least that a person is entitled to the help of a lawyer at or after the time that judicial proceedings have been initiated against him—"whether by way of formal charge, preliminary hearing, indictment, information, or arraignment."...

There can be no doubt in the present case that judicial proceedings had been initiated against Williams before the start of the automobile ride from Davenport to Des Moines. A warrant håd been issued for his arrest, he had been arraigned on that warrant before a judge in a Davenport courtroom, and he had been committed by the court to confinement in jail. The State does not contend otherwise.

There can be no serious doubt, either, that Detective Leaming deliberately and designedly set out to elicit information from Williams just as surely as—and perhaps more effectively than—if he had formally interrogated him. Detective Leaming was fully aware before departing for Des Moines that Williams was being represented in Davenport by Kelly and in Des Moines by McKnight. Yet he purposely sought during Williams' isolation from his lawyers to obtain as much incriminating information as possible.

The state courts clearly proceeded upon the hypothesis that Detective Leaming's "Christian burial speech" had been tantamount to interrogation. Both courts recognized that Williams had been entitled to the assistance of counsel at the time he made the incriminating statements. Yet no such constitutional protection would have come into play if there had been no interrogation.

The circumstances of this case are thus constitutionally indistinguishable from those presented in *Massiah* v. *United States...*[1963]. The petitioner in that case was indicted for violating the federal narcotics law. He retained a lawyer, pleaded not guilty, and was released on bail. While he was free on bail a federal agent succeeded by surreptitious means in listening to incriminating statements made by him. Evidence of these statements was introduced against the petitioner at his trial, and he was convicted. This Court reversed the conviction, holding "that the petitioner was denied the basic protections of that guarantee [the right to counsel] when there was used against him at his trial evidence of his own incriminating words, which federal agents had deliberately solicited from him after he had been indicted and in the absence of his counsel."...

That the incriminating statements were elicited surreptitiously in the *Massiah* case, and otherwise here, is constitutionally irrelevant.... Rather, the clear rule of *Massiah* is that once adversary proceedings have commenced against an individual, he has a right to legal representation when the government interrogates him. It thus requires no wooden or technical application of the *Massiah* doctrine to conclude that Williams was entitled to the assistance of counsel guaranteed to him by the Sixth and Fourteenth Amendments.

III

...We conclude, finally, that the Court of Appeals was correct in holding that, judged by these standards, the record in this case falls far short of sustaining the State's burden. It is true that Williams had been informed of and appeared to understand his right to counsel. But waiver requires not merely comprehension but relinquishment, and Williams' consistent reliance upon the advice of counsel in dealing with the authorities refutes any suggestion that he waived that right. He consulted McKnight by long distance telephone before turning himself in. He spoke with McKnight by telephone again shortly after being booked. After he was arraigned, Williams sought out and obtained legal advice from Kelly. Williams again consulted with Kelly after Detective Leaming and his fellow officer arrived in Davenport. Throughout, Williams was advised not to make any statements before seeing McKnight in Des Moines, and was assured that the police had agreed not to question him. His statements while in the car that he would tell the whole story *after* seeing McKnight in Des Moines were the clearest expressions by Williams himself that he desired the presence of an attorney before any interrogation took place. But even before making these statements, Williams had effectively asserted his right to counsel by having secured attorneys at both ends of the automobile trip, both of whom, acting as his agents, had made clear to the police that no interrogation was to occur during the journey. Williams knew of that agreement and, particularly in view of his consistent reliance on counsel, there is no basis for concluding that he disavowed it.

Despite Williams' express and implicit assertions of his right to counsel, Detective Leaming proceeded to elicit incriminating statements from Williams. Leaming did not preface this effort by telling Williams that he had a right to the presence of a lawyer, and made no effort at all to ascertain whether Williams wished to relinquish that right. The circumstances of record in this case thus provide no reasonable basis for finding that Williams waived his right to the assistance of counsel.

The Court of Appeals did not hold, nor do we, that under the circumstances of this case Williams *could not,* without notice to counsel, have waived his rights under the Sixth and Fourteenth Amendments. It only held, as do we, that he did not.

IV

The crime of which Williams was convicted was senseless and brutal, calling for swift and energetic action by the police to apprehend the perpetrator and gather evidence with which he could be convicted. No mission of law enforcement officials is more important. Yet "[d]isinterested zeal for the public good does not assure either wisdom or right in the methods it pursues."... Although we do not lightly affirm the issuance of a writ of habeas corpus in this case, so clear a violation of the Sixth and Fourteenth Amendments as here occurred cannot be condoned. The pressures on state executive and judicial officers charged with the administration of the criminal law are great, especially when the crime is murder and the victim a small child. But it is precisely the predictability of those pressures that makes imperative a resolute loyalty to the guarantees that the Constitution extends to us all.

The judgment of the Court of Appeals is affirmed.

It is so ordered.

MR. JUSTICE MARSHALL, concurring.

I concur wholeheartedly in my Brother STEWART's opinion for the Court, but add these words in light of the dissenting opinions filed today. The dissenters have, I believe, lost sight of the fundamental constitutional backbone of our criminal law. They seem to think that Detective Leaming's actions were perfectly proper, indeed laudable, examples of "good police work." In my view, good police work is something far different from catching the criminal at any price. It is equally important that the police, as guardians of the law, fulfill their responsibility to obey its commands scrupulously. For "in the end life and liberty can be as much endangered from illegal methods used to convict those thought to be criminals as from the actual criminals themselves."...

In this case, there can be no doubt that Detective Leaming consciously and knowingly set out to violate Williams' Sixth Amendment right to counsel and his Fifth Amendment privilege against self-incrimination, as Leaming himself understood those rights....

MR. JUSTICE POWELL, concurring.

As the dissenting opinion of THE CHIEF JUSTICE sharply illustrates, resolution of the issues in this case turns primarily on one's perception of the facts. There is little difference of opinion, among the several courts (and numerous judges) who have reviewed the case, as to the relevant constitutional principles: (i) Williams had the right to assistance of counsel; (ii) once that right attached (it is conceded that it had in this case), the State could not properly interrogate Williams in the absence of counsel unless he voluntarily and knowingly waived the right; and (iii) the burden was on the State to show that Williams in fact had waived the right before the police interrogated him.

The critical factual issue is whether there had been a voluntary waiver, and this turns in large part upon whether there was interrogation....

...Significantly, the recognition by the police of the status of counsel was evidenced by the *express agreement* between McKnight and the appropriate police officials that the officers who would drive Williams to Des Moines would not interrogate him in the absence of counsel.

The incriminating statements were made by Williams during the long ride while in the custody of two police officers, and in the absence of his retained counsel. The dissent of THE CHIEF JUSTICE concludes that prior to these statements, Williams had "made a valid waiver" of his right to have counsel present.... This view disregards the record evidence clearly indicating that the police engaged in interrogation of Williams....

...I join the opinion of the Court which also finds that the efforts of Detective Leaming "to elicit information from Williams," as conceded by counsel for the State at oral argument...were a skillful and effective form of interrogation. Moreover, the entire setting was conducive to the psychological coercion that was successfully exploited. Williams was known by the police to be a young man with quixotic religious convictions and a history of mental disorders. The date was Christmas eve, the weather was ominous, and the setting appropriate for Detective Leaming's talk of snow concealing the body and preventing a "Christian burial." Williams was alone in the automobile with two police officers for several hours. It is clear from the record, as both of the federal courts below found, that there was no evidence of a knowing and voluntary waiver of the right to have counsel present beyond the fact that Williams ultimately confessed....

The dissenting opinion of THE CHIEF JUSTICE states that the Court's holding today "conclusively presumes a suspect is legally incompetent to change his mind and tell the truth until an attorney is present."... I find no justification for this view. On the contrary, the opinion of the Court is explicitly clear that the right to assistance of counsel may be waived, after it has attached, without notice to or consultation with counsel.... We would have such a case here if the State had proved that the police officers refrained from coercion and interrogation, as they have agreed, and that Williams freely on his own initiative had confessed the crime....

MR. JUSTICE STEVENS, concurring....

...Underlying the surface issues in this case is the question whether a fugitive from justice can rely on his lawyer's advice given in connection with a decision to surrender voluntarily. The defendant placed his trust in an experienced Iowa trial lawyer who in turn trusted the Iowa law enforcement authorities to honor a commitment made during negotiations which led to the apprehension of a potentially dangerous person. Under any analysis, this was a critical stage of the proceeding in which the participation of an independent professional was of vital importance to the accused and to society. At this stage—as in countless others in which the law profoundly affects the life of the individual—the lawyer is the essential medium through which the demands and commitments of the sovereign are communicated to the citizen. If, in the long run, we are seriously concerned about the individual's effective representation by counsel, the State cannot be permitted to dishonor its promise to this lawyer.

MR. CHIEF JUSTICE BURGER, dissenting.

The result reached by the Court in this case ought to be intolerable in any society which purports to call itself an organized society. It continues the court—by the narrowest margin—on the much criticized course of punishing the public for the mistakes and misdeeds of law enforcement officers, instead of punishing the officer directly, if in fact he is guilty of wrongdoing. It mechanically and blindly keeps reliable evidence from juries whether the claimed constitutional violation involves gross police misconduct or honest human error. Williams is guilty of the savage murder of a small child; no Member of the Court contends he is not. While in custody, and after no fewer than *five* warnings of his rights to silence and to counsel, he led police to the place where he had buried the body of his victim. The Court now holds the jury must not be told how the police found the body.

The Court concedes Williams was not threatened or coerced and that he acted voluntarily and with full awareness of his constitutional rights when he guided police to the body. In the face of all this, the Court now holds that because Williams was prompted by the detective's statement—not interrogation but a statement—his disclosure cannot be given to the jury.

The effect of this is to fulfill Justice Cardozo's grim prophecy that some-day some court might carry the exclusionary rule to the absurd extent that its operative effect would exclude evidence relating to the body of a murder victim because of the means by which it was found. In so doing the Court regresses to playing a grisly game of "hide and seek," once more exalting the sporting theory of criminal justice which has been experiencing a decline in our jurisprudence. With JUSTICES WHITE and BLACKMUN, I categorically reject the remarkable notion that the police in this case were guilty of unconstitutional misconduct, or any conduct justifying the bizarre result reached by the Court. Apart from a brief comment on the merits, however, I wish to focus on the irrationality of applying the in-creasingly discredited exclusionary rule to this case.

The Court Concedes Williams' Disclosures Were Voluntary

Under well-settled precedents which the Court freely acknowledges, it is very clear that Williams had made a valid waiver of his Fifth Amendment right to silence and his Sixth Amendment right to counsel when he led police to the child's body. Indeed, even under the Court's analysis I do not understand how a contrary conclusion is possible.

The Court purports to apply as the appropriate constitutional waiver standard the familiar "intentional relinquishment or abandonment of a known right or privilege" test of *Johnson* v. *Zerbst*...[1938]. The Court assumes, without deciding that Williams' conduct and statements were voluntary.... It concedes, as it must...that Williams had been informed of and fully understood his constitutional rights and the consequences of their waiver. Then, having either assumed or found every element necessary to make out a valid waiver under its own test, the Court reaches the astonishing conclusion that no valid waiver has been demonstrated....

...The evidence is uncontradicted that Williams had abundant knowledge of his right to have counsel present and of his right to silence. Since the Court does not question Williams' mental competence, it boggles the mind to suggest that he could not understand that leading police to the child's body would have other than the most serious consequences. All of the elements necessary to make out a valid waiver are shown by the record and, paradoxically, acknowledged by the Court; we thus are left to guess how the Court reached its holding.

One plausible but unarticulated basis for the result reached is that once a suspect has asserted his right not to talk without the presence of an at-torney, it becomes legally impossible to waive that right until the suspect has seen an attorney. But constitutional rights are *personal,* and an otherwise valid waiver should not be brushed aside by judges simply because an attorney was not present. The Court's holding operates to "imprison a man in his privileges"...; it conclusively presumes a suspect is legally incompetent to change his mind and tell the truth until an attorney is present. It denigrates an individual to some sort of nonperson whose free will has become hostage to a lawyer so that until a lawyer consents, the suspect is deprived of any legal right or power to decide for himself that he wishes to make a disclosure. It denies that the rights to counsel and silence are *personal*, nondelegable, and subject to a waiver only by that individual. The opinions in support of the Court's judgment do not enlighten us as to why police conduct—whether good or bad—should operate to suspend Williams' right to change his mind and "tell all" at once rather than waiting until he reached Des Moines.

In his concurring opinion MR. JUSTICE POWELL suggests that the result in this case turns on whether Detective Leaming's remarks constituted "interrogation," as he views them, or whether they were "statements" intended to prick the conscience of the accused. I find it most remarkable that a murder case should turn on judicial interpretation that a statement becomes a question simply because it is followed by an incriminating disclosure from the suspect. The Court seems to be saying that since Williams said he would "tell the whole story" at Des Moines, the police should have been content and waited; of course, that would have been the wiser course, especially in light of the nuances of constitutional jurisprudence applied by the Court, but a murder case ought not turn on such tenuous strands.

In any case, the Court assures us...this is not at all what it intends and that a valid waiver was *possible* in these circumstances, but was not quite made. Here of course Williams did not confess to the murder in so many words; it was his conduct in guiding police to the body, not his words, which incriminated him. And the record is replete with evidence that Williams knew precisely what he was doing when he guided police to the body. The human urge to confess wrongdoing is, of course, normal in all save hardened, professional criminals, as psychiatrists and analysts have demonstrated....

The Exclusionary Rule Should Not Be Applied to Non-egregious Police Conduct

Even if there was no waiver, and assuming a technical violation occurred, the Court errs gravely in mechanically applying the exclusionary rule without considering whether that draconian judicial doctrine should be invoked in these circumstances, or indeed whether any of its conceivable goals will be furthered by its application here.

The obvious flaws of the exclusionary rule as a judical remedy are familiar.... Today's holding interrupts what has been a more rational perception of the constitutional and social utility of excluding reliable evidence from the truth-seeking process. In its Fourth Amendment context, we have now recognized that the exclusionary rule is in no sense a *personal* constitutional right, but a judicially conceived remedial device designed to safeguard and effectuate guaranteed legal rights generally.... We have repeatedly emphasized that deterrence of unconstitutional or otherwise unlawful police conduct is the only valid justification for excluding reliable and probative evidence from the criminal factfinding process....

Accordingly, unlawfully obtained evidence is not automatically excluded from the factfinding process in all circumstances. In a variety of contexts we inquire whether application of the rule will promote its objectives sufficiently to justify the enormous cost it imposes on society....

...Against this background, it is striking that the Court fails even to consider whether the benefits secured by application of the exclusionary rule in this case outweigh its obvious social costs. Perhaps the failure is due to the fact that this case arises not under the Fourth Amendment, but under *Miranda* v. *Arizona*...and the Sixth Amendment right to counsel. The Court apparently perceives the function of the exclusionary rule to be so different in these varying contexts that it must be mechanically and uncritically applied in all cases arising outside the Fourth Amendment.

But this is demonstrably not the case where police conduct collides with *Miranda*'s procedural safeguards rather than with the Fifth Amendment privilege against compulsory self-incrimination. Involuntary and coerced admissions are suppressed because of the inherent unreliability of a confession wrung from an unwilling suspect by threats, brutality, or other coercion....

But use of Williams' disclosures and their fruits carries no risk whatever of unreliability, for the body was found where he said it would be found. Moreover, since the Court makes no issue of voluntariness, no dangers are posed to individual dignity or free will. *Miranda's* safeguards are premised on presumed unreliability long associated with confessions extorted by brutality or threats; they are not personal constitutional rights, but are simply judicially created prophylactic measures.... It will not do to brush this off by calling this a Sixth Amendment right-to-counsel case.

Thus, in cases where incriminating disclosures are voluntarily made without coercion, and hence not violative of the Fifth Amendment, but are obtained in violation of one of the *Miranda* prophylaxis, suppression is no longer automatic. Rather, we weigh the deterrent effect on unlawful police conduct, together with the normative Fifth Amendment justifications for suppression, against "the strong interest under any system of justice of making available to the trier of fact all concededly relevant and trustworthy evidence which either party seeks to adduce.... We also 'must consider society's interest in the effective prosecution of criminals....' " *Michigan* v. *Tucker*...[1974]. This individualized consideration or balancing process with respect to the exclusionary sanction is possible in this case, as in others, because Williams' incriminating disclosures are not infected with any element of compulsion the Fifth Amendment forbids; nor, as noted earlier, does this evidence pose any danger of unreliability to the factfinding process. In short, there is no reason to exclude this evidence.

Similarly, the exclusionary rule is not uniformly implicated in the Sixth Amendment, particularly its pretrial aspects.... Thus, the right to counsel is fundamentally a "trial" right necessitated by the legal complexities of a criminal prosecution and the need to offset, to the trier of fact, the power of the State as prosecutor.... It is now thought that modern law enforcement involves pretrial confrontations at which the defendant's fate might effectively be sealed before the right of counsel could attach. In order to make meaningful the defendant's opportunity to a fair trial and to assistance of counsel at that trial—the core purposes of the counsel guarantee—the Court formulated a *per se* rule guaranteeing counsel at what it has characterized as "critical" pretrial preceedings where substantial rights might be endangered....

As we have seen in the Fifth Amendment setting, violations of prophylactic rules designed to safeguard other constitutional guarantees and deter impermissible police conduct need not call for the automatic suppression of evidence without regard to the purposes served by exclusion; nor do Fourth Amendment violations merit uncritical suppression of evidence. In other situations we decline to suppress eyewitness identification which violates a defendant is right to due process"..., we exclude photo displays unless there is a "very substantial likelihood of irreparable misidentification."... Recognizing that "[i]t is the likelihood of misidentification which violates a defendant's right to due process," ...we exclude evidence only when essential to safeguard the integrity of the truth-seeking process. The test, in short, is the reliability of the evidence.

So too in the Sixth Amendment sphere failure to have counsel in a pretrial setting should not lead to the "knee-jerk" suppression of relevant and reliable evidence. Just as even uncounselled "critical" pretrial confrontations may often be conducted fairly and not in derogation of Sixth Amendment values..., evidence obtained in such proceedings should be suppressed only when its use would imperil the core values the Amendment was written to protect. Having extended Sixth Amendment concepts originally thought to relate to the trial itself to earlier periods when a criminal investigation is focused on a suspect, application of the drastic bar of exclusion should be approached with caution.

In any event, the fundamental purpose of the Sixth Amendment is to safeguard the fairness of the trial and the integrity of the factfinding process. In this case, where the evidence of how the child's body was found is of unquestioned reliability, and since the Court accepts Williams' disclosures as voluntary and uncoerced, there is no issue either of fairness or evidentiary reliability to justify suppression of truth. It appears suppression is mandated here for no other reason than the Court's general impression that it may have a beneficial effect on future police conduct; indeed, the Court fails to say even that much in defense of its holding.

Thus, whether considered under *Miranda* or the Sixth Amendment, there is no more reason to exclude the evidence in this case than there was in *Stone* v. *Powell*...[1976]; that holding was premised on the utter reliability of evidence sought to be suppressed, the irrelevancy of the constitutional claim to the criminal defendant's factual guilt or innocence, and the minimal deterrent effect of habeas corpus on police misconduct. This case, like *Stone* v. *Powell,* comes to us by way of habeas corpus after a fair trial and appeal in the state courts. Relevant factors in this case are thus indistinguishable from those in *Stone,* and from those in other Fourth Amendment cases suggesting a balancing approach toward utilization of the exclusionary sanction. Rather than adopting a formalistic analysis varying with the constitutional provision invoked, we should apply the exclusionary rule on the basis of its benefits and costs, at least in those cases where the police conduct at issue is far from being "outrageous" or "egregious."...

...I cannot possibly agree with the Court.

MR. JUSTICE WHITE, with whom MR. JUSTICE BLACKMUN and MR. JUSTICE REHNQUIST join, dissenting.

The respondent in this case killed a 10-year-old child. The majority sets aside his conviction, holding that certain statements of unquestioned reliability were unconstitutionally obtained from him, and under the circumstances probably makes it impossible to retry him. Because there is nothing in the Constitution or in our previous cases which requires the Court's action, I dissent....

...The strictest test of waiver which might be applied to this case is that set forth in *Johnson* v. *Zerbst...*[1938]. In order to show that a right has been waived under this test, the State must prove "an intentional relinquishment or abandonment of a known right or privilege." The majority creates no new rule preventing an accused who has retained a lawyer from waiving his right to the lawyer's presence during questioning. The majority simply finds that no waiver was *proved* in this case. I disagree. That respondent knew of his right not to say anything to the officers without advice and presence of counsel is established on this record to a moral certainty. He was advised of the right by three officials of the State—telling at least one that he understood the right—and by two lawyers. Finally, he further demonstrated his knowledge of the right by informing the police that he would tell them the story in the presence of McKnight when they arrived in Des Moines. The issue in this case, then, is whether respondent relinquished that right intentionally.

Respondent relinquished his right not to talk to the police about his crime when the car approached the place where he had hidden the victim's clothes. Men usually intend to do what they do and there is nothing in the record to support the proposition that respondent's decision to talk was anything but an exercise of his own free will. Apparently, without any prodding from the officers, respondent—who had earlier said that he would tell the whole story when he arrived in Des Moines—spontaneously changed his mind about the timing of his disclosures when the car approached the places where he had hidden the evidence. However, even if his statements were influenced by Detective Leaming's above-quoted statement, respondent's decision to talk in the absence of counsel can hardly be viewed as the product of an overborn will. The statement by

Leaming was not coercive; it was accompanied by a request that respondent not respond to it; and it was delivered hours before respondent decided to make any statement. Respondent's waiver was thus knowing and intentional.

The majority's contrary conclusion seems to rest on the fact that respondent "asserted" his right to counsel by retaining and consulting with one lawyer and by consulting with another. How this supports the conclusion that respondent's later relinquishment of his right not to talk in the absence of counsel was unintentional is a mystery. The fact that respondent consulted with counsel on the question whether he should talk to the police in counsel's absence makes his later decision to talk in counsel's absence *better* informed and, if anything, more intelligent.

The majority recognizes that even after this "assertion" of his right to counsel, it would have found that respondent waived his right not to talk in counsel's absence if his waiver had been express—*i.e.,* if the officers had asked him in the car whether he would be willing to answer questions in counsel's absence and if he had answered "yes."... But waiver is not a formalistic concept. Waiver is shown whenever the facts establish that an accused knew of a right and intended to relinquish it. Such waiver, even if not express, was plainly shown here. The only other conceivable basis for the majority's holding is the implicit suggestion...that the right involved in *Massiah* v. *United States*...as distinguished from the right involved in *Miranda* v. *Arizona*...is a right not to be *asked* any questions in counsel's absence rather than a right not to *answer* any questions in counsel's absence, and that the right not to be *asked* questions must be waived *before* the questions are asked. Such wafer thin distinctions cannot determine whether a guilty murderer should go free. The only conceivable purpose for the presence of counsel during questioning is to protect an accused from making incriminating *answers*. Questions, unanswered, have no significance at all. Absent coercion—no matter how the right involved is defined—an accused is amply protected by a rule requiring waiver before or simultaneously with the giving by him of an answer or the making by him of a statement.

The consequence of the majority's decision is, as the majority recognizes, extremely serious. A mentally disturbed killer whose guilt is not in question may be released. Why? Apparently, the answer is that the majority believes that the law enforcement officers acted in a way which involves some risk of injury to society and that such conduct should be deterred. However, the officers' conduct did not and was not likely to, jeopardize the fairness of respondent's trial or in any way risk the conviction of an innocent man—the risk against which the Sixth Amendment guaranty of assistance of counsel is designed to protect.... The police did nothing "wrong," let alone anything "unconstitutional." To anyone not lost in the intricacies of the prophylactic rules of *Miranda* v. *Arizona*...the result in this case seems utterly senseless.... In light of these considerations, the majority's protest that the result in this case is justified by a "clear violation" of the Sixth and Fourteenth Amendments has a distressing hollow ring. I respectfully dissent.

▼▼▼

NEW GOVERNMENT IN INDIA
March 28, 1977

Voters in India hailed the resignation of Indira Gandhi as Prime Minister on March 22 as a victory for parliamentary democracy in that nation. Gandhi stepped down after her Congress Party lost the nationwide election for the lower house of Parliament March 16-20. The contest had become a national referendum on the emergency rule imposed by Gandhi June 26, 1975.

The policies of Gandhi's successor, Morarji R. Desai, were outlined in an address March 28 at the opening session of Parliament. Desai, the 81-year-old leader of the victorious Janata Party, was Gandhi's Deputy Prime Minister and Minister of Finance from 1967 until his resignation in July 1969. Desai was among the top leaders to be detained when the emergency rule went into effect in June 1975.

The Desai government's policy address was read by B. D. Jatti, the ceremonial head of state during the transition of governments. The speech stressed personal liberties and condemned the action of the Gandhi government's experiment in "executive arbitrariness" and the emergence of a "personality cult and extra-constitutional centres of power." The Janata Party promised to remove the curbs on civil rights, repeal the press censorship laws, and amend the constitution to prevent abuse of the power to declare emergency rule. The new government also promised to review, and perhaps repeal, the Maintenance of Internal Security Act, under which thousands of political prisoners had been held without trial. The speech expressed the new government's desire to pursue a policy of moderation, to return power to local and state administrative units and to become fully nonaligned in foreign policy.

"The people have given a clear verdict in favor of individual freedom, democracy and the rule of law...," Jatti stated. "The most urgent task is to remove the remaining curbs on the fundamental freedoms and civil rights of the people, to restore the rule of law and the right of free expression to the press," the Acting President read as the new Prime Minister listened approvingly.

Background

Indira Gandhi became Prime Minister in 1966. Lal Bahadur Shastri bridged the interim as Prime Minister between Indira Gandhi and her father Jawaharlal Nehru who held the office from 1947 until his death in 1964. For nine years Gandhi's government followed the democratic socialist path set forth by Nehru.

Gandhi's government moved away from parliamentary democracy when Raj Narain, Gandhi's defeated opponent in her 1971 election to Parliament, won a court ruling June 12, 1975, which found Gandhi in violation of the election laws for using government civil servants in her campaign. Claiming that a "deep and widespread conspiracy" existed to oust her from office, Gandhi declared a state of emergency June 26, 1975, before the Supreme Court had ruled on her appeal of the conviction. The Prime Minister imprisoned leaders of the political opposition July 4, censored the press, suspended court proceedings on civil rights cases and placed her actions beyond judicial remedy July 23. Gandhi Aug. 5-6 rewrote the election laws retroactively to invalidate her conviction for campaign law violations.

Additional unrest was caused by the government-sponsored birth control program introduced April 16, 1975. The attempt to impose a "voluntary" sterilization program for men angered broad sections of the population and caused widespread rioting in the Moslem district of New Delhi April 19. Prime Minister Gandhi's son, Sanjay Gandhi, was yet another cause of dissatisfaction among the Indian people. Opposition leaders, many of whom were among the more than 55,000 people held or detained in the government's roundup of political dissidents, accused Sanjay Gandhi of using his position as the Prime Minister's son for personal gain.

Faced with mounting domestic criticism, Gandhi eased press censorship Jan. 18, 1977, released political prisoners, including Morarji Desai, and announced that parliamentary elections would be held March 16. Gandhi's Agriculture Minister Jagjivan Ram, leader of India's 85 million untouchables, the lowest order in the Hindu caste system, resigned his post Feb. 2 and formed the Congress for Democracy Party in opposition to Gandhi's rule. Ram's defection, and the Janata Party campaign against the authoritarian laws, put Gandhi on the defensive in the election. The Prime Minister began to apologize for the excesses of the emergency rule and promised to remove overzealous officials.

Victory Margin

The Janata Party won a clear majority in the lower house of Parliament. The party had built its victory in the so-called Hindi Belt in the northeastern states of Uttar Pradesh and Bihar which, with a combined population of 160 million, elected more than one-fourth of the seats in Parliament. In the new Parliament the Janata Party controlled 271 seats. Ram's Congress for Democracy Party held 28 seats and the Congress Party of Indira Gandhi retained 157 seats.

Desai, sworn in as India's fourth Prime Minister in 30 years March 24, pledged "to drive fear out of the society." Indira Gandhi, in her message of resignation March 22 said, "the collective judgment of the people must be respected. My colleagues and I accept their verdict unreservedly in a spirit of humility." She promised "constructive cooperation" with Desai.

Gandhi Arrested and Released

Four days after the start of an official government inquiry Sept. 29 into alleged excesses during her regime, Indira Gandhi was arrested on charges of being involved in official corruption during her term of office as Prime Minister. She was released the following day after the magistrate determined that there was insufficient evidence presented against her.

Before leaving her home after the arrest, Gandhi issued a statement saying that the arrest was "political. It is to prevent me from going to the people." Prior to her release Oct. 4, her supporters rioted in several cities. Gandhi's immediate release, according to press reports, proved politically embarrassing to the Desai government which was attempting to consolidate its coalition in Parliament and gain the confidence of the people.

> *Following is the text of the speech delivered March 28, 1977 by B. D. Jatti, in which he outlined the programs of the newly-elected Desai government; transcript provided by the Information Service of the Embassy of India. (Boldface headings in brackets have been added by Congressional Quarterly to highlight the organization of the text.):*

Honorable Members,

I extend my felicitations to the Members of the new Lok Sabha and welcome you to the joint session of the Sixth Parliament....

...The general election, just concluded, has effectively and decisively demonstrated the power of the people, the vitality of the democratic process in India and the deep root that it has taken. The people have given a clear verdict in favor of individual freedom, democracy and the rule of law, and against executive arbitrariness, the emergence of a personality cult and extra-constitutional centres of power. The election marks an important milestone in the evolution of our democratic polity into a healthy and two-party system.

...In doing so, it will not take the people for granted or assume that they know nothing and that the government alone knows all the answers and solutions. The traumatic experience of the last two years during which many atrocities were committed on the people and they had to undergo untold sufferings and some have even died, has brought home the relevance of this.

Honorable Members, the new government has taken charge only three days ago. It has not had the time to work out the details of the various measures it intends to adopt. This will be done in due course during the year and placed before you. Nevertheless, there are some urgent tasks to be attended to and the government will take them in hand immediately.

[Restore Freedom and Civil Rights]

The most urgent task is to remove the remaining curbs on the fundamental freedoms and civil rights of the people to restore the rule of law and the right of free expression to the press. The External Emergency proclaimed in 1971 has been revoked by me yesterday. The government will also take the following measures:

(1) Having regard to the gross abuse to which the Maintenance of Internal Security Act has been put during the last two years, a thorough review of the Act will be undertaken with a view to repealing it and examining whether the existing laws need further strengthening to deal with economic offences and the security of the country without denying the right of approach to courts.

(2) Legislation will be introduced...[so that] no political or social organization is banned except on adequate grounds and after an independent judicial enquiry.

(3) The Prevention of Publication of Objectionable Matters Act will be repealed. Immunity which the press enjoyed in reporting the proceedings of legislatures will be restored.

(4) The amendment to the Representation of the [P]eople's Act, which redefined corrupt practices and afforded protection to electoral offences by certain individuals by placing them beyond the scrutiny of courts, will be repealed.

During the course of the year, a comprehensive measure will be placed before you to amend the constitution to restore the balance between the people and Parliament and the judiciary, the judiciary and the Executive, the states and the center, the citizen and the government, that the founding fathers of our constitution worked out. This will include provisions to amend Article 352 to prevent the abuse of the power to declare emergency and of the relevant articles to ensure that [the] President's rule is imposed strictly in accordance with the objectives mentioned in the constitution and not for extraneous purposes.

One of the very serious developments in the recent past was the erosion of the freedom of impartiality of the media, of publicity and information. My government will take steps to restore to the media their due place in a democracy. Steps will also be taken to ensure that All India Radio, Door-darshan, Films Division and other government media function in a fair and objective manner.

Nothing has roused the public anger and resentment so much as the manner in which the family planning program was implemented last year in several parts of the country. This has caused a major set-back to the program which is vital for the welfare of the nation. Family planning will be pursued vigorously as a wholly voluntary program and as an integral part of a comprehensive policy covering education, health, maternity and child-care, family welfare, women's rights and nutrition.

[Economic Program]

In the economic sphere, the government is pledged to the removal of destitution within a definite time frame of ten years. Relative neglect of the rural sector has created a dangerous imbalance in the economy leading to migration of people from rural areas to urban centers. The farmer has been denied a reasonable and fair price for his products. Allocations for agriculture and related developments [have] been grossly inadequate and the need to improve conditions in the villages has received scarce attention. More than 100,000 of the villages do not even have the most elementary facilities for drinking water. My government will follow an employment oriented strategy in which primacy will be given to the development of agriculture, agro-industries, small and cottage industries, especially in the rural areas. High priority will also be given to the provisions of minimum needs in rural areas and to integrated rural development. To the extent possible, at this point of time, the Fifth Five Year Plan will be reviewed. The planning process will be revitalized and work on the Sixth Five Year Plan will be taken up without delay. My government will announce, at the time of the presentation of the final budget later this year, the details of the economic program that is proposed to be followed.

I now come to external relations. My government will honour all the commitments made by the previous government. It stands for friendship with all our neighbors and other nations of the world on the basis of equality and reciprocity, and will follow a path of genuine non-alignment. I am glad to say that my government will be hosting a meeting of the non-aligned Co-ordinating Bureau early next month. My government will also give very special attention to the strengthening of ties and economic and technical cooperation with all developing nations.

Honorable Members....[a] heavy and busy schedule lies ahead of you in the coming months. There is, today, a mood of expectancy in the country.... I commend you to your tasks and wish you all success.

MOSCOW SALT NEGOTIATIONS
March 28-30, 1977

A new Strategic Arms Limitation Talks (SALT) agreement to reduce the number of offensive nuclear missiles and strategic bombers remained elusive throughout 1977. U.S.-Soviet differences over SALT were evident during three days of talks held in Moscow March 28-30 in an effort to reach agreement on a new treaty prior to the expiration Oct. 1 of the 1972 SALT I interim agreement.

The negotiating climate at the March meeting had been clouded by disagreement over the interpretation of the November 1974 Vladivostok Accords which had set guidelines for a SALT II agreement and by the intensified U.S.-Soviet confrontation over human rights. A joint communiqué issued March 31 papered over U.S.-Soviet differences on SALT but they emerged during news conferences held by Secretary of State Cyrus R. Vance, President Jimmy Carter and Soviet Foreign Minister Andrei A. Gromyko at the conclusion of the talks. (Carter's UN speech, p. 189; Historic Documents of 1974, p. 967; 1972, p. 431)

U.S.-Soviet Differences on SALT

Vance March 30 told reporters the Soviet government rejected two U.S. proposals: a comprehensive plan which proposed overall reductions in the 2,400-missile limit already imposed by the 1974 agreement, a ban on testing and development of new missile systems and a "list of measures" to assure the United States that the Russian backfire bomber was indeed an intermediate-range weapon, as the Russians had claimed, and not a long-range bomber. The second plan, the so-called deferral plan, accepted the

2,400-missile limit and postponed discussion of the Backfire bomber and the U.S. cruise missile.

The Soviets claimed that the cruise missile had been included in the missile limitation agreement signed at Vladivostok. [The cruise missile was an air, land or submarine-launched low-flying nuclear missile capable of avoiding low altitude radar detection by following the topographical contours of the land.] The U.S. position, restated by Vance during the press briefing, was that neither the cruise missile nor the Backfire bomber figured in the Vladivostok talks and were items still to be negotiated.

Within hours of Vance's press conference, President Carter, at a White House press conference, promised to "hang tough" in pressing the Soviet Union for an arms agreement that was not just "a superficial ratification of rules by which we can continue the arms race." Carter told the press that former President Gerald R. Ford and former Secretary of State Henry A. Kissinger had said "publicly and to me privately" that no agreement or secret understanding to prohibit the development or deployment of the cruise missile had been made at Vladivostok. The President said he would accept restrictions on the cruise missile "if it is part of an overall balanced package." Carter told reporters he did not believe the talks failed because of U.S. initiatives on the human rights issue.

Gromyko Press Conference

In an unusual departure from Soviet practice Soviet Foreign Minister Gromyko held a televised news conference for Soviet and foreign correspondents in Moscow March 31 to explain the Soviet rejection of the two strategic arms limitation proposals. Gromyko said the Carter administration's proposals were "false" and "unrealistic." The Foreign Minister expressed displeasure at Carter's public style of diplomacy and said it was "a dubious, if not cheap" move for the President to present disarmament plans that "would give advantages to the United States, with the Soviet Union finding itself in a worse position." There were substantial differences between the Soviet and American views, Gromyko said, but there were no "insurmountable obstacles" to continued negotiations. The Russian Foreign Minister noted that all that had been said about human rights "naturally poisons the atmosphere and aggravates the political climate."

Negotiations Continued

Although no SALT agreement was reached in 1977, progress toward a treaty was made. A meeting in Geneva May 18-21 between Vance and Gromyko produced guidelines for a resumption of SALT negotiations in Geneva. A May 21 joint communiqué outlined "a framework for further negotiations" which included the following points for discussion:

• *A U.S.-Soviet treaty to run until 1985 based on the 1974 Vladivostok accords;*

• *A slight reduction in missile launcher and bomber production;*

• *A three-year protocol to cover the controversial issues of the U.S. cruise missile and the Soviet Backfire bomber;*

• *A statement of general principles to guide the negotiations leading to a SALT II treaty.*

President Carter and Soviet President Leonid I. Brezhnev gave assurances during the summer that negotiations would proceed toward a new SALT pact despite disagreement over human rights matters. Both nations announced in September that they would abide by the SALT I arms quotas until a new pact had been signed. [In a move to affirm the congressional role in foreign policy-making, the Senate Oct. 3 took up a resolution endorsing the Carter administration's decision to continue to abide by the SALT I agreement. But conservatives called for clarification of the resolution's language and for more time to study it, and a final vote was delayed when the chair ruled that a quorum had not been present for committee approval of the measure. The resolution was not taken up again in 1977.]

Arms Control and Disarmament Agency director Paul C. Warnke, chief U.S. arms talks representative, told reporters Dec. 13 that the SALT and concurrent atomic test ban negotiations had made progress. In a Dec. 28 interview with network reporters, President Carter predicted a new SALT treaty in 1978 and said that he thought Congress would approve it.

> *Following are the texts of the press conferences of Secretary of State Vance in Moscow March 30, 1977; President Carter's Washington press conference March 30; and Foreign Minister Gromyko's Moscow press conference March 31, 1977, as released by the Soviet Embassy Information Department. (Boldface headings in brackets have been added by Congressional Quarterly to highlight the organization of the text.):*

VANCE PRESS CONFERENCE

Good evening. Let me fill you in on our meeting of this afternoon. We met this afternoon with General Secretary Brezhnev and Foreign Minister Gromyko and other officials.

At the meeting, the Soviets told us that they had examined our two proposals and did not find either acceptable. They proposed nothing new on their side. Let me give you a brief outline, as I promised I would when we reached this point, on the nature of the two proposals which we put forward.

[Deferral Proposal]

We first proposed what we have called our deferral proposal. Under this proposal we suggested the deferral of consideration of the cruise missile and Backfire bomber issues and that we resolve all other remaining issues under the Vladivostok accord and sign a new treaty.

That proposal is wholly consistent with the agreement reached at Vladivostok. As you know, there was no agreement reached at Vladivostok with respect to either cruise missiles or the Backfire bomber.... So in essence our proposal was "let's sign up what has been agreed at Vladivostok and put aside the cruise issue and get on with SALT III."

[Comprehensive Proposal]

As an alternative, and what we have referred to as a comprehensive proposal and the one which we prefer and urged that they give serious consideration to, was a proposal which would have really made substantive progress toward true arms control.

It had in it four elements, or it has in it four elements. Let me run through them with you. The first deals with aggregates. We proposed that there be a substantial reduction in the overall aggregates of strategic delivery vehicles.

Second, we proposed that there be a reduction in the number of what are called modern large ballistic-missile launchers. Thirdly, we proposed that there by a reduction in the MIRV [multiple independently targeted reentry vehicle] launcher aggregate. And fourth, we proposed that there be a limit on the launchers of ICBM's [intercontinental ballistic missiles] equipped with MIRV's—in other words, we proposed a sublimit in that area.

Going on to ICBM restrictions, we proposed that there continue to be a ban on the construction of new ICBM launchers. We proposed in addition a ban on modification of existing ICBM's. In addition to that, we proposed a limit on the number of flight tests for existing ICBM's. We proposed in addition a ban on the development, the testing and deployment of new ICBM's. In addition to that, we proposed a ban on the development, the testing and deployment of mobile ICBM launchers.

With respect to cruise missiles, we proposed a ban on the development, testing and deployment of all cruise missiles whether nuclear armed or conventionally armed, with ranges that were not intercontinental ranges, in other words, we set a limit—I'm not going to give you that precise number, but there was a specific number—over which they would be banned and that limit was a limit between intercontinental and nonintercontinental.

Finally, with respect to the Backfire bomber, we indicated that we wanted them to provide us with a list of measure to assure the Backfire bomber could not be used as [a] strategic bomber. That in essence is the comprehensive package which we put forward. We have agreed to continue discussions in the future. Foreign Minister Gromyko and I will be meeting in May to discuss Middle East and other items including strategic arms limitations.

[Agenda for Working Groups]

In addition to that, we have agreed to set up a number of working groups in various areas to follow-on on the discussions which we have had here in Moscow. Let me give you a list of the areas in which we will have these working groups. They include the area of comprehensive test ban, the area of chemical weapons, the area of notification of missile test firings, the area of antisatellite weapons, the area of civil defense, the area of possible military limitations in the Indian Ocean, the area of radiological weapons, the area of conventional weapons, and we agreed to set up a regular schedule of meetings to deal with the whole question of proliferation.

This is the summary of where we are at this point.

Yes?

Q: Mr. Secretary, what effect do you think the outcome of these negotiations will have on U.S.-Soviet relations?

[VANCE]: I think we made progress in these negotiations. They were useful. I think that U.S.-Soviet relations will continue to be good. I hope in the future that we can strengthen those relations. Needless to say I am disappointed that we have failed to make progress in what I consider to be the most essential of all these areas, namely the area of strategic nuclear arms, but I think our relationship will continue good. We will certainly do everything we can to continue to try and strengthen the relationship. Yes?

Q: Mr. Secretary, sir, it must be very evident, sir, that without the specifics of the proposal that the United States presented, it will be impossible for any rational person to draw a conclusion as to whether the United States proposal was plausible or not as a proposal made between adversary nations. Is there nothing that you can do, sir, to give us the specifics that would tell the American public whether the proposal made by the United States was a plausible proposal?

A: I cannot give you at this point any specific numbers. I think that you have enough in terms of the outline of the proposals to answer the question which you put....

Q: I would defer with due respect, sir.

Q: Sir, did the Soviet side give you any reason to hope that there may be some further negotiations on your proposal and on their proposals, that you might find a bridge between the two of them?

A: Yes, we agreed that we would continue discussions. That's all I...

[Human Rights Issue]

Q: Mr. Secretary, to what extent do you think that the issue of human rights might have played a role in the failure of the negotiations?

A: Well, human rights did not come up after the first day. We never discussed it again.

Q: You don't think it in any way affected their thinking on your proposals?

A: I don't believe it did, no. I think it stood on its own feet, but you'll have to ask them.

Q: Mr. Secretary, I'm not clear what happens next. Is one side supposed to come up with a new proposal, or where do you go from here specifically?

A: Where we go from here is that I would hope that they would consider the proposals which we have made. We think that they provide a reasonable basis for further discussions. We will be meeting again and I hope that by that time there will be something put on the table which will permit us to make progress.

Q: Is it still possible, sir, do you think to replace SALT I by October when it expires?

A: Yes, I think it's still possible. I would come back to the point that the deferral proposal is a proposal which is based upon what was agreed upon at Vladivostok and simply puts aside the very difficult issues of Backfire and the cruise missile and one could sign that and move immediately on to the more complex problems which are contained in the comprehensive proposal and SALT III.

Q: Could you amplify, sir, on the meetings that are continuing tonight?

A: No, the only meeting is on the drafting of the communiqué.

Q: Mr. Secretary, then you leave Moscow without having achieved that general framework?

A: This is correct. I do leave it without having achieved that general framework, and I'm very disappointed that we were unable to do so.

Q: You said that the Soviets have put on the table a slightly modified version of the January 1976 proposal. Is that still on the table in their point of view?

A: Yes.

Q: We have two American proposals and a Soviet proposal?

A: That's correct.

Q: Mr. Secretary, do you think that today's failure will result in an acceleration of the arms race on the part of both countries?

A: I would certainly hope not. I think that this would be a tragedy if there should be an acceleration of the arms race. This would be in the interests of neither side, nor in the interests of peace.

[U.S.-Soviet Relations]

Q: You were saying that you thought relations were nevertheless good despite your inability to reach an agreement on SALT. I must say it seems to strain credibility, that statement. It would seem to, I think, most of us that the main topic here was SALT. There was a collapse in SALT negotiations. There seems to be no possible compromise on this and I would think that relations look worse than at any time in recent years. Where is the relation good, given the fact that on the central question there is absolutely no agreement?

A: Well, I think...that we have made, as I indicated earlier, progress in a number of other areas as outlined to you. The nature of the talks was at no time acrimonious or unbusinesslike. I think that the task remains before us to try and find a way to reach agreement in the state[d] area and we both should bend our efforts to that end.

Q: Mr. Secretary, could you help here on some physical things?

A: Yes, sure.

Q: How long did the meeting last?

A: You mean this afternoon? I think about an hour.

Q: Did Mr. Brezhnev—was he present all the time?

A: Yes, he was.

Q: Did he participate much in the discussions?

A: Yes, he did. He did all the talking.

Q: Mr. Secretary, what was the central reason—perhaps you might answer in some way—in this discussion that the Soviets gave you for their rejection of both proposals that the United States put forth?

A: It was their view that the deferral proposal did not accord with Vladivostok. It is our very clear view that it does accord with Vladivostok because Backfire and the cruise missile were not included in the Vladivostok accord. They remained unsettled issues, so that there was a difference of view between the Soviets and ourselves on that matter.

Q: Was there a central dispute, sir, on the difference between the two aides-mémoire out of Vladivostok, the one on ballistic missiles and the American version mentioning ballistic missiles and the Soviet version mentioning just missiles?

A: There was discussion of the aides-mémoire, yes.

Q: [Unintelligible words] sir, and tell us what their reason was for rejecting the comprehensive package, sir?

A: They really should speak to this themselves, but I will tell you that their indication is that they do not feel that, as they put it, that it is an equitable package. We believe that it is equitable and it does attack the central questions which are involved in seeking a real arms-control agreement.

Q: Is that proposal still on the table?

A: It is. All proposals are still on the table.

Q: Is it in your view negotiable after they have rejected the basic form, in general?

A: I would hope that as they reflect on it they will find merit in it, and we'll find a way to get back together again and start talking further.

Q: Sir, did you formally tell the Soviets that we also found their proposal unacceptable and could you tell us why we do find their proposal unacceptable?

A: The reason that we have found their proposal unacceptable is that it does not deal properly with the cruise missile issue.

Q: Did you discuss the possibility of extending your SALT I agreement?

A: We did not discuss that, no. Let's try a couple of more questions and then we'll go.

Q: Any indication that they would settle for a reduction of less deep than the one we proposed, a smaller reduction?

A: As I say, no counterproposals were made by them today.

Q: Mr. Secretary, was it suggested at all that at any time between now and, let's say, the next several months, that you would return to Moscow to continue to negotiate on this subject?

A: No, but as I indicated, Mr. Gromyko and I are going to be meeting in May and one of the subjects which will come up at that time will be the subject of strategic-arms limitations. Thank you very much.

CARTER PRESS CONFERENCE

THE PRESIDENT: Good afternoon.

This has been an afternoon devoted to receiving dispatches from Moscow, and I would like to make a report to the American people about what has occurred.

We have proposed to the Soviet leaders in the last two days a comprehensive package of agreements which, if concluded, will lay a permanent groundwork for a more peaceful world, an alleviation of the great threat of atomic weapons that will retain the political and strategic weapon capability and balance between the United States and the Soviet Union.

One of our proposals on this nuclear weapons talks was very brief and it was our second option. It was in effect to ratify the Vladivostok Agreement that had already been reached.

The difference between us and the Soviet Union on this point is that the Soviets claim that Secretary Kissinger and my predecessors in the White House—President Ford and earlier Nixon—did agree to forego the deployment of cruise missiles. Our position is that we have never agreed to any such thing. But we asked the Soviet Union to accept an agreement on all other matters and postpone the cruise missile and the Russians' new bomber, the Backfire Bomber, until continuing later discussions. They rejected that proposal.

The other one was much more far-reaching and has profound consequences that are beneficial, I think, to our own Nation and to the rest of the world. It was to have substantial reductions in the level of deployment of missile launchers and the MIRV missiles below the 2400 level and the 1320 level that were established under the Vladivostok Agreements—substantial reductions.

Secondly, to stop the development and deployment of any new weapons systems. A third point was to freeze at the present level about 550 intercontinental ballistic missiles, our Minuteman and their missiles known as the SS-17, -18, and -19.

Another was to ban the deployment of all mobile missiles, their SS-16 and others, or ours—that is under the development stage, the MX.

Another one is to have a strict limit on the deployment of the Backfire Bomber and a strict limit on the range that would be permitted on cruise missiles.

Another element of the proposal was to limit the number of test firings of missiles to six firings per year of the intercontinental range and also of the medium range missiles, and to ask the Soviet Union to give us some assured mechanism by which we could distinguish between their intercontinental mobile missile, the SS-16, and their limited range mobile missile, the SS-20.

The sum total of all of this proposal was a fair, balanced, substantial reduction in the arms race which would have guaranteed, I believe, a permanent lessening of tension and of mutual benefit to both our countries. The Soviets at least at this point have not accepted this proposal, either.

Both parties, which will be promulgated in a joint communiqué tomorrow, have agreed to continue the discussions the first half of May in Geneva.

You might be interested in knowing that a few other points that we proposed were to have adequate verification, an end of concealment and the establishment of a so-called data base by which we would tell the Soviet Union the level of our own armaments at this point and they would tell us their level of armaments at this point so we would have an assured mutually agreed level of weapon capability.

[Eight Study Groups]

I might cover just a few more things. In addition to discussing the SALT agreements in Geneva early in May, we have agreed to discuss other matters—South Africa, the upcoming possible Middle Eastern talks—and we have agreed to set up eight study groups, one to develop an agreement where we might forego the development of capability of destroying satellite observation vehicles so that we could have an assured way to watch the Soviets; they can have an assured way of watching us from satellite.

The second is to discuss the terms of a possible comprehensive test ban so that we don't test in the future any more nuclear weapons. And we have also asked the Soviets to join with us in a prohibition against testing of peaceful nuclear devices.

Another study group that has been mutually agreed to be established is to discuss the terms by which we might demilitarize or reduce the military effort in the Indian Ocean.

Another group will be set up of experts to discuss the terms by which we can agree on advanced notice on all missile test firings so that perhaps 24 hours ahead of time we would notify the Soviets when we were going to test fire one of our missiles, they would do the same for us.

Another group will be studying a way to initiate comprehensive arms control in conventional weapons to third countries, particularly the developing nations of the world.

Another is to discuss how we might contribute mutually toward non-proliferation of nuclear weapon capability. Nations do need a way to produce atomic power for electricity, but we hope that the Soviets will join with us and our allies and friends in cutting down the capability of nations to use spent nuclear fuels to develop explosives.

Another item that we agreed to discuss at the Soviets' request was the termination in the capability of waging radiological or chemical warfare.

And the eighth study group that we agreed to establish is to study the means by which we could mutually agree on foregoing major efforts in civil defense. We feel that the Soviets have done a great deal on civil defense capability. We have done less amount but we would like for both of us to agree not to expend large sums of money on this effort. So the sum total of the discussions has been to lay out a firm proposal which the Soviets have not yet responded to on drastic reductions in nuclear capability in the future—these discussions will continue early in May—and to set up study groups to continue with the analysis of the other eight items that I described to you.

I would be glad to answer a few questions.

Q: Mr. President, pardon me if I don't stand, but I will block the camera there.

Do you still believe that the Soviets in no way linked your human rights crusade with arms control negotiations?

[PRESIDENT CARTER]: I can't certify to you that there is no linkage in the Soviets' minds between the human rights effort and this SALT limitations. We have no evidence that this was the case.

Secretary Vance thought it was quite significant, for instance, that when General Secretary Brezhnev presented a prepared statement on the human rights issue that it was done in a different meeting entirely from the meeting in which the SALT negotiations occurred.

So our assessment is that there was no linkage, but I can't certify that there is no linkage in the Soviets' minds.

Q: Mr. President, you have said that the Soviets contend that Secretary Kissinger and your predecessors had promised that we would not deploy, I believe, the cruise missile.

A: Yes.

Q: Just where and how did they contend that this promise was given, and have you checked with them to see if in fact it was?

A: Yes. Both President Ford and Secretary Kissinger have maintained publicly and to me privately that there was never any agreement on the part of the United States to contain or to prohibit the deployment or development of cruise missiles.

[Vladivostok Agreement Language]

The language that was used in the early Vladivostok Agreement which, as you know, has not yet been ratified, was prohibition against air-launched missiles.

Secretary Kissinger's position has been—and he is much better able to speak than I am to speak for him—that that meant ballistic missiles, which was the subject of the Vladivostok Agreements.

Two and a half years ago when these talks took place, the cruise missile capability was not well-understood and there was no detailed discussion at all of the cruise missile. The Soviets claimed that when they did discuss air launch missiles that they were talking about cruise missiles.

Secretary Kissinger said he was not talking about cruise missiles.

Q: Sir, the point, just to follow, they are not contending there was any secret understanding or discussion or anything?

A: No.

Q: They are talking about the language in the Vladivostok Agreement?

A: Exactly.

Q: Did the Russians have a counter-proposal on SALT that they offered us, or were they content to listen to our proposals?

A: They listened to our two proposals. Of course, their proposal has been to ratify their understanding of the Vladivostok Agreement which includes their capability of developing the backfire bomber and our incapability of developing cruise missiles. That is an agreement that we never understood to be part of the Vladivostok Agreement.

[Human Rights Position]

Q: Mr. Carter, if necessary to achieve any progress, are you willing to modify your human rights statements?

A: No.

Q: Or will you continue to speak out?

A: No. I will not modify my human rights statements. My human rights statements are compatible with the consciousness of this country. I think that there has been repeated recognition in international law that verbal statements or any sort of public expression of a nation's beliefs is not an intrusion in other nations' affairs.

The Soviets have in effect ratified the rights of human beings when they adopted the United Nations' Charter. The Helsinki Agreement, which will be assessed at Belgrade later on this year, also includes references to human rights themselves. So I don't intend to modify my position. It is a position that I think accurately represents the attitude of this country.

I don't think it is accurate to link the human rights concept with the SALT negotiations. I think that is an incorrect linkage. The SALT negotiations, I hope, will be successful as we pursue in laborious detail those discussions the rest of this year. They will be successful only if the Soviets are convinced that it is to their advantage to forego a continued commitment and a very expensive commitment and a very threatening commitment to the arms race. And only if our own people believe that we derive the same advantage. That is what we hope for.

Q: Mr. President, how would you characterize what happened today? How serious a setback is this? Did we expect that the Soviets might be more receptive to our positions?

A: We had no indications either in direct or indirect communications with Brezhnev that they were ready to accept our positions. We carefully prepared over a period of five or six weeks what we thought was a balanced and what we still think is a balanced proposal with drastic reductions.

I might say that there is a unanimous agreement among the key Members of Congress, the State Department, my own staff, the Secretary of Defense, the Joint Chiefs, that this is a good and fair proposal. I have hoped that the substance of our proposal will be accepted by the Soviet Union in the future because it is to their advantage and ours to do so.

But I am not discouraged at all. Cy Vance sent back word that he was disappointed that we didn't reach immediate agreement, but he was not discouraged. I think the fact that a joint communiqué has been prepared and will be released tomorrow morning spelling out the fact that our nations will continue without interruption these discussions is very encouraging, also.

[Cruise Missile Restrictions]

Q: Mr. President, would it be fair to say that the talks broke down because the United States is now not prepared to accept restrictions on cruise missiles?

A: No.

Q: Isn't that the heart of it?

A: That is not the heart of it at all. We are prepared to accept restrictions on the cruise missile, if it is part of an overall balanced package. We are not prepared to accept a unilateral prohibition against the development of or deployment of the cruise missile absent some equivalent response from the Soviet Union including the Backfire Bomber. But we put together a package which was fair and balanced, but we are not prepared unilaterally to forego an opportunity unless it is equivalent to a Soviet Union response.

Q: I didn't mean unilaterally, but on the January 1976 trip by Secretary Kissinger to the Soviet Union there was active negotiation regarding a balanced reduction involving some limitations on cruise missiles.

So when you say, sir, that the Soviets say we agreed to restrict cruise missiles, aren't they referring to 1976 and not to Vladivostok when indeed the cruise missile was on the drawing board and not a real thing?

A: I don't believe that—I don't want to get myself into the position of speaking for Secretary Kissinger—there has never been an insinuation of American agreement that the Soviets could build and deploy the Backfire Bomber without limitation while we limited cruise missiles. That is the position that the Soviets adopted in the Vladivostok Agreement.

Q: Mr. President, have the Russians explained why they were turning down the comprehensive proposal? Was it because they didn't want such drastic reductions as you proposed or was it because they felt the limitations on cruise were not adequate? Did they give any reasons?

A: I do not know yet. I have not received a definitive analysis from Secretary Vance. He a few minutes ago was in the American Embassy in Moscow preparing for me a detailed report on what has occurred. So far as

I know, at this point, there were not any specific reasons given for the Soviets turning down our proposal.

My guess is that this proposal is so substantive and such a radical departure in putting strict limits and reductions on existing missiles and a prohibition against the development or deployment of new missiles in the future that the Soviets simply need more time to consider it.

Whether they will accept it or not, at the May meetings in Geneva or subsequently, I don't have any way to know yet.

Q: The May meetings are to be between Mr. Gromyko and Mr. Vance?

A: That is correct.

Q: Mr. President, Senator [Howard] Baker, just outside a few moments ago said that during your briefing of the Congressional leadership you said you intended to "hang tough." Did you say that and what did you mean by that?

A: Yes. I do. I think that it is important for us to take advantage of an opportunity this year to negotiate not just a superficial ratification of rules by which we can continue the arms race, but to have a freeze on deployment and development of new missiles and an actual reduction in launchers and MIRV missiles below what was agreed to previously.

On those items I intend to remain very strong in my position. I don't think it is to our Nation's advantage to put forward in piecemeal fashion additional proposals. Our experience in the past has been that the Soviet Union extracts from those comprehensive proposals those items that are favorable to them and want to continue to negotiate the other parts of the proposal that might not be so favorable to them.

So I do intend to continue strong negotiations to let the leaders of our country know what we are proposing, and I am not in any hurry. It is important enough to proceed methodically and carefully but I would hope that the Soviets will agree with us to drastic reductions and strict limitations in the future which have never been part of previous agreements.

Q: Mr. President, could I follow that?

A: Please.

Q: When you say you intend to continue negotiations, is there a chance that you might go to Geneva in May since you will already be in Europe in the early part of May?

A: As a matter of fact, I am already scheduled to go to Europe, not just to meet with the allies in London, but to meet with President Assad of Syria and where that meeting will be taking place I don't know. But I have no intentions at this time to meet with any Soviet leaders on that trip.

Q: Mr. President, how will this data base work? Will that include all conventional armaments as well?

A: That would be a separate matter of discussion. The data base has been for a long period of time a matter of dispute in the mutually balanced force reductions taking place in Vienna where we have asked the Soviets to give us an inventory of their arsenal among the Warsaw Pact nations. These are conventional weapons primarily.

[Nuclear Weapons Inventory]

But the data base to which I was referring this afternoon is an inventory of nuclear weapons that have been included in the SALT talks—the strategic nuclear weapons. So far we have a fairly good way on both sides of inventorying weapons that are actually deployed. But we would like to have a free and accurate exchange with the Soviet Union about how many weapons they have and how many we have so that we can monitor much more closely any deviations from those figures.

Q: If I could follow, would that include any kind of verification?

A: Yes. We would like to have the subject of verification opened up dramatically. For instance, in a comprehensive test ban we would like to have on-sight inspection. The Soviets have never agreed to this principle, but they have mentioned it a couple of times in the discussions. Foreign Minister Gromyko last year filed a statement at the United Nations that mentioned the possibility of on-sight inspection. But we feel the verification is a very crucial element in a comprehensive arms limitation agreement. Verification obviously includes an absence of concealment and verification to a lesser degree also includes the data base to which I just referred.

One more question.

Q: May I ask, please? Has the breakdown of these talks in any way influenced your thinking on development of future U.S. weaponry; that is, will you be now more inclined to go for full production of the B-1 or any other advanced weapon systems?

A: Obviously, if we feel at the conclusion of next month's discussions that the Soviets are not acting in good faith with us, and that an agreement is unlikely, then I would be forced to consider a much more deep commitment to the development and deployment of additional weapons. But I would like to forego that decision until I am convinced the Soviets are not acting in good faith. I hope they will....

Q: Mr. President, one question about the deep cuts. Because the Soviets seem to have more delivery systems today than we do, is there objection that they would have to destroy more weapons than we would have to if you did get those deep cuts?

A: Deep cuts would affect both of us about the same. Shallow cuts, say, from 2400 down to 2200 on launchers would affect the Soviets much more adversely than it would us. Part of our package involves the very heavy missiles, the SS-9, and SS-18 which now stand at a 308 level.

We included in our package a substantial reduction below that figure. I think that the details of our proposal would probably best be revealed later. I am a little constrained about the details because Secretary Vance and Mr. Gromyko still have agreements among themselves about revelations of the negotiations with which I am not yet familiar. But I think later on those exact figures can be made available.

Thank you.

THE PRESS: Thank you.

GROMYKO PRESS CONFERENCE

Andrei Gromyko, member of the Political Bureau of the Central Committee of the Communist Party of the Soviet Union and Foreign Minister of the USSR made the following statement.

In connection with the visit of U.S. Secretary of State Cyrus Vance in Moscow, rumors appeared abroad, chiefly in the United States, as well as all sorts of versions in regard to the outcome of the talks held.

It will be recalled that U.S. President Carter also made a statement without even waiting for the Secretary of State's arrival in Washington. I must say that the rumors do not accord with the actual state of affairs. What is more, some of them distort the actual situation and that is why there is need for appropriate explanations and clarifications from our side.

I believe that everyone of those present here guesses that one of the main questions discussed during the talks held by Leonid Brezhnev with U.S. Secretary of State Cyrus Vance and also during my own meetings with the Secretary of State, was the question of concluding a new agreement on the limitation of strategic arms, since the agreement now in force expires in October of this year.

[Vladivostok Accord]

What is the essence of the Vladivostok accord? For example, what is the essence of the main question which was considered? It would not be out of place to recall this.

Way back in Vladivostok, an accord was reached that the Soviet Union and the United States will each have 2,400 strategic arms carriers, including 1,320 MIRVs. This is the main content of the Vladivostok accord.

You know that there were many reports—both official and semiofficial—saying that there was progress after Vladivostok. There were also more moderate reports. But, in general, it is true that quite a few steps forward have been made. There were opportunities to bring things to completion. This, however, did not happen. Then all of a sudden the question arose of the so-called cruise missiles. What does this mean? There is hardly need to dwell on the technical aspect of the matter. They tried to prove that the Vladivostok accord did not refer to the cruise missiles, that these missiles, don't you see, are generally not subject to any limitations and that the Vladivostok accord concerns ballistic missiles only. We resolutely objected to this attempt. At Vladivostok the question was posed differently. No green light was given there to the cruise missiles. The question was posed thus—to achieve such an agreement that would shut off all channels of the strategic arms race and reduce the threat of nuclear war.

The United States of America and the Soviet Union exchanged relevant official documents which sealed the Vladivostok accords. Everything, it seemed, was clear and it remained to carry the matter forward to the signing of an agreement. Working on some of the questions, including the juridical wording of the agreement, were the delegations of the USSR and the USA at Geneva. At first, things were moving. But all of a sudden, a wall had risen and everything was frozen. Apparently somebody, some influential forces in the U.S., found all this not to their liking. And you know that great difficulties arose and these difficulties have not been removed. If one is to speak frankly, of late these difficulties have increased. What should we call this situation and this kind of position, which certain people in the United States began taking after Vladivostok? This is the line of revision, a line of revising the commitments taken in Vladivostok.

We are categorically opposed to this. We are all for the edifice that was built by such hard work in Vladivostok, an edifice on which such intellectual and other resources were spent, not only to be preserved, but that things should be brought to a conclusion and a new agreement on limiting strategic arms should be concluded between the USSR and the USA.

We were told, and it was said to us even in the last days when the talks were on in Moscow, that one of the obstacles is the Soviet Union's possession of a certain type of bomber (it is called "Backfire" in the United States) which, it was said, can be used as a strategic weapon and that this plane absolutely must be taken into consideration in the agreement. We categorically rejected it and continue rejecting such attempts. Time and again Leonid Brezhnev personally explained to President Ford, specifically during the meeting in Helsinki, and later to President Carter, that it concerns a medium-range bomber and not a strategic bomber. Nevertheless, this question was tossed at us once again. Somebody evidently needs to artificially create this additional obstacle. It is better known to the Americans at what level these obstacles are being created. We note that this question is being artificially introduced to complicate the situation along the road of concluding an agreement.

[Moscow Talks]

During the first talk with Mr. Vance, Leonid Brezhnev set forth our position on all the basic questions of limiting strategic arms and concluding a new agreement. In several public statements Leonid Brezhnev furthermore set forth the Soviet Union's policy on that question, underlining its readiness to work for this agreement. It was emphasized that this agreement accords with the interests of the United States and the Soviet Union, as well as with the interests of the whole world. Throughout the talks here in Moscow, our side emphasized the main idea that the foundation for a new agreement, that has been built up, should not be destroyed, but that it should be preserved at all cost.

And truly, what will happen if the arrival of a new leadership in some country will scrap all the constructive things that were achieved in relations with other countries? What stability in relations with other countries can be talked about in such a case? What stability can be talked about in relations between the USA and the USSR in this case? We, our side, would like to see precisely stability in our relations and that these relations should be as good as possible and based on the principles of peaceful coexistence and, even better, that they should be friendly. This is our stand and we would like to see similar actions in reply from the other side, that is the United States of America.

A version is now being circulated in the USA, alleging that the U.S. representatives at the Moscow talks proposed some broad program for disarmament, but that the Soviet leadership did not accept this program. I must say that this version does not accord with reality. This version is essentially false. Nobody proposed such a program to us.

I am dwelling on some facts from which you, certainly, will draw for yourselves some conclusions. For example, it is proposed to us now to reduce the total number of strategic arms carriers to 2,000 to even to 1,800 units, and MIRVs to 1,200-1,100. What is more, it is simultaneously proposed to liquidate half of those rockets in our possession which are simply disliked by somebody in the United States. They are described differently: sometimes "too heavy" or "excessively effective." They dislike these rockets and that is why the Soviet Union must be deprived of half of these weapons. So the question is whether such a unilateral way of putting the question is a way to agreement? No, it only damages the Vladivostok accord, breaks the balance of limitations concerning which agreement was reached in Vladivostok. What changed after Vladivostok? Nothing, absolutely nothing changed.

Call this as you like, but this is no way of solving problems. It is a way of piling one unresolved problem on another unresolved problem. Unfortunately, there are quite a few such problems as yet, especially if we take the broad area of the arms race. Here too, we are all for the accord earlier reached between the USA and the Soviet Union, being meticulously observed as it was intended when this accord was achieved.

Advancing such kind of proposals, attempts are made to depict them as all but "general and complete disarmament."

If one really was to speak of general and complete disarmament, the American president and the governments of the other NATO countries and the governments of all states of the world have before them a broad plan of general and complete disarmament with strict and effective control. Control, especially in the post-war period, has been mentioned a great deal. Broad control with the dispatch of foreign inspectors to other states, etc. We replied to all these statements: Yes, we are prepared to accept complete and general control, given general and complete disarmament. Well, was there any advance after this? No, there was no advance. There was an increase in the number of resolutions adopted by various UN agencies and at various international disarmament conferences, but this did not reduce the scope of the arms race.

Next, in the talks with Cyrus Vance it was suggested that we revise the right of the two sides to modernize existing missiles as laid down in the present agreement, just as in the Vladivostok accord. This was taken for granted. No problems arose here. But no, it is now proposed to break up the agreement also in this respect, and to do so in a way that would give advantages to the United States, with the Soviet Union finding itself in a worse position. Clearly, we shall not depart from the principle of equality also in this respect. And to put forward such demands is a dubious if not a cheap move.

One more fact. It was proposed to us to include in the agreement a clause prohibiting the development of new types of weapons. At a first glance, it would seem that there is nothing wrong with this. But I would like to recall that the Soviet Union itself has long ago made the proposal on banning the manufacture of new types and new systems of weapons of mass extermination. Moreover, we have submitted to the United Nations a draft of the relevant international treaty. And what was the response? Maybe the U.S. Government supported this treaty? No, it did not say a single word in support of this treaty.

Indeed, at the Moscow talks too, only the most general words were uttered to the effect that such a clause should be included into the agreement, in a "package" at that, or geared to other obviously unacceptable proposals. All this made a very dubious impression. If there is a serious intention in this matter then, as I have already said, there is a concrete proposal. At first, when we raised the question of banning new types of weapons we were asked: What do you have in mind? Can one really invent a new nuclear weapon? When we cited relevant facts, and they are known not only to us but also to scientists of other countries, the attitude to our proposal somewhat changed. That is why I cannot say that our proposal met with a negative attitude on the part of all other states. No. But unfortunately, it did not enlist support from the big states, from the USA.

[Soviet Draft Treaty]

Let us speak frankly. If both our countries stand for banning new types of weapons of mass extermination, then let us discuss the draft treaty we have. If you have amendments to the Soviet draft, put them forth. Let us discuss these amendments. If you have no amendments, then let us conclude this treaty. I repeat, our draft treaty is in the hands of the U.S. Government. And would it not be better to reply concretely to the question: Is the U.S. Government ready to sign such a treaty or is it not ready? And to attach this idea to other questions and to propose that all this be considered in the single "package" means to bury both the "package" and to bury the idea together with the "package." This, of course, is no new method. It has long been practiced by somebody. It seems to us that in international affairs in general, including relations between the USA and the Soviet Union, it would be better to examine relevant problems on a more realistic, or an honest basis. The more attempts there are to play a game in this matter, to tread on the foot of the partner, the more difficulties there will be. This will not promote an improvement in Soviet-American relations, the cause of detente, consolidation of peace. This should be said especially in connection with recent statements appearing in the United States in newspapers and, unfortunately, not only in newspapers.

[B-1 Bomber and Trident Submarine]

I should like to add a few more words. If the USA is prepared to ban new types of weapons, why then, is the need to produce the "B-1" strategic bomber, so beloved by some people in the USA, defended all that much. The same is true of the manufacture of the "Trident" atomic submarine. Leonid Brezhnev spoke of these new American weapons systems both in his public speeches and in his remarks during the official negotiations with the American side, and did so repeatedly. So what we have is that certain declarations by the American side do not tally with the actual readiness to ban new types of weapons of mass extermination.

One would rather not speak on this theme, but one has to. In his last statement, the President of the United States used the word "sincerity" when referring to the Soviet leaderships' attitude to questions of strategic arms limitation. I would like to say: We do not lack sincerity. We have plenty of it. It is on this basis that we are building all our policy and would want all to build their policies on the same basis, so that the deeds would not differ from the words.

U.S. representative Cyrus Vance described his proposals as the basis for a broad and all-encompassing agreement. But it is easy, after an objective study of these proposals, to draw the conclusion that they pursue the aim of getting unilateral advantages for the USA to the detriment of the Soviet Union, its security and the security of its friends and allies. The Soviet Union will never be able to agree to this. This was openly said by Leonid Brezhnev to the U.S. Secretary of State during the first talk. He said the same during the last talk which was held yesterday.

[U.S. "Narrow Proposal"]

Reading some of the statements made in the USA you probably noticed that not only what some people call all-encompassing proposals, but also an alternative "narrow proposal" has been made to us. But what is the essence of this "narrow proposal"? Here it is: We are simply told, let us conclude an agreement that will concern ballistic missiles and strategic bombers. At the same time, it is proposed to leave aside the cruise missiles and the Soviet bomber referred to as "Backfire" which, as I have already mentioned, is not strategic at all. It looks as if a concession is being made to us, but this is an extremely strange concession. We are offered what does not belong to the United States. A non-strategic aircraft was named a strategic one, and they say: We are ready not to include this bomber in the agreement now, if the Soviet Union consents to give a green light for the manufacture and deployment of the U.S. cruise missiles. So according to this narrower agreement, the cruise missiles would be totally excluded from an agreement. Such a decision would mean that, while plugging one gap—the ballistic missiles—a new gap, maybe an even wider and deeper one, would be simultaneously opening—nuclear weapons carriers.

I stress nuclear weapons carriers. But it is our objective to prevent an outbreak of a nuclear war, to deliver mankind from nuclear war. Is it not the same for a human being to die of a weapon from a cruise missile, as from a weapon from a ballistic missile. The result is the same. Apart from it, the manufacture of cruise missiles will swallow up no less funds, dollars, pounds, sterling, rubles, francs, lire, etc. Do people stand to gain from it? One cannot help asking what such an agreement will give for security? And is it going to be security in general? No, it will not be security, which peoples sincerely want. It will not even be a semblance of security. That is why we rejected, frankly speaking, this so-called narrow agreement too. We declared that it does not present a solution to the problem and does not even come close to solving this problem. This is what the U.S. Secretary of State took back when he left Moscow.

["Distorted" Account of Talks]

We do not know how all this will be presented to public opinion in the USA. Judging by the first symptoms, the actual state of things is distorted. The results of the exchange of opinions and the statements that were made to the U.S. Secretary of State were also distorted. Leonid Brezhnev's statements were distorted too.

All this does not help towards a productive solution of problems, though we would sincerely wish so. But we are ready to continue talks on all these problems. The Soviet leaders have enough patience. We would like the discussions, regardless of where they are held—here in Moscow, in Washington or in other places—to finally come to a favorable conclusion.

Leonid Brezhnev strongly emphasized: We firmly stand for good relations with the United States just as with other countries in the world. We stand for relations based on the principles of peaceful coexistence, for friendly relations. And the possibilities for it are far from having been exhausted. They have not been exhausted because the point at issue is the United States and the Soviet Union.

We do not intend to belittle the substantial differences that now exist between the stands of the USA and the Soviet Union. The Secretary of State was told about it frankly. But does this mean that there are insurmountable obstacles? No, it does not. We would like to express the hope that the leadership of the United States will take up a more realistic stand, that it will give greater consideration to the interests of the security of the Soviet Union and its allies and will not strive for unilateral advantages.

I would like to touch upon one more problem. It is the question of military budgets. Our Central Committee, the Supreme Soviet, the Soviet Government and Leonid Brezhnev, personally, many times put forward the question of a cut in military budgets in their public statements, in confidential talks with the leaders of the countries concerned belonging to the other social system. We have also tabled this proposal for discussion by all states of the world. And, like the proposal on a ban on the manufacture of new types of mass destruction weapons, this proposal has also met with wide support. Regrettably, we see how the budgets of some states, the USA included, crawl up and follow the ascending line. It is a broad subject, and I would not want to go deep into it, but I would want to give every emphasis to the fact that military budgets must be reduced and the funds in question be rechanneled to peaceful purposes.

[Recent Soviet Proposals]

I will not give you the full list of the proposals that have been tabled by the Soviet Union in recent years for consideration by the international organizations concerned, for consideration by other governments, the proposals that are [aimed] at an easing of tension, at ensuring peace, at disarmament, at improving relations among states. This list includes more than 70 such proposals. I will only name some of them in order to put things into their right places, to restore the truth and refute the falsehood which has been, with persistence, spread recently by some newspapers abroad and some political figures, saying that the Soviet Union is allegedly responsible for spurring on the arms race. It was as far back as 1946, right after the war, that the Soviet Union tabled a proposal on concluding a convention banning the use of nuclear energy for military purposes. And who tabled the proposal on nonproliferation of nuclear weapons? The Soviet Union, the Soviet state did and not the country which today declares itself to be almost an advocate of general and complete disarmament.

Such a treaty has been concluded. But regrettably, not all the states have acceded to it. This is bad.

It was on the Soviet Union's initiative that the Moscow treaty banning nuclear weapon tests in three elements was concluded. Moreover, we tabled a proposal on general and complete prohibition of nuclear weapons tests. This proposal has met with most wide support in the United Nations organization. Do you think the United States has supported our proposal? No, it has not. It is even today on the table of the governments concerned. If the administration of the United States and its allies want to do a good thing, they must, in accordance with the will of an overwhelming majority of states, conclude an all-encompassing agreement on a full ban on nuclear weapons tests. We will actively carry on the struggle for a positive solution to this question.

Our country has tabled a proposal on the prohibition of modification of the natural environment for military purposes. I must note here that the USA has, in general, acceded to this proposal, although some provisions of our draft treaty were weakened by them, which arouses dissatisfaction among a number of states. But nevertheless, the general, ultimate outcome is a positive one, and an international convention to this effect will probably be signed soon.

Take the proposal to ban the bacteriological weapon. Who tabled this proposal? Maybe those who declare now that it is precisely they who are advocates of a radical disarmament and curbing the arms race? No, this proposal has also been put forward by the Soviet Union. We place on record, with satisfaction, that a relevant agreement has been concluded.

We have also tabled a proposal on nonuse of force in international relations. Although an overwhelming majority of states of the world have voted for this proposal of the Soviet Union, some individual countries, without which it is impossible to make this agreement effective, show a sharply negative attitude to it until now. What reasons are advanced against this proposal? They say that there is the UN Charter, which already deals with it. To this I will answer: The Charter is the general trend, but of importance is not only the general trend, but the practical policy of governments. Therefore, the conclusion of such an agreement that we are proposing means a big step forward, and we would like to express the hope that the administration of the United States and its allies will take into consideration the opinion of a majority of the states of the world, and that, in the long run, this idea will materialize in the form of an international agreement.

Not so long ago, during the session of the Political Consultative Committee in Bucharest, the Warsaw Treaty member-states jointly proposed that the participating countries of the All-European Conference take commitments not to be the first to use nuclear weapons one against the other. One cannot help asking: Is there anything bad in that proposal?

[And] if nuclear weapons are not used first, there will be no state that would be second and, consequently, third, fourth and fifth to use it. This would mean a removal of the threat of a nuclear war. It is one of the most effective proposals aimed at a strengthening of peace and easing of tension.

The NATO member-states, however, without any particular discussions, although they say there was a difference of views, declared their negative attitude to this proposal. We do not regard the discussion of this matter to be over. This question may not officially be on the agenda of NATO, but it remains in life, and it will be discussed until the problem of nonuse of nuclear energy for military purposes is resolved.

We stand for the United States joining more effectively and more actively in a positive solution of relevant problems. We are trying to convince the United States, and our explanations today are aimed precisely at it.

The Soviet Union is pursuing a consistent policy of peace, the easing of international tension, the policy of curbing the nuclear arms race, the policy of disarmament. It is a Leninist peace-loving policy. You heard about it from the rostrums of our Party congresses, the Plenary Meetings of the Party Central Committee. It is our basic line and we will pursue it persistently and nobody will be able to sidetrack us from this road. But we will also give a rebuff to those who are trying to mend their affairs to the detriment of our interests, the interests of our friends and allies.

It is precisely on such a just basis that we are dealing and would like to further deal with the United States.

Do not think that the critical remarks addressed to the USA, in particular in connection with the question of strategic arms, diminish to some degree our wish to see the relations between the USA and the Soviet Union to be good, and what is even better—friendly. But this does not depend only on us. We will be covering and will cover our part of the way. But there is also the other part of the way that must be covered by the United States. I would like to believe that they will cover their part of the way.

I shall touch on two more questions. Some people pretend that they are not directly concerned with the problem that was discussed as the basic one during the stay of the U.S. Secretary of State in Moscow. But it is far from being so.

I would like to formulate the first question thus: This is the question of not handing strategic weapons over to third countries and of taking no actions whatever to evade the agreement, the signing of which we are now concerned. On this question we formulated a concrete proposal. It was discussed. At any rate, we put it forward in Geneva in the course of the talks between the U.S. and Soviet delegations. But our representatives as a matter of fact received no substantive reply.

We attach no small importance to the solution of this matter.

[U.S. Nuclear Weapons in Europe]

The second question is about the advance deployment of U.S. nuclear weapons in Europe, around Europe and in other areas, from where the Soviet territory is within reach. In concluding the first agreement on the limitation of strategic weapons we made official statements to the effect that we must return to this question. In the interests of reaching an agreement, we did not propose in Vladivostok that the provision of liquidation of U.S. nuclear weapons of advance deployment be included into an agreement as a compulsory term. But now we have a different view of this issue in the light of the latest U.S. proposals. This is a matter of our security and the security of our allies. We are entitled to pose the question of liquidating U.S. advance deployment means. This concerns atomic powered submarines, bombers capable of carrying nuclear weapons and aircraft carriers in the corresponding region of Europe (you well know which region is meant). Call it what you may: a toughening of position, a change of position. But I have to say it again: This question now faces us in connection with the latest U.S. proposals.

In conclusion of my statement, I would like to stress that we are invariably loyal in our peace policy and will unswervingly pursue this policy. It is the policy of our Party, its Central Committee and the policy of the whole Soviet people. It was spoken of on many occasions by Leonid Brezhnev in his speeches from the rostrum of the Central Committee and in many other speeches, including those in Tula and at the recent Congress of Trade Unions.

But we will never cede our legitimate interests and our security. We can do business only on the basis of equality, including the transaction of business with the United States of America, with no damage to our legitimate interests. If the other side does the same, I think that both sides can look into the future with optimism.

We have a preliminary understanding about a meeting of foreign ministers of the two countries in Geneva. I think we will have plenty to talk about.

[Questions from the Press]

Q: What can you say about the statements from the White House that, in case of a failure of the talks on the limitation of strategic arms, the USA will create and deploy new strategic weapons?

[GROMYKO]: I can say only one thing: If anyone takes this road, he would assume the whole responsibility for the consequences of such actions.

In our opinion, every effort must be made to curb the arms race, to achieve positive results in the talks.

Q: What other questions of arms limitation and disarmament were examined during the talks with Cyrus Vance and what is the USSR's stand on this score?

A: I gave a sufficiently full list of questions that were examined. I can only add, concerning some issues that remain open at the present time—and the USA has objections on most of them—we agreed that our representatives will evidently have to meet, and maybe more than once in order to remove the existing disagreements. Such meetings can prove to be useful. This is a positive side of Cyrus Vance's visit.

Q: Does the line by the U.S. President on the question of "human rights" affect resolving of the strategic arms problem?

Don't you think that the campaign being waged in the USA by certain circles on the far fetched "human rights" question is a deliberate building up of tension?

A: The second question helps me to answer the first one. I will not say that, in discussing any aspect of the problems of preparing a new agreement on the limitation of strategic arms, we talked about "rights". Of course not. But the thing is that all that is lately said in the USA about "human rights," and those present here know what and how much is said on this subject there, naturally poisons the atmosphere and aggravates the political climate. But does this help to solve other issues, including those related to strategic arms? No, it does not. On the contrary, it hinders it. And speaking on the essence of the matter, I would like to say as follows: We do not claim to be teachers of anybody since the domestic affairs of states are concerned and only the states themselves can decide on their domestic affairs. I stress "domestic affairs." But we will not allow anybody to assume the pose of teachers and decide how to solve our internal affairs, I stress "our internal affairs."

I shall recall the documents which were exchanged in 1933 by President Roosevelt and the then USSR Minister of Foreign Affairs Litvinov on the establishment of normal diplomatic relations between the Soviet Union and the United States. It clearly says that one of the basic conditions for a normalization of relations between the USA and the Soviet Union is non-interference in the internal affairs of each other. This, by the way, was placed on record on the initiative of the U.S. side. This does not mean that we would not have proposed it ourselves. If this principle was right then, it is right today too. The tenet about noninterference in the internal affairs of states is an integral part of the general line in our Leninist foreign policy. We shall not retreat from it. No noise, howling or screeching will sidetrack us from this road. We shall follow our own road and need no aid of the teachers, of whom I have just spoken.

Q: What do you think about the sale of arms and military technology by the great powers to the developing countries?

A: I would like to note in the first place that U.S. President Carter himself said that the United States is No. 1 supplier of arms to other countries. A lot of U.S., Soviet and other countries' arms are traveling in the world at the present time. Why? Because there are many seats of tension and there are many places in which people are waging a legitimate struggle either for the liberation of their territory, as is the case in the Middle East, or for their other inalienable rights. Where is the sage or the sages who, under the situation existing today, can solve the question of stopping the arms trade, while leaving aside the solution of problems that create seats of tension? If this question means anything, it means that an effort should be made to solve these problems.

Take Rhodesia for example. There, twenty-four out of every twenty-five people are black Africans and only one is white. Who must wield power in that country? I think that the answer is clear from these figures. I would expand on this idea. What order that country would have must be decided by the people itself, not by outside forces, not by some instructors and not by all kinds of persons who like to travel about and teach the peoples how they should arrange their internal affairs.

[Geneva Agenda]

Q: Could you say in greater detail about the purpose of your possible meeting with the U.S. Secretary of State in Geneva in May?

A: We agreed to discuss in detail and meticulously the Middle East problem. I must say in passing that Cyrus Vance and the U.S. Government stressed the role of the two powers, as cochairmen of the Geneva Conference, in settling this problem. I mentioned in my statement that we do not rule out the emergence by that time of questions on which an exchange of views may take place.

Q: Can you say what was, in your view, the use of the meeting with the U.S. Secretary of State Mr. Vance, meaning the use for a better understanding between the USSR and the USA?

A: I would answer the question as follows: The visit of the Secretary of State was necessary and indeed useful because we must know each other well. I mean not a superficial acquaintance, but the knowledge of positions, the knowledge of the policies of the countries on the problems concerned. We also diverge on questions, and important questions they are. I have already spoken about it and I don't think that there is a necessity to repeat it. Some agreement was reached to continue discussions of unsolved matters, on which we could not find a common language with the USA. An exchange of views may be held, not necessarily at a high level, but, say, at the level of experts, counsellors. Then we will be able to see where we stand. We hope that the U.S. side will show a serious attitude to these efforts. On our part we guarantee this.

Q: Were any exceptions made with regard to cruise missiles in the Vladivostok accord?

A: No, there were not.

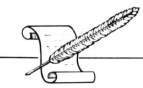
April

CARTER NUCLEAR POLICY
April 7, 27, 1977

President Jimmy Carter April 7 and 27 outlined a nuclear power policy for the United States and proposed legislation designed to halt nuclear proliferation. The President hoped to secure the establishment of adequate safeguards to ensure that nations used nuclear technology for peaceful purposes and not to make atomic weapons. (Historic Documents of 1975, p. 361)

Carter's policy declaration may have marked an historic turning point in American nuclear power development. The President deferred "indefinitely commercial reprocessing of plutonium used in the U.S. nuclear power programs." He said: "The benefits of nuclear power are very real and practical. But a serious risk accompanies worldwide use of nuclear power—the risk that components of the nuclear process will be turned to providing weapons."

In his message, Carter also stressed the need to:
● Redirect the U.S. breeder-reactor program to emphasize research on reactors that did not produce weapons grade material;
● Direct the funding of research for programs involving non-weapons grade fuel;
● Increase production of enriched uranium, the fuel used in conventional power plants, to meet domestic and foreign nuclear power needs;
● Guarantee other nations a nuclear fuel supply so they would not build their own nuclear fuel producing and reprocessing plants;
● Continue the U.S. embargo on the exportation of equipment and technology that permitted uranium enrichment and chemical reprocessing;

● *Press other nations to cooperate in meeting world energy needs and in curbing nuclear fuel and weapons proliferation.*

Plutonium Policy

Plutonium is a highly radioactive by-product of nuclear fission. Conventional nuclear reactors which generate electricity have been fueled by uranium, an expensive and scarce commodity. Once the uranium is burned, it can be chemically reprocessed to separate out plutonium. For decades American scientists and public policymakers had been committed to a next generation of nuclear reactors fueled by plutonium that, once activated, would generate more plutonium than they consumed. Such reactors, long hailed as the world's answer to future energy supply problems, are known as "breeder" reactors. The problem has been that plutonium is the key ingredient in atomic weapons.

Carter's decision on reactors fueled by plutonium collided with the nuclear power plans of other nations. Great Britain, France and West Germany had placed heavy reliance on breeder reactor development as a solution to their mounting energy needs. Carter underscored his determination to keep the United States out of the plutonium business when he vetoed legislation Nov. 5 authorizing funds to continue work on a plutonium-producing breeder reactor at Clinch River, Tenn. However, another showdown on the Clinch River prototype breeder was expected in 1978, when Congress was to take up the conference version of a supplemental appropriations bill that contained funds for the project.

Nuclear Proliferation

President Carter submitted legislation to Congress April 27 to grant him authority to tighten controls on nations using U.S. nuclear fuel and equipment and to withhold nuclear materials from nations that used U.S. nuclear fuels and technology to make atomic weapons. Carter called the need to halt nuclear proliferation "one of mankind's most pressing challenges."

Carter's bill prevented the export of nuclear material until the executive branch notified the Nuclear Regulatory Commission that the sale would not be inimical to common defense and national security. The tough legislation reflected the United States' considerable leverage in the international bargaining over nonproliferation of nuclear weapons. Many nations using U.S. technology depended on the United States for supplies of enriched uranium fuel.

Responding to President Carter's efforts to limit the spread of nuclear weapons, the House of Representatives Sept. 28 overwhelmingly approved legislation placing strict controls on the export of nuclear fuels and technology. The vote was 411-0. In the Senate, legislation was reported out of committee but there was no floor action on the measure in 1977.

Other Initiatives

U.S. initiatives led to further efforts to control the export of nuclear technology. Representatives of 15 supplier nations attending the Conference of Atomic Energy Suppliers in London agreed Sept. 21 to require strict safety controls from their customers before exporting additional nuclear technology.

President Carter in an Oct. 19 speech proposed the establishment of an international nuclear fuel repository as a way to lessen the chance of the further spread of nuclear weapons. He told the International Fuel Cycle Evaluation Conference that creation of an assured supply of enriched uranium would encourage energy-short nations to avoid development of fuel reprocessing and fast breeder technologies.

Following are the texts of Carter's April 7, 1977, statement on the use of plutonium in the U.S. nuclear power development program, and his April 27, 1977, message to Congress proposing safeguards to be followed by the U.S. nuclear technology and materials exporters. (Boldface headings in brackets have been added by Congressional Quarterly to highlight the organization of the text.):

NUCLEAR POWER POLICY TEXT

There is no dilemma today more difficult to resolve than that connected with the use of nuclear power. Many countries see nuclear power as the only real opportunity, at least in this century, to reduce the dependence of their economic well-being on foreign oil—an energy source of uncertain availability, growing price, and ultimate exhaustion. The U.S., by contrast, has a major domestic energy source—coal—but its use is not without penalties and our plans also call for the use of nuclear power as a share in our energy production.

The benefits of nuclear power are thus very real and practical. But a serious risk accompanies world-wide use of nuclear power—the risk that components of the nuclear power process will be turned to providing atomic weapons.

We took an important step in reducing the risk of expanding possession of atomic weapons through the Non-Proliferation Treaty, whereby more than 100 nations have agreed not to develop such explosives. But we must go further. The U.S. is deeply concerned about the consequences for all nations of a further spread of nuclear weapons or explosive capabilities. We believe that these risks would be vastly increased by the further spread of sensitive technologies which entail direct access to plutonium, highly enriched uranium or other weapons useable material. The question I have had under review from my first day in office is how can that be accomplished without foregoing the tangible benefits of nuclear power.

We are now completing an extremely thorough review of all the issues that bear on the use of nuclear power. We have concluded that the serious consequences of proliferation and direct implications for peace and security—as well as strong scientific and economic evidence—require:

● a major change in U.S. domestic nuclear energy policies and programs; and

● a concerted effort among all nations to find better answers to the problems and risks accompanying the increased use of nuclear power.

Presidential Decisions

I am announcing today some of my decisions resulting from that review.

First, we will defer indefinitely the commercial reprocessing and recycling of the plutonium produced in the U.S. nuclear power programs. From our own experience we have concluded that a viable and economic nuclear power program can be sustained without such reprocessing and recycling. The plant at Barnwell, South Carolina, will receive neither federal encouragement nor funding for its completion as a reprocessing facility.

Second, we will restructure the U.S. breeder reactor program to give greater priority to alternative designs of the breeder, and to defer the date when breeder reactors would be put into commercial use.

Third, we will redirect funding of U.S. nuclear research and development programs to accelerate our research into alternative nuclear fuel cycles which do not involve direct access to materials useable in nuclear weapons.

Fourth, we will increase U.S. production capacity for enriched uranium to provide adequate and timely supply of nuclear fuels for domestic and foreign needs.

Fifth, we will propose the necessary legislative steps to permit the U.S. to offer nuclear fuel supply contracts and guarantee delivery of such nuclear fuel to other countries.

Sixth, we will continue to embargo the export of equipment or technology that would permit uranium enrichment and chemical reprocessing.

Seventh, we will continue discussions with supplying and recipient countries alike, of a wide range of international approaches and frameworks that will permit all nations to achieve their energy objectives while reducing the spread of nuclear explosive capability. Among other things, we will explore the establishment of an international nuclear fuel cycle evaluation program aimed at developing alternative fuel cycles and a variety of international and U.S. measures to assure access to nuclear fuel supplies and spent fuel storage for nations sharing common non-proliferation objectives.

We will continue to consult very closely with a number of governments regarding the most desirable multilateral and bilateral arrangements for assuring that nuclear energy is creatively harnessed for peaceful economic purposes. Our intent is to develop wider international cooperation in regard to this vital issue through systematic and thorough international consultations.

NUCLEAR NONPROLIFERATION POLICY

To the Congress of the United States:

The need to halt nuclear proliferation is one of mankind's most pressing challenges. Members of my Administration are now engaged in international discussions to find ways of controlling the spread of nuclear explosive capability without depriving any nation of the means to satisfy its energy needs. The domestic nuclear policies which I have already put forward will place our nation in a leadership position, setting a positive example for other nuclear suppliers as well as demonstrating the strength of our concern here at home for the hazards of a plutonium economy. Today I am submitting to the Congress a bill which would establish for the United States a strong and effective non-proliferation policy.

This bill relies heavily upon work which the Congress has already done, and I commend the Congress for these valuable initiatives. I look forward to working with the Congress to establish a strong, responsible legislative framework from which we can continue strengthened efforts to halt the spread of nuclear weapons.

Among our shared goals are: an increase in the effectiveness of international safeguards and controls on peaceful nuclear activities to prevent further proliferation of nuclear explosive devices, the establishment of common international sanctions to prevent such proliferation, an effort to encourage nations which have not ratified the Non-Proliferation Treaty to do so at the earliest possible date, and adoption of programs to enhance the reliability of the United States as a supplier of nuclear fuel.

This bill differs from pending proposals, however, in several respects:

1. It defines the immediate nuclear export conditions which we can reasonably ask other nations to meet while we negotiate stricter arrangements. The proposals currently before Congress would impose criteria that could force an immediate moratorium on our nuclear exports, adversely affecting certain allies whose cooperation is needed if we are to achieve our ultimate objective of non-proliferation.

2. It defines additional nuclear export conditions which will be required in new agreements for civil nuclear cooperation. In particular, we will require as a continuing condition of U.S. supply that recipients have

all their nuclear activities under IAEA [International Atomic Energy Agency] safeguards. I view this as an interim measure and shall make it clear to all potential recipients and to other nuclear suppliers that our first preference, and continuing objective, is universal adherence to the Non-Proliferation Treaty.

3. For the near future, it attempts to tighten the conditions for U.S. nuclear cooperation through renegotiation of existing agreements to meet the same standards as those we will require in new agreements. I believe that this approach will better meet our non-proliferation objectives than will the unilateral imposition of new export licensing conditions.

4. It increases the flexibility we need to deal with an extremely complex subject. For example, instead of requiring countries that want our nuclear exports to foreswear fuel enrichment and reprocessing for all time, it allows us to draft new agreements using incentives to encourage countries not to acquire such facilities. It also permits me to grant exceptions when doing so would further our basic aim of non-proliferation. All new cooperation agreements would, of course, be subject to Congressional review.

This bill is intended to reassure other nations that the United States will be a reliable supplier of nuclear fuel and equipment for those who genuinely share our desire for non-proliferation. It will insure that when all statutory standards have been met, export licenses will be issued—or, if the judgment of the Executive Branch and the independent Nuclear Regulatory Commission should differ, that a workable mechanism exists for resolving the dispute.

Since I intend personally to oversee Executive Branch actions affecting non-proliferation, I do not think a substantial reorganization of the responsibility for nuclear exports within the Executive Branch is necessary. This conclusion is shared by the Nuclear Regulatory Commission.

The need for prompt action is great. Until domestic legislation is enacted, other countries will be reluctant to renegotiate their agreements with us, because they will fear that new legislation might suddenly change the terms of cooperation. If the incentives we offer them to renegotiate with us are not attractive enough, the United States could lose important existing safeguards and controls. And if our policy is too weak, we could find ourselves powerless to restrain a deadly world-wide expansion of nuclear explosive capability. I believe the legislation now submitted to you strikes the necessary balance.

JIMMY CARTER

The White House
April 27, 1977

CARTER ENERGY PROGRAM
April 18, 20, 1977

Early in his administration, President Jimmy Carter proposed a far-reaching national energy policy designed to conserve dwindling supplies of fuel. In a speech to a joint session of Congress, in other nationally televised speeches and in news conferences, the President pounded away at his theme that the time had come for Americans to draw limits on their prodigious use of the world's energy resources. He asserted that energy was "the most important domestic issue that we will face while I am in office."

Carter fired the opening salvos of his campaign for conservation in a televised speech delivered from the White House April 18. He warned that the United States faced a possible "national catastrophe" unless it waged the "moral equivalent of war" against the specter of crippling energy shortages. Two days later, on April 20, the President delivered another barrage in a televised speech to Congress. In it, he proposed a comprehensive energy plan that would increase the cost of fuels, penalize wasteful consumption of oil and natural gas and bring about important changes in the ways Americans live. Fashioning the new energy policy, he told Congress, was "a thankless job, but it is our job."

By the end of 1977, the President's goal of having an acceptable energy package enacted quickly had not been achieved and it appeared that, at best, energy legislation would not be passed until early in 1978. Some observers thought that contributing to the slow pace of legislative activity on the energy proposals was inattention and ineptitude on the part of the White House itself. President Carter acknowledged in October that he might have done a more effective job of advancing his program in the

Senate. After winning an early success in the House of Representatives, which approved the bulk of the President's recommendations, the administration faced senators with intense beliefs about such issues as the price of natural gas. But underlying the delay seemed to be a simple lack of public and political support for legislation which would change basic patterns in the American way of life. For all the President's rhetoric, his energy program commanded little public enthusiasm in 1977.

Conservation and Sacrifice

The President's approach to the energy crisis emphasized conservation and sacrifice on the part of every sector of the economy and every segment of the population. Tax rebates for the individual consumer and the tax credits for industry built into the Carter plan were intended to cushion the blow of higher energy costs. While encouraging voluntary cooperation to implement the program, the President acknowledged that some coercive measures would be necessary to prevent the depletion of oil and natural gas. "The heart of our energy problem is that our demand for fuel keeps rising more quickly than our production," Carter told Congress, "and our primary means of solving this problem is to reduce waste and inefficiency."

The major components of Carter's energy package had been discussed in the energy conscious 93rd and 94th Congresses but no comprehensive plan of action had emerged from their deliberations. Presidents Nixon and Ford proposed energy plans that called for the United States to achieve "energy independence" by deregulating U.S. oil prices to stimulate production. (Historic Documents of 1973, p. 913; 1975, p. 3) But both Nixon and Ford avoided mandatory measures to enforce energy conservation. Oil consumption continued to rise and domestic production declined until the United States was relying on a higher percentage of imported oil for its needs in 1977 than it had at the time of the Arab oil embargo in 1973.

Highlights of Proposals

President Carter's energy program contained these principal elements:

● A new gasoline tax beginning Jan. 15, 1979, that could escalate from five cents per gallon in the first year to 50 cents a gallon after 10 years if Americans failed to reduce consumption in accordance with an established federal timetable. Funds collected from the tax would be rebated to the American people.

● A "gas guzzler" tax starting with model year 1978 cars and light trucks. By 1985, vehicles exceeding federal fuel consumption standards would pay a tax of up to $2,488 per year; fuel efficient cars would earn rebates of up to $493.

● United States crude oil would be taxed at the wellhead. This "equalization" tax would raise U.S. crude oil prices to world market levels by 1980 and thus stimulate domestic crude oil production. Oil tax funds would be rebated to the public.

• *Federal control over the sale of natural gas would be extended to the intrastate sale of gas for all new gas production. The higher priced "new" gas would be sold for industrial use. The cheaper "old" gas remaining under existing controls would be reserved for residential and commercial users.*

• *Taxes would be levied on industries burning gas or oil for boiler fuel to encourage a shift to coal. Coal would be the required fuel source in new plants. Tax credits would offset conversion costs for existing plants that shift to coal.*

• *Enriched uranium production would be expanded. Licensing for conventional reactors would be speeded up.*

• *Tax credits of up to $2,000 would be offered for the home installation of solar heating equipment. Tax credits would be extended to homeowners who installed energy saving items such as home insulation, storm windows and weather stripping.*

Oil Companies

The President, at a nationally televised news conference on Oct. 13, tried to breathe new life into his energy program by identifying the petroleum lobby as the major source of opposition to his programs. "...[A]s is the case in time of war," Carter said, "there is potential war profiteering in the impending energy crisis. This could develop with the passing months as the biggest ripoff in history.... The package...ensured that the oil companies get enough incentive to ensure adequate exploration and production. But the oil companies apparently want it all. And we are talking about enormous amounts of money." Figures that the President projected at his news conference were challenged by the oil companies.

Carter applied further pressure, but in a markedly lower key, in a televised address on Nov. 8. Notably conciliatory toward Congress, he said, "The choices facing the members of Congress are not easy.... [T]hey will need your support and understanding." He pledged, however, to veto final energy legislation unless it met three broad tests. The bills, he said, must be fair to both consumers and producers. They must be effective in encouraging conservation, conversion away from oil and gas, and production. And they must not place "any unreasonable financial burden" on the federal budget.

Following are the prepared texts of President Carter's televised speech delivered from the White House April 18, 1977, outlining the critical nature of the energy crisis, and his address to a joint session of Congress April 20, 1977, recommending legislation to deal with the issue. (Boldface headings in brackets have been added by Congressional Quarterly to highlight the organization of the text.):

ENERGY BROADCAST TEXT

Tonight I want to have an unpleasant talk with you about a problem unprecedented in our history. With the exception of preventing war, this is the greatest challenge our country will face during our lifetimes. The energy crisis has not yet overwhelmed us, but it will if we do not act quickly.

It's a problem we will not solve in the next few years, and it is likely to get progressively worse through the rest of this century.

We must not be selfish or timid if we hope to have a decent world for our children and grandchildren. We simply must balance our demand for energy with our rapidly shrinking resources. By acting now we can control our future instead of letting the future control us.

Two days from now, I will present to the Congress my energy proposals. Its members will be my partners and they have already given me a great deal of valuable advice.

Many of these proposals will be unpopular. Some will cause you to put up with inconveniences and to make sacrifices. The most important thing about these proposals is that the alternative may be a national catastrophe. Further delay can affect our strength and our power as a nation.

Our decision about energy will test the character of the American people and the ability of the President and the Congress to govern this nation. This difficult effort will be the "moral equivalent of war"—except that we will be uniting our efforts to build and not to destroy.

[Public Skepticism]

I know that some of you may doubt that we face real energy shortages. The 1973 gas lines are gone, and with the springtime weather our homes are warm again.

But our energy problem is worse tonight than it was in 1973 or a few weeks ago in the dead of winter. It is worse because more waste has occurred, and more time has passed by without our planning for the future. And it will get worse every day until we act.

The oil and natural gas we rely on for 75 per cent of our energy are simply running out. In spite of increased effort, domestic production has been dropping steadily at about 6 per cent a year. Imports have doubled in the last five years. And our nation's independence of economic and political action is becoming increasingly constrained. Unless profound changes are made to lower oil consumption, we now believe that early in the 1980s the world will be demanding more oil than it can produce.

The world now uses about 60 million barrels of oil a day, and demand increases each year about 5 per cent. This means that just to stay even we need the production of a new Texas every year, an Alaskan North Slope every nine months, or a new Saudi Arabia every three years. Obviously this cannot continue.

We must look back into history to understand our energy problem. Twice in the last several hundred years there has been a transition in the way people use energy. The first was about 200 years ago, when we changed away from wood—which had provided about 90 per cent of all fuel—to coal, which was more efficient. This change became the basis of the Industrial Revolution.

The second change took place in this century, with the growing use of oil and natural gas. They were more convenient and cheaper than coal, and the supply seemed to be almost without limit. They made possible the age of automobile and airplane travel. Nearly everyone who is alive today grew up during this age and we have never known anything different.

Because we are now running out of gas and oil, we must prepare quickly for a third change, to strict conservation and to the renewed use of coal and permanent renewable energy sources, like solar power.

The world has not prepared for the future. During the 1950s, people used twice as much oil as during the 1940s. During the 1960s, we used twice as much as during the 1950s. And in each of those decades, more oil was consumed than in all of mankind's previous history combined.

World consumption of oil is still going up. If it were possible to keep it rising during the 1970s and 1980s by 5 per cent a year as it has in the past, we could use up all the proven reserves of oil in the entire world by the end of the next decade.

I know that many of you have suspected that some supplies of oil and gas are being withheld. You may be right, but suspicions about the oil companies cannot change the fact that we are running out of petroleum. All of us have heard about the large oil fields on Alaska's North Slope. In a few years when the North Slope is producing fully, its total output will be just about equal to two years' increase in our own nation's energy demand.

Each new inventory of world oil reserves has been more disturbing than the last. World oil production can probably keep going up for another six or eight years. But sometime in the 1980s it can't go up any more.

Demand will overtake production. We have no choice about that. But we do have a choice about how we will spend the next few years. Each American uses the energy equivalent of 60 barrels of oil per person each year. Ours is the most wasteful nation on earth. We waste more energy than we import. With about the same standard of living, we use twice as much energy per person as do other countries like Germany, Japan and Sweden.

[Consequences of Drift]

One choice is to continue doing what we have been doing before. We can drift along for a few more years. Our consumption of oil would keep going up every year. Our cars would continue to be too large and inefficient. Three-quarters of them would carry only one person—the driver—while our public transportation system continues to decline. We can delay insulating our houses, and they will continue to lose about 50 per cent of their heat in waste.

We can continue using scarce oil and natural gas to generate electricity, and continue wasting two-thirds of their fuel value in the process. If we do not act, then by 1985 we will be using 33 per cent more energy than we do use today.

We can't substantially increase our domestic production, so we would need to import twice as much oil as we do now. Supplies will be uncertain. The cost will keep going up. Six years ago, we paid $3.7-billion for imported oil. Last year we spent $36-billion—nearly ten times as much—and this year we may spend $45-billion.

Unless we act, we will spend more than $550-billion for imported oil by 1985—more than $2,500 for every man, woman, and child in America. Along with that money—that we transport overseas—we will continue losing American jobs and becoming increasingly vulnerable to supply interruptions.

Now we have a choice. But if we wait, we will live in fear of embargoes. We could endanger our freedom as a sovereign nation to act in foreign affairs. Within ten years we would not be able to import enough oil—from any country, at any acceptable price.

If we wait, and do not act, then our factories will not be able to keep our people on the job with reduced supplies of fuel. Too few of our utilities will have switched to coal, which is our most abundant energy source. We will not be ready to keep our transportation system running with smaller, more efficient cars and a better network of buses, trains, and public transportation.

We will feel mounting pressure to plunder the environment. We would have a crash program to build more nuclear plants, strip-mine and burn more coal, and drill more off-shore wells than if we begin to conserve now. Inflation will soar, production will go down, people will lose their jobs. Intense competition for oil will build up among nations, and among the different regions within our own country. If we fail to act soon, we will face an economic, social and political crisis that will threaten our free institutions.

But we still have another choice. We can begin to prepare right now. We can decide to act while there is still time. That is the concept of the energy policy we will present on Wednesday.

[Ten Principles]

Our national energy plan is based on ten fundamental principles.

—The first principle is that we can have an effective and comprehensive energy policy only if the government takes responsibility for it and if the people understand the seriousness of the challenge and are willing to make sacrifices.

—The second principle is that healthy economic growth must continue. Only by saving energy can we maintain our standard of living and keep our people at work. An effective conservation program will create hundreds of thousands of new jobs.

—The third principle is that we must protect the environment. Our energy problems have the same cause as our environmental problems—wasteful use of resources. Conservation helps us solve both problems at once.

—The fourth principle is that we must reduce our vulnerability to potentially devastating embargoes. We can protect ourselves from uncertain supplies by reducing our demand for oil, making the most of our abundant resources such as coal, and by developing a strategic petroleum reserve.

—The fifth principle is that we must be fair. Our solutions must ask equal sacrifices from every region, every class of people, and every interest group. Industry will have to do its part to conserve, just as consumers will. The energy producers deserve fair treatment, but we will not let the oil companies profiteer.

—The sixth principle, and the cornerstone of our policy, is to reduce demand through conservation. Our emphasis on conservation is a clear difference between this plan and others which merely encouraged crash production efforts. Conservation is the quickest, cheapest, most practical source of energy. Conservation is the only way we can buy a barrel of oil for a few dollars, for about $2. It costs about $13 to waste it.

—The seventh principle is that prices should generally reflect the true replacement cost of energy. We are only cheating ourselves if we make energy artifically cheap and use more than we can really afford.

—The eighth principle is that government policies must be predictable and certain. Both consumers and producers need policies they can count on so they can plan ahead. This is one reason I am working with the Congress to create a new Department of Energy, to replace more than 50 different agencies that now have some control over energy.

—The ninth principle is that we must conserve the fuels that are scarcest and making the most of those that are plentiful. We can't continue to use oil and gas for 75 per cent of our consumption as we do now when they make up only 7 per cent of our domestic reserves. We need to shift to plentiful coal while taking care to protect the environment, and to apply stricter safety standards to nuclear energy.

—The tenth and last principle is that we must start now to develop the new, unconventional sources of energy that we will rely on in the next century.

Now, these ten principles have guided the development of the policy I will describe to you and the Congress on Wednesday night.

[Goals for 1985]

Our energy plan will also include a number of specific goals, to measure our progress toward a stable energy system. These are the goals that we set for 1985:

● To reduce the annual growth rate in our energy demand to less than 2 per cent.

- To reduce gasoline consumption by 10 per cent below its current level.
- To cut in half the portion of U.S. oil which is imported—from a potential level of 16 million barrels to 6 million barrels a day.
- To establish a strategic petroleum reserve of one billion barrels, more than a six-month supply.
- To increase our coal production by about two-thirds to more than 1 billion tons a year.
- To insulate 90 per cent of American homes and all new buildings.
- To use solar energy in more than two and one-half million houses.

We will monitor our progress toward these goals year by year. Our plan will call for strict conservation measures if we fall behind.

I can't tell you that these measures will be easy, nor will they be popular. But I think most of you realize that a policy which does not ask for changes or sacrifices would not be an effective policy at this late date. This plan is essential to protect our jobs, our environment, our standard of living, and our future.

Whether this plan truly makes a difference will not be decided now here in Washington, but in every town and every factory, in every home and on every highway and every farm.

I believe this can be a positive challenge. There is something especially American in the kinds of changes that we have to make. We have been proud, through our history, of being efficient people.

We have been proud of our ingenuity, our skill at answering questions. We need efficiency and ingenuity more than ever. We have been proud of our leadership in the world. And now we have a chance again to give the world a positive example.

And we've always been proud of our vision of the future. We have always wanted to give our children and grandchildren a world richer in possibilities than we've had. They are the ones we must provide for now. They are the ones who will suffer most if we don't act.

I've given you some of the principles of the plan.

I am sure each of you will find something you don't like about the specifics of our proposal. It will demand that we make sacrifices and changes in every life. To some degree the sacrifices will be painful—but so is any meaningful sacrifice. It will lead to some higher costs, and to some greater inconveniences for everyone.

But the sacrifices can be gradual, realistic, and they are necessary. Above all, they will be fair. No one will gain an unfair advantage through this plan. No one will be asked to bear an unfair burden. We will monitor the accuracy of data from the oil and natural gas companies for the first time, so that we will know their true production, supplies, reserves, and profits.

Those citizens who insist on driving large, unnecessarily powerful cars must expect to pay more for that luxury.

We can be sure that all the special interest groups in the country will attack the part of this plan that affects them directly. They will say that sacrifice is fine, as long as other people do it, but that their sacrifice is unreasonable, or unfair, or harmful to the country. If they succeed with this approach, then the burden on the ordinary citizen, who is not organized into an interest group, would be crushing.

There should be only one test for this program—whether it will help our country. Other generations of Americans have faced and mastered great challenges. I have faith that meeting this challenge will make our own lives even richer. If you will join me so that we can work together with patriotism and courage, we will again prove that our great nation can lead the world into an age of peace, independence, and freedom. Thank you very much and good night.

ENERGY SPEECH TO CONGRESS

Mr. President, Mr. Speaker, Members of the Congress, and guests:
The last time we met as a group was exactly three months ago on Inauguration day. We've had a good beginning as partners in addressing our nation's problems.

But in the months ahead, we must work together even more closely, for we have to deal with the greatest domestic challenge our nation will face in our lifetime. We must act now—together—to devise and to implement a comprehensive national energy plan to cope with a crisis that otherwise could overwhelm us.

This cannot be an inspirational speech tonight. It is a sober and difficult presentation. During the last three months, I have come to realize very clearly why a comprehensive energy policy has not already been evolved. It is a thankless job, but it is our job, and I believe we have a fair, well balanced and effective plan to present to you. It can lead to an even better life for the people of America.

The heart of our energy problem is that our demand for fuel keeps rising more quickly than our production, and our primary means of solving this problem is to reduce waste and inefficiency.

Oil and natural gas make up 75 per cent of our consumption in this country, but they represent only about 7 per cent of our reserves. Our demand for oil has been rising by more than 5 per cent each year, but domestic oil production has been falling lately by more than 6 per cent. Our imports of oil have risen sharply—making us more vulnerable if supplies are interrupted—but early in the 1980's even foreign oil will become increasingly scarce. If it were possible for world demand to continue rising during the 1980's at the present rate of 5 per cent a year, we could use up all the proven reserves of oil in the entire world by the end of the next decade.

Our trade deficits are growing. We imported more than $35-billion worth of oil last year, and we will spend much more than that this year. The time has come to draw the line.

We could continue to ignore this problem—but to do so would subject our people to an impending catastrophe.

That is why we need a comprehensive national energy policy. Your advice has been an important influence as this plan has taken shape. Many of its proposals will build on your own legislative initiatives.

Two nights ago, I spoke to the American people about the principles behind our plan and our goals for 1985:

- to reduce the annual growth rate in our energy demand to less than 2 per cent;
- to reduce gasoline consumption by 10 per cent;
- to cut imports of foreign oil to 6 million barrels a day, less than half the level it would be if we did not conserve;
- to establish a strategic petroleum reserve of one billion barrels, about a ten months' supply;
- to increase our coal production by more than two-thirds, to over one billion tons a year;
- to insulate 90 per cent of American homes and all new buildings; and
- to use solar energy in more than two and a half million homes.

I hope that the Congress will adopt these goals by joint resolution as a demonstration of our mutual commitment to achieve them.

Tonight I want to outline the specific steps by which we can reach those goals. The proposals fall into these central categories:

- conservation
- production
- conversion
- development, and
- fairness, which is a primary consideration in all our proposals.

We prefer to reach these goals through voluntary cooperation with a minimum of coercion. In many cases, we propose financial incentives, which will encourage people to save energy and will harness the power of our free economy to meet our needs.

But I must say to you that voluntary compliance will not be enough—the problem is too large and the time is too short.

In a few cases, penalties and restrictions to reduce waste are essential.

[Conservation]

Our first goal is conservation. It is the cheapest, most practical way to meet our energy needs and to reduce our growing dependence on foreign supplies of oil.

With proper planning, economic growth, enhanced job opportunities and higher quality of life can result even while we eliminate the waste of energy.

The two areas where we waste most of our energy are transportation and our heating and cooling systems.

Transportation consumes 26 per cent of our energy—and as much as half of that is waste. In Europe the average automobile weighs 2,700 pounds; in our country 4,100 pounds.

The Congress has already adopted fuel efficiency standards, which will require new cars to average 27.5 miles per gallon by 1985 instead of the 18 they average today.

To insure that this existing Congressional mandate is met, I am proposing a graduated excise tax on new gas guzzlers that do not meet federal average mileage standards. The tax will start low and then rise each year until 1985. In 1978, a tax of $180 will be levied on a car getting 15 miles per gallon, and for an 11 mile-per-gallon car the tax will be $450. By 1985 on wasteful new cars with the same low mileage, the taxes will have risen to $1,600 and $2,500.

All of the money collected by this tax on wasteful automobiles will be returned to consumers, through rebates on cars that are more efficient than the mileage standard. We expect that both efficiency and total automobile production and sales will increase under this proposal. We will insure that American automobile workers and their families do not bear an unfair share of the burden.

[Gasoline Tax]

Now I want to discuss one of the most controversial and misunderstood parts of the energy proposal—a standby tax on gasoline. Gasoline consumption represents half of our total oil usage.

We simply must save gasoline, and I believe that the American people can meet this challenge. It is a matter of patriotism and commitment.

Between now and 1980 we expect gasoline consumption to rise slightly above the present level. For the following five years, when we have more efficient automobiles we need to reduce consumption each year to reach our targets for 1985.

I propose that we commit ourselves to these fair, reasonable and necessary goals and at the same time write into law a gasoline tax of an additional 5 cents per gallon that will automatically take effect every year that we fail to meet our annual targets. As an added incentive, if we miss one year but are back on track the next, the additional tax would come off. If the American people respond to our challenge, we can meet these targets, and this gasoline tax will never be imposed. I know and you know it can be done.

As with other taxes, we must minimize the adverse effects of our economy—reward those who conserve—and penalize those who waste. Therefore, any proceeds from the tax—if it is triggered—should be returned to the general public in an equitable manner.

I will also propose a variety of other measures to make our transportation system more efficient.

One of the side effects of conserving gasoline is that state governments collect less money through gasoline taxes. To reduce their hardships and to insure adequate highway maintenance, we should compensate states for this loss through the highway trust fund.

[Homes and Buildings]

The second major area where we can reduce waste is in our homes and buildings. Some buildings waste half the energy used for heating and cooling. From now on, we must make sure that new buildings are as efficient as possible, and that old buildings are equipped—or "retrofitted"—with insulation and heating systems that dramatically reduce the use of fuel.

The federal government should set an example. I will issue an executive order establishing strict conservation goals for both new and old federal buildings—a 45 per cent increase in energy efficiency for new buildings, and a 20 per cent increase for existing buildings by 1985.

We also need incentives to help those who own homes and businesses to conserve.

Those who weatherize buildings would be eligible for a tax credit of 25 per cent of the first $800 invested in conservation, and 15 per cent of the next $1,400.

If homeowners prefer, they may take advantage of a weatherization service which all regulated utility companies will be required to offer. The utilities would arrange for the contractors and provide reasonable financing. The customer would pay for the improvements through small, regular additions to monthly utility bills. In many cases, these additional charges would be almost entirely offset by lower energy consumption brought about by energy savings.

Other proposals for conservation in home and buildings include:

- direct federal help for low-income residents;
- an additional 10 per cent tax credit for business investments;
- federal matching grants to non-profit schools and hospitals; and
- public works money for weatherizing state and local government buildings.

While improving the efficiency of our businesses and homes, we must also make electrical home appliances more efficient. I propose legislation that would, for the first time, impose stringent efficiency standards for household appliances by 1980.

We must also reform our utility rate structure. For many years we have rewarded waste by offering the cheapest rates to the largest users. It is difficult for individual states to make such reforms because of the competition for new industry. The only fair way is to adopt a set of principles to be applied nationwide.

I am therefore proposing legislation which would require the following steps over the next two years:

- phasing out promotional rates and other pricing systems that make natural gas and electricity artificially cheap for high-volume users and which do not accurately reflect costs.

• offering users peak-load pricing techniques which set higher charges during the day when demand is great and lower charges when demand is small; and

• individual meters for each apartment in new buildings instead of one master meter.

Plans are already being discussed for the TVA System to act as a model for implementing such new programs to conserve energy.

One final step toward conservation is to encourage industries and utilities to expand "cogeneration" projects, which capture much of the steam that is now wasted in generating electricity. In Germany, 29 per cent of total energy comes from cogeneration, but only 4 per cent in the United States.

I propose a special 10 per cent tax credit for investments in cogeneration.

[Production and Pricing]

Along with conservation, our second major strategy is production and rational pricing.

We can never increase our production of oil and natural gas by enough to meet our demand, but we must be sure that our pricing system is sensible, discourages waste and encourages exploration and new production.

One of the principles of our energy policy is that the price of energy should reflect its true replacement cost, as a means of bringing supply and demand into balance over the long-run. Realistic pricing is especially important for our scarcest fuels, oil and natural gas. However, proposals for immediate and total decontrol of domestic oil and natural gas prices would be disastrous for our economy and for working Americans, and would not solve long range problems of dwindling supplies.

The price of newly discovered oil will be allowed to rise, over a three-year period, to the 1977 world market price, with allowances for inflation. The current return to producers for previously discovered oil would remain the same, except for adjustments because of inflation.

Because fairness is an essential strategy of our energy program, we do not want to give producers windfall profits, beyond the incentives they need for exploration and production. But we are misleading ourselves if we do not recognize the replacement costs of energy in our pricing system.

Therefore, I propose that we phase in a wellhead tax on existing supplies of domestic oil, equal to the difference between the present controlled price of oil and the world price, and return the money collected by this tax to the consumers and workers of America.

We should also end the artificial distortions in natural gas prices in different parts of the country which have caused people in the producing states to pay exorbitant prices, while creating shortages, unemployment and economic stagnation, particularly in the Northeast. We must not permit energy shortages to balkanize our nation.

I want to work with the Congress to give gas producers an adequate incentive for exploration, working carefully toward deregulation of newly discovered natural gas as market conditions permit.

I propose now that the price limit for all new gas sold anywhere in the country be set at the price of the equivalent energy value of domestic crude oil, beginning in 1978. This proposal will apply both to new gas and to expiring intrastate contracts. It would not affect existing contracts.

[Conversion]

We must be sure that oil and natural gas are not wasted by industries and utilities that could use coal instead. Our third strategy will be conversion from scarce fuels to coal wherever possible.

Although coal now provides only 18 per cent of our energy needs, it makes up 90 per cent of our energy reserves. Its production and use create environmental difficulties, but we can cope with them through strict strip-mining and clean air standards.

To increase the use of coal by 400 million tons, or 65 per cent, in industry and utilities by 1985, I propose a sliding scale tax, starting in 1979, on large industrial users of oil and natural gas. Fertilizer manufacturers and crop dryers which must use gas would be exempt from the tax. Utilities would not be subject to these taxes until 1983, because it will take them longer to convert to coal.

I will also submit proposals for expanded research and development in coal. We need to find better ways to mine it safely and burn it cleanly, and to use it to produce other clean energy sources. We have spent billions on research and development of nuclear power, but very little on coal. Investments here can pay rich dividends.

Even with this conversion effort, we will still face a gap-—between the energy we need and the energy we can produce and import. Therefore, as a last resort we must continue to use increasing amounts of nuclear energy.

We now have 63 nuclear power plants, producing about 3 per cent of our total energy and about 70 more are licensed for construction. Domestic uranium supplies can support this number of plants for another 75 years. Effective conservation efforts can minimize the shift toward nuclear power. There is no need to enter the plutonium age by licensing or building a fast breeder reactor such as the proposed demonstration plant at Clinch River.

We must, however, increase our capacity to produce enriched uranium for light water nuclear power plants, using the new centrifuge technology, which consumes only about 1/10th the energy of existing gaseous diffusion plants.

We must also reform the nuclear licensing procedures. New plants should not be located near earthquake fault zones or near population centers, safety standards should be strengthened and enforced, designs standardized as much as possible, and more adequate storage for spent fuel assured.

However, even with the most thorough safeguards, it should not take ten years to license a plant. I propose that we establish reasonable, objective criteria for licensing, and that plants which are based on a standard design not require extensive individual design studies for licensing.

[Development]

Our fourth strategy is to develop permanent and reliable new energy sources.

The most promising is solar energy, for which much of the technology is already available. Solar water heaters and space heaters are ready for commercialization. All they need is some incentive to initiate the growth of a large market.

Therefore, I am proposing a gradually decreasing tax credit, to run from now through 1984, for those who purchase approved solar heating equipment. Initially, it would be 40 per cent of the first $1,000 and 25 per cent of the next $6,400 invested.

Increased production of geothermal energy can be insured by providing the same tax incentives as for gas and oil drilling operations.

[Fairness]

Our guiding principle, as we developed this plan, was that above all it must be fair.

None of our people must make an unfair sacrifice.

None should reap an unfair benefit.

The desire for equity is reflected throughout our plan:

● in the wellhead tax, which encourages conservation but is returned to the public;

● in a dollar-for-dollar refund of the wellhead tax as it affects home heating oil;

● in reducing the unfairness of natural gas pricing;

● in ensuring that homes will have the oil and natural gas they need, while industry turns toward the more abundant coal that can also suit its needs;

● in basing utility prices on true cost, so every user pays a fair share;

● in the automobile tax and rebate system, which rewards those who save our energy and penalizes those who waste it.

I propose one other step to insure proper balance in our plan. We need more accurate information about our supplies of energy, and about the companies that produce it.

If we are asking sacrifices of ourselves, we need facts we can count on. We need an independent information system that will give us reliable data about energy reserves and production, emergency capabilities and financial data from the energy producers.

I happen to believe in competition, and we don't have enough of it.

During this time of increasing scarcity, competition among energy producers and distributors must be guaranteed. I recommend that individual accounting be required from energy companies for production, refining, distribution and marketing—separately for domestic and foreign operations. Strict enforcement of the anti-trust laws can be based on this data, and may prevent the need for divestiture.

Profiteering through tax shelters should be prevented, and independent drillers should have the same intangible tax credits as the major corporations.

The energy industry should not reap large unearned profits. Increasing prices on existing inventories of oil should not result in windfall gains but should be captured for the people of our country.

We must make it clear to everyone that our people, through their government, will now be setting our energy policy.

The new Department of Energy should be established without delay. Continued fragmentation of government authority and responsibility for our nation's energy program is dangerous and unnecessary.

Two nights ago, I said that this difficult effort would be the moral equivalent of war. If successful, this effort will protect our jobs, our environment, our national independence, our standard of living, and our future. Our energy policy will be innovative, but fair and predictable, it will not be easy. It will demand the best of us—our vision, our dedication, our courage, and our sense of common purpose.

This is a carefully balanced program, depending for its fairness on all its major component parts. It will be a test of our basic political strength and ability.

But we have met challenges before, and our nation has been the stronger for it. That is the responsibility that we face—you in the Congress, the members of my administration, and all the people of our country. I am confident that together we will succeed.

COURT ON CORPORAL PUNISHMENT
April 19, 1977

The Supreme Court in a 5-4 decision April 19 refused to rule that paddlings in a public school were "cruel and unusual punishment" in violation of the Eighth Amendment. The court also said that students were not required to be given a hearing before the punishment was administered.

The court rejected the argument of two junior high school students from Miami, Fla., who claimed that they had received "excessively harsh" paddlings at school in violation of their constitutional rights. (Ingraham v. Wright)

Majority Opinion

Justice Lewis F. Powell Jr. wrote the majority opinion, joined by Chief Justice Warren E. Burger, Justices Potter Stewart, Harry A. Blackmun and William H. Rehnquist. Justices Byron R. White, William J. Brennan Jr., Thurgood Marshall and John Paul Stevens dissented.

"The use of corporal punishment in this country as a means of disciplining school children dates back to the colonial period," wrote Powell. Since before the American Revolution, it has been established in common law that "teachers may impose reasonable but not excessive force to discipline a child.... To the extent that the force is excessive or unreasonable, the educator in virtually all states is subject to possible civil and criminal liability."

The Eighth Amendment ban on cruel and unusual punishment did not apply here, held the majority, because it was "designed to protect those convicted of crimes," and not school children. "The prisoner and the school child stand in wholly different circumstances," wrote Powell. "The openness of the public school and its supervision by the community afford significant safeguards against the kinds of abuses from which the Eighth Amendment protects the prisoner."

In a 1975 ruling (Goss v. Lopez), the court had held that the constitutional guarantee of due process required that students be given a hearing before they were suspended. In Ingraham, the two pupils had argued that students deserved a similar hearing before they were spanked. (Historic Documents of 1975, p. 67)

Although the majority agreed that one's right to liberty, which is protected by the due process guarantee of the Fourteenth Amendment, was involved in corporal punishment, it refused to require a hearing before the infliction of such punishment.

To do so "would significantly burden the use of corporal punishment as a disciplinary measure," wrote Powell, and that was not justified in light of "the low incidence of abuse, the openness of our schools and the common law safeguards that already exist."

Dissenting Opinion

"I am not suggesting that spanking in the public schools is in every instance prohibited by the Eighth Amendment," wrote Justice White for the four dissenters. "I only take issue with the extreme view of the majority that corporal punishment in public schools, no matter how barbaric, inhumane or severe, is never limited by the Eighth Amendment."

Neither the openness of the public schools nor the availability of damage suits under state law affected the constitutional validity of excessive corporal punishment, he continued. "If there are some punishments that are so barbaric that they may not be imposed for the commission of crimes...similar punishments may not be imposed on persons for less culpable acts, such as breaches of school discipline. Thus, if it is constitutionally impermissible to cut off someone's ear for the commission of murder, it must be unconstitutional to cut off a child's ear for being late to class. Although there were no ears cut off in this case, the record reveals beatings so severe that if they were inflicted on a hardened criminal, they might not pass constitutional muster."

The dissenters also would hold that due process required the disciplinarian to stop before punishment to give the student notice of the charges against him and, if he denied them, an opportunity to give his side of the story.

Background

The court had been sharply divided on issues that involved the rights of public school students. Justice White, who wrote the dissenting opinion in the present case, had written for the majority of the court in two previous student rights cases. In the 1975 Goss v. Lopez *decision, White wrote that public school students had a right to a hearing on charges which school officials felt merited their expulsion or suspension. "The claimed right of the state to determine unilaterally and without process whether that misconduct has occurred immediately collides with the requirements of the Constitution," White wrote.*

In a subsequent decision, White again spoke for the court's majority holding school officials liable to damage suits from students whose constitutional rights they had violated by disciplinary action. An official was liable, White wrote, "if he knew or reasonably should have known that the action he took...would violate the constitutional rights of the student affected, or if he took the action with the malicious intention" of injuring the student. (Wood v. Strickland)

Following are excerpts from the Supreme Court's opinion, delivered April 19, 1977, upholding the right of school officials to administer corporal punishment in the public schools:

No. 75-6527

| James Ingraham, by his Mother and Next Friend, Eloise Ingraham, et al., Petitioners, *v.* Willie J. Wright, I, et. al. | On Writ of Certiorari to the United States Court of Appeals for the Fifth Circuit. |

[April 19, 1977]

MR. JUSTICE POWELL delivered the opinion of the Court.

This case presents questions concerning the use of corporal punishment in public schools: first, whether the paddling of students as a means of maintaining school discipline constitutes cruel and unusual punishment in violation of the Eighth Amendment; and second, to the extent that paddling is constitutionally permissible, whether the Due Process Clause of the Fourteenth Amendment requires prior notice and an opportunity to be heard.

I

Petitioners James Ingraham and Roosevelt Andrews filed the complaint in this case on January 7, 1971, in the United States District Court for the

District of Florida. At the time both were enrolled in the Charles R. Drew Junior High School in Dade County, Fla., Ingraham in the eighth grade and Andrews in the ninth. The complaint contained three counts, each alleging a separate cause of action for deprivation of constitutional rights.... Counts one and two were individual damage actions by Ingraham and Andrews based on paddling incidents that allegedly occurred in October 1970 at Drew Junior High School. Count three was a class action for declaratory and injunctive relief filed on behalf of all students in the Dade County schools. Named as defendants in all counts were respondents Willie J. Wright (principal at Drew Junior High School), Lemmie Deliford (an assistant principal), Solomon Barnes (an assistant to the principal), and Edward L. Whigham (superintendent of the Dade County School System).

Petitioners presented their evidence at a week-long trial before the District Court. At the close of the petitioners' case, respondents moved for dismissal of count three "on the ground that upon the facts and the law the plaintiff has shown no right to relief," ...and for a ruling that the evidence would be insufficient to go to a jury on counts one and two. The District Court granted the motion as to all three counts, and dismissed the complaint without hearing evidence on behalf of the school authorities....

Petitioners' evidence may be summarized briefly. In the 1970-1971 school year many of the 237 schools in Dade County used corporal punishment as a means of maintaining discipline pursuant to Florida legislation and a local school board regulation. The statute then in effect authorized limited corporal punishment by negative inference, proscribing punishment which was "degrading or unduly severe" or which was inflicted without prior consultation with the principal or the teacher in charge of the school.... The regulation, Dade County School Board Policy 5144, contained explicit directions and limitations. The authorized punishment consisted of paddling the recalcitrant student on the buttocks with a flat wooden paddle measuring less than two feet long, three to four inches wide, and about one-half inch thick. The normal punishment was limited to one to five "licks" or blows with the paddle and resulted in no apparent physical injury to the student. School authorities viewed corporal punishment as a less drastic means of discipline than suspension or expulsion. Contrary to the procedural requirements of the statute and regulation, teachers often paddled students on their own authority without first consulting the principal.

Petitioners focused on Drew Junior High School, the school in which both Ingraham and Andrews were enrolled in the fall of 1970. In an apparent reference to Drew, the District Court found that "[t]he instances of punishment which could be characterized as severe, accepting the students' testimony as credible, took place in one junior high school."... The evidence, consisting mainly of the testimony of 16 students, suggests that the regime at Drew was exceptionally harsh. The testimony of Ingraham and Andrews, in support of their individual claims for damages, is illustrative. Because he was slow to respond to his teacher's instructions,

Ingraham was subjected to more than 20 licks with a paddle while being held over a table in the principal's office. The paddling was so severe that he suffered a hematoma requiring medical attention and keeping him out of school for 11 days. Andrews was paddled several times for minor infractions. On two occasions he was struck on his arms, once depriving him of the full use of his arm for a week.

The District Court made no findings on the credibility of the students' testimony. Rather, assuming their testimony to be credible, the court found no constitutional basis for relief. With respect to count three, the class action, the court concluded that the punishment authorized and practiced generally in the county schools violated no constitutional right.... With respect to counts one and two, the individual damage actions, the court concluded that while corporal punishment could in some cases violate the Eighth Amendment, in this case a jury could not lawfully find "the elements of severity, arbitrary infliction, unacceptability in terms of contemporary standards, or gross disproportion which are necessary to bring 'punishment' to the constitutional level of 'cruel and unusual punishment.' "...

A panel of the Court of Appeals voted to reverse.... The panel concluded that the punishment was so severe and oppressive as to violate the Eighth and Fourteenth Amendments, and that the procedures outlined in Policy 5144-failed to satisfy the requirements of the Due Process Clause. Upon rehearing, the en banc court rejected these conclusions and affirmed the judgment of the District Court... The full court held that the Due Process Clause did not require notice or an opportunity to be heard:

> "In essence, we refuse to set forth, as constitutionally mandated, procedural standards for an activity which is not substantial enough, on a constitutional level, to justify the time and effort which would have to be expended by the school in adhering to those procedures or to justify further interference by federal courts into the internal affairs of public schools."...

The court also rejected the petitioners' substantive contentions. The Eighth Amendment, in the court's view, was simply inapplicable to corporal punishment in public schools. Stressing the likelihood of civil and criminal liability in state law, if petitioners' evidence were believed, the court held that "[t]he administration of corporal punishment in public schools, whether or not excessively administered, does not come within the scope of Eighth Amendment protection." ...Nor was there any substantive violation of the Due Process Clause. The court noted that "[p]addling of recalcitrant children has long been an acceptable method of promoting good behavior and instilling notions of responsibility and decorum into the mischievous heads of school children." ...The court refused to examine instances of punishment individually:

> "We think it a misuse of our judicial power to determine, for example, whether a teacher has acted arbitrarily in paddling a par-

ticular child for certain behavior or whether in a particular instance
of misconduct five licks would have been more appropriate punishment than ten licks...."

We granted certiorari, limited to the questions of cruel and unusual
punishment and procedural due process....

II

In addressing the scope of the Eighth Amendment's prohibition on cruel
and unusual punishment, this Court has found it useful to refer to
"[t]raditional common law concepts," ...and to the "attitude[s] which our
society has traditionally taken."... So too, in defining the requirements of
procedural due process under the Fifth and Fourteenth Amendments, the
Court has been attuned to what "has always been the law of the land"
...and to "traditional ideas of fair procedure." ... We therefore begin by examining the way in which our traditions and our laws have responded to
the use of corporal punishment in public schools.

The use of corporal punishment in this country as a means of disciplining schoolchildren dates back to the colonial period. It has survived the
transformation of primary and secondary education from the colonials'
reliance on optional private arrangements to our present system of compulsory education and dependence on public schools. Despite the general
abandonment of corporal punishment as a means of punishing criminal
offenders, the practice continues to play a role in the public education of
schoolchildren in most parts of the country. Professional and public
opinion is sharply divided on the practice, and has been for more than
a century. Yet we can discern no trend toward its elimination.

At common law a single principle has governed the use of corporal
punishment since before the American Revolution: teachers may impose
reasonable but not excessive force to discipline a child.... The basic
doctrine has not changed. The prevelant rule in this country today
privileges such force as a teacher or administrator "reasonably believes to
be necessary for [the child's] proper control, training, or education."... To
the extent that the force is excessive or unreasonable, the educator in virtually all States is subject to possible civil and criminal liability.

Although the early cases viewed the authority of the teacher as deriving
from the parents, the concept of parental delegation has been replaced by
the view—more consonant with compulsory education laws—that the
State itself may impose such corporal punishment as is reasonably
necessary "for the proper education of the child and for the maintenance of
group discipline."... All of the circumstances are to be taken into account
in determining whether the punishment is reasonable in a particular case.
Among the most important considerations are the seriousness of the
offense, the attitude and past behavior of the child, the nature and severity
of the punishment, the age and strength of the child, and the availability of
less severe but equally effective means of discipline....

Of the 23 States that have addressed the problem through legislation, 21 have authorized the moderate use of corporal punishment in public schools. Of these States only a few have elaborated on the common law test of reasonableness, typically providing for approval or notification of the child's parents, or for infliction of punishment only by the principal or in the presence of an adult witness. Only two States, Massachusetts and New Jersey, have prohibited all corporal punishment in their public schools. Where the legislatures have not acted, the state courts have uniformly preserved the common law rule permitting teachers to use reasonable force in disciplining children in their charge.

Against this background of historical and contemporary approval of reasonable corporal punishment, we turn to the constitutional questions before us.

III

The Eighth Amendment provides, "Excessive bail shall not be required, nor excessive fines imposed, nor cruel and unusual punishments inflicted." Bail, fines and punishment traditionally have been associated with the criminal process, and by subjecting the three to parallel limitations the text of the Amendment suggests an intention to limit the power of those entrusted with the criminal law function of government. An examination of the history of the Amendment and the decisions of this Court construing the proscription against cruel and unusual punishment confirms that it was designed to protect those convicted of crimes. We adhere to this long-standing limitation and hold that the Eighth Amendment does not apply to the paddling of children as a means of maintaining discipline in public schools....

[Eighth Amendment Does Not Apply]

Petitioners acknowledge that the original design of the Cruel and Unusual Punishments Clause was to limit criminal punishments, but urge nonetheless that the prohibition should be extended to ban the paddling of school children. Observing that the Framers of the Eighth Amendment could not have envisioned our present system of public and compulsory education, with its opportunities for noncriminal punishments, petitioners contend that extension of the prohibition against cruel punishments is necessary lest we afford greater protection to criminals than to schoolchildren. It would be anomalous, they say, if schoolchildren could be beaten without constitutional redress, while hardened criminals suffering the same beatings at the hands of their jailors might have a valid claim under the Eighth Amendment.... Whatever force this logic may have in other settings, we find it an inadequate basis for wrenching the Eighth Amendment from its historical context and extending it to traditional disciplinary practices in the public schools.

The prisoner and the schoolchild stand in wholly different circumstances, separated by the harsh facts of criminal conviction and incarceration. The prisoner's conviction entitles the State to classify him as a "criminal," and his incarceration deprives him of the freedom "to be with family and friends and to form the other enduring attachments of normal life." ...Prison brutality, as the Court of Appeals observed in this case, is "part of the total punishment to which the individual is subjected for his crime and, as such, is a proper subject for Eighth Amendment scrutiny."... Even so, the protection afforded by the Eighth Amendment is limited. After incarceration, only the "unnecessary and wanton infliction of pain" ...constitutes cruel and unusual punishment forbidden by the Eighth Amendment.

The schoolchild has little need for the protection of the Eighth Amendment. Though attendance may not always be voluntary, the public school remains an open institution. Except perhaps when very young, the child is not physically restrained from leaving school during school hours; and at the end of the school day, the child is invariably free to return home. Even while at school, the child brings with him the support of family and friends and is rarely apart from teachers and other pupils who may witness and protest any instances of mistreatment.

The openness of the public school and its supervision by the community afford significant safeguards against the kinds of abuses from which the Eighth Amendment protects the prisoner. In virtually every community where corporal punishment is permitted in the schools, these safeguards are reinforced by the legal constraints of the common law. Public school teachers and administrators are privileged at common law to inflict only such corporal punishment as is reasonably necessary for the proper education and discipline of the child; any punishment going beyond the privilege may result in both civil and criminal liability.... As long as the schools are open to public scrutiny, there is no reason to believe that the common law constraints will not effectively remedy and deter excesses such as those alleged in this case.

We conclude that when public school teachers or administrators impose disciplinary corporal punishment, the Eighth Amendment is inapplicable. The pertinent constitutional question is whether the imposition is consonant with the requirements of due process.

IV

The Fourteenth Amendment prohibits any State deprivation of life, liberty or property without due process of law. Application of this prohibition requires the familiar two-stage analysis: we must first ask whether the asserted individual interests are encompassed within the Fourteenth Amendment's protection of "life, liberty or property"; if protected interests are implicated, we then must decide what procedures constitute "due process of law."... Following that analysis here, we find that corporal punishment in public school implicates a constitutionally protected liberty interest, but we hold that the traditional common law remedies are fully adequate to afford due process.

"[T]he range of interests protected by procedural due process is not infinite."... We have repeatedly rejected "the notion that *any* grievous loss visited upon a person by the State is sufficient to invoke the procedural protections of the Due Process Clause."... Due process is required only when a decision of the State implicates an interest within the protection of the Fourteenth Amendment. And "to determine whether due process requirements apply in the first place, we must look not to the 'weight' but to the *nature* of the interest at stake."...

The Due Process Clause of the Fifth Amendment, later incorporated into the Fourteenth, was intended to give Americans at least the protection against governmental power that they had enjoyed as Englishmen against the power of the Crown. The liberty preserved from deprivation without due process included the right "generally to enjoy those privileges long recognized at common law as essential to the orderly pursuit of happiness by free men."... Among the historic liberties so protected was a right to be free from, and to obtain judicial relief for, unjustified intrusions on personal security.

While the contours of this historic liberty interest in the context of our federal system of government have not been defined precisely, they always have been thought to encompass freedom from bodily restraint and punishment.... It is fundamental that the state cannot hold and physically punish an individual except in accordance with due process of law.

This constitutionally protected liberty interest is at stake in this case. There is, of course, a *de minimis* level of imposition with which the Constitution is not concerned. But at least where school authorities, acting under color of state law, deliberately decide to punish a child for misconduct by restraining the child and inflicting appreciable physical pain, we hold that Fourteenth Amendment liberty interests are implicated.

"[T]he question remains what process is due."...Were it not for the common law privilege permitting teachers to inflict reasonable corporal punishment on children in their care, and the availability of the traditional remedies for abuse, the case for requiring advance procedural safeguards would be strong indeed. But here we deal with a punishment—paddling—within that tradition, and the question is whether the common law remedies are adequate to afford due process.... Whether in this case the common law remedies for excessive corporal punishment constitute due process of law must turn on an analysis of the competing interests at stake, viewed against the background of "history, reason, [and] the past course of decisions." The analysis requires consideration of three distinct factors: "first, the private interest that will be affected...; second, the risk of an erroneous deprivation of such interest...and the probable value, if any, of additional or substitute procedural safeguards; and, finally, the [state] interest, including the function involved and the fiscal and administrative burdens that the additional or substitute procedural requirement would entail."...

Because it is rooted in history, the child's liberty interest in avoiding corporal punishment while in the care of public school authorities is subject to historical limitations. Under the common law, an invasion of personal security gave rise to a right to recover damages in a subsequent judicial proceeding.... But the right of recovery was qualified by the concept of justification. Thus, there could be no recovery against a teacher who gave only "moderate correction" to a child.... To the extent that the force used was reasonable in light of its purpose, it was not wrongful, but rather "justifiable or lawful."...

The concept that reasonable corporal punishment in school is justifiable continues to be recognized in the laws of most States.... It represents "the balance struck by this country," ...between the child's interest in personal security and the traditional view that some limited corporal punishment may be necessary in the course of a child's education. Under that longstanding accommodation of interests, there can be no deprivation of substantive rights as long as disciplinary corporal punishment is within the limits of the common law privilege.

This is not to say that the child's interest in procedural safeguards is insubstantial. The school disciplinary process is not "a totally accurate, unerring process, never mistaken and never unfair...." *Goss* v. *Lopez*... (1975). In any deliberate infliction of corporal punishment on a child who is restrained for that purpose, there is some risk that the intrusion on the child's liberty will be unjustified and therefore unlawful. In these circumstances the child has a strong interest in procedural safeguards that minimize the risk of wrongful punishment and provide for the resolution of disputed questions of justification....

...But even if the need for advance procedural safeguards were clear, the question would remain whether the incremental benefit could justify the cost. Acceptance of petitioners' claims would work a transformation in the law governing corporal punishment in Florida and most other States. Given the impracticability of formulating a rule of procedural due process that varies with the severity of the particular imposition, the prior hearing petitioners seek would have to precede *any* paddling, however moderate or trivial.

Such a universal constitutional requirement would significantly burden the use of corporal punishment as a disciplinary measure. Hearings—even informal hearings—require time, personnel, and a diversion of attention from normal school pursuits. School authorities may well choose to abandon corporal punishment rather than incur the burdens of complying with the procedural requirements. Teachers, properly concerned with maintaining authority in the classroom, may well prefer to rely on other disciplinary measures—which they may view as less effective—rather than confront the possible disruption that prior notice and a hearing may entail. Paradoxically, such an alteration of disciplinary policy is most likely to occur in the ordinary case where the contemplated punishment is well within the common law privilege.

Elimination or curtailment of corporal punishment would be welcomed by many as a societal advance. But when such a policy choice may result from this Court's determination of an asserted right to due process, rather than from the normal processes of community debate and legislative action, the societal costs cannot be dismissed as insubstantial. We are reviewing here a legislative judgment, rooted in history and reaffirmed in the laws of many States, that corporal punishment serves important educational interests. This judgment must be viewed in light of the disciplinary problems commonplace in the schools. As noted in *Goss* v. *Lopez*,..."[e]vents calling for discipline are frequent occurrences and sometimes require immediate, effective action." Assessment of the need for, and the appropriate means of maintaining, school discipline is committed generally to the discretion of school authorities subject to state law. "[T]he court has repeatedly emphasized the need for affirming the comprehensive authority of the States and of school officials, consistent with fundamental constitutional safeguards, to prescribe and control conduct in the schools." *Tinker* v. *Des Moines School District*...(1969).

"At some point the benefit of an additional safeguard to the individual affected...and to society in terms of increased assurance that the action is just, may be outweighed by the cost."... We think that point has been reached in this case. In view of the low incidence of abuse, the openness of our schools, and the common law safeguards that already exist, the risk of error that may result in violation of a schoolchild's substantive rights can only be regarded as minimal. Imposing additional administrative safeguards as a constitutional requirement might reduce that risk marginally, but would also entail a significant intrusion into an area of primary educational responsibility. We conclude that the Due Process Clause does not require notice and a hearing prior to the imposition of corporal punishment in the public schools, as that practice is authorized and limited by the common law.

V

Petitioners cannot prevail on either of the theories before us in this case. The Eighth Amendment's prohibition against cruel and unusual punishments is inapplicable to school paddlings, and the Fourteenth Amendment's requirement of procedural due process is satisfied by Florida's preservation of common law constraints and remedies. We therefore agree with the Court of Appeals that petitioners' evidence affords no basis for injunctive relief, and that petitioners cannot recover damages on the basis of any Eighth Amendment or procedural due process violation.

Affirmed.

MR. JUSTICE WHITE, with whom MR. JUSTICE BRENNAN, MR. JUSTICE MARSHALL, and MR. JUSTICE STEVENS join, dissenting.

Today the Court holds that corporal punishment in public schools, no matter how severe, can never be the subject of the protections afforded by the Eighth Amendment. It also holds that students in the public school systems are not constitutionally entitled to a hearing of any sort before beatings can be inflicted on them. Because I believe that these holdings are inconsistent with the prior decisions of this Court and are contrary to a reasoned analysis of the constitutional provisions involved, I respectfully dissent.

I

A

The Eighth Amendment places a flat prohibition against the infliction of "cruel and unusual punishment." This reflects a societal judgment that there are some punishments that are so barbaric and inhumane that we will not permit them to be imposed on anyone, no matter how opprobrious the offense.... If there are some punishments that are so barbaric that they may not be imposed for the commission of crimes, designated by our social system as the most thoroughly reprehensible acts an individual can commit, then *a fortiori,* similar punishments may not be imposed on persons for less culpable acts, such as breaches of school discipline. Thus, if it is constitutionally impermissible to cut off someone's ear for the commission of murder, it must be unconstitutional to cut off a child's ear for being late to class. Although there were no ears cut off in this case, the record reveals beatings so severe that if they were inflicted on a hardened criminal for the commission of a serious crime, they might not pass constitutional muster.

Nevertheless, the majority holds that the Eighth Amendment "was designed to protect [only] those convicted of crimes,"...relying on a vague and inconclusive recitation of the history of the Amendment. Yet the constitutional prohibition is against cruel and unusual *punishments;* nowhere is that prohibition limited or modified by the language of the Constitution. Certainly, the fact that the Framers did not choose to insert the word "criminal" into the language of the Eighth Amendment is strong evidence that the Amendment was designed to prohibit all inhumane or barbaric punishments, no matter what the nature of the offense for which the punishment is imposed.

No one can deny that spanking of school children is "punishment" under any reasonable reading of the word, for the similarities between spanking in public schools and other forms of punishment are too obvious to ignore. Like other forms of punishment, spanking of school children involves an institutionalized response to the violation of some official rule or regulation proscribing certain conduct and is imposed for the purpose of rehabilitating the offender, deterring the offender and others like him from committing the violation in the future, and inflicting some measure of social retribution for the harm that has been done.

B

We are fortunate that in our society punishments that are severe enough to raise a doubt as to their constitutional validity are ordinarily not imposed without first affording the accused the full panoply of procedural safeguards provided by the criminal process. The effect has been that "every decision of this Court considering whether a punishment is 'cruel and unusual' within the meaning of the Eighth and Fourteenth Amendments has dealt with a criminal punishment.".... The Court would have us believe from this fact that there is a recognized distinction between criminal and noncriminal punishment for purposes of the Eighth Amendment. This is plainly wrong. "[E]ven a clear legislative classification of a statute as 'non-penal' would not alter the fundamental nature of a plainly penal statute."... The relevant inquiry is not whether the offense for which a punishment is inflicted has been labeled as criminal, but whether the purpose of the deprivation is among those ordinarily associated with punishment, such as retribution, rehabilitation, or deterrence....

If this purposive approach were followed in the present case, it would be clear that spanking in the Florida public schools is punishment within the meaning of the Eighth Amendment. The District Court found that "corporal punishment is one of a variety of measures employed in the school system for the correction of pupil behavior and the preservation of order."... Behavior correction and preservation of order are purposes ordinarily associated with punishment.

Without even mentioning the purposive analysis applied in the prior decisions of this Court, the majority adopts a rule that turns on the label given to the offense for which the punishment is inflicted. Thus, the record in this case reveals that one student at Drew Junior High School received 50 licks with a paddle for allegedly making an obscene telephone call.... The majority holds that the Eighth Amendment does not prohibit such punishment since it was only inflicted for a breach of school discipline. However, that same conduct is punishable as a misdemeanor under Florida law...and there can be little doubt that if that same "punishment" had been inflicted by an officer of the state courts...it would have had to satisfy the requirements of the Eighth Amendment.

C

In fact, as the Court recognizes, the Eighth Amendment has never been confined to criminal punishments. Nevertheless, the majority adheres to its view that any protections afforded by the Eighth Amendment must have something to do with criminals, and it would therefore confine any exceptions to its general rule that only criminal punishments are covered by the Eighth Amendment to abuses inflicted on prisoners. Thus, if a prisoner is beaten mercilessly for a breach of discipline, he is entitled to the protection of the Eighth Amendment, while a school child who commits the same breach of discipline and is similarly beaten is simply not covered.

The purported explanation of this anomaly is the assertion that school children have no need for the Eighth Amendment. We are told that schools are open institutions, subject to constant public scrutiny; that school children have adequate remedies under state law; and that prisoners suffer the social stigma of being labeled as criminals. How any of these policy considerations got into the Constitution is difficult to discern, for the Court has never considered any of these factors in determining the scope of the Eighth Amendment.

The essence of the majority's argument is that school children do not need Eighth Amendment protection because corporal punishment is less subject to abuse in the public schools than it is in the prison system. However, it cannot be reasonably suggested that just because cruel and unusual punishments may occur less frequently under public scrutiny, they will not occur at all. The mere fact that a public flogging or a public execution would be available for all to see would not render the punishment constitutional if it were otherwise impermissible. Similarly, the majority would not suggest that a prisoner who is placed in a minimum security prison and permitted to go home to his family on the weekends should be any less entitled to Eighth Amendment protections than his counterpart in a maximum security prison. In short, if a punishment is so barbaric and inhumane that it goes beyond the tolerance of a civilized society, its openness to public scrutiny should have nothing to do with its constitutional validity.

Nor is it an adequate answer that school children may have other state and constitutional remedies available to them. Even assuming that the remedies available to public school students are adequate under Florida law, the availability of state remedies has never been determinative of the coverage or of the protections afforded by the Eighth Amendment. The reason is obvious. The fact that a person may have a state-law cause of action against a public official who tortures him with a thumb screw for the commission of an antisocial act has nothing to do with the fact that such official conduct is cruel and unusual punishment prohibited by the Eighth Amendment. Indeed, the majority's view was implicitly rejected this Term...when the Court held that failure to provide for the medical needs of prisoners could constitute cruel and unusual punishment even though a medical malpractice remedy in tort was available to prisoners under state law....

D

By holding that the Eighth Amendment protects only criminals, the majority adopts the view that one is entitled to the protections afforded by the Eighth Amendment only if he is punished for acts that are sufficiently opprobrious for society to make them "criminal." This is a curious holding in view of the fact that the more culpable the offender the more likely it is that the punishment will not be disproportionate to the offense, and consequently, the less likely it is that the punishment will be cruel and unusual. Conversely, a public school student who is spanked for a mere breach of discipline may sometimes have a strong argument that the punishment does not fit the offense, depending upon the severity of the beating, and therefore that it is cruel and unusual. Yet the majority would afford the student no protection no matter how inhumane and barbaric the punishment inflicted on him might be.

The issue presented in this phase of the case is limited to whether corporal punishment in public schools can *ever* be prohibited by the Eighth Amendment. İ am therefore not suggesting that spanking in the public schools is in every instance prohibited by the Eighth Amendment. My own view is that it is not. I only take issue with the extreme view of the majority that corporal punishment in public schools, no matter how barbaric, inhumane, or severe, is never limited by the Eighth Amendment. Where corporal punishment becomes so severe as to be unacceptable in a civilized society, I can see no reason that it should become any more acceptable just because it is inflicted on children in the public schools.

II

The majority concedes that corporal punishment in the public schools implicates an interest protected by the Due Process Clause—the liberty interest of the student to be free from "bodily restraint and punishment" involving "appreciable physical pain" inflicted by persons acting under color of state law.... The question remaining, as the majority recognizes, is what process is due.

The reason that the Constitution requires a State to provide "due process of law" when it punishes an individual for misconduct is to protect the individual from erroneous or mistaken punishment that the State would not have inflicted had it found the facts in a more reliable way.... [T]he Court applied this principle to the school disciplinary process, holding that a student must be given an informal opportunity to be heard before he is finally suspended from public school.... To guard against this risk of punishing an innocent child, the Due Process Clause requires, not an "elaborate hearing" before a neutral party, but simply "an informal give-and-take between student and disciplinarian" which gives the student "an opportunity to explain his version of the facts."...

The Court now holds that these "rudimentary precautions against unfair or mistaken findings of misconduct" ...are not required if the student is punished with "appreciable physical pain" rather than with a suspension, even though both punishments deprive the student of a constitutionally protected interest. Although the respondent school authorities provide absolutely *no* process to the student before the punishment is finally inflicted, the majority concludes that the student is nonetheless given due process because he can later sue the teacher and recover damages if the punishment was "excessive."

This tort action is utterly inadequate to protect against erroneous infliction of punishment for two reasons. First, under Florida law, a student punished for an act he did not commit cannot recover damages from a teacher "proceeding in utmost good faith...on the reports and advice of others[.]" ...[T]he student has no remedy at all for punishment imposed on the basis of mistaken facts, at least as long as the punishment was reasonable from the point of view of the disciplinarian, uninformed by any prior hearing. The "traditional common law remedies" on which the majority relies...thus do nothing to protect the student from the danger that concerned the Court in *Goss*—the risk of reasonable, good faith mistake in the school disciplinary process.

Second, and more important, even if the student could sue for good faith error in the infliction of punishment, the lawsuit occurs after the punishment has been finally imposed. The infliction of physical pain is final and irreparable; it cannot be undone in a subsequent proceeding. There is every reason to require, as the Court did in *Goss*, a few minutes of "informal give-and-take between student and disciplinarian" as a "meaningful hedge" against the erroneous infliction of irreparable injury....

The majority's conclusion that a damage remedy for excessive corporal punishment affords adequate process rests on the novel theory that the State may punish an individual without giving him any opportunity to present his side of the story, as long as he can later recover damages from a state official if he is innocent. The logic of this theory would permit a State that punished speeding with a one-day jail sentence to make a driver serve his sentence first without a trial and then sue to recover damages for wrongful imprisonment. Similarly, the State could finally take away a prisoner's good time credits for alleged disciplinary infractions and require him to bring a damage suit after he was eventually released. There is no authority for this theory, nor does the majority purport to find any, in the procedural due process decisions of this Court. Those cases have "consistently held that *some kind of hearing is required at some time before a person is finally deprived* of his property interests... [and that] a person's liberty is equally protected...."

The majority attempts to support its novel theory by drawing an analogy to warrantless arrests on probable cause, which the Court has held reasonable under the Fourth Amendment.... This analogy fails for two reasons. First, the particular requirements of the Fourth Amendment, rooted in the "ancient common-law rule[s]" regulating police practices...must be understood in the context of the criminal justice system for which that Amendment was explicitly tailored. Thus...the Court...rejected the argument that procedural protections required in *Goss* and other due process cases should be afforded to a criminal suspect arrested without a warrant....

...There is, in short, no basis in logic or authority for the majority's suggestion that an action to recover damages for excessive corporal punishment "afford[s] substantially greater protection to the child than the informal conference mandated by *Goss.*" The majority purports to follow the settled principle that what process is due depends on " 'the risk of an erroneous deprivation of [the protected] interest...and the probable value, if any, of additional or substitute procedural safeguards' "; it recognizes, as did *Goss*, the risk of error in the school disciplinary process and concedes that "the child has a strong interest in procedural safeguards that minimize the risk of wrongful punishment...," ...but it somehow concludes that this risk is adequately reduced by a damage remedy that never has been recognized by a Florida court, that leaves unprotected the innocent student punished by mistake, and that allows the State to punish first and hear the student's version of events later. I cannot agree.

The majority emphasizes, as did the dissenters in *Goss,* that even the "rudimentary precautions" required by that decision would impose some burden on the school disciplinary process. But those costs are no greater if the student is paddled rather than suspended; the risk of error in the punishment is no smaller; and the fear of "a significant intrusion" into the disciplinary process...is just as exaggerated. The disciplinarian need only take a few minutes to give the student "notice of the charges against him and, if he denies them, an explanation of the evidence the authorities have and an opportunity to present his side of the story."... In this context the Constitution requires, "if anything, less than a fair-minded principal would impose upon himself" in order to avoid injustice....

I would reverse the judgment below.

MR. JUSTICE STEVENS, dissenting....

...The constitutional prohibition of state deprivations of life, liberty, or property without due process of law does not, by its express language, require that a hearing be provided *before* any deprivation may occur. To be sure, the timing of the process may be a critical element in determining its adequacy—that is, in deciding what process is due in a particular context. Generally, adequate notice and a fair opportunity to be heard in advance of any deprivation of a constitutionally protected interest are essential. The Court has recognized, however, that the wording of the command that there shall be no deprivation "without" due process of law is consistent with the conclusion that a postdeprivation remedy is sometimes constitutionally sufficient.

When only an invasion of a property interest is involved, there is a greater likelihood that a damage award will make a person completely whole than when an invasion of the individual's interest in freedom from bodily restraint and punishment has occurred. In the property context, therefore, frequently a postdeprivation state remedy may be all the process that the Fourteenth Amendment requires. It may also be true—although I do not express an opinion on the point—that an adequate state remedy for defamation may satisfy the due process requirement when a State has impaired an individual's interest in his reputation. On that hypothesis, the Court's analysis today gives rise to the thought that *Paul* v. *Davis*...[1976] may have been correctly decided on an incorrect rationale. Perhaps the Court will one day agree with MR. JUSTICE BRENNAN's appraisal of the importance of the constitutional interest at stake in *Paul* v. *Davis*...and nevertheless conclude that an adequate state remedy may prevent every state inflicted injury to a person's reputation....

▼▼▼

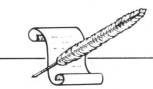

May

COURT ON "FOR SALE" SIGN BAN

May 2, 1977

The Supreme Court May 2 ruled 8-0 that the First Amendment forbade town officials from prohibiting the posting of "For Sale" or "Sold" signs on real estate.

Fearful that the racially integrated community of Willingboro, N.J.—a town near Fort Dix—would experience the flight of white homeowners from the community, the town council in 1974 passed a resolution that forbade the use of lawn signs advertising real estate transactions in the town. Linmark Associates, owning real estate it wished to sell in Willingboro, challenged the law as unconstitutional.

The town's goal was an important one, wrote Justice Thurgood Marshall for the court, but the council must find other ways to implement it. Until 1975, commercial speech—such as advertisements—was thought to be outside the First Amendment's protection of free speech. In 1975 the court invalidated a Virginia law under which a newspaper publisher could be punished for running ads for abortion services in his newspaper (Bigelow v. Virginia). In 1976, the court struck down another Virginia law which forbade the advertising of prescription drug prices. (Historic Documents of 1976, p. 351)

Citing those decisions, Marshall wrote that the First Amendment interest of persons wishing to buy or sell a home was no less than that of persons wishing to buy and sell prescription drugs. "And the societal interest in the free flow of commercial information,...is in no way lessened by the fact that the subject of the commercial information here is realty rather than abortion or drugs," Marshall wrote.

"There can be no question about the importance of achieving this goal" of stable racially integrated housing—the objective of the ordinance—Marshall wrote. But the town did not prove that the ordinance was necessary to assure that it would remain an integrated community.

And the constitutional problem presented by the ban on "For Sale" signs was basic, Marshall said. Through the ban, the city council acted "to prevent its residents from obtaining certain information...of vital interest to Willingboro residents, since it may bear on one of the most important decisions they have a right to make: where to live and raise their families. The Council has sought to restrict the free flow of this data because it fears that otherwise, homeowners will make decisions inimical to what the Council views as the homeowners' self-interest and the corporate interest of the township: They will choose to leave the town. The Council's concern...was not with any commercial aspect of 'For Sale' signs...but with the substance of the information communicated to Willingboro citizens."

"If dissemination of this information can be restricted, then every locality in the country can suppress any facts that reflect poorly on the locality so long as a plausible claim can be made that disclosure would cause the recipients of the information to act 'irrationally,'" Marshall said.

The decision reversed a ruling by the Third U.S. Circuit Court of Appeals that had upheld the ordinance. The decision extended a recent trend in Supreme Court decisions regarding certain forms of "commercial" expression permitted under the right of free speech.

Following are excerpts from the Supreme Court decision delivered May 2, 1977 extending First Amendment protection to upholding an individual's right to post "For Sale" signs on real estate:

No. 76-357

| Linmark Associates, Inc. and William Mellman, Petitioners, *v.* Township of Willingboro and Gerald Daly. | On Writ of Certiorari to the United States Court of Appeals for the Third Circuit. |

[May 2, 1977]

MR. JUSTICE MARSHALL delivered the opinion of the Court. [MR. JUSTICE REHNQUIST took no part in the consideration or decision of this case.]

This case presents the question whether the First Amendment permits a municipality to prohibit the posting of "For Sale" or "Sold" signs when the municipality acts to stem what it perceives as the flight of white homeowners from a racially integrated community.

Petitioner Linmark Associates, a New Jersey corporation, owned a piece of realty in the Township of Willingboro, N.J. Petitioner decided to sell its property, and on March 26, 1974, listed it with petitioner Mellman, a real estate agent. To attract interest in the property, petitioners desired to place a "For Sale" sign on the lawn. Willingboro, however, narrowly limits the types of signs that can be erected on land in the township. Although prior to March of 1974 "For Sale" and "Sold" signs were permitted subject to certain restrictions not at issue here, on March 18, 1974, the Township Council enacted Ordinance 5-1974, repealing the statutory authorization for such signs on all but model homes. Petitioners brought this action against both the township and the building inspector charged with enforcing the ban on "For Sale" signs, seeking declaratory and injunctive relief. The District Court granted a declaration of unconstitutionality, but a divided court of appeals reversed.... We granted certiorari and reverse the judgment of the Court of Appeals.

I

The Township of Willingboro is a residential community located in southern New Jersey near Fort Dix, McGuire Air Force Base, and offices of several national corporations. The township was developed as a middle income community by Levitt and Sons, beginning in the late 1950's. It is served by over 80 realtors.

During the 1960's Willingboro underwent rapid growth. The white population increased by almost 350%, and the nonwhite population rose from 60 to over 5,000, or from .005% of the population to 11.7%. As of the 1970 census, almost 44,000 people resided in Willingboro. In the 1970's, however, the population growth slowed; from 1970 to 1973, the latest year for which figures were available at the time of trial, Willingboro's population rose by only 3%. More significantly, the white population actually declined by almost 2,000 in this interval, a drop of over 5%, while the nonwhite population grew by more than 3,000, an increase of approximately 60%. By 1973, nonwhites constituted 18.2% of the township's population.

At the trial in this case respondent presented testimony from two realtors, two members of the Township Council, and three members of the Human Relations Commission, all of whom agreed that a major cause in the decline in the white population was "panic selling"—that is, selling by whites who feared that the Township was becoming all black, and that property values would decline. One realtor estimated that the reason 80% of the sellers gave for their decision to sell was that "the whole town was for sale, and they didn't want to be caught in any bind."... Respondents' witnesses also testified that in their view "For Sale" and "Sold" signs were a major catalyst of these fears.

William Kearns, the Mayor of Willingboro during the year preceding enactment of the ordinance and a member of the Council when the ordinance was enacted, testified concerning the events leading up to its passage.... According to Kearns, beginning at least in 1973 the community became concerned about the changing population. At a town meeting in February 1973, called to discuss "Willingboro, to sell or not to sell," a member of the community suggested that real estate signs be banned. The suggestion received the overwhelming support of those attending the meeting. Kearns brought the proposal to the Township Council, which requested the Township Solicitor to study it. The Council also contacted National Neighbors, a nationwide organization promoting integrated housing, and obtained the names of other communities that had prohibited "For Sale" signs. After obtaining a favorable report from Shaker Heights, Ohio, on its ordinance, and after receiving an endorsement of the proposed ban from the Willingboro Human Relations Commission, the Council began drafting legislation.

Rather than following its usual procedure of conducting a public hearing only after the proposed law had received preliminary Council approval, the Council scheduled two public meetings on Ordinance 5-1974. The first took place in February 1974, before the initial Council vote, and the second in March 1974, after the vote. At the conclusion of the second hearing, the Ordinance was approved unanimously.

The transcripts of the Council hearings were introduced into evidence at trial. They reveal that at the hearings the Council received important information bearing on the need for and likely impact of the ordinance. With respect to the justification for the ordinance, the Council was told (a) that a study of Willingboro home sales in 1973 revealed that the turnover rate was roughly 11%; ...(b) that in February 1974—a typical month—230 "For Sale" signs were posted among the 11,000 houses in the community; ...and (c) that the Willingboro Tax Assessor had reported that "by and large the increased value of Willingboro properties was way ahead of...comparable communities."... With respect to the projected effect of the ordinance, several realtors reported that 30%-35% of their purchaser-clients came to them because they had seen one of the realtor's "For Sale" or "Sold" signs...and one realtor estimated, based on his experience in a neighboring community that already banned signs, that selling realty without signs takes twice as long as selling with signs....

The transcripts of the Council hearings also reveal that the hearings provided useful barometers of public sentiment towards the proposed ordinance. The Council was told, for example, that surveys in two areas of the township found overwhelming support for the law.... In addition, at least at the second meeting, the nonrealtor citizens who spoke favored the proposed ordinance by a sizeable margin. Interestingly, however, at both meetings those defending the ordinance focused primarily on aesthetic considerations and on the effect of signs—and transiency generally—on property values. Few speakers directly referred to the changing racial composition of Willingboro in supporting the proposed law.

Although the ordinance had been in effect for nine months prior to trial, no statistical data was presented concerning its impact. Respondents' witnesses all agreed, however, that the number of persons selling or considering selling their houses because of racial fears had declined sharply. But several of these witnesses also testified that the number of sales in Willingboro had not declined since the ordinance was enacted. Moreover, respondents' realtor-witnesses both stated that their business had increased by 25% since the ordinance was enacted...and one of these realtors reported that the racial composition of his clientele remained unchanged....

The District Court did not make specific findings of fact. In the course of its opinion, however, the court stated that Willingboro "is to a large extent a transient community, partly due to its proximity to the military facility at Fort Dix and in part due to the numerous transfers of real estate." The court also stated that there was "no evidence" that whites were leaving Willingboro *en masse* as "For Sale" signs appeared, but "merely an indication that its residents are concerned that there may be a large influx of minority groups moving in to the town with the resultant effect being a reduction in property values." The Court of Appeals essentially accepted these "findings," although it found that Willingboro was experiencing "incipient" panic selling...and that a "fear psychology [had] developed."...

II

A

The starting point for analysis of petitioners' First Amendment claim must be the two recent decisions in which this Court has eroded the "commercial speech" exception to the First Amendment. In *Bigelow* v. *Virginia*...(1975), decided just two years ago, this Court for the first time expressed its dissatisfaction with the then-prevalent approach of resolving a class of First Amendment claims simply by categorizing the speech as commercial."... "Regardless of the particular label," we stated, "a court may not escape the task of assessing the First Amendment interest at stake and weighing it against the public interest allegedly served by the regulation."... After conducting such an analysis in *Bigelow* we concluded that Virginia could not constitutionally punish the publisher of a newspaper for printing an abortion referral agency's paid advertisement which not only promoted the agency's services but also contained information about the availability of abortions.

One year later, in *Virginia State Board of Pharmacy* v. *Virginia Citizens Consumer Council, Inc.*...(1976), we went further. Conceding that "[s]ome fragment of hope for the continuing validity of a 'commercial speech' exception arguably might have persisted because of the subject matter in the advertisement in *Bigelow*," ...we held quite simply, that commercial speech is not "wholly outside the protection of the First Amendment."... Although recognizing that "[s]ome forms of commercial speech regulation"—such as regulation of false or misleading speech—"are surely permissible"...we had little difficulty in finding that Virginia's ban on the advertising of prescription drug prices by pharmacists was unconstitutional.

Respondents contend, as they must, that the "For Sale" signs banned in Willingboro are constitutionally distinguishable from the abortion and drug advertisements we have previously considered. It is to the distinctions respondents advance that we now turn.

B

If the Willingboro law is to be treated differently from those invalidated in *Bigelow* and *Virginia Pharmacy,* it cannot be because the speakers—or listeners—have a lesser First Amendment interest in the subject matter of the speech that is regulated here. Persons desiring to sell their homes are just as interested in communicating that fact as are sellers of other goods and services. Similarly, would-be-purchasers of realty are no less interested in receiving information about available property than are purchasers of other commodities in receiving like information about those commodities. And the societal interest in "the free flow of commercial information"...is in no way lessened by the fact that the subject of the commercial information here is realty rather than abortions or drugs.

Respondents nevertheless argue that First Amendment concerns are less directly implicated by Willingboro's ordinance because it restricts only one method of communication. This distinction is not without significance to First Amendment analysis, since laws regulating the time, place or manner of speech stand on a different footing than laws prohibiting speech altogether.... Respondents effort to defend the ordinance on this ground is unpersuasive, however, for two reasons.

First, serious questions exist as to whether the ordinance "leave[s] open ample alternative channels for communication."... Although in theory sellers remain free to employ a number of different alternatives, in practice realty is not marketed through leaflets, sound trucks, demonstrations or the like. The options to which sellers realistically are relegated—primarily newspaper advertising and listing with realtors—involve more cost and less autonomy than "For Sale" signs...are less likely to reach persons not deliberately seeking sales information...and may be less effective media for communicating the message that is conveyed by a "For Sale" sign in front of the house to be sold.... The alternatives, then, are far from satisfactory.

Second, the Willingboro ordinance is not genuinely concerned with the place of the speech—front lawns—or the manner of the speech—signs. The township has not prohibited all lawn signs—or all lawn signs of a particular size or shape—in order to promote aesthetic values or any other value "unrelated to the suppression of free expression."... Nor has it acted to restrict a mode of communication that "intrudes on the privacy of the home, ...makes it impractical for the unwilling viewer or auditor to avoid exposure"...or otherwise reaches a group the township has a right to protect. And respondents have not demonstrated that the place or manner

of the speech produces a detrimental "secondary effect" on society....
Rather, Willingboro has proscribed particular types of signs based on their
content because it fears their "primary" effect—that they will cause those
receiving the information to act upon it. That the proscription applies only
to one mode of communication, therefore, does not transform this into a
"time, place, or manner" case.... If the ordinance is to be sustained, it
must be on the basis of the township's interest in regulating the content of
the communication, and not on any interest in regulating the form.

C

Respondents do seek to distinguish *Bigelow* and *Virginia Pharmacy* by
relying on the vital goal this ordinance serves: namely, promoting stable,
racially integrated housing. There can be no question about the importance of achieving this goal. This Court has expressly recognized that substantial benefits flow to both whites and blacks from interracial association
and that Congress has made a strong national commitment to promoting
integrated housing. *Trafficante* v. *Metropolitan Life Insurance Co...*
(1972).

That this ordinance was enacted to achieve an important governmental
objective, however, does not distinguish the case from *Virginia Pharmacy*.
In *Virginia Pharmacy* the State argued that its prohibition on prescription
drug price advertising furthered the health and safety of state residents by
preventing low cost, low quality pharmacists from driving reputable pharmacists out of business. We expressly recognized the "strong interest" of a
State in maintaining "professionalism on the part of licensed pharmacists."... But we nevertheless found the Virginia law unconstitutional
because we were unpersuaded that the law was necessary to achieve this
objective, and were convinced that in any event, the First Amendment
disabled the State from achieving its goal by restricting the free flow of
truthful information. For the same reasons we conclude that the
Willingboro ordinance at issue here is also constitutionally infirm.

The record here demonstrates that respondents failed to establish that
this ordinance is needed to assure that Willingboro remains an integrated
community. As the District Court concluded, the evidence does not support the Council's apparent fears that Willingboro was experiencing a substantial incidence of panic selling by white homeowners. *A fortiori*, the
evidence does not establish that "For Sale" signs in front of 2% of
Willingboro homes were a major cause of panic selling. And the record does
not confirm the township's assumption that proscribing such signs will
reduce public awareness of realty sales and thereby decrease public concern over selling.

The constitutional defect in this ordinance, however, is far more basic.
The Township Council here, like the Virginia Assembly in *Virginia Pharmacy*, acted to prevent its residents from obtaining certain information.
That information, which pertains to sales activity in Willingboro, is of vital
interest to Willingboro residents, since it may bear on one of the most im-

portant decisions they have a right to make: where to live and raise their families. The Council has sought to restrict the free flow of this data because it fears that otherwise, homeowners will make decisions inimical to what the Council views as the homeowners' self-interest and the corporate interest of the township: they will choose to leave town. The Council's concern, then, was not with any commercial aspect of "For Sale" signs—with offerors communicating offers to offerees—but with the substance of the information communicated to Willingboro citizens. If dissemination of this information can be restricted, then every locality in the country can suppress any facts that reflect poorly on the locality, so long as a plausible claim can be made that disclosure would cause the recipients of the information to act "irrationally." *Virginia Pharmacy* denies government such sweeping powers....

...Since we can find no meaningful distinction between Ordinance 5-1974 and the statute overturned in *Virginia Pharmacy,* we must conclude this ordinance violates the First Amendment.

III

In invalidating this law, we by no means leave Willingboro defenseless in its effort to promote integrated housing. The township obviously remains free to continue "the process of education" it has already begun. It can give widespread publicity—through "Not for Sale" signs or other methods—to the number of whites remaining in Willingboro. And it surely can endeavor to create inducements to retain individuals who are considering selling their homes.

Beyond this, we reaffirm our statement in *Virginia Pharmacy* that the "commonsense differences between speech that 'does no more than propose a commercial transaction'...and other varieties...suggest that a different degree of protection is necessary to insure that the flow of truthful and legitimate commercial information is unimpaired."... Laws dealing with false or misleading signs, and laws requiring such signs to "appear in such a form, or include such additional information...as [is] necessary to prevent [their] being deceptive,"...therefore, would raise very different constitutional questions. We leave those questions for another day, and simply hold that the ordinance under review here, which impairs "the flow of truthful and legitimate commercial information" is constitutionally infirm.

Reversed.

NIXON-FROST INTERVIEWS

May 4, 12, 19, 25; September 3, 1977

Former President Richard M. Nixon broke his self-imposed silence on the Watergate affair May 4, 1977, in the first of a series of interviews conducted by British television personality David Frost.

The former President, in a statement that fell short of an outright admission of wrongdoing, said he had "let the American people down" by abetting the Watergate coverup and not meeting his constitutional duty to see that the laws were enforced.

"I brought myself down," Nixon told Frost. "I have impeached myself," he said, "by resigning." During the course of the 90-minute interview, Nixon said that his conduct did not amount to an obstruction of justice. The former President denied any prior knowledge of the June 17, 1972, burglary at the Democratic National Committee offices in the plush Watergate complex.

Watergate Scandal

In a series of long and sometimes sharp exchanges with Frost, Nixon denied that he had condoned payment of hush money to the Watergate burglars. Mr. Nixon said that his mistake after March 21, 1973—the date White House counsel John Dean III informed him of the deep involvement of White House personnel and Nixon campaign officials in the coverup—was to act as a lawyer for the defense of his close personal associates on the White House staff, and that perhaps he had not met fully the responsibility of his oath of office to enforce the law.

The former President told Frost that he had interpreted the Watergate burglary as a political problem and tried to contain it. By early 1973 the Senate Watergate Committee, the Special Prosecutor, the media and the House Judiciary Committee—all partisan and set against him, Nixon alleged—had caused events to "snowball." "I brought myself down. I gave 'em a sword. And they stuck it in and they twisted it with relish. And I guess, if I'd been in their position, I'd [have] done the same thing."

The former President reiterated his view that his actions had not been illegal or unconstitutional because his motives had been rooted in humanitarian impulses. Despite Frost's objection to Nixon's definition, the former President contended that the charge of obstruction of justice required evidence of corrupt intention. On that basis, Nixon observed, "I did not have a corrupt motive." He noted that "political containment is not a corrupt motive."

At an emotional peak in the telecast Nixon admitted that his handling of Watergate-related matters had caused him considerable anguish. Nixon said, "I let down my friends. I let down the country. I let down our system of government.... I let the American people down, and I have to carry that burden with me for the rest of my life.... I made so many bad judgments. The worse one [sic], mistakes of the heart, rather than the head...."

Foreign Policy

In the May 12 interview, which was devoted to foreign policy, the former President told Frost he had rejected an Egyptian plan to impose a cease-fire in the 1973 Middle East war. It would have been "sheer madness," he said, to pose a big power confrontation in such a strategic area. When the Soviet Union threatened intervention on Egypt's side, Nixon ordered a U.S. military alert as, he said, "a message that would get through to Moscow."

The U.S. diplomatic "tilt" toward Pakistan in the 1971 India-Pakistan War was the result of big power rivalry, Nixon recounted. He had received reliable information that India, supported diplomatically by the Soviet Union, planned an attack on West Pakistan after the struggle for control of East Pakistan (Bangladesh) ended. "We saved West Pakistan," Nixon told Frost. Moreover, U.S. support of Pakistan "built up a lot of credibility with the Chinese," the former President added.

Frost asked Nixon to give an appraisal of former Secretary of State Henry A. Kissinger. Nixon responded that he thought Kissinger was "less fatalistic" and more emotional than he was. He told Frost that Kissinger, perhaps half a dozen times during their working relationship, offered his resignation as Secretary of State because he thought he was no longer useful to the administration. Kissinger's impulse to resign, Nixon said, occurred at times of disappointment and frustration over matters of state.

Defense of Indochina Policies

Nixon May 19 defended the 1970 invasion of Cambodia, saying that his action had kept that nation out of Communist hands for five years. Nixon said his foreign policy brought North Vietnam to the negotiating table and won an honorable peace that "lasted for at least two...years." The political costs of the policy lay at home, Nixon said, but he denied a suggestion by Frost that his political objective, once it was determined that the war would continue with widening dissent at home, included policies aimed at dividing the American people and isolating the dissidents.

Nixon compared his situation to that faced by Abraham Lincoln during the Civil War, saying that the nation was torn apart "in an ideological way" in the 1970s as it was divided North and South during the Civil War. While Nixon conceded to Frost that the Constitution did not specifically grant the power to act above the law simply because a President considered an action necessary, he said that in wartime, "a President does have extraordinary powers which would make acts that would otherwise be unlawful, lawful if undertaken for the purpose of preserving the nation...."

Comments on Resignation, Chile, Agnew

In the telecast interview aired May 25 Nixon said that he regretted that he was unable to clear his name "through the agony of a trial" and that life had become "almost unbearable" after resigning the presidency. Americans were understandably incensed that he was "able to get off with a pardon," Nixon observed, but he explained that he was physically and mentally exhausted. Moreover, Nixon claimed, he would not have received a fair trial in the prevailing climate of opinion. Nixon denied that there had been any discussion with incoming President Gerald R. Ford regarding the pardon.

In the discussion of the legal proceedings against Vice President Spiro T. Agnew on charges of bribery and corruption, Nixon told Frost that Agnew had maintained his innocence throughout their conversations on the matter. Nixon said he treated the question of Agnew's guilt or innocence in a pragmatic way, because he knew that Agnew had to consider the resignation option in any case.

When questioned about the role of the Central Intelligence Agency (CIA) in the downfall of President Salvador Allende Gossens of Chile, Nixon turned aside any suggestions of U.S. wrongdoing and presented the picture of a President defending the hemisphere against the establishment of Marxist governments. Nixon said Allende was overthrown "...not because of anything that was done from the outside, but because his system didn't work in Chile and Chile decided to throw it out."

Nixon's concluding statement in the May 25 interview captured the inner turmoil and personal ambivalence of the controversial former

President: "No one can know how it feels to resign the presidency of the United States. Is that punishment enough? Oh, probably not. But whether it is or isn't...we have to live with not only the past, but for the future, and I don't know what the future brings, but whatever it brings, I'll still be fighting."

White House Tapes

Former President Nixon told David Frost in the interview broadcast Sept. 3 that he thought he had ordered the White House chief of staff, H. R. Haldeman, to destroy all but the most historical of the taped conversations of the President and his staff before the Watergate investigators had learned of the recordings. The former President also said he did not believe that there was anything detrimental to him on the tapes. "If the tapes had been destroyed," Nixon told Frost, "I believe that it is likely that I would not have had to go through the agony of the resignation."

The 18½-minute erasure gap on a potentially key tape of a conversation between him and Haldeman three days after the Watergate burglary remained a mystery. "I didn't do it...," Nixon said. He supported the testimony of his longtime personal secretary Rose Mary Woods who testified during the Watergate inquiry that she might have been responsible for the accidental erasure of four and a half minutes. If she meant to do it, Nixon remarked, "she's so smart...she'd [have] destroyed a lot more."

Following are excerpts from the telecast transcripts, as printed by The New York Times, *of the May 4, 12, 19, 25 and Sept. 3, 1977, interviews by David Frost with former President Richard M. Nixon. (Boldface headings in brackets have been added by Congressional Quarterly to highlight the organization of the text.):*

May 4, 1977

[Watergate Coverup]

[FROST]:....So, beginning with June 20th, then, what did [H. R.] Haldeman [former White House chief of staff] tell you during the 18½ minute gap?

[NIXON]: Haldeman's notes are the only recollection I have of what he told me. Haldeman was a, a very good notetaker, because, of course, we've had other opportunities to look at his notes and he was very... He was making the notes for my Presidential files. The notes indicated—

Q P.R. offensive and...

A. That's right.

Q. But, as far as your general state of knowledge that evening, when you were talking with Chuck Colson [former special counsel to the President] on the evening of June the 20th, it suggests that from somewhere your knowledge has gone much further. You say, "If we didn't know better, we'd have thought the whole thing had been deliberately botched." Colson tells you, "Bob is pulling it all together. Thus far, I think we've done the right things to date." And you say, "Ba . . . ah, basic. . ." He says, "Basically, they're all pretty hard-line guys." Ah, and you say, "You mean, Hunt?" [E. Howard Hunt Jr., a former White House consultant] and, he says...and you say, "Of course, we're just gonna leave this where it is with the Cubans...at times, I just stonewall it." And, you also say, "We gotta have lawyers smart enough to have our people delay." Now, somewhere you were pretty well informed by that conversation on June 20th.

A. As far as my information on June 20th is concerned, I had been informed by...with regard to the possibility of Hunt's involvement, whether I knew on the 20th or the 21st or 22nd, I knew something...I learned in that period about the possibility of [G. Gordon] Liddy's involvement. [Liddy was a staff member of the Finance Committee to Re-elect the President]. Of course, I knew about the Cubans and [James W.] McCord [a security adviser for the committee], who were all picked up at the scene of the crime. Now, ah you have read here, excerpts out of a conversation with Colson. And, let me say as far as my motive was concerned, and that's the important thing. My motive was, in everything I was saying, or certainly thinking at the time, was not to try to cover up a criminal action. But, to be sure that as far as any slip-over, or should I say, "slop-over," I think, would be a better word. Any slop-over in a way that would damage innocent people, or blow it into political proportions...it was that that I certainly wanted to avoid.

Q. So, you invented the C.I.A. thing on the 23rd as a cover?

A. No. Now, let's use the word "cover-up" through in the sense that it had—should be used and should not be used. If a cover-up is for the purpose of covering up criminal activities, it is illegal. If, however, a cover-up as you have called it, is for a motive that is not criminal, that is something else again. And my motive was not criminal. I didn't believe that we were covering any criminal activities.

I didn't believe that [Attorney General] John Mitchell was involved. I didn't believe that, for that matter, anybody else was. I was trying to contain it politically. And that's a very different motive from the motive of attempting to cover up criminal activities of an individual.

And so, there was no cover-up of any criminal activities; that was not my motive.

Q. But surely, in all you've said, you have proved exactly that that was the case; that there was a cover-up of criminal activity because you've already said, and the record shows, that you knew that Hunt and Liddy were involved; you'd been told that Hunt and Liddy were involved.

At the moment when you told the C.I.A. to tell the F.B.I. to "stop period," as you put it, at that point, only five people had been arrested.

Liddy was not even under suspicion. And so you knew, in terms of intent and you knew in terms of foreseeable consequence that the result would be that, in fact, criminals would be protected. Hunt and Liddy, who were criminally liable, would be protected. You knew about them.

The whole statement says that "we, we're gonna...." Haldeman says, "We don't want you to go any further on it. Get them to stop. They don't need to pursue it; they've already got their case." Walters [Lt. Gen. Vernon A. Walters, deputy director of the C.I.A.] notes that he said, "Five suspects had been arrested, this should be sufficient." You said, "Tell them, don't go any further into this case period."

By definition, by what you've said and by what the record shows, that, per se, was a conspiracy to obstruct justice, because you were limiting it to five people, when, even if we grant the point that you weren't sure about Mitchell, you already knew about Hunt and Liddy and had talked about both, so that is obstruction of justice—

A. Now just a moment—

Q. —period.

A. Ah, that's your conclusion.

Q. It is.

A. But now let's look at the facts. The fact is, that as far as Liddy was concerned, what I knew was, was only the fact that, ah, he was the man on the committee who was in charge of intelligence operations.

As far as Hunt is, was, concerned, and if you read that tape you will find I told them to tell the F.B.I. they didn't know, apparently, and the C.I.A. that Hunt was involved.

And so, there wasn't any, any attempt to keep them from knowing that Hunt was involved. The other important point to bear in mind when you ask "What happened?" and so forth, is that what happened two weeks later.

[Obstruction of Justice]

Two weeks later when I was here in San Clemente, I called Pat Gray, the then-F.B.I. Director, on the phone to congratulate the F.B.I. on a very successful operation they had in apprehending some hijackers in San Francisco, or some place abroad.

He then brought up the subject of the Watergate investigation. He said that there are some people around you who are mortally wounding you, or would, might, mortally wound you, because they're trying to restrict this investigation.

And, I said, "Well, have you talked to Walters about this matter?" And he said, "Yes." I said, "Does he agree?" He said, "Yes." I said, "Well, Pat, I know him," had known him very well, of course, over the years—I did call him by his first name. I said, "Pat, you go right ahead with your investigation." He has so testified, and he did go ahead with the investigation.

Q. Yes, but the point is that obstruction of justice is obstruction of justice, if it's for a minute, or five minutes, much less for the period June

23rd to July the 5th, when I think it was when he talked to Walters and decided to go ahead. The day before he spoke to you on July the 6th. It's obstruction of justice how, for however long a period, isn't it?

And, also, it's no defense to say that the plan failed, that the C.I.A. didn't go along with it, refused to go along with it, that it was transparent....

I mean, if I try and rob a bank and fail, that's no defense. I still tried to rob a bank. I would say, you still tried to obstruct justice, and succeeded for that period. He's testified they didn't interview [Manuel] Ogarrio [a Mexican lawyer], they didn't do all of this. And so, I would have said it was a successful attempt to obstruct justice for that brief period.

A. Now just a moment. You're again making the case, which of course is your responsibility, as the attorney for the prosecution.

Let me make the case as it should be made, even if I were not the one who was involved for the defense.

The case for the defense here is this: You use the term "obstruction of justice." You perhaps have not read the statute with regard to, respect—ah, obstruction of justice.

Q. Well, I have.

A. Obstruction...well, oh, I'm sorry, of course, you probably have read it. But possibly you might have missed it, because when I read it many years ago in, perhaps when I was studying law, although the statute didn't even exist then, because it's a relatively new statute, as you know.

But in any event, when I read it even in recent times, I was not familiar with all of the implications of it. The statute doesn't require just an act. The statute has the specific provision one must corruptly impede a judicial—

Q. Well, you, a corrupt—

A. —matter.

Q. Endeavor is enough.

A. A con—all right, we'll—a conduct—endeavor—corrupt intent. But it must be corrupt, and that gets to the point of motive. One must have a corrupt motive. Now, I did not have a corrupt motive.

Q. You, you were—

A. My motive was pure political containment. And political containment is not a corrupt motive. If so, for example, we—President Truman would have been impeached.

Q. ...Motive can be helpful when intent is not clear. Your intent is absolutely clear. [I]t's stated, again: "Stop this investigation here period."

The foreseeable, inevitable consequence, if you'd been successful, would have been that Hunt and Liddy would not have been brought to justice. How can that not be a conspiracy to obstruct justice?

A. No. Wait a minute. "Stop the investigation." You still have to get back to the point that I have made previously, that, when I, that my concern there, which was conveyed to them, and the decision then was in their hands, my concern was having the investigation spread further than it needed to.

And, as far as that was concerned, I don't believe, as I said, we turned over the fact that we knew that Hunt was involved; that a possibility that Liddy was involved; ah, but under the circumstances—

Q. You didn't turn that over though did you?

A. What?

Q. You didn't turn that over.

A. No, no, no, no, no. We turned over the fact that Hunt, that, that Hunt was, was involved.

Q. You never told anyone about Liddy though.

A. No, not at that point.

Q. Now after the Gray conversation, the cover-up went on. You would say, I think, that you were not aware of it. I, I think, was arguing that you were a part of it as a result of the June the 23rd conversations. But you say that you were—

A. —Are you sure I was a part of it, as a result of the June 23rd conversations?

Q. Yes.

A. After July 6th, when I talked to Gray?

Q. I would have said that you joined the conspiracy, which you therefore never left.

A. Yes. No. Well, then we totally disagree on that

Q. But, I mean, that, that's, those are the two positions.

A. That's right.

Q. Now, you, in fact, however, would say that you first learned of the cover-up on March the 21st. Is that right?

A. On March 21st—was the date when I was first informed of the fact. The important fact, to me, in that conversation, was of the blackmail threat that was being made by Howard Hunt, who was one of the Watergate, ah, ah, participants, but not about Watergate.

Q. So, during the period between those two dates, between the end of June, beginning of July, and March the 21st, while lots of elements of the cover-up as we now know were continuing, were you ever made aware of any of them?

A. No. I, I don't know what you're referring to.

[Hunt "Hush-money"]

Q. Well, for instance, the, your personal lawyer, Herbert Kalmbach, coming to Washington to start the raising of $219,000 of hush-money, approved by Haldeman and [John D.] Ehrlichman [Assistant to the President]. They went ahead but without—without clearing it with you?

A. That was one of the statements that I've made, which, after all of the checking we can possibly do...we checked with Haldeman, we checked with Ehrlichman.

I wondered, for example, if I had been informed, if I had been informed that money was being raised for humanitarian purposes, to help these people with their defense, I would certainly have approved it.

If I had been told that the purpose of the money was to raise it for the purpose of keeping them quiet, I would have been—disapproved it. But the truth of the matter is that I was not told. I did not learn of it until the March period.

Q. But in that case, if that was the first occasion, why did you say, in, ah, such strong terms to Colson, on February the 14th, which is more than a month before, you said to him: "The cover-up is the main ingredient; that's where we gotta cut our losses; my losses are to be cut; the President's loss has gotta be cut on the cover-up deal."

A. Why did I say that? Well, because I read the American papers. And, in January, the stories that came out, they're not, not just from The Washington Post, the famous series by some unnamed correspondents, who have written a best-selling book since then, but The New York Times, the networks and so forth.

We're talking about "hush-money." They were talking about clemency pay, ah, ah, for cover-up, and all the rest. It was that that I was referring to at that point. I was referring to the fact that there was a lot of talk about cover-up, and that this must be avoided at all cost.

Q. But, there's one very clear, self-contained quote, and I read the whole of this conversation of February the 13th, which I don't think's ever been published, but, and there was one very clear quote in it that I thought was—

A. It hasn't been published, you say?

Q. No, I think it's, it's available to anybody who consults the records, but, ah—

A. Oh, yes.

Q. But people don't consult all the records.

A. Just wondered if we'd seen it.

Q. Well, I'm, I'm sure you have, yes, but,—where the President says this, on February the 13th:

"When I'm speaking about Wa—" This is to Colson: "When I'm speaking about Watergate, though, that's the whole point of, of the election. This tremendous investigation rests unless one of the seven begins to talk. That's the problem."

Now, in that remark, it seems to me that someone running the cover-up couldn't have expressed it more clearly than that, could they?

A. What do we mean by "one of the seven beginning to talk?"

I've—how many times do I have to tell you that as far as these seven were concerned, the concern that we had, certainly that I had, was that men who worked in this kind of a covert activity, men who, of course, realize it's dangerous activity to work in, particularly since it involves illegal entry, that once they're apprehended, they are likely to say anything.

And the question was, I didn't know of anybody at that point—nobody on the White House staff, not John Mitchell, anybody else, that I believed was involved, ah criminally.

But on the other hand, I certainly could believe that a man like Howard Hunt, who was a prolific bookwriter, or anyone of the others under the pressures of the moment, could have started blowing, and putting out all sorts of stories to embarrass the Administration, and as it later turned out, in Hunt's case, to blackmail the President to provide clemency, or to provide money, or both.

Q. I still just think, though, that one has to go contrary to the, ah, normal usage of language of almost 10,000 gangster movies to interpret "this tremendous investigation rests, unless one of the seven begins to talk; that's the problem," as anything other than some sort of conspiracy to stop him talking about something damaging—

A. Well, you can, you can state—

Q. —to the press, and making the speech—

A. You can state your conclusion, and I've stated my views.

Q. That's fair.

A. So now we go on with the rest of it....

Q. ...Looking back on the record now, of that [March 21, 1973 conversation with John W. Dean 3d], as I'm sure you've done, in addition to the overall details, which we'll come to in a minute. Bearing in mind that a payment probably was set in motion prior to the meeting and was certainly not completed until late the evening of the meeting, wouldn't you say that the record of the meeting does show that you endorsed, or ratified, what was going on with regard to payment to Hunt?

A. No, the record doesn't show that at all. In fact, the record actually is ambiguous until you get to the end, and then it's quite clear. And, what I said later in the day, and what I said the following day, shows [what] the facts really are, and completely contradicts the fact, the point, that has been made....

Let me say, I did consider the payment of $120,000 to Hunt's lawyer and to Hunt for his attorney's fees and for support. I considered it not because Hunt was "gonna blow," using our gangster language here, on Watergate, because as the record clearly shows, Dean says, "It isn't about Watergate, but [he's] going to talk about some of the things he's done for Ehrlichman."

As far as the payment of the money was concerned, when the total record is read, you will find that it seems to end on a basis which is indecisive. But I clearly remember, and you undoubtedly have it in your notes there, my saying that the White House can't do it," I think, for my, was my last words.

Because I had gone through the whole scenario with Dean, and I laid it out. I said, "Look, what would it co—I mean, when you're talking about all of these people, what would it cost to take care of them for—and we talked about a million dollars.

['Question of Clemency']

And, I said, "Well, you could raise the money, but doesn't it finally get down to a question of clemency?" And, he said, "Yes."

I said, "Well, you can't provide clemency and that would be wrong for sure." Now, if clemency's the bottom line, then providing money isn't going to make any sense....

Q. You [were] talking on April the 20th, and you were recollecting this meeting and you said that you said to Dean and to Haldeman, "Christ, turn over any cash we got." That's your recollection of the meeting on April 20 when you didn't know you were on television.

A. Of course I didn't know I was on television. On April the 20th, it could well have been my recollection. But, my point is: I wonder why, again, we haven't followed up with what happened after the meeting? Let me tell you what happened after the meeting. And you were, incidentally, very fair to point out—and the record clearly shows—that Dean did not follow up in any way on this. The payment that was made... Dean didn't know it. I didn't know it. Nobody else knew it, apparently, was being made contemporaneously that day through another source.

Q. The next...the next...

A. Yeah.

Q. The next morning, Mitchell told Haldeman that it had been paid.

A. Yeah.

Q. And in a later transcript you agree with Haldeman, that he told you. You say, you say, "Yes, you reported that to me."

A. Yes. I understand.

Q. You were very soon aware it had gone through.

['Blackmail']

A. That's right. But my point is: The question we have is whether or not the payment was made as a result of a direction given by the President for that purpose. And, the point is: It was not. And the point is that the next morning—you talk about the conversation, and here again you probably don't have it on your notes here, but on the 22nd, I raised the whole question of payments. And I said, and I'm compressing it all so we don't take too much of our time on this, I said:

"As far as these fellows in jail are concerned, you can help them for humanitarian reasons; but you can't pay—but that Hunt thing goes too far. That's just damn blackmail."

It would have been damn blackmail if Dean had done it. Now, that's in the record. And that's certainly an indication that it wasn't paid.

Q. But later on that day at some point, according to your later words to Haldeman, you were told that it had been paid.

A. I agree that I was told that it had been paid. But what I am saying here is that the charge has been made that I directed it, and that it was paid as a result of what I said at that meeting.

That charge is not true, and it's proved by the tapes, which in so many cases, can be damaging. In this case, they're helpful.

Q. Well, there's two concerns to be said to that. One is: I think that the, the, my reading of the tapes tells me, trying to read in an openminded way, that the writing, not just between the lines, but on so many of the lines that I quoted, is very, very clear: that you were in fact, endorsing at least the short-term solution of paying this sum of money to buy time. That would be my reading of it.

But the other point to be said is: Here's Dean, talking about his hush-money for Hunt; talking about blackmail and all of that. I would say that you endorsed to ratify it. But let's leave that on one side.

A. I didn't endorse or ratify it.

Q. Why didn't you stop it?

A. Because at that point I had nothing to—no knowledge of the fact that it was going to be paid. I'd had no knowledge of the fact that the, what you have mentioned in the transcript of the next day, where Mitchell said he "thought it'd been taken care of."

I think that was what the words were or words to that effect. I wasn't there. I didn't, I don't remember what he said. That was only reported to me.

The point that I made is this: It's possible, it's a mistake that I didn't stop it. The point that I make is that I did consider it. I've told you that I considered it. I considered it for reasons that I thought were very good ones. I would not consider it for the other reasons, which would have been in my view, bad ones....

Q. One of the other things that people find very difficult to take in the Oval Office on March the 21st, is the, is the coaching that you gave Dean and Haldeman on how to deal with the Grand Jury without getting caught, and saying that, "perjury's a tough rap to prove," as you'd said earlier, "just be damned sure you say, 'I don't remember. I can't recall.' "

Is that the sort of conversation that ought to have been going on in the Oval Office, do you think?

['Attorney for the Defense']

A. I think that kind of advice is proper advice for one who, as I was at that time, beginning to put myself in the position of an attorney for the defense—something that I wish I hadn't felt I had the responsibility to, to do.

But I would like the opportunity, when the question arises, to tell you why I felt as deeply as I did on that point. Every lawyer, when he talks to a witness who's going before a Grand Jury, says, "Be sure that you don't volunteer anything. Be sure if you have any questions about anything, say that you don't recollect. Be sure that everything—that you state only the facts that you're absolutely sure of."

Ah, now, on the other hand, I didn't tell them to say, "Don't—forget, if you do remember." That then would be suborning perjury. And, I did not say that.

[Dean Report]

Q. One of the things you repeated many times, but I suppose most memorably or most clearly on August the 15th, 1973. You said:

"If anyone at the White House or high up in my campaign had been involved in wrongdoing of any kind, I wanted that White House to take the lead in making that known. On March the 21st I instructed Dean to write a complete report of all that he knew on the entire Watergate matter."

Now, when one looks through the record of what had gone on, just before and after March the 21st, on March the 17th, the written statement from Dean, you asked for a "self-serving God-damned statement denying culpability of principal figures." When he told you that the original Liddy plan had involved bugging, you told him to omit that fact in his document and state it was for, the plan was for totally legal intelligence operation.

March 20th, as I'm sure you know, you said, "You want a complete statement, but make it very incomplete." On March the 21st, after his revelations to you, you say, "Understand, I don't want to get all that God-damned specific." And, Ehrlichman and you, when you're talking on the 22nd, and he's talking of the Dean report, he says, "And the report says, 'Nobody was involved.' " And, there's several other quotes to that effect. Was that the Dean report that you described? It wasn't the same as what you described on August the 15th was it?

A. Well, what you're leaving out, of course, which is in that same tape that you've just quoted from, is a very, very significant statement.

I said, that "John Dean should make a report." And, I said, "We've, er, we have to have a statement." And then I went on to say, "And, if it opens doors, let it open doors."

Now with regard to the report being complete, but incomplete, what I meant was this, very simply. I meant that he should state what he was sure of, what he knew. Because, one day, he would say one day one thing, another day, he'd say something else....

I didn't want him to answer, and you'll find that also in one of the tapes, I said: "Don't go into every charge that has been made. Go into only what you know." And particularly, go in hard on the fact, which he had consistently repeated over and over again, "No one in the White House is involved." That's what I wanted him to do.

['A Modified, Limited Hang-out']

Q. But, then you have a discussion in the meeting with Haldeman, Ehrlichman, Mitchell, Dean, where you're deciding what the policy's going to be:

"Is it going to be a hang-out," i.e., is it going to be the whole of the truth? And, in the end, it's decided that it's going to be one of the great phrases of Watergate—"a modified, limited hang-out." Which is why I suggest the other quotes that I've quoted to you, are decisive.

And then Ehrlichman goes on to say, "I'm looking at the future." And he says, "Now we already know it's a modified, limited version of the truth, I mean it's obviously not going to be the whole of the truth. I am looking at the future. Assuming some corner of this thing comes unstuck at some time, you [that's you] are in a position [t]o say, 'Look, that document I've published is a document I relied on, that is the report I relied on.' "

And, you respond, "That's right." Now you've decided the document's going to be modified. It's going to be limited, and then you're going to rely on that document, and so you're going to be able to blame it on Dean. And, it seems to me that, that is consistent with all the quotes that I have quoted, and not the open-door quote that you have quoted.

A. That's your opinion, and I have my opinion. Dean was sent to write a report. He worked on it, and he certainly would have remembered, ah, a phrase that was, let me say, a lot more easy to understand than "modified hang-out" or whatever Ehrlichman said. He would have remembered, "If it opens doors, it opens doors."

I meant by that I was prepared to hear the worst as well as the good.

And he says, "I disagree with your decision totally." He said, "I think it's going to eventually, you're going to live to regret it, but I will.".....

...And, I suppose you could sum it all up the way one of your British Prime Ministers summed it up, Gladstone, when he said that "the first requirement for a Prime Minister is to be a good butcher." Well, I think the great story as far as summary of Watergate is concerned, I, ah, I did some of the big things rather well.

I screwed up terribly in what was a little thing and became a big thing. But I still have to admit, I wasn't a good butcher....

...I would say that the statements that I made afterwards were, on the big issues, true; that I was not involved in the matters that I have spoken to, about—not involved in the breakin; that I did not engage in the, and participate in, or approve the payment of money or the authorization of clemency, which of course were the essential elements of the cover-up. That was true.

But the statements were misleading in exaggerating, in that enormous political attack I was under. It was a five-front war with a fifth column. I had a partisan Senate Committee staff. We had a partisan Special Prosecutor staff. We had a partisan media. We had a partisan judiciary committee staff in the fifth column.

Now under all these circumstances, my reactions in some of the statements and press conferences and so forth after that, I want to say right here and now, I said things that were not true. Most of them were fundamentally true on the big issues, but without going as far as I should have gone, and saying perhaps that I had considered other things but had not done them.

And for all those things I have a very deep regret.

Q. You got caught up in something—

A. Yeah.

Q. And then it snowballed.

A. It snowballed. And it was my fault. I'm not blaming anybody else. I'm simply saying to you that, as far as I'm concerned, I not only regret it, I indicated my own beliefs in this matter when I resigned. People didn't think it was enough to admit mistakes, fine. If they want me to get down and grovel on the floor, no. Never, because I don't believe I should.

On the other hand, there are some friends who say, "Just face them down. There is a conspiracy to get you." There may have been. I don't know what the C.I.A. had to do. Some of their shenanigans have yet to be told, according to a book I read recently. I don't know what was going on in some Republican, some Democratic circles, as far as the so-called impeachment lobby was concerned. However, I don't go with the idea that there...that what brought me down was a coup, a conspiracy, et cetera, et cetera, et cetera.

I brought myself down. I gave 'em a sword. And they stuck it in, and they twisted it with relish. And I guess if I'd been in their position, I'd have done the same thing....

A. The lawyers can argue that. I did not commit, in my view, an impeachable offense. Now, the House has ruled overwhelmingly that I did; of course, there was only an indictment and would have to be tried in the Senate. I might have won. I might have lost. But, even if I'd won in the Senate by a vote or two, I would have been crippled and the...for six months the country couldn't afford having the President in the dock in the United States Senate, and there can never be an impeachment in the future in this country without voluntarily impeaching himself. I have impeached myself. That speaks for itself.

Q. How do you mean, "I have impeached myself?"

[Voluntary Impeachment]

A. By resigning. That was a voluntary impeachment. And, now what does that mean in terms of whether I, ah...you're wanting me to say that I...participated in an illegal cover-up? No. Now, when you come to the period—and this is the critical period—that when you come to the period of March 21st, on, when Dean gave his legal opinion, that certain things, actions taken by Haldeman, Ehrlichman, Mitchell, et cetera, and even by himself, amounted to a legal cover-up and so forth; then I was in a very different position, and during that period, I will admit that I started acting as lawyer for their defense.

I will admit that, acting as lawyer for their defense, I was not prosecuting the case. I will admit that during that period, rather than acting primarily in my role as the chief law enforcement officer in the United States of America, or at least with responsibility for the law enforcement, because the Attorney General is the chief law enforcement officer, but as the one with the chief responsibility for seeing that the laws of the United States are enforced, that I did not meet that responsibility. And, to the extent that I did not meet that responsibility, to the extent that within the law, and in some cases going right to the edge of the law in trying to advise Ehrlichman and Haldeman and all the rest as to how best to present their cases—because I thought they were legally innocent—that I came to the edge and, under the circumstances, I would have to say that a reasonable person could call that a cover-up.

I didn't think of it as a cover-up. I didn't intend it to cover up. Let me say, if I intended to cover up, believe me, I'd have done it. You know how I could have done it? So easily? I could have done it immediately after the election, simply by giving clemency to everybody, and the whole thing would have gone away. I couldn't do that because I said, "Clemency was wrong."

But now we come down to the key point. And let me answer it my own way about, "How do I feel about the American people?" I mean, how, ah, whether I should have resigned earlier, or what I should say to them now. Well, that forces me to rationalize now and give you a carefully prepared and cropped statement. I didn't expect this question, frankly though, so I'm not going to give you that, but I can tell you this....

Q. Nor did I.

A. ...I can tell you this: I think I said it all, in, in one of those moments that, that you're not thinking. Sometimes you say the things that are really in your heart. When you're thinking in advance, then you say things, you know, that are tailored to the audience. I had a lot of difficult meetings those last days before I resigned, and the most difficult one and the only one where I broke into tears, frankly, except for that very brief session with Ehrlichman up at Camp David; it was the first time I cried since Eisenhower died. I met with all of my key supporters just a half-hour before going on television....

...Well, when I said, "I just hope I haven't let you down," that said it all. I had. I let down my friends. I let down the country. I let down our system of government and the dreams of all those young people that ought to get into government, but think it's all too corrupt and the rest.

[Lost Opportunity]

Most of all, I let down an opportunity that I would have had for two and a half more years to proceed on great projects and programs for building a lasting peace, which has been my dream, as you know from our first interview in 1968, before I had any...thought I might even win that year. I didn't tell you I didn't think I might win, but I wasn't sure. Yep, I...I let the American people down, and I have to carry that burden with me for the rest of my life. My political life is over. I will never yet, and never again have an opportunity to serve in any official position. Maybe I can give a little advice from time to time.

And so, I can only say that in answer to your question, that while technically, I did not commit a crime, an impeachable offense...these are legalisms, as far as the handling of this matter is concerned; it was so botched up. I made so many bad judgments. The worst one, mistakes of the heart, rather than the head, as I pointed out. But let me say, a man in that top judge...top job—he's got to have a heart, but his head must always rule his heart.

Q. This has, ah...this been more—

A. Been tough for you? (laughter)

Q. Well, no, but I was going to say that I feel we've....

A. Covered a lot of ground.

Q. ...Been through life almost, rather than an interview...thank you.

May 12, 1977

[Mao and the China Initiative]

[FROST]: Whose idea was the initiative to China? Was it yours? Henry Kissinger's? Or whose?

[NIXON]: I do not know when Dr. Kissinger may have conceived of the possibility of an initiative toward China. I do know that I conceived it before I ever met him and that I pushed it very very hard from the first days of the Administration. I was the one, as he of course agrees, who raised the issue and kept pressing the issue, but he pursued it with enormous enthusiasm.

Q. Chairman Mao very close there to the end of his life. Was he still compos mentis at the meeting? Was he still speaking clearly?

A. Well, I should point out that in 1972, ah, Chairman Mao had already suffered, in my view, a partial stroke. He had to be helped to stand up for the hand shake, but he was very proud that way. In this case they were girl aides as you see—these rather pretty Chinese girls that were his—lifted him up and helped him walk over, and—but, once they—once those lights turned on, ah, he got turned away. Another interesting thing I noticed from that picture is that when I went to visit him the first time, I noticed he lived very simply.

[Mao's Health]

Q. When the conversation began in '76, did you feel it was still Mao talking or that the interpreter was doing the work?

A. No question about it. Ah, he talked, ah, almost monosyllabically. It was obvious that he was having terrible problems of getting the words out. They were sort of grunts and groans, but the interpreter took things down. But, then, whenever the interpretation was made, he would listen, and then he would nod his head, no, and he would reach over and take a pad from her and then he would write out the answer—right to the last in that conversation, as of course was true in 1972.

Ah, while he had greater problems—great problems in '72 and much greater ones in '76 of communication, Mao was in charge of himself and he was in charge in China. And, all of those around him referred to him as being the one in charge.

Ah, he was a colossus as you can see in this last picture, shriveled, old. But, if you watched his hands, the things that I remembered in both cases, in '72 and '76: His hands never got old. They were very fine, delicate hands. Ah, and yet, we must recognize here had been a tough, ruthless leader, but it didn't show in his hands.

He knew he was going to die. He talked fatalistically. He said, " 'How long will peace last?' Ah, ah, 'One generation?' " He held his finger up like that, and I said, "No, I think longer." And then he, without saying, held up another. I said, "No longer than that." And, then he smiled rather ironically, skeptically. "No, I think maybe a hundred years." And, then he—it would be very difficult, and I said, I quoted one of his poems to him, I said, "Well, Mr. Chairman, as you have written, 'Nothing is hard if one dares to scale the heights.' " And I said, "Of course, it is difficult, but the stakes are so great here." And, he reached over and grasped his cup at that point, as you saw on the film and we raised our hands in a toast. And, at the—he seemed to be quite moved by that thought.

[1973 Yom Kippur War]

Q. When, for instance in '73, the Russians were supplying Egypt and leading up to the Yom Kippur October War, would you have said that that was contrary to the intent of SALT, which refers to not increasing international tension, and so on? Or, what you would have expected as a Russian tactic towards what was then a client?

A. Well, let us look at what led up to that particular event. Ah, at Summit II, which occurred in Washington at Camp David, and in San Clemente. Ah, there had been a very spirited, and I must say at times, heated discussion of the Mideast. It started in my home, ah, where we'd had dinner for Brezhnev. For three hours, until past midnight, Brezhnev hammered me on the Mideast, Mideast. He said, "You must force the Israelis to withdraw from all of the occupied territories and they must do it soon." And, I told him, "We can't do that." I said, "We cannot impose a settlement," and I said, "You can't impose a settlement." He said: "It is my concern that unless the Israelis do withdraw that the Egyptians and Syrians are going to attack and they're going to attack soon." I said, "If they do attack," I said, "we will not let Israel go down the tube." Or words to that effect....

Q. There were a lot of reports in Israel that you had a key phone conversation with Golda Meir [Prime Minister of Israel] soon after the war began over supplies?

A. Oh, yes, I had several conservations with her. The main point of the matter was this: I can tell the story on the war very briefly. What happened was that because Egyptians and the Syrians struck first, and also because they fought better, not as well as the Israelis, but much better than they had in previous wars—they're learning to fight, and that's one thing the Israelis have got to be worried about as far as the future. They won four wars, but each time they've had more casualties. And they'll win the next one, but, in the end, three million Israelis cannot defeat 100 million Arabs, 'cause Arabs can also learn to fight. That's the problem.

Now, as far as Mrs. Meir—here's the essence of what happened: Ah, her concern was that because of the strike, they were losing a great deal of equipment. She needed equipment. Then came the Russian airlift. It was then that I made a very critical decision in the early time of the war—that if the Russians were sending an airlift in, as they were, to help the Egyptians and to help the Syrians, that we would airlift to help Israel.

I remember the conversation very well when, ah, I'd asked the Defense Department, and they prepared an option paper, what have you, for Kissinger to provide the, ah, method for doing it. At first, we wanted to cover the situation, or they did, and send the—paint some planes differently and make it appear as if they were El Al [Israeli airline] planes, I mean, Israeli planes or something like that, or have a chartered plane. And, I finally cut through all of the red tape and I said, "Look, I mean, it isn't going to fool anybody."

[Nixon Orders Airlift]

Q. But, what you're saying is that in the end, in terms of the delay in the airlift, you in a sense, had to overrule the views of both Dr. Kissinger and Mr. Schlesinger on timing, on tactics.

A. Yeah. As far as Dr. Kissinger is concerned, I would have to say I didn't overrule his views. The way that we worked was that he would come in with options, and the option that he presented was that the Defense Department thought we should send three of these big cargo planes and then, of course, he gave his own opinion as to their reasons and reasons which he thought I ought to have before me—that politically it would be, ah, perhaps, ah, dangerous for us to send a greater number and that it would, ah, destroy the chances for negotiations in the future if our profile was too high.

And, my view, I felt in the political area, ah, that, ah, my expertise was somewhat more than Dr. Kissinger's and he understood that, just as I understood that his expertise in certain diplomatic areas was considerably more than mine. And, I said, "Look, Henry, we're gonna get just as much blame for sending three, if we send 30, or a hundred, or whatever we've got, so send everything that flies. The main thing is make it work."

Q. What was the bottom line [on a cease-fire] then really? That you had the leverage?

A. Well, no, we didn't put the Israelis in the spot where we were trying to threaten them, because they won't take it. I mean, they're—they're not—they'll never take it. And, we wouldn't put them in that spot. What we did was to reason with them, but to reason with them in a way, well, we in effect, if I may paraphrase from the "Godfather," "We gave 'em an offer, ah, that they, ah, could not refuse." And, the offer basically was: "Look, the United States will continue to stand by you. We have demonstrated that we will come to your aid with arms if you come under attack, but third, on your side, if we will take such great risks, including, not only the airlift but an alert in order to save you, you must listen to us, at least, in terms of being reasonable in talking to your potential enemies."

[India-Pakistan War]

Q. There was another regional war during your Presidency that could well have embroiled the big powers and that was the war between India and Pakistan over Bangladesh, what had been East Pakistan. How closely was the United States involved in that particular conflict?

A. In the first phase of the Pakistan-Indian clash, Pakistan clearly, ah, was the party that was—has to take the major responsibility and blame, ah, because of the cruelty with which they put down the Bangladesh, East Pakistan rebellion. As a result of that, ah, this brought India into the conflict, and India, despite warnings from us, and we think even from the Soviet Union, ah, declared war on Pakistan—or they didn't declare war on Pakistan, they entered, ah, Bangladesh ah, fighting the Pakistan army in Bangladesh without a declaration of war.

In the meantime, messages are going back and forth between the United States and Moscow. We ask—tell the Russians how important it is for them to restrain the Indians. Ah, they tell us how important it is for Pakistanis to give up East Pakistan, and, ah, there were a number of issues. But, in any event, we both got across to each other, ah, our points of view. And, our point of view was very strongly stated that we thought that if the Russians allowed their client, India, using Soviet arms, ah, to destroy Pakistan, ah, both East and West, that this would imperil our future relationship. And, we put it down just as hard as that. Now, what happened was that after the Bangladesh phase of it, ah, began to be worked out, even though India as you recall, ah, would not adhere to a U.N. cease-fire resolution there. Then, from a source that we consider to be totally reliable, we learned that Prime Minister Indira Ghandi, in a meeting of her Cabinet, had directed that a military operation be put in place to attack West Pakistan, and we had, as I said, information that we knew was completely reliable.

It was then that we made the move that we did make. It was then that I ordered the carrier task force into the Indian Ocean. We sent a very sharp note, of course, to the Russians, ah, and, ah, the Indians, ah, ah according to the Russians, ah, this was [Leonid I.] Brezhnev's, I thought very weak response, he says: "Well, they're very difficult to deal with. We find that our influence on them at this point, once they have tasted the victory in East Pakistan, is very little." But I knew that we had to help try to save West Pakistan.

Now, unless we had brought pressure to bear on the Russians, unless we had basically conditioned our continued progress toward the summit, détente, etc., on their restraining their clients, and we of course by the same token, would restrain, to the extent we could, the Pakistanis, who didn't need to be restrained; they were defeated. Unless that had happened, I believe, ah, I believe, that, ah, she would have taken West Pakistan. She would have gobbled it up and that would have had dramatic consequences: an effect on the Chinese, on American-Soviet relations, for reasons that I've mentioned, as well as of course, the point is: It would have been wrong and totally wrong. And, so basically, we saved West Pakistan because it was right. We also saved it, it's true, because it had something to do with our China initiative. The Chinese were putting a lot of pressure on us to do something. They couldn't do anything. They didn't want to get involved in a war with India at that point, although they had utter contempt for the Indians.

What we did in saving West Pakistan built up a lot of credibility with the Chinese.

[Khrushchev and Brezhnev]

Q. We've talked a lot about your dealing with Brezhnev and we've talked about the various material confrontations and so on with him, but we haven't really talked about what your impressions and memories of Brezhnev as a man were. What sort of a man was Brezhnev to deal with?

A. Well, let me compare him with Khrushchev, because I think people have a more vivid picture of Khrushchev, even today, people of our generation at least, than they do of Brezhnev. Khrushchev was, ah, boorish, crude, brilliant, ah, ruthless, potentially rash, terrible inferiority complex....

With Brezhnev, you had a man, not as quick as Khrushchev, intellectually, ah, a man far better mannered, ah, than Khrushchev, a man who did not have the inferiority complex, even though he knew they were inferior in certain ways, he knew as Khrushchev did not know, that the Soviet Union by that time, when Brezhnev was in power, had—was, frankly, dealing equally across the table, whereas Khrushchev knew he was behind, and therefore, had to put on this big bravado act or the big macho act to prove, ah, that he was ahead of everybody and everything.

Another difference is—and this appears not to be too important, but it's interesting, ah, Khrushchev tried to put on the air of being just a common peasant-like person. He would dress with the sloppy hat and, and, ah, collar wouldn't be too clean and this and that, or clean. Ah, whereas Brezhnev was somewhat of a fashion plate. He liked beautiful cars. He liked beautiful women. Ah, a small thing. Brezhnev, [Nikolai V.] Podgorny and [Alexei] Kosygin all wore cufflinks. None of the Soviet party in 1959 wore cufflinks. Ah, things had changed. Ah, the new class in the Soviet Union is doin' pretty good.

Ah, now let's get to the kind of a man he is: Ah, intellectually, not as quick as Khrushchev, but smart. Ah, as far as his temperament is concerned; not as rash as Khrushchev, more cautious, one who consults with people before acting rather than moving off impulsively on his own; not as volatile as Khrushchev, and in that way, a much safer man to have sitting there with his finger on the button than Khrushchev.

He is basically very much a, ah, physical kind of person. Ah, he has a lot of animal magnetism, as distinguished from Podgorny, or particularly from Kosygin, who's rather cold, more aristocratic in bearing. Ah, he's a man who's very earthy in his humor. I won't go into how earthy he is—let's just leave it there. Ah, but, also not as crude, not as boorish as Khrushchev in some of the expletives that he would use; better mannered.

When I said that he was cautious, I would not like to leave the impression that he was timid. Ah, I think that he had read and practices the doctrine of Lenin, which is, as you may recall, "Probe with bayonets; if you encounter mush, proceed; if you encounter steel, withdraw." And, that's the way Brezhnev will be. That's the way the Communist leaders will be all over the world. Because as Communists, they have to go forward spreading the gospel. That's what they believe. They want just not a Communist Russia or what have you; they want a Communist world.

I'm not sure that's the Chinese view at the present time, but it may come that way in the future, and they may want to accomplish it in different ways. But I remember one incident that perhaps tells Brezhnev's deeper sense better than anything else. I'll never forget the day that we were riding on his yacht. His yacht makes that old Sequoia, that President Carter's now put in mothballs, look like a rowboat next to a 100-foot yacht. But anyway, here's this marvelous Russian Navy yacht, and we had a beautiful luncheon on the yacht with the other members of the party, with caviar and champagne and everything else. And, as we were—went up the tour, up by the Black Sea, he pointed out Yalta; he pointed to where Roosevelt had stayed and where Stalin had stayed and where Churchill had stayed. And as he pointed this out to me, all of a sudden, impulsively, he reached over and grabbed me. He was kind of like Johnson that way—he likes to grab people. He and Johnson would have had a lot of fun. They're much alike. And, he put his arm around me and he said, "You know, my friend, President Nixon." He said, "I only hope the day will come when every Russian and every American can sit together as we are sitting now, and we can be friends."

[Nixon and Kissinger]

Q. When you first selected Henry Kissinger for the [National Security Council], did you expect him to become as much of an international star as he did or did you intend it originally to be a back-room role?

A. No, I don't think I expected, and I don't think he expected it either. Ah, however, I knew that we were going to deal with great events. I didn't know at the time I met him, ah, I didn't know enough about his background; I didn't know him enough personally to know what a dramatic impact his personality would have as he executed his role quite brilliantly.

Q. You must have had disagreements, I suppose. What were the most important ones?

A. Ah, I'm a fatalist, basically. Ah, Kissinger is more, despite his enormous intellectual capabilities, ah, one who, ah, ah, is, ah, perhaps, ah, somewhat less fatalistic, and ah—or determinist in his views. More emotional, interestingly enough. Ah, although, I, too, have emotions. I tend to hide them perhaps more than he does, or submerge them or suppress them, ah, but, ah, be that as it may we won't try to psychoanalyze each other at the moment.

Ah, but Kissinger, I will remember, after we went into Cambodia. He was going in, ah, but here I made a decision on the spot which we had not discussed before. He wondered about it at the time, but he totally supported it once it was made. We went to the Pentagon, and the day after the first movement into two sanctuaries and I asked the people at the Pentagon how many there were, and they said there were six. And, I said, "Let's move into all of them." I remember [General William C.] Westmoreland raised the point that he didn't know whether or not we could even handle two.

However, the other chiefs and the rest felt maybe we could handle all of them, particularly with the way the, ah, South Vietnamese, in the early days were fighting. So, right then, the decision was made to go into six, and it was one of the best decisions we made. Then came Kent State, which was a terrible emotional shock to me, ah, and a very great shock to Kissinger. And, of course, a torrent of abuse because the implication was that because we did Cambodia, three [*sic*] students were killed in Kent State—that one followed the other, although the student body president of Kent State pointed out when he came to see me at the White House that while the Kent State tragedy partly was due to the disagreement about the war, that long before the war there were other issues that were stirring people up.

But, I remember right after that Henry came in one day and he said, "You know, I'm not sure that we should have gone into this Cambodian thing, and perhaps now has come the time that we should shorten the time and get out a little sooner." Ah, he wasn't seriously considering it, but he says, "I think," and he used to always preface it by saying, "I must warn you, Mr. President, that the situation that I hear from my colleagues from the colleges and universities is very, very serious, and, ah, Cambodia is—it could have been a mistake." And, I said, "Henry," I said, "We've done it." I said: "Remember Lot's wife. Never look back." I don't know whether Henry had read the Old Testament or not, but I had, and he got the point.

Henry and I often had a little joke between us after that. Whenever he would come in and say, "Well, I'm not sure we should have done this, or that, or the other thing." I would say, "Henry, remember Lot's wife." And, that would end the conversation.

[Kissinger Resignation Hints]

Q. How many times did he say he might resign?

A. Oh, to me he would hint it on occasion. How many times, ah, ah, not many, not often. He would come in and say, "Well, I—I just wonder if my usefulness isn't finished. I wonder if I shouldn't resign." He had a tendency, too, to get highly elated by some piece of good news and very depressed by something that he considered to be bad news. Ah, that doesn't mean that he was emotionally unstable: it simply meant, that having the kind of wide-ranging mind that he was—he had the imagination that any genius, and he was a genius in this area, or intellectual has—and, ah, one of the, one of the characteristics of an individual with an exceptional mind is that he can see the heights and also see the depths, and he feels them both. And, Henry, was that way.

Well, I of course, don't contend that I'm a genius, ah, and so forth. I usually could see the heights, and could be—feel somewhat elated, although I tried to restrain elation, because I always know that the, ah, as [Winston S.] Churchill once said, that the brightest moments are those that flash away the fastest. And, so that when you're up today, you may be down tomorrow. Ah, but, ah, many times I think that the way that the instant historians write about the Kissinger-Nixon relationship that they misread it to an extent because they, they take for example, an emotional statement, ah, ah, which, ah, he may not really mean. He would never come in and threaten to resign. He would come in and suggest that maybe he should because he was no longer useful. I, of course, then would say, "Now, look here, just stop all that talk, I'm not gonna want to hear any more of it, let's talk about the real thing."

Q. How many times did he come in and say that maybe, maybe he should resign?

A. Maybe a half a dozen. But, to others, more often. He would talk to [Gen. Alexander M.] Haig and to, ah, [H. R.] Haldeman about this. And, this would be when he would be in fights with the bureaucracy. He couldn't stand the bureaucratic infighting. He had differences, as you know, with Secretary [of State, William P.] Rogers. And incidentally, this was a very painful thing for me because Rogers had been my friend. He was a personal friend. Henry, of course, was not a personal friend. We were, we were associates, but not personal frineds; not enemies, but not personal friends. Rogers was a personal friend. But, ah, Henry was fighting—first, they were—they were two very proud men. They were two very intelligent men.

[Kissinger-Rogers Feud]

There could be only one person to handle some of these major issues, and where secrecy was involved, I mean, secret negotiations, it had to be Henry ah, in the areas like Vietnam, China, Russia and the Mideast. Now in the case of Rogers, on the other hand, being a very proud man, ah, he did not resent Henry handling such things but he objected to the fact that Henry got too much credit, and he felt was taking too much credit, and also he objected, and here I think he had a good case, and I think Henry would have to agree, that he, Rogers, who had to make public statements all the time and testify and answer questions before the Congress, wasn't informed about things. He wanted to be informed.

Well, Henry would come to me and we had several arguments about it. He would say, "I will not inform Rogers because he'll leak." I said, "Henry," and I must have told him this a dozen times, I says: "Henry, the State Department bureaucracy will leak. It always has. It always will," I said, "but, Bill Rogers will never leak, if we—if I tell him it's in confidence." "Well, I'm not so sure." See, he didn't know Rogers as well as I did. I knew that Rogers was a man of honor and I knew he wouldn't leak. And that was why on the China initiative, for example, we had a very good—we had quite an argument about that. Henry didn't want to tell anybody, of course, except those on a need-to-know basis. And I said, "Rogers has gotta know." And he said, "Well, he'll leak, or he'll object to it." I said: "You cannot have the Secretary of State not be informed, because he has got to take off the day that announcement was made."

Q. Did Henry say that he's resign if John [B.] Connally was appointed Secretary of State?

A. Not to me. I, ah, I have read reports to that effect, and I do know, ah, he, ah, ah, that his views with regard to Connally were mixed. Ah, he had—he respected him as a political leader. However, I think Henry saw in Connally—let's face it, a potential rival. Ah, Connally basically—everything that Connally touches, ah, in the political area, Connally controls. And so Connally would be a very formidable person to have around. Ah, I could sense that he would have preferred somebody else—let's put it that way.

Q. Were you actually considering John Connally as Secretary of State?

A. Yes, I thought he would have made a very good Secretary of State. However, in this case, while Henry did not have a veto power where the President is concerned, ah, any President—but, while he didn't have a veto power, it was indispensable that whoever was Secretary of State be able to work with Henry and Henry be able to work with him because he had his fingers in so many pies, ah, which were in various stages of development, ah, and consequently, we couldn't possibly have a situation where he'd be at odds.

In other words, I'd gone through, ah, the Rogers-Kissinger feud for four years, and I didn't want to buy another feud with another Secretary of State for the—for the rest of the four years, and that's why I finally made Henry—gave Henry both hats, which I, ah, in retrospect, probably would not have done, had, ah, we—could we have found some individual who would be Henry's equal. That didn't mean that from time as we did at the time of the May 8th bombing when, ah, we got advice from Connally and took his rather than Henry's ah, with regard to go ahead with the bombing and don't cancel the summit, rather than the other way around which is the way Henry first recommended it, and the way I first approved it.

[Nixon's View of Kissinger]

Q. Didn't you sometimes feel, "Why is he saying all those terrible things about me?"

A. Well, to answer the question quite candidly, it drives my family up the wall. And it's only because that it bothers them that it would bother me at all. Ah, after such accounts appear, I know that, ah, I always get a call from Henry on the phone, ah, ah, explaining that, ah, that there's been either a misquotation, or misinterpretation or what have you. And I have always said to him, ah, "Forget it." I said, I said, ah, ah: "What your opinion of me is, is, ah, not, ah, however you express it, isn't going to affect our relationship unless you express it to me personally. I mean, what you say about me to other people isn't going to bother me." That's what I said. But in all candor I would have to admit my family didn't share that, and I think what we have to understand, too, is that Henry likes to say outrageous things.

Ah, most, ah, people with great intellectual ability couldn't care less about the so-called Hollywood celebrity set or celebrities of any kind. I mean, basically, they're only interested in a person's brains, and not particularly whether or not they have a lot of money or a lot of a—of good news clippings, or what have you. But, Henry, on the other hand, was fascinated first by the celebrity set, and second, he liked being one himself. Not at first, but people would start coming up for his autograph and he was invited more and more to the Hollywood parties and the rest. I used to like them, but Henry will learn to despise them, too, after he's been through a few more. But, be that as it may, so he goes to a party, and I can see exactly what happened in Canada. He runs into a lady who, ah, has a very low opinion of me, and ah, ah, so Henry feels that really he's defending me and that the way to defend is to concede that, "Well, he's sort of an odd person, he's an artificial person," and so forth and so on, and ah, the only problem was that he didn't think to turn the microphone off, but on the other hand, I didn't turn it off either in the Oval Office on occasions, so I never held him for that.

May 19, 1977

[Cambodia]

[NIXON]: Between April 20th and April 30th [1970], the North Vietnamese launched a massive offensive. A massive offensive; I meant, in terms of...Launched a massive build-up, I should say. A build-up which all of our intelligence detected. A build-up in the sanctuary area, and and in that period of time we had then to make the decision as to whether or not we could take the attack that was to follow.

[FROST]: Yes, the only thing that they could find between April the 20th and April the 30th, was that you'd seen "Patton" twice, so they thought that might be the reason.

A. Yes, yes.

Q. Did that have an influence on you?

A. Well, I've seen the "Sound of Music" twice, and it hasn't made me a writer either. Patton's an interesting movie, I recommend it, curiously enough, not so much for what it tells about Patton, but in a sense it's like Tolstoy's "War and Peace," or any Tolstoian novel—"War and Peace," "Anna Karenina." The war part of the Patton movie didn't particularly interest me. The character sketch was fascinating. And so far as that was concerned, it had no effect whatever on my decisions.

Q. On the subject of Cambodia, let me put a philosophical thought to you, which I put to you particularly in a sense as a Quaker. In the sense that a lot of the philosophical studies that I've read of Cambodia and this little nation that started, perhaps 6,000 members of the Khmer Rouge and a population of seven million, in neutrality, or flawed neutrality. That, nevertheless, with that flawed neutrality, was somehow surviving in the midst of a holocaust. And, the concatenation of events that the Administration were involved in; starting with the bombing; the armed incursion; the driving of people, the North Vietnamese and others, back across Cambodia; the continued bombing and twice the tonnage we dropped on North Vietnam....

[A.] ...Let us understand that in this war, it was never the policy of the United States to bomb civilian installations. If we had had that policy we could have ended the war in a very, certainly a tragic way, but ended it much, much sooner. The cost of Cambodia, which I'm sure you will want to get into, was very much at home, very high at home in terms of what happened at Kent State, the campuses and all the rest, the feeling that we had done something immoral, and all the rest.

Although, as far as the American people were concerned, Gallup reported within a week afterwards, before the Kent State thing, of course, came off, that, it had about 65 per cent support. And, as far as Cambodia is concerned, as Laos is concerned, I know I feel strongly about this, and I know many disagree, but, I say it again, I only regret that I didn't act stronger sooner....

[Firm Line on Dissent]

Q. Now, where...would you put the Damocles moment? When you realized that all hope of speaking quietly and bringing everybody together, was, was hopeless, and that, in fact, you had a war on your hands at home as well? When was the moment when, in effect, you said, 'O.K., no more Mr. Nice Guy'?

A. Well, as far as being no more Mr. Nice Guy. I would not claim that, I never received that particular description before. I tried to be what I am, and that is: I do the job that has to be done and I do it as fairly as I can, and if it requires being firm, I'm firm.

Now, when you say, 'When was the time that I became convinced that we had to take, what I would say a firmer line with demonstrations. I would say that after having met Thieu at Midway and started the process of withdrawal; after having made a speech in May, North Vietnamese, and, also to the Vietcong, ah, for a peace settlement; and to negotiate on some reasonable terms; when in spite of those efforts and our efforts to bring the war to a peaceful conclusion as quickly as possible, there continued to be a rising, ah, tide, not just of quickly as possible, ah, there continued to be a rising tide, not just of dissent, peaceful dissent, that's one thing. But, dissent coupled with violence, and advocacy of violence, then I had to make a choice.

I had to make a choice: Are we going to allow this group to first, where they were violent—violence prone, to endanger the lives of others within; but, second, even more important, are we going to allow our potential enemies, those that we were negotiating with in Paris, gain the impression that they represent a majority? In other words, are we going to have a situation where this war would be lost in Washington as the French lost, in 1954 in Paris, rather than in Dien Bien Phu?

Q. And so when did you make that decision, that you had to speak back; that you had to rally your own support?

A. I reached the conclusion after receiving reports from Kissinger on his first secret negotiations; after getting reports from the negotiations in Paris; after seeing the developments within this country; after reading, for example, in magazines and so forth, and so on, that statements by various people, that, having broken [President Lyndon B.] Johnson, that, the dissenters, many of them were now out to break Nixon.

Q. Right. And that you saw those divisions, and that you realized that the war would continue with dissent; continue with a divided America; and, that also wherever you could in other policies, you tried to build that group that were your support, play to them politically, to increase your majority in '72, ...an America that was already divided, you divided even more on a principle of...divide and rule.

A. You can make that charge, and I don't say that in any personal sense. You can make it, and you should, because a lot of your constituency in the media do think that. But, they're wrong. In my view, I had a responsibility which was, above everything else, to bring that war to the earliest possible conclusion, and I did it. And we got it finished, and we got it finished on what I would say again was an honorable basis and a peace that lasted for at least two, over two years.

The second point was that in the meantime I had to deal with the problem of dissent at home. Now, the reason.... Another thing, point, that has to be made: Without having enough support at home, the enemy, in my opinion, would never have negotiated in Paris, as they did....

[The Huston Plan]

[**Q.**]: The wave of dissent, occasionally violent, which followed in the wake of the Cambodian incursion prompted President Nixon to demand better intelligence about the people who were opposing him. To this end, the Deputy White House Counsel, Tom Huston, arranged a series of meetings with representatives of the C.I.A., the F.B.I. and other police and intelligence agencies.

These meetings produced a plan, the Huston Plan, which advocated the systematic use of wiretappings, burglaries, or so-called black bag jobs, mail openings and infiltration against antiwar groups and others. Some of these activities, as Huston emphasized to Nixon, were clearly illegal. Nevertheless, the President approved the plan. Five days later, after opposition from J. Edgar Hoover [Director, Federal Bureau of Investigation], the plan was withdrawn, but the President's approval was later to be listed in the articles of Impeachment as an alleged abuse of Presidential power....

[Presidential Power]

Q. So what in a sense, you're saying is that there are certain situations, and the Huston Plan or that part of it was one of them, where the President can decide that it's in the best interests of the nation or something, and do something illegal.

A. Well, when the President does it, that means that it is not illegal.

Q. By definition.

A. Exactly. Exactly. If the President, for example, approves something because of the national security, or in this case because of a threat to internal peace and order of significant magnitude, then the President's decision in that instance is one that enables those who carry it out, to carry it out without violating a law. Otherwise they're in an impossible position.

Q. So, that in other words, really you were saying in that answer, really, between the burglary and murder, again, there's no subtle way to say that there was murder of a dissenter in this country because I don't know any evidence to that effect at all. But, the point is: just the dividing line, is that in fact, the dividing line is the President's judgment?

A. Yes, and the dividing line and, just so that one does not get the impression, that a President can run amok in this country and get away with it, we have to have in mind that a President has to come up before the electorate. We also have to have in mind, that a President has to get appropriations from the Congress. We have to have in mind, for example, that as far as the C.I.A.'s covert operations are concerned, as far as the F.B.I.'s covert operations are concerned, through the years, they have been disclosed on a very, very limited basis to trusted members of Congress. I don't know whether it can be done today or not....

Q. Also at the same time, there were enemies lists circulating, and conversations about the use of the I.R.S. and all of that, also moving against opponents of the Administration.

And in the September the 15th tape, for instance, Haldeman says that Dean's moving ruthlessly on the investigation and the [Sen. George] McGovern [D S.D.] people, and working the thing through the I.R.S., and Schultz has been a bit difficult and you say, "I don't want George Schultz to ever raise the question because it'd put me in the position of having to throw him out of the office. He didn't get to be Secretary of the Treasury because he had nice blue eyes. It was a God damned favor to get him that job." And so on.

And then you talk about using the I.R.S. and you say, "I want the most comprehensive notes on all of those who've tried to do us in because they didn't have to do it; they're asking for it; they're gonna get it."

A. Well, let me say this: They were more successful, they may have been, but let me say, what was put out; what we're talking about here is this: that, they shouldn't have gone into this, yes. I have never seen, let me say this, and except for Eisenhower, I think I'm the only President in recent times...I have never seen anybody else's tax return except my own.

Q. But, as we look at the overall picture and those things about the comprehensive notes "on those who've tried to do us in" and all that, and, talking in that same conversation about Edward Bennett Williams [prominent attorney], and Haldeman says, "That's the guy we've got to ruin." And you say, "Yes, I think we're going to fix the S.O.B., ah, believe me we're going to." And, so on. Isn't there in that whole conversation....

A. A paranoic attitude?

Q. Yes.

A. Yeah, I know. I understand that and it gets back to the statement that I made, rather an emotional statement the day I left office and I said, "Don't hate other people because hatred destroys yourself." Yeah, I, I want to say here, that I, I have a temper, I control it publicly rather well. Ah, sometimes privately I blow off some steam, but also as I've indicated, if, and this is very hard to believe, but I think you can believe it after our session a few hours ago. My weakness is perhaps, where personal factors are concerned....

[Comparison With Lincoln]

Q. Pulling some of our discussions together, as it were; speaking of the Presidency and in an interrogatory filed with the Church Committee [Senate Select Committee to Study Governmental Operations with Respect to Intelligence Activities chaired by Sen. Frank Church (D Idaho)], you stated, quote, "It's quite obvious that there are certain inherently government activities, which, if undertaken by the sovereign in protection of the interests of the nation's security are lawful, but which if undertaken by private persons, are not."

What, at root, did you have in mind there?

A. Well, what I, at root I had in mind I think was perhaps much better stated by Lincoln during the War between the States. Lincoln said, and I think I can remember the quote almost exactly, he said, "Actions which otherwise would be unconstitutional, could become lawful if undertaken for the purpose of preserving the Constitution and the Nation."

Now that's the kind of action I'm referring to. Of course in Lincoln's case it was the survival of the Union in war time, it's the defense of the nation and, who knows, perhaps the survival of the nation.

Q. But there was no comparison, was there, between the situation you faced and the situation Lincoln faced, for instance?

A. This nation was torn apart in an ideological way by the war in Vietnam, as much as the Civil War tore apart the nation when Lincoln was President. Now it's true that we didn't have the North and South—

Q. But when you said, as you said when we were talking about the Huston Plan, you know, "If the President orders it, that makes it legal," as it were: Is the President in that sense—is there anything in the Constitution or the Bill of Rights that suggests the President is that far of a sovereign, that far above the law?

A. No, there isn't. There's nothing specific that the Constitution contemplates in that respect. I haven't read every word, every jot and every title, but I do know this: That it has been, however, argued that as far as a

President is concerned, that in war time, a President does have certain extraordinary powers which would make acts that would otherwise be unlawful, lawful if undertaken for the purpose of preserving the nation and the Constitution, which is essential for the rights we're all talking about....

May 25, 1977

[Chile and Allende]

[FROST]: On September the 16th, 1970, after Salvador Allende had won the most votes in the Chilean Presidential elections, Henry Kissinger glumly remarked that if the Chilean Congress confirmed Allende as President over the non-Marxist runner-up candidate, his rule could spell the end of democracy in Chile. What Kissinger did not reveal was that on the day before he spoke, Richard Nixon had himself taken action to subvert Chile's democratic process by ordering the C.I.A. to prevent Allende's accession to power not even excluding a coup d'etat. Whether or not the subsequent actions of the C.I.A. did, by themselves, prevent the overthrow of Allende, three years later, is in dispute. That the C.I.A. did take action is not. The Church Committee reported the following facts:

The U.S. collaborated with groups that kidnapped and murdered General Renee Schneider, a Chilean whose belief in constitutional democracy outweighed his opposition to Allende.

Between 1970 and 1973 the C.I.A. spent some $8 million in Chile supporting the political opposition and establishing a network of those committed to Allende's downfall. And, when the coup occurred, the C.I.A. used additional funds to support a public relations effort on behalf of the newly installed right-wing government headed by General [Augusto] Pinochet.

Can you think of any other example of where the United States, in recent United States history, attempted to interrupt the constitutional processes of a democratic government?

[NIXON]: You mean the last four or five years? No, I can't think of any.

Q. What did you have in mind, in Chile, when you said that you wanted the C.I.A., or you wanted America to make the economy scream?

A. Chile, of course, is interested in obtaining loans from international organizations where we have a vote, and I indicated that wherever we had a vote, where Chile was involved, that unless there were strong considerations on the other side that we would vote against them. I felt that as far as Chile was concerned, since they were expropriating American property, they expropriated, Allende did...it took him only three years to expropriate 275 firms.

Q. He hadn't done that on September the 15th.

A. I know. I know, but I knew that was coming. All you had to do was read his campaign speeches. There wasn't any question but that he was cooperating with [Cuban premier Fidel] Castro. There wasn't any question that Chile was being used by some of Castro's agents as a base to export terrorism to Argentina, to Bolivia, to Brazil. We knew all of that. I am not here to defend, and will not defend repression by any government, be it a friend of the United States, or one that is opposed to the United States. But, in terms of national security, in terms of our own self-interest, the right-wing dictatorship, if it is not exporting its revolution, if it is not interfering with its neighbors, if it is not taking action against the United States, it is therefore of no security concern to us. It is of a human-rights concern. A left-wing dictatorship, on the other hand, we find that they do engage in trying to export their subversion to other countries, and that does involve our security interests. As far as the situation in Chile was concerned, he was engaging in dictatorial actions which eventually would have allowed him to impose a dictatorship. That was his goal.

Q. But the C.I.A. reported, shortly before his death, that he was no threat to democracy; he wasn't planning to abolish democracy and he was going to lose in the next election.

A. Based on the C.I.A.'s record of accuracy in their reports, I would take all of that with a grain of salt. They didn't even predict that he was going to win this time. They didn't predict what was going to happen in Cambodia. They didn't predict there was going to be the Yom Kippur War. As far as the C.I.A. was concerned, at that point, and now I understand it is being improved, and I trust it will be under the new leadership, at that point it's intelligence estimates were not very good on Latin America. I also go back to the point that in terms of what we really have here in Chile. I remember months before Allende came to power in 1970. An Italian businessman came to call on me in the Oval Office and he said, "If Allende should win the election in Chile, and then you have Castro in Cuba, what you will in effect have in Latin America is a red sandwich, and eventually it will all be red." And that's what we confronted.

Q. But that's madness of him to say that.

A. It isn't madness at all. It shows somebody cutting through the hypocritical double standard of those who can see all the dangers on the right and don't look at the dangers on the left.

Q. ...What I really wanted to say was that Allende won the election as you said, albeit with 36 per cent. We wanted to prevent him coming to power. In retrospect, don't you think that the Chileans were a better judge of what would preserve their democracy than you were?

A. Who do you think overthrew Allende? You see, there's the point you've missed. Allende, at the time he had been in charge of the government, with his programs that destroyed agriculture, with his programs of confiscating property and discouraging foreign investment, because obviously I wasn't going to approve any American loans to companies to invest in Chile when it might be expropriated. That was one of the economic squeezes we put on them. Allende lost eventually. Allende was overthrown eventually, not because of anything that was done from the outside, but because his system didn't work in Chile and Chile decided to throw it out....

[Agnew Resignation]

Q. When the Attorney General told you (on Aug. 7, 1973), that there was a strong case against Agnew, what did you say?

A. I told [Attorney General Elliott] Richardson what I had earlier had Haig convey to him, that I felt that in this case, that he, Richardson had to be very sure not only that the case was strong, because of the rights of the individual involved and the position that he held, but very sure that he, Richardson, was not in a position where it would look as if this were a political motivation on his part.

I mean, there was no secret Richardson and Agnew didn't like each other. There was no secret that Richardson had ambitions to be Vice President or President in 1976, and earlier if possible if somebody had picked him. But on the other hand I didn't want his judgment to be the judgment, which I would use as the final word in making recommendations to Agnew or in discussions with Agnew. And I suggested at that point that Henry Petersen, the Assistant Attorney General in charge of the Criminal Division, a Democrat, conduct an independent investigation.

...I got in [Robert] Bork, the Solicitor General, a great Constitutional lawyer, and that was about three days later on the 28th of September, and Bork said that it was his opinion, as he interpreted the Constitution, that since the Constitution did not specifically include the Vice President in the clause with regard to impeachment being the only recourse against a President, that, therefore, a Vice President could be tried on charges by the regular court.

When we got this news, then frankly, Agnew had come to the point, and he realized that he had no alternative but to do everything that he possibly could to avoid going into a court.

And therefore the resignation option became absolutely indispensable. The point here was not that resignation would lead to no charges, but the point is that resignation was a step that if it were not taken, would probably mean that he would get a tougher rap.

Q. When you met on October the 9th, the farewell meeting, did he still maintain his total innocence?

A. Yes, there was not a time during the course of this whole period that I met with Agnew that he did not maintain that he was innocent.

Now, we have to understand what he was talking about. What he was talking about was being innocent of bribery. He said that for years contractors who did business with the state of Maryland contributed to expenses that the Governor, or the county official, or what have you, might have. That was common practice.

But Agnew always made the point, that there was never an instance where a contract did not go to a highly qualified and in his view, the most qualified individual. In other words, his point being that he did not, in effect, accept money from somebody who would not have otherwise been entitled to the contract. I was very pragmatic. In my view, it didn't really make any difference. There wasn't any question after hearing Petersen and his version that he was frankly going to get it. So under the circumstances, it became an irrelevant point. I'm not going to sit here and judge Spiro Agnew. I know that he feels he didn't get enough support from the White House. I know that he feels that some people were undercutting him. I know that he has bitter feelings, certainly, about me in this respect. All that I can say is that it was a no-win proposition.

Q. When you say that he has bitter feelings toward the White House and toward you, does that mean, really, there's been no contact with you since he left office?

A. No, we have not had any contact.

[Mrs. Nixon's Health]

Q. There's one question that a great many people have asked me about Mrs. Nixon's recovery. How is Mrs. Nixon, in fact?

A. Mrs. Nixon is coming along remarkably well. She's been through a very difficult time, but she has a strong character. That's what you have to have when you have a stroke. And this will please all of our audience who remember her, all of the paralysis is gone from her face. And all of it from her left leg. She still has some in her left arm, and the doctors think that within a few months, that will be gone. So, she will have a complete recovery. I've mentioned the stories that have been written, and some written by some book authors, and so forth, which reflected even on her on occasion, and what her alleged weaknesses were. They haven't helped, and, as far as my attitude toward the press is concerned, I respect some, but for those who write history as fiction on third-hand knowledge, I have nothing but utter contempt. And, I will never forgive them. Never.

And, let me say another thing on that point. You have to bear in mind, you and the media, you and your friends in America, not in Britain, but you have here a very interesting decision of the Supreme Court, *Sullivan* vs. *New York Times,* which is really a license for the media to lie.

And, so my point is: let's just not have all this sanctimonious business about the poor repressed press. I went through it through all the years I've been in public life, and they never have been repressed as far as I am concerned....

[Final Meeting With Kissinger]

Q. Reading the account of the last days, it seems almost as though your more emotional moment was, in fact, on the Wednesday evening in that heart-to-heart that you had with Henry Kissinger.

A. Yes. It was, perhaps, as an emotional moment as I have had. Henry came over and we began to reminisce and we reminisced about all the great decisions we'd participated in. He said "Well, Mr. President, I just (wanted) you to know," he said, "It is a crime that you are leaving office. It's a disservice to the peace in the world which you helped to build, and history is going to record that you were a great President."

I said, "Henry, that depends on who writes the history."

And, then he said, "I just want you to know that if they harass you after you leave office, I am going to resign, and I'm going to tell the reason why."

And, his voice broke and I said, "Henry, you're not going to resign. Don't ever talk that way again." I said, "The country needs you. Jerry Ford needs you and you have got to stay and continue the work that we have begun, because if we don't have continuity, everything that we have done could be lost."

And then, Henry said, "Well, that's the way I feel about it."

And at that time, I just can't stand to see somebody else with tears in their eyes, crying. And, I started to cry. And here we were, two grown men who'd been through mountain-top experiences and great crises and so forth. We were crying.

When that was over I said, "Well, Henry, let us understand, you're going to stay on. Never talk about that resigning again." And, I put my arm around him and said, "You've got to go home now. Go back. Go over to the office, and I've got to work on this speech."

And then on impulse, I said, "You know, let me tell you something that I've never told anybody before. About something I've done. There we were in the Lincoln sitting room. I said, "When I've had these really tough decisions I've come into this room for the purpose of praying."

I said, "Now, Henry, I know you and I are both alike in one way. We don't wear our religion on our sleeve. I'm a Quaker and you're a Jew and neither of us is very orthodox, but I think both of us probably have a deeper religious sensitivity than some of those that are so loudly proclaiming it all the time." I said, "If you don't mind, could we just have a moment of silent prayer?" So we knelt down in front of that table where Lincoln had signed the Emancipation Proclamation: where I used to pray. And then we got up. We were only there a minute.

Q. Did either of you speak?

A. No. Not a word. That's not the Quaker fashion.

Q. No it isn't. There was one report that afterwards you called him and said, "Henry, please don't ever tell anyone that I cried and that I was not strong." Did you do that?

A. Yeah, I did call him. I felt, you know, and probably I may have been wrong about this in terms of my appraisal, but I thought Henry might have been a bit embarrassed about kneeling down and praying, and frankly, I was a bit embarrassed about having even asked him to do so. And of course, I don't like to show my emotions. And he doesn't like to show his, either. And under the circumstances, I just by impulse picked up the phone and I said, "Henry, if you don't mind, why don't we just keep that incident to ourselves."

[Nixon Pardon]

Q. Were there any discussion on the subject of pardon, in fact, between you or your representatives and Vice President Ford and his representatives before you left office?

A. Absolutely not. No. No. President Ford has answered that question under oath, and I consider that I'm responding here, in effect, under oath. There were no such discussions. The White House lawyer, Mr. [Philip W.] Buchen, got ahold of Jack Miller, who was my attorney; informed them of it; and Miller flew out to California and talked to me about it. It was a terribly difficult decision for me. Almost as difficult as resigning. I said, "A signing of this pardon, acceptance of this pardon, is going to be interpreted as a confession of guilt." Well, Miller's answer, as a good lawyer, I guess he is, was that, he said, "First," he said, "a pardon isn't necessarily an admission of guilt." Of course, that's legalistic, pettifogging. It isn't, of course. Sometimes, people are pardoned because there's a question about guilt, but my point was: it didn't make any difference. I said, "Most people, including even President Ford, considered that the pardon was, in effect, an admission of guilt."

I sat for an hour in the chair by myself; I asked Miller to leave the room; and here in my office in San Clemente; and, I called him back in and I said, "Well, I will sign it." I said, "I'm not sure that it's the right thing to do because the process has to go forward." And then he, Miller's a rather sensitive man, apparently, and he could rather sense that I wasn't quite up to par physically. I didn't realize that I was quite beaten down mentally, and frankly, I was so emotionally drawn; mentally beaten down; physically not up to par; that I said, "Well, ok, I'll do it." And, so I signed it. And it had exactly the effect that I expected. It exacerbated the issue. It was embarrassing to Ford. It cost him a great deal. I called him a couple of days afterwards, or the day afterwards, and I said I was terribly concerned about the criticism he was getting and I was sorry that he was receiving such criticism, and he was so very nice about it. He said, "You know," he says, "I don't give a damn about the criticism. I did it because it was right." That's the way he is.

Q. And, did you, in a sense, feel that resignation was worse than death?

A. In some ways. I had nothing more to contribute to the causes I so deeply believed in. And also, I felt that resignation meant that I would be in a position of, of not having really anything to live for. I mean, you see, people, the average person, and I understand this, I do not consider myself to be other than an average person, and none of us should really. We all think we're a little smarter than we are, but you feel that, "Well, gee isn't it just great to, you know, to have enough money to afford to live in a very nice house and to be able to play golf and to have nice parties, and to wear good clothes, and shoes, and suits, et cetera, et cetera, et cetera, or travel if you want to."

They don't know life, because what makes life mean something is purpose; a goal; the battle; the struggle; even if you don't win it.

I can only say, that no one in the world, and no one in our history could know how I felt. No one can know how it feels to resign the Presidency of the United States. Is that punishment enough? Oh, probably not. But, whether it is or isn't, as I have said earlier in our interview, we have to live with not only the past, but for the future, and I don't know what the future brings, but whatever it brings, I'll still be fighting.

[September 3, 1977]

[Nixon Tapes; Martha Mitchell]

[FROST]: The first question I put to Richard Nixon was: "Why didn't you burn the tapes?" This was his response:

[NIXON]: Now as a matter of fact, curiously enough I did not only consider, ah, but I even suggested and I believe, ah directed, that Mr. Haldeman, ah, take the taping system out, ah, not take it out, ah, but go through the tapes, ah, and, as I put it to him, ah, to make the search that would be necessary to retain all those that had historical value, and to destroy the, those that had no historical value; those that involved the family; those that involved political or other friends; and so forth and so on, those that really shouldn't be in the public domain.

I pointed out that, ah, the, ah, that the we, if we waited until after I left office to do it that either only he or I would be able to listen to all of it; it would be a monumental task and that we should do it now, and I suggested then that the taping system be changed because I found out then for the first time, that it was one that recorded everything; changed so that I could turn it on and off with a switch.

This was in April [1973], early April; early April before we were considering, for example, the, ah, the situation with regard to the possibility of Haldeman or Ehrlichman resigning, and that sort of thing. But, I said, "Let's have a system whereby we can only record and will only record those that really have historical significance."

Now, his recollection, I understand, is that while we discussed it, he didn't feel that he had been ordered to take it out, and so that time passed. But, on June the 4th of 1973 after Mr. Dean had made some charges that I knew were untrue, ah, certainly in part and probably substantially in many other respects, I, ah, ah, it was suggested by Al Haig, who was then chief of staff in 1973 after Haldeman and Ehrlichman resigned, that I listen to the tapes, and so I did, and it was a very tough experience.

I'll conclude on this point: I didn't destroy the tapes because first, I didn't believe that the, ah, there was a reason to destroy them, ah, I didn't believe that there was anything on them that would, ah, ah, be detrimental to me. Ah, I also, I must admit....

Q. Do you still feel that?

A. In all candor I don't believe that they were going to come out. The second point was that I didn't destroy them because I felt, ah, that ah, if at, at a later time, that had I done so, it would have been an open admission, or at least appeared to be an admission, "Well, I'm trying to cover something up."

[Nixon Orders Tapes Destroyed]

Q. But, looking back on it now, don't you wish you'd destroyed them?

A. Well, as a matter of fact, if the tapes had been destroyed, I believe that it is likely that I would not have had to go through the agony of the resignation, and, ah, consequently, I wish that Mr. Haldeman perhaps, had either taken my instruction, if it was an instruction, ah, or suggestion, and gone further on it and done [what] I had suggested, ah, destroyed those except those that had major significance from a policy standpoint.

Now, it's true at the time I didn't think that the tapes might, I thought the tapes might not come out. At the time, I felt that as far as the tapes are concerned, if they did come out, that possibly they would contradict some of the worst statements were, were being made at the other time, other side. On the other hand, if I had thought that on those tapes, with the possibility, which there always was that they would come out, that there was conversation that was criminal, I sure as the, the dickens—I could use stronger expletives, but not before this home audience—I sure as the dickens would have destroyed them.

[Tape Erasure]

Q. The record is replete with reports, ah, that only three people had access to the tapes during the key period when the erasure may have been made, the 18½ minutes. And that was yourself and Rose Mary Woods [Nixon's personal secretary] and, ah, Stephen Bull [presidential aide]. Em, who did erase the tape?

A. Let me say first, I cannot answer the question as to who did the race, who did erase the tape. Ah, assuming that all of it was erased, the portion that was missing. Or whether because of a defect part was not recorded. That of course can, as, not even, not even been established. I do know this: I didn't do it because I never had access—and this is the important thing here—to the machine on which the experts said the accident or erasure occurred. I never touched it. I never saw the tape, or touch, touched the machine or put the earphones on or anything because she was able to, ah, complete her work on that machine.

Q. You're asking us to take an awful lot on trust, aren't you?

A. All right. Let's get away from trust. Ah, because I don't ask you or anybody else to take anything on trust. Let me say that as far as that 18½ minutes is concerned, I have no recollection of the conversation, ah, beyond what Haldeman's notes had indicated, ah, to refresh me on it. Ah, I, I will be glad to tell you what else I recall I was told in that period by Haldeman, by others. As far as that is concerned, I have no recollection.

Let me also make this other point. It isn't just a matter of trust, ah, Miss Woods testified, and this is, this is pretty tough for even a strong person as she is, she testified under oath for 20½ hours under this situation. Ah, hundreds of thousands of dollars was spent on the investigation. Other witnesses were called. What is also perhaps not known, is that I testified under oath here at San Clemente, ah, before a Federal grand jury on this matter.

Now, of course, the immediate, ah, ah, reaction as far as my testimony is concerned, might be, after all, you have a pardon, and, and, so why do you have to worry? Ah, of course, as you know, a pardon, does not cover anything you do after the pardon. And, I was testifying under oath. And, I swore both as to my own noninvolvement and my own belief as to why, as her nonresponsibility, ah, for what could have been a deliberate erasure. Ah, as, now what has happened on the legal side, believe me.

If the group at the special prosecutor's office thought that they could get me after all the uproar about the pardon or perjury about this issue; if they had other evidence; if they had any evidence; ah, they would have tried, but they didn't. If they had thought, for example, that they could get my secretary; there's nothing they would have loved more.

If they had thought, as they did in other cases, they could get my best friend, Mr. [Charles G. Bebe] Rebozo [personal friend of Nixon], whom they spent $5 million on investigating; they and the Senate committees and the rest, around that much at least. OK, but, they didn't do it. Let us understand just so that the record is clear. You say it's just a question of trust; let us say from a legal standpoint, no incident, so insignificant where you had the notes to show that it was an insignificant conversation. No incident has ever been so, been blown out of proportion to create an appearance of guilt, ah, as this incident.

And, as far as the investigation is concerned, ah, Mr. [Leon] Jaworski [Special Prosecutor] did not bring charges against Miss Woods. As far as I am concerned, no charges have been brought against me and they could do it if they felt that, had any proof.

Q. Do you have any idea who caused the accident?

A. All that I know is that Miss Woods told me that she caused the accident, because she reported it immediately and noticed it immediately, ah, for a portion of it. That it was her, ah, belief, that, however, the part that had been knocked off when she picked up the telephone and the tape was still running, the part that she knocked off, she said, and this was her belief, and I believe her totally, was 4 to 4½ minutes.

Ah, now as to who caused the rest of it, ah, I simply can't say except that I don't know anybody who deliberately could have done it. I didn't do it, cause I didn't touch the machine. Rose Woods did have the machine, but I know she would tell the truth and has always told the truth. And, that if she had done it, ah, she, and if she frankly was venal which she couldn't possibly be, because she's a great person, that, ah, she's so smart, she'd [laughter] a done a, she'd a destroyed a lot more.

[China Breakthrough]

Q. The subjects of Mao Tse-tung and Chou En-lai are subjects on which Richard Nixon can speak with special authority and information. But, early in one session before delving into those topics we began by talking about the lead-up to the China breakthrough. And, in particular, the importance of the role of then President of Pakistan, Yahya Khan. Together with a somewhat macabre reference to the way that the Chinese dealt with dissent, at least in the matter of the Nixon visit to China. But, first it was Yahya Khan, the intermediary.

A. Yahya Khan, ah, ah, had talked at great length with the Chinese, ah, about this matter, and ah, ah, finally, ah, he sent a message to us in either December of 1970 or early January of 1970, ah, 1971. And, that message was, ah, to the effect, again very conciliatory, very warm from Chou En-lai himself. The other messages had been more at the ambassadorial or lower levels, or quoting Chou En-lai. But, this was a message directly from Chou En-lai, ah, ah, to me as President. And, in that message he said that they would be, ah, willing to accept, ah, a, ah, a visit by, a high level representative to discuss again the, and, then with a nice grace note, which was so typical of Chou En-lai, one of the most sophisticated and subtle diplomats in world history.

He said, ah, "this is the first time in history when a message has been sent, ah, from a head through a head, to a head." He had pointed out incidentally in his message that he was sending this message with the knowledge and approval of Mao Tse-tung, and also Lin Piao, who later, as you know, was, ah....

[Lin Piao's death]

Q. Somewhat discredited.

A. That's right. He took an airplane flight and they couldn't find the remains. Let's put it that way.

Q. That's right. And, ah, I think the general conclusion is that, ah, that there was deliberateness in that. Wasn't there?

A. Well, they referred to it in a rather, ah, in their usual subtle and, ah, humorous way, only in passing by saying that there were some who opposed the idea of my coming, ah, to the P.R.C. [Peoples Republic of China]. This was in some, in the, my first visit in 1972. And, he said, ah, "They got into a plane and, ah, it disappeared, ah, and, ah, we have not been able to find it since." And then he just smiled.

Q. That said it all really, didn't it?

A. That's right. That, that, when talking with the Chinese, you often learn far more from what they don't say than from what they do say.

And, one thing that I constantly had to tell our staff and others, not Kissinger, who of course, was aware of this, but others. I said, ah, "Don't go into meetings with the Chinese and just blab about the, ah, usual, ah, line that we're for peace and friendship and all that sort of thing." I said, "It's fine to refer to the fact that we are natural friends, which we are. The Americans and the Chinese, except for the sad incident of the Korean War, have never fought each other. Ah, we have a natural tendency to like each other, wherever we meet them in the world. Whether in the P.R.C. or in the non-Communist areas like Singapore and Taiwan and, ah, for that matter New York City, which is a major Chinese city at the present time.

But, on the other hand, as far as the Communist Chinese are concerned, ah, once you put your case on the basis of just peace or friendship, ah, first they consider you to be a fool and second, they consider you to be wrong. Because they constantly talk about struggle. They're still Communists. Ah, and, they will continue to be Communists. Ah, and as long as there is what they call imperialism in the world, and incidentally, now they think among the major imperialists are the Soviet Union, among others, ah, as long as there is imperialism in the world, there must be not just peace, but there must be struggle.

Q. Did Mao regard the Russian Communists as another branch of the same church, or what?

A. Ah, he considered himself to be a Communist who was true to the doctrines of the original gospel, Marx and Lenin. He was like an early Christian basically. Ah, he considered the Russians, on the other hand, to be deviations, ah, by that, of course, ah, he meant that no longer were they following the doctrines of Marx and Lenin and, ah, at one point he and Hua in a conversation I had with him made the same point.

He said, "The trouble with Russia today, the Soviet Union, in its foreign policy is that it has become a capitalist country at home and therefore is acting like a capitalist country in its policies abroad." Well, in any event, he felt that basically Brezhnev, Kosygin, Podgorny were frankly, fallen away Communist or fallen away Marxists. And were no longer, therefore, ones who should be followed by those who still were true believers.

[Nixon and Kissinger]

Q. Now, as one looks at the Nixon-Kissinger relationship, and it's a fascinating thing to note who did what and with which and to whom. And, there was continually in the press this image of you as the, a hard guy, the taking.

A. Or as the British say, "The ornery guy."

Q. The ornery guy, yes. And, the ah, the British, yes. Ah, and at the same time of Kissinger and his conversations with the press, and so on, ah, seeming to take a softer line. Em, was that, a deliberate?

A. Quite deliberate. And, ah, with both his knowledge and mine and, ah, ah, with our joint cooperation. It was a quite different relationship than [Dwight D.] Eisenhower had with [John F.] Dulles [Eisenhower's Secretary of State]. Dulles was, a 'Mister Bad Guy,' basically. He was not a bad man, but on the other hand, he was tough and strong, ah, he testified before the Congress; he made the hard-line speeches and the rest.

Ah, President Eisenhower was always portrayed as the 'Good Guy.' Ah, restraining Dulles from taking as hard a line, here, there or someplace else. Now actually, I think both Eisenhower and Dulles knew what the game was.

Dulles willingly played that game, and Eisenhower, of course, graciously and probably quite gladly accepted the role because politically it was much better for him to appear as the 'Good Guy.' Now, the point that I make with regard to Kissinger and my relationship: It was almost directly the opposite.

People who think that Kissinger was basically a soft-liner and I was a hard-liner, ah, just don't know what each of us believed. For example, in the soft-line-hard-line dialogue, the first crisis, so-called crisis, I say, as we should say, 'cause we had so many that this gets down to perspective; ah, was·very early in the Administration when the EC-121, you may remember, transport was shot down by the North Koreans, ah, and ah, all the crewmen were lost.

It was an unarmed reconnaissance plane and it was shot down over international waters. Ah, options were presented, ah, the, everything from doing nothing to, ah, taking out two or three airfields. Kissinger came down hard, this is in that very, in about the third month of the Administration, for the hard option.

He said, "that the Russians or basic, possibly, or the North Koreans were testing us. If the Russians weren't testing us, the North Koreans and the Chinese, and the Vietnamese are all going to be watching to see how we reacted to this." And, he said, "We must react strongly." And, he advocated the option of taking out two or three North Korean airfields as a result of this.

Ah, I considered the option. Frankly, I tilted toward it. Ah, Bill [William P.] Rogers, Mel [Melvin R.] Laird thought it was too early in the Administration for us to take such an option of this sort. Our Ambassador in South Korea thought it would be a mistake; that it would have [Kim Il] Sung, the North Korean [Premier], take some action against us. There was the question of what would happen and this is what I think probably delayed me more than anything else, or at least brought me to the conclusion not to take the hard option.

I was concerned not so much about the effect on the Russians, but I was concerned by the effect on the Chinese. After all, we had fought the Chinese in Korea. As a matter of fact, did you know that one of Mao's sons was killed in Korea fighting Americans? He never mentioned it to me, but I knew that that had happened. Ah, and I was concerned about that. And, my other reason for not taking the hard option at that point, the other major reason, ah, I didn't know whether that kind of, of action, protective reaction after they had shot down the plane, taking out an airfield, might escalate into a war, and, I figured having one war on our hands was enough without getting another war on our hands, particularly one in which the Chinese were very close and the Russians too.

[John and Martha Mitchell]

Q. Well, we've covered a lot of ground in this program and there's time now only for postscript, which is not inappropriate because Richard Nixon himself volunteered what follows, almost as a postscript to our discussions. It's a remarkable story he obviously wanted to tell about John and Martha Mitchell. But, we found it personally revealing about Richard Nixon himself. Perhaps you will too.

A. Let me tell you John, John Mitchell. Do you mind? Just a second? It's never been told before, and I haven't asked John whether I can tell it, ah, but I, he is too, I suppose, as decent a man to ever tell it. You see, John's problem was not Watergate. It was Martha. And, it's one of the personal tragedies of our time.

I was the only one in the Administration who knew, except for Rose Woods, my secretary, of the Martha problem. All the people in Washington who knew about the Martha problem, knew that she was, you know, an interesting person who'd make midnight telephone calls to Helen Thomas [reporter] or somebody else, and put out some tidbit of a story and raise hell about [Sen. J. W.] Fulbright [D Ark.] or this or that, or the other thing, and, you know, a good thing to yuk, yuk, yuk about. But, in 1968, during the campaign, John had to send Martha away for about five or six weeks. I didn't know it at the time. She was an emotionally disturbed person.

[The 'Martha Problem']

I asked John to come down to be Attorney General. I spent a day with him working on it. I didn't know why he wouldn't do it. As a matter of fact, he didn't even want to come down for the election night business and all that sort of thing. And, he told me a little about Martha's problem, only saying, "You know she's, she's not really up to it emotionally." I said, "Look," not be, being an amateur psychiatrist, we all are, aren't we? I said, "If you move her to Washington, she may be better." So he brought her to Washington. She was much better for a while.

Then the midnight calls came, and so forth and so on. And, then came the campaign. And, then it began to go up and up, and up. I mean the tempo of her calls and she busted her hand through a window out in, here in California, and all the rest. And said that she was going to blow the whistle on everybody and that John was doing this and being made a scapegoat or words to that effect.

But, we don't need to go into that. All right. This sets the stage for why I feel about John. I asked Bebe about it. Bebe Rebozo. John and Martha used to go down and stay with him on their vacations. And, Bebe said, "You know, I talked to John about Martha." This was, incidentally, ah, during the campaign, shortly before the election, and she was acting up a bit then. This is after he left the committee. And, he said, "John"—and they'd had a couple of drinks, and John was talking a little freely to him—and he said, "John, why don't you put her away like you did in '68?" Bebe said, "Tears came into John's eyes and he says, 'Well, because I love her.'"

Well, you can't fault a guy like that. Sure, great stone face. But he loved her. He knew she was emotionally disturbed. He knew it wasn't just booze. Sometimes she could be this way with no drinks. And sometimes be perfect with a lot of drinks. And so I'll never forget the campaign. I called one day. I was very busy. It was toward the end of the campaign, September or October.

Hadn't heard from John; called to say, "John, how's the campaign going?" And, he sounded very depressed. Said, "Oh, the campaign's going great." And, I thought, "God, maybe he's depressed about Watergate or something?" No. And I could hear on the phone somebody come into the room; he said, "Mr. President, would you mind saying 'hello' to my girl?" I said, "Sure." I thought he meant Marne, that's his daughter—sweet, lovely girl. He adores her. I said, "Sure."

Martha came on the phone. Her voice, and you know, she could be just as charming, wonderful when she talks. She says, "Mr. President, I just want you to know, that there are only three men in the world I love: I love John; I love Bebe and I love you." The next night she was on the phone at midnight raisin' hell about everything. OK. We come to the Watergate period. I mean, when the Watergate had already happened by that time. We're coming now to the period when the ax is going to fall on John, and I must say, I made some statement then when Dean came in and said, you know, "Draw the wagons up around the White House, Mitchell is the guy."

And Haldeman and Ehrlichman wanted to put it on Mitchell and all the rest. I said, "Well, it does look that way to me, and indict him and I said, it'll be a hell of a tough couple of weeks." And, all that sort of thing, but, ah, "That's the way we have to go." This is in April [1973].

Q. Hors d'oeuvres.

A. And, then, ah, but that they'd want more. As I knew they'd want more. Somebody said it was an hors d'oeuvre, I says, "Oh, no, they won't stop at Mitchell, they'll want more." Just as I told Ray Price [Nixon speechwriter] when Haldeman and Ehrlichman, when he says, "You know, when Haldeman and Ehrlichman leave," this is on April 29th, he says, "That'll be enough for 'em." I said, "No, Ray, you know writing, but you don't know politics. They're just going to raise the ante."

But, I understood it. I didn't like it. But, in any event, here's Martha in this period; here's John. I knew that he was strong. He never lets his emotions show, except he does have a quiver in his hand at times. It's better now I understand. But, I just didn't know what was going to break the man, or her. I didn't know how bad the situation was.

[Blame for Watergate]

I've talked too long about it, but just let me summarize it by saying: I'm convinced that if it hadn't been for Martha, and God rest her soul, because she, in her heart, was a good person. She just had a mental and emotional problem that nobody knew about.

If it hadn't been for Martha, there'd have been no Watergate, because John wasn't mindin' that store. He was practically out of his mind about Martha in the spring of 1972. He was letting [Jeb S.] Magruder and all these boys, these kids, these nuts run this thing. The point of the matter is that if John had been watchin' that store, Watergate would never have happened.

Now, am I saying here, at this late juncture, that Watergate is, should be blamed on Martha Mitchell? Of course not. It might have happened anyway. Other things might have brought it on. Who knows? I do say this: I'm trying to explain my feeling of compassion for my friend, John Mitchell.

John Mitchell is a smart man. He's too smart to ever get involved in a stupid jackass thing like Watergate. And, John Mitchell also knew, he was smart enough to know the dangers of cover-ups and that sort of thing. On the other hand, John Mitchell could only think of that poor Martha and that lovely child, Marne, and so, that's the human side of this story, which I don't, I know that you and the press, you can't be interested in that. You can only be interested in "Who shot John?" Well, go ahead.

DOWNING STREET SUMMIT
May 7-8, 1977

The leaders of the world's seven major non-Communist industrialized nations, at an economic summit meeting in London May 7-8, pledged in a joint declaration to work together to resolve common economic problems and to strengthen appropriate international institutions. The leaders said their "most urgent task" was "to create more jobs while continuing to reduce inflation." No agreement was reached, however, on the issue of the spread of nuclear technology.

The London meeting continued discussions begun in November 1975 in France and held again a year later in Puerto Rico June 27-28, 1976. (Historic Documents of 1976, p. 425)

Joining Prime Minister James Callaghan at 10 Downing Street were U.S. President Jimmy Carter, West German Chancellor Helmut Schmidt, Canadian Prime Minister Pierre Elliot Trudeau, Japanese Premier Takeo Fukuda, Italian Premier Giulio Andreotti and French President Valery Giscard d'Estaing. The representatives at the conference expressed a sense of shared goals and mutual interdependence in dealing with economic issues. "The world economy has to be seen as a whole.... We are determined to respond collectively to the challenges of the future," they declared.

Noting that there had been a "meeting of the minds" on devising a common strategy to deal with unemployment and inflation, the declaration said that the stronger Western economies had pledged to meet internal economic growth targets in 1977 to stimulate the recovery of other Western industrial nations suffering from recessions. The United States targeted its growth rate at 5.8-6 per cent; West Germany, 5 per cent; and Japan, 6-7 per cent.

Rejecting the high tariff protectionist policies that crippled world economic response to depression in the 1930s, the leaders pledged to reduce internal trade barriers and promote freer economic trade. The members of the conference urged that "irregular practices and improper conduct should be eliminated from international trade, banking and commerce, and we welcome the work being done toward international agreements prohibiting illicit payments."

Unemployment among young people was a major topic at the conference. Recognizing the politically unsettling effect of having high unemployment among young workers, the leaders expressed their concern about the political threat that a substantial increase in mass unemployment could bring during a slowdown in economic recovery.

In an effort to spur lagging economic growth, the conference members agreed to seek improved financing facilities through the International Monetary Fund (IMF), so that nations suffering balance-of-payments deficits because of soaring energy costs could obtain more aid. The creation of a multibillion-dollar cushion through the IMF to offset trade deficits to the oil-producing countries would be used to help nations hardest hit by rising energy costs. The declaration further stated that the conference members supported measures that would increase the resources of multilateral lending institutions, such as the World Bank, to permit the level of lending to rise in real terms to keep pace with inflation. The leaders of the seven nations noted that they would seek cooperation with the United Nations, and agreed to "give a new impetus" to the Geneva talks under the auspices of the General Agreement on Tariffs and Trade (GATT). The goal of the GATT negotiations was to reduce barriers to free trade.

The declaration expressed the general concern of the participants about the increasing level of energy dependence of the industrial democracies on imported oil. The seven heads of state declared their intention to "further conserve energy and increase and diversify energy production so that we reduce our dependence on oil." There was general agreement among the conference members on the need to develop nuclear energy to meet the world's energy requirements.

Nuclear Technology Issue

The members of the summit conference established a seven-nation study group on the development, use and exportation of nuclear technology. The study group was asked to submit a preliminary plan on how to reconcile the need for greater reliance on nuclear energy with the need to avoid the spread of nuclear weapons. The decision to form a study group was a compromise measure that reflected differences among the seven on assisting other nations in developing breeder reactors. Glossing over their differences on nuclear policy, the statesmen said they hoped to "meet the world's energy requirements...while reducing the risks of nuclear proliferation."

In an appendix to the declaration the leaders of the western nations noted that the world economic situation had improved. The appendix spelled out the plans for meeting the payments deficits of oil-importing nations, expanding opportunities for world trade, conserving energy and sharing an "open market system" with the agricultural economies of the developing countries.

Following are the texts of the Declaration of the Downing Street Summit Conference and the appendix to the declaration May 7-8, 1977, in which the leaders of seven industrial democracies pledged to work together to reduce inflation and unemployment.

DOWNING STREET SUMMIT DECLARATION

In two days of intensive discussion at Downing Street we have agreed on how we can best help to promote the well-being both of our own countries and of others.

The world economy has to be seen as a whole; it involves not only cooperation among national Governments but also strengthening appropriate international organizations. We were reinforced in our awareness of the interrelationship of all the issues before us, as well as our own interdependence. We are determined to respond collectively to the challenges of the future.

—Our most urgent task is to create more jobs while continuing to reduce inflation. Inflation does not reduce unemployment. On the contrary it is one of its major causes. We are particularly concerned about the problem of unemployment among young people. We have agreed that there will be an exchange of experience and ideas on providing the young with job opportunities.

—We commit our governments to stated economic growth targets or to stabilization policies which, taken as a whole, should provide a basis for sustained non-inflationary growth, in our own countries and world-wide and for reduction of imbalances in international payments.

—Improved financing facilities are needed. The International Monetary Fund must play a prominent role. We commit ourselves to seek additional resources for the IMF and support the linkage of its lending practices to the adoption of appropriate stabilization policies.

369

—We will provide strong political leadership to expand opportunities for trade to strengthen the open international trading system, which will increase job opportunities. We reject protectionism: it would foster unemployment, increase inflation and undermine the welfare of our peoples. We will give a new impetus to the Tokyo Round of Multilateral Trade Negotiations. Our objective is to make substantive progress in key areas in 1977. In this field structural changes in the world economy must be taken into consideration.

—We will further conserve energy and increase and diversify energy production, so that we reduce our dependence on oil. We agree on the need to increase nuclear energy to help meet the world's energy requirements. We commit ourselves to do this while reducing the risks of nuclear proliferation. We are launching an urgent study to determine how best to fulfil these purposes.

—The world economy can only grow on a sustained and equitable basis if developing countries share in that growth. We are agreed to do all in our power to achieve a successful conclusion of the CIEC [Conference on International Economic Cooperation] and we commit ourselves to a continued constructive dialogue with developing countries. We aim to increase the flow of aid and other real resources to those countries. We invite the COMECON [Council for Mutual Economic Cooperation] countries to do the same. We support multilateral institutions such as the World Bank, whose general resources should be increased sufficiently to permit its lending to rise in real terms. We stress the importance of secure private investments to foster world economic progress.

To carry out these tasks we need the assistance and cooperation in appropriate international institutions, such as the United Nations, the World Bank, the IMF, the GATT [General Agreement on Tariffs and Trade] and OECD [Organization for Economic Cooperation and Development]. Those among us whose countries are members of the European Economic Community intend to make their efforts within its framework.

In our discussions we have reached substantial agreement. Our firm purpose is now to put that agreement into action. We shall review progress on all the measures we have discussed here at Downing Street in order to maintain the momentum of recovery.

The message of the Downing Street Summit is thus one of confidence:

—in the continuing strength of our societies and the proven democratic principles that give them vitality;

—that we are undertaking the measures needed to overcome problems and achieve a more prosperous future.

APPENDIX TO DOWNING STREET
SUMMIT DECLARATION

World Economic Prospects

Since 1975 the world economic situation has been improving gradually. Serious problems, however, still persist in all of our countries. Our most urgent task is to create jobs while continuing to reduce inflation. Inflation is not a remedy to unemployment but one of its major causes. Progress in the fight against inflation has been uneven. The needs for adjustment between surplus and deficit countries remain large. The world has not yet fully adjusted to the depressive effects of the 1974 oil price rise.

We commit our Governments to targets for growth and stabilization which vary from country to country but which, taken as a whole, should provide a basis for sustained non-inflationary growth world-wide.

Some of our countries have adopted reasonably expansionist growth targets for 1977. The governments of these countries will keep their policies under review, and commit themselves to adopt further policies, if needed to achieve their stated target rates and to contribute to the adjustment of payments imbalances. Others are pursuing stabilization policies designed to provide a basis for sustained growth without increasing inflationary expectations. The governments of these countries will continue to pursue those goals.

These two sets of policies are interrelated. Those of the first group of countries should help to create an environment conducive to expansion in the others without adding to inflation. Only if growth rates can be maintained in the first group and increased in the second, and inflation tackled successfully in both, can unemployment be reduced.

We are particularly concerned about the problem of unemployment among young people. Therefore we shall promote the training of young people in order to build a skilled and flexible labor force so that they can be ready to take advantage of the upturn in economic activity as it develops. All of our governments, individually or collectively, are taking appropriate measures to this end. We must learn as much as possible from each other and agree to exchange experiences and ideas.

Success in managing our domestic economies will not only strengthen world economic growth but also contribute to success in four other main economic fields to which we now turn—balance of payments financing, trade, energy and North/South relations. Progress in these fields will in turn contribute to world economic recovery.

Balance of Payments Financing

For some years to come oil-importing nations, as a group, will be facing substantial payments deficits and importing capital from OPEC [Organization of Petroleum Exporting Countries] nations to finance them. The deficit for the current year could run as high as $45-billion. Only through a reduction in our dependence on imported oil and a rise in the capacity of oil-producing nations to import can that deficit be reduced.

This deficit needs to be distributed among the oil-consuming nations in a pattern compatible with their ability to attract capital on a continuing basis. The need for adjustment to this pattern remains large, and it will take much international cooperation, and determined action by surplus as well as deficit countries, if continuing progress is to be made. Strategies of adjustment in the deficit countries must include emphasis on elimination of domestic sources of inflation and improvement in international cost-price relationships. It is important that industrial countries in relatively strong payments positions should ensure continued adequate expansion of domestic demand, within prudent limits. Moreover these countries, as well as other countries in strong payments positions, should promote increased flows of long-term capital exports.

The International Monetary Fund must play a prominent role in balance of payments financing and adjustment. We therefore strongly endorse the recent agreement of the Interim Committee of the IMF to seek additional resources for that organization and to link IMF lending to the adoption of appropriate stabilization policies. These added resources will strengthen the ability of the IMF to encourage and assist member countries in adopting policies which will limit payments deficits and warrant their financing through the private markets. These resources should be used with the conditionality and flexibility required to encourage an appropriate pace of adjustment.

This IMF proposal should facilitate the maintenance of reasonable levels of economic activity and reduce the danger of resort to trade and payments restrictions. It demonstrates co-operation between oil-exporting nations, industrial nations in stronger financial positions, and the IMF. It will contribute materially to the health and progress of the world economy. In pursuit of this objective, we also reaffirm our intention to strive to increase monetary stability.

We agreed that the international monetary and financial system, in its new and agreed legal framework, should be strengthened by the early implementation of the increase in quotas. We will work towards an early agreement within the IMF on another increase in the quotas of that organization.

Trade

We are committed to providing strong political leadership for the global effort to expand opportunities for trade and to strengthen the open international trading system. Achievement of these goals is central to world economic prosperity and the effective resolution of economic problems faced by both developed and developing countries throughout the world.

Policies on protectionism foster unemployment, increase inflation and undermine the welfare of our peoples. We are therefore agreed on the need to maintain our political commitment to an open and non-discriminatory world trading system. We will seek both nationally and through the appropriate international institutions to promote solutions that create new jobs and consumer benefits through expanded trade and to avoid approaches which restrict trade.

The Tokyo Round of multilateral trade negotiations must be pursued vigorously. The continuing economic difficulties make it even more essential to achieve the objective of the Tokyo Declaration and to negotiate a comprehensive set of agreements to the maximum benefit of all. Toward this end, we will seek this year to achieve substantive progress in such key areas as:

(i)   a tariff reduction plan of broadest possible application designed to achieve a substantial cut and harmonization and in certain cases the elimination of tariffs;

(ii) codes, agreements and other measures that will facilitate a significant reduction of nontariff barriers to trade and the avoidance of new barriers in the future and that will take into account the structural changes which have taken place in the world economy;

(iii) a mutually acceptable approach to agriculture that will achieve increased expansion and stabilization of trade, and greater assurance of world food supplies.

Such progress should not remove the right of individual countries under existing international agreements to avoid significant market disruption.

While seeking to conclude comprehensive and balanced agreements on the basis of reciprocity among all industrial countries we are determined, in accordance with the aims of the Tokyo Declaration, to ensure that the agreements provide special benefits to developing countries.

We welcome the action taken by Governments to reduce counterproductive competition in officially supported export credits and propose that substantial further efforts be made this year to improve and extend the present consensus in this area.

We consider that irregular practices and improper conduct should be eliminated from international trade, banking and commerce, and we welcome the work being done toward international agreements prohibiting illicit payments.

Energy

We welcome the measures taken by a number of Governments to increase energy conservation. The increase in demand for energy and oil imports continues at a rate which places excessive pressure on the world's depleting hydrocarbon resources. We agree therefore on the need to do everything possible to strengthen our efforts still further.

We are committed to national and joint efforts to limit energy demand and to increase and diversify supplies. There will need to be greater exchanges of technology and joint research and development aimed at more efficient energy use, improved recovery and use of coal and other conventional resources, and the development of new energy sources.

373

Increasing reliance will have to be placed on nuclear energy to satisfy growing energy requirements and to help diversify sources of energy. This should be done with the utmost precaution with respect to the generation and dissemination of material that can be used for nuclear weapons. Our objective is to meet the world's energy needs and to make peaceful use of nuclear energy widely available, while avoiding the danger of the spread of nuclear weapons. We are also agreed that, in order to be effective, non-proliferation policies should as far as possible be acceptable to both industrialized and developing countries alike. To this end, we are undertaking a preliminary analysis to be completed within two months of the best means of advancing these objectives, including the study of terms of reference for international fuel cycle evaluation.

The oil-importing developing countries have special problems both in securing and in paying for the energy supplies needed to sustain their economic development programs. They require additional help in expanding their domestic energy production and to this end we hope the World Bank, as its resources grow, will give special emphasis to projects that serve this purpose.

We intend to do our utmost to ensure, during this transitional period, that the energy market functions harmoniously, in particular through strict conservation measures and the development of all our energy resources. We hope very much that the oil-producing countries will take these efforts into account and will make their contribution as well.

We believe that these activities are essential to enable all countries to have continuing energy supplies now and for the future at reasonable prices consistent with sustained noninflationary economic growth, and we intend through all useful channels to concert our policies in continued consultation and cooperation with each other and with other countries.

North/South Relations

The world economy can only grow on a sustained and equitable basis if developing countries share in that growth. Progress has been made. The industrial countries have maintained an open market system despite a deep recession. They have increased aid flows, especially to poorer nations. Some $8-billion will be available from the IDA [International Development Association] for these nations over the next three years, as we join others in fulfilling pledges to its Fifth Replenishment. The IMF has made available to developing countries, under its compensatory financing facility nearly an additional $2-billion last year. An International Fund for Agricultural Development has been created, based on common efforts by the developed OPEC, and other developing nations.

The progress and the spirit of cooperation that have emerged can serve as an excellent base for further steps. The next step will be the successful conclusion of the Conference on International Economic Cooperation [CIEC] and we agreed to do all in our power to achieve this.

We shall work:

(i)   to increase the flow of aid and other real resources from the industrial to developing countries, particularly to the 800 million people who now live in absolute poverty; and to improve the effectiveness of aid;

(ii) to facilitate developing countries' access to sources of international finance;

(iii) to support such multilateral lending institutions as the World Bank, whose lending capacity we believe will have to be increased in the years ahead to permit its lending to increase in real terms and widen in scope;

(iv) to promote the secure investment needed to foster world economic development;

(v) to secure productive results from negotiations about the stabilization of commodity prices and the creation of a Common Fund for individual buffer stock agreements and to consider problems of the stabilization of export earnings of developing countries; and

(vi) to continue to improve access in a non-disruptive way to the markets of industrial countries for the products of developing nations.

It is desirable that these actions by developed and developing countries be assessed and concerted in relation to each other and to the larger goals that our countries share. We hope that the World Bank, together with the IMF, will consult with other developed and developing countries in exploring how this could best be done.

The well-being of the developed and developing nations are bound up together. The developing countries' growing prosperity benefit industrial countries, as the latter's growth benefits developing nations. Both developed and developing nations have a mutual interest in maintaining a climate conducive to stable growth worldwide.

CARTER PROPOSALS FOR SOCIAL SECURITY REFORM
May 9, 1977

Addressing himself to the generally agreed need for major revisions in Social Security financing, President Carter May 9 unveiled the administration's plan to rescue the deficit-ridden system.

The most controversial parts of the administration's proposal called for higher Social Security taxes on employers and temporary use of income tax revenues to build up Social Security trust fund reserves. The full eight-point plan aimed to provide an additional $83-billion to the Old Age, Survivors and Disability Insurance (OASDI) trust funds by 1982, eliminating the current operating deficits and reducing the potential for serious strain on the system in the longer run.

Although the House originally approved limited authority for the Social Security system to borrow from general funds and the Senate initially required employers to pay Social Security taxes on a higher wage base than would employees, both these provisions were dropped from the final Social Security financing bill which Congress cleared Dec. 15.

"Taken together, the actions I am recommending today will eliminate the Social Security deficit for the remainder of this century," said Carter in his message to Congress. He further emphasized that his plan would accomplish that without raising payroll taxes for low- and middle-income workers—a promise of Carter's in his presidential campaign. The President said that more than 33 million Americans receive benefits; another 104 million are making contributions and expect to receive benefits when they retire or become disabled.

Summary of Plan

The main elements of the plan included:

* *A "countercyclical" transfer of general revenues to the Social Security trust funds when the national unemployment rate exceeded 6 per cent to supplement depressed payroll tax collections.*

* *A phased-in elimination of the ceiling on the wages on which employers pay Social Security taxes.*

* *A series of smaller increases ($600 each) in the wage base for employees, occurring in 1979, 1981, 1983 and 1985.*

* *An increase, to 7.5 per cent from 7 per cent, in the payroll tax rate levied on self-employed persons.*

* *A shift of approximately $7-billion of revenues from already scheduled Medicare tax rate increases into the OASDI trust fund. The administration claimed that enactment of its proposed hospital cost containment plan would save the government at least $10-billion in Medicare and Medicaid payments, leaving the hospital insurance trust fund with money to spare.*

* *New eligibility requirements for dependents' benefits, to bring the Social Security system into compliance with a recent Supreme Court ruling that found previous dependency tests discriminated against men.* (Sex Bias in Social Security, p. 169)

* *"Decoupling" procedures to change a costly feature in the current method of adjusting Social Security benefits for inflation.*

* *Earlier imposition of an additional 1 per cent increase in the payroll tax rate each for employers and employees scheduled under existing law for 2011. Under the administration's plan, one quarter of this increase would occur in 1985 and the rest in 1990.*

> *Following is the text of President Carter's May 9, 1977, message to Congress on financing of the Social Security system:*

To the Congress of the United States:

The Social Security system affects the lives of more Americans than almost any other function of government. More than 33 million people currently receive benefits. Another 104 million people are making contributions with the expectation that they will receive benefits when they retire or become disabled, or when their survivors need help.

Today, the Board of Trustees of the Social Security Trust Funds is submitting its 1977 report to the Congress. The report tells us that the system critically needs financial support in the short term. The high unemployment of recent years has curtailed Social Security's revenues, while benefits have risen with inflation. Since 1975 expenditures have exceeded income; and existing reserves will soon be exhausted.

Unless we act now, the Disability Insurance Trust (DI) Fund will be exhausted in 1979 and the Old Age and Survivors Insurance (OASI) Trust Fund will run out in 1983.

The Trustees' Report indicates that there are serious longer term problems as well. Under current law the Social Security system will have an estimated deficit of 8.2 per cent of taxable payroll over the next seventy-five years. About half of this deficit is due to changes in the projected composition of our population over those years. Higher life expectancy and lower birthrates will make the nation older as a whole. About half is due to a technical flaw in the automatic cost of living formula adopted in 1972.

While campaigning for President, I stressed my commitment to restore the financial integrity of the Social Security system. I pledged I would do my best to avoid increases above those already scheduled in tax rates, which fall most heavily on moderate- and lower-income workers. I also promised to correct the technical flaw in the system which exaggerates the adjustment for inflation, and to do so without reducing the relative value of retirement benefits as compared with pre-retirement earnings.

I am announcing today a set of proposals which meet those commitments and which solve both the short-term and long-term problems in the Social Security system through the end of the twentieth century. These proposals are designed to:

● Prevent the default of the trust funds now predicted to occur.

● Bring income and expenses into balance in 1978 and keep them that way through the end of the century.

● Create sufficient reserves to protect the system against sudden declines in revenue caused by unemployment or other economic uncertainties.

● Protect the system's integrity beyond the turn of the century to the extent we can predict what will happen in the next 75 years.

● Provide for an orderly review and examination of the system's basic structure.

My proposals are the result of a number of hard choices. I am convinced that action is needed now, and that these steps will restore the financial integrity of the Social Security system.

I will ask the Congress to take the following specific actions:

1. Compensate the Social Security trust funds from general revenues for a share of revenues lost during severe recessions. General revenues would be used in a countercyclical fashion to replace the payroll tax receipts lost as a result of that portion of unemployment in excess of six per cent. General revenues would be used *only* in these carefully limited situations. Because this is an innovative measure, the legislation we submit will provide this feature only through 1982. The next Social Security Advisory Council will be asked to review this countercyclical mechanism to determine whether it should be made permanent.

2. Remove the wage-base ceiling for employers. Under present law employers and employees pay a tax only on the first $16,500 in wages. Under this proposal the employer ceiling would be raised over a three-year period, so that by 1981 the ceiling would be removed. This action will provide a significant source of revenue without increasing long-term benefit liabilities.

3. Increase the wage base subject to the employee tax by $600 in 1979, 1981, 1983, and 1985, beyond the automatic increases in current law. This will provide a progressive source of financing.

4. Shift revenues from the Hospital Insurance Trust Fund to the Old Age, Survivors, and Disability Trust Funds. In part, this shift will be made possible because of substantial savings to the Medicare system from the hospital cost containment legislation that I have proposed.

5. Increase the tax rate on the self-employed from 7 per cent to 7.5 per cent. This will restore the historical relationship between the OASI and the DI rates paid by the self-employed to one and one-half times that paid by employees.

6. Correct certain technical provisions of the Social Security Act which differentiate on the basis of sex. This will include a new eligibility test for dependent benefits. Recent Supreme Court decisions would result in unfinanced increases in the cost of the system and some inequities without this change.

These six steps, along with measures already contained in existing law will eliminate the short-term financing problem and improve the overall equity of the Social Security system.

In order to guarantee the financial integrity of the system into the next century, two additional steps must be taken. I will be asking the Congress to:

1. Modify the Social Security benefit formula to eliminate the inflation over-adjustment now in law. This modification, known as "decoupling," should be done in a way that maintains the current ratio of retirement benefits to pre-retirement wages.

2. Adjust the timing of a tax rate increase already contained in current law. The one per cent tax rate increase presently scheduled for the year 2011 would be moved forward so that .25 per cent would occur in 1985 and the remainder in 1990.

Taken together, the actions I am recommending today will eliminate the Social Security deficit for the remainder of this century. They will reduce the estimated 75-year deficit from the Trustee Report forecast of 8.2 per cent of payroll to a manageable 1.9 per cent.

Prompt enactment of the measure I have recommended will provide the Social Security system with financial stability. This is an overriding immediate objective.

In addition, I am instructing the Secretary of Health, Education and Welfare to appoint the independent Social Security Advisory Council required by law to meet each four years. I will ask the Council to conduct a thorough reexamination of the structure of the system, the adequacy of its benefits, the effectiveness and equity of disability definitions, and the efficiency and responsiveness of its administration. Their report, which will be issued within the next two years, will provide the basis for further improvements.

I call upon the Congress to act favorably on these major reform initiatives.

COURT ON SENIORITY AND EMPLOYMENT DISCRIMINATION

May 31, 1977

Seniority systems perpetuating the effect of racial discrimination which occurred before the 1964 Civil Rights Act were upheld by the Supreme Court May 31 by a 7-2 vote.

In a case involving a nationwide motor freight company, T.I.M.E.-D.C. Inc., and the International Brotherhood of Teamsters, the court found that the Congress in the 1964 Act, specifically immunized bona fide *seniority systems from challenge.*

Justice Potter Stewart, writing for the majority, noted that the court did not dispute the finding of the lower courts that the trucking company indeed had systematically denied the line-driver jobs (driving trucks between cities rather than within cities) to black and Spanish-surnamed employees and applicants.

The seniority issue arose in determining the remedy which should be provided to victims of discrimination. For competitive purposes such as job assignment and lay-off order (not matters such as vacation time and other benefits), seniority counted from the time he took the post, not from the time he joined the company in another position. Thus, a black employee who earlier had been denied a line-driver post would have to surrender his existing seniority if he now moved into a line-driver position.

Citing its 1976 ruling in the case of Franks v. Bowman Transportation Co., *the court upheld unanimously that persons discriminated against by the company after July 2, 1965, the effective date of the 1964 law, should be awarded seniority retroactively as far back as that date.*

But the court refused to order changes in the seniority system as it existed when the 1964 law took effect, declining to order seniority awards for persons discriminated against by the company before that date. In so ruling the court rejected the argument of the Justice Department, which filed the cases initially, that any seniority system which perpetuated the effects of pre-1965 discrimination was not a bona fide *seniority system within the immunity granted by the 1964 Act.*

Were it not for that immunity provision and the legislative history surrounding it, wrote Justice Stewart, the seniority system challenged in this case would probably be found invalid. The advantages of the seniority system "flow disproportionately" to the white employees, Stewart noted. This "disproportionate distribution of advantages" operated to freeze the status quo of prior discriminatory practices, he observed. Stewart wrote: "But both the literal terms of...that provision and the legislative history of Title VII demonstrate that Congress considered this very effect of many seniority systems and extended a measure of immunity to them.... The congressional judgment was that Title VII should not outlaw the use of existing seniority lists and thereby destroy or water down the vested seniority rights of employees simply because their employer had engaged in discrimination prior to the passage of the Act...."

"We hold that an otherwise neutral, legitimate seniority system does not become unlawful under Title VII simply because it may perpetuate pre-Act discrimination. Congress did not intend to make it illegal for employees with vested seniority rights to exercise those rights, even at the expense of pre-Act discriminatees," Stewart said.

Persons suffering discrimination only prior to the 1964 Act were not entitled to any award of seniority, and no one could be given seniority dating back to a date earlier than July 2, 1965. But the court did hold that seniority awards could be made not only to persons actually denied line-driver jobs after July 2, 1965, but also to those who did not apply for line driver jobs but who could prove that they would have, in the absence of the company's clear policy of discrimination.

Justices Thurgood Marshall and William J. Brennan Jr. dissented, agreeing with the Justice Department's position that a system perpetuating the effect of pre-1965 discrimination was not a bona fide *system covered by the immunity provisions of the 1964 law. They pointed out that their interpretation of the 1964 Act coincided with the holding of eight Courts of Appeals and the Equal Employment Opportunity Commission.*

Following are excerpts from the decision of the Supreme Court upholding the validity of certain seniority systems which may have discriminated against minority employees, delivered May 31, 1977. (Boldface headings in brackets have been added by Congressional Quarterly to highlight the organization of the text.):

Nos. 75-636 and 75-672

International Brotherhood of
    Teamsters, Petitioner,
75-636   *v.*
        United States et al.

        T.I.M.E.-D.C., Inc.,
            Petitioner,
75-672   *v.*
        United States et al.

On Writs of Certiorari to the
United States Court of Appeals for the Fifth Circuit.

[May 31, 1977]

MR. JUSTICE STEWART delivered the opinion of the Court.

This litigation brings here several important questions under Title VII of the Civil Rights Act of 1964.... The issues grow out of alleged unlawful employment practices engaged in by an employer and a union. The employer is a common carrier of motor freight with nationwide operations, and the union represents a large group of its employees. The District Court and the Court of Appeals held that the employer had violated Title VII by engaging in a pattern and practice of employment discrimination against Negroes and Spanish-surnamed Americans, and that the union had violated the Act by agreeing with the employer to create and maintain a seniority system that perpetuated the effects of past racial and ethnic discrimination. In addition to the basic questions presented by these two rulings, other subsidiary issues must be resolved if violations of Title VII occurred—issues concerning the nature of the relief to which aggrieved individuals may be entitled.

I

The United States brought an action in a Tennessee federal court against the petitioner T.I.M.E.-D.C., Inc.... The complaint charged that the company had followed discriminatory hiring, assignment, and promotion policies against Negroes at its terminal in Nashville, Tenn. The Government brought a second action against the company almost three years later in a federal district court in Texas, charging a pattern and practice of employment discrimination against Negroes and Spanish-surnamed persons throughout the company's transportation system. The petitioner International Brotherhood of Teamsters (the union) was joined as a defendant in that suit. The two actions were consolidated for trial in the Northern District of Texas.

The central claim in both lawsuits was that the company had engaged in a pattern or practice of discriminating against minorities in hiring so-called line drivers. Those Negroes and Spanish-surnamed persons who had been hired, the Government alleged, were given lower paying, less

385

desirable jobs as servicemen or local city drivers, and were thereafter discriminated against with respect to promotions and transfers. In this connection the complaint also challenged the seniority system established by the collective-bargaining agreements between the employer and the union. The Government sought a general injunctive remedy and specific "make whole" relief for all individual discriminatees, which would allow them an opportunity to transfer to line-driver jobs with full company seniority for all purposes....

II

In this Court the company and the unions contend that their conduct did not violate Title VII in any respect, asserting first that the evidence introduced at trial was insufficient to show that the company engaged in a "pattern or practice" of employment discrimination. The union further contends that the seniority system contained in the collective-bargaining agreements in no way violated Title VII. If these contentions are correct, it is unnecessary, of course, to reach any of the issues concerning remedies that so occupied the attention of the Court of Appeals.

Consideration of the question whether the company engaged in a pattern or practice of discriminatory hiring practices involves controlling legal principles that are relatively clear. The Government's theory of discrimination was simply that the company, in violation of...Title VII regularly and purposefully treated Negroes and Spanish-surnamed Americans less favorably than white persons. The disparity in treatment allegedly involved the refusal to recruit, hire, transfer, or promote minority group members on an equal basis with white people, particularly with respect to line-driving positions. The ultimate factual issues are thus simply whether there was a pattern or practice of such disparate treatment and, if so, whether the differences were "racially premised."...

As the plaintiff, the Government bore the initial burden of making out a prima facie case of discrimination.... And, because it alleged a systemwide pattern or practice of resistance to the full enjoyment of Title VII rights, the Government ultimately had to prove more than the mere occurrence of isolated or "accidental" or sporadic discriminatory acts. It had to establish by a preponderance of the evidence that racial discrimination was the company's standard operating procedure—the regular rather than the unusual practice.

We agree with the District Court and the Court of Appeals that the Government carried its burden of proof. As of March 31, 1971, shortly after the Government filed its complaint alleging systemwide discrimination, the company had 6,472 employees. Of these, 314 (5%) were Negroes and 257 (4%) were Spanish-surnamed Americans. Of the 1,828 line drivers, however, there were only 8 (0.4%) Negroes and 5 (0.3%) Spanish-surnamed persons, and all of the Negroes had been hired after the litigation had commenced. With one exception—a man who worked as a line driver at the Chicago terminal from 1950 to 1959—the company and its predecessors *did not employ a Negro on a regular basis as a line driver until 1969.* And, as the Government showed, even in 1971 there were terminals in areas of substantial Negro population where all of the company's line drivers were white. A great majority of the Negroes (83%) and Spanish-surnamed Americans (78%) who did work for the company held the lower-paying city operations and serviceman jobs, whereas only 39% of the nonminority employees held jobs in those categories.

The Government bolstered its statistical evidence with the testimony of individuals who recounted over 40 specific instances of discrimination. Upon the basis of this testimony the District Court found that "[n]umerous qualified black and Spanish-surnamed American applicants who sought line-driving jobs at the company over the years had their requests ignored, were given false or misleading information about requirements, opportunities, and application procedures, or were not considered and hired on the same basis that whites were considered and hired." Minority employees who wanted to transfer to line-driver jobs met with similar difficulties.

The company's principal response to this evidence is that statistics can never in and of themselves prove the existence of a pattern or practice of discrimination, or even establish a prima facie case shifting to the employer the burden of rebutting...the figures. But...this was not a case in which the Government relief on "statistics alone," The individuals who testified about their personal experiences with the company brought the cold numbers convincingly to life.

In any event, our cases make it unmistakably clear that "[s]tatistical analyses have served and will continue to serve an important role" in cases in which the existance of discrimination is a disputed issue.... We have repeatedly approved the use of statistical proof, where it reached proportions comparable to those in this case, to establish a prima facie case of racial discrimination in jury selection cases.... Statistics are equally competent in proving employment discrimination. We caution only that statistics are not irrefutable; they come in an infinite variety and, like any other kind of evidence, they may be rebutted. In short, their usefulness depends on all of the surrounding facts and circumstances....

In addition to its general protest against the use of statistics in Title VII cases, the company claims that in this case the statistics revealing racial imbalance are misleading because they fail to take into account the company's particular business situation as of the effective date of Title VII. The company concedes that its line drivers were virtually all white in July 1965, but it claims that thereafter business conditions were such that its work force dropped. Its argument is that low personnel turnover, rather than post-Act discrimination, accounts for more recent statistical disparities. It points to substantial minority hiring in later years, especially after 1971, as showing that any pre-Act patterns of discrimination were broken.

The argument would be a forceful one if this were an employer who, at the time of suit, had done virtually no new hiring since the effective date of

Title VII. But it is not. Although the company's total number of employees apparently dropped somewhat during the late 1960's, the record shows that many line drivers continued to be hired throughout this period, and that almost all of them were white. To be sure, there were improvements in the company's hiring practices. The Court of Appeals commented that "T.I.M.E.-D.C.'s recent minority hiring progress stands as a laudable good faith effort to eradicate the effects of past discrimination in the area of hiring and initial assignment."... But the District Court and the Court of Appeals found upon substantial evidence that the company had engaged in a course of discrimination that continued well after the effective date of Title VII. The company's later changes in its hiring and promotion policies could be little comfort to the victims of the earlier post-Act discrimination, and could not erase its previous illegal conduct or its obligation to afford relief to those who suffered because of it....

The District Court and the Court of Appeals, on the basis of substantial evidence, held that the governnment had proved a prima facie case of systematic and purposeful employment discrimination, continuing well beyond the effective date of Title VII. The company's attempts to rebut that conclusion were held to be inadequate. For the reasons we have summarized, there is no warrant for this Court to disturb the findings of the District Court and the Court of Appeals on this basic issue....

The District Court and the Court of Appeals also found that the seniority system contained in the collective-bargaining agreements between the company and the union operated to violate Title VII of the Act.

For purposes of calculating benefits, such as vacations, pensions, and other fringe benefits, an employee's seniority under this system runs from the date he joins the company, and takes into account his total service in all jobs and bargaining units. For competitive purposes, however, such as determining the order in which employees may bid for particular jobs, are laid off, or are recalled from layoff, it is bargaining-unit seniority that controls. Thus, a line driver's seniority, for purposes of bidding for particular runs and protection against layoff, takes into account only the length of time he has been a line driver at a particular terminal. The practical effect is that a city driver or serviceman who transfers to a line-driver job must forfeit all the competitive seniority he has accumulated in his previous bargaining unit and start at the bottom of the line-drivers' "board."

The vice of this arrangement, as found by the District Court and the Court of Appeals, was that it "locked" minority workers into inferior jobs and perpetuated prior discrimination by discouraging transfers to jobs as line drivers. While the disincentive applied to all workers, including whites, it was Negroes and Spanish-surnamed persons who, those courts found, suffered the most because many of them had been denied the equal opportunity to become line drivers when they were initially hired, whereas whites either had not sought or were refused line-driver positions for reasons unrelated to their race or national origin.

The linchpin of the theory embraced by the District Court and the Court of Appeals was that a discriminatee who must forfeit his competitive seniority in order finally to obtain a line-driver job will never be able to "catch up" to the seniority level of his contemporary who was not subject to discrimination. Accordingly, this continued, built-in disadvantage to the prior discriminatee who transfers to a line-driver job was held to constitute a continuing violation of Title VII, for which both the employer and the union who jointly created and maintain the seniority system were liable.

The union, while acknowledging that the seniority system may in some sense perpetuate the effects of prior discrimination, asserts that the system is immunized from a finding of illegality....

It argues that the seniority system in this case is "bona fide"...when judged in light of its history, intent, application, and all of the circumstances under which it was created and is maintained. More specifically, the union claims that the central purpose...is to ensure that mere perpetuation of *pre-Act* discrimination is not unlawful under Title VII. And...the union claims that the seniority system in this case has no such effect. Its position in this Court...is that the seniority system presents no hurdle to post-Act discriminatees who seek retroactive seniority to the date they would have become line drivers but for the company's discrimination. Indeed, the union asserts that under its collective-bargaining agreements the union will itself take up the cause of the post-Act victim and attempt, through grievance procedures, to gain for him full "make whole" relief, including appropriate seniority.

The Government responds that a seniority system that perpetuates the effects of prior discrimination—pre- or post-Act—can never be "bona fide"...; at a minimum Title VII prohibits those applications of a seniority system that perpetuate the effects on incumbent employees of prior discriminatory job assignments....

...Because the company discriminated both before and after the enactment of Title VII, the seniority system is said to have operated to perpetuate the effects of both pre- and post-Act discrimination. Post-Act discriminatees, however, may obtain full "make whole" relief, including retroactive seniority under *Franks* v. *Bowman [Transportation Co.* (1976)]...without attacking the legality of the seniority system as applied to them. *Franks* made clear and the union acknowledges that retroactive seniority may be awarded as relief from an employer's discriminatory hiring and assignment policies even if the seniority system agreement itself makes no provision for such relief.... Here the Government has proved that the company engaged in a post-Act pattern of discriminatory hiring, assignment, transfer, and promotion policies. Any Negro or Spanish-surnamed American injured by those policies may receive all appropriate relief as a direct remedy for this discrimination.

What remains for review is the judgment that the seniority system unlawfully perpetuated the effects of *pre-Act* discrimination. We must decide, in short whether...[Title VII] invalidates otherwise bona fide seniority systems that afford no constructive seniority to victims discriminated against prior to the effective date of Title VII, and it is to that issue that we now turn.

The primary purpose of Title VII was "to assure equality of employment opportunities and to eliminate those discriminatory practices and devices which have fostered racially stratified job environments to the disadvantage of minority citizens."...

One kind of practice "fair in form, but discriminatory in operation" is that which perpetuates the effects of prior discrimination. As the Court held in *Griggs* [v. *Duke Power Co.* (1971)]...: "Under the Act, practices, procedures or tests neutral on their face, and even neutral in terms of intent, cannot be maintained if they operate to 'freeze' the status quo of prior discriminatory employment practices."...

...The heart of the system is its allocation of the choicest jobs, the greatest protection against layoffs, and other advantages to those employees who have been line drivers for the longest time. Where, because of the employer's prior intentional discrimination, the line drivers with the longest tenure are without exception white, the advantages of the seniority system flow disproportionately to them and away from Negro and Spanish-surnamed employees who might by now have enjoyed those advantages had not the employer discriminated before the passage of the Act. This disproportionate distribution of advantages does in a very real sense "operate to 'freeze' the status quo of prior discriminatory employment practices."... But both the literal terms...and the legislative history of Title VII demonstrate that Congress considered this every effect of many seniority systems and extended a measure of immunity to them....

...In sum, the unmistakable purpose...was to make clear that the routine application of a bona fide seniority system would not be unlawful under Title VII. As the legislative history shows, this was the intended result even where the employer's pre-Act discrimination resulted in whites having greater existing seniority rights than Negroes. Although a seniority system inevitably tends to perpetuate the effects of pre-Act discrimination in such cases, the congressional judgment was that Title VII should not outlaw the use of existing seniority lists and thereby destroy or water down the vested seniority rights of employees simply because their employer had engaged in discrimination prior to the passage of the Act....

...It refers only to "bona fide" systems, and a proviso requires that any differences in treatment not be "the result of an intention to discriminate because of race...or national origin...." But our reading of the legislative history compels us to reject the Government's broad argument that no seniority system that tends to perpetuate pre-Act discrimination can be "bona fide." To accept the argument would require us to hold that a seniority system becomes illegal simply because it allows the full exercise of the pre-Act seniority rights of employees of a company that discriminated before Title VII was enacted. It would place an affirmative obligation on the parties to the seniority agreement to subordinate those rights in favor of the claims of pre-Act discriminatees without seniority. The consequence would be a perversion of the congressional purpose. We cannot accept the invitation to disembowel...by reading the words "bona fide" as the Government would have us do. Accordingly, we hold that an otherwise neutral, legitimate seniority system does not become unlawful under Title VII simply because it may perpetuate pre-Act discrimination. Congress did not intend to make it illegal for employees with vested seniority rights to continue to exercise those rights, even at the expense of pre-Act discriminatees.

That conclusion is inescapable even in a case, such as this one, where the pre-Act discriminatees are incumbent employees who accumulated seniority in other bargaining units. Although there seems to be no explicit reference in the legislative history to pre-Act discriminatees already employed in less desirable jobs, there can be no rational basis for distinguishing their claims from those of persons initially denied *any* job but hired later with less seniority than they might have had in the absence of pre-Act discrimination....

The seniority system in this case is entirely bona fide. It applies equally to all races and ethnic groups. To the extent that it "locks" employees into nonline-driver jobs, it does so for all. The city drivers and servicemen who are discouraged from transferring to line-driver jobs are not all Negroes or Spanish-surnamed Americans; to the contrary, the overwhelming majority are white. The placing of line drivers in a separate bargaining unit from other employees is rational, in accord with the industry practice, and consistent with NLRB [National Labor Relations Board] precedents. It is conceded that the seniority system did not have its genesis in racial discrimination, and that it was negotiated and has been maintained free from any illegal purpose. In these circumstances, the single fact that the system extends no retroactive seniority to pre-Act discriminatees does not make it unlawful.

Because the seniority system was protected...the union's conduct in agreeing to and maintaining the system did not violate Title VII....

III

...After the evidentiary hearings to be conducted on remand, both the size and the composition of the class of minority employees entitled to relief may be altered substantially. Until those hearings have been conducted and both the number of identifiable victims and the consequent extent of necessary relief have been determined, it is not possible to evaluate abstract claims concerning the equitable balance that should be struck between the statutory rights of victims and the contractual rights of nonvictim employees. That determination is best left, in the first instance, to the sound equitable discretion of the trial court.... We observe only that when the court exercises its discretion in dealing with the problem of laid-off employees in light of the facts developed at the hearings on remand, it should clearly state its reasons so that meaningful review may be had on appeal....

For all the reasons we have discussed, the judgment of the Court of Appeals is vacated, and the cases are remanded to the District Court for further proceedings consistent with this opinion.

It is so ordered.

MR. JUSTICE MARSHALL, with whom MR. JUSTICE BRENNAN joins, concurring in part and dissenting in part.

I agree with the Court that the United States proved that petitioner T.I.M.E.-D.C. was guilty of a pattern or practice of discriminating against blacks and Spanish-speaking Americans in hiring line drivers. I also agree that incumbent minority-group employees who show that they applied for a line-driving job or that they would have applied but for petitioner's unlawful acts are presumptively entitled to the full measure of relief set forth in our decision last Term in *Franks* v. *Bowman*.... But I do not agree that Title VII permits petitioners to treat non-Anglo line drivers differently from Anglo drivers who were hired by the company at the same time simply because the non-Anglo drivers were prevented by the company from acquiring seniority over the road. I therefore dissent from that aspect of the Court's holding, and from the limitations on the scope of the remedy that follow from it.

...Even if I were to agree that this case properly can be decided on the basis of inferences as to Congress' intent, I still could not accept the Court's holding. In my view, the legislative history of the 1964 Civil Rights Act does not support the conclusion that Congress intended to legalize seniority systems that perpetuate discrimination, and administrative and legislative developments since 1964 positively refute that conclusion....

...Our task, then, assuming still that the case properly can be decided on the basis of imputed legislative intent, is "to put to ourselves the question, which choice is it more likely that Congress would have made"...had it focused on the problem: would it have validated or invalidated seniority systems that perpetuate pre-Act discrimination? To answer that question, the devastating impact of today's holding validating such systems must be fully understood. Prior to 1965 blacks and Spanish-speaking Americans who were able to find employment were assigned the lowest paid, most menial jobs in many industries throughout the Nation but especially in the South. In many factories, blacks were hired as laborers while whites were trained and given skilled positions; in the transportation industry blacks could only become porters; and in steel plants blacks were assigned to the coke ovens and blasting furnaces, "the hotter and dirtier" places of employment. The Court holds, in essence, that while after 1965 these incumbent employees are entitled to an equal opportunity to advance to more desirable jobs, to take advantage of that opportunity they must pay a price: they must surrender the seniority they have accumulated in their old jobs. For many, the price will be too high, and they will be locked-in to their previous positions. Even those willing to pay the price will have to reconcile themselves to being forever behind subsequently hired whites who were not discriminatorily assigned. Thus equal opportunity will remain a distant dream for all incumbent employees.

I am aware of nothing in the legislative history of the 1964 Civil Rights Act to suggest that if Congress had focused on this fact it nonetheless would have decided to write off an entire generation of minority group employees. Nor can I believe that the Congress that enacted Title VII would have agreed to postpone for one generation the achievement of economic equality. The backers of that Title viewed economic equality as both a practical necessity and a moral imperative. They were well aware of the corrosive impact employment discrimination has on its victims, and on the society generally. They sought, therefore, "to eliminate those discriminatory practices and devices which have fostered racially stratified job environments to the disadvantage of minority citizens"...and "to make persons whole for injuries suffered on account of unlawful employment discrimination."... In short, Congress wanted to enable black workers to assume their rightful place in society....

...Only last Term, we concluded that the legislative materials reviewed above "completely answer the argument that Congress somehow intended seniority relief to be less available" than backpay as a remedy for discrimination. *Franks* v. *Bowman....* If anything, the materials provide an even more complete answer to the argument that Congress somehow intended to immunize seniority systems that perpetuate past discrimination. To the extent that today's decision grants immunity to such systems, I respectfully dissent.

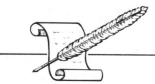

June

COURT ON DEATH PENALTY FOR MURDER OF POLICE
June 6, 1977

The Supreme Court June 6 further narrowed the possibility that any mandatory death penalty law might survive constitutional challenge when it ruled that Louisiana could not make death the mandatory sentence for anyone convicted of murdering an on-duty policeman. The vote was 5-4; the opinion was unsigned (per curiam). (Roberts v. Louisiana) (Court on death penalty for rapists, p. 517)

The majority left for a later day the decision on whether it might be permissible to make death the mandatory sentence for a person already serving a life sentence and then convicted of killing a prison guard or police officer.

The court divided on this issue just as it had in striking down mandatory death penalties for all first-degree murderers in July 1976. The majority consisted of Justices William J. Brennan Jr., Thurgood Marshall, Potter Stewart, Lewis F. Powell Jr. and John Paul Stevens. The dissenters were Chief Justice Warren Burger, Justices Harry A. Blackmun, Byron R. White and William H. Rehnquist. (Historic Documents of 1976, p. 917)

The June 6 decision spared the life of Harry Roberts, a Louisiana resident, who was convicted of killing a New Orleans policeman in 1974 and was sentenced to death under the mandatory death penalty law for first-degree murder then prevailing in the state.

The Louisiana law was unconstitutional—as violating the Eighth Amendment ban on cruel and unusual punishment—because it provided

*no opportunity for consideration of mitigating circumstances which might
exist for an individual defendant or in an individual offense, the majority
said. "The fact that the murder victim was a peace officer performing his
regular duties may be regarded as an aggravating circumstance.... But it is
incorrect to suppose that no mitigating circumstances can exist when the
victim is a police officer." Among the possible mitigating factors which
could exist, the court said, were the age of the murderer, his being under
the influence of drugs, alcohol or extreme emotional disturbance or even
his reasonable belief that "circumstances...provided a moral justification
for his conduct."*

*In a footnote, the majority noted that more than twice as many on-duty
policemen were killed in 1975 as in 1966.*

Dissenting Opinion

*"Policemen are both symbols and outriders of our ordered society and
they literally risk their lives in an effort to preserve it," wrote Rehnquist for
the dissenters. "To a degree unequalled in the ordinary first-degree
murder...the state therefore has an interest in making unmistakably clear
that those who are convicted of deliberately killing police officers acting in
the line of duty be forewarned that punishment, in the form of death, will
be inexorable."*

*"We are dealing here...with what sanctions the state is entitled to bring
into play to assure that there will be a police force to see that the criminal
laws are enforced at all," continued Rehnquist. "It is no service to individual rights or to individual liberty, to undermine what is surely the
fundamental right and responsibility of any civilized government: the
maintenance of order so that all may enjoy liberty and security."*

> *Following are excerpts from the majority and dissenting
> opinions in the Supreme Court's June 6, 1977, ruling on
> mandatory death penalty for police killers:*

No. 76-5206

Harry Roberts, Petitioner,   On Writ of Certiorari to the
          v.   Supreme Court of Louisiana.
State of Louisiana.

[June 6, 1977]

PER CURIAM.

Petitioner Harry Roberts was indicted, tried, and convicted of the first-
degree murder of Police Officer Dennis McInerney, who at the time of his
death was engaged in the performance of his lawful duties. As required by
Louisiana statute, petitioner was sentenced to death.... On appeal, the
Supreme Court of Louisiana affirmed his conviction and sentence....
Roberts then filed a petition for a writ of certiorari in this Court. The peti-

tion presented the question of whether Louisiana's mandatory death penalty could be imposed pursuant to his conviction of first-degree murder....

Shortly before that petition was filed, we held in another case (involving a different petitioner named Roberts) that Louisiana could not enforce its mandatory death penalty for a conviction of first-degree murder.... In the plurality opinion in that case, the precise question presented in this case was explicitly answered.

This precise question was again answered by the Court in *Washington* v. *Louisiana*...(1976). The petitioner in the *Washington* case had killed a policeman and was tried and sentenced to death under the same provision of the Louisiana statute as was the petitioner in the present case. We vacated the death sentence, holding: "The imposition and carrying out of the death penalty [in this case] constitute cruel and unusual punishment in violation of the Eighth and Fourteenth Amendments. [*Stanislaus*] *Roberts* v. *Louisiana*...."....

Recognizing that this Court had already decided that a mandatory death sentence could not be imposed for the crime that Harry Roberts committed, the Attorney General of Louisiana initially conceded that "under this Court's decision in *Stanislaus Roberts* v. *Louisiana,* No. 75-5844, [the sentence of death in the present case] cannot be carried out unless, of course, this Court grants Louisiana's Application for Rehearing and modifies its Former holding." ...The Court nevertheless granted certiorari on November 8, 1976...and on November 29 limited the grant to the question "[w]hether the imposition and carrying out of the sentence of death for the crime of first-degree murder of a police officer under the law of Louisiana violates the Eighth and Fourteenth Amendments to the Constitution of the United States."...

In *Woodson* v. *North Carolina*...this Court held that "...the fundamental respect for humanity underlying the Eighth Amendment...requires consideration of the character and record of the individual offender and the circumstances of a particular offense as a constitutionally indispensable part of the process of inflicing the penalty of death." In *Roberts* v. *Louisiana,* ...we made clear that this principle applies even where the crime of first-degree murder is narrowly defined....

To be sure, the fact that the murder victim was a peace officer performing his regular duties may be regarded as an aggravating circumstance. There is a special interest in affording protection to these public servants who regularly must risk their lives in order to guard the safety of other persons and property. But it is incorrect to suppose that no mitigating circumstances can exist when the victim is a police officer. Circumstances such as the youth of the offender, the absence of any prior conviction, the influence of drugs, alcohol or extreme emotional disturbance, and even the existence of circumstances which the offender reasonably believed provided a moral justification for his conduct are all examples of mitigating facts which might attend the killing of a peace officer and which are considered relevant in other jurisdictions.

As we emphasized repeatedly in *Roberts* and its companion cases decided last Term, it is essential that the capital sentencing decision allow for consideration of whatever mitigating circumstances may be relevant to either the particular offender or the particular offense. Because the Louisiana statute does not allow consideration of particularized mitigating factors, it is unconstitutional.

Accordingly, we hold that the death sentence imposed upon this petitioner violates the Eighth and Fourteenth Amendments and must be set aside. The judgment of the Supreme Court of Louisiana is reversed insofar as it upholds the death sentence upon petitioner. The case is remanded for further proceedings not inconsistent with this opinion.

It is so ordered.

MR. CHIEF JUSTICE BURGER, dissenting.

I would sustain the Louisiana statute and I therefore dissent on the basis of my dissenting statement in *Roberts* v. *Louisiana*...and that of MR. JUSTICE WHITE in *Woodson* v. *North Carolina*...(1976).

MR. JUSTICE BLACKMUN, with whom MR. JUSTICE WHITE and MR. JUSTICE REHNQUIST join, dissenting.

The Court, feeling itself bound by the plurality opinion in *Stanislaus Roberts* v. *Louisiana*...(1976), has painted itself into a corner. I did not join that plurality opinion, and I decline to be so confined. I therefore dissent from the Court's disposition of the present case and from its holding that the mandatory imposition of the death penalty for killing a peace officer, engaged in the performance of his lawful duties, constitutes cruel and unusual punishment in violation of the Eighth and Fourteenth Amendments. I would uphold the State's power to impose such a punishment...and I would reject any statements or intimations to the contrary in the Court's prior cases.

The *per curiam* opinion asserts that "the precise question presented in this case was explicitly answered" in *Stanislaus Roberts*.... It also relies on the summary disposition of *Washington* v. *Louisiana*...(1976), where a death sentence that had been imposed...was vacated and where it was stated that the imposition and carrying out of the death penalty constituted cruel and unusual punishment.... Finally, the *per curiam* states that "it is essential that the capital sentencing decision allow for consideration of whatever mitigating circumstances may be relevant to either the particular offender or the particular offense."... Since [the statute] does not allow for consideration of mitigating factors, the *per curiam* strikes down the death sentence imposed on petitioner.

In my view, the question of the constitutionality of Louisiana's mandatory death penalty for killing a police officer was not answered in *Stanislaus Roberts*. *Washington* may be said to be a summary ruling on the merits, but that case was decided without the benefit of plenary consideration, and without focusing on the identity and activity of the victim. I believe its result to be incorrect as a constitutional matter and I would disapprove and withhold its further application.

Stanislaus Roberts was charged and convicted under a different subsection...of the Louisiana first-degree murder statute.... Subsection (1)
provided a mandatory death penalty in the case where the killer had a
specific intent to kill or to inflict great bodily harm and was engaged in the
perpetration or attempted perpetration of aggravated kidnapping,
aggravated rape, or armed robbery.... Subsection (2), in contrast, provides
that first-degree murder is committed when the killer has a specific intent
to kill, or to inflict great bodily harm upon, a fireman or a peace officer who
is engaged in the performance of his lawful duties.... The two subsections
obviously should involve quite different considerations with regard to the
lawfulness of a mandatory death penalty, even accepting the analysis set
forth in the plurality opinions of last Term. Thus, to the extent that the
plurality in *Stanislaus Roberts* alluded to subsections of the Louisiana law
that were not before the Court, those statements are nonbinding dicta. It is
indisputable that carefully focused consideration was not given to the
special problem of a mandatory death sentence for one who has intentionally killed a police officer engaged in the performance of his lawful
duties. I therefore approach this case as a new one, not predetermined and
governed by the plurality in *Stanislaus Roberts.*

Washington may present a different problem.... I would simply inquire,
as to *Washington,* whether its holding should not be overruled, now that
the Court has had the benefit of more careful and complete consideration
of the issue.

...Since the decision in *Washington* is inconsistent with this view, I
would overrule it.

I should note that I do not read the *per curiam* opinion today as one
deciding the issue of the constitutionality of a mandatory death sentence
for a killer of a peace officer for all cases and all times. Reference to the
plurality opinion in *Stanislaus Roberts* reveals that the Louisiana statute
contained what that opinion regarded as two fatal defects: lack of an opportunity to consider mitigating factors, and standardless jury discretion
inherent in the Louisiana responsive verdict system. Without the latter, as
here, a different case surely is presented. Furthermore, it is evident,
despite the *per curiam's* general statement to the contrary, that mitigating
factors need not be considered in every case; even the *per curiam* continues
to reserve the issue of a mandatory death sentence for murder by a prisoner
already serving a life sentence.... For me, therefore, today's decision must
be viewed in the context of the Court's previous criticism of the Louisiana
system; it need not freeze the Court into a position that condemns every
statute with a mandatory death penalty for the intentional killing of a
peace officer.

MR. JUSTICE REHNQUIST, with whom MR. JUSTICE WHITE
joins, dissenting.

The Court today holds that the State of Louisiana is not entitled to vin-
dicate its substantial interests in protecting the foot soldiers of an ordered
society by mandatorily sentencing their murderers to death. This is so even

though the State has demonstrated to a jury in a fair trial, beyond a reasonable doubt, that a particular defendant was the murderer, and that he committed the act while possessing "a specific intent to kill, or to inflict great bodily harm upon, a fireman or a peace officer who was engaged in the performance of his lawful duties...." That holding would have shocked those who drafted the Bill of Rights on which it purports to rest, and would commend itself only to the most imaginative observer as being required by today's "evolving standards of decency."

I am unable to agree that a mandatory death sentence under such circumstances violates the Eighth Amendment's proscription against "cruel and unusual punishment." I am equally unable to see how this limited application of the mandatory death statute violates even the scope of the Eighth Amendment as seen through the eyes of last Term's plurality in *Stanislaus Roberts* v. *Louisiana*...(1976). Nor does the brief *per curiam* opinion issued today demonstrate why the application of a mandatory death sentence to the criminal who intentionally murders a peace officer performing his official duties should be considered "cruel and unusual punishment" in light of either the view of society when the Eighth Amendment was passed, ...the "objective indicia that reflect the public attitude" today, ...or even the more generalized "basic concept of human dignity" test relied upon last Term by the plurality in striking down several more general mandatory statutes.

While the arguments weighing in favor of individualized consideration for the convicted defendant are much the same here as they are for one accused of any homicide, the arguments weighing in favor of society's determination to impose a mandatory sentence for the murder of a police officer in the line of duty are far stronger than in the case of an ordinary homicide. Thus the Court's intimation that this particular issue was *considered* and *decided* last Term in *Stanislaus Roberts* v. *Louisiana*...simply does not wash. A footnoted dictum in *Stanislaus Roberts* discussing a different section of the Louisiana law than the one now before us scarcely rises to the level of plenary, deliberate consideration which has traditionally preceded a declaration of unconstitutionality....

Five Terms ago, in *Furman* v. *Georgia*...(1972), this Court invalidated the then-current system of capital punishments, condemning jury discretion as resulting in "freakish" punishment. The Louisiana Legislature has conscientiously determined, in an effort to respond to that holding, that the death sentence would be made mandatory upon the conviction of particular types of offenses, including, as in the case before us, the intentional killing of a peace officer while in the performance of his duties. For the reasons stated by MR. JUSTICE WHITE for himself, THE CHIEF JUSTICE, MR. JUSTICE BLACKMUN, and me in his dissent in *Stanislaus Roberts* v. *Louisiana*...and by me in my dissent in *Woodson* v. *North Carolina*...(1976), I am no more persuaded now than I was then that a mandatory death sentence for all, let alone for a limited class of, persons who commit premeditated murder constitutes "cruel and unusual punishment" under the Eighth and Fourteenth Amendments.

...Louisiana's decision to impose a mandatory death sentence upon one convicted of the particular offense of premeditated murder of a peace officer engaged in the performance of his lawful duties is clearly not governed by the holding of *Stanislaus Roberts,* and I do not believe that it is controlled by the reasoning of the plurality's opinion in that case. Today's opinion assumes, without analysis, that the faults of the generalized mandatory death sentence under review in *Stanislaus Roberts,* must necessarily inhere in such a sentence imposed on those who commit this much more carefully limited and far more serious crime....

Under the analysis of last Term's plurality opinion, a State, before it is constitutionally entitled to put a murderer to death, must consider aggravating and mitigating circumstances. It is possible to agree with the plurality in the general case without at all conceding that it follows that a mandatory death sentence is impermissible in the specific case we have before us: the deliberate killing of a peace officer. The opinion today is willing to concede that "the fact that the murder victim was a peace officer performing his regular duties may be regarded as an aggravating circumstance."... But it seems to me that the factors which entitle a State to consider it as an aggravating circumstance also entitle the State to consider it so grave an aggravating circumstance that no permutation of mitigating factors exists which would disable it from constitutionally sentencing the murderer to death. If the State would be constitutionally entitled, due to the nature of the offense, to sentence the murderer to death *after* going through such a limited version of the plurality's "balancing" approach. I see no constitutional reason why the "cruel and unusual punishment" clause precludes the State from doing so without engaging in that process.

The elements that differentiate this case from the *Stanislaus Roberts* case are easy to state. In both cases, the factors weighing on the defendant's side of the scale are constant. It is consideration of these factors alone that the opinion today apparently relies on for its holding. But this ignores the significantly different factors which weigh on the State's side of the scale. In all murder cases, and of course this one, the State has an interest in protecting its citizens from such ultimate attacks; this surely is at the core of the Lockean "social contract" idea. But other, and important, state interests exist where the victim was a peace officer performing his lawful duties. Policemen on the beat are exposed, in the service of society, to all the risks which the constant effort to prevent crime and apprehend criminals entails. Because these people are literally the foot soldiers of society's defense of ordered liberty, the State has an especial interest in their protection.

We are dealing here not merely with the State's determination as to whether particular conduct on the part of an individual should be punished, and in what manner, but also with what sanctions the State is entitled to bring into play to assure that there will be a police force to see that the criminal laws are enforced at all. It is no service to individual rights, or to individual liberty, to undermine what is surely the fundamental right and responsibility of any civilized government: the maintenance of order so that all may enjoy liberty and security.... Policemen are both symbols and outriders of our ordered society, and they literally risk their lives in an effort to preserve it. To a degree unequaled in the ordinary first-degree murder presented in the *Stanislaus Roberts* case, the State therefore has an interest in making unmistakably clear that those who are convicted of deliberately killing police officers acting in the line of duty be forewarned that punishment, in the form of death, will be inexorable.

This interest of the State, I think, entitled the Louisiana Legislature, in its considered judgment, to make the death penalty mandatory for those convicted of the intentional murder of a police officer. I had thought the plurality had conceded that this response—this need for a mandatory penalty—could be permissible when, focusing on the crime, not the criminal, it wrote last Term...that

> "the decision that capital punishment may be the appropriate sanction in extreme cases is an expression of the community's belief that certain *crimes* are themselves so grievous an affront to humanity that the only adequate response may be the penalty of death." (Emphasis added.)

I am quite unable to decipher why the Court today concludes that the intentional murder of a police officer is not one of these "certain crimes." The Court's answer appears to lie in its observation that "it is incorrect to suppose that no mitigating circumstances can exist when the victim is a police officer."... The Court, however, has asked the wrong question. The question is not whether mitigating factors might *exist,* but, rather, whether whatever "mitigating" factors that might exist are of sufficient *force* so as to constitutionally require their consideration as counterweights to the admitted aggravating circumstance. Like MR. JUSTICE WHITE, I am unable to believe that a State is not entitled to determine that the premeditated murder of a peace officer is so heinous and intolerable a crime that no combination of mitigating factors can overcome the demonstration "that the criminal's character is such that he deserves death."...

As an example of a mitigating factor which, presumably, may "overcome" the aggravating factor inherent in the murder of a peace officer.... I cannot believe that States are constitutionally required to allow a defense, even at the sentencing stage, which depends on nothing more than the convict's moral belief that he was entitled to kill a peace officer in cold blood. John Wilkes Booth may well have thought he was morally justified in murdering Abraham Lincoln, whom, while fleeing from the stage of Ford's Theater, he characterized as a "tyrant"; I am appalled to believe that the Constitution would have *required* the government to allow him to argue that as a "mitigating factor" before it could sentence him to death if he were found guilty. I am equally appalled that a State should be required to instruct a jury that such individual beliefs must or should be considered as a possible balancing factor against the admittedly proper aggravating factor.

The historical and legal content of the "cruel and unusual punishment" clause was stretched to the breaking point by the plurality's opinion in the

Stanislaus Roberts case last Term. Today this judicially created superstructure, designed and erected more than 180 years after the Bill of Rights was adopted, is tortured beyond permissible limits of judicial review. There is nothing in the Constitution's prohibition against cruel and unusual punishment which disables a legislature from imposing a mandatory death sentence on a defendant convicted after a fair trial of deliberately murdering a police officer.

COURT ON PUBLIC
FUNDS FOR ABORTIONS

June 20, 1977

In a major setback for pro-abortion and women's rights groups, the Supreme Court June 20 ruled that states and cities did not have to spend public funds for abortions of an elective or nontherapeutic nature.

Dividing 6 to 3 in three cases involving state and local laws in Connecticut, Pennsylvania and Missouri, the court held that the spending bans and certain other restrictions on access to elective abortions violated neither the Constitution nor existing federal law. The decisions appeared to smooth the way for moves in Congress to restrict the use of federal funds for abortions nationwide. The rulings did not mean, however, that states were required to ban funds for abortions. But they did permit states and localities, if they desired and if their state laws and constitutions allowed, to bar the use of public funds and facilities for so-called "nontherapeutic" abortions.

Background

The main anti-abortion efforts had been aimed at the Medicaid program, which pays for health care for the poor. Funded by the federal government and administered by the states, Medicaid annually financed an estimated 300,000 abortions—most of them elective—at a cost of $50-million.

Congress attempted to curb this practice in 1976 by including, as part of fiscal 1977 appropriations for the Departments of Labor, Health, Education and Welfare (HEW) and related agencies, a ban on the use of federal funds for abortion except when the mother's life would be endangered by continued pregnancy. Named the "Hyde amendment" after its chief sponsor, Rep. Henry J. Hyde (R Ill.), the ban was stayed after opponents won a challenge to it at the U.S. District Court level. However, on June 29, 1977, the Supreme Court gave U.S. District Court Judge John F. Dooling 25 days to lift the stay; the Hyde amendment went into effect Aug. 4.

With the existing ban set to expire Sept. 30 in any event, the House June 17 attached a new, tougher Hyde amendment barring any federal expenditures on abortions to the fiscal 1978 Labor-HEW appropriations bill. The Senate adopted a more moderate anti-abortion amendment that permitted publicly-financed abortions in certain instances. The refusal of either house to accept the other's position held up appropriation of fiscal 1978 Labor-HEW funds until December.

In each of the three cases decided June 20, lower courts had found the state and local abortion restrictions unconstitutional, based on their interpretations of a landmark Supreme Court ruling on abortion in 1973. In those cases, the court struck down state laws forbidding abortions, arguing that privacy considerations gave women the right to choose to have abortions during the early months of pregnancy without interference from the state. (Historic Documents of 1973, pp. 101-114)

Opinions, Dissents

The Supreme Court majority insisted that its June 20 rulings were consistent with the 1973 decisions. Writing the majority opinion in the Connecticut case, Justice Lewis F. Powell Jr. denied that the court had granted any absolute rights to an abortion in 1973. The right to an abortion only "protects the woman from unduly burdensome interference with her freedom to decide whether to terminate her pregnancy," said Powell. "It implies no limitation on the authority of a state to make a value judgment favoring childbirth over abortion, and to implement that judgment by allocation of public funds."

Dissenting Justices William J. Brennan Jr., Harry A. Blackmun and Thurgood Marshall attacked the three rulings as signaling a major departure from the court's stand in 1973. In his dissent to the Pennsylvania case, Blackmun argued that the new decisions allowed states to "accomplish indirectly what the Court...said they could not do directly" and impose the preferences of abortion opponents on the rest of society.

The dissenters vigorously disputed the distinction that the state and local restrictions were not outright bans on abortions, that the poor could rely on "private sources" to pay for or perform these operations. "As a practical matter, many indigent women will feel they have no choice but to carry their pregnancies to term because the State will pay for the associated medical services, even though they would have [otherwise]

408

chosen to have abortions," wrote Brennan. The majority's assumptions were "almost reminiscent of 'let them eat cake,'" wrote Blackmun.

The Three Cases

Though hailed as a victory by right-to-life groups around the country, the three rulings were not likely to be the final word from the court on the subject of abortion. By limiting its discussion to the issue of elective abortions, the court appeared to leave room for considerable dispute over the types of "medically necessary" abortions that might qualify for public funding.

Briefly, the three June 20 cases involved:

● *A Pennsylvania Medicaid program that denied funds for abortions not certified by physicians as medically necessary. The court held that the federal law authorizing the Medicaid program, Title XIX of the Social Security Act, allowed states to determine the scope of medical coverage. Because a state has a valid interest in encouraging childbirth, restrictions on financing elective abortions were not unreasonable, the majority said. (Beal v. Doe)*

● *A Connecticut Medicaid program that paid medical expenses related to childbirth but restricted the use of funds for abortion to medically necessary operations occurring during the first three months of pregnancy. The court found that these regulations did not violate the equal protection clause of the Constitution but simply encouraged one policy choice without flatly eliminating the right to obtain an abortion by other means. (Maher v. Roe)*

● *A St. Louis, Mo., public hospital that, under a directive from the mayor, refused to perform nontherapeutic abortions. Upholding the city's practice with the same equal protection arguments as in the Connecticut case, the court said the hospital policy issues were matters for local residents to decide at the polls. (Poelker v. Doe)*

Administration Position

In a statement that drew immediate criticism from pro-abortion interests, President Jimmy Carter July 12 repeated his opposition to abortions paid for with federal funds—"except when the woman's life is threatened or when the pregnancy was a result of rape or incest." Carter, whose comments on the issue were made at a nationally televised news conference, said he thought the Supreme Court's June 20 rulings on abortion were "adequate" and "reasonably fair." When asked how fair he thought it was to deny poor women access to abortions that wealthier women could afford, Carter answered, "There are many things in life that are not fair, that wealthy people can afford and poor people can't. But I don't believe that the federal government should take action to try to make these opportunities exactly equal, particularly when there is a moral factor involved." Carter also noted that HEW Secretary Joseph A. Califano Jr. "agrees with me completely, and we are trying to make it possible for the people of this nation to understand how to prevent unwanted pregnancies with education programs and with the availability of contraceptives and other devices when they believe in their use as an alternative to abortion."

Congressional Action

A bitter five-month struggle over what restrictions should be placed on the use of federal funds for abortion ended Dec. 7, 1977, when the House and Senate finally agreed on a compromise position. The breakthrough came when the House voted 181-167 to partially loosen restrictions on payment of Medicaid money for abortions for low-income women in cases of rape, incest and severe physical illness. The Senate, despite its long-standing preference for a more lenient policy, quickly approved the new wording by voice vote the same day.

In their long search for compromise language on abortion, members of both houses agonized over practically every word and punctuation mark. While the House adamantly resisted major changes in the 1976 Hyde amendment, the Senate wanted to make exceptions for women with medical reasons for seeking abortion as well as for victims of rape and incest.

Briefly, the final provision:

● Prohibited the use of any funds in the bill to pay for abortions unless continued pregnancy would endanger the mother's life or, in the opinion of two doctors, cause the woman to suffer "severe and long-lasting physical health damage."

● Permitted funds for "medical procedures" to treat victims of rape or incest if the offenses have been promptly reported to police or to a public health agency.

● Permitted payments for birth control drugs or devices and for operations to terminate tubal pregnancies.

● Required the Secretary of HEW to promptly issue regulations "rigorously" enforcing the provision.

Pro-abortion groups generally denounced the provision claiming that all the compromising had been done by their side. They were also concerned that HEW Secretary Califano, an outspoken opponent of abortion, might use the contradictory statements from the two chambers to interpret the provision as narrowly as possible and, as a result, write highly restrictive regulations.

Right-to-life groups also had reservations about the final provision. "It's maybe a two-thirds victory for us," said William Cox, executive director of *the National Committee for a Human Life Amendment. "But by holding the House over a long period of time, we brought the Senate through a series of stricter amendments."*

Hyde and his pro-life supporters vowed to continue to press for more restrictive language in 1978, on the Labor-HEW appropriations bill or other legislative vehicles. Meanwhile the new provision was expected to face at least one court challenge.

Following are excerpts from the Supreme Court's majority and dissenting opinions on state use of public funds to assist in financing abortions, handed down June 20, 1977:

No. 75-554

Frank S. Beal, etc., et al., Petitioners, *v.* Ann Doe et al.	On Writ of Certiorari to the United States Court of Appeals for the Third Circuit.

[June 20, 1977]

MR. JUSTICE POWELL delivered the opinion of the Court.

The issue in this case is whether Title XIX of the Social Security Act...requires States that participate in the Medical Assistance Program (Medicaid) to fund the cost of nontherapeutic abortions.

I

Title XIX establishes a Medical Assistance Program under which participating States may provide federally funded medical assistance to needy persons. The statute requires participating States to provide qualified individuals with financial assistance in five general categories of medical treatment.... Although Title XIX does not require States to provide funding for all medical treatment falling within the five general categories, it does require that State medicaid plans establish "reasonable standards...for determining...the extent of medical assistance under the plan which...are consistent with the objectives of [Title XIX]."...

Respondents, who are eligible for medical assistance under Pennsylvania's federally approved medicaid plan, were denied financial assistance for desired abortions pursuant to Pennsylvania regulations limiting such assistance to those abortions that are certified by physicians as medically necessary. When respondents' applications for medicaid assistance were denied because of their failure to furnish the required certificates, they filed this action in United States District Court for the Western District of Pennsylvania seeking declaratory and injunctive relief.

Their complaint alleged that Pennsylvania's requirement of a certificate of medical necessity contravened relevant provisions of Title XIX and denied them equal protection of the law in violation of the Fourteenth Amendment.

...After resolving the statutory issue against respondents, the District Court held that Pennsylvania's medical necessity restriction denied respondents equal protection of the law.... Accordingly, the court granted a declaratory judgment that the Pennsylvania requirement was unconstitutional as applied during the first trimester. The United States Court of Appeals for the Third Circuit, sitting en banc, reversed on the statutory issue, holding that Title XIX prohibits participating States from requiring a physician's certificate of medical necessity as a condition for funding during both the first and second trimesters of pregnancy.... The Court of Appeals therefore did not reach the constitutional issue.

We granted certiorari to resolve a conflict among the federal courts as to the requirements of Title XIX....

II

The only question before us is one of statutory construction: whether Title XIX requires Pennsylvania to fund under its medicaid program the cost of *all* abortions that are permissible under state law. "The starting point in every case involving construction of a statute is the language itself." [*Blue Chip Stamps* v. *Manor Drug Stores* (1975)] ...Title XIX makes no reference to abortions, or, for that matter, to any other particular medical procedure. Instead, the statute is cast in terms that require participating States to provide financial assistance with respect to five broad categories of medical treatment.... But nothing in the statute suggests that participating States are required to fund every medical procedure that falls within the delineated categories of medical care. Indeed, the statute expressly provides that:

> "A State plan for medical assistance must...include reasonable standards...for determining eligibility for and the extent of medical assistance under the plan...which are consistent with the objectives of this [Title]..."

This language confers broad discretion on the States to adopt standards for determining the extent of medical assistance, requiring only that such standards be "reasonable" and "consistent with the objectives" of the Act.

Pennsylvania's regulation comports fully with Title XIX's broadly stated primary objective to "enabl[e] each State, as far as practicable under the conditions in such State, to furnish...medical assistance [to] individuals...whose income and resources are insufficient to meet the costs of necessary medical services."... Although serious statutory questions might be presented if a state medicaid plan excluded necessary medical treatment from its coverage, it is hardly inconsistent with the objectives of the

Act for a State to refuse to fund *unnecessary*—though perhaps desirable—medical services.

The thrust of respondents' argument is that the exclusion of non-therapeutic abortions from medicaid coverage is unreasonable on both economic and health grounds. The economic argument is grounded on the view that abortion is generally a less expensive medical procedure than childbirth. Since a pregnant woman normally will either have an abortion or carry her child full term, a State that elects not to fund nontherapeutic abortions will eventually be confronted with the greater expenses associated with childbirth. The corresponding health argument is based on the view that an early abortion poses less of a risk to the woman's health than childbirth. Consequently, respondents argue, the economic and health considerations that ordinarily support the reasonableness of state limitations on financing of unnecessary medical services are not applicable to pregnancy.

Accepting respondents' assumptions as accurate, we do not agree that the exclusion of nontherapeutic abortions from medicaid coverage is unreasonable under Title XIX. As we acknowledged in *Roe* v. *Wade*...(1973), the State has a valid and important interest in encouraging childbirth. We expressly recognized in *Roe* the "important and legitimate interest [of the State] in protecting the potentiality of human life."... That interest alone does not, at least until approximately the third trimester, become sufficiently compelling to justify unduly burdensome state interference with the woman's constitutionally protected private interest. But it is a significant state interest existing throughout the course of the woman's pregnancy. Respondents point to nothing in either the language or the legislative history of Title XIX that suggests that it is unreasonable for a participating State to further this unquestionably strong and legitimate interest in encouraging normal childbirth. Absent such a showing, we will not presume that Congress intended to condition a State's participation in the Medicaid Program on its willingness to undercut this important interest by subsidizing the costs of nontherapeutic abortions.

Our interpretation of the statute is reinforced by two other relevant considerations. First, when Congress passed Title XIX in 1965, non-therapeutic abortions were unlawful in most States. In view of the then prevailing state law, the contention that Congress intended to require—rather than permit—participating States to fund nontherapeutic abortions requires far more convincing proof than respondents have offered. Second, the Department of Health, Education, and Welfare, the agency charged with the administration of this complicated statute, takes the position that Title XIX allows—but does not mandate—funding for such abortions. "[W]e must be mindful that 'the construction of a statute by those charged with its execution should be followed unless there are compelling indications that it is wrong....' " *New York Department of Social Services* v. *Dublino*...(1973), quoting *Red Lion Broadcasting Co.* v. *FCC*...(1969). Here, such indications are completely absent.

We therefore hold that Pennsylvania's refusal to extend medicaid coverage to nontherapeutic abortions is not inconsistent with Title XIX. We make clear, however, that the federal statute leaves a State free to provide such coverage if it so desires.

III

There is one feature of the Pennsylvania medicaid program, not addressed by the Court of Appeals, that may conflict with Title XIX. Under the Pennsylvania program, financial assistance is not provided for medically necessary abortions unless two physicians in addition to the attending physician have examined the patient and have concurred in writing that the abortion is medically necessary.... On this record, we are unable to determine the precise role played by these two additional physicians, and consequently we are unable to ascertain whether this requirement interferes with the attending physician's medical judgment in a manner not contemplated by the Congress. The judgment of the Court of Appeals is therefore vacated, and the case is remanded for consideration of this requirement.

It is so ordered.

MR. JUSTICE BRENNAN, with whom MR. JUSTICE MARSHALL and MR. JUSTICE BLACKMUN join, dissenting.

The Court holds that the "necessary medical services" which Pennsylvania must fund for individuals eligible for Medicaid do not include services connected with elective abortions. I dissent.

Though the question presented by this case is one of statutory interpretation, a difficult constitutional question would be raised if the Act were read not to require funding of elective abortions.... Since the Court should "first ascertain whether a construction of the statute is fairly possible by which the [constitutional] question may be avoided," *Ashwander* v. *TVA*...(1936),...the Act, in my view, read fairly in light of the principle of avoidance of unnecessary constitutional decisions, requires agreement with the Court of Appeals that the legislative history of the Medicaid statute and our abortion cases compel the conclusion that elective abortions constitute medically necessary treatment for the condition of pregnancy. I would therefore find that Title XIX of the Social Security Act...requires that Pennsylvania pay the costs of elective abortions for women who are eligible participants in the Medicaid program....

...[S]ignificantly, the Senate Committee Report on the Medicaid bill expressly stated that the "physician is to be the key figure in determining utilization of health service." ...Thus the very heart of the congressional scheme is that the physician and patient should have complete freedom to choose those medical procedures for a given condition which are best suited to the needs of the patient.

The Court's original abortion decisions dovetail precisely with the congressional purpose under Medicaid to avoid interference with the decision of the woman and her physician. *Roe* v. *Wade*...(1973), held that "[t]he attending physician, in consultation with his patient, is free to determine without regulation by the State, that in his medical judgment the patient's pregnancy should be terminated." And *Doe* v. *Bolton*...(1973), held that "the medical judgment may be exercised in the light of all factors—physical, emotional, psychological, familial, and the woman's age—relevant to the well-being of the patient. All these factors may relate to health. This allows the attending physician the room he needs to make his best medical judgment. And it is room that operates for the benefit, not the disadvantage of the pregnant woman." Once medical treatment of some sort is necessary, the Act does not dictate what the treatment should be. In the face of the Act's emphasis upon the joint autonomy of the physician and patient in the decision of how to treat the condition of pregnancy, it is beyond comprehension how treatment for therapeutic abortions and live births constitutes "necessary medical services" under the Act, but that for elective abortions does not.

If Pennsylvania is not obligated to fund medical services rendered in performing elective abortions because they are not "necessary" within the meaning of § 1396 [of the Medicaid Statutes], it must follow that Pennsylvania also would not violate the statute if it refused to fund medical services for "therapeutic" abortions or live births. For if the availability of therapeutic abortions and live births make elective abortions "unnecessary," the converse must also be true. This highlights the violence done the congressional mandate by today's decision. If the State must pay the costs of therapeutic abortions and of live birth as constituting medically necessary responses to the condition of pregnancy, it must, under the command of § 1396, also pay the costs of elective abortions; the procedures in each case constitute necessary medical treatment for the condition of pregnancy....

...It is no answer that abortions were illegal in 1965 when Medicaid was enacted, and in 1972 when the family planning amendment was adopted. Medicaid deals with general categories of medical services, not with specific procedures, and nothing in the statute even suggests that Medicaid is designed to assist in payment for only those medical services that were legally permissible in 1965 and 1972. I fully agree with the Court of Appeals that

> "It is impossible to believe that in enacting Title XIX Congress intended to freeze the medical services available to recipients at those which were legal in 1965. Congress surely intended Medicaid to pay for drugs not legally marketable under the FDA's regulations in 1965 which are subsequently found to be marketable. We can see no reason why the same analysis should not apply to the Supreme Court's legalization of elective abortion in 1973."...

Finally, there is certainly no affirmative policy justification of the State that aids the Court's construction of "necessary medical services" as not including medical services rendered in performing elective abortions. The

State cannot contend that it protects its fiscal interests in not funding elective abortions when it incurs far greater expense in paying for the more costly medical services performed in carrying pregnancies to term, and, after birth, paying the increased welfare bill incurred to support the mother and child. Nor can the State contend that it protects the mother's health by discouraging an abortion, for not only may Pennsylvania's exclusion force the pregnant woman to use of measures dangerous to her life and health but *Roe* v. *Wade*...concluded that elective abortions by competent licensed physicians are now "relatively safe" and the risks to women undergoing abortions by such means "appear to be as low or lower...than for normal childbirth."

The Court's construction can only result as a practical matter in forcing penniless pregnant women to have children they would not have borne if the State had not weighted the scales to make their choice to have abortions substantially more onerous. Indeed, as the Court said only last Term, "For a doctor who cannot afford to work for nothing, and a woman who cannot afford to pay him, the State's refusal to fund an abortion is as effective an 'interdiction' of it as would ever be necessary." *Singleton* v. *Wulff*... (1976). The Court's construction thus makes a mockery of the congressional mandate that States provide "care and services...in a manner consistent with...the best interests of the recipients." We should respect the congressional plan by...requiring States to pay the costs of the "necessary medical services" rendered in performing elective abortions, chosen by physicians and their women patients who participate in Medicaid as the appropriate treatment for their pregnancies.

The Court does not address the question whether the provision requiring the concurrence in writing of two physicians in addition to the attending physician conflicts with Title XIX. I would hold that the provision is invalid as clearly in conflict with Title XIX under my view of the paramount role played by the attending physician in the abortion decision, and in any event is constitutionally invalid under *Doe v. Bolton*....

I would affirm the judgment of the Court of Appeals.

MR. JUSTICE MARSHALL, dissenting.

It is all too obvious that the governmental actions in these cases, ostensibly taken to "encourage" women to carry pregnancies to term, are in reality intended to impose a moral viewpoint that no State may constitutionally enforce. *Roe* v. *Wade*...(1973); *Doe* v. *Bolton*...(1973). Since efforts to overturn those decisions have been unsuccessful, the opponents of abortion have attempted every imaginable means to circumvent the commands of the Constitution and impose their moral choices upon the rest of society. See, *e.g.*, *Planned Parenthood of Missouri* v. *Danforth*...(1976); *Singleton* v. *Wulff*...[Aid to Families with Dependent Children] (1976); *Bellotti* v. *Baird*...(1976). The present cases involve the most vicious attacks yet devised. The impact of the regulations here falls tragically upon those among us least able to help or defend ourselves. As the Court well knows, these regulations inevitably will have the practical effect of preventing nearly all poor women from obtaining safe and legal abortions.

The enactments challenged here brutally coerce poor women to bear children whom society will scorn for every day of their lives. Many thousands of unwanted minority and mixed race children now spend blighted lives in foster homes, orphanges, and "reform" schools. Cf. *Smith* v. *Organization of Foster Families*...(1977). Many children of the poor will sadly attend second-rate segregated schools. Cf. *Milliken* v. *Bradley*...(1974). And opposition remains strong against increasing AFDC benefits for impoverished mothers and children, so that there is little chance for the children to grow up in a decent environment.... I am appalled at the ethical bankruptcy of those who preach a "right to life" that means, under present social policies, a bare existence in utter misery for so many poor women and their children.

I

The Court's insensitivity to the human dimension of these decisions is particularly obvious in its cursory discussion of respondents' equal protection claims in *Maher* v. *Roe* [1977]. That case points up once again the need for this Court to repudiate its outdated and intellectually disingenuous "two-tier" equal protection analysis.... As I have suggested before, this "model's two fixed modes of analysis, strict scrutiny and mere rationality, simply do not describe the inquiry the Court has undertaken—or should undertake—in equal protection cases.".... In the present case, in its evident desire to avoid strict scrutiny—or indeed any meaningful scrutiny—of the challenged legislation, which would almost surely result in its invalidation,... the Court pulls from thin air a distinction between laws that absolutely prevent exercise of the fundamental right to abortion and those that "merely" make its exercise difficult for some people.... MR. JUSTICE BRENNAN demonstrates that our cases support no such distinction...and I have argued above that the challenged regulations are little different from a total prohibition from the viewpoint of the poor. But the Court's legal legerdemain has produced the desired result: a fundamental right is no longer at stake and mere rationality becomes the appropriate mode of analysis. To no one's surprise, application of that test—combined with misreading of *Roe* v. *Wade* to generate a "strong" state interest in "potential life" during the first trimester of pregnancy...—"leaves little doubt about the outcome; the challenged legislation is [as] always upheld." *Massachusetts [Board of Retirement]* v. *Murgia*...[1976]. And once again, "relevant factors [are] misapplied or ignored" while the Court "forego[es] all judicial protection against discriminatory legislation bearing upon" a right "vital to the flourishing of a free society" and a class "unfairly burdened by invidious discrimination unrelated to the individual worth of [its] members."...

...It is no less disturbing that the effect of the challenged regulations will fall with great disparity upon women of minority races. Nonwhite women now obtain abortions at nearly twice the rate of whites, and it appears that almost 40 per cent of minority women—more than five times the proportion of whites—are dependent upon medicaid for their health care. Even if this strongly disparate racial impact does not alone violate the Equal Protection Clause..."at some point a showing that state action has a devastating impact on the lives of minority racial groups must be relevant." [*Jefferson* v. *Hackney* (1972)]....

Against the brutal effect that the challenged laws will have must be weighed the asserted state interest. The Court describes this as a "strong interest in protecting the potential life of the fetus."... Yet in *Doe* v. *Bolton,*...the Court expressly held that any state interest during the first trimester of pregnancy, when 88 per cent of all abortions occur...was wholly insufficient to justify state interference with the right to abortion.... If a State's interest in potential human life before the point of viability is insufficient to justify requiring several physicians' concurrence for an abortion...I cannot comprehend how it magically becomes adequate to allow the present infringement on rights of disfavored classes. If there is any state interest in potential life before the point of viability, it certainly does not outweigh the deprivation or serious discouragement of a vital constitutional right of especial importance to poor and minority women.

Thus, taking account of all relevant factors under the flexible standard of equal protection review, I would hold the Connecticut and Pennsylvania medicaid regulations and the St. Louis public hospital policy violative of the Fourteenth Amendment.

II

When this Court decided *Roe* v. *Wade* and *Doe* v. *Bolton,* it properly embarked on a course of constitutional adjudication no less controversial than that begun by *Brown* v. *Board of Education*...(1954). The abortion decisions are sound law and undoubtedly good policy. They have never been questioned by the Court and we are told that today's cases "signal[ ] no retreat from *Roe* or the cases applying it."... The logic of those cases inexorably requires invalidation of the present enactments. Yet I fear that the Court's decisions will be an invitation to public officials, already under extraordinary pressure from well financed and carefully orchestrated lobbying campaigns, to approve more such restrictions. The effect will be to relegate millions of people to lives of poverty and despair. When elected leaders cower before public pressure, this Court, more than ever, must not shirk its duty to enforce the Constitution for the benefit of the poor and powerless.

MR. JUSTICE BLACKMUN, with whom MR. JUSTICE BRENNAN and MR. JUSTICE MARSHALL join dissenting.

The Court today, by its decisions in these cases, allows the States and municipalities.as choose to do so, to accomplish indirectly what the Court in *Roe* v. *Wade*...(1973), and *Doe* v. *Bolton*...(1973)—by a substantial majority and with some emphasis, I had thought—said they could not do directly. The Court concedes the existence of a constitutional right but denies the realization and enjoyment of that right on the ground that existence and realization are separate and distinct. For the individual woman concerned, indigent and financially helpless, as the Court's opinions in the three cases concede her to be, the result is punitive and tragic. Implicit in the Court's holdings is the condescension that she may go elsewhere for her abortion. I find that disingenuous and alarming, almost reminiscent of "let them eat cake."

The result the Court reaches is particularly distressing in *Poelker* v. *Doe* [1975], where a presumed majority, in electing as mayor one whom the record shows campaigned on the issue of closing public hospitals to nontherapeutic abortions, punitively impresses upon a needy minority its own concepts of the socially desirable, the publicly acceptable, and the morally sound, with a touch of the devil-take-the-hindmost. This is not the kind of thing for which our Constitution stands.

The Court's financial argument, of course, is specious. To be sure, welfare funds are limited and welfare must be spread perhaps as best meets the community's concept of its needs. But the cost of a nontherapeutic abortion is far less than the cost of maternity care and delivery, and holds no comparison whatsoever with the welfare costs that will burden the State for the new indigents and their support in the long, long years ahead.

Neither is it an acceptable answer, as the Court well knows, to say that the Congress and the States are free to authorize the use of funds for nontherapeutic abortions. Why should any politician incur the demonstrated wrath and noise of the abortion opponents when mere silence and nonactivity accomplish the results the opponents want?

There is another world "out there," the existence of which the Court, I suspect, either chooses to ignore or fears to recognize. And so the cancer of poverty will continue to grow. This is a sad day for those who regard the Constitution as a force that would serve justice to all evenhandedly and, in so doing, would better the lot of the poorest among us.

Following are excerpts from the Supreme Court decision June 20, 1977, restricting use of public funds for abortion to medically necessary operations during the first three months of pregnancy:

No. 75-1440

| Edward W. Maher, Commissioner of Social Services of Connecticut, Appellant, *v.* Susan Roe et al. | On Appeal from the United States District Court for the District of Connecticut. |

[June 20, 1977]

MR. JUSTICE POWELL delivered the opinion of the Court.

In *Beal* v. *Doe...*, we hold today that Title XIX of the Social Security Act does not require the funding of nontherapeutic abortions as a condition of participation in the joint federal-state medicaid program established by that statute. In this case, as a result of our decision in *Beal,* we must decide whether the Constitution requires a participating State to pay for nontherapeutic abortions when it pays for childbirth.

I

A regulation of the Connecticut Welfare Department limits state medicaid benefits for first trimester abortions to those that are "medically necessary," a term defined to include psychiatric necessity.... Connecticut enforces this limitation through a system of prior authorization from its Department of Social Services. In order to obtain authorization for a first trimester abortion, the hospital or clinic where the abortion is to be performed must submit, among other things, a certificate from the patient's attending physician stating that the abortion is medically necessary.

This attack on the validity of the Connecticut regulation was brought against Appellant Maher, the Commissioner of Social Services, by Appellees Poe and Roe, two indigent women who were unable to obtain a physician's certificate of medical necessity. In a complaint filed in the United States District Court for the District of Connecticut, they challenged the regulation both as inconsistent with the requirements of Title XIX of the Social Security Act...and as violative of their constitutional rights, including the Fourteenth Amendment's guarantees of due process and equal protection. Connecticut originally defended its regulation on the theory that Title XIX of the Social Security Act prohibited the funding of abortions that were not medically necessary. After certifying a class of women unable to obtain medicaid assistance for abortions because of the regulation, the District Court held that the Social Security Act not only allowed state funding of nontherapeutic abortions but also required it.... On appeal, the Court of Appeals for the Second Circuit read the Social Security Act to allow, but not to require, state funding of such abortions.... Upon remand for consideration of the constitutional issues raised in the complaint, a three-judge District Court was convened. That court invalidated the Connecticut regulation....

Although it found no independent constitutional right to a state-financed abortion, the District Court held that the Equal Protection Clause forbids the exclusion of nontherapeutic abortions from a state welfare program that generally subsidizes the medical expenses incident to pregnancy and childbirth. The court found implicit in *Roe* v. *Wade...*(1973), and *Doe* v. *Bolton...*(1973), the view that "abortion and childbirth, when stripped of the sensitive moral arguments surrounding the abortion controversy, are simply two alternative medical methods of dealing with pregnancy...." Relying also on *Shapiro* v. *Thompson...*(1969), and *Memorial Hospital* v. *Maricopa County...*(1974), the court held that the Connecticut program "weights the choice of the pregnant mother against choosing to exercise her constitutionally protected right" to a non-therapeutic abortion and "thus infringes upon a fundamental interest."... The court found no state interest to justify this infringement. The State's fiscal interest was held to be "wholly chimerical because abortion is the least expensive medical response to a pregnancy."... And any moral objection to abortion was deemed constitutionally irrelevant....

The District Court enjoined the State from requiring the certificate of medical necessity for medicaid-funded abortions. The court also struck down the related requirements of prior written request by the pregnant woman and prior authorization by the Department of Social Services, holding that the State could not impose any requirements on medicaid payments for abortions that are not "equally applicable to medicaid payments for childbirth, if such conditions or requirements tend to discourage a woman from choosing an abortion or to delay the occurrence of an abortion that she has asked her physician to perform."... We noted probable jurisdiction to consider the constitutionality of the Connecticut regulation....

II

The Constitution imposes no obligation on the States to pay the pregnancy-related medical expenses of indigent women, or indeed to pay any of the medical expenses of indigents. But when a State decides to alleviate some of the hardships of poverty by providing medical care, the manner in which it dispenses benefits is subject to constitutional limitations. Appellees' claim is that Connecticut must accord equal treatment to both abortion and childbirth, and may not evidence a policy preference by funding only the medical expenses incident to childbirth. This challenge to the classifications established by the Connecticut regulation presents a question arising under the Equal Protection Clause of the Fourteenth Amendment....

...[W]e think the District Court erred in holding that the Connecticut regulation violated the Equal Protection Clause of the Fourteenth Amendment.

A

This case involves no discrimination against a suspect class. An indigent woman desiring an abortion does not come within the limited category of disadvantaged classes so recognized by our cases. Nor does the fact that the impact of the regulation falls upon those who cannot pay lead to a different conclusion. In a sense, every denial of welfare to an indigent creates a wealth classification as compared to nonindigents who are able to pay for the desired goods or services. But this Court has never held that financial need alone identifies a suspect class for purposes of equal protection analysis.... Accordingly, the central question in this case is whether the regulation "impinges upon a fundamental right explicitly or implicitly protected by the Constitution." The District Court read our decisions in *Roe* v. *Wade*...and the subsequent cases applying it, as established a fundamental right to abortion and therefore concluded that nothing less than a compelling state interest would justify Connecticut's different treatment of abortion and childbirth. We think the District Court misconceived the nature and scope of the fundamental right recognized in *Roe*.

B

At issue in *Roe* was the constitutionality of a Texas law making it a crime to procure or attempt to procure an abortion, except on medical advice for the purpose of saving the life of the mother. Drawing on a group of disparate cases restricting governmental intrusion, physical coercion, and criminal prohibition of certain activities, we concluded that the Fourteenth Amendment's concept of personal liberty affords constitutional protection against state interference with certain aspects of an individual's personal "privacy," including a woman's decision to terminate her pregnancy....

The Texas statute imposed severe criminal sanctions on the physicians and other medical personnel who performed abortions, thus drastically limiting the availability and safety of the desired service. As MR. JUSTICE STEWART observed, "it is difficult to imagine a more complete abridgement of a constitutional freedom...." We held that only a compelling state interest would justify such a sweeping restriction on a constitutionally protected interest, and we found no such state interest during the first trimester. Even when judged against this demanding standard, however, the State's dual interests in the health of the pregnant woman and the potential life of the fetus were deemed sufficient to justify substantial regulation of abortions in the second and third trimesters. "These interests are separate and distinct. Each grows in substantiality as the woman approaches term and, at a point during pregnancy, each becomes 'compelling.' "... In the second trimester, the State's interest in the health of the pregnant woman justifies state regulation reasonably related to that concern.... At viability, usually in the third trimester, the State's interest in the potential life of the fetus justifies prohibition with criminal penalties, except where the life or health of the mother is threatened....

The Texas law in *Roe* was a stark example of impermissible interference with the pregnant woman's decision to terminate her pregnancy. In subsequent cases, we have invalidated other types of restrictions, different in form but similar in effect, on the woman's freedom of choice....

...The Connecticut regulation before us is different in kind from the laws invalidated in our previous abortion decisions. The Connecticut regulation places no obstacles—absolute or otherwise—in the pregnant woman's path to an abortion. An indigent woman who desires an abortion suffers no disadvantage as a consequence of Connecticut's decision to fund childbirth; she continues as before to be dependent on private sources for the service she desires. The State may have made childbirth a more attractive alternative, thereby influencing the woman's decision, but it has imposed no restriction on access to abortions that was not already there. The indigency that may make it difficult—and in some cases, perhaps impossible—for some women to have abortions is neither created nor in any way affected by the Connecticut regulation. We conclude that the Connecticut regulation does not impinge upon the fundamental right recognized in *Roe*.

C

Our conclusion signals no retreat from *Roe* or the cases applying it. There is a basic difference between direct state interference with a protected activity and state encouragement of an alternative activity consonant with legislative policy. Constitutional concerns are greatest when the State attempts to impose its will by force of law; the State's power to encourage actions deemed to be in the public interest is necessarily far broader....

D

The question remains whether Connecticut's regulation can be sustained under the less demanding test of rationality that applies in the absence of a suspect classification or the impingement of a fundamental right. This test requires that the distinction drawn between childbirth and nontherapeutic abortion by the regulation be "rationally related" to a "constitutionally permissible" purpose.... We hold that the Connecticut funding scheme satisfies this standard.

Roe itself explicitly acknowledged the State's strong interest in protecting the potential life of the fetus. That interest exists throughout the pregnancy, "grow[ing] in substantiality as the woman approaches term."... Because the pregnant woman carries a potential human being, she "cannot be isolated in her privacy.... [Her] privacy is no longer sole and any right of privacy she possesses must be measured accordingly."... The State unquestionably has a "strong and legitimate interest in encouraging normal childbirth," *Beal* v. *Doe*..., an interest honored over the centuries. Nor can there be any question that the Connecticut regulation rationally furthers that interest. The medical costs associated with childbirth are substantial, and have increased significantly in recent years. As recognized by the District Court in this case, such costs are significantly greater than those normally associated with elective abortions during the first trimester. The subsidizing of costs incident to childbirth is a rational means of encouraging childbirth.

We certainly are not unsympathetic to the plight of an indigent woman who desires an abortion, but "the Constitution does not provide judicial remedies for every social and economic ill."... Our cases uniformly have accorded the States a wide latitude in choosing among competing demands for limited public funds. In *Dandridge* v. *Williams*...(1970), despite recognition that laws and regulations allocating welfare funds involve "the most basic economic needs of impoverished human beings," we held that classifications survive equal protection challenge when a "reasonable basis" for the classification is shown. As the preceding discussion makes clear, the state interest in encouraging normal childbirth exceeds this minimal level.

The decision whether to expend state funds for nontherapeutic abortion is fraught with judgments of policy and value over which opinions are sharply divided. Our conclusion that the Connecticut regulation is constitutional is not based on a weighing of its wisdom or social desirability, for this Court does not strike down state laws "because they may be unwise, improvident, or out of harmony with a particular school of thought." *Williamson* v. *Lee Optical Co...* (1955).... Indeed, when an issue involves policy choices as sensitive as those implicated by public funding of nontherapeutic abortions, the appropriate forum for their resolution in a democracy is the legislature. We should not forget that "legislatures are ultimate guardians of the liberties and welfare of the people in quite as great a degree as the courts." *Missouri, Kansas and Texas Ry. Co.* v. *May...* (1904).

In conclusion, we emphasize that our decision today does not proscribe government funding of nontherapeutic abortions. It is open to Congress to require provision of medicaid benefits for such abortions as a condition of state participation in the medicaid program. Also, under Title XIX as construed in *Beal* v. *Doe*, Connecticut is free—through normal democratic processes—to decide that such benefits should be provided. We hold only that the Constitution does not require a judicially imposed resolution of these difficult issues.

III

The District Court also invalidated Connecticut's requirements of prior written request by the pregnant woman and prior authorization by the Department of Social Services. Our analysis above rejects the basic premise that prompted invalidation of these procedural requirements. It is not unreasonable for a State to insist upon a prior showing of medical necessity to insure that its money is being spent only for authorized purposes. The simple answer to the argument that similar requirements are not imposed for other medical procedures is that such procedures do not involve the termination of a potential human life. In *Planned Parenthood of Missouri* v. *Danforth* [1976]..., we held that the woman's written consent to an abortion was not an impermissible burden under *Roe*. We think that decision is controlling on the similar issue here.

The judgment of the District Court is reversed, and the case is remanded for further proceedings consistent with this opinion.

MR. CHIEF JUSTICE BURGER, concurring.

I join the Court's opinion. Like the Court, I do not read any decision of this Court as requiring a State to finance a nontherapeutic abortion. The Court's holdings in *Roe* and *Doe...* simply require that a State not create an absolute barrier to a woman's decision to have an abortion. These precedents do not suggest that the State is constitutionally required to assist her in procuring it.

From time to time, every state legislature determines that, as a matter of sound public policy, the government ought to provide certain health and social services to its citizens. Encouragement of childbirth and child care is not a novel undertaking in this regard. Various governments, both in this country and in others, have made such a determination for centuries. In recent times, they have similarly provided educational services. The decision to provide any one of these services—or not to provide them—is not required by the Federal Constitution. Nor does the providing of a particular service require, as a matter of federal constitutional law, the provision of another.

Here, the State of Connecticut has determined that it will finance certain childbirth expenses. That legislative determination places no state-created barrier to a woman's choice to procure an abortion, and it does not require the State to provide it. Accordingly, I concur in the judgment.

MR. JUSTICE BRENNAN, with whom MR. JUSTICE MARSHALL and MR. JUSTICE BLACKMUN join dissenting....

...[A] distressing insensitivity to the plight of impoverished pregnant women is inherent in the Court's analysis. The stark reality for too many, not just "some," indigent pregnant women is that indigency makes access to competent licensed physicians not merely "difficult" but "impossible." As a practical matter, many indigent women will feel they have no choice but to carry their pregnancies to term because the State will pay for the associated medical services, even though they would have chosen to have abortions if the State had also provided funds for that procedure, or indeed if the State had provided funds for neither procedure. This disparity in funding by the State clearly operates to coerce indigent pregnant women to bear children they would not otherwise choose to have, and just as clearly, this coercion can only operate upon the poor, who are uniquely the victims of this form of financial pressure....

...The Court's premise is that only an equal protection claim is presented here. Claims of interference with enjoyment of fundamental rights have, however, occupied a rather protean position in our constitutional jurisprudence. Whether or not the Court's analysis may reasonably proceed under the Equal Protection Clause, the Court plainly errs in ignoring, as it does, the unanswerable argument of appellee, and holding of the District Court, that the regulation unconstitutionally impinges upon her claim of privacy derived from the Due Process Clause.

Roe v. *Wade* [1973] and cases following it hold that an area of privacy invulnerable to the State's intrusion surrounds the decision of a pregnant women whether or not to carry her pregnancy to term. The Connecticut scheme clearly infringes upon that area of privacy by bringing financial pressures on indigent women that force them to bear children they would not otherwise have. That is an obvious impairment of the fundamental right established by *Roe*. Yet the Court concludes that "the Connecticut regulation does not impinge upon [that] fundamental right."... This conclusion is based on a perceived distinction, on the one hand, between the imposition of criminal penalties for the procurement of an abortion present in *Roe* v. *Wade* and *Doe* v. *Bolton* [1973] and the absolute prohibition present in *Planned Parenthood of Missouri* v. *Danforth*...(1976), and, on the other, the assertedly lesser inhibition imposed by the Connecticut scheme...

The last time our Brother POWELL espoused the concept in an abortion case that "there is a basic difference between direct State interference with a protected activity and State encouragement of an alternative activity concurrent with legislative policy," ...the Court refused to adopt it....

...[C]ases involving other fundamental rights also make clear that the Court's concept of what constitutes an impermissible infringement upon the fundamental right of a pregnant woman to choose to have an abortion makes new law. We have repeatedly found that infringements of fundamental rights are not limited to outright denials of those rights. First Amendment decisions have consistently held in a wide variety of contexts that the compelling state interest test is applicable not only to outright denials but also to restraints that make exercise of those rights more difficult.... The compelling state interest test has been applied in voting cases, even where only relatively small infringements upon voting power, such as dilution of voting strength caused by malapportionment, have been involved.... Similarly, cases involving the right to travel have consistently held that statutes penalizing the fundamental right to travel must pass muster under the compelling state interest test, irrespective of whether the statutes actually deter travel.... And indigents asserting a fundamental right of access to the courts have been excused payment of entry costs without being required first to show that their indigency was an absolute bar to access....

Until today, I had not thought the nature of the fundamental right established in *Roe* was open to question, let alone susceptible to the interpretation advanced by the Court. The fact that the Connecticut scheme may not operate as an absolute bar preventing all indigent women from having abortions is not critical. What is critical is that the State has inhibited their fundamental right to make that choice free from state interference.

Nor does the manner in which Connecticut has burdened the right freely to choose to have an abortion save its Medicaid program. The Connecticut scheme cannot be distinguished from other grants and withholdings of financial benefits that we have held unconstitutionally burdened a fundamental right....

...*Belloti* v. *Baird*...(1976), held, and the Court today agrees...that a state requirement is unconstitutional if it "unduly burdens the right to seek an abortion." Connecticut has "unduly" burdened the fundamental right of pregnant women to be free to choose to have an abortion because the State has advanced no compelling state interest to justify its interference in that choice.

Although Connecticut does not argue it as justification, the Court concludes that the State's interest "in protecting the potential life of the fetus" suffices.... Since only the first trimester of pregnancy is involved in this case, that justification is totally foreclosed if the Court is not overruling the holding of *Roe* v. *Wade* that "[w]ith respect to the State's important and legitimate interest in potential life, the compelling point is at viability," occurring at about the end of the second trimester.... The State also argues a further justification not relied upon by the Court, namely, that it needs "to control the amount of its limited public funds which will be allocated to its public welfare budget."... The District Court correctly held, however, that the asserted interest was "wholly chimerical" because the "state's assertion that it saves money when it declines to pay the cost of a welfare mother's abortion is simply contrary to indisputed facts."...

Finally, the reasons that render the Connecticut regulation unconstitutional also render invalid in my view the requirement of a prior written certification by the woman's attending physician that the abortion is "medically necessary," and the requirement that the hospital submit a Request for Authorization of Professional Services including a "statement indicating the medical need for the abortion."... For the same reasons, I would also strike down the requirement for prior authorization of payment by the Connecticut Department of Social Services.

Excerpts from the Court's decision June 20, 1977, ruling that hospital policy issues with respect to performing abortions were matters for local residents to decide at the polls.

No. 75-442

| John H. Poelker, etc., et al.,
Petitioners,
v.
Jane Doe, etc. | On Writ of Certiorari to
the United States Court
of Appeals for the
Eighth Circuit. |

[June 20, 1977]

PER CURIAM.

Respondent Jane Doe, an indigent, sought unsuccessfully to obtain a nontherapeutic abortion at Starkloff Hospital, one of two city-owned public hospitals in St. Louis, Mo. She subsequently brought this class action...against the Mayor of St. Louis and the Director of Health and Hospitals, alleging that the refusal by Starkloff Hospital to provide the desired abortion violated her constitutional rights. Although the District Court ruled against Doe following a trial, the Court of Appeals for the Eighth Circuit reversed in an opinion that accepted both her factual and legal arguments. *Doe* v. *Poelker*...(1975).

The Court of Appeals concluded that Doe's inability to obtain an abortion resulted from a combination of a policy directive by the Mayor and a longstanding staffing practice at Starkloff Hospital. The directive, communicated to the Director of Health and Hospitals by the Mayor, prohibited the performance of abortions in the city hospitals except when there was a threat of grave physiological injury or death to the mother. Under the staffing practice, the doctors and medical students at the obstetrics-gynecology clinic at the hospital are drawn from the faculty and students at the St. Louis University School of Medicine, a Jesuit-operated institution opposed to abortion. Relying on our decisions in *Roe* v. *Wade*...(1973), and *Doe* v. *Bolton*...(1973), the Court of Appeals held that the city's policy and the hospital's staffing practice denied the "constitutional rights of indigent pregnant women...long after those rights had been clearly enunciated" in *Roe* and *Doe*.... The court cast the issue in an equal protection mold, finding that the provision of publicly financed hospital services for childbirth but not for elective abortions constituted invidious discrimination. In support of its equal protection analysis, the court also emphasized the contrast between nonindigent women who can afford to obtain abortions in private hospitals and indigent women who cannot....

We agree that the constitutional question presented here is identical in principle with that presented by a State's refusal to provide medicaid benefits for abortions while providing them for childbirth. This was the issue before us in *Maher* v. *Roe*...[1977]. For the reasons set forth in our opinion in that case, we find no constitutional violation by the city of St. Louis in electing, as a policy choice, to provide publicly financed hospital services for childbirth without providing corresponding services for nontherapeutic abortions....

...The judgment of the Court of Appeals for the Eighth Circuit is reversed, and the case is remanded for further proceedings consistent with this opinion.

MR. JUSTICE BRENNAN, with whom MR. JUSTICE MARSHALL and MR. JUSTICE BLACKMUN join, dissenting.

The Court holds that St. Louis may constitutionally refuse to permit the performance of elective abortions in its city-owned hospitals while providing hospital services to women who carry their pregnancies to term....

The Court of Appeals held that St. Louis could not in this way "interfer[e] in her decision of whether to bear a child or have an abortion simply because she is indigent and unable to afford private treatment,"...because it was constitutionally impermissible that indigent women be " 'subjected to State coercion to bear children which they do not wish to bear [while] no other women similarly situated are so coerced.' "...

For the reasons set forth in my dissent in *Maher* v. *Roe*,...I would affirm the Court of Appeals. Here the fundamental right of a woman freely to choose to terminate her pregnancy has been infringed by the city of St.

Louis through a deliberate policy based on opposition to elective abortions on moral grounds by city officials. While it may still be possible for some indigent women to obtain abortions in clinics or private hospitals, it is clear that the city policy is a significant, and in some cases insurmountable, obstacle to indigent pregnant women who cannot pay for abortions in those private facilities. Nor is the closing of St. Louis' public hospitals an isolated instance with little practical significance. The importance of today's decision is greatly magnified by the fact that during 1975 and the first quarter of 1976 only about 18% of all public hospitals in the country provided abortion services, and in 10 States there were no public hospitals providing such services.

A number of difficulties lie beneath the surface of the Court's holding. Public hospitals that do not permit the performance of elective abortions will frequently have physicians on their staffs who would willingly perform them. This may operate in some communities significantly to reduce the number of physicians who are both willing and able to perform abortions in a hospital setting. It is not a complete answer that many abortions may safely be performed in clinics, for some physicians will not be affiliated with those clinics, and some abortions may pose unacceptable risks if performed outside a hospital. Indeed, such an answer would be ironic, for if the result is to force some abortions to be performed in a clinic that properly should be performed in a hospital, the city policy will have operated to increase rather than reduce health risks associated with abortions; and in *Roe* the Court permitted regulation by the State solely to *protect* maternal health....

The Court's holding will also pose difficulties in small communities where the public hospital is the only nearby health care facility. If such a public hospital is closed to abortions, any woman—rich or poor—will be seriously inconvenienced; and for some women—particularly poor women—the unavailability of abortions in the public hospital will be an insuperable obstacle. Indeed, a recent survey suggests that the decision in this case will be felt most strongly in rural areas, where the public hospital will in all likelihood be closed elective abortions, and where there will not be sufficient demand to support a separate abortion clinic.

Because the city policy constitutes "coercion [of women] to bear children they do not wish to bear," *Roe* v. *Wade* and the cases following it require that the city show a compelling state interest that justifies this infringement upon the fundamental right to choose to have an abortion. "[E]xpressing a preference for normal childbirth,"...does not satisfy that standard. *Roe* explicitly held that during the first trimester no state interest in regulating abortions was compelling, and that during the second trimester the State's interest was compelling only insofar as it protected maternal health.... Under *Roe,* the State's "important and legitimate interest in potential life"...—which I take to be another way of referring to a State's "preference for normal childbirth"—becomes compelling only at the end of the second trimester. Thus it is clear that St. Louis' policy preference is insufficient to justify its infringement on the right of women to choose to have abortions during the first two trimesters of pregnancy without interference by the State on the ground of moral opposition to abortions. St. Louis' policy therefore "unduly burdens the right to seek an abortion," *Belloti* v. *Baird*...(1976).

I would affirm the Court of Appeals.

COURT ON AID TO
PAROCHIAL SCHOOLS
June 24, 1977

The Supreme Court June 29 adjourned its 1976-77 session, which began on Oct. 4, 1976, with the traditional burst of activity in the last weeks of a term. Decisions in more than three dozen cases were announced, among them a ruling dealing with state aid to parochial schools (Wolman v. Walter).

"We have acknowledged before, and we do so again here, that the wall of separation that must be maintained between church and state 'is a blurred, indistinct, and variable barrier depending on all the circumstances of a particular relationship,' " wrote Justice Harry A. Blackmun for the court June 24. Justice Potter Stewart was the only justice to concur with Blackmun in every aspect of the case.

To determine its validity under the First Amendment ban on establishment of religion, the justices applied a three-part test to an Ohio law setting up various forms of state aid to nonpublic schools and their students. The court's test required that such a law "in order to pass muster...must have a secular legislative purpose, must have a principal or primary effect that neither advances nor inhibits religion, and must not foster an excessive government entanglement with religion."

Under this test, the court upheld the provisions of the Ohio law permitting:
● The loan of secular textbooks to nonpublic school students or their parents. The vote was 6-3; Justices William J. Brennan Jr., Thurgood Marshall and John Paul Stevens found this aid impermissible.

431

● *The provision of standardized test and scoring services to nonpublic schools. The vote was 6-3; Justices Brennan, Marshall and Stevens again dissented.*

● *The provision of speech and hearing and psychological diagnostic services to nonpublic schools. The vote was 8-1; only Justice Brennan dissented.*

● *The provision of therapeutic, guidance and remedial services on nonpublic school premises. The vote was 8-1 on the therapeutic services; only Justice Brennan dissented. The vote was 7-2 on the guidance and remedial services; Justice Marshall joined Justice Brennan in dissent.*

The court struck down as impermissible the provisions of the law allowing:

● *State-supplied instructional materials for nonpublic schools and their students. The vote was 9-0. This aid "inescapably had the primary effect of providing a direct and substantial advancement of the sectarian enterprise," wrote Justice Blackmun.*

● *State-supplied field trip transportation and services. The vote was 5-4. This was impermissable direct aid to sectarian education, wrote Justice Blackmun, and would create excessive entanglement of church and state if the state tried to ensure that the field trip funds were all used for secular purposes. Chief Justice Warren E. Burger and Justice Lewis F. Powell Jr., William H. Rehnquist and Byron R. White dissented.*

● *State-lent classroom materials such as projectors, maps or instructional equipment other than textbooks. The vote was 6-3, with Chief Justice Burger and Justices Rehnquist and White dissenting.*

Justice Brennan, the only justice to dissent in every aspect of the case, criticized his colleagues for not evaluating the cost of these services to the taxpayers of Ohio, estimated to be $88.8-million over a two-year period.

Previous Cases

Several aspects of the June 24 decisions had been touched on in earlier decisions. In 1975, referring to the First Amendment's ban on church-state relations, the court struck down a Pennsylvania plan for loaning instructional equipment to nonpublic schools (Meek v. Pittinger). The plan provided those schools with the staff and services to run supportive programs such as remedial instruction, testing and counseling. The majority, with Stewart speaking on their behalf, did approve a program of textbook loans to students at nonpublic as well as public schools. But the other two forms of aid, said Stewart for the court, would lead to excessive entanglement of church and state.

In vigorous dissent, Chief Justice Warren E. Burger, Byron R. White and William H. Rehnquist charged the majority with insensitivity to the impact of the decision, saying that it would penalize children who needed those services, not the nonpublic institutions which they attended.

In its 1977 ruling, however, the court noted that the 1975 ruling specifically stated that the diagnostic speech and hearing services in the Pennsylvania plan appeared to fall under the category of "general welfare" services for children that were permissible. The provision of those services was banned in the 1975 case, noted the court two years later, only because it was "unseverable" from the rest of the plan.

Continuing its effort to "police the constitutional boundary between church and state," the court June 21, 1976, in a 5-4 decision, upheld Maryland's program of general annual grants to private colleges, including several which were church-related. The aid was given with only one condition, that it not be used for sectarian purposes (Roemer v. Board of Public Works of Maryland).

Following are excerpts from the Supreme Court's opinion, decided June 24, 1977, holding that certain forms of public aid and services could be provided to parochial schools without violating the constitutional separation of church and state:

No. 76-496

Benson A. Wolman et al.,
Appellants,

v.

Franklin B. Walter et al.

On Appeal from the United States District Court for the Southern District of Ohio.

[June 24, 1977]

MR. JUSTICE BLACKMUN delivered the opinion of the Court (Parts I, V, VI, VII, and VIII), together with an opinion (Parts II, III, and IV), in which THE CHIEF JUSTICE, MR. JUSTICE STEWART, and MR. JUSTICE POWELL joined.

This is still another case presenting the recurrent issue of the limitations imposed by the Establishment Clause of the First Amendment, made applicable to the States by the Fourteenth Amendment, *Meek* v. *Pittenger...* (1975), on state aid to pupils in church-related elementary and secondary schools. Appellants are citizens and taxpayers of Ohio. They challenge all but one of the provisions of Ohio Rev. Code § 3317.06 (Supp. 1976) which authorize various forms of aid. The appellees are the State Superintendent of Public Instruction, the State Treasurer, the State Auditor, the Board of Education of the City School District of Columbus, Ohio, and, at their request, certain representative potential beneficiaries of the statutory program. A three-judge court was convened. It held the statute constitutional in all respects.... We noted probable jurisdiction.

I

Section 3317.06 was enacted after this Court's May 1975 decision in *Meek* v. *Pittenger*...and obviously is an attempt to conform to the teachings of that decision. The state appellees so acknowledged at oral argument. In broad outline, the statute authorizes the State to provide nonpublic school pupils with books, instructional materials and equipment, standardized testing and scoring, diagnostic services, therapeutic services, and field trip transportation.

The initial biennial appropriation by the Ohio Legislature for implementation of the statute was the sum of $88,800,000.... Funds so appropriated are paid to the State's public school districts and are then expended by them. All disbursements made with respect to nonpublic schools have their equivalents in disbursements for public schools, and the amount expended per pupil in nonpublic schools may not exceed the amount expended per pupil in the public schools.

The parties stipulated that during the 1974-1975 school year there were 720 chartered nonpublic schools in Ohio. Of these, all but 29 were sectarian. More than 96% of the nonpublic enrollment attended sectarian schools, and more than 92% attended Catholic schools.... It was also stipulated that, if they were called, officials of representative Catholic schools would testify that such schools operate under the general supervision of the Bishop of their Diocese; that most principals are members of a religious order within the Catholic Church; that a little less than one-third of the teachers are members of such religious orders; that "in all probability a majority of the teachers are members of the Catholic faith"; and that many of the rooms and hallways in these schools are decorated with a Christian symbol.... All such schools teach the secular subjects required to meet the State's minimum standards. The state-mandated five-hour day is expanded to include, usually, one-half hour of religious instruction. Pupils who are not members of the Catholic faith are not required to attend religion classes or to participate in religious exercises or activities, and no teacher is required to teach religious doctrine as a part of the secular courses taught in the schools....

The parties also stipulated that nonpublic school officials, if called, would testify that none of the schools covered by the statute discriminate in the admission of pupils or in the hiring of teachers on the basis of race, creed, color, or national origin....

II

The mode of analysis for Establishment Clause questions is defined by the three-part test that has emerged from the Court's decisions. In order to pass muster, a statute must have a secular legislative purpose, must have a principal or primary effect that neither advances nor inhibits religion, and must not foster an excessive government entanglement with religion....

In the present case we have no difficulty with the first prong of this three-part test. We are satisfied that the challenged statute reflects Ohio's legitimate interest in protecting the health of its youth and in providing a fertile educational environment for all the school children of the State. As is usual in our cases, the analytical difficulty has to do with the effect and entanglement criteria.

We have acknowledged before, and we do so again here, that the wall of separation that must be maintained between church and state "is a blurred, indistinct, and variable barrier depending on all the circumstances of a particular relationship."... Nonetheless, the Court's numerous precedents "have become firmly rooted" and now provide substantial guidance. We therefore turn to the task of applying the rules derived from our decisions to the respective provisions of the statute at issue.

III

Textbooks

...This system for the loan of textbooks to individual students bears a striking resemblance to the systems approved in *Board of Education* v. *Allen*...(1968), and in *Meek* v. *Pittenger*.... Indeed, the only distinction offered by appellants is that the challenged statute defines "textbook" as "any book or book substitute." Appellants argue that a "book substitute" might include auxiliary equipment and materials that, they assert, may not constitutionally be loaned.... We find this argument untenable in light of the statute's separate treatment of instructional materials and equipment in its subsections (B) and (C), and in light of the stipulation defining textbooks as "limited to books, reusable workbooks, or manuals." Appellants claim that the stipulation shows only the intent of the Department of Education,... and that the statute is so vague as to fail to insure against sectarian abuse of the assistance programs.... We find no grounds, however, to doubt the Board of Education's reading of the statute, or to fear that the Board is using the stipulations as a subterfuge. As read, the statute provides the same protections against abuse as were provided in the text book programs under consideration in *Allen* and in *Meek*.

In the alternative, appellants urge that we overrule *Allen* and *Meek*. This we decline to do. Accordingly, we conclude that § 3317.06 (A) is constitutional.

IV

Testing and Scoring

...These tests "are used to measure the progress of students in secular subjects."... Nonpublic school personnel are not involved in either the drafting or scoring of the tests.... The statute does not authorize any payment to nonpublic school personnel for the costs of administering the tests.

In *Levitt* v. *Committee for Public Education*...(1973), this Court invalidated a New York statutory scheme for reimbursement of church-sponsored schools for the expenses of teacher-prepared testing. The reasoning behind that decision was straightforward. The system was held unconstitutional because "no means are available, to assure that internally prepared tests are free of religious instruction."....

There is no question that the State has a substantial and legitimate interest in insuring that its youth receive an adequate secular education.... The State may require that schools that are utilized to fulfill the State's compulsory education requirement meet certain standards of instruction...and may examine both teachers and pupils to ensure that the State's legitimate interest is being fulfilled.... Under the section at issue, the State provides both the schools and the school district with the means of ensuring that the minimum standards are met. The nonpublic school does not control the content of the test or its result. This serves to prevent the use of the test as a part of religious teaching, and thus avoids that kind of direct aid to religion found present in *Levitt*. Similarly, the inability of the school to control the test eliminates the need for the supervision that gives rise to excessive entanglement. We therefore agree with the District Court's conclusion that § 3317.06 (J) is constitutional....

V

Diagnostic Services

...It will be observed that these speech and hearing and psychological diagnostic services are to be provided within the nonpublic school. It is stipulated, however, that the personnel (with the exception of physicians) who perform the services are employees of the local board of education; that physicians may be hired on a contract basis; that the purpose of these services is to determine the pupil's deficiency or need of assistance; and that treatment of any defect so found would take place off the nonpublic school premises....

Appellants assert that the funding of these services is constitutionally impermissible. They argue that the speech and hearing staff might engage in unrestricted conversation with the pupil and, on occasion, might fail to separate religious instruction from secular responsibilities. They further assert that the communication between the psychological diagnostician and the pupil will provide an impermissible opportunity for the instrusion of religious influence.

The District Court found these dangers so insubstantial as not to render the statute unconstitutional.... We agree. This Court's decisions contain a common thread to the effect that the provision of health services to all school children—public and nonpublic—does not have the primary effect of aiding religion....

...We perceive no basis for drawing a different conclusion with respect to diagnostic speech and hearing services and diagnostic psychological services....

...The reason for considering diagnostic services to be different from teaching or counseling is readily apparent. First, diagnostic services, unlike teaching or counseling, have little or no educational content and are not closely associated with the educational mission of the nonpublic school. Accordingly, any pressure on the public diagnostician to allow the intrusion of sectarian views is greatly reduced. Second, the diagnostician has only limited contact with the child, and that contact involves chiefly the use of objective and professional testing methods to detect students in need of treatment. The nature of the relationship between the diagnostician and the pupil does not provide the same opportunity for the transmission of sectarian views as attends the relationship between teacher and student or that between counselor and student.

We conclude that providing diagnostic services on the nonpublic school premises will not create an impermissible risk of the fostering of ideological views. It follows that there is no need for excessive surveillance, and there will not be impermissible entanglement. We therefore hold that § § 3317.06 (D) and (F) are constitutional....

VI

Therapeutic Services

...Appellants concede that the provision of remedial, therapeutic, and guidance services in public schools, public centers, or mobile units is constitutional if both public and nonpublic school students are served simultaneously.... Their challenge is limited to the situation where a facility is used to service only nonpublic school students. They argue that any program that isolates the sectarian pupils is impermissible because the public employee providing the service might tailor his approach to reflect and reinforce the ideological view of the sectarian school attended by the children. Such action by the employee, it is claimed, renders direct aid to the sectarian institution. Appellants express particular concern over mobile units because they perceive a danger that such a unit might operate merely as an annex of the school or schools it services.

At the outset, we note that in its present posture the case does not properly present any issue concerning the use of a public facility as an adjunct of a sectarian educational enterprise. The District Court construed the statute, as do we, to authorize services only on sites that are "neither physically nor educationally identified with the functions of the nonpublic school."... Thus, the services are to be offered under circumstances that reflect their religious neutrality.

We recognize that, unlike the diagnostician, the therapist may establish a relationship with the pupil in which there might be opportunities to transmit ideological views. In *Meek* the Court acknowledged the danger that publicly employed personnel who provide services analogous to those at issue here might transmit religious instruction and advance religious beliefs in their activities. But, as discussed in Part V, ...the Court emphasized that this danger arose from the fact that the services were performed in the pervasively sectarian atmosphere of the church-related school.... The danger existed there not because the public employee was likely deliberately to subvert his task to the service of religion, but rather because the pressures of the environment might alter his behavior from its normal course. So long as these types of services are offered at truly religiously neutral locations, the danger perceived in *Meek* does not arise.

The fact that a unit on a neutral site on occasion may serve only sectarian pupils does not provoke the same concerns that troubled the Court in *Meek*. The influence on a therapist's behavior that is exerted by the fact that he serves a sectarian pupil is qualitatively different from the influence of the pervasive atmosphere of a religious institution. The dangers perceived in *Meek* arose from the nature of the institution, not from the nature of the pupils.

Accordingly, we hold that providing therapeutic and remedial services at a neutral site off the premises of the nonpublic schools will not have the impermissible effect of advancing religion. Neither will there be any excessive entanglement arising from supervision of public employees to insure that they maintain a neutral stance. It can hardly be said that the supervision of public employees performing public functions on public property creates an excessive entanglement between church and state. Sections 3317.06 (G), (H), (I), and (K) are constitutional.

VII

Instructional Materials and Equipment

Sections 3317.06 (B) and (C) authorize expenditures of funds for the purchase and loan to pupils or their parents upon individual request of instructional materials and instructional equipment of the kind in use in the public schools within the district and which is "incapable of diversion to religious use." Section 3717.06 also provides that the materials and equipment may be stored on the premises of a nonpublic school and that publicly hired personnel who administer the lending program may perform their services upon the nonpublic school premises when necessary "for efficient implementation of the lending program."

Although the exact nature of the material and equipment is not clearly revealed, the parties have stipulated: "It is expected that materials and equipment loaned to pupils or parents under the new law will be similar to such former materials and equipment except that to the extent that the law requires that materials and equipment capable of diversion to religious issues will not be supplied."... Equipment provided under the predecessor statute...included projectors, tape recorders, record players, maps and globes, science kits, weather forecasting charts, and the like. The District

Court...found the new statute, as now limited, constitutional because the Court could not distinguish the loan of material and equipment from the textbook provisions upheld in *Meek*...and in *Allen*....

In *Meek*, however, the Court considered the constitutional validity of a direct loan to nonpublic schools of instructional material and equipment, and, despite the apparent secular nature of the goods, held the loan impermissible.... Thus, even though the loan ostensibly was limited to neutral and secular instructional material and equipment, it inescapably had the primary effect of providing a direct and substantial advancement of the sectarian enterprise.

Appellees seek to avoid *Meek* by emphasizing that it involved a program of direct loans to nonpublic schools. In contrast, the material and equipment at issue under the Ohio statute are loaned to the pupil or his parent. In our view, however, it would exalt form over substance if this distinction were found to justify a result different from that in *Meek*. Before *Meek* was decided by this Court, Ohio authorized the loan of material and equipment directly to the nonpublic schools. Then, in light of *Meek*, the state legislature decided to channel the goods through the parents and pupils. Despite the technical change in legal bailee, the program in substance is the same; it will receive the same use by the students; and it may still be stored and distributed on the nonpublic school premises. In view of the impossibility of separating the secular education function from the sectarian, the state aid inevitably flows in part in support of the religious role of the schools....

...Accordingly, we hold § § 3316.06 (B) and (C) to be unconstitutional.

VIII

Field Trips

...There is no restriction on the timing of field trips; the only restriction on number lies in the parallel the statute draws to field trips provided to public school students in the district. The parties have stipulated that the trips "would consist of visits to governmental, industrial, cultural, and scientific centers designed to enrich the secular studies of students."... The choice of destination, however, will be made by the nonpublic school teacher from a wide range of locations.

The District Court...held this feature to be constitutionally indistinguishable from that with which the Court was concerned in *Everson* v. *Board of Education*...(1947). We do not agree. In *Everson* the Court approved a system under which a New Jersey board of education reimbursed parents for the cost of sending their children to and from school, public or parochial, by public carrier. The Court analogized the reimbursement to situations where a municipal common carrier is ordered to carry all school children at a reduced rate, or where the police force is ordered to protect all children on their way to and from school.... The critical factors in these examples, as in the *Everson* reimbursement system, are that the school has no control over the expenditure of the funds and the effect of the expenditure is unrelated to the content of the education provided. Thus, the bus fare program in *Everson* passed constitutional muster because the school did not determine how often the pupil traveled between home and school—every child must make one round trip every day—and because the travel was unrelated to any aspect of the curriculum.

The Ohio situation is in sharp contrast. First, the nonpublic school controls the timing of the trips and, within a certain range, their frequency and destinations. Thus, the schools, rather than the children, truly are the recipients of the service and, as this Court has recognized, this fact alone may be sufficient to invalidate the program as impermissiible direct aid.... Second, although a trip may be to a location that would be of interest to those in public schools, it is the individual teacher who makes a field trip meaningful. The experience begins with the study and discussion of the place to be visited; it continues on location with the teacher pointing out items of interest and stimulating the imagination; and it ends with a discussion of the experience. The field trips are an integral part of the educational experience, and where the teacher works within and for a sectarian institution, an unacceptable risk of fostering of religion is an inevitable byproduct.... Funding of field trips, therefore, must be treated as was the funding of maps and charts in *Meek* v. *Pittenger*,...the funding of buildings and tuition in *Committee for Public Education* v. *Nyquist*,...and the funding of teacher-prepared tests in *Levitt* v. *Committee for Public Education;* it must be declared an impermissible direct aid to sectarian education.

Moreover, the public school authorities will be unable adequately to insure secular use of the field trip funds without close supervision of the nonpublic teachers....

We hold § 3317.06 (L) to be unconstitutional.

IX

In summary, we hold constitutional those portions of the Ohio statute authorizing the State to provide nonpublic school pupils with books, standardized testing and scoring, diagnostic services, and therapeutic and remedial services. We hold unconstitutional those portions relating to instructional materials and equipment and field trip services.

The judgment of the District Court is therefore affirmed in part and reversed in part.

It is so ordered.

THE CHIEF JUSTICE dissents from Parts VII and VIII of the Court's opinion....

...MR. JUSTICE WHITE and MR. JUSTICE REHNQUIST concur in the judgment with respect to textbooks, testing, and scoring, and diagnostic and therapeutic services (Parts III, IV, V and VI of the opinion) and dissent from the judgment with respect to instructional materials and equipment and field trips (Parts VII and VIII of the opinion).

MR. JUSTICE BRENNAN, concurring and dissenting.

I join Parts I, VII, and VIII of the Court's opinion, and the reversal of the District Court's judgment insofar as that judgment upheld the constitutionality of § § 3317.06 (B), (C), and (L).

I dissent however from Parts II, III, IV, V, and VI of the opinion and the affirmance of the District Court's judgment insofar as it sustained the constitutionality of § § 3317.06 (A), (D), (F), (G), (H), (I), (J), and (K). The Court holds that Ohio has managed in these respects to fashion a statute that avoids an effect or entanglement condemned by the Establishment Clause. But "The [First] Amendment nullifies sophisticated as well as simple-minded..." attempts to avoid its prohibitions *Land* v. *Wilson...* (1939), and, in any event, ingenuity in draftsmanship cannot obscure the fact that this subsidy to sectarian schools amounts to $88,800,-000 (less now the sums appropriated to finance § § 3317.06 (B) and (C) which today are invalidated) just for the initial biennium. The Court nowhere evaluates this factor in determining the compatibility of the statute with the Establishment Clause....

MR. JUSTICE MARSHALL, concurring and dissenting.

I join Parts I, V, VII, and VIII of the Court's opinion. For the reasons stated below, however, I am unable to join the remainder of the Court's opinion or its judgment upholding the constitutionality of § § 3317.06 (A), (G), (H), (I), (J), and (K).

The Court upholds the textbook loan provision, § 3317.06 (A), on precedent of *Board of Education* v. *Allen...*(1968).... It also recognizes, however, that there is "a tension" between *Allen* and the reasoning of the Court in *Meek* v. *Pittenger...*(1975). I would resolve that tension by overruling *Allen*. I am now convinced that *Allen* is largely responsible for reducing the "high and impregnable" wall between church and state erected by the First Amendment, *Everson* v. *Board of Education...*(1947), to "a blurred, indistinct, and variable barrier," *Lemon* v. *Kurtzman...*, incapable of performing its vital functions of protecting both church and state.

In *Allen,* we upheld a textbook loan program on the assumption that the sectarian school's twin functions of religious instruction and secular education were separable.... In *Meek,* we flatly rejected that assumption as a basis for allowing a State to loan secular teaching materials and equipment to such schools.... Thus, although *Meek* upheld a textbook loan program on the strength of *Allen,* it left the rationale of *Allen* undamaged only if there is a constitutionally significant difference between a loan of pedagogical materials directly to a sectarian school and a loan of those materials to students for use in sectarian schools. As the Court convincingly demonstrates...there is no such difference....

...By overruling *Allen*, we would free ourselves to draw a line between acceptable and unacceptable forms of aid that would be both capable of consistent application and responsive to the concerns discussed above. That line, I believe, should be placed between general welfare programs that serve children in sectarian schools because the schools happen to be a convenient place to reach the programs' target populations and programs of education assistance. General welfare programs, in contrast to programs of educational assistance, do not provide "[s]ubstantial aid to the educational function" of schools, whether secular or sectarian, and therefore do not provide the kind of assistance to the religious mission of sectarian schools we found impermissible in *Meek*. Moreover, because general welfare programs do not assist the sectarian functions of denominational schools, there is no reason to expect that political disputes over the merits of those programs will divide the public along religious lines....

The Court upholds paragraphs (H), (I), and (K), which it groups with paragraph (G), under the rubric of "therapeutic services."... I cannot agree that the services authorized by these three paragraphs should be treated like the psychological services provided by paragraph (G). Paragraph (H) authorizes the provision of guidance and counseling services. The parties stipulated that the functions to be performed by the guidance and counseling personnel would include assisting students in "developing meaningful educational and career goals," and "planning school programs of study." In addition, these personnel will discuss with parents "their children's a) educational progress and needs, b) course selections, c) educational and vocational opportunities and plans, and d) study skills." The counselors will also collect and organize information for use by parents, teachers, and students.... This description makes clear that paragraph (H) authorizes services that would directly support the educational programs of sectarian schools. It is, therefore, in violation of the First Amendment.

Paragraphs (I) and (K) provide remedial services and programs for disabled children. The stipulation of the parties indicates that these paragraphs will fund specialized teachers who will both provide instruction themselves and create instructional plans for use in the students' regular classrooms.... These "therapeutic services" are clearly intended to aid the sectarian schools to improve the performance of their students in the classroom. I would not treat them as if they were programs of physical or psychological therapy.

Finally, the Court upholds paragraph (J), which provides standardized tests and scoring services, on the ground that these tests are clearly non-ideological and that the State has an interest in assuring that the education received by sectarian school students meets minimum standards. I do not question the legitimacy of this interest, and if Ohio required students to obtain specified scores on certain tests before being promoted or graduated, I would agree that it could administer those tests to sectarian school students to ensure that its standards were being met. The record indicates, however, only that the tests "are used to measure the progress of students in secular subjects."... It contains no indication that the measurements are taken to assure compliance with state standards rather than for internal administrative purposes of the schools. To the extent that the testing is done to serve the purposes of the sectarian schools rather than the State, I would hold that its provision by the State violates the First Amendment.

MR. JUSTICE POWELL, concurring in part and dissenting in part.

Our decisions in this troubling area draw lines that often must seem arbitrary. No doubt we could achieve greater analytical tidiness if we were to accept the broadest implications of the observation in *Meek* v. *Pittenger*...(1975), that "[s]ubstantial aid to the educational function of [sectarian] schools...necessarily results in aid to the sectarian enterprise as a whole." If we took that course, it would become impossible to sustain state aid of any kind—even if the aid is wholly secular in character and is supplied to the pupils rather than the institutions. *Meek* itself would have to be overruled along with *Board of Education* v. *Allen*... (1968) and even perhaps *Everson* v. *Board of Education*...(1947). The persistent desire of a number of States to find proper means of helping sectarian education to survive would be doomed. This Court has not yet thought that such a harsh result is required by the Establishment Clause. Certainly few would consider it in the public interest. Parochial schools, quite apart from their sectarian purpose, have provided an educational alternative for millions of young Americans; they often afford wholesome competition with our public schools; and in some States they relieve substantially the tax burden incident to the operation of public schools. The State has, moreover, a legitimate interest in facilitating education of the highest quality for all children within its boundaries, whatever school their parents have chosen for them.

It is important to keep these issues in perspective. At this point in the 20th century we are quite far removed from the dangers that prompted the Framers to include the Establishment Clause in the Bill of Rights.... The risk of significant religious or denominational control over our democratic processes—or even of deep political division along religious lines—is remote, and when viewed against the positive contributions of sectarian schools, any such risk seems entirely tolerable in light of the continuing oversight of this Court. Our decisions have sought to establish principles that preserve the cherished safeguard of the Establishment Clause without resort to blind absolutism. If this endeavor means a loss of some analytical tidiness, then that too is entirely tolerable. Most of the Court's decision today follows in this tradition, and I join Parts I through VI of its opinion.

With respect to Part VII, I concur only in the judgment. I am not persuaded, nor did *Meek* hold, that all loans of secular instructional material and equipment "inescapably [have] the primary effect of providing a direct and substantial advancement of the sectarian enterprise."... If that were the case, then *Meek* surely would have overruled *Allen.* Instead the Court reaffirmed *Allen,* thereby necessarily holding that at least some such loans of materials helpful in the educational process are permissible—so long as the aid is incapable of diversion to religious uses...and so long as the materials are lent to the individual students or their parents and not to the sectarian institutions. Here the statute is expressly limited to materials incapable of diversion. Therefore the relevant question is whether the materials are such that they are "furnished for the use of *individual* students and at their request."...

The Ohio statute includes some materials such as wall maps, charts and other classroom paraphernalia for which the concept of a loan to individuals is a transparent fiction. A loan of these items is indistinguishable from forbidden "direct aid" to the sectarian institution itself, whoever the technical bailee.... Since the provision makes no attempt to separate these instructional materials from others meaningfully lent to individuals, I agree with the Court that it cannot be sustained under our precedents. But I would find no constitutional defect in a properly limited provision lending to the individuals themselves only appropriate instructional materials and equipment similar to that customarily used in public schools.

I dissent as to Part VIII, concerning field trip transportation. The Court writes as though the statute funded the salary of the teacher who takes the students on the outing. In fact only the bus and driver are provided for the limited purpose of physical movement between the school and the secular destination of the field trip. As I find this aid indistinguishable in principle from that upheld in *Everson*...I would sustain the District Court's judgment approving this part of the Ohio statute.

MR. JUSTICE STEVENS, concurring in part and dissenting in part.
The distinction between the religious and secular is a fundamental one. To quote from Clarence Darrow's argument in the *Scopes* case:
"The realm of religion...is where knowledge leaves off, and where faith begins, and it never has needed the arm of the State for support, and wherever it has received it, it has harmed both the public and the religion that it would pretend to serve."

The line drawn by the Establishment Clause of the First Amendment must also have a fundamental character. It should not differentiate between direct and indirect subsidies, or between instructional materials like globes and maps on the one hand and instructional materials like textbooks on the other....
...The financing of buildings, field trips, instructional materials, educational tests, and school books are all equally invalid. For all give aid

to the school's educational mission, which at heart is religious. On the other hand, I am not prepared to exclude the possibility that some parts of the statute before us may be administered in a constitutional manner. The State can plainly provide public health services to children attending non-public schools. The diagnostic and therapeutic services described in Parts V and VI of the Court's opinion may fall into this category. Although I have some misgivings on this point, I am not prepared to hold this part of the statute invalid on its face.

This Court's efforts to improve on the *Everson* test have not proved successful. "Corrosive precedents" have left us without firm principles on which to decide these cases. As this case demonstrates, the States have been encouraged to search for new ways of achieving forbidden ends.... What should be a "high and impregnable" wall between church and state, has been reduced to a "blurred, indistinct, and variable barrier."... The result has been, as Clarence Darrow predicted, harm to "both the public and the religion that [this aid] would pretend to serve."

Accordingly, I dissent from Parts II, III, and IV of the Court's opinion.

COURT ON SCHOOL DESEGREGATION
June 27, 1977

In two separate cases, decided June 27, the Supreme Court upheld the power of federal courts to order citywide desegregation plans, including citywide busing, to remedy illegal segregation, and reaffirmed the power of federal courts to order school districts to devise remedial courses for the victims of educational bias.

In the first case (Dayton Board of Education v. Brinkman), *the court voted 8-0 to vacate an appeals court ruling upholding a broad desegregation plan for Dayton, Ohio. Writing for the seven-man majority (Justice William J. Brennan Jr. joined only in the result, not the opinion, and Justice Thurgood Marshall did not participate), Justice William H. Rehnquist said that the imposition of a "system-wide remedy" was too broad and was not justified in view of the relatively narrow scope of the constitutional violations that the district court had found to exist. However, the court restated its June 21, 1973, decision that when school segregation had a citywide impact and was the result of illegal actions by authorities, citywide busing could be ordered. In that case, involving Denver* (Keyes v. School District No. 1, Denver), *the court ruled, 7-1, that school board policies that fostered segregation even in limited parts of a metropolitan area might affect the whole system, and the whole system required desegregation, "root and branch."*

In its 1977 ruling in the Dayton case, the Supreme Court left the city's desegregation plan in effect, pending further proceedings by the lower courts, stating that those courts could reconsider the evidence to determine whether broader violations existed than had been outlined in the district court's opinion.

Remedial Course Order

In a second case, Millikin v. Bradley, *the court ruled, 9-0, that federal courts could order school districts to provide educational programs, such as remedial reading classes, to help children recover from the effects of attending illegally segregated schools. Specifically, the ruling upheld a court-ordered desegregation plan for Detroit, Michigan, and also ordered the state to pay part of the cost of remedial programs for the victims of Detroit school segregation. The remedial programs had been ordered in addition to the extensive busing plan for the city inaugurated in January 1976.*

Writing for the court, Chief Justice Warren E. Burger contended that children who had been "educationally and culturally set apart from the larger community [would] inevitably acquire habits of speech, conduct and attitudes reflecting cultural isolation." He said the need for remedial courses in Detroit "flowed directly from constitutional violations by state and local officials."

The court's 1977 decision reaffirmed the basic finding in the 1954 ruling on school desegregation, Brown v. *Board of Education, that "separate educational facilities are inherently unequal." "Speech habits acquired in a segregated system do not vanish simply by moving the child to a desegregated school," the court wrote in 1977. "The root condition shown by this record must be treated directly by special training at the hands of teachers prepared for that task."*

Background

The Supreme Court had previously ruled on another aspect of the Detroit school system, holding in 1974 that a city-suburban desegregation plan that crossed the city limits was too extensive and not justified by the facts of the case. (Historic Documents of 1974, pp. 639-654)

In the case of Dayton, the federal district court in its first ruling on the matter, found circumstances adding up to what it called a "cumulative violation" of the Constitution and ordered a desegregation plan to remedy the situation. However, an appeals court reversed on the ground that the remedy was insufficient. The district court then devised another plan, which the appeals court again reversed as too narrow. The district court then imposed the plan involved in the 1977 case, requiring the busing of about 15,000 students. The appeals court affirmed the plan.

The Justice Department and civil rights groups then filed friend-of-the-court briefs requesting the Supreme Court to affirm the decision. In its ruling, the court stated that federal courts must enumerate specific findings regarding illegal segregation and then devise a suitable remedy. Although the lower court's finding of "cumulative violation" did not justify a broad remedy, the Supreme Court majority did not hold that there was not enough potentially available evidence in the Dayton case to support a broad remedy in subsequent court actions.

Following are excerpts from the Supreme Court's June 27, 1977, majority opinion upholding the power of federal courts to order citywide desegregation plans:

No. 76-539

Dayton Board of Education et al., Petitioners, *v.* Mark Brinkman et al.	On Writ of Certiorari to the United States Court of Appeals for the Sixth Circuit.

[June 27, 1977]

MR. JUSTICE REHNQUIST delivered the opinion of the Court.

[MR. JUSTICE MARSHALL took no part in the consideration or decision of this case.]

This school desegregation action comes to us after five years and two round trips through the lower federal courts. Those protracted proceedings have been devoted to the formulation of a remedy for actions of the Dayton Board of Education found to be in violation of the Equal Protection Clause of the Fourteenth Amendment. In the decision now under review, the Court of Appeals for the Sixth Circuit finally approved a plan involving districtwide racial distribution requirements, after rejecting two previous, less sweeping orders by the District Court. The plan required, beginning with the 1976-1977 school year, that the racial distribution of each school in the district be brought within 15 per cent of the 48-52 per cent black-white population ratio of Dayton. As finally formulated, the plan employed a variety of desegregation techniques, including the "pairing" of schools, the redefinition of attendance zones, and a variety of centralized special programs and "magnet schools." We granted certiorari...(Jan. 17, 1976), to consider the propriety of this court-ordered remedy in light of the constitutional violations which were found by the courts below.

Whatever public notice this case has received as it wended its way from the United States District Court for the Southern District of Ohio to this Court has been due to the fact that it represented an effort by minority plaintiffs to obtain relief from alleged unconstitutional segregation of the Dayton public schools said to have resulted from actions by the respondent School Board. While we would by no means discount the importance of this aspect of the case, we think that the case is every bit as important for the issues it raises as to the proper allocation of functions between the district courts and the courts of appeals within the federal judicial system.

Indeed, the importance of the judicial administration aspects of the case are heightened by the presence of the substantive issues on which it turns. The proper observance of the division of functions between the federal trial courts and the federal appellate courts is important in every case. It is especially important in a case such as this where the District Court for the Southern District of Ohio was not simply asked to render judgment in accordance with the law of Ohio in favor of one private party against another; it was asked by the plaintiffs, students in the public school system of a large city, to restructure the administration of that system.

There is no doubt that federal courts have authority to grant appropriate relief of this sort when constitutional violations on the part of school officials are proven.... But our cases have just as firmly recognized that local autonomy of school districts is a vital national tradition.... It is for this reason that the case for displacement of the local authorities by a federal court in a school desegregation case must be satisfactorily established by factual proof and justified by a reasoned statement of legal principles....

The lawsuit was begun in April 1972, and the District Court filed its original decision on February 7, 1973. The District Court first surveyed the past conduct of affairs by the Dayton School Board, and found "isolated but repeated instances of failure by the Dayton School Board to meet the standards of the Ohio law mandating an integrated school system." It cited instances of physical segregation in the schools during the early decades of this century, but concluded that "[b]oth by reason of the substantial time that had elapsed and because these practices have ceased,...the foregoing will not necessarily be deemed to be evidence of a continuing segregative policy."

The District Court also found that as recently as the 1950s, faculty hiring had not been on a racially neutral basis, but that "by 1963, under a policy designated as one of 'dynamic gradualism,' at least one black teacher had been assigned to all eleven high schools and to 35 of the 66 schools in the entire system." It further found that by 1969 each school in the Dayton system had an integrated teaching staff consisting of at least one black faculty member. The Court's conclusion with respect to faculty hiring was that pursuant to a 1971 agreement with the Department of HEW, "the teaching staff of the Dayton public schools became and still remains substantially integrated."

The District Court noted that Dunbar High School had been established in 1933 as a black high school, taught by black teachers and attended by black pupils. At the time of its creation there were no attendance zones in Dayton and students were permitted liberal transfers, so that attendance at Dunbar was voluntary. The court found that Dunbar continued to exist as a citywide all-black high school until it closed in 1962.

Turning to more recent operations of the Dayton public schools, the District Court found that the "great majority" of the 66 schools were imbalanced and that, with one exception, the Dayton School Board had made no affirmative effort to achieve racial balance within those schools. But the court stated that there was no evidence of racial discrimination in the establishment or alteration of attendance boundaries or in the site selection and construction of new schools and school additions. It considered the use of optional attendance zones within the District, and concluded that in the majority of cases the "optional zones had no racial significance at the time of their creation." It made a somewhat ambiguous finding as to the effect of some of the zones in the past, and concluded that although none of the elementary optional school attendance zones today "have any significant potential effects in terms of increased racial separation," the same cannot be said of the high school optional zones. Two zones in particular, "those between Roosevelt and Colonel White and between Kiser and Colonel White, are by far the largest in the system and have had the most demonstrable racial effects in the past."

The court found no evidence that the District's "freedom of enrollment" policy had been unfairly operated or that black students [had] been denied transfers because of their race." Finally the court considered action by a newly elected Board on January 3, 1972, rescinding resolutions, passed by the previous Board, which had acknowledged a role played by the Board in the creation of segregative racial patterns and had called for various types of remedial measures. The District Court's ultimate conclusion was that the "racially imbalanced schools, optional attendance zones, and recent Board action...are cumulatively a violation of the Equal Protection Clause."

The District Court's use of the phrase "cumulative violation" is unfortunately not free from ambiguity. Treated most favorably to the respondents, it may be said to represent the District Court's opinion that there were three separate although relatively isolated instances of unconstitutional action on the part of petitioners. Treated most favorably to the petitioners, however, they must be viewed in quite a different light. The finding that the pupil population in the various Dayton schools is not homogeneous, standing by itself, is not a violation of the Fourteenth Amendment in the absence of a showing that this condition resulted from intentionally segregative actions on the part of the Board. *Washington* v. *Davis*...(1976). The District Court's finding as to the effect of the optional attendance zones for the three Dayton high schools, assuming that it was a violation under the standards of *Washington* v. *Davis*,..., appears to be so only with respect to high school districting. *Swann* [v. *Charlotte Mecklenburg Board of Education* (1971)]. The District Court's conclusion that the Board's recision of previously adopted school board resolutions was itself a constitutional violation is also of questionable validity.

The Board had not acted to undo operative regulations affecting the assignment of pupils or other aspects of the management of school affairs..., but simply repudiated a resolution of a predecessor Board stating that it recognized its own fault in not taking affirmative action at an earlier date....

Judged most favorably to the Petitioners, then, the District Court's findings of constitutional violations did not, under our cases, suffice to justify the remedy imposed. Nor is light cast upon the District Court's finding by its repeated use of the phrase "cumulative violation." We realize, of course, that the task of factfinding in a case such as this is a good deal more difficult than is typically the case in a more orthodox lawsuit. Findings as to the motivations of multimembered public bodies are of necessity difficult...and the question of whether demographic changes resulting in racial concentration occurred from purely neutral public actions or were instead the intended result of actions which appeared neutral on their face but were in fact invidiously discriminatory is not an easy one to resolve.

We think it accurate to say that the District Court's formulation of a remedy on the basis of the three part "cumulative violation" was certainly not based on an unduly cautious understanding of its authority in such a situation. The remedy which it originally propounded in light of these findings of fact included requirements that optional attendance zones be eliminated, and that faculty assignment practices and hiring policies with respect to classified personnel be tailored to achieve representative racial distribution in all schools. The one portion of the remedial plan submitted by the School Board which the District Court refused to accept without change was that which dealt with so-called "freedom of enrollment priorities." The court ordered that, as applied to high schools, new students at each school be chosen at random from those wishing to attend. The Board was required to furnish transportation for all students who chose to attend a high school outside the attendance area of their residence.

Both the plaintiffs and the defendant School Board appealed the order of the District Court to the United States Court of Appeals for the Sixth Circuit.... That court considered at somewhat greater length than had the District Court both the historical instances of alleged racial discrimination by the Dayton School Board and the circumstances surrounding the adoption of the Board's resolutions and the subsequent rescission of those resolutions. This consideration was in a purely descriptive vein: no findings of fact made by the District Court were reversed as having been clearly erroneous, and the Court of Appeals engaged in no factfinding of its own based on evidence adduced before the District Court. The Court of Appeals then focused on the District Court's finding of a three-part "cumulative" constitutional violation consisting of racially imbalanced schools, optional attendance zones, and the rescission of the Board resolutions. It found these to be "amply supported by the evidence."

Plaintiffs in the District Court, respondents here, had cross-appealed from the order of the District Court, contending that the District Court had erred in failing to make further findings tending to show segregative actions on the part of the Dayton School Board, but the Court of Appeals found it unnecessary to pass on these contentions. The Court of Appeals also stated that it was unnecessary to "pass on the question of whether the rescission [of the Board resolutions] by itself was a violation of" constitutional rights. It did discuss at length what it described as "serious questions" as to whether Board conduct relating to staff assignment, school construction, grade structure and reorganization, and transfers and transportation, should have been included within the "cumulative violation" found by the District Court. But it did no more than discuss these questions; it neither upset the factual findings of the District Court nor did it reverse the District Court's conclusions of law.

Thus the Court of Appeals, over and above its historical discussion of the Dayton school situation, dealt with and upheld only the three-part "cumulative violation" found by the District Court. But it nonetheless reversed the District Court's approval of the school board plan as modified by the District Court, because the Court of Appeals concluded that "the remedy ordered...is inadequate, considering the scope of the cumulative violations." While it did not discuss the specifics of any plan to be adopted on remand, it repeated the admonition that the court's duty is to eliminate "all vestiges of state-imposed school segregation." *Keyes...*[v. *School District No. 1, Denver, Colorado* (1973)]; *Swann...*[1971].

Viewing the findings of the District Court as to the three-part "cumulative violation" in the strongest light for the respondents, the Court of Appeals simply had no warrant in our cases for imposing the systemwide remedy which it apparently did. There had been no showing that such a remedy was necessary to "eliminate all vestiges of the state-imposed school segregation." It is clear from the findings of the District Court that Dayton is a racially mixed community, and that many of its schools are either predominantly white or predominantly black. This fact without more, of course, does not offend the Constitution. *Spencer* v. *Kugler...*(1972); *Swann...*[1971]. The Court of Appeals seems to have viewed the present structure of the Dayton School system as a sort of "fruit of the poisonous tree," since some of the racial imbalance that presently obtains may have resulted in some part from the three instances of segregative action found by the District Court. But instead of tailoring a remedy commensurate to the three specific violations, the Court of Appeals imposed a systemwide remedy going beyond their scope.

On appeal, the task of a Court of Appeals is defined with relative clarity; it is confined by law and precedent, just as are those of the district courts and of this Court. If it concludes that the findings of the District Court are clearly erroneous, it may reverse them.... If it decides that the District Court has misapprehended the law, it may accept that court's findings of fact but reverse its judgment because of legal errors. Here, however, as we conceive the situation, the Court of Appeals did neither. It was vaguely dissatisfied with the limited character of the remedy which the District Court had afforded plaintiffs, and proceeded to institute a far more sweeping one of its own, without in any way upsetting the District Court's findings of fact or reversing its conclusions of law.

The Court of Appeals did not actually specify a remedy, but did, in increasingly strong language in subsequent opinions require that any plan eliminate systemwide patterns of one-race schools predominant in the district.... In the face of this commandment, the District Court, after twice being reversed, observed:

> "This court now reaches the reluctant conclusion that there exists no feasible method of complying with the mandate of the United States Court of Appeals for the Sixth Circuit without the transportation of a substantial number of stu-

> dents in the Dayton school system. Based upon the plans of
> both the plaintiff and defendant the assumption must be
> that the transportation of approximately 15,000 students
> on a regular and permanent basis will be required."

We think that the District Court would have been insensitive indeed
to the nuances of the repeated reversals of its orders by the Court
of Appeals had it not reached this conclusion. In effect, the Court of
Appeals imposed a remedy which we think is entirely out of proportion to the constitutional violations found by the District Court, taking
those findings of violations in the light most favorable to respondents.

   This is not to say that the last word has been spoken as to the correctness
of the District Court's findings as to unconstitutionally segregative actions
on the part of the petitioners. As we have noted, respondents appealed
from the initial decision and order of the District Court, asserting that additional violations should have been found by that court. The Court of
Appeals found it unnecessary to pass upon the respondents' contentions in
its first decision, and respondents have not cross-petitioned for certiorari
from decision of the Court of Appeals in this Court. Nonetheless, they are
entitled under our precedents to urge any grounds which would lend support to the judgment below, and we think that their contentions of unconstitutionally segregative actions, in addition to those found as fact by the
District Court, fall into this category. In view of the confusion at various
stages in this case, evident from the opinions both of the Court of Appeals
and the District Court, as to the applicable principles and appropriate
relief, the case must be remanded to the District Court for the making of
more specific findings and, if necessary, the taking of additional evidence.

   If the only deficiency in the record before us were the failure of the Court
of Appeals to pass on respondents' assignments of error respecting the initial rulings of the District Court, it would be appropriate to remand the
case to that court. But we think it evident that supplementation of the
record will be necessary. Apart from what has been said above with respect
to the use of the ambiguous phrase "cumulative violation" by both courts,
the disparity between the evidence of constitutional violations and the
sweeping remedy finally decreed requires supplementation of the record
and additional findings addressed specifically to the scope of the remedy.
It is clear that the presently mandated remedy cannot stand upon the basis
of the violations found by the District Court.

   The District Court, in the first instance, subject to review by the Court of
Appeals, must make new findings and conclusions as to violations in the
light of this opinion.... It must then fashion a remedy in the light of the
rule laid down in *Swann*...[1971] and elaborated upon in *Hills* v.
Gautreaux...(1976). The power of the federal courts to restructure the
operation of local and state governmental entities "is not plenary. It 'may
be exercised only on the basis of a constitutional violation.' *[Milliken* v.
Bradley]...quoting *Swann*.... Once a constitutional violation is found, a
federal court is required to tailor 'the scope of the remedy' to fit 'the nature
of the violation.'...*Swann"*....

The duty of both the District Court and of the Court of Appeals in a case such as this, where mandatory segregation by law of the races in the schools has long since ceased, is to first determine whether there was any action in the conduct of the business of the school board which was intended to and did in fact, discriminate against minority pupils, teachers or staff. *Washington* v. *Davis*.... All parties should be free to introduce such additional testimony and other evidence as the District Court may deem appropriate. If such violations are found, the District Court in the first instance, subject to review by the Court of Appeals, must determine how much incremental segregative effect these violations had on the racial distribution of the Dayton school population as presently constituted, when that distribution is compared to what it would have been in the absence of such constitutional violations. The remedy must be designed to redress that difference, and only if there has been a system-wide impact may there be a systemwide remedy. *Keyes*...[1973].

We realize that this is a difficult task, and that it is much easier for a reviewing court to fault ambiguous phrases such as "cumulative violation" than it is for the finder of fact to make the complex factual determinations in the first instance. Nonetheless, that is what the Constitution and our cases call for, and that is what must be done in this case.

While we have found that the plan implicitly, if not explicitly, imposed by the Court of Appeals was erroneous on the present state of the record, it is undisputed that it has been in effect in the Dayton school system during the present year without creating serious problems. While a school board and a school constituency which attempt to comply with a plan to the best of their ability should not be penalized, we think that the plan finally adopted by the District Court should remain in effect for the coming school year subject to such further orders of the District Court as it may find warranted following the hearings mandated by this opinion.

The judgment of the Court of Appeals is vacated, and the cause is remanded for further proceedings consistent with this opinion.

It is so ordered.

MR. JUSTICE BRENNAN, concurring in the judgment.

The Court today reaffirms the authority of the federal courts "to grant appropriate relief of this sort [i.e., busing] when constitutional violations on the part of school officials are proven. *Keyes* v. *School District No. 1, Denver, Colorado*...(1973)...." In this case, however, the violations actually found by the District Court were not sufficient to justify the remedy imposed. Indeed, none of the parties contends otherwise. Respondents nowhere argue that the three "cumulative violations" should by themselves be sufficient to support the comprehensive, systemwide busing order imposed. Instead, they urge us to find that other, additional actions by the school board appearing in the record should be used to support the result. The United States, as *amicus curiae,* concedes that the "three-part 'cumulative' violation found by the district court does not support its remedial order"...and also urges us to affirm the busing order by resort to other, additional evidence in the record. Under this circumstance, I agree with the result reached by the Court. I do so because it is clear from the holding in this case, and that in *Milliken* v. *Bradley*...(1977), also decided today, that the "broad and flexible equity powers" of district courts to remedy unlawful school segregation continue unimpaired.

This case thus does not turn upon any doubt of power in the federal courts to remedy state-imposed segregation. Rather, as the Court points out, it turns upon the "proper allocation of functions between the district courts and the courts of appeals within the federal judicial system.".... As the Court recognizes, the task of the district courts and courts of appeals is a particularly difficult one in school desegregation cases.... Although the efforts of both the District Court and the Court of Appeals in this protracted litigation deserve our commendation, it is plain that the proceedings in the two courts resulted in a remedy going beyond the violations so far found.

On remand, the task of the District Court, subject to review by the Court of Appeals, will be to make further findings of fact from evidence already in the record, and, if appropriate, as supplemented by additional evidence. The additional facts, combined with those upon which the violations already found are based, must then be evaluated to determine what relief is appropriate to remedy the resulting unconstitutional segregation. In making this determination, the courts of course "need not, and cannot, close their eyes to inequalities, shown by the record, which flow from a long-standing segregated system." *Milliken* v. *Bradley*....

Although the three violations already found are not of themselves sufficient to support the broad remedial order entered below, this is not to say that the three violations are insignificant. While they are not sufficient to justify the remedy imposed when considered solely as unconstitutional *actions,* they clearly are very significant as indicia of *intent* on the part of the school board. As we emphasized in *Keyes*..., "Plainly, a finding of intentional segregation as to a portion of a school system is not devoid of probative value in assessing the school authorities' intent with respect to other parts of the same school system." Once segregative intent is found, the District Court may more readily conclude that not only blatant, but also subtle actions—and in some circumstances even inaction—justify a finding of unconstitutional segregation that must be redressed by a remedial busing order such as that imposed in this case.

If it is determined on remand that the school board's unconstitutional actions had a "systemwide impact," then the court should order a "systemwide remedy.".... Under *Keyes,* once a school board's actions have created a segregated dual school system, then the school board "has the affirmative duty to desegregate the entire system 'root and branch.' "... Or, as stated by the Court today in *Milliken,* the school board must "take the necessary steps 'to eliminate from the public schools all vestiges of state-imposed segregation.' " ...[*Keyes*] quoting *Swann* v. *Charlotte-Mecklenburg Board of Education*...(1971). A judicial decree to accomplish this result must be formulated with great sensitivity to the practicalities of the situation, without ever losing sight of the paramount importance of the constitutional rights being enforced. The District Court must be mindful not only of its "authority to grant appropriate relief,"... but also of its duty to remedy fully those constitutional violations it finds. It should be flexible but unflinching in its use of its equitable powers, always conscious that it is the rights of individual school children that are at stake, and that it is the constitutional right to equal treatment for all races that is being protected.

MR. JUSTICE STEVENS, concurring.

With the caveat that the relevant finding of intent in a case of this kind necessarily depends primarily on objective evidence concerning the effect of the Board's action, rather than the subjective motivation of one or more members of the Board, see *Washington* v. *Davis*...[1976].

(STEVENS, J., concurring), I join the Court's opinion.

Following are excerpts from the Supreme Court's decision June 27, 1977, ruling that federal courts could order school districts to provide remedial educational programs to overcome the effects of attending illegally segregated schools:

No. 76-447

William G. Milliken, Governor of the State of Michigan, et al., Petitioners, *v.* Ronald Bradley et al.	On Writ of Certiorari to the United States Court of Appeals for the Sixth Circuit.

[June 27, 1977]

MR. CHIEF JUSTICE BURGER delivered the opinion of the Court.

We granted certiorari in this case to consider two questions concerning the remedial powers of federal district courts in school desegregation cases, namely, whether a District Court can, as part of a desegregation decree, order compensatory or remedial educational programs for schoolchildren who have been subjected to past acts of *de jure* segregation, and whether, consistent with the Eleventh Amendment, a federal court can require state officials found responsible for constitutional violations to bear part of the costs of those programs.

457

I

This case is before the Court for the second time following our remand, *Milliken* v. *Bradley*...(1974) *(Milliken I);* it marks the culmination of seven years of litigation over *de jure* school segregation in the Detroit Public School System. For almost six years, the litigation has focused exclusively on the appropriate remedy to correct official acts of racial discrimination committed by both the Detroit School Board and the State of Michigan. No challenge is now made by the state or the local school board to the prior findings of *de jure* segregation.

In the first stage of the remedy proceedings, which we reviewed in *Milliken I*...the District Court, after reviewing several "Detroit-only" desegregation plans, concluded that an interdistrict plan was required to " 'achieve the greatest degree of actual desegregation...[so that] no school, grade or classroom [would be] substantially disproportionate to the overall pupil racial composition.' "... On those premises, the District Court ordered the parties to submit plans for "metropolitan desegregation" and appointed a nine-member panel to formulate a desegregation plan, which would encompass a "desegregation area" consisting of 54 school districts.

In June 1973, a divided Court of Appeals, sitting en banc, upheld the District Court's determination that a metropolitan-wide plan was essential to bring about what the District Court had described as "the greatest degree of actual desegregation...." We reversed, holding that the order exceeded appropriate limits of federal equitable authority as defined in *Swann* v. *Charlotte-Mecklenburg Board of Educ*....(1971), by concluding that "as a matter of substantive constitutional right, [a] particular degree of racial balance" is required, and by subjecting other school districts, uninvolved with and unaffected by any constitutional violations, to the court's remedial powers.... Proceeding from the *Swann* standard "that the scope of the remedy is determined by the nature and extent of the constitutional violation," we held that, on the record before us, there was no interdistrict violation calling for an interdistrict remedy. Because the District Court's "metropolitan remedy" went beyond the constitutional violation, we remanded the case for further proceedings "leading to prompt formulation of a decree directed to eliminating the segregation found to exist in the Detroit city schools, a remedy which has been delayed since 1970."... On April 1, 1975, both parties submitted their proposed plans. Respondent Bradley's plan was limited solely to pupil reassignment; the proposal called for extensive transportation of students to achieve the plan's ultimate goal of assuring that every school within the district reflected, within 15 percentage points, the racial ratio of the school district as a whole. In contrast to respondent Bradley's proposal, the Detroit Board's plan provided for sufficient pupil reassignment to eliminate "racially identifiable white schools," while ensuring that "every child will spend at least a portion of his education in either a neighborhood elementary school or a neighborhood junior and senior high school."... By eschewing racial ratios for each school, the Board's plan contemplated transportation of fewer students for shorter distances than respondent Bradley's proposal.

In addition to student reassignments, the Board's plan called for implementation of 13 remedial or compensatory programs, referred to in the record as "educational components." These compensatory programs, which were proposed in addition to the plan's provisions for magnet schools and vocational high schools, included three of the four components at issue in this case—in service training for teachers and administrators, guidance and counseling programs, and revised testing procedures. Pursuant to the District Court's direction, the State Department of Education on April 21, 1975, submitted a critique of the Detroit Board's desegregation plan; in its report, the Department opined that, although "[i]t is possible that none of the thirteen 'quality education' components is essential...to correct the constitutional violation....", eight of the 13 proposed programs nonetheless deserved special consideration in the desegregation setting....

II

This Court has not previously addressed directly the question whether federal courts can order remedial education programs as part of a school desegregation decree. However, the general principles governing our resolution of this issue are well settled by the prior decisions of this Court. In the first case concerning federal courts' remedial powers in eliminating *de jure* school segregation, the Court laid down the basic rule which governs to this day: "In fashioning and effectuating the [desegregation] decrees, the courts will be guided by equitable principles." *Brown* v. *Board of Education*...(1955) *(Brown II).*

Application of those "equitable principles," we have held, requires federal courts to focus upon three factors. In the first place, like other equitable remedies, the nature of the desegregation remedy is to be determined by the nature and scope of the constitutional violation. *Swann* v. *Charlotte-Mecklenburg Board of Education....* The remedy must therefore be related to "the *condition* alleged to offend the Constitution...." *Milliken I....* Second, the decree must indeed be *remedial* in nature, that is, it must be designed as nearly as possible "to restore the victims of discriminatory conduct to the position they would have occupied in the absence of such conduct."... Third, the federal courts in devising a remedy must take into account the interests of state and local authorities in managing their own affairs, consistent with the Constitution. In *Brown II* the Court squarely held that "[s]chool authorities have the *primary* responsibility for elucidating, assessing, and solving these problems...." If, however, "school authorities fail in their affirmative obligations...judicial authority may be invoked."... Once invoked, "the scope of a district court's equitable powers to remedy past wrongs is broad, for breadth and flexibility are inherent in equitable remedies."...

In challenging the order before us, petitioners do not specifically question that the District Court's mandated programs are designed, as nearly as practicable, to restore the schoolchildren of Detroit to the position they would have enjoyed absent constitutional violations by state and local officials. And, petitioners do not contend, nor could they, that the prerogatives of the Detroit School Board have been abrogated by the decree, since of course the Detroit School Board itself proposed incorporation of these programs in the first place. Petitioners' sole contention is that, under *Swann,* the District Court's order exceeds the scope of the constitutional violation. Invoking our holding in *Milliken I...,* petitioners claim that, since the constitutional violation found by the District Court was the unlawful segregation of students on the basis of race, the court's decree must be limited to remedying unlawful pupil assignments. This contention misconceives the principle petitioners seek to invoke, and we reject their argument.

The well-settled principle that the nature and scope of the remedy is to be determined by the violation means simply that federal court decrees must directly address and relate to the constitutional violation itself. Because of this inherent limitation upon federal judicial authority, federal court decrees exceed appropriate limits if they are aimed at eliminating a condition that does not violate the Constitution or does not flow from such a violation, see *Pasadena City Board of Education* v. *Spangler...*[1976], or if they are imposed upon governmental units that were neither involved in nor affected by the constitutional violation, as in *Milliken I.... Hills* v. *Gautreaux...*(1976). But where, as here, a constitutional violation has been found, the remedy does not "exceed" the violation if the remedy is tailored to cure the *"condition* that offends the Constitution." *Milliken I....*

The "condition" offending the Constitution is Detroit's *de jure* segregated school system, which was so pervasively and persistently segregated that the District Court found that the need for the educational components flowed directly from constitutional violations by both state and local officials. These specific educational remedies, although normally left to the discretion of the elected school board and professional educators, were deemed necessary to restore the victims of discriminatory conduct to the position they would have enjoyed in terms of education had these four components been provided in a nondiscriminatory manner in a school system free from pervasive *de jure* racial segregation.

In the first case invalidating a *de jure* system, a unanimous Court, speaking through Chief Justice Warren, held in *Brown I:* "Separate educational facilities are inherently unequal." *Brown* v. *Board of Education...*(1954). And in *United States* v. *Montgomery County Board of Education...*(1969), the Court concerned itself not with pupil assignment, but with the desegregation of faculty and staff as part of the process of dismantling a dual system. In doing so, the Court, there speaking through Mr. Justice Black, focused on the reason for judicial concerns going beyond pupil assignment: "The dispute...deals with faculty and staff desegregation, a goal that we have recognized to be an important aspect of *the basic task of achieving a public school system wholly free from racial discrimination."...*

Montgomery County therefore stands firmly for the proposition that matters other than pupil assignment must on occasion be addressed by federal courts to eliminate the effects of prior segregation. Similarly, in *Swann* we reaffirmed the principle laid down in *Green* v. *County School Board* [of New Kenty County (1968)] that "existing policy and practice with respect to faculty, staff, transportation, extracurricular activities, and facilities were among the most important indicia of a segregated system."... In a word, discriminatory student assignment policies can themselves manifest and breed other inequalities built into a dual system founded on racial discrimination. Federal courts need not, and cannot, close their eyes to inequalities, shown by the record, which flow from a longstanding segregated system.

In light of the mandate of *Brown I* and *Brown II,* federal courts have, over the years, often required the inclusion of remedial programs in desegregation plans to overcome the inequalities inherent in dual school systems....

...[I]n addition to other remedial programs, which could, if circumstances warranted, include programs to remedy deficiencies, particularly in reading and communication skills, federal courts have expressly ordered special in-service training for teachers,...and have altered or even suspended testing programs employed by school systems undergoing desegregation....

...We do not, of course, imply that the order here is a blueprint for other cases. That cannot be; in school desegregation cases, "[t]here is no universal answer to complex problems...; there is obviously no plan that will do the job in every case." *Green....* On this record, however, we are bound to conclude that the decree before us was aptly tailored to remedy the consequences of the constitutional violation. Children who have been thus educationally and culturally set apart from the larger community will inevitably acquire habits of speech, conduct, and attitudes reflecting their cultural isolation. They are likely to acquire speech habits, for example, which vary from the environment in which they must ultimately function and compete, if they are to enter and be a part of that community. This is not peculiar to race; in this setting, it can affect any children who, as a group, are isolated by force of law from the mainstream....

Pupil assignment alone does not automatically remedy the impact of previous, unlawful educational isolation; the consequences linger and can be dealt with only by independent measures. In short, speech habits acquired in a segregated system do not vanish simply by moving the child to a desegregated school. The root condition shown by this record must be treated directly by special training at the hands of teachers prepared for that task. This is what the District Judge in the case drew from the record before him as to the consequences of Detroit's *de jure* system, and we cannot conclude that the remedies decreed exceeded the scope of the violations found.

Nor do we find any other reason to believe that the broad and flexible equity powers of the court were abused in this case. The established role of local school authorities was maintained inviolate,. and the remedy is indeed remedial. The order does not punish anyone, nor does it impair or jeopardize the educational system in Detroit....

III

Petitioners also contend that the District Court's order, even if otherwise proper, violates the Eleventh Amendment. In their view, the requirement that the state defendants pay one-half the additional costs attributable to the four educational components is, "in practical effect, indistinguishable from an award of money damages against the state based upon the asserted prior misconduct of state officials."... Arguing from this premise, petitioners conclude that the "award" in this case is barred under this Court's holding in *Edelman* v. *Jordan....* (1974).

...The decree to share the future costs of educational components in this case fits squarely within the prospective-compliance exception reaffirmed by *Edelman*. That exception...permits federal courts to enjoin state officials to conform their conduct to requirements of federal law, notwithstanding a direct and substantial impact on the state treasury.... The order challenged here does no more than that. The decree requires state officials, held responsible for unconstitutional conduct, in findings which are not challenged, to eliminate a *de jure* segregated school system. More precisely, the burden of state officials is that set forth in *Swann*—to take the necessary steps "to eliminate from the public schools all vestiges of state-imposed segregation."... The educational components, which the District Court ordered into effect *prospectively,* are plainly designed to wipe out continuing conditions of inequality produced by the inherently unequal dual school system long maintained by Detroit.

These programs were not, and as a practical matter could not be, intended to wipe the slate clean by one bold stroke, as could a retroactive award of money in *Edelman*. Rather, by the nature of the antecedent violation, which on this record caused significant deficiencies in communications skills—reading and speaking—the victims of Detroit's *de jure* segregated system will continue to experience the effects of segregation until such future time as the remedial programs can help dissipate the continuing effects of past misconduct. Reading and speech deficiencies cannot be eliminated by judicial fiat; they will require time, patience, and the skills of specially trained teachers. That the programs are also "compensatory" in nature does not change the fact that they are part of a plan that operates *prospectively* to bring about the delayed benefits of a unitary school system. We therefore hold that such prospective relief is not barred by the Eleventh Amendment.

Finally, there is no merit to petitioners' claims that the relief ordered here violates the Tenth Amendment and general principles of federalism. The Tenth Amendment's reservation of nondelegated powers to the States is not implicated by a federal court judgment enforcing the express prohibitions of unlawful state conduct enacted by the Fourteenth

Amendment.... Nor are principles of federalism abrogated by the decree. The District Court has neither attempted to restructure local governmental entities nor to mandate a particular method or structure of state or local financing.... The District Court has, rather, properly enforced the guarantees of the Fourteenth Amendment consistent with our prior holdings, and in a manner that does not jeopardize the integrity of the structure or functions of state and local government.

The judgement of the Court of Appeals is therefore affirmed.

Affirmed.

MR. JUSTICE MARSHALL, concurring.

I wholeheartedly join THE CHIEF JUSTICE's opinion for the Court. My Brother POWELL's opinion prompts these additional comments.

What is, to me, most tragic about this case is that in all relevant respects it is in no way unique. That a northern school board has been found guilty of intentionally discriminatory acts is, unfortunately, not unusual. That the academic development of black children has been impaired by this wrongdoing is to be expected. And, therefore, that a program of remediation is necessary to supplement the primary remedy of pupil reassignment is inevitable.

It is of course true, as MR. JUSTICE POWELL notes, that the Detroit School Board has belatedly recognized its responsibility for the injuries that Negroes have suffered, and has joined in the effort to remedy them. He may be right—although I hope not—that this makes the case "wholly different from any prior case.".... But I think it worth noting that the legal issues would be no different if the Detroit School Board came to this Court on the other side. The question before us still would be the one posed by the State: Is the remedy tailored to fit the scope of the violation. And as THE CHIEF JUSTICE convincingly demonstrates, that question would have to be answered in the affirmative in light of the findings of the District Court, supported by abundant evidence....

MR. JUSTICE POWELL, concurring in the judgment.

The Court's opinion addresses this case as if it were conventional desegregation litigation. The wide-ranging opinion reiterates the familiar general principles drawn from the line of precedents commencing with *Brown* v. *Board of Education*...(1954).... One has to read the opinion closely to understand that the case, as it finally reaches us, is wholly different from any prior case. I write to emphasize its uniqueness, and the consequent limited precedential effect of much of the Court's opinion.

Normally, the plaintiffs in this type of litigation are students, parents and supporting organizations who desire to desegregate a school system alleged to be the product, in whole or in apart, of *de jure* segregative action by the public school authorities. The principal defendant is usually the local board of education or school board. Occasionally the state board of education and state officials are joined as defendants. This protracted litigation commenced in 1970 in this conventional mold. In the intervening years, however, the posture of the litigation has changed so drastically as to leave it largely a friendly suit between the plaintiffs (respondents Bradley, *et al.*) and the original principal defendant, the Detroit School Board. These parties, antagonistic for years, have now joined forces apparently for the purpose of extracting funds from the state treasury. As between the original principal parties—the plaintiffs and the Detroit School Board—no case or controversy remains on the issues now before us. The Board enthusiastically supports the entire desegregation decree even though the decree intrudes deeply on the Board's own decisionmaking powers. Indeed, the present School Board *proposed* most of the educational components included in the District Court's decree. The plaintiffs originally favored a desegregation plan that would have required more extensive transportation of pupils, and they did not initially propose or endorse the educational components. In this Court, however, the plaintiffs also support the decree of the District Court as affirmed by the Court of Appeals.

Thus the only complaining party is the State of Michigan (acting through state officials), and its basic complaint concerns *money,* not desegregation. It has been ordered to pay about $5,800,000 to the Detroit School Board. This is one-half the estimated "excess cost" of four of the 11 educational components included in the desegregation decree: remedial reading, in-service training of teachers, testing, and counseling. The State, understandably anxious to preserve the state budget from federal court control or interference, now contests the decree....

...Given the foregoing unique circumstances, it seems to me that the proper disposition of this case is to dismiss the writ of certiorari as improvidently granted. But as the Court has chosen to decide the case here, I join in the judgment as a result less likely to prolong the disruption of education in Detroit than a reversal or remand. Despite wide-ranging dicta in the Court's opinion, the only issue decided is that the District Court's findings as to specific constitutional violations justified the four remedial educational components included in the desegregation decree. In my view, it is at least arguable that the findings in this respect were too generalized to meet the standards prescribed by this Court.... But the majority views the record as justifying the conclusion that "the need for educational components flowed directly from constitutional violations by both state and local officials."... On that view of the record, our settled doctrine requiring that the remedy be carefully tailored to fit identified constitutional violations is reaffirmed by today's result. I therefore concur in the judgment.

COURT ON NIXON
TAPES AND PAPERS

June 28, 1977

The Supreme Court June 28 upheld as constitutional the 1974 Act of Congress placing the tapes and papers of the Nixon administration in the custody of the federal government, not the former President. Nixon had challenged the Presidential Recordings and Materials Preservation Act of 1974 (PL 93-526) as violating the separation of powers, presidential privilege, his personal privacy, his First Amendment rights, his Fourth Amendment right to be free from unreasonable search and seizure, his right to equal protection of the laws and the constitutional ban on bills of attainder—laws enacted to punish a specific individual.

The court's decision came in a lawsuit filed by Nixon on Dec. 20, 1974, the day after President Ford signed the bill. On Jan. 7, 1976, a special panel made up of three federal judges in Washington, D.C., upheld the 1974 law. Nixon's lawyers then appealed the decision to the Supreme Court.

In its June 28 ruling, the Supreme Court left unresolved, but set for argument before the justices in the 1977-1978 term, the question of the copying, sale and broadcasting of the Nixon tapes used as evidence at the Watergate coverup trial. Those tapes were the subject of the Supreme Court's 1974 decision in the Watergate matter. In that ruling, the court resoundingly rejected Nixon's claim of absolute privilege to withhold evidence from the Watergate prosecutor. The President's general need to preserve the confidentiality of his conversations was not strong enough to justify Nixon's withholding of evidence relevant to a criminal trial, the unanimous court held July 24. (Historic Documents of 1974, pp. 621-628)

The 1974 act was enacted by Congress primarily to override the agreement reached by Nixon, soon after his resignation, with the General Ser-

465

vices Administrator, providing that his papers and tapes would be shipped to California, placed in Nixon's custody, and that some of them would eventually be destroyed.

By a vote of 7-2, the justices rejected Nixon's many-pronged attack on the law placing the papers and tapes in federal custody. The majority opinion was written by Justice William J. Brennan Jr.; Chief Justice Warren E. Burger and William H. Rehnquist dissented. (Richard M. Nixon, Appellant, v. Administrator of General Services et al.)

The material consisted of some 42 million pages and 880 tape recordings.

Majority Opinion

The majority did not deny that some of the rights which Nixon asserted might be infringed by the law, but it saw those encroachments as minor in light of the public interest in preserving the materials from the Nixon administration. The dissenters, on the other hand, viewed that need as insufficient to justify such an intrusion by one branch of the government into the affairs of another.

Dealing first with Nixon's argument that the act did violate the separation of powers, Brennan wrote that the former President's claim was based on "an archaic view of the separation of powers as requiring three airtight departments of government." The act did not so intrude on executive branch prerogatives that it hindered that branch's accomplishment of its constitutional functions, he continued, and so was upheld against that challenge.

Executive privilege would no more be infringed by the screening of these materials by executive branch archivists, as the law directed, wrote Brennan, than it was by federal Judge John J. Sirica's private screening of the White House tapes which Nixon turned over to him for use as evidence at the coverup trial.

There was no reason to believe now that the still unissued regulations to govern public access to the Nixon materials after screening would not be carefully drawn to protect presidential privacy. Furthermore, all the purely personal materials contained in the mass of material would be immediately returned to Nixon once they were separated out, the court stated. The screening of Nixon's papers by the archivists would be very little different, Brennan wrote, from the screening of any President's papers before they were moved into a presidential library.

And the 1974 law was not a bill of attainder to punish Nixon, the majority held. The fact that it affected him alone was justified because he "constituted a legitimate class of one, and this provides a basis for Congress' decision to proceed with dispatch with respect to his materials, while accepting the status of his successor's papers and ordering the further consideration of generalized standards to govern his successors."

Justice John Paul Stevens, in concurring, noted that Nixon "resigned his office under unique circumstances and accepted a pardon for offenses committed while in office. By so doing he placed himself in a different class from all other Presidents."

In Dissent

Justice Rehnquist warned that this decision "will daily stand as a veritable sword of Damocles over every succeeding President and his advisers." The law was "a clear violation of the constitutional separation of powers," he wrote. "I find no support in the Constitution or in our cases for the court's pronouncement that the operations of the Office of the President may be severely impeded by Congress simply because Congress had a good reason for doing so."

This decision, wrote Chief Justice Burger, was "a grave repudiation of nearly 200 years of judicial precedent and historical practice.... To 'punish' one person, Congress—and now the Court—tears into the fabric of our constitutional framework." Criticizing the majority's analysis of the separation-of-powers issue as "superficial in the extreme," Burger continued: "Separation-of-powers principles are no less eroded simply because Congress goes through a 'minuet' of directing Executive Department employees rather than the Secretary of the Senate...to possess and control presidential papers. Whether there has been a violation of separation-of-powers principles depends not on the identity of the custodians, but upon which branch has commanded the custodians to act. Here, Congress has given the command."

The law would severely affect the conduct of executive branch matters, Burger continued; it would "be a 'ghost' at future White House conferences with conferees choosing their words more cautiously because of the enlarged prospect of compelled disclosure to others."

> *Following are excerpts from the Supreme Court's ruling, delivered June 28, 1977, on the Nixon tapes and papers placing the documents in the custody of the federal government. (Boldface headings in brackets have been added by Congressional Quarterly to highlight the organization of the text.):*

No. 75-1605

Richard M. Nixon, Appellant,	On Appeal from the United
v.	States District Court for the
Administrator of General	District of Columbia.
Services et al.	

[June 28, 1977]

MR. JUSTICE BRENNAN delivered the opinion of the Court.

Title I of Pub. L. 93-526 (1974)..., the "Presidential Recordings and Materials Preservation Act," directs the Administrator of General Services, an official of the Executive Branch, to take custody of the Presidential papers and tape recordings of appellant, former President Richard M. Nixon, and promulgate regulations that (1) provide for the orderly processing and screening by Executive Branch archivists of such materials for the purpose of returning to appellant those that are personal and private in nature, and (2) determine the terms and conditions upon which public access may eventually be had to those materials that are retained. The question for decision is whether Title I is unconstitutional on its face as a violation of (1) separation of powers; (2) Presidential privilege doctrines; (3) appellant's privacy interests; (4) appellant's First Amendment associational rights; or (5) the Bill of Attainder Clause.

On December 19, 1974, four months after appellant resigned as President of the United States, his successor, President Gerald R. Ford, signed Pub. L. 93-526 into law.... The next day, December 20, 1974, appellant filed this action in the District Court for the District of Columbia, which under § 105 (a) of the Act has exclusive jurisdiction to entertain complaints challenging the Act's legal or constitutional validity, or that of any regulation promulgated by the Administrator. Appellant's complaint challenged the Act's constitutionality on a number of grounds and sought declaratory and injunctive relief against its enforcement. A three-judge District Court was convened.... Because regulations required by...the Act governing public access to the materials were not yet effective, the District Court held that questions going to the possibility of future public release under regulations yet to be published were not ripe for review. It found that there was "no need and no justification for this court now to reach constitutional claims directed at the regulations...the promulgation of [which] might eliminate, limit or cast [the constitutional claims] in a different light."... Accordingly, the District Court limited review "to consideration of the propriety of injunctive relief against the alleged facial unconstitutionality of the statute"...and held that the challenges to the facial constitutionality of the Act were without merit. It therefore dismissed the complaint.... We noted probable jurisdiction.... We affirm.

The Background

The materials at issue consist of some 42 million pages of documents and some 880 tape recordings of conversations. Upon his resignation, appellant directed government archivists to pack and ship the materials to him in California. This shipment was delayed when the Watergate Special Prosecutor advised President Ford of his continuing need for the materials. At the same time, President Ford requested that the Attorney General give his opinion respecting ownership of the materials. The Attorney General advised that the historical practice of former Presidents and the absence of any governing statute to the contrary supported ownership in the appellant, with a possible limited exception..... The Attorney General's opinion emphasized, however, that

> "[h]istorically, there has been consistent acknowledgement that Presidential materials are peculiarly affected by a public interest

which may justify subjecting the absolute ownership rights of the
ex-President to certain limitations directly related to the character
of the documents as records of government activity."

On September 8, 1974, after issuance of the Attorney General's opinion,
the Administrator of General Services, Arthur F. Sampson, announced
that he had signed a depository agreement with appellant.... We shall
refer to the agreement as the Nixon-Sampson agreement.... The agreement
recited that appellant retained "all legal and equitable title to the
Materials, including all literary property rights," and that the materials
accordingly were to be "deposited temporarily" near appellant's California
home in an "existing facility belonging to the United States." The agreement stated further that appellant's purpose was "to donate" the
materials to the United States "with appropriate restrictions." It was
provided that all of the materials "shall be placed within secure storage
areas to which access can be gained only by use of two keys," one in
appellant's possession and the other in the possession of the Archivist of
the United States or members of his staff. With exceptions not material
here, appellant agreed "not to withdraw from deposit any originals of the
materials" for a period of three years, but reserved the right to "make
reproductions" and to authorize other persons to have access on conditions
prescribed by him. After three years, appellant might exercise the "right to
withdraw from deposit without formality any or all of the Materials...and
to retain...[them] for any purpose..." determined by him.

The Nixon-Sampson agreement treated the tape recordings separately.
They were donated to the United States "effective September 1, 1979" and
meanwhile "shall remain on deposit." It was provided however that
"subsequent to September 1, 1979 the administrator shall destroy such
tapes as [Mr. Nixon] shall direct" and in any event the tapes "shall be
destroyed at the time of [his] death or on September 1, 1984, whichever
event shall first occur." Otherwise the tapes were not to be withdrawn, and
reproductions would be made only by "mutual agreement." Access until
September 1, 1979, was expressly reserved to appellant, except as he might
authorize access by others on terms prescribed by him.

Public announcement of the agreement was followed 10 days later,
September 18, by the introduction of S. 4016 by 13 Senators in the United
States Senate. The bill, which became Pub. L. 93-526 and was
designed...to abrogate the Nixon-Sampson agreement, passed the Senate
on October 4, 1974. It was awaiting action in the House of Representatives
when on October 17, 1974, appellant filed suit in the District Court seeking
specific enforcement of the Nixon-Sampson agreement. That action was
consolidated with other suits seeking access to Presidential materials pursuant to the Freedom of Information Act...and also seeking injunctive
relief against enforcement of the agreement.... The House passed its version of the Senate bill on December 3, 1974. Following conference committee action, both Houses of Congress passed the conference version of S.
4016 on December 9, 1974, and President Ford signed it into law on
December 19....

The Scope of the Inquiry

The District Court correctly focused on the Act's requirement that the Administrator of General Services administer the tape recordings and materials placed in his custody only under regulations promulgated by him providing for the orderly processing of such materials for the purpose of returning to appellant such of them as are personal and private in nature, and of determining the terms and conditions upon which public access may eventually be had to those remaining in the Government's possession. The District Court also noted that in designing the regulations, the Administrator must consider the need to protect the constitutional rights of appellant and other individuals against infringement by the processing itself or, ultimately, by public access to the materials retained....

...The constitutional questions to be decided are, of course, of considerable importance. They touch the relationship between two of the three coordinate branches of the Federal Government, the Executive and the Legislative, and the relationship of appellant to his Government. They arise in a context unique in the history of the Presidency and present issues that this Court has had no occasion heretofore to address. Judge McGowan, speaking for the District Court, comprehensively canvassed all the claims, and in a thorough opinion, concluded that none had merit. Our independent examination of the issues brings us to the same conclusion, although our analysis differs somewhat on some questions.

Claims Concerning the Autonomy of the Executive Branch

The Act was the product of joint action by the Congress and President Ford, who signed the bill into law. It is therefore urged by intervenor-appellees that, in this circumstance, the case does not truly present a controversy concerning the separation of powers, or a controversy concerning the Presidential privilege of confidentiality, because, it is argued, such claims may be asserted only by incumbents who are presently responsible to the American people for their action. We reject the argument that only an incumbent President may assert such claims and hold that appellant, as a former President, may also be heard to assert them. We further hold, however, that neither his separation of powers claim nor his claim of breach of constitutional privilege has merit.

Appellant argues broadly that the Act encroaches upon the Presidential prerogative to control internal operations of the Presidential office and therefore offends the autonomy of the Executive Branch. The argument is divided into separate but interrelated parts.

First, appellant contends that Congress is without power to delegate to a subordinate officer of the Executive Branch the decision whether to disclose Presidential materials and to prescribe the terms that govern any disclosure. To do so, appellant contends, constitutes, without more, an impermissible interference by the Legislative Branch into matters inherently the business solely of the Executive Branch.

Second, appellant contends, somewhat more narrowly, that by authorizing the Administrator to take custody of all Presidential materials in a "broad, undifferentiated" manner, and authorizing future publication except where a privilege is affirmatively established, the Act offends the presumptive confidentiality of Presidential communications recognized in *United States* v. *Nixon...* (1974). He argues that the District Court erred in two respects in rejecting this contention. Initially, he contends that the District Court erred in distinguishing incumbent from former Presidents in evaluating appellant's claim of confidentiality. Appellant asserts that, unlike the very specific privilege protecting against disclosure of state secrets and sensitive information concerning military or diplomatic matters, which appellant concedes may be asserted only by an incumbent President, a more generalized Presidential privilege survives the termination of the President-advisor relationship much as the attorney-client privilege survives the relationship that creates it. Appellant further argues that the District Court erred in applying a balancing test to his claim of Presidential privilege and in concluding that, notwithstanding the fact that some of the materials might legitimately be included within a claim of Presidential confidentiality, substantial public interests outweighed and justified the limited inroads on Presidential confidentiality necessitated by the Act's provision for government custody and screening of the materials. Finally, appellant contends that the Act's authorization of the process of screening the materials itself violates the privilege and will chill the future exercise of constitutionally protected executive functions, thereby impairing the ability of future Presidents to obtain the candid advice necessary to the conduct of their constitutionally imposed duties.

Separation of Powers

We reject at the outset appellant's argument that the Act's regulation of the disposition of Presidential materials within the Executive Branch constitutes, without more, a violation of the principle of separation of powers. Neither President Ford nor President Carter supports this claim. The Executive Branch became a party to the Act's regulation when President Ford signed the Act into law, and the administration of President Carter, acting through the Solicitor General, vigorously supports affirmance of the District Court's judgment sustaining its constitutionality. Moreover, the control over the materials remains in the Executive Branch. The Administrator of the General Services Administration, who must promulgate and administer the regulations that are the keystone of the statutory scheme, is himself an official of the Executive Branch, appointed by the President. The career archivists appointed to do the initial screening for the purpose of selecting out and returning to appellant his private and personal papers similarly are Executive Branch employees.

Appellant's argument is in any event based on an interpretation of the separation of powers doctrine inconsistent with the origins of that doctrine, recent decisions of the Court, and the contemporary realities of our political system. True, it has been said that "each of the three general departments of government [must remain] entirely free from the control of coercive influence, direct or indirect, of either of the others...and that "[t]he sound application of a principle that makes one master in his own house precludes him from imposing his control in the house of another who is master there."... Like the District Court, we therefore find that appellant's argument rests upon an "archaic view of the separation of powers as requiring three airtight departments of Government,"... Rather, in determining whether the Act disrupts the proper balance between the coordinate branches, the proper inquiry focuses on the extent to which it prevents the Executive Branch from accomplishing its constitutionally assigned functions. *United States* v. *Nixon*.... Only where the potential for disruption is present must we then determine whether that impact is justified by an overriding need to promote objectives within the constitutional authority of Congress....

...The Executive Branch remains in full control of the Presidential materials, and the Act facially is designed to ensure that the materials can be released only when release is not barred by some applicable privilege inherent in that branch.

Thus, whatever are the future possibilities for constitutional conflict in the promulgation of regulations respecting public access to particular documents, nothing contained in the Act renders it unduly disruptive of the Executive Branch and, therefore, unconstitutional on its face. And, of course, there is abundant statutory precedent for the regulation and mandatory disclosure of documents in the possession of the Executive Branch.... Such regulation of material generated in the Executive Branch has never been considered invalid as has invasion of its privacy.... Similar congressional power to regulate Executive Branch documents exists in this instance, a power augmented by the important interests that the Act seeks to attain....

Presidential Privilege

Having concluded that the separation of powers principle is not necessarily violated by the Administrator's taking custody and screening appellant's papers, we next consider appellant's more narrowly defined claim that the Presidential privilege shields these records from archival scrutiny. We start with what was established in *United States* v. *Nixon*... —that the privilege is a qualified one. Appellant had argued in that case that *in camera* inspection by the District Court of Presidential documents and materials subpoenaed by the Special Prosecutor would itself violate the privilege without regard to whether the documents were protected from public disclosure. The Court disagreed, stating that "neither the doctrine of separation of powers nor the generalized need for confidentiality of high-level communications, without more, can sustain an absolute, unqualified Presidential privilege...." The Court recognized that the privilege of confidentiality of Presidential communications derives from the supremacy of the Executive Branch within its assigned area of constitutional responsibilities, but distinguished a President's "broad, undifferentiated claim of public interest in the confidentiality of such [communications]" from the more particularized and less qualified privilege relating to the need "to protect military, diplomatic, or sensitive national security secrets...." The Court held that in the case of the general privilege of confidentiality of Presidential communications, its importance must be balanced against the inroads of the privilege upon the effective functioning of the Judicial Branch. This balance was struck against the claim of privilege in that case because the Court determined that the intrusion into the confidentiality of Presidential communications resulting from *in camera* inspection by the District Court, "with all the protection that a District Court will be obliged to provide," would be minimal and therefore that the claim was outweighed by "[t]he impediment that an absolute, unqualified privilege would place in the way of the primary constitutional duty of the Judicial Branch...."

Unlike *United States* v. *Nixon,* in which appellant asserted a claim of absolute Presidential privilege against inquiry by the coordinate Judicial Branch, this case initially involves appellant's assertion of a privilege against the very Executive Branch in whose name the privilege is invoked. The nonfederal appellees rely on this apparent anomaly to contend that only an incumbent President can assert the privilege of the Presidency. Acceptance of that proposition would, of course, end this inquiry. The contention draws on *United States* v. *Reynolds...* (1953), where it was said that the privilege "belongs to the Government and must be asserted by it: it can neither be claimed nor waived by a private party." The District Court believed that this statement was strong support for the contention, but found resolution of the issue unnecessary.... It sufficed, said the District Court, that the privilege, if available to a former President, was at least one that "carries much less weight than a claim asserted by the incumbent himself." [*District of Columbia District Court decision*]...

It is true that only the incumbent is charged with performance of the executive duty under the Constitution. And an incumbent may be inhibited in disclosing confidences of a predecessor when he believes that the effect may be to discourage candid presentation of views by his contemporary advisors. Moreover, to the extent that the privilege serves as a shield for executive officials against burdensome requests for information which might interfere with the proper performance of their duties, see *United States* v. *Nixon...Eastland* v. *United States Servicemen's Fund...* (1975); *Dombrowski* v. *Eastland...* (1967) *(per curiam)*, a former President is in less need of it than an incumbent. In addition, there are obvious political checks against an incumbent's abuse of the privilege....

Nevertheless, we think that the Solicitor General states the sounder view, and we adopt it....

...At the same time, however, the fact that neither President Ford nor President Carter supports appellant's claim detracts from the weight of his contention that the Act impermissibly intrudes into the executive function and the needs of the Executive Branch. This necessarily follows, for it must be presumed that the incumbent President is vitally concerned with and in the best position to assess the present and future needs of the Executive Branch, and to support invocation of the privilege accordingly.

The appellant may legitimately assert the Presidential privilege, of course, only as to those materials whose contents fall within the scope of the privilege recognized in *United States* v. *Nixon....* In that case the Court held that the privilege is limited to communications "in performance of [a President's] responsibilities"..."of his office",...and made "in the process of shaping policies and making decisions."...[*United States* v. *Nixon* (1974)] Of the estimated 42 million pages of documents and 880 tape recordings whose custody is at stake, the District Court concluded that the appellant's claim of Presidential privilege could apply at most to the 200,-000 items with which the appellant was personally familiar.

The appellant bases his claim of Presidential privilege in this case on the assertion that the potential disclosure of communications given to the appellant in confidence would adversely affect the ability of future Presidents to obtain the candid advice necessary for effective decision-making. We are called upon to adjudicate that claim, however, only with respect to the process by which the materials will be screened and catalogued by professional archivists. For any eventual public access will be governed by the guidelines...which direct the Administrator to take into account "the need to protect any party's opportunity to assert any constitutionally based right or privilege"...and the need to return purely private materials to the appellant....

In view of these specific directions, there is no reason to believe that the restriction on public access ultimately established by regulation will not be adequate to preserve executive confidentiality. An absolute barrier to all outside disclosure is not practically or constitutionally necessary. As the careful research by the District Court clearly demonstrates, there has never been an expectation that the confidences of the Executive Office are absolute and unyielding. All former Presidents since President Hoover have deposited their papers in Presidential libraries (an example appellant has said he intended to follow) for governmental preservation and eventual disclosure. The screening processes for sorting materials for lodgment in these libraries also involved comprehensive review by archivists, often involving materials upon which access restrictions ultimately have been imposed [*District of Columbia District Court decision*].... The expectation of the confidentiality of executive communications thus has always been limited and subject to erosion over time after an administration leaves office.

We are thus left with the bare claim that the mere screening of the materials by the archivists will impermissibly interfere with candid communication of views by Presidential advisors. We agree with the District Court that, thus framed, the question is readily resolved. The screening constitutes a very limited intrusion by personnel in the Executive Branch sensitive to executive concerns. These very personnel have performed the identical task in each of the Presidential libraries without any suggestion that such activity has in any way interfered with executive confidentiality. Indeed, in light of this consistent historical practice, past and present executive officials must be well aware of the possibility that, at some time in the future, their communications may be reviewed on a confidential basis by professional archivists. Appellant has suggested no reason why review under the instant Act, rather than the Presidential Libraries Act, is significantly more likely to impair confidentiality, nor has he called into question the District Court's finding that the archivists' "record for discretion in handling confidential material is unblemished."...

Moreover, adequate justifications are shown for this limited intrusion into executive confidentiality comparable to those held to justify the *in camera* inspection of the District Court sustained in *United States* v. *Nixon*.... Congress' purposes in enacting the Act are exhaustively treated in the opinion of the District Court. The legislative history of the Act clearly reveals that, among other purposes, Congress acted to establish regular procedures to deal with the perceived need to preserve the materials for legitimate historical and governmental purposes. An incumbent President should not be dependent on happenstance or the whim of a prior President when he seeks access to records of past decisions that define or channel current governmental obligations. Nor should the American people's ability to reconstruct and come to terms with their history be truncated by an analysis of Presidential privilege that focuses only on the needs of the present. Congress can legitimately act to rectify the hit-or-miss approach that has characterized past attempts to protect these substantial interests by entrusting the materials to expert handling by trusted and disinterested professionals.

Other substantial public interests that led Congress to seek to preserve appellant's materials were the desire to restore public confidence in our political processes by preserving the materials as a source for facilitating a full airing of the events leading to appellant's resignation, and Congress' need to understand how those political processes had in fact operated in order to gauge the necessity for remedial legislation. Thus by preserving these materials, the Act may be thought to aid the legislative process and thus to be within the scope of Congress' broad investigative power, see...*Eastland* v. *United States Servicemen's Fund*.... And, of course, the Congress repeatedly referred to the importance of the materials to the Judiciary in the event that they shed light upon issues in civil or criminal litigation, a social interest that cannot be doubted. See *United States* v. *Nixon*....

In light of these objectives, the scheme adopted by Congress for preservation of the appellant's Presidential materials cannot be said to be overbroad. It is true that among the voluminous materials to be screened by archivists are some materials that bear no relationship to any of these objectives (and whose prompt return to appellant is therefore mandated).... But these materials are commingled with other materials whose preservation the Act requires, for the appellant, like his predecessors, made no

systematic attempt to segregate official, personal, and private materials....
Even individual documents and tapes often intermingle communications
relating to governmental duties, and of great interest to historians or future
policymakers, with private and confidential communications....

Thus, as in the Presidential libraries, the intermingled state of the
materials requires the comprehensive review and classification contemplated by the Act if Congress' important objectives are to be furthered.
In the course of that process, the archivists will be required to view the
small fraction of the materials that implicate Presidential confidentiality,
as well as personal and private materials to be returned to appellant. But
given the safeguards built into the Act to prevent disclosure of such
materials and the minimal nature of the intrusion into the confidentiality
of the Presidency, we believe that the claims of Presidential privilege clearly must yield to the important congressional purposes of preserving the
materials and maintaining access to them for lawful government and
historical purposes.

In short, we conclude that the screening process contemplated by the
Act will not constitute a more severe intrusion into Presidential confidentiality than the *in camera* inspection by the District Court approved in
United States v. *Nixon....* We must of course presume that the Administrator and the career archivists concerned will carry out the duties
assigned to them by the Act. Thus, there is no basis for appellant's claim
that the Act "reverses" the presumption in favor of confidentiality of
Presidential papers recognized in *United States* v. *Nixon.* Appellant's right
to assert the privilege is specifically preserved by the Act. The guideline
provisions on their face are as broad as the privilege itself. If the broadly
written protections of the Act should nevertheless prove inadequate to
safeguard appellant's rights or to prevent usurpation of executive powers,
there will be time enough to consider that problem in a specific factual
context. For the present, we hold, in agreement with the District Court,
that the Act on its face does not violate the Presidential privilege.

Privacy

Appellant concedes that when he entered public life he voluntarily surrendered the privacy secured by law for those who elect not to place
themselves in the public spotlight. See, *e.g., New York Times Co.* v.
Sullivan...(1964). He argues, however, that he was not thereby stripped of
all legal protection for his privacy, and contends that the Act violates fundamental rights of expression and privacy guaranteed to him by the First,
Fourth and Fifth Amendments.

The District Court treated appellant's argument as addressed only to the
process by which the screening of the materials will be performed. "Since
any claim by [appellant] that his privacy will be invaded by public access
to private materials must be considered premature when it must actually
be directed to the regulations once they become effective, we need not consider how the materials will be treated after they are reviewed...."

Although denominating the privacy claim "[t]he most troublesome challenge that plaintiff raises...," [*District of Columbia District Court decision*], the District Court concluded that the claim was without merit. The court reasoned that the proportion of the 42 million pages of documents and 880 tape recordings implicating appellant's privacy interests was quite small since the great bulk of the materials related to appellant's conduct of his duties as President, and were therefore materials to which great public interest attached. The touchstone of the legality of the archival processing, in the District Court's view, was its reasonableness. Balancing the public interest in preserving the materials touching appellant's performance of his official duties against the invasion of appellant's privacy that archival screening necessarily entails, the District Court concluded that the Act was not unreasonable and hence not facially unconstitutional....

Thus, the Act "is a reasonable response to the difficult problem caused by the mingling of personal and private documents and conversations in the midst of a vastly greater number of nonprivate documents and materials related to government objectives. The processing contemplated by the Act—at least as narrowed by carefully tailored regulations—represents the least intrusive manner in which to protect an adequate level of promotion of government interests of overriding importance." [*District of Columbia District Court decision*]... We agree with the District Court that the Act does not unconstitutionally invade appellant's right of privacy....

We may agree with appellant that, at least when government intervention is at stake, public officials, including the President, are not wholly without constitutionally protected privacy rights in matters of personal life unrelated to any acts done by them in their public capacity. Presidents who have established Presidential libraries have usually withheld matters concerned with family or personal finances, or have deposited such materials with restrictions on their screening.... We may assume with the District Court, for the purposes of this case, that this pattern of *de facto* Presidential control and congressional acquiescence gives rise to appellant's legitimate expectation of privacy in such materials. *Katz* v. *United States*...(1967). This expectation is independent of the question of ownership of the materials, an issue we do not reach.... But the merit of appellant's claim of invasion of his privacy cannot be considered in the abstract; rather, the claim must be considered in light of the specific provisions of the Act, and any intrusion must be weighed against the public interest in subjecting the Presidential materials of appellant's administration to archival screening. *Camara* v. *Municipal Court*...(1967); *Terry* v. *Ohio*...(1968). Under this test, the privacy interest asserted by appellant is weaker than that found wanting in the recent decision of *Whalen* v. *Roe*.... Emphasizing the precautions utilized by New York State to prevent the unwarranted disclosure of private medical information retained in a state computer bank system, *Whalen* rejected a constitutional objection to New York's program on privacy grounds. Not only does the Act challenged here mandate regulations similarly aimed at preventing undue dissemination of private materials but, unlike *Whalen*, the Government will not even retain long-term control over such private information; rather, purely private papers and recordings will be returned to appellant....

The overwhelming bulk of the 42 million documents and the 880 tape recordings pertain, not to appellant's private communications, but to the official conduct of his Presidency. Most of the 42 million papers were prepared and seen by others and were widely circulated within the Government. Appellant concedes that he saw no more than 200,000, and we do not understand him to suggest that his privacy claim extends to items he never saw. See *United States* v. *Miller*...(1976). Further, it is logical to assume that the tape recordings made in the Presidential offices primarily relate to the conduct and business of the Presidency. And, of course, appellant cannot assert any privacy claim as to the documents and tape recordings that he has already disclosed to the public. *United States* v. *Dionisio*...(1973); *Katz* v. *United States*...[1967]. Therefore appellant's privacy claim embracing, for example, "extremely private communications between [him] and, among others, his wife, his daughters, his physician, lawyer and clergyman, and his close friends as well as personal diary dictabelts and his wife's personal files,"...relates only to a very small fraction of the massive volume of official materials with which they are presently commingled.

The fact that appellant may assert his privacy claim as to only a small fraction of the materials of his Presidency is plainly relevant in judging the reasonableness of the screening process contemplated by the Act, but this of course does not without more, require rejection of his privacy argument [*District of Columbia, District Court decision*]. Although the Act requires that the regulations promulgated by the Administrator under § 104 (a) take into account appellant's legally and constitutionally based rights and privileges, presumably including his privacy rights, § 104 (a)(5), and also take into account the need to return to appellant his private materials, §104, the identity and separation of these purely private matters can be achieved, as all parties concede, only by screening all of the materials.

Appellant contends that the Act therefore is tantamount to a general warrant authorizing search and seizure of all of his Presidential "papers, and effects." Such "blanket authority," appellant contends, is precisely the kind of abuse that the Fourth Amendment was intended to prevent, for "the real evil aimed [at] by the Fourth Amendment is the search itself, that invasion of a man's privacy which consists of rummaging about his personal effects to secure evidence against him."...

Appellant principally relies on *Stanford* v. *Texas*...(1965), but that reliance is misplaced. *Stanford* invalidated a search aimed at obtaining evidence that an individual had violated a "sweeping and many-faceted law which, among other things, outlaws the Communist Party and creates various individual criminal offenses, each punishable by imprisonment for up to 20 years."... The search warrant authorized a search of his private home for books, records, and other materials concerning illegal Communist activities. After spending more than four hours in Stanford's house, police officers seized half of his books which included works by Sartre, Marx, Pope John XXIII, Justice Hugo Black, Theodore Draper, and Earl Browder, as well as private documents including a marriage certificate, insurance policies, household bills and receipts, and personal correspondence.... *Stanford* held this to be an unconstitutional general search.

The District Court concluded that the Act's provision for custody and screening could not be analogized to a general search and that *Stanford*, therefore, did not require the Act's invalidation [*District of Columbia District Court decision*].... We agree. Only a few documents among the vast quantity of materials seized in *Stanford* were even remotely related to any legitimate government interest. This case presents precisely the opposite situation: the vast proportion of appellant's Presidential materials are official documents or records in which appellant concedes the public has a recognized interest. Moreover, the Act provides procedures and orders the promulgation of regulations expressly for the purpose of minimizing the intrusion into appellant's private and personal materials. Finally, the search in *Stanford* was an intrusion into an individual's home to search and seize personal papers in furtherance of a criminal investigation and designed for exposure in a criminal trial. In contrast, any intrusion by archivists into appellant's private papers and effects is undertaken with the sole purpose of separating private materials to be returned to appellant from nonprivate materials to be retained and preserved by the Government as a record of appellant's Presidency.

Moreover, the screening will be undertaken by government archivists with as the District Court noted, "an unblemished record for discretion." [*District of Columbia, District Court decision*]... That review can hardly differ materially from that contemplated by appellant's intention to establish a President Library, for Presidents who have established such libraries have found that screening by professional archivists was essential. Although the District Court recognized that this contemplation of archival review would not defeat appellant's expectation of privacy, the court held that it does indicate that "in the special situation of documents accumulated by a President during his tenure and reviewed by professional government personnel, pursuant to a practice employed by past Presidents, any intrusion into privacy interests is less substantial than it might appear at first."...

The District Court analogized the screening process contemplated by the Act to electronic surveillance conducted pursuant to Title III of the Omnibus Crime Control and Safe Streets Act of 1968...[*District of Columbia, District Court decision*] We think the analogy is apt. There are obvious similarities between the two procedures. Both involve the problem of separating intermingled communications, (1) some of which are expected to be related to legitimate government objectives, (2) some of which are not and (3) for which there is no means to segregate the one from the other except by reviewing them all. Thus the screening process under the Act, like electronic surveillance, requires some intrusion into private communications unconnected with any legitimate governmental objectives. Yet this fact has not been thought to render surveillance under the Omnibus Act unconstitutional.... *United States* v. *Donovan*....(1977); *Berger* v. *New York*...(1967). [*District of Columbia, District Court decision*]

Appellant argues that this analogy is inappropriate because the electronic surveillance procedure was carefully designed to meet the constitutional requirements enumerated in *Berger* v. *New York*..., including (1) prior judicial authorization, (2) specification of particular offenses said to justify the intrusion, (3) specification "with particularity" of the conversations sought to be seized, (4) minimization of the duration of the wiretap, (5) termination once the conversation sought is seized, and (6) a showing of exigent circumstances justifying use of the wiretap procedure.... Although the parallel is far from perfect, we agree with the District Court that many considerations supporting the constitutionality of the Omnibus Act also argue for the constitutionality of this Act's materials screening process. For example, the Omnibus Act permits electronic surveillance only to investigate designated crimes that are serious in nature...and only when normal investigative techniques have failed or are likely to do so.... Similarly, the archival review procedure involved here is designed to serve important national interests asserted by Congress, and the unavailability of less restrictive means necessarily follows from the commingling of the documents. Similarly, just as the Omnibus Act expressly requires that interception of nonrelevant communications be minimized...the Act's screening process is designed to minimize any privacy intrusions, a goal that is further reinforced by regulations which must take those interests into account. The fact that apparently only a minute portion of the materials implicates appellant's privacy interests also negates any conclusion that the screening process is an unreasonable solution to the problem of separating commingled communications.

In sum, appellant has a legitimate expectation of privacy in his personal communications. But the constitutionality of the Act must be viewed in the context of the limited intrusion of the screening process, of appellant's status as a public figure, of his lack of any expectation of privacy in the overwhelming majority of the materials, and of the virtual impossibility of segregating the small quantity of private materials without comprehensive screening. When this is combined with the Act's sensitivity to appellant's legitimate privacy interests...the unblemished record of the archivists for discretion, and the likelihood that the regulations to be promulgated by the Administrator will further moot appellant's fears that his materials will be reviewed by "a host of persons..." we are compelled to agree with the District Court that appellant's privacy claim is without merit.

First Amendment

During his Presidency appellant served also as head of his national political party and spent a substantial portion of his working time on partisan political matters. Records arising from his political activities, like his private and personal records, are not segregated from the great mass of materials. He argues that the Act's archival screening process therefore necessarily entails invasion of his constitutionally protected rights of associational privacy and political speech. As summarized by the District Court, "It is alleged that the Act invades the private formulation of political thought critical to free speech and association, imposing sanctions upon past expressive activity, and more significantly, limiting that of the future because individuals who learn the substance of certain private communications by [him]—especially those critical of themselves—will refuse to associate with him. The Act is furthermore said to chill [his] expression because he will be 'saddled' with prior positions communicated in private, leaving him unable to take inconsistent positions in the future." [*District of Columbia, District Court decision*]

The District Court, viewing these arguments as in essence a claim that disclosure of the materials violated appellant's associational privacy, and therefore as not significantly different in structure from appellant's privacy claim, again treated the arguments as limited to the constitutionality of the Act's screening process.... As was true with respect to the more general privacy challenge, only a fraction of the materials can be said to raise a First Amendment claim. Nevertheless, the District Court acknowledged that appellant "would appear to have a legitimate expectation that he would have an opportunity to remove some of the sensitive political documents before any government screening took place...." The District Court concluded, however, that there was no reason to believe that the mandated regulations when promulgated would not adequately protect against public access to materials implicating appellant's privacy in political association, and that "any burden arising solely from review by professional and discreet archivists is not significant." The court therefore held that the Act does not significantly interfere with or chill appellant's First Amendment rights.... We agree with the District Court's conclusion.

It is of course true that involvement in partisan politics is closely protected by the First Amendment, *Buckley* v. *Valeo*...(1976), and that "compelled disclosure in itself can seriously infringe on privacy and belief guaranteed by the First Amendment...." But a compelling public need that cannot be met in a less restrictive way will override those interests, *Kusper* v. *Pontikes*...(1973); *United States* v. *O'Brien*...(1968); *Shelton* v. *Tucker*...(1966), "particularly when the 'free functioning of our national institutions' is involved." *Buckley* v. *Valeo*.... Since no less restrictive way than archival screening has been suggested as a means for identification of materials to be returned to appellant, the burden of that screening is presently the measure of his First Amendment claim.... The extent of any such burden, however, is speculative in light of the Act's terms protecting appellant from improper public disclosures and guaranteeing him full judicial review before any public access is permitted.... As the District Court concluded, the First Amendment claim is clearly outweighed by the important governmental interests promoted by the Act.

For the same reasons, we find no merit in appellant's argument that the Act's scheme for custody and archival screening of the materials "necessarily inhibits [the] freedom of political activity [of future Presidents] and thereby reduces the 'quantity and diversity' of the political speech and association that the Nation will be receiving from its leaders...." It is significant, moreover, that this concern has not deterred President Ford from signing the Act into law, or President Carter from urging this Court's affirmance of the judgment of the District Court.

Bill of Attainder Clause

A

Finally, we address appellant's argument that the Act constitutes a bill of attainder proscribed by Art. I, § 9 of the Constitution. His argument is that Congress acted on the premise that he had engaged in "misconduct," was an "unreliable custodian" of his own documents, and generally was deserving of a "legislative judgment of blameworthiness," Brief for Appellant 132-133. Thus, he argues, the Act is pervaded with the key features of a bill of attainder: a law that legislatively determines guilt and inflicts punishment upon an identifiable individual without provision of the protections of a judicial trial. See *United States* v. *Brown*...(1965); *United States* v. *Lovett*...(1946); *Ex Parte Garland*...(1866); *Cummings* v. *Missouri*...(1866).

Appellant's argument relies almost entirely upon *United States* v. *Brown*...the Court's most recent decision addressing the scope of the Bill of Attainder Clause. It is instructive, therefore, to sketch the broad outline of that case. *Brown* invalidated § 504 of the Labor-Management Reporting and Disclosure Act of 1959...that made it a crime for a Communist Party member to serve as an officer of a labor union. After detailing the infamous history of bills of attainder, the Court found that the Bill of Attainder Clause was an important ingredient of the doctrine of "separation of powers," one of the organizing principles of our system of government.... Just as Art. III confines the judiciary to the task of adjudicating concrete "cases or controversies," so too the Bill of Attainder Clause was found to "reflect...the Framers' belief that the Legislative Branch is not so well suited as politically independent judges and juries to the task of ruling upon the blameworthiness of, and levying appropriate punishment upon, specific persons...." *Brown* thus held that § 504 worked a bill of attainder by focusing upon easily identifiable members of a class, members of the Communist Party, and imposing on them the sanction of mandatory forfeiture of a job or office, long deemed to be punishment within the contemplation of the Bill of Attainder Clause....

Brown, Lovett, and earlier cases unquestionably gave broad and generous meaning to the constitutional protection against bills of attainder. But appellant's proposed reading is far broader still. In essence, he argues that *Brown* establishes that the Constitution is offended whenever a law imposes undesired consequences on an individual or on a class that is not defined at a proper level of generality. The Act in question therefore is faulted for singling out appellant, as opposed to all other Presidents or members of the government, for disfavored treatment.

Appellant's characterization of the meaning of a bill of attainder obviously proves far too much. By arguing that an individual or defined group is attainted whenever it is compelled to bear burdens which the individual or group dislikes, appellant removes the anchor that ties the bill of attainder guarantee to realistic conceptions of classification and punishment. His view would cripple the very process of legislating, for any individual or group that is made the subject of adverse legislation can complain that the lawmakers could and should have defined the relevant affected class at a greater level of generality. Furthermore, every person or group made subject to legislation which it finds burdensome may subjectively feel, and can complain, that it is being subjected to unwarranted punishment. *United States* v. *Lovett*.... However expansive is the prohibition against bills of attainder, it surely was not intended to serve as a variant of the Equal Protection Clause, invalidating every act of Congress or the States that legislatively burdens some persons or groups but not all other plausible individuals. In short, while the Bill of Attainder Clause serves as an important "bulwark against tyranny," *United States* v. *Brown*...it does not do so by limiting Congress to the choice of legislating for the universe, or legislating only benefits, or not legislating at all.

Thus, in the present case, the Act's specificity—the fact that it refers to appellant by name—does not automatically offend the Bill of Attainder Clause. Indeed, viewed in context, the focus of the enactment can be fairly and rationally understood. It is true that Title I deals exclusively with appellant's papers. But Title II casts a wider net by establishing a special commission to study and recommend appropriate legislation regarding the preservation of the records of future Presidents and all other federal officials. In this light, Congress' action to preserve only appellant's records is easily explained by the fact that at the time of the Act's passage, only his materials demanded immediate attention. The Presidential papers of all former Presidents from Hoover to Johnson were already housed in functioning Presidential libraries. Congress had reason for concern solely with the preservation of appellant's materials, for he alone had entered into a depository agreement, the Nixon-Sampson agreement, which by terms called for the destruction of certain of the materials. Indeed, as the Government argues, "appellant's depository agreement...created an imminent danger that the tape recordings would be destroyed if appellant, who had contracted phlebitis, were to die." Brief for Federal Appellee 41. In short, appellant constituted a legitimate class of one, and this provides a basis for Congress' decision to proceed with dispatch with respect to his materials while accepting the status of his predecessors' papers and ordering the further consideration of generalized standards to govern his successors.

Moreover, even if the specificity element were deemed to be satisfied here, the Bill of Attainder Clause would not automatically be implicated.

Forbidden legislative punishment is not involved merely because the Act imposes burdensome consequences. Rather, we must inquire further whether Congress, by lodging appellant's materials in the custody of the General Services Administration pending their screening by government archivists and the promulgation of further regulations, "inflict[ed] punishment" within the constitutional proscription against bills of attainder. *United States* v. *Lovett...United States* v. *Brown...Cummings* v. *Missouri....*

B

The infamous history of bills of attainder is a useful starting point in the inquiry whether the Act fairly can be characterized as a form of punishment leveled against appellant. For the substantial experience of both England and the United States with such abuses of parliamentary and legislative power offer a ready checklist of deprivations and disabilities so disproportionately severe and so inappropriate to nonpunitive ends that they unquestionably have been held to fall within the proscription of Art. I, § 9. A statutory enactment that imposes any of those sanctions on named or identifiable individuals would be immediately constitutionally suspect.

In England a bill of attainder originally connoted a parliamentary act sentencing a named individual or identifiable members of a group to death. Article I, § 9, however, also proscribes enactments originally characterized as bills of pains and penalties, that is, legislative acts inflicting punishment other than execution. *United States* v. *Lovett...; Cummings* v. *Missouri...*Z. Chafee, Three Human Rights in the Constitution...(1956). Generally addressed to persons considered disloyal to the Crown or State, "pains and penalties" historically consisted of a wide array of punishments: commonly included were imprisonment, banishment, and the punitive confiscation of property by the sovereign. Our country's own experience with bills of attainder resulted in the addition of another sanction to the list of impermissible legislative punishments: a legislative enactment barring designated individuals or groups from participation in specified employments or vocations, a mode of punishment commonly deployed against those legislatively branded as disloyal. See...*Cummings* v. *Missouri...*(barring clergymen from ministry in the absence of subscribing to a loyalty oath); *United States* v. *Lovett...*(barring named individuals from government employment); *United States* v. *Brown...*(barring Communist Party members from offices in labor unions).

Needless to say, appellant cannot claim to have suffered any of these forbidden deprivations at the hands of the Congress. While it is true that Congress ordered the General Services Administration to retain control over records that appellant claims as his property, § 105 of the Act makes provision for an award by the District Court of "just compensation." This undercuts even a colorable contention that the Government has punitively confiscated appellant's property, for the "owner [thereby] is put in the same position monetarily as he would have occupied if his property had not been taken." *United States* v. *Reynolds*...(1970); accord *United States* v. *Miller*...(1943). Thus, no feature of the challenged Act falls within the historical meaning of legislative punishment.

But our inquiry is not ended by the determination that the Act imposes no punishment traditionally judged to be prohibited by the Bill of Attainder Clause. Our treatment of the scope of the Clause has never precluded the possibility that new burdens and deprivations might be legislatively fashioned that are inconsistent with the bill of attainder guarantee. The Court, therefore, often has looked beyond mere historical experience and has applied a functional test of the existence of punishment, analyzing whether the law under challenge, viewed in terms of the type and severity of burdens imposed, reasonably can be said to further nonpunitive legislative purposes. *Cummings* v. *Missouri*...; *Hawker v. New York*...(1898); *Dent* v. *West Virginia*...(1889); *Trap* v. *Dulles*...(1958) (Warren, C. J.); *Kennedy* v. *Mendoza-Martinez*...(1963). Where such legitimate legislative purposes do not appear, it is reasonable to conclude that punishment of individuals disadvantaged by the enactment was the purpose of the decisionmakers....

Evaluated in terms of these asserted purposes, the law plainly must be held to be an act of nonpunitive legislative policymaking. Legislation designed to guarantee the availability of evidence for use at criminal trials is a fair exercise of Congress' responsibility to the "due process of law in the fair administration of justice," *United States* v. *Nixon*...(1974), and to the functioning of our adversary legal system which depends upon the availability of relevant evidence in carrying out its commitments both to fair play and to the discovery of truth within the bounds set by law. *Branzburg* v. *Hayes*...(1972); *Blackmer* v. *United States*...(1932); *Blair* v. *United States*...(1919). Similarly, Congress' interest in and expansive authority to act in preservation of monuments and records of historical value to our national heritage are fully established. *United States* v. *Gettysburg Electric R. Co.*...(1896); *Roe* v. *Kansas*...(1929). A legislature thus acts responsibly in seeking to accomplish either of these objectives. Neither supports an implication of a legislature policy designed to inflict punishment on an individual.

A third recognized test of punishment is strictly a motivational one: inquiring whether the legislative record evinces a congressional intent to punish. See, *e.g., United States* v. *Lovett*...; *Kennedy* v. *Mendoza-Martinez*.... The District Court unequivocally found that "[t]here is no evidence presented to us, nor is there any to be found in the legislative record, to indicate that Congress' design was to impose a penalty upon Mr. Nixon...as punishment for alleged wrongdoings.... The legislative history leads to only one conclusion, namely, that the Act before us is regulatory and not punitive in character [*District of Columbia, District Court decision*]." We find no cogent reason for disagreeing with this conclusion.

We also agree with the District Court that "specific aspects of the Act... just do not square with the claim that the Act was a punitive measure."...

Whereas appellant complains that the Act has for some two years deprived him of control over the materials in question...the Congress placed the materials under the auspices of the General Services Administration...the same agency designated in the Nixon-Sampson agreement as depository of the documents for a minimum three-year period.... Whereas appellant complains that the Act deprives him of "ready access" to the materials...the Act provides that "Richard M. Nixon, or any person whom he may designate in writing, shall at all times have access to the tape records and other materials...," § 102 (C). The District Court correctly construed this as safeguarding appellant's right to inspect, copy, and use the materials in issue...paralleling the right to "make reproductions" contained in the Sampson agreement.... And even if we assumed that there is merit in appellant's complaint that his property has been confiscated...the Act expressly provides for the payment of just compensation....

One final consideration should be mentioned in light of the unique posture of this controversy. In determining whether a legislature sought to inflict punishment on an individual, it is often useful to inquire into the existence of less burdensome alternatives by which the Congress could have achieved its legitimate nonpunitive objectives. Today, in framing his challenge to the Act, appellant contends that such an alternative was readily available....

We have no doubt that Congress might have selected this course. It very well may be, however, that Congress chose not to do so on the view that a full-fledged judicial inquiry into appellant's conduct and reliability would be no less punitive and intrusive than the solution actually adopted. For Congress doubtless was well aware that just three months earlier, appellant had resisted efforts to subject himself and his records to the scrutiny of the Judicial Branch, *United States* v. *Nixon*,...a position apparently maintained to this day. A rational and fairminded Congress, therefore, might well have decided that the carefully tailored law that it enacted would be less objectionable to appellant than the alternative that he today appears to endorse. To be sure, if the record were unambiguously to demonstrate that the Act represents the infliction of legislative punishment, the fact that the judicial alternative poses its own difficulties would be of no constitutional significance. But the record suggests the contrary, and the unique choice that Congress faced buttresses our conclusion that the Act cannot fairly be read to inflict legislative punishment as forbidden by the Constitution.

We, of course, are not blind to appellant's plea that we recognize the social and political realities of 1974. It was a period of political turbulence unprecedented in our history. But this Court is not free to invalidate acts of Congress based upon inferences that we may be asked to draw from our personalized reading of the contemporary scene or recent history. In judging the constitutionality of the Act, we may only look to its terms, to the intent expressed by Members of Congress who voted its passage, and to the existence or non-existence of legitimate explanations for its apparent effects. We are persuaded that none of these factors is suggestive that the

Act is a punitive bill of attainder, or otherwise facially unconstitutional. The judgment of the District Court is

Affirmed.

MR. JUSTICE WHITE, concurring.

I concur in the judgment and, except for Part VII, in the Court's opinion. With respect to the bill of attainder issue, I concur in the result reached in Part VII; the statute does not impose "punishment" and is not, therefore, a bill of attainder. See *United States* v. *Brown*...(1965) (WHITE, J., dissenting). I also append the following observations with respect to one of the many issues in this case.

It is conceded by all concerned that a very small portion of the vast collection of presidential material now in possession of the Administrator consists of purely private materials, such as diaries, recordings of family conversations, private correspondence—"personal property of any kind not involving the actual transaction of government business...."

...[A]s I see it, the validity of the Act would be questionable if mere historical significance sufficed to withhold purely private letters or diaries; and in view of the other provisions of the Act, particularly § 104 (a)(5), it need not be so construed. Purely private materials, whether or not of historical interest, are to be delivered to Mr. Nixon. The United States and the other respondents conceded as much at oral argument.

Similarly, although the Court relies to some extent on the statutory recognition of the constitutional right to compensation in the event it is determined that the Government has confiscated Mr. Nixon's property, I would question whether a mere historical interest in purely private communications would be a sufficient predicate for taking them for public use. Historical considerations are normally sufficient grounds for condemning property, *United States* v. *Gettysburg Electric Ry*...(1896); *Roe* v. *Kansas*...(1929); but whatever may be true of the great bulk of the materials in the event they are declared to be Mr. Nixon's property. I doubt that the Government is entitled to his purely private communications merely because it wants to preserve them and offers compensation.

MR. JUSTICE BLACKMUN, concurring in part and concurring in the judgment.

My posture in this case is essentially that of MR. JUSTICE POWELL.... I refrain from joining his opinion, however, because I fall somewhat short of sharing his view...that the incumbent President's submission, made through the Solicitor General, that the Act serves rather than hinders the Chief Executive's Article II functions, is *dispositive* of the separation of powers issue. I would be willing to agree that it is significant and that it is entitled to serious consideration, but I am not convinced that it is dispositive. The fact that President Ford signed the Act does not mean that he necessarily approved of its every detail. Political realities often guide a President to a decision not to veto.

One must remind oneself that our Nation's history reveals a number of instances where presidential transition has not been particularly friendly or easy. On occasion it has been openly hostile. It is my hope and anticipation—as it obviously is of the others who have written in this case—that this Act, concerned as it is with what the Court describes...as "a legitimate class of one," will not become a model for the disposition of the papers of each President who leaves office at a time when his successor or the Congress is not of his political persuasion.

I agree fully with my BROTHER POWELL when he observes...that the "difficult constitutional questions lie ahead" for resolution in the future. Reserving judgment on those issues for a more appropriate time—certainly not now—I, too, join in the judgment of the Court and agree with much of its opinion. I specifically join Part VII of the Court's opinion.

MR. JUSTICE POWELL, concurring in part and concurring in the judgment.

I join the judgment of the Court and all but Parts IV and V of its opinion. For substantially the reasons stated by the Court, I agree that the Act on its face does not violate appellant's rights under the First, Fourth, and Fifth Amendments and the Bill of Attainder Clause. For reasons quite different from those stated by the Court, I also would hold that the Act is consistent on its face with the separation of powers.

I

The Court begins its analysis of the issues by limiting its inquiry to those constitutional claims that are addressed to "the facial validity of the provisions of the Act requiring the Administrator to take the recordings and materials into the Government's custody subject to screening by Government archivists...." I agree that the inquiry must be limited in this manner, but I would add two qualifications that in my view further restrict the reach of today's decision.

First, Title I of the Act does not purport to be a generalized provision addressed to the complex problem of disposition of the accumulated papers of Presidents or other federal officers. Unlike Title II, which authorizes a study of that problem, Title I is addressed specifically and narrowly to the need to preserve the papers of former President Nixon after his resignation under threat of impeachment. It is legislation, as the Court properly observes, directed against "a legitimate class of one...."

...Those who drafted and sponsored Title I of the Presidential Recordings and Materials Preservation Act in Congress uniformly viewed its provisions as emergency legislation, necessitated by the extraordinary events that led to the resignation and pardon and to the former President's arrangement for the disposition of his papers....

...It is essential in addressing the constitutional issues before us not to lose sight of the limited justification for and objectives of this legislation. The extraordinary events that led to the resignation and pardon, and the agreement providing that the record of those events might be destroyed by President Nixon, created an impetus for congressional action that may—without overstatement—be termed unique. I therefore do not share my BROTHER REHNQUIST's foreboding that this Act "will daily stand as a veritable sword of Damocles over every succeeding President and his advisors...." If the study authorized by Title II of the Act should lead to more general legislation, there will be time enough to consider its validity if a proper case comes before us.

My second reservation follows from the first. Because Congress acted in what it perceived to be an emergency, it concentrated on the immediate problem of establishing governmental custody for the purpose of safeguarding the materials. It deliberately left to the rulemaking process, and to subsequent judicial review, the difficult and sensitive task of reconciling the long-range interests of President Nixon, his advisors, the three branches of Government, and the American public, once custody was established....

No regulations have yet taken effect.... In these circumstances, I believe it is appropriate to address appellant's constitutional claims, as did the District Court, with an eye toward the kind of regulations and screening practices that would be consistent with the Act and yet that would afford protection to the important constitutional interests asserted....

I have no doubt that procedural safeguards and substantive restrictions such as these are within the authority of the Administrator to adopt under the broad mandate of § 104 (a). While there can be no positive assurance that such protections will in fact be afforded, we nonetheless may assume, in reviewing the facial validity of the Act, that all constitutional and legal rights will be given full protection. Indeed, that assumption is the basis on which I join today's judgment upholding the facial validity of the Act. As the Court makes clear in its opinion, the Act plainly requires the Administrator, in designing the regulations, to "consider the need to protect the constitutional rights of appellant and other individuals against infringement by the processing itself or, ultimately, by public access to the materials retained...."

II

I agree that Title I of the Act cannot be held unconstitutional on its face as a violation of the principle of separation of powers or of the Presidential privilege that derives from that principle. This is not a case in which the Legislative Branch has exceeded its enumerated powers by assuming a function reserved to the Executive under Art. II. *E. g., Buckley* v. *Valeo...* (1976); *Myers* v. *United States,...* (1926). The question of governmental power in this case is whether the Act, by mandating seizure and eventual public access to the papers of the Nixon Presidency, impermissibly interferes with the President's power to carry out his Art. II obligations. In concluding that the Act is not facially invalid on this ground, I consider it dispositive in the circumstances of this case that the President has represented to this Court, through the Solicitor General, that the Act serves rather than hinders the Art. II functions of the Chief Executive.

I would begin by asking whether, putting to one side other limiting provisions of the Constitution, Congress has acted beyond the scope of its enumerated powers. Cf. *Reid* v. *Covert*...(1957) (Harlan, J., concurring). Apart from the legislative concerns mentioned by the Court...I believe that Congress unquestionably has acted within the ambit of its broad authority to investigate, to inform the public, and ultimately, to legislate against suspected corruption and abuse of power in the Executive Branch.

This Court has recognized inherent power in Congress to pass appropriate legislation to "preserve the departments and institutions of the general government from impairment or destruction, whether threatened by force or by corruption," *Burroughs* v. *United States*...(1934). Congress has the power, for example, to restrict the political activities of civil servants, *e.g. CSC* v. *Letter Carriers*...(1973); to punish bribery and conflicts of interest, *e.g.*, *Burton* v. *United States*...(1906), to punish obstructions of lawful governmental functions, *Haas* v. *Henkel*...(1910), and—with important exceptions—to make Executive documents available to the public, *EPA* v. *Mink*...(1973). The Court also has recognized that in aid of such legislation Congress has a broad power "to inquire into and publicize corruption, maladministration or inefficiency in the agencies of the Government." *Watkins* v. *United States*...(1957). See also *Buckley* v. *Valeo;...Eastland* v. *United States Servicemen's Fund*...(1975).

The legislation before us rationally serves these investigative and informative powers. Congress legitimately could conclude that the Nixon-Sampson agreement, following the recommendation of impeachment and the resignation of President Nixon, might lead to destruction of those of the former President's papers that would be most likely to assure public understanding of the unprecedented events that led to the premature termination of the Nixon Administration. Congress similarly could conclude that preservation of the papers was important to its own eventual understanding of whether that Administration had been characterized by deficiencies susceptible of legislative correction. Providing for retention of the materials by the Administrator and for the selection of appropriate materials for eventual disclosure to the public was a rational means of serving these legitimate congressional objectives.

Congress still might be said to have exceeded its enumerated powers, however, if the Act could be viewed as an assumption by the Legislative Branch of functions reserved exclusively to the Executive by Art. II. In *Youngstown Sheet & Tube Co.* v. *Sawyer*... (1952), for example, the Court buttressed its conclusion that the President had acted beyond his power under Art. II by characterizing his seizure of the steel mills as an exercise of a "legislative" function reserved exclusively to Congress by Art. I.... And last Term we reaffirmed the fundamental principle that the appointment of executive officers is an "executive" function that Congress is without power to vest in itself. *Buckley* v. *Valeo*.... But the Act before us presumptively avoids these difficulties by entrusting the task of ensuring that its provisions are faithfully executed to an officer of the Executive Branch.

I therefore conclude that the Act cannot be held invalid on the ground that Congress has exceeded its affirmative grant of power under the Constitution. But it is further argued that Congress nonetheless has contravened the limitations on legislative power implicitly imposed by the creation of a coequal Executive Branch in Art. II. It is said that by opening up the operations of a past Administration to eventual public scrutiny, the Act impairs the ability of present and future Presidents to obtain unfettered information and candid advice and thereby limits executive power in contravention of Art. II and the principle of separation of powers. I see no material distinction between such an argument and the collateral claim that the Act violates the Presidential privilege in confidential communications.

In *United States* v. *Nixon*...(1974), we recognized a presumptive, yet qualified, privilege for confidential communications between the President and his advisors. Observing that "those who expect public dissemination of their remarks may well temper candor with a concern for appearances and for their own interests to the detriment of the decisionmaking process"...we recognized that a President's generalized interest in confidentiality is "constitutionally based" to the extent that it relates to "the effective discharge of a President's powers...." We held nonetheless that "[t]he generalized assertion of privilege must yield to the demonstrated, specified need for evidence in a pending criminal trial."...

Appellant understandably relies on *Nixon I*. Comparing the narrow scope of the judicial subpoenas considered there with the comprehensive reach of this Act—encompassing all of the communications of his Administration—appellant argues that there is no "demonstrated, specific need" here that can outweigh the extraordinary intrusion worked by this legislation. On the ground that the result will be to destroy "the effective discharge of the President's powers," appellant urges that the Act be held unconstitutional on its face.

These arguments undoubtedly have considerable force, but I do not think they can support a decision invalidating this Act on its face. Section 1 of Art. II vests all of the executive power in the sitting President and limits his term of office to four years. It is his sole responsibility to "take Care that the Laws be faithfully executed." Art. II., § 3. Here, President Carter has represented to this Court through the Solicitor General that the Act is consistent with "the effective discharge of the President's powers"....

This representation is similar to one made earlier on behalf of President Ford, who signed the Act.... I would hold that these representations must be given precedence over appellant's claim of Presidential privilege. Since the incumbent President views this Act as furthering rather than hindering effective execution of the laws, I do not believe it is within the province of this Court to hold otherwise.

This is not to say that a former President lacks standing to assert a claim of Presidential privilege. I agree with the Court that the former President may raise such a claim, whether before a court or a congressional committee. In some circumstances the intervention of the incumbent President will be impractical or his views unknown, and in such a case I assume that the former President's views on the effective operation of the Executive

Branch would be entitled to the greatest deference. It is uncontroverted, I believe, that the privilege in confidential Presidential communications survives a change in administrations. I would only hold that in the circumstances here presented the incumbent, having made clear in the appropriate forum his opposition to the former President's claim, alone can speak for the Executive Branch.... My position is simply that a decision to waive the privileges inhering in the Office of the President with respect to an otherwise valid Act of Congress is the President's alone to make under the Constitution.

III

The difficult constitutional questions lie ahead. The President no doubt will see to it that the interests in confidentiality so forcefully urged by THE CHIEF JUSTICE and MR. JUSTICE REHNQUIST in their dissenting opinions are taken into account in the final regulations that are promulgated under § 104 (a). While the President has supported the constitutionality of the Act as it is written, there is no indication that he will oppose appellant's assertions of Presidential privilege as they relate to the rules that will govern the screening process and the timing of disclosure, and particularly the restrictions that may be placed on certain documents and recordings. I emphasize that the validity of such assertions of Presidential privilege is not properly before us at this time.

Similarly, difficult and important questions concerning individual rights remain to be resolved. At stake are not only the rights of appellant but also those of other individuals whose First, Fourth, and Fifth Amendment interests may be implicated by disclosure of communications as to which a legitimate expectation of privacy existed. I agree with the Court that even in the councils of government an individual "has a legitimate expectation of privacy in his personal communications"...and also that compelled disclosure of an individual's political associations, in and out of government, can be justified only by "a compelling public need that cannot be met in a less restrictive way...." Today's decision is limited to the facial validity of the Act's provisions for retention and screening of the materials. The Court's discussion of the interests served by those provisions should not foreclose in any way the search that must yet be undertaken for means of assuring eventual access to important historical records without infringing individual rights protected by the First, Fourth and Fifth Amendments.

MR. JUSTICE STEVENS, concurring.

The statute before the Court does not apply to all Presidents or former Presidents. It singles out one, by name, for special treatment. Unlike all other former Presidents in our history, he is denied custody of his own Presidential papers; he is subjected to the burden of prolonged litigation over the administration of the statute; and his most private papers and conversations are to be scrutinized by government archivists. The statute implicitly condemns him as an unreliable custodian of his papers. Legislation which subjects a named individual to this humiliating treatment must raise serious questions under the Bill of Attainder Clause.

Bills of Attainder were typically directed at once powerful leaders of government. By special legislative acts, Parliament deprived one statesman after another of his reputation, his property, and his potential for future leadership. The motivation for such bills was as much political as it was punitive—and often the victims were those who had been the most relentless in attacking their political enemies at the height of their own power. In light of this history, legislation like that before us must be scrutinized with great care.

Our cases "stand for the proposition that legislative acts, no matter what their form, that apply either to named individuals or to easily ascertainable members of a group in such a way as to inflict punishment on them without a judicial trial are bills of attainder prohibited by the Constitution." *United States* v. *Lovett....* The concept of punishment involves not only the character of the deprivation, but also the manner in which that deprivation is imposed. It has been held permissible for Congress to deprive Communist deportees, as a group, of their social security benefits, *Flemming* v. *Nestor...* but it would surely be a bill of attainder for Congress to deprive a single, named individual of the same benefit.... The very specificity of the statute would mark it as punishment, for there is rarely any valid reason for such narrow legislation; and normally, the Constitution requires Congress to proceed by general rulemaking rather than by deciding individual cases. *United States* v. *Brown....*

Like the Court, however, I am persuaded that "appellant constituted a legitimate class of one...." The opinion of the Court leaves unmentioned the two facts which I consider decisive in this regard. Appellant resigned his office under unique circumstances and accepted a pardon for offenses committed while in office. By so doing, he placed himself in a different class from all other Presidents.... Even though unmentioned, it would be unrealistic to assume that historic facts of this consequence did not affect the legislative decision.

Since these facts provide a legitimate justification for the specificity of the statute, they also avoid the conclusion that this otherwise nonpunitive statute is made punitive by its specificity. If I did not consider it appropriate to take judicial notice of those facts, I would be unwilling to uphold the power of Congress to enact special legislation directed only at one former President at a time when his popularity was at its nadir. For even when it deals with Presidents or former Presidents, the legislative focus should be upon "the calling" rather than "the person...." In short, in my view, this case will not be a precedent for future legislation which relates, not to the Office of President, but just to one of its occupants.

Without imputing a similar reservation to the Court, I join its opinion with the qualification that these unmentioned facts have had a critical influence on my vote to affirm.

MR. CHIEF JUSTICE BURGER, dissenting.

In my view, the Court's holding is a grave repudiation of nearly 200 years of judicial precedent and historical practice. That repudiation arises out of an Act of Congress passed in the aftermath of a great national crisis which culminated in the resignation of a President. The Act violates firmly established constitutional principles in several respects.

I find it very disturbing that fundamental principles of constitutional law are subordinated to what seems the needs of a particular situation. That moments of great national distress give rise to passions reminds us why the three Branches of government were created as separate and co-equal, each intended as a check, in turn, on possible excesses by one or both of the others. The Court, however, has now joined a Congress, in haste to "do something," and has invaded historic, fundamental principles of the separate powers of coequal Branches of government. To "punish" one person, Congress—and now the Court—tears into the fabric of our constitutional framework.

Any case in this Court calling upon principles of separation of powers, rights of privacy, and the prohibitions against bills of attainder, whether urged by a former President—or any citizen—is inevitably a major constitutional holding....

I

Separation of Powers

Appellant urges that Title I is an unconstitutional intrusion by Congress into the internal workings of the Office of the President, in violation of the constitutional principle of separation of powers. Three reasons support that conclusion. The well-established principles of separation of powers, as developed in the decisions of this Court, are violated if Congress compels or coerces the President, in matters relating to the operation and conduct of his office. Next, the Act is an exercise of executive—not legislative—power by the Legislative Branch. Finally, Title I works a sweeping modification of the constitutional privilege and historical practice of confidentiality of every Chief Executive since 1789.

A

As a threshold matter, we should first establish the standard of constitutional review by which Title I is to be judged. In the usual case, of course, legislation challenged in this Court benefits from a presumption of constitutionality. To survive judicial scrutiny a statutory enactment need only have a reasonable relationship to the promotion of an objective which the Constitution does not independently forbid, unless the legislation trenches on fundamental constitutional rights.

But where challenged legislation implicates fundamental constitutional guarantees, a far more demanding scrutiny is required. For example, this Court has held that the presumption of constitutionality does not apply with equal force where the very legitimacy of the composition of representative institutions is at stake. *Reynolds* v. *Sims*...(1964). Similarly, the presumption of constitutionality is lessened when the Court reviews legislation endangering fundamental constitutional rights, such as freedom of speech, or which denies persons governmental rights or benefits because of race. Legislation touching substantially on these areas comes here bearing a heavy burden which its proponents must carry.

Long ago, this Court found the ordinary presumption of constitutionality inappropriate in measuring legislation directly impinging on the basic tripartite structure of our government. In *Kilbourn* v. *Thompson...*(1880), Mr. Justice Miller observed for the Court that encroachments by Congress posed the greatest threat to the continued independence of the other branches. Accordingly, he cautioned that the exercise of power by one branch directly affecting the potential independence of another "should be watched with vigilance, and when called in question before any other tribunal...should receive *the most careful scrutiny....*" See also *Buckley* v. *Valeo...*(1976).

Our role in reviewing legislation which touches on the fundamental structure of our government is therefore akin to that which obtains when reviewing legislation touching on other fundamental constitutional guarantees. Because separation of powers is the base framework of our governmental system and the means by which all our liberties depend, Title I can be upheld only if it is necessary to secure some overriding governmental objective, and if there is no reasonable alternative which will trench less heavily on separation-of-powers principles.

B

Separation of powers is in no sense a formalism. It is the characteristic that distinguished our system from all others conceived up to the time of our Constitution. With federalism, separation of powers is "one of the two great structural principles of the American constitutional system...." E. Corwin, The President 9 (1957). See also *Griswold* v. *Connecticut....*

In pursuit of that principle, executive power was vested in the President; no other offices in the Executive Branch, other than the Presidency and Vice Presidency, were mandated by the Constitution. Only two Executive Branch offices, therefore, are creatures of the Constitution; all other departments and agencies, from the State Department to the General Services Administration, are creatures of the Congress and owe their very existence to the Legislative Branch.

The Presidency, in contrast, stands on a very different footing. Unlike the vast array of departments which the President oversees, the Presidency is in no sense a creature of the Legislature. The President's powers originate not from statute, but from the constitutional command to "take Care that the Laws be faithfully executed...." These independent, constitutional origins of the Presidency have an important bearing on determining the appropriate extent of congressional power over the Chief Executive or his records and work papers. For, although the branches of government are obviously not divided into "watertight compartments," *Springer* v. *Philippine Islands...*(1928) (Holmes, J.), the office of the Presidency, as a constitutional equal of Congress, must as a general proposition be free from Congress' *coercive* powers. This is not simply an abstract proposition of political philosophy; it is a fundamental prohibition plainly established by the decisions of this Court...

Part of our constitutional fabric, then, from the beginning has been the President's freedom from control or coercion by Congress, including attempts to procure documents that, though clearly pertaining to matters of important governmental interests, belong and pertain to the President. This freedom from Congress' coercive influence, in the words of *Humphrey's Executor* [v. *United States* (1935)], "is implied in the very fact of separation of powers...." Moreover, it is not constitutionally significant that Congress has not directed that the papers be turned over to it for examination or retention, rather than to GSA. Separation of powers is fully implicated simply by Congress' mandating what disposition is to be made of the papers of another Branch.

This independence of the three Branches of government, including control over the papers of each, lies at the heart of this Court's broad holdings concerning the immunity of *congressional* papers from outside scrutiny. The Constitution, of course, expressly grants immunity to Members of Congress as to any "Speech or Debate in either House...."; yet, the Court has refused to confine the Clause literally "to words spoken in debate...." *Powell* v. *McCormack*...(1969). Congressional papers, including Congressional reports, have been held protected by the Clause in order "to prevent intimidation [of legislators] by the executive and accountability before a possibly hostile judiciary...." In a word, to preserve the constitutionally rooted independence of each Branch of government, each Branch must be able to control its own papers.

Title I is an unprecedented departure from the constitutional tradition of noncompulsion. The statute commands the head of a *legislatively* created department to take and maintain custody of appellant's Presidential papers, including many purely personal papers wholly unrelated to any operations of the Government. Title I does not concern itself in any way with materials belonging to departments of the Executive Branch created and controlled by Congress.

The Court brushes aside the fundamental principle of noncompulsion, abandoning outright the careful, previously unchallenged holdings of this Court in [*Massachusetts* v.] *Mellon* [1923], *O'Donoghue* [v. *United States* (1933)] and *Humphrey's Executor.* In place of this firmly established doctrine, the Court substitutes, without analysis, an ill-defined "pragmatic, flexible approach...." Recasting, for the immediate purposes of this case, our narrow holding in *United States* v. *Nixon*...(1974)...the Court distills separation-of-powers principles into a simplistic rule which requires a "potential for disruption" or an "unduly disruptive" intrusion, before a measure will be held to trench on President powers.

The Court's approach patently ignores *Buckley* v. *Valeo,* where, only one year ago, we *unanimously* found a separation-of-powers violation without any allegation, much less a showing, of "undue disruption." There, we held that Congress could not impinge, even to the modest extent of six appointments to the Federal Election Commission, on the appointing powers of the President. We reached this conclusion in the face of the fact that President Ford had signed the bill into law and that the Department of Justice itself supported the Act as not posing any separation-of-powers problems.

But even taking the "undue disruption" test as postulated, the Court engages in a facile analysis, as MR. JUSTICE REHNQUIST so well demonstrates. We are told, under the Court's view, that no "undue disruption" arises because GSA officials have taken custody of appellant's Presidential papers, and since, for the time being, only GSA and other Executive Branch officials will have access to them....

This analysis is superficial in the extreme. Separation-of-powers principles are no less eroded simply because *Congress* goes through a "minuet" of directing Executive Department employees, rather than the Secretary of the Senate or the Doorkeeper of the House, to possess and control Presidential papers. Whether there has been a violation of separation-of-powers principles depends not on the identity of the custodians, but upon which Branch has commanded the custodians to act. Here, Congress has given the command.

If separation-of-powers principles can be so easily evaded, then the constitutional separation is a sham.

Congress' power to regulate Executive Department *documents,* as contrasted with Presidential *papers,* under such measures as the Freedom of Information Act...does not bear on the question. No one challenges Congress' power to provide for access to records of the Executive Departments which Congress itself created. But the Freedom of Information Act, the Privacy Act, and similar measures never contemplated mandatory production of Presidential papers. What is instructive, by contrast, is the nonmandatory noncoercive manner in which Congress has previously legislated with respect to Presidential papers, by providing for Presidential Libraries *at the option* of every former President. Title I, however, breaches the nonmandatory tradition that has long been a vital incident of separation of powers.

C

The statute, therefore, violates separation-of-powers principles because it exercises a coercive influence by another Branch over the Presidency. The legislation is also invalid on another ground pertaining to separation of power; it is an attempt by Congress to exercise powers vested exclusively in the President—the power to control files, records and papers of the office, which are comparable to the internal work papers of Members of the House and Senate....

...In the 1975 Term, in the face of a holding by a Court of Appeals that the separation-of-powers challenge was meritless, we unanimously invalidated an attempt by Congress to exercise appointing powers constitutionally vested in the Chief Executive. *Buckley* v. *Valeo*...(1976).

The Constitution does not speak of Presidential papers, just as it does not speak of work papers of Members of Congress or of judges. But there can be no room for doubt that, up to now, it has been the implied prerogative of the President—as of Members of Congress and of judges—to memorialize matters, establish filing systems, and to provide unilaterally for disposition of his work papers. Control of Presidential papers is, obviously, a natural and necessary incident of the broad discretion vested in the President in order for him to discharge his duties. To be sure, we recognized a narrowly limited exception to Presidential control of Presidential papers in *United States* v. *Nixon...* (1974). But that case permits compulsory judicial intrusions only when a vital constitutional function, *i.e.,* the conduct of criminal proceedings, would be impaired *and* when the President makes no more "than a generalized claim of...public interest..." in maintaining complete control of papers and in preserving confidentiality. That case, in short, was essentially a conflict between the Judicial Branch and the President, where the effective functional of both Branches demanded an accommodation and where the prosecutorial and judicial demands upon the President were very narrowly restricted with great specificity "to a limited number of conversations...." Moreover, the request for production there was limited to materials that might themselves contain evidence of criminal activity of persons then under inquiry or indictment. Finally, the intrusion was carefully limited to an *in camera* examination, under strict limits, by a single United States District Judge. That case does not stand for the proposition that the Judiciary is at liberty to order *all* papers of a President into custody of United States Marshals.

United States v. *Nixon,* therefore, provides no authority for Congress' mandatory regulation of Presidential papers simply "to promote the General Welfare" which, of course, is a generalized purpose. No showing has been made, nor could it, that Congress' functions will be impaired by the former President's being allowed to control his own Presidential papers. Without any threat whatever to its own functions, Congress has by this statute, as in *Buckley* v. *Valeo,* exercised authority entrusted to the Executive Branch.

D

Finally, in my view, the Act violates principles of separation of powers by intruding into the confidentiality of Presidential communications protected by the constitutionally based doctrine of Presidential privilege. A unanimous Court in *United States* v. *Nixon* could not have been clearer in holding that the privilege guaranteeing confidentiality of such communications derives from the Constitution, subject to compelled disclosure only in narrowly limited circumstances....

...As a constitutionally based prerogative, Presidential privilege inures to the President himself; it is personal in the same sense as the privilege against compelled self-incrimination. Presidential privilege would therefore be largely illusory unless it could be interposed by the President against the countless thousands of persons in the Executive Branch, and most certainly if the Executive officials are acting, as this statute contemplates, at the command of a different branch of government.

This statute requires that persons not designated or approved by the former President will review all Presidential papers. Even if the government agents, in culling through the materials, follow the "advisory" suggestions offered by the District Court, the fact remains that their function abrogates the Presidential privilege. Congress has, in essence, commanded them to review and catalog thousands of papers and recordings that are undoubtedly privileged. Given that fact, it is clear that the Presidential privilege of one occupant of that office will have been rendered a nullity.

E

There remains another inquiry under the issue of separation of powers. Does the fact that the Act applies only to a former President, described as "a legitimate class of one," after he has left office, justify what would otherwise be unconstitutional if applicable to an incumbent President?

On the face of it, congressional regulation of the papers of a former President obviously will have less disruptive impact on the operations of an incumbent President than an effort at regulation or control over the same papers of an incumbent President. But this "remoteness" does not eliminate the separation-of-powers defects. First, the principle that a President must be free from coercion should apply to a former President, so long as Congress is inquiring or acting with respect to operations of the government while the former President was in office.

To the extent Congress is empowered to coerce a *former* President, every future President is at risk of denial of a large measure of the autonomy and independence contemplated by the Constitution and of the confidentiality attending it. *Myers* v. *United States*...(1926). Indeed, the President, if he is to have autonomy while in office, needs the assurance that Congress will not immediately be free to coerce him to open all his files and records and give an account of Presidential actions at the instant his successor is sworn in. Absent the validity of the expectation of privacy of such papers...future Presidents and those they consult will be well advised to take into account the possibility that their most confidential correspondence, work papers, and diaries may well be open to congressionally mandated review, with no time limit, should some political issue give rise to an interbranch conflict.

The Need For Confidentiality

The consequences of this development on what a President expresses to others in writing and orally are incalculable; perhaps even more crucial is the inhibiting impact on those to whom the President turns for information and for counsel, whether they are officials in the government, business or labor leaders, or foreign diplomats and statesmen. I have little doubt that Title I—and the Court's opinion—will be the subject of careful scrutiny and analysis in the foreign offices of other countries whose representatives speak to a President on matters they prefer not to put in writing, but which may be memorialized by a President or an aide. Similarly, Title I may well be a "ghost" at future White House conferences, with conferees choosing their words more cautiously because of the enlarged prospect of compelled disclosure to others. A unanimous Court carefully took this into account in *United States* v. *Nixon....*

In this same vein, MR. JUSTICE POWELL argues that the Solicitor General's representation to the Court that Title I enhances the efficiency of the Executive Branch is dispositive of appellant's separation-of-powers claim. This deference to the views of one Administration, expressed approximately 100 days after its inception, as to the permanent structure of our government is not supported by precedent and conflicts with 188 years of history. First, there is no principled basis for limiting this unique deference. If and when the one-House veto issue, for example, comes before us, are we to accept the opinion of the Department of Justice as to the effects of that legislative device on the Executive Branch's operations? Second, if Title I is thus efficacious, why did the President who signed this bill into law decide to establish a Presidential Library in Ann Arbor, Michigan, rather than turn all of his Presidential materials over to GSA for screening and retention in Washington, D.C., where the materials would be readily accessible to officials of the Executive Branch? And why, suddenly, is Congress' acquiescence in President Ford's actions consistent with the supposed foundation of Title I?

Third, as pointed out by MR. JUSTICE BLACKMUN..."[p]olitical realities often guide a President to a decision not to veto" or indeed, a decision not to challenge in court the action of Congress.... Finally, it is perhaps not inappropriate to note that, on occasion, Presidents disagree with their predecessors on issues of policy. Some have believed in "Congressional Government"; others adhered to expansive notions of Presidential power. It is, I respectfully submit, a unique idea that this Court accept as controlling the representations of any Administration on a constitutional question going to the permanent structure of government.

Title I is also objectionable on separation-of-powers grounds, despite its applicability only to a former President, because compelling the disposition of all of a former President's papers is a legislative exercise of what have historically been regarded as executive powers. Presidential papers do not, after all, instantly lose their nature quadrennially at high noon on January 20. Moreover, under Title I it is now the Congress, not the incumbent President, that has decided what to do with *all* the papers of one entire Administration.

Finally, the Government concedes that Presidential privilege, a vital incident of our separation-of-powers system, does not terminate instantly upon a President's departure from office. The Government candidly acknowledges "the privilege survives the individual President's tenure..." because of the vital public interests underlying the privilege. This principle, as all parties concede, finds explicit support in history; former President Truman in 1953 refused to provide information to the Congress on matters occurring during his Administration....

To ensure institutional integrity and confidentiality, Presidents and their advisers must have assurance, as do judges and Members of Congress, that their internal communications will not become subject to retroactive legislation mandating intrusions into matters as to which there was a well-founded expectation of privacy when the communications took place. Just as Mr. Truman rejected congressional efforts to inquire of him, after he left office, as to his activities while President, this Court has always assumed that the immunity conferred by the Speech or Debate Clause is available to a Member of Congress after he leaves office. *United States* v. *Brewster*...[1972].... It would therefore be illogical to conclude that the President loses all immunity from legislative coercion as to his Presidential papers from the moment he leaves office.

The Court correctly concedes that a former President retains the Presidential privilege after leaving office...; but it then concludes that several considerations cut against recognition of the privilege as to one former President. First, the Court places great emphasis on the fact that neither President Ford nor President Carter "supports appellant's claim....

...The relevance of that fact is not immediately clear. The validity of one person's constitutional privilege does not depend on whether some other holder of the same privilege supports his claim. The fact that an *incumbent* President has signed or supports a particular measure cannot defeat a *former* President's claim of privilege. If the Court is correct today, it was wrong one year ago in *Buckley* v. *Valeo*, when we unanimously held that Presidential approval of the Federal Elections Act could not validate an unconstitutional invasion of Presidential appointing authority.

Second, the Court suggests that many of the papers are unprivileged. Of the great volume of pages, appellant estimated that he saw only about 200,000 items while he was President. Several points are relevant in this regard. We do not know how many pages the 200,000 items represent; the critical factor is that all papers are presumptively privileged. Regardless of the number of pages, the fact remains that the 200,000 items that the President personally reviewed or prepared while in office obviously have greater historical value than the mass of routine papers coming to the White House. Mountains of government reports tucked away in Presidential files will not likely engage the interest of archivists or historians, since most such reports are not historically important and are, in any event, available elsewhere. Rather, archivists and historians will want to find and preserve the materials that reflect the President's internal decisionmaking processes. Those are precisely the papers which will be subjected to the most intensive review and which have always been afforded absolute protection. The Court's analytically void invocation of sheer numbers cannot mask the fact that the targets of the review are privileged papers, diaries and conversations.

I agree that, under *United States* v. *Nixon*, the Presidential privilege is qualified. From that premise, however, the Court leaps to the conclusion that future regulations governing *public access* to the materials are sufficient to protect that qualified privilege. The Act does indeed provide for a number of safeguards before the public at large obtains access to the materials.... But the Court cannot have it both ways. The opinion expressly recognizes again and again that *public access is not now the issue.* The constitutionality of a statute cannot rest on the presumed validity of regulations not yet issued; moreover, no regulations governing public access can remedy the statute's basic flaw of permitting Congress to seize the confidential papers of a President.

F

In concluding that Title I on its face violates the principle of separation of powers, I do not address the issue whether some circumstances might justify legislation for the disposition of Presidential papers without the President's consent. Here, nothing remotely like the *particularized need* we found in *United States* v. *Nixon* has been shown with respect to these Presidential papers. No one has suggested that Congress will find its own "core" functioning impaired by lack of the impounded papers, as we expressly found the judicial function would be impaired by lack of the material subpoenaed in *United States* v. *Nixon.*

I leave to another day the question whether, under exigent circumstances, a *narrowly defined* congressional demand for Presidential materials might be justified. But Title I fails to satisfy either the required narrowness demanded by *United States* v. *Nixon* or the requirement that the coequal powers of the Presidency not be injured by congressional legislation.

II

Privacy

The discussion of separation of powers concerns, of course, the structure of government, not the rights of the sole individual ostensibly affected by this legislation. But Title I of the Act before us touches not only upon the independence of a coordinate branch of government, it also affects, in the most direct way, the basic rights of one named individual. The statute provides, as we have seen, for governmental custody over—and review of—all of the former President's written and recorded materials at the time he left office, including diary recordings and conversations in his private residences outside Washington, D.C....

The District Court was deeply troubled by this admittedly unprecedented intrusion. Its opinion candidly acknowledged that the personal-privacy claim was the "most troublesome" point raised by this unique statute. In addition to communications and memoranda reflecting the President's confidential deliberations, the District Court admitted that the materials subject to GSA review included highly personal communications....

A

Given this admitted intrusion, the legislation before us must be subjected to the most searching kind of judicial scrutiny. Statutes that trench on fundamental liberties, like those affecting significantly the structure of our government, are not entitled to the same presumption of constitutionality we normally accord legislation. *Moore* v. *City of East Cleveland*...[1977]. The burden of justification is reversed; the burden rests upon government, not on the individual whose liberties are affected, to justify the measure. *Abood* v. *Detroit Board of Education*...[1977]. We recently reaffirmed the standard or review in such cases as one of "exacting scrutiny...."

B

Constitutional analysis must, of course, take fully into account the nature of the Government's interests underlying challenged legislation. Once those interests are identified, we must then focus on the nature of the individual interests affected by the statute.... Finally, we must decide whether the Government's interests are of sufficient weight to subordinate the individual's interests, and, if so, whether the Government has nonetheless employed unnecessarily broad means for achieving its purposes. *Lamont* v. *Postmaster General*...(1965)....

Two governmental interests are asserted as the justification for this statute: to ensure the general efficiency of the Executive Branch's operations and to preserve historically significant papers and tape recordings for posterity. Both these purposes are legitimate and important. Yet, there was no serious suggestion by Congress that the operations of the Executive Branch would actually be impaired unless, contrary to nearly 200 years' past practice, all Presidential papers of the one named incumbent were required by law to be impounded in the sole control of government agents. The statute on its face, moreover, does not purport to address a particularized need, such as the need to secure Presidential papers concerning the Middle East, the SALT talks, or problems in Panama. Indeed, the congressionally perceived "need" is a far more "generalized need" than that rejected in *United States* v. *Nixon* by a unanimous Court.

As to the interest in preserving historical materials, there is nothing whatever in our national experience to suggest that existing mechanisms, such as the 20-year-old Presidential Libraries Act, were insufficient to achieve that purpose. In any event, the interest in preserving "historical materials" cannot justify seizing, without notice or hearing, private papers preliminary to a line-by-line examination by government agents.

In contrast to Congress' purposes underlying the statute, this Act intrudes significantly on two areas of traditional privacy interests of Presidents. One embraces Presidential papers relating to his decisions, development of policies, appointments, and communications in his role as leader of a political party; the other encompasses purely private matters of family, property, investments, diaries and intimate conversations. Both interests are of the highest order, with perhaps some primacy for family papers. *Moore* v. *City of East Cleveland.*

One point emerges clearly: the papers here involve the most fundamental First and Fourth Amendment interests. Since the Act asserts *exclusive* government custody over *all* papers of a former President, the Fourth Amendment's prohibition against unreasonable searches and seizures is surely implicated. Indeed, where papers or books are the subject of a government intrusion, our cases uniformly hold that the Fourth Amendment prohibition against a general search requires that warrants contain descriptions reflecting "the most scrupulous exactitude...," *Stanford* v. *Texas*.... (1965). Those cases proscribe general language in a warrant—or a statute—of "indiscriminate sweep...." Title I, commanding seizure followed by permanent control of all materials having "historical or commemorative value," evidences the "indiscriminate sweep" we have long denounced. This "broad broom" statute provides virtually no standard at all to guide the government agents combing through the papers; the agents are left to roam at large through confidential materials, something to which no other President, no Member of Congress or of the Judicial Branch has been subjected.

The Court, while recognizing that government agents will necessarily be reviewing the most private kinds of communications covering a period of five and one-half years, tells us that *Stanford* is inapposite. Several reasons are given. The Court suggests that, unlike the instant case, the seizure in *Stanford* includes vast quantities of materials unrelated to any legitimate government objective; in addition, the *Stanford* intrusion constituted an invasion of the home in connection with a criminal investigation. That last consideration relied on by the Court can be disposed of quickly, for by its terms, just as in *Stanford*, Title I commands seizure and reviewing of papers from appellant's *private residences* outside Washington, D.C.,...for the purpose, among others, of criminal proceedings brought by the Special Prosecutor...and to make the materials available more broadly "for use in judicial proceedings...." § 104(a)(12). Title I is not needed for this purpose, since a narrowly defined subpoena can accomplish those purposes under *United States* v. *Nixon.* Title I is in effect a "legislative warrant" reminiscent of the odious general warrants of the colonial era.

As to the Court's first consideration, its "quantity" test is fallacious. The intrusion in *Stanford* was unlawful not because the Government had an interest in only part of many items in Stanford's home, but rather because the warrant failed to describe the objects of seizure with the "most scrupulous exactitude." *Stanford* is not a "numbers" test, the protection of which vanishes if unprotected materials outnumber protected materials; it is, rather, a test designed to ensure *that protected materials are not seized at all.* Title I on its face commands that protected materials be seized wherever found—including the private residences mentioned—reviewed, and returned only if the government agents decide that certain protected materials lack historical significance. The Act plainly accomplishes exactly what *Stanford* expressly forbids.

In addition to Fourth Amendment considerations, highly important First Amendment interests pervade all Presidential papers, since they include expressions of privately held views about politics, diplomacy or people of all walks of life, within and outside this country. Appellant's freedom of association is also implicated, since his recordings and papers will likely reveal much about his relationships with both individuals and organizations....

The fact that the former President was an important national and world political figure obviously does not diminish the traditional privacy interest in his papers. Forced disclosure of private information, even to Government officials, is by no means sanctioned by this Court's decisions, except for the most compelling reasons. ...*Whalen* v. *Roe*...(1977). I do not think, for example, that this Court would readily sustain, as a condition to holding public office, a requirement that a candidate reveal publicly membership in every organization whether religious, social, or political. After all, our decision in *NAACP* v. *Alabama*...[1958] was presumably intended to protect from compelled disclosure members of the organization who were actively involved in public affairs or who held public office in Alabama.

The Court's reliance on *Whalen* v. *Roe*...in rejecting appellant's privacy claim is surprising. That case dealt with the State's undoubted police power to regulate dispensing of dangerous drugs, the very use or possession of which the State could forbid.... Hence, we had no difficulty whatever in reaching a unanimous holding that the public interest in regulating *dangerous drugs* outweighed any privacy interest in reporting to the State all prescriptions, those reports being made confidential by statute. No personal, private business, or political confidences were involved.

C

In short, a former President up to now has had essentially the same expectation of privacy with respect to his papers and records as every other person. This expectation is soundly based on two factors: first, under our constitutional traditions, Presidential papers have been, for more than 180 years, deemed by the Congress to belong to the President. Congress ratified this tradition by specific acts: (a) Congressional appropriations following authorization to purchase Presidential papers; (b) Congressional enactment of a nonmandatory system of Presidential Libraries; and (c) statutes permitting, until 1969, a charitable-contribution deduction for papers of Presidents donated to the United States or to nonprofit institutions.

Second, in the absence of any legislation to the contrary, there was no reason whatever for a President to take time from his official duties to ensure that there was no "commingling" of "public" and private papers. Indeed, the fact that the former President commingled Presidential and private family papers, absent any then-existing laws to the contrary, points strongly to the conclusion that he did in fact have an expectation of privacy with respect to both categories of papers.

On the basis of this Court's holdings, I cannot understand why the former President's privacy interests do not outweigh the generalized, undifferentiated goals sought to be achieved by Title I. Without a more carefully defined focus, these legislative goals do not represent "paramount government interests," nor is this particular piece of legislation needed to achieve those goals, even if we assume, *arguendo,* that they are of a "compelling" or "overriding" nature. But even if other Members of the Court strike the balance differently, the Government has nonetheless failed to choose narrowly tailored means of carrying out its purposes so as not to invade unnecessarily important First and Fourth Amendment liberties. The Court demanded no less in *Buckley* v. *Valeo*...and nothing less will do here. Cf. *Hynes* v. *Mayor of Borough of Oradell*...(1976).

The Government points to two factors as mitigating the effects of this admitted intrusion: first, in its view, most of the President's papers and conversations relate to the business of government, rather than to personal, family or political matters; second, it is said that the intrusion is limited as much as possible, since the review will be carried out by specially trained government agents.

Even accepting the Government's interest in identifying and preserving governmentally related papers in order to preserve them for historical purposes, that interest cannot justify a seizure and search of *all* the papers taken here. Since compulsory review of personal and family papers and tape recordings is an admittedly improper invasion of privacy, no constitutional principle justifies an intrusion into indisputably protected areas in order to carry out the "generalized" statutory objectives.

Second, the intrusion cannot be saved by the credentials, however impeccable, of the government agents. The initial problem with this justification is that no one knows whether these agents are, as the Government contends, uniformly discreet. Despite the lip service paid by the District Court and appellees to the record of archivists generally, there is nothing before us to justify the conclusion that each of the more than 100 persons who apparently will have access to, and will monitor and examine, the materials is indeed reliably discreet.

The Act, furthermore, provides GSA with no meaningful standards to minimize the extent of intrusions upon appellant's privacy. We are thus faced with precisely the same standardless discretion vested in governmental officials which this Court has unhesitatingly struck down in other First Amendment areas.... In the absence of any meaningful statutory standards, which might help secure the privacy interests at stake, I question whether we can assume, as a matter of law, that government agents will be able to formulate for themselves constitutionally valid standards of review in examining, segregating and cataloging the papers of the former President.

Nor does the possibility that, had Title I not been passed, appellant would perhaps use government specialists to help classify and catalog his papers eliminate the objections to this intrusion. Had appellant, like all his recent predecessors, been permitted to deposit his papers in a Presidential library, government archivists would have been working directly under appellant's guidance and direction, not solely that of Congress or GSA. He, not Congress, would have established standards for preservation, to ensure that his privacy would be protected. Similarly, he would have been able to participate personally in the reviewing process and could thus assure that any governmental review of purely personal papers was minimized or entirely eliminated. He, not Congress, would have controlled the selection of which experts, if any, would have access to his papers. Finally, and most important, the "intrusion" would have been consented to, eliminating any constitutional question. But the *possibility* of a consent intrusion cannot, under our law, justify a nonconsensual invasion. Actual consent is required, cf. *Schneckloth* v. *Bustamonte...* (1973), not the mere possibility of consent under drastically different circumstances.

Finally, even if the government agents are completely discreet, they are still government officials charged with reviewing highly private papers and tape recordings. Unless we are to say that a police seizure and examination of private papers is justified by the "impeccable" record of a discreet police officer, I have considerable difficulty understanding how a compulsory review of admittedly private papers, in which there is no conceivable governmental interest, by government agents is constitutionally permissible.

III

Bill of Attainder

Under Art. I, § 9, cl. 3, as construed and applied by this Court since the time of Chief Justice Marshall, Title I violates the Bill of Attainder Clause. In contrast to Title II of the Act, which establishes a National Study Commission to study questions concerning the preservation of records of *all* Federal officials, Title I commands the Administrator to seize all tape recordings "involv[ing] former President Richard M. Nixon and all Presidential historical materials of Richard M. Nixon...." § 101 (a)(1), (b)(1). By contrast with Title II, which is general legislation, Title I is special legislation singling out one individual as the target.

Although the prohibition against bills of attainder has been addressed only infrequently by this Court, it is now settled beyond dispute that a bill of attainder, within the meaning of Art. I, is by no means the same as a bill of attainder at common law. The definition departed from the common-law concept very early in our history, in a most fundamental way. At common law, the bill was a death sentence imposed by legislative act. Anything less than death was not a bill of attainder, but was, rather, "a bill of pains and penalties." This restrictive definition was recognized tangentially in *Marbury* v. *Madison...* (1803), but the Court soon thereafter rejected conclusively any notion that only a legislative death sentence or even incarceration imposed on named individuals fell within the prohibition. Chief Justice Marshall firmly settled the matter in 1810, holding that legislative punishment in the form of a deprivation of property was prohibited by the Bill of Attainder Clause.... The same point was made 17 years later in *Ogden* v. *Saunders...* (1827).... More than 100 years ago this Court struck down statutes which had the effect of preventing defined categories of persons from practicing their professions. *Cummings*

v. *Missouri*...(1866) (a priest); *Ex parte Garland*,...[1866] (a lawyer). Those two cases established more broadly that "punishment" for purposes of bills of attainder is not limited to criminal sanctions; rather, "[t]he deprivation of *any rights, civil,* or political, *previously enjoyed,* may be punishment...."

Chief Justice Warren pointed out that the Constitution, in prohibiting bills of attainder, did not envision "a narrow, technical (and therefore soon to be outmoded) prohibition...." *United States* v. *Brown*...(1965). To the contrary, the evil was a *legislatively imposed* deprivation of existing rights, including property rights, directed at named individuals...*United States* v. *Lovett*...(1946).... The only "punishment" in *Lovett*, in fact, was the deprivation of Lovett's salary as a government employee—an indirect punishment for his "bad" associations.

Under our cases, therefore, bills of attainder require two elements: first, a specific designation of persons or groups as subjects of the legislation, and, second, a *Garland, Cummings, Lovett-Brown*-type arbitrary deprivation, including deprivation of property rights, without notice, trial or other hearing. No one disputes that Title I of the Act before us suffers from the first infirmity, since it applies only to one former President. The issue that remains is whether there has been a legislatively mandated deprivation of an existing right....

...I see no escape, therefore, from the conclusion that, on the basis of more than 180 years' history, the appellant has been deprived of a property right enjoyed by all Presidents after leaving office, namely, the control of his Presidential papers.

Even more starkly, Title I deprives only one former President of the right *vested by statute* in other former Presidents by the 1955 Act—the right to have a Presidential Library at a facility of his own choosing for the deposit of such Presidential papers as he unilaterally selects. Title I did not purport to repeal the Presidential Libraries Act; that statute remains in effect, available to present and future Presidents, and has already been availed of by former President Ford. The operative effect of Title I, therefore, is to exclude, by name, one former President and deprive him of what his predecessors—and his successor—have already been allowed....

But apart from Presidential papers generally, Title I on its face contemplates that even the former President's purely family and personal papers and tape recordings are likewise to be taken into custody for whatever period of time is required for review. Some items, such as the originals of tape recordings of the former President's conversations, will never be returned to him under the Act.

I need not, and do not, inquire into the motives of Congress in imposing this deprivation on only one named person. Our cases plainly hold that retribution and vindictiveness are not requisite elements of a bill of attainder. The Court appears to overlook that Chief Justice Warren in *Brown* v. *United States*...concluded that retributive motives on the part of Congress were irrelevant to bill-of-attainder analysis. To the contrary, he said flatly: "It would be archaic to limit the definition of punishment to 'retribution.' " Indeed, he expressly noted that the bills of attainder had historically been enacted for regulatory or preventive purposes....

Under the long line of our decisions, therefore, the Court has the heavy burden of demonstrating that legislation which singles out one named individual for deprivation—without any procedural safeguards—of what had for nearly 200 years been treated by all three Branches of government as private property, can survive the prohibition of the Bill of Attainder Clause. In deciding this case, the Court provides the basis for a future Congress to enact yet another Title I, directed at some future former President, or a Member of the House or the Senate because the individual has incurred public disfavor, and that of the Congress. *Powell* v. *McCormack*...(1969). As in *Brown* v. *United States*,...Title I of the present statute...is beyond doubt special legislation doing precisely the evil against which the prohibitions of the "bill of attainder, *ex post facto* laws and laws impairing the obligation of contracts..." were aimed....

The concurring opinions make explicit what is implicit throughout the Court's opinion, *i.e.*, (a) that Title I would be unconstitutional under separation-of-powers principles if it applied to any other President; (b) that the Court's holding rests on appellant's being a "legitimate class of one,..." and (c) that the Court's holding "will not be a precedent...."

Nothing in our cases supports the analysis of MR. JUSTICE STEVENS.... Under his view, appellant's resignation and subsequent acceptance of a pardon set him apart as a " 'legitimate class of one.' " The two events upon which he relies, however, are beside the point. Correct analysis under the Bill of Attainder Clause focuses solely upon the nature of the measure adopted by Congress, not upon the actions of the target of the legislation. Even if this approach were analytically sound, the two events singled out are relevant only to two possible theories: first, that appellant is culpably deserving of punishment by virtue of his resignation and pardon; or second, that appellant's actions were so unique as to justify legislation confiscating his Presidential materials but not those of any other President. The first point can be disposed of quickly, since the Bill of Attainder Clause was of course intended to prevent legislatively imposed deprivations of rights upon persons who the Legislature thought to be culpably deserving of punishment.

The remaining question, then, is whether appellant's "uniqueness" permits individualized legislation of the sort passed here. It does not. The point is not that Congress is powerless to act as to exigencies arising during or in the immediate aftermath of a particular Administration; rather, the point is that Congress cannot *punish* a particular individual on account of his "uniqueness." If Congress had declared forfeited appellant's retirement pay to which he otherwise would be entitled, instead of confiscating his Presidential materials, it would not avoid the bill-of-attainder prohibition to say that appellant was guilty of unprecedented actions setting him apart from his predecessors in office. In short, appellant's uniqueness does not justify serious deprivations of existing rights, including the statutory right abrogated by Title I to establish a Presidential Library.

The novel arguments advanced in the several concurring opinions serve to emphasize how clearly Title I violates the Bill of Attainder Clause; MR. JUSTICE STEVENS although finding no violation of the Clause, admirably states the case which, for me, demonstrates the unconstitutionality of Title I....

IV

The immediate consequences of the Court's holding may be discounted by some on the grounds it is justified by the uniqueness of the circumstances—in short, that the end justifies the means—and that, after all, the Court's holding is really not to be regarded as precedent. Yet the reported decisions of this Court reflect other instances in which unique situations confronted the Judicial Branch, for example, the alleged treason of one of the Founding Fathers. *United States* v. *Burr...* (1807). Burr may or may not have been blameless; Father Cummings and Lawyer Garland, in common with hundreds of thousands of others, may have been technically guilty of "carrying on rebellion" against the United States. But this Court did not weigh the culpability of Cummings, Garland, or of Lovett or Brown in according to each of them the full measure of the protection guaranteed by the literal language of the Constitution. For nearly 200 years this Court has not viewed either a "class" or a "class of one" as "legitimate" under the Bill of Attainder Clause.

It may be, as three Justices intimate in their concurring opinions, that today's holding will be confined to this particular "class of one"; if so it may not do great harm to our constitutional jurisprudence but neither will it enhance the Court's credit in terms of adherence to *stare decisis.* Only with future analysis, in perspective, and free from the "hydraulic pressure" Holmes spoke of, will we be able to render judgment on whether the Court has today enforced the Constitution or eroded it.

MR. JUSTICE REHNQUIST, dissenting.

Appellant resigned the Office of the Presidency nearly three years ago, and if the issue here were limited to the right of Congress to dispose of his particular Presidential papers, this case would not be of major constitutional significance. Unfortunately, however, today's decision countenances the power of any future Congress to seize the official papers of an out-going President as he leaves the inaugural stand. In so doing, it poses a real threat to the ability of future Presidents to receive candid advice and to give candid instructions. This result, so at odds with our previous case law on the separation of powers, will daily stand as a veritable sword of Damocles over every succeeding President and his advisors. Believing as I do that the Act is a clear violation of the constitutional principle separation of powers, I need not address the other issues considered by the Court.

My conclusion that the Act violates the principle of separation of powers is based upon three fundamental propositions. First, candid and open discourse among the President, his advisors, foreign heads of state and Ambassadors, Members of Congress, and the others who deal with the White House on a sensitive basis is an absolute prerequisite to the effective discharge of the duties of that high office. Second, the effect of the Act, and of this Court's decision upholding its constitutionality, will undoubtedly restrain the necessary free flow of information to and from present and future Presidents. Third, any substantial intrusion upon the effective discharge of the duties of the President is sufficient to violate the principle of separation of powers, and our prior cases do not permit the sustaining of an Act such as this by "balancing" an intrusion of substantial magnitude against the interests assertedly fostered by the Act.

With respect to the second point, it is of course true that the Act is directed solely at the papers of former President Nixon. Although the terms of the Act, therefore, have no direct application to present or future occupants of the Office, the effect upon candid communication to and from these future Presidents depends, in the long run, not upon the limited nature of the present Act, but upon the precedential effect of today's decision. Unless the authority of Congress to seize the papers of this appellant is limited only to him in some principled way, future Presidents and their advisors will be wary of a similar Act directed at their papers out of pure political hostility.

We are dealing with a privilege, albeit a qualified one, that both the Court and the Solicitor General concede may be asserted by an ex-President. It is a privilege which has been relied upon by chief executives since the time of George Washington.... Unfortunately, the Court's opinion upholding the constitutionality of this Act is obscure, to say the least, as to the circumstances that will justify Congress in seizing the papers of an ex-President. A potpourri of reasons is advanced as to why the Act is not an unconstitutional infringement upon the principle of separation of powers, but the weight to be attached to any of the factors is left wholly unclear.

The Court speaks of the need to establish procedures to preserve Presidential materials, to allow a successor President access to the papers of the prior President, to grant the American public historical access, and to rectify the present "hit-or-miss" approach by entrusting the materials to the expert handling of the archivists.... These justifications are equally applicable to each and every future President, and other than one cryptic paragraph...the Court's treatment contains no suggestion that Congress might not permissibly seize the papers of any outgoing future President. The unclear scope of today's opinion will cause future Presidents and their advisors to be uneasy over the confidentiality of their communications, thereby restraining those communications.

The position of my BROTHERS POWELL and BLACKMUN is that today's opinion will not result in an impediment to future Presidential communications since this case is "unique"—appellant resigned in disgrace from the Presidency during events unique in the history of our Nation. MR. JUSTICE POWELL recognizes that this position is quite different from that of the Court.... Unfortunately his concurring view that the authority of Congress is limited to the situation he describes does not itself change the expansive scope of the Court's opinion, and will serve as scant consolation to future Presidential advisors. For so long as the Court's opinion represents a threat to confidential communications, the concurrences of MR. JUSTICE POWELL and MR. JUSTICE BLACKMUN, I fear, are based on no more than wishful thinking.

Were the Court to advance a principled justification for affirming the judgment solely on the facts surrounding appellant's fall from office, the effect of its decision upon future presidential communications would be far less serious. But the Court does not advance any such justification.

A

It would require far more of a discourse than could profitably be included in an opinion such as this to fully describe the pre-eminent position that the President of the United States occupies with respect to our Republic. Suffice it to say that the President is made the sole repository of the executive powers of the United States, and the powers entrusted to him as well as the duties imposed upon him are awesome indeed. Given the vast spectrum of the decisions that confront him—domestic affairs, relationships with foreign powers, direction of the military as Commander-in-Chief—it is by no means an overstatement to conclude that current, accurate, and absolutely candid information is essential to the proper performance of his office. Nor is it an overstatement to conclude that the President must be free to give frank and candid instructions to his subordinates. It cannot be denied that one of the principal determinants of the quality of the information furnished to the President will be the degree of trust placed in him by those who confide in him....

...There simply can be no doubt that it is of the utmost importance for sensitive communications to the President to be viewed as confidential, and generally unreachable without the President's consent.

B

In order to fully understand the impact of this Act upon the confidential communications in the White House, it must be understood that the Act will affect not merely former President Nixon, but the present and future Presidents. As discussed above, while this Act itself addresses only the papers of former President Nixon, today's decision upholding its constitutionality renders uncertain the constitutionality of future congressional action directed at any ex-President. Thus Presidential confidants will assume, correctly, that any records of communications to the President could be subject to "appropriation" in much the same manner as the present Act seized the records of confidential communications to and from President Nixon. When advice is sought by future Presidents, no one will be unmindful of the fact that, as a result of the uncertainty engendered by today's decision, all confidential communications of any ex-President could be subject to seizure over his objection, as he leaves the inaugural stand on January 20.

And Presidential communications will undoubtedly be impeded by the recognition that there is a substantial probability of public disclosure of material seized under this Act, which, by today's decision, is a constitutional blueprint for future Acts. First, the Act on its face requires that 100-odd government archivists study and review Presidential papers, heretofore accessible only with the specific consent of the President. Second, the Act requires that public access is to be granted by future regulations consistent with "the need to provide public access to those materials which have general historical significance...." Section 104 (a)(6). Either of these provisions is sufficient to detract markedly from the candor of communications to and from the President.

In brushing aside the fact that the archivists are empowered to review the papers, the Court concludes that the archivists will be "discrete."... But there is no foundation for the Court's assumption that there will be no leaks. Any reviews that the archivists have made of Presidential papers in the past have been done only after authorization by the President, and after the President has had an opportunity to cull the most sensitive documents. It strikes me as extremely naive, and I dare say that this view will be shared by a large number of potential confidants of future Presidents, to suppose that each and every one of the archivists who might participate in a similar screening by virtue of a future Act would remain completely silent with respect to those portions of the Presidential papers which are extremely newsworthy. The Solicitor General, supporting the constitutionality of the Act, candidly conceded as much in oral argument....

It borders on the absurd for the Court to cite our recent decision in *Whalen* v. *Roe*..., as a precedent for the proposition that government officials will invariably honor provisions in a law dedicated to the preservation of privacy. It is quite doubtful, at least to my mind, that columnists or investigative reporters will be avidly searching for what doctor prescribed what drug for what patient in the State of New York, which was the information required to be furnished in *Whalen* v. *Roe*. But with respect to the advice received by a President, or the instructions given by him, on highly sensitive matters of great historical significance, the case is quite the opposite. Hence, at the minimum, today's decision upholding the constitutionality of this Act, mandating review by archivists, will engender the expectation that future confidential communications to the President may be subject to leaks or public disclosure without his consent.

In addition to this review by archivists, Presidential papers may now be seized and shown to the public if they are of "general historical significance." The Court attempts to avoid this problem with the wishful expectation that the regulations regarding public access, when promulgated, will be narrowly drawn. However, this assumes that a Presidential advisor will speak candidly based upon this same wishful assumption that the regulations, when ultimately issued and interpreted, will protect his confidences. But the current Act is over two and one-half years old and no binding regulations have yet been promulgated. And it is anyone's guess as to how long it will take before such ambiguous terms as "historical significance" are definitively interpreted, and as to whether some future administrator as yet unknown might issue a broader definition. Thus, the public access required by this Act will at the very least engender substantial uncertainty regarding whether future confidential communications will, in fact, remain confidential.

The critical factor in all of this is not that confidential material might be disclosed, since the President himself might choose to "go public" with it. The critical factor is that the determination as to whether to disclose is wrested by the Act from the President. When one speaks in confidence to a President, he necessarily relies upon the President's discretion not to disclose the sensitive. The President similarly relies on the discretion of a subordinate when instructing him. Thus it is no answer to suggest, as does the Court,...that the expectation of confidentiality has always been limited because Presidential papers have in the past been turned over to Presidential libraries or otherwise subsequently disclosed. In those cases, ultimate reliance was upon the discretion of the President to cull the sensitive before disclosure. But when, as is the case under this Act, the decision whether to disclose no longer resides in the President, communication will inevitably be restrained.

The Court, as does MR. JUSTICE POWELL, seeks to diminish the impact of this Act on the Office of the President by virtue of the fact that neither President Ford nor President Carter support appellant's claim.... It is quite true that President Ford signed the Act into law, and that the Solicitor General, representing President Carter, supports its constitutionality. While we must give due regard to the fact that these Presidents have not opposed the Act, we must also give due regard to the unusual political forces that have contributed to making this situation "unique...." MR. JUSTICE POWELL refers to the stance of the current executive as "dispositive"...and the Court places great emphasis upon it. I think this analysis is mistaken.

The current occupant of the Presidency cannot by signing into law a bill passed by Congress waive the claim of a successor President that the Act violates the separation of powers. We so held in *Myers* v. *United States*...(1926). And only last Term we unanimously held in *Buckley* v. *Valeo*...(1976), that persons with no connection to the Executive Branch of the Government may attack the constitutionality of a law signed by the President on the ground that it invaded authority reserved for the Executive Branch under the principle of the separation of powers. This principle, perhaps the most fundamental in our constitutional framework, may not be signed away by the temporary incumbent of the office which it was designed to protect.

MR. JUSTICE POWELL's view that the incumbent President must join the challenge of the ex-President places Presidential communications in limbo, since advisors, at the time of the communication, cannot know who the successor will be or what his stance will be regarding seizure by Congress of his predecessor's papers. Since the advisors cannot be sure that the President to whom they are communicating can protect their confidences, communication will be inhibited. MR. JUSTICE POWELL's view, requiring an ex-President to depend upon his successor, blinks at political and historical reality. The tripartite system of government established by the Constitution has on more than one occasion bred political hostility not merely between Congress and a lame duck President, but between the latter and his successor. To substantiate this view one need only recall the relationship at the time of the transfer to the reins of power from John Adams to Thomas Jefferson, from James Buchanan to Abraham Lincoln, from Herbert Hoover to Franklin Roosevelt, and from Harry Truman to Dwight Eisenhower. Thus while the Court's decision is an invitation for a hostile Congress to legislate against an unpopular lame duck President, MR. JUSTICE POWELL's position places the ultimate disposition of a challenge to such legislation in the hands of what history has shown may be a hostile incoming President. I cannot believe that the Constitution countenances this result. One may ascribe no such motives to Congress and the successor Presidents in this case, without nevertheless harboring a fear that they may play a part in some succeeding case.

The shadow that today's decision casts upon the daily operation of the Office of the President during his entire four-year term sharply differentiates it from our previous separation of powers decisions, which have dealt with much more specific and limitation intrusions. These cases have focused upon unique aspects of the operation of a particular branch of government, rather than upon an intrusion, such as the present one, that permeates the entire decisionmaking process of the Office of the President. For example, in *Youngstown Sheet & Tube Co.* v. *Sawyer*...(1952) (the *"Steel Seizure Cases"*), this Court held that the President could not by Executive order seize steel mills in order to prevent a work stoppage when Congress had provided other methods for dealing with such an eventuality. In *Myers* v. *United States*...(1926), the Court struck down an 1876 statute which had attempted to restrict the President's power to remove Postmasters without congressional approval. In *Buckley* v. *Valeo*...(1976), the Court struck down Congress' attempt to vest the power to appoint members of the Federal Election Commission in persons other than the President.

To say that these cases dealt with discrete instances of governmental action is by no means to disparage their importance in the development of our constitutional law. But it does contrast them quite sharply with the issue involved in the present case. To uphold the "Presidential Recordings and Materials Preservation Act" is not simply to sustain or invalidate a particular instance of the exercise of governmental power by Congress or by the President; it has the much more far reaching effect of significantly hampering the President, during his entire term of office, in his ability to gather the necessary information to perform the countless discrete acts which are the prerogative of his office under Art. II of the Constitution.

C

It thus appears to me indisputable that this Act is a significant intrusion into the operations of the Presidency. I do not think that this severe dampening of free communication to and from the President may be discounted by the Court's adoption of a novel "balancing" test for determining whether it is constitutional. I agree with the Court that the three branches of government need not be airtight, and that the separate branches are not intended to operate with absolute independence, *United States* v. *Nixon...* (1974). But I find no support in the Constitution or in our cases for the Court's pronouncement that the operations of the Office of the President may be severely impeded by Congress simply because Congress had a good reason for doing so.

Surely if ever there were a case for "balancing," and giving weight to the asserted "national interest" to sustain governmental action, it was in the *Steel Seizure Cases....* There the challenged Presidential proclamation recited, without contradiction by its challengers, that "American fighting men and fighting men of other nations of the United [Nations] are now engaged in deadly combat with the forces of aggression in Korea"; that "the weapons and other materials needed by our armed forces and by those joined with us in the defense of the free world are produced to a great extent in this country, and steel is an indispensable component of substantially all of such weapons and materials"; and that a work stoppage in the steel industry "would immediately jeopardize and imperil our national defense and those joined with us in resisting aggression, and would add to the continuing danger of our soldiers, sailors, and air men engaged in combat in the field...." Although the "legislative" actions by the President could have been quickly overridden by an act of Congress...this Court struck down the executive order as violative of the separation of powers principle with nary a mention of the national interest to be fostered by what could have been characterized as a relatively minimal and temporary intrusion upon the role of Congress. The analysis was simple and straightforward: Congress had exclusive authority to legislate; the President's Executive order was an exercise of legislative power that impinged upon that authority of Congress, and was therefore unconstitutional....

I think that not only the Executive Branch of the Federal Government, but the Legislative and Judicial Branches as well, will come to regret this day when the Court has upheld an Act of Congress that trenches so significantly on the functioning of the Office of the Presidency. I dissent.

COURT ON DEATH
PENALTY FOR RAPISTS

June 29, 1977

Continuing to make clear that death can constitutionally be the penalty for only a small category of crimes, the Supreme Court June 29 struck down a Georgia law which allowed the death sentence to be imposed upon rapists. (Coker v. Georgia)

The court divided 7-2. Justice Byron R. White announced the decision in an opinion joined by three other justices—less than a majority: Justices Potter Stewart, Harry A. Blackmun and John Paul Stevens. Justices William J. Brennan Jr. and Thurgood Marshall agreed with simple restatements of their view that the death penalty was always cruel and unusual and, hence, unconstitutional. Justice Lewis F. Powell Jr. said he agreed that the death penalty should not be imposed on this particular rapist, but that he would not hold that death should never be the penalty for rape. Chief Justice Warren E. Burger and Justice William H. Rehnquist dissented.

The penalty of death is disproportionate to the crime of rape, wrote White, noting that Georgia was the only state which allowed imposition of the death penalty for rape.

Rape is "highly reprehensible," wrote White. "Short of homicide, it is the 'ultimate violation of self.' It is also a violent crime....

"Rape is without doubt deserving of serious punishment; but in terms of moral depravity and of the injury to the person and to the public, it does not compare with murder.... Life is over for the victim of the murderers; for the rape victim, life may not be nearly so happy as it was, but is not over and normally is not beyond repair," continued White.

Burger and Rehnquist argued that "the court has overstepped the bounds of proper constitutional adjudication by substituting its policy judgment for that of the state legislature. I accept that the Eighth Amendment's concept of disproportionality bars the death penalty for minor crimes. But rape is not a minor crime...."

The defendant in this case, Ehrlich Anthony Coker, stated Burger, had already raped and killed one woman, raped and attempted to kill another woman, and then escaped from prison to commit the rape for which the death sentence was imposed. "It seriously impinges upon the state's legislative judgment to hold that it may not impose such a sentence upon an individual who has shown total and repeated disregard for the welfare, personal integrity and human worth of others and who seemingly cannot be deterred from continuing such conduct."

Georgia, Florida and Mississippi were the only states in which rapists could be condemned to death. (Laws in the latter two states pertained only to the rape of children. The Supreme Court ruling did not address those laws.)

Background

In June 1972, the Supreme Court, 5-4, invalidated all existing state laws allowing the imposition of capital punishment. Those laws, held the majority, violated the Eighth Amendment by giving judge and jury so much discretion in deciding when and upon whom to impose the death sentence that it was imposed "wantonly and freakishly." The laws directly involved in the 1972 cases were those of Georgia and Texas. (Historic Documents of 1972, p. 499)

Following the 1972 decision, the legislatures of 35 states passed new capital punishment laws, adopting procedures designed to avoid the constitutional defects which the court had pointed out. And in 1974 Congress passed a law (PL 93-366) allowing imposition of the death penalty for hijacking when someone died as a result of the aircraft piracy.

Four years after its 1972 ruling, the Supreme Court July 2, 1976, upheld the constitutionality of the newly drafted state laws which imposed the death penalty in certain cases. The court's action came on five cases, all of them brought by men convicted of murder. Three of the cases involved two-part, trial-and-penalty-procedure laws enacted by Georgia, Florida and Texas. The court held, 7-2, that these laws were constitutional. The other two cases challenged newly drafted mandatory death penalty laws of North Carolina and Louisiana. The court held, 5-4, that these were unconstitutional. (Historic Documents of 1976, p. 489)

On Oct. 4, 1976, the first day of its new term, the Supreme Court refused to reconsider its July 2 decision. And on Dec. 13, by a 5-4 vote, the court lifted a stay of execution of the death sentence of Gary Mark Gilmore in Utah. (Historic Documents of 1976, p. 917)

Florida Statute Upheld

Until mid-1972, Florida law authorized the death penalty for persons convicted of murder. This statute, like similar ones in almost all other states, was invalidated by the Supreme Court's June 1972 ruling in Furman v. Georgia *that all these laws allowed the death penalty to be unfairly imposed. Subsequently, the Florida legislature enacted a new law authorizing the death penalty for persons convicted of murder. This new statute was upheld by the Supreme Court in 1976* (Proffitt v. Florida).

*In 1971 and early 1972, two of Ernest John Dobbert Jr.'s children were tortured and killed. Dobbert was charged with their murder, tried under the post-*Furman *law, convicted and sentenced to death. He challenged his sentence arguing that it violated the constitutional ban on* ex post facto *laws, laws enacted after the crime, for him to be sentenced under the new law when, at the time of the murders, the state did not have a valid death penalty statute.* (Dobbert v. Florida)

By a 6-3 vote, the Supreme Court June 17, 1977, upheld Dobbert's death sentence. Justice Rehnquist wrote the opinion; Justices Brennan, Marshall and Stevens dissented.

*The major difference between the pre-*Furman *and post-*Furman *Florida laws was procedural; wrote Rehnquist. And procedural changes do not fall under the* ex post facto *ban. Furthermore, the changes incorporated in the new law actually benefitted Dobbert, giving him more safeguards than he would have under the old law. Despite the fact that the Florida capital punishment law at the time of the crimes was invalid, Rehnquist continued, it served to give Dobbert fair warning of the seriousness with which the state viewed the crime of murder and the sort of penalty it found appropriate.*

Following are excerpts from the majority, concurring and dissenting opinions of the Supreme Court in the capital punishment case of Coker v. Georgia, *decided June 29, 1977:*

No. 75-5444

Ehrlich Anthony Coker, Petitioner, *v.* State of Georgia.	On Writ of Certiorari to the Supreme Court of Georgia.

[June 29, 1977]

MR. JUSTICE WHITE announced the judgment of the Court and filed an opinion in which MR. JUSTICE STEWART, MR. JUSTICE BLACKMUN, and MR. JUSTICE STEVENS, joined.

Georgia Code...provides that "[a] person convicted of rape shall be punished by death or by imprisonment for life, or by imprisonment for not less than 20 years." Punishment is determined by a jury in a separate sentencing proceeding in which at least one of the statutory aggravating circumstances must be found before the death penalty may be imposed. Petitioner Coker was convicted of rape and sentenced to death. Both conviction and sentence were affirmed by the Georgia Supreme Court. Coker was granted a writ of certiorari...limited to the single claim, rejected by the Georgia court, that the punishment of death for rape violates the Eighth Amendment, which proscribes "cruel and unusual punishments" and which must be observed by the States as well as the Federal Government....

I

While serving various sentences for murder, rape, kidnapping, and aggravated assault, petitioner escaped from the Ware Correctional Institution near Waycross, Ga., on September 2, 1974. At approximately 11 p.m. that night, petitioner entered the house of Allen and Elnita Carver through an unlocked kitchen door. Threatening the couple with a "board," he tied up Mr. Carver in the bathroom, obtained a knife from the kitchen, and took Mr. Carver's money and the keys to the family car. Brandishing the knife and saying "you know what's going to happen to you if you try anything, don't you," Coker then raped Mrs. Carver. Soon thereafter, petitioner drove away in the Carver car, taking Mrs. Carver with him. Mr. Carver, freeing himself, notified the police; and not long thereafter petitioner was apprehended. Mrs. Carver was unharmed.

Petitioner was charged with escape, armed robbery, motor vehicle theft, kidnapping, and rape. Counsel was appointed to represent him. Having been found competent to stand trial, he was tried. The jury returned a verdict of guilty, rejecting his general plea of insanity. A sentencing hearing was then conducted in accordance with the procedures dealt with at length in *Gregg* v. *Georgia*...(1976), where this Court sustained the death penalty for murder when imposed pursuant to the statutory procedures. The jury was instructed that it could consider as aggravating circumstances whether the rape had been committed by a person with a prior record of conviction for a capital felony and whether the rape had been committed in the course of committing another capital felony, namely, the armed robbery of Allen Carver. The court also instructed, pursuant to statute, that even if aggravating circumstances were present, the death penalty need not be imposed if the jury found they were outweighed by mitigating circumstances, that is, circumstances not constituting justification or excuse for the offense in question, "but which, in fairness and mercy, may be considered as extenuating or reducing the degree" of moral culpability or punishment.... The jury's verdict on the rape count was death by electrocution. Both aggravating circumstances on which the court instructed were found to be present by the jury.

II

Furman v. *Georgia*...(1972), and the Court's decisions last Term in *Gregg* v. *Georgia*...[1976]; *Proffit* v. *Florida*...(1976); *Jurek* v. *Texas*...(1976); *Woodson* v. *North Carolina*...(1976); and *Roberts* v. *Louisiana*...(1976), make unnecessary the recanvassing of certain critical aspects of the controversy about the constitutionality of capital punishment. It is now settled that the death penalty is not invariably cruel and unusual punishment within the meaning of the Eighth Amendment; it is not inherently barbaric or an unacceptable mode of punishment for crime; neither is it always disproportionate to the crime for which it is imposed. It is also established that imposing capital punishment, at least for murder, in accordance with the procedures provided under the Georgia statutes saves the sentence from the infirmities which led the Court to invalidate the prior Georgia capital punishment statute in *Furman* v. *Georgia*....

In sustaining the imposition of the death penalty in *Gregg*, however, the Court firmly embraced the holdings and dicta from prior cases..., to the effect that the Eighth Amendment bars not only those punishments that are "barbaric" but also those that are "excessive" in relation to the crime committed. Under *Gregg*, a punishment is "excessive" and unconstitutional if it (1) makes no measurable contribution to acceptable goals of punishment and hence is nothing more than the purposeless and needless imposition of pain and suffering; or (2) is grossly out of proportion to the severity of the crime. A punishment might fail the test on either ground. Furthermore, these Eighth Amendment judgments should not be, or appear to be, merely the subjective views of individual Justices; judgment should be informed by objective factors to the maximum possible extent. To this end, attention must be given to the public attitudes concerning a particular sentence—history and precedent, legislative attitudes, and the response of juries reflected in their sentencing decisions are to be consulted. In *Gregg*, after giving due regard to such sources, the Court's judgment was that the death penalty for deliberate murder was neither the purposeless imposition of severe punishment nor a punishment grossly disproportionate to the crime. But the Court reserved the question of the constitutionality of the death penalty when imposed for other crimes....

III

That question, with respect to rape of an adult woman, is now before us. We have concluded that a sentence of death is grossly disproportionate and excessive punishment for the crime of rape and is therefore forbidden by the Eighth Amendment as cruel and unusual punishment.

A

As advised by recent cases, we seek guidance in history and from the objective evidence of the country's present judgment concerning the acceptability of death as a penalty of rape of an adult woman. At no time in the last 50 years has a majority of the States authorized death as a punishment for rape. In 1925, 18 States, the District of Columbia, and the Federal Government authorized capital' punishment for the rape of an adult female. By 1971 just prior to the decision in *Furman* v. *Georgia,* that number had declined, but not substantially, to 16 States plus the Federal Government. *Furman* then invalidated most of the capital punishment statutes in this country, including the rape statutes, because, among other reasons, of the manner in which the death penalty was imposed and utilized under those laws.

With their death penalty statutes for the most part invalidated, the States were faced with the choice of enacting modified capital punishment laws in an attempt to satisfy the requirements of *Furman* or of being satisfied with life imprisonment as the ultimate punishment for *any* offense. Thirty-five States immediately reinstituted the death penalty for at least limited kinds of crime.... This public judgment as to the acceptability of capital punishment, evidenced by the immediate, post-*Furman* legislative reaction in a large majority of the States, heavily influenced the Court to sustain the death penalty for murder in *Gregg* v. *Georgia*....

But if the "most marked indication of a society's endorsement of the death penalty for murder is the legislative response to *Furman*," *Gregg* v. *Georgia*..., it should also be a telling datum that the public judgment with respect to rape, as reflected in the statutes providing the punishment for that crime, has been dramatically different. In reviving death penalty laws to satisfy *Furman's* mandate, none of the States that had not previously authorized death for rape chose to include rape among capital felonies. Of the 16 States in which rape had been a capital offense, only three provided the death penalty for rape of an adult woman in their revised statutes—Georgia, North Carolina, and Louisiana. In the latter two States, the death penalty was mandatory for those found guilty, and those laws were invalidated by *Woodson* and *Roberts.* When Louisiana and North Carolina, responding to those decisions, again revised their capital punishment laws, they reenacted the death penalty for murder but not for rape; none of the seven other legislatures that to our knowledge have amended or replaced their death penalty statutes since July 2, 1976, including four States (in addition to Louisiana and North Carolina) that had authorized the death sentence for rape prior to 1972 and had reacted to *Furman* with mandatory statutes, included rape among the crimes for which death was an authorized punishment.

Georgia argues that 11 of the 16 States that authorized death for rape in 1972 attempted to comply with *Furman* by enacting arguably mandatory death penalty legislation and that it is very likely that aside from Louisiana and North Carolina, these States simply chose to eliminate rape as a capital offense rather than to *require* death for *each* and *every* instance of rape. The argument is not without force; but four of the 16 States did not take the mandatory course and also did *not* continue rape of an adult woman as a capital offense. Further, as we have indicated, the legislatures of six of the 11 arguably mandatory States have revised their death penalty laws since *Woodson* and *Roberts* without enacting a new death penalty for rape. And this is to say nothing of 19 other States that enacted nonmandatory, post-*Furman* statutes and chose not to sentence rapists to death.

It should be noted that Florida, Mississippi, and Tennessee also authorized the death penalty in some rape cases, but only where the victim was a child and the rapist an adult. The Tennessee statute has since been invalidated because the death sentence was mandatory. *Collins* v. *State,* ...(1977). The upshot is that Georgia is the sole jurisdiction in the United States at the present time that authorizes a sentence of death when the rape victim is an adult woman, and only two other jurisdictions provide capital punishment when the victim is a child.

The current judgment with respect to the death penalty for rape is not wholly unanimous among state legislatures, but it obviously weighs very heavily on the side of rejecting capital punishment as a suitable penalty for raping an adult woman.

B

...According to the factual submissions in this Court, out of all rape convictions in Georgia since 1973—and that total number has not been tendered—63 cases had been reviewed by the Georgia Supreme Court as of the time of oral argument; and of these, six involved a death sentence, one of which was set aside, leaving five convicted rapists now under sentence of death in the State of Georgia. Georgia juries have thus sentenced rapists to death six times since 1973. This obviously is not a negligible number; and the State argues that as a practical matter juries simply reserve the extreme sanction for extreme cases of rape and that recent experience surely does not prove that jurors consider the death penalty to be a disproportionate punishment for every conceivable instance of rape, no matter how aggravated. Nevertheless, it is true that in the vast majority of cases, at least nine out of 10, juries have not imposed the death sentence.

IV

The recent events evidencing the attitude of state legislatures and sentencing juries do not wholly determine this controversy, for the Constitution contemplates that in the end our own judgment will be brought to bear on the question of the acceptability of the death penalty under the Eighth Amendment. Nevertheless, the legislative rejection of capital punishment for rape strongly confirms our own judgment, which is that death is indeed a disproportionate penalty for the crime of raping an adult woman.

We do not discount the seriousness of rape as a crime. It is highly reprehensible, both in a moral sense and in its almost total contempt for the personal integrity and autonomy of the female victim and for the latter's privilege of choosing those with whom intimate relationships are to be established. Short of homicide, it is the "ultimate violation of self." It is also a violent crime because it normally involves force, or the threat of force or intimidation, to overcome the will and the capacity of the victim to resist. Rape is very often accompanied by physical injury to the female and can also inflict mental and psychological damage. Because it undermines the community's sense of security, there is public injury as well.

Rape is without doubt deserving of serious punishment; but in terms of moral depravity and of the injury to the person and to the public, it does not compare with murder, which does involve the unjustified taking of human life. Although it may be accompanied by another crime, rape by definition does not include the death or even the serious injury to another person. The murderer kills; the rapist, if no more than that, does not. Life is over for the victim of the murderers; for the rape victim, life may not be nearly so happy as it was, but it is not over and normally is not beyond repair. We have the abiding conviction that the death penalty, which "is unique in its severity and revocability," ...is an excessive penalty for the rapist who, as such, does not take human life.

This does not end the matter; for under Georgia law, death may not be imposed for any capital offense, including rape, unless the jury or judge finds one of the statutory aggravating circumstances and then elects to impose that sentence.... For the rapist to be executed in Georgia, it must therefore be found not only that he committed rape but also that one or more of the following aggravating circumstances were present: (1) that the rape was committed by a person with a prior record of conviction for a capital felony; (2) that the rape was committed while the offender was engaged in the commission of another capital felony, or aggravated battery; or (3) the rape "was outrageously or wantonly vile, horrible or inhuman in that it involved torture, depravity of mind, or aggravated battery to the victim." Here, the first two of these aggravating circumstances were alleged and found by the jury.

Neither of these circumstances, nor both of them together, change our conclusion that the death sentence imposed on Coker is a disproportionate punishment for rape. Coker had prior convictions for capital felonies—rape, murder and kidnapping—but these prior convictions do not change the fact that the instant crime being punished is a rape not involving the taking of life.

It is also true that the present rape occurred while Coker was committing armed robbery, a felony for which the Georgia statutes authorize the death penalty. But Coker was tried for the robbery offense as well as for rape and received a separate life sentence for this crime; the jury did not deem the robbery itself deserving of the death penalty, even though accompanied by the aggravating circumstance, which was stipulated, that Coker had been convicted of a prior capital crime.

We note finally that in Georgia a person commits murder when he unlawfully and with malice aforethought, either express or implied, causes the death of another human being. He also commits that crime when in the commission of a felony he causes the death of another human being, irrespective of malice. But even where the killing is deliberate, it is not punishable by death absent proof of aggravating circumstances. It is difficult to accept the notion, and we do not, that the rape, with or without aggravating circumstances, should be punished more heavily than the deliberate killer as long as the rapist does not himself take the life of his victim. The judgment of the Georgia Supreme Court upholding the death sentence is reversed and the case is remanded to that court for further proceedings not inconsistent with this opinion.

So ordered.

MR. JUSTICE BRENNAN, concurring in the judgment.

Adhering to my view that the death penalty is in all circumstances cruel and unusual punishment prohibited by the Eighth and Fourteenth Amendments, *Gregg* v. *Georgia,* ...(1976), I concur in the judgment of the Court setting aside the death sentence imposed under the Georgia rape statute.

MR. JUSTICE MARSHALL concurring in the judgment of the Court.

In *Gregg* v. *Georgia,* ...(1976), I stated, "In *Furman* v. *Georgia,* ...(1972) (concurring), I set forth at some length my views on the basic issue presented to the Court in these cases. The death penalty, I concluded, is a cruel and unusual punishment prohibited by the Eighth and Fourteenth Amendments. That continues to be my view."

I then explained in some detail my reasons for reaffirming my position. I continue to adhere to those views in concurring in the judgment of the Court in this case.

MR. CHIEF JUSTICE BURGER, with whom MR. JUSTICE REHNQUIST joins, dissenting.

In a case such as this, confusion often arises as to the Court's proper role in reaching a decision. Our task is not to give effect to our individual views on capital punishment; rather, we must determine what the Constitution permits a State to do under its reserved powers. In striking down the death penalty imposed upon the petitioner in this case, the Court has overstepped the bounds of proper constitutional adjudication by substituting its policy judgment for that of the state legislature. I accept that the Eighth Amendment's concept of disproportionality bars the death penalty for minor crimes. But rape is not a minor crime; hence the Cruel and Unusual Punishment Clause does not give the Members of this Court license to engraft their conceptions of proper public policy onto the considered legislative judgments of the States. Since I cannot agree that Georgia lacked the constitutional power to impose the penalty of death for rape, I dissent from the Court's judgment.

...My first disagreement with the Court's holding is its unnecessary breadth. The narrow issue here presented is whether the State of Georgia may constitutionally execute this petitioner for the particular rape which he has committed, in light of all the facts and circumstances shown by this record. The plurality opinion goes to great lengths to consider societal mores and attitudes toward the generic crime of rape and the punishment for it; however, the opinion gives little attention on the special circumstances which bear directly on whether imposition of the death penalty is an appropriate societal response to Coker's criminal acts: (1) On account of his prior offenses, Coker is already serving such lengthy prison sentences that imposition of additional periods of imprisonment would have no incremental punitive effect; (b) by his life pattern Coker has shown that he presents a particular danger to the safety, welfare and chastity of women, and on his record the likelihood is therefore great that he will repeat his crime at first opportunity; (c) petitioner escaped from prison, only a year and a half after he commenced serving his latest sentences; he has nothing to lose by further escape attempts; and (d) should he again succeed in escaping from prison, it is reasonably predictable that he will repeat his pattern of attacks on women—and with impunity since the threat of added prison sentences will be no deterrent.

Unlike the Court, I would narrow the inquiry in this case to the question actually presented: Does the Eighth Amendment's ban against cruel and unusual punishment prohibit the State of Georgia from executing a person who has, within the space of three years, raped three separate women, killing one and attempting to kill another, who is serving prison terms exceeding his probable lifetime and who has not hesitated to escape confinement at the first available opportunity? Whatever one's view may be as to the State's constitutional power to impose the death penalty upon a rapist who stands before a court convicted for the first time, this case reveals a chronic rapist whose continuing danger to the community is abundantly clear.

MR. JUSTICE POWELL would hold the death sentence inappropriate in *this* case because "there is no indication that petitioner's offense was committed with excessive brutality or that the victim sustained serious or lasting injury." ...Apart from the reality that rape is inherently one of the most egregiously brutal acts one human being can inflict upon another, there is nothing in the Eighth Amendment that so narrowly limits the factors which may be considered by a state legislature in determining whether a particular punishment is grossly excessive. Surely recidivism, especially the repeated commission of heinous crimes, is a factor which may properly be weighed as an aggravating circumstance, permitting the imposition of a punishment more severe than for one isolated offense. For example, as a matter of national policy, Congress has expressed its will that a person who has committed two felonies will suffer enhanced punishment for a third one...; Congress has also declared that a second conviction for assault on a mail carrier may be punished more seriously than a first such conviction.... Many states provide an increased penalty for habitual criminality.... As a factual matter, the plurality opinion is correct in stating the Coker's "prior convictions do not change the fact that the instant crime being punished is rape not involving the taking of life,"...; however, it cannot be disputed that the existence of these prior convictions make Coker a substantially more serious menace to society than a first-time offender....

...In my view, the Eighth Amendment does not prevent the State from taking an individual's "well demonstrated propensity for life-endangering behavior" into account in devising punitive measures which will prevent inflicting further harm upon innocent victims....

In sum, once the Court has held that "the punishment of death does not invariably violate the Constitution," ...it seriously impinges upon the State's legislative judgment to hold that it may not impose such sentence upon an individual who has shown total and repeated disregard for the welfare, safety, personal integrity and human worth of others, and who seemingly cannot be deterred from continuing such conduct. I therefore would hold that the death sentence here imposed is within the power reserved to the State and leave for another day the question of whether such sanction would be proper under other circumstances. The dangers which inhere whenever the Court casts its constitutional decisions in terms sweeping beyond the facts of the case presented, are magnified in the context of the Eighth Amendment.... Since the Court now invalidates the death penalty as a sanction for all rapes of adults at all times under all circumstances, I reluctantly turn to what I see as the broader issues raised by this holding.

The plurality...acknowledges the gross nature of the crime of rape. A rapist not only violates a victim's privacy and personal integrity, but inevitably causes serious psychological as well as physical harm in the process. The long-range effect upon the victim's life and health is likely to be irreparable; it is impossible to measure the harm which results. Volumes have been written by victims, physicians and psychiatric specialists on the lasting injury suffered by rape victims. Rape is not a mere physical attack—it is destructive of the human personality. The remainder of the victim's life may be gravely affected, and this in turn may have a serious detrimental effect upon her husband and any children she may have. I therefore wholly agree with MR. JUSTICE WHITE's conclusion as far as it goes—that "[s]hort of homicide, [rape] is the 'ultimate violation of the self' ".... Victims may recover from the physical damage of knife or bullet wounds, or a beating with fists or a club, but recovery from such a gross assault on the human personality is not healed by medicine or surgery. To speak blandly, as the plurality does, of rape victims which are "unharmed," or, as the concurrence, to classify the human outrage of rape in terms of "excessively brutal," ...versus "moderately brutal," takes too little account of the profound suffering the crime imposes upon the victims and their loved ones.

Despite its strong condemnation of rape, the Court reaches the inexplicable conclusion that "the death penalty...is an excessive penalty" for the perpetrator of this heinous offense. This, the Court holds, is true even though in Georgia the death penalty may be imposed only where the rape is coupled with one or more aggravating circumstances. The process by which this conclusion is reached is as startling as it is disquieting. It represents a clear departure from precedent by making this Court "under the aegis of the Cruel and Unusual Punishment Clause, the ultimate arbiter of the standards of criminal responsibility in diverse areas of the criminal law, throughout the country." *Powell* v. *Texas,* ...(1968).... This seriously strains and distorts our federal system, removing much of the flexibility from which it has drawn strength for two centuries....

MR. JUSTICE POWELL, concurring in part and dissenting in part.

I concur in the judgment of the Court on the facts of this case, and also in its reasoning supporting the view that ordinarily death is disproportionate punishment for the crime of raping an adult woman. Although rape invariably is a reprehensible crime, there is no indication that petitioner's offense was committed with excessive brutality or that the victim sustained serious or lasting injury. The plurality, however, does not limit its holding to the case before us or to similar cases. Rather, in an opinion that ranges well beyond what is necessary, it holds that capital punishment *always*—regardless of the circumstances—is a disproportionate penalty for the crime of rape.

...Today, in a case that does not require such an expansive pronouncement, the plurality draws a bright line between murder and all rapes—regardless of the degree of brutality of the rape or the effect upon the victim. I dissent because I am not persuaded that such a bright line is appropriate. As noted in *Snider* v. *Peyton*..."[t]here is extreme variation in the degree of culpability of rapists." The deliberate viciousness of the rapist may be greater than that of the murderer. Rape is never an act committed accidentally. Rarely can it be said to be unpremeditated. There also is wide variation in the effect on the victim. The plurality opinion says that "[l]ife is over for the victim of the murderer; for the rape victim, life may not be nearly so happy as it was, but it is not over and normally is not beyond repair".... But there is indeed "extreme variation" in the crime of rape. Some victims are so grievously injured physically or psychologically that life *is* beyond repair.

Thus it may be that the death penalty is not disproportionate punishment for the crime of aggravated rape. Final resolution of the question must await careful inquiry into objective indicators of society's "evolving standards of decency," particularly legislative enactments and the responses of juries in capital cases.... The plurality properly examines these indicia, which do support the conclusion that society finds the death penalty unacceptable for the crime of rape in the absence of excessive brutality or severe injury. But it has not been shown that society finds the penalty disproportionate for all rapists. In a proper case a more discriminating inquiry than the plurality undertakes well might discover that both juries and legislatures have reserved the ultimate penalty for the case of an outrageous rape resulting in serious, lasting harm to the victim. I would not prejudge the issue. To this extent, I respectfully dissent.

CARTER ON THE B-1 BOMBER
June 30, 1977

Calling it "one of the most difficult decisions that I've made," President Carter announced at a June 30 press conference that instead of putting the controversial B-1 bomber into production he favored equipping existing B-52 bombers with air-launched cruise missiles—small drone jet powered aircraft that could carry a nuclear warhead several hundred miles to within yards of the target. The President called for continued research on the B-1 so that the United States would retain the option of producing the planes "in the unlikely event that more cost-effective alternative systems should run into difficulty."

Carter said the decision did not adversely alter the triad concept on which U.S. nuclear defense policy was predicated, that is, the concept of maintaining three nuclear warhead delivery systems: submarine-launched ballistic missiles, intercontinental ballistic missiles and the manned bomber fleet. "We will continue thereby to have an effective and flexible strategic force whose capability is fully sufficient for our national defense," Carter said.

President Carter also said that he made his decision "on my analysis that, within a given budgetary limit for the defense of our country, which I am sure will always be adequate...we should have the optimum capability to defend ourselves." He added: "But this is a matter that is of so very great importance, and if at the end of a few years the relations with the Soviets should deteriorate drastically, which I don't anticipate, then it may be necessary for me to change my mind. But I don't expect that to oc-cur...." (SALT talks, p. 243)

Reaction

President Carter's announcement came as a surprise to the officers of the Strategic Air Command (SAC) who, according to press reports, did not anticipate outright rejection of the B-1. SAC officers expected approval for construction of at least 140 B-1s. Moreover, Rockwell International Corporation of California, which would have produced the aircraft, was stunned by the Carter announcement. The company said that about two-thirds of the 16,000 employees working on the project would be laid off.

Former President Ford called Carter's rejection of the B-1 "a very risky gamble." Ford said, "I strongly disagree with the President's decision.... He is relying on a B-52 that is 20 years or more old, an aircraft that was developed in the 1950s."

Controversy

The B-1 bomber was designed to fly fast and low to avoid radar detection. The B-1 project had grown out of an earlier B-70 bomber program. In contrast to the B-1, the B-70 was engineered to fly fast and high. The concept of flying fast and high to penetrate an enemy's defenses, however, was abandoned after Francis Gary Powers' high altitude U-2 reconnaissance plane was shot down by Soviet ground-to-air missiles during an overflight inside Russian territory in 1960. Like the B-1, the B-70 bomber was never put into production.

The cost of the B-1 program—amounting to $24.8-billion for 244 planes or about $100-million for each plane—and the continuing debate over U.S. nuclear strategy kept the B-1 on the drawing board for nearly 10 years.

Basically, the debate was over how much and what kind of military power the nation needed to deter a Soviet attack. According to B-1 opponents, the plane, though better able to penetrate Soviet defenses than the existing B-52, soon would become vulnerable to Soviet airborne radar detection planes. Cruise missile advocates contended that, on the other hand, Soviet defenses in the foreseeable future would be swamped by swarms of the small (14 feet in length) cruise missiles carried in large numbers by existing bombers or by modified cargo jets.

While conceding that the cruise missile would in many cases frustrate Soviet defenses, supporters of the B-1 argued that the missile's subsonic speed and its lack of self-defense equipment would allow the Soviets to beat back attacks on heavily defended targets. Only a bomber equipped with electronic gear and a human crew to outmaneuver Soviet defenses would suffice, they insisted.

Congressional Action

Two days before Carter's announcement, the House of Representatives June 28 voted against deleting funds for B-1 production from the 1978 defense appropriations bill. The Senate version of the appropriations bill dropped the B-1 production money, and the House concurred with the Senate action Sept. 8. In October B-1 supporters made another effort to revive the project by adding the fiscal 1978 production money to a supplemental appropriations bill. The House rejected the attempt on Oct. 20. Congress adjourned Dec. 15 without taking final action on President Carter's request to cancel fiscal 1977 appropriations for B-1 production, thus terminating the B-1 program.

Following are excerpts from the White House Press Office transcript of President Carter's press conference June 30, 1977, announcing his decision to reject production of the B-1 bomber. (Boldface headings in brackets have been added by Congressional Quarterly to highlight the organization of the text.):

THE PRESIDENT: I have a brief statement to make before we begin the questions.

This has been one of the most difficult decisions that I have made since I have been in office. During the last few months, I have done my best to assess all the factors involving production of the B-1 bomber. My decision is that we should not continue with deployment of the B-1, and I am directing that we discontinue plans for production of this weapons system. The Secretary of Defense [Harold G. Brown] agrees that this is a preferable decision, and he will have a news conference tomorrow morning to discuss this issue in whatever detail you consider necessary.

The existing testing and development program now underway on the B-1 should continue to provide us with the needed technical base in the unlikely event that more cost-effective alternative systems should run into difficulty. Continued efforts at the research and development stage will give us better answers about the cost and effectiveness of the bomber and support system, including electronic countermeasures techniques.

During the coming months, we will also be able to assess the progress toward agreements on strategic arms limitations in order to determine the need for any additional investments in nuclear weapons delivery systems. In the meantime, we should begin deployment of cruise missiles using air-launched platforms, such as our B-52s, modernized as necessary. Our triad concept of attaining three basic delivery systems will be continued with submarine-launched ballistic missiles, intercontinental ballistic missiles and a bomber fleet, including cruise missiles as one of its elements. We will continue thereby to have an effective and flexible strategic force whose capability is fully sufficient for our national defense.

Thank you.

Q: Mr. President, the House at least seems bent on providing money for the B-1. Does this put you on a collision course with them on this subject?

P: No. I think not. The Congress took action last year to delay a final decision on the B-1 bomber pending my ability to analyze its needs.

When I came into office, I tried to deliberately have an open mind. I have spent weeks studying all the aspects of our strategic defense forces. I have met with Congressional leaders; I have spent a great deal of time with the Secretary of Defense and others in trying to understand all the ramifications of this very important decision.

The leaders in the House and Senate this morning have been informed of my decision, both by Frank Moore [President's congressional liaison] and by the Secretary of Defense.

My belief is that the Congress will be supportive knowing that our previous request for limited production funds were based on a previous decision. But my decision is that this production is not now necessary. And I believe that the House and the Senate will confirm my decision....

[Major Factors in Decision]

Q: Mr. President, what were the major factors that led to your decision against the B-1 bomber?

P: There are a number of factors. One is obviously the recent evolution of the cruise missile as an effective weapon itself. The tests of this system have been very successful so far.

Another one, of course, is the continued ability to use the B-52 bombers, particularly the G's and H's up well into the 1980s, and the belief on my part that our defense capability using the submarine-launched missile and intercontinental ballistic missiles combined with the B-52 cruise missile combination is adequate.

We will also explore the possibility of cruise missile carriers, perhaps using existing airplanes or others as a stand-off launching base.

But I think in toto the B-1, a very expensive weapons system, basically conceived in the absence of the cruise missile factor is not necessary.

Those are the major reasons.

Q: Mr. President, the Soviet Union has shown great concern about the cruise missile capability of the United States.

P: Yes.

Q: What limits are you ready to accept, if any, on air-launched cruise missiles so far as their range, and secondly, are you willing to accept the proposition that an airplane carrying cruise will be counted as a MIRV [multiple independently targeted reentry vehicle] under the limits that you would set in the SALT [strategic arms limitation talks] agreement?

P: Those questions are being negotiated now. We have a fairly compatible position with the Soviets on maximum range of air-launched cruise missiles carried over from the Vladivostok discussions. I don't think there is any particular difference in that. It is an adequate range in my opinion for the cruise missiles to be launched as a stand-off weapon without the carrying airplane having to encroach into the Soviet territory. This, though, is a matter that has not yet been finally resolved.

Also, the definition of what is a MIRVd weapon is one that is still in dispute. We don't believe that a bomber equipped with cruise missiles as a weapon ought to be classified as a MIRVd weapon. But depending upon the Soviets' attitude in reaching an overall comprehensive settlement, those matters are still open for discussion.

Q: Mr. President, in listening to factors involving your decision, sir, you didn't mention or I didn't hear the fact that you had made a commitment or what many people took to be a commitment during the campaign against the bomber; I think particularly in the submission to the Democratic Platform Committee. Was that a factor, sir?

P: Well, when I went into office, as I think I said earlier, I tried to take the position of complete open-mindedness, because obviously I have had available to me as President much of the classified analyses and information about weapons systems, which I did not have before. And I tried to approach this question with an open mind.

I have spent many hours reading those detailed technical reports, the advice of specialists on both sides, the analysis of ultimate cost of weapons. Although, obviously, opinions are always hard to change, I deliberately tried not to let my campaign statements be the factor in this decision. I have made it I think recently with an original very open mind, after carefully considering all aspects of the question and consulting very closely with the Secretary of Defense.

I might say with the advent of the cruise missile as a possible alternative, that the Secretary of Defense agrees with me that this is a preferable decision.

Q: Can I follow that up, Mr. President?

P: Yes.

Q: This open-mindedness that you describe, is that applied to other campaign commitments you made in other areas outside of defense?

P: I will always try to keep an open mind and make a decision on what I think is best for our country.

Q: Mr. President, is this decision on your part not to go ahead with the B-1 intended as any kind of a signal to the Soviets that you are willing to—that you want to do something quickly in the strategic arms talks?

P: I can't deny that that is a potential factor. But that has not been a reason for my decision. I think if I looked upon the B-1 as simply a bargaining chip for the Soviets, then my decision would have been to go ahead with the weapon. But I made my decision on my analysis that, within a given budgetary limit for the defense of our country, which I am sure will always be adequate, that we should have the optimum capability to defend ourselves.

But this is a matter that is of so very great importance, and if at the end of a few years the relations with the Soviets should deteriorate drastically, which I don't anticipate, then it may be necessary for me to change my mind. But I don't expect that to occur....

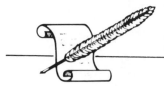

July

PAKISTANI ARMY COUP
July 5, 1977

The Pakistani army July 5, 1977, overthrew the government of Prime Minister Zulfikar Ali Bhutto, imposed martial law and promised new elections in October. "The Bhutto regime is ended," the army chief of staff, Gen. Mohammad Zia ul-Haq, said in a nationwide broadcast after the army acted to end four months of political violence that claimed more than 300 lives.

The army acted as Bhutto and the opposition party, the Pakistan National Alliance (PNA), remained deadlocked in their efforts to resolve the political crisis that stemmed from the March 7 elections, which the PNA had charged were rigged. Bhutto, eight members of his cabinet and six PNA leaders were taken into "temporary protective custody," Zia announced. Zia also dissolved the National Assembly and state assemblies and removed from office all cabinet ministers and state governors. All political parties were banned, and some provisions of the constitution were suspended. Zia said he and his colleagues had decided to seize power in order to "fill the vacuum created by the political leaders."

Background

The turmoil that preceded the military takeover had its roots in PNA attempts to reverse the results of the March 7 National Assembly elections, in which Bhutto won a landslide victory. On June 14, the Bhutto government and PNA announced they had agreed to hold new elections before the end of the year. However, the talks broke down, leading to the July 5 army coup.

537

Bhutto had been installed as leader of Pakistan in December 1971, after 13 years of military rule and after East Pakistan seceded from the nation in a war with India to become the independent country of Bangladesh. Bhutto had appointed Zia as chief of staff in 1976. (Historic Documents of 1972, pp. 23, 163)

In his July 5 broadcast, Zia said he wanted to make it "absolutely clear" that he had no personal political ambitions. "My sole aim is to organize free and fair elections which would be held in October of this year," he said. "Soon after the polls, power will be transferred to the elected representatives of the people. I give a solemn assurance that I will not deviate from this schedule." Zia concluded his address by pledging that the Moslem nation of 70 million would remain an "Islamic state."

Bhutto Arrested; Elections Postponed

On July 8, Zia said he had informed Bhutto of the military's plan more than a month before the coup. He rejected demands by religious leaders that Bhutto be tried and punished under Islamic law for actions taken since Bhutto became Prime Minister in 1971. Bhutto was freed from detention July 28, as were other leaders of his Pakistan People's Party and the rival PNA. The military government re-arrested Bhutto in Karachi Sept. 3 in connection with his alleged complicity in the murders of two political opponents while he was in office.

After a meeting with Zia Oct. 13, PNA President Maulana Mufti Malmoud said that Zia had told him that the elections had been called off because the campaign "threatens law and order" and that a new election date would be set for 1978—60 days after the completion of the trial of Bhutto for conspiracy and murder. At a pre-trial hearing Oct. 11, Bhutto pleaded not guilty. The trial was expected to last four months.

> *Following are excerpts from the July 5, 1977, nationally broadcast address of Gen. Mohammad Zia ul-Haq announcing the army ouster of the Bhutto government. Text provided by the Embassy of Pakistan. (Boldface headings in brackets have been added by Congressional Quarterly to highlight the organization of the text.):*

I deem it a singular honour to address the great people of this great country. I am grateful to God Almighty for this. You must have learnt by now that the Government of Mr. Zulfikar Ali Bhutto has ceased to exist and an Interim Government has been established in its place. This change-over which began at about midnight last night, was completed by this morning. I am grateful to God Almighty that the process of change-over has been accomplished smoothly and peacefully. This action was carried out on my orders.

During this period the former Prime Minister, Zulfikar Ali Bhutto, and some of his colleagues have been taken into protective custody. Likewise, all the prominent leaders of the Pakistan National Alliance except Begum Nasim Wali Khan have also been taken into custody.

The reactions to this take-over have so far been very encouraging. A stream of congratulatory messages has been pouring in from different quarters. I am grateful for this to my nation as well as to the buoyant and 'MOMIN' [Arabic word meaning "true Muslim"] armed forces of Pakistan.

It is necessary to add here that some people have expressed misgivings that the army take-over may have been at the behest of someone. Could it be that General [Mohammad] Zia [-ul-Haq] had secretly concerted with the former Prime Minister?

On this I can only say that truth can never remain unexposed. In fact, such an air of distrust has been created during the past few months that even well-meaning people also get bogged down in doubts and apprehensions.

You must have heard from the morning news bulletin that the armed forces of Pakistan have taken over the administration of the country. The army take-over is never a pleasant act because the armed forces of Pakistan genuinely want that the Administration of the country should remain in the hands of representatives of the people who are its real masters. The people exercise this right through their elected representatives who are chosen in every democratic country through periodic elections. The elections were held in our beloved homeland on March 7, last. The results, however, were rejected by one of the contending parties (The Pakistan National Alliance) [PNA]. They alleged that the elections had been rigged on a large scale and have demanded fresh elections.

To press their demand for re-elections, they launched a movement which assumed such dimensions that people even started saying that democracy was not workable in Pakistan. But, I genuinely feel that the survival of this country lies in democracy and democracy alone. It is mainly due to this belief that the armed forces resisted the temptation to take-over during the recent provocative circumstances in spite of...massive political pressures.

[Role of the Military]

The armed forces have always desired and sought political solution to political problems. That is why the armed forces stressed on the then government that it should reach a compromise with its political rivals without any loss of time. The government needed time to hold these talks so the armed forces bought them this valuable period of time by maintaining law and order in the country.

The armed forces were subjected to criticism from certain quarters for their role in aid of the civil administration but we tolerated this criticism in the hope that it was a passing phase. We hoped that when this climate of agitational frenzy came to an end, the nation would be able to appreciate the correct and constitutional role of the armed forces and all fears would be allayed.

I have just given you a very broad outline picture of the situation obtaining in the country. It must be quite clear to you now that when the political leaders failed to steer the country out of a crisis, it is an inexcusable sin for the armed forces to sit as silent spectators. It is primarily, for this reason, that the army had to intervene to save the country.

I would like to point out here that I saw no prospect of a compromise between the People's Party [PPP] and the PNA, because of their mutual distrust and lack of faith. It was feared that the failure of the PNA and PPP to reach a compromise would throw the country into chaos and thus plunged [sic] it into more serious crisis.

This risk could not be taken in view of the larger interest of the country. The army had, therefore, to act and as a result of which the government of Mr. Bhutto has ceased to exist.

Martial law had been imposed thoughout the country. The National and Provincial Assemblies have been dissolved and the Provincial Governors and Ministers have been removed. But the Constitution has not been abrogated. Only the operation of certain parts of the Constitution has been held in abeyance.

Mr. Fazal Elahi Chaudhry has very kindly consented to continue to discharge his duties as President of Pakistan as heretofore under the same Constitution. I am grateful to him for this.

To assist him in the discharge of his national duties, a Four-Member Military Council has been formed. The Council consists of the Chairman, Joint Chiefs of Staff and Chiefs of Staff of the Army, Navy and Air Force.

I will discharge the duties of the Chief of Army Staff and Chief Martial Law Administrator. Martial law orders and instructions, as and when required, will be issued under my orders. I met Mr. Justice Yagub Ali, Chief Justice of Pakistan this morning. I am grateful to him for the advise [sic] and guidance on legal matters.

[Political Ambitions Denied]

I want to make it absolutely clear that neither I have any political ambitions nor does the Army want to be detracted from its profession of soldiering. I was obliged to step in to fill in the vacuum created by the political leaders. I have accepted this challenge as a true soldier of Islam. My sole aim is to organize free and fair elections which would be held in October this year. Soon after the polls power will be transferred to the elected representatives of the people.

I give a solemn assurance that I will not deviate from this schedule. During the next three months my total attention will be concentrated on the holding of elections and I would not like to dissipate my powers and energies as Chief Martial Law Administrator on anything else.

It will not be out of place to mention here that I hold the Judiciary of the country in high esteem. I will do my best to refrain from doing anything which is likely to restrict the power of the Judiciary.

However, under unavoidable circumstances, if and when martial law orders and martial law regulations are issued, they will not be challenged in any court of law.

I will soon announce the modalities and detailed timetable for holding of elections. I hope and expect that all political parties will cooperate....

A good measure of tension had been created in the country during the recent political confrontation. It had, therefore, become imperative to allow time to cool off human emotions. I have, therefore, banned all political activities from today till further orders. Political activities, however, will be allowed before the polls.

My dear countrymen, I have expressed my real feelings and intentions, without the slightest ambiguity. I have also taken you into confidence about my future plans.

I seek guidance from God Almighty and help and cooperation from my countrymen to achieve this nobel [sic] mission. I also hope that the Judiciary, the adminitration and the common man will extend whole hearted cooperation to me. It would be my utmost endeavour to ensure that the martial law administration not only treats the people in a spirit of justice and equality, but also make [sic] them feel so. The civil administration, too, has to play an important role in this behalf.

I am, therefore, pleased to announce that the Chief Justices of the Provincial High Courts have, on my request, consented to become the acting governors of their respective provinces. The officers in the civil administration, who have any apprehensions about their future, are hereby assured that no victimization will take place. However, if any public servant fails in the discharge of his duties, shows partiality or betrays the confidence of the nation, he will be given exemplary punishment. Similarly, if any citizen disturbs law and order in the country, he will also be severely dealt with.

So far as foreign relations are concerned, I want to make it absolutely clear that I will honour all the agreements.

In the end, I would appeal to all of [sic] officers and men of the armed forces to discharge their duties justly and impartially. I hope they will also expect them to forgive those who have ridiculed or harassed them. This will be in the true Islamic tradition. I call upon them to preserve their honour and that of their profession in the discharge of their duties. I am sure they will acquit themselves of their new responsibility honorably. This will certainly enhance their prestige and position in the society....

...I want to assure you that the frontiers of Pakistan are fully guarded and the armed forces are there to discharge their duties. Authorized traffic across the borders is continuing.

To conclude, I must say that the spirit of Islam, demonstrated during the recent movement, was commendable. It proves that Pakistan, which was created in the name of Islam, will continue to survive only if it sticks to Islam. That is why, I consider the introduction of Islamic system as an essential pre-requisite for the country.

 HISTORIC DOCUMENTS OF 1977

August

FPC REPORT ON
NEW YORK CITY BLACKOUT
August 4, 1977

The Federal Power Commission (FPC), in a report issued Aug. 4, said the Consolidated Edison Company of New York, the city's electrical power supplier, bore heavy responsibility for failing to prevent a massive power failure in New York City's five boroughs and Westchester County. The blackout left nine million people without electrical power for up to 25 hours July 13-14. It was reminiscent of the power blackout suffered by the whole northeastern region Nov. 9, 1965.

President Carter July 14 directed the FPC to investigate the cause of the New York blackout. The power outage, Carter said in his memorandum to FPC chairman Richard L. Dunham ordering the inquiry, "is another dramatic reminder of the total dependence of this nation on reliable energy supplies."

The resultant FPC report said: "The massive outage experienced by Con Edison on July 13, 1977, indicates obvious flaws in the ability of the company to provide continuous service without prolonged interruptions." The transmission network and devices designed to protect the system were inadequate, the report concluded, and failed "to operate in the manner for which they were designed."

Con Ed president Arthur Hauspurg denounced the FPC report for what he termed "inaccurate statements and unsupported conclusions." Hauspurg said that many of the steps recommended in the report had been taken and "would do little to help prevent another system outage, given the extraordinary set of circumstances experienced by our system on the night of July 13."

New York Mayor Abraham D. Beame, at the time a candidate for re-election, in a press statement Aug. 4 said the FPC report "confirms my judgment that Con Edison failed in its responsibility to the consumers." Con Edison, the mayor stated, "wasn't prepared to prevent a major failure. It moved too late to prevent the blackout from spreading throughout the system. And it was guilty of inordinate delays in restoring service."

Blackout Investigations

The power shutdown apparently was caused by a succession of lightning bolts that struck two of Con Edison's major 345,000-volt transmission lines, which in turn caused the automatic equipment to halt power generation in two of the city's largest generating facilities.

Lightning first struck a substation transformer at 8:30 p.m. in Buchanan, N.Y., 12 miles north of the city and caused the Indian Point No. 3 nuclear power facility to cut off. A second lightning strike caused a series of overloads and short circuits that severed power from another plant, the Ravenswood No. 3, in Astoria, Queens. The entire city went dark at 9:34 p.m.

New York Gov. Hugh L. Carey and Mayor Beame ordered separate investigations of the breakdown and the inadequacy of the safeguards that had been implemented following the 1965 northeast blackout. Con Edison said that it would conduct its own study of the power failure.

Heated exchanges among the mayor, other public officials and officers of Con Edison obscured the fact that wide areas of agreement existed among all of the agencies investigating the blackout. Con Edison, the New York State Power Commission and the FPC all agreed on the chronology of events that led to the blackout. Moreover, the three suggested similar remedies to prevent a recurrence.

Shortly after the blackout occurred, a Con Edison spokesman had attributed the blackout to an "act of God." But when Con Edison released its report Aug. 24, the company concluded that the blackout was due to human and mechanical failures within its own system. The report stated: "Although it cannot be stated with certainty, it appears that on July 13, 1977, the equipment may not have been operated properly," because, Con Edison added, "early in the sequence, the system operator, believing he had other options, did not take actions soon enough to increase generation and reclose feeders. Later on, unaware of the exact condition of the system, he did not act to reduce voltage or shed load soon enough to prevent the overloading failures of two major interties." Further, the report concluded, "Had in-city generation been increased more rapidly, it would have reduced the loading on the remaining ties and might have prevented or deferred the tripping of two 345,000-volt feeders."

Looting and Vandalism

A city in darkness invited rampant looting, vandalism and other criminal activity. In many neighborhoods of Brooklyn, Harlem and the South Bronx, police reported that more than 3,700 persons were arrested and 100 policemen injured in attempts to prevent looting. Fire officials reported at least 500 fires during the blackout. Mayor Beame said that the blackout had subjected New Yorkers to a "night of terror." The city's Planning Department estimated that 1,328 stores were damaged in the looting. Repair of the damage would cost $14.1-million, the department calculated.

New York Gov. Hugh L. Carey July 22 requested aid for New York City under the 1974 Federal Disaster Relief Act. The Carter administration denied the request, but the White House July 30 announced an $11.3-million program of grants and loans to help the city recover. Although Mayor Beame called the federal money an "important contribution" to the city's recovery, it was less than would have been available under the disaster relief program. The program announced by Labor Secretary F. Ray Marshall provided:

● *$2-million for 2,000 jobs under the Comprehensive Employment and Training Act to hire unemployed youths to clean up areas worst hit by looting;*

● *$3.1-million for the demolition of burned-out and hazardous buildings;*

● *$5-million for Department of Housing and Urban Development rehabilitation loans for commercial development;*

● *$1-million to relieve congestion in the criminal justice system as a result of the record number of arrests for looting and vandalism;*

● *$250,000 for anti-poverty and community organization programs to encourage community-based economic development.*

> *Following are excerpts from the Federal Power Commission report of Aug. 4, 1977, citing the Con Edison's responsibility for the electrical blackout in New York City July 13-14, 1977:*

A sequence of events apparently initiated by lightning storm activity on the evening of July 13, 1977, in the lower Hudson Valley of New York State resulted in loss of all electric load by the Consolidated Edison Company of New York, Inc. (Con Edison). Electric service was interrupted to more than 8 million people in the New York City metropolitan area for periods ranging from 5 hours to 25 hours. By 9:30 p.m. elevators had stopped, trains had stopped, air conditioners had stopped, tv sets had blackened and the city had been plunged into darkness. While efforts to restore service commenced immediately, many were without service during the entire night and the following day. The health and safety of many thousands of persons were jeopardized and the losses of property through looting and vandalism were very large. The occurrence was incredible. The results were intolerable.

In the short period of time since the failure, it has not been possible to complete a definitive analysis of all the circumstances surrounding and bearing upon the causes of the failure and the delay in the restoration of service. It is evident that Con Edison personnel strained every resource to restore service to the system as rapidly as possible. While they are to be commended for this effort the fact remains that the City suffered outages stretching to as long as 25 hours. The difficulties of restoring service in a complex system serving such a densely populated area in which a high proportion of facilities are underground were immense.

While the geographic extent of the July 13 blackout was much less than that of the power failure of November 1965, it was in some respects much more serious. In part, this was caused by the fact that the 1965 blackout occurred in the cold month of November whereas the July 13 blackout occurred in the midst of one of the worst heat waves to strike the Northeast for many years. More important, perhaps, was the extent of the disorder and lawbreaking that occurred out of control in several areas of the City. Again, it should not be overlooked that the great bulk of the population took the disturbance calmly and remained entirely orderly and law abiding. A small proportion of the population lost control creating a disturbance with concomitant robbing and destruction of property as well as danger to the public safety. The social costs of a power outage of this sort have risen to a new order of magnitude. In issuing this report, the FPC staff has not sought to assess any legal cause and effect relationship between social losses and power supply interruptions....

Conclusions and Preliminary Recommendations

The massive outage experienced by Con Edison on July 13, 1977, indicates obvious flaws in the ability of the Company to provide continuous service without prolonged interruptions. It is evident from the nature of the incidents that led to the ultimate disruption of the system that the design of the transmission network and the protective devices designed to protect the system were inadequate and failed to operate in the manner for which they were designed. It is also apparent that the existing interconnections with neighboring utilities, notably, Public Service Electric and Gas Company (PSE&G) and Long Island Lighting Company (LILCO), are not strong enough to provide the necessary support needed in times of emergency. Additionally, another major tie with PSE&G (Farragut-Hudson interconnection) has been out of service since September 4, 1976, and this contributed to Con Edison's inability to import some of the power that would have been necessary to maintain its system on July 13.

Other indications of Con Edison's inability to provide reliable service are apparent from the fact that (a) adequate emergency measures were not employed in time to automatically shed sufficient load, (b) Con Edison failed to put into operation all of its idle combustion turbine units, and (c) it did not communicate quickly to its customers the necessity to reduce the demand on the system.

The difficulties experienced by Con Edison in restoring service and the inordinate time required to bring service to all of its customers demonstrate shortcomings in the planning of its system, such as the absence of an auxiliary power source necessary to maintain oil pressure in underground cables.

We are cognizant of the aforementioned deficiencies even though our review and analysis of the July 13 failure is as yet sketchy and far from complete. Nonetheless, based on our preliminary study made to date, we recommend that the following actions should be immediately taken by Con Edison:

(1) Proceed to restore to service as promptly as possible the Hudson-Farragut tie with PSE&G, and advise the Commission within 15 days as to the plans for such restoration.

(2) Advance to an earlier date the construction now scheduled for completion in 1981 (which recently slipped from 1980) of a new Hudson-Farragut...interconnection and a new Linden-Geothals ...interconnection with PSE&G. The inadequacy of existing interconnections forcefully points to the need for acceleration of the construction schedules and avoidance of further delays.

(3) Advance to an earlier date the projected Farragut-Whiteside ...interconnection with LILCO now scheduled for 1984, for the same reason indicated in (2) above.

(4) Automate all small combustion turbine units for quick start-up by remote control, and until that can be accomplished, all such units should be manned full-time. Unmanned and inoperative generating units have little or no value in preserving system operability under conditions of extreme emergency.

(5) Since the existing load shedding procedures and the related equipment failed to fulfill their intended mission, Con Edison must reassess and revise its emergency procedures and upgrade the ability of its system to shed load quickly and to the degree necessary to maintain the integrity of its system.

(6) Con Edison's internal emergency procedures and training of personnel to cope with emergency situations evidently have to be reassessed. Serious questions remain as to the adequacy of manpower at the Control Center at times of emergency, management's standing instructions to its operators, and the soundness of judgment exercised by the Company's personnel as to the actions that could have been taken, but were not taken, that might have enabled the system to withstand the initial disturbances.

(7) The extraordinary length of time needed to restore service indicates a serious deficiency in planning, for example, by failing to provide standby auxiliary power sources to maintain oil pressure in underground cables. Con Edison must take immediate steps to provide such a standby power source as well as all necessary measures that would permit quick restoration of service. Further,

549

to shorten the time required to restore service to its customers, Con Edison must find ways to reconnect distribution circuits faster than its present procedures.

(8) It is obvious that had Con Edison more spinning reserve on its own system at the time of the outage and had it been generating more of its power requirements rather than purchasing less expensive power, it may have been able to withstand the initial disturbances. Con Edison must reassess, in conjunction with the other members of NYPP and the New York Public Service Commission, the existing provisions of the Pool Agreement and the directives of the New York Public Service Commission in order to provide for a greater degree of local area security generation even though it may be more costly.

(9) Because of the apparent failure of equipment protecting major facilities, Con Edison must reassess the adequacy of such protective equipment and revise its procedures to test it more.

(10) Because of its dependence on a long, narrow transmission corridor, Con Edison must reassess its plans for the location of new generating facilities. The location of generation closer to load centers would tend to minimize the possibility of outages due to disruption of some components of the transmission network. As another example, had the Cornwall Project, which was first authorized by the Federal Power Commission in 1965, been in operation, the operating schedule for July 13 would have been different and the effects of the initial disturbance could have been minimized.

The foregoing recommendations are tentative and subject to revision when the further studies contemplated in this report have been completed. We make them also in the knowledge that some of them may involve substantial outlays by Con Edison for facilities and other purposes. Compliance with such recommendations may then, of course, result in material increases in the cost of electricity by a system whose electric rates are already nearly twice the national average. Nevertheless, the extreme vulnerability of New York City to a power failure and the cost to the City in terms of damage to the public safety, economic loss, and destruction of property make it all the more essential that the increased expenditures for improvement of reliability should be committed immediately....

...In light of the above, it is essential that a thorough reexamination be made of the reliability of bulk power supply systems in New York and throughout the balance of the nation. If the July 13 failure serves to stimulate a painful reexamination of all of those aspects of power system planning, maintenance, monitoring, and operation that bear upon service reliability, some positive good may be salvaged from an otherwise intolerable event.

CARTER WELFARE REFORM PLAN
August 6, 1977

Following up on a campaign pledge to undertake a "complete overhaul" of the nation's welfare system, President Carter Aug. 6 sent Congress his proposals to scrap the existing melange of welfare programs and replace them with a "Program for Better Jobs and Income." The program would, according to Carter, provide jobs for those who need work, provide fairer and more uniform cash benefits, promote family stability and improve the self-respect of recipients.

It would accomplish those goals by spending $31.1-billion to create 1.4 million public service jobs, provide a basic cash benefit to the needy, relieve the financial burden on every state by at least 10 per cent the first year of the plan in fiscal 1981 and include benefits for the first time for the so-called working poor.

Carter's Aug. 6 proposals followed the broad outline the President sketched for Congress in a May 2 statement in which he pledged a job for welfare recipients who could work and a "decent income" for those who could not.

In his May 2 statement, Carter said a three-month study of the welfare system initiated shortly after his inauguration had led to the conclusion that the system was "worse than we thought. The most important unanimous conclusion is that the present welfare programs should be scrapped and a totally new system implemented." The President criticized existing programs as "overly wasteful, capricious and subject to fraud; they violate many desirable and necessary principles."

"Welfare Reform"

"Welfare reform" has had almost as many definitions as there are individuals and groups trying to redo the system. "Reform" can mean any number of things, ranging from broadening eligibility and increasing benefits to tightening requirements in order to keep people off the rolls.

The need for welfare programs depends largely on the success of employment, private savings and government social insurance programs in meeting basic income needs.

The Department of Health, Education and Welfare (HEW) classifies seven government programs as "social insurance" programs—Social Security, Railroad Retirement, Workmen's Compensation, Black Lung, Unemployment Insurance, Veterans' Compensation and Medicare. Although not designed specifically for the poor, these programs redistribute among the population 2½ times as many dollars as the welfare programs do, according to HEW figures. By themselves they reduce the percentage of the U.S. population considered "poor" to 14 per cent, from 25 per cent. In fiscal 1977, benefits from the seven programs were expected to exceed $130-billion. (Social Security reform proposals, p. 377)

There are nine basic income assistance programs which HEW considers part of the welfare structure and which were the programs included in studies of welfare reform. With these programs, the percentage of poverty-level persons in the United States is reduced to less than 7 per cent of the population if in-kind transfers such as Medicaid and housing subsidies are included as part of income. The nine programs cost federal, state and local governments about $50-billion a year.

Growth of Programs

The 1930s saw the birth of veterans' pensions (1933), Aid to Families with Dependent Children (AFDC) (1935) and housing assistance (1937). In the ensuing 27 years there were changes in the programs—AFDC coverage was extended to needy parents in 1950 and to families with unemployed fathers at states' option in 1961—but no new ones were enacted until 1964. In 1964 and 1965 the two largest programs were created by Congress: food stamps and Medicaid. Two more programs were added in 1972: Basic Educational Opportunity Grants and Supplemental Security Income (SSI). Earned income tax credits were enacted in 1975.

The irregular growth of the programs led to wide disparities in benefit levels among states and to a cumbersome administrative structure. In the AFDC program, for example, annual benefit levels for a four-person family varied in June 1976 from $5,964 in Hawaii to $720 in Mississippi. At the same time, the federal share of those benefits equaled $2,982 in Hawaii compared to $600 in Mississippi.

12 Goals Outlined

Promising to complete legislative proposals by August, the President May 2 set forward the following 12 goals for welfare reform:

1. *No higher initial cost than the present system.*
2. *Access to a job for every family with children and a member able to work.*
3. *Incentives to take full-time and part-time jobs in the private sector.*
4. *Public training and jobs "when private employment is unavailable."*
5. *More income for a family "if it works than if it does not."*
6. *Incentives to keep families together.*
7. *Continuation of earned income tax credits for the working poor.*
8. *A decent income for those unable to work or earn adequate income, "with federal benefits consolidated into a simple cash payment, varying in amount only to accommodate differences in costs of living from one area to another."*
9. *Simpler and easier administration.*
10. *Incentives "to be honest and to eliminate fraud."*
11. *Reduction of "the unpredictable and growing financial burden on state and local governments" as soon as federal resources permitted.*
12. *Emphasis on local administration of public job programs.*

The Plan

The Carter welfare plan resembled in many ways Richard Nixon's Family Assistance Plan (FAP) proposed eight years earlier almost to the day. However, the two plans had one major difference—while Nixon's required recipients to work, it did not provide any jobs.

Although Carter's Aug. 6 proposals followed up on his May 2 statement, the major departure from his earlier pronouncement was the price of the program. He originally stipulated that the administration's welfare revisions would have "no higher initial cost than the present systems." That would have set a ceiling of more than $23-billion in 1978 dollars on the welfare reform plan.

As Carter outlined his plan, it would cost $30.7-billion in 1978 dollars. But later estimates presented by HEW Secretary Joseph A. Califano Jr. to a House subcommittee put the cost at $31.1-billion. The administration calculated that $28.3-billion of that amount would come from existing programs or savings and $2.8-billion would be additional cost.

The "no higher initial cost" statement had drawn heavy fire from numerous quarters, especially from financially pressed state and local governments looking to Washington for relief. Carter pledged to reduce the financial burdens on those governments "as rapidly as federal resources permit," but they told him clearly that was not soon enough.

In his Aug. 6 statement, Carter said the decision to add more money came after careful consultation with state and local leaders. The additional funds would provide more than $2.1-billion in fiscal relief to the states, particularly those that had borne the heaviest burdens. As proposed, New York and California alone would receive more than $1-billion of that money.

A special House subcommittee, comprised of the Ways and Means Subcommittee on Public Assistance and Unemployment Compensation and members from the Agriculture and Education and Labor Committees, began consideration of the reform proposal Sept. 19 but did not complete work in 1977.

> *Following is the text of President Carter's Aug. 6 message to Congress proposing a new welfare system for the United States.* (Boldface headings in brackets have been added by Congressional Quarterly to highlight the organization of the text.):

To the Congress of the United States:

As I pledged during my campaign for the Presidency I am asking the Congress to abolish our existing welfare system, and replace it with a job-oriented program for those able to work and a simplified, uniform, equitable cash assistance program for those in need who are unable to work by virtue of disability, age or family circumstance. The Program for Better Jobs and Income I am proposing will transform the manner in which the Federal government deals with the income needs of the poor, and begin to break the welfare cycle:

The program I propose will provide:

- Job opportunities for those who need work.
- A Work Benefit for those who work but whose incomes are inadequate to support their families.
- Income Support for those able to work part-time or who are unable to work due to age, physical disability or the need to care for children six years of age or younger.

This new program will accomplish the following:

- Dramatically reduce reliance on welfare payments by doubling the number of single-parent family heads who support their families primarily through earnings from work.
- Ensure that work will always be more profitable than welfare, and that a private or non-subsidized public job will always be more profitable than a special federally-funded public service job.
- Combine effective work requirements and strong work incentives with improved private sector placement services, and create up to 1.4 million public service jobs. Forty-two per cent of those jobs may be taken by

current AFDC recipients. Those who can work will work, and every family with a full-time worker will have an income substantially above the poverty line.

● Provide increased benefits and more sensitive treatment to those most in need.

● Reduce complexity by consolidating the current AFDC, Supplemental Security Income (SSI), and Food Stamp programs, all of which have differing eligibility requirements, into a single cash assistance program, providing for the first time a uniform minimum Federal payment for the poor.

● Provide strong incentives to keep families together rather than tear them apart, by offering the dignity of useful work to family heads and by ending rules which prohibit assistance when the father of a family remains within the household.

● Reduce fraud and error and accelerate efforts to assure that deserting fathers meet their obligations to their families.

● Give significant financial relief to hard-pressed state and local governments.

[The Need for Reform]

In May, after almost four months of study, I said that the welfare system was worse than I expected. I stand by that conclusion. Each program has a high purpose and serves many needy people; but taken as a whole the system is neither rational nor fair. The welfare system is anti-work, anti-family, inequitable in its treatment of the poor and wasteful of taxpayers' dollars. The defects of the current system are clear:

● It treats people with similar needs in different fashion with separate eligibility requirements for each program.

● It creates exaggerated difference in benefits based on state of residence. Current combined state and federal AFDC benefits for a family of four with no income vary from $720 per year in Mississippi to $5,954 in Hawaii.

● It provides incentives for family breakup. In most cases two-parent families are not eligible for cash assistance and, therefore, a working father often can increase his family's income by leaving home. In Michigan a two-parent family with the father working at the minimum wage has a total income, including tax credits and food stamps, of $5,922. But if the father leaves, the family will be eligible for benefits totalling $7,076.

● It discourages work. In one Midwestern state, for example, a father who leaves part-time employment paying $2,400 for a full-time job paying $4,800 reduces his family's income by $1,250.

● Efforts to find jobs for current recipients have floundered.

● The complexity of current programs leads to waste, fraud, red tape, and errors. HEW has recently discovered even government workers unlawfully receiving benefits, and numbers of people receive benefits in more than one jurisdiction at the same time.

The solutions to these problems are not easy—and no solution can be perfect; but it is time to begin. The welfare system is too hopeless to be cured by minor modifcations. We must make a complete and clean break with the past.

People in poverty want to work, and most of them do. This program is intended to give them the opportunity for self-support by providing jobs for those who need them, and by increasing the rewards from working for those who earn low wages.

[Program Summary]

The Program for Better Jobs and Income has the following major elements:

● Strengthened services through the employment and training system for placement in the private sector jobs.

● Creation of up to 1.4 million public service and training positions for principal earners in families with children, at or slightly above the minimum wage through state and local government and non-profit sponsors.

● An expansion of the Earned Income Tax Credit to provide an income supplement of up to a maximum of well over $600 for a family of four through the tax system, by a 10% credit for earnings up to $4,000, a 5% credit for earnings from $4,000 to the entry point of the positive tax system, and a declining 10% credit thereafter until phase-out. A major share of the benefit will accrue to hard-pressed workers with modest incomes struggling successfully to avoid welfare.

● Strong work requirements applying to single persons, childless couples and family heads, with work requirements of a more flexible nature for single-parent family heads with children aged 7 to 14. Single-parent family heads with pre-school aged children are not required to work.

● A Work Benefit for two-parent families, single-parent families with older children, singles and childless couples. The Federal benefit for a family of four would be a maximum of $2,300 and, after $3,800 of earnings, would be reduced fifty cents for each dollar of earnings.

● Income Support for single-parent families with younger children and aged, blind or disabled persons. The federal benefit would be a base of $4,200 for a family of four and would be reduced fifty cents for each dollar of earnings.

● New eligibility requirements for cash assistance which insure that benefits go to those most in need.

● Fiscal relief to States and localities of $2-billion in the first year, growing in subsequent years.

● Simple rules for state supplements to the basic program, in which the Federal government will bear a share of the cost.

[Costs]

In my May 2, 1977, statement I established as a goal that the new reformed system involve no higher initial cost than the present system. It was my belief that fundamental reform was possible within the confines of current expenditures if the system were made more rational and efficient. That belief has been borne out in our planning. Thereafter, Secretary Califano outlined a tentative no cost plan which embodied the major reform we have been seeking:

- Consolidation of programs.
- Incentives to work.
- Provision of jobs.
- Establishment of a national minimum payment.
- Streamlined administration.
- Incentives to keep families together.
- Some fiscal relief for State and local governments.

Subsequently, we have consulted with state and local officials and others who are knowledgeable in this area. As a result of those consultations we have gone beyond the no cost plan to one with modest additional cost in order to provide more jobs, particularly for current AFDC family heads, additional work incentives, broader coverage for needy families and greater fiscal relief for states and localities.

The Program for Better Jobs and Income will replace $26.3-billion in current programs which provide income assistance to low-income people. In addition, the program will produce savings in other programs amounting to $1.6-billion. The total amount available from replaced programs and savings is $27.9-billion.

Current Federal Expenditures and Savings*

(1978 Dollars)

EXPENDITURES

AFDC	$6.4-billion
SSI	$5.7-billion
Food Stamps	$5.0-billion
Earned Income Tax Credit	$1.3-billion
Stimulus Portion of CETA Public Jobs	$5.5-billion
WIN Program	$0.4-billion
Extended Unemployment Insurance Benefits (27-39 weeks)	$0.7-billion
Rebates of per capita share of Wellhead Tax Revenues to Low-Income People if Passed by Congress[1]	$1.3-billion
Sub-Total	$26.3-billion

SAVINGS (1978 DOLLARS)

Decreased Unemployment Insurance Expenditures	$0.4-billion

* Figures subsequently revised by Carter administration; see p. 564.

1 The National Energy plan calls for rebate of the wellhead tax revenues to taxpayers through the income tax system and to "the poor who do not pay taxes" in effect through income maintenance programs.

HEW Program to Reduce Fraud and Abuse	$0.4-billion
Decrease in Required Housing Subsidies Due to Increased Income[2]	$0.5-billion
Increases in Social Security Contributions[3]	$0.3-billion
Sub-total	$1.6-billion
Total	$27.9-billion

The new Program for Better Jobs and Income will have a total cost of $30.7-billion. The additional cost of the program above existing costs is $2.8-billion in spending. In addition, $3.3-billion of tax relief is given to working low and moderate income taxpayers through an expanded income tax credit.

Cost of New Program

Work Benefit and Income Support	$20.4-billion
Earned Income Tax Credit[4]	$1.5-billion
Employment and Training	$8.8-billion
Total	$30.7-billion

The additional cost above current expenditures has been used to make important improvements in our original plan:

• Increased fiscal relief has been provided for states and localities, particularly for those which have borne the greatest financial burdens.

• Incentives which strengthen family ties have been improved by adopting a broader definition of eligible applicants to permit more generous payment than in the earlier plan to older persons and young mothers with children who live in extended families.

• Work incentives for low wage workers have been increased by expanding the Earned Income Tax Credit for those in private and non-subsidized public work to cover and supplement approximately twice the income covered by the existing EITC.

• A deduction for child care will permit and encourage single parents to take work which will lift them out of poverty.

• Up to 300,000 additional part-time jobs have been added for single parent families with school age children (if adequate day care is available, such parents will be expected to accept full-time jobs).

2 This does not decrease housing programs nor reduce the amount of cash assistance paid to residents of subsidized housing. It is merely an estimate of the savings to the Department of Housing and Urban Development's housing subsidy programs on account of higher incomes going to tenants under the new program.

3 This does not increase anyone's Social Security Tax, nor does it take any money out of the Social Security Trust Funds. It merely recognizes that the millions of people taken off of dependence on welfare and given a job will become contributors to the Social Security System.

4 This is the cost of the portion of the expanded EITC which will be received by those who do not pay income taxes. Income taxpayers with families will receive benefits totaling $3.3-billion.

With these improvements the Program for Better Jobs and Income will help turn low income Americans away from welfare dependence with a system that is fair, and fundamentally based on work for those who can and should work.

Employment Services and Job Search

A central element of this proposal is a new effort to match low-income persons with available work in the private and public sector. It will be the responsibility of state and local officials to assure an unbroken sequence of employment and training services, including job search, training, and placement. Prime sponsors under the Comprehensive Employment and Training Act, state employment service agencies, and community-based organizations will play major roles in this effort.

Jobs for Families

A major component of the program is a national effort to secure jobs for the principal wage earners in low-income families with children. The majority of poor families—including many who are on welfare for brief periods of time—depend upon earnings from work for most of their income. People want to support themselves and we should help them do so. I propose that the federal government assist workers from low income families to find regular employment in the private and public sectors. When such employment cannot be found I propose to provide up to 1.4 million public service jobs (including part-time jobs and training) paying at the minimum wage, or slightly above where states supplement the basic Federal program.

This program represents a commitment by my Administration to ensure that families will have both the skills and the opportunity for self-support.

This new Public Service Employment Program is carefully designed to avoid disruptive effects to the regular economy:

• Applicants will be required to engage in an intensive 5-week search for regular employment before becoming eligible for a public service job. Those working in public service employment will be required to engage in a period of intensive job search every 12 months.

• In order to encourage participants to seek employment in the regular economy, the basic wage rate will be kept at, or where states supplement, slightly above, the minimum wage.

• Every effort will be made to emphasize job activities which lead to the acquisition of useful skills by participants, to help them obtain employment in the regular economy. Training activities will be a regular component of most job placements.

The development of this job program is clearly a substantial undertaking requiring close cooperation of all levels of government. I am confident it will succeed. Thousands of unmet needs for public goods and services exist in our country. Through an imaginative program of job creation we can insure that the goals of human development and community development are approached simultaneously. Public service jobs will be created in areas such as public safety, recreational facilities and programs, facilities for the handicapped, environmental monitoring, child care, waste treatment and recycling, clean-up and pest and insect control, home services for the elderly and ill, weatherization of homes and buildings and other energy-saving activities, teachers' aides and other paraprofessionals in schools, school facilities improvements, and cultural arts activities.

Earned Income Tax Credit

The current Earned Income Tax Credit (EITC) is an excellent mechanism to provide tax relief to the working poor. I propose to expand this concept to provide benefits to more families and provide relief to low- and modest-income working people hard hit by payroll tax increases, improve work incentives, and integrate the Program for Better Jobs and Income with the income tax system. The expanded EITC, which will apply to private and non-subsidized public employment, will have the following features:

● A 10% credit on earnings up to $4,000 per year as under current law.

● A 5% credit on earnings between $4,000 and approximately $9,000 for a family of four (the point at which the family will become liable for federal income taxes).

● A phase-out of the credit beyond roughly $9,000 of earnings at ten per cent. The credit will provide benefits to a family of four up to $15,600 of income.

● The credit will be paid by the Treasury Department and the maximum credit for a family of four would be well over $600.

Work Benefit and Income Support

I propose to scrap and completely overhaul the current public assistance programs, combining them into a simplified, uniform, integrated system of cash assistance. ADFC, SSI and Food Stamps will be abolished. In their place will be a new program providing: (1) a Work Benefit for two-parent families, single people, childless couples and single parents with no child under 14, all of whom are expected to work full-time and required to accept available work; and (2) Income Support for those who are aged, blind or disabled, and for single parents of children under age 14. Single parents with children aged 7 to 14 will be required to accept part-time work which does not interfere with caring for the children, and will be expected to accept full-time work where appropriate day care is available.

These two levels of assistance are coordinated parts of a unified system which maintains incentives to work and simplifies administration.

● For those qualifying for income support the basic benefit for a family of four with no other income will be $4,200 in 1978 dollars. Benefits will be reduced fifty cents for each dollar of earnings, phasing out completely at $8,400 of earnings. Added benefits would accrue to those in regular private or public employment through the Earned Income Tax Credit.

• An aged, blind, or disabled individual would receive a Federal benefit of $2,500 and a couple would receive $3,750—more than they are now receiving. That is higher than the projected SSI benefit for either group—about $100 higher than for a couple and $120 higher for a single person.

• For those persons required to work who receive a Work Benefit, the basic benefit for a family of four with no other income will be $2,300. To encourage continued work, benefits will not be reduced at all for the first $3,800 of earnings and will thereafter be reduced by fifty cents for each dollar earned up to $8,400. Again, the Earned Income Tax Credit will provide added benefits to persons in regular private or public employment.

• We are committed to assure that inflation will not erode the value of the benefits, and that real benefits will be increased over time as federal resources grow. To preserve flexibility in the initial transition period, however, we do not at this time propose automatic indexing of benefits or automatic increases in their real value. (The figures contained in this message expressed in 1978 dollars will be adjusted to retain their real purchasing power at the time of implementation.)

• Single parent family heads will be able to deduct up to 20% of earned income up to an amount of $150 per month to pay for child care expenses required for the parent to go to work.

• No limits are placed on the right of states to supplement these basic benefits. However, only if states adopt supplements which complement the structure and incentives of the federal program will the federal government share in the cost.

Eligibility rules for the Work Benefit and Income Support will be tightened to insure that the assistance goes to those who are most in need.

• To reduce error and direct assistance to those most in need, benefits will be calculated based on a retrospective accounting period, rather than on the prospective accounting period used in existing programs. The income of the applicant over the previous six-month period will determine the amount of benefits.

• The value of assets will be reviewed to insure that those with substantial bank accounts or other resources do not receive benefits. The value of certain assets will be imputed as income to the family in determining the amount of benefits.

• Eligibility has been tightened in cases where related individuals share the same household, while preserving the ability of the aged, disabled and young mothers to file for benefits separately.

[State Role and Fiscal Relief For States and Communities]

Public assistance has been a shared federal and state responsibility for forty years. The program I propose will significantly increase federal participation but maintain an important role for the states.

• Every state will be assured that it will save at least ten per cent of its current welfare expenses in the first year of the program, with substantially increased fiscal relief thereafter.

• Every state is required to pay ten per cent of the basic federal income benefits provided to its residents except where it will exceed 90 per cent of its prior welfare expenditures.

• Every state is free to supplement the basic benefits, and is eligible for federal matching payments for supplements structured to complement and maintain the incentives of the federal program. The federal government will pay 75% of the first $500 supplement and 25% of any additional supplement up to the poverty line. These state supplements will be required to follow federal eligibility criteria to help achieve nation-wide uniformity.

• Where states supplement the income support they must also proportionally supplement the work benefit and the public service wage.

• There will be a three-year period during which states will be required to maintain a share of their current effort in order to ease the transition of those now receiving benefits. These resources must be directed to payment of the state's 10% share of the basic benefit, to supplements complementary to the basic program, and to grandfathering of existing SSI and partially grandfathering AFDC beneficiaries. The Federal government will guarantee a state that its total cost for these expenditures will not exceed 90% of current welfare costs. States can retain any amounts under the 90% requirement not actually needed for the mandated expenditures. In the second year of the program states will be *required* to maintain only 60% of current expenditures, in the third year, only 30%. In the fourth year, they will only be required to spend enough to meet their 10% share of the basic benefit.

• States will have the option to assist in the administration of the program. They will be able to operate the crucial intake function serving applicants, making possible effective coordination with social service programs. The federal government will operate the data processing system, calculate benefits, and issue payments.

• The federal government will provide a $600-million block grant to the states to provide for emergency needs. These grants will assist the states in responding to sudden and drastic changes in family circumstances.

• The federal government will provide 30% above the basic wage for fringe benefits and administrative costs of the jobs program, and will reimburse the states for costs of administration of the work benefit and income support program.

In the first year of this program, states and localities would recieve $2-billion in fiscal relief, while at the same time ensuring that no current SSI beneficiary receives a reduced benefit and that over 90 per cent of current AFDC beneficiaries receive similar protection.

In subsequent years as current recipients leave the rolls and as the maintenance of state effort requirement declines from 90 per cent to zero within 3 years, the opportunities for increased fiscal relief will grow.

Under our program for fiscal relief, states will be required to pass through their fiscal relief to municipal and county governments in full proportion to their contributions. Thus, for example, in New York State, where New York City pays 33% of the state's share, New York City would receive 33% of the state's fiscal relief or $174-million.

Reduction of Fraud and Abuse

The few providers and recipients guilty of fraud and abuse in our welfare programs not only rob the taxpayers but cheat the vast majority of honest recipients. One of the most significant benefits of consolidation of existing cash assistance programs is the opportunity to apply sophisticated management techniques to improve their operation. The use of a central computer facility will permit more efficient processing of claims, reduce the incidence of error in calculating benefits, and facilitate the detection of fraud. No longer will people easily claim benefits in more than one jurisdiction.

We will strongly enforce current programs directed at assisting local officials in obtaining child support payments from run-away parents, as determined by judicial proceedings.

We will ensure that the Department of Health, Education, and Welfare will vigorously root out abuses and fraud in our social programs.

We will work for passage of current legislation designed to crack down on fraud and abuse in our Medicaid and Medicare Program. The administration of these programs will be a major challenge for federal and state officials. It provides a valuable opportunity to demonstrate that government can be made to work, particularly in its operation of programs which serve those in our society most in need.

Implementation

Because of the complexity of integrating the different welfare systems of the 50 states and the District of Columbia into a more unified national system, we estimate that this program will be effective in Fiscal Year 1981. Moreover, we recognize that the National Health Insurance plan which will be submitted next year must contain fundamental reform and rationalization of the Medicaid program, carefully coordinated with the structure of this proposal. However, we are anxious to achieve the swiftest implementation possible and will work with the Congress and state and local government to accelerate this timetable if at all possible.

Given the present complex system, welfare reform inevitably involves difficult choices. Simplicity and uniformity and improved benefits for the great majority inevitably require reduction of special benefits for some who receive favored treatment now. Providing the dignity of a job to those who at present are denied work opportunities will require all the creativity and ingenuity that private business and government at all levels can bring to bear. But the effort will be worthwhile both for the individual and for the country. The Program for Better Jobs and Income stresses the fundamental American commitment to work, strengthens the family, respects the less advantaged in our society, and makes a far more efficient and effective use of our hard-earned tax dollars.

I hope the Congress will move expeditiously and pass this program early next year.

JIMMY CARTER

The White House,
August 6, 1977

Following are the revisions in the costs estimates as presented to a House subcommittee Sept. 19 by HEW Secretary Joseph A. Califano Jr.:

Current Federal Expenditures and Savings
(1978 DOLLARS)

EXPENDITURES

AFDC	$6.4-billion
SSI	$5.7-billion
Food Stamps	$5.5-billion
Earned Income Tax Credit	$1.1-billion
Stimulus Portion of CETA Public Jobs	$5.5 billion
WIN Program	$0.4-billion
Extended Unemployment Insurance Benefits (27-39 weeks)	$0.7-billion
Rebates of per capita share of Wellhead Tax Revenues to Low-Income People if Passed by Congress	$1.3-billion
Sub-Total	$26.6-billion

SAVINGS (1978 DOLLARS)

Decreased Unemployment Insurance Expenditures	$0.3-billion
HEW Program to Reduce Fraud and Abuse	$0.4-billion
Decrease in Required Housing Subsidies Due to Increased Income	$0.3-billion
Increases in Social Security Contributions	$0.7-billion
Sub-Total	$1.7-billion
TOTAL	$28.3-billion

The new Program for Better Jobs and Income will have a total cost of $31.07-billion. Thus, the additional cost of the above existing costs is $2.8-billion in spending.

Cost of New Program

Work Benefit and Income Support	$20.8-billion
Earned Income Tax Credit	$ 1.5-billion
Employment and Training	$ 8.8-billion
TOTAL	$31.1-billion

▼▼▼

SEC REPORT ON NEW YORK CITY FISCAL CRISIS

August 26, 1977

A Securities and Exchange Commission (SEC) report charged Aug. 26 that New York City Mayor Abraham D. Beame, City Comptroller Harrison J. Goldin, six city banks and the nation's largest brokerage firm, Merrill Lynch, Pierce, Fenner and Smith Inc., misled investors in city securities in 1974-1975 by failing to disclose the city's precarious financial situation. The Commission report alleged that Beame and Goldin engaged in "deceptive practices masking the city's true and disastrous financial condition." It said that Beame and Goldin "made numerous reassuring public statements" to sell the securities while the city verged on collapse. No charges of deliberate fraud or criminal intent were made in the report, nor did it include recommendations for formal action by the Justice Department.

The 800-page Staff Report of Transactions in the Securities of the City of New York, transmitted to Congress, was the product of a 19-month investigation of the period from October 1974 through April 1975, when the city faced a fiscal crisis and issued large offerings of short-term securities.

The report also concluded that:

● The city used unsound budgeting practices that it knew distorted the true financial picture. City officials employed a variety of accounting and financial gimmicks to produce a balanced budget that rested on a hidden deficit totaling $5-billion.

● Six leading New York banks and the Merrill Lynch firm failed to inform investors that the city was in financial trouble when they promoted sale of the securities. The banks named were: Citibank, Morgan Guaranty

Trust Co., Banker's Trust Co., Chase Manhattan Bank, Manufacturer's Hanover Trust Co. and Chemical Bank.

●All but one of the banks named, Chemical Bank, reduced their own holdings of city obligations while selling them as a good investment to the public.

●The nation's two major bond rating services, Standard and Poor's Corp. and Moody's Investors Service Inc., together with four bond counsel firms failed to verify the city's financial reports.

●Faced with a deepening fiscal crisis, the minimum face amount of the short-term securities was reduced from $100,000 to $10,000 to attract individual investors.

●Failure to disclose the city's true financial condition "impaired" the liquidity of several New York banks and prolonged the effect of the crisis.

Reaction to the SEC Report

Mayor Beame Aug. 26 called the report a "shameless, vicious political document...a hatchet job." Beame went on to say: "The SEC's criticism is nothing more than 20-20 hindsight.... And rather than question my integrity, the SEC must explain its own cover-up and non-disclosure. For more than a year it withheld and covered up the fact that the banks secretly dumped city securities from their own portfolios on the market, robbing the small investor, and accelerating the city's credit crisis.... No mayor can be expected to speak to his people in the language of an investment prospectus. The city must assure the well-being of its citizens and provide for their future. To turn off this spigot of hope is just as devastating to a city as the denial of credit."

The SEC report quickly became an issue in the Democratic mayoral primary in New York City. Expecting the report to be critical of Mayor Beame's administration, the mayor's opponents pressed for its early release. Beame, on the other hand, tried to blunt its impact. Observers thought that it had an impact on the election outcome Sept. 8 when Rep. Edward I. Koch (D N.Y.) defeated Beame.

On Capitol Hill, after the report was released, Sen. Harrison A. Williams Jr. (D N.J.), chairman of the Senate Banking, Housing and Urban Affairs Committee's Subcommittee on Securities, said that he planned to introduce legislation to require full disclosure by municipal bond issuers. Sen. William Proxmire (D Wis.), chairman of the full Senate Banking Committee, said that he also favored tougher disclosure rules but doubted that Congress would pass a new law.

Proxmire urged New York Gov. Hugh L. Carey Sept. 22 to summon the New York state legislature into session to pass legislation permitting the city to re-enter the public credit market before the end of the year. In letters to both Carey and U.S. Treasury Secretary Michael W.

Blumenthal, Proxmire said there was no assurance Congress would continue to extend credit to New York City beyond the June 30, 1978, deadline, particularly if the state of New York failed to show that it had done all it could do to help the city. It was a test of good faith, Proxmire noted, to permit the re-entry of the city into the securities market.

Wrongdoing Denied

During state legislative hearings on the banks' role during the fiscal crisis, Walter B. Wriston, chairman of Citicorp, denied Oct. 11 that a subsidiary, Citibank, had acted in bad faith in the marketing of city securities in 1974-1975. Wriston accused the SEC of distortion and omissions in its report on the city's fiscal crisis. Citibank did not "dump" city securities and at no time possessed "inside" knowledge of the city's deteriorating finances other than the information available to the general public, Wriston said.

David Rockefeller, chairman of the Chase Manhattan Bank, acknowledged Oct. 17 during the same hearings that Chase sold New York City bonds from its own portfolio in late 1974—at the time New York was having difficulty issuing new notes to the public. Rockefeller was the first bank officer to admit that the banks had sold off city bonds during the fiscal crisis. However, he denied having any "material inside information" not available to public investors. Heavy overseas earnings, resulting in deductible tax payments to foreign governments, forced the bank to increase its taxable income portfolio starting in late 1974, and therefore tax-exempt holdings were reduced, Rockefeller said.

William F. Haddad, director of the New York Assembly's Office of Legislative Oversight, charged that the banks had dumped the city bonds. During the hearings Haddad produced memoranda written by a member of Chase's Municipal Credit Department recommending that city security holdings "be reduced." Thomas G. Labrecque, an executive vice president at Chase, said the memoranda represented the opinion of one analyst and had nothing to do with the final decision to reduce the bank's holdings. Rockefeller, in an interview after the hearings, said he was unaware of the memoranda.

> *Following are excerpts from the report of the Securities and Exchange Commission investigation into the role of New York City banks and city officials in the marketing of municipal bonds during the city's fiscal crisis, released Aug. 27, 1977. (Boldface headings in brackets have been added by Congressional Quarterly to highlight the organization of the text.):*

The investigation which underlies the Report, conducted by the New York Regional Office, was one of the most complex in the Commission's history and involved collection of more than 250,000 documents and over 12,000 pages of sworn testimony. It sought to—

(1) determine the nature and extent of the knowledge of City officials, underwriters, and bond counsel with respect to the steadily-worsening financial condition of the City; and

(2) compare the knowledge of these parties to the disclosures made to the public from October, 1974 through April, 1975—a period during which approximately $4 billion worth of City short-term debt securities were sold to the public.

The federal securities laws administered by the Securities and Exchange Commission have as their principal purpose the protection of public investors," the Report declares. "Accordingly, our inquiry has been to determine whether, in the offer, sale and distribution of the City's debt securities, under the circumstances, there was provided the measure of disclosure mandated under the federal securities laws in the interests of the investing public. We conclude that it was not...."

[Background]

The last offer of securities by the City of New York to the general public was made in March, 1975. Since that time, the public debt market has been closed to the City. On November 15, 1975, the New York State Legislature enacted the Moratorium Act, which suspended the enforcement of the City's short-term debt, because the City was unable to meet its maturing obligations. Thousands of small investors had purchased a substantial part of the approximately $4 billion of short-term securities sold during the six months preceding March 31, 1975. On November 5, 1975, ten days before the passage of the Moratorium Act, certain short-term notes actually traded at a 35 percent discount from their principal face amount. On December 31, 1975, after the Moratorium Act was passed, but before it was declared unconstitutional, prices of certain short-term notes had declined to a 45 percent discount from their principal face amount.

[The Investigation]

In January, 1976, the Commission commenced an investigation into transactions in securities of the City. The staff's inquiry principally focused on the period from October 1, 1974, to March 31, 1975—the period during which the City's reliance on short-term borrowing increased dramatically over prior comparable periods, and the period during which the City issued substantial amounts of certain debt instruments to the investing public that remained outstanding at the time of the passage of the Moratorium Act.

During its 19-month investigation, the staff obtained over 250,000 documents and compiled over 12,000 pages of investigative testimony. The staff's Report is a distillation, analysis and evaluation of the evidence that has been obtained to date. The investigation, which is a continuing one, is in no sense an adjudicatory proceeding. Nor is the investigation or this Report a determination of the rights or liabilities of any person.

[City Financial Practices]

For a number of years, the City was incurring increasing deficits in its operations. In order to finance these deficits, and to appear to comply with the legal requirement that it balance its operating budget, the City, among other things, increasingly resorted to the sale of "short-term" debt securities.[1]

On March 31, 1975, the City had outstanding debt in excess of $14 billion, as follows:

$ 7,887,733,170	Funded Debt
1,102,000,000	TANs
1,767,655,000	BANs
3,185,000,000	RANs
107,610,000	Other short-term debt
$14,049,998,170	TOTAL

The City employed budgetary, accounting and financing practices which it knew distorted its true financial condition. These practices enabled the City to issue about $4 billion of short-term securities during the six-month period preceding its preclusion from the Nation's securities markets.[1] This record amount of securities was issued at the very time the City was on the brink of financial collapse.

In fact, the City dramatically increased its short-term debt six-fold—from $747 million to $4.5 billion—in the six years from 1969 to June 30, 1975. The New York State Charter Revision Commission primarily attributed this "enormous increase" in the City's debt to:

> ...the City's refusal to soundly finance its expense budget. Since 1970-71, every expense budget has been balanced with an array of gim-micks—revenue accruals, capitalization of expenses, raiding reserves, appropriation of illusory fund balances, suspension of payments, carry-forward of deficits of questionable receivables, and finally, the creation of a public benefit corporation whose purpose is to borrow funds to bail out the expense budget.

These practices, it was concluded, did not "produce any cash in themselves; they simply enable[d] the City to borrow to pay current expenses."

The June 30, 1975 deficit, as later adjusted by the City, exceeded $5 billion. Reliable financial information was unavailable, and the adjusted deficit could only be estimated because, among other things, the City's internal accounting control system had been deficient in material respects.

---

[1] The "short-term" debt securities offered by the City, with stated maturities of one year or less, included: Tax Anticipation Notes ("TANs"), issued by the City in anticipation of the collection of real estate taxes; Revenue Anticipation Notes ("RANs"), issued in anticipation of the collection of estimated taxes (other than real estate taxes), monies that were estimated to be received from the New York State and federal governments and certain other kinds of revenue; and Bond Anticipation Notes ("BANs"), issued in the anticipation of revenues from subsequent sales of bonds.

The estimates of receivables, which formed the basis for the huge amount of RANs and TANs offered in the October, 1974 - March, 1975 period, were overstated by the accrual of revenues, including federal and New York State aid receivables and real estate and other local taxes which were unearned, uncollectible or non-existent.... Subsequent reports of New York State and City officials disclosed yet additional, significant areas in which the City's actual financial condition during the October, 1974 - March, 1975 period was vastly different from that claimed by the City and its officials.

During this period, the City continued to issue debt securities to investors throughout the United States and in foreign countries. As the City's financial plight worsened, it reduced the minimum face amount of the instruments it issued from $100,000 to $10,000, in order to penetrate the individual investor market more effectively. City securities were also placed with the City's pension funds and with a bond sinking fund—funds under the management of City officials, who were acting in fiduciary capacities on behalf of the beneficiaries of such funds....

...The functioning of the process by which City securities were brought to the market place depended not only upon the issuer, but also upon the principal underwriters, bond counsel and rating agencies. As is evident from the facts set forth in this Report, in varying degrees, they also failed to meet their responsibilities. Thus, public investors were denied the protections to which they were entitled....

[Accounting And Reporting Practices]

...[C]ertain of the City's unsound accounting and reporting practices...successfully obscured the City's real revenues, costs and financial position. Substantial weaknesses in the City's system of internal accounting control caused its financial information to be inherently unreliable. Many of the City's accounting practices were specifically designed to assist the City in its budget-balancing exercises by prematurely recognizing revenues and postponing expenses to unrelated future periods. The increase in revenue recognition was accomplished by the accrual of revenues, including federal and New York State aid receivables and real estate and other local taxes which were unearned, uncollectible or nonexistent. The essentially cash-basis accounting for City expenditures failed to recognize significant costs incurred but unpaid during the year, including millions of dollars annually in pension costs, which were calculated based on outdated actuarial assumptions and paid two years later. These were significant factors which contributed to the City's financial difficulties and enabled it to borrow funds from the public which could not be supported by its sources of revenue.

...[The report in discussing] the role of the City and its officials in the events surrounding the City's fiscal crisis.... concludes that:

(1) City officials were aware that there was an ever-growing disparity between revenues and expenses;

(2) City officials employed certain unsound budgetary, accounting and financial reporting practices which created the appearance that revenues and expenses were in balance;

(3) City officials prepared and published various reports which did not, individually or in the aggregate, clearly and accurately describe such practices or reveal the City's true financial condition; and

(4) The Mayor and the Comptroller made numerous reassuring public statements concerning the City's financial condition and the safety of investments in the City's debt securities, which statements facilitated the sale of the City's securities, and which did not provide adequate disclosure of the facts.

In sum, the Mayor and the Comptroller misled public investors in the offer, sale and distribution of billions of dollars of the City's municipal securities from October, 1974, through at least March, 1975.

...[The report also] focuses upon the key role played by the underwriters in the distribution of the City's securities. It discusses the underwriters' knowledge of the financial crisis and the City's related problems, the inadequacies of their disclosure of materially adverse information regarding the budgetary and financial problems of the City, and their failure to fulfill their responsibilities to the investing public. It also discusses the realization of these underwriters, and their failure to disclose, that their capacity to distribute substantial additional quantities of securities successfully was significantly impaired because of the City's financial crisis and that the market had become saturated with City securities. As the City's fiscal crisis further deteriorated, the public was subjected to a confusing and contradictory financial picture, with the result that public investors were misled.

[Security Rating Agencies]

...[The security rating] agencies rate the creditworthiness of municipal obligations. Their ratings have a significant impact upon investment decisions and access by municipalities to the capital markets. The agencies appear to have failed, in a number of respects, to make either diligent inquiry into data which called for further investigation, or to adjust their ratings of the City's securities based on known data in a manner consistent with standards upon which prior ratings had been based.

[Bond Counsel]

...During October, 1974, through March, 1975, four firms issued opinions on the validity of the issuance of New York City securities. The Report examines the engagement of the firms and the procedures they used in providing their opinions. The Report also explores bond counsel's awareness of circumstances relating to the City's fiscal problems that affected matters basic to bond counsel's opinions. In addition, the Report examines the knowledge of bond counsel of other matters that should have been, but were not, disclosed to investors. The Report concludes that bond counsel, when on notice of circumstances that called into question matters basic to their opinions, should have conducted additional investigation. It also concludes that bond counsel, who continued with their engagement having knowledge of information material to investors, should, in view of the particular circumstances, have taken reasonable steps to satisfy themselves that such material facts were disclosed to the public.

[Investor Survey]

...[A]nalyses of the responses received from questionnaires sent to individual investors, syndicate members and managing underwriters... indicate that the majority had never invested in municipal securities before, and 90 percent responded that a factor in their investment was their belief that an investment in City securities was "safe and secure." The survey also found that, at the time they made their investments:

—78 percent of the investors believed the City's bookkeeping and accounting practices to be excellent or good; and

—79 percent of the investors believed that the City was in good or excellent financial condition.

Additional comments volunteered by a number of these individual investors concerning their experiences with these investments were overwhelmingly negative, and indicated quite clearly that, in their purchase of City securities, they had been "misled."

[SEC Mandate]

The Commission's mandate is to assure that investors in securities, whether issued by municipalities or others, receive the protections afforded by the federal securities laws. This Report concludes that investors in the securities of New York City did not receive those protections.

On a number of occasions, the key participants had a clear opportunity to prevent further serious damage to public investors. However, they did not do so. As the City's financial condition deteriorated, additional steps were taken to sell its notes to individual investors, thus unfairly and improperly shifting the inherent risks. At a minimum, before such a shifting of risk was attempted, the key participants had the duty to assure adequate disclosure upon which investment decisions could be predicated.

Depriving investors of their clearly defined rights cannot be justified by the need to provide vital services to New York's citizens. Rather than serving the salutary goals the City sought to effect, the failure to make meaningful disclosure prolonged the agony of the City's fiscal crisis, and delayed major necessary corrective efforts. This failure caused undue risks and substantial injury to investors in the City's securities. It also impaired the liquidity of a number of the City's major banks, which are leading financial institutions in the United States, and cast a pall on the capacity of municipalities generally to utilize the Nation's securities markets to fund their essential operations.

It is imperative that persons with responsibilities in the marketing of municipal securities reassess their roles to assure that, when required, they will meet the demands of such occasions. It is hoped that this Report will be studied by the various participants in municipal financing, and that they will commence a critical review of the facts as the first step in the development of a program designed to place into effect at the earliest possible time the necessary remedial measures, not only to prevent a recurrence of what took place in New York City, but also to install a system that will assure municipalities vital access to the Nation's securities markets and the protection of those who invest in municipal securities.

[The Role of City Officials]

...This Report has described the knowledge of the City and its officials, particularly the Mayor and the Comptroller, as to the events surrounding the City's fiscal crisis. The following conclusions appear to be warranted, based on the evidence gathered by the staff: (1) the City consistently spent more than it received in revenues; (2) City officials were aware that there was an ever-growing disparity between revenues and expenses; (3) City officials employed certain unsound budgetary, accounting and financial reporting practices which created the appearance that revenues and expenses were in balance; (4) City officials prepared and published various reports which did not, individually or in the aggregate, clearly, fully and accurately describe such practices or reveal the City's true financial condition; and (5) the Mayor and the Comptroller made numerous reassuring public statements concerning the City's financial condition and the safety of investments in the City's debt securities, which statements facilitated the sale of the City's securities, and which did not provide adequate disclosure of the facts. In sum, the Mayor and the Comptroller misled public investors in the offer, sale and distribution of billions of dollars of the City's municipal securities from October 1974 through at least March 1975.

The Mayor and the Comptroller had knowledge of the facts. The Mayor controlled the budgetary process, and was fully aware of the gamut of unsound budgetary, accounting and financial reporting practices utilized by the City. Prior to assuming office as Mayor, Mr. Beame had spent 15 years in the City's Office of Management and Budget and eight years as Comptroller. After assuming office in January, 1974, Comptroller Goldin quickly became aware of the facts. Comptroller Goldin's consultants and assistants, particularly Steven Clifford, provided him with detailed memoranda as to these unsound practices and their effectiveness, often in terms of actual dollar amounts, in masking the City's true and disastrous financial condition.

To the extent that the City's budget overestimated revenues and under-stated expenses, borrowing was needed to cover the resulting "budget gap." To the extent that the budget employed other practices to mask the further disparities between anticipated receipts and expenditures, even greater borrowing "authority" was needed from the State. The City's true finan-cial needs were overwhelming, and for this reason the need for fair dis-closure was compelling.

Furthermore, the City's inadequate internal accounting controls resulted in unreliable and inaccurate financial information. The Mayor and Comptroller knew this. The inaccurate information was utilized in the City's fragmented official reports issued throughout the fiscal year. More importantly, this data was selectively reproduced in parts of the City's Notices of Sale and Reports of Essential Facts in connection with the offer-ing of the City's data securities.

Investors were injured by these practices, particularly when the New York State Legislature imposed a moratorium on the payment of principal and interest on the City's short-term debt maturing subsequent to November 15, 1975. After March, 1975 and prior to and during the moratorium, certain investors sustained large losses by selling into the declining and severely restricted secondary markets for the City's debt securities. For example, by December 31, 1975 certain RANs had declined 45% in principal amount in actual trading.

The political, economic and social pressures which assailed the City did not erupt overnight, but were burgeoning for many years. The City was only partially successful in obtaining increased federal and state aid; on the state level, additional City borrowing "authority" in lieu of an equivalent amount of state aid was provided in many instances. In ad-dition, the City's ability to raise revenue through taxation had apparently been extended to the point where further increases might have adversely impacted the City's economy. The City's officials were apparently unwill-ing or unable to reduce expenses to reflect the lack of needed revenues.

Even if one could assert that the City was motivated in good faith by these factors to seek out new investors to keep itself "afloat," that would constitute no excuse for misleading them in connection with the offer and sale of City securities. The City faced hard choices. But it was not appropriate to shift a large part of the risk inherent in the City's predica-ment to public investors without adequate disclosure of what that risk en-tailed.

Such deceptive practices proved counter-productive, insofar as they postponed the hard choices which had to be made and exacerbated the City's pyramiding deficits. Once revealed, such practices could not have aided the City's credibility as an issuer in a market where investor con-fidence plays a key role.

Insofar as the socio-economic conditions of the City impact its finances, they become items of importance to be disclosed to investors. After the crisis, the City itself recognized this obligation....

The federal securities laws administered by the Securities and Exchange Commission have as their principal purpose the protection of public investors. Accordingly, our inquiry has been to determine whether, under the circumstances, the measure of disclosure mandated under the federal securities laws was provided in connection with the offer, sale and distribution of the City's debt securities. We conclude that it was not....

[The Role of the Underwriters]

...The City's financial crisis was primarily the result of insufficient revenues to meet mounting City expenses. The growing gap between City revenues and City expenses was bridged through the resort to constant and unprecedented levels of short-term borrowings. Years of questionable and unsound budgetary, accounting and financial reporting practices helped mask the City's true financial condition from public view. In the Spring of 1975, however, these policies culminated in the virtual collapse of the market for City securities, ending the City's ability to raise more funds through issuance of short-term notes.

A key role in the nationwide distribution of the City's securities was played by the City's principal underwriters: Chase, Citibank, Morgan, Manufacturers, Chemical, Bankers and Merrill Lynch. The underwriters, through their own investments and by selling the City's securities to the investing public, enabled the City to raise billions of dollars in short-term debt issues through the Spring of 1975.

Approximately four billion dollars of City notes were underwritten during the period October 1974 through March 1975, a time when the City's fiscal condition was critical. Faced with a marketing problem, caused by the saturation of the market through previous billions of dollars of city issues and the growing doubts of the financial community as to the city's financial status, the City and the underwriters reached out for the smaller investor.

Thus, beginning in the winter of 1974, City notes began to be marketed in denominations as small as $10,000. This had the effect, at least in part, of shifting the risk for financing the City from the City's major banks and large institutional investors to individual investors.

As the City's fiscal crisis worsened, the public was subjected to a confusing and contradictory financial picture, with the result that the public, unlike the City and its underwriters, was deprived of a basic understanding of the City's finances. While the public was left largely uninformed, the City's underwriters had an increasing awareness of the range of problems underlying the City's fiscal crisis.

During 1974 and early 1975, certain of the underwriters of City securities ceased purchasing City securities for their fiduciary accounts. Despite the shift of investment policy, they continued as underwriters to market these securities to the public. The underwriters did not disclose this significant change in their investment strategy and policy.

The problems of the City came to a head in February and March 1975. A $260 million TAN offering in February 1975 was cancelled when the City was unable to certify certain current information that the underwriters had requested from the City. At about the same time the City's major banks informed the Mayor and the Comptroller that the underwriters would be unable to continue to support the City by taking down City securities unless the City took immediate remedial action.

The City's securities offerings were carried out without adequate disclosure. As a result, the public's principal source of information, besides the stream of confusing and contradictory statements in the press, was the representations by the City and the underwriters attesting to the safety and security of City notes.

Indeed, as one of the underwriters' attorneys stated in April 1975 to the City's principal underwriters, "the adverse information which would be required in...(a disclosure document)...would in all likelihood render the City securities unsaleable."

Despite the needs of the City for funds to meet the urgent demands of its citizenry, these needs do not justify the tapping of the public debt markets when neither the City nor its underwriters were willing or able to make adequate disclosures to investors....

[The Role of the Bond Counsel]

...The practice of municipal securities law is little understood by other lawyers, and probably not understood at all by the investing public. Yet, it is a role so vital that, without the closely-worded opinion provided by municipal bond counsel, municipalities would be unable to secure the tens of billions of dollars of yearly financings which they seek from the public capital markets.

Until late February, 1975 bond counsel passing upon New York City securities did little if any independent investigation and relied almost exclusively on City officials. Even during the period when events began to point to a fiscal crisis, bond counsel did not critically analyze the financial information provided by the issuer.

Bond counsel were not expected to investigate the creditworthiness of the City. However, when put on notice of circumstances that called into question matters basic to the issuance of their opinion, bond counsel should have conducted an additional investigation. And bond counsel with knowledge of information material to investors should have taken all reasonable steps to satisfy themselves that those material facts were disclosed to the public. Even in the maelstrom of the City's difficulties, some bond counsel recognized the duty of participants in the distribution to disclose material facts—and so advised them. Unfortunately, there was a gap between the recognition of that duty and its implementation.

Of course, there are others who had a key role in the disclosure process, particularly the City and its officials. This did not relieve bond counsel of the duty to obtain background information substantiating their opinions, and to take reasonable steps to bring about disclosure of material facts which were known to them. If they had taken reasonable steps to bring about disclosure and if that disclosure had not been forthcoming, bond counsel should not have associated themselves with the offering.

The Commission has indicated in another matter (In the Matter of Jo M. Ferguson, Securities Act Release No. 5523, August 21, 1974), that when the role of bond counsel is expanded to include preparation of disclosure documents such as an official statement, bond counsel is obliged to see to it that all material facts that bond counsel knew or should have known are included in the official statement.

When testifying during the investigation, at least two bond counsel stated it would not be appropriate to issue an approving opinion if there was significant danger that the City could not pay the obligation when due. But, since bond counsel relied almost exclusively on information provided by officials of the City it appears they relied on chance to determine whether that danger existed.

Nor are bond counsel relieved of their obligations because some issues were discussed in the press. The City's problems were discussed in the press but these discussions did not constitute full and fair disclosure. Bond counsel knew or should have known this. Furthermore, investors are entitled to and did rely on participants in the process for full disclosure of material facts concerning the issuer.

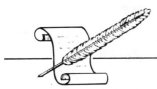

September

ANGLO-AMERICAN PLAN FOR RHODESIAN SETTLEMENT

September 1, 1977

Britain and the United States Sept. 1 offered a plan designed to bring about a peaceful transition to majority rule in Rhodesia. British Foreign Secretary David Owen and Andrew J. Young, U.S. ambassador to the United Nations, presented the constitutional white paper on behalf of their governments to Ian D. Smith, Rhodesian prime minister. One day later Smith rejected key sections of the proposal.

The Anglo-American plan called for Smith to surrender power voluntarily to a British administrator until free elections based on universal adult suffrage could be held. Rhodesia had been a self-governing colony under British sovereignty until 1965 when the colony unilaterally declared its independence.

At issue in the impasse was the insistence on the part of Britain and the United States that Rhodesia's six million blacks be brought into the country's political processes. At that time, only the 268,000 whites in Rhodesia could participate fully in the white minority political system.

Anglo-American initiatives failed to arrange a peaceful settlement acceptable to Smith's minority government and the black nationalists. By year's end Smith had called the joint British-American plan a failure and had decided to seek an internal settlement calling for a multiracial government in Rhodesia. Smith excluded any negotiations with the black nationalist guerrilla forces of the Patriotic Front.

The key proposals in the British-American plan were:
• Creation of an interim government during the transition headed by a British administrator for a period of not more than six months;

• *Deployment of a United Nations peacekeeping force to oversee a cease-fire between black nationalists and the white-led Rhodesian army;*

• *Creation of a Zimbabwe (Rhodesia) National Army comprised of black nationalist forces and troops loyal to Smith's government;*

• *Free elections based on universal adult suffrage held before the end of 1978;*

• *A constitution for Zimbabwe that would establish a democratic system of government, abolish discrimination, protect individual human rights and create an independent judiciary;*

• *A development fund to restore the nation's economy.*

A major obstacle that prevented a negotiated settlement was the inability of the negotiators to find common grounds for a settlement between Smith's white minority government and the Patriotic Front. The front, supported by the five Front-Line States bordering Rhodesia—Angola, Botswana, Mozambique, Tanzania and Zambia—conducted guerrilla raids in Rhodesia from bases in Mozambique and Zambia. The front's leaders, Joshua Nkomo and Robert Mugabe, had demanded that front troops serve as Rhodesia's security force during the transition to majority rule. Smith rejected the proposal to create a national army from black liberation forces because, he said, it inadequately safeguarded whites against reprisals during the transition. Smith also balked at a one-man, one-vote basis for national elections.

Smith Proposal

Then, in a dramatic reversal of policy, Smith Nov. 24 told reporters he was prepared to accept the principle of majority rule based on the one-man, one-vote principle as the basis for negotiations with black leaders living within Rhodesia. Smith said he had received assurances from black leaders that would safeguard whites. Talks were scheduled to begin in Salisbury, Rhodesia, with representatives of moderate groups including the United African Council headed by Bishop Abel Muzorewa, the African National Council led by the Rev. Ndananingi Sithole and the Zimbabwe People's Organization, a group of tribal leaders headed by Chief Jeremiah Cirau.

British Foreign Secretary Owen said Nov. 25 that Smith's new proposal might be acceptable to Britain if it involved "a genuine transfer of power to a government representing the majority of the people...following elections on the basis of universal adult suffrage." That objective was not achieved in 1977 although meetings with moderate black leaders began in Salisbury in December. Meanwhile, the guerrilla war between the Patriotic Front and Smith's government forces along the Rhodesia-Mozambique border continued as the year ended.

Despite rejection of the Anglo-American peace initiative by Smith and the Patriotic Front, the United Nations Security Council Sept. 29 approved a motion by Britain to appoint a special United Nations representative to oversee the transition to black majority rule. The cease-fire agreement was to be the first step in the transfer of power. The United Nations appointed Lt. Gen. Prem Chand of India to serve as its envoy. Chand's appointment followed the naming of Field Marshall Lord Carver as Britain's choice for resident commissioner. Chand and Carver toured African capitals Oct. 30-Nov. 9 to discuss the Anglo-American plan. Talks with Smith Nov. 6 produced no progress on a framework for a settlement that would be acceptable to Britain and the United States.

Background

Smith on Jan. 21, 1977, had rejected a peace plan proposed by Ivor Richard, the British chairman of the adjourned Geneva talks on a Rhodesian settlement. That plan had called for a resident commissioner, a council of ministers and a separate security council, with each of the councils having two-thirds black representation. The Richard plan differed from a 1976 peace proposal made by then U.S. Secretary of State Henry A. Kissinger, and accepted by Smith Sept. 24, 1976, as the basis for the abortive Geneva talks held Oct. 24, 1976 - Jan. 24, 1977. At the breakup of the Geneva meetings Smith said his government intended to seek an internal settlement of the problem of Rhodesian independence. (Historic Documents of 1976, p. 721)

A joint team of U.S.-British diplomats toured African capitals May 17-June 1 and July 5-10, 1977, to rekindle interest in a negotiated settlement. But Patriotic Front leader Nkomo said July 7 that no conference was possible until Britain handed over power to the front, and Smith July 8-10 ruled out any plan for a British interim administration in Rhodesia. U.S.-British insistence on the one-man, one-vote principle for representation and the failure to provide guarantees for the safety of the white minority, Smith said, led him to dissolve Parliament July 18. He called for new elections Aug. 31. In the elections, Smith's party scored an overwhelming victory, sweeping all 50 white seats in the 66-seat Parliament. Smith called the victory a popular mandate from which to negotiate with black moderate leaders in order to form a multiracial government under a new constitution.

Following is the text of the Proposals for a Settlement as presented to Rhodesian Prime Minister Ian D. Smith Sept. 1, 1977, by British Foreign Secretary David Owen and Ambassador Andrew Young. Text provided by the Embassy of Great Britain, Public Information Office:

The British Government, with the full agreement of the United States Government and after consulting all the parties concerned, have drawn up certain proposals for the restoration of legality in Rhodesia and the settlement of the Rhodesian problem. These proposals are based on the following elements:

1. The surrender of power by the illegal regime and a return to legality.

2. An orderly and peaceful transition to independence in the course of 1978.

3. Free and impartial elections on the basis of universal adult suffrage.

4. The establishment by the British Government of a transitional administration, with the task of conducting the elections for an independent government.

5. A United Nations presence, including a United Nations force, during the transition period.

6. An Independence Constitution providing for a democratically elected government, the abolition of discrimination, the protection of individual human rights and the independence of the judiciary.

7. A Development Fund to revive the economy of the country which the United Kingdom and the United States view as predicated upon the implementation of the settlement as a whole....

...The precise provisions of the Independence Constitution will have to be elaborated in further detailed discussions with the parties and in due course will be considered at a Constitutional Conference to be held during the transition period.

It is impossible at this stage to lay down an exact timetable: but it is the intention of the British Government that elections should be held, and that Rhodesia should become independent as Zimbabwe, not later than six months after the return to legality. To achieve this it will be necessary to proceed as quickly as possible after the return to legality to the registration of voters, the delimitation of constituencies, the detailed drafting of the Constitution and its enactment under the authority of the British Parliament.

Proposals for a Settlement in Rhodesia

1. On 10 March 1977 the British and United States Governments agreed to work together on a joint peace initiative to achieve a negotiated settlement in Rhodesia. The objective was an independent Zimbabwe with majority rule in 1978.

2. To succeed, any settlement must command the support of those people of goodwill of all races and creeds who intend to live together in peace as citizens of Zimbabwe. Amongst these people there are now many conflicting interests and views. There is an atmosphere of deep distrust. The armed struggle has led to the loss of many lives and to much human suffering. The economy has been gravely weakened. But there is surely one

overriding common interest, that peace should be restored and that government with the consent and in the interest of all the people should be established.

3. In April the British Foreign and Commonwealth Secretary, Dr. [David] Owen, toured the area and met all the parties to the problem as well as the Presidents of the five Front-Line States [the Presidents are: Julius K. Nyerere, Tanzania; Kenneth Kaunda, Zambia; Samora Machel, Mozambique; Seretse Khama, Botswana; Agostinho Neto, Angola.], the Prime Minister of South Africa [John Vorster] and the Commissioner for External Affairs of Nigeria [Brig. Joseph Garba]. He set out the elements which, taken together, could in the view of the two Governments comprise a negotiated settlement, as follows:

(a) A Constitution for an independent Zimbabwe which would provide for—

    (1) a democratically-elected government, with the widest possible franchise;

    (2) a Bill of Rights to protect individual human rights on the basis of the Universal Declaration of Human Rights. The Bill would be "entrenched" so that amendment of it would be made subject to special legislative procedures and it would give the right to an individual who believed his rights were being infringed to seek redress through the courts;

    (3) an independent judiciary.

(b) A transition period covering the surrender of power by the present regime, the installation of a neutral caretaker administration whose primary role, in addition to administering the country, would be the organisation and conduct of elections in conditions of peace and security and the preparation of the country for the transition to independence. This period, it was envisaged, would be as short as possible, and in any case not more than six months.

(c) The establishment of an internationally constituted and managed development fund (the Zimbabwe Development Fund).

4. Following that tour, Dr. [David] Owen [British foreign secretary] and the United States Secretary of State, Mr. [Cyrus R.] Vance, met in London on 6 May and agreed to carry forward their consultations with the parties on the basis of these proposals. To this end they established a joint consultative group. The group met all the parties on a number of occasions in London and in Africa and carried out detailed technical discussions with them. In parallel, the Governments of interested countries have been kept informed generally of the progress of the consultations.

5. On the basis of these consultations the British Government, in full agreement with the United States Government, have now decided to put firm proposals forward, covering the three aspects of the problem described in paragraph 3 above. In doing so they emphasise that the three aspects are intimately linked and must be judged as a whole. It is impossible for every single aspect of a settlement to be acceptable to everyone. The best, if not the only, hope for a settlement is a balanced and fair package in which,

though no one may achieve all their aims, everyone can see hope for the future.

The Constitution

6. It is proposed that the Independence Constitution should provide that Zimbabwe would be a sovereign republic. Provision would be made for democratic elections on the basis of one man, one vote and one woman, one vote, for a single-chamber National Assembly. Elections would be on the basis of single-member constituencies. Detailed constitutional proposals are set out at Annex A. The proposals should not necessarily be taken as excluding alternative possibilities in certain areas which do not go to the heart of the Constitution: *e.g.* provision is made for an executive President with a Vice-President, but there might instead be a constitutional President and a Prime Minister, in which case many of the powers which it is proposed to vest in the President would be vested in the Prime Minister or would be exercised by the President on the advice of the Prime Minister.

7. Discrimination would be forbidden by a Bill of Rights protecting the rights of individuals. As described above (para. 3(a)(2)), this Bill of Rights would be entrenched in the Constitution and would be justiciable so that aggrieved individuals could enforce their rights through the courts. The Bill of Rights would permit the Government of Zimbabwe to introduce measures of land reform while guaranteeing the right to private property. The Constitution would also establish an independent judiciary and an independent Public Service Commission to ensure an efficient and non-political civil service.

8. The Government of Zimbabwe would inherit the assets and debts of the Government of Southern Rhodesia and would take over past and present pensions obligations in the public sector, the rights of the pensioners being guaranteed by the Constitution. The Constitution would contain the basic provisions regulating Zimbabwe citizenship and these would be entrenched. The question whether there should be any restrictions on the possession of dual citizenship and, if so, whether there should be an extended period during which the choice would have to be made would be a matter for further discussion with the parties.

9. The Commonwealth Governments in London expressed the unanimous hope that Zimbabwe would soon become a member of the Commonwealth. The British Government will do everything to facilitate this.

The Transition

10. It is a basic premise of the British and United States Governments that the present illegal regime will surrender power so that the transitional administration may be installed peacefully. The two Governments will take such steps as seem to them appropriate to secure the transfer of power by Mr. [Ian D.] Smith [Rhodesian prime minister] (or his successor) on a day to be agreed.

11. The British Government will place before the Security Council their proposal for the Independence Constitution...and also their proposal for the administration of the territory of Rhodesia during the transition period leading up to independence. The latter will comprise the following elements:

(a) The appointment by the British Government, either under existing statutory powers or under new powers enacted for the purpose, of a Resident Commissioner and a Deputy. The role of the Resident Commissioner will be to administer the country, to organise and conduct the general election which, within a period not exceeding six months, will lead to independence for Zimbabwe, and to take command, as Commander-in-Chief, of all armed forces in Rhodesia, apart from the United Nations Zimbabwe Force (see below).

(b) The appointment by the Secretary-General of the United Nations, on the authority of the Security Council, of a Special Representative whose role will be to work with the Resident Commissioner and to observe that the administration of the country and the organisation and conduct of the elections are fair and impartial.

(c) The establishment by resolution of the Security Council of a United Nations Zimbabwe Force whose role may include:
(1) the supervision of the cease-fire (see below);
(2) support for the civil power;
(3) liaison with the existing Rhodesian armed forces and with the forces of the Liberation Armies.
The Secretary-General will be invited to appoint a representative to enter into discussions, before the transition period, with the British Resident Commissioner designate and with all the parties with a view to establishing in detail the respective roles of all the forces in Rhodesia.

(d) The primary responsibility for the maintenance of law and order during the transition period will lie with the police forces. They will be under the command of a Commissioner of Police who will be appointed by and responsible to the Resident Commissioner. The Special Representative of the Secretary-General of the United Nations may appoint liaison officers to the police forces.

(e) The formation, as soon as possible after the establishment of the transitional administration, of a new Zimbabwe National Army which will in due course replace all existing armed forces in Rhodesia and will be the army of the future independent State of Zimbabwe.

(f) The establishment by the Resident Commissioner of an electoral and boundary commission, with the role of carrying out the registration of voters, the delimitation of constituencies and the holding of a general election for the purposes of the Independence Constitution.

On the agreed day on which power is transferred to the transitional administration (para. 10 above), a cease-fire will come into effect within Rhodesia and measures will be taken to lift sanctions....

The Zimbabwe Development Fund

13. The Zimbabwe Development Fund, jointly sponsored by the British and United States Governments, will have as a target a minimum approaching US$1,000 million and a maximum rather less than US$1,500 million to which Governments in many parts of the world will be asked to contribute. Its purpose will be to provide funds for the economic stability and development of an independent Zimbabwe through assistance to various sectors and programmes such as rural development, education, health, social and economic infrastructure, and resettlement and training schemes for Africans, including those affected by the present conflict. The operations of the Fund would help to ensure that the obligations of the Zimbabwe Government under the settlement will not inhibit economic development in Zimbabwe for lack of foreign exchange and would thereby also help to reassure those who might fear that the new Government might be unable to carry out these obligations. The establishment and continued operation of the Fund are predicated upon the acceptance and implementation of the terms of the settlement as a whole....

Conclusion

14. The British and United States Governments believe that the above proposals provide for all the citizens of the independent Zimbabwe security, but not privilege, under the rule of law, equal political rights without discrimination, and the right to be governed by a government of their own choice. They also believe that the proposed arrangements for the transfer of power are calculated to ensure a quick, orderly and peaceful transition to independence. They have agreed to use their joint influence to the full to put the proposals into effect. But a lasting settlement cannot be imposed from outside: it is the people of Zimbabwe who must achieve their own independence. These proposals offer them a way. The two Governments urge them to seize the opportunity.

PANAMA CANAL TREATIES AND STATEMENT OF UNDERSTANDING
September 7; October 14, 1977

President Carter and Panamanian ruler Brig. Gen. Omar Torrijos Herrera signed two controversial treaties Sept. 7 that would give Panama control of the Panama Canal by the year 2000 and would guarantee the canal's permanent neutrality. Representatives from 26 Western Hemisphere nations joined scores of federal officials and other prominent Americans invited by President Carter to demonstrate support for the pacts at brief signing ceremonies in Washington at the Organization of American States (OAS).

Despite this orchestrated unity, opposition to U.S. ratification of the treaties was strong. The question of whether or not the treaties would be approved by the U.S. Senate remained unanswered. [For ratification of a treaty, the Constitution requires that the Senate approve the treaty by a two-thirds majority vote of those senators present.] In a national referendum Oct. 23, Panamanians voted 2-1 in favor of the treaties.

In his remarks at the OAS ceremonies, Carter said the agreements "mark the commitment of the United States to the belief that fairness, not force, should lie at the heart of our dealings with the nations of the world." Moreover, he said, the 1903 canal treaty, because it was "drafted in a world so different from ours today, has become an obstacle to better relations with Latin America."

Details of Treaties

Under the terms of the basic treaty governing the operation and defense of the canal, the United States would have the primary responsibility to protect and defend the canal for the rest of the century, with Panama guaranteeing American access to its land and waters for the canal's defense. After the United States relinquished control of the canal at the end of 1999, the nation still would have the permanent right to defend the canal indefinitely as specified by the companion treaty guaranteeing the canal's permanent neutrality. In addition, U.S. warships would have the permanent right to move through the canal without restrictions.

On the effective date of the treaties, Panama would assume general territorial jurisdiction over the Canal Zone and the country could use portions of the area not needed for the operation and defense of the canal. The United States would maintain control over all lands, waters and installations necessary to manage, operate and defend the canal until 1999, acting through a new U.S. government agency that would replace the Panama Canal Company. Panamanians would participate increasingly in the canal's operations; until 1990, the canal administrator would be an American and the deputy, Panamanian. Thereafter, the positions would be reversed.

During the treaty's life, Panama would receive from canal revenues 30 cents per ton shipped through the canal, $10-million from annual toll revenues and up to an additional $10-million if canal revenues were high enough. The United States also pledged $200-million in Export-Import Bank credits; $75-million in housing guarantees and $20-million in Overseas Private Investment Corporation guarantees.

Under the basic treaty terms, all U.S. civilians employed in the canal could continue to hold their federal jobs until retirement or could opt for early retirement. Those displaced from their jobs by the terms of the treaty could transfer to other U.S. Civil Service jobs. The treaty recognized the continued right of canal employees to bargain collectively, a key factor in winning AFL-CIO support for the pacts.

Proponents and Opponents

Building the case for approval of the treaties at Senate Foreign Relations Committee hearings, administration leaders stressed that the pacts would win the United States worldwide respect and "help set the tone" of inter-American relations for years to come. If the Senate rejected the treaties, Secretary of State Cyrus R. Vance said, "our relations with Panama would be shattered, our standing in Latin America damaged immeasurably, and the security of the canal itself placed in jeopardy." The practical advantage of the treaties for the United States, Vance explained, was that the canal would be open, neutral, secure and efficiently operated without cost to U.S. taxpayers. And for Panama, according to Vance, there would be economic benefits from toll revenues and, most important, full jurisdiction over its own territory.

Both State Department and Pentagon officials bore down on a major contention of treaty critics that if the United States relinquished control of the canal, it would not be able to protect the waterway from attack. The canal's operation could best be maintained, Secretary of Defense Harold Brown said, "by a cooperative effort with a friendly Panama" rather than by an "American garrison amid hostile surroundings." Witnesses also said the treaties would protect commercial shipping, but they maintained that the commercial value of the canal had dwindled.

The Carter administration had some highly influential backers of the treaties in the persons of former President Gerald R. Ford and former Secretaries of State Henry A. Kissinger and Dean Rusk. AFL-CIO President George Meany endorsed the pacts and joined with several other influential statesmen and businessmen to form a Committee of Americans for the Canal Treaties.

Those opposed to the treaties tried to convince undecided senators that the financial arrangements with Panama were unfair to the United States; that the neutrality treaty was too vague and unclear about U.S. rights; that the canal's security would be jeopardized if the agreements were ratified, and that it was "hypocritical" for the Carter administration to call for other Latin American nations to improve their human rights practices while at the same time agreeing to a treaty with a government headed by the allegedly repressive Torrijos regime.

"From a military viewpoint," American Legion spokesman William J. Rogers told the House International Relations Committee, "a commander never gives away strategic territory which he may have to fight to regain." Former California Gov. Ronald Reagan, the figure probably most closely identified with the opposition to the treaties, urged that the pacts be rejected because of the possibility that the Soviet Union and Cuba might increase their influence in Panama. "It should never surprise us that whenever the United States withdraws its presence or its strong interest from any areas, the Soviets are ready, willing and often able to exploit the situation. Can we believe that the Panama Canal is any exception?" he said Sept. 9.

The opposition outside the Senate was coordinated by the Emergency Coalition to Save the Panama Canal. An umbrella group inspired by the American Conservative Union, the coalition counted among its members the Conservative Caucus, the American Security Council and the Committee for the Survival of a Free Congress.

Treaty Clarification Issue

After three weeks of hearings on the canal treaties, members of the Senate Foreign Relations Committee told President Carter Oct. 11 that the treaties would never be approved without clarification of Article IV of the neutrality guarantee treaty, which stated that the United States and Panama "agree to maintain the regime of neutrality." Testimony during the committee hearings raised questions as to how the bilateral agreement *permitted a prompt U.S. response to keep the waterway open if a political upheaval in Panama led to an attempt to nationalize the canal.*

To clarify the interpretation of the wording, Carter again met with Gen. Torrijos Oct. 14 and they issued a Statement of Understanding saying: "the correct interpretation of this principle is that each of the two countries shall, in accordance with their respective constitutional processes, defend the canal against any threat to the regime of neutrality...." But, the statement said, "this does not nor shall it be interpreted as a right of intervention of the United States in the internal affairs of Panama." The understanding clarified another disputed article in the neutrality pact—the language giving the U.S. and Panamanian warships the right to "transit the canal expeditiously." In case of need or emergency, the statement said, the two nations' vessels "can go to the head of the line of vessels in order to transit the canal rapidly."

Following are the texts of the Panama Canal treaties signed Sept. 7, 1977, by President Carter and Brig. Gen. Omar Torrijos Herrera at ceremonies in Washington, D.C., at the Organization of American States, and the Statement of Clarification issued Oct. 14 by Carter and Torrijos:

PANAMA CANAL TREATY

The United States of America and the Republic of Panama,

Acting in the spirit of the Joint Declaration of April 3, 1964, by the Representatives of the Governments of the United States of America and the Republic of Panama, and of the Joint Statement of Principles of February 7, 1974, initialed by the Secretary of State of the United States of America and the Foreign Minister of the Republic of Panama, and

Acknowledging the Republic of Panama's sovereignty over its territory,

Have decided to terminate the prior Treaties pertaining to the Panama Canal and to conclude a new Treaty to serve as the basis for a new relationship between them and, accordingly, have agreed upon the following:

ARTICLE I

Abrogation of Prior Treaties
and Establishment
of a New Relationship

1. Upon its entry into force, this Treaty terminates and supersedes:

   (a) The Isthmian Canal Convention between the United States of America and the Republic of Panama, signed at Washington, November 18, 1903;

(b) The Treaty of Friendship and Cooperation signed at Washington, March 2, 1936, and the Treaty of Mutual Understanding and Cooperation and the related Memorandum of Understandings Reached, signed at Panama, January 25, 1955, between the United States of America and the Republic of Panama;

(c) All other treaties, conventions, agreements and exchanges of notes between the United States of America and the Republic of Panama, concerning the Panama Canal which were in force prior to the entry into force of this Treaty; and

(d) Provisions concerning the Panama Canal which appear in other treaties, conventions, agreements and exchanges of notes between the United States of America and the Republic of Panama which were in force prior to the entry into force of this Treaty.

2. In accordance with the terms of this Treaty and related agreements, the Republic of Panama, as territorial sovereign, grants to the United States of America, for the duration of this Treaty, the rights necessary to regulate the transit of ships through the Panama Canal, and to manage, operate, maintain, improve, protect and defend the Canal. The Republic of Panama guarantees to the United States of America the peaceful use of the land and water areas which it has been granted the rights to use for such purposes [pursuant] to this Treaty and related agreements.

3. The Republic of Panama shall participate increasingly in the management and protection and defense of the Canal, as provided in this Treaty.

4. In view of the special relationship established by this Treaty, the United States of America and the Republic of Panama shall cooperate to assure the uninterrupted and efficient operation of the Panama Canal.

ARTICLE II

Ratification, Entry into
Force, and Termination

1. This Treaty shall be subject to ratification in accordance with the constitutional procedures of the two Parties. The instruments of ratification of this Treaty shall be exchanged at Panama at the same time as the instruments of ratification of the Treaty Concerning the Permanent Neutrality and Operation of the Panama Canal, signed this date, are exchanged. This Treaty shall enter into force, simultaneously with the Treaty Concerning the Permanent Neutrality and Operation of the Panama Canal, six calendar months from the date of the exchange of the instruments of ratification.

2. This Treaty shall terminate at noon, Panama time, December 31, 1999.

ARTICLE III

Canal Operation and Management

1. The Republic of Panama, as territorial sovereign, grants to the United States of America the rights to manage, operate, and maintain the Panama Canal, its complementary works, installations and equipment and to provide for the orderly transit of vessels through the Panama Canal. The United States of America accepts the grant of such rights and undertakes to exercise them in accordance with this Treaty and related agreements.

2. In carrying out the foregoing responsibilities, the United States of America may:

(a) Use for the aforementioned purposes, without cost except as provided in this Treaty, the various installations and areas (including the Panama Canal) and waters, described in the Agreement in Implementation of this Article, signed this date, as well as such other areas and installations as are made available to the United States of America under this Treaty and related agreements, and take the measures necessary to ensure sanitation of such areas;

(b) Make such improvements and alterations to the aforesaid installations and areas as it deems appropriate, consistent with the terms of this Treaty;

(c) Make and enforce all rules pertaining to the passage of vessels through the Canal and other rules with respect to navigation and maritime matters, in accordance with this Treaty and related agreements. The Republic of Panama will lend its cooperation, when necessary, in the enforcement of such rules;

(d) Establish, modify, collect and retain tolls for the use of the Panama Canal, and other charges, and establish and modify methods of their assessment;

(e) Regulate relations with employees of the United States Government;

(f) Provide supporting services to facilitate the performance of its responsibilities under this Article;

(g) Issue and enforce regulations for the effective exercise of the rights and responsibilities of the United States of America under this Treaty and related agreements. The Republic of Panama will lend its cooperation, when necessary, in the enforcement of such rules; and

(h) Exercise any other right granted under this Treaty, or otherwise agreed upon between the two Parties.

3. Pursuant to the foregoing grant of rights, the United States of America shall, in accordance with the terms of this Treaty and the provisions of United States law, carry out its responsibilities by means of a United States Government agency called the Panama Canal Commission, which shall be constituted by and in conformity with the laws of the United States of America.

(a) The Panama Canal Commission shall be supervised by a Board composed of nine members, five of whom shall be nationals of the United States of America, and four of whom shall be Panamanian nationals proposed by the Republic of Panama for appointment to such positions by the United States of America in a timely manner.

(b) Should the Republic of Panama request the United States of America to remove a Panamanian national from membership on the Board, the United States of America shall agree to such a request. In that event, the Republic of Panama shall propose another Panamanian national for appointment by the United States of America to such position in a timely manner. In case of removal of a Panamanian member of the Board at the initiative of the United States of America, both Parties will consult in advance in order to reach agreement concerning such removal, and the Republic of Panama shall propose another Panamanian national for appointment by the United States of America in his stead.

(c) The United States of America shall employ a national of the United States of America as Administrator of the Panama Canal Commission, and a Panamanian national as Deputy Administrator, through December 31, 1989. Beginning January 1, 1990, a Panamanian national shall be employed as the Administrator and a national of the United States of America shall occupy the position of Deputy Administrator. Such Panamanian nationals shall be proposed to the United States of America by the Republic of Panama for appointment to such positions by the United States of America.

(d) Should the United States of America remove the Panamanian national from his position as Deputy Administrator, or Administrator, the Republic of Panama shall propose another Panamanian national for appointment to such position by the United States of America.

4. An illustrative description of the activities the Panama Canal Commission will perform in carrying out the responsibilities and rights of the United States of America under this Article is set forth at the Annex. Also set forth in the Annex are procedures for the discontinuance or transfer of those activities performed prior to the entry into force of this Treaty by the Panama Canal Company or the Canal Zone Government which are not to be carried out by the Panama Canal Commission.

5. The Panama Canal Commission shall reimburse the Republic of Panama for the costs incurred by the Republic of Panama in providing the following public services in the Canal operating areas and in housing areas

set forth in the Agreement in Implementation of Article III of this Treaty and occupied by both United States and Panamanian citizen employees of the Panama Canal Commission: police, fire protection, street maintenance, street lighting, street cleaning, traffic management and garbage collection. The Panama Canal Commission shall pay the Republic of Panama the sum of ten million United States dollars ($10,000,000) per annum for the foregoing services. It is agreed that every three years from the date that this Treaty enters into force, the costs involved in furnishing said services shall be reexamined to determine whether adjustment of the annual payment should be made because of inflation and other relevant factors affecting the cost of such services.

6. The Republic of Panama shall be responsible for providing, in all areas comprising the former Canal Zone, services of a general jurisdictional nature such as customs and immigration, postal services, courts and licensing, in accordance with this Treaty and related agreements.

7. The United States of America and the Republic of Panama shall establish a Panama Canal Consultative Committee, composed of an equal number of high-level representatives of the United States of America and the Republic of Panama, and which may appoint such subcommittees as it may deem appropriate. This Committee shall advise the United States of America and the Republic of Panama on matters of policy affecting the Canal's operation. In view of both Parties' special interest in the continuity and efficiency of the Canal operation in the future, the Committee shall advise on matters such as general tolls policy, employment and training policies to increase the participation of Panamanian nationals in the operation of the Canal, and international policies on matters concerning the Canal. The Committee's recommendations shall be transmitted to the two Governments, which shall give such recommendations full consideration in the formulation of such policy decisions.

8. In addition to the participation of Panamanian nationals at high management levels of the Panama Canal Commission, as provided for in paragraph 3 of this Article, there shall be growing participation of Panamanian nationals at all other levels and areas of employment in the aforesaid Commission, with the objective of preparing, in an orderly and efficient fashion, for the assumption by the Republic of Panama of full responsibility for the management, operation and maintenance of the Canal upon the termination of this Treaty.

9. The use of the areas, waters and installations with respect to which the United States of America is granted rights pursuant to this Article, and the rights and legal status of United States Government agencies and employees operating in the Republic of Panama pursuant to this Article, shall be governed by the Agreement in Implementation of this Article, signed this date.

10. Upon entry into force of this Treaty, the United States Government agencies known as the Panama Canal Company and the Canal Zone Government shall cease to operate within the territory of the Republic of Panama that formerly constituted the Canal Zone.

ARTICLE IV

Protection and Defense

1. The United States of America and the Republic of.Panama commit themselves to protect and defend the Panama Canal. Each Party shall act, in accordance with its constitutional processes, to meet the danger resulting from an armed attack or other actions which threaten the security of the Panama Canal or of ships transiting it.

2. For the duration of this Treaty, the United States of America shall have primary responsibility to protect and defend the Canal. The rights of the United States of America to station, train, and move military forces within the Republic of Panama are described in the Agreement in Implementation of this Article, signed this date. The use of areas and installations and the legal status of the armed forces of the United States of America in the Republic of Panama shall be governed by the aforesaid Agreement.

3. In order to facilitate the participation and cooperation of the armed forces of both Parties in the protection and defense of the Canal, the United States of America and the Republic of Panama shall establish a Combined Board comprised of an equal number of senior military representatives of each Party. These representatives shall be charged by their respective governments with consulting and cooperating on all matters pertaining to the protection and defense of the Canal, and with planning for actions to be taken in concert for that purpose. Such combined protection and defense arrangements shall not inhibit the identity or lines of authority of the armed forces of the United States of America or the Republic of Panama. The Combined Board shall provide for coordination and cooperation concerning such matters as:

(a) The preparation of contingency plans for the protection and defense of the Canal based upon the cooperative efforts of the armed forces of both Parties;

(b) The planning and conduct of combined military exercises; and

(c) The conduct of United States and Panamanian military operations with respect to the protection and defense of the Canal.

4. The Combined Board shall, at five-year intervals throughout the duration of this Treaty, review the resources being made available by the two Parties for the protection and defense of the Canal. Also, the Combined Board shall make appropriate recommendations to the two Governments respecting projected requirements, the efficient utilization of available resources of the two Parties, and other matters of mutual interest with respect to the protection and defense of the Canal.

5. To the extent possible consistent with its primary responsibility for the protection and defense of the Panama Canal, the United States of America will endeavor to maintain its armed forces in the Republic of Panama in normal times at a level not in excess of that of the armed forces

of the United States of America in the territory of the former Canal Zone immediately prior to the entry into force of this Treaty.

ARTICLE V

Principle of Non-Intervention

Employees of the Panama Canal Commission, their dependents and designated contractors of the Panama Canal Commission, who are nationals of the United States of America, shall respect the laws of the Republic of Panama and shall abstain from any activity incompatible with the spirit of this Treaty. Accordingly, they shall abstain from any political activity in the Republic of Panama as well as from any intervention in the internal affairs of the Republic of Panama. The United States of America shall take all measures within its authority to ensure that the provisions of this Article are fulfilled.

ARTICLE VI

Protection of the Environment

1. The United States of America and the Republic of Panama commit themselves to implement this Treaty in a manner consistent with the protection of the natural environment of the Republic of Panama. To this end, they shall consult and cooperate with each other in all appropriate ways to ensure that they shall give due regard to the protection and conservation of the environment.

2. A Joint Commission on the Environment shall be established with equal representation from the United States of America and the Republic of Panama, which shall periodically review the implementation of this Treaty and shall recommend as appropriate to the two Governments ways to avoid or, should this not be possible, to mitigate the adverse environmental impacts which might result from their respective actions pursuant to the Treaty.

3. The United States of America and the Republic of Panama shall furnish the Joint Commission on the Environment complete information on any action taken in accordance with this Treaty which, in the judgment of both, might have a significant effect on the environment. Such information shall be made available to the Commission as far in advance of the contemplated action as possible to facilitate the study by the Commission of any potential environmental problems and to allow for consideration of the recommendation of the Commission before the contemplated action is carried out.

ARTICLE VII

Flags

1. The entire territory of the Republic of Panama, including the areas the use of which the Republic of Panama makes available to the United States of America pursuant to this Treaty and related agreements, shall be under the flag of the Republic of Panama, and consequently such flag always shall occupy the position of honor.

2. The flag of the United States of America may be displayed, together with the flag of the Republic of Panama, at the headquarters of the Panama Canal Commission, at the site of the Combined Board, and as provided in the Agreement in Implementation of Article IV of this Treaty.

3. The flag of the United States of America also may be displayed at other places and on some occasions, as agreed by both Parties.

ARTICLE VIII

Privileges and Immunities

1. The installations owned or used by the agencies or instrumentalities of the United States of America operating in the Republic of Panama pursuant to this Treaty and related agreements, and their official archives and documents, shall be inviolable. The two Parties shall agree on procedures to be followed in the conduct of any criminal investigation at such locations by the Republic of Panama.

2. Agencies and instrumentalities of the Government of the United States of America operating in the Republic of Panama pursuant to this Treaty and related agreements shall be immune from the jurisdiction of the Republic of Panama.

3. In addition to such other privileges and immunities as are afforded to employees of the United States Government and their dependents pursuant to this Treaty, the United States of America may designate up to twenty officials of the Panama Canal Commission who, along with their dependents, shall enjoy the privileges and immunities accorded to diplomatic agents and their dependents under international law and practice. The United States of America shall furnish to the Republic of Panama a list of the names of said officials and their dependents, identifying the positions they occupy in the Government of the United States of America, and shall keep such list current at all times.

ARTICLE IX

Applicable Laws and
Law Enforcement

1. In accordance with the provisions of this Treaty and related agreements, the law of the Republic of Panama shall apply in the areas

made available for the use of the United States of America pursuant to this Treaty. The law of the Republic of Panama shall be applied to matters or events which occurred in the former Canal Zone prior to the entry into force of this Treaty only to the extent specifically provided in prior treaties and agreements.

2. Natural or juridical persons who, on the date of entry into force of this Treaty, are engaged in business or non-profit activities at locations in the former Canal Zone may continue such business or activities at those locations under the same terms and conditions prevailing prior to the entry into force of this Treaty for a thirty-month transition period from its entry into force. The Republic of Panama shall maintain the same operating conditions as those applicable to the aforementioned enterprises prior to the entry into force of this Treaty in order that they may receive licenses to do business in the Republic of Panama subject to their compliance with the requirements of its law. Thereafter, such persons shall receive the same treatment under the law of the Republic of Panama as similar enterprises already established in the rest of the territory of the Republic of Panama without discrimination.

3. The rights of ownership, as recognized by the United States of America, enjoyed by natural or juridical private persons in buildings and other improvements to real property located in the former Canal Zone shall be recognized by the Republic of Panama in conformity with its laws.

4. With respect to buildings and other improvements to real property located in the Canal operating areas, housing areas or other areas subject to the licensing procedure established in Article IV of the Agreement in Implementation of Article III of this Treaty, the owners shall be authorized to continue using the land upon which their property is located in accordance with the procedures established in that Article.

5. With respect to buildings and other improvements to real property located in areas of the former Canal Zone to which the aforesaid licensing procedure is not applicable, or may cease to be applicable during the lifetime or upon termination of this Treaty, the owners may continue to use the land upon which their property is located, subject to the payment of a reasonable charge to the Republic of Panama. Should the Republic of Panama decide to sell such land, the owners of the buildings or other improvements located thereon shall be offered a first option to purchase such land at a reasonable cost. In the case of non-profit enterprises, such as churches and fraternal organizations, the cost of purchase will be nominal in accordance with the prevailing practice in the rest of the territory of the Republic of Panama.

6. If any of the aforementioned persons are required by the Republic of Panama to discontinue their activities or vacate their property for public purposes, they shall be compensated at fair market value by the Republic of Panama.

7. The provisions of paragraphs 2-6 above shall apply to natural or juridical persons who have been engaged in business or non-profit ac-

tivities at locations in the former Canal Zone for at least six months prior to the date of signature of this Treaty.

8. The Republic of Panama shall not issue, adopt or enforce any law, decree, regulation, or international agreement or take any other action which purports to regulate or would otherwise interfere with the exercise on the part of the United States of America of any right granted under this Treaty or related agreements.

9. Vessels transiting the Canal, and cargo, passengers and crews carried on such vessels shall be exempt from any taxes, fees, or other charges by the Republic of Panama. However, in the event such vessels call at a Panamanian port, they may be assessed charges incident thereto, such as charges for services provided to the vessel. The Republic of Panama may also require the passengers and crew disembarking from such vessels to pay such taxes, fees and charges as are established under Panamanian law for persons entering its territory. Such taxes, fees and charges shall be assessed on a nondiscriminatory basis.

10. The United States of America and the Republic of Panama will cooperate in taking such steps as may from time to time be necessary to guarantee the security of the Panama Canal Commission, its property, its employees and their dependents, and their property, for Forces of the United States of America and the members thereof, the civilian component of the United States Forces, the dependents of members of the Forces and the civilian component, and their property, and the contractors of the Panama Canal Commission and of the United States Forces, their dependents, and their property. The Republic of Panama will seek from its Legislative Branch such legislation as may be needed to carry out the foregoing purposes and to punish any offenders.

11. The Parties shall conclude an agreement whereby nationals of either State, who are sentenced by the courts of the other State, and who are not domiciled therein, may elect to serve their sentences in their State of nationality.

ARTICLE X

Employment with the
Panama Canal Commission

1. In exercising its right and fulfilling its responsibilities as the employer, the United States of America shall establish employment and labor regulations which shall contain the terms, conditions and prerequisites for all categories of employees of the Panama Canal Commission. These regulations shall be provided to the Republic of Panama prior to their entry into force.

2. (a) The regulations shall establish a system of preference when hiring employees, for Panamanian applicants possessing the skills and qualifications required for employment by the Panama Canal Com-

mission. The United States of America shall endeavor to ensure that the number of Panamanian nationals employed by the Panama Canal Commission in relation to the total number of its employees will conform to the proportion established for foreign enterprises under the law of the Republic of Panama.

(b) The terms and conditions of employment to be established will in general be no less favorable to persons already employed by the Panama Canal Company or Canal Zone Government prior to the entry into force of this Treaty, than those in effect immediately prior to that date.

3. (a) The United States of America shall establish an employment policy for the Panama Canal Commission that shall generally limit the recruitment of personnel outside the Republic of Panama to persons possessing requisite skills and qualifications which are not available in the Republic of Panama.

(b) The United States of America will establish training programs for Panamanian employees and apprentices in order to increase the number of Panamanian nationals qualified to assume positions with the Panama Canal Commission, as positions become available.

(c) Within five years from the entry into force of this Treaty, the number of United States nationals employed by the Panama Canal Commission who were previously employed by the Panama Canal Company shall be at least twenty percent less than the total number of United States nationals working for the Panama Canal Company immediately prior to the entry into force of this Treaty.

(d) The United States of America shall periodically inform the Republic of Panama, through the Coordinating Committee, established pursuant to the Agreement in Implementation of Article III of this Treaty, of available positions within the Panama Canal Commission. The Republic of Panama shall similarly provide the United States of America any information it may have as to the availability of Panamanian nationals claiming to have skills and qualifications that might be required by the Panama Canal Commission, in order that the United States of America may take this information into account.

4. The United States of America will establish qualification standards for skills, training and experience required by the Panama Canal Commission. In establishing such standards, to the extent they include a requirement for a professional license, the United States of America, without prejudice to its right to require additional professional skills and qualifications, shall recognize the professional licenses issued by the Republic of Panama.

5. The United States of America shall establish a policy for the periodic rotation, at a maximum of every five years, of United States citizen employees and other non-Panamanian employees, hired after the entry into force of this Treaty. It is recognized that certain exceptions to the said policy of rotation may be made for sound administrative reasons, such as in the case of employees holding positions requiring certain non-transferable or non-recruitable skills.

6. With regard to wages and fringe benefits, there shall be no discrimination on the basis of nationality, sex, or race. Payments by the Panama Canal Commission of additional remuneration, or the provision of other benefits, such as home leave benefits, to United States nationals employed prior to entry into force of this Treaty, or to persons of any nationality, including Panamanian nationals who are thereafter recruited outside of the Republic of Panama and who change their place of residence, shall not be considered to be discrimination for the purpose of this paragraph.

7. Persons employed by the Panama Canal Company or Canal Zone Government prior to the entry into force of this Treaty, who are displaced from their employment as a result of the discontinuance by the United States of America of certain activities pursuant to this Treaty, will be placed by the United States of America, to the maximum extent feasible, in other appropriate jobs with the Government of the United States in accordance with United States Civil Service regulations. For such persons who are not United States nationals, placement efforts will be confined to United States Government activities located within the Republic of Panama. Likewise, persons previously employed in activities for which the Republic of Panama assumes responsibility as a result of this Treaty will be continued in their employment to the maximum extent feasible by the Republic of Panama. The Republic of Panama shall, to the maximum extent feasible, ensure that the terms and conditions of employment applicable to personnel employed in the activities for which it assumes responsibility are no less favorable than those in effect immediately prior to the entry into force of this Treaty. Non-United States nationals employed by the Panama Canal Company or Canal Zone Government prior to the entry into force of this Treaty who are involuntarily separated from their positions because of the discontinuance of an activity by reason of this Treaty, who are not entitled to an immediate annuity under the United States Civil Service Retirement System, and for whom continued employment in the Republic of Panama by the Government of the United States of America is not practicable, will be provided special job placement assistance by the Republic of Panama for employment in positions for which they may be qualified by experience and training.

8. The Parties agree to establish a system whereby the Panama Canal Commission may, if deemed mutually convenient or desirable by the two Parties, assign certain employees of the Panama Canal Commission, for a limited period of time, to assist in the operation of activities transferred to the responsibility of the Republic of Panama as a result of this Treaty or related agreements. The salaries and other costs of employment of any such persons assigned to provide such assistance shall be reimbursed to the United States of America by the Republic of Panama.

9. (a) The right of employees to negotiate collective contracts with the Panama Canal Commission is recognized. Labor relations with employees of the Panama Canal Commission shall be conducted in accor-

dance with forms of collective bargaining established by the United States of America after consultation with employee unions.

(b) Employee unions shall have the right to affiliate with international labor organizations.

10. The United States of America will provide an appropriate early optional retirement program for all persons employed by the Panama Canal Company or Canal Zone Government immediately prior to the entry into force of this Treaty. In this regard, taking into account the unique circumstances created by the provisions of this Treaty, including its duration, and their effect upon such employees, the United States of America shall, with respect to them:

(a) determine that conditions exist which invoke applicable United States law permitting early retirement annuities and apply such law for a substantial period of the duration of the Treaty;

(b) seek special legislation to provide more liberal entitlement to, and calculation of, retirement annuities than is currently provided for by law.

ARTICLE XI

Provisions for the
Transition Period

1. The Republic of Panama shall reassume plenary jurisdiction over the former Canal Zone upon entry into force of this Treaty and in accordance with its terms. In order to provide for an orderly transition to the full application of the jurisdictional arrangements established by this Treaty and related agreements, the provisions of this Article shall become applicable upon the date this Treaty enters into force, and shall remain in effect for thirty calendar months. The authority granted in this Article to the United States of America for this transition period shall supplement, and is not intended to limit, the full application and effect of the rights and authority granted to the United States of America elsewhere in this Treaty and in related agreements.

2. During this transition period, the criminal and civil laws of the United States of America shall apply concurrently with those of the Republic of Panama in certain of the areas and installations made available for the use of the United States of America pursuant to this Treaty, in accordance with the following provisions:

(a) The Republic of Panama permits the authorities of the United States of America to have the primary right to exercise criminal jurisdiction over United States citizen employees of the Panama Canal Commission and their dependents, and members of the United States Forces and civilian component and their dependents, in the following cases:

(i) for any offense committed during the transition period within such areas and installations, and

(ii) for any offense committed prior to that period in the former Canal Zone.

The Republic of Panama shall have the primary right to exercise jurisdiction over all other offenses committed by such persons, except as otherwise provided in this Treaty and related agreements or as may be otherwise agreed.

(b) Either Party may waive its primary right to exercise jurisdiction in a specific case or category of cases.

3. The United States of America shall retain the right to exercise jurisdiction in criminal cases relating to offenses committed prior to the entry into force of this Treaty in violation of the laws applicable in the former Canal Zone.

4. For the transition period, the United States of America shall retain police authority and maintain a police force in the aforementioned areas and installations. In such areas, the police authorities of the United States of America may take into custody any person not subject to their primary jurisdiction if such person is believed to have committed or to be committing an offense against applicable laws or regulations, and shall promptly transfer custody to the police authorities of the Republic of Panama. The United States of America and the Republic of Panama shall establish joint police patrols in agreed areas. Any arrests conducted by a joint patrol shall be the responsibility of the patrol member or members representing the party having primary jurisdiction over the person or persons arrested.

5. The courts of the United States of America and related personnel, functioning in the former Canal Zone immediately prior to the entry into force of this Treaty, may continue to function during the transition period for the judicial enforcement of the jurisdiction to be exercised by the United States of America in accordance with this Article.

6. In civil cases, the civilian courts of the United States of America in the Republic of Panama shall have no jurisdiction over new cases of a private civil nature, but shall retain full jurisdiction during the transition period to dispose of any civil cases, including admiralty cases, already instituted and pending before the courts prior to the entry into force of this Treaty.

7. The laws, regulations, and administrative authority of the United States of America applicable in the former Canal Zone immediately prior to the entry into force of this Treaty shall, to the extent not inconsistent with this Treaty and related agreements, continue in force for the purpose of the exercise by the United States of America of law enforcement and judicial jurisdiction only during the transition period. The United States of America may amend, repeal or otherwise change such laws, regulations and administrative authority. The two Parties shall consult concerning procedural and substantive matters relative to the implementation of this Article, including the disposition of cases pending at the end of the transition period and, in this respect, may enter into appropriate agreements by an exchange of notes or other instrument.

8. During this transition period, the United States of America may continue to incarcerate individuals in the areas and installations made

available for the use of the United States of America by the Republic of Panama pursuant to this Treaty and related agreements, or to transfer them to penal facilities in the United States of America to serve their sentences.

ARTICLE XII

A Sea-Level Canal or
a Third Lane of Locks

1. The United States of America and the Republic of Panama recognize that a sea-level canal may be important for international navigation in the future. Consequently, during the duration of this Treaty, both Parties commit themselves to study jointly the feasibility of a sea-level canal in the Republic of Panama, and in the event they determine that such a waterway is necessary, they shall negotiate terms, agreeable to both Parties, for its construction.

2. The United States of America and the Republic of Panama agree on the following:

(a) No new interoceanic canal shall be constructed in the territory of the Republic of Panama during the duration of this Treaty, except in accordance with the provisions of this Treaty, or as the two Parties may otherwise agree; and

(b) During the duration of this Treaty, the United States of America shall not negotiate with third States for the right to construct an interoceanic canal on any other route in the Western Hemisphere, except as the two Parties may otherwise agree.

3. The Republic of Panama grants to the United States of America the right to add a third lane of locks to the existing Panama Canal. This right may be exercised at any time during the duration of this Treaty, provided that the United States of America has delivered to the Republic of Panama copies of the plans for such construction.

4. In the event the United States of America exercises the right granted in paragraph 3 above, it may use for that purpose, in addition to the areas otherwise made available to the United States of America pursuant to this Treaty, such other areas as the two Parties may agree upon. The terms and conditions applicable to Canal operating areas made available by the Republic of Panama for the use of the United States of America pursuant to Article III of this Treaty shall apply in a similar manner to such additional areas.

5. In the construction of the aforesaid works, the United States of America shall not use nuclear excavation techniques without the previous consent of the Republic of Panama.

ARTICLE XIII

Property Transfer and
Economic Participation
by the Republic of Panama

1. Upon termination of this Treaty, the Republic of Panama shall assume total responsibility for the management, operation, and maintenance of the Panama Canal, which shall be turned over in operating condition and free of liens and debts, except as the two Parties may otherwise agree.

2. The United States of America transfers, without charge, to the Republic of Panama all right, title and interest the United States of America may have with respect to all real property, including non-removable improvements thereon, as set forth below:

(a) Upon the entry into force of this Treaty, the Panama Railroad and such property that was located in the former Canal Zone but that is not within the land and water areas the use of which is made available to the United States of America pursuant to this Treaty. However, it is agreed that the transfer on such date shall not include buildings and other facilities, except housing, the use of which is retained by the United States of America pursuant to this Treaty and related agreements, outside such areas;

(b) Such property located in an area or a portion thereof at such time as the use by the United States of America of such area or portion thereof ceases pursuant to agreement between the two Parties.

(c) Housing units made available for occupancy by members of the Armed Forces of the Republic of Panama in accordance with paragraph 5(b) of Annex B to the Agreement in Implementation of Article IV of this Treaty at such time as such units are made available to the Republic of Panama.

(d) Upon termination of this Treaty, all real property, and non-removable improvements that were used by the United States of America for the purposes of this Treaty and related agreements, and equipment related to the management, operation and maintenance of the Canal remaining in the Republic of Panama.

3. The Republic of Panama agrees to hold the United States of America harmless with respect to any claims which may be made by third parties relating to rights, title and interest in such property.

4. The Republic of Panama shall receive, in addition, from the Panama Canal Commission a just and equitable return on the national resources which it has dedicated to the efficient management, operation, maintenance, protection and defense of the Panama Canal, in accordance with the following:

(a) An annual amount to be paid out of Canal operating revenues computed at a rate of thirty hundredths of a United States dollar ($0.30) per Panama Canal net ton, or its equivalence, for each vessel transiting the Canal, after the entry into force of this Treaty, for which tolls are charged. The rate of thirty hundredths of a United States dollar ($0.30) per Panama Canal net ton, or its equivalency, will be adjusted to reflect changes in the United States wholesale price index for total manufactured goods during biennial periods. The first adjustment shall take place five years after entry into force of this Treaty, taking into account the changes that occurred in such price index during the preceding two years. Thereafter successive adjustments shall take place at the end of each biennial period. If the United States of America should decide that another indexing method is preferable, such method shall be proposed to the Republic of Panama and applied if mutually agreed.

(b) A fixed annuity of ten million United States dollars ($10,000,-000) to be paid out of Canal operating revenues. This amount shall constitute a fixed expense of the Panama Canal Commission.

(c) An annual amount of up to ten million United States dollars ($10,000,000) per year, to be paid out of Canal operating revenues to the extent that such revenues exceed expenditures of the Panama Canal Commission including amounts paid pursuant to this Treaty. In the event Canal operating revenues in any year do not produce a surplus sufficient to cover this payment, the unpaid balance shall be paid from operating surpluses in future years in a manner to be mutually agreed.

ARTICLE XIV

Settlement of Disputes

In the event that any question should arise between the Parties concerning the interpretation of this Treaty or related agreements, they shall make every effort to resolve the matter through consultation in the appropriate committees established pursuant to this Treaty and related agreements, or, if appropriate, through diplomatic channels. In the event the Parties are unable to resolve a particular matter through such means, they may, in appropriate cases, agree to submit the matter to reconciliation, mediation, arbitration, or such other procedure for the peaceful settlement of the dispute as they may mutually deem appropriate.

ANNEX

Procedures for the Cessation or Transfer of Activities Carried out by the Panama Canal Company and the Canal Zone Government and Illustrative List of the Functions that may be Performed by the Panama Canal Commission

1. The laws of the Republic of Panama shall regulate the exercise of private economic activities within the areas made available by the

Republic of Panama for the use of the United States of America pursuant to this Treaty. Natural or juridical persons who, at least six months prior to the date of signature of this Treaty, were legally established and engaged in the exercise of economic activities in the former Canal Zone, may continue such activities in accordance with the provisions of paragraphs 2-7 of Article IX of this Treaty.

2. The Panama Canal Commission shall not perform governmental or commercial functions as stipulated in paragraph 4 of this Annex, provided, however, that this shall not be deemed to limit in any way the right of the United States of America to perform those functions that may be necessary for the efficient management, operation and maintenance of the Canal.

3. It is understood that the Panama Canal Commission, in the exercise of the rights of the United States of America with respect to the management, operation and maintenance of the Canal, may perform functions such as are set forth below by way of illustration:

  a. Management of the Canal enterprise.

  b. Aids to navigation in Canal waters and in proximity thereto.

  c. Control of vessel movement.

  d. Operation and maintenance of the locks.

  e. Tug service for the transit of vessels and dredging for the piers and docks of the Panama Canal Commission.

  f. Control of the water levels in Gatun, Alajuela (Madden) and Miraflores Lakes.

  g. Non-commercial transportation services in Canal waters.

  h. Meteorological and hydrographic services.

  i. Admeasurement.

  j. Non-commercial motor transport and maintenance.

  k. Industrial security through the use of watchmen.

  l. Procurement and warehousing.

  m. Telecommunications.

  n. Protection of the environment by preventing and controlling the spillage of oil and substances harmful to human or animal life and of the ecological equilibrium in areas used in operation of the Canal and the anchorages.

  o. Non-commercial vessel repair.

  p. Air conditioning services in Canal installations.

  q. Industrial sanitation and health services.

  r. Engineering design, construction and maintenance of Panama Canal Commission installations.

  s. Dredging of the Canal channel, terminal ports and adjacent waters.

  t. Control of the banks and stabilizing of the slopes of the Canal.

  u. Non-commercial handling of cargo on the piers and docks of the Panama Canal Commission.

  v. Maintenance of public areas of the Panama Canal Commission, such as parks and gardens.

  w. Generation of electric power.

x. Purification and supply of water.

y. Marine salvage in Canal waters.

z. Such other functions as may be necessary or appropriate to carry out, in conformity with this Treaty and related agreements, the rights and responsibilities of the United States of America with respect to the management, operation and maintenance of the Panama Canal.

4. The following activities and operations carried out by the Panama Canal Company and the Canal Zone Government shall not be carried out by the Panama Canal Commission, effective upon the dates indicated herein:

(a) Upon the date of entry into force of this Treaty:

(i) Wholesale and retail sales, including those through commissaries, food stores, department stores, optical shops and pastry shops;

(ii) The production of food and drink, including milk products and bakery products;

(iii) The operation of public restaurants and cafeterias and the sale of articles through vending machines;

(iv) The operation of movie theaters, bowling alleys, pool rooms and other recreational and amusement facilities for the use of which a charge is payable;

(v) The operation of laundry and dry cleaning plants other than those operated for official use;

(vi) The repair and service of privately owned automobiles or the sale of petroleum or lubricants, including the operation of gasoline stations, repair garages and tire repair and recapping facilities, and the repair and service of other privately owned property, including appliances, electronic devices, boats, motors, and furniture;

(vii) The operation of cold storage and freezer plants other than those operated for official use;

(viii) The operation of freight houses other than those operated for official use;

(ix) Commercial services to and supply of privately owned and operated vessels, including the construction of vessels, the sale of petroleum and lubricants and the provision of water, tug services not related to the Canal or other United States Government operations, and repair of such vessels, except in situations where repairs may be necessary to remove disabled vessels from the Canal;

(x) Printing services other than for official use;

(xi) Maritime transportation for the use of the general public;

(xii) Health and medical services provided to individuals, including hospitals, leprosariums, veterinary, mortuary and cemetery services;

(xiii) Educational services not for professional training, including schools and libraries;

(xiv) Postal services;

(xv) Immigration, customs and quarantine controls, except those measures necessary to ensure the sanitation of the Canal;

(xvi) Commercial pier and dock services, such as the handling of cargo and passengers; and

(xvii) Any other commercial activity of a similar nature, not related to the management, operation or maintenance of the Canal.

(b) Within thirty calendar months from the date of entry into force of this Treaty, governmental services such as:

(i) Police;

(ii) Courts; and

(iii) Prison system.

5. (a) With respect to those activities or functions described in paragraph 4 above, or otherwise agreed upon by the two Parties, which are to be assumed by the Government of the Republic of Panama or by private persons subject to its authority, the two Parties shall consult prior to the discontinuance of such activities or functions by the Panama Canal Commission to develop appropriate arrangements for the orderly transfer and continued efficient operation or conduct thereof.

(b) In the event that appropriate arrangements cannot be arrived at to ensure the continued performance of a particular activity or function described in paragraph 4 above which is necessary to the efficient management, operation or maintenance of the Canal, the Panama Canal Commission may, to the extent consistent with the other provisions of this Treaty and related agreements, continue to perform such activity or function until such arrangements can be made.

AGREED MINUTE TO THE
PANAMA CANAL TREATY

1. With reference to paragraph 1(c) of Article I (Abrogation of Prior Treaties and Establishment of a New Relationship), it is understood that the treaties, conventions, agreements and exchanges of notes, or portions thereof, abrogated and superseded thereby include:

(a) The Agreement delimiting the Canal Zone referred to in Article II of the Interoceanic Canal Convention of November 18, 1903, signed at Panama on June 15, 1904.

(b) The Boundary Convention signed at Panama on Sept. 2, 1914.

(c) The Convention regarding the Colon Corridor and certain other corridors through the Canal Zone signed at Panama on May 24, 1950.

(d) The Trans-Isthmian Highway Convention signed at Washington on March 2, 1936, the Agreement supplementing that Convention entered into through an exchange of notes signed at Washington on August 31 and September 6, 1940, and the arrangement between the United States of America and Panama respecting the Trans-Isthmian Joint Highway Board, entered into through an exchange of notes at Panama on October 19 and 23, 1939.

(e) The Highway Convention between the United States and Panama signed at Panama on September 14, 1950.

(f) The Convention regulating the transit of alcoholic liquors through the Canal Zone signed at Panama on March 14, 1932.

(g) The Protocol of an Agreement restricting use of Panama and Canal Zone waters by belligerents signed at Washington on October 10, 1914.

(h) The Agreement providing for the reciprocal recognition of motor vehicle license plates in Panama and the Canal Zone entered into through an exchange of notes at Panama on December 7 and December 12, 1950, and the Agreement establishing procedures for the reciprocal recognition of motor vehicle operator's licenses in the Canal Zone and Panama entered into through an exchange of notes at Panama on October 31, 1960.

(i) The General Relations Agreement entered into through an exchange of notes at Washington on May 18, 1942.

(j) Any other treaty, convention, agreement or exchange of notes between the United States and the Republic of Panama, or portions thereof, concerning the Panama Canal which was entered into prior to the entry into force of the Panama Canal Treaty.

2. It is further understood that the following treaties, conventions, agreements and exchanges of notes between the two Parties are not affected by paragraph 1 of Article I of the Panama Canal Treaty:

(a) The Agreement confirming the cooperative agreement between the Panamanian Ministry of Agriculture and Livestock and the United States Department of Agriculture for the prevention of foot-and-mouth disease and rinderpest in Panama, entered into by an exchange of notes signed at Panama on June 21 and October 5, 1972, and amended May 28 and June 12, 1974.

(b) The Loan Agreement to assist Panama in executing public marketing programs in basic grains and perishables, with annex, signed at Panama on September 10, 1975.

(c) The Agreement concerning the regulation of commercial aviation in the Republic of Panama, entered into by an exchange of notes signed at Panama on April 22, 1929.

(d) The Air Transport Agreement signed at Panama on March 31, 1949, and amended May 29 and June 3, 1952, June 5, 1967, December 23, 1974, and March 6, 1975.

(e) The Agreement relating to the establishment of headquarters in Panama for a civil aviation technical assistance group for the Latin American area, entered into by an exchange of notes signed at Panama on August 8, 1952.

(f) The Agreement relating to the furnishing by the Federal Aviation Agency of certain services and materials for air navigation aids, entered into by an exchange of notes signed at Panama on December 5, 1967, and February 22, 1968.

(g) The Declaration permitting consuls to take note in person, or by authorized representatives, of declarations of values of exports made by shippers before customs officers, entered into by an exchange of notes signed at Washington on April 17, 1913.

(h) The Agreement relating to customs privileges for consular officers, entered into by an exchange of notes signed at Panama on January 7 and 31, 1935.

(i) The Agreement relating to the sale of military equipment, materials, and services to Panama, entered into by an exchange of notes signed at Panama on May 20, 1959.

(j) The Agreement relating to the furnishing of defense articles and services to Panama for the purpose of contributing to its internal security, entered into by an exchange of notes signed at Panama on March 26 and May 23, 1962.

(k) The Agreement relating to the deposit by Panama of ten percent of the value of grant military assistance and excess defense articles furnished by the United States, entered into by an exchange of notes signed at Panama on April 4 and May 9, 1972.

(l) The Agreement concerning payment to the United States of net proceeds from the sale of defense articles furnished under the military assistance program, entered into by an exchange of notes signed at Panama on May 20 and December 6, 1974.

(m) The General Agreement for Technical and Economic Cooperation, signed at Panama on December 11, 1961.

(n) The Loan Agreement relating to the Panama City water supply system, with annex, signed at Panama on May 6, 1969, and amended September 30, 1971.

(o) The Loan Agreement for rural municipal development in Panama, signed at Panama on November 28, 1975.

(p) The Loan Agreement relating to a project for the modernization, restructuring and orientation of Panama's educational programs, signed at Panama on November 19, 1975.

(q) The Treaty providing for the extradition of criminals, signed at Panama on May 25, 1904.

(r) The Agreement relating to legal tender and fractional silver coinage by Panama, entered into by an exchange of notes signed at Washington and New York on June 20, 1904, and amended March 26 and April 2, 1930, May 28 and June 6, 1931, March 2, 1936, June 17, 1946, May 9 and 24, 1950, September 11 and October 22, 1953, August 23 and October 25, 1961, and September 26 and October 23, 1962.

(s) The Agreement for enlargement and use by Canal Zone of sewerage facilities in Colon Free Zone Area, entered into by an exchange of notes signed at Panama on March 8 and 25, 1954.

(t) The Agreement relating to the construction of the inter-American highway, entered into by an exchange of notes signed at Panama on May 15 and June 7, 1943.

(u) The Agreement for cooperation in the construction of the Panama segment of the Darien Gap highway, signed at Washington on May 6, 1971.

(v) The Agreement relating to investment guaranties under sec. 413(b) (4) of the Mutual Security Act of 1954, as amended, entered into by an exchange of notes signed at Washington on January 23, 1961.

(w) The Informal Arrangement relating to cooperation between the American Embassy, or Consulate, and Panamanian authorities when American merchant seamen or tourists are brought before a magistrate's court, entered into by an exchange of notes signed at Panama on September 18 and October 15, 1947.

(x) The Agreement relating to the mutual recognition of ship measurement certificates, entered into by an exchange of notes signed at Washington on August 17, 1937.

(y) The Agreement relating to the detail of a military officer to serve as adviser to the Minister of Foreign Affairs of Panama, signed at Washington on July 7, 1942, and extended and amended February 17, March 23, September 22 and November 6, 1959, March 26 and July 6, 1962, and September 20 and October 8, 1962.

(z) The Agreement relating to the exchange of official publications, entered into by an exchange of notes signed at Panama on November 27, 1941 and March 7, 1942.

(aa) The Convention for the Prevention of Smuggling of Intoxicating Liquors, signed at Washington on June 6, 1924.

(bb) The Arrangement providing for relief from double income tax on shipping profits, entered into by an exchange of notes signed at Washington on January 15, February 8, and March 28, 1941.

(cc) The Agreement for withholding of Panamanian income tax from compensation paid to Panamanians employed within Canal Zone by the canal, railroad, or auxiliary works, entered into by an exchange of notes signed at Panama on August 12 and 30, 1963.

(dd) The Agreement relating to the withholding of contributions for educational insurance from salaries paid to certain Canal Zone employees, entered into by an exchange of notes signed at Panama on September 8 and October 13, 1972.

(ee) The Agreement for radio communications between amateur stations on behalf of third parties, entered into by an exchange of notes signed at Panama on July 19 and August 1, 1956.

(ff) The Agreement relating to the granting of reciprocal authorizations to permit licensed amateur radio operators of either country to operate their stations in the other country, entered into by an exchange of notes signed at Panama on November 16, 1966.

(gg) The Convention facilitating the work of traveling salesmen, signed at Washington on February 8, 1919.

(hh) The Reciprocal Agreement for gratis nonimmigrant visas, entered into by an exchange of notes signed at Panama on March 27 and May 22 and 25, 1956.

(ii) The Agreement modifying the Agreement of March 27 and May 22 and 25, 1956 for gratis nonimmigrant visas, entered into by an exchange of notes signed at Panama on June 14 and 17, 1971.

(jj) Any other treaty, convention, agreement or exchange of notes, or portions thereof, which does not concern the Panama Canal and which is in force immediately prior to the entry into force of the Panama Canal Treaty.

3. With reference to paragraph 2 of Article X (Employment with the Panama Canal Commission), concerning the endeavor to ensure that the number of Panamanian nationals employed in relation to the total number of employees will conform to the proportion established under Panamanian law for foreign business enterprises, it is recognized that progress in this regard may require an extended period in consonance with the concept of a growing and orderly Panamanian participation, through training programs and otherwise, and that progress may be affected from time to time by such actions as the transfer or discontinuance of functions and activities.

4. With reference to paragraph 10(a) of Article X, it is understood that the currently applicable United States law is that contained in Section 8336 of Title 5, United States Code.

5. With reference to paragraph 2 of Article XI (Transitional Provisions), the areas and installations in which the jurisdictional arrangements therein described shall apply during the transition period are as follows:

(a) The Canal operating areas and housing areas described in Annex A to the Agreement in Implementation of Article III of the Panama Canal Treaty.

(b) The Defense Sites and Areas of Military Coordination described in the Agreement in Implementation of Article IV of the Panama Canal Treaty.

(c) The Ports of Balboa and Cristobal described in Annex B of the Agreement in Implementation of Article III of the Panama Canal Treaty.

6. With reference to paragraph 4 of Article XI, the areas in which the police authorities of the Republic of Panama may conduct joint police patrols with the police authorities of the United States of America during the transition period are as follows:

(a) Those portions of the Canal operating areas open to the general public, the housing areas and the Ports of Balboa and Cristobal.

(b) Those areas of military coordination in which joint police patrols are established pursuant to the provisions of the Agreement in Implementation of Article IV of this Treaty, signed this date. The two police authorities shall develop appropriate administrative arrangements for the scheduling and conduct of such joint police patrols.

DONE at Washington, this 7th day of September, 1977, in duplicate, in the English and Spanish languages, both texts being equally authentic.

TREATY
CONCERNING THE PERMANENT NEUTRALITY
AND OPERATION OF THE PANAMA CANAL

The United States of America and the Republic of Panama have agreed upon the following:

ARTICLE I

The Republic of Panama declares that the Canal, as an international transit waterway, shall be permanently neutral in accordance with the regime established in this Treaty. The same regime of neutrality shall apply to any other international waterway that may be built either partially or wholly in the territory of the Republic of Panama.

ARTICLE II

The Republic of Panama declares the neutrality of the Canal in order that both in time of peace and in time of war it shall remain secure and open to peaceful transit by the vessels of all nations on terms of entire equality, so that there will be no discrimination against any nation, or its citizens or subjects, concerning the conditions or charges of transit, or for any other reason, and so that the Canal, and therefore the Isthmus of Panama, shall not be the target of reprisals in any armed conflict between other nations of the world. The foregoing shall be subject to the following requirements:

(a) Payment of tolls and other charges for transit and ancillary services, provided they have been fixed in conformity with the provisions of Article III (c);

(b) Compliance with applicable rules and regulations, provided such rules and regulations are applied in conformity with the provisions of Article III;

(c) The requirement that transiting vessels commit no acts of hostility while in the Canal; and

(d) Such other conditions and restrictions as are established by this Treaty.

ARTICLE III

1. For purposes of the security, efficiency and proper maintenance of the Canal the following rules shall apply:

(a) The Canal shall be operated efficiently in accordance with conditions of transit through the Canal, and rules and regulations that shall be just, equitable and reasonable, and limited to those necessary for safe navigation and efficient, sanitary operation of the Canal;

(b) Ancillary services necessary for transit through the Canal shall be provided;

(c) Tolls and other charges for transit and ancillary services shall be just, reasonable, equitable and consistent with the principles of international law;

(d) As a pre-condition of transit, vessels may be required to establish clearly the financial responsibility and guarantees for payment of reasonable and adequate indemnification, consistent with international practice and standards, for damages resulting from acts or omissions of such vessels when passing through the Canal. In the case of vessels owned or operated by a State or for which it has acknowledged responsibility, a certification by that State that it shall observe its obligations under international law to pay for damages resulting from the act or omission of such vessels when passing through the Canal shall be deemed sufficient to establish such financial responsibility;

(e) Vessels of war and auxiliary vessels of all nations shall at all times be entitled to transit the Canal, irrespective of their internal operation, means of propulsion, origin, destination or armament, without being subjected, as a condition of transit, to inspection, search or surveillance. However, such vessels may be required to certify that they have complied with all applicable health, sanitation and quarantine regulations. In addition, such vessels shall be entitled to refuse to disclose their internal operation, origin, armament, cargo or destination. However, auxiliary vessels may be required to present written assurances, certified by an official at a high level of the government of the State requesting the exemption, that they are owned or operated by that government and in this case are being used only on government non-commercial service.

2. For the purposes of this Treaty, the terms "Canal," "vessel of war," "auxiliary vessel," "internal operation," "armament" and "inspection" shall have the meanings assigned them in Annex A to this Treaty.

ARTICLE IV

The United States of America and the Republic of Panama agree to maintain the regime of neutrality established in this Treaty, which shall be maintained in order that the Canal shall remain permanently neutral, notwithstanding the termination of any other treaties entered into by the two Contracting Parties.

ARTICLE V

After the termination of the Panama Canal Treaty, only the Republic of Panama shall operate the Canal and maintain military forces, defense sites and military installations within its national territory.

ARTICLE VI

1. In recognition of the important contributions of the United States of America and of the Republic of Panama to the construction, operation, maintenance, and protection and defense of the Canal, vessels of war and auxiliary vessels of those nations shall, notwithstanding any other provisions of this Treaty, be entitled to transit the Canal irrespective of their internal operation, means of propulsion, origin, destination, armament or cargo carried. Such vessels of war and auxiliary vessels will be entitled to transit the Canal expeditiously.

2. The United States of America, so long as it has responsibility for the operation of the Canal, may continue to provide the Republic of Colombia toll-free transit through the Canal for its troops, vessels and materials of war. Thereafter, the Republic of Panama may provide the Republic of Colombia and the Republic of Costa Rica with the right of toll-free transit.

ARTICLE VII

1. The United States of America and the Republic of Panama shall jointly sponsor a resolution in the Organization of American States opening to accession by all States of the world the Protocol to this Treaty whereby all the signatories will adhere to the objectives of this Treaty, agreeing to respect the regime of neutrality set forth herein.

2. The Organization of American States shall act as the depository for this Treaty and related instruments.

ARTICLE VIII

This Treaty shall be subject to ratification in accordance with the constitutional procedures of the two Parties. The instruments of ratification of this Treaty shall be exchanged at Panama at the same time as the instruments of ratification of the Panama Canal Treaty, signed this date, are exchanged. This Treaty shall enter into force, simultaneously with the Panama Canal Treaty, six calendar months from the date of the exchange of the instruments of ratification.

DONE at Washington, this 7th day of September, 1977, in duplicate, in the English and Spanish languages, both texts being equally authentic.

ANNEX A

1. "Canal" includes the existing Panama Canal, the entrances thereto and the territorial seas of the Republic of Panama adjacent thereto, as defined on the map annexed hereto (Annex B), and any other inter-oceanic

waterway in which the United States of America is a participant or in which the United States of America has participated in connection with the construction or financing, that may be operated wholly or partially within the territory of the Republic of Panama, the entrances thereto and the territorial seas adjacent thereto.

2. "Vessel of war" means a ship belonging to the naval forces of a State, and bearing the external marks distinguishing warships of its nationality, under the command of an officer duly commissioned by the government and whose name appears in the Navy List, and manned by a crew which is under regular naval discipline.

3. "Auxiliary vessel" means any ship, not a vessel of war, that is owned or operated by a State and used, for the time being, exclusively on government non-commercial service.

4. "Internal operation" encompasses all machinery and propulsion systems, as well as the management and control of the vessel, including its crew. It does not include the measures necessary to transit vessels under the control of pilots while such vessels are in the Canal.

5. "Armament" means arms, ammunitions, implements of war and other equipment of a vessel which possesses characteristics appropriate for use for warlike purposes.

6. "Inspection" includes on-board examination of vessel structure, cargo, armament and internal operation. It does not include those measures strictly necessary for admeasurement, nor those measures strictly necessary to assure safe, sanitary transit and navigation, including examination of deck and visual navigation equipment, nor in the case of live cargoes, such as cattle or other livestock, that may carry communicable diseases, those measures necessary to assure that health and sanitation requirements are satisfied.

PROTOCOL

TO THE TREATY CONCERNING THE PERMANENT NEUTRALITY AND OPERATION OF THE PANAMA CANAL

Whereas the maintenance of the neutrality of the Panama Canal is important not only to the commerce and security of the United States of America and the Republic of Panama, but to the peace and security of the Western Hemisphere and to the interests of world commerce as well;

Whereas the regime of neutrality which the United States of America and the Republic of Panama have agreed to maintain will ensure permanent access to the Canal by vessels of all nations on the basis of entire equality;

Whereas the said regime of effective neutrality shall constitute the best protection for the Canal and shall ensure the absence of any hostile act against it;

The Contracting Parties to this Protocol have agreed upon the following:

ARTICLE I

The Contracting Parties hereby acknowledge the regime of permanent neutrality for the Canal established in the Treaty Concerning the Permanent Neutrality and Operation of the Panama Canal and associate themselves with its objectives.

ARTICLE II

The Contracting Parties agree to observe and respect the regime of permanent neutrality of the Canal in time of war as in time of peace, and to ensure that vessels of their registry strictly observe the applicable rules.

ARTICLE III

This Protocol shall be open to accession by all states of the world, and shall enter into force for each State at the time of deposit of its instrument of accession with the Secretary General of the Organization of American States.

STATEMENT OF UNDERSTANDING
October 14, 1977

Under the treaty concerning the permanent neutrality and operation of the Panama Canal (The Neutrality Treaty), Panama and the United States have the responsibility to assure that the Panama Canal will remain open and secure to ships of all nations. The correct interpretation of this principle is that each of the two countries shall, in accordance with their respective Constitutional processes, defend the Canal against any threat to the regime of neutrality, and consequently shall have the right to act against any aggression or threat directed against the Canal or against the peaceful transit of vessels through the Canal.

This does not mean, nor shall it be interpreted as a right of intervention of the United States in the internal affairs of Panama. Any United States action will be directed at insuring that the Canal will remain open, secure and accessible, and it shall never be directed against the territorial integrity or political independence of Panama.

The Neutrality Treaty provides that the vessels of war and auxiliary vessels of the United States and Panama will be entitled to transit the

Canal expeditiously. This is intended, and it shall be so interpreted, to assure the transit of such vessels through the Canal as quickly as possible, without any impediment, with expedited treatment, and in case of need or emergency, to go to the head of the line of vessels in order to transit the Canal rapidly.

BERT LANCE RESIGNATION
September 21, 1977

Bert Lance had been director of the Office of Management and Budget (OMB), one of the most powerful positions in the federal government, for only eight months when President Carter felt compelled to accept his friend's resignation. Close to tears, the President read Lance's letter of resignation and answered questions at a televised news conference on Sept. 21. "Bert Lance is my friend," Carter said. "I know him personally as well as if he was my own brother. I know him without any doubt in my mind or heart to be a good and an honorable man."

Lance was brought down by persistent questions over whether or not some of his past banking practices were ethical. Many people were concerned that a man whose own financial affairs seemed to be in a convoluted mess was managing the public budget. The resignation followed nearly four months of controversy and investigation by government agencies and the press into Lance's personal dealings while he was the head of the Calhoun (Ga.) National Bank and the First National Bank of Georgia in Atlanta.

None of the criticism was directed at Lance's performance as director of the OMB. His resignation removed from White House counsels not only one of the President's closest friends and advisers but also a man who had been serving with some success as a bridge between the administration and business community. (Historic Documents of 1976, p. 877)

Among the allegations investigated were the following:
• That Lance had withheld pertinent information about his banking history during confirmation hearings in January 1977;

• *That he had backdated checks to take illegal tax deductions on his 1976 return [a charge made by Sen. Charles H. Percy (R Ill.); Percy later said that there was no substance to the charge and apologized for it to Lance].*

• *That credit practices of the Calhoun bank had permitted Lance and members of his family extensive overdraft privileges amounting to hundreds of thousands of dollars;*

• *That Lance used improper influence to clear his record prior to his appointment to the OMB;*

• *That the same block of stock was used by Lance to secure two loans from different banks in 1975 and 1976;*

• *That during his campaign for election as governor of Georgia Lance persistently overdrew his campaign account with the Calhoun bank;*

• *That he used aircraft belonging to the National Bank of Georgia for personal and political purposes while he was the bank's president.*

Background

While Lance's problems surfaced during the summer of 1977, they actually began in the early 1970s at the First National Bank of Calhoun where, with Lance as president and chairman, the bank was troubled by an embezzlement and by problems of management. In 1974 it was discovered that the bank permitted large overdrafts on Lance's gubernatorial campaign account and had permitted members of his family to run up no-interest or low-interest overdrafts—actions which might have violated a federal statute prohibiting loans to a bank officer in excess of $5,000.

The Atlanta office of the U.S. Comptroller of the Currency secured on Dec. 2, 1975, an agreement from the Calhoun bank to terminate overdraft privileges to Lance and others and to refrain from assisting political campaigns. The comptroller referred Lance's campaign fund case to the Justice Department for possible criminal prosecution. Shortly after Carter's election in November 1976, a series of events eased Lance's immediate problems but ultimately led to his downfall. The most damaging charge was that Lance had used his political influence to persuade Donald G. Tarleton, director of the Comptroller's Altanta office, to rescind the overdraft agreement with the Calhoun bank. Tarleton ordered the agreement dropped Nov. 22, 1976. U.S. Attorney John Stokes Jr. Dec. 1 dropped the Justice Department investigation of Lance. Carter nominated Lance as director of OMB on Dec. 3, 1976.

Lance was confirmed Jan. 20 despite news stories about the quashed Justice Department inquiry and the overdraft agreement. Throughout the spring and summer occasional reports elaborated on the allegations or described a new problem but these, like earlier stories, were overlooked or dismissed.

Comptroller's Inquiry

In July new details about Lance's finances surfaced. Press reports revealed that the National Bank of Georgia had opened a "correspondent" account with the First National Bank of Chicago only one month before Lance obtained a $3.4-million loan from the Chicago bank. Lance used the loan to pay off an earlier loan from the Manufacturer's Hanover Trust Co. of New York which had financed his purchase of Georgia bank stock. Lance testified July 25 before the Senate Governmental Affairs Committee that there was no relationship between the "correspondent" account and the loan he received. (A "correspondent" account is usually a non-interest bearing account placed by one bank with another bank in exchange for check clearing and other financial services.)

The Chicago loan was one of the targets of an investigation conducted by the Office of the Comptroller of the Currency. Comptroller John G. Heimann Aug. 18 released the initial report on his inquiry into Lance's affairs. Heimann's report cleared Lance of criminal wrongdoing while president of the National Bank of Georgia. But the report did say that some of his practices "posed serious problems of banking ethics."

The comptroller's inquiry had questioned whether Lance had obtained another large loan from the Manufacturer's Hanover Trust Co. of New York in June 1975 while establishing a "correspondent" account at that bank. Heimann concluded that, lacking controverted testimony, "there appears to be no violation of any applicable laws or regulations." The report asserted that Lance's dealings with a third New York bank, Chemical Bank, produced "no evidence...indicating that loans to Mr. Lance...were preferential in treatment because of a correspondent relationship."

The report showed that Lance's wife, LaBelle Lance, was overdrawn generally from $25,000 to $100,000 between September and December 1974, and it disclosed that other Lance relatives were also overdrawn by large sums ranging up to $450,000 between September 1974 and April 1975. The comptroller's report judged the overdraft privileges at the Calhoun bank "unsafe and unsound banking practices."

Release of the report prompted Carter to deliver a warm endorsement of Lance at a televised news conference on Aug. 18. "My faith in the character and competence of Bert Lance has been reconfirmed," the President said, adding "Bert, I'm proud of you." Lance, at Carter's side at the news conference, called the report "very favorable" and said that it had not impeded his ability to serve as OMB director.

Lance's Resignation

New revelations about Lance's financial affairs appeared almost daily during the next two weeks. On Sept. 5, after meeting with President Carter *at the White House, Sen. Abraham Ribicoff (D Conn.), chairman of the Governmental Affairs Committee, and Sen. Percy publicly called for Lance to step down. By Sept. 8 six federal units were investigating Lance—the Office of the Comptroller of the Currency, the Internal Revenue Service, the Securities and Exchange Commission, the Federal Elections Commission, the Federal Deposit Insurance Corp. and the Justice Department.*

In testimony Sept. 15-17 before the Senate Governmental Affairs Committee, Lance attempted to refute, point-by-point, allegations flowing from his financial dealings. Lance's 49-page prepared statement called the allegations "erroneous," "misrepresented," "exaggerated," and "completely misunderstood." In a counterattack against his critics, Lance said he had been deprived of his rights and had been treated "in the most irresponsible and destructive manner. The basic American principle of justice and fair play has been pointedly ignored by certain members of this committee." "Certain persons," Lance said, "have publicly, in effect, brought in a verdict of guilty before I have been given an opportunity to present my side of the case. It has been a saddening and disillusioning experience."

With Clark M. Clifford, a prominent Washington, D.C., attorney and former Secretary of Defense seated beside him as counsel, Lance appealed, in the televised hearings, to all the American people. "I welcome them as the jury in this proceeding," he said, "for I am secure and comfortable knowing that my conscience is clear and that the people's verdict will be a fair and just one."

Lance rebutted all the allegations that had been lodged against him during the hearings, making no admission of any kind of misconduct and giving no hint of imminent resignation. Four days later, however, on Sept. 21, President Carter accepted Lance's resignation. Lance returned to his native Georgia, but the press reported that he remained one of the President's advisers. Investigations by a number of agencies of the federal government into Lance's tangled affairs continued.

Carter Dec. 27 announced that acting budget director James T. McIntyre, a 37-year-old Georgia lawyer had been named OMB director. McIntyre served as Carter's budget chief when Carter was governor of Georgia.

Following are excerpts from the Comptroller of the Currency's report Aug. 18, 1977; Lance's statement before the Senate Governmental Affairs Committee, Sept. 15, 1977, and excerpts from that committee's inquiry, Sept. 15-17, 1977; and Carter's news conference announcing Lance's resignation Sept. 21, 1977. (Boldface headings in brackets have been added by Congressional Quarterly to highlight the organization of the text.):

[Letter of Transmittal]

August 18, 1977

Honorable Abraham A. Ribicoff
Chairman
Committee on Governmental Affairs
United States Senate
Room 337, Russell Office Building
Washington, D.C. 20510

Dear Mr. Chairman:

On July 12, 1977 when I assumed office as Comptroller of the Currency, I was aware of allegations from various quarters that T. Bertram Lance, Director, Office of Management and Budget, prior to his assumption of that office, may have committed infractions of laws or regulations relating to national banks. An inquiry was begun by my office into these allegations on July 14, 1977 and the Secretary of the Treasury was so informed. On July 21, 1977 the Secretary told me that the President expected me to take such action as was appropriate to carry out the responsibilities of my office.

Prior to the hearing of your Committee on July 25, 1977, at which Mr. Lance testified, you inquired as to the actions the Office of the Comptroller was taking concerning such allegations. I informed you that I had initiated an inquiry into such allegations, and you asked to be supplied with the results of that inquiry as promptly as practicable. That request was confirmed at the July 25, 1977 public hearing of the Committee. Subsequently, I have received requests for a report from the Chairmen and the ranking minority members of the U.S. Senate Committee on Banking, Housing and Urban Affairs and the Committee on Banking, Finance and Urban Affairs of the U.S. House of Representatives. I have also received requests for specific information from several other members of the Congress.

As you know, the general responsibility of this Office is to supervise the activities of, and to enforce the laws and regulations relating to national banks. The Office has no authority to prosecute violations of criminal statutes or to enforce the laws that do not relate to national banks. Prior to becoming Director of the Office of Management and Budget, Mr. Lance had served as an executive of two national banks, The National Bank of Georgia and The Calhoun First National Bank. Since the allegations involved activities relating to these two national banks, the Comptroller clearly had a duty to make an appropriate inquiry. In order to produce a report within a reasonable time, this inquiry has covered principally the period since January 1975. I also want to stress that it has not dealt with matters which fall outside of the general jurisdiction of this Office, that is, matters that do not relate to national banks.

This report has been compiled from the files of this Office, extensive examination of the records of banks through the use of this Office's bank examination process, and depositions under oath of a number of individuals.

Assistance was rendered by several other state and federal banking agencies. As you know, there are statutory restrictions on the public disclosure of material from bank examinations. Mr. Lance has informed me that he has no objection to the public release of any information relating to him. However, questions about the rights of privacy of other individuals are raised by some portions of this inquiry and the propriety of the public release of information previously supplied to the Department of Justice. Accordingly, this report has been divided into (i) an extensive summary of the data generated by the inquiry and certain conclusions that the Office has drawn from the data, and (ii) exhibits consisting of copies of documents that provide the basis for the statements in the summary.

To accommodate unique circumstances here involved, we have attempted to write the summaries so that their public release would not unacceptably compromise the privacy of individuals or raise any question about the release of bank examination material. While none of the exhibits raises any substantial question concerning the solvency or condition of any bank, you and the Chairmen of the other Committees to whom I am transmitting copies of this report may wish to review the exhibits to determine whether the benefits from their public release outweigh individuals' rights to privacy and the general principles protecting bank examination material from public release. In addition, we are not transmitting to you at this time transcripts of depositions taken and copies of material previously transmitted to the Department of Justice on December 24, 1975. Should you desire such material, I will be glad to undertake arrangements to make it available to you.

While we have endeavored to complete this inquiry expeditiously, the following areas remain to be concluded.

(i) It became clear to me in the first days of this inquiry that certain parts of the inquiry involved questions as to whether employees of this Office had correctly followed the internal rules and regulations of our Office and of the Department of the Treasury and as to whether they had properly performed their responsibilities. Accordingly I requested the assistance of the Secretary of the Treasury, to whom this Office is responsible, since I felt an inquiry into this subject could not properly be conducted by personnel of this Office. On July 18, 1977 the Secretary directed the Assistant Commissioner for Inspection of the Internal Revenue Service to conduct such an inquiry under my general supervision. The Inspection Service has had extensive experience in conducting such inquiries, and I am informed that the Department of the Treasury has followed this procedure in the past in analogous situations. The results of this inquiry will not be available for several weeks, but I have no reason to believe it will reveal any violation of any applicable law or regulation by Mr. Lance not covered by this report.

(ii) Allegations have been made that The National Bank of Georgia may not have adequately controlled the accounts relating to owned or leased aircraft in the period from February 1975 to the present. The inquiry thus far conducted (which has included examination of available records and deposition of one witness) has not progressed to a point where any conclusions may properly be drawn.

(iii) In the course of this inquiry thus far, it has not been possible to resolve all matters that have come to the attention of this Office, particularly where they relate to periods prior to 1975. We expect to pursue as appropriate all open matters but I did not believe it desirable to delay reporting on those areas which I believe have been the focus of your Committee.

In addition to the conclusions stated in the body of the report, I believe that it might be helpful to add a few general comments:

(1) We do not believe the information developed to date in the inquiry warrants the prosecution of any individuals.

(2) It is clear from the summary of information that Mr. Lance made his principal borrowings from banking institutions which had a correspondent relationship, including deposit balances, with the banks in which Mr. Lance served as officer and director. This recurring pattern of shifting bank relationships and personal borrowing raises unresolved questions as to what constitutes acceptable banking practice. The Office intends to address the question of whether its regulations under the Securities Exchange Act of 1934 or under other statutes should be amended to require public disclosure of such practices or other remedial action.

(3) The report recites that the management of The Calhoun First National Bank from 1973 to 1975 permitted officers, directors, some employees and their families to overdraw checking accounts in substantial amounts for considerable periods of time. In the case of the Lance for Governor Campaign account, the facts were referred to the Department of Justice on December 24, 1975. On December 2, 1975, the Office entered into an agreement pursuant to the Financial Institutions Supervisory Act of 1966 with the board of directors of Calhoun which, among other things, required management to cease permitting insiders to maintain overdrafts. The questionable overdraft practices were corrected in compliance with the agreement. The agreement itself was terminated by the Regional Administrator on November 22, 1976.

(4) As is developed fully in this summary, Mr. Lance did not file with the banks of which he was an officer certain reports of outside business interests and personal borrowing and of borrowing by his affiliates as required by statute or regulation in the years covered in this inquiry. If Mr. Lance were still with the banks, the normal action of this Office would be to direct that the reports forthwith be filed.

I look forward to continued cooperation with you and your Committee, as well as the other interested Committees of the Congress, in this matter. If there is any way you feel this Office can be of assistance to you in your deliberations, I know you will call on us....

[COMPTROLLER OF THE CURRENCY'S REPORT]

Inquiry into Certain Matters Relating to
T. Bertram Lance and Various Financial Institutions

[Section A]

Scope of Inquiry: Review of: (a) documents at FNBC [First National Bank of Chicago] and NBG [National Bank of Georgia] relating to Mr. Lance's personal loan and NBG's correspondent balance account; (b) records of hearings before the Committee on Governmental Affairs, U.S. Senate; and (c) public statements reported in newspaper articles....

Conclusion: ...Mr. Lance actively participated in establishing the correspondent relationship between NBG and FNBC in November 1976. There is no record of discussion at that time of the possibility of a loan to Mr. Lance. FNBC memoranda relating to the granting of Mr. Lance's loans in January 1977 specifically state that no compensating balance was expected. FNBC anticipated the loans to Mr. Lance would be fully secured, and, as such, its terms were not more favorable than terms offered to other borrowers on secured loans. FNBC has a well documented file of correspondent services offered to NBG. On the basis of the information currently available to the Office of the Comptroller of the Currency, there appears to be no violation of applicable laws or regulations relating to national banks in the establishment or operation of these loan and deposit accounts.

[Section B]

Scope of Inquiry: The Office of the Comptroller of the Currency (OCC) reviewed documents obtained from the files of MHT [Manufacturers Hanover Trust Company] and NBG relating to: (a) the correspondent balances maintained by NBG and Calhoun First National Bank (Calhoun) at MHT; (b) the services provided to NBG by MHT and the costs of those services; and (c) a loan by MHT to Bert Lance. Records reviewed included credit files, collateral registers, correspondent account statements, correspondent bank memoranda, profitability analyses, interest payment records and individual deposit accounts in which either Mr. Lance or Mrs. LaBelle Lance had an interest....

Conclusion: ...There is some documentary and circumstantial evidence suggesting the possibility that a 20 percent compensating balance from NBG was a condition of the loan to Mr. Lance from MHT. However, all the principals involved denied under oath (a) that such an arrangement existed and (b) that such an arrangement was ever discussed. Based upon the information available to the Office of the Comptroller of the Currency at this time, evaluated in light of the uncontroverted testimony, there appears to be no violation of any applicable laws or regulations relating to national banks.

[Section C]

Scope of Inquiry: Citibank records pertaining to NBG and Mr. Lance were reviewed. Records showing deposit activity in NBG's correspondent balance at Citibank were reviewed at both NBG and Citibank. NBG board of directors and executive committee minutes pertaining to any correspondent relationship were reviewed and copied at NBG. A comparative review of deposit relationships of NBG with all New York banks was made....

Conclusion: ...The NBG correspondent relationship with Citibank was an unprofitable one for Citibank. Operational problems also led to expressions of dissatisfaction with the account by both Citibank and NBG officials. Those problems appear to have contributed to the movement by NBG of its principal correspondent relationship to MHT in the summer of 1975, eventually resulting in the closing of the account. Based on the information available to the Office of the Comptroller of the Currency, there appears to be no violation of the applicable laws and regulations relating to national banks.

[Section D]

Scope of Inquiry: The Office of the Comptroller of the Currency (OCC) reviewed correspondent account records of NBG and Calhoun [First National Bank] at C&S [Citizens and Southern National Bank] and the C&S records

of loans to Bert Lance, Lancelot and Company, Bert
Lance for Governor Campaign Committee, Inc., and
Calhoun Unifirst, Inc....

Conclusion: ...There is no discernible relationship between the
loans to Mr. Lance and his associated interests and
the deposit accounts maintained by NBG and Calhoun at C&S. Based on the information currently
available to the Office of the Comptroller of the
Currency, there appears to be no violation of
statutes or regulations applicable to national banks
in the establishment or operation of these loan and
deposit accounts.

[Section E]

Scope of Inquiry: The Office of the Comptroller of the Currency (OCC)
reviewed loan records of UAB [United American
Bank]-Knoxville and United American Bank, Nashville (UAB-Nashville) and correspondent account
records of The National Bank of Georgia (NBG)
and The Calhoun First National Bank (Calhoun) at
both UAB banks.

Conclusion: The files of the banks involved contain no evidence
of connections between the UAB-Knoxville loan to
Mr. Lance and the deposit accounts maintained by
NBG and Calhoun at UAB-Knoxville or UAB-
Nashville. Based on the information currently available to the Comptroller of the Currency, there appears to be no violation of applicable laws or
regulations relating to national banks in the establishment or operation of these loan and deposit
accounts.

[Section F]

Scope of Inquiry: The Office of the Comptroller of the Currency (OCC)
reviewed documents at Chemical [Chemical Bank,
New York] relating to Bert Lance's personal loan, a
loan to Gwinnett Industries, Inc. and NBG's correspondent balance account with Chemical....

Conclusion: ...Although it appears that Chemical became a correspondent bank of NBG in part because Chemical
lent money to Mr. Lance and to Mr. Pattillo's company [Gwinnett Industries], no evidence was discovered indicating that loans to Mr. Lance or Gwinett
Industries, Inc. were preferential in treatment because of the correspondent balance relationship.

Based on the information currently available to the Office of the Comptroller of the Currency, there appears to be no violation of the applicable laws and regulations relating to national banks in the establishment or operation of their loan and deposit accounts.

[Section G]

Scope of Inquiry: The Office of the Comptroller of the Currency (OCC) reviewed NBG records relating to the acquisition and administration of the trust account and OCC examination reports pertinent to the operations of NBG's trust department....

Conclusions:
1. Mr. Lance participated to some degree in acquiring the Teamster's Pension Fund account for NBG, but he did not participate in the detailed negotiation of the agreement.
2. Based on the information available to the Office of the Comptroller of the Currency, there appears to be no violation of any statutes or regulations applicable to national banks in connection with NBG's investment management agreement with the Teamster's Pension Fund.

[Section H]

Scope of Inquiry: The Office of the Comptroller of the Currency (OCC) reviewed all available documents from Calhoun [First National Bank] and OCC Washington and regional office files which related to correspondent balances by Calhoun. In some instances, OCC also reviewed records of other banks to verify correspondent activity....

Conclusion: ...No relationship appears between borrowings by Mr. Lance and correspondent balances maintained by Calhoun. Based on the information currently available to the Office of the Comptroller of the Currency, there appears to be no violation of statutes or regulations applicable to national banks in the establishment or operation of these loan and deposit accounts.

[Section I]

Scope of Inquiry: A review was made of the two checking accounts maintained by the "Bert Lance for Governor Campaign" and of various other accounts on the general ledger of Calhoun from August 1973 through December 1974. Testimony of certain Calhoun [First National Bank] officials was also taken in August 1975....

Conclusion: ...The Comptroller's Office concluded that both administrative proceedings and a criminal referral were appropriate. Calhoun's board of directors was asked to, and did, on December 2, 1975, enter into a written agreement under the Financial Institutions Supervisory Act of 1966, agreeing, among other things, to cease allowing the campaign committee to overdraw its account. A referral of the matter to the Department of Justice was made on December 24, 1975.

[Section J]

Scope of Inquiry: All checking accounts of Mr. and Mrs. Lance and their children and other known relatives at Calhoun for the period January 1, 1972 through January 1976 were reviewed....

Conclusion: ...The overdrafts permitted to bank directors, officers and their families (including Mr. Lance) by Calhoun constituted unsafe and unsound banking practices. Certain of the overdrafts amounted to extensions of credit to executive officers (including Mr. Lance) in excess of the amounts permissible under 12 USC [United States Code] 375a. During 1976, Calhoun's policies, procedures and practices concerning overdrafts were corrected in keeping with the terms of the formal written agreement executed under the Financial Institutions Supervisory Act of 1966 on December 2, 1975.

[Section K]

Scope of Inquiry: Documents of record in Hartford Indemnity v. Calhoun First National Bank, [Docket] No. C76-35R ([Northern District], Ga., filed March 16, 1976), were reviewed. A copy of the FBI report of investigation relative to the defalcations of Bill L. Campbell was obtained and reviewed, as were records of Campbell's deposit account activity in Calhoun. Data compiled from the records of NBG concerning loans to Mr. Campbell on February 18, 1975 and July 14, 1975 were examined. The current president of Calhoun, Y.A. Henderson, was interviewed concerning the matter....

Conclusion: ...Based on the information available to the Office of the Comptroller of the Currency, there appears to be no violations of the statutes or regulations applicable to national banks except those provisions involved in the criminal proceedings brought against Mr. Campbell.

[Section L]

Scope of Inquiry: All reports of borrowings from other banks filed by Bert Lance with the board of directors of The Calhoun First National Bank (Calhoun) and The National Bank of Georgia (NBG) over the period January 1, 1970 to January 23, 1977 were examined. The reports were compared with reports prepared by bank regulatory agencies (Federal Deposit Insurance Corporation, Federal Reserve, Comptroller of the Currency, and State of Georgia) on extensions of credit to Mr. Lance over the same time period, as those extensions of credit were reflected in the records of the lending banks....

Conclusion: ...Mr. Lance did not file with the banks of which he was an executive officer certain reports of personal borrowing as required by statute. If Mr. Lance were still an executive officer with the banks, the normal action of this Office would be to direct that the reports be filed forthwith.

[Section M]

Scope of Inquiry: National Bank of Georgia (NBG) and Calhoun First National Bank (Calhoun) records of Bert Lance's Part 23 filings [a required statement of interest form filed by directors and principal officers of national banks] were compared with information furnished by Mr. Lance to the U.S. Senate Committee on Governmental Affairs at the time of the hearings on his confirmation as Director of the Office of Management and Budget (OMB)....

Conclusion: ...Mr. Lance's Part 23 filings failed to disclose information on some business interests required to be disclosed by Part 23; a new and complex regulation. On the basis of the information currently available the Office cannot conclude that Mr. Lance knowingly made incomplete and inaccurate filings. If

Mr. Lance were still a director of NBG or Calhoun, the Office of the Comptroller of the Currency would routinely request that corrected filings be made.

[Lance Checking Accounts]

Scope of Inquiry: The Office of the Comptroller of the Currency (OCC) examiners reviewed records of the Calhoun First National Bank (Calhoun) and of The National Bank of Georgia (NBG) for the period December 1, 1975 through August 22, 1977 relating to the checking accounts of Mr. Lance and to the correspondent account maintained by Calhoun at NBG....

Conclusion: ...The processing of checks through the unposted transactions account enabled Calhoun to avoid placing Mr. Lance's demand deposit account in a one day overdraft status while funds were in the process of being transferred from NBG. It appears that a similar opportunity to avoid overdrafts when funds were immediately available had been provided by Calhoun to other customers, including directors, for some time. This practice essentially causes the bank to lose the opportunity to earn one day's interest on items accorded such special handling. The interest and processing costs could be offset by collection of service charges. No service charges were made by Calhoun on Mr. Lance's transactions. With profitable accounts, such service charges are frequently waived by bank management.

The procedures followed by Calhoun...were not subject to sufficient controls to insure that overdrafts would not occur at Calhoun. On some occasions, one-day overdrafts did occur in Mr. Lance's account in Calhoun even though funds were available in accounts at NBG. In addition, it is unknown whether Mr. Lance's relationship with Calhoun was sufficiently profitable to warrant the waiving of service charges on the special handling accorded his transactions. If such a practice were detected during the course of regular examinations, the OCC would criticize the management.

[Lancelot Company]

Scope of Inquiry: The Office of the Comptroller of the Currency (OCC) reviewed documents obtained from the files of Calhoun and Fulton relating to (a) loans made by Fulton to Mr. and Mrs. Lance and directors of Calhoun, (b) correspondent balances maintained at Fulton [National Bank] by Calhoun [National Bank], Cohutta [Banking Company], and Ringgold [The Northwest Georgia Bank, Ringgold], and (c) Fulton's profitability analysis of the Calhoun, Cohutta, and Ringgold accounts. OCC also reviewed a limited number of documents from Federal Deposit Insurance Corporation (FDIC) files pertaining to Cohutta and Ringgold. Several Fulton employees were questioned by examiners with regard to matters referred to in the documents....

Conclusion: ...The Fulton-Calhoun transactions show a pattern of loans to Mr. and Mrs. Lance and associates from a correspondent bank. The correspondent bank looked in some measure to the maintenance of satisfactory correspondent balances in determining whether to make the loans and in calculating the profitability of loans after they were made. In addition, there is some evidence tending to support the view that, but for the correspondent accounts, the loans would not have been made.

Notwithstanding Fulton's possible expectations, available information discloses that the services provided by Fulton exceeded Fulton's calculated return on the Calhoun deposits. In fact, Fulton provided Calhoun with correspondent services at a net loss. In September 1970, the Department of Justice advised OCC that only when a potential compensating balance case shows both "clear detriment to the bank and concomitant benefit to its officers, the activity might in certain situations warrant prosecutive action." Therefore, based on the information currently available to the Office of the Comptroller of the Currency, with regard to the transactions between Fulton and Calhoun, we do not believe that the prosecution of any individuals is warranted. The correspondent accounts maintained by the Cohutta and Ringgold banks, on the other hand, appear to have resulted in some profits to Fulton to the possible detriment of Ringgold and Cohutta. These banks are not under the jurisdiction of the OCC and it is therefore clear that additional inquiry by the FDIC or the Commissioner of Banking and Finance of the State of Georgia will be required to evaluate this matter fully. Accordingly, the OCC has brought the circumstances of these transactions to the attention of the FDIC for analysis and such further inquiry as it may deem appropriate.

LANCE STATEMENT BEFORE SENATE COMMITTEE

I'm here today not only to make this statement and to answer any questions that you may have but also to speak directly to the American people.

Many charges and accusations involving me have been brought to their attention until I am sure they wonder what kind of man I really am.

They will know me much better when I have finished testifying before this committee because I intend to answer every charge that has been made and I shall answer every question that is asked, to the best of my ability.

I have infinite faith in the fairness of the American people. I welcome them as the jury in this proceeding, for I am secure and comfortable knowing that my conscience is clear and that the people's verdict will be a fair and just one....

[Lance as Bank Manager]

...Much has been said in the press recently about my management of the Calhoun Bank and the National Bank of Georgia. Let me recite some facts which have not been brought to the attention of the public.

During the period I served as president and chairman of the Calhoun Bank, its deposits increased from $11 million to $49 million. Its assets increased from $11.9 million to $54.1 million.

At the National Bank of Georgia, the results were even more dramatic. In the two years of 1975 and 1976, its deposits increased 50 per cent and its assets increased from $254 million to $404 million.

Because of the volume of unfavorable publicity these past weeks, it may come as a surprise when I say that no depositor in either the Calhoun Bank or the National Bank of Georgia ever lost a cent while I was with those banks.

In addition, I have read many critical stories devoted to family loans and overdrafts. I want you to know and understand that every overdraft has been paid in full.

From January 1975 to the end of 1976 I served as president of the National Bank of Georgia. Following his election, President-elect Carter asked me to serve in his new Administration as Director of the Office of Management and Budget. In January of 1977, I was confirmed by this committee and the Senate.

[Lance Criticizes Committee]

Then in late May, the questions began and gradually grew into a full-fledged investigation. Now, today, after weeks of accusations I have my opportunity to tell you how I feel about these events.

We have been hearing a great deal lately about the subject of human rights. We have been outspoken in our criticism of certain totalitarian governments for the manner in which the rights of their citizens have been violated.

Implicit in our criticism has been the suggestion that it is different in our country. We proudly point to our Constitution and our Bill of Rights and smugly compare our shining record in this field with the harsh and oppressive actions of other nations.

I wonder. I wonder because my experience these last few weeks has been one of profound shock and disappointment.

The rights that I thought I had as an American have been treated in the most irresponsible and destructive manner. The basic American principle of justice and fair play has been pointedly ignored by certain members of this committee.

Certain persons have publicly, in effect, brought in a verdict of "guilty" before I had been given the opportunity to present my side of the case. It has been a saddening and disillusioning experience.

Let me be more specific.

The Fifth Amendment to the Constitution provides that no person shall be deprived of life, liberty or property without due process of law. All my adult life I have been a banker. My reputation, in effect, has been my life and my property. I have had the confidence and respect of the people of my state and the two banks with which I have been associated.

But now my reputation has been questioned. Charge has followed charge. Accusations have poured forth, accompanied by prompt and destructive interpretations, by certain members of this body. Ready-made opinions have been offered affecting my character, my ability and my integrity.

And yet, not until today have I been given the opportunity to answer the charges that have been made. Some of the claims are erroneous, some are misrepresented, some are exaggerated and some are completely misunderstood because those making the charge do not have all the facts.

And in the process, the rights that I thought that I possessed have, one by one, gone down the drain.

[Lance Cites Example of Unfair Treatment]

Let me give you a dramatic example of what I am referring to.

On Monday, Sept. 5 (Labor Day) The Atlanta Journal and Constitution carried a major front page story with the lurid headline, "Swindler Implicates Lance."

In the body of the story, it appeared that investigators of this committee had gone to the Federal prison in which one Bill Lee Campbell is incarcerated. The Atlanta paper's story stated that there were three investigators from this committee and that they had obtained an affidavit from Campbell asserting that Lance was implicated in the bank embezzlement which had sent Campbell to prison for eight years. The story further stated that the three investigators had returned promptly to Washington and had consulted immediately with this committee.

On the same day, Sept. 5, that the story appeared in the Atlanta paper, Senators [Abraham] Ribicoff and [Charles H.] Percy made a much publicized call upon President Carter. They asked President Carter to force Lance to resign and gave as the reason that they had received "allegations of illegality" involving Lance.

Much attention was given in the press to the Billy Lee Campbell accusation. The New York Times subhead was "Illinois Senator Says Some Charges Were Made by Banker Now In Jail" (New York Times, Tuesday, Sept. 6, 1977).

The net result of the developments of Labor Day, 1977, was to inform the American people that Lance, who was already under attack, was now involved in some "serious illegality" that had something to do with "embezzlement," that was of such sinister proportions that the two senators felt compelled to ask that Lance be fired.

This was the last straw for many people. Even some of my friends felt there must be something to the charge, or it would not have been uttered by a United States senator. Now the question is were my human rights protected? Were the rights of a citizen to fair and decent treatment properly accorded?

You will let the American people answer that question.

Here are the facts.

The accusations by members of this committee which were passed on to the President and which were so damaging to me, were based upon the unsupported and unverified statement of a man in the Federal penitentiary.

Did the three committee investigators attempt to verify the extremely serious charge made by this convicted felon before the story was leaked to the press? Not so far as we can ascertain.

If someone were searching for the facts instead of a "smear" the obvious first step would be to go to the Assistant U.S. Attorney who prosecuted Billy Lee Campbell. His name is Jeffrey B. Bogart. He would have been easy to find for he was still the Assistant U.S. Attorney at that time.

If they had talked with Mr. Bogart, they would have learned from him that Campbell at no time attempted to implicate Lance or anyone else. Mr. Bogart has been quoted as saying: "It's my recollection that he said he took it all. At no time in open court did he indicate, in mitigation, that there were any people involved."

If, by chance, any possible skepticism remained, the investigator could have called upon the lawyer who defended Campbell in the embezzlement case. He would have learned from him that in the many months he represented Campbell, and in innumerable conferences, Campbell never in any way implicated Lance in the embezzlement.

[Embezzlement Investigation Result]

The transcripts in Federal court show that the judge questioned Campbell in great detail, but Campbell again did not involve Lance in any embezzlement.

Apparently, no steps of this kind were taken by the investigators. They talked to Campbell, received an unsupported accusation, brought it to the committee, two of whose members promptly took it to the White House and then, at a press conference, informed the American people that they had reported the Campbell charge to the President.

A curious epilogue should be mentioned. Although the Atlanta paper reported that the committee investigators obtained an affidavit from Campbell, this proved to be untrue. Not only would Campbell not give an affidavit, he would not even permit his conversation to be taped.

This is the background of the accusation that has brought such pain to me, to my wife, and to members of my family. And the entire tragic and irresponsible incident could have been prevented by one simple telephone call. If I had been called, I could have in five minutes told them who should be seen to get the true story.

One lesson I have learned from this experience is to be mighty careful in the future when I am discussing basic human rights.

Over these past weeks, as charge after charge has been leveled against me, I have attempted to keep a record of them. I have carefully checked my own knowledge and recollection. I have consulted with others who have been involved and I have read many records casting light on the circumstance of the various incidents.

I now wish, in as warily a manner as possible, to designate the accusation and to supply the answer as I know it.

[Lance Responds to Confirmation Cover-Up Charge]

Perhaps the most fundamental charge to be discussed at this hearing is the allegation that I failed to disclose all pertinent facts to this committee at the time of my confirmation hearing. This oft-repeated accusation by certain members of this committee was readily seized upon by the press who sought to denigrate me—and indeed the Carter Administration—with suggestions of a "cover-up."

Members of this committee have been quoted in the national press as having said the committee had been "misled" prior to my confirmation.

Senator Ribicoff is reported in The New York Times as saying: "My feeling is that if the committee had all the information we now have, it would have been very difficult for him to have been confirmed." (Wednesday, Sept. 7.) His theme has been echoed by other members of the committee during these hearings.

The newspapers have made this allegation their favorite theme. James Reston, for example, states in his column of Sept. 7, 1977, "Either Lance deceived Carter by withholding information from him or Carter, if he had the information, deceived the Congress."

On Monday of this week, The Washington Post quotes Senator [Henry M.] Jackson, who asserted that "the major item of inquiry" at the hearing is whether damaging information about me was withheld from the committee during my confirmation hearings. I quite agree with the Senator.

At the time this committee commenced its investigation of my qualifications to be director of the Office of Management and Budget, I submitted detailed written information outlining my personal and financial background. In addition, I specifically authorized this committee to obtain any further "written opinions as you may deem appropriate in investigating my nomination."

Prior to a confirmation hearing, it is customary for the nominee to meet with Senate investigators to explore his qualifications for the office, provide explanation and information as to his personal and financial background, and in general, answer any questions that are raised.

[Lance Meeting with Committee Staff]

I attended such a meeting with Senate investigators on Jan. 13, 1977. Also present at the meeting were my attorney, Harvey Hill, and Mr. Thomas Mitchell, the man who was to be the trustee of the blind trust which would be established under the Administration's new guidelines.

The Senate investigators of this committee who attended that meeting included Mr. Richard Wegman, chief counsel and staff director, John B. Childers, chief counsel to the minority, and David R. Schaeffer, former counsel to the committee and special assistant to Senator Ribicoff.

During the course of that meeting, I disclosed to the representatives of this committee the various financial matters which now are the focus of this hearing.

At our meeting on Jan. 13, I discussed with the committee investigators my previous relationship with the National Bank of Georgia and the Calhoun First National Bank.

We discussed my financial assets and liabilities, including loans I had obtained from various banks.

We discussed in detail the entire matter concerning the Calhoun First National Bank's involvement in my 1974 gubernatorial race, including overdrafts incurred by my campaign committee, the investigation by the Comptroller's office and the subsequent referral of this case to the Department of Justice.

[Personal Overdrafts Disclosed by Lance]

I advised them of my personal overdrafts. We discussed previous financial problems of the Calhoun First National Bank and their current status.

Specifically, I disclosed and we discussed the agreement between the Office of the Comptroller of the Currency and the Calhoun First National Bank. We further discussed the fact that the agreement had been removed in November, 1976, by the regional administrator of the Comptroller's Office.

Statements taken in the recent I.R.S. [Internal Revenue Service] investigation of the Comptroller's office confirms my present testimony. Mr. Childers, who was present at the Jan. 13 meeting, was interviewed during the I.R.S. investigation.

His statement, which was released last Friday, reveals that Mr. Childers and Mr. Schaeffer of the committee had telephone conversations on Jan. 17 and 18 with Mr. Robert Bloom, then acting Comptroller of the Currency, during which the committee investigators asked Mr. Bloom "about the campaign and personal overdrafts of Mr. Lance and his family."

Mr. Bloom indicated to them that overdrafts of $100,000 to $200,000 would be "in the ballpark." In those conversations Mr. Bloom also advised the Senate investigators that "the campaign overdrafts were referred to the Department of Justice and Justice declined prosecution."

Finally, Mr. Bloom told the Senate investigators "that personal overdrafts of the Lance, David, and Chance families had been handled internally and administratively, and had been paid with interest."

Mr. Schaeffer's testimony in connection with the Internal Revenue Service investigation again confirms that Senate investigators of this committee were fully cognizant at the time of my confirmation hearing of "possible problems involving overdrafts by Mr. Lance and his family at the Calhoun National Bank and possible campaign violations."

Mr. Schaeffer testified that On Jan. 17, 1977, he made a report about these matters to Senators Percy and Ribicoff. That Senators Percy and Ribicoff later professed lack of knowledge as to this information is thus, to say the least somewhat puzzling.

The New York Times on Sunday, Jan. 16, 1977, the day before my hearing, published a story entitled "Lance Ran Bank Criticized in 1974 in Federal Study."

The article discussed the entire question of overdrafts as well as the Federal investigation into campaign law violations. With respect to the latter issue, the article comments on the timing of the decision to close the case one day before my nomination.

Further, it should be noted that the record of this committee reflects that the very question posed to me at my confirmation hearing by the chairman of this committee, Senator Ribicoff, concerned the Department of Justice investigation of my 1974 campaign committee and the overdrafts honored by the Calhoun National Bank.

The issue of overdrafts by members of my family and others was also discussed at the hearings. Those who claim that I was withholding information from this committee at my confirmation hearings have, under the most charitable interpretation, ignorec the information that was made readily available.

Admittedly, discussions I had in mid-January with the Senate investigators regarding the matters which have now taken on such importance did not include a microscopic review of my affairs. The failure to review additional financial data was not due to any hesitation on my part to disclose anything of interest to the committee.

I apprised this committee in some detail of my past financial and personal background and answered fully and accurately all questions that any senator or staff member asked.

[Personal Loans and Correspondent Accounts]

At the time of my confirmation hearings, I submitted a financial statement which set forth various personal loans I had obtained. A great controversy has since arisen regarding my "pattern of borrowing" from certain banks in which the National Bank of Georgia and Calhoun First National Bank had correspondent accounts.

It has been alleged that I maintained certain correspondent accounts as compensating balances to help me secure personal loans. It is said that I used depositors' money in the banks of which I was an officer for my own personal benefit in order to obtain more favorable loans from the correspondent banks. There is no truth to this charge.

Bank Circular No. 31...states that the use of compensating balances would be a violation of law "where the facts demonstrate a clear detriment to the bank and a concomitant benefit to its officers."

The Comptroller has investigated three instances involving me where such violations were alleged to have existed. They involved loans from the First National Bank of Chicago, Manufacturers Hanover Trust Company and the Fulton National Bank.

In no instance was there a finding that the terms of my loans were more favorable because the lending institution was a correspondent bank. In all cases it was determined that the interest rate that had been charged on the loan was at least the market rate.

Further, the Comptroller's report reveals that in all instances the banks with which I was associated received services for the deposit which fully justified the correspondent relationship. In other words, neither side of the equation outlined by the Comptroller in Banking Circular No. 31 was found to exist.

[Backdated Checks Allegation]

Given the politically charged atmosphere in hearings of this kind, I suppose it is natural to expect that the progress of the hearing would be accompanied by an occasional savage charge. Yet that expectation does not fully prepare one to confront the reality of the accusation when it is carried by the national press. So I learned last Friday.

Last Friday this committee heard testimony about Exhibit 4 of Section B of the Comptroller's report of Sept. 7, 1977, which contains an analysis of a series of my checking transactions for the period Dec. 31, 1976 to Jan. 15, 1977. The exhibit was included by the Comptroller in his description of the banking arrangement between the Calhoun First National Bank and the National Bank of Georgia through which deposits in my account in the latter bank would be used to cover checks drawn on the Calhoun Bank that might otherwise cause an overdraft.

In the course of his examination of Mr. [John G.] Heimann about this material, Senator Percy made the charge that the documents suggested that Bert Lance might have committed tax fraud. Not surprisingly, the wire services and newspapers immediately circulated the accusation.

The Associated Press carried the story that evening that "Percy suggested that Lance may have backdated the checks to allow him to take income tax deductions for 1976."

The New York Times on Saturday repeated the charge: "Percy Suggests That Lance Sought an Improper '76 Tax Deduction—Senator Hints 3 Checks Were Backdated." I deeply regret that Senator Percy saw fit to act in this regrettable manner in making a charge that has no merit....

The exhibit at issue contained copies of five checks numbered 917 through 921 and payable in varying amounts. Senator Percy notes that the checks numbered 918 through 921 were dated prior to the checks numbered 917 and 918. With this so-called "evidence," Senator Percy suggested to the American people that I had backdated checks to take illegal tax deductions. The facts disprove such a charge.

[Lance Explanation]

The checks numbered 919 through 921 were written on Dec. 31, 1976, as indicated on the checks themselves. No backdating of the checks occurred. The explanation why checks numbered 919 through 921 were dated prior to checks containing the serial numbers 917 and 918 is a simple one.

The checks numbered 917 and 918 had been removed from the checkbook while blank and kept by me for possible use in my briefcase. I frequently tear out checks from the checkbook in this manner so that I will have checks with me when I need them.

On Dec. 31, 1976, I used the checks in the checkbook, numbered 919 through 921, and wrote the checks referred to in the Comptroller's report. A week later I used the two checks numbered 917 and 918 which I had removed from the checkbook to draw checks payable to Citizens and Southern Bank.

Senator Percy noted in support of his accusation that on Dec. 31, 1976, my personal checking account at the National Bank of Georgia had a closing balance of $26,731.99.

The question is then asked: If the dates on the checks did in fact reflect the day they were written, how could I be certain I would have funds sufficient to cover checks totaling some $195,000?

He intended that the clear implication of the question would be that the checks were backdated so that I could take illegal income tax deductions for 1976.

[Income Tax Evasion Charge]

Again, the answer to Senator Percy's question is a simple one. Had he investigated before publicizing the charge, he would have learned the following:

On Dec. 30, 1976 I sold three blocks of stock for a total of $250,000. I was paid by check but the funds were not actually deposited in my account until after New Year's Day.

Accordingly, I held the checks I had written on Dec. 31, 1976 until I had deposited adequate funds to cover them. Even at the time the three checks were written, however, I had funds in my possession in excess of their face amount. As a footnote, let me add that I reported the gain on the sale of the stock as income on my 1976 return.

I find some irony in the fact that such importance was placed on the dates contained on my checks. These dates had no bearing on income tax deductions that were taken by me for 1976.

As is true of many persons today, I do not personally prepare my own tax returns. In determining interest deductions to which I am entitled, however, my accountant makes no reference to dates contained on checks I have written.

Instead, interest deductions claimed by me are based on information provided by the bank, which sends a written statement as the amount of principal and interest paid during the year in question.

Interest deductions taken by me in 1976 for interest paid to National City Bank mentioned in Exhibit 4 as the payee of checks 920 and 921 totaled $8,985.57. That figure was obtained from the bank and was based on seven interest payments I made to the National City Bank during 1976, the last of which was made on the 10th of November.

Interest paid to the Chemical Bank (the payee mentioned on check 919) which was deducted on my 1976 tax return, totaled $7,160.96. Again the figure was provided by the bank and was based on two interest payments I made, one in July 1976 and the other in November 1976.

None of the checks in question, i.e., Nos. 919-921, was included in calculating any interest expense for my 1976 tax return.

This is another charge by Senator Percy which is unfounded. The knowledge of my innocence, however, does little to lessen the shock and anguish caused me and my family when the charge is published all over the country. Here again is an instance in which the Senator failed to ascertain the facts before making accusations that challenged my honesty and impugned my integrity.

[Overdrafts]

Much criticism has been directed at me by certain members of this committee regarding the large overdrafts in checking accounts maintained at the Calhoun First National Bank by me and my family. It has been said that this practice was an unsound banking practice, that its adoption constituted an abuse of my position at the bank, and that it was engaged in to the detriment of other depositors and stockholders.

Reports of my overdrafts at the bank have led to the further charge that I considered the Calhoun Bank to be a "playpen"—to be used as I pleased.

The overdraft policy of a bank simply involves the decision to extend credit to depositors, and the policy varies from bank to bank. Some banks have special overdraft services which they advertise in an effort to attract customers.

Though the record has become confused with respect to this issue, there is nothing illegal about overdrafts. Nothing in the banking laws prohibits their use. The issue as to overdrafts thus becomes a question of degree—a subjective determination.

The overdrafts which occurred at the Calhoun Bank are a matter of record. However, I do find it curious that the news stories have grouped all overdrafts incurred by me, by my family, and by relatives and in-laws and imply that I personally had overdrafts of $450,000. This is a gross distortion of the truth.

The Calhoun First National Bank for years followed a liberal policy with respect to overdrafts. I make no apology for this practice. It was believed by the bank's management that a liberal overdraft policy was a valuable tool for the bank to use in attracting and retaining customers.

Despite the characterization of the bank as my "personal toy," members of the Lance family were not accorded special favors regarding overdrafts. The liberal overdraft policy of the bank was available to all depositors.

It was not uncommon for many depositors in the bank, including those who held no position as an officer or member of the board, to sustain large overdrafts in their checking accounts.

In a small rural bank such as Calhoun, this was an acceptable practice because the bank personnel knew all the customers at the bank and could readily determine whether a given check ultimately would be covered.

Considerations such as earnings lost were simply not as important as rendering this service to our customers.

The financial history of the bank reflects the fact that our overdraft policy was not in fact unsafe or unsound. The following information confirms this view:

[Bank Overdraft Record]

● In 1972, losses charged off on overdrafts totaled only $3,999—for all accounts combined. This compared to service charge income on deposit accounts totaling $102,562.

● In 1973, losses charged off on overdrafts totaled only $5,570—for all accounts combined. This compared to service charge income on deposit accounts totaling $123,399.

● In 1974, losses charged off on overdrafts totaled only $6,409—for all accounts combined. This compared to service charge income on deposit accounts totaling $249,113.

● In 1975, losses charged off on overdrafts totaled only $7,307—for all accounts combined. This compared to service charge income on deposit accounts totaling $185,000.

● In 1976, losses charged off on overdrafts totaled only $5,757—for all accounts combined. This compared to service charge income on deposit accounts totaling $180,000.

I would add that during that period total deposits averaged more than $47 million.

[Overdrafts Paid in Full]

It is also to be emphasized that all overdrafts attributable to me, my family or any of my relatives which have been widely reported in the press were paid in full. Not one penny was ever charged off as a loss.

I believe our loss experience proved that our overdrafts were not excessive or unusual. Federal bank examiners, nevertheless, criticized the bank's overdraft policy in their reports of examination for the years 1972, 1973 and 1975. It is noted that criticism of this type is not unusual in reports of Federal bank examiners.

However, the 1972 report of examination for Calhoun criticized not only overdrafts of directors and officers but also noted that the bank overdraft policies for all customers were extremely lenient. The report further indicates that no charge for overdrafts was generally imposed on any bank customer.

The report of examination for 1973 again noted that the overdraft policy of the bank was lenient for all customers.

The 1974 report of examination did not criticize the bank for its overdrafts. In June of that year the bank adopted a policy to charge interest at 1½ per cent over prime on all accounts which became overdrawn.

Despite the 1974 modification of the bank's overdraft policy, the examiners decided in April 1975 that the bank's liberal policy toward overdrawn. ...I do not mean to avoid responsibility for what occurred at the bank but merely to make all circumstances known to the committee.

The period when the liberal overdraft policy of the bank became, in the view of the examiners, excessive, was a time when I was not working on a daily basis at the bank.

I have explained that I headed the State Highway Department from 1971 to 1973 and then from October 1973 to December 1974, I was campaigning for the gubernatorial race. At the time of the 1975 examination report I had joined the National Bank of Georgia.

I thus did not supervise the daily status of accounts which were overdrawn. ...I do not mean to avoid responsibility for what occurred at the bank but merely to make all circumstances known to the committee.

Following the 1975 report of examination in which bank management was criticized for overdrafts and other policies, the board of directors voluntarily signed an agreement with the Office of the Comptroller of the Currency to undertake various changes in bank operations.

This was not a "cease and desist" order as it has erroneously been called in these hearings. Rather, it was a voluntary agreement by the bank to change certain practices which the Comptroller's office had criticized.

What was the result? Did the overdrafts continue unabated or did the bank management make a serious effort to stop excessive overdrafts? Here is what the April 5, 1976 annual report of examination states:

"Overdraft abuses which were so prevalent during the previous examination and for years before, involving certain officers and directors and members of their families, have ceased completely."

[Personal Overdraft Record]

Let us now turn to the subject of my personal overdrafts. It has been charged that overdrafts I had in my personal accounts constituted a loan to an officer of the bank in excess of $5,000 and was therefore prohibited under Section 375 (a).

Section 375 (a) is, of course, a civil statute. Mr. Heimann last week is reported to have said that my personal overdrafts constituted a "serious violation."

The reports of examination which are written by the Comptroller's office list violations of Section 375 (a). What does a review of the reports of examination for the Calhoun Bank for the years 1972-76 indicate in this regard? The reports by Comptroller's office at no time cite me as having violated Section 375 (a).

The Comptroller's report notes various overdrafts in my personal checking account in 1972. Despite press stories that my personal overdrafts amounted to $450,000, the highest overdraft reported during that period was $8,799.

Further, what the report fails to mention is that during that same period of time, I always had funds on deposit in the bank in other accounts—available as an offset—which would exceed the overdrafts. The monthly average of all funds I had on deposit for the year was more than $44,080, not counting any funds of my wife or any of her relatives.

The Comptroller's report also details personal overdrafts I incurred in 1973, with a high of $16,845. What the report does not point out is that at all times during 1973 I had funds on deposit in all accounts with the bank which would exceed any overdraft. My monthly average of all funds on deposit for the year was more than $69,000.

The Comptroller's report sets forth my personal overdrafts for 1974. Again, during the first half of 1974, I had at all times funds on deposit in other accounts sufficient to cover any overdrafts.

As I have noted, in June 1974 the bank adopted the policy of charging interest on overdrafts at the rate of 1½ over prime. Overdrafts incurred by me from that time forward were repaid with interest.

In the last half of 1974 and in 1975, I had overdrafts on occasion. The highest amount I was overdrawn in those years was $26,272 in 1974 and $24,147 in 1975. All such overdrafts were repaid in full, with interest.

The Comptroller has suggested to the committee that a liberal overdraft policy may constitute an unsafe and unsound banking practice. There is concern that a liberal overdraft policy can result in significant loss to the bank.

I have recounted the overdraft loss experience at the Calhoun First National Bank. It was negligible—both in absolute terms and in comparison to income earned on deposit accounts. And, as you are well aware, the bank, while I was chairman of the board, was brought into full compliance with the overdraft policy guidelines proposed by the Comptroller.

[Improper Influence Allegation]

Circumstances surrounding the removal of the agreement between the Calhoun First National Bank and the Comptroller of the Currency as well as the decision by the U.S. Attorney's office in Atlanta to terminate an investigation into possible violations of law arising out of the financing of my 1974 gubernatorial campaign have given rise to charges in the press that I used my relationship with President Carter to exert improper influences on these decisions.

No evidence is offered to support the charge. Apparently there are those who feel that the mere making of an accusation is sufficient to shift the burden to the accused to disprove it. The effort to convict me on the charge of undue influence is based on mere circumstances and ignores uncontroverted sworn testimony by those involved who state that I had nothing to do with either decision.

I will first address the issue with respect to the removal of the agreement by the Comptroller's Office. The Calhoun First National Bank on Dec. 2, 1975 entered into an agreement with the Comptroller of the Currency in which the bank agreed to take certain steps to remedy practices of the bank which had been criticized in examination reports of the Comptroller's office.

[OCC-Calhoun Agreement]

The agreement was not a "cease and desist order" as has been reported in the press. Rather it was a voluntary agreement between the directors of the bank and the Comptroller of the Currency which was undertaken in an effort to improve the bank operations and protect the interests of depositors, customers and shareholders of the bank.

The terms of the agreement provided that the bank was to raise additional capital, hire a new senior lending officer to supplement the existing staff, prohibit overdrafts in excess of 30 days or any overdrafts by me and certain other persons, prohibit participation in any manner in any campaign for political office that might be conducted, and various other requirements.

It is to be noted that agreements of this type between the Comptroller's office and national banks were not unusual during that period in which we were going through a recession.

Following the signing of the agreement, the bank immediately undertook to comply with all its provisions. The April 1976 report of examination of the Office of the Comptroller notes the improvement in the bank's operation, including the fact that all overdrafts had ceased. Management continued to comply meticulously with the provisions of the agreement throughout the year and filed progress reports with the Comptroller's office in accordance with its terms.

This affirmative action by the bank soon resulted in substantial compliance with the...agreement. The only remaining provision...was the obligation of filing monthly reports with the Comptroller's office. Accordingly, the agreement became of little concern to me.

In September 1975, Donald Tarleton was assigned to Atlanta as the regional administrator of the Office of the Comptroller. I had occasion to meet Mr. Tarleton in the fall of 1975 as a result of his duties as regional administrator. We thereafter maintained a business relationship.

[Meeting with Tarleton]

On Nov. 22, 1976 I made a courtesy call to Mr. Tarleton's office to advise him that I had been asked by President Carter to serve in the Administration and would be leaving the National Bank of Georgia.

During the course of that meeting we briefly mentioned the greatly improved condition of the Calhoun First National Bank and in that context made passing reference to the agreement which had been entered into between the Comptroller's office and the Calhoun First National Bank.

Mention of the agreement was made simply as a reference in discussing in a general way the improvements that had taken place at the bank.

I am aware that Mr. Tarleton has testified during the recent Internal Revenue Service investigation that he did not recall ever discussing anything relating to Calhoun Bank.

It is understandable that he might not remember this since our discussion was both general and brief and only concerned in a general way the significant progress the bank had made during the past year.

I did not ask or tell Mr. Tarleton to remove the agreement between the Calhoun First National Bank and the Office of the Comptroller nor did I suggest or imply in any way that the agreement should be rescinded. Mr. Tarleton's sworn testimony confirms this fact. He stated that "Lance did not on that or any other date request release of the Calhoun agreement."

[Lance Comments on Tarleton's Testimony]

The testimony that has been taken regarding this matter establishes that in September 1976, prior to the election, Mr. Tarleton in a telephone conversation with First Deputy Comptroller of the Currency H. Joe Selby said that they discussed progress of the Calhoun Bank and that "both felt the agreement had served its purpose."

Mr. Tarleton states that a visitation at the bank had been scheduled to take place in October 1976, and he and Mr. Selby decided to await the results of that examination in making a determination whether to remove the agreement.

Following review of the visitation report which was received by Mr. Tarleton on Nov. 2, 1976, and which indicated marked improvement by the bank in areas which had been criticized by examiners, Mr. Tarleton decided the agreement should be removed. Mr. Selby's affidavit confirms Mr. Tarleton's recollection as to these events.

Since the bank had already complied with its terms, the agreement was essentially of no consequence to me. As I noted, the only matter of concern was the paperwork involved in filing monthly progress reports by the bank to the Comptroller's office.

I find it curious that in all the discussion that has ensued regarding the removal of this agreement there has been no mention of the fact that the reporting requirement was not lifted.

Mr. Tarleton's letter of Nov. 22, 1976 continued the requirement that the bank forward monthly progress reports to the Comptroller's office to enable it to monitor future progress.

In other words, in my opinion, the only condition of any consequence in the agreement as of Nov. 22, 1976 remained after the agreement was rescinded. The sworn testimony of the persons involved is uncontroverted that at no time did I request or suggest to Mr. Tarleton that the agreement between the Comptroller's office and the National Bank of Georgia be rescinded.

[Gubernatorial Campaign Finance Practices]

Similar charges of improper influence have been made in connection with the U.S. Attorney's termination of an investigation of the questions of finances in my 1974 gubernatorial race. Once again the false impression has been created that something sinister was involved in the closing of that case.

I discussed the subject of the termination of that investigation with this committee at the time of my confirmation. I am prepared to repeat for the record the facts of this matter.

Following my unsuccessful campaign for Governor in 1974, I was the subject of a private investigation conducted by the Office of the Comptroller of the Currency which was checking to ascertain whether there had been any violation of law in the financing of my campaign. The investigation focused on two accounts maintained by my campaign committee at the Calhoun First National Bank. The Comptroller's office was seeking to determine whether there had been illegal contributions to the campaign made by the bank.

I gave a deposition on this matter in August 1975. I heard nothing further from the Comptroller for over a year and assumed the case had been closed.

In early December 1976 my attorney, Judge Sidney Smith of Atlanta, had several telephone conversations with then Acting Comptroller Robert Bloom concerning the release of confidential information contained in the agreement between the Calhoun First National Bank and the Comptroller's office.

It is my understanding that during the course of those conversations, Judge Smith learned that the investigation of the accounts maintained by my campaign committee at the Calhoun Bank had been referred to the Department of Justice for a determination whether any legal violations had occurred. The referral had been made because the Comptroller's office did not have jurisdiction to make a determination regarding this type of matter.

Mr. Bloom advised Judge Smith that the Justice Department in Washington had closed the case because they had determined that no violation had occurred. The file had then been sent in March 1976 to the U.S. Attorney in Atlanta, Ga., for further determination by that office whether there was any violation of law that warranted prosecution.

Judge Smith advised me of this matter in December. To the best of my knowledge, that was the first time that I learned about this particular investigation.

Judge Smith offered to call the U.S. Attorney in Atlanta and inquire as to the status of the case. It is my understanding that Judge Smith talked with John Stokes, who was in charge of the office and who said that he would check on the matter and report back.

Mr. Stokes concluded that no prosecution was appropriate and thereafter he advised Judge Smith that the investigation had been terminated.

I am aware of no testimony that in any way links me with Mr. Stokes' decision to close this case. I did not talk to Mr. Stokes. I did not ask that the investigation be terminated, nor was such a request made on my behalf by Judge Smith. Mr. Stokes has stated that he had concluded there was no merit to the case and that his decision was supported by Justice Department officials in Washington.

[Double Pledge of Collateral Charge]

Another issue which has been raised involves an accusation that I "pledged the same collateral twice for separate loans" at two different lending institutions. The impression created in the press is that I pledged stock as security for a loan from Manufacturers Hanover Trust, then somehow obtained the stock back from that bank and pledged it again for a loan from the Chemical Bank. The charge is not true.

When I obtained a loan in 1975 from Manufacturers Hanover Trust Company in the amount of $2,625,000, it was based upon the understanding that the bank would lend me 90 per cent of the purchase price for 148,118 shares of stock of the National Bank of Georgia. The bank noted that it was customary for them to lend 90 per cent of book value in these circumstances. The book value amounted to $17.74 per share.

The following computation reflects the transaction: 148,118 shares of N.B.G. stock at $17.74 per share totals $2,627,613.30. Ninety per cent of that amount, or $2,364,851, was the collateral valuation at the time the loan was made.

A collateral shortfall of $260,148.10 thus remained. To cover that shortfall, I pledged 8,375 shares of Calhoun First National Bank stock. I also pledged as collateral certain life insurance policies. Since the book value of Calhoun would not have reflected the stock's true worth as collateral, the bank and I agreed to value the stock at its market rate measured as of the date of its last sale. The stock's market value at the time was approximately $30 per share for a collateral valuation of $259,625.

I signed a secured note for the loan which was held by the bank. No written loan agreement was executed. The bank held total collateral equal at least to the value of the loan.

In December 1975, I received a stock dividend of 14,657 shares of stock from the National Bank of Georgia. I obtained a loan from Chemical Bank in February 1976 and pledged as collateral the 14,657 National Bank of Georgia shares I had received. At the time this loan was obtained, the loan from Manufacturers Hanover Trust remained fully collateralized.

[Lance Explanation of Collateral Pledge]

In June 1976, I began to receive requests from Manufacturers Hanover Trust for additional collateral. ...[T]he bank requested a pledge of the N.B.G. stock I had received as a stock dividend.

The financial reports of the National Bank of Georgia indicated that on June 30, 1976, the book value of its stock totaled $17.72. This, of course, constituted only a 2 cent difference per share from the value attributed to the stock when the loan was first obtained from Manufacturers Hanover Trust.

It is noted that this value was derived after the 10 per cent stock dividend. The dividend did not cause a material per share dilution of collateral value of the National Bank of Georgia stock. In other words, the loan from the Manufacturers Hanover Trust Company remained fully collateralized, in my opinion.

There is an explanation for the bank's request for additional collateral. The loan officers at Manufacturers Hanover Trust unilaterally wished to modify our oral agreement with respect to the valuation of the Calhoun Bank stock. They had decided that the value of this collateral should also be computed at book value.

The written memoranda and letters included as exhibits in the Comptroller's report reflect only a part of the discussions and understandings reached between the bank and me with respect to this loan. I had numerous telephone conversations with officers of the bank during which I challenged their request for additional collateral. In my opinion, the loan was as fully collateralized as it was when it was obtained a year earlier.

The matter was resolved when I refinanced the loan in January 1977 with the First National Bank of Chicago. The loan from Manufacturers Hanover Trust was then paid in full. In short, the so-called issue as to "a double pledge of stock" involved a dispute as to collateral adequacy with Manufacturers Hanover. Unfortunately, only the bank's side of that dispute was included in the Comptroller's report.

[Lance Refutes Embezzlement Allegation]

I have already mentioned the totally irresponsible charge by certain members of this committee that I was involved in an embezzlement scheme at the Calhoun First National Bank during the years 1971 through 1975. To complete the record, I feel it appropriate to add my personal statement regarding this matter.

I met Billy Lee Campbell when I was president of the Calhoun First National Bank. He joined the bank at my request in April 1968. He had been engaged in the tractor business in Calhoun for a few years and possessed a good reputation among the farmers of the area. We were interested in developing new approaches in the area of agricultural development and business development at the bank. We felt it was important to have someone who would specialize in that particular area.

In January 1969, Bill Campbell became a loan officer of the bank. He remained with the bank in that capacity until he was discharged in 1975.

In addition to his work at the bank, Campbell established his own cattle operation. He devoted great time and effort to this venture in an effort to make it profitable. As a result of poor market conditions in 1974, however, Campbell suffered severe cash flow problems.

[Billy Lee Campbell Loan]

In February 1975, after I had joined the National Bank of Georgia, Campbell sought a loan from me of $100,000. He needed the cash to invest in his cattle operation, and he said he intended to pay the loan out of the proceeds of a government-guaranteed disaster loan for which he had made application.

In July 1975, Campbell again advised me that he was having cash flow problems and asked if the National Bank of Georgia would be willing to increase his loan. In mid-July, the bank lent him an additional $150,000 on a secured basis. This was to be a temporary loan which would be refinanced by the loan from the Government. I might add, then as now, that these Government-guaranteed loans were extremely hard to finalize.

It is to be noted that during the time in which Mr. Campbell engaged in his unlawful conduct, I was not present at the bank on a daily basis. From December 1970-March 1973, I worked in the State Highway Department of Georgia. Then in October 1973 I began my campaign for Governor of Georgia, to which I devoted the majority of my time until December 1974.

Following the campaign in 1974, I joined the National Bank of Georgia in January 1975 as president. Although I remained chairman of the Calhoun First National Bank, my daily activities required me to be present at the National Bank of Georgia.

[Lance Investigates Campbell's Performance]

In the last week of July 1975, while I was working at the National Bank of Georgia, I received a telephone call from Atkins Henderson, the president of the Calhoun First National Bank. Mr. Henderson said he was concerned about the performance of Mr. Campbell.

Apparently Mr. Campbell had not consulted with Mr. Henderson about making certain loans as required by bank procedures. I said to Mr.

Henderson that I would come down and review Mr. Campbell's performance. I studied the loan files carefully and detected what appeared to be certain imprudent loans that he had made.

At this time, I still did not suspect that Mr. Campbell had engaged in any illegal activity, but merely thought he had exercised poor judgment. Both Mr. Henderson and I talked to Mr. Campbell about the loans he had made and told him that certain borrowers should be asked to meet with Mr. Henderson in the bank the next morning to discuss their lines of credit.

The next day Mr. Campbell did not arrange for Mr. Henderson to see the people I had mentioned. Mr. Henderson called me again at the National Bank of Georgia and advised me of these developments.

I started calling some of the people to whom Mr. Campbell had made loans in order to get a better feel for the situation. I continued my investigation and worked late into the night reviewing files and telephoning persons to whom Mr. Campbell indicated he had made loans.

It became increasingly apparent after talking with various borrowers and studying the files that something improper had occurred. I concluded that Mr. Campbell had been embezzling funds from the bank.

I decided to confront Mr. Campbell with my accusation. He did not come to work the next day, and in the afternoon I went to his house together with Mr. Henderson and J. Beverley Langford, a director of the bank. I spoke with Mr. Campbell and told him of my findings.

I informed him that I was going to call the proper authorities and did so, including the regional administrator, the Federal Bureau of Investigation and the agent for the bonding company.

Following an investigation of this matter by the authorities, Mr. Campbell was arrested and charged with embezzlement, to which he entered a plea of guilty. Mr. Campbell's conviction was delayed due to the fact that he suffered from various mental disorders and had to be hospitalized for psychiatric examination for several months.

With the single exception of the man convicted of the crime, all persons connected with this case, including the U.S. Attorney who prosecuted it, Mr. Campbell's attorney, and the attorney for the bonding firm, Hartford Accident and Indemnity Company, have unanimously concluded that Mr. Campbell alone had embezzled the funds of the bank.

[Lance's 1974 Campaign Accounts]

A charge which received attention at the time of my confirmation hearing in January has again been revived during these hearings. This matter involves allegations of illegality surrounding the finances for my 1974 gubernatorial campaign.

While the members of this committee are hardly ignorant of this matter—the very first question posed to me by Senator Ribicoff at my confirmation hearing involved the subject—I will briefly provide some factual background that I trust will be helpful.

In May 1973, I made a decision to enter the primary race for the Democratic nomination for Governor of Georgia. From that time until August of 1974 I was actively engaged in campaigning in my efforts to seek that office. A campaign committee was established and accounts were opened at the Calhoun First National Bank for the payment of expenses which would be incurred.

On Oct. 13, 1973 I wrote a letter to the bank enclosing a check in the amount of $5,000 as a credit to the campaign committee account. I further asked the bank to calculate any amounts due if there were insufficient funds to cover expenses and to notify me regarding payment.

During the campaign, expense vouchers were sent directly to the bank. The bank would pay them and then bill the campaign committee account for reimbursements at the beginning of the following month. On several occasions the campaign committee issued checks to reimburse the bank when the account did not have sufficient funds to cover the checks.

I was not personally involved in these transactions as I was actively engaged in campaigning. In addition, on one occasion in August 1974 the bank sent an expense voucher to the committee for $4,779.93 but was not reimbursed.

The bank entered the amount on its ledger as an account receivable from the campaign committee.

Following the termination of the campaign, I paid all expenses that were outstanding plus interest.

[Justice Department Ruling]

During an examination of the bank in April 1975 the Comptroller's office reviewed the activities of the campaign committee and commenced an investigation to determine whether the bank's activity had constituted illegal contributions to a political campaign. I gave a deposition to the Comptroller's office in late August 1975 and heard nothing further about the matter. I assumed the case had been closed.

In December 1976 I was advised by Judge Sidney Smith following a telephone conversation he had had with Robert Bloom, then acting Comptroller of the Currency, that the Comptroller's office had made a routine referral of this matter to the Department of Justice on December 24, 1975 to check on possible violations.

The Department of Justice determined that no prosecution was warranted. In March 1976 the department forwarded the entire file to the U.S. Attorney in Atlanta, Ga., to determine whether other violations of law were present. On Dec. 2, 1976 the case was closed.

The following factors...made prosecution of the case inappropriate:

(1) Separate accurate records of campaign expenses were maintained by the bank at all times. No attempt was made to hide, disguise, or destroy relevant records.

(2) Full disclosure was made as to the extent bank employees would or could participate in the political campaign, both in minutes of the board meeting and in a memorandum to employees.

(3) No loss was suffered by the bank. All amounts were repaid.

(4) The bank had been given my signed, unlimited guarantee to cover any.

(5) I have a savings certificate pledged at the bank in the amount of $110,000.

As I testified previously, I had absolutely no participation in the decision by the U.S. Attorney's office to close this case.

[Use of Bank's Airplane]

Questions with respect to my use of bank-owned airplanes have received much attention in the press. Allegations have been made that airplanes owned by the National Bank of Georgia were improperly used by me for personal rather than business purposes.

The Office of the Comptroller conducted an investigation into this matter and...it is under review by the Department of Justice.

While I was president of the Calhoun First National Bank, it leased a Piper Seneca airplane from a fixed based operator in Calhoun, Ga. Thereafter, when I began campaigning in the Democratic primary in 1973, I leased the airplane from the bank and paid rent on a monthly basis.

In early 1974, Lancelot & Company, a partnership consisting of my wife and me, bought a Beechcraft Queen Air airplane. We used the plane in 1974 during the remainder of my campaign. I paid all expenses incurred in connection with the use of the plane. Moreover, I continued to pay the bank a rental fee for the Piper airplane although, in fact, I did not use it.

In 1975, I was approached by the National Bank of Georgia and asked to join it as president and chief operating officer. I had various other employment possibilities at the time but was intrigued by the bank's offer because I felt that a real opportunity existed to expand greatly the bank's market area and establish it as a major financial institution in Atlanta.

My plans for the bank included a program to develop a network of correspondent banking relationships, establish a national account department, conduct an aggressive agribusiness program and become involved in international banking.

I discussed my expansion program with the executive committee of the bank, which made me an offer of employment. It was clear that to accomplish these objectives, extensive travel on a flexible basis would be necessary. Accordingly, we agreed at the time I joined the bank that it would purchase a plane for my extensive use.

I continued to own the Beechcraft Queen Air at that time. The National Bank of Georgia offered to purchase it from me and use it as a company plane. Although the propriety of this sale has been questioned in the press, the transaction was perfectly legitimate.

The purchase price was determined after having the plane appraised by two independent appraisers. The bank initially leased the plane from me and in July 1975 purchased it. Subsequently, in November 1976 the bank sold the Queen Air and purchased a Beechcraft King Air airplane.

No specific guidelines were established by the bank for the use of the plane. It was generally understood that I was to be creating a new image for the bank and would be seeking new business whenever and wherever I traveled.

While one might not be able to connect a particular plane trip to a specific piece of new business that was obtained as a result, it was understood that the achievement of the bank's growth objective would depend largely on the new image we could create for the bank. This required extensive plane travel.

I did advise the Comptroller of the bank that he was to charge me for any purely personal use of the plane and on occasion I made payments to the bank in accordance with this understanding.

There was nothing covert about my arrangement with the bank. It was understood that I would use the plane in the manner I concluded was most appropriate. The bank believed that use of the plane would generate substantial new business. The record clearly reflects that it did.

To assume that one can readily distinguish personal use of the plane from business use simply ignores the realities involved in developing new business. Such ready pigeonholing of the plane's use is impossible.

["Sloppy Banking" Practices]

In apparent recognition of the lack of evidence to support any of the more serious charges against me, certain critics take refuge in the more ambiguous allegation that I have engaged in "sloppy" banking practices. The question is asked, "How can Lance possibly run the Office of Management and Budget when he could not even manage a small bank in Georgia?" The objective facts which answer this charge are found in the financial records of the two banks with which I have been associated.

I have already testified that I became president of the Calhoun First National Bank in 1963 and I remained in that position for 10 years. In May 1974, I assumed the position of chairman of the bank which I held until my resignation in January 1977, when I joined the Administration. It is interesting to note what happened at the bank during the period of my stewardship.

Financial data of the bank reveals that total assets grew from $11.9 million in 1964 to $54.1 million by the end of 1976. Deposits which amounted to only $11 million when I became president increased dramatically to $49 million by the time I was ready to leave the bank.

Our loan portfolio expanded from only $5.9 million in 1964 to over $32 million last year. I submit that this is a record of successful and sustained growth.

Various banking practices and particularly the policy regarding overdrafts at the Calhoun First National Bank have been widely criticized in these hearings during testimony by representatives of the Office of the Comptroller. It has been said that bank management permitted unsafe and unsound banking practices to exist. That is a subject for debate. But in all the years I was at the Calhoun First National Bank, no depositor has ever lost a cent.

[Bank Performance Record]

In January 1975 I became president of the National Bank of Georgia. It is perhaps more difficult to assess my performance there since I was with the bank for only two years.

But what do the records disclose? In the two years I was at the bank as president, the total assets increased 60 per cent from $254 million to $404 million. During the same period, the bank's loan portfolio grew significantly, and this growth was supported by a 50 per cent increase in deposits and a 38 per cent increase in capital.

That the growth was controlled is indicated by the bank's maintenance of reasonable loan to deposit ratios and capital to asset ratios. And these successes came at a time of serious financial difficulty for many banks throughout the country.

It is ironic in one sense that I am defending my record as a bank manager against charges that I was inept. On three separate occasions while I was at the National Bank of Georgia, the bank was asked by the Comptroller's office to take over failing banks in the area and thus protect depositors. We did so.

I do not contend that I made no mistakes when running these banks. But to accept the assertion that I could not even manage a small country bank one must ignore the objective facts.

We have witnessed a flood of accusations about me which has dominated the front pages of our newspapers in recent weeks. My financial affairs have been examined in minute detail. Investigators have taken sworn testimony regarding my relationships with various people. Information in Government agencies which was once thought confidential has been widely publicized.

So many allegations have been made that it has been difficult to maintain a complete list of them. Thus, if I have failed to address any allegation, it is due only to the fact that it was overlooked and not for any lack of explanation on my part.

I did not ask for this fight, but now that I am in it I am fighting not only for myself but also for our system. I was a successful businessman in my home state, and I thought I had an important contribution to make by coming into Government service.

I have worked hard these past eight months in Washington, and I am proud of the job I have done in O.M.B. But is it part of our American system that a man can be drummed out of Government by a series of false charges, half-truths, misrepresentations, innuendos and the like?

I have long felt that businessmen should be willing to take positions in our Government. They can bring new ideas, new attitudes, new philosophies and, as a result, our Government can be more responsive to the views of all our people.

I speak, more in sorrow than in anger, when I suggest that it won't be any easier to get these men and women to volunteer for public service after my experience of these past weeks.

[Lance Quotes Lincoln]

Abraham Lincoln had a rare facility for putting into words what many men have felt through the ages. Let me close with this famous quotation from President Lincoln:

"If I were to try to read, much less answer, all the attacks made on me, this shop might as well be closed for any other business. I do the very best I know how, the very best I can; and I mean to keep doing so until the end. If the end brings me out all right, what is said against me won't amount to anything. If the end brings me out wrong, 10 angels swearing I was right would make no difference."

EXCERPTS FROM SENATE COMMITTEE INQUIRY

Q. [ABRAHAM RIBICOFF (D Conn.)]. Mr. Lance, I'm very troubled by a number of statements in your presentation this morning which failed to give us the full picture. For example, on page 25 of your statement you say that at all times during the first half of 1974, you had sufficient funds on deposit in other accounts to cover any overdrafts.

However, the Comptroller has provided information to the committee which indicates that after June of 1974, overdrafts by you, your wife and your campaign consistently exceeded amounts on deposit in other accounts through December 1974. According to the Comptroller, overdrafts exceeded deposits by $55,108 in July 1974, by $25,015 during August 1974, by $100,844 during September 1974, by $185,988 during October 1974, by $189,733 during November 1974, by $137,939 during December 1974. Is this correct?

[LANCE]. Mr. Chairman, what I said in my statement was, that up until the first half of 1974, that I had sufficient funds in my accounts to cover any overdrawn situation in any other account. I, being Bert Lance. Now, in the second half of 1974, it was obvious when you took the campaign overdraft, that that exceeded at times the balances that were in all other accounts.

Q. Well then, in other words, the impression that we get from your statement, which was very carefully drafted, that's for the first half of '74, but during the second half of '74 the accounts were very, very heavily overdrafted and there were no sufficient funds in any other accounts to cover. Isn't that correct?

L. No sir, I don't think that is correct per se when you consider the fact that there was $110,000 in savings certificate that was there that had been pledged to the bank to cover any campaign overdraft. And what I said in my statement, Mr. Chairman, was, in the last half of 1974 and in 1975, I, Bert Lance, had overdrafts on occasion. The highest amount I was overdrawn, in those years, was $26,272 in 1974 and $24,147 in 1975. Now, what I had said further in my statement was that the charge has turned into an allegation that I was personally overdrawn $450,000. And my comment in my statement relates to my personal account.

[Personal and Political Account Overdrafts]

Q. Well let me, will someone give Mr. Lance a copy of the statement from the Comptroller of the Currency.

Would you look at that? And may I note that reading from the record, Mr. Heimann said, I believe to Mr. [Jim] Sasser [D Tenn.], 'I also, I also, just so there is no confusion it combines all related overdrafts. This includes political overdrafts and the personal overdrafts. Senator Sasser, 'Well does this also include the $100,000 certificate of deposit?' 'Yes it does. As a net offset.' And the Comptroller of the Currency, who has made a combined totaling of all your assets and accounts, including, and he itemizes that, the $100,000 certificate of deposit, indicates that you had these consistently high overdrafts during the second half of 1974. Do you want to look at that statement and tell me whether the Comptroller of the Currency is right or wrong?

L. Mr. Chairman, in the overdraft report exhibit of the Comptroller of the Currency, on the Bert Lance account, the overdraft of the high was $26,272 in November of 1974 and that's what I said in my statement.

Q. Well, you and I read the Comptroller of the Currency absolutely opposite. I am talking about all accounts. Yours, your wife's and the campaign.

L. Yes sir, Mr. Chairman, again. In response to your question, my statement was referring to the personal overdrafts that I had in late 1974 and 1975. That's what my statement said. You obviously are referring to a combined total that appears outside the Comptroller's report as it related to the campaign overdraft as well.

Q. Some of the most disturbing matters that have come out during this entire affair concern overdrafts to you, to your wife, to your relatives and to your campaign for Governor of Georgia in 1974. Now let me ask you, were there anyone else beside Mr. Lance, Mrs. Lance and the Lance relatives who had any overdrafts out of the Calhoun bank in the magnitude of these overdrafts?

L. There were overdrafts to customers for good and sufficient reasons as they related to the business of the bank, that I can't respond to, as to the amount of any high overdraft, or any low overdraft during that period of time from memory. We have a lot of corporate customers that there may well have significant and large overdrafts involved. There's no way I can respond to that question, as to the degree.

Q. [JACOB K. JAVITS (R N.Y.)]. Did you feel as principal executive officer of the Calhoun National Bank that it was proper for a bank to pay campaign bills, whether it was paid as a loan or overdrafts or anything else—the mere appearance to a depositor of a campaign bill going to a bank and being paid by it—did that trouble you?

L. The intent was very clear throughout—that there would be cases where it would be hard to distinguish what expenses were involved in the normal course of business for the bank and what might be related to a campaign expense. And that was the reason that that was handled that way and it was the intent of me; it was the intent of those who were involved in the campaign committee; it was the intent of those who were involved as directors of the bank that there not be any question about that. And that was the way that it was handled. As I said in my statement, very careful records were kept about those expenses.

Q. If you had this to do again would you do it the same way? Do you still feel that there was nothing concerning in terms of ethics about having a bank pay campaign bills?

L. The bank did not pay campaign bills specifically. Now I think that's where we would be engaged in a matter of semantics about who was paying what, because the campaign ultimately paid the bank, as I said there in that statement.

Now, if I would do it over again, you know the answer to that, that because of the fact that it has been looked at and scrutinized and certain things that have come about as a result of that, certainly, I would say to you that if given my druthers and given my choices I would even make sure that it was even more of arms'-length transaction than it actually was and we tried our very best under the circumstances of what my role was in the State of Georgia during that period of time and what my role still was as a banker during that period of time to make sure it was handled on that sort of a basis.

That in no way says that it was improper or unethical. It says that in the light of hindsight, in the light of retrospect, then certainly we'd take a different look at it.

[Overdraft]

Q. Let's trace this out. In the first place, there's no question about the fact that the campaign committee operated on an overdraft basis, correct?

L. There's no question about it....

Q. Beginning Aug. 9, '74, the account was in continuous overdraft status, which accumulated to $152,161.20 on Dec. 16, '74. On Dec. 16, '74 a zero balance appeared, date of last posting. Calhoun records indicate that the depositor was charged overdraft service charges beginning June '74 through December '74, which aggregated $6,230.69, collected by Calhoun on Sept. 2, '74. Rate charged by Calhoun varied from 12 per cent to 13.5 per cent.

And I'd like you to turn, if you would, in the same document to Page 376 headed BL to wit, I assume, Bert Lance, LaBelle and Campaign. Days overdraft and expenses exceeding $110,000, that being your principal contention that you had that certificate of deposit. And the list starts with June 27, 1974 at $111,000 and ends with Dec. 15, 1974 at $152,000 and all of that is long before April 1975.

Now in '75 the examiner reported—and we must assume, I certainly feel we must assume—that you knew what that report said. It said overdrafts. "It is readily apparent that the situation has become abusive especially involving members and relatives of the David Family, who represent some of the largest shareholders in the bank." And went on to say the age and size of the overdrafts is appalling, especially considering the people involved, whose every association with the bank should be on an exemplary basis.

As a matter of fact, Mr. Lance, as chief executive officer when you read that didn't you—weren't you conscious of the fact that one of the biggest overdrafters in this little bank was your own campaign committee?

L. This was in April 28, 1975, Senator.

Q. Right, right. They were criticizing the way in which your bank had operated.

L. But the campaign committee had paid its overdrafts in full. There'd been no loss to the bank. The interest had been paid on it at the rates which you read, which a small bank such as you refer to—12 per cent to 13.5 percent—are pretty high rates.

It sounds to me like I don't think that there are many loans that Calhoun had that bore that sort of interest rate during that period of time because of trying to extend credit to people who were deserving of credit at reasonable rates so that they could continue to make it through the recession of 1974 and 1975 and there's no reference in the examination report of 1975 to the campaign situation.

Q. Now, was it your understanding of President Carter's standard for his Cabinet, and Cabinet-level officials, that the standard of ethics would be what everybody's doing? The average? Or that the standard would be higher than that? Were you, when you sought to qualify before us, seeking to meet a standard of "well, everybody does it, so I do it, too?" Or were you trying to meet President Carter's standard that "my people shall be superior in terms of their ethical standards and their observance of ethics."?

L. Senator, I've always tried to conduct myself in that way, and I have 27 years of reputation as a businessman and a banker in both a small community and a large city. And I think, on balance, without exception and even with the allegations that have been raised with regard to these circumstances that I'm considered to be a man of ethics and good reputation. And I stand on that.

[Conflict of Interest]

Q. [WILLIAM V. ROTH JR. (R Del.)]. Did it seem strange, perhaps a conflict of interest, for the same law firm to have one lawyer representing the incoming Administration on ethics and another lawyer representing you on being confirmed?

L. It was not strange to me, Senator, because I was dealing with different people in the law firm and I didn't know what Mr. Moore's situation was with regard as the technical circumstance. I'm sure that attorneys, because of their high standard of ethics, that they make sure that in that sort of situation that there is no conflict and they judge for themselves in that regard. I'm sure that if they'd felt that there was a conflict that they would have said so.

Q. But it seems to me that it raises a serious question of conflict of interest to have—because there is potentially a conflict of interest between your position and being confirmed and the incoming Administration making certain that whoever comes into the Administration meets his high standard of ethics.

Q. [JAVITS]. I'd like to read to you from an affidavit which [Robert] Bloom made in respect of the F.B.I. inquiry. "On the matter of the agreement, he, Lance, said he did not have any objection to the F.B.I. seeing it but he thought that the F.B.I. report would become part of the confirmation hearing record and made public. He, Lance, was concerned about possible negative effects on the Calhoun Bank if the existence of the agreement became public record. He, Lance, preferred therefore that the enforcement agreement not be disclosed to the F.B.I. unless they insisted on seeing it." Is that a correct report of the conversation?

L. No, sir, my only concern was in response to any question about the agreement, and anything about anybody seeing it was related to other people who might be involved in it. And that was my only concern, because that was a confidential record. And some of the names that you read out in that section this morning out of the agreement, I think violate everything that stands as a result of the confidential process of the Comptroller's Office, because they're not members of my family, they're people, citizens of Calhoun, Ga., whose name is being spread across the country in relationship to something that may or may not be accurate in regard to an agreement.

And that was my concern about anything of the agreement as it related to being made a part of the public record. I didn't care what they said about me, Senator. And I didn't care what they disclosed about me.

Q. [JAVITS]. Now as to those who were named in the agreement, the fact is they were named in the agreement. We didn't put them in there. And the fact is that the agreement is a critically important element in what we're talking about. So we have no choice; neither have you, neither have they. They only question I'd like to ask you, therefore, and I'll read it again, is this paragraph—which you didn't answer yet—a correct version of the conversation that you had with Bloom and Judge Smith?

L. I answered it for you before and I'll answer it again. I had no objection at all to the F.B.I. seeing the agreement.

Q. Is this the correct version of—.

L. That's Mr. Bloom's recollection.

Q. But is it or isn't it correct? Is it or isn't it correct?

L. My recollection of the situation is that I had no objection whatsoever to anybody seeing the agreement as it related to me. And any part of that process. Anbody else, I thought they had a problem about the confidential nature of the Comptroller's Office.

Q. I take it, therefore, that you do not wish to tell me whether it is or it is not correct?

[Overdrafts and Loans]

Q. [ROTH]. In your testimony yesterday in answer to some of my questions whether your overdrafts in excess of $5,000 violated the insider loan provisions of 12 U.S.C. 375-A, I understood you to say that overdrafts were not loans. Later that afternoon, when Senator [Charles McC.] Mathias [Jr. (R Md.)] was questioning you, you said that the Lance campaign overdrafts did not violate 18 U.S.C. 610 because the statute does not prohibit loans and that overdrafts are loans. Now, Mr. Lance, I don't think you can have it both ways. Are overdrafts loans or are they not loans.

L. I don't recall exactly what my response was or what your question was in response to overdrafts and loans. I think basically my response has been that overdrafts are considered as extensions of credit.

Q. I would like to ask you the specific question: Do you consider overdrafts loans? Yes or no?

L. You have to draw a distinction between loans and overdrafts in relationship to what you're really talking about, Senator. Overdrafts are for generally a brief duration of time, even though some of these in this instance were for a longer duration of time. Loans are for a specific period of time with specific due dates and dates certain. Now I think that in every case—I'm not sure about this, but I think in ever case that I've responded that an overdraft is considered to be an extension of credit. Now a loan is also an extension of credit, so if you want to draw that analogy then you could say that the two are the same. But in trying to specifically delineate what one is and what one is not, there is that fine line between them....

[Violation of Banking Regulation]

Q. ...[I]t's been read into the record earlier, but I want to read it again, that this Regulation O says that the extension of credit, the terms extension of credit and extend credit means the making of a loan or the extending of credit...include (1) any advance by means of an overdraft, cash item or otherwise.

So the regulation is very clear, is it not, Mr. Lance, that at least as the Government, the Federal Government, the agencies responsible for administering the Federal law construe an overdraft as a loan?

L. In regard to that section, yes, sir.

Q. Now, Mr. Lance, you have agreed that there have been a number of overdrafts on your part?

L. Senator, I don't think there's any question that I've agreed about that for three days.

Q. [I]t appears perfectly clear that your practice of overdrafts does raise a serious question under Regulation O.

L. I think the way that I would have to answer that would be to go back and take my balances in the account on a day by day basis and see how many days there actually were times when the overdraft exceeded those balances. Now technically, what is an overdraft? If you've got three accounts in the bank and you're overdrawn—

Q. Mr. Lance, I don't want to interrupt. We did go over that yesterday. To my knowledge you have not yet supplied the information asked by the chairman with respect to what other balances you had. You do each time this matter comes up want to limit it to a discussion of your overdrafts. There are, of course, overdrafts of your wife; there are are the overdrafts of the campaign which you guaranteed. There is in the record, uncontroverted, the fact that the Comptroller—and again I must mention that it's Mr. Heimann, who as appointed by Carter, has said that there were not funds in excess of the overdrafts by you, by your wife and by the campaign overfund.

L. Senator, you raised your question in response to Regulation O, which relates to loans to executive officers. Now that's what I was trying to respond to in saying to you exactly what the circumstances were. Now once again the reports of the Comptroller for the year '72 through '76, in view of the overdrafts he criticized them but didn't cite me for violation of 375-A. Now let me raise one other thing in response to your question, because you say you're not talking about a violation of law. But the analogy and the example that you gave yesterday related to the running of red light, which is a violation of law.

And the situation is not the same and I think that I ought to point that out in regard to what you said yesterday. Because the overdraft is not illegal, its not a violation of the law according to what the Comptroller says and what you heard testimony from.

Yet the running of a red light is, and the situations are not the same. And I just think that if we're going to draw comparisons that we ought to be consistent in what we're trying to draw.

Q. Well, Mr. Lance, I would again like to point out that the Comptroller's report specifically states that certain of your overdrafts, and I'm quoting, amounted to extensions of credit to executive officers including Mr. Lance in excess of the amounts permissible under 12 U.S.C. 375-A. Would you agree that that is a serious conclusion to be made by the current Comptroller, Mr. Heimann?

Would you agree, the director of O.M.B., who has responsibility in the area of banks, that that is a very serious conclusion?

L. I would agree that it's a conclusion of criticism that needed to be corrected, and it was corrected. And his own report says it was corrected.

Q. I'd like to move on to an area that Senator Javits covered in considerable detail. I do have just a question or two there. But it was my understanding, in answer to a question by Senator Javits that you said the bank did not pay campaign expenses. Is that correct?

L. I said the bank did not pay campaign expenses unless it was reimbursed by the campaign committee. Now if you're speaking of strictly a technical situation where there may have a bill for printing or something of that type that related to the campaign, the bank may well have written a check for it and in turn was reimbursed by the committee. I'm not familiar with all the circumstances; I did not deal with it from the mechanical standpoint.

[Sherry Memorandum]

Q. Nevertheless, Mr. Lance, as has been brought out and we all understand and I agree that there are many problems in trying to run a campaign, that you cannot be advised of every activity every day. But the fact remains that when you ran for Governor, you were also chairman of a bank and a system was set up at your bank that is really contrary as to what the law permits.

Let me read—you're familiar with the Sherry memorandum. From October of 1973 through August 1974, the bank paid directly by a bank check certain expenses incurred during each month by the campaign committee. At the close of the month, the bank would present a statement of expenses paid to the campaign committee.

Further checks written by the committee to reimburse the bank for expenses paid for the months December 1973 through May 1974, and for July 1974, were drawn on committee accounts at the bank with insufficient balances. Therefore, Mr. Sherry concluded, the committee was reimbursing the bank with hot checks. That is from the I.R.S.—the Sherry memorandum.

The point, Mr. Lance, is that, in fact, the bank did for a period of time directly pay campaign expenses. The bank in turn did draw checks for which there were insufficient balances. So that as Mr. Sherry did indicate at one time, in fact in testimony contained in the I.R.S., raised a very serious question of violation of the law.

How can you say in your testimony on Jan. 17th that there appeared to be no cause that there was anything wrong? Now if there was nothing wrong with these overdrafts, why were they the subject matter of agreement between your bank and O.C.C.?

L. I think it's obvious that they had looked into the case, and my reference was to the fact that it had been thoroughly investigated. Now I assume that when there is a charge of wrongdoing and an allegation of wrongdoing, at some point you get to the point where it is finally dealt with. You know, how long do you keep going on judging the guilt or innocence of somebody?

Q. Let me ask you this simple question. If there was nothing wrong with the agreement—I mean, if there was nothing wrong with respect to the campaign overdrafts, why did the agreement cover those overdrafts?

L. Well, you'll have to ask the Comptroller about why he drew that into the agreement because those facts were not present in December of 1975. I wasn't running for any political office, didn't intend to run for any political office in December of 1975, so I can't respond to that. You ask me specifically about this question and my response there—in the January hearing—and my response there to that question was that the case had been fully investigated, fully looked into, and a determination had been made that there was nothing wrong.

[Campbell Investigation]

Q. [H. JOHN HEINZ III (R Pa.)]. In light of the information about Billy Lee Campbell provided to you through bank examinations and through the memorandum that we referred to the other day from the bank employee, didn't you have enough reason to be extremely suspicious of Mr. Campbell's activities. And if not, why not?

[LANCE]. Again, I think that in relationship to anybody who is in the business of lending money to anybody else that there is always a question about what is good judgment, what is poor judgment and what is somewhere in between. Now I think that it's very obvious that in any given situation there always is the possibility that there'll be loans that are criticized by the bank examiners. They criticize them for various numbers of reasons, as you well know, that we've already talked about.

Now in relationship to the Campbell situation, again I think I said to you yesterday that I had no reason to doubt his integrity and his honesty at that time. You always try to measure a man's competence and judgment in the process, and wherever there was criticism we tried to clear it up.

Q. So that there's no misunderstanding, let me tell you why I raise the question. It just seems reasonable to me that instead of forwarding an unsecured $100,000 note to Mr. Campbell and then a quarter of a million dollar loan on top of that in which N.B.G. subsequently took at least a partial loss, that it would have been a more reasonable, prudent course of conduct for you at that time, particularly in light of all the other red flags that had been raised about Mr. Campbell, for you to be investigating him earlier. Why wouldn't that be a reasonable statement?

L. I don't think that just the circumstances relating to the criticism by a bank examiner would raise the red flag. Let me call to your attention, Senator, and I think this is something that you can direct questions to somebody else about also, in the April 1975 reported condition that has been the topic of much conversation over the last three days, the bank was examined...very carefully, very minutely in that regard.

Q. This is the National Bank of Georgia?

L. No, sir, the Calhoun First National Bank.

Q. At this time we're talking about the National Bank of Georgia, which is where you were lending the money from.

L. But you were asking me about his activities in being criticized for loans that he was making at the Calhoun National in his capacity as a lending officer. Now if we can draw a clear distinction about where we are and what we're talking about, then I'll respond to each one of them. But let me finish with what I was saying about Calhoun, because I think this is important. We were examined in April of '75. Did the examiners discover the embezzlement and the defalcation? No. I discovered the embezzlement. I discovered the defalcation.

Q. Were there criticisms of Mr. Campbell at that time, though?

L. You gave us a copy yesterday of something I don't have before me. There were criticisms of Mr. Campbell in that report but they were not criticisms that would lead one to doubt his integrity and his honesty. Or if it were, certainly then the examiners from the Comptroller's Office should have discovered the defalcation instead of me discovering it three months later.

Q. Well, Mr. Lance, didn't Atkins Henderson get a tipoff in 1975 that things were not right with Mr. Campbell's credit? And what's the difference between the tipoff Mr. Henderson got in 1975 and the one that you got later on?

L. Well, that was also in 1975 and I assume at the same time those events were very, very close together. In fact I think I said, again in response to you or in my statement, that he called me whenever that occurred....

Q. Mr. Lance you seem to take some solace in the fact that the U.S. Attorney decided not to prosecute your campaign overdraft case and that solace is understandable. But having become familiar, as the committee did earlier, with the handling of that case, it's clear to me that this shouldn't be a special point of pride because it's clear to me the case was bungled. I don't know for sure what went on in phone conversations between your lawyer and John Stokes, but it is clear to me that even if the case was not closed because of what you or Mr. Stokes said or did, it was closed in my judgment because of who you were and because John Stokes was afraid of rocking the boat.

I say that because three Assistant U.S. Attorneys came before this committee and they told the committee that they believed the investigation was not—should not have been closed and they felt that it was proper and right to reopen the Title 18 U.S.C. 610 violation. Do you believe that a reopening of this case would help clear the air? And, if so, would you join with me in making a request for the reopening of the political overdraft case?

L. Senator, I don't see anything to be gained from the reopening of that case at all. It has been decided at all levels in government about the process. If you read in the Post, on one occasion Mr. Thornburgh, who was the Washington Deputy Attorney General, or Assistant Attorney General in charge of that matter, said that he reviewed the case after it was closed by Mr. Stokes and that in order to make certain that there was no question about it that he had two of his associates review the case. And they all came to the conclusion that the case should have been closed, that they had merely sent it to Mr. Stokes in March of 1976 because that was within his jurisdiction. Now I don't know what would possibly benefit from reopening that under those circumstances when those folks have made that decision.

Q. [SASSER]. I think, to be perfectly fair here, we might set the record straight on one assertion which has I think just been made. My colleague, Senator Heinz, asserted that all three Assistant United States

Attorneys indicated that this case should not have been closed. Now my recollection of that testimony—and I think the record will reflect this—is that Miss Glenna Stone, who was Mr. Bogart's supervisor, agreed on the merits that the case was not prosecutable. And of course Mr. Stokes also agreed with this. And apparently this has been the agreement all up through the chain of command of the Justice Department that the case simply was not prosecutable on its merits and could not be substantiated in front of a jury.

[Failure to Report Loans]

Q. [CHARLES McC. MATHIAS JR. (R Md.)]. Banking regulations require bank directors to inform their fellow directors of money that they borrow from other institutions. The Comptroller's report cites 12 U.S. Code 375—A6 in this respect. And the Comptroller reports that on five occasions you did make these reports to your fellow directors while you were at the Calhoun Bank and with the National Bank of Georgia. But the Comptroller notes that on 50 other occasions you did not do so, and I'm wondering why you met the requirement of the law on one occasion and not on others.

L. I did not do a good job in meeting the reporting requirements. Most of these situations related to guarantees or endorsements or indirect liabilities rather than any direct liability.

Yesterday we had some conversation about the dates on the F.B.I. report, and when it was filed, and I asked them to go back and check on their records and see. And if I just might read this statement for the record I think it may clear up totally the question that you had yesterday.

My appointment was announced on December the third, as you mentioned earlier, of 1976. Apparently I signed a consent form for the F.B.I. investigation on December the 15th. The investigation started on Dec. 23rd, the F.B.I. report was filed on Jan. 6th and a later supplement was filed on Jan. 31st.

I recall that my appointment and that of [Secretary of State] Cyrus [R.] Vance were announced at the same day in Plains, Ga. I checked with his record in this regard because he has been free from the type of charges and accusations that have been directed against me.

He signed his consent form on Dec. 9th and the F.B.I. did not start his investigation until Jan. 7th. His investigation was completed on Feb. 4th. My investigation started 20 days after the announcement of my appointment, whereas Mr. Vance's investigation started some 34 days after his appointment.

[Lancelot Company]

Q. [RIBICOFF]. The financial questionnaire sent to you by the committee at the time of confirmation, requested—and I quote—"A complete current financial net worth statement which itemizes in detail all assets, including but not limited to bank accounts, real estate, securities,

trust investments and other financial holdings; and all liabilities including, but not limited to debts, mortgages, loans and other financial
obligations of yourself and your spouse."

Your financial statement dated Jan. 7th, 1977, in response to this
questionnaire, listed partnerships interests of $75,000. After receiving your
responses, the committee requested a list of the partnerships in which you
have a financial interest which were included in the $75,000 figure on your
financial statement.

Now I'd like to ask you some questions about Lancelot and Company.
Who are the partners of Lancelot?

[LANCE]. My wife and I.

Q. Just the two of you?

L. Yes, sir.

Q. For what purpose was the partnership of Lancelot and Company set
up, and when?

L. The purpose was for my wife and I to be able to handle certain
aspects of investment as it relates to ownership of the Calhoun National
Bank and also other relationships within the family.

Q. Specifically, what were the assets and liabilities of Lancelot and
Company, as of Jan. 7th, 1977?

L. Senator, I'll have to develop that for you at the appropriate time.

Q. Do you have any ideas, any estimate of what it was?

L. Well, Senator, let me explain the item on my financial statement,
because I think that's of importance. We talked about this at the staff
meeting, as I recall, about my financial statement as we went into it. We
talked about the disclosure of indirect liabilities. And in the partnership
case, I said I was doing as has normally been the case, that I was showing a
net asset value. Now there are liabilities, there are assets involved in those
partnerships. Nobody seemed to think that was an issue with regard to the
circumstance, and that's the way that it was held.

Q. But didn't the staff ask you specifically to list the partnership assets
of you and your wife?

L. Not that I recall, or I would have.

Q. Didn't they specifically talk about this?

L. We talked about the partnership assets.

Q. Did Lancelot own any securities or real estate?

L. Yes.

Q. Did Lancelot ever borrow money?

L. Yes.

Q. In borrowing money in the name of Lancelot and Company over the
past five years, did you every submit a financial statement for Lancelot
and Company to a bank from which you were seeking such a loan?

L. I don't recall submitting one, Senator.

Q. In other words, when borrowing money in the name of Lancelot and
Company, isn't it true that money was principally based and the money
loaned upon the financial position of you and your wife, and not the financial statement of Lancelot?

L. Well, as a guarantee from me about Lancelot, yes, sir.

Q. That's right. Is it not true that you and your wife are personally liable for the liabilities of Lancelot and Company?

L. If, in fact, the assets of Lancelot are not sufficient to pay them, then yes.

Q. Yes, they were. Mr. Lance, did you ever inform this committee that the only partners of Lancelot and Company were you and your wife?

L. I cannot recall specifically, in response to the question that was asked me by the staff about who the partners were of the various partnerships that were listed in response to the question.

Q. Since it was clear from the questionnaire that the committee was interested in obtaining a complete listing of all assets and liabilities, why didn't you list the assets and liabilities for Lancelot, for which you were solely responsible?

L. Because I was not solely responsible except as it related to the inability of the assets in those partnerships to be able to take care of any liabilities, Mr. Chairman.

Q. Yes, but generally a partnership, the partners—unless it's a limited partnership—are liable for the liabilities.

L. But I was liable after the asset liquidation in the event that that was necessary, Senator.

Q. But there was a contingent responsibility—

L. And that's exactly my point, it was contingent liability, Senator, and that's the reason I didn't list it.

CARTER NEWS CONFERENCE

THE PRESIDENT: I would like to read first a letter that I have just received from Bert Lance.

"My Dear Mr. President: There is no need for me to go into the events of the last few weeks. You know them well, as do the American people. You also know that previously I had said three things to you about the importance of a so-called Lance affair. I will recall those for you.

"First, it was, and is, important that my name and reputation be cleared, for me, my wife, my children, my grandchildren and those who have trust and faith in me. And I believe that this has been done. As I said at the Senate hearings, my conscience is clear.

"Second, it was, and is, important for me to be able to say that people should be willing to make the necessary sacrifices and be willing to serve their government and country. This I can still say and say proudly.

"Third, I believe in the absolute need for Government to be able to attract good people from the private sector. We must find ways to encourage these people.

"As to my position as Director of the Office of Management and Budget, I hope the American people feel that during my eight months in office I have met well my responsibilities and performed well my tasks. This has been an important aspect of the entire matter. However, I have to ask the question, at what price do I remain?

"My only intention in coming to Washington in the first place was to make a contribution to this country and to you. I am convinced that I can continue to be an effective Director of the Office of Management and Budget. However, because of the amount of controversy and the continuing nature of it, I have decided to submit my resignation as Director of OMB. I desire to return to my native State of Georgia.

"It has been a high privilege and honor to be a part of your Administration. Hopefully I have made a contribution which will be of lasting value.

"Respectfully yours," signed, Bert Lance.

Bert Lance is my friend. I know him personally, as well as if he was my own brother. I know him without any doubt in my mind or heart to be a good and an honorable man.

He was given this past weekend a chance to answer thousands of questions that have been raised against him, unproven allegations that have been raised against him, and he did it well. He told the truth. I think he proved that our system of government works because when he was given a chance to testify on his own behalf he was able to clear his name.

My responsibility along with Bert's has been, and is, to make sure that the American people can have justified confidence in our own government. We also have an additional responsibility which is just as difficult, and that is to protect the reputation of decent men and women. Nothing that I have heard or read has shaken my belief in Bert's ability or his integrity.

There have been numerous allegations which I admit are true, that a lot of the problem has been brought on Bert Lance by me because of the extraordinary standards that we have tried to set in government and the expectations of the American people that were engendered during my own campaign in my inauguration statement, and as has been so strongly supported by Bert in his voluntary sacrifice, financially and otherwise, to come to Washington.

It was I who insisted that Bert agree to sell his substantial holdings in bank stock. Had he stayed there in a selfish fashion and enriched himself and his own family financially, I am sure he would have been spared any allegations of impropriety, but he wanted to come to Washington and serve his government because I asked him to, and he did.

I accept Bert's resignation with the greatest sense of regret and sorrow. He is a good man. Even those who have made other statements about Bert have never alleged on any occasion that he did not do a good job as the Director of the Office of Management and Budget. He is close to me and always will be, and I think he has made the right decision, because it would be difficult for him to devote full time to his responsibilities in the future. And although I regret his resignation, I do accept it.

I would be glad to answer any questions you might have about this or any others....

[Was Resignation Asked?]

Q: Mr. President, there have been reports that you knew early on what the charges were, that Mr. Lance had told you some of the allegations last January. Is that so, and can you tell us what you knew? And also did you ask for his resignation or encourage it, and what made you accept it?

P: I did not ask for Bert's resignation. Bert Lance and I communicate without embarrassment, without restraint and without evasion of issues. I thought Bert did a superb job Thursday, Friday, and Saturday in answering all the questions that had been leveled about him and against him.

Monday morning about 6:00 o'clock, Bert came to my office and we spent about 45 minutes going over all of the present questions that still remain, the prospects for the future. I told Bert I thought he had exonerated himself completely, proven our system worked, and asked him to make his own decision about what his choice would be.

He told me yesterday afternoon that he had decided that it would be best to resign. He wanted to talk to his wife again. He wanted to discuss the question with his attorney, Clark Clifford, before he made a final judgment. Mr. Clifford was in Detroit, came back this afternoon, and that was why the press conference was delayed.

This was a decision that Bert made. I did not disagree with it, and I think he has made a very unselfish and wise judgment.

The other question that you asked was whether and when I knew about charges that were made against Bert. The only thing that I ever heard about before Bert became OMB Director was last fall I knew that there had been questions about the Calhoun National Bank and overdrafts. My understanding at that time was that the overdraft question referred to his 1974 campaign debt.

The first time I heard about it was when Bert mentioned it to me in Plains about two weeks later. I think the date is now determined to be the 1st of December. I was called from Atlanta and told that the matter had been resolved by the Comptroller's Office and by the Justice Department.

On that date was the first time that either Bert or I knew that the Justice Department had been involved at all. And my understanding then was that it was an oversight and had the oversight not occurred, that the Justice Department would have resolved the issue long before. So I would hope that in the future the complete FBI report might be made available. That is a decision for Bert Lance to make. But I think if any of you would read it, you would see that approximately a hundred people were interviewed, three of them from the Justice Department, three of them from the Comptroller's Department.

All of the analyses of Bert Lance's character and ability were good and favorable, and I don't think that any mistake was made. I think he was qualified then; I think he is qualified now. And there was no attempt to conceal anything from me nor my staff.

[Drummed Out?]

Q: Mr. President, you have spoken so highly of Mr. Lance again this afternoon. I wonder if you feel that he was unfairly drummed out of the government?

P: That is a difficult question for me to answer. I have had personal knowledge of many of the statements and happenings that have been widely publicized. Some of them were greatly exaggerated. Some of them were actually untrue. On some occasions the report of an incident was not unbiased, but unfair. In general, I think the media have been fair. There are some exceptions. In general, I think that the Senate committee has been fair.

Bert has now had a chance to let his own positions be known and I think that at this point his resignation is voluntary. He needs to go home and take care of his own business.

I think it is obvious that if he stayed here he couldn't serve completely and with full commitment to his job. And I think his honor and integrity have been proven.

[Successor]

Q: Mr. President, Mr. Lance was in charge of some very important subjects: the Federal budget, of course, and government reorganization.

What are your plans for short-term continuity in those areas and in the long-term do you have a successor in mind?

P: I have not thought about a successor because the vacancy has just become apparent to me recently. I haven't given any thought to that yet.

If there is one agency of the government in which the President is daily involved, not only with the director, but also with immediate subordinates, it is the Office of Management and Budget. This is in effect an extension of the Oval Office.

I happen to know Bert Lance's immediate subordinates much better than I do the subordinates of any other department in government. They are highly competent. They have been chosen by him and me, long-time professionals there, and there has been in the past few weeks absolutely no slippage in the schedules that Bert and I and others had evolved earlier this year.

There has been no instance where a major question has been ignored, nor where responsibility has been delayed. And for the time being, I and those assistants that Bert and I have chosen together will continue.

I have not yet had a chance to talk to Bert about how quickly he can leave, how long he can stay. I would guess he will be wanting to leave fairly shortly, but there will be an orderly transition and I will decide beginning after today on who a successor might be.

Q: Mr. President, you said, sir, that you did not ask for the resignation. But you said it was, you felt, the right decision. Does that mean, sir, that you really came down to feel that he could no longer be an effective advocate for the Administration on Capitol Hill?

P: No, I think it would be a mistake to attribute Bert's decision to the fact that he could not be an effective advocate of the Administration's positions. There are so many advocates that even if one were completely incapacitated, other advocates could put forth the arguments for the Administration's position.

I think that it would be better to let Bert answer this question, because some of it involved his own personal affairs back home. But he has suffered greatly in a financial way. The value of his stock, if purchased, and his major holdings in the National Bank of Georgia is quite greatly above the market value because it involves a substantial controlling interest in the bank itself. Several would-be purchasers, I understand, in the last few days have come forward wanting to buy the stock, but are reluctant to do so because of the high focus of publicity on the sale. They would be scrutinized thoroughly. And I think that is expectable. And I don't deplore that. So they have been reluctant to do it.

I think Bert can very quickly get his own financial affairs back in order if he takes care of them himself. He has complied stringently in removing himself from his own affairs in the blind trust arrangement. He could have cheated on that arrangement. He did not. So part of his reasons for resigning, with which I have an understanding, is to help himself to get his own family affairs and financial affairs back in good shape. I don't know what the future might hold if he couldn't do that. I'm afraid it might get even worse than it is now.

This is no fault of his. If there is any fault there, it is mine because of the strict requirements we placed on him. Obviously, it takes a great deal of Bert's time to look up ancient data that goes back to '72, '73, '74. Did you have a power of attorney? How many overdrafts did your in-laws have? How many trips did you take on the plane to your home in Sea Island, and so forth. This has required an enormous amount of Bert's time.

My expectation, along with Bert's, is that this kind of investigation and demand on his time might continue. Bert is the kind of person who comes to work at 5:00 o'clock in the morning. He puts in, even in these past few weeks, I would say 12 hours a day or more on his OMB job. But it is obviously disconcerting to him.

I think, to be perfectly frank, the constant high publicity that has accrued to this case, even if completely unfair and unbiased, creates doubt among the news media, among the people of this country about the integrity of me and our Government, even though I think there is no doubt about Bert's being a man of complete integrity.

So there are multiple reasons for his decision. And I don't think any of them should be interpreted as being a reflection on him.

Q: There is an obvious follow-up, Mr. President, and that is if he had not offered to resign, would you have wanted him to stay on?

P: That is hard to say. As I have said several times in brief, impromptu news encounters in the last few weeks, the decision that Bert

Lance and I make together will be acceptable to the American people. And I have had large numbers of people who have asked me not to let Bert Lance resign. A group from Tennessee and North Carolina were in the White House this afternoon for a briefing on the Panama Canal Treaty. They rose, and the Governor of Tennessee, said, "We all hope Bert Lance will not resign." I had twelve speakers of the House of State Legislatures here last Friday. They unanimously voted and importuned me not to let Bert resign. I felt, and still feel, it is basically a decision for him.

I don't know the details of Bert's financial dealings back home. I don't have the time, nor the inclination to learn them. All I know about it is what I have had a chance to read in the news media. So the decision was Bert's. And when he discussed it with me, it was not from a posture of a subordinate talking to a superior; it was in the posture of friends who understood one another, discussing mutually what ought to be done about a difficult situation.

I think it was a courageous and also a patriotic gesture on Bert's part to resign.

[Credibility]

Q: Mr. President, how much has your credibility been damaged by this incident and by Mr. Lance's resignation?

P: I don't know. I think that as best I could from one hour to another, one day to another, and as best Bert could from one hour and one day to another, we have done what was right as judged by what we knew at that time.

We have been partners in every sense of the word, since he has been here, and you having covered the government of Georgia know that we were equally close partners in Georgia.

I have never known the head of a State or Federal agency who is more competent and has better judgment and who understands me better, and can work in close harmony with me. But whether my own credibility has been damaged, I can't say. I would guess to some degree an unpleasant situation like this would be damaging somewhat, but I just have to accept that if it comes.

[Relationship]

Q: How will you replace the kind of close relationship that you have had with him, and how much does that concern you?

P: I don't think there is any way that I could find anyone to replace Bert Lance that would be in my judgment as competent, as strong, as decent and as close to me as a friend and adviser as he has been. And, obviously, the government will continue, and I hope to do a good job as President, and I am sure a successor will be adequate.

But there has been a special relationship between me and Bert Lance that transcended official responsibilities or duties or even governmental service over the last six or seven years.

So he has occupied a special place in my governmental career, in my political career, and in my personal life. I don't think there is any way anyone could replace him now.

[Integrity]

Q: Mr. President, apart from Mr. Lance's reasons for resigning, can you share more of your thoughts for accepting his resignation? You said your belief in his integrity has not been shaken.

P: That is correct.

[Effectiveness]

Q: Just recently, House Speaker [Thomas P.] O'Neill [D Mass.] said he can be an effective Budget Director in the future. Why do you feel, sir, that Mr. Lance did have to go?

P: I have described to you my assessment of Bert Lance's reasons and I have read his letter, which I am sure was very carefully prepared by Bert to emphasize the most important reasons for his resignation. I don't have any way to know anything further beyond that answer.

[Impropriety]

Q: Mr. President, you have referred to the high standards you set for your people during the campaign. You said often you would not tolerate impropriety or even the appearance of impropriety.

I think now a lot of people are looking at your standards against the Bert Lance case.

You know what the charges and allegations were. I would like to ask you whether you feel now today Bert Lance has avoided the appearance of impropriety or whether a new standard is now in operation?

P: The standards were high at the beginning. The standards are still high, and the standards have been high in the service of Bert Lance. There has been not even one allegation that I have ever heard of that Bert Lance did not perform his duties as Director of OMB in a superlative way.

There has not been one allegation that he violated his responsibility or his oath when he was sworn in, that he has done anything improper at all, that he has violated any law. And even those allegations that were made about his life several years ago, in my opinion, have been proven false and without foundation.

I think there has been an adequate opportunity for Bert, after some unfortunate delay, in presenting his answers in the Senate hearings this past week. So I don't think any blame should accrue to Bert Lance for having acted improperly or having lowered the standards of our government.

[How Justify Support?]

Q: Mr. President, I would like to follow that up with a little more specific question. During the campaign you not only campaigned on the promise that your appointees would avoid the appearance of impropriety, but you also campaigned against the privileged few who had too much influence and against expense account matters and that sort of thing.

Mr. Lance, by his own admission—I think this isn't in doubt—overdrew his checking account by thousands of dollars on a regular basis. He flew on corporate planes for what appears to be political and personal reasons.

What I think many of us are interested in, sir, is your justification for reaffirming your belief in his integrity given the positions you took as a candidate.

P: My impression is that I have answered that already, but I would be glad to reaffirm what I have said. I have seen the statements about him. I have read the charges against him. I have heard the allegations about him, even criminal acts. I have seen some of his accusers apologize publicly for having made a serious mistake, for having made a peremptory and a preliminary judgment without hearing his explanation which, when it came, was adequate.

I just don't feel that I can preserve just the appearance of the White House to the exclusion of everything else. I also have a responsibility as President to be interested in justice and fairness and in giving someone who is accused erroneously a chance to answer the questions.

There has always been a possibility that in the last week's Senate hearings that Bert could not answer the allegations adequately, that he would prove to have violated a law. That was not the case. And I think my judgment that Bert had a right to officially answer every question in three hard days of interrogation by highly competent Senators and well-qualified staffs after they have had months to prepare was justified.

He has answered them adequately. So it would not be possible for me, just because one of my leaders or employees was accused of something, to discharge them or demand their resignation on the basis of an accusation about which I had doubt and which later proved to be false.

[Any Illegality?]

Q: Mr. President, sir, I would like to ask you about your statement, repeated statement that Mr. Lance never did anything illegal. The Comptroller of the Currency reported that Mr. Lance's overdraft loans of more than $5,000 violated the banking law and Mr. Lance I think conceded that his failure to report loans to board of directors of the two banks he ran also was an infraction of the banking statutes.

It is true, I know, civil, there are civil statutes; there are no criminal penalties. But how do you justify this with your statement that he never broke any law?

P: My assessment is that you are trying to succeed where the Senate Committee failed. There was no judgment made that Bert Lance did anything illegal. The only Comptroller's report that I saw specifically said that he had done nothing illegal and I think that he has adequately explained his position. He had three days to do it in. I think he did it well. I have no information to add to what Bert has already revealed to the Senators and to the public.

[Did Feelings Influence Actions?]

Q: Mr. President, I would like to follow up.... Not directly on how this may have damaged you, at the first meeting of your Cabinet appointees, Cabinet designees at St. Simons Island, there was a meeting at which Mr. Lance attended and you were there.

It was pointed out to every Member of this Cabinet a feeling on your part and those of some of the staff closest to you that because of the recent past political history in the country, and partly because of the expectations that had been raised by your campaign, that this was sort of a last chance, that if the public became disappointed and disallusioned in your Administration, that the result would be very, very damaging.

Early in this press conference you said Bert Lance is my friend, I have known him personally as well as my own brother and without any doubt in my mind or heart that he could be, that he was a good and honorable man.

P: That is correct.

Q: Do you think that you may have been, if only slightly, less than fully prudent and diligent because of your feeling towards Mr. Lance in the way you read some of these things, when he talked to you on November 15th, when he talked to you on December 1st, when the FBI report which I understand has also an appendix with some of these judgmental matters about the propriety of some of Mr. Lance's banking practices, in retrospect do you feel that in effect two standards were applied: One, a very firm, strong standard which you set and one for Mr. Lance who you knew so well, that you felt you didn't have to examine it that closely?

P: No. I don't think I have been remiss in that incident at all, even looking at it from this retrospective point of view.

Obviously, you can make a much better judgment on someone who comes in as a Member of a Cabinet if you yourself have known that person for years, if you know that person's general reputation, if you have worked intimately with that person in matters of times of stress and matters of challenge and have seen the basic competence, courage, honesty, unselfishness there. This existed in Bert Lance.

And I don't think there is any doubt that the FBI check of Bert Lance was just as thorough as was the FBI investigation of any other Member of the Cabinet. I think that if you examine the entire FBI report now, that you would confirm that if that was all you knew about him and had never seen Bert Lance before, you would agree that he was superlatively qualified to be a Cabinet level officer.

So I don't think there is any feeling on my part that my friendship with him distorted my point of view in assessing his competence. My friendship for Bert Lance, my long knowledge of him just confirmed a very favorable assessment of his qualifications by those who did not know him.

[Impact on Government]

Q: Has the Lance case diverted your attention at all away from important matters at home and abroad? Has there been a price that you have had to pay there and the American public has had to pay because of the Lance case, any heavy attention being placed upon it?

P: Well, I have to admit that there has been some diversion of my attention. I have been deeply concerned about the case. I have been concerned about Bert Lance personally. I have been concerned about the impact on my Administration if some of those serious allegations proved to be true. And it hasn't taken nearly so much of my own time as it has, say, of Jody Powell, who has had to face this questioning every day, which I think was a good thing.

Bob Lipshutz on my staff has had to confirm the accuracy of the answers to questions that were raised by the Comptroller's report and by other testimony that has come forward. Some of my staff have put a lot of time on it. I don't think their effort was misplaced. I think it was good for us to be informed. I think it was good for Jody, in his daily briefings to you, to be accurate. And I think had we, through error, or through neglect, given you a false statement, even though it might have been completely unintentional, that would have been a very serious matter.

But as far as my own time and effort was concerned, it had a slight but detectable effect of diverting me from some things. I don't think the country has suffered, and I think that is one of the reasons that Bert decided to resign, not for his own benefit, but to make sure that I didn't have this potential problem in the future.

[Would You Have Kept Him?]

Q: If Mr. Lance had not decided to resign, were you prepared to have him stay on or would you have tried to persuade him to resign?

P: I can't answer that question because it is, first of all, hypothetical. As I said before, it wasn't a matter of Bert Lance operating in isolation from me. We had thorough discussions about the matter. I left it completely up to him. He and I talked about the advantages of his staying, the disadvantages of his staying, to him, to my Administration, to the government, to his family, and Bert consulted with his own attorney, he consulted with several Members of the Congress, he consulted with people back home.

He talked it over with members of his family and he came to me and said he had decided it was best for him and for me if he resigned. And as has always been the case between me and Bert, I was honest with him. I didn't artificially try to talk him out of it because as we discussed the same facts and the same issues and the same prospects for the future, I think that our minds were working in the same direction.

I have always trusted Bert Lance to do the proper and the unselfish thing. And my guess is that he was much more concerned about me and my Administration and the reputation of the government and the diversion of our attention to his case away from things that were important for the people. I think that was by far the most important factor in his decision.

THE PRESS: Thank you very much.

IMF-WORLD BANK CONFERENCE
September 26-30, 1977

At the 32nd annual joint meetings of the International Monetary Fund and the World Bank held in Washington Sept. 26-30, discussions focused on the faltering pace of economic recovery and the consequences of the recovery slowdown for world trade. Keynote speakers pinpointed the recent lag in industrial output—not inflation—as the biggest obstacle to economic recovery.

During the four-day conference 3,000 finance ministers, representatives of central banks and private bankers discussed world economic conditions. They heard optimistic welcoming remarks from U.S. President Jimmy Carter and keynote speeches by H. Johannes Witteveen, the IMF's managing director, and World Bank President Robert S. McNamara.

Carter's Remarks

President Carter ignored the evidence of economic slowdown discussed by other conference speakers and painted a rosier picture of the U.S. economy, which he described as "healthy and growing." Carter said the U.S. economy is expected to grow at a "vigorous" pace in 1978 and that he is committed to meeting the U.S. economic growth target of 6 per cent after inflation. The two major goals, Carter told the conference members, were the restoration and maintenance of a "steady, noninflationary" expansion of the world economy and an "increase in the pace of growth" in the developing countries.

The general view developed at the IMF-World Bank 1976 Manila meeting and in London May 7-8, 1977, was that the countries with the *strongest economies—the United States, West Germany and Japan—would expand their economies at a more rapid rate to pull the weaker industrial and less-developed nations out of the recession. (London summit, p. 367; Historic Documents of 1976, p. 425)*

Witteveen Keynote Speech

Witteveen called attention to the faltering pace of recovery during the "past few months," noting that the gross national product (GNP) in West Germany failed to show any increase and that in Japan, while there was a "fairly rapid expansion" of real GNP during the first two quarters of 1977, the growth of "private domestic demand and of the volume of imports was not satisfactory." The IMF director asserted that inflation and unemployment remained "much too high to be considered acceptable."

Witteveen said the economic difficulties of the past few years had "given rise to pressures for protectionist measures in some of the major trading countries." The pressures had been resisted, but "there seems to have been a weakening in the commitment of some countries to a system of international trade free from restrictions and discrimination."

Countries in a strong economic position have an "international responsibility" to maintain an adequate growth of domestic demand, and during the process of international adjustment, Witteveen told the audience, "we may expect an increasing number of countries...to bring their inflation and balance of payments problems under control, and thus be strong enough to contribute to growth of the world economy."

In an unexpected announcement Sept. 21 Witteveen said that he would resign as director of the IMF at the end of his five-year term in August 1978. He cited personal reasons for his decision.

McNamara's Address

World Bank President Robert S. McNamara urged continued expansion of trade between the developed and less-developed nations. Trade expansion, McNamara said, "would benefit both consumers and producers in the industrialized countries and would expand incomes in the less-advantaged ones."

McNamara called for a sharp rise in the level of manufactured goods that industrialized countries imported from developing nations. Developing countries could triple their exports of manufactured goods between 1975 and 1985 if no new restrictions were placed on trade, McNamara said. The developing countries then could attain export earning levels of $94-billion by 1985. Gains in export earnings had been a major factor in the increase in economic growth among developing countries from a 3.7 per cent *level in 1975 to 4.7 per cent in 1976. McNamara noted, however, that the industrial nations had allowed the percentage of their GNPs committed to foreign aid programs to drop in 1976.*

World Bank Lending Limits

President Carter publicly supported McNamara's request for an increase in the World Bank's capital resources, which were estimated at $39-billion. While private banks were permitted to loan up to 20 times their capital, the World Bank could only make loans to the extent of its capital. An increase in capitalization would permit an increase in the World Bank's lending operations. At the 1976 meetings the Ford administration had opposed McNamara's request for an increase in capitalization.

The United States also supported an increase in the IMF's lending operations. In Paris Aug. 6, 14 countries agreed to contribute the equivalent of $8.4-billion in special drawing rights to a special fund for nations with severe balance of payments deficits. U.S. support marked another shift in policy. The Ford administration had opposed the increase and suggested instead the creation of a $25-billion safety net fund for industrialized countries.

Following are excerpts from the remarks of President Jimmy Carter and the keynote speeches of IMF managing director H. Johannes Witteveen and World Bank President Robert S. McNamara, delivered Sept. 26 at the 32nd annual joint meetings of the IMF and World Bank in Washington, D.C. (Boldface headings in brackets have been added by Congressional Quarterly to highlight the organization of the text.):

[PRESIDENT CARTER'S REMARKS]

...This meeting is important to all of us because the partnership that exists among nations and among people is so evident in this room. These meetings provide an opportunity for the leaders of the world's financial institutions, both public and private, to consider the economic problems and also the economic opportunities that our nations share. And through the [World] Bank and the [International Monetary] Fund, we are able to meet the challenges to our shared well-being.

[Economic Challenges]

The two greatest challenges we face are to restore and to maintain steady, non-inflationary expansion of the world economy and to increase the pace of growth in the developing nations of the world, with the benefits of the growth among us all more widely and equitably shared.

The health of the international economic system depends upon the health of our individual domestic economies. Just as none of us can prosper without a stable system, so the system will not be sound unless we act responsibly at home.

I am pleased that the United States economy is healthy and growing. Our rate of inflation, while still too high for our liking—about 6 per cent—is moderating and is below that, of course, in most other countries.

We will meet our economic growth targets for this year—about 6 per cent in real terms. And we will also maintain a vigorous and noninflationary growth next year.

And I am committed to take such actions as are necessary as President to insure that this optimistic prediction comes true. We will do so principally because it is good for our own country, but also because it contributes to the economic health of the rest of the world.

[U.S. Unemployment]

Our unemployment rate is steadily going down. We have very little doubt about this. And there's a sense of commitment in our country and a strength of our economic system. They bode us good for the future. Strong economic growth in the United States and a slowing pace of growth in other countries, combined with an excessive United States import of oil, have all led to a rise this year in the United States trade deficit, which has continued even through last month.

[Oil Imports and Energy]

With respect to oil imports, I have proposed to the Congress—really for the first time in the history of our country—a comprehensive energy program, which in the years ahead, is designed to reduce our oil imports substantially below what they are now and to less than one-half the previous projections for the next 8 years.

We know that it is critical that the Congress enact strong and effective energy measures. The U.S. must have a credible program to limit the growth of oil consumption and, therefore, to reduce oil imports.

I urge all nations, and especially the major industrial countries, to reduce energy waste along with us and to pursue economic growth and stabilization policies along with us, leading to an expanding, noninflationary world economy, growing international trade, and an improved pattern of world trade balances.

The International Monetary Fund has played already a vital role in keeping the international monetary system both flexible and effective. I'm particularly grateful for the enlightened fiscal discipline which the Fund and the [World] Bank encourage throughout the world with their loans. The present system is working well.

The United States has ratified the amendments to the Articles of Agreement of the IMF, and we hope that other nations, other members will do the same so as to increase the Fund's resources and strengthen its capacity for surveillance of exchange rate policies and the oversight of monetary agreements....

...The United States remains firmly committed to policies that will promote freer and wider trade without the deleterious consequences of protectionism. My country joins others in pledging to seek substantive progress in the ongoing multinational trade negotiations by the end of this year.

[The World Economy]

Restoring health to the world economy will help us toward what we all recognize is a vital, human obligation—assisting poor countries in the task of human development. If the roughly 1 billion people who now live in extreme poverty are to have their chance, every nation must take more effective action. And the United States is ready to join such an international campaign.

The study of world development issues now being undertaken by the Bank and the Fund should provide a framework in which all nations can expand our efforts toward common development efforts.

Of course, the developing countries are ultimately responsible for their own growth. Only they can mobilize the skills and the resources necessary for development. Only they can be sure that the benefits of growth, when and if it does come, extends [sic] throughout the country involved, to those who need it most. But the industrialized countries like our own must provide more outside capital.

I'm glad to report that the United States Congress has authorized more than twice as much money for the World Bank and the regional development banks this year as we did last year.

I hope that the negotiations for a major, general capital increase will permit the World Bank to increase the level of its lending in real terms.

All this will take time. Our goals will not be achieved overnight. Perseverance will be the key to success. There will be many difficulties to overcome, many complicated questions to answer, many national interests that might separate countries to be overwhelmed by a common commitment to mutual responsibility.

The United States wants to cooperate with all of you. We are prepared to stay the course, and you can depend upon us.

Thank you very much.

[STATEMENT BY H. JOHANNES WITTEVEEN]

...First, let me comment on the pace of recovery from the severe international recession of 1974-75. It may be recalled that expansion of production in the industrial countries proceeded on a generally satisfactory course in the initial phase of the recovery, that the rate of expansion showed an unexpectedly sharp slowdown during the latter part of 1976, and that this "pause" was then followed by a fairly widespread pickup in the tempo of economic activity. Now, it is evident that during the past few months the pace of recovery has faltered again in a number of the industrial countries, especially in Europe. In the Federal Republic of Germany, real GNP [gross national product] in the second quarter failed to show any increase. Economic expansion has continued to conform closely to expectations in the United States, while easing markedly in Canada. In Japan, there was a fairly rapid expansion of real GNP during the first two quarters of 1977; but this centered on export gains and higher government expenditures, and the growth of private domestic demand and of the volume of imports was not satisfactory. Several of the industrial countries, including both the Federal Republic of Germany and Japan, have responded to these unexpected developments by adopting stimulative measures.

One distressing aspect of the current situation is the prevalence of high unemployment. For the industrial countries as a group, the overall rate of unemployment remains close to its recession peak of two years ago and is substantially above the levels that prevailed during the 1960s and early 1970s. This is rightly a matter of serious concern for national governments. Various types of specific measures now in widespread use may help to deal with the structural aspects of unemployment, but any major reduction in unemployment levels can only stem from markedly higher rates of economic expansion. The situation presents an acute dilemma, since the harsh experience of recent years has made governments understandably reluctant to switch from anti-inflation policies to a more aggressive stimulation of domestic demand.

[Inflation Levels High]

On the inflation front, rates of price increase in most member countries have been brought down from their exceptional levels of 1974 and 1975 but are still much too high to be considered acceptable. National authorities will agree, I believe, that inflation remains a generally severe problem. In a longer-term perspective, as I observed at last year's Annual Meeting, inflation redistributes wealth and income arbitrarily, undermines confidence, reduces investment incentives, and misallocates resources.

Among the industrial countries, the overall rate of price increase is still running at an annual rate of almost 7 per cent this year—only about half as high as in the second half of 1974 but well above historical standards. This overall rate conceals wide differences among individual countries. As measured by the comprehensive GNP deflators, the rate of inflation is relatively quite low in the Federal Republic of Germany and Japan, and it is also below the industrial-country average in the United States. Within the industrial world, inflation rates are by far the highest in Italy and the United Kingdom, although the stabilization programs adopted by those two countries in the course of 1976 have begun to produce some significant declines.

[The Developing Countries]

Among the nonindustrial, or primary producing countries, the economic picture is very mixed. In the more developed countries, the growth of total output lags well behind that of the industrial group, and this year's increase in their consumer prices is expected to average some 15 per cent. The non-oil developing countries, which were less affected by the global recession than other groups of oil importing countries, achieved a growth rate of about 5 per cent in 1976 and are likely to show a still higher rate for the current year. The record of these developing countries with respect to inflation is quite uneven, but most of them have achieved some success in reducing their rates of increase in consumer prices. For the oil exporting countries, growth of output in recent years has averaged about 9 per cent annually, whereas consumer prices have been rising at a rate of over 15 per cent.

[Protectionist Measures Rejected]

The domestic and external economic difficulties of the past few years, particularly the high level of unemployment, have given rise to pressures for protectionist measures in some of the major trading countries. These countries have generally managed to resist such pressures, and have avoided imposing across-the-board trade restrictions to safeguard the balance of payments. Lately, however, there seems to have been a weakening in the commitment of some countries to a system of international trade free from restrictions and discrimination. One sign of this has been a gradual but definite spreading of selective restrictions on imports; other signs have been the negotiation of so-called voluntary restraints on exports and the interest being expressed in the organization of markets. Such restrictions add to the difficulties of adjustment for weaker countries, and particularly for those developing countries that have increased their manufacturing capacity and now depend heavily on an open and expanding system of world trade.

Although protectionist measures may be a natural response to high unemployment and low growth rates, such measures are unlikely to provide anything other than very short-term relief for these problems. The growth of international trade would undoubtedly be impeded by a proliferation of trade restrictions, with inevitable repercussions on the countries imposing them. It is, however, encouraging that on several occasions governments have publicly reaffirmed their opposition to protectionism and stressed their intention to pursue vigorously the wide-ranging trade negotiations in Geneva. I very much hope that these negotiations will be successful, and that they will provide a new impetus to the expansion of world trade.

Mr. Chairman, I have noted that members of the Fund are confronted by the problems of generally subnormal growth rates, high unemployment, and rising protectionism. These problems prevail in an economic environment dominated by the persistence of inflation, coupled in some countries with weakness of the external position.

In this situation, the industrial countries, and most other member countries as well, have been placing a primary emphasis in their demand policies on combating inflation and, where necessary, strengthening the external position over the next few years. This priority is based on the firm belief that such an approach will yield the best results for economic growth and employment in the longer run. At the same time, the approach being followed envisaged, at least for the industrial countries as a group, achievement of a rate of economic growth sufficient to permit a gradual reduction in unemployment.

This general strategy of policy was recommended in last year's Annual Report, and national targets and expectations were broadly consistent with it. The difficulty that is now emerging very clearly is that these expectations have not been realized. The pace of economic recovery in the industrial countries as a group has become so slow that it is adversely affecting employment and foreign trade (including the exports of developing countries) while encouraging protectionism. This is a matter for serious concern.

['Pause' in Cyclical Recovery]

One question that immediately arises concerns the reasons for the "pause" in cyclical recovery and expansion during the second half of 1976 and of the further slackening in the pace of activity that has occurred in recent months. In part, the explanation can be traced to the conduct of fiscal policy. Throughout the industrial world, some of the fiscal stimulus supplied in 1975 was withdrawn in accordance with the plan of exercising restraint over the rise in aggregate demand during the recovery phase of the cycle. However, in a number of industrial countries, the shift of fiscal policy in the direction of restraint has turned out to be greater than was intended. The latest surprising "shortfall" in fiscal expenditures has appeared in the Federal Republic of Germany, where indications are that the reduction in the public sector deficit this year will again be larger than planned.

The decision of industrial countries to shift the stance of fiscal policy in 1976 was based on one key assumption: that fixed investment would soon resume expansion and would become a major factor in sustaining the rise of general economic activity during the second half of 1976 and beyond. In the event, as is well known, the behavior of business fixed investment has been very disappointing—quite contrary to the pattern of previous economic recoveries. In retrospect, this is not surprising in the case of those countries which found it necessary to adopt very restrictive demand policies in order to deal with large payments imbalances and severe inflation. But the growth of investment also has been lagging in economically stronger countries, although in the United States it has gained momentum over the past few quarters.

Immediate explanations of the unusual behavior of investment can be sought, of course, in the depressed level of profits and the relatively low rates of capacity utilization. But such factors were also present in earlier recessions. It is clear that a number of somewhat different influences must underlie the depressed state of fixed investment. Of basic importance, I believe, is the cautiousness of the business community in the face of various kinds of uncertainty. In differing degrees among countries, there is uncertainty with respect to the future rate of inflation, the extent and character of government regulations, the movement of exchange rates, the risk of further trade restrictions, and the maintenance of political stability. In addition, cost-price relationships—notably with respect to the sharply higher cost of energy—have probably had an unusually depressive effect on the profitability of investment in recent years. For many industrial countries, certain structural changes in the world economy may also be hampering investment; for example, the success achieved by developing countries in the expansion of their manufacturing capacity means that some sectors of industry in industrial countries are becoming unprofitable and should contract.

In the present complex situation, there are no easy solutions to the problems posed by lagging investment and slow economic growth. The problems are interrelated, and the emphasis of any policy approach is bound to vary from country to country. But a few guidelines may be suggested.

[Economic Guidelines Suggested]

First, let me emphasize that steadiness in pursuing a certain strategy of policy is highly desirable from the standpoint of reducing uncertainty and encouraging investment. Such a steadiness does not call for the "fine tuning" of policies, which is neither feasible nor conducive to the restoration of public confidence in government policies. But it does imply the need to adjust policies in time to avoid cumulative deviations from an equilibrium path over the medium term. As I mentioned earlier, the [International Monetary] Fund supported the strategy of economic policy that has been followed by the industrial countries, and we recommended that, in the current inflationary environment, governments should not shade policy risks on the side of growth, as they had done in the past. This recommendation was followed by most governments, but national targets and expectations now seem to have been missed in a downward direction. The growth of domestic demand has been significantly less than that required by our strategy, particularly in countries with strong external positions. This lag in demand growth should now be decisively corrected. In addition, I believe that some special efforts could and should now be made to reduce inflation.

In the current environment of high inflation combined with economic slack, it would seem especially necessary for governments to do whatever they can in the difficult field of incomes policy. In this context, the marked declines in primary commodity prices that occurred in the middle months of 1977 provide a good opportunity to bring about a deceleration of wage and price increases. This could be strengthened by providing fiscal stimulus, in the countries where needed, in the form of tax reductions. In the design and operation of incomes policies, an effort could be made to take these two elements into account in such a way as to have a maximum effect on wage and price movements.

Even if a general strategy of policy is pursued steadily, and special efforts are made to reduce inflation, some additional steps will still need to be taken. These might include, for example, policies designed to improve supply conditions and alleviate cost pressures. Also, in view of the structural difficulties being encountered in a number of sectors, many industrial countries need to develop an active policy for structural reorientation and rationalization of manufacturing industries; this should be done with a clear objective of providing more room for imports from developing countries and helping to bring about a favorable climate for the international division of labor in a free trade system. Finally, even though the essential prerequisites of higher investment are a further reduction in inflation and return to a more stable economic environment, investment can and should be strengthened by policies to improve the rate of return on capital. In developing countries, the incentives to invest, especially in manufacturing capacity, would be enhanced if their products had freer access to the markets of industrial countries. Also, the very fact that developing countries find it difficult to generate sufficient domestic saving for investment programs underlines the importance of raising the flow of capital and aid from the industrial countries to the developing world; this, in turn, would lead to additional demand for the exports of the industrial countries themselves.

I have discussed the question of an appropriate general strategy of policy largely by reference to the industrial countries as a group. However, as my remarks may have already indicated, the strategy cannot be applied uniformly to all countries, but rather must take into account the strength or weakness of the external position. This consideration brings us to a vitally important subject—the working of the international adjustment process.

[Reducing Payments Deficits]

The importance of the adjustment process in present circumstances is evident in two respects. The first is that a number of countries are now facing large payments imbalances. In the absence of satisfactory programs of domestic and external adjustment, their situations would simply deteriorate. These countries badly need to adopt policies ensuring a reduction of their current account deficits to levels that can be financed by sustainable capital flows and with a manageable structure of external debt. The second important aspect of the adjustment process concerns countries in relatively strong external positions; for these countries, the appropriate course of policy is to take expansionary measures strong enough to ensure meeting their own domestic objectives, thus helping to restore a satisfactory growth of world trade and assisting the adjustment efforts of deficit countries.

By last year's Annual Meeting, it was evident that the time had come —as I said in Manila—to lay more stress on the adjustment of external positions and less on the mere financing of deficits. Since then, a number of deficit countries have taken important actions to adjust, and other such countries urgently need to follow suit. However, the functioning of the adjustment process has been impaired by the failure of domestic demand in some of the relatively strong countries to show adequate rates of expansion.

I would emphasize that all countries in a relatively strong position have an international responsibility to maintain an adequate growth of domestic demand. As the process of international adjustment evolves, we may expect an increasing number of countries—both developed and developing—to bring their inflation and balance of payments problems under control, and thus to be strong enough to contribute to growth of the world economy. Meanwhile, in the circumstances that have prevailed in recent years, particular attention has inevitably focused on the United States, the Federal Republic of Germany, and Japan—which because of their economic size can have a substantial impact on the pace of trade and activity throughout the world.

[West German and Japanese Economies]

The German and Japanese economies exhibit several common features: relatively low rates of inflation, exceptional strength of the external position, sluggish growth of domestic demand, and a tendency for the exchange rate to appreciate. Since early 1976, the external value of the deutsche mark and of the yen has appreciated by some 15 per cent in relation to a composite of other major currencies—a development that, in and of itself, tends to depress domestic demand.

The stimulative measures recently adopted by the Federal Republic of Germany and Japan are essential for the purpose of meeting domestic objectives, and they are certainly very welcome from an international standpoint. In view of the difficulties and imponderables involved in directing economic policy in a modern industrial economy, I know that the German and Japanese authorities will be carefully assessing developments over the coming year. And I trust that they will be prepared to take further measures of stimulus in the event that the performance of their domestic economies does not improve substantially.

[U.S. Economy]

When attention is turned to the United States, it should first be noted that the U.S. economy experienced rapid growth of real GNP during the first two quarters of this year. The rate of growth achieved—averaging close to 7 per cent in those quarters—was neither meant nor expected to be

697

sustained, and the economy is now in the process of shifting to a more moderate pace of expansion. Let me emphasize the importance for the rest of the world that expansion of the U.S. economy be maintained at a satisfactory rate. In this connection, developments on the external side do not indicate a need for U.S. fiscal and monetary restraint beyond that required on domestic grounds for the purpose of reducing inflation. I base this view, among other things, on the fact that the deficit of the United States on current account is accompanied by large inflows of capital.

In these remarks on the adjustment process, I have stressed the need for countries in relatively strong external positions to achieve faster growth of domestic demand. Another important requirement of the adjustment process relates to the provision of official financing to deficit countries—financing that is provided in sufficiently large amounts, over long enough periods, and with appropriate conditionality....

...Mr. Chairman, I have focused my remarks on the problems and difficulties confronting us in order to promote discussion of how they might be solved. In doing so, I do not want to minimize the improvement in the general economic picture that we have seen over the past year or two. We have only to remember the gloomy outlook in 1974 to appreciate how much has been achieved. This should encourage us to tackle the remaining difficulties with determination and in a continuing spirit of international cooperation.

[ROBERT McNAMARA'S SPEECH]

If one surveys what has taken place in the developing world since we last met in this forum, there are, I believe, two important points that emerge.

The first and more obvious one is that the immediate economic outlook, although still clouded, has measurably improved.

You will recall the situation twelve months ago.

The 1975 performance figures for the developing nations were in, and confirmed that their average GNP growth rate did not exceed 3.7%, down sharply from the averages of the 1960s.

The per capita income of the poorest nations—inadequate in the best of years—had simply stagnated.

The middle-income developing nations were faced with mounting external debt, and stubborn problems of adjustment.

And serious difficulties threatened the future operations of the World Bank itself: there were repeated delays in the IDA-V [International Development Association] negotiations, and considerable uncertainty over the IBRD [International Bank for Reconstruction and Development] capital increase.

It was not a very reassuring situation.

Today, as we meet, the prospects are brighter.

The 1976 performance figures indicate that the average growth rate of the developing countries moved up to 4.7%....

There are, then, discernibly better prospects for the period ahead than there were twelve months ago.

And yet beneath this immediate and short-term improvement in the global development scene—and partially obscured by it—lies a more profound and troubling problem.

It is this.

A certain restive and uneasy interlude has followed on the international community's unsuccessful efforts to reach fundamental agreements. There is a pervasive and growing sense of dissatisfaction with the outcome of the lengthy discussions that have taken place over the past two years in various international forums....

And yet the most urgent issues remain largely unresolved.

Some partial agreements have been reached, some differences have been narrowed, and some willingness to compromise has emerged.

But it is evident that neither the developed nor the developing nations, neither the capital-surplus nor the capital-deficit countries, neither the North nor the South are really satisfied with the outcome. The atmosphere today is at best one of regret and disappointment, and at worst one of frustration and disillusionment.

It is not a promising climate in which to achieve what is needed most of all: a basic understanding of development issues and how to resolve them.

Now, there are two types of actions that can be taken to improve that climate.

[Establish Commission]

One is to prevent the political aspects of the situation from hardening further into stalemate.

That, of course, is essentially a political matter, and as such beyond the mandate of the Bank itself. And it was for this reason that last January I suggested that there be organized a wholly independent, high-level, but deliberately unofficial commission of experienced political leaders—drawn from the developed and developing countries alike—that could assess and recommend feasible alternatives to the current North-South deadlock.

I recommended that someone of the political experience and stature of Willy Brandt, former Chancellor of the Federal Republic of Germany, be the convener and chairman of such a commission.

I continue to hope that Herr Brandt will accept the task, assemble a distinguished group of commissioners, recruit an expert staff, and begin the work.

It would be an important effort to help remove the roadblocks to more effective international development cooperation.

And there is a second type of action that would be useful today: action that would be ongoing and complementary to the political effort.

[Analysis of Development Problems]

What is needed is a comprehensive and continuing analysis of development problems: a practical and sustained effort to integrate the diverse components of development experience into a more understandable pattern; an effort to explore and evaluate the critical linkages among such components, linkages that often interact in strongly supportive or seriously disruptive ways not readily apparent; an analysis that would clearly state the costs and benefits to both developed and developing countries of alternative ways of dealing with the central issues.

The truth is that the lack of such systematic, detailed knowledge often makes it difficult for governments to design appropriate long-term development policies with full understanding of their broader impact. The result is that effective international cooperation is hampered....

The international community today has no fully adequate analytical mechanism for assessing complex development phenomena and hence no fully adequate means of evaluating alternative ways of dealing with them. Nor does it have a satisfactory yardstick by which to measure progress in the cooperative effort.

Earlier this year a number of political leaders of both developed and developing countries proposed that the World Bank should initiate work on such a project—on what might be termed a "World Development Report."

I believe the proposal has merit....

This morning I want to explore it further with you. But before doing so, I would like to examine some of the fundamental development issues that need to be integrated into such a general framework.

Specifically, I want to:

● Briefly review what we can learn from the past record of development;

● Discuss the elements of an effective strategy to accelerate economic growth in both the poorest and the middle-income developing countries;

● Suggest how the benefits of that growth can be better channeled to meet the basic human needs of the absolute poor;

● Indicate for the near term the projected financial operations of the Bank required to support accelerated growth and the attack on absolute poverty;

● And, finally, outline the initial steps that can be taken to organize the proposed "World Development Report."

Let me begin, then, with what we can learn from the past record.

[Past Record of Development]

It is a very impressive record.

Indeed, historically, it is without precedent. Never has so large a group of human beings—two billion people—achieved so much economic growth in so short a time.

In the quarter century from 1950 to 1975 the average per capita income of the developing world grew at over 3% a year. The present industrialized countries, at a comparable stage in their own development, required a much longer time to advance as far, and attained an annual per capita income growth of only about 2%.

Nor was the achievement exclusively economic. Important social progress was made as well. Average life expectancy, for example, was expanded from about 40 years to 50 years. Though 50 is still 30% lower than the longevity currently enjoyed in the industrialized nations, it took Western Europe a century to achieve what the developing nations did in 25 years.

So successful were the developing countries in reducing their death rates—by either eradicating or severely reducing a number of major diseases—that as an unintended result, their populations began to grow at unacceptably high rates.

In the period 1950-1975 more people were added to the population of the developing world than the present total population of the developed world. It was the demographic effect, not of expanded birth rates, but of diminished death rates.

Excluding the People's Republic of China, the population of the developing countries increased from 1.1 billion in 1950 to 2 billion in 1975: an annual rate of growth of 2.4%—about double the rate in the developed countries.

That birth rates must come more rapidly into balance with death rates is an urgent imperative of our era....

[Remarkable Advances Made]

But the fact remains that it was a staggering feat for the developing world to absorb 900 million people into their population in so short a time, and still effect some improvement in their average standard of living. Had the population growth not been so rapid, the improvement would have been even more impressive.

As it is, despite the immense increase in numbers, marginally more food per person is available there today, on average, than it was a quarter century ago. And during the last ten years in particular, calorie consumption per capita appears to have increased in at least 47 developing countries.

These emerging societies have also succeeded in increasing the literacy of their peoples. Twenty-five years ago 65 million children were in primary school. Today 260 million are. Then, only 7 million were in secondary and higher institutions. Today 65 million are. In 1950 only a third of their adult population could read and write. Today more than a half can.

Much of this social progress was possible because the real per capita income of the developing world...had more than doubled during the period....

It was, then, in spite of its difficulties, a quarter century of remarkable advance.

And yet, it is very often not perceived as such.

To many people, indeed perhaps to most people in the developed nations, the problems of the developing world seem far more real than its progress.

Nor is that a view shared exclusively by outside observers.

To many within the developing countries themselves, progress seems tortuously slow. And hopes fade and disillusionment grows as the distance between expectation and achievement lengthens.

There are, of course, many reasons for this attitude: some valid, but others quite misleading and unrealistic.

Let me single out two common characterizations that are made about international development today, and briefly examine their validity.

Closing the Gap

The first proposition is that development, despite all the efforts of the past 25 years, has failed to close the gap in per capita incomes between the developed and developing countries—a gap that at its extremes ranges in money terms to more than $8,000 per capita.

The proposition is true. But the conclusion to be drawn from it is not that development efforts have failed, but rather that "closing the gap" was never a realistic objective in the first place. Given the immense differences in the capital and technological base of the industrialized nations as compared with that of the developing countries, it was simply not a feasible goal. Nor is it one today....

Income gaps are not unimportant. They tell us a great deal about inequalities in the world, both between nations and within nations. And they make it obvious that the wealthy nations can clearly afford greater financial assistance to the poor nations.

But for the developing nations to make closing the gap their primary development objective is simply a prescription for needless frustration.

What is far more important as an objective is to seek to narrow the gaps between themselves and the developed nations in terms of the quality of life: in nutrition, literacy, life expectancy, and the physical and social environment.

These gaps are already narrowing, and can be narrowed much further in a reasonable period of time. Just how this can be done, I will discuss in a few moments.

Eliminating Poverty

Another characterization of the performance of the developing countries over the past quarter century is that they have failed to eliminate, or even significantly reduce the massive poverty in their societies.

Again, the proposition is true, but misleading.

Unlike "closing the gap," reducing poverty is a realistic objective, indeed an absolutely essential one. And it is true that some developing societies have had ineffective policies in this matter. In retrospect, it is clear that too much confidence was based on the belief that rapid economic growth would automatically result in the reduction of poverty—the so-called "trickle down" theory. For several years now the Bank and the countries it serves have been striving to develop effective strategies for dealing directly with the poorest elements in society.

The strategies which are now emerging must, of course, be applied in very different ways for different poverty groups. What is effective for the small farmer with half a hectare of land in the countryside may be irrelevant for the unemployed laborer in the urban slums.

There are ways of dealing with massive poverty effectively, but none of them can completely finish the task in one simple burst of activity, or in one specialized five-year plan, or even in one determined decade of effort.

The time span required depends largely on the institutional structures available through which appropriate policies can be applied. In many of the developing countries those structures are just now coming into place.

There are in the developing world today more trained people, a broader economic and social infrastructure, and a greater practical experience with the development process than these societies have ever enjoyed before. That is a result of their past 25 years of investment and hard work, and it provides the basis for turning the final quarter of the twentieth century into an even more remarkable period.

The characterizations, then, that development has failed because it has not "closed the gap" or "eliminated poverty" are superficial and misleading.

A far more realistic appraisal is that the impressive overall economic growth achieved by the developing world in fact obscures profound differences in the performance of various economic groups. There has been both uneven growth among countries, and misdirected growth within countries.

Uneven Growth Among Countries

Consider the following:

● For 32 poor countries, chiefly in South Asia and Sub-Saharan Africa, the rate of increase in per capita income was 1.5% or less per annum—less than half the average rate. Together these countries contain more than 950 million people: 46% of the total in the developing world.

● Not only have the poorest nations experienced substantially slower growth, but...their growth performance has continued to fall further and further behind from one decade to the next. It fell from 2.6% in the 1950s to 1.8% in the 1960s, and to 1.1% in the first half of the 1970s....

Economic growth is a necessary condition of development in any society, but in itself it is never a sufficient condition. And the reason is clear. Economic growth cannot assist the poor if it does not reach the poor.

The truth is that in every developing country the poor are trapped in a set of circumstances that makes it virtually impossible for them either to contribute to the economic development of their nation, or to share equitably in its benefits.

They are condemned by their situation to remain largely outside the development process. It simply passes them by.

Nor are we talking here about an insignificant minority. We are talking about hundreds of millions of people. They are what I have termed the absolute poor: those trapped in conditions so limited by illiteracy, malnutrition, disease, high infant mortality, and low life expectancy as to be denied the very potential of the genes with which they were born. Their basic human needs are simply not met.

1.2 billion do not have access to safe drinking water or to a public health facility. 700 million are seriously malnourished. 550 million are unable to read or write. 250 million living in urban areas do not have adequate shelter. Hundreds of millions are without sufficient employment.

These are not simply large rounded numbers. They are individual human beings.

Most tragic of all, many of them are children. For of the total of two billion people in the developing countries, some 860 million are under the age of 15.

They are the chief hope of their societies' future. And yet almost half of them suffer from some debilitating disease likely to have long-lasting effects. Well over a third of them are undernourished. 290 million of them are not in school.

That is the profile of absolute poverty in the developing world. And that profile cannot be altered by a development strategy that ignores it.

The problem is not so much that we do not know what to do about all of this.

We do know what to do. We must design an effective overall development strategy that can both:

● Accelerate economic growth;

● And channel more of the benefits of that growth toward meeting the basic human needs of the absolute poor.

The problem is that doing this requires changes in both developed and developing countries which may cut across the personal interests of a privileged minority who are more affluent and more politically influential.

Let me try, then, to analyze the two major elements of such a strategy in more detail.

Policies for Accelerating Economic Growth

In view of the global economic turbulence of the last five years, are there actions which the international community can take that will give reasonable assurance of achieving higher rates of economic growth in the developing countries?

I believe there are.

The adjustment processes, as painful as they have been, have not broken down.

The OECD [Organization for Economic Cooperation and Development] nations are displaying signs of recovery—though it remains slower than had earlier been expected—and growth in the poorest and middle-income developing countries is moving in the direction of more normal historical levels.

The developed nations, in all but a few cases, have resisted the temptation to resort to increased protectionism.

The private capital markets responded well to the emergency needs of the developing countries for credit, and despite a major rise in external debt, the situation has remained manageable.

What is needed now is determination in the international community to assist the developing countries to continue the adjustment process, and to accelerate their present pace of growth.

Let me review with you, briefly, our appraisal of the prospects for growth in the developing countries in the 1977-85 period, and the actions necessary to realize them. We can begin with the poorest countries.

[Growth Prospects for Poor Countries, 1977-85]

An optimistic program for the poorest countries suggests that they may be able to reverse the declining trend of recent years, and achieve an annual growth rate in per capita income, for the 1977-85 period, of about 2%.

This would be a substantial improvement compared to 1970-75, but would do no more than restore their growth to the average level they experienced in the 1950s and 1960s.

In terms of their immense needs, this is disappointing. It would mean an addition of only about $30 to their per capita incomes by 1985.

But we must be realistic. Even this modest advance requires the following difficult actions:

● The poorest countries must save and reinvest at least one-fifth of the small increase in their per capita income;

● They must achieve a 25% increase in efficiency in their capital utilization, through better investment, pricing, and management policies;

● They must double their export growth in relation to the historical trends;

● And there must be a 50% increase, in real terms, in Official Development Assistance flows to the poorest nations between 1976 and 1985.

Now these policy actions are urgent.

Without them, the outlook is dismal. Even with them, the per capita incomes of these already disadvantaged countries would reach only $185 by 1985. I will return to this matter a bit later on.

Prospects for the Middle-Income Developing Countries, 1977-85

The growth prospects for the middle-income developing nations are more favorable. During the adjustment period from 1973 to 1976 they managed to maintain a per capita growth of almost 3% per year, and now appear to be poised for a major expansion in their exports; particularly of manufactured goods.

If they continue to improve their efforts to mobilize internal resources, and if the recovery quickens in the developed nations, and world trade expands, it would be reasonable to expect that the middle-income countries could achieve during the 1977-85 period an annual increase in per capita income of nearly 4%.

That would mean about a 40% increase in average incomes over current levels. And if these growth rates could be maintained until the end of the century, these countries as a group would achieve an average per capita income then of about $2,100.

But these favorable prospects cannot become a reality unless there is the will to take appropriate policy actions.

Many of these actions, of course, can be taken only by the developing countries themselves: greater mobilization of internal resources; increased efficiency in their use; better incentives for export promotion.

It is their task to fashion and implement these policies, and the Bank will do all that it can to assist them.

But these actions, as necessary as they are, cannot succeed if the prospects for world trade expansion, and the access to international capital markets, do not improve at the same time.

It is these latter policy actions, both as they relate to the poorest and to the middle-income countries, that I want to examine now.

Trade Expansion

The per capita growth rates of 2% for the poorest countries and 4% for the middle-income nations for the years 1977-85 are based on a continuation of the set of policies that produced the expansion in their export earnings in the last decade.

With such policies we believe the developing countries could increase the volume of primary commodity exports by about 50%, and, more importantly, that they could nearly triple manufactured exports, increasing them from $33 billion in 1975 to about $94 billion by 1985.

To increase exports of manufactured goods at that rate—11% per year—would require a major effort on their part. And the success of this effort assumes a continued tolerance on the part of the developed world to accept such a rapid expansion in imports from the developing countries.

But achievement of the $94 billion level would not exhaust the trade potential of the developing nations. As I pointed out last year in Manila, if the OECD countries were completely to dismantle their trade barriers against the manufactured goods of the developing countries, the latter could, by 1985, earn $24 billion per year beyond the amounts projected above.

And this represents only one part of the additional trading opportunities available to the developing countries. A recent Bank study indicates that if these countries themselves were to remove all of their own supply constraints on exportable manufactures, they could earn yet another $21 billion per year by 1985.

In other words, if fully rational policies were pursued by importers and exporters alike, the developing countries' export earnings from manufactured goods would increase by $45-billion per year above the levels which will result from a continuation of past policies.

It is, of course, unrealistic to expect that the developed world, even over a ten-year period, could dismantle all trade barriers, or that the developing countries over the same period, could remove all supply constraints. That would mean that the developed countries would quickly have to shift capital and labor away from those industries that can no longer compete with imports, and the developing countries would quickly have to shift more of their effort from older, less efficient production into the newer export lines.

Now, neither of these adjustments is going to happen immediately, but they do illustrate the immense contribution to development that greater efforts to liberalize trade can bring about. Would it not be a reasonable goal for both the developed and developing nations to try to achieve one-half of that potential by 1985? ...[T]his goal can be achieved if:

● First, the Tokyo Round of trade negotiations leads to a tariff reduction of 50%. This would add $4 billion to the developing countries' manufactured exports by 1985.

● Second, the non-tariff trade barriers of the industrial countries are partially relaxed. This could add $6 billion per year to these earnings.

● And third, the developing countries exploit at least half of their remaining unused export potential—through greater efficiency and further reduction of supply constraints—and the developed countries pledge not to react by increasing their levels of protection. This would boost export earnings by an additional $10 billion per year....

The truth is, of course, that these policy actions are in the larger interest of both the developed and developing nations.

The increased imports from the developing countries would be matched by increased exports from the developed countries. Thus the expanded trade would benefit both consumers and producers in the industrialized countries, and would expand incomes in the less-advantaged countries.

It would require, however, practical adjustment assistance for those industries affected in the developed nations, adjustment assistance which would shift the burden from the displaced labor and capital to society as a whole. And it would mean that the developing countries must move to a more outward-looking economic stance so as not to inhibit the trade expansion that the international markets are willing to absorb.

In short, it would call for enlightened attitudes on both sides, and a mutual measure of political courage.

Greater Access to Capital

Better, more realistic trade policies are clearly essential. But foreign exchange earnings will supply only part of the financing required for acceptable levels of growth in the developing countries. They must also have continued access to international capital markets.

...[T]he bulk of the external capital flow to the poorest countries has come from official sources, including the World Bank, rather than commercial banks. It must continue to do so.

The essential problem in these countries is that the resources used to service external debt diminish the already inadequate resources available to support their development efforts. Thus the problem of debt is linked closely to the need for increased transfers of real resources on concessional terms....

[Middle-Income Developing Countries]

The middle-income developing countries, on the other hand, have relied extensively on private external capital sources....

...[P]rivate credits to middle-income countries increased rapidly—by $35 billion—in the 1973-76 period. There has been concern that this dramatic growth in external borrowing—particularly the borrowing from commercial banks—is unsustainable, and that if it is allowed to continue there will eventually be a generalized debt crisis.

A year ago I argued that such a crisis was not inevitable, and could be avoided through a series of interrelated actions to be taken by the developing countries themselves, by the international banking community, and by the international financial institutions. And the record of the past year indicates that corrective action has in fact been taken.

Thus during 1976 the ten nations which account for three-quarters of all the debt owed to private sources by the oil-importing developing countries managed to reduce their total current deficit by more than one-third: from $22.5 billion in 1975, to approximately $14.2 billion in 1976. This improvement exceeded by a substantial margin the Bank's own projections.

Export performance during 1976 was enhanced by unanticipated increases in certain commodity prices—coffee, for example—but this was far from the whole story. Rates of growth of manufactured exports were also higher than expected. Moreover, as a group these ten countries exercised substantial restraint on imports. In several cases, imports were kept constant, or even reduced in real terms.

In addition, the middle-income countries, as a group, raised their real domestic savings last year by 15%.

These impressive overall figures do, of course, tend to obscure the less than satisfactory performance of a few countries. But on balance the adjustment record of the major borrowing countries this past year has been a good one.

Further there is increased public awareness that the debt problem cannot sensibly be measured by simply charting the growth of the developing world's debt. Such global statistics reflect a "money illusion" in the sense that much of the apparent growth is simply a consequence of the high rates of inflation experienced in recent years.

If debt is deflated by the borrowing countries' export price index, the real rate of growth of developing countries' debt was actually slower in the last few years (1973-1976) than in the late 1960s. And as a proportion of export earnings, the disbursed debt of the middle-income developing countries increased only 12% over the last decade: from 84% in 1967 to 96% in 1976.

[New Lending Anticipated]

Based on a series of consultations between World Bank staff and the major international banks in North America and Europe, it appears that the commercial banks anticipate continued growth in their net lending to developing countries, though at a more moderate rate: perhaps 10 to 15% per annum in current dollars, as compared to more than 30% over the last three years. Such a pace in new lending would be consistent with the requirements for private credit which we project for the developing countries over the next few years. And it means, in effect, that the major lending banks and the major borrowing countries are operating on assumptions which are broadly consistent with one another.

Another critical element in the middle-income countries' debt prospects is the outlook for official finance. For the middle-income countries, the major source of long-term official finance is the World Bank and the Regional Banks. A year ago there were major uncertainties about the prospects for future growth in lending from these institutions, particularly for the World Bank itself. Those uncertainties are now largely resolved.

For all these reasons we are even more confident today than we were a year ago that the debt problem is indeed manageable, and need not stand in the way of desirable rates of growth for the developing countries.

But in stating this conclusion, I would not want to create the impression that the debt issue may simply be ignored. It cannot.

Although the adjustment process has been successfully completed by many of the developing countries that are major borrowers in private markets, there are a few cases that clearly need further corrective action. And though the net requirements of the developing countries for private borrowings will not rise much in real terms in the years ahead, large amounts of recent medium-term loans will fall due. In 1980, half of all gross borrowings will be needed for amortization payments.

Past experience suggests that liquidity problems will be encountered by at least a few borrowers in the coming years. The challenge to the international community is to ensure that these isolated occurrences do not undermine the stability of the system as a whole. The IMF's recently approved Supplementary Financing Facility is clearly welcome in this connection.

But the World Bank itself also has a role to play. As I have stressed, there is a need for a better balance between official and private flows over the next few years. This shift would promote greater stability, both by lengthening the debt structure of borrowing countries and by spreading the burden and risk of lending to individual developing countries more broadly throughout the international community.

In summary, then, the goals of expanded trade, and greater access to capital—and the policy actions that will make this possible—are key ingredients of accelerated economic growth in the developing countries.

That growth is absolutely essential to development.

But growth, no matter what its magnitude, cannot assist the hundreds of millions of absolute poor in the developing societies unless it reaches them.

It is not reaching them adequately today, and it is to that issue that I want to turn now.

Policies for Redirecting Growth

The aggregate economic growth the developing countries have achieved over the past 25 years—as remarkable as it has been—has not been very effective in reducing poverty.

The poorest countries, as I have noted, participated only modestly in the general trend of rapid growth since 1950. In the last few years, their growth rates have lagged even further behind.

Even in those developing countries that have enjoyed rapid growth, the poorest income groups have not shared in it equitably. Their incomes have risen only one-third as fast as the national average.

Taken together, these two tendencies explain why there has been so little increase in the living standards of the absolute poor throughout the developing world.

It is clear there must be a more equitable and effective sharing of the benefits of growth within both groups of developing countries.

[Development Objectives]

Formulating development objectives in these terms avoids the misconception that because economic growth has not always been effective in increasing the incomes of the poor, it is somehow not really necessary.

It is very necessary.

In the countries with the greatest concentrations of the absolute poor—particularly those in South Asia and Sub-Saharan Africa—economic growth has been particularly slow relative to the growth of population. In these conditions, there is little scope for improving the quality of life through income redistribution alone. The total national income is simply not adequate.

But let us suppose that these poorest nations were now to double the average rate of per capita growth that they experienced in the last 25 years. This is clearly an improbable target, and even if they were able to reach it, their average per capita income, by the end of the century, would only be about $400.

But in the absence of effective government policies to moderate skewed income distribution, such an average level of income in itself cannot effect an extensive reduction in absolute poverty. And that would mean that hundreds of millions of the absolute poor in Asia and Africa have an interminable wait ahead of them before they can begin to lead decent lives in which their basic human needs are met.

The poorest countries, then, must do everything they can to increase per capita income growth, but they must do something else as well. They must fashion ways in which basic human needs can be met earlier in the development process.

Is that feasible?

It is. A number of countries have made progress towards that goal. Not always very effectively, and never without some setbacks. But progress nevertheless.

Even the middle-income developing countries must not rely solely on rising average levels of per capita income to solve problems of absolute poverty. Like the poorest societies, they must attack it directly. They have far more resources with which to do so, and can cut short the time period in which their least-advantaged citizens must wait to have basic needs met.

The strategy we are discussing for attacking absolute poverty applies, therefore, both to the poorest nations and to the middle-income countries. But it obviously applies with much greater force to the poorest nations since they have no other viable alternatives.

What are the components of those basic needs which must be satisfied if absolute poverty is to be overcome? It is not difficult to list them, although the characteristics of each will vary from country to country, from culture to culture, and from society to society. They include:

• Food with sufficient nutritional value to avoid the debilitating effects of malnutrition, and to meet the physical requirements of a productive life;

• Shelter and clothing to ensure reasonable protection against the rigors of climate and environment; and

• Public services that make available the education, clean water, and health care that all members of society need if they are to become fully productive.

The first requirement for meeting these basic needs is that the absolute poor must be able to earn an adequate income with which to purchase on the market such essential goods as the market can supply: food, for example, and shelter.

Enhancing the Productivity of the Poor

Assisting the poorest groups in the society to find earning opportunities and to enhance their own productivity is essential since they are the very groups that are so often bypassed by the traditional development process.

To the extent that the poor possess some tangible assets, however meager—a small farm, a cottage industry, or a small-scale commercial operation in the urban sector—it is possible to help them to become more productive through better access to credit, extension assistance, and production inputs.

The experience of Malaysia, Kenya, Malawi, Taiwan, Korea, Nigeria, and other countries, demonstrates that the productivity of small farms can be significantly enhanced through such programs, and the Bank itself is committed to this objective through its new rural development projects. We have over the last three years initiated projects which will approximately double the incomes of about 40 million individuals living below the poverty line in both the poorest and middle-income countries.

Both the developing countries themselves, and the Bank, have had less experience in creating off-farm earning opportunities and in assisting cottage industries and small-scale entrepreneurs, but it is clearly important to try to do so. Two-thirds of the employment in the industrial sector of the developing world still originates in small-scale enterprises. Their expansion and increased productivity is vital to the overall growth of the economy, and to the incomes of the poor.

We in the Bank are still in the early stages of launching an increased effort to finance such labor-intensive activities—activities that can provide productive employment at low unit capital costs. By 1980 we intend to increase our annual financial commitments to these types of operations to roughly $300-million. We plan to work through and, where necessary, to create local financial institutions for that purpose. Urban and rural development projects will increasingly include such operations as components of the investment plan.

This is already being done in projects in Tanzania, India, and Indonesia. In Madras, for example, an urban development project will create 5,000 jobs in cottage industry activities in slum areas at an average investment cost of $225 per job. Thus, the earning capacity of the urban poor will be increased with only a modest investment of scarce capital.

Redesigning Public Services

Equally essential to expanding the capacity of the absolute poor to purchase market goods are the redesign and expansion of public services.

Health care, education, public transportation, water supply, electricity, and similar public services are of course the concern of developing countries everywhere. Over the past 25 years their governments have been faced with increasing pressures to satisfy demand as overall populations have nearly doubled, and urban inhabitants have quadrupled.

Inevitably some mistakes have been made. Wealthy urban and rural families, often constituting a very small but politically influential and elite group, have frequently managed to preempt a disproportionate share of scarce public services.

It is a very old story in human affairs, and far from being an attribute of developing countries only. But wealth and privilege have made their influence felt in these matters, and almost always at the expense of the poor.

Piped water allocation, the availability of electricity, the cost and routing of public transportation, the location of schools, the accessibility of public health facilities—all of these are national and local government decisions that are critical to the living standards of the very poor, who have no margin for alternatives, and no political access to policymakers.

Not only are essential public services often out of financial and geographical reach of the poor, but such facilities as are in place may be so inappropriately designed as to be virtually irrelevant to their needs: impressive four-lane highways, but too few market roads; elaborate curative-care urban hospitals, but too few preventive-care rural clinics; prestigious institutions of higher learning, but too few village literacy programs.

Public services that are not designed modestly and at low cost per unit will almost certainly end by serving the privileged few rather than the deprived many.

To reverse this trend, governments must be prepared to make tough and politically sensitive decisions, and to reallocate scarce resources into less elaborate—but more broadly based—delivery systems that can get the services to the poor, and the poor to the services....

[Worldwide Struggle Against Poverty]

It always comes down to a question of priorities: more foreign exchange for importing private automobiles; or an expanded bus fleet. Elaborate government offices; or squatter settlement upgrading. A new generation of jet fighters for the air force; or a new generation of infants who will live beyond their fifth birthday.

No government can do everything. To govern is to choose. But poverty will persist and grow if the choice too often favors the peripheral extravagance over the critical need.

Basic human needs are by definition critical. And for governments to assist the poor to satisfy them is not public philanthropy, but a wise investment in human capital formation.

It is the poverty itself that is a social liability. Not the people who happen to be poor. They represent immense human potential. Investing in their future productivity—if it is done effectively—is very sound economics.

Certainly what is very unsound economics is to permit a culture of poverty to so expand and grow within a nation that it begins to infect and erode the entire social fabric.

Poverty at its worst is like a virus. It spreads the contagion of bitterness, cynicism, frustration, and despair. And little wonder. Few human experiences are more embittering than the gradual perception of oneself as a trapped victim of gross social injustice.

No government wants to perpetuate poverty. But not all governments are persuaded that there is much that they can really do against so vast a problem.

But there is.

Moving against the roots of poverty; assisting the poor to become more productive, and hence more an integral part of the whole development process; redirecting economic growth and public services more toward meeting basic human needs: these are practical and attainable objectives.

Last year I suggested that developed and developing nations alike establish as one of their major goals the meeting of the basic human needs of the majority of the absolute poor within a reasonable period of time—say, by the end of the century. I continue to believe such a goal is both fundamental and feasible. Moreover, we see more clearly now, than we did then, the means by which it can be achieved.

[Time Schedule for Action Against Poverty]

Should not, then, the developing nations individually, and the world community collectively, formulate the specific actions that must be taken to accomplish such an objective, lay out the time schedule for these actions, and monitor the progress of the program?

Most of the task must, of course, be done by the developing countries themselves. Only they are in a position to adjust their national priorities. Only they can create the necessary economic and political framework in which to reach their own poor. Only they can mobilize the creative energies of their own citizenry.

But the task is too vast for national efforts alone. If it is left exclusively to these countries—if they are refused reasonable outside assistance—either the time period may stretch so far into the future that it outruns the patience of their own people, or they may be confronted with such critical economic strains in the short term that they are forced to give up the longer-term effort.

Surely, the developing societies that make a determined commitment to meeting the basic human needs of all their people deserve broader alternatives than those.

That is why—as I have pointed out—the international community must help in this matter by expanding trading opportunities, and by increasing capital flows. What we all must grasp is that the task itself is neither unrealistic nor naive. Indeed, it is clearly manageable in purely technical and supply terms since the shortfalls are quite modest in comparison to total world production.

It is rather the institutional and political constraints—not physical or technological limits—that are the greatest obstacle.

In this overall effort, the World Bank itself must, of course, do all it can through its own financial operations to be helpful....

Summary and Conclusions

Let me now summarize and conclude the central points I have made this morning.

If one looks objectively at the developing world's economic record during the past quarter century, it is impressive. It surpasses the performance of the present industrialized nations for any comparable period of their own development.

But the unexpectedly high average rate of growth conceals significant differences between groups of countries.

The poorest nations have done only half as well as the middle-income group. Crippled by serious disadvantages, these societies have witnessed their growth gradually diminish. And collectively they contain more than half the total population of the developing world.

In the middle-income countries, the rates of growth have been better, but here too the averages obscure sharply skewed income patterns. Far too many in these societies—as in the poorest nations—have been able neither to contribute much to economic growth, nor to share equitably in its benefits. Development has passed them by.

The tragedy of the absolute poor is that they are trapped in a set of social and economic circumstances that they cannot break out of by their own efforts alone. Hundreds of millions of them cannot read or write; are seriously malnourished; have no access to adequate medical care; are without adequate shelter; and have no meaningful work.

Their basic human needs are simply not met.

For these hundreds of millions, development has failed.

It will continue to fail unless the dynamics of absolute poverty are dealt with directly, and reversed.

There are two essential things that must be done. The rate of economic growth of the developing nations must be accelerated. And more of the benefits of that growth must be channeled towards helping the absolute poor meet their basic human needs.

The task facing the poorest nations of restoring their earlier per capita income growth rates is going to be arduous. Even to return to their average historical level of 2% will require a doubling of their growth in export earnings, and a 50% increase, in real terms, of the current ODA capital flows to them over the next eight years.

Without these two complementary actions, the outlook for the poorest nations...is grim indeed.

The middle-income nations have considerably higher prospects. But they too will be unable to accelerate their present growth rates without greater export earnings, and continued access to capital.

The required increase in export earnings can be realized if the developed countries will make modest concessions in the removal of tariff and non-tariff barriers and if the developing countries reduce their own export constraints.

Economic growth clearly is a necessary condition of development. But it is not in itself a sufficient condition. Little can be done without growth. But much, unfortunately, can be left undone even with growth.

That is what has happened in many of the developing societies over the past 25 years. There has been growth; in some countries very rapid growth. But it has not notably helped the severely disadvantaged break out of their poverty.

What is required, then, is that developing country governments adopt policies that will assist the poor to enhance their own productivity, and that will assure them more equitable access to essential public services.

But the developing countries cannot achieve these immense tasks alone. They will need greater assistance from the developed nations.

The World Bank's contribution to this can at best be only a part of the larger effort of the international community as a whole. But its contribution will not be insignificant. Over the next five years the Bank should be able to provide its member developing countries between $30 and $35 billion in net financing.

Further, the Bank will initiate work on a detailed analysis of major development issues, and of the cost and benefits of alternative policies to deal with them. The objective of this ongoing "World Development Report" will be both to improve the Bank's own grasp of these complexities, and gradually to develop a framework that can better assist developed and developing nations alike in their own decisions.

In the end, development is always complex and exacting.

None of it is easy. None of it is without cost. And none of it is without some risk.

But the attack on absolute poverty—basic human needs and their satisfaction—cannot be forgotten, cannot be forever delayed, and cannot be finally denied by any global society that hopes tranquilly to endure.

JOINT ECONOMIC REPORT
September 30, 1977

A pessimistic assessment of the economic outlook for 1978 was offered by the Joint Economic Committee of Congress in a report issued Sept. 30. The report, The 1977 Midyear Review of the Economy, *predicted that economic growth would fall short of levels projected by the Carter administration. In a secondary conclusion which drew written statements from most of the committee members, the report largely blamed the monetary policies of the Federal Reserve Board for a "sluggish" economic recovery.*

The report also criticized what it termed the administration's "unadventuresome" budget policy and predicted a 4 to 4.5 per cent economic growth rate during 1978. The administration earlier had projected a 5 per cent rate of growth. (President's budget message, p. 57; President's economic report, economic advisers' report, p. 65; Carter budget revisions, p. 125)

The impact of the report, written by the committee staff, was lessened by the fact that the committee's 12 Democratic members gave it only shaky support while the eight Republican members rejected outright many of its conclusions.

Federal Reserve Board

The report called the Federal Reserve Board the "perennial source of obstruction to recovery" since the 1974-1975 recession. "Our view," the report said, "is that monetary policy in the past three years has been too restrictive; that this has severely impeded recovery; and that it is past time to reverse this posture and to support economic growth."

Tight money policies had run counter to needed business investment and construction of housing, the report said, and also had frustrated the administration's goal of reducing unemployment. It recommended that Federal Reserve Board and administration officials develop a consensus economic forecast and that they include in the projection "a clearly defined rate of monetary growth."

Burns and the White House

Arthur F. Burns, the chairman of the Federal Reserve Board since 1970, was singled out by the Joint Economic Committee report as having an "obsession with inflation." Indeed, Burns, although having only one vote in the seven-member Board of Governors and one vote in the 12-member Federal Open Market Committee of the Federal Reserve Board, had become a focus of the larger debate in the country over appropriate policies for overcoming economic problems.

An outspoken critic of the administration's economic policies, Burns enjoyed strong support from bankers, businessmen, finance ministers and many economists for his relentless fight against inflation. He was criticized by many liberals, on the other hand, for giving insufficient attention to the problem of unemployment.

With Burns' term as chairman expiring Jan. 31, 1978, a large amount of speculation built up as to whether President Carter would reappoint Burns or name a new chairman of the independent Federal Reserve Board. The speculation ended Dec. 28 with the announcement by Carter that he would replace Burns with G. William Miller, the head of a diversified manufacturing company based in Providence, R.I. Miller was largely unknown outside New England, where he was regarded as a progressive businessman.

Committee Members

Among the six Democratic members of the Joint Economic Committee who wrote additional views which were attached to the report were Rep. Henry S. Reuss (Wis.) and Sen. William Proxmire (Wis.). Reuss wrote that "what is now called for is a steady hand on general economic policies—monetary and fiscal—together with specific rifle shot programs aimed at inner cities and improving employment opportunities for minority youth."

Proxmire wrote, "For my part, I would put much greater stress on a combination of tax cuts to stimulate demand and consumption in the private sector, plus a reduction in public spending for a wide spectrum of programs. These should include military, and military aid, space, highway, and big project foreign aid programs, as well as funds for those education, health and welfare programs which seem to have had no influence on increasing education excellence or health or decreasing welfare."

Committee Republicans unanimously refused to endorse the report. Led by the ranking minority member, Sen. Jacob K. Javits (N.Y.), the minority said that the failure of the Federal Reserve Board to increase rapidly the money supply would not result in a recession. The Republicans contended that the report was too concerned with short-term interest rates and did not emphasize sufficiently the significance of long-term business savings and investment.

> *Following are excerpts from The 1977 Midyear Review of the Economy report of the Joint Economic Committee issued September 30, 1977, forecasting a shortfall in U.S. economic growth from levels projected by the Carter administration. (Boldface headings in brackets have been added by Congressional Quarterly to highlight the organization of the text.):*

The sub-par condition of the American economy continues to be a source of serious concern to the Joint Economic Committee. We are alarmed by the continuation of unacceptably high rates of unemployment more than two years after the bottom of the recent recession, and by the failure of inflation to slow to a tolerable rate. For this reason, this report pays particular attention to the sources of our economic difficulties and to measures that would make it possible to combine a reduction in inflation with increases in production and employment....

The Congress recently directed the Joint Economic to undertake an extensive study of economic change, past and prospective, and to provide the Congress with recommendations for meeting the future economic policy requirements of the Nation.... These changes have reduced the relevance of traditional economic doctrine to the problems of today. More knowledge and better insight are needed. The JEC will be addressing these matters in the months ahead.

This Report begins with a review of the progress, and lack thereof, of the recovery from our deepest post-war recession. It moves from there to the presentation of our rather pessimistic forecast for the remainder of 1977 and for 1978. ...[T]he Report identifies the continuation of rapid inflation as the chief obstacle to speedy recovery. However, the view that inflation must be stopped at all costs—including the cost of higher unemployment and slower growth—is firmly rejected as primitive and ineffective. Instead, we propose an agenda for study and action that is intended to shift the burden of inflation control away from those persons—the poor, minorities, teenagers, the aged—who have tended to be the principal victims of the traditional method of slowing inflation by restricting demand.

[Recession and Recovery]

The recent recession is by far the deepest of the post-World War II era. It began in late 1973 and reached bottom in the spring of 1975. However, more than two years later unemployment still hovers at about 7 per cent of the labor force. Prior to this recession, the year 1958 was the worst year of the post-war era; yet unemployment that year was only 6.8 per cent as compared with the 7.7 per cent of 1976—a year of recovery—and the 7 plus per cent that will be registered this year.

Meanwhile, inflation has failed to respond either as hoped or as predicted to the slack in the economy. Although the 9.1 per cent increase in the Consumer Price Index (CPI) of 1975 gave way to a more modest 5.8 per cent in 1976, this rate is still alarmingly high by historical standards, and it jumped once again to an annual rate of 8.9 per cent in the first half of this year.

That recovery from a recession as deep as the recent one should take several years does not come as a surprise. Raising output to its past peak only gets us a small part of the way back to full employment. The inexorable arithmetic of labor force and productivity growth keeps pushing up potential output at a rate between 3.5 and 4.0 per cent a year. Recovery requires actual output to grow faster than potential output—about 3 per cent faster to reduce unemployment by 1 percentage point in a year. And this must be kept up...to reduce the unemployment rate to tolerable levels.

Had real growth proceeded rapidly and steadily, full recovery would have taken about four years. However, actual growth has been uneven and not firmly based and the economy has therefore fallen far short of the targets that the JEC set forth in "The 1975 Joint Economic Report." The Carter Administration's present long-range goal of a 4-3/4 per cent unemployment rate by 1981 is far less ambitious than the goal established by the Committee. Yet the halting progress of the recovery, combined with the bleakness of the outlook for the immediate future, makes even this modest target seem remote and overly optimistic.

[1976 Slowdown]

The economy rebounded rapidly in the last half of 1975 and early 1976. But in the spring of 1976 the Federal budget began showing an expenditure shortfall that continued throughout 1977 in an amount likely to produce outlays that are approximately $15-billion below the approved budget for fiscal year 1977. This expenditure shortfall, inventory over-building in early 1976, the persistent failure of business fixed investment to revive, and the constant drag caused by the failure of other industrial countries to expand, stalled the recovery and produced a slowdown in the last half of 1976 that brought the unemployment rate to a level exceeding that of the beginning of the year. Thus, 1976 proved to be a throwaway on the road to recovery, and...it will take longer to return to full employment.

[Recovery Momentum]

The recovery again picked up momentum in the first half of 1977 as the real growth rate rose from the 2.5 per cent of the second half of 1976, to a rate of 6.8 per cent. This very rapidly reduced the unemployment rate from the 7.8 per cent of last December, to an average rate of 7.0 per cent in the second quarter of 1977. Unfortunately, the rate of inflation has also accelerated. After rising at a rate of 5.3 per cent in 1976, the GNP deflator moved along at a 6.2 per cent annual clip during the first half of this year.

The current recovery is lagging behind the progress of recovery of previous recessions in most relevant respects. ...[D]uring the recent recession real final sales—the best measure of overall demand in the economy—fell much more than in the earlier recessions. Although real final sales have actually risen at about the average rate for recovery periods, the gap caused by the original greater than normal decline of 1974-1975 has not been made up.

Similarly, when measured as a per cent of the levels achieved at the cyclical peak prior to recession, the current recovery lags the average of the past four recessions in all expenditure components except personal consumption and single-family home construction.... The most serious shortfall has been investment in nonresidential structures. State and local purchases have not been nearly as great a source of stimulus as in earlier recoveries. And the failure of other industrial countries to achieve rapid expansion has caused the growth of our exports to be sluggish....

[Unemployment]

The response of the unemployment rate to the forces of recovery has been particularly disheartening. More than two years after the recession trough, the unemployment rate still exceeds the 6.8 per cent rate recorded in 1958, the worst post war year our economy experienced prior to the recent recession.

Some would attribute our unemployment miseries to changes in the composition of the labor force. Because of rising labor force participation rates and the baby boom of the 1940s and 1950s, the proportion of the civilian labor force composed of teenagers and young adults has increased from 15 per cent in 1955 to 24 per cent in 1976. At the same time, labor force participation rates for adult women have risen sharply.

It is an established fact that teenagers and women suffer higher unemployment rates than adult males. Therefore, the change in the composition of the labor force has tended to pull up the overall unemployment rate, and it has caused the degree of labor market tightness associated with any given unemployment rate to increase.

Although the changing composition of the labor force probably means that it will be more difficult to achieve a 4 per cent unemployment rate than in the past, it does not follow, as some now find it fashionable to contend, that the change in the composition of the labor force makes it more difficult to lower unemployment by the use of expansionary fiscal and monetary policies.... Our present 7 per cent unemployment rate cannot, therefore, be explained by changes in the composition of the labor force.

The unemployment rate for teenagers reached 17.5 per cent in August—almost 3½ times the rate for adult males. This very high unemployment rate for all teenagers obscures the even higher rates for certain categories of the teenage population and for teenagers in many large cities. The unemployment rate for black teenagers is now about 40 per cent, whereas the rate for all teenagers is just over 17 per cent. In many urban areas the deviations from the average are even more pronounced.

[Problems of Recovery]

The experience of the last two years has made several very hard facts clear:

First, recovery is still a problem that extends well beyond the next fiscal year even though three and one-half years have passed since the recession began, and more than two years have passed since it touched bottom. Planning for full employment still requires looking ahead four or five years.

Second, one of the principal reasons for the anemia displayed by the recovery is the continuation of a rapid rate of inflation.... [I]t is the inflation, more than any other factor, that sucks the lifeblood of expansion out of the economy and that continues to cause the road back to full employment to be so long and so difficult.

Third,...attempting to control inflation by restricting aggregate demand has proven to be an abysmal and costly failure. The main consequence of such policy has been to reduce production, to increase unemployment, and to cast doubt upon the ability of policy makers to manage a free economy effectively. Alternative methods of slowing inflation—methods that do not place the entire burden of inflation control on production and employment—are urgently needed....

[Short-term Economic Outlook]

The outlook for the remainder of 1977 and for 1978 is unfavorable. We expect the economy to slow down in the last half of 1977, and we would consider ourselves fortunate if we were able to sustain a real growth rate in 1978 high enough to prevent unemployment from rising. Specifically, we project a year-over-year increase in real GNP of from 5 to 5½ per cent in 1977, and an increase in 1978 of from 4 to 4½ per cent. The unemployment rate may fall to the 6.5-6.8 per cent range by the fourth quarter of this year, but only because of recently enacted job creation programs. Thereafter little improvement is to be expected.

Although the forecast is pessimistic, the assumptions that underpin it are, for the most part, reasonably optimistic. For example, we have assumed that the personal saving rate will remain below 6 per cent during 1978, even though this is well below the 7.4 per cent average of the first half of this decade, and even though consumers depleted their savings and increased their debt, partly in anticipation of the income tax rebate that never materialized. We have also assumed that housing starts will remain in the 1.7-1.9 million range over the forecast period even though we expect the cost and availability of mortgage financing to move adversely in response to monetary policies that have been dominated by an obsessive concern with inflation. We have also assumed that Federal Government purchases of goods and services—which have been flat in real terms for the last year and a half—will pick up as the 1978 budget goes into operation.

A certain amount of stimulus may result from the spending of State and local governments, although it is very difficult to be certain about this. According to data for the first half of 1977, State and local governments are running a surplus of about $26-billion at an annual rate in 1977. However, some $15-billion of this surplus represents social insurance funds that are not available to finance capital projects or operating deficits. Further, much of the remaining $11-billion consists of surpluses in only two States—Texas and California. With negligible surpluses in most of the States, any Federal grants to State and local governments are likely to result in speedy increases in government spending.

[Investment and Inflation]

The areas of greatest uncertainty in the economic outlook are business fixed investment, the rate of inflation, and the foreign sector. We have projected a rise in business fixed investment in real terms of about 10 per cent for 1977 and 8 to 9 per cent for 1978. If we achieve growth rates in capital spending of this magnitude, we will have done very well by historical standards. Unfortunately, there are a number of uncertainties that becloud this projection.

On the sunny side, many forecasters have been predicting the imminent arrival of a capital spending spree. While this boom has not as yet materialized, there are reasons for supposing that a pickup in capital spending may come along soon. First of all, there is some new evidence which suggests that capacity utilization measures overstate the amount of unused plant and equipment currently available....

Environmental legislation is accelerating the rate at which our capital stock is becoming obsolete, and the conversion of oil and gas fired facilities to coal-burning facilities will require some investment of a one-shot nature. But whether this will happen quickly or drag on over a period of years is anyone's guess.

[Production Capacity Underused]

Although the factors above make for an optimistic investment picture, there is at least as much reason to be pessimistic. Revisions of capacity utilization and potential output indices notwithstanding, it is clear that the productive facilities of the economy are still badly underutilized. Until increased demand raises operating rates to near full capacity levels, hopes for a capital spending boom are apt to be in vain.

Second, the acute depression of the stock market does not bode well for capital spending. Stock prices are now very low relative to the replacement costs of the physical assets of business enterprise. To say the same thing differently, the cost of raising new capital in financial markets relative to the cost of the physical assets is extremely high. This is a situation that could, perhaps, be corrected by more expansionary monetary policy. However, as long as depression of the stock market persists, it will tend to keep the level of capital spending below desirable levels.

[Negative Factors]

Finally, there is a group of unique negative factors to be considered. Uncertainties surrounding the tax policy changes which Congress will be considering next year could easily cause investment decisions to be delayed until these uncertainties are eliminated. Similarly, investment associated with the energy conservation program are not likely to be undertaken until it is clear what the terms of that program are. In addition, these investments could be stretched out over several years, thereby minimizing their immediate impact.

Surveys of investment intentions are pessimistic about the prospects for capital spending in 1978. We take these surveys seriously, but also are sufficiently impressed by the arguments that predict expansion to project a growth rate in the 8-10 per cent range in real terms. As mentioned earlier, and as will be emphasized throughout this report, such ambitious levels of activity will require the active support of monetary policy.

[Continued High Inflation Rate]

One of the most discouraging results of our forecasting exercise is the likelihood of a continued high rate of inflation. As indicated earlier, inflation decelerated between 1974 and 1976, but has picked up again in the first half of 1977. The implicit price deflator for GNP increased at a 5.3 per cent annual rate in the first quarter of 1977, and at a 7.1 per cent annual rate in the second quarter.

Although the real spendable earning of a typical wage earner has risen very little, unit labor cost continues to rise rapidly, and it is unit labor cost that represents the basic cost-push force that underlies the ongoing inflation....

...In the second quarter of 1977, unit labor cost in nonfinancial corporations was 7.2 per cent above its level of a year ago. Because unit labor cost has continued to rise at an annual rate in excess of 6 per cent, it is difficult to foresee any speedy abatement in the rate of price inflation.

There is no particular reason to expect productivity developments in the near future to deviate much from their longer term trends. In addition, we anticipate that money wages will continue to rise at rates that attempt to make up for past losses in purchasing power. In combination, these trends suggest that unit labor costs and prices will continue to rise at the 6 to 8 per cent trend that has come to be denoted as the "underlying rate of inflation."

...[A] high rate of inflation has a seriously dampening effect on real expenditures in various sectors of the economy. For example, personal income and personal consumption are expected to increase at about 10 per cent next year; but when adjusted for the anticipated inflation, these increases will come to only 3.3 per cent in real terms. Thus, while growth in nominal terms may be quite substantial, the level of real activity will not proceed at a rate nearly rapid enough to reduce unemployment. Indeed, a "growth recession,"—a situation in which real growth remains positive but yet is so slow that unemployment rises—is quite a distinct possibility in the near future.

[Monetary Policy]

One of the greatest unknowns which will affect the outcome is the conduct of monetary policy. Our view is that monetary policy in the past three years has been too restrictive; that this has severely impeded recovery; and that it is past time to reverse this posture and to support economic growth. Our present forecast is based on the assumption that monetary policy will accommodate the limited growth that is being projected. This implies rates of growth in M_1 [money supply term; calculated as currency in circulation plus demand deposits in commercial banks] in a range of 7.0 to 8.0 per cent. If monetary policy fails to provide such accommodation, as we and several of our witnesses fear may happen, interest rates will surely rise, and this will slow investment spending, especially in the presently strong housing sector. As explained below, it will also add an additional deflationary impulse by further weakening the current account of our balance of payments.

As indicated earlier, the foreign sector has become a very serious question mark in the outlook for the American economy. Foreign demand for U.S. goods can provide an important stimulus to our economy. On the other hand, when our consumers purchase foreign rather than domestic automobiles and TV sets this employs foreign workers rather than our own workers. An excess of exports over imports provides a net stimulus in employment to our economy, whereas an excess of imports over exports does the opposite.

During the present economic recovery the foreign sector has been a burdensome drag. The reason is that recovery in the United States began sooner and proved to be brisker than in other industrial countries. The effect has been to cause our imports to grow much more rapidly than our exports. The differential growth rates have, in fact, been so huge that we are very likely to run up a record trade deficit of $25-$30-billion in 1977.

[Sluggish Worldwide Recovery]

A deterrent to our own recovery is the circumstance that recovery remains sluggish in the major industrial countries, especially West Germany and Japan. Neither of these countries is likely to achieve the growth targets that they announced earlier this year. Although Japan has recently indicated the intention to stimulate its economy, this can hardly be expected to have much impact on our massive trade deficit.

[U.S. Trade Deficits to Continue]

The United States is very likely to continue to have substantial trade deficits in the next two or three years. Petroleum imports are sure to continue at high levels. And much will depend on the movement of international capital. A large part of the trade deficit has been financed by reinvestment of OPEC surpluses and by other capital movements. Although these inflows helped to finance our oil bill, they have held up the value of the dollar in relation to foreign currencies and this has made our exports relatively expensive, our imports relatively cheap, and has therefore prevented our trade gap from narrowing. If these capital inflows persist, as may happen if tight money raises interest rates or the political situation abroad deteriorates, the dollar will continue to be strong, but at the same time this will perpetuate the trade deficit and therefore have a depressing effect on our economy....

Long Range Projections

The Joint Economic Committee has stated on many occasions that the way to achieve optimal economic progress is to begin by setting forth clearly defined economic targets with respect to employment, growth, and the rate of inflation. We have gone on to say that policy should be designed in a way that attempts to attain those goals. Two and a half years ago the Committee recommended that policy be redirected in an expansionary manner so as to reduce the unemployment rate below 6 per cent by the end of 1977. That advice was not heeded, and the failure to adopt expansionary policies has resulted in an unemployment rate that is expected to remain well above 6 per cent at the end of the year.

The Carter Administration's targets for 1981, as amended in its Mid-Year Review of the Budget, are as follows:

- reduction of the unemployment rate to 4¾ per cent;
- reduction of the inflation rate to 4-3/10 per cent;
- balance of the Federal budget at expenditure and revenue levels equal to 21 per cent of GNP.

As indicated earlier the JEC has always supported the idea of establishing economic targets toward which policy should strive. Furthermore, our bias has been to adopt targets that are relatively ambitious because we have felt that only by working toward ambitious goals could we hope to sustain sufficient momentum to maintain real growth and employment at high levels. President Carter's decision to establish targets and his determination to look into the economic future are therefore entirely commendable decisions that are wholly in tune with the type of approach that this Committee has long been urging.

[Carter's Goals Not Achievable]

Although we have urged the delineation of clear but ambitious goals, we have also stressed that these goals must be achievable in response to reasonable policies. Unfortunately, our recent staff study, "The Macroeconomic Goals of the Administration for 1981: Targets and Realizations," found that only a very unusual combination of extremely good luck such as bumper harvests and cheap and plentiful new energy supplies, combined with rapid expansion of the money supply, would allow all of these goals to be achieved simultaneously. The major conclusions of the study were as follows:

(1) To reach the inflation target of 4.3 per cent by using fiscal and monetary policies would necessitate such restrictive policies that the unemployment rate would rise well above its present level of 7 per cent. The Administration's present anti-inflation program is not nearly powerful enough to change this picture in any significant way.

(2) To reach the full employment and balanced budget targets, non-residential fixed investment would have to grow by 10 per cent per year in real terms for five consecutive years. This target is beyond reach unless monetary policy becomes sharply more expansionary and this would make it most unlikely that the inflation target could be reached.

(3) The balanced budget and full employment targets are very likely to be incompatible because of structural changes in the economy that have weakened aggregate demand and that will make it necessary to run a budget deficit if the economy is to achieve full employment. The report singled out the foreign sector and State and local spending as sectors that were apt to be particularly weak.

The testimony of witnesses before the Committee generally confirmed the conclusions of the staff report. We commend the Administration for focusing attention on the longer term horizon but feel that Congress should revise these targets in a way that makes them more realistic goals at which to aim policies.

[Inflation and Recovery]

Recovery from the present recession has been seriously hampered because the recession has been accompanied by an alarmingly rapid and seemingly intractable rate of inflation. Other recovery periods were not marred by the confusion and indecision caused by the difficulty of knowing whether to pursue expansionary policy to spur recovery, or restrictive policy to slow inflation. This confusion is but one of the reasons why inflation is showing itself to be the principal impediment to speedy recovery. It is this theme that provides the subject matter for the remainder of this report.

[Unemployment and Inflation]

The conventional view of the relationship between unemployment and inflation is that expansionary policies which reduce unemployment will also add to inflation. This is because such policies raise total demand in the economy and cause a price pull effect. Simultaneously, there is a tightening of labor markets which raises wages and unit labor costs and tends, therefore, to cause an upward price push. In this view there is a trade-off between unemployment and inflation. The economy can enjoy lower unemployment, but only at the cost of a higher rate of inflation; or it can reduce the rate of inflation, but only at the cost of higher unemployment....

In summary: Inflation causes the competitive position of the economy to deteriorate and this has an adverse effect on the current account of the balance of payments and on the level of domestic employment. These effects will tend to be offset if rates of international currency exchange are free to fluctuate. If, however, it is the policy of the Fed to prevent the dollar from falling in response to market forces, it will pursue foreign exchange intervention policies and/or restrictive domestic monetary policies. These policies will raise interest rates, attract foreign capital, prevent the exchange rate from falling, and thus perpetuate the purchasing power drain that comes from an excess of imports over exports.

Since 1973, this Committee has been on record as opposing official intervention in foreign exchange markets for the purpose of achieving domestic economic objectives. Because of the very close parallel between the economic effects of foreign exchange intervention and domestic monetary policies under the flexible exchange rate system, it is important to add that monetary policies should not be used to achieve exchange rate objectives.

[Monetary and Fiscal Policies]

...[B]oth fiscal and monetary policies have been deterred from promoting recovery aggressively because of the fear that expansionary policies will raise the rate of inflation. This situation has also produced added potential for conflict between fiscal and monetary policy. There is little doubt that fiscal policy has been inhibited by the fear that any effort by Congress or the Administration to hasten recovery by an expansionary fiscal action will be negated by restrictive Federal Reserve monetary policy. Such policy conflicts are most unfortunate. If the Fed offsets the aggregate expenditure effect of the fiscal action, there will be no increase in employment to show for the effort, but there will be a larger deficit. Worse still, a movement towards fiscal ease combined with increasing monetary tightness raises interest rates, reduces the rate of capital formation, and impairs the economy's long-range growth potential.

[Federal Reserve Board]

The Fed [Federal Reserve Board] is supposed to conduct monetary policy. To the extent that it is able to prod Congress and the Administration into the adoption of restrictive budget policies, it controls fiscal policy as well. The Fed wishes to protect its independence. But as matters stand at the present time, that independence gives the impression of being a one-way street.

This Committee does not subscribe to the view that an independent monetary authority is a necessary last line of defense against the inflationary spending proclivities of the Executive and the Legislature. Indeed, the budgets that have been approved by Congress since the inception of the Budget Act bear witness to the fact that Congress is quite capable of conducting fiscal policy in a responsible manner. Congress cannot, and should not, remain forever tolerant of monetary policies that are clearly at variance with the economic goals toward which Congress is striving. Rational fiscal policy cannot be planned in a vacuum separate from monetary policy. Yet, that is the way economic policy is currently conducted.

[Macroeconomic Strategy]

This Committee is strongly of the opinion that it is time to coordinate and integrate monetary and fiscal policies. The macroeconomic strategy we propose is as follows:

1) Officials of the Administration and the Fed should begin the annual economic program by establishing a set of targets for the coming fiscal year. These targets would include, as a minimum, the rate of unemployment, the rate of growth of real output, the rate of inflation, and the distribution of the national product between consumption, capital formation, government purchases, and the net export of goods and services. The Administration and the Fed should be obliged to agree to a common set of target values prior to the undertaking of the next step. Otherwise, further steps are apt to be futile and policy will work at cross-purposes.

2) The second step is for the Administration and the Fed to develop a consensus forecast of economic activity for the coming fiscal year. This forecast should be a baseline projection which incorporates the current services budget and also a clearly defined rate of monetary growth. It must be emphasized that this must be a consensus projection, and it should be made public.

3) The baseline projection should then be compared with the targets previously established. Policy decisions may then be made that, when implemented, will eliminate the discrepancies between the projected and the target values. In the absence of such a cooperative program, it will continue to be difficult for Congress to evaluate the adequacy of monetary-fiscal policies.

This planning step will also involve consideration of the important issue of policy mix. The expenditure requirements of new programs must be considered here. If more stimulus is needed, a joint decision must be made whether this should be provided by monetary policy in order to stimulate capital formation and growth, or by tax reduction in the hope that this might ease wage pressures and create fewer balance-of-payments problems. Economic conditions might be such that balanced monetary-fiscal expansion is advisable.

4) The national economic strategy having been agreed to, the next step is to see to its implementation. The results should be monitored as often as possible, but no less frequently than each calendar quarter as GNP data become available. Provision must also be made for altering the plan in a way that will provide offsets for unexpected deviations between the original forecast and the actual outcome.

It will require a cooperative sequence of this sort to introduce rational macroeconomic policymaking. As we have indicated earlier, it is obsolete and much too costly to preserve the antiquated fiction that politicians are irresponsible spenders, in consequence of which an authoritarian central bank is required as a last line of defense against inflation. A last line of defense against unemployment needs to be given similar priority.

Summary and Conclusions

The economic outlook for the remainder of 1977 and for 1978 is for a slowing down in the rate of real economic growth. Further substantial reductions in unemployment seem unlikely to occur in the near future, and the inflation rate will continue to be high and dominated by the rapid growth of unit labor costs. Even with rather optimistic assumptions about consumer and government spending, the continuing weakness of fixed investment and the sharp deterioration in our international trade position seem likely to ensure fairly sluggish performance in our economy.

[Federal Reserve Policy]

One of the most serious question marks concerns the future course of monetary policy. The obsession with inflation has caused the Fed to reduce real M_1 by about 9 per cent since the end of 1972. This disastrous policy was a principal cause of the magnitude and length of the recession; it has been a perennial source of obstruction to recovery; and it now threatens to abort the recovery entirely if the policy is continued. It is difficult to predict how monetary policy will behave in the next few months. On the one hand, M_1 growth has accelerated in the last six months. But on the other hand, short-term interest rates have been rising and the Fed recently raised its rediscount rate to discourage member bank borrowing. Moreover, the view expressed by the Fed that monetary growth rates are excessive, and that the declining international value of the dollar may require Fed intervention, are strong signals that tightening is in the offing. Such tightening, at this time, would be inappropriate. It would abort the very healthy recovery of homebuilding, it would keep the stock market depressed and further delay the long-awaited revival of capital spending, and because it would artificially lift the international value of the dollar, would cause a further deterioration in our international trade position.

Because inflation has been such an enormous deterrent to the recovery of the economy, we have devoted a sizeable portion of this report to this problem. While we may agree that inflation retards recovery and causes unemployment, we most definitely reject the conclusion that some draw from this fact, namely, that stabilization policy should devote itself exclusively to the elimination of inflation.

Our conclusion is quite the opposite. At present the entire burden of inflation control falls on production and employment. This burden should be shifted, and this report has indicated some ways in which this can be done. The disruptions and inequities caused by inflation can be eased by judicious changes in the income tax laws. Inflation can be reduced and [employment] simultaneously increased by replacing payroll taxes with alternative means of financing social insurance. And tax incentives can be designed that provide business and labor with economic incentives to moderate their wage-price demands.

[Coordinated Policy Recommended]

To support orderly economic growth and to eliminate potential policy conflict, the Committee recommends the establishment of a procedure that would require the Administration and the Federal Reserve to come forward each year with a coherent monetary-fiscal program. This program should include a consensus forecast, a set of mutually agreed upon targets for policy, and a plan for reconciling the forecast with the target values.

[Republican Minority Report]

Because of our differences over monetary policy and the international sector and the recommendations emanating therefrom, the Minority cannot issue a joint report with the Majority. However, we do have substantial areas of agreement, which are outlined below.... These differences lead to our desire to discuss saving and social security in more detail than is done in the Majority views. Our chief point of disagreement...[is] the Majority chapter on monetary policy....

Areas of Agreement

(1) Recovery is still a problem that extends well beyond the next fiscal year.

(2) We expect the economy to slow down in the last half of 1977, and in 1978.

(3) One of the principal reasons for the anemia displayed by the recovery is the continuation of a rapid rate of inflation.

(4) Many Government policies, including the energy program, higher social security taxes, import quotas and tariffs, increased price supports, certain OSHA [Occupational Safety and Health Administration] regulations, the proposed minimum wage legislation, and other regulations

and red tape, whatever their other merits or demerits, do affect the rate of inflation. Congress should take every opportunity to rationalize regulation of business and to liberalized trade.

(5) The exemptions and bracket structure of the tax system must be adjusted annually to prevent the now-automatic increase in tax rates due to inflation from destabilizing the economy.

(6) Taxation of nominal (unadjusted for inflation) capital gains should be ended. Only real gains should be taxed. The current practice of taxing that part of capital gains due only to inflation is a senseless capital levy.

(7) Congress should discontinue the taxation of nominal (unadjusted for inflation) interest rates. Tax only real interest earned in excess of the inflation rate to allow people a true return on their savings.

(8) Congress should examine seriously the problem of underdepreciation due to inflation and develop a workable formula for replacement cost depreciation.

(9) Capacity utilization measures overstate the amount of unused plant and equipment currently available. This is partly due to restricted energy supplies. In addition, certain environmental legislation is accelerating the rate at which our capital stock is becoming obsolete.

Finally, the conversion of oil and gas fired facilities to use coal will require billions of dollars of investment.

(10) The Congress should act promptly to end the uncertainties surrounding proposed tax changes, uncertainties which could easily cause investment decisions to be delayed:

While we join with the Majority report with the exception of the monetary and international economic policy recommendations, the Minority Members wish to sharpen a few points contained in the Majority report.

[Deficit Spending]

While the Majority fails to point out the importance of excessive deficit spending as a cause of inflation, they are to be commended for facing up to the inflationary consequences of Federal regulation, restraint of trade, and the taxes contained in the Carter energy plan.

We also commend the Majority report for its analysis of the tax consequences of inflation. The Minority has repeatedly warned, in reports and in proposed legislation, that inflation has boosted taxpayers into higher brackets, raising taxes even in recessions and destabilizing the economy.

The report's warning against taxation of illusory inflation-induced capital gains is most timely. If, as is rumored, the Administration will seek to tax capital gains as if they were ordinary income (a practice no other major nation follows), then at most only real gains should be taxed. Otherwise, saving, investment, and the growth of jobs and income could be severely crippled.

The Majority recommendation that only real interest be taxed is also welcome. Today, a typical saver in the 20 per cent tax bracket may get 5 per cent interest on his savings. This is completely wiped out by the erosion of his savings by 5 per cent inflation. To add insult to injury, the saver must turn one-fifth of that interest over to the government. He gets 5 per cent interest, and loses 6 per cent to inflation and taxes, for a net loss of 1 per cent. Considering that savings (whether personal or corporate) is our only source of investment money, and our main source of job creation and productivity growth, this negative return is a disgrace.

The Majority discusses the underdepreciation of plant and equipment caused by inflation. This could be costing business as much as $20-$30-billion per year, roughly one-quarter of corporate profits. It is, in effect, a tax on capital equipment, retarding growth and reducing real wages by limiting the supply of capital with which labor can work. Some form of replacement cost depreciation is essential. Otherwise, corporate saving will be inadequate to sustain the growth we need to bring down unemployment.

October

CARTER U.N. SPEECH ON
ARMS CONTROL AND DISARMAMENT
October 4, 1977

The issue of disarmament dominated President Carter's Oct. 4 address to the 32nd United Nations General Assembly. The President spoke on the control of both nuclear and conventional arms.

Carter announced that the United States and the Soviet Union were "within sight of a significant agreement." The announcement came one day after the original SALT agreement between the two countries expired. Both sides agreed to maintain the original agreement's ceilings on intercontinental missiles until a new agreement was reached.

As a step toward his goal of a "world truly free of nuclear weapons," Carter pledged American willingness to reduce nuclear weapons levels by as much as 50 per cent if the Soviets reciprocated. Warning that nuclear weapons proliferation posed "one of the greatest challenges" facing humanity, Carter reiterated U.S. support for efforts by supplier nations to ensure that the peaceful use of atomic power not become the basis for the production of explosives. (SALT talks, p. 243; Carter nuclear policy, p. 271)

Nuclear Testing

On the issue of nuclear testing, Carter proposed a ban on "all explosions of nuclear devices, no matter what their claimed justification—peaceful or military." Carter added: "We appreciate the efforts of other nations to reach this same goal." Soviet President Leonid I. Brezhnev responded to Carter's appeal to halt all nuclear testing in a Nov. 2 speech marking the 60th anniversary of the Bolshevik revolution. Brezhnev said the Soviet

Union was "prepared to reach agreement on a moratorium covering nuclear explosions for peaceful purposes along with a ban on all nuclear weapons tests for a definite period." The statement marked a shift in the position of the Soviet Union which had previously insisted that any suspension of nuclear explosions exclude low-yield tests for peaceful purposes.

Carter made explicit for the first time U.S. policy against a first strike with nuclear weapons unless attacked. "I hereby solemnly declare on behalf of the United States that we will not use nuclear weapons except in self-defense," he said.

The President said the United States had begun to curb the trade in conventional arms and that the U.S. aim was "to reduce both the quantity and the deadliness of the weapons that we sell. We have taken the first few steps, but we cannot go very far alone." The President also said he hoped to work with other supplier nations "to decrease the need for more numerous, more deadly and ever more expensive weapons."

Commitment to Israel

Turning to the Middle East, Carter took pains to re-emphasize that the U.S. commitment "to Israel's security is unquestionable." Carter's pledge followed a period of strained relations between the United States and Israel that came to a head Oct. 1 with the release of a joint U.S.-Soviet declaration on the proposed Geneva peace conference on the Middle East. Announcement of the U.S.-Soviet agreement brought an angry response from Israel and its American supporters. Despite assurances that the statement did not represent a change in U.S. policy, the Israeli government of Prime Minister Menahem Begin made clear it viewed the announcement as a sharp turn for the worse in relations with its vital ally.

*The President told the U.N. members "the legitimate rights of the Palestinian people must be recognized." He went on to say: "How these rights are to be defined and implemented is, of course, for the interested parties to decide in detailed negotiations and not for us to dictate." Carter noted that the United States did "not intend to impose from the outside a settlement on nations of the Middle East." (*Sadat and Begin speeches, p. 827)

Other Issues

Carter said he supported efforts in southern Africa to effect a peaceful and rapid transition to majority rule and independence. He referred to the regions by names used by black nationalists—Zimbabwe (Rhodesia) and Namibia (Southwest Africa). (Rhodesian settlement proposal, p. 583; Historic Documents of 1976, pp. 611, 721)

On the topic of the Indian Ocean, the President said that neither the United States nor the Soviet Union had a large military presence there, "nor is there a rapidly mounting competition between us." Carter stated: "Restraint in the area may well begin with a mutual effort to stabilize our presence and to avoid an escalation in military competition."

> *Following is the prepared text of President Carter's Oct. 4, 1977, speech to the United Nations General Assembly urging stronger efforts toward disarmament and arms control. (Boldface headings in brackets have been added by Congressional Quarterly to highlight the organization of the text.):*

Thirty-two years ago, in the cold dawn of the Atomic Age, this Organization came into being. Its first and most urgent purpose has been to secure peace for an exhausted and ravaged world.

Present conditions in some respects appear quite hopeful.

Yet the assurance of peace still eludes us. Before the end of this century, a score of nations could possess nuclear weapons. If this should happen, the world we leave our children will mock our hopes for peace.

● The level of nuclear armaments could grow by tens of thousands, and the same situation could well occur with advanced conventional weapons. The temptation to use them, or fear that someone else will do it first, will be almost irresistible.

● The ever-growing trade in conventional arms subverts international commerce from a force for peace to a caterer for war.

● Violence, terrorism, assassination, undeclared wars—all threaten to destroy the restraint and moderation that must become the dominant characteristic of our age.

Unless we establish a code of international behavior in which the resort to violence becomes increasingly irrelevant to the pursuit of national interests, we will crush the world's dreams for human development and the full flowering of human freedom.

We have already become a global community—but only in the sense that we face common problems and share, for good or ill, a common future. In this community, power to solve the world's problems—particularly economic and political power—no longer lies solely in the hands of a few nations. Power is now widely shared among many nations with different cultures, histories and aspirations. The question is whether we will allow our differences to defeat us or whether we will work together to realize our common hopes for peace.

Today, I want to address the major dimensions of peace, and the role the United States intends to play in limiting and reducing all armaments, controlling nuclear technology, restricting the arms trade, and settling disputes by peaceful means.

[The Control of Nuclear Arms]

Winston Churchill, upon first hearing of the splitting of the atom, described that awesome discovery as "knowledge which until now has been mercifully withheld from Man." Since then we have learned in Dürren-

739

matt's chilling words, that "what has once been thought can never be unthought."

If we are to have any assurance that our children are to live out their lives in a world which satisfies our hopes—or that they will have a chance to live at all—we must finally come to terms with this enormous force and turn it to beneficial ends.

Peace will not be assured until the weapons of war are finally put away. While we work toward that goal, nations will want sufficient arms to preserve their security. The United States' purpose is to ensure peace. It is for that reason that our military posture and our alliances will remain as strong as necessary to deter attack.

However, the security of the global community cannot forever rest on a balance of terror. In the past, war has been accepted as the ultimate arbiter of disputes among nations.

In the nuclear era, we can no longer think of war as merely the continuation of diplomacy by other means. Nuclear war cannot be measured by archaic standards of "victory" and "defeat." This stark reality imposes on the United States and the Soviet Union an awesome and special responsibility.

The United States is engaged along with other nations in a broad range of negotiations. In Strategic Arms Limitation Talks, we and the Soviets are within sight of a significant agreement in limiting the total numbers of weapons and in restricting certain categories of weapons of special concern to each of us. We can also start the crucial process of curbing the relentless march of technological development which makes nuclear weapons ever more difficult to control.

We must look beyond the present, and work to prevent the critical threats and instabilities of the future. If the principles of self-restraint, reciprocity, and mutual accommodation of interests are observed, then the United States and the Soviet Union will not only succeed in limiting weapons, but will also create a foundation for better relations in other spheres.

The United States is willing to go as far as possible, consistent with our security interests, in limiting and reducing our nuclear weapons. On a reciprocal basis we are willing now to reduce them by 10 per cent, by 20 per cent, even by 50 per cent. Then we will work for further reductions to a world truly free of nuclear weapons.

The United States also recognizes the threat of continued testing of nuclear explosives.

Negotiations for a comprehensive ban on nuclear explosions are now being conducted by the United States, the United Kingdom and the Soviet Union. As in other areas where vital national security interests are engaged, agreements must be verifiable and fair. They must be seen by all the parties as serving a longer term interest that justifies the restraints of the moment.

That longer term interest in this instance is to close one more avenue of nuclear competition, and thereby demonstrate to all the world that the major nuclear powers take seriously our obligations to reduce the threat of nuclear catastrophe.

My country believes that the time has come to end all explosions of nuclear devices, no matter what their claimed justification—peaceful or military. We appreciate the efforts of other nations to reach this same goal.

During the past nine months, I have expressed the special importance we attach to controlling nuclear proliferation. But I fear that many do not understand why the United States feels as it does.

Why is it so important to avoid the chance that one or two or ten other nations might acquire one or two or ten nuclear weapons of their own? Let me try to explain, for I deeply believe that this is one of the greatest challenges that we face in the next quarter of a century.

It is a truism that nuclear weapons are a powerful deterrent. They are a deterrent because they threaten. They could be used for terrorism or blackmail as well as war. But they threaten not just the intended enemy, they threaten every nation—combatant and non-combatant alike. This is why all of us must be concerned.

Let me be frank. The existence of nuclear weapons in the US and USSR, and in Great Britain, France and China, is something we cannot undo except by the painstaking process of negotiation. But the existence of these weapons does not mean that other nations need to develop their own weapons, any more than it provides a reason for those of us who have them to share them with others.

Rather it imposes two solemn obligations on the nations which have the capacity to export nuclear fuels and technologies—the obligations to meet legitimate energy needs and, in doing so, to ensure that nothing we export contributes—directly or indirectly—to the production of nuclear explosives. That is why the supplier nations are seeking a common policy, and that is why the United States and the Soviet Union, even as we struggle to find common ground in the SALT talks, have already moved closer toward agreement and cooperation in our efforts to limit nuclear proliferation.

I believe that the London Suppliers Group must conclude its work as it is presently constituted, so that world security will be safeguarded from the pressures of commercial competition. We have learned that it is not enough to safeguard just some facilities, or some materials. Full scope comprehensive safeguards are necessary.

Two weeks from now, more than thirty supplier and consuming nations will convene for the International Fuel Cycle Evaluation which we proposed last spring. For the next several years experts will work together on every facet of the nuclear fuel cycle.

The scientists and policymakers of these nations face a tremendous challenge. We know that by the year 2000, nuclear power reactors could be producing enough plutonium to make tens of thousands of bombs every year. I believe, from my personal knowledge of this issue, that there are ways to solve the problems we face. I believe that there are alternative fuel cycles that can be managed safely on a global basis. I hope therefore that the International Fuel Cycle Evaluation will have the support and encouragement of every nation.

I have heard it said that efforts to control nuclear proliferation are futile; that the genie is already out of the bottle. I do not believe this to be true. It should not be forgotten that for 25 years the nuclear club did not expand its membership. By genuine cooperation we can make certain that it grows no further.

[Conventional Arms]

I have talked about the special problems of nuclear arms control and nuclear proliferation at some length. Now let me turn to the problem of conventional arms control. This is not a matter of the future—not even of the near future—but of the immediate present. Worldwide military expenditures are now in the neighborhood of $300-billion a year. Last year the nations of the world spent more than 60 times as much equipping each soldier as we did educating each child. The industrialized nations spend the most money, but the rate of growth in military spending is faster in the developing world. And while only a handful of states produce sophisticated weapons, the number of nations which seek to purchase them is increasing rapidly.

The conventional arms race both causes and feeds on the threat of larger and more deadly wars. It levies an enormous burden on an already troubled world economy.

For its part, the United States has now begun to constrain its arms exports. Our aim is to reduce both the quantity and deadliness of the weapons we sell. We have taken the first few steps, but we cannot go very far alone. Nations whose neighbors are purchasing large quantities of arms feel constrained to do the same. Supplier nations who practice restraint in arms sales sometimes find that they simply lose valuable commercial markets to other suppliers.

We hope to work with other suppliers to cut back on the flow of arms and to reduce the rate at which the most advanced and sophisticated weapon technologies spread around the world. We do not expect this task to be easy or to produce instant results. But we are committed to stop the spiral of increasing sales.

Equally important, we hope that purchaser nations, individually and through regional organizations, will limit their arms imports. We are ready to provide to some nations the necessary means for legitimate self-defense, but we are also eager to work with any nation or region in order to decrease the need for more numerous, more deadly and ever more expensive weapons.

[Regional Conflict]

Fourteen years ago, one of my predecessors spoke in this room under circumstances that in certain ways resembled these. It was a time, he said, of comparative calm and there was an atmosphere of rising hopes about the prospect of controlling nuclear energy. The first specific step had been taken to limit the nuclear arms race—a test-ban treaty signed by nearly a hundred nations.

But the succeeding years did not live up to the optimistic prospect John F. Kennedy placed before this Assembly because, as a community of nations, we failed to address the deepest sources of potential conflict among us.

As we seek to establish the principles of detente among the major nuclear powers, we believe that these principles must also apply in regional conflicts. The United States is committed to the peaceful settlement of differences. We are committed to the strengthening of the peace-making capabilities of the United Nations and regional organizations, such as the Organization of African Unity and the Organization of American States.

The United States supports Great Britain's efforts to bring about a peaceful, rapid transition to majority rule and independence in Zimbabwe. We have joined other members of the Security Council and the Secretary General in efforts to bring about independence and democratic rule in Namibia. We are pleased with the level of cooperation we have achieved with the leaders of the nations in the area, as well as those people who are struggling for independence. We urge South Africa and other nations to support the proposed solution to the problems in Zimbabwe, and to cooperate still more closely in providing for a smooth and prompt transition in Namibia.

But it is essential that all outside nations exercise restraint in their actions in Zimbabwe and Namibia, so that we can bring about majority rule and avoid a widening war that could engulf the southern half of the African continent.

Of all the regional conflicts in the world, none holds more menace than the Middle East. War there has carried the world to the edge of nuclear confrontation. It has disrupted the world economy and imposed severe hardships on the people in the developed and developing nations alike. So true peace—peace embodied in binding treaties—is essential. It will be in the interest of the Israelis and the Arabs. It is in the interest of the American people. It is in the interest of the entire world.

The United Nations Security Council has provided the basis for peace in Resolutions 242 and 338, but negotiation in good faith by all parties is needed to give substance to peace.

Such good faith negotiations must be inspired by a recognition that all nations in the area—Israel and the Arab countries—have a right to exist in peace, with early establishment of normal diplomatic relations, economic and cultural exchanges. Peace must include a process in which the bitter divisions of generations—hatreds and suspicions—can be overcome. Negotiations cannot be successful if any of the parties harbor the deceitful view that peace is simply an interlude in which to prepare for war.

Good faith negotiations also require acceptance by all sides of the fundamental rights and interests of everyone involved.

• For Israel, this must mean borders that are recognized and secure. Security arrangements are crucial to a nation that has fought for its survival in each of the last four decades. The commitment of the United States to Israel's security is unquestionable.

• For the Arabs, the legitimate rights of the Palestinians must be recognized. One of the things that binds the American people to Israel is our shared respect for human rights and the courage with which Israel has defended such rights. It is clear that a true and lasting peace in the Middle East must also respect the rights of all the peoples of the area. How these rights are to be defined and implemented is, of course, for the interested parties to decide in negotiations, and not for us to dictate.

We do not intend to impose from the outside a settlement on the nations of the Middle East.

The United States has been meeting with the Foreign Ministers of Israel and the Arab nations involved in the search for peace. We are staying in close contact with the Soviet Union, with whom we share responsibility for reconvening the Geneva Conference. As a result of these consultations, the Soviet Union and the United States have agreed to call for the resumption of the Geneva Conference before the end of this year. While a number of procedural questions remain, if the parties continue to act in good faith, I believe they can be answered.

The major powers have a special responsibility to act with restraint in areas of the world where they have competing interests because the association of these interests with local rivalries and conflicts can lead to confrontation. In the Indian Ocean area neither we nor the Soviet Union has a large military presence, nor is there a rapidly mounting competition between us. Restraint in the area may well begin with a mutual effort to stabilize our presence and to avoid an escalation in military competition. Then both sides can consider how our military activities in the Indian Ocean area might be even further reduced.

The peaceful settlement of differences is, of course, essential. The United States is willing to abide by that principle, as in the case of the recently signed Panama Canal Treaties. Once ratified, these treaties can transform the US-Panama relationship into one that permanently protects the interests and respects the sovereignty of both countries.

We have survived and surmounted major challenges since the UN was founded, but we can accelerate progress even in a world of ever increasing diversity. A commitment to strengthen international institutions is vital, but progress lies also in our national policies. We can work together and form a community of peace if we accept the kind of obligations I have suggested:

• First, an obligation to remove the threat of nuclear weaponry, to reverse the build-up of armaments and their trade, and to conclude bilateral and multilateral arms control agreements that can bring security to all of us.

• To reduce the reliance of nations on nuclear weaponry I hereby solemnly declare on behalf of the United States that we will not use nuclear weapons except in self-defense; that is, in circumstances of an actual nuclear or conventional attack on the United States, our territories or armed forces or such an attack on our allies.

● In addition, we hope that initiatives by the Western nations to secure mutual and balanced force reductions in Europe will be met by equal response from the Warsaw Pact countries.

● Second, an obligation to show restraint in areas of tension, to negotiate disputes and to settle them peacefully, and to strengthen peacemaking capabilities of the United Nations and regional organizations.

● And, finally, an effort by all nations, East as well as West, North as well as South, to fulfill mankind's aspirations for human development and human freedom. It is to meet these basic demands that we build governments and seek peace.

We must share these obligations for our mutual survival and prosperity.

We can see a world at peace. We can work for a world without want. We can build a global community dedicated to these purposes and to human dignity.

The view that I have sketched for you, today, is that of one leader in only one nation. However wealthy and powerful the United States may be—however capable of leadership—this power is increasingly relative, the leadership increasingly in need of being shared. No nation has a monopoly of vision, of creativity, of idea. Bringing these together from many nations is our common responsibility and challenge. For only in these ways can the idea of a peaceful global community grow and prosper.

SOVIET UNION ADOPTS
NEW CONSTITUTION
October 4-7, 1977

The parliament of the Soviet Union Oct. 7 approved unanimously a new Soviet constitution to replace the one enacted under Joseph Stalin in 1936. The new document differed little from its predecessor, although it did create the position of First Deputy Chairman of the Presidium, codify for the first time the role of the Communist Party and add a new section on foreign policy. The document became the law of the land after ratification by the 1,517-member Supreme Soviet, or parliament, which had taken a series of 22 votes on various sections of the charter but had made only minor changes.

Soviet President Leonid I. Brezhnev's speech Oct. 4 opened four days of deliberations on the draft constitution which had first been made public June 4. He praised the new document as a "true reflection of our gains, our aspirations and hopes, which gives a correct definition of our rights and duties." Brezhnev noted that the new constitution signaled the onset of a mature socialist society which, "while formalizing what has been achieved...opens up a perspective for the further advance of Communist construction." There had been three previous constitutions: in 1918, 1924 and 1936.

He scored the "shameless fabrications and blatant lies about the Soviet Union" promulgated in the West. "What real rights and freedoms are guaranteed to the masses in present-day imperialist society?" Brezhnev asked. The Soviet President defined Western rights as unemployment, costly health care, racial discrimination, organized crime, and the Western media "going out of their way to educate the younger generation in a spirit of selfishness, cruelty and violence." It could not be denied, he concluded, "that socialism has long cured these social sores."

Brezhnev also said that during public discussion of the Soviet constitution he had received reports of "...deception of the state...cheating...bribe taking...[of] a superficial approach to the working people's requirements and instances of harassment for criticism." He said all such reports would be investigated and the offenders punished "with the full severity of the law."

The Constitution's Provisions

The charter codified the role of the Communist Party as the "leading and guiding force of Soviet society and the nucleus of its political system." The statement in the constitution thereby removed the contradiction of having the nation's source of political power—the Communist Party—unnoticed in its basic law.

The new charter made no basic changes in the relationship between the individual and the state. It rested on the premise that rights were granted by the state to its citizens and therefore could be limited or suspended by the state. It stressed certain economic guarantees such as rights to employment, leisure time, health care, old age and disability care, housing and education. The constitution contained a section on women's rights advocating equal access to employment, education and job promotions, and paid maternity leave. A clause added to the original draft called for "the gradual reduction of working hours for women with small children."

The document also included guarantees of various political freedoms, such as freedom of conscience, inviolability of the person and the home, rights of citizens to privacy and the "right to lodge complaints against actions of officials in state organs and public organizations." An amendment to Article 48 strengthened the right of the citizen to criticize the state. The original draft said, "Persecutions for criticism shall be prohibited"; the final version added, "Persons guilty of such persecution shall be called to account." But Article 59 stated that the exercise of rights and freedoms under the Soviet constitution was "inseparable from the performance by citizens of their duties...."

Changes in U.S.S.R. Leadership

The new constitution created the position of First Deputy Chairman of the Presidium of the Supreme Soviet—in effect, a Vice President. The new position permitted Brezhnev to assume the presidency of the U.S.S.R. June 16 while remaining in his key post as General Secretary of the Communist Party. The change relieved Brezhnev of the routine ceremonial duties associated with being head of state. Signs of impending changes had been apparent May 24 when Brezhnev's predecessor as President, Nikolai V. Podgorny, was ousted from the Politburo, the party's highest decision-

*making body. The Supreme Soviet Oct. 7 approved the nomination of 76-
year old Deputy Foreign Minister Vasily V. Kusnetsov for the newly
created post of first deputy chairman.*

> *Following are excerpts from President Leonid I. Brezhnev's
> Oct. 4, 1977 speech outlining the changes in the draft con-
> stitution and excerpts from the constitution ratified by the
> Supreme Soviet Oct. 7, 1977, as provided by the Information
> Office of the Embassy of the Soviet Union.* (Boldface
> headings in brackets have been added by Congressional
> Quarterly to highlight the organization of the text.):

BREZHNEV SPEECH

Esteemed Comrade Delegates,

The present session of the Supreme Soviet has before it a task that is
historic in the full sense of the word: adoption of a new Constitution of the
Union of Soviet Socialist Republics.

We are about to adopt the new Constitution on the eve of the 60th Anniversary of the Great October Socialist Revolution. This is not a mere
coincidence in time of two major events in the life of the country. The connection between them goes much deeper. The new Constitution, one might
say, epitomizes the whole 60 years of the Soviet state's development. It is
striking evidence of the fact that the ideas proclaimed by the October
Revolution and Lenin's precepts are being successfully translated into life.

The Draft Constitution, placed before the Supreme Soviet for its consideration, is the result of many years of intense effort by a large group of
men and women. The Constitution Commission, set up by the USSR
Supreme Soviet, includes experienced Party and government workers,
representatives of the working class, the collective farm peasantry, the
people's intelligentsia and the country's numerous nations. Prominent
scientists, specialists and men and women working in state agencies and
social organizations have been involved in working out the Draft. It has
been twice considered by Plenary meetings of the CPSU [Communist Party Soviet Union] Central Committee.

I think that we have every right to say that the important tasks which we
faced in the preparation, discussion and adoption of the Constitution have
been fulfilled in the most conscientious way and with the most consistent
observance of all the principles of socialist democracy.

The discussion of the Draft Constitution by the whole people has been
the crucial test of the quality of all the preparatory work. It went on for
nearly four months and was nationwide in the true sense of the word.
Altogether it involved over 140 million men and women, that is, more than
80 per cent of the adult population of this country. Never before has this
country had popular activity on such a scale.

The main political result of the nationwide discussion consists in the fact
that the Soviet people have said: Yes, this is the Fundamental Law we expected. It is a true reflection of our gains, of our aspirations and hopes, and

gives a correct definition of our rights and duties. While formalizing what has been achieved, it opens up a perspective for the further advance of Communist construction.

The Draft was discussed at nearly 1.5 million meetings of working people at enterprises and collective farms and in military units and residential areas. It was discussed at Plenary meetings, meetings of activists and other meetings in the trade unions, the Young Communist League, cooperative associations and artists', writers', musicians' and other unions. The whole Party was involved in its discussion. More than 450,000 open Party meetings were held, and these were addressed by over three million men and women. The Draft was considered by all the Soviets, starting from the rural Soviets and all the way to the Supreme Soviets of the union republics, which means more than two million deputies, representing the whole of our people. Each of these forums approved the Draft Constitution....

[Letters from the Soviet People]

The vast majority of these letters are marked by patriotism, wholehearted approval of the policy of our Party and Soviet Government, breadth of vision and maturity of judgment and a high standard of exactingness upon oneself and one's comrades. Their authors, like those who took part in the discussion at meetings, people from all walks of life and different age groups, representing all our nations and nationalities, are Party and non-Party men and women, and all of them, like the masters of the country which they are, have thoroughly analyzed the Draft Constitution, made proposals for improving the text and also expressed other considerations bearing on various aspects of life in our society.

Pondering such statements and letters one comes to the conclusion that they are a reflection of the tremendous victory scored by socialism—the emergence of the new man, who does not separate himself from the state and espouses the interests of the state and of the whole people as his own....

The Constitution Commission reports that the nationwide discussion has made it possible to markedly improve the Draft Constitution and to write into it a number of useful additions, clarifications and amendments.

[Proposals for Amendments]

Altogether about 400,000 proposals for amendments to individual articles have been made for the purpose of clarifying, improving and adding to the language of the Draft. Having made a careful study of these amendments—many of which, of course, recur—the Constitution Commission recommends that 110 articles of the Draft should be amended and one new article added. The Commission's recommendations have been circulated to all deputies. My task is to substantiate the Commission's proposals on the most essential matters.

Let me start by saying that the greatest number of proposals that have come in bear on the vital question of the role of labor under socialism. The comrades suggest that the character of our society as a society of working people should be described in much more explicit terms in the Constitution.

I think that this proposal is highly meaningful. Soviet society consists only of working classes and social groups. In view of this it is proposed that Article I of the Constitution should say that the Soviet state of the whole people shall express the will and interests of the workers, peasants and intelligentsia, of the working people of all the nations and nationalities of the country. Simultaneously, we should evidently accept this other proposal: to define in the Constitution not only the political foundation of the USSR, not only the foundation of our economic system, but also the social foundation of our state. We now have as such a foundation of the USSR, not only the foundation of our economic system, but also the social foundation of our state. We now have as such a foundation the unbreakable alliance of the working class, the collective farm peasantry and the people's intelligentsia, and this needs to be clearly stated.

The comrades have also proposed more precise language for the article dealing with the foundation of the economic system of the USSR, so as to bring out in greater detail the fact that this foundation consists of state and collective farm cooperative property.

This is quite correct. After all it is these two forms of socialist property in the means of production that determine the character of our economy and the division of Soviet society into the two friendly classes of workers and peasants. Such clarification has been provided for....

[Importance of the Communist Party]

The Party conducts its policy on state matters primarily through the Communists elected by the people to the Soviet and working in state organs. It believes that one of its most important tasks is to do its utmost to consolidate and perfect the power of the Soviets and to display concern for the further development of socialist democracy. This is a principled line to which we have adhered and to which we shall always adhere.

Comrades, the discussion of the Draft Constitution has largely gone well beyond the framework of an analysis of the text itself. It has developed into a frank and truly popular conversation on the key aspects of our life which are of stirring concern to all Soviet people. Collectives of working people and individual citizens have made just and—not infrequently—sharp critical remarks on various aspects of the activity of state organs and social organizations, proposing measures for improving the work and eliminating the existing shortcomings.

[Abuses by Officials Reported]

Many letters call for a stiffer drive against parasitism, deliberate breaches of labor discipline, hard drinking and other anti-social phenomena which cut across the very substance of our socialist way of life.

From this persistent demand voiced by the working people concrete conclusions should be drawn by all state and social organizations.

Some letters report revolting facts of abuse by some persons in office of their position, facts of deception of the state by means of doctoring records and cheating, of bribe-taking, of indifference and a superficial approach to the working people's requirements and of instances of harassment for criticism.

I should like to stress, comrades, that all reports of this kind are being thoroughly verified for the purpose of taking the necessary measures, including punishment of the guilty persons with the full severity of the law. In general, I must say that our society has a large reserve for its development in the establishment of due order wherever it is violated in this country—in production, government or social life. By putting an end to phenomena like sloppy work, waste of socialist property, red-tape and bureaucratic attitudes to one's work and to citizens, we shall considerably accelerate the country's advance and improve the life of the whole people.

Many letters and speeches suggest the further strengthening and improvement of the people's control. That is right. And it will be promoted, in particular, by the law on the people's control in the USSR, whose adoption is provided for by the new Constitution....

[Constitution Focus of World Attention]

The Draft Constitution and its nationwide discussions have long been in the focus of world attention. Moreover, the discussion has virtually assumed an international scale. This is fresh evidence of the immense role of socialism in the world today.

Our friends in the fraternal socialist countries have widely discussed and enthusiastically supported the Draft Constitution. They have exhibited full and exacting attention to it in a comradely and businesslike spirit. They have analyzed it in detail and shared their experience with us. For this we are sincerely grateful to them.

The press in the socialist countries has given the Draft wide coverage. It has assessed it as a document telling the world "the truth about socialism and mankind's future," as "a manifesto of the epoch of Communist construction." The leaders of the socialist community of nations—our comrades-in-arms—have emphasized the great importance of the Draft in outlining the development prospects for their countries.

It is acknowledged with satisfaction in the socialist countries that the Draft Constitution reflects in various forms elements characteristic of their constitutions, just as the latter reflect the earlier experience of Soviet legislation. In this way collective experience is gained in developing socialist statehood.

The new Soviet Draft Constitution has been studied with keen interest in the countries newly liberated from colonial bondage and now choosing their path. Their prominent leaders have told Soviet representatives of their hopes to benefit substantially by this Draft summing up the 60-year experience in developing the state institution of the world's first socialist country. The press in many African, Asian and Latin American countries has widely commented on the Draft and underscored in particular that the Soviet Union's accomplishments which it reflects are an inspiring example to all the peoples taking the socialist orientation.

[Reaction of the Western Press]

The working people in the capitalist countries and, above all, their vanguard—the Communist and workers' parties—have shown an exceptional interest in the Draft Constitution. The Communist press has published detailed accounts of the Draft, analyzed its contents and highly assessed its significance. The fraternal parties have emphasized that it is a document of crucial importance demonstrating the essence and goals of developed socialism today. The Soviet Union has made a giant leap forward in its democratic development, and the Soviet people have proved in practice the truth of the great ideas of Marx, Engels and Lenin. The Draft Constitution contains extensive material for study, reflection and debate—such are the comments of Communists in the capitalist world for whom the new Constitution of the land of the October Revolution means support for their just struggle for the working people's cause.

On the whole, the lively comments, the great and sincere interest and warm approval of the Draft Constitution by the working masses of the world fill our hearts with pride in the Soviet people's achievements and illustrate even more strikingly their great international significance.

Nor has the Draft Constitution been ignored by the bourgeois press and other mass media in the capitalist world. Some of them have given more or less objective coverage of its content.

A number of Western newspapers have pointed out that the new Constitution of the USSR signifies further development of democracy in the Soviet Union, a widening of the rights of citizens and public organizations and an increase in their influence on national policy. The American *Baltimore Sun* has frankly acknowledged that the Draft guarantees Soviet citizens wider rights compared with any Western constitution: the right to work, rest, choice of occupation, social security, housing, education and free medical aid.

Statesmen, political leaders and the press in the capitalist countries have admitted the importance of the fact that in the chapter on foreign policy of the Constitution, the Soviet Union has reaffirmed by statutory law its allegiance to the cause of peace and international cooperation....

The masterminds of imperialist propaganda, however, obviously became worried when the discussion of the Draft Constitution assumed a broad international scale....

This is a repetition of what we have seen time out of number in the history of the Soviet state: a striking picture of the methods of imperialist propaganda. It is blind to the achievements of our great country, with its heroic history, vivid and many-sided culture, one of the world's best educational standards, and the vigorous joint creative activity of its numerous nations and peoples. "Psychological warfare" experts take very little interest in this. Their only goal is to obstruct the growth of the influence of socialism on human minds, to induce distrust and hostility towards it by whatever means. Hence the stereotyped inventions, shameless fabrications and blatant lies about the Soviet Union intended for misinformed audiences and gullible readers, listeners and spectators. Hence the tendency not so much to give information about the new Soviet Constitution as to distort its content, play down its importance and, whenever possible, ignore its major provisions altogether.

[Human Rights]

The clauses on the rights, freedoms and duties of Soviet citizens have been attacked with special vehemence.

This has, of course, its inner logic: Indeed, it is precisely the idea of "concern" for human rights that prominent leaders of the capitalist world have lately chosen as the main thrust of their ideological crusade against the socialist countries. The critics of the Soviet Constitution, however, have found themselves in an unenviable situation. They cannot escape the fact that the Soviet Draft Constitution defines the social, economic and political rights and freedoms of citizens and the specific guarantees of these rights more widely, clearly and fully than ever and anywhere else.

What, indeed, can the apologists of the capitalist system oppose in these real achievements of developed socialism? What real rights and freedoms are guaranteed to the masses in present-day imperialist society?

The "right" of tens of millions to unemployment? Or the "right" of sick people to do without medical aid, which costs a vast sum of money? Or else, the "right" of ethnic minorities to humiliating discrimination in employment and education, in political and everyday life? Or is it the "right" to live in perpetual fear of the omnipotent underworld of organized crime and to see how the press, cinema, TV and radio services are going out of their way to educate the younger generation in a spirit of selfishness, cruelty and violence?

Propagandists and ideologists of capitalism cannot deny the fact that socialism has long cured these social sores. They have resorted, therefore, to another maneuver. They have concentrated their attacks on the constitutional provisions which say that the enjoyment by citizens of their rights and freedoms should not prejudice the interests of society and the state, the rights of other citizens and that the exercise of one's rights and freedoms is inseparable from the fulfillment of one's civic duty....

Speaking in general, it seems that from the standpoint of our class adversaries, Soviet citizens should evidently be granted only the "right" to fight against the Soviet state and the socialist system so as to gladden the hearts of the imperialists. However, we must disappoint such "critics" of our Constitution: Their wish will never be satisfied by the Soviet people.

Our "critics" pretend to be unaware of the fact that the clauses in the Draft Constitution causing their discontent fully conform to fundamental international documents. Let us remind them of this fact: The UN Universal Declaration of Human Rights says unequivocally that "Everyone has duties to the community in which alone the free and full development of his personality is possible," and that the exercise of rights and freedoms by citizens requires "due recognition and respect for the rights and freedoms of others and of meeting the just requirements of morality, public order and the general welfare in a democratic society."

Such is the principle of democratic social life recognized throughout the world. It may be useful for our "critics" to know that nothing else is contained in the provisions of the new Constitution of the USSR, which has aroused their sham indignation.

[The Party and Society]

The majority of bourgeois analysts have also criticized the provisions defining the role of the CPSU in the life of Soviet society. They have clamored about the alleged "proclamation of the dictatorship of the Communist Party," "the primacy of the Party over the state," "a dangerous integration of the Party and government institutions," and "the obliteration of the boundaries between the Party and the State."

How is one to regard this? The motives for this attack are clear enough. The Communist Party is the vanguard of the Soviet people, their most conscious and progressive section inseparably united with the people as a whole. The Party has no other interests at heart but the interests of the people. To try and separate the Party from the people by talking about the "dictatorship of the Party" is tantamount to trying to separate, say, the heart from the body.

As I have already said, the Communist Party operates within the framework of the USSR Constitution. Bourgeois critics, however, do not care about this. They would like to undermine the role of the Party in Soviet society since they hope to weaken our country, our socialist system and stamp out our Communist ideals. Fortunately, this is beyond their power. As the Soviet people will increasingly tackle the complex and responsible tasks of building communism, the Communist Party will have a growing role to play. This leads not to restriction but to increasingly profound development of socialist democracy in full conformity with our Party's program.

Here is another point. Some Western critics of our new Constitution have tried to attack it "from the left," as it were, going into theoretical discussions about the authors of the Draft being inconsistent in their loyalty to the Marxist doctrine of the withering away of the state under communism....

Such concern of ideologists of capitalism for our socialist state developing in accordance with the Marxist-Leninist doctrine is truly touching. However, their anxiety is groundless. Developments are running the precise course predicted by the classics of Marxism and formulated by our Party in its policy statements.

Our critics from the bourgeois camp (and, speaking frankly, some comrades in the ranks of the international working class movement along with them) are unable or unwilling to see the main thing—the dialectics of the development of our state and society. It means that with the development and advancement of the socialist state millions of citizens are increasingly involved in the activities of the government and people's control bodies, in the management of production and distribution, in social and cultural policies and in the administration of justice. In short, our statehood is gradually transformed into Communist social self-government along with the development of socialist democracy.

This is, of course, a long process, but it is running a steady course. We are convinced that the new Soviet Constitution will contribute effectively to attaining this important goal of Communist construction.

[Mature Socialism Attained]

The new Constitution is justly called "the law of the life of developed socialist society." This is the society that has actually been built in the Soviet Union. Such a developed, mature socialist society is also being built successfully in other countries of the socialist community. And it is very important to have a clear idea of its characteristic features and its place in the historical process of the emergence of the Communist system.

It will be recalled that in the early Soviet years Lenin, taking a look into the future, spoke and wrote of "complete," "full" and "developed" socialism, as a prospect, a goal of socialist construction.

This goal has now been attained. The experience of the Soviet Union, followed by other socialist countries, has demonstrated that laying the foundations of socialism, that is, the abolition of the exploiter classes and the establishment of social property in all the sectors of the national economy, does not yet allow a direct transition to communism. Triumphant socialism should pass through definite stages of maturation, and only developed socialist society makes it possible to embark on Communist construction. What is more as you know today, the development and advancement of socialism is a task that is no less complicated and responsible than the laying of its foundations....

Such are the processes which entitle us to say that developed socialism has been built in the USSR—a stage of maturity of the new society at which the entire system of social relations has been restructured on the collectivist principles intrinsic to socialism. Hence, the full scope for the operation of the laws of socialism, for bringing into play its advantages in all the spheres of social life. Hence, the organic integrity and dynamic force of the social system, its political stability and its indestructible inner unit. Hence, the growing integration of all the classes and social groups and all the nations and nationalities into a historically new social and international entity, the Soviet people. Hence, the emergence of a new, socialist culture and the establishment of a new, socialist way of life.

Of course, only that socialist society can be described as developed which is based on powerful, advanced industry and on large-scale, highly mechanized agriculture, which practically permits an increasingly complete satisfaction of the varied requirements of citizens to become the central and direct goal of social development. In the situation prevailing in our country the task of building up such a material and technological base indispensable for mature socialism had to be tackled after laying the foundations of the new system. Other countries which have taken the path of socialism with an underdeveloped or moderately developed economy will evidently have to work on these problems in the same way.

In countries where highly developed productive forces will be available at the time of a victorious socialist revolution the situation will be different. But even they will have to handle such complicated tasks of building mature socialism as learning the sophisticated science of planning and management of the economy and the cultivation of socialist consciousness in citizens.

In short, whatever specific conditions may prevail in the countries building socialism, the stage of its perfection on its own basis, the stage of mature, developed socialist society is an indispensable element of social transformations and a relatively long stretch on the path from capitalism to communism. At the same time, bringing out and using all the potential of developed socialism also means a transition to building communism. The future does not lie beyond the limits of the present. The future lies in the present. And by fulfilling the tasks of the present day, of the socialist present, we are gradually approaching the morrow, the Communist future.

As our experience has shown, the gradual development of the state of proletarian dictatorship into a state of the whole people is one of the results of the complete triumph of socialist social relations. The Soviet Union today is a legitimate stage in the development of the state born of the October Revolution—a stage characteristic of mature socialism. Consequently, the tasks of the state institutions, their structure, functions and work procedure should conform to the stage attained in the development of society.

The new Constitution of the USSR guarantees such conformity. Having adopted it we shall be fully entitled to say that another important step has been taken to bring our country nearer to the great goals of our Party and people.

[Sputnik Recalled]

Comrades, just 20 years ago, on October 4, mankind took its first step into outer space. This was heralded by the artificial earth satellite created by the genius and hands of Soviet people. The whole world could see the achievement of the "alliance of representatives of science, the proletariat and technology" which Lenin had envisaged at the dawn of the Soviet period. This alliance was embodied in the practices of socialist construction in our country and has become a mainspring of the spectacular accomplishments of developed socialism.

The discussion of the Draft Constitution has once again demonstrated the strength and vitality of the unity of all classes and social groups. All nations and nationalities, all generations of Soviet society rallied behind the Communist Party.

Millions upon millions of working people in town and country have supported the new Constitution by word and by deed. They compared every line in the Draft with their own practical work and with the work of their labor collectives. They made increased socialist pledges, amended production plans, discovered new reserves for enhancing production efficiency and improving work performance and met their new Constitution with great labor exploits. In short, our people have again shown themselves to be full masters of the socialist homeland. Honor and glory to the heroic Soviet people, the builders of communism!

Comrade deputies, I want to express my confidence that the Supreme Soviet, having discussed the Draft Constitution of the USSR, will approve it, thereby equipping the Soviet people with a new powerful instrument for building communism!

[CONSTITUTION OF THE SOVIET UNION]

The Soviet people, guided by the ideas of scientific communism and remaining true to their revolutionary traditions, resting on the great social, economic and political achievements of socialism, striving to further develop socialist democracy, taking into account the international position of the USSR as part of the world socialist system and conscious of their international responsibility, preserving the continuity of the ideas and principles of the 1918 Constitution of the RSFSR, the 1924 Constitution of the USSR and the 1936 Constitution of the USSR, proclaim the aims and principles, define the foundations of the organization of the socialist state of the whole people, and formalize them in this Constitution....

The Political System

Article 1. The Union of Soviet Socialist Republics is a socialist state of the whole people, expressing the will and interests of the working class, the peasantry and the intelligentsia, of all the nations and nationalities in the country.

Article 2. All power in the USSR shall be vested in the people.

The people shall exercise state power through the Soviets of People's Deputies, which constitute the political foundation of the USSR.

All other organs of state shall be under the control of and accountable to the Soviets.

Article 3. The Soviet state shall be organized and shall function in accordance with the principle of democratic centralism: electivity of all organs of state power from top to bottom, their accountability to the people, and mandatory fulfillment of the decisions of higher organs by lower organs. Democratic centralism shall combine single leadership with local initiative and creative activity, with the responsibility of each state organ and each official for the work at hand.

Article 4. The Soviet state, in all its organs, shall function on the basis of socialist legality and ensure the protection of law and order, the interests of society and the rights of citizens. State institutions, public organizations and officials shall observe the Constitution of the USSR and Soviet laws....

Article 6. The Communist Party of the Soviet Union is the leading and guiding force of Soviet society and the nucleus of its political system, of all state and public organizations. The CPSU exists for the people and serves the people.

Armed with the Marxist-Leninist (body of) teaching, the Communist Party shall determine the general perspective of society's development and the guidelines for the internal and external policy of the USSR, give guidance to the great creative endeavor of the Soviet people, and place their struggle for the triumph of communism on a planned, scientific basis....

[The Economic System]

Article 9. Socialist ownership of the means of production shall be the foundation of the economic system of the USSR. Socialist ownership shall comprise: state property (belonging to the whole people), property of collective farms and other cooperative organizations (collective farm-cooperative property), and property of trade unions and other public organizations.

The state shall protect socialist property and create the conditions for augmenting it.

No one shall have the right to use socialist property for personal gain.

Article 10. State property, i.e., property belonging to the whole people, shall be the principal form of socialist ownership.

The land, its minerals, waters and forests shall be the exclusive property of the state. The state shall be in possession of the basic means of production: industrial, building and agricultural enterprises, means of transport and communication, and also the banks, distributive enterprises and community services and the bulk of urban housing....

Article 13. The free labor of Soviet people shall be the basis of the growth of social wealth and the welfare of the people, of every Soviet citizen.

The state shall control the measure of labor and consumption in accordance with the principle: "From each according to his ability, to each according to his work." It shall determine the rates of the income tax and establish the level of wages exempted from taxes.

Socially useful work and its results shall determine a citizen's status in society. By combining material and moral incentives the state shall help turn labor into the prime need in the life of every Soviet citizen....

Article 15. The economy of the USSR shall be an integral economic complex embracing all the elements of social production, distribution and exchange on the territory of the USSR.

The economy shall be managed on the basis of state plans for economic, social and cultural development with due account taken of the branch and territorial principles, and combining centralized leadership with the economic independence and initiative of enterprises, associations and other organizations. Here active use shall be made of cost accounting, profit and production costs....

Social Development and Culture

Article 19. The Soviet state shall create the conditions for enhancing society's social homogeneity, erasing the essential distinctions between town and countryside and between mental and manual labor, and further developing and drawing together all the nations and nationalities of the USSR.

Article 20. In accordance with the communist ideal, "the free development of each is the condition for the free development of all," the Soviet state shall pursue the aim of expanding the actual possibilities for citizens to develop and apply their creative strength, abilities and talents, for the all-around development of the individual....

[Foreign Policy]

Article 28. The Soviet state shall consistently pursue the Leninist policy of peace and stand for the consolidation of the security of peoples and broad international cooperation.

The foreign policy of the USSR shall be aimed at ensuring favorable international conditions for the building of communism in the USSR, at strengthening the positions of world socialism, supporting the struggle of peoples for national liberation and social progress, preventing wars of aggression, and consistently implementing the principle of peaceful coexistence of states with different social systems.

In the USSR war propaganda shall be prohibited by law.

Article 29. The relations of the USSR with other states shall be based on the observance of the principle of mutual renunciation of the use or threats of force, and of the principles of sovereign equality, inviolability of frontiers, territorial integrity of states, peaceful settlement of disputes, noninterference in internal affairs, respect for human rights and basic freedoms, equality and the right of peoples to decide their own destiny, cooperation between states, scrupulous fulfillment of commitments emanating from universally recognized principles and norms of international law, and the international treaties signed by the USSR.

Article 30. As part of the world socialist system, of the socialist community, the Soviet Union shall promote and strengthen friendship, cooperation and comradely mutual assistance with the other socialist countries on the basis of socialist internationalism, and shall actively participate in economic integration and in the international socialist division of labor....

[The State and the Individual]

Article 33. Soviet citizenship shall be uniform for the whole Union of Soviet Socialist Republics. Every citizen of a Union Republic shall be a citizen of the USSR.

The grounds and procedure of acquiring or losing Soviet citizenship shall be established by the law of the USSR.

Citizens of the USSR living abroad shall have the protection and guardianship of the Soviet state.

Article 34. Citizens of the USSR shall be equal before the law, irrespective of origin, social and property status, nationality or race, sex, education, language, attitude to religion, type or character of occupation, domicile, or other particulars.

Equality of rights of citizens of the USSR shall be ensured in all fields of economic, political, social, and cultural life.

Article 35. In the USSR women shall have equal rights with men.

Exercise of these rights shall be ensured by according to women equal opportunities (with men) for education and professional training, for employment, remuneration and promotion, for social, political and cultural activity, and likewise by special measures for the protection of the labor and health of women; by legal protection, material and moral support of mother and child, including paid leaves and other benefits to mothers and expectant mothers, and state aid to unmarried mothers.

Article 36. Soviet citizens of different nationalities and races shall have equal rights.

The exercise of these rights shall be ensured by the policy of all-around development and drawing together of all nations and nationalities of the USSR, education of citizens in the spirit of Soviet patriotism and socialist internationalism, and the opportunity for using their mother tongue as well as the languages of the other peoples of the USSR.

Any and all direct or indirect restriction of the rights of, or the establishment of direct or indirect privileges for, citizens on grounds of race or nationality, and likewise any advocacy of racial or national exclusiveness, hostility or contempt, shall be punishable by law.

Article 37. In the USSR citizens of other countries and stateless persons shall be guaranteed the rights and freedoms provided for by law, including the right of instituting proceedings in law courts and other state organs in protection of personal, proprietary, family and other rights accorded to them by law.

On the territory of the USSR, citizens of other countries and stateless persons shall be obliged to respect the Constitution of the USSR and to observe Soviet laws.

Article 38. The USSR shall afford the right of asylum to foreign nationals persecuted for upholding the interests of the working people and the cause of peace, or for participating in a revolutionary or national liberation movement, or for progressive social, political, scientific or other creative activity.

[Rights, Freedoms and Duties]

Article 39. Citizens of the USSR shall enjoy in their entirety the social, economic, political and personal rights and freedoms proclaimed and guaranteed by the Constitution of the USSR and Soviet laws. The socialist system shall ensure extension of rights and freedoms and unintermittent improvement of the conditions of life of citizens relative to the fulfillment of programs of social, economic and cultural development.

Exercise by citizens of rights and freedoms must not injure the interests of society and the state, or the rights of other citizens.

Article 40. Citizens of the USSR shall have the right to work, that is, to guaranteed employment and remuneration for their work in accordance with its quantity and quality, including the right to choice of profession, type of occupation and employment, in accordance with their vocation, abilities, training, education, and with due account taken of the needs of society....

Article 41. Citizens of the USSR shall have the right to rest and leisure....

Article 42. Citizens of the USSR shall have the right to health protection....

Article 43. Citizens of the USSR shall have the right to maintenance in old age, in the event of sickness, and likewise in the event of complete or partial disability or loss of breadwinner....

Article 44. Citizens of the USSR shall have the right to housing. This right shall be ensured by the development and protection of state and public housing, assistance to co-operative and individual house-building, fair distribution under public control of housing, allotted with reference to the implementation of the housing program, and likewise by low rent.

Article 45. Citizens of the USSR shall have the right to education....

Article 46. Citizens of the USSR shall have the right to make use of the achievements of culture....

Article 48. Citizens of the USSR shall have the right to take part in the administration of state and public affairs....

Article 49. Every citizen of the USSR shall have the right to submit to state organs and public organizations proposals for improving their activity, to criticize shortcomings in their work. Officials shall be bound, within terms established by law, to examine proposals and requests made by citizens, reply to them and take due action.

Persecution for criticism shall be prohibited.

Article 50. In conformity with the interests of the working people and for the purpose of strengthening the socialist system, citizens of the USSR shall be guaranteed freedom of speech, press, assembly, meetings, street processions and demonstrations. Exercise of these political freedoms shall be ensured by putting at the disposal of the working people and their organizations public buildings, streets and squares, by broad dissemination of information, and by the opportunity to use the press, television and radio....

Article 52. Freedom of conscience, that is, the right to profess any religion and perform religious rites, or not to profess any religion and to conduct atheistic propaganda, shall be recognized for all citizens of the USSR. Incitement of hostility and hatred on religious grounds shall be prohibited.

The church in the USSR shall be separated from the state, and the school from the church.

Article 53. The family shall be under the protection of the state.

Marriage shall be entered into with the free consent of the intending spouses; spouses shall be completely equal in their matrimonial relations....

Article 54. Citizens of the USSR shall be guaranteed inviolability of the person. No person shall be subjected to arrest other than by decision of a court of law, or with the sanction of a prosecutor.

Article 55. Citizens of the USSR shall be guaranteed inviolability of the home. No person shall without lawful grounds enter a home against the will of the persons residing in it.

Article 56. The privacy of citizens, of correspondence, telephone conversations and telegraphic messages shall be protected by law.

Article 57. Respect for the individual and protection of the rights and freedoms of Soviet citizens shall be the duty of all state organs, public organizations and officials....

Article 58. Citizens of the USSR shall have the right to lodge complaints against actions of officials in state organs and public organizations. These complaints shall be examined in the manner and within the terms defined by law....

Citizens of the USSR shall have the right to compensation for damage inflicted by unlawful actions of state institutions and public organizations, and likewise by officials in the performance of their duties, in the manner and within the limits defined by law.

Article 59. Exercise of rights and freedoms shall be inseparable from the performance by citizens of their duties....

Article 62. The citizens of the USSR shall be obliged to safeguard the interests of the Soviet state, to contribute to the strengthening of its might and prestige.

Defense of the socialist motherland shall be the sacred duty of every citizen of the USSR.

High treason shall be the gravest crime against the people....

Article 64. It shall be the duty of every citizen of the USSR to respect the national dignity of other citizens, to strengthen the friendship of the nations and nationalities of the Soviet multinational state....

Article 67. Citizens of the USSR shall be obligated to protect nature, to safeguard its wealth.

Concern for the preservation of historical monuments and other cultural values shall be the duty of citizens of the USSR.

Article 68. It shall be the internationalist duty of citizens of the USSR to further the development of friendship and cooperation with the peoples of other countries and the maintenance and consolidation of world peace....

The USSR—A Federal State

Article 69. The Union of Soviet Socialist Republics is an integral federal multinational state formed on the basis of the free self-determination of nations and the voluntary union of equal Soviet Socialist Republics.

The USSR embodies the state unity of the Soviet people and brings all the nations and nationalities together for the joint building of communism....

Article 71. Every Union Republic shall retain the right freely to secede from the USSR....

[The Soviets of People's Deputies]

Article 88. The Soviets of People's Deputies—the Supreme Soviet of the USSR, the Supreme Soviet of the Union Republics, the Supreme Soviets of the Autonomous Republics, the Territorial and Regional Soviets of People's Deputies, the Soviets of People's Deputies of Autonomous Regions and Autonomous Areas, and the city, district, city district, township and village Soviets of People's Deputies—shall comprise an integral system of organs of state power....

Article 101. Deputies shall be authorized representatives of the people in the Soviets of People's Deputies.

By participating in the work of the Soviets, deputies shall resolve matters related to state, economic, social and cultural development, organize the execution of the decisions of the Soviets, and exercise control over the work of state organs, enterprises, institutions and organizations....

Article 103. A deputy shall have the right to address an inquiry to the appropriate state organs and officials, who shall be obliged to reply to the inquiry at a session of the Soviet.

Deputies shall have the right to address an inquiry to any state or public organ, enterprise, institution or organization on questions within their terms of reference as deputies and to take part in considering the questions thus raised. The heads of the respective state or public organs, enterprises, institutions or organizations shall be obliged to receive deputies without delay and consider their recommendations within the period established by law.

Article 104. Deputies shall be assured conditions for the unobstructed and effective exercise of their rights and duties.

The immunity of deputies, as well as other guarantees of their functions as deputies, shall be defined in the Law on the Status of Deputies and other legislation of the USSR and of the Union and Autonomous Republics....

[The Supreme Soviet]

Article 106. The Supreme Soviet of the USSR shall be the highest organ of state power in the USSR.

The Supreme Soviet of the USSR shall be empowered to deal with all matters placed within the jurisdiction of the Union of Soviet Socialist Republics by the present Constitution.

The adoption of the Constitution of the USSR and amendments to it, the admission of new Republics to the USSR, approval of the formation of new Autonomous Republics and Autonomous Regions, endorsement of state plans of economic, social and cultural development and of the State Budget of the USSR, and of reports on their execution, and the formation of organs of the USSR accountable to it shall be the exclusive competence of the Supreme Soviet of the USSR.

Laws of the USSR shall be enacted solely by the Supreme Soviet of the USSR.

Article 107. The Supreme Soviet of the USSR shall consist of two chambers: the Soviet of the Union and the Soviet of Nationalities.

The two chambers of the Supreme Soviet of the USSR shall have equal rights.

Article 108. The Soviet of the Union and the Soviet of Nationalities shall have an equal number of deputies.

The Soviet of the Union shall be elected by constituencies with equal populations.

The Soviet of Nationalities shall be elected on the basis of the following quotas: 32 deputies from each Union Republic, 11 deputies from each Autonomous Republic, 5 deputies from each Autonomous Region, and one deputy from each Autonomous Area.

Upon representation by the credentials commissions elected by them, the Soviet of the Union and the Soviet of Nationalities shall recognize the credentials of deputies, and in cases where the election law has been violated, declare the election of individual deputies invalid....

Article 111. The right to initiate legislation in the Supreme Soviet of the USSR shall be exercised by the Soviet of the Union and the Soviet of Nationalities, the Presidium of the Supreme Soviet of the USSR, the Council of Ministers of the USSR, the Union Republics represented by their higher organs of state power, the commissions of the Supreme Soviet of the USSR and the standing commissions of its chambers, deputies of the Supreme Soviet of the USSR, the Supreme Court of the USSR, and the Prosecutor-General of the USSR.

The right to initiate legislation shall be enjoyed also by mass public organizations represented by their all-Union organs....

Article 117. The Supreme Soviet of the USSR at a joint sitting of the two chambers shall elect the Presidium of the Supreme Soviet of the USSR, the continuously functioning organ of the Supreme Soviet of the USSR accountable to it in all its activities.

Article 118. The Presidium of the Supreme Soviet of the USSR shall be elected from among deputies and shall consist of a President, a First Vice-

President, 15 Vice Presidents, i.e., one from each Union Republic, a Secretary of the Presidium, and 21 members of the Presidium of the Supreme Soviet of the USSR....

The Council of Ministers of the USSR

Article 127. The Council of Ministers of the USSR—the Government of the USSR—shall be the highest executive and administrative organ of state power in the USSR.

Article 128. The Council of Ministers of the USSR shall be formed by the Supreme Soviet of the USSR at a joint sitting of the Soviet of the Union and the Soviet of Nationalities and consist of: the Chairman of the Council of Ministers of the USSR, First Vice-Chairmen and Vice-Chairmen of the Council of Ministers of the USSR, the Ministers of the USSR, the Chairmen of state committees of the USSR.

The Council of Ministers of the USSR shall include, by virtue of their office, the Chairmen of the Councils of Ministers of Union Republics.

Upon submission by the Chairman of the Council of Ministers of the USSR, the Supreme Soviet of the USSR may include in the Government of the USSR leaders of other organs and organizations of the USSR.

Article 129. The Council of Ministers of the USSR shall be responsible and accountable to the Supreme Soviet of the USSR, and between sessions of the Supreme Soviet of the USSR to the Presidium of the Supreme Soviet of the USSR, to which it shall be accountable.

The Council of Ministers of the USSR shall regularly report on its work to the Supreme Soviet of the USSR....

Article 131. The Presidium of the Council of Ministers of the USSR, consisting of the Chairman of the Council of Ministers of the USSR and the First Vice-Chairmen and Vice-Chairmen of the Council of Ministers of the USSR, shall function as a permanent organ of the Council of Ministers of the USSR for the purpose of dealing with matters related to the administration of the economy and to other questions of state administration....

Courts of Law and Arbitration

Article 150. In the USSR justice shall be administered exclusively by courts of law.

In the USSR the court system shall consist of the following: the Supreme Court of the USSR, Supreme Courts of Union Republics, Supreme Courts of Autonomous Republics, territorial, regional and city courts, courts of Autonomous Regions, courts of Autonomous Areas, district (city) people's courts, and military tribunals in the Armed Forces.

Article 151. All courts in the USSR shall be formed on the principle of electivity of judges and people's assessors....

The Prosecutor's Office

Article 163. Supreme supervisory power over the precise and uniform execution of laws by all ministries, state committees and departments, enterprises, institutions and organizations, executive and administrative organs of local Soviets of People's Deputies, collective farms, cooperative and other public organizations, officials and citizens, shall be exercised by the Prosecutor General of the USSR and prosecutors subordinate to him.

Article 164. The Prosecutor General of the USSR shall be appointed by the Supreme Soviet of the USSR and shall be responsible and accountable to it, or between sessions of the Supreme Soviet to the Presidium of the Supreme Soviet of the USSR, to which he is accountable....

[Amendment of the Constitution of the USSR]

Article 172. The Constitution of the USSR shall have supreme legal force. All laws and other acts of state organs shall be issued on the basis of, and in conformity with, the Constitution of the USSR.

The Constitution of the USSR shall be effective from the time of its adoption.

Article 173. Amendment of the Constitution of the USSR shall be by decision of the Supreme Soviet of the USSR, adopted by a majority of not less than two-thirds of the total number of deputies of each of its chambers.

▼▼▼

KOREAN INFLUENCE INVESTIGATION
October 19-21, 1977

Details of a master plan devised by the South Korean Intelligence Agency (KCIA) and South Korean government officials to buy influence in the U.S. Congress emerged in public hearings held Oct. 19-21 by the House Committee on Standards of Official Conduct. Committee Chairman John J. Flynt (D Ga.) and the committee's special counsel, Leon Jaworski, told of attempts by the Korean ambassador to the United States and the KCIA station chief in Washington, D.C., to purchase congressional good will with cash, free trips and other favors.

In opening remarks before the committee, Jaworski said the plan was "to be implemented personally by the ambassador, Kim Dong Jo, and by the KCIA station chief, Yang Doo Wan." Jaworski's deputy counsel, Peter A. White, said the hearings would prove there was substance to the reports of illicit lobbying that first surfaced in a story in The Washington Post *Oct. 24, 1976. "The question of whether these things took place is, very simply, a dead issue," White said.*

Flynt said the committee staff had interviewed more than 200 witnesses and reviewed over 10,000 pages of documents and materials. The investigation "has established by convincing evidence...that there were efforts made by elements in the government of the Republic of Korea to influence members of Congress by giving them cash; and that further and intensified efforts to determine which members of Congress received it are more than warranted," Flynt asserted.

The House committee in 1977 did not release names of any members of Congress who might have been compromised by the acceptance of cash or *other favors. However, three persons were indicted by a federal grand jury in connection with the lobbying scandal. They were Tongsun Park, a South Korean described in an indictment as the Washington operative in the KCIA plan; former U.S. Rep. Richard T. Hanna (D Calif., 1963-1974), described as Park's partner in the illicit scheme; and Hancho Kim, a Korean-born Washington businessman who was charged with having received about $600,000 through the KCIA to pursue an influence-buying operation. The indictments were disclosed in September and October.*

Uncertainty

Although most of the South Korean plan apparently was never implemented, great uncertainty persisted in Washington throughout 1977 as to the extent of involvement in the scheme by members of Congress and possibly other U.S. officials. The central figure in the scandal, Park, was well-known in Washington business and social circles. In 1966 he had opened the George Town Club in the city which had become a popular gathering place for members of Congress and other prominent persons.

Jaworski was named as special counsel of the Committee on Standards of Official Conduct after House Speaker Thomas P. O'Neill Jr. (D Mass.) urged that a counsel of "national reputation" be appointed. Jaworski, who had served as the Watergate special prosecutor in 1973-1974, accepted the appointment July 20. The following day the committee agreed that it would issue any subpoenas that Jaworski requested and that he could be removed only by a majority vote of the full House rather than merely by action of the committee.

Park abruptly left the United States and went to London after the bribery story broke. Returning to South Korea Aug. 18, 1977, he refused to cooperate with U.S. Justice Department officials who attempted to persuade him to return to the United States to testify. He could not be extradited from South Korea. After long and difficult negotiations between the government of South Korea, Park's lawyers and U.S. Justice Department officials, Park agreed to testify in return for full immunity from prosecution. He signed an agreement Jan. 11, 1978, to tell all he knew about the congressional pay-off scheme. Hanna, who had acknowledged that he had been Park's silent partner in a 1971 business venture to export American rice to Korea, denied any illegality in the arrangement and in any other accusation of wrongdoing. Hanna's trial on charges stemming from the South Korea bribery scandal was scheduled to begin Jan. 9, 1978.

Hearings

In the three days of hearings conducted by the House Committee on Standards of Official Conduct, witnesses recounted tales of the South Korean ambassador to the United States personally stuffing envelopes with $100 bills and leaving them in congressional offices, of wives of representatives being handed cash to spend while traveling in Korea with *their husbands (they returned the money), and of at least $9.2-million in commissions on rice sales flowing through the hands of Tongsun Park.*

The plan allegedly had its beginnings in 1967 when Park met with KCIA officials in Seoul and convinced them he should be made the middleman in the purchase of U.S.-grown rice exported to Korea. Commissions from the sales went to Park, who, as the exclusive Korean rice-export agent in the United States, used the money to distribute to members of the U.S. Congress to buy good will for South Korea, it was alleged.

Corroboration of the bribery plan occurred Nov. 29 when the House International Relations Subcommittee on International Organizations made public a 23-page KCIA master plan that projected elaborate intelligence operations including "implementation of an intelligence network in the White House" and a "network of collaboration" in Congress.

Following are the texts of opening remarks made by Rep. John J. Flynt (D Ga.), chairman of the House Committee on Standards of Official Conduct; excerpts from special counsel Leon Jaworski's statement and excerpts from the testimony of witnesses at the hearings held Oct. 19-21, 1977. (Boldface headings in brackets have been added by Congressional Quarterly to highlight the organization of the text.):

REP. FLYNT'S REMARKS

Mr. Flynt. In the course of pursuing the task mandated by House Resolution 252 [authorizes the committee to conduct hearings], this investigation has divided itself into two principal phases.

The first phase which is now largely completed—but let me emphasize that it is not entirely complete—has involved the gathering of background information relevant to the question of whether there were, in the words of House Resolution 252, efforts made by the government of a foreign country to influence Members of Congress by conferring things of value upon them or their immediate families, or associates.

This phase is thorough, accurate and complete except for interviewing and taking depositions of individuals who are beyond the reach of compulsory processes within the subpoena power of this committee.

During this phase the committee and/or the committee staff have interviewed over 200 persons. Many of those have been interviewed voluntarily. The committee has issued a total of more than 160 subpoenas for named persons for the taking of sworn testimony and has interviewed many others without subpoenas or with subpoenas issued but not actually served.

We have issued 194 subpoenas duces tecum for the production of documents and other materials, including over 50 since September 1, and in response to such subpoenas duces tecum we have received and reviewed more than 10,000 pages of documents and other material.

The committee has approved requests by counsel for authority to go into the U.S. district court to request orders of immunity from prosecution in 11 instances.

In connection with these immunity orders, the Department of Justice is always notified in advance so it may intervene and either concur in or object to such immunity orders. I am unaware of any instance in which the Department of Justice has filed an objection to such an order.

The committee has interviewed or subpoenaed every document and every person which it has reason to believe is relevant to this inquiry. Many leads have produced information which was based on facts and such information has been verified and corroborated.

Other leads have turned out to be totally false and some appeared to have been inspired by malicious or deranged minds. But all leads have been pursued.

It is the purpose of this first series of hearings to present information relating to the first phase of the investigation.

The committee believes that the investigation has established by convincing evidence, which will be developed at these hearings, that there were efforts made by elements in the Government of the Republic of Korea to influence Members of Congress by giving them cash; and that further and intensified efforts to determine which Members of Congress received it are more than warranted.

As would be expected, it is not an easy task to uncover evidence of a plan to pay cash to Members of Congress. Where the cash is accepted, neither party to the transaction has any motive to disclose that the transaction occurred and the transaction may be unknown to anyone else.

Fortunately, there are at least three Members of Congress, about whom you will hear during the hearings, who refused the efforts of the Koreans to give them cash.

Because of their upright conduct at the time of the offer of the money and because of their subsequent cooperation with this investigation, we are able to present tangible proof that the plans to influence Congress were not only formulated but implemented.

Since on or about August 1 the investigation has been directed by Leon Jaworski, Esquire, as Special Counsel, and Peter A. White, Esquire, as Deputy Special Counsel. Mr. White began his duties and functions as Deputy Special Counsel on July 21 and Mr. Jaworski assumed active leadership of the investigation on August 15 and has directed it competently and effectively since that time.

The relationship between the legal and the investigative divisions of the special staff on the one hand, and the committee and its permanent staff on the other hand, has been at an absolute optimum since August 1, without which optimum relationship the work of the committee could not have reached the point at which we find ourselves today.

Every effort has been made and is continuing to be made to move this inquiry as fast as practical consistent with accuracy, thoroughness, and completeness.

Let me emphasize that there are witnesses whom the committee would like to interview and whom we would like to subpoena. This we shall do if such compulsory process can be served and/or voluntary interviews can be accomplished.

This committee has received full cooperation from the Secretary of State [Cyrus R. Vance] and the Attorney General [Griffin B. Bell] in these efforts. In return we have extended plenary cooperation to the Department of Justice, the Department of State, and other agencies of Government.

This committee has made certain oral and written assurances to the intelligence community that this committee and its staff would treat in the closest confidence certain information furnished the committee pursuant to such assurances that the contents would not be made available to any person on or off the committee except on a demonstrated need to know basis.

These assurances were made in good faith and, in spite of repeated efforts to violate the terms of this commitment, the majority of the committee has on more than one occasion decided that it should not, and with propriety could not, make any changes in these assurances and agreements. The cooperation between the committee and the intelligence community has been mutual and exemplary.

During the time that this committee has been engaged in this investigation, there have arisen many obstacles to the orderly conduct of this investigation. Some of the obstacles have been generally internally, others externally. On the whole, the committee believes it has overcome all such obstacles.

This committee has conducted its investigation without fear, favor, affection, reward, or the hope thereof and we intend to continue this investigation to its conclusion in precisely the same manner.

I want to emphasize that every avenue which would lead to the discovery of pertinent facts, information, and evidence has been and will be explored as thoroughly as possible. The investigation is on course and while we shall take as much time as necessary to complete our job, it appears now that the job will be thoroughly completed in the foreseeable future.

The principal objective of this investigation is the ascertainment of the truth.

The scope of these hearings will not include proof relating to the second phase of our investigation. This is for two reasons.

First, until that phase is complete, premature presentation of evidence relating to it holds a risk of defaming persons who may eventually be exonerated, and the rules of the House preclude release of such untested information in open session.

Second, it will be very difficult to complete the second phase in a satisfactory manner without cooperation by the Government of Korea. In light of the proof to be presented at this set of hearings, we have a right to expect such cooperation from one of our allies will be forthcoming.

In the course of this investigation, which is beyond the normal scope of the jurisdiction of this committee, the committee has been cast in the role of investigator, prosecutor, judge and jury, neither of which alone is an easy or a pleasant assignment.

The combination of all four is close to impossible. In spite of both internal and external obstacles, the committee has proceeded undeterred by the charges, allegations, and innuendoes which have been directed at this committee and its staff....

The role of a prosecutor is never an easy role. It is manyfold more difficult when that role is combined with the role of investigator, judge, and jury.

During the course of this investigation, we have received unsolicited advice and suggestions from many sources. Since such sources have no responsibility for the final end product of this investigation, they could enjoy the luxury of inaccuracy, recklessness, and occasional falsehood which we who shoulder responsibility cannot afford.

The qualities of a good investigation are as elusive and impossible to define as the qualities which mark a gentleman. Those who need to be told would not understand it anyway....

JAWORSKI STATEMENT

Mr. Jaworski. Mr. Chairman and members of the committee. As you, Mr. Chairman, and other members of the committee, explained in your statements of the scope and the purpose of these hearings, our objective this week is to focus upon the activities of South Korean nationals and elements in the Government of the Republic of Korea in formulating, but not only in formulating, but also carrying out a plan to influence Members of Congress.

I think, Mr. Chairman, that you pointed to this with clarity. But, it is worth repeating.

The first phase of our investigation has been to piece together the facts regarding these activities, and it is my belief that we are now prepared to lay those facts, as we have them, before you.

As your counsel, I must advise you that we cannot assign absolute veracity to every element of the testimony to be addressed or to the authenticity of every instrument to be presented in the course of these hearings.

But, we conceive it to be our duty to pass on to you information that we believe to be reliable unless we explicitly inform you to the contrary.

Of course, we leave to you the assessment of its worthiness and its probative force. To be sure, of course, I should add parenthetically perhaps that we will not burden you with matters that are obviously frivolous.

It should also be emphasized, I think, that we do not consider the first phase of our investigation to be complete in every respect. In the weaving of the pattern of South Korean activities with some Members of Congress, we are confronted with a need to use certain links in forging the chain, some of which are circumstantial in nature and some of which, to be sure, are hearsay.

I point this out to suggest that final evaluation must await the completion of all hearings concerning our investigation. We feel, however, that the facts developed thus far are sufficiently compelling, and that this phase of our investigation is sufficiently completed to warrant this presentation to you and through you to the American people.

Now, the second phase of our investigation, which is now progressing, will focus upon the activities of specific Members of Congress to determine whether they received money or other things of value in violation of the Constitution, of applicable statutes, or of ethical standards.

The identities of any such Congressmen will not be the subject of this hearing, for two reasons.

If I may elaborate, and perhaps repeat to some extent—but I do so designedly because of its importance—under the rules of the House incriminating information as to a Congressman cannot be presented in public unless and until the person incriminated has been given an opportunity in executive session to refute the allegations by his own testimony and by the testimony of other witnesses he chooses to call.

It is interesting to me that this rule has been ignored, perhaps overlooked by some, in commenting on today's hearing. I assure you that I can well understand the eagerness with which names of possible offenders are sought. But this must be done with fairness and with justice; the same standard some of our critics would want used in instances that might involve themselves.

We are now engaged in investigating allegations against individual Congressmen, to be sure, in obtaining their testimony and obtaining the testimony of other witnesses. When that task is completed, but not before, the committee will decide what information regarding Congressmen will be publicized.

Now, next, the identities of all the Congressmen alleged to have engaged in illegal or unethical conduct cannot be known without the cooperation of the Korean Government and Korean nationals who know the facts.

I believe you will be persuaded from the evidence to be presented in these hearings that officials of the Korean Government and that some Korean nationals are in possession of facts which are absolutely essential to the completion of our assigned task.

The testimony to be rendered here will tend to establish the following facts: In the spring of 1973 representatives of the Korean Embassy here in Washington were told of a plan to "buy off"—and I am using these words in quotes—to "buy off" American Congressmen.

The [plan] was explained by the Washington station chief of the Korean Central Intelligence Agency [KCIA], a man named Yang Du Hwon, who operated here under the alias of Lee Sang Ho. The plan was to be implemented personally by the Ambassador, Kim Dong Jo, and by the KCIA station chief, Yang Du Hwon.

The plan was shrouded in extreme secrecy. The testimony you will hear will refer to code words, to the use of diplomatic privilege to avoid detection, and the destruction of documents.

Nevertheless, the evidence we have been able to gather indicates that a plan was adopted, and at least in part carried out.

A former Korean Embassy official will testify that in the spring of 1973 he chanced to enter the office of the Ambassador, the Ambassador of South Korea, where he saw the Ambassador of South Korea stuffing envelopes with $100 bills.

The Ambassador told this official that he was going to deliver these envelopes to Capitol Hill.

The testimony will also show that a Member of Congress, following the dictates of the law, as well as conscience, refused to accept an envelope full of cash tendered at his office by an emissary from the Korean Embassy.

By late 1974 the KCIA station chief, Yang Du Hwon, had returned to Korea. His departure did not, however, terminate further implementation of the plan.

In late 1974 a Korean-born businessman who resided in the Washington area, named Hancho Kim, was recruited to carry on the plan. Thereafter, $600,000 in cash was transferred from Korean sources to Hancho Kim through a KCIA officer stationed in this country named Kim Sang Keun.

We will have Kim Sang Keun's testimony, which discloses, among other things, that a very substantial part of the $600,000 was to be used to influence Congressmen.

Washington was not the only place where the influence-buying plan was implemented. In August of 1975 eight Congressmen, accompanied by their wives, visited Korea.

Testimony will show that while in Korea two of the wives were offered envelopes full of cash. One envelope was tendered by the wife of Kim Dong Jo, who had been the Korean Ambassador in Washington when the plan was formulated.

This evidence can be presented to you because of the proper and forthright action by these Congressmen and their wives who rejected the money and later reported the incident to the committee.

The testimony that you will hear will also tend to establish another aspect of the plan to gain influence in Congress by elements in the Korean Government.

In 1967 Tongsun Park, of whom you have heard, a Korean national who resided primarily in Washington, met in Seoul with officials of the Korean Central Intelligence Agency. Mr. Park eventually convinced the KCIA that he should be made the middleman in purchase of rice from American sellers by the Korean Government.

He proposed that commissions that would flow to him as the exclusive agent of American rice sellers could be used to create a more favorable atmosphere for South Korea in Congress.

Mr. Park was in fact made the middleman and received rice commissions from 1968 through 1970 and, following a significant gap in 1971 and the early part of 1972, continued on through January 1976.

Now, the commissions paid to Mr. Park during this 7-year period amounted to more than $9 million—$9 million.

Evidence will be adduced to show that the KCIA directed Mr. Park to use the rice commissions to buy influence and that Mr. Park made reports to the KCIA claiming great success in his efforts to influence Congressmen.

One document purporting to be a report of Mr. Park's activities will be presented to you. We cannot vouch for the accuracies or ultimate probative value of this report. Indeed, we believe that at least parts of it are inaccurate or exaggerated in substantial respects.

The testimony and documents to be brought out will, however, lead to the reasonable inference that money was intended to be paid and may in fact have been paid to Members of Congress.

The witnesses whose testimony you will have during these hearings are among those who have contributed, whether voluntarily or pursuant to subpoena, to our ascertaining the truth.

For the most part, their testimony will paint a grim picture. But, it is worth noting that some of the evidence will show the commendable conduct of persons who refused to receive moneys in violation of the Constitution, other laws, and the code of ethics.

We must also appreciate the forthrightness of those witnesses who appear to regret sincerely any misconduct or error in judgment that has taken place.

Now, as we begin these hearings, I emphasize, as I have done before, that the Government of Korea is not the subject of our investigation. Nor is it our intent to castigate or to embarrass, or in any way pass judgment on that government, its policies, its principles, its concepts, and its precepts.

South Korea is a sovereign nation, and as such has a right to judge the conduct of its citizens and public officials by its own standards, which may be different from ours.

The methods used by the Korean Government to conduct its foreign policy are, under principles of diplomatic immunity, not subject to question under our laws.

But we do have the right, and I think we have the duty, to judge the conduct of our elected officials, and the Republic of Korea, as our ally and the beneficiary of our historic friendship, has no right to coverup and to obstruct our investigation of any conduct by our public officials of which we may disapprove.

All we desire is access to the facts, and I believe firmly that the American Government and the American people have the right to expect cooperation in this regard.

The obstacle to establishing a full and true disclosure of Tongsun Park's activities with Members of Congress, as well as those of other South Korean representatives and emissaries, rests in the unwillingness of the South Korean Government to cooperate.

Not only has there been no tender of cooperation, but efforts to resist our progress in ascertaining the facts have been encountered.

When South Korean dispatches from Seoul indicated a willingness to extend us an opportunity to interview Tongsun Park, I offered to meet with the foreign minister during his recent visit here to assure ourselves that the session with Mr. Park would be more than a social visit and would involve a full discussion of the relevant facts.

Nothing further was heard from South Korea until the Attorney General disclosed that contacts had been made with his office for his nominee and for me to meet with South Korean authorities in Seoul regarding an interview of Tongsun Park.

On further inquiry, however, it was learned that the South Korean Government was willing for Mr. Park to be interviewed only under such stringent conditions as to make the confrontation worthless, in my judgment.

Any restrictions and limitations such as the South Korean Government wished to impose would make a farce of the responsibilities entrusted to this committee by the House of Representatives.

Because of what has come to light in our investigation, buttressed by the present attitude of the South Korean Government, there are compelling indications that the South Korean Government not only through Tongsun Park, but as well through some elements in the government itself, were engaged in an effort to influence Members of Congress by giving them valuable gifts.

Mr. Chairman, members of the committee, forgive me for making this additional comment, but I think that the time has come for this committee to go on record to recommend that the House pass a resolution calling on South Korea to extend full and unlimited cooperation in a total disclosure of the activities, not only of Tongsun Park as a functionary in seeking congressional favors, but as well of the activities of those who were operating out of the South Korean Embassy and other agencies and other instrumentalities of that Government whether or not authorized by their superiors. I so strongly recommend.

This, Mr. Chairman, concludes the opening statement....

Testimony of Nan Elder

Mr. [John W.] Nields [Jr., Chief Counsel]. Mrs. Elder, how are you presently employed?

Mrs. Elder. I am personal secretary to Congressman Larry Winn [R] of Kansas.

Mr. Nields. How long have you had that job?

Mrs. Elder. Eight and a half years.

Mr. Nields. And how long has Congressman Winn been a Member of Congress?

Mrs. Elder. Ten years....

Mr. Nields. Directing your attention, Mrs. Elder, to September or October of 1972, did you receive a call concerning an emissary from the Embassy of the Government of the Republic of Korea?

Mrs. Elder. Yes, we did.

Mr. Nields. Did you personally receive that call?

Mrs. Elder. Yes, I did.

Mr. Nields. Would you describe it?

Mrs. Elder. The gentleman calling said that an official of the Korean Embassy was in the building and would like to come by and pay a courtesy call on the Congressman. I said that would be fine.

Mr. Nields. Did the person who called name the official who was to appear?

Mrs. Elder. He did, but I don't remember the name.

Mr. Nields. Did he give a title?

Mrs. Elder. He did, but I don't remember that, either.

Mr. Nields. Did a Korean gentleman appear in your office soon thereafter?

Mrs. Elder. Yes, he did, within the next few minutes he arrived.

Mr. Nields. And what did you do when he arrived?

Mr. Elder. I showed him into the Congressman's office, and they shook hands, and I left and closed the door.

Mr. Nields. What happened after that?

Mrs. Elder. The Congressman and the Korean gentleman both left shortly thereafter. They were not there more than, oh, a minute or two, and then they both left the office. I think the Korean gentleman left first, and then Congressman Winn left shortly thereafter.

Mr. Nields. Do you know where Congressman Winn went?

Mrs. Elder. It was in the morning, as I recall, and he either went to a committee meeting or to the floor, and I am not certain now, but one or the other.

Mr. Nields. Did you receive a call from the Congressman soon thereafter?

Mrs. Elder. Yes. He asked me if I would go into his office and look in the top drawer of his desk and see—he had a habit of leaving the top drawer of his desk open—and see what was in the white envelope that was in the desk.

Mr. Nields. Was there a reason for his habit of leaving the top drawer of his desk open?

Mrs. Elder. He leaned his foot on it.

Mr. Nields. Did you go into his room?

Mrs. Elder. Pardon?

Mr. Nields. Did you then go into his office?

Mrs. Elder. Yes, I went into his office, and I looked—there was a white envelope in the top drawer, and I took it out and I opened it and then I picked up the telephone in his office.

Mr. Nields. Did you say something to the Congressman when you picked up the telephone?

Mrs. Elder. Yes. I said there was more money in the envelope than I had ever seen in my life.

Mr. Nields. And what exactly did you see in the envelope, Mrs. Elder.

Mrs. Elder. There was a stack of $100 bills, about that many.

Mr. Nields. Is that about an inch high?

Mrs. Elder. I would guess about an inch.

Mr. Nields. What did Congressman Winn say to you?

Mrs. Elder. Something to the effect of return it or get rid of it. I said don't worry, I will take care of it.

Mr. Nields. And what did you do?

Mrs. Elder. I went out to the front office, and I looked up the Korean Embassy in the Congressional Directory, and I called the Embassy and asked—a young woman answered the telephone, and I asked her if she could tell me where I might be able to locate this gentleman who had been in our office. She referred me to a gentleman and he told me where I might find him.

Mr. Nields. When you say referred you, do you mean she transferred the call?

Mrs. Elder. Yes, she transferred the call to a gentleman in the Embassy.

Mr. Nields. And what did the man that you spoke to at the Embassy say?

Mrs. Elder. He told me where the next appointment was, and I called there and asked if I might speak to the gentleman when he was through.

Mr. Nields. Now, when you say he told you where the next appointment was, do you mean that he told you where the emissary could be found in the House Office Building?

Mrs. Elder. That is right.

Mr. Nields. And what did you do after you finished your conversation with the man from the Korean Embassy?

Mrs. Elder. I called that Member's office and asked that if they would advise him it was imperative I get in touch with him, and please as soon as he was finished to call me. He did.

Mr. Nields. Now, you say as soon as he was finished. Did the person in the other Congressman's office say where he was or what he was doing?

Mrs. Elder. No, no.

Mr. Nields. Was he immediately available to talk to you?

Mrs. Elder. It was very shortly thereafter he called me, and I asked him if I could meet him someplace and he said he could come back up to the office, which he did.

Mr. Nields. What did you do when he came back into the office?

Mrs. Elder. I showed him into the Congressman's office. I gave him the envelope and said thank you very much, but we can't accept this.

Mr. Nields. By the way, what did the envelope look like?

Mrs. Elder. Just a plain white envelope, and it was not sealed.

Mr. Nields. Did he take the envelope?

Mrs. Elder. Yes.

Mr. Nields. What did he do?

Mrs. Elder. He left.

Mr. Nields. Mrs. Elder, have you seen this gentleman since?

Mrs. Elder. No, I have not.

Mr. Nields. And had you seen him before?

Mrs. Elder. No, I had not.

Mr. Nields. Have you seen a picture of him since?

Mrs. Elder. Yes, I have.

Mr. Nields. And when did you first see a picture of him?

Mrs. Elder. Last Friday in your office.

Mr. Nields. Would you show the witness committee exhibit A?

Mrs. Elder. Thank you.

Mr. Nields. Just leave it there.

Mrs. Elder, would you look at committee exhibit A and first tell the committee whether that is a picture of the man whom you saw in my office last Thursday.

Mrs. Elder. It's the picture I saw last Thursday.

Mr. Nields. And is that, in fact, a picture of the man who came into Congressman Winn's office in the fall of 1972?

Mrs. Elder. Yes, it is.

Mr. Nields. And when you saw his picture in my office, was that together with a spread of about 14 other photographs?

Mrs. Elder. Yes, at least.

Mr. Nields. And did you pick out that photograph?

Mrs. Elder. Yes, I did.

Mr. Nields. At that time?

Mrs. Elder. Yes, I did.

Mr. Nields. Mrs. Elder, can you be a little bit more certain as to the date on which this emissary from the Korean Embassy entered your office?

Mrs. Elder. As nearly as I can remember, I checked back on the appointment book, and on September 27 Congressman and Mrs. Winn were invited to a reception at the Korean Embassy, and the meeting with the Korean gentleman was within a day or so after that. I would say in all probability the next day.

Mr. Nields. What committee was Congressman Winn a member of at the time of the visit?

Mrs. Elder. He was a member of the Committee on Science and Astronautics, now the Committee on Science and Technology, and of the Veterans' Affairs Committee.

Mr. Nields. Did he soon thereafter become a member of the Foreign Affairs Committee?

Mrs. Elder. In January of 1973 he was appointed to the International Relations Committee.

Mr. Nields. Had he previously made known around Congress his intent in being named to the International Relations Committee?

Mrs. Elder. Ever since he had come to Congress he had made known to the minority leader that should a vacancy for a middle westerner be on the International Relations Committee, he would like to be considered for it.

Mr. Nields. Mr. Chairman, I have no further questions of this witness at this time....

Testimony of Dr. Jai Hyon Lee

Mr. Nields. What position did you hold at the Korean Embassy?

Dr. Lee. I was chief counsel and information attaché, concurrently the director of the Korean Information Office in the United States.

Mr. Nields. What were your duties as director of the Korean Information Office?

Dr. Lee. My duties included being the official spokesman for the Embassy, and for the Korean Government in the United States. I used to put out news releases, answer inquiries from the press and other people in the United States. I maintained a rental film library which gave out films to those who wanted to use them.

Mr. Nields. Would you give the committee a brief description of the manner in which the Korean Embassy was organized?

Dr. Lee. Under the Ambassador there were at that time eight different services. All internal divisions: Political, economic, commercial, counselor, general affairs, education, defense, and culture and information.

Mr. Nields. And were you the director of the last division that you just named?

Dr. Lee. Exactly.

Mr. Nields. And were there any employees in the Embassy who were not assigned to any particular division?

Dr. Lee. Yes, there were.

Mr. Nields. And what were those employees?

Dr. Lee. Those were the members of the Korean Central Intelligence Agency.

Mr. Nields. Approximately how many Korean Central Intelligence Agency agents were employed in the Korean Embassy when you first arrived there?

Dr. Lee. When I first arrived there I thought there were four, and later I noticed there were five. At one point there were six.

Mr. Nields. Did the number increase to about 12 shortly after you left the Embassy?

Dr. Lee. Yes.

Mr. Nields. Approximately how many employees were there in the Embassy as a whole?

Dr. Lee. I could count about 12 of those KCIA agents.

Mr. Nields. Do you know of any KCIA agent who was also assigned to one of the divisions that you have described?

Dr. Lee. Yes. There was one military personnel who was assigned to the office of the defense attaché.

Mr. Nields. What was his name?

Dr. Lee. His name was Col. Lim Kyu-Il.

Mr. Nields. What were his functions?

Dr. Lee. He was responsible for operating on Capitol Hill.

Mr. Nields. Do you know precisely what he did on Capitol Hill?

Dr. Lee. I have no idea.

Mr. Nields. Dr. Lee, who was the KCIA station chief when you first arrived at the Embassy?

Dr. Lee. When I first arrived in the Embassy, in January 1970, that was Yoon Seung Kook.

Mr. Nields. And was he replaced by another KCIA station chief before you left?

Dr. Lee. Yes. About a year and one-half or so later he was replaced by a new man.

Mr. Nields. What was that man's name?

Dr. Lee. His name was Lee Sang Ho.

Mr. Nields. Was that his real name?

Dr. Lee. No; that was his alias; his real name was Yang, Du Hwon.

Mr. Nields. And approximately when did he arrive at the Embassy?

Dr. Lee. I believe it was sometime in 1972.

Mr. Nields. Dr. Lee, during the period of time you were at the Embassy, who was the Ambassador?

Dr. Lee. He was Kim Dong Jo.

Mr. Nields. Ms. Pavelic [committee staff member], would you show this witness committee exhibit A?

[Exhibit shown to witness.]

Mr. Nields. Dr. Lee, can you identify the man in the committee exhibit A?

Dr. Lee. Yes. This is Kim Dong Jo.

Mr. Nields. Mr. Chairman, I would like the record to reflect that committee exhibit A is the picture that was identified by Nan Elder, the previous witness.

Mr. Flynt. The record will so reflect.

Mr. Nidleds. Dr. Lee, directing your attention to the spring of 1973, do you recall any unusual meetings that occurred in the Embassy?

Dr. Lee. Yes. I was called to a series of meetings.

Mr. Nields. Who called the meetings?

Dr. Lee. The Ambassador called.

Mr. Nields. Who did most of the talking at the meetings?

Dr. Lee. After the Ambassador made a very brief remark, then the meeting was passed on to the KCIA station chief, Lee Sang Ho, and thereafter he did most of the talking.

Mr. Nields. How frequent were these meetings?

Dr. Lee. It was virtually every other day, or sometimes 2 days in a row, but approximately two or three times a week.

Mr. Nields. And for how long did these meetings continue?

Dr. Lee. The meetings continued until the day I resigned, I left the Embassy.

Mr. Nields. At first what was discussed at these meetings?

Dr. Lee. The first things in that first meeting, what the KCIA station chief most emphatically pointed out, was that the meetings are going to be strictly secret, and nothing discussed in that room should be discussed outside that room, even within the chancellory building.

Mr. Nields. What else was discussed, Dr. Lee?

Dr. Lee. Then he began to explain very vaguely sort of an outline of the KCIA operation plan in the United States.

Mr. Nields. In general terms, can you tell us what that was?

Dr. Lee. As the meetings went on, after a number of sessions, I could piece together what he was describing to us. Those included in the scheme, for instance, to put pressure, covert pressure, on American businesses, which have vested interest in Korea, to use their influence in the American Government in support of the Park government's new policies, known as Yushim policies.

Mr. Nields. Dr. Lee, had you shortly before these meetings commenced been to Korea?

Dr. Lee. Yes. I was back in Korea in March 1973, to attend another series of meetings.

Mr. Nields. And what did these meetings concern?

Dr. Lee. These meetings were to reorient us, those information officers serving abroad, to the new policies under the new constitution, and also they instructed us to carry out certain activities. In my case that was to disseminate false information in the United States, to improve or rather enhance the image of these dictatorial policies known as the Yushim.

Mr. Nields. Dr. Lee, did there come a time during the course of the meetings in Washington when a document was passed around to the people who attended the meeting with a series of proposals listed on the document?

Dr. Lee. Yes. After a number of sessions, the KCIA station chief began to distribute documents to discuss about. Some of the documents included the listing of their schemes or proposals, what they were going to do in the United States. The list was more like in the form of a table of contents.

Mr. Nields. How were these documents handled?

Dr. Lee. These documents were serially numbered, and again, these documents were given out only in that conference room, and we were allowed to look at the documents only in that room and instructed not to take them out, even to our own offices in the Embassy.

Mr. Nields. And who was allowed to attend these meetings?

Dr. Lee. Only key personnel of the Embassy. About 10 people including the Ambassador were allowed.

Mr. Nields. Do you recall a particular item on this document you have described as a table of contents?

Dr. Lee. Yes. There was one item which referred to seduction and buying off of American leaders, particularly in the Congress.

Mr. Nields. Did Lee Sang Ho say anything about that item?

Dr. Lee. When we were going through these items, as we reached this point, he briefly made a remark that this part of the operation would be more or less left to the Ambassador and us. So, you don't have to know about it, or something of that nature. Then went over to the next item.

Mr. Nields. To whom did he refer by the word "us"?

Dr. Lee. I assumed that was the Ambassador and himself, or if not, some of his own staff. KCIA people.

Mr. Nields. Dr. Lee, did anything ever occur, to your knowledge, indicating that this plan to buy off American leaders, particularly in Congress, was actually implemented?

Dr. Lee. By sheer accident one day I discovered the Ambassador stuffing $100 bills into plain white envelopes.

Mr. Nields. Will you describe how that came about?

Dr. Lee. I entered into his office one day, in spring, 1973.

Mr. Nields. Were you announced?

Dr. Lee. No.

Mr. Nields. Were people in the Embassy permitted to enter the Ambassador's office unannounced?

Dr. Lee. There were four or five key people who could walk in and out of the Ambassador's office unannounced; yes.

Mr. Nields. Would you describe as precisely as you can, Dr. Lee, exactly what you saw as you walked into his office?

Dr. Lee. When I entered his office he was at his desk. He was stuffing something into envelopes. As I walked over to his desk I could see $100 bills on his desk and also in the attaché case atop his desk, and he was stuffing $100 bills in the envelopes. And he looked at me and said, "What do you have in mind; speak up, I have to deliver these things."

Mr. Nields. Now, were these plain white envelopes?

Dr. Lee. Yes.

Mr. Nields. And how many of them did you see?

Dr. Lee. Approximately two dozen of them.

Mr. Nields. And how do you arrive at a figure "two dozen"?

Dr. Lee. Well, I could see the envelopes already stuffed in the attaché case, also I could see a few on the desk, and I could also see broken bands which tied the envelopes, a bundle of envelopes around.

Mr. Nields. Is this paper bands you are referring to?

Dr. Lee. Yes; that is paper band.

Mr. Nields. Of the type that are around envelopes when you but them at a store in bunches?

Dr. Lee. Exactly. So there was usually 1 bundle contains 12 envelopes, so I can say there were approximately 2 dozen.

Mr. Nields. And what did you say to the Ambassador?

Dr. Lee. Well, he was almost finishing his packing and he started to put the envelopes into his pocket, and the rest of the envelopes were in his attaché case he closed, and he stood up and started to walk out of the room, so I walked out with him. But I asked him where he was going. He said, "To the Capitol."

Mr. Nields. Did you have any further conversations with the Ambassador or with the KCIA station chief?

Dr. Lee. No; I did not.

Mr. Nields. Concerning the payment of money to Congress or the subject of cash?

Dr. Lee. Right. I did not discuss any further.

Mr. Nields. Dr. Lee, do you know of any methods whereby U.S. currency was brought into the Embassy?

Dr. Lee. Yes. On a number of occasions I noticed U.S. currencies were brought in from Korea by diplomatic pouch.

Mr. Nields. And how did you notice this?

Dr. Lee. I was discussing with the Ambassador in his office, then a man in the general affairs section downstairs brought in a small cube.

Mr. Nields. A cubic package?

Dr. Lee. A cubic package packed with brown paper and he told the Ambassador that this was the money from Seoul, came by pouch.

Mr. Nields. Dr. Lee, is the diplomatic pouch subject to inspection by customs?

Dr. Lee. No, not at all....

Testimony of Kim San Keun

Mr. [Thomas M.] Fortuin [committee counsel]. Mr. Kim [former employee, Korean embassy], do you know a man by the name of Hancho Kim?

Mr. Kim. Yes, I know him.

Mr. Fortuin. When did you meet him for the first time?

Mr. Kim. I believe it was in the fall of 1972.

Mr. Fortuin. Where did you meet him?

Mr. Kim. I met him at the office of Minister Lee Sang Ho.

Mr. Fortuin. Who was at that time the KCIA station chief; is that correct?

Mr. Kim. That is correct.

Mr. Fortuin. What was said on that occasion?

Mr. Kim. It was my first meeting with Mr. Hancho Kim, and on the occasion I was merely introduced to Mr. Kim.

Mr. Fortuin. Thereafter, did you meet Mr. Hancho Kim on another occasion?

Mr. Kim. Yes.

Mr. Fortuin. Where did you meet him on that occasion?

Mr. Kim. I met him at the residence of Ambassador Kim Dong Jo.

Mr. Fortuin. What was he doing there on that occasion?

Mr. Kim. I believe it was in 1973, and at that particular time there was a meeting of the chiefs of Korean delegations stationed throughout the United States. At that time the consul generals from Korea gathered in Washington for the meeting, and it was on the occasion of a dinner party Ambassador Kim Dong Jo hosted for the delegation chiefs. To the dinner party invited were several Korean residents, and Mr. Hancho Kim was one of them invited.

Mr. Fortuin. Did you have a conversation with Mr. Hancho Kim on that occasion?

Mr. Kim. No; I did not.

Mr. Fortuin. I want to direct your attention to late August of 1974, and ask you whether you had a conversation with Hancho Kim on that occasion?

Mr. An [Korean translator]. Did you ask whether did Mr. Kim see him?

Mr. Fortuin. Did he have a conversation with him in August of 1974?

Mr. Kim. He called me at my office at the Embassy over the phone.

Mr. Fortuin. Tell us what he said and what you said.

Mr. Kim. First he said he had visited Korea on the occasion of August 15, National Independence Day. He said over the phone that while he was visiting Korea the wife of President Park [Chung Hee, President of South Korea] was assassinated. And he said again over the phone that I was going to work with him on a very important mission, and he said I would be, later, I would be referred to as Professor Kim.

Mr. Fortuin. I don't understand.

Mr. Kim. He told me over the phone that I would be, that is me, I would be referred to as Professor Kim.

Mr. Fortuin. Was anything else said?

Mr. Kim. Then he requested me to come over to his home sometime later. Then he gave me directions to get to his home....

Mr. Fortuin. ...[D]id you then have a conversation with Mr. Kim Hancho?

Mr. Kim. Yes. I visited Mr. Hancho [sic] at his home.

Mr. Fortuin. And approximately when would this be?

Mr. Kim. I believe it was either on September 5 or September 6.

Mr. Fortuin. And when you talked with Mr. Hancho Kim was anyone else present?

Mr. Kim. No, no one was there except himself and I.

Mr. Fortuin. Tell us what you said and what Mr. Kim Hancho [sic] said on that occasion?

Mr. Kim. Mr. Hancho Kim repeated what he had said over the phone. He later told me why and as to how he had gotten the very important task he was going to carry out.

Mr. Fortuin. Tell us what he said.

Mr. Kim. He said that whenever he visited Korea, Mrs. Park, Chung Hee, the wife of the President, had asked of me that I contribute my effort for the interest of Korea, that was what he said. He continued saying that. However, whenever he had this request from Mrs. Park he had declined by saying that he was merely a businessman and not a political figure, and, therefore, he said he declined. However, he says since now Mrs. Park passed away he would take what Mrs. Park told me as her will, and, therefore, he would now carry that task out. And he said to me that he needed, he wanted, my cooperation in carrying out this task. And he asked me whether I have received a letter from Seoul. I said, yes, I did, and he said whether the letter indicated I would be referred as Professor Kim, I said yes.

Then he said, "You see, what I told you was right." And he said he was a successful man making a million in this country.

Then he told me that soon afterward there will be a very important article coming from Korea. I asked him what was that important article. He said that was money. Those are the gist he made related to me.

Mr. Fortuin. And what you have just told us is a second conversation you had with Mr. Hancho Kim; is that correct?

Mr. Kim. Yes....

Mr. Fortuin. Tell us what you did on September 12, 1974.

Mr. Kim. Following the instruction as specified..., I went to my bank, where I had a personal account, checking account, that is Dupont Circle Riggs Bank, and I withdrew from my checking account $44,000. Then I stopped in at my office at the Embassy.

Mr. Fortuin. Mr. Kim, let me show you what has been premarked committee exhibit No. 3 and ask you if you can identify that.

Mr. Kim. This is a canceled check of $44,000 with which I had withdrawn from my bank account, which was mentioned by you just now.

Mr. Fortuin. Mr. Chairman, I supplied the committee with copies of exhibit 3. The record should reflect that it is a copy of a check made from bank microfilm on the Riggs National Bank at Dupont Circle. It is dated September 12, 1974, and it is in the amount of $44,000 drawn on the account of Mr. Kim Sang Keun. The endorsements on the check indicate that it was cashed at the bank on September 12, 1974.

What did you do with the $44,000 after you got it, Mr. Kim?

Mr. Kim. After staying in the Embassy for some 30 minutes, I took that money to my apartment.

Mr. Fortuin. What happened when you got there?

Mr. Kim. I put this money—that is $44,000—together with the money Mr. Kim, Hak Chin brought me the day before in the amount of $256,000 making altogether $300,000 and I wrapped it.

Mr. Fortuin. I am sorry. What did you do with it?

Mr. Kim. I put $44,000 together with $256,000, which was brought by Mr. Kim, Hak Chin the day before, put together and made it into $300,000, and I wrapped it.

Mr. Fortuin. What did you do with the $300,000 after you wrapped it?

Mr. Kim. Then I went to the house of Mr. Hancho Kim with it.

Mr. Fortuin. What happened when you got there?

Mr. Kim. Then I met with Mr. Hancho Kim.

Mr. Fortuin. Tell us what was said when you met with Mr. Kim.

Mr. Kim. I gave the money to Mr. Hancho Kim. Then he said the money was really big size. He said it was a preciously large sum of money particularly for a country like Korea, which is quite poor.

He said according to newspaper accounts, some of the village children omit their lunch. He said in that view the money was all the more precious.

Then he began to count the money. He chose at random some bundles and began to count each bundle. At that moment, Mrs. Hancho Kim came into the room. She looked quite surprised at the sight of the money.

Mr. Hancho Kim told his wife that that was the money to be delivered early in the morning next day. Then he repeated that he was a millionaire.

He said he had plants. Then he showed me many clips of American newspapers in which he was mentioned. The articles were of the content commenting how successful Hancho Kim was in this country as a businessman.

He said there was more money to come forth later in relation to that particular money. He said when he discussed things in Seoul, it was a mission worth $1 million. He said he would be needing more money in order to carry out his mission.

Those are the major points we discussed on that particular night.

Mr. Fortuin. Did you discuss what the mission was, Mr. Kim?

Mr. Kim. Since the detailed discussion was made in Seoul, I was not asking what it was about in detail. However, he said, Mr. Kim said, that by using that money, he would expand his activities through the Congress.

Mr. Fortuin. Mr. Kim, I directed you not to mention the name of any Congressman heretoday, is that correct?

Mr. Kim. Yes; I remember that.

Mr. Fortuin. But did Mr. Hancho Kim mention the name of a particular Congressman on this occasion in September 1974; when you delivered the $300,000 to him?

Mr. Kim. Yes, he mentioned the name of a specific Member of the Congress and he said he had been friends of that particular Congressman for a long time.

Mr. Fortuin. Did he also indicate to you that he would attempt to gain influence with this particular Member of Congress?

Mr. Kim. Yes, he said he would secure or gain further acquaintances within the Congress through this particular Congressman.

Mr. Fortuin. Mr. Kim, these are statements made to you by Mr. Hancho Kim, and you don't know whether they are true or not; is that accurate?

Mr. Kim. That is right; I do not know....

Testimony of Mrs. Kika de la Garza

Mr. Nields. Mrs. de la Garza, how is your husband employed?

Mrs. de la Garza. He is the Representative for the 15th District of Texas in the House of Representatives....

Mr. Nields. Have you ever been to Korea?

Mrs. de la Garza. Yes, sir.

Mr. Nields. How many times?

Mrs. de la Garza. Three times.

Mr. Nields. And was your most recent trip there in August 1975?

Mrs. de la Garza. Yes, sir.

Mr. Nields. Did you go with your husband?

Mrs. de la Garza. Yes, sir.

Mr. Nields. And were there other Members of Congress on the trip?

Mrs. de la Garza. Yes, sir.

Mr. Nields. Can you tell us their names, if you remember them?

Mrs. de la Garza. Congressman and Mrs. [Paul] Simon [D Ill.]; Congressman and Mrs. [Gus] Yatron [D Pa.]; Congressman and Mrs. John [T.] Myers [R Ind.]; Congressman and Mrs. [Tennyson] Guyer [R Ohio]; Congressman and Mrs. [Norman Y.] Mineta [D Calif.]; former Congressman and Mrs. [Donald D.] Clancy [R Ohio] and Congressman [Stephen J.] Solarz [D N.Y.].

Mr. Nields. Was he with his wife?

Mrs. de la Garza. Right, and Congressman and Mrs. Lester Wolff [D N.Y.], who was chairman of the delegation that we went with, and Congressman and Mrs. Ben Gilman [R N.Y.], and Congressman and Mrs. Herman Badillo [D N.Y.], as far as I can remember.

Mr. Nields. Now, Mrs. de la Garza, do you know what the purpose of this trip was?

Mrs. de la Garza. I think it was a protocol trip; I am not sure. But it could have been with the Select Committee on Narcotics.

Mr. Nields. Mrs. de la Garza, did the delegation go straight to Korea, or did it stop in other countries?

Mrs. de la Garza. No, we went to other countries first.

Mr. Nields. Would you tell us which they were?

Mrs. de la Garza. We went to the Philippines; we went to Indonesia, and then we went to Korea, and then to Japan, and then back to the States.

Mr. Nields. How many days and nights did you spend in Korea?

Mrs. de la Garza. As far as I can remember, it was either two or three nights, I am not sure. And maybe it would have been 2½ days, probably.

Mr. Nields. Where did you stay while you were in Korea?

Mrs. de la Garza. We stayed at the Chosun Hotel.

Mr. Nields. Is that in Seoul?

Mrs. de la Garza. Yes.

Mr. Nields. Do you remember an evening at which you attended a social function at which there was a floor show?

Mrs. de la Garza. Yes, sir, I do.

Mr. Nields. And was that a floor show and dinner?

Mrs. de la Garza. Yes, sir.

Mr. Nields. Can you describe the room in which this floor show occurred?

Mrs. de la Garza. It was at another hotel, not the hotel we were staying at, but it was at another hotel, and it was a large room and it had two levels. The place where we had dinner was on the top level, and it was like a semicircle, and we had dinner with the Members of Congress from Korea, and in the lower level I imagine there were hotel guests or other guests, because they were also having dinner there, and it was in the lower level.

Mr. Nields. And was the place where the floor show occurred beyond the lower level from where you were?

Mrs. de la Garza. Yes, sir.

Mr. Nields. Mrs. de la Garza, do you know a woman named Kim Dong Jo?

Mrs. de la Garza. Yes, I do.

Mr. Nields. And did you know her at that time?

Mrs. de la Garza. Yes, sir.

Mr. Nields. Where had you met her before your trip to Korea in August of 1975?

Mrs. de la Garza. My husband and I were invited to a reception at the Korean Embassy, I don't remember exactly the day, but it was, oh, maybe like 6, 7 years ago, probably.

Mr. Nields. Was this when her husband was the Ambassador?

Mrs. de la Garza. Yes, sir.

Mr. Nields. And was her husband still the Ambassador in August of 1975?

Mrs. de la Garza. No, sir.

Mr. Nields. Had you ever met her at anything other than an official function of some kind?

Mrs. de la Garza. No, sir.

Mr. Nields. Was Mrs. Kim Dong Jo present at this dinner and the floor show to follow?

Mrs. de la Garza. Yes, she was.

Mr. Nields. Did you speak to her at any time during the evening?

Mrs. de la Garza. We saw her when we arrived at this hotel where we went to the dinner, and she was in the lobby of the hotel, and we greeted her.

Mr. Nields. Did you speak to her at the dinner?

Mrs. de la Garza. No, sir. We were seated at another table with other Congressmen.

Mr. Nields. Where did you go following the dinner?

Mrs. de la Garza. We went back to the hotel, to the Chosun Hotel where we were staying.

Mr. Nields. Did you go to your hotel room?

Mrs. de la Garza. Yes, we did.

Mr. Nields. Do you know whether the other members of the delegation also went back to their hotel rooms?

Mrs. de la Garza. No, sir. I couldn't tell you.

Mr. Nields. Approximately what time did you return to your room?

Mrs. de la Garza. Probably 11:30 or 12 o'clock.

Mr. Nields. Can you tell the committee what happened after you got back to your hotel room?

Mrs. de la Garza. Yes, sir. At the dinner the Congressman that we were seated with asked us to have coffee with him after the dinner at the hotel where we were staying. So we were going to come to the lobby to meet them. But before, when we arrived at the hotel, my husband and I went back to our room to freshen up, and while we were there someone knocked at the door and it was Mrs. Kim.

Mr. Nields. Who opened the door?

Mrs. de la Garza. I did.

Mr. Nields. When you say Mrs. Kim, is that Mrs. Kim Dong Jo?

Mrs. de la Garza. Yes, sir.

Mr. Nields. What happened after you opened the door?

Mrs. de la Garza. We asked her in, and asked her to have a seat. We just visited. She asked about Washington and how everything was and how we had enjoyed the show, and how we were enjoying our trip to Korea, just things like that.

Mr. Nields. Did there come a time when the telephone rang?

Mrs. de la Garza. Yes, sir. While we were visiting with her the phone rang, and it was the—my husband answered the phone—and it was the Congressman that we were going to meet to have coffee, to tell us that they were already in the lobby waiting for us.

Mr. Nields. Did Mrs. Kim Dong Jo say something or do anything while your husband was on the telephone?

Mrs. de la Garza. Yes; while he was on the phone she says, well someone is waiting for you, so I have to leave. And so I saw her to the door, and before she left she turned around and opened her purse and she says, "Oh, I have something for your husband's campaign," and she handed me an envelope.

Mr. Nields. Will you describe the envelope?

Mrs. de la Garza. It was a small size envelope, and it had my name written on it.

Mr. Nields. Was it a white envelope?

Mrs. de la Garza. Yes, sir.

Mr. Nields. Will you describe her pocketbook?

Mrs. de la Garza. It was an evening bag, like a clutch type small evening bag.

Mr. Nields. What color was it?

Mrs. de la Garza. It was black.

Mr. Nields. Was it approximately rectangular in shape?

Mrs. de la Garza. Yes, sir, with the rounded corners.

Mr. Nields. What did you do when she handed you the envelope?

Mrs. de la Garza. When she handed me the envelope, and when she said this is something I have for your husband's campaign and she handed it to me and I looked at it, then at that she said goodnight and walked out the door and left. Then when my husband hung up the telephone he came and he asked, he said, what did she give you? And I said I don't know, she gave me this envelope. So, then I opened it on the side of the envelope and then I looked in and I saw that there was money in it.

Mr. Nields. Could you tell whether it was U.S. money?

Mrs. de la Garza. Yes.

Mr. Nields. Could you tell what the denominations were?

Mrs. de la Garza. No, sir, because I didn't take it out. I just looked at it and I didn't want to have a thing to do with it.

Mr. Nields. How did you feel, Mrs. de la Garza, about the visit of Mrs. Kim Dong Jo to your hotel room, late at night, and the gift of the envelope full of cash?

Mrs. de la Garza. Well, I was shocked, and I was hurt. I felt insulted, really, In 25 years my husband has been a public servant, which is all our married life, this is the first experience I have had like that.

Mr. Nields. What did you do with the envelope after you tore off one side of it?

Mrs. de la Garza. When we both saw what it was, I guess simultaneously we both said, "we can't take this," and then my husband asked me where did she go, and I said I don't know, she walked out the door. So he said, I am going to go look for her, and he walked out the door and went out to the hall and toward the elevators, and she was nowhere around. So then he came back into the room and we put the envelope in the suitcase, and he said "Well, we have to go down and meet these friends, so then we will return it tomorrow." So we locked the suitcase and left.

Mr. Nields. And what happened the next morning?

Mrs. de la Garza. Well, the men had meetings there at the hotel, and my husband got up early and dressed, and he went down to the lobby to see if he could find Ambassador Kim to return the money.

Mr. Nields. What did you do?

Mrs. de la Garza. Well, while my husband went down and I was getting dressed, I was in the shower, and then I was getting out of the bathroom when I heard his voice, my husband's voice, in the hall talking to someone, so I immediately went, got back into the bathroom. Then I heard my husband tell him your wife was here last night and he gave me—she gave my wife this envelope, and told her that it was a contribution for my campaign, but we cannot accept this and I heard him say, "Oh," and so he says, no, I am very sorry, but we just can't take it, and he said, but if you want to do something for me why don't you make a contribution to a school that is run by a friend of mine outside of Osan Air Base; it's a village called Pyong Taek.

Mr. Nields. And to your knowledge, did the other person in the room leave and did you eventually emerge from the bathroom?

Mrs. de la Garza. Pardon me? I didn't hear.

Mr. Nields. When you emerged from the bathroom, was the second gentleman gone?

Mrs. de la Garza. Oh, yes, sir.

Mr. Nields. Would you tell the committee what your husband's and your interest was in this school?

Mrs. de la Garza. The principal of this school served, during the Korean war, he was, he came to Fort Sill, Okla., for training, and my husband was stationed there at the artillery school, and my husband helped him with his English, and how to, and to get around there at the base, so they became friends. Then they had lost track of each other, and when my husband made his first trip to Korea, I think in 1969, I am not sure, he took a picture with him that my husband had taken with his Korean friend in front of the barracks where they lived at Fort Sill, and asked one of the gentlemen from the Korean war veterans to see if they could find his friend.

Mr. Nields. Is this using the picture?

Mrs. de la Garza. Yes. And all my husband read was that his name was Kim. So, then, about, oh, I would say about 4 months later, my husband received a letter from his friend saying that to his surprise this man from the Korean war veterans had contacted him and told him that my husband had asked about him, and then he knew their acquaintance, and corresponded back and forth and sent pictures of his family and told him that now he was a principal of a Catholic vocational school outside of Osan at this village, and so that was our interest with the school, and we have visited the school twice.

Mr. Nields. And did you visit the school again on your trip in August of 1975?

Mrs. de la Garza. Yes, sir.

Mr. Nields. Do you know whether any money was given to this school?

Mrs. de la Garza. Yes, sir, because 3 weeks after we arrived back in Washington my husband had a letter from his friend telling him that he was very happy to have received a $2,000 donation to the school, and that this had been given to him by someone, we don't know who, at the Foreign Ministry in Seoul....

Statement of Gen. Kim Hyung Wook

Mr. Nields. General Kim, will you state and spell your full name for the record, please?

General Kim. My name is Kim, Hyung Wook....

Mr. Nields. Were you closely associated with Park Chung Hee's coup in 1961 which resulted in his taking over control of the Government of the Republic of South Korea?

General Kim. That is correct.

Mr. Nields. Did Park Chung Hee then name you Director of the Korean Central Intelligence Agency in 1963?

General Kim. That is correct.

Mr. Nields. How long did you hold that post?

General Kim. I was on that post until October 1969.

Mr. Nields. Has anyone else held that post as long as you have, General Kim?

General Kim. No.

Mr. Nields. Were you, as Director of the Korean Central Intelligence Agency, responsible to anyone other than the President of South Korea?

General Kim. Legally I was responsible only to the President. However, in practice I had also to coordinate with other Government officers.

Mr. Nields. Did that include the Prime Minister?

General Kim. Yes. I was referring to the Prime Minister.

Mr. Nields. After you left the directorship of the Korean Central Intelligence Agency in October of 1969, did you spend approximately a year and a half out of Government service?

General Kim. That is correct.

Mr. Nields. Did you in May of 1971 become a member of the Korean National Assembly?

General Kim. Yes.

Mr. Nields. Did you subsequently leave the National Assembly in October of 1972?

General Kim. Yes.

Mr. Nields. Did you subsequently fall out of favor with the Park Chung Hee regime in Korea?

General Kim. Yes.

Mr. Nields. Did you leave Korea in the spring of 1973 and come to this country?

General Kim. That is correct.

Mr. Nields. Is it fair to say, General Kim, that you left in something of a hurry?

General Kim. Of course.

Mr. Nields. Have you remained in this country ever since?

General Kim. Yes....

Mr. Nields. General Kim, do you know a man named Tongsun Park?

General Kim. Yes; I do.

Mr. Nields. When did you first hear of him?

General Kim. I believe it was sometime in the latter part of 1966.

Mr. Nields. How did you hear of him?

General Kim. I received a letter from the Kim Hyun Chul stationed in Washington, D.C.

Mr. Nields. Who succeeded him as Ambassador?

General Kim. I think it was Mr. Kim Dong Jo.

Mr. Nields. When did Kim Dong Jo succeed him as Ambassador?

General Kim. I can't remember the exact date. I think it is sometime in the first or middle part of 1967.

Mr. Nields. Referring you again to the letter that you received from Kim Hyun Chul, would you tell the committee what the letter said.

General Kim. The letter stated that a person by the name of Tongsun Park was impersonating the Korean Ambassador in the States and he was claiming to be a relative of President Park Chung Hee. The letter stated Mr. Tongsun Park was coming to visit Korea, and I was to have him arrested and have him warned concerning these allegations.

Mr. Nields. What did you do after you received the letter?

General Kim. I called Hong Pil Yong, who was then the director of the fifth bureau. I showed the letter to him and said, "Since Tongsun Park is coming to Korea, have him investigated."

Mr. Nields. Once again, is the fifth bureau the investigations bureau?

General Kim. Yes.

Mr. Nields. Did you later learn that your orders to the director of the investigations bureau had been carried out?

General Kim. Yes. I received a report.

Mr. Nields. Did you receive the report in person?

General Kim. Yes.

Mr. Nields. From whom?

General Kim. Mr. Hong Pil Yong, director of the bureau.

Mr. Nields. Would you tell the committee what the director of the investigating bureau told you.

General Kim. He reported to me that Mr. Park was arrested at the airport when he set his foot in Korea, and he was investigated throughout the night. And Mr. Park stated that he never had claimed to be an ambassador from Korea.

Concerning his allegations as a relative to the President, he said when American friends asked whether he was related, since he had same surname as that of the President, he said, "Yes, I belong to same clan, and somehow Americans took it as I claiming to be a relative to the President."

Mr. Nields. Did you give the director of the investigations bureau any instructions as to what to do next?

General Kim. The bureau director suggested to me since there was no legal basis to prosecute him, it was better to have him sternly warned and briefed.

Mr. Nields. Was this conversation with the director of the investigations bureau the morning after the interrogation of Tongsun Park?

General Kim. Yes.

Mr. Nields. Did you tell the director of the investigations bureau to do as he had suggested?

General Kim. Yes, I did. And I also instructed him that he write a report to the station chief of KCIA in Washington, D.C., and also make a report to the Ambassador in Washington, D.C., and I told him to tell them to watch over Mr. Tongsun Park in the future time.

Mr. Nields. What was the name of the then KCIA station chief in Washington?

General Kim. Mr. Kim Yoon Ho.

Mr. Nields. Shortly thereafter did you receive a telephone call from the Prime Minister as to Tongsun Park?

General Kim. Yes.

Mr. Nields. Approximately how long thereafter?

General Kim. I think it was some three days after.

Mr. Nields. What did the Prime Minister say on the telephone?

General Kim. He said over the phone that he had known Mr. Tongsun Park while he was the ambassador in Washington, D.C., and he said Tongsun Park was after all not such a bad character and once you get to know him you will find his usefulness.

Mr. Nields. Did he suggest that you meet with Tongsun Park?

General Kim. Yes.

Mr. Nields. Did you later meet with Tongsun Park?

General Kim. Yes. I called the Prime Minister to send him over here.

Mr. Nields. When did you meet with Tongsun Park?

General Kim. I saw him next day.

Mr. Nields. Where?

General Kim. In my office.

Mr. Nields. Did you have a conversation with him?

General Kim. Yes, of course.

Mr. Nields. Would you describe the conversation please.

General Kim. First he repeated what he told to the investigators. Second, he said, "As the Prime Minister told you, I know many prominent figures in Washington, D.C., and therefore Embassy staff are jealous of me."

He said, "With the assistance from you, I could work for the benefit or interest of Korea."

So I said, "What kind of assistance do you need?"

He answered he did not need any assistance at the moment but he would say at a later time.

So I said to him once, "When you return to Washington, D.C., you maintain contact with the station chief in Washington, D.C." This is the essence of my conversation with him.

Mr. Nields. A few days later did the Prime Minister, Chung Il Kwon, invite you to a dinner at a private Kaesang house?

General Kim. Yes.

Mr. Nields. Who was present at the dinner?

General Kim. I went there merely because I was invited and I found there Mr. Tongsun Park.

Mr. Nields. Anyone else besides Tongsun Park, Chung Il Kwon, and yourself?

General Kim. No.

Mr. Nields. What was said during the course of the dinner?

General Kim. Mainly Mr. Chung Il Kwon praised Mr. Tongsun Park.

Mr. Nields. Anything else?

General Kim. In the beginning it was mostly concentrated on how great Mr. Park was.

Mr. Nields. At the time, did you tell Tongsun Park once again if he needed help, he should see you?

General Kim. Yes, I did say that.

Mr. Nields. Did Tongsun Park ever seek your help after that?

General Kim. Yes.

Mr. Nields. How did that come about?

General Kim. I believe it was sometime the first part of 1967 I received a letter from KCIA station chief.

Mr. Nields. Who was then the KCIA station chief?

General Kim. Minister Kim Yoon Ho.

Mr. Nields. What did the letter say?

General Kim. He said there is a club by the name of the George Town Club who was operated by Mrs. Chenault, who was a lobbyist for Taiwan. The suggestion was that Mr. Tongsun take over the operation of that particular club and use it for the purpose of lobbying for Korea. However, Mr. Tongsun Park lacked funds to operate, and in the meantime Korea had its foreign currency holdings deposited in foreign banks. The suggestion of Mr. Tongsun Park was this: If the Korean Government would transfer $3 million from one bank to a bank Mr. Tongsun Park designates, then Mr. Tongsun Park, by putting out his own collateral, will secure loan from that particular bank and use those funds for operating the club.

That is the gist of the letter.

Mr. Nields. What did you do after you received the letter?

General Kim. I called in my chief secretary, Mr. Mun Han Lim, and give him the letter.

I asked him to look into this matter unless it is out of line. My secretary, Mr. Mun, had looked into the affair and gave me this report. He said it could be done without too much difficulty. He said there was some deposit made in the States which will expire on its time deposit agreement, which would expire in 1 to 1½ months. He said the Korean exchange bank would be able to transfer that money from one bank to the other, not that moment but within a month or month and a half, to the bank designated by Tongsun Park.

So we had contacted Mr. Kim Yoon Ho and asked whether we could do it, not at the time but month or a month and a half later.

Mr. Nields. Once again, was Kim Yoon Ho the then KCIA station chief in Washington?

General Kim. Yes.

Mr. Nields. Did you receive a reply from him?

General Kim. Yes. A letter came for me stating affirmatively it could be carried out. Then I instructed Secretary Mun to carry it out.

Mr. Nields. Did the letter from Kim Yoon Ho say anything about what Tongsun Park would do with the George Town Club?

General Kim. The letter said that Mr. Tongsun Park promised he would do his best to lobby for the interest of Korea.

Mr. Nields. Did you ever receive a report back from your chief secretary after you told him to take care of the matter?

General Kim. Yes. I received a report that all actions had been taken.

Mr. Nields. Did you later talk with Tongsun Park about this loan?

General Kim. After the action was taken, Mr. Tongsun Park came to Korea and met with me and thanked me for my assistance and said he would do his best.

Mr. Nields. Did he say what he would do his best for?

General Kim. He said he would seek for membership to the club U.S. Congressmen, high officials of the executive branch, business people in the States, and diplomats of foreign countries, and through this membership setup he would make effort to further interest of Korea.

Mr. Nields. Did you see Tongsun Park again a few months later?

General Kim. Yes.

Mr. Nields. Where?

General Kim. He came back to Korea some 3 months later, and I met him at my office.

Mr. Nields. What was discussed?

General Kim. He said, once he had started operation of the George Town Club, he was suffering from shortage of funds.

He said that he had in his assets in Korea $100,000 in U.S. currency. He said since he could not exchange his property into U.S. currency, he asked me whether I could help him having the money sent into U.S. currency in the black market and have the money forwarded to the States.

So I called in Secretary Mun and I asked him whether this request could be carried out. He said it could not be done in short period but it could be done in 2 weeks to 1 month. Mr. Mun said after exchange is done then he could send it through station chief in Washington.

Mr. Nields. Did you tell your secretary to carry it out?

General Kim. Yes. I instructed him to that effect.

Mr. Nields. Did he later tell you that it had been carried out?

General Kim. Yes.

Mr. Nields. How was the money sent to Tongsun Park?

General Kim. According to the report of Mr. Mun, the money was sent by diplomatic pouch.

In the meantime, Mr. Kim Yoon Ho was replaced by Mr. Hang Su Hwan.

Mr. Nields. As KCIA Chief?

General Kim. That is correct.

Mr. Nields. Was the money sent to Yang Du Hwon?

General Kim. Yes; money was sent to Mr. Yang Du Hwon and he, in turn, handed the money to Tongsun Park and I received the receipt.

Mr. Nields. Was Yang Du Hwon using his own name while KCIA Chief in Washington?

General Kim. He used the name Lee Sang Ho.

Mr. Nields. Did you later receive a letter from Tongsun Park?

General Kim. Yes.

Mr. Nields. What did it say?

General Kim. It said money came just in time; and the money, he said, helped the operation of the George Town Club.

Mr. Nields. General Kim, once again, how much U.S. currency was sent through the diplomatic pouch?

General Kim. It was $100,000....

Mr. Nields. Did there come a time, General Kim, when you saw Tongsun Park in the presence of a Member of Congress?

General Kim. Yes.

Mr. Nields. When?

General Kim. I believe it was in the early part of 1968.

Mr. Nields. Where?

General Kim. The Prime Minister, Chung Il Kwon, had invited me to a dinner, saying he was having dinner with a U.S. Congressman.

Mr. Nields. Did you go to the dinner?

General Kim. Yes, I did.

Mr. Nields. Where was it.

General Kim. It was a restaurant by the name of Daeha.

Mr. Nields. Who was the Member of Congress?

Mr. An. Am I supposed to tell the name or not.

Mr. Nields. Yes.

General Kim. It was Mr. Richard Hanna.

Mr. Nields. Did you have a conversation with him and Tongsun Park during the course of that evening?

General Kim. Yes, I went there knowing that we were to have dinner with a U.S. Congressman and I found Mr. Tongsun Park in the place, himself.

Mr. Nields. Did you have a conversation with either Tongsun Park or Mr. Hanna?

General Kim. Yes, we exchanged greetings and introduction. Prime Minister Chung introduced Mr. Hanna to me as a wonderful person.

Mr. Nields. Did you tell Mr. Hanna that he could come see you at anytime?

General Kim. Yes. Mr. Hanna first asked us that he wanted to see my office and I answered he could come to my office at any time.

Mr. Nields. Did he subsequently come to your office?

General Kim. Yes, he came to my office the next day, together with Mr. Tongsun Park.

Mr. Nields. Will you describe the conversation which took place?

General Kim. Mostly it was Mr. Hanna's praise of Mr. Tongsun Park; and he said that if we extended our assistance to Mr. Tongsun Park that would help the cause of Korea. This is what we talked about in that meeting.

Mr. Nields. Did you see Tongsun Park again after that?

General Kim. Several months later, Mr. Hanna and Mr. Tongsun Park came to Korea.

Mr. Nields. Can you be a little bit more explicit about the date?

General Kim. Sometime in August 1968.

Mr. Nields. Did they come to your office and talk with you?

General Kim. Yes.

Mr. Nields. Where?

General Kim. My office.

Mr. Nields. Was there anyone else besides you, Congressman Hanna and Tongsun Park?

General Kim. Yes, my interpreter was also present.

Mr. Nields. Did someone raise the subject of rice?

General Kim. Yes, both mentioned rice and Mr. Tongsun Park first spoke of rice.

Mr. Nields. What did he say about rice?

General Kim. He said that Korea was to purchase rice from United States; and he said Mr. Hanna wanted Korea to buy rice from his district.

Then Mr. Hanna told me that his State was California and California produces a lot of rice and should Korea buy rice anyway, he said he wanted Korea to buy rice from his State.

I told him since I was not familiar with rice transaction, I said I would look into the matter.

Mr. Hanna suggested that if we appointed Mr. Tongsun Park as a middleman of the transaction, the office could move more smoothly.

I said, since I was not familiar with the matter, I said I would look into the matter. He said once Mr. Tongsun Park is appointed as a middleman, he could earn some money in terms of commission.

Then he said once that is done, he, together with Mr. Tongsun Park, would distribute that money among U.S. Congressmen and have them help Korea's cause.

I then promised I would look into the matter and I would let them know.

Mr. Nields. Did you subsequently look into the matter?

General Kim. Then I called in Mr. Kim Won Hee, the Director of the Office of Supply.

Mr. Nields. Was the Director of the Office of Supply under your official control?

General Kim. No.

Mr. Nields. Is it fair to say, however, General Kim, that as Director of the Korean Central Intelligence Agency, you wielded a tremendous amount of unofficial power?

General Kim. That is correct.

Mr. Nields. Will you describe your conversation with Kim Won Hee, the director of the Office of Supply?

General Kim. I asked him there was a request by a U.S. Congressman. "Can you help him in this regard?"

He said if that was to be done it could be done without much difficulty.

Mr. Nields. Just one item of clarification, General Kim: Is the Office of Supply the agency in Korea which would purchase the rice?

General Kim. Yes, the Office of Supply is responsible for purchase of all materials or goods from overseas, using the national budget.

Mr. Nields. What, if anything, did you do after your meeting with Kim Won Hee?

General Kim. Mr. Kim called me that he wanted to see the two gentlemen at his office.

So, I told Mr. Tongsun Park things seemed to be working out; and I told him to visit Mr. Kim Won Hee's office. Mr. Tongsun Park, after his visit to Mr. Kim Won Hee's office, came to me and said that things would be well carried out.

Mr. Nields. Did you later learn that things had been carried out? That Tongsun Park had been named the middleman; and that a purchase of rice was to occur?

General Kim. Yes, both Mr. Tongsun Park and the director of the Office of Supply reported to me to that effect and I also received a letter from Mr. Hanna stating to that effect....

Mr. Nields. Do you know whether Tongsun Park continued to report to officials in the Government of Korea as to his activities?

General Kim. Yes, of course.

Mr. Nields. Did he?

General Kim. Yes.

Mr. Nields. General Kim, did you have occasion to meet with Tongsun Park after you became a member of the National Assembly in May of 1971?

General Kim. Yes, many times.

Mr. Nields. Was there an occasion on which you met him and talked about a rice commission?

General Kim. Yes. In the tone of bragging, he said that he was continuing his activities, having contact with the U.S. Congressmen and that he had been reporting his activities to the officials of the Government....

Mr. [James H. (Jimmy)] Quillen [R Tenn.]. General Kim, in your official capacity as KCIA Director, do you, to your personal knowledge, know, as a private citizen, that these activities were carried on for the exact purpose of influencing favoritism to the Government of South Korea on the part of the U.S. officials, or Members of Congress, or anyone here that had the power to offer that favoritism?

General Kim. Yes. During this period the U.S. Government was preoccupied by the war in Vietnam. And Korea then sent two divisions and one combat engineer corps to Vietnam. During the years 1967 to 1968 North Korea had engaged in very active guerrilla warfare in South Korea in order to keep South Korea from sending its troops to Vietnam.

Frankly speaking, Korean armed forces are equipped with the weapons supplied by the United States. However, the weapons are left over from the time of the Korean War. In the meantime, North Korea had accomplished by 1965, through the aid of Soviet Russia and Communist China, the modernization of their armed forces and was capable of producing their own weapons. Of course, I don't believe the United States was negligent of this equipment in South Korea. However, because of this preoccupation on the Vietnamese War, we felt that certain, that there was a certain lack of direct concern on the part of the United States vis-a-vis Korea.

Our purpose and our desire at that time was to have U.S. Congress not to reduce its military and other aid to Korea. Even until 1969 Korea could not manufacture even a single bullet. And I thought it was a good idea. I thought it was a very conducive idea that this Congressman from the United States and others would help Korea in furthering Korea's interest in terms of security. However, the direction took another course, since the revision of October revitalization of the Constitution. Otherwise, there is no support from the United States; no one in Korea would be able to sustain its power. And, therefore, the effort of the Korean Government shifted from our original desire, to maintaining U.S. support for the dictatorial policies that were carried out in Korea. While I was in the office I had offered my help in terms of rice concession only once. That is all I want to say about that....

Statement of Joseph Alioto

Ms. [Barbara Ann] Rowan [committee counsel]. Mr. Alioto, how were you employed in 1968?

Mr. Alioto. In 1968 I was the Mayor of San Francisco, beginning in January 1968, and prior to that time—I was also at that point the president of the Rice Growers Association—prior to that time I had been the chief executive officer of the Rice Growers Association, but that stopped in January 1968.

Ms. Rowan. How long did you remain in office as Mayor of San Francisco?

Mr. Alioto. Eight years.

Ms. Rowan. And have you been able to find employment since?

Mr. Alioto. I have been able to find gainful employment after leaving the mayor's office, as a matter of fact. I am an attorney, of course, and I have been the chief executive officer of the Rice Growers Association after having been the attorney for the Rice Growers Association. I am presently engaged as an attorney and involved in the shipping business.

Ms. Rowan. In fact, you represent the next witness here today, Mr. Freeland?

Mr. Alioto. I represent the Rice Growers Association. I have always represented them. My office even represented them at the time I was in the mayor's office. There was no conflict between agriculture and urban problems.

Ms. Rowan. In connection with your representation of the rice growers and your position as president of the rice growers in 1968, did you have occasion to have an appointment with former Congressman Hanna?

Mr. Alioto. Yes, I did.

Ms. Rowan. Will you tell us how that appointment was arranged?

Mr. Alioto. Shortly after the Democratic Convention, Congressman Hanna—I met him at or about that time—in 1968 Congressman Hanna and I were engaged in the Humphrey campaign. I nominated Mr. Humphrey at that convention. And he called me or called my office, rather, made an appointment to see me sometime in September 1968, as best I can fix it. It would either be September or October 1968.

My appointments secretary told me that Congressman Hanna had made this appointment. So he came in for his appointment.

Ms. Rowan. And where was the appointment to take place?

Mr. Alioto. I met him in the mayor's office.

Ms. Rowan. Can you tell us whether Mr. Hanna was alone or whether he was accompanied by anyone?

Mr. Alioto. I am not sure whether he came in alone, but during the course of the meeting with him—the meeting was between Mr. Hanna and me, Mr. Tongsun Park and, I believe, one of my assistants.

Ms. Rowan. Will you tell us, to the best of your recollection, what was said by each person at that meeting?

Mr. Alioto. I first assumed that he was coming in for political purposes. I had no idea what the meeting was about. He came in to see me and said that he was on one of the banking committees, that the banking committee was interested in foreign trade between California and Korea, that the Koreans were about to buy a huge quantity of rice, that at that point the

Japanese had become competitive with us. Up until that time we had sold the Japanese huge quantities of our rice.

I might mention, Mr. [Bruce F.] Caputo [R N.Y.], that the Koreans grow the same kind of rice as the Californians, so there has always been a historical preference for California rice in those two countries. As you get farther south the preference is for long-grain, nonglutinous rice. Those two countries, Korea and Japan, have always purchased California rice as a matter of preference and up until very lately didn't purchase anything but California rice, and they would find similar rice throughout the world but they couldn't get it.

Ms. Rowan. Let me interrupt for a moment. Is Mr. Hanna from a rice-growing district?

Mr. Alioto. He is from Orange County. They don't grow any rice. They used to grow oranges. They are now growing instant suburbs, as you know. But they don't grow rice and never have grown rice in Orange County. But he was on the foreign—or banking committee, rather, on some business that had to do with foreign trade. He simply said the Koreans were about to buy rice, the Japanese were in contention against California, and he was trying to arrange it for California, and he had a man named Tongsun Park, who I had never met before, who I didn't expect to see at the conference. And he said to me Mr. Tongsun Park is the man who can open the doors for us in Korea in connection with the competitive struggle with the Japanese.

I told him that before becoming mayor I had personally negotiated through one Woodward-Dickerson [international heavy commodity sales company] the 250,000 tons of rice for Korea, the sale made in 1967.

I had also been involved in the sale of Korean rice earlier in 1967. There were some 60,000 tons of rice left over from the preceding crop and we had sold that to Korea as well. In connection with the sale of 250,000 tons, I told him we were represented by Woodward-Dickerson. We were very happy with them. It was the policy of the Rice Growers Association not to change representatives when we were satisfied with those representatives.

I also told him that Woodward-Dickerson, in addition to being the representatives of the rice growers—of the California rice industry, rather—incidentally, 50 per cent of the crop, California rice growers handle, the rest was handled by other sections of the California industry on these foreign sales.

I told him Woodward-Dickerson had arranged for the financing, rather elaborate, intricate financing that made that sale possible, and therefore we felt we would stick with them.

Ms. Rowan. What was the response of Mr. Hanna or Mr. Park, if any?

Mr. Alioto. Both of them said they thought Mr. Park would do a better job for us and Mr. Park would open doors better for us in Korea, and perhaps Woodward-Dickerson did not have the position now in Korea that they had at the time I negotiated the first sale.

Ms. Rowan. Were you then aware of any change in position with regard to Woodward-Dickerson and Korea?

Mr. Alioto. No. We—I assumed at the time—remember I had not been the chief executive officer for approximately 8 months. Mr. [Robert] Freeland [chief executive officer, Rice Growers Association of California], who is going to testify next, became the chief executive officer. At the time of the conference I said I was quite satisfied with Woodward-Dickerson's status in Korea, they had done well by us and it was our policy to stick by loyal representatives. So I rejected the request.

Ms. Rowan. Had you ever had any complaints from the Government of Korea about the performance of Woodward-Dickerson?

Mr. Alioto. Not at that time. But as they kept pressing me and saying Mr. Park was the man who can open the doors and Woodward-Dickerson was persona non grata now in Korea, I said, "If that is true, get me a cable to that effect with the buying mission." We had dealt with the buying mission on a regular basis. So I said, "Get me a letter." I assumed that would be the end of it because rice growers get requests twice a week from people who want to be brokers or representatives, and we get lots of people who make those requests. We finally ended by saying our policy is to stick by our old alliances. Secondly, I said, "If that is the situation, get me a letter," believing that was going to be the end of it.

Ms. Rowan. What happened?

Mr. Alioto. To my surprise I got a cable a couple of days later saying in substance that Tongsun Park was well thought of in Korea, that Tongsun Park had a great deal of good will in Korea, that Tongsun Park would be instrumental in diverting the sale from Japan to California and in substance Woodward-Dickerson were persona non grata.

Ms. Rowan. What happened to that cable?

Mr. Alioto. I simply passed the cable on to Mr. Freeland, who was then the chief executive officer, with my recommendation that Woodward-Dickerson be retained, and Mr. Freeland agreed on that. As a matter of fact, he went to Korea with Woodward-Dickerson to negotiate the transaction.

Ms. Rowan. From whom did the cable come?

Mr. Alioto. I believe it was OSROK, the buying mission.

Ms. Rowan. OSROK being the Office of Supply in the Republic of Korea?

Mr. Alioto. That is correct....

Testimony of Cheryl Holmes

Mr. [David H.] Belkin [Deputy Chief Counsel]. Will you state your name for the record?

Ms. Holmes. Cheryl Holmes.

Mr. Belkin. ...What is your occupation?

Ms. Holmes. I am the intelligence analyst for the special staff of the House Committee on Standards of Official Conduct.

Mr. Belkin. You were hired for the purpose of this Korean influence investigation?

Ms. Holmes. Yes; I was.

Mr. Belkin. Have you ever worked for Congress?

Ms. Holmes. No.

Mr. Belkin. What is your education?

Ms. Holmes. I have a bachelor of arts degree from Luther College in Decorah, Iowa, with majors in sociology and political science.

Mr. Belkin. What is your work background?

Ms. Holmes. Prior to joining the special staff of the committee, I worked for the Department of Justice for over 7 years, 3½ for the Criminal Division, over 2 with the Watergate Special Prosecution Force, and nearly 2 with the Drug Enforcement Administration.

Mr. Belkin. What did you do for the Department of Justice?

Ms. Holmes. I was a research analyst and compiled information on possible criminal activities of various individuals.

Mr. Belkin. What about the Watergate prosecutor position?

Ms. Holmes. I reviewed testimony and documents to develop information concerning possible criminal activities surrounding the 1972 Presidential elections.

Mr. Belkin. What work did you do for the Drug Enforcement Administration?

Ms. Holmes. I developed intelligence about possible criminal activities relating to narcotics.

Mr. Belkin. Have you in the past reviewed financial information as to persons, companies, and/or individuals?

Ms. Holmes. Yes; I have.

Mr. Belkin. In what respect have you done this?

Ms. Holmes. For the Watergate special prosecutor I reviewed testimony and documents to analyze the cash flow from the Committee to Reelect the President to the persons involved in the break-in at the Democratic National Committee headquarters at Watergate and their counsel. At DEA I reviewed Dun & Bradstreet reports, tax records, and any other documents available, including investigative reports, to analyze the cash flow of suspected narcotics violators.

Mr. Belkin. In connection with your work for this committee, have you reviewed any financial information relating to Tongsun Park?

Ms. Holmes. Yes; I have.

Mr. Belkin. What have you reviewed?

Ms. Holmes. I reviewed Rice Grower's Association of California and Connell Rice and Sugar Co. records concerning payments of rice commissions to Tongsun Park and his companies. I also reviewed records of bank accounts maintained by Park for himself and his companies. These include: Equitable Trust; National Bank of Washington; American Security and Trust; Riggs National Bank; Bank of Virginia, formerly American Bank; Guaranty Bank and Trust; Industrial Bank of Japan; and Korea Exchange Bank of California.

I also reviewed records of Purolator Security, an armored car company used by Tongsun Park.

Mr. Belkin. What was the purpose of the review?

Ms. Holmes. Simply to determine how much money Tongsun Park was paid annually in rice commissions and how much money he withdrew from his various bank accounts and converted into cash.

Mr. Belkin. Have you reviewed all of Tongsun Park's bank records?

Ms. Holmes. No; because of the secrecy laws of foreign countries, the committee does not have access to Park's foreign bank accounts. The committee has information that Park has bank accounts in England, Bermuda, and Korea.

He may have other accounts of which we are unaware at this point. Also, because banks are not legally required to maintain records and deposit transactions over a certain length of time, and since some of the information we are interested in is quite old, some records have already legally been destroyed by the banks but we have reviewed everything that has been available to the committee to date.

Mr. Belkin. I believe you have with you exhibits which have been premarked as committee exhibits 27-36. I would like you with respect to each exhibit to identify the exhibit. Mr. Chairman, because of the voluminous nature of these exhibits, which are about to be identified, I have not made copies for each committee member. However, I have copies available here and there are certain summary exhibits which have been distributed to the committee members.

Ms. Holmes. Exhibits 27(a) and 27(b) are commission checks from Rice Growers' Association of California to Tongsun Park in 1969.

Exhibits 28(a) through (h) are letters from Rice Growers' Association indicating that checks were enclosed for deposit in one of Park's accounts which was maintained at Equitable Trust Co.; 28(i) and (j) are copies of rice commission advance checks from Rice Growers' Association to Tongsun Park in 1969 and 1970.

Mr. Flynt. I wonder if I could request the witness to speak out in a little stronger voice, if she can.

Ms. Holmes. Exhibit 29 is a schedule of activities in Tongsun Park's Equitable Trust Co. account from 1970 to 1976.

Committee exhibits 30 (a) through (l) are records of Connell Rice & Sugar Co., reflecting payments to Park and repayment of advances to the Rice Growers' Association of California.

Exhibit 31 is a check dated June 12, 1974, from Connell Rice & Sugar Co. to Tongsun Park for $30,000.

Exhibit 32(a) is a copy of a summary.

Mr. Flynt. Will you give the total on that summary, please, Ms. Holmes?

Ms. Holmes. $1,537,715.

Mr. Flynt. And 50 cents.

Ms. Holmes. And 50 cents.

Mr. Flynt. Are (b) through (u) the exact documents which make up the summary on 32(a)?

Ms. Holmes. Yes; they are.

They transfer funds from Connell Rice & Sugar Co. to Daihan Nongsan accounts at the American Security & Trust Bank and the Bank of Bermuda.

Exhibit 33(a) is a summary for $883,585 and (b) through (g) are copies indicating transfers from Connell to the Bowsprit account at the Bank of Bermuda.

Mr. Belkin. Ms. Holmes, to shorten this have these documents been subpoenaed or required by the committee in connection with this investigation?

Ms. Holmes. Yes.

Mr. Belkin. Do these documents represent records of either Tongsun Park or his company reflecting payment of commissions into his various bank accounts?

Ms. Holmes. Yes; they do.

Mr. Belkin. Have you analyzed these documents and prepared a chart or charts which summarize these documents?

Ms. Holmes. Yes; I have.

Mr. Belkin. Mr. Chairman, I ask that exhibits 27 through 36 be made part of the record and that we move on to the summaries to shorten this.

Mr. Flynt. Exhibits 27 through 36, with each of the appendices, thereto.

Mr. Belkin. Correct.

Mr. Flynt. Without objection.

Mr. Belkin. May we have exhibit 37 put up on the easel?

You have in front of you, I believe, a document marked as exhibit 37. I have taken the liberty of having exhibit 37 blown up so that everyone in the room can see it. Could you explain to us, Ms. Holmes, what exhibit 37 represents?

Ms. Holmes. Exhibit 37 is entitled, "Rice Commission Payments Made by Connell Rice & Sugar Co. and Rice Growers' Association of California to Tongsun Park and his Companies (1969-76)." Exhibit 37 indicates that Rice Growers' Association of California paid rice commissions to Tongsun Park's companies, Korea Development Fund and to Tongsun Park personally. They paid $105,816 to the Korea Development Fund account at Equitable Trust Co. which includes $25,600 in expense moneys, and $105,-450 to Tongsun Park's personal account at Equitable Trust Co. The exhibit also reflects that Connell Rice & Sugar Co. provided payments to Tongsun Park through numerous companies. They paid $202,500 to the Korea Development Fund account at Equitable Trust Co.; $202,310 to Park's personal account at Equitable Trust; $30,000 to Tongsun Park's personal account at Riggs National Bank; $860,965 to the Daihan Nongsan account at American Security & Trust; $676,850 to the Daihan Nongsan account at the Bank of Bermuda; $371,250 to the Five Star Navigation Co. account at the Bank of Bermuda; $5,640,125 to the Three Star Navigation Co. account at the Bank of Bermuda; $883,585 to the Bowsprit account at the Bank of Bermuda; and $110,000 to Pacific Development Co. account at Riggs National Bank. The Rice Growers' Association of California, also paid

$16,062 to Tongsun Park, but we have not established which bank accounts that went into.

This totals to $9,204,815 paid to Tongsun Park between 1969 and 1976 by Rice Growers' Association of California and Connell Rice & Sugar Co.

Mr. Belkin. Have you prepared another chart which reflects payments by year to Tongsun Park?

Ms. Holmes. Yes, I have.

Mr. Belkin. May we please have that set up.

Is exhibit 38 a copy of that chart?

Ms. Holmes. Yes, it is.

Mr. Belkin. Mr. Chairman, I request that exhibits 37 and 38 be made a part of the record.

Mr. Flynt. Without objection, so ordered.

Mr. Belkin. Now, I notice from the chart that we have marked as exhibit 38, which is the payments to Tongsun Park or his companies by year, that, according to the committee's record, he received no commissions in 1971. Is that the same year in which, according to the testimony of Gen. Kim Chung Uk this morning, that Park Chung Kyu took rice commissions which Tongsun Park told the general belonged to Tongsun Park?

Ms. Holmes. Yes, it is.

Mr. Belkin. Have you analyzed documents which reflect whether or not Tongsun Park converted money—funds that he had in his banks—into cash currency?

Ms. Holmes. Yes, I have.

Mr. Belkin. Can you tell us what you have reviewed, what bank accounts?

Ms. Holmes. I reviewed Equitable Trust, National Bank of Washington, American Security & Trust, Riggs National Bank, Bank of Virginia, formerly American Bank, Guaranty Bank & Trust, Industrial Bank of Japan, Korea Exchange Bank of California and, again, Purolator Security records.

Mr. Belkin. Mr. Chairman, we have premarked as exhibits 39 through 46, copies of checks and other records which reflect conversion of funds into cash. We would like to have these marked as part of the record of these hearings.

Mr. Flynt. Exhibits 39 through 46?

Mr. Belkin. And 61. Excuse me.

Mr. Flynt. I didn't understand you.

Mr. Belkin. Exhibits 39 through 46 and exhibit 61.

Mr. Flynt. Without objection, exhibits 39 through 46 and exhibit 61 will be made a part of the record.

Mr. Belkin. Have you summarized these exhibits?

Ms. Holmes. Yes, I have.

Mr. Belkin. Can you tell us what they show?

Ms. Holmes. In 1969 Park converted $9,750 into cash from his bank accounts; in 1970, he converted $57,700 into cash; in 1971 he converted $34,-900 into cash; in 1972 he converted $236,270 into cash; in 1973 he converted

$153,850; in 1974 he converted $426,905; in 1975 he converted $596,917; in 1976 he converted $121,360.

Mr. Belkin. Now, how much money from 1969 to 1976 has Tongsun Park converted from funds that he had in banks into American currency?

Ms. Holmes. $1,637,652.

Mr. Belkin. According to the figures you have read into the record, Tongsun Park converted funds he had in his banks in certain years into currency in excess of what he had actually received in rice commissions. Do you have any reason—can you explain that?

Ms. Holmes. We know that Tongsun Park had funds left over at the end of a particular year for his use in the next year. The committee also has information of two significant transactions that occurred during periods when he was not earning rice commissions—in 1971, and in early 1972. In July 1971, shortly after returning from Korea, he went to the Equitable Trust Bank with an employee of his and deposited $350,000 in cash.

In March 1972—which may relate to the $200,000 in rice commissions which, according to General Kim's testimony, was originally taken by Park Chung Kyu from Tongsun Park, and then returned by Kyu to Tongsun Park—that transaction involved Park sending an employee on a short-notice trip to Switzerland, with written authority to transfer $190,000 from a Swiss bank into Park's personal account at Equitable and this happened during periods when Park was not earning rice commissions.

Mr. Belkin. We also have marked exhibits 47, 48, 49, and 50, and exhibit 62. Will you identify those exhibits for us, Ms. Holmes?

Ms. Holmes. They are checks to S. Lee drawn on Park's personal account. One check is for $4,000, dated January 10, 1972; one is for $5,000, dated January 25, 1972; one dated April 28, 1972, is for $2,000; one dated July 20, 1973, is for $2,000; and then a check dated April 4, 1969, payable to the Riggs National Bank for $5,200 was endorsed on the back for cashier's check for S.H. Lee.

Mr. Belkin. Exhibits 47 through 50, and 62, are there endorsements on the reverse of the check which are a part of the exhibit?

Ms. Holmes. Yes.

Mr. Belkin. And what is the name of the endorsement?

Ms. Holmes. S. Lee.

Mr. Belkin. Is it Sang Ho Lee?

Ms. Holmes. Sang Ho Lee.

Mr. Belkin. Is that Sang Ho Lee the same person whose name is General Yang or Yang Du Hwon, as far as you know?

Ms. Holmes. Yes.

Mr. Belkin. Do you have any idea why Park was paying Sang Ho Lee?

Ms. Holmes. Neither Park nor Lee has been available to the committee for interviews so we have no idea.

Mr. Belkin. I have no further questions, Mr. Chairman.

Mr. Flynt. Do you want those last exhibits entered in the record?

Mr. Belkin. Excuse me, I would like to have exhibits 47 through 50 and exhibit 62 in the record.

Mr. Flynt. Without objection, exhibits 47 through 50 and exhibit 62 will be entered in the record....

Mr. [Richardson] Preyer [D N.C.]. ...That was a very impressive presentation. It takes a brave man to ask any questions about that presentation, but I want to see if I understand a little bit about it.

You have been able to account for all of the rice payments going to Mr. Park into these various accounts except for $16,000, is that right?

Ms. Holmes. Yes; and that was in 1969 and the records have probably been destroyed.

Mr. Preyer. Then from those different bank accounts, have you literally traced the $9,204,000 to Tongsun Park or is that a schematic diagram that it would have been possible for him to draw all that from those accounts?

Ms. Holmes. Tongsun Park was either a signatory on all those accounts or as on the one account we don't have a signature card for yet, he frequently wrote checks on the account. We know that he had access to all that money and those were his companies.

Mr. Preyer. You say there were several substantial deposits. Are those the only evidence you have of accounts that might have existed in other banks, that haven't been available to you?

Ms. Holmes. I don't know of any others at this time....

Mr. [Walter] Flowers [D Ala.]. ...Do you have any canceled checks which would represent or tend to represent checks made to Members of the U.S. Congress or other Government officials drawn on any one of Tongsun Park's companies?

Ms. Holmes. I did not review the checks for that purpose but I think there are such checks.

Mr. Flowers. There are checks made out to either Members of Congress, former or sitting and/or Government officials?

Ms. Holmes. Yes.

Mr. Flowers. I have no further questions, Mr. Chairman....

Mrs. [Millicent] Fenwick [R N.J.]. You testified there are checks drawn on Mr. Tongsun Park's account by Mr. Park made payable to Members of Congress. Have you given those checks to the legal staff?

Ms. Holmes. Yes.

Mrs. Fenwick. What was the total, if you totaled it up, amount of those checks?

Ms. Holmes. I have not totaled them up.

Mrs. Fenwick. Have you a rough idea as to what they might add up to?

Ms. Holmes. I have no idea.

Mrs. Fenwick. How many are there would you say? How many checks?

Ms. Holmes. I have seen—not to different Congressmen, but sometimes repeating Congressmen, about 40 to 50.

Mrs. Fenwick. And—

Ms. Holmes. Some to former Congressmen.

Testimony of Dennis Robert Hazelton

Ms. [Martha] Talley [committee counsel]. What is your present occupation, Mr. Hazelton?

Mr. Hazelton. I am an operations officer with the U.S. Customs Service.

Ms. Talley. And you are stationed here in Washington?

Ms. Hazelton. Yes, I am.

Ms. Talley. How long have you been with the Customs Service?

Mr. Hazelton. I have been with the U.S. Customs Service since 1969.

Ms. Talley. Were you with the Customs Service in December of 1973?

Mr. Hazelton. I was.

Ms. Talley. What was your job at that time?

Mr. Hazelton. At that time I was a supervisory customs inspector in Anchorage, Alaska.

Ms. Talley. Have you ever met Tongsun Park, Mr. Hazelton?

Mr. Hazelton. Yes, I have.

Ms. Talley. And, to your knowledge, was your first contact with him on December 8, 1973?

Mr. Hazelton. Yes.

Ms. Talley. At that time were you supervising customs inspections of passengers deplaning Northwestern flight 6?

Mr. Hazelton. Yes, I was.

Ms. Talley. Can you explain to the committee exactly what you were doing at that time?

Mr. Hazelton. My duties during that flight routinely consisted of watching the passengers as they emerged into the package claim area from the immigration area, and, in general, to observe whether or not they appeared suspicious, and as I observed them going to particular belts to be processed by certain inspectors, I would advise inspectors of any suspicions I had about those passengers, and as a supervisor perhaps direct that they conduct complete examinations.

Ms. Talley. Did Mr. Park come to your attention?

Mr. Hazelton. Very definitely.

Ms. Talley. Why did he attract your attention?

Mr. Hazelton. He had a number of parcels with him, including a plastic camera bag that is normally given out with large purchases of camera equipment or optical gear. These are usually plastic, bright yellow or bright orange, and very attractive. They attract the senses. When we see one of those bags we know that that person has made some recent expensive purchases, and we wonder whether or not those purchases are declared to Customs.

Ms. Talley. What did you do when he attracted your attention in this way?

Mr. Hazelton. If I operated according to my normal procedure, I would have tried to view his declaration to determine whether or not he had already declared the items. In this case, I am certain I found that he hadn't, so when I saw that he was going to a certain inspection belt, I advised the inspector to conduct a thorough examination.

Ms. Talley. Who was that inspector?

Mr. Hazelton. That was inspector Robert Lynes.

Ms. Talley. And what did he do in response to your instructions?

Mr. Hazelton. The next time I saw Mr. Lynes with Mr. Park, Mr. Park's large suitcase was open and Mr. Lynes was advising Mr. Park that he must declare all gifts that he was bringing for persons in the United States.

Ms. Talley. Now, would you explain why that was necessary?

Mr. Hazelton. Yes. Basically, all articles coming into the United States from foreign countries are subject to duty, unless exempted by some provision of law. In Mr. Park's case it was determined he was a nonresident and that he was, therefore, limited to a $100 gift exemption. Many of the articles he had were brand new, and although typical to travelers not typical to a traveler going back and forth as often as Mr. Park did.

In other words, he had a lot of new articles that had been purchased on this trip, many of them identical to each other. Not really reasonable and appropriate for his personal use while travelling, you know, two cameras, two razors, two hair dryers, things like that.

Ms. Talley. Did he acknowledge that some items in his luggage, in fact, were gifts?

Mr. Hazelton. He acknowledged that some things, scarves, to be specific, were gifts; however, he denied any of the expensive optical equipment were gifts.

Ms. Talley. He insisted they were for his personal use?

Mr. Hazelton. Yes, he insisted that they were.

Ms. Talley. What did you do to determine whether, in fact, these were gifts or not?

Mr. Hazelton. We asked him whether he had any guarantees or any proof that he could offer showing that they were for his personal use.

Ms. Talley. And how did he respond?

Mr. Hazelton. He said that he had a guarantee for, I believe, it was a Nikomat camera. Nikon 50-millimeter lens. He produced a guarantee; we examined it, and the reason we examined it is that usually when there is a purchase of this nature made the guarantee is filled out with the proper name of the person who will be using the item to expedite warranty repairs, et cetera.

Mr. Park did produce a guarantee, but it turned out it was either for a razor or hair dryer or perhaps a calculator. It was not for the camera.

Ms. Talley. Did you search his luggage for additional documentation?

Mr. Hazelton. Yes. While Mr. Lynes searched his bag for additional items or receipts, I opened and proceeded to examine Mr. Park's briefcase.

Ms. Talley. What did you find in his briefcase?

Mr. Hazelton. In the briefcase I found a number of folders, as I remember, they were legal size manila-type folders, and most of them contained import-export documents, agreements, shipping information, things like this.

Ms. Talley. Was there another folder?

Mr. Hazelton. Yes. There was another folder which I started to pull out as I had the other folders, and when I did I encountered quite strong resistance from Mr. Park.

Ms. Talley. What did he do?

Mr. Hazelton. He used both of his hands to grab, I believe, my left hand and arm, to keep me from pulling this folder out of the briefcase.

Ms. Talley. And—

Mr. Hazelton. And it was forcible. It lingered, it was forcible. I couldn't move my arm while his hands were holding me.

Ms. Talley. How did you respond?

Mr. Hazelton. I had enough time to think about how I should respond because it hadn't happened before. I had been there about 4 years by then, and I hadn't encountered this. I finally ended up deciding that I should advise Mr. Park that I was entitled, as a customs officer, to inspect that bag; that I was going to inspect it, and that if he continued any forcible resistance to the inspection, he could find himself under arrest.

Ms. Talley. And did you eventually look in the folder?

Mr. Hazelton. Yes. After I advised him of his obligation and of my rights, well, he removed his hands.

Ms. Talley. And—

Mr. Hazelton. And then I pulled out the folder, and I saw that it was entitled "Congressional List."

Ms. Talley. And what was in it?

Mr. Hazelton. The list was about 3½ pages long. It was double spaced, that time Mr. Park made a very quick grab to try to get it back. He tore two of the uppermost papers, but I held tighter, and I proceeded to examine the folder.

Ms. Talley. Can you describe what you saw?

Mr. Hazelton. Yes. It was a folder that contained a number of papers; it turned out that there was a list that was entitled "Congressional List," and there were two letters also. The list was broken down into five major headings; there was the name, party, political affiliation, party, State, committee, and contributions. And there were names and notations under each of these headings.

Ms. Talley. I am sorry; did you indicate how long the list was?

Mr. Hazelton. The list was about 3½ pages long. It was double spaced, typewritten.

Ms. Talley. And was it written in English?

Mr. Hazelton. It was typed in English; I estimate 70, 80 names were on the list.

Ms. Talley. Now, you mentioned there were two letters as well in the folder. Can you describe the letters?

Mr. Hazelton. Yes. There were two letters which I remember being from a U.S. Congressman to President Park, speaking of rice, the export of rice from the United States to Korea. These letters were almost like en-

814

dorsements to Tongsun Park. They spoke very well and very highly of Mr. Park to President Park.

Ms. Talley. What did Mr. Park do while you examined the list?

Mr. Hazelton. He continued to voice verbal resistance throughout the examination. I couldn't conduct a reasonable examination because of the repeated interruptions.

Ms. Talley. Did you decide to consult with your superior about this?

Mr. Hazelton. Very definitely.

Ms. Talley. Who was that?

Mr. Hazelton. That was Chief Inspector Gene Lowrance.

Ms. Talley. Where was he located?

Mr. Hazelton. He was at the entry control desk, which is about 30 or 40 feet from where I was.

Ms. Talley. What happened when you tried to consult with Mr. Lowrance?

Mr. Hazelton. As I approached Mr. Lowrance, Mr. Park kept trying to interrupt that approach, not forcibly, but he was trying to divert my attention from going to consult with Mr. Lowrance. He tried to step in front of me. He tried to draw my attention away from what I wanted to do.

Ms. Talley. But you did, in fact, consult with Mr. Lowrance?

Mr. Hazleton. With Mr. Park as a witness; yes.

Ms. Talley. There did come a time when you decided to consult with Mr. Lowrance and Mr. Park in private?

Mr. Hazelton. I thought I could consult in private right there. But Mr. Park, even though I directed him away and back to Mr. Lowrance and back to his baggage several times, he continued to interrupt, so Mr. Lowrance suggested that perhaps we were creating a scene in the baggage inspection area, and suggested we move into the privacy of his office.

Ms. Talley. Now, can you tell us what happened when you went into the supervisor's office?

Mr. Hazelton. We went into the supervisor's office. Mr. Park was still very strong in his objections to our examination of the list, still demanding that we not look at it. He continued to interrupt us as we looked over the list, but after a few moments we decided we had seen enough of the list that we appreciated its contents.

Ms. Talley. Did you question him about the list?

Mr. Hazelton. Yes; we did. We asked him several questions about it, what it represented. He said that it was contributions. Under the contributions column were either single or double digits, like 5, 10, 15, and the numbers ranged between 5 and 50. I asked Mr. Park what these single and double digits meant. He said that they represented hundreds of dollars.

Ms. Talley. Did Mr. Park say anything to indicate to you whether these contributions were contributions that he had made or intended to make.

Mr. Hazelton. I can't say that he said anything definite that they were contributions which had been made, but the whole tone, the whole substance of the entire examination, including the viewing of the list, his explanation of its contents, left no doubt in my mind that they were payments or contributions that had been made in the past. There was nothing futuristic about the list.

Ms. Talley. Mr. Park, have you been shown by the staff a document entitled the "T.S. Report"?

Mr. Hazelton. Please, I am Mr. Hazelton.

Ms. Talley. I am sorry, Mr. Hazelton.

Mr. Hazelton, you have been shown by the staff a document entitled the "T.S. Report" with a list attached; is that right?

Mr. Hazelton. Yes; I have.

Ms. Talley. And is that the same list as the one that Mr. Park had on the night of December 8, as far as you can recall?

Mr. Hazelton. It is very similar in substance, but the format is different. It is not the same list that I saw.

Ms. Talley. Did there come a time when you left Mr. Park alone in the office with his list?

Mr. Hazelton. Yes; Mr. Lowrance and I decided since we had Mr. Park under our control, mostly, and since we had the list under our control, we could leave him with the list while we went into the inspector's office to determine what we should do next.

Ms. Talley. So did you go just outside the office when you left Mr. Park?

Mr. Hazelton. We left the supervisor's office, went into the inspector's office, closed the door behind us, to talk about, "My God, what are we going to do now?"

Ms. Talley. And you were standing just outside the closed door?

Mr. Hazelton. That is correct.

Ms. Talley. What happened when you closed the door?

Mr. Hazelton. Probably within a few seconds or within 1 minute after we closed the door, we heard the sound of tearing paper through the door.

Ms. Talley. Did you immediately return to the office?

Mr. Hazelton. Yes.

Ms. Talley. And what did you see?

Mr. Hazelton. We saw Mr. Park hurriedly and very guiltily, I think, removing his left hand from his left trouser pocket.

Ms. Talley. What did you do?

Mr. Hazelton. We decided at that point that an examination of Mr. Park's person was in order, so we directed that Mr. Park should empty all of his pockets onto the table.

Ms. Talley. Did you "pat down" search him also?

Mr. Hazelton. After he stated his pockets were empty, we patted him down, crinkled his pockets to make sure they were empty. They were, and we looked there at the items that he had removed from his pockets.

Ms. Talley. What did Mr. Park remove from his left trouser pocket?

Mr. Hazelton. Among pocket change, probably some keys and other things that people normally keep in pockets, there were a number of pieces of torn paper.

Ms. Talley. Can you describe the paper? What kind of paper was it?

Mr. Hazelton. I would say it was like white bond paper.

Ms. Talley. Did you ask him whether these were the pieces of paper he had torn in your absence?

Mr. Hazelton. Yes; we did. He denied that those were the papers he had torn up.

Ms. Talley. How did he explain the tearing noise?

Mr. Hazelton. He affirmed that there had been a tearing noise and he picked up a green kleenex from the table and he tore it up and he said that's what the tearing noise was, but there was only one piece of green kleenex.

Ms. Talley. Was it torn before he picked it up and tore it in your presence?

Mr. Hazelton. No; it wasn't.

Ms. Talley. Did it make any noise?

Mr. Hazelton. Not that we noticed.

Ms. Talley. But he said that was what you heard tearing through the door?

Mr. Hazelton. That is what he claimed. We didn't believe him.

Ms. Talley. Did you have the opportunity to examine the pieces of torn bond paper that Mr. Park had removed from his pocket?

Mr. Hazelton. Yes; we did. We had several things to do then. For one, we wanted to see what was on the torn paper.

We had also decided at this time that we should consult higher authority and we wanted to retain Mr. Park, so as I remember, I left the supervisor's office with Mr. Park. Mr. Lowrance at about this time called the district director, the district director of customs, our immediate superior, and we wanted to find out more about what should happen next. During this time period after we left the office—Mr. Park, incidentally, had picked up the goods from his pockets and put them back in, leaving the torn pieces of paper on the desk—another inspector—or I forget exactly how it happened, but we started piecing the pieces of torn paper back together and we did so. We secured them together with tape.

Ms. Talley. Did you make an effort to have the writing on the paper translated?

Mr. Hazelton. Yes; we did. There is an inspector, Al Knapp, who had some proficiency in reading Asian languages.

Ms. Talley. There appeared to be Asian language written on the paper?

Mr. Hazelton. Right.

Ms. Talley. Was there some English as well?

Mr. Hazelton. There was some.

Ms. Talley. Do you remember the English?

Mr. Hazelton. There were two dates, I believe, January and June, abbreviated, and the word "Contribution".

Ms. Talley. Were you able to get a translation of the rest of the writing?

Mr. Hazelton. Mr. Knapp was able to translate some of the wording on the documents. Oh, I forgot to mention, there were also large dollar figures on this torn piece of paper. Mr. Knapp was able to translate some of the wording but, as I remember, not enough that we were satisfied as to whether or not it was meaningful to our inspection or meaningful with relation to the other list.

Ms. Talley. Did you keep and copy that piece of torn paper?

Mr. Hazelton. Yes; we did.

Ms. Talley. A member of the staff is going to show you committee exhibit 51. Is that a copy of the reconstituted torn paper that Mr. Park abandoned in your office?

Mr. Hazelton. It looks the same; yes. I would say it is.

Ms. Talley. And are you comparing it to a copy that you personally made of the original torn paper?

Mr. Hazelton. I am.

Ms. Talley. Thank you.

Now did there come a time when you made a tentative decision, pending consulting higher authority, that you had no reason to hold Mr. Park or his list, and you completed his processing?

Mr. Hazelton. Yes; there was. We looked at the list. We recognized what we thought it was, but we, in our own minds, determined that there was no recognizable violation of U.S. law which had taken place or which was taking place by the presence of that list, and we determined in our own minds that it was probably not subject to seizure or detention; so in our own mind we had decided we didn't think we should hold it, but we also felt from the nature of the list and the nature of some of the comments Mr. Park was making that we should refer to higher authority.

Ms. Talley. But pending that consultation did you return with Mr. Park to the examination building?

Mr. Hazelton. Yes. While we were waiting word from above about what to do next, I returned with Mr. Park out to the inspection area. We allowed him to proceed with repacking his baggage. He, at this point still had his list with him and the letters in the folder, and I went ahead and started getting the information I would need for my search report and send in a report.

Ms. Talley. Would you describe the conversation you had with him at that time?

Mr. Hazelton. Yes. Basically my goal at that point was to get Mr. Park's full name, passport number, date of birth, country of birth, routine identifying information, so that I would identify him should it become later necessary.

Mr. Park apparently also felt the responsibility at this time because he was asking me for my name and my badge number and my supervisor's number. He was also quite forcefully declaring that he was a true friend of the United States, he had studied law in the United States, he had been through customs many times and never been so badly treated; and while he was telling me all of this, it was laced with the idea that he was going to meet with the Vice President the next night and he was meeting with a Member of Congress to arrange for rice dealings between Korea and the United States. He was very forceful and I felt I should remember as much as I could.

Ms. Talley. In the course of this conversation did Mr. Park use the term "diplomatic"?

Mr. Hazelton. Yes. In fact, one of the better factors about this whole thing was that he was almost as mad at himself as he was at me. He made reference to the fact that he should have gone, or should have used diplomatic—the implication to me being that he had access either to diplomatic immunity or to a diplomatic pouch, in which case anything he had in the case of diplomatic immunity on his person or in his bag or in the case of diplomatic pouch, in the pouch, would not be subject to inspection by Customs.

Ms. Talley. But he was not traveling under a diplomatic passport?

Mr. Hazelton. He was not, but he apparently wished he were.

Ms. Talley. After you completed processing Mr. Park, did he reboard his aircraft?

Mr. Hazelton. To the best of my knowledge, he did.

Ms. Talley. To backtrack for a moment, you and your colleagues consulted with higher authorities. You said a call was made to the district director to confirm your decision that it was all right to let him go?

Mr. Hazelton. That is correct.

Ms. Talley. Was that decision confirmed?

Mr. Hazelton. Yes; it was.

Ms. Talley. Do you know whether or not anyone else was consulted about that?

Mr. Hazelton. I don't know personally; however, knowing my organization, I am quite sure that there were calls made above the district director.

Ms. Talley. You allowed Mr. Park to leave with his copy of the list and you have no copy; is that correct?

Mr. Hazelton. That is correct.

Ms. Talley. But after this incident did you write up a report giving all the details that you could remember?

Mr. Hazelton. Yes, very definitely.

Ms. Talley. And did you write down all of the names of Members of Congress on the list that you could remember?

Mr. Hazelton. Yes. Later that same day; in fact, I would say within an hour after he left, I sat down with my typewriter and typed out notes and then typed out a report listing all of the names that I could definitely remember.

Ms. Talley. Have you provided the committee with a copy of that report?

Mr. Hazelton. Yes, I have....

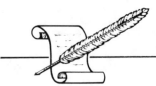
November

U.N. ARMS EMBARGO
AGAINST SOUTH AFRICA
November 4, 1977

The United Nations Security Council Nov. 4 voted unanimously to impose an embargo on shipments of arms and military materiel to South Africa. The 15-member council approved a resolution that for the first time ordered sanctions against a member state. The resolution condemned the South African government "for its acts of repression, its defiant continuance of the system of apartheid and its attacks against neighboring independent states...."

The embargo called upon the member states of the United Nations to "cease forthwith" providing South Africa with arms, ammunition, military vehicles and spare parts and to review existing contract and licensing agreements with a view toward terminating them. The resolution requested a report from U.N. Secretary General Kurt Waldheim on its implementation by May 1, 1978. The resolution also asked non-member states to observe the embargo. The mandatory embargo could be lifted only by a Security Council vote.

The United States, Great Britain and France in 1975 and 1976 had vetoed mandatory arms embargo resolutions on grounds that the internal situation in South Africa did not constitute a "threat to peace." Thus, acceptance by the Western powers of sanctions represented a major shift in policy.

Secretary General Waldheim termed the Security Council action "an historic occasion," and Andrew Young, the U.S. ambassador to the United Nations, called the resolution "a very clear message to the government of South Africa."

Roelof F. Botha, the South African foreign minister, on the other hand, said that the action was "an incitement to violence" and that it would not succeed in weakening his government's position. South Africa produced 75 per cent of its military equipment and required only aircraft, parts, vehicles and patrol boats as imported military materiel.

Background

African members of the United Nations had brought pressure on member countries to take action after an Oct. 19 massive crackdown on black protest by the South African government resulted in the arrest of black leaders, the closing of two black newspapers and the banning of 18 organizations critical of the government's race-separation policies.

The United States, Great Britain and France Oct. 31 had vetoed three resolutions in the Security Council that called for broad economic sanctions against South Africa. The resolutions, introduced by representatives of African states, would have imposed bans on foreign investments in South Africa and on arms sales to that country. The Western nations then sponsored a resolution calling for a six-month arms embargo. Objecting to the wording of the African-sponsored resolution which called South Africa's government "a threat to international peace and security," the Western powers gave up the six-month time limit on the embargo in return for milder wording which stated that South Africa's actions "were fraught with danger to international peace and security."

Following is the text of the U.N. Security Council resolution, approved Nov. 4, 1977, calling for an arms embargo against the government of South Africa:

The Security Council,

Recalling its Resolution 392 (1976) strongly condemning the South African government for its resort to massive violence against and killings of the African people, including schoolchildren and students and others opposing racial discrimination, and calling upon that government urgently to end violence against the African people and take urgent steps to eliminate apartheid and racial discrimination.

Recognizing that the military buildup and persistent acts of aggression by South Africa against the neighboring states seriously disturb the security of those states.

Further recognizing that the existing arms embargo must be strengthened and universally applied, without any reservations or qualifications whatsoever, in order to prevent a further aggravation of the grave situation in South Africa.

Taking note of the Lagos Declaration for Action Against Apartheid [United Nations conference held in Lagos, Nigeria Aug. 22-26, 1977],

Gravely concerned that South Africa is at the threshold of producing nuclear weapons,

Strongly condemning the South African government for its acts of repression, its defiant continuance of the system of apartheid and its attacks against neighboring independent states,

Considering that the policies and acts of the South African government are fraught with danger to international peace and security,

Recalling its Resolution 181 (1963) and other resolutions concerning a voluntary arms embargo against South Africa,

Convinced that a mandatory arms embargo needs to be universally applied against South Africa in the first instance,

Acting therefore under Chapter VII of the Charter of the United Nations:

1. Determines, having regard to the policies and acts of the South African government, that the acquisition by South Africa of arms and related materiel constitutes a threat to the maintenance of international peace and security;

2. Decides that all states shall cease forthwith any provision to South Africa of arms and related materiel of all types, including the sale or transfer of weapons and ammunition, military vehicles and equipment, paramilitary police equipment, and spare parts for the aforementioned, and shall cease as well the provision of all types of equipment and supplies, and grants of licensing arrangements for the manufacture or maintenance of the aforementioned.

3. Calls on all states to review, having regard to the objectives of this resolution, all existing contractual arrangements with and licenses granted to South Africa relating to the manufacture and maintenance of arms, ammunition of all types and military equipment and vehicles, with a view to terminating them;

4. Further decides that all states shall refrain from any cooperation with South Africa in the manufacture and development of nuclear weapons;

5. Calls upon all states, including states non-members of the United Nations, to act strictly in accordance with the provisions of this resolution;

6. Requests the secretary general to report to the Council on the progress of the implementation of this resolution, the first report to be submitted not later than 1 May 1978;

7. Decides to keep this item on its agenda for further action, as appropriate, in the light of developments.

SADAT'S PEACE INITIATIVE
November 19-21, 1977

Egyptian President Anwar el-Sadat in November startled the world by offering to go to Jerusalem and address the Israeli Knesset. Prime Minister Menahem Begin of Israel immediately sent Sadat a formal invitation. For three euphoric days Nov. 19-21, while millions over the world watched on television, Sadat visited Jerusalem. He was the first Arab leader to be welcomed to Israel since the creation of the Jewish state in 1948. Four wars in 30 years had prevented peace.

In his speech to the Knesset (Israel's parliament) Nov. 20, Sadat said he had come "to deliver a message," not to sign a separate peace agreement between Egypt and Israel. "If you want to live with us in this part of the world, in sincerity I tell you that we welcome you among us with all security and safety."

Sadat's historic journey to Jerusalem and his warm welcome by the Israelis raised expectations that a dramatic breakthrough might occur in the deadlocked Middle East peace negotiations. Indeed, Begin traveled to Ismailia, Egypt, for return talks with Sadat Dec. 25-26, and plans were made for a meeting of the Israeli and Egyptian foreign ministers in Jerusalem early in 1978.

As 1977 ended, however, some of the earlier sense of buoyancy had given way to a more realistic view of the many difficulties that remained to be resolved concerning relations between Israel and the Arab states. But while the basic issues dividing the Middle East had not changed in 1977, there seemed to be little doubt that Sadat's dramatic initiative had, at the very least, increased the willingness of the adversaries to try to discover a common ground for peace.

Historic Journey

The spectacular series of events began Nov. 9 when Sadat told the Egyptian parliament that he was ready to go "to the ends of the world" in search of peace. Interviewed by Walter Cronkite on CBS television Nov. 14, Sadat said that he was prepared to address the Knesset within a week from the time he received an invitation from Prime Minister Begin. Begin, also appearing on television with Cronkite, announced within hours that he would ask the United States ambassador to convey his invitation to Sadat.

If television served as a catalyst in bringing Sadat and Begin together, it played an enormous role in conveying the drama of Sadat's visit to the world. Huge audiences were glued to television sets in the Middle East, Western Europe and the United States. News accounts said that people in Cairo seemed transfixed as they watched their president being welcomed in Israel, address the Knesset and make his way about the city of Jerusalem. In Israel, schools, shops and theaters closed while Israelis watched the events unfold on television.

Speaking in Arabic, Sadat pledged to the Knesset that a peace settlement would include the recognition of Israel's right to exist within secure boundaries. But he warned that there could be no peace "without the Palestinians." He also called for the surrender of all lands occupied during the 1967 war, and he reminded Israel that the price of peace included recognition of a West Bank homeland for the Palestinians. Comprehensive peace in the region, Sadat said, must be "based on justice and not on the occupation of the land of others.... You have to give up once and for all the dreams of conquest and the belief that force is the best method of dealing with the Arabs." In his reply, Prime Minister Begin avoided direct reference to Sadat's terms. He praised the Egyptian president's "courage" in visiting Israel, and he invited other Arab leaders to join in peace talks.

In a joint press conference Nov. 21, prior to his departure for Egypt, Sadat said the chief accomplishment of his trip had been "to get rid of the psychological barrier, which in my idea was more than 70 [per cent] of the whole conflict, and the other 30 [per cent] is substance." Begin said, "We agreed we are going to continue our dialogue, and ultimately out of it will come peace." He called Sadat's visit "a great moral achievement."

Stubborn Issues

Despite the stunning effect of Sadat's journey to Jerusalem, 30 years of hostility between Israel and the Arab countries, punctuated by four wars, prevented a sudden peace settlement in the Middle East. Chiefly at issue in 1977 were the return to Arab control of territories captured by Israel in the Six Day War of 1967 and the degree of autonomy or independence of a homeland for the Palestinians.

The Arab position called for return of all Arab lands including the West Bank of the Jordan River, the Sinai peninsula, the Gaza Strip and the Golan Heights. It also insisted that the Palestine Liberation Organization (PLO), which had called for armed struggle against Israel to secure a Palestinian homeland, was the sole legitimate representative of the Palestinians in any peace talks.

Israel, on the other hand, considered the PLO an armed terrorist group pledged to the destruction of the Jewish state and flatly rejected any negotiations with the PLO on the Palestinian question. Moreover, the Israelis insisted that the creation of a Palestinian state on their borders, coupled with a return of all lands captured in the 1967 war, ignored Israeli requirements for secure and defensible borders and constituted a threat to their future security.

Arab Reaction

The Egyptian president received a hero's welcome when he returned to Cairo Nov. 21, but other Arab leaders condemned his visit. Sadat's foreign minister, Ismail Fahmy, resigned Nov. 17 in protest over the trip. Other Arab states, fearing that Egypt would make a separate peace with Israel, echoed Syrian President Hafez al-Assad's statement that the journey was "very dangerous to the Arab cause." Libya Nov. 18 called for Egypt's expulsion from the Arab League. The PLO denounced Sadat's trip as a violation of the 1974 Arab summit agreement made at Rabat, Morocco, where the Arab states recognized the PLO as the voice of the Palestinian peoples in any negotiated settlement.

Arab hard-line states held an anti-Sadat conference Dec. 2-5 in Tripoli where they reaffirmed Arab unity, froze diplomatic relations with Egypt and reiterated opposition to Sadat's peace talks with Israel. Egypt Dec. 5, in retaliation for attempts to disrupt the talks, broke diplomatic relations with five Arab states—Syria, Iraq, Libya, Algeria and South Yemen. Sadat Dec. 7 also ordered Russian cultural centers and some consulates closed because of the Soviet Union's support of the hard-line Arab states.

Second Meeting

At his meeting with Sadat in Ismailia, Egypt, Dec. 25-26 Begin proposed a plan that called for administrative autonomy of the West Bank under Israeli jurisdiction. The Egyptian president rejected the plan and reiterated his call for a separate Palestinian state. The two leaders agreed to set up two separate joint committees to negotiate the political and military terms for a settlement. There was, however, no longer any suggestion of a quick breakthrough to peace.

U.S. Role

Diplomatic initiatives by the Carter administration in 1977 tried to break the deadlock over Palestinian representation that had blocked the reconvening of a peace conference in Geneva, Switzerland. The U.S. State Department in a new policy statement Sept. 12 supported PLO representation in the peacemaking process. However, Carter said Dec. 15 that the PLO had removed itself from "serious consideration" for a place in the peace talks by its refusal to accept Israel's existence. In a Dec. 28 broadcast interview after the Ismailia meeting, President Carter praised Begin's plan for Palestinian self-rule on the West Bank and stated that he opposed creation of a separate Palestinian state as a threat to Israel's security.

When Egyptian President Sadat took exception to Carter's remarks Dec. 29 and called the Palestinian issue "...the core and the crux of the whole problem," Carter arranged a visit with Sadat during the U.S. President's world trip. Carter and Sadat Jan. 4, 1978, smoothed over their differences, with Carter saying that the Palestinians should play a role in determining their own future. (Carter trip, p. 897) Carter clarified the U.S. position Jan. 7, 1978, endorsing a limited-choice referendum for Palestinians on the West Bank and in the Gaza Strip. He said that a limited-choice plan might include alignment with Jordan or a U.S.-backed plan for an international administration of the two regions.

Western powers considered United Nations Security Council Resolutions 242 (approved in 1967) and 338 (approved in 1973) as the basis for a negotiated settlement. Resolution 242 called for withdrawal of all Israeli troops from territories occupied in the Six Day War of 1967. Resolution 338, approved after the Yom Kippur War of 1973, reaffirmed terms of Resolution 242. The PLO considered United Nations General Assembly Resolution 3236 (approved in 1974), which recognized Palestinian rights of self-determination and called for an independent state on the West Bank, as the proper basis for peace talks.

> *Following are the texts of the speeches by Egyptian President Anwar el-Sadat and Israeli Prime Minister Menahem Begin before the Israeli Knesset Nov. 20, 1977; excerpts from the Sadat-Begin joint press conference Nov. 21, 1977; the text of the Israeli plan for the West Bank-Gaza Strip presented to Sadat Dec. 26, 1977, and remarks by Prime Minister Begin Dec. 26, 1977. (Boldface headings in brackets have been added by Congressional Quarterly to highlight the organization of the text.):*

SADAT'S ADDRESS

In the name of God, Mr. Speaker of the Knesset, ladies and gentlemen, allow me first to thank deeply the Speaker of the Knesset for affording me this opportunity to address you.

As I begin my address I wish to say, peace and the mercy of God Almighty be upon you and may peace be with us all, God willing. Peace for us all, of the Arab lands and in Israel, as well as in every part of this big world, which is so beset by conflicts, perturbed by its deep contradictions, menaced now and then by destructive wars launched by man to annihilate his fellow men.

Finally, amidst the ruins of what man has built among the remains of the victims of mankind there emerges neither victor nor vanquished. The only vanquished remains always a man, God's most sublime creation. Man, whom God has created, as Gandhi, the apostle of peace puts it, to forge ahead, to mold the way of life and to worship God Almighty.

I come to you today on solid ground to shape a new life and to establish peace. We all love this land, the land of God, we all, Moslems, Christians and Jews, all worship God.

Under God, God's teachings and commandments are love, sincerity, security and peace.

I do not blame all those who received my decision when I announced it to the entire world before the Egyptian People's Assembly. I do not blame all those who received my decision with surprise and even with amazement, some gripped even by violent surprise. Still others interpreted it as political, to camouflage my intentions of launching a new war.

I would go so far as to tell you that one of my aides at the presidential office contacted me at a late hour following my return home from the People's Assembly and sounded worried as he asked me: "Mr. President, what would be our reaction if Israel actually extended an invitation to you?"

I replied calmly: "I would accept it immediately. I have declared that I would go to the end of the earth. I would go to Israel, for I want to put before the people of Israel all the facts."

I can see the faces of all those who were astounded by my decision and had doubts as to the sincerity of the intentions behind the declaration of my decision. No one could have ever conceived that the president of the biggest Arab state, which bears the heaviest burden and the main responsibility pertaining to the cause of war and peace in the Middle East, should declare his readiness to go to the land of the adversary while we were still in a state of war.

We all still bear the consequences of four fierce wars waged within 30 years. All this at the time when the families of the 1973 October war are still mourning under the cruel pain of bereavement of father, son, husband and brother.

As I have already declared, I have not consulted as far as this decision is concerned with any of my colleagues or brothers, the Arab heads of state or the confrontation states.

Most of those who contacted me following the declaration of this decision expressed their objection because of the feeling of utter suspicion and absolute lack of confidence between the Arab states and the Palestine people on the one hand and Israel on the other that still surges in us all.

Many months in which peace could have been brought about have been wasted over differences and fruitless discussions on the procedure of convening the Geneva conference. All have shared suspicion and absolute lack of confidence.

[Decision to Make Peace]

But to be absolutely frank with you, I took this decision after long thought, knowing that it constitutes a great risk, for God Almighty has made it my fate to assume responsibility on behalf of the Egyptian people, to share in the responsibility of the Arab nation, the main duty of which, dictated by responsibility, is to exploit all and every means in a bid to save my Egyptian Arab people and the pan-Arab nation from the horrors of new suffering and destructive wars, the dimensions of which are foreseen only by God Himself.

After long thinking, I was convinced that the obligation of responsibility before God and before the people make it incumbent upon me that I should go to the far corners of the world—even to Jerusalem to address members of the Knesset and acquaint them with all the facts surging in me, then I would let you decide for yourselves.

Following this, may God Almighty determine our fate.

Ladies and gentlemen, there are moments in the lives of nations and peoples when it is incumbent upon those known for their wisdom and clarity of vision to survey the problem, with all its complexities and vain memories, in a bold drive towards new horizons.

Those who like us are shouldering the same responsibilities entrusted to us are the first who should have the courage to make determining decisions that are consonant with the magnitude of the circumstances. We must all rise above all forms of obsolete theories of superiority, and the most important thing is never to forget that infallibility is the prerogative of God alone.

If I said that I wanted to avert from all the Arab people the horrors of shocking and destructive wars I must sincerely declare before you that I have the same feelings and bear the same responsibility towards all and every man on earth, and certainly toward the Israeli people.

Any life that is lost in war is a human life, be it that of an Arab or an Israeli. A wife who becomes a widow is a human being entitled to a happy family life, whether she be an Arab or an Israeli.

Innocent children who are deprived of the care and compassion of their parents are ours. They are ours, be they living on Arab or Israeli land.

They command our full responsibility to afford them a comfortable life today and tomorrow.

For the sake of them all, for the sake of the lives of all our sons and brothers, for the sake of affording our communities the opportunity to work for the progress and happiness of man, feeling secure and with the right to a dignified life, for the generations to come, for a smile on the face of every child born in our land—for all that I have taken my decision to come to you, despite all the hazards, to deliver my address.

I have shouldered the prerequisites of the historic responsibility and therefore I declared on Feb. 4, 1971, that I was willing to sign a peace agreement with Israel. This was the first declaration made by a responsible Arab official since the outbreak of the Arab-Israeli conflict. Motivated by all these factors dictated by the responsibilities of leadership, on Oct. 16, 1973, before the Egyptian People's Assembly, I called for an international conference to establish permanent peace based on justice. I was not heard.

I was in the position of [a] man pleading for peace or asking for a cease-fire, motivated by the duties of history and leadership, I signed the first disengagement agreement, followed by the second disengagement agreement in Sinai.

Then we proceeded, trying both open and closed doors in a bid to find a certain road leading to a durable and just peace.

We opened our heart to the peoples of the entire world to make them understand our motivations and objectives and actually to convince them of the fact that we are advocates of justice and peacemakers. Motivated by all these factors, I also decided to come to you with an open mind and an open heart and with a conscious determination so that we might establish permanent peace based on justice.

It is so fated that my trip to you, which is a journey of peace, coincided with the Islamic feast, the holy Feast of the Sacrifice when Abraham— peace be upon him—forefather of the Arabs and Jews, submitted to God, I say, when God Almighty ordered him, not out of weakness, but through a giant spiritual force and by free will to sacrifice his very own son, personified a firm and unshakeable belief in ideals that had for mankind a profound significance.

Ladies and gentlemen, let us be frank with each other. Using straightforward words and a clear conception with no ambiguity, let us be frank with each other today while the entire world, both East and West, follows these unparalleled moments, which could prove to be a radical turning point in the history of this part of the world if not in the history of the world as a whole.

[Permanent Peace with Justice]

Let us be frank with each other, let us be frank with each other as we answer this important question.

How can we achieve permanent peace based on justice? Well, I have come to you carrying my clear and frank answer to this big question, so that the people in Israel as well as the entire world may hear it. All those devoted prayers ring in my ears, pleading to God Almighty that this historic meeting may eventually lead to the result aspired to by millions.

Before I prolcaim my answer, I wish to assure you that in my clear and frank answer I am availing myself of a number of facts that no one can deny.

The first fact is that no one can build this happiness at the expense of the misery of others.

The second fact: never have I spoken, nor will I ever speak, with two tongues; never have I adopted, nor will I ever adopt, two policies. I never deal with anyone except in one tongue, one policy and with one face.

The third fact: direct confrontation is the nearest and most successful method to reach a clear objective.

The fourth fact: the call for permanent and just peace based on respect for United Nations resolutions has now become the call of the entire world. It has become the expression of the will of the international community, whether in official capitals where policies are made and decisions taken, or at the level of the world public opinion, which influences policymaking and decision-taking.

The fifth fact, and this is probably the clearest and most prominent, is that the Arab nation, in its drive for permanent peace based on justice, does not proceed from a position of weakness. On the contrary, it has the power and stability for a sincere will for peace.

The Arab declared intention stems from an awareness prompted by a heritage of civilization, that to avoid an inevitable disaster that will befall us, you and the whole world, there is no alternative to the establishment of permanent peace based on justice, peace that is not swayed by suspicion or jeopardized by ill intentions.

In the light of these facts, which I meant to place before you the way I see them, I would also wish to warn you, in all sincerity I warn you, against some thoughts that could cross your minds.

Frankness makes it incumbent upon me to tell you the following:

[No Interim Peace Pact]

First, I have not come here for a separate agreement between Egypt and Israel. This is not part of the policy of Egypt. The problem is not that of Egypt and Israel.

An interim peace between Egypt and Israel, or between any Arab confrontation state and Israel, will not bring permanent peace based on justice in the entire region.

Rather, even if peace between all the confrontation states and Israel were achieved in the absence of a just solution of the Palestinian problem, never will there be that durable and just peace upon which the entire world insists.

Second, I have not come to you to seek a partial peace, namely to terminate the state of belligerency at this stage and put off the entire problem to a subsequent stage. This is not the radical solution that would steer us to permanent peace.

Equally, I have not come to you for a third disengagement agreement in Sinai or in Golan or the West Bank.

For this would mean that we are merely delaying the ignition of the fuse. It would also mean that we are lacking the courage to face peace, that we are too weak to shoulder the burdens and responsibilities of a durable peace based upon justice.

I have come to you so that together we should build a durable peace based on justice to avoid the shedding of one single drop of blood by both sides. It is for this reason that I have proclaimed my readiness to go to the farthest corner of the earth.

Here I would go back to the big question.

How can we achieve a durable peace based on justice? In my opinion, and I declare it to the whole world, from this forum, the answer is neither difficult nor is it impossible despite long years of feuds, blood, faction, strife, hatreds and deep-rooted animosity.

The answer is not difficult, nor is it impossible, if we sincerely and faithfully follow a straight line.

You want to live with us, in this part of the world.

In all sincerity I tell you we welcome you among us with full security and safety. This in itself is a tremendous turning point, one of the landmarks of a decisive historical change. We used to reject you. We had our reasons and our fears, yes.

We refused to meet with you, anywhere, yes.

We were together in international conferences and organizations and our representatives did not, and still do not, exchange greetings with you. Yes. This has happened and is still happening.

It is also true that we used to set as a precondition for any negotiations with you a mediator who would meet separately with each party.

Yes. Through this procedure, the talks of the first and second disengagement agreements took place.

Our delegates met in the first Geneva conference without exchanging a direct word, yes, this has happened.

Yet today I tell you, and I declare it to the whole world, that we accept to live with you in permanent peace based on justice. We do not want to encircle you or be encircled ourselves by destructive missiles ready for launching, nor by the shells of grudges and hatreds.

I have announced on more than one occasion that Israel has become a *fait accompli*, recognized by the world, and that the two superpowers have undertaken the responsibility for its existence. As we really and truly seek peace we really and truly welcome you to live among us in peace and security.

There was a huge wall between us that you tried to build up over a quarter of a century but it was destroyed in 1973. It was the wall of an implacable and escalating psychological warfare.

It was a wall of the fear of the force that could sweep the entire Arab nation. It was a wall of propaganda that we were a nation reduced to immobility. Some of you have gone as far as to say that even for 50 years to come, the Arabs will not regain their strength. It was a wall that always threatened with a long arm that could reach and strike anywhere. It was a wall that warned us of extermination and annihilation if we tried to use our legitimate rights to liberate the occupied territories.

Together we have to admit that that wall fell and collapsed in 1973. Yet, there remains another wall. This wall constitutes a psychological barrier between us, a barrier of suspicion, a barrier of rejection; a barrier of fear, of deception, a barrier of hallucination without any action, deed or decision.

A barrier of distorted and eroded interpretation of every event and statement. It is this psychological barrier that I described in official statements as constituting 70 per cent of the whole problem.

Today, through my visit to you, I ask why don't we stretch out our hands with faith and sincerity so that together we might destroy this barrier? Why shouldn't our and your will meet with faith and sincerity so that together we might remove all suspicion of fear, betrayal and bad intentions?

Why don't we stand together with the courage of men and the boldness of heroes who dedicate themselves to a sublime aim? Why don't we stand together with the same courage and daring to erect a huge edifice of peace?

An edifice that builds and does not destroy. An edifice that serves as a beacon for generations to come with the human message for construction, development and the dignity of man.

Why should we bequeath to the coming generations the plight of bloodshed, yes, orphans, widowhood, family disintegration and the wailing of victims?

Why don't we believe in the wisdom of God conveyed to us by the wisdom of the proverbs of Solomon. [Sadat quoted from the proverbs.]

[Withdrawal to 1967 Borders]

Ladies and gentlemen, to tell you the truth, peace cannot be worth its name unless it is based on justice and not on the occupation of the land of others. It would not be right for you to demand for yourselves what you deny to others. With all frankness and in the spirit that has prompted me to come to you today, I tell you you have to give up once and for all the dreams of conquest and give up the belief that force is the best method for dealing with the Arabs.

You should clearly understand the lesson of confrontation between you and us. Expansion does not pay. To speak frankly, our land does not yield itself to bargaining, it is not even open to argument. To us, the nation's soil is equal to the holy valley where God Almighty spoke to Moses. Peace be upon him.

We cannot accept any attempt to take away or accept to seek one inch of it nor can we accept the principle of debating or bargaining over it.

I sincerely tell you also that before us today lies the appropriate chance for peace. If we are really serious in our endeavor for peace, it is a chance that may never come again. It is a chance that if lost or wasted, the resulting slaughter would bear the curse of humanity and of history.

What is peace for Israel? It means that Israel lives in the region with her Arab neighbors in security and safety. Is that logical? I say yes. It means that Israel lives within its borders, secure against any aggression. Is that logical? And I say yes. It means that Isreal obtains all kinds of guarantees that will ensure these two factors. To this demand, I say yes.

Beyond that we declare that we accept all the international guarantees you envisage and accept. We declare that we accept all the guarantees you want from the two superpowers or from either of them or from the Big Five or from some of them. Once again, I declare clearly and unequivocally that we agree to any guarantees you accept, because in return we shall receive the same guarantees.

In short then, when we ask what is peace for Israel, the answer would be that Israel lives within her borders, among her Arab neighbors in safety and security, within the framework of all the guarantees she accepts and that are offered to her.

But, how can this be achieved? How can we reach this conclusion that would lead us to permanent peace based on justice? There are facts that should be faced with courage and clarity. There are Arab territories that Israel has occupied and still occupies by force. We insist on complete withdrawal from these territories, including Arab Jerusalem.

I have come to Jerusalem, the city of peace, which will always remain as a living embodiment of coexistence among believers of the three religions. It is inadmissible that anyone should conceive the special status of the city of Jerusalem within the framework of annexation or expansionism. It should be a free and open city for all believers.

Above all, this city should not be severed from those who have made it their abode for centuries. Instead of reviving the precedent of the Crusades, we should revive the spirit of Omar Emil Khtah [Muslim caliph A.D. 634-644, one of Mohammed's chief advisers] and Saladin [Sultan of Egypt and Syria, A.D. 1183-93], namely the spirit of tolerance and respect for right.

The holy shrines of Islam and Christianity are not only places of worship but a living testimony of our interrupted presence here. Politically, spiritually and intellectually, here let us make no mistake about the importance and reverence we Christians and Moslems attach to Jerusalem.

Let me tell you without the slightest hesitation that I have not come to you under this roof to make a request that your troops evacuate the occupied territories. Complete withdrawal from the Arab territories occupied after 1967 is a logical and undisputed fact. Nobody should plead for that. Any talk about permanent peace based on justice and any move to ensure our coexistence in peace and security in this part of the world would become meaningless while you occupy Arab territories by force of arms.

For there is no peace that could be built on the occupation of the land of others, otherwise it would not be a serious peace. Yet this is a foregone conclusion that is not open to the passion of debate if intentions are sincere or if endeavors to establish a just and durable peace for our and for generations to come are genuine.

[The Palestine Cause]

As for the Palestine cause—nobody could deny that it is the crux of the entire problem. Nobody in the world could accept today slogans propagated here in Israel, ignoring the existence of a Palestinian people and questioning even their whereabouts. Because the Palestine people and their legitimate rights are no longer denied today by anybody; that is nobody who has the ability of judgment can deny or ignore it.

It is an acknowledged fact, perceived by the world community, both in the East and in the West, with support and recognition in international documents and official statements. It is of no use to anybody to turn deaf ears to its resounding voice, which is being heard day and night, or to overlook its historical reality.

Even the United States of America, your first ally, which is absolutely committed to safeguard Israel's security and existence and which offered and still offers Israel every moral, material and military support—I say, even the United States has opted to face up to reality and admit that the Palestinian people are entitled to legitimate rights and that the Palestine problem is the cause and essence of the conflict and that so long as it continues to be unresolved, the conflict will continue to aggravate, reaching new dimension.

In all sincerity I tell you that there can be no peace without the Palestinians. It is a grave error of unpredictable consequences to overlook or brush aside this cause.

I shall not indulge in past events such as the Balfour Declaration [Arthur James Balfour, 1848-1930, British statesman who authored the agreement to create a Jewish state in Palestine after W.W. I.] 60 years ago. You are well acquainted with the relevant text. If you have found the moral and legal justification to set up a national home on a land that did not all belong to you, it is incumbent upon you to show understanding of the insistence of the people of Palestine for establishment once again of a state on their land. When some extremists ask the Palestinians to give up this sublime objective, this in fact means asking them to renounce their identity and every hope for the future.

I hail the Israeli voices that called for the recognition of the Palestinian people's right to achieve and safeguard peace.

Here I tell you, ladies and gentlemen, that it is no use to refrain from recognizing the Palestinian people and their right to statehood as their right of return. We, the Arabs, have faced this experience before, with you. And with the reality of the Israeli existence, the struggle that took us from war to war, from victims to more victims, until you and we have today reached the edge of a horrible abyss and a terrifying disaster unless, together, we seize this opportunity today of a durable peace based on justice.

You have to face reality bravely, as I have done. There can never be any solution to a problem by evading it or turning a deaf ear to it. Peace cannot last if attempts are made to impose fantasy concepts on which the world has turned its back and announced its unanimous call for the respect of rights and facts.

There is no need to enter a vicious circle as to Palestinian rights. It is useless to create obstacles, otherwise the march of peace will be impeded or peace will be blown up. As I have told you, there is no happiness [based on] the detriment of others.

Direct confrontation and straightforwardness are the shortcuts and the most successful way to reach a clear objective. Direct confrontation concerning the Palestinian problem and tackling it in one single language with a view to achieving a durable and just peace lie in the establishment of that peace. With all the guarantees you demand, there should be no fear of a newly born state that needs the assistance of all countries of the world.

When the bells of peace ring there will be no hands to beat the drums of war. Even if they existed, they would be stilled.

[Peace Terms]

Conceive with me a peace agreement in Geneva that we would herald to a world thirsting for peace. A peace agreement based on the following points:

Ending the occupation of the Arab territories occupied in 1967.

Achievement of the fundamental rights of the Palestinian people and their right to self-determination, including their right to establish their own state.

The right of all states in the area to live in peace within their boundaries, their secure boundaries, which will be secured and guaranteed through procedures to be agreed upon, which will provide appropriate security to international boundaries in addition to appropriate international guarantees.

Commitment of all states in the region to administer the relations among them in accordance with the objectives and principles of the United Nations Charter. Particularly the principles concerning the nonuse of force and a solution of differences among them by peaceful means.

Ending the state of belligerence in the region.

Ladies and gentlemen, peace is not a mere endorsement of written lines. Rather it is a rewriting of history. Peace is not a game of calling for peace to defend certain whims or hide certain admissions. Peace in its essence is a dire struggle against all and every ambition and whim.

Perhaps the example taken and experienced, taken from ancient and modern history, teaches that missiles, warships and nuclear weapons cannot establish security. Instead they destroy what peace and security build.

For the sake of our peoples and for the sake of the civilization made by man, we have to defend man everywhere against rule by the force of arms so that we may endow the rule of humanity with all the power of the values and principles that further the sublime position of mankind.

Allow me to address my call from this rostrum to the people of Israel. I pledge myself with true and sincere words to every man, woman and child in Israel. I tell them, from the Egyptian people who bless this sacred mission of peace, I convey to you the message of peace of the Egyptian people, who do not harbor fanatacism and whose sons, Moslems, Christians and Jews, live together in a state of cordiality, love and tolerance.

[A Message of Security]

This is Egypt, whose people have entrusted me with their sacred message. A message of security, safety and peace to every man, woman and child in Israel. I say, encourage your leadership to struggle for peace. Let all endeavors be channeled towards building a huge stronghold for peace instead of building destructive rockets.

Introduce to the entire world the image of the new man in this area so that he might set an example to the man of our age, the man of peace everywhere. Ring the bells for your sons. Tell them that those wars were the last of wars and the end of sorrows. Tell them that we are entering upon a new beginning, a new life, a life of love, prosperity, freedom and peace.

You, sorrowing mother, you, widowed wife, you, the son who lost a brother or a father, all the victims of wars, fill the air and space with recitals of peace, fill bosoms and hearts with the aspirations of peace. Make a reality that blossoms and lives. Make hope a code of conduct and endeavor.

The will of peoples is part of the will of God. Ladies and gentlemen, before I came to this place, with every beat of my heart and with every sentiment, I prayed to God Almighty. While performing the prayers at the Al Aksa mosque and while visiting the Holy Sepulcher I asked the Almighty to give me strength and to confirm my belief that this visit may achieve the objective I look forward to for a happy present and a happier future.

I have chosen to set aside all precedents and traditions known by warring countries. In spite of the fact that occupation of Arab territories is still there, the declaration of my readiness to proceed to Israel came as a great surprise that stirred many feelings and confounded many minds. Some of them even doubted its intent.

Despite all that, the decision was inspired by all the clarity and purity of belief and with all the true passions of my people's will and intentions and I have chosen this road, considered by many to be the most difficult road.

I have chosen to come to you with an open heart and an open mind. I have chosen to give this great impetus to all international efforts exerted for peace. I have chosen to present to you, in your own home, the realities, devoid of any scheme or whim. Not to maneuver, or win a round, but for us to win together, the most dangerous of rounds embattled in modern history, the battle of permanent peace based on justice.

It is not my battle alone. Nor is it the battle of the leadership in Israel alone. It is the battle of all and every citizen in all our territories, whose right it is to live in peace. It is the commitment of conscience and responsibility in the hearts of millions.

When I put forward this initiative, many asked what is it that I conceived as possible to achieve during this visit and what my expectations were. And as I answer the questions, I announce before you that I have not thought of carrying out this initiative from the precepts of what could be achieved during this visit. And I have come here to deliver a message. I have delivered the message and may God be my witness.

I repeat with Zachariah: Love, right and justice. From the holy Koran I quote the following verses: "We believe in God and in what has been revealed to us and what was revealed to Abraham, Ishmael, Isaac, Jacob and the 13 Jewish tribes. And in the books given to Moses and Jesus and the prophets from their Lord, who made no distinction between them." So we agree. Salam Aleikum—peace be upon you.

BEGIN'S SPEECH

Mr. Speaker, Honourable President of the State of Israel, Honourable President of the Arab Republic of Egypt, Worthy and Learned Knesset Members:

We send our greetings to the President and to all adherents of the Islamic faith, in our own country and wherever they may be, on the occasion of the Feast of Sacrifice, Id el-Adha.

This feast reminds us of the binding of Isaac on the altar, the test with which the Creator tried the faith of our forefather Abraham—our common father; the challenge which Abraham met. But, from the point of view of morality and the advancement of Mankind, this event heralded the principle of a ban on human sacrifice. Our two Peoples, in their ancient tradition, learned and taught that humanitarian prohibition, while the nations around us continued to offer human sacrifices to their idols. Thus we, the People of Israel and the Arab People, contributed to the advancement of Mankind, and we continue to contribute to human civilization until this very day.

I greet the President of Egypt on the occasion of his visit to our country and his participation in this session of the Knesset. The duration of the flight from Cairo to Jerusalem is short but, until last night, the distance between them was infinite. President Sadat showed courage in crossing this distance. We Jews can appreciate courage, as exhibited by our guest, because it is with courage that we arose, and with it we shall continue to exist.

Mr. Speaker, this small People, the surviving remnant of the Jewish People which returned to our historic Homeland, always sought peace. And, when the dawn of our freedom rose on the 14th of May, 1948, the 4th of Iyyar, 5708, David Ben-Gurion [Prime Minister of Israel, 1949-53; 1955-63] said, in the Declaration of Independence, the charter of our national independence:

> "We extend our hand to all neighbouring states and their peoples in an offer of peace and good neighbourliness, and appeal to them to establish bonds of cooperation and mutual help with the sovereign Jewish People settled in its own Land."

A year earlier, in the midst of the fateful struggle for the liberation of the Land and the redemption of the Nation, while still in the underground, we issued the following call to our neighbours:

"Let us live together in this Land and together advance towards a life of freedom and happiness. Our Arab neighbours—do not reject the hand which is outstretched to you in peace."

But it is my duty—my duty Mr. Speaker, and not only my privilege—to assert today in truth that our hand, extended in peace, was rejected. And, one day after our independence was renewed, in accordance with our eternal and indisputable right, we were attacked on three fronts, and we stood virtually without arms—few against many, weak against strong. One day after the declaration of our independence, an attempt was made to strangle it with enmity, and to extinguish the last hope of the Jewish People in the generation of Holocaust and Resurrection.

No, we do not believe in might, and we have never based our relations with the Arab Nation on force. On the contrary, force was exercised against us. Throughout all the years of this generation we have never ceased to be attacked with brute force in order to destroy our Nation, to demolish our independence, to annul our right. And we defended ourselves.

True, we defended our right, our existence, our honour, our women and our children against recurrent attempts to crush us by brute force, and not on one front alone. This, too, is true: with the help of God we overcame the forces of aggression and assured the survival of our nation, not only for this generation, but for all those to come.

We do not believe in might; we believe in right, only in right. And that is why our aspiration, from the depths of our hearts, from time immemorial until this very day, is peace.

Mr. President, in this democratic chamber sit commanders of all the Hebrew underground fighting organizations. They were compelled to conduct a battle of few against many, against a mighty world power. Here sit our top military commanders, who led their forces in a battle that was imposed on them, and to a victory that was inevitable, because they defended right. They belong to various parties, and have different outlooks. But I am sure, Mr. President, that I am expressing the views of them all, without exception, when I say that we have one aspiration at heart, one desire in our souls, and we are all united in this aspiration and this desire—to bring peace: peace to our nation which has not known it for even one day since the beginning of the Return to Zion; and peace to our neighbours to whom we wish all the best. And we believe that if we achieve peace, true peace, we shall be able to assist one another in all realms of life, and a new era will be opened in the Middle East: an era of flourishing and growth, of development and progress and advancement, as in ancient times.

[A True, Full Peace]

Therefore, allow me today to define the meaning of peace as we understand it. We seek a true, full peace, with absolute reconciliation between the Jewish People and the Arab People. We must not permit memories of the past to stand in our way. There have been wars; blood has been shed; our wonderful sons have fallen in battle on both sides. We shall always cherish the memory of our heroes who gave their lives so that this day, yea even this day, might come. We respect the valour of an adversary, and we pay tribute to all members of the young generation of the Arab Nation who have fallen as well.

Let us not be daunted by memories of the past, even if they are bitter to us all. We must overcome them, and focus on what lies ahead: on our Peoples, on our children, on our common future. For, in this region, we shall all live together—the Great Arab Nation in its States and its countries, and the Jewish People in its Land, Eretz Israel—forever and ever. For this reason the meaning of peace must be defined.

As free men, Mr. President, let us conduct negotiations for a peace treaty and, with the help of God, so we believe with all our hearts, the day will come when we will sign it, with mutual respect. Then will we know that the era of wars has ended, that we have extended a hand to one another, that we have shaken each other's hand, and that the future will be glorious for all the Peoples of the region. Of prime significance, therefore, in the context of a peace treaty, is a termination of the state of war.

I agree, Mr. President, that you have not come here and we did not invite you to our country in order, as has been suggested in recent days, to drive a wedge between the Arab Peoples, or, expressed more cleverly in accord with the ancient saying, *"divide et impera."* Israel has no desire to rule and does not wish to divide. We want peace with all our neighbours—with Egypt and with Jordan, with Syria and with Lebanon.

There is no need to differentiate between a peace treaty and the termination of the state of war. We neither propose this, nor do we seek it. On the contrary, the first article of a peace treaty determines the end of the state of war, forever. We wish to establish normal relations between us, as exist among all nations after all wars. We have learned from history, Mr. President, that war is avoidable. It is peace that is inevitable.

Many nations have waged war against one another, and sometimes they have made use of the foolish term "eternal enemy." There are no eternal enemies. After all wars comes the inevitable—peace. Therefore, in the context of a peace treaty, we seek to stipulate the establishment of diplomatic relations, as is customary among civilized nations.

Today, Jerusalem is bedecked with two flags—the Egyptian and the Israeli. Together, Mr. President, we have seen our little children waving both flags. Let us sign a peace treaty and establish such a situation forever, both in Jerusalem and in Cairo. I hope the day will come when Egyptian children will wave Israeli and Egyptian flags together, just as the Israeli children are waving both of these flags together in Jerusalem; when you, Mr. President, will be represented by a loyal Ambassador in Jerusalem, and we, by an Ambassador in Cairo and, should differences of opinion arise between us, we will clarify them, like civilized peoples, through our authorized emissaries.

We propose economic cooperation for the development of our countries. God created marvelous lands in the Middle East—virtual oases in the desert—but there are also deserts, and these can be made fertile. Let us join hands in facing this challenge, and cooperate in developing our countries, in abolishing poverty, hunger and homelessness. Let us raise our nations to the status of developed countries, so that we may no longer be called developing states.

With all due respect, I am prepared to endorse the words of His Highness, the King of Morocco [Hassan II], who said, publicly, that, if peace were to be established in the Middle East, the combination of Arab and Jewish genius can together convert the region into a paradise on earth.

Let us open our countries to free movement, so that you shall come to us and we will visit you. I am prepared today to announce, Mr. Speaker, that our country is open to the citizens of Egypt, and I do not qualify this announcement with any condition on our part. I think it would be only proper and just that there be a mutual announcement on this matter. And, just as Egyptian flags are flying in our streets, there is also an honoured Egyptian delegation in our capital and in our country today. Let there be many visitors. Our border will be open to you, just as will be all the other borders, for, as I noted, we would like the same situation to prevail in the south, in the north and in the east.

Therefore, I renew my invitation to the President of Syria [Hafez al-Assad] to follow in your footsteps, Mr. President, and to come to our country to begin negotiations on the establishment of peace between Israel and Syria and on the signing of a peace treaty between us. I am sorry to say, there is no justification for the mourning that has been decreed on the other side of our northern border. On the contrary, such visits, such contacts and discussions, can and should be a cause of happiness, a cause of elation for all peoples.

I invite King Hussein [of Jordan] to come here and we shall discuss with him all the problems that exist between us. I also invite genuine spokesmen of the Palestinian Arabs to come and to hold talks with us on our common future, on guaranteeing human freedom, social justice, peace and mutual respect.

And, if they should invite us to come to their capitals, we shall respond to their invitation. Should they invite us to begin negotiations in Damascus, Amman or Beirut, we shall go to those capitals in order to negotiate there. We do not wish to divide. We seek true peace with all our neighbours, to be expressed in peace treaties, the context of which shall be as I have already clarified.

[Balfour Declaration]

Mr. Speaker, it is my duty today to tell our guests and all the nations who are watching and listening to our words about the bond between our People and this Land. The President mentioned the Balfour Declaration. No, sir, we took no foreign land. We returned to our Homeland. The bond between our People and this Land is eternal. It was created at the dawn of human history. It was never severed. In this Land we established our civilization; here our prophets spoke those holy words you cited this very day; here the Kings of Judah and Israel prostrated themselves; here we became a nation; here we established our Kingdom and, when we were exiled from our country by the force that was exercised against us, even when we were far away, we did not forget this Land, not even for a single day. We prayed for it; we longed for it; we have believed in our return to it ever since the day these words were spoken:

"When the Lord brought back the captivity of Zion we were like those who dream. Then our mouth was filled with laughter and our tongue with joyful shouting."

That song applies to all our exiles, to all our sufferings, and to the consolation that the Return to Zion would surely come.

This, our right, has been recognized. The Balfour Declaration was included in the Mandate which was recognized by the nations of the world, including the United States of America. And the preamble to that authoritative international document states:

"Whereas recognition has thereby been given to the historical connection of the Jewish People with Palestine...and to the grounds for reconstituting their National Home in that country...."

In 1919, we also gained recognition of this right from the spokesman of the Arab people. The agreement of 3 January 1919, signed by Emir Feisal [1885-1933, King of Syria (1920), of Iraq (1921-1933)] and Chaim Weizman [1874-1952, Zionist leader and first President of Israel], states:

"Mindful of the racial kinship and ancient bonds existing between the Arabs and the Jewish People, and realizing that the surest means of working out the consummation of their national aspirations is through the closest possible collaboration in the development of the Arab State and of Palestine..."

Afterwards, follow all the articles on cooperation between the Arab State and Eretz Israel. That is our right; its fulfilment—the truth.

What happened to us when our Homeland was taken from us? I accompanied you this morning, Mr. President, to Yad Vashem [Israeli shrine to W.W. II victims]. With your own eyes you saw what the fate of our People was when this Homeland was taken from it. It is an incredible story. We both agreed, Mr. President, that whoever has not himself seen what is found in Yad Vashem cannot understand what befell this People when it was homeless, robbed of its own Homeland. And we both read a document, dated 30 January 1939, in which the word *"vernichtung"* appears—"if war breaks out the Jewish race in Europe will be annihilated." Then, too, we were told to pay no heed to such words. The whole world heard. No one came to our rescue; not during the nine critical, fateful months following this announcement—the likes of which had never been heard since God created man and man created Satan—and not during those six years when millions of our people, among them a million and a half small Jewish children were slaughtered in every possible way.

No one came to our rescue, not from the East and not from the West. And therefore we, this entire generation, the generation of Holocaust and Resurrection, swore an oath of allegiance: never again shall we endanger our People; never again will our wives and our children—whom it is our duty to defend, if need be even at the cost of our own lives—be put in the devastating range of enemy fire.

And further: ever since then it has been, and will continue to be, our duty, for generations to come, to remember that certain things said about our People are to be related to with all seriousness. We must not, Heaven forbid, for the future of our People, accept any advice suggesting that we not take such words seriously.

[Everything Is Negotiable]

President Sadat knows, as he knew from us before he came to Jerusalem, that our position concerning permanent borders between us and our neighbours differs from his. However, I call upon the President of Egypt and upon all our neighbours: do not rule out negotiations on any subject whatsoever. I propose, in the name of the overwhelming majority of this Parliament, that everything will be negotiable. Anybody who says that, in the relationship between the Arab People—or the Arab Nations in the area—and the State of Israel there are subjects that should be excluded from negotiations, is assuming an awesome responsibility. Everything is negotiable. No side shall say the contrary. No side shall present prior conditions. We will conduct the negotiations with respect.

If there are differences of opinion between us, that is not exceptional. Anyone who has studied the history of wars and the annals of peace treaties knows that all negotiations for peace treaties have begun with differences of opinion between the parties concerned, and that, in the course of the negotiations, they have reached solutions which have made possible the signing of agreements or peace treaties. That is the path we propose to follow.

We shall conduct the negotiations as equals. There are no vanquished and there are no victors. All the Peoples of the region are equal, and all will relate to each other with respect. In this spirit of openness, of readiness of each to listen to the other—to facts, reasons, explanations—with every reasonable attempt at mutual persuasion—let us conduct the negotiations as I have asked and propose to open them, to conduct them, to continue them persistently until we succeed, in good time, in signing a peace treaty between us.

We are prepared, not only, to sit with representatives of Egypt and with representatives of Jordan, Syria and Lebanon—if it so desires—at a Peace Conference in Geneva. We proposed that the Geneva Conference be renewed on the basis of Resolutions 242 [Nov. 22, 1967; calls for a return to pre-1967 borders] and 338 [Oct. 22, 1973; cease-fire agreement to end Yom Kippur War] of the Security Council. However, should problems arise between us prior to the convening of the Geneva Conference, we will clarify them today and tomorrow and, if the President of Egypt will be interested in continuing to clarify them in Cairo—all the better; if on neutral ground—no opposition. Anywhere. Let us clarify—even before the Geneva Conference convenes—the problems that should be made clear before it meets, with open eyes and a readiness to listen to all suggestions.

Allow me to say a word about Jerusalem. Mr. President, today you prayed in a house of worship sacred to the Islamic faith, and from there you went to the Church of the Holy Sepulchre. You witnessed the fact, known to all who come from throughout the world, that ever since this city was joined together, there is absolutely free access, without any interference or obstacle, for the members of all religions to their holy places. This positive phenomenon did not exist for 19 years. It has existed now for about 11 years, and we can assure the Moslem world and the Christian world—all the nations—that there will always be free access to the holy places of every faith. We shall defend this right of free access, for it is something in which we believe—in the equality of rights for every man and every citizen, and in respect for every faith.

Mr. Speaker, this is a special day for our Parliament, and it will undoubtedly be remembered for many years in the annals of our Nation, in the history of the Egyptian People, and perhaps, also, in the history of nations.

And on this day, with your permission, worthy and learned Members of the Knesset, I wish to offer a prayer that the God of our common ancestors will grant us the requisite wisdom of heart in order to overcome the difficulties and obstacles, the calumnies and slanders. With the help of God, may we arrive at the longed-for day for which all our people pray—the day of peace.

For indeed, as the Psalmist of Israel said, *"Righteousness and peace have kissed,"* and, as the prophet Zacharia said, *"Love truth and peace."*

JOINT NEWS CONFERENCE

[Sadat]: In the name of God, let me seize this opportunity to express my gratitude for the efforts you have done to cover the historical moments here in Ismailia. As you know, after my visit to Jerusalem on Nov. 20, a new spirit prevails in the area and we have agreed in Jerusalem and in Ismailia also to continue our efforts toward achieving a comprehensive settlement.

We have agreed upon raising the level of the representation in the Cairo conference to ministerial level and, as you have heard yesterday, we have agreed upon two committees—a political committee and a military committee headed by ministers of foreign affairs and ministers of defense. The military committee will convene in Cairo. The political committee will convene in Jerusalem.

Those committees shall work in the context of the Cairo conference, meaning that they will report to the plenary whenever they reach any decision. On the question of the withdrawal we have made progress, but not on the Palestinian question, which we consider the core and crux of the problem here in this area.

The Egyptian and Israeli delegations here discussed the Palestinian problem. The position of Egypt is that on the West Bank and the Gaza Strip a Palestinian state should be established. The position of Israel is that Palestinian Arabs in Judea, Samaria, the West Bank of Jordan and the Gaza Strip should enjoy self-rule.

We have agreed that, because we have differed on the issue, the issue will be discussed in the political committee of the Cairo preparatory conference.

I hope I have given you some light upon our work and thank you again.

[Begin]: Mr. President, ladies and gentlemen. I have come here a hopeful Prime Minister and I am leaving a happy man. The conference in Ismailia has been successful. We will continue with the momentum of the peace-making process.

Now starts the phase of the most serious negotiations: how to establish peace between Egypt and Israel as part of a comprehensive settlement throughout the Middle East. These two days are very good days for Egypt, Israel and for peace.

May I express our gratitude to the President for his gracious hospitality he bestowed upon me, upon my friends and colleagues, the Foreign Minister, Moshe Dayan, and the Defense Minister, Ezer Weizman, and our collaborators and advisers.

This is the second meeting between President Sadat and myself after the historic event of his breakthrough visit to Jerusalem.

Here, too, may I say, we spoke as friends. We want to establish real peace. There are problems to discuss and in these two committees the chairmanship of which we will rotate between our respective ministers, those serious negotiations and talks will take place.

Now my friends and I will leave Ismailia and Egypt with the faith that we contributed to the peace-making process and there is hope that, with God's help, President Sadat and I and our friends will establish peace.

Thank you, ladies and gentlemen.

[Comprehensive Settlement]

Q: Mr. Begin, what are the advantages of two or three committees working in tandem rather than a cohesive peace forum and, since you and President Sadat obviously coordinated these discussions, do you expect to meet soon and frequently?

[Begin]: The committees will start with their work quite soon. In the first week of January, they will work every day. We hope for good and concrete results. President Sadat and I also agreed during our private talks that, if necessary, from time to time we shall meet again.

Q: Mr. Begin and Mr. Sadat, would you say Egypt and Israel are about to achieve a peace treaty in a couple of months?

[Sadat]: We are working towards a comprehensive settlement. As I said before, we want to establish peace in the area. Without a comprehensive settlement we can't achieve peace.

[Begin]: I agree with the President.

Q: To Begin. What about the declaration of intention you were both to announce? And how do the proposals you submitted to President Carter differ from those you brought here?

[Begin]: The statement made by the President is an agreed upon statement. So we don't need now an additional written declaration. We agreed to continue the efforts to establish a comprehensive peace settlement in the Middle East on the basis of U.N. Security Council resolutions 242 and 338 and to establish these committees. This is the basic agreement. This is the most important development at the Ismailia conference.

Our colleagues and friends will continue with the efforts, as the President and I explained. We have presented to President Sadat the proposals I took to President Carter. There were a few amendments not of decisive importance. And yesterday at the conference I presented all our proposals in detail. The President listened very attentively and now the committees may have counterproposals by Egypt, as is natural in the process of negotiating peace treaties.

Q: Looking beyond a peace settlement, can you tell us something about your long-term grand designs for peace? How to satisfy your people's expectations of a better life, of a renaissance in this Middle East cradle of civilization? Are you in favor of cooperation in science, education, agriculture, industry, trade and cultural exchanges between your two countries and eventually between Israel and the Arab world as a whole?

[Sadat]: Well, the committees will start, and, as I said, will report to the plenary. Let me say this: We are working towards a comprehensive settlement in the area here and the nature of peace is on the agenda between both sides of the two committees, and all that you have mentioned will be discussed in the committees.

[Begin]: May I congratulate you, Mr. Carr, on the poetry you read to us and I think this is a very good vision and when we establish peace all those good things you put into your question will be put into realization.

Q: Mr. President, is the gap on the Palestinians unabridgeable?

[Sadat]: Inasmuch as we shall be continuing in the Cairo conference to discuss whatever points of difference between us, we shall continue. As Prime Minister Begin has said, if need be, we shall meet again. I don't think there is any gap that cannot be bridged between us.

Q: Mr. President, do you agree not only that Egypt holds the key to peace in the Middle East but also that no combination of Arab countries can wage war in the foreseeable future against Israel?

[Sadat]: Well, maybe you have heard my speech. We were sincere in war and we are sincere for peace. Since my visit to Jerusalem last November we have agreed upon the facts that let us sit together like civilized people and discuss whatever problem between us. Let us agree upon the fact that the

October war should be the last war. We did not differ upon this at all. The continuation of our efforts will answer all this.

Q: What about waging war without Egypt?

[Sadat]: Well, we have here, for sure, in the Arab world, in this area here, the key to war and peace, in Egypt here. This is a fact, a historic fact. Well, I can't speak for anyone but I can say this.

Q: Mr. President, can the West Bank Palestinian issue be solved without a role for the P.L.O. [Palestine Liberation Organization]?

[Sadat]: There should be a solution for this problem. We have passed it to the political committee that we have agreed upon in the Cairo conference. For sure, we shall find a solution. Because, as I have said before, the Palestinian question is the crux of the whole problem. Maybe in the future after the political committee works and the discussions start a new situation will develop.

[Begin]: The organization called the P.L.O. is bent on the destruction of Israel. It is written in its charter. They never changed their position. As I stated time and again, from our point of view everything is negotiable except the destruction of Israel. Therefore this organization is no partner to our negotiations.

Now, as I read before I reached Ismailia, the spokesman of this organization threatened the life of President Sadat, speaking about one bullet that may change the course of events. So now we have a situation, after Tripoli, in which such threats are issued both against Israel and Egypt. We want to discuss the problem of the Palestinian Arabs with our Egyptian friends. We want to negotiate with the representatives of the Palestinian Arabs and this we are going to do in the first week of January.

Q: Is there any possibility that other Arab countries will join the conference? Will you keep King Hussein of Jordan informed?

[Sadat]: For sure, I will be informing King Hussein of all the developments that have taken place here in Ismailia and let us hope that others will join yet in the next stage.

Q: In view of the dramatic changes that have taken place, have you, Mr. President, changed your mind about delaying diplomatic relations for future generations?

[Sadat]: As I have said before, the nature of peace is one of the important points that is on the agenda. For the two committees and for the plenary session after that. Let me tell you this: It is now not more than 35 or 40 days since my visit to Jerusalem. Everything has changed. Everything has changed since that visit took place. I quite agree with those who say that the world after the Jerusalem visit is completely different to the world before the visit.

Q: Seven years ago the United States and China started Ping-Pong diplomacy. Will you open the borders to allow sportsmen of both sides, even at this stage, and in that way to allow people to know each other and play together?

[Sadat]: It is not yet ripe. But, for sure, we shall be continuing our discussions in our meetings. As you have heard there will be a committee here and a committee there and gradually we shall be in a position to reach agreement upon all what you are proposing here.

[Begin]: Until the day the President agrees to exchange our sportsmen on both sides, do something to strengthen our football team!

Q: Mr. President, in view of the disagreement on the Palestinians, can an interim accord be reached between Egypt and Israel?

[Sadat]: The differences should be overcome in the committees. It is a fact.

Q: You are not seeking an alternative to peace?

[Sadat]: As I have already stated before the Knesset, this time we are not, either for a disengagement agreement or for a partial agreement, trying to reach some stages and then postponing other steps after that. No. This time we are for peace. Genuine peace. Comprehensive settlement.

[Begin]: May I add...the President and I agreed that there is no alternative to peace.

[Sadat]: Aha, right.

Q: How do you explain the abrupt change from years of enmity and distrust to friendliness and trust?

[Sadat]: It is not abrupt. It must have been in the subconscious of all of us and when I made my step in my calculation, really, I knew my people would agree to it. But I never thought that they will go to this extent. It is a natural feeling and there is no fear at all. There will be no revival of anything that has happened in the past.

Q: Mr. President, Mr. Begin, have you reached the stage where mutual troop reductions in the Sinai are possible?

[Sadat]: Let us hope that in a few weeks we shall be in a position to report.

[Begin]: Yes, yes, we hope so. When peace comes, both countries, all countries, in the Middle East will be able to reduce their military forces and expenditure, which is eating up our sustenance, and rather devote our sources and resources to the liquidation of poverty, development of agriculture and industry. This is our common aim.

Q: I was asking about troop reduction at this stage.

[Begin]: We do hope for the possibility of reducing troops from all sides.

Q: On what moral grounds, Mr. Begin, are you denying the Palestinians, the West Bank and Gaza, their right to self-determination? And you, Mr. President, on what moral grounds can you negotiate about the future of the Palestinians without a single Palestinian representative present?

[Begin]: One correction, my friend, I belong to the Palestinian people, too. Because I am a Palestinian Jew and there are Palestinian Arabs. But, of course, we want to live in human dignity, in liberty, justice and equality of rights. Therefore I brought the President a proposal of self-rule for the first time in the history of the Palestinian Arabs. Now we have established a political committee. We stated our positions clearly and the political committee will continue the discussion of this very serious problem.

[Sadat]: What we are discussing really is within the Arab strategy that was agreed upon in the Arab summit conference. But in the details I shall not negotiate for the Palestinians. So they should take their share. But in this Arab strategy, what I am doing really is that I am not speaking for myself but for this strategy in its principles. But I shall not put myself as a spokesman for them or speak for them. They should join in the next stage.

Q: Is Israel's demand for a military presence in the West Bank a major stumbling block?

[Sadat]: I do not want to reveal what we have already discussed in the proposals that have been made by Prime Minister Begin. He has shown his will to end the military government on the West Bank. But we differ upon the issue, as I have told you, of a Palestinian state on the West Bank and the Gaza Strip. That means self-determination.

[Golan Heights Issue]

Q: Did you discuss the future of the Golan Heights?

[Sadat]: I cannot speak for Syria on the Golan Heights. As I told you now we are concerned with the main principles in the Arab strategy. And whenever we reach agreement upon those points between us in the committees, in the political and military committees, after that everyone should negotiate for himself.

[Begin]: I do want to express the hope that President Assad will join our common effort. We want a comprehensive peace treaty. We want peace with all our neighbors to the south, to the north and to the east, and when President Assad agrees to negotiate with us, we will be willing to negotiate with him. This is a problem of the northern border of Israel and the common border of Israel and Syria.

Q: I am an Egyptian journalist and I want to ask Mr. Begin in his language—

[Begin]: You want to speak to me in Hebrew? I understand Hebrew!

Q: [In Hebrew] Mr. Prime Minister, I want to ask you whether the initiative of President Sadat brought about profound changes in your thinking and outlook and also how you see the future of Israel and the Middle East after peace.

[Begin]: [In Hebrew] First, I want to tell you you speak better Hebrew than I do. [In English, to Mr. Sadat] I want you to know he speaks better Hebrew than I do. Congratulations. No, I want to answer. [In Hebrew] I thank you for your question. I want to say that the visit of President Sadat to Jerusalem was a visit of historic significance, for the whole Israeli people, for the whole Egyptian people, for all the peoples, and we appreciate it. Since the visit we have worked well on a peace plan, and I brought this peace plan before the President and we explained it in detail yesterday in the joint meeting, when we were alone, and when the two delegations met.

The future of Israel after peace is achieved, as in the case of Egypt, I have no doubt, will be glorious. Peace will be achieved between the peoples, the Middle East will develop, and, as His Majesty the King of

Morocco [Hassan II] has said, it can become a sort of paradise on earth. This is the cradle of human civilization and from here came the tidings of peace and progress.

Therefore I was very happy to hear your question and that is my answer. Now I shall translate into English with a Hebrew accent. [Mr. Begin then translated his remarks into English for Mr. Sadat.]

[United States' Role in Talks]

Q: Now that you have raised the level of the talks, how do you see the role of the United States? Will you be inviting Secretary of State Vance to take part in some of your talks and is there a role for the Soviet Union?

[Sadat]: I foresee for the United States and the United Nations a role in the political committee, but the military committee will be bilateral. As for the United States, it will be in the political committee without the Soviet Union. We didn't exclude them. They excluded themselves.

Q: Mr. President, will you call an Arab summit, and will the other parties be invited to the Cairo conference when the level is upgraded?

[Sadat]: Until we reach in the committee agreement on the main issues and mainly the Palestinian issue, on which we have differed, until we reach this point, as it is part of our Arab strategy, I shall not be in a position to ask for an Arab summit meeting. But whenever we reach this, I think that after that I shall be in a position to discuss with my Arab colleagues the possibility of a summit.

Q: Do you feel that Mr. Begin's proposals contain sufficient concessions to have justified your trip to Jerusalem?

[Sadat]: Well, we have agreed on certain points. We have made progress on the withdrawal. We have differed among us on certain points, namely the Palestinian question. These proposals that have been made by Premier Begin will be put before the committee, political or military, and other counterproposals will be submitted to these committees, and until we reach them we think that the momentum that we have given to the peace process is continuing.

[Sinai]

Q: What do you think of Begin's proposals?

[Sadat]: Well, as I have told you, we have points of difference and points of agreement.

Q: Can you be more specific on what progress was made on Sinai? And does this mean foreign ministers exclusively in the Cairo conference?

[Sadat]: I have stated before that in the political committee there will be the foreign ministers, and in the military committee there will be the defense ministers. For the first part that you have asked, I have heard the proposals Premier Begin told us about and we are preparing our counterproposal in the military committee, but really what concerns us in this respect is a comprehensive settlement, this is not the Sinai that is the problem now, because as I told you, after peace, after a genuine peace in the area, regarding Sinai, this is a side issue. And of course, in a comprehensive settlement it will be part of it. And as I told you, I prefer not to reveal anything, and leave the military committee to work on the details and discuss proposals and counterproposals until we reach agreement.

Q: Mr. President, what about the P.L.O.? Don't you feel the Palestinians have the right to choose their representatives? What role do you think the P.L.O. should play in the peace-making process?

[Sadat]: I have stated before the Knesset that the Palestinians should be a part of this settlement because, as I said, the Palestinian question is the core of the whole problem. The P.L.O. is now in the rejection camp. I sent them an invitation, and they refused and excluded themselves. Well, I didn't exclude them. For the future, let us wait for what will develop.

[East Jerusalem]

Q: Mr. President, is it still your position that Israel must withdraw from all occupied land, including East Jerusalem?

[Sadat]: That's right.

Q: When you speak of progress on the question of withdrawal, may I ask Mr. Begin how he interprets that progress?

[Begin]: Well, Resolution 242 doesn't commit Israel to total withdrawal, and therefore this matter is a matter for negotiation, to establish those secure and recognized boundaries which are mentioned in the second paragraph of Resolution 242. And this is the crux of our problem—to negotiate the conditions of peace in order to establish peace throughout the Middle East. This is what we are going to do in the next few weeks and months.

Q: Will Syria eventually join the talks, and what would be the effect?

[Sadat]: I can't answer this. You should ask President Assad. I can't speak for him.... Whenever they...join, we shall welcome them.

Q: Will the Cairo conference reconvene simultaneously with the two ministerial committees? Or alternately?

[Sadat]: It has always been my position that without good preparation, Geneva will be a failure. I said this during my visit last April in the United States. I made my first proposal for a working group under Vance to start contacting all the parties concerned and a meeting to be prepared before Geneva for the preparation. What we are doing here in Cairo is the preparation for Geneva. Geneva is not excluded.

Q: But what about simultaneous meetings of the two committees?

[Sadat]: They will be working in the context of the Cairo conference, and as I said, they will report to the plenary.

Q: Does this mean the Cairo conference will continue on the foreign minister level, that Mr. Vance and Mr. Waldheim will come here?

[Sadat]: Let us hope so. ...[W]e shall not go back. We are going forward.

Q: But the political committee is meeting in Jerusalem. Does this mean that Mr. [Cyrus R.] Vance [U.S. Secretary of State] and Mr. [Kurt] Waldheim [U.N. Secretary General] will also be in Jerusalem?

[Sadat]: Well, we shall leave this to them.

Q: Mr. Begin, do you accept the principle of nonacquisition of territory by force and are you going to apply it to a comprehensive settlement?

[Begin]: Yes, we are for a comprehensive settlement and I accept the principle established under law attesting that there mustn't be any acquisition of territory in the wake of a war of aggression. The war of the six days was a war of legitimate self-defense, and the President told me yesterday, yes, he does remember the slogans issued in those days to throw the Israelis into the sea and so we defended ourselves and this is my reply to you, in complete accordance with international law and practice. Thank you.

ISRAELI PLAN FOR THE WEST BANK

AND GAZA STRIP

[1]

The administration of the military government in Judea, Samaria and the Gaza district will be abolished.

[2]

In Judea, Samaria and the Gaza district, administrative autonomy of the residents, by and for them, will be established.

[3]

The residents of Judea, Samaria and the Gaza district will elect an administrative council composed of 11 members. The administrative council will operate in accordance with the principles laid down in this paper.

[4]

Any resident, 18 years old and above, without distinction of citizenship, or if stateless, is entitled to vote in the elections to the administrative council.

[5]

Any resident whose name is included in the list of candidates for the administrative council and who, on the day the list is submitted, is 25 years old or above, is entitled to be elected to the council.

[6]

The administrative council will be elected by general, direct, personal, equal and secret ballot.

[7]

The period of office of the administrative council will be four years from the day of its election.

[8]

The administrative council will sit in Bethlehem.

[9]

All the administrative affairs relating to the Arab residents of the areas of Judea, Samaria and the Gaza district, will be under the direction and within the competence of the administrative council.

[10]

The administrative council will operate the following departments: education, religious affairs, finance, transportation, construction and housing, industry, commerce and tourism, agriculture, health, labor and social welfare, rehabilitation of refugees and the department for the administration of justice and the supervision of the local police forces, and promulgate regulations relating to the operations of these departments.

[11]

Security and public order in the areas of Judea, Samaria and the Gaza district will be the responsibility of the Israeli authorities.

[12]

The administrative council will elect its own chairman.

[13]

The first session of the administrative council will be convened 30 days after the publication of the elections results.

[14]

Residents of Judea, Samaria and the Gaza district, without distinction of citizenship, or if stateless, will be granted free choice (option) of either Israeli or Jordanian citizenship.

[15]

A resident of the areas of Judea, Samaria and the Gaza district who requests Israeli citizenship will be granted such citizenship in accordance with the citizenship law of the state.

[16]

Residents of Judea, Samaria and the Gaza district who, in accordance with the right of free option, choose Israeli citizenship, will be entitled to vote for, and be elected to the Knesset in accordance with the election law.

[17]

Residents of Judea, Samaria and the Gaza district who are citizens of Jordan or who, in accordance with the right of free option will become citizens of Jordan, will elect and be eligible for election to the Parliament of the Hashemite Kingdom of Jordan in accordance with the election law of that country.

[18]

Questions arising from the vote to the Jordanian Parliament by residents of Judea, Samaria and the Gaza district will be clarified in negotiations between Israel and Jordan.

[19]

A committee will be established of representatives of Israel, Jordan and the administrative council to examine existing legislation in Judea, Samaria and the Gaza district and to determine which legislation will continue in force, which will be abolished and what will be the competence of the administrative council to promulgate regulations. The rulings of the committee will be adopted by unanimous decisions.

[20]

Residents of Israel will be entitled to acquire land and settle in the areas of Judea, Samaria and the Gaza district. Arabs, residents of Judea, Samaria and the Gaza district who, in accordance with the free options granted them, will become Israeli citizens, will be entitled to acquire land and settle in Israel.

[21]

A committee will be established of representatives of Israel, Jordan and the administrative council to determine norms of immigration to the areas of Judea, Samaria and the Gaza district. The committee will determine the norms whereby Arab refugees residing outside Judea, Samaria and the Gaza district will be permitted to immigrate to these areas in reasonable numbers. The ruling of the committee will be adopted by unanimous decision.

[22]

Residents of Israel and residents of Judea, Samaria and the Gaza district will be assured of movement and freedom of economic activity in Israel, Judea, Samaria and the Gaza district.

[23]

The administrative council will appoint one of its members to represent the council before the Government of Israel for deliberation on matters of common interest; and one of its members to represent the council before the Government of Jordan for deliberation on matters of common interest.

[24]

Israel stands by its right and its claim of sovereignty to Judea, Samaria and the Gaza district. In the knowledge that other claims exist, it proposes for the sake of the agreement and the peace, that the question of sovereignty be left open.

[25]

With regard to the administration of the holy places of the three religions in Jerusalem, a special proposal will be drawn up and submitted that will include the guarantee of freedom of access to members of all faiths to the shrines holy to them.

[26]

These principles will be subject to review after a five-year period.

BEGIN STATEMENT ON ISMAILIA TALKS

Ladies and gentlemen, citizens of Israel, if, as I requested, you prayed for our success, your prayers were heard. The meeting at Ismailia between the Egyptian delegation and the Defense Minister [Ezer Weizman], the Foreign Minister [Moshe Dayan] and myself, that meeting was crowned with success.

Yesterday, immediately after our arrival in Ismailia, I held a personal talk with President Sadat, and within a few minutes we agreed to set up two committees, one political, the other military. We thus lent added momentum to the peace-making process in the Middle East. We agreed that the two committees would be chaired by the foreign ministers of the two countries and the defense ministers of the two countries.

We agreed that one committee—the political committee—would sit in Jerusalem, and the military committee in Cairo. That is a just division. We also agreed that the chairmanship of the committees would be on a rotating basis. In Cairo, in the first week of the discussions, General [Mohammed Abdel Ghany el-]Gamasy, whom we respect as a courageous soldier, will lead off, and after a week Defense Minister Ezer Weizman, whom Egypt respects as a courageous soldier, will take over.

In Jerusalem, the political committee will be chaired first by the Foreign Minister, and after a week the new Foreign Minister of Egypt [Butros Ghali] will take over as chairman. By the way, we were present at the swearing-in of the new Foreign Minister.

These committees will start working in mid-January, probably on Jan. 14 or 15. We have set no date for the conclusion of their work, but it may be expected that they will work for between two and three months. We hope they will bring us an agreement. If there is an agreement it will serve as the basis for the peace treaties.

[Palestinian Issue]

There was a proposal that we issue a joint declaration, and we discussed that proposal. Many things were agreed upon, but what was not agreed upon, as regards content and formulations, had to do with the Palestinian Arabs. An Egyptian formulation, which we could not accept, was presented to us, and we put forth our own formulation, and the Egyptians could not accept it.

For several hours we discussed how to find a joint formulation, and last night between 10 and 10:30 P.M., we had not yet attained the agreed and joint formulation. We therefore decided to put off the session until this morning, out of the assumption that, after the night, following further thought, we would...find a formulation acceptable to both sides.

[Fundamental Differences]

But it emerged that the differences of opinion on this matter are fundamental, as everyone knows. The Egyptians propose establishing a

Palestinian state in Judea, Samaria and Gaza. We unreservedly reject such a proposal, and not just us. The United States of America also unreservedly rejects the idea of establishing a Palestinian state in Judea, Samaria and Gaza, and other factors also reject its establishment. And the Egyptians did not accept our proposal that the solution be found in self-rule, or, in its Hebrew, actually Greek version, administrative autonomy.

Well, when you don't find a joint formulation, you must look for the accepted path, on the basis of the precedents in the international conferences, to wit: each side will determine its stand, according to its content and its own terminology.

And following consultation by the Israeli delegation, we agreed that we would present such a formulation to President Sadat, and he accepted it without hesitation, on the spot. Thus did we overcome that point past which it was, ostensibly, impossible to move, and we proposed the following formulation, which expressed the stands of the two sides:

"The Egyptian and the Israeli delegations discussed the Palestinian problem. The Egyptian position is that in the West Bank and in the Gaza Strip a Palestinian state should be established. The Israeli position is that the Palestinian Arabs residing in Judea, Samaria and the Gaza district should enjoy self-rule, and this issue will be discussed in the political committee."

At the press conference, which you no doubt watched, President Sadat read out both parts and both formulations of this statement, as they were accepted.

We may now sum up that the momentum is continuing. In another three weeks or so, serious negotiations will open in two working committees, one in Cairo and one in Jerusalem, at ministerial level, and these committees will submit their conclusions and their recommendations. Hence I was able to say, at the press conference in Ismailia, "I have come a hopeful Prime Minister and I am leaving a happy man." There is a basis for this feeling.

Ladies and gentlemen, only a few months ago this entire development would have seemed to me utterly fantastic: the meeting in Jerusalem and in Ismailia between President Sadat and myself, between the foreign ministers, between the defense ministers, in a very friendly, warm atmosphere, of hospitality, of understanding, with mutual assurance that we would continue to see each other and together seek a way to establish peace.

Of course there are differences, no one will ignore them. But the mutual desire is to overcome them, bridge them, and reach peace. And there is indeed good hope that, God willing, we shall attain that peace quickly and those are the tidings I bring from the meeting in Ismailia with President Sadat.

NATIONAL WOMEN'S CONFERENCE
November 19-21, 1977

Attended by all the hoopla of a political convention, delegates to the National Women's Conference endorsed a 25-point program calling for equal treatment and an end to sex discrimination in the economic, social, cultural and political arenas. It was the first national meeting of women since 1848 when suffragists gathered in Seneca Falls, N.Y., to push for voting rights for women.

Nearly 2,000 women, including 1,442 voting delegates, convened in Houston, Texas, Nov. 19-21. During the conference, delegates ratified resolutions urging federal, state and local governments, private business and labor unions to provide equal opportunities for women in education, employment and health care; to give special attention to the economic and social problems encountered by older, disabled, rural and minority women; to involve women fully in international affairs; and to encourage women to seek elective and appointive office.

The most controversial planks were those endorsing adoption of the Equal Rights Amendment (ERA), civil rights and child custody for lesbians, abortion and federally-funded child care. Despite protests by opponents that these planks were being railroaded through the conference, the resolutions were passed with relative ease. Only one resolution put before the conference was rejected. It urged creation of a Cabinet-level Women's Department. The delegates, however, did approve a resolution calling for a second conference to assess progress toward reaching the recommendations made in Houston.

Conference Mandate

The conference, organized by the National Commission on the Observance of International Women's Year, had been mandated by a 1975 federal law (PL 94-167). The conference's goal was to "identify the barriers that prevent women from participating fully and equally in all aspects of national life and develop recommendations for means by which such barriers can be removed." A total of $5-million had been authorized to fund state and territorial meetings to select delegates and to pay for the travel and lodging expenses of the national conferees. Delegates to the state meetings also had adopted positions on pending issues which had then been distilled into a "National Plan of Action" by the 46 presidentially-appointed national commissioners, headed by former U.S. Rep. Bella S. Abzug (D N.Y. 1971-77). The plan was placed before the national conference for ratification. (Historic Documents of 1975, p. 507)

The approved resolutions and report on the conference were to be submitted to President Carter and Congress by March 1, 1978. Carter then was to have 120 days to submit his own legislative recommendations to Congress.

While Carter had not revealed what his recommendations might be, his wife, Rosalynn, told the Nov. 19 opening session that the President's "concern about the outcome of your agenda is deep." Joined by former first ladies Betty Ford and Lady Bird Johnson and several other prominent women, Mrs. Carter said she was "proud to be a part of the National Women's Conference. Never before in our history has there been such a women's meeting—in numbers, in preparation, in diversity, in long-range effect. The breadth of opinion, ethnic groups, income and occupation represented here is remarkably reflective of our whole country."

Controversial Resolutions

Endorsement of the Equal Rights Amendment was considered one of the most significant developments of the conference, and supporters hoped it would give the drive for ratification of the proposed constitutional amendment new momentum. ERA advocates found at the end of 1977 that their ratification drive was stalled at 35 states—three short of the number needed for ratification. But a move was underway in Congress to extend the ratification deadline from March 1979 to 1986. Phyllis Schlafly, leader of the anti-ERA forces, called that extension effort "an act of desperation" and said she would fight it through lobbying and in court.

The conference also put itself on record in favor of federally-funded abortions. Earlier in the year, pro-abortion groups suffered a setback on this issue when the Supreme Court ruled that states and local governments did not have to spend public funds for abortions of an elective or nontherapeutic nature. Only two weeks after the women's conference con-

cluded, Congress Dec. 7 approved language that prohibited the payment of Medicaid to low-income women for abortions unless continued pregnancy would endanger the life of the mother or cause her "severe and long-lasting physical health damage." (Supreme Court on abortion, p. 407)

As expected, about 300 delegates actively opposed adoption of various resolutions including the ERA and abortion resolutions. They were supported outside the convention hall by a Nov. 19 counter-rally organized by Schlafly to demonstrate support for the traditional roles of women. "The American people do not want the ERA. And they do not want government-funded abortion, lesbian privileges or the federal government to set up institutions for universal child care," Schlafly told an estimated 10,000 people.

Long-Term Effect

While the dissenting delegates were unsuccessful in blocking adoption of the controversial resolutions, it remained to be seen what long-term effect the conference would have on women's rights. According to several surveys, Americans as a whole remained deeply divided over the role of women in society. In 1976 more than 56 per cent of American women aged 20 to 64 worked outside the home. Yet one national survey conducted that year found that the overwhelming majority of American parents—including three-fourths of the working mothers interviewed—believed that women with small children should not work unless the additional income was really needed. Nearly 70 per cent of the parents said that children were better off when their mothers did not work.

The public's ambivalence about the women's movement was evident in the results of an April 1977 Harris Poll. On the one hand, the poll showed that between 1970 and 1977 the number of Americans favoring "efforts to strengthen and change women's status in society today" grew from 42 to 64 per cent. On the other hand, the poll showed a sharp drop in the proportion of those favoring passage of the ERA. Between 1976 and 1977 the number of Americans favoring the amendment dropped from 65 to 56 per cent.

Following are excerpts from the resolutions approved by the National Women's Conference Nov. 19-21 in Houston, Texas:

...The President and Congress should declare the elimination of violence in the home to be a national goal. To help achieve this, Congress should establish a national clearinghouse for information and technical and financial assistance to locally controlled public and private nonprofit organizations providing emergency shelter and other support services for battered women and their children....

Business

The President should issue an Executive Order establishing as national policy:

● The full integration of women entrepreneurs in government-wide business-related and procurement activities, including a directive to all government agencies to assess the impact of these activities on women business owners.

● The development of outreach and action programs to bring about the full integration of women entrepreneurs into business-related government activities and procurement.

● The development of evaluation and monitoring programs to assess progress periodically and to develop new programs....

Child Care

The Federal government should assume a major role in directing and providing comprehensive, voluntary, flexible hour, bias-free, non-sexist, quality child care and developmental programs, including child care facilities for Federal employees, and should request and support adequate legislation and funding for these programs.

Federally funded child care and developmental programs should have low-cost, ability-to-pay fee schedules that make these services accessible to all who need them, regardless of income....

Employment

The President and Congress should support a policy of full employment so that all women who are able and willing to work may do so.

...The Equal Employment Opportunity Commission should receive the necessary funding and staff to process complaints and to carry out its duties speedily and effectively....

...Federal laws prohibiting discrimination in employment should be extended to include the legislative branch of the Federal government....

...Title VII of the 1964 Civil Rights Act should be amended to prohibit discrimination on the basis of pregnancy, childbirth or related medical conditions....

...Federal and State governments should promote Flexitime jobs, and pro-rated benefits should be provided for part-time workers....

Equal Rights Amendment

The Equal Rights Amendment should be ratified....

Homemakers

The Federal Government and State legislatures should base their laws relating to marital property, inheritance, and domestic relations on the principle that marriage is a partnership in which the contribution of each spouse is of equal importance and value.

The President and Congress should support a practical plan of covering homemakers in their own right under Social Security and facilitate its enactment....

...Loss of pension rights because of divorce should be considered in property divisions....

Minority Women

Minority women share with all women the experience of sexism as a barrier to their full rights of citizenship....

But institutionalized bias based on race, language, culture and/or ethnic origin or governance of territories or localities have led to the additional oppression and exclusion of minority women and to the conditions of poverty from which they disproportionately suffer....

Legislation, the enforcement of existing laws and all levels of government action should be directed especially toward such problem areas as involuntary sterilization; monolingual education and services; high infant and maternal mortality rates; bias toward minority women's children; confinement to low level jobs; confinement to poor, ghettoized housing; culturally biased educational, psychological and employment testing (for instance, civil service); failure to enforce affirmative action and special admission programs; combined sex and race bias in insurance; and failure to gather statistical data based on both sex and race so that the needs and conditions of minority women may be accurately understood....

Rape

Federal, State and local governments should revise their criminal codes and case law dealing with rape and related offenses to provide for graduated degrees of the crime with graduated penalties depending on the amount of force or coercion occurring with the activity; to apply to assult by or upon both sexes, including spouses as victims; to include all types of sexual assault against adults, including oral and anal contact and use of objects; to enlarge beyond traditional common law concepts the circumstances under which the act will be considered to have occurred without the victim's consent; to specify that the past sexual conduct of the victim cannot be introduced into evidence; to require no more corroborative evidence than is required in the prosecution of any other type of violent assault, and to prohibit the Hale instruction where it has been required by law or is customary....

Reproductive Freedom

We support the U.S. Supreme Court decisions which guarantee reproductive freedom to women.

We urge all branches of Federal, State and local governments to give the highest priority to complying with these Supreme Court decisions and to making available all methods of family planning to women unable to take advantage of private facilities.

We oppose the exclusion of abortion or childbirth and pregnancy-related care from Federal, State or local funding of medical services or from privately financed medical services....

We oppose involuntary sterilization and urge strict compliance by all doctors, medical and family planning facilities with the Dept. of Health, Education and Welfare's minimum April 1974 regulations requiring that consent to sterilization be truly voluntary, informed and competent. Spousal consent should not be a requirement upon which sterilization procedures are contingent....

Sexual Preference

Congress, State, and local legislatures should enact legislation to eliminate discrimination on the basis of sexual and affectional preference in areas including, but not limited to, employment, housing, public accommodations, credit, public facilities, government funding, and the military.

State legislatures should reform their penal codes or repeal State laws that restrict private sexual behavior between consenting adults.

State legislatures should enact legislation that would prohibit consideration of sexual or affectional orientation as a factor in any judicial determination of child custody or visitation rights. Rather, child custody cases should be evaluated solely on the merits of which party is the better parent, without regard to that person's sexual and affectional orientation....

Women, Welfare and Poverty

The Federal and State governments should assume a role in focusing on welfare and poverty as major women's issues. All welfare reform proposals should be examined specifically for their impact on women. Inequality of opportunity for women must be recognized as a primary factor contributing to the growth of welfare roles....

...Along with major improvements in the welfare system, elimination of poverty for women must include improvements in social security and retirement systems, universal minimum wage, nontraditional job opportunities, quality child care, comprehensive health insurance, and comprehensive legal services. A concerted effort must be made to educate the public about the realities of welfare, the plight of the blind, the aged, the disabled, single-parent families and other low income women....

We oppose the Carter Administration proposal for welfare reform (HR 9030), which among other things eliminates food stamps, CETA training and CETA jobs paying more than minimum wage, adequate day care and introduces "workfare" where welfare mothers would be forced to "work off" their grants which is work without wage, without fringe benefits or bargaining rights, and without dignity. HR 9030 further requires those individuals and families without income to wait weeks or even months before even the inadequate grant is available. We strongly support a welfare reform program developed from on-going consultation with persons who will be impacted. This program should be consistent with the National Academy of Science[s'] recommendations that no individual or family living standard should be lower than half the median family level (after taxes); should not fall below the government defined poverty level of family income even for shorter periods; that help sustain the family unit; and that women on welfare and other low income women who choose to work not be forced into jobs paying less than the prevailing wage....

December

COURT ON SENIORITY RIGHTS AFTER MATERNITY LEAVE
December 6, 1977

The Supreme Court ruled Dec. 6 that an employer could not deprive an employee of accumulated seniority because she took uncompensated maternity leave. The court, however, reaffirmed a 1976 ruling that employers were not required to provide pregnancy or childbirth sick leave benefits in their company health plans.

The case involved Nora Satty, an employee of the Nashville Gas Company, who took uncompensated maternity leave. Company policy stipulated that pregnancy leave was not paid for as a sickness or disability. When Satty returned to work she found that she had lost three and one-half years' seniority and her regular position. She was placed in a temporary position at a pay rate $10 below her previous pay scale. She applied for three permanent positions with the company during the time of her temporary employment, and each time the position went to a woman who had come to work for the company after she had. Nashville Gas fired Satty after the temporary work project ended.

Two lower courts held that both the denial of sick pay and the divestiture of seniority violated Title VII of the 1964 Civil Rights Act. The company appealed. (Nashville Gas Co. v. Satty)

Writing for the court Justice William H. Rehnquist said an employer could deny pregnancy benefits but could not "burden female employees in such a way as to deprive them of employment opportunities because of their different roles." The company's policy violated Title VII of the 1964 Civil Rights Act, Rehnquist said, because the policy discriminated against female workers, leaving them "permanently disadvantaged as compared to

HISTORIC DOCUMENTS OF 1977   DECEMBER

the rest of the work force." He observed that employees who lost their seniority rights were condemned to "less desirable and lower paying jobs." The employer "has not merely refused to extend to women a benefit that men cannot and do not receive but has imposed on women a substantial burden that men need not suffer," Rehnquist wrote.

Justice John Paul Stevens, in a separate concurring opinion, said that the legal distinction between permissible discrimination and impermissible discrimination against pregnant or formerly pregnant employees had caused "some confusion." A dissenter in the 1976 decision upholding the General Electric Company's refusal to provide sick pay to women workers absent due to pregnancy and childbirth (General Electric v. Gilbert), Stevens said that in that case the court upheld a disability plan that "did not attach any consequences to the condition of pregnancy that extended beyond the period of maternity leave." In the Nashville Gas Company *opinion, the court invalidated a plan because it had "an adverse impact on the employee's status after pregnancy leave...terminated" and left the female worker "permanently disadvantaged as compared to the rest of the work force," Stevens said. (Historic Documents of 1976, p. 891)*

The court sent the case back to the lower court for consideration in light of Gilbert. *In a concurring opinion Justices Lewis F. Powell Jr., William J. Brennan Jr., and Thurgood Marshall suggested that the lower court might find that the combination of the seniority and sick pay policies did violate Title VII by resulting in less net compensation for women than for men. Marshall said the sick pay issue required further factual development and argued that Rehnquist's opinion had "constricted unnecessarily the scope of the inquiry on remand."*

In a related decision Dec. 6, the court nullified and sent back to the lower court a ruling that the Richmond, Calif., school board had violated the civil rights law by refusing to pay sick leave benefits to employees disabled by pregnancy and childbirth.

In September 1977, the U.S. Senate voted 75-11 to require employers to include pregnancy benefits in any disability plans they offered. A House Education and Labor subcommittee held hearings on a bill with a similar requirement but no further action was taken in 1977.

> *Following are excerpts from the Supreme Court's Dec. 6,*
> *1977, ruling restoring seniority rights to female employees*
> *who return to work after pregnancy and childbirth leave:*

No. 75-536

Nashville Gas Company, Petitioner, *v.* Nora D. Satty.	On Writ of Certiorari to the United States Court of Appeals for the Sixth Circuit.

[December 6, 1977]

MR. JUSTICE REHNQUIST delivered the opinion of the Court.

Petitioner requires pregnant employees to take a formal leave of absence. The employee does not receive sick pay while on pregnancy leave. She also loses all accumulated job seniority; as a result, while petitioner attempts to provide the employee with temporary work upon her return, she will be employed in a permanent job position only if no employee presently working for petitioner also applies for the position. The United States District Court for the Middle District of Tennessee held that these policies violate Title VII of the Civil Rights Act of 1965.... The Court of Appeals for the Sixth Circuit affirmed. ...(1975). We granted certiorari to decide, in light of our opinion last Term in *General Electric Co.* v. *Gilbert*...(1976), whether the lower courts properly applied Title VII to petitioner's policies respecting pregnancy.

Two separate policies are at issue in this case. The first is petitioner's practice of giving sick pay to employees disabled by reason of nonoccupational sickness or injury but not to those disabled by pregnancy. The second is petitioner's practice of denying accumulated seniority to female employees returning to work following disability caused by childbirth. We shall discuss them in reverse order.

I

Petitioner requires an employee who is about to give birth to take a pregnancy leave of indeterminate length. Such an employee does not accumulate seniority while absent, but instead actually loses any job seniority accrued before the leave commenced. Petitioner will not hold the employee's job open for her awaiting her return from pregnancy leave. An employee who wishes to return to work from such leave will be placed in any open position for which she is qualified and for which no individual currently employed is bidding; before such time as a permanent position becomes available, the company attempts to find temporary work for the employee. If and when the employee acquires a permanent position, she regains previous accumulated seniority for purposes of pension, vacation, and the like, but does not regain it for the purpose of bidding on future job openings.

Respondent began work for petitioner on March 24, 1969, as a clerk in its Customer Accounting Department. She commenced maternity leave on December 29, 1972, and gave birth to her child on January 23, 1973. Seven weeks later she sought re-employment with petitioner. The position that she had previously held had been eliminated as a result of bona fide cutbacks in her department. Temporary employment was found for her at a lower salary than she had earned prior to taking leave. While holding this temporary employment, respondent unsuccessfully applied for three permanent positions with petitioner. Each position was awarded to another employee who had begun to work for petitioner before respondent had returned from leave; if respondent had been credited with the seniority that she had accumulated prior to leave, she would have been awarded each of the positions for which she applied. After the temporary assignment was completed, respondent requested, "due to lack of work and job openings," that petitioner change her status from maternity leave to termination in order that she could draw unemployment compensation.

We conclude that petitioner's policy of denying accumulated seniority to female employees returning from pregnancy leave violates of Title VII.... That section declares it to be an unlawful employment practice for an employer to:

> "limit, segregate, or classify his employees or applicants for employment in any way which would deprive or tend to deprive any individual of employment opportunities or otherwise adversely affect his status as an employee because of such individual's...sex...."

On its face, petitioner's seniority policy appears to be neutral in its treatment of male and female employees. If an employee is forced to take a leave of absence from his job because of disease or any disability other than pregnancy, the employee, whether male or female, retains accumulated seniority and, indeed, continues to acrue seniority while on leave. If the employee takes a leave of absence for any other reason, including pregnancy, accumulated seniority is divested. Petitioner's decision not to treat pregnancy as a disease or disability for purposes of seniority retention is not on its face a discriminatory policy. "Pregnancy is, of course, confined to women, but it is in other ways significantly different from the typical covered disease or disability." *Gilbert....*

We have recognized, however, that both intentional discrimination and policies neutral on their face but having a discriminatory effect may run afoul of § 703 (a)(2). *Griggs* v. *Duke Power Co....*(1971). It is beyond dispute that petitioner's policy of depriving employees returning from pregnancy leave of their accumulated seniority acts both to deprive them "of employment opportunities" and to "adversely affect [their] status as an employee." It is apparent from the previous recitation of the events which occurred following respondent's return from pregnancy leave that petitioner's policy denied her specific employment opportunities that she otherwise would have obtained. Even if she had ultimately been able to regain a permanent position with petitioner, she would have felt the effects of a lower seniority level, with its attendant relegation to less desirable and lower paying jobs, for the remainder of her career with petitioner.

In *Gilbert...*there was no showing that General Electric's policy of compensating for all nonjob-related disabilities except pregnancy favored men over women. No evidence was produced to suggest that men received more benefits from General Electric's disability insurance fund than did women; both men and women were subject generally to the disabilities covered and presumably drew similar amounts from the insurance fund. We therefore upheld the plan under Title VII.

> "As there is no proof that the package is in fact worth more to men than to women, it is impossible to find any gender-based discriminatory effect in this scheme simply because women disabled as a result of pregnancy do not receive benefits; that is to say, gender-based discrimination does not result simply because an employer's disability benefits plan is less than all-inclusive. For all that appears, pregnancy-related disabilities constitute an *additional* risk, unique to women, and the failure to compensate them for this risk does not destroy the presumed parity of the benefits, accruing to men and women alike, which results from the facially evenhanded *inclusion* of risks."...

Here, by comparison, petitioner has not merely refused to extend to women a benefit that men cannot and do not receive, but has imposed on women a substantial burden that men need not suffer. The distinction between benefits and burdens is more than one of semantics. We held in *Gilbert* that § 703 (a)(1) did not require that greater economic benefits be paid to one sex or the other "because of their different roles in the scheme of existence." *Gilbert*.... But that holding does not allow us to read § 703 (a)(2) to permit an employer to burden female employees in such a way as to deprive them of employment opportunities because of their different role.

Recognition that petitioner's facially neutral seniority system does deprive women of employment opportunities because of their sex does not end the inquiry under § 703 (a)(2) of Title VII. If a company's business necessitates the adoption of particular leave policies, Title VII does not prohibit the company from applying these policies to all leaves of absence, including pregnancy leaves; Title VII is not violated even though the policies may burden female employees. *Griggs...Dothard* v. *Rawlinson*...(1977). But we agree with the District Court in this case that since there was no proof of any business necessity adduced with respect to the policies in question, that court was entitled to "assume no justification exists."...

II

On the basis of the evidence presented to the District Court, petitioner's policy of not awarding sick-leave pay to pregnant employees is legally indistinguishable from the disability insurance program upheld in *Gilbert*.... As in *Gilbert,* petitioner compensates employees for limited periods of time during which the employee must miss work because of a non-job related illness or disability. As in *Gilbert,* the compensation is not extended to pregnancy-related absences. We emphasized in *Gilbert* that exclusions of this kind are not *per se* violations of Title VII: "an exclusion of pregnancy from a disability-benefits plan providing general coverage is not a gender-based discrimination at all.''... Only if a plaintiff through the presentation of other evidence can demonstrate that exclusion of pregnancy from the compensated conditions is a mere "[pretext] designed to effect an invidious discrimination against the members of one sex or the other'' does Title VII apply....

In *Gilbert,* evidence had been introduced indicating that women drew substantially greater sums than did men from *General Electric's* disability insurance program, even though it excluded pregnancy.... But our holding did not depend on this evidence. The District Court in *Gilbert* expressly declined to find "that the present actuarial value of the coverage was equal as between men and women." We upheld the disability program on the ground "that neither [was] there a finding, nor was there any evidence which would support a finding, that the financial benefits of the Plan 'worked to discriminate against any definable group or class in terms of the aggregate risk protection derived by that group or class from the program.' ''... When confronted by a facially neutral plan, whose only fault is underinclusiveness, the burden is on the plaintiff to show that the plan discriminates on the basis of sex in violation of Title VII. *Albemarle Paper Co.* v. *Moody...*(1975); *McDonnell Douglas Corp.* v. *Green...*(1973).

We again need not decide whether, when confronted by a facially neutral plan, it is necessary to prove intent to establish a prima facie violation of § 703 (a)(1). *McDonnell Douglas Corp....*(1973). *Griggs...* held that a violation of § 703 (a)(2) can be established by proof of a discriminatory effect. But it is difficult to perceive how exclusion of pregnancy from a disability insurance plan or sick leave compensation program "deprives an individual of employment opportunities" or "otherwise adversely affects his status as an employee" in violation of § 703 (a)(2). The direct effect of the exclusion is merely a loss of income for the period the employee is not at work; such an exclusion has no direct effect upon either employment opportunities or job status. Plaintiff's attack in *Gilbert...*was brought under § 703 (a)(1), which would appear to be the proper section of Title VII under which to analyze questions of sick leave or disability payments.

Respondent failed to prove even a discriminatory effect with respect to petitioner's sick-leave plan. She candidly concedes in her brief before this Court that "petitioner's Sick Leave benefit plan is, in and of itself, for all intents and purposes, the same as the Weekly Sickness and Accident Insurance Plan examined in *Gilbert*" and that "if the exclusion of sick pay was the only manner in which respondent had been treated differently by petitioner, *Gilbert* would control." Respondent, however, contends that because petitioner has violated Title VII by its policy respecting seniority following return from pregnancy leave, the sick-leave pay differentiation must also fall.

But this conclusion by no means follows from the premise. Respondent herself abandoned attacks on other aspects of petitioner's employment policies following rulings adverse to her by the District Court, a position scarcely consistent with her present one. We of course recognized in both *Geduldig* v. *Aiello...*(1974), and in *Gilbert...*that the facial neutrality of an employee benefit plan would not end analysis if it could be shown "that distinctions involving pregnancy are mere pretexts designed to effect an invidious discrimination against the members of one sex or the other...." *Gilbert....* Petitioner's refusal to allow pregnant employees to retain their accumulated seniority may be deemed relevant by the trier of fact in deciding whether petitioner's sick-leave plan was such a pretext. But it most certainly does not require such a finding by a trier of fact, to say nothing of the making of such a finding as an original matter by this Court.

The District Court sitting as a trier of fact made no such finding in this case, and we are not advised whether it was requested to or not. The decision of the Court of Appeals was not based on any such finding, but instead embodied generally the same line of reasoning as the Court of Appeals for the Fourth Circuit followed in its opinion in *General Electric Co.* v. *Gilbert...* (1975). Since we rejected that line of reasoning in our opinion in *Gilbert...*, the judgment of the Court of Appeals with respect to petitioner's sick pay policies must be vacated. That court and the District Court are in a better position than we are to know whether respondent adequately preserved in those courts the right to proceed further in the District Court on the theory which we have just described.

Affirmed in part, vacated in part, and remanded.

MR. JUSTICE POWELL, with whom MR. JUSTICE BRENNAN and MR. JUSTICE MARSHALL join, concurring in the result and concurring in part.

I join Part I of the opinion of the Court affirming the decision of the Court of Appeals that petitioner's policy denying accumulated seniority for job-bidding purposes to female employees returning from pregnancy leave violates Title VII.

I also concur in the result in Part II, for the legal status under Title VII of petitioner's policy of denying accumulated sick-pay benefits to female employees while on pregnancy leave requires further factual development in light of *General Electric Co.* v. *Gilbert...*(1976). I write separately, however, because the Court appears to have constricted unnecessarily the scope of inquiry on remand by holding prematurely that respondent has failed to meet her burden of establishing a prima facie case that petitioner's sick-leave policy is discriminatory under Title VII. This case was tried in the District Court and reviewed in the Court of Appeals before our decision in *Gilbert.* The appellate court upheld her claim in accord with the then uniform view of the courts of appeals that any disability plan that treated pregnancy differently from other disabilities was *per se* violative of Title VII. Since respondent had no reason to make the showing of gender-based discrimination required by *Gilbert,* I would follow our usual practice of vacating the judgment below and remanding to permit the lower court to reconsider its sick-leave ruling in light of our intervening decision.

The issue is not simply one of burden of proof, which properly rests with the Title VII plaintiff, *Albemarle Paper Co.* v. *Moody*...(1975); *McDonnell Douglas Corp.* v. *Green*...(1973), but of a "full opportunity for presentation of the relevant facts," *Harris* v. *Nelson*...(1969). Given the meandering course that Title VII adjudication has taken, final resolution of a lawsuit in this Court often has not been possible because the parties or the lower courts proceeded on what was ultimately an erroneous theory of the case. Where the mistaken theory is premised on the pre-existing understanding of the law, and where the record as constituted does not foreclose the arguments made necessary by our ruling, I would prefer to remand the controversy and permit the lower courts to pass on the new contentions in light of whatever additional evidence is deemed necessary.

For example, in *Albemarle Paper Co.* v. *Moody*...the Court approved the Court of Appeals' conclusion that the employer had not proved the job relatedness of its testing program, but declined to permit immediate issuance of an injunction against all use of testing in the plant. The Court thought that a remand to the District Court was indicated in part because "[t]he appropriate standard of proof for job relatedness has not been clarified until today," and the plaintiffs "have not until today been specifically apprised of their opportunity to present evidence that even validated tests might be a 'pretext' for discrimination in light of alternative selection procedures available to the Company."

Similarly, in *International Bhd. of Teamsters* v. *United States*...(1977), we found a remand for further factual development appropriate because the Government had employed an erroneous evidentiary approach that precluded satisfaction of its burden of identifying which nonapplicant employees were victims of the employer's unlawful discrimination and thus entitled to a retroactive seniority award. "While it may be true that many of the nonapplicant employees desired and would have applied for line-driver jobs but for their knowledge of the company's policy of discrimination, the Government must carry its burden of proof, with respect to each specific individual, at the remedial hearings to be conducted by the District Court on remand."...*Brown* v. *Illinois*...(1975) (Powell, Jr., concurring in part).

Here, respondent has abandoned the theory that enabled her to prevail in the District Court and the Court of Appeals. Instead, she urges that her case is distinguishable from *Gilbert:*

> "Respondent submits that because the exclusion of sick pay is only one of the many ways in which female employees who experience pregnancy are treated differently by petitioner, the holding in *Gilbert* is not controlling. Upon examination of the overall manner in which female employees who experience pregnancy are treated by petitioner, it becomes plain that petitioner's policies are much more pervasive than the mere under-inclusiveness of the Sickness and Accident Insurance Plan in *Gilbert.*"...

At least two distinguishing characteristics are identified by respondent. First, as found by the District Court, only pregnant women are required to take a leave of absence and are denied sick-leave benefits while in all other cases of nonoccupational disability sick-leave benefits are available.... Second, the sick-leave policy is necessarily related to petitioner's discriminatory denial of job-bidding seniority to pregnant women on mandatory maternity leave, presumably because both policies flow from the premise that a female employee is no longer in active service when she becomes pregnant.

Although respondent's theory is not fully articulated, she presents a plausible contention, one not required to have been raised until *Gilbert* and not foreclosed by the stipulated evidence of record, see *Gilbert*, ...or the concurrent findings of the lower courts, see *Village of Arlington Heights* v. *Metropolitan Housing Development Corp*....(1977). It is not inconceivable that on remand respondent will be able to show that the combined operation of petitioner's mandatory maternity leave policy and denial of accumulated sick-pay benefits yielded significantly less net compensation for petitioner's female employees than for the class of male employees. A number of the former, but not the latter, endured forced absence from work without sick pay or other compensation. The parties stipulated that between July 2, 1965, and August 27, 1974, petitioner had placed 12 employees on pregnancy leave, and that some of these employees were on leave for periods of two months or more.... It is possible that these women had not exhausted their sick-pay benefits at the time they were compelled to take a maternity leave, and that the denial of sick pay for this period of absence resulted in a relative loss of net compensation for petitioner's female workforce. Petitioner's male employees, on the other hand, are not subject to a mandatory leave policy, and are eligible to receive compensation in some form for any period of absence from work due to sickness or disability.

In short, I would not foreclose the possibility that the facts as developed on remand will support a finding that "the package is in fact worth more to men than to women." *Gilbert*.... If such a finding were made, I would view respondent's case as not barred by *Gilbert*. In that case, the Court related: "[t]he District Court noted the evidence introduced at trial, a good deal of it stipulated, concerning the relative cost to General Electric of providing benefits under the Plan to male and female employees, all of which indicated that, with pregnancy-related disabilities excluded, the cost to the plan was at least as high, if not substantially higher, than the cost per male employee."... The District Court also "found that the inclusion of pregnancy-related disabilities within the scope of Plan would "increase G. E.'s (disability benefits plan) costs by an amount which, though large, is at this time undeterminable.'... While the District Court declined to make an explicit finding that the actuarial value of the coverage was equal between men and women, it may have been referring simply to the quantum and specificity of proof necessary to establish a "business necessity" defense....(ED Va. 1974). In any event, in *Gilbert* this Court viewed the evidence of record as precluding a prima facie showing of discrimination in "compensation" contrary to § 703 (a)(1). "Whatever the ultimate probative value of the evidence introduced before the District Court on this subject...at the very least it tended to illustrate that the selection of risks covered by the Plan did not operate, in fact, to discriminate against women."... As the record had developed in *Gilbert,* there was no basis for a remand.

I di not view the record in this case as precluding a finding of discrimination in compensation within the principles enunciated in *Gilbert.* I would simply remand the sick-pay issue for further proceedings in light of our decision in that case.

MR. JUSTICE STEVENS, concurring in the judgment.

Petitioner enforces two policies that treat pregnant employees less favorably than other employees who incur a temporary disability. First, they are denied seniority benefits during their absence from work and thereafter; second, they are denied sick pay during their absence. The Court holds that the former policy is unlawful whereas the latter is lawful. I concur in the Court's judgment, but because I believe that its explanation of the legal distinction between the two policies may engender some confusion among those who must make compliance decisions on a day-to-day basis, I advance a separate, and rather pragmatic, basis for reconciling the two parts of the decision with each other and with *General Electric Co.* v. *Gilbert....*

The general problem is to decide when a company policy which attaches a special burden to the risk of absenteeism caused by pregnancy is a prima facie violation of the statutory prohibition against sex discrimination. The answer "always," which I had thought quite plainly correct, is foreclosed by the Court's holding in *Gilbert.* The answer "never" would seem to be dictated by the Court's view that a discrimination against pregnancy is "not a gender-based discrimination at all." The Court has, however, made it clear that the correct answer is "sometimes." Even though a plan which frankly and unambiguously discriminates against pregnancy is "facially neutral," the Court will find it unlawful if it has a "discriminatory effect." The question, then, is how to identify this discriminatory effect.

Two possible answers are suggested by the Court. The Court seems to rely on (a) the difference between a benefit and a burden, and (b) the difference between § 703 (a)(2) and § 703 (a)(1). In my judgment, both of these differences are illusory. I agree with the Court that the effect of the respondent's seniority plan is significantly different from that of the General Electric disability plan in *Gilbert,* but I suggest that the difference may be described in this way: although the *Gilbert* Court was unwilling to hold that discrimination against pregnancy—as compared with other physical disabilities—is discrimination on account of sex, it may nevertheless be true that discrimination against pregnant or formerly pregnant employees—as compared with other employees—does constitute sex discrimination. This distinction may be pragmatically expressed in terms of whether the employer has a policy which adversely affects a woman beyond the term of her pregnancy leave.

Although the opinion in *Gilbert* characterizes as "facially neutral" a company policy which differentiates between an absence caused by pregnancy and an absence caused by illness, the factual context of *Gilbert* limits the reach of that broad characterization. Under the Court's reasoning, the disability plan in *Gilbert* did not discriminate against pregnant employees or formerly pregnant employees while they were working for the company. If an employee, whether pregnant or non-pregnant, contracted the measles, he or she would receive disability benefits; moreover, an employee returning from maternity leave would also receive those benefits. On the other hand, pregnancy, or an illness occurring while absent on maternity leave, was not covered. During that period of maternity leave, the pregnant woman was temporarily cut off from the benefits extended by the Company's plan. At all other times, the woman was treated the same as other employees in terms of her eligibility for...benefits.

The Company's seniority plan in this case has a markedly different effect. In attempting to return to work, the formerly pregnant woman is deprived of all previously accumulated seniority. The policy affects both her ability to re-enter the work force, and her compensation when she does return. The Company argues that these effects are permissible because they flow from its initial decision to treat pregnancy as an unexcused absence. But this argument misconceives the scope of the protection afforded by *Gilbert* to such initial decisions. For the General Electric plan did not attach any consequences to the condition of pregnancy that extended beyond the period of maternity leave. *Gilbert* allowed the employer to treat pregnancy leave as a temporal gap in the full employment status of a woman. During that period, the employer may treat the employee in a manner consistent with the determination that pregnancy is not an illness. In this case, however, the Company's seniority policy has an adverse impact on the employee's status after pregnancy leave is terminated. The formerly pregnant person is permanently disadvantaged as compared to the rest of the work force. And since the persons adversely affected by this policy comprise an exclusively female class, the Company's plan has an obvious discriminatory effect.

Under this analysis, it is clear that petitioner's seniority rule discriminating against formerly pregnant employees is invalid. It is equally clear that the denial of sick pay during maternity leave is consistent with the *Gilbert* rationale, since the Company was free to withhold those benefits during that period.

As is evident from my dissent in *Gilbert,* I would prefer to decide this case on a simpler rationale. Since that preference is foreclosed by *Gilbert,* I concur in the Court's judgment on the understanding that as the law now stands, although some discrimination against pregnancy—as compared with other physical disabilities—is permissible, discrimination against pregnant or formerly pregnant employees is not.

COURT ON PHONE
SURVEILLANCE ORDERS
December 7, 1977

A sharply divided Supreme Court ruled Dec. 7 that federal district courts had the authority to order a telephone company to install surveillance equipment as part of a federal criminal investigation. The vote was 5-4. In a second major issue raised by the case—whether the district court had the authority at all to permit such surveillance—the Supreme Court divided 6-3, upholding the federal court's power to authorize surveillance.

Justice Byron R. White, writing for the majority, said that the federal rule governing search warrants was "sufficiently flexible to include within its scope electronic intrusions authorized upon a finding of probable cause." White based the decision on the rules for criminal procedure and on the 1789 All Writs Act which authorized federal judges to issue orders "necessary or appropriate in aid of their respective jurisdictions." The majority opinion said that, once the court found probable cause to believe that phone lines facilitated criminal activities, the telephone company must assist in the investigation as the court required. "For the company with this knowledge to refuse to supply the meager assistance required by the FBI...to put an end to this venture threatened obstruction of an investigation which would determine whether the company's facilities were being lawfully used," White said. The New York Telephone Company was, he said, "a highly regulated public utility with a duty to serve the public...."

Justice Potter Stewart voted with the minority against requiring telephone company cooperation and joined with the majority upholding the authority of federal court judges to issue surveillance orders. Justices

Thurgood Marshall and William J. Brennan Jr. dissented on both questions raised in the case.

At the request of the FBI, U.S. District Court Judge Charles Tenney in 1976 ordered the New York Telephone Co. to install devices known as pen registers on two phones in Manhattan where an FBI agent's affadavit indicated that an illegal gambling enterprise operated. [Pen registers recorded the telephone numbers dialed on a telephone but did not record conversations. The telephone company noted, however, that with the use of headphones and a tape recorder, pen registers could be converted to a wiretap at any terminal on the line.] The phone company refused to cooperate, arguing that compliance invaded customer privacy. A Circuit Court of Appeals voided the Tenney order.

Sharp Dissent

In a sharp dissent four justices, with Justice John Paul Stevens writing for the minority, said the majority opinion was a first step toward the "accretion of arbitrary police powers in the Federal courts no less dangerous and unprecedented because the first step appears to be only minimally obtrusive." The majority's reliance upon the All Writs Act of 1789 "made it absurd to suppose that its draftsmen thought they were authorizing any form of electronic surveillance," Stevens wrote. "This is an extraordinary judicial effort in such a sensitive area and I can only regard it as most unwise." Moreover, Stevens said, federal rules for criminal procedure did not grant "open-ended authority" to federal courts to issue search warrants.

Limits of Authority

By this decision the court, in effect, made it easier for federal agents to enlist public and private corporate cooperation in the conduct of a criminal investigation. All the justices agreed that Congress had not intended to subject pen register use to the same strict requirements imposed on wiretaps by the Omnibus Crime Control and Safe Streets Act of 1968. The law specified that all electronic surveillance by the FBI had to be approved in writing by the U.S. Attorney General and then sanctioned by a federal judge.

The Dec. 7 decision left unanswered questions as to the limits of the authority of federal judges to compel private citizens to cooperate with federal investigators. The Supreme Court, in the New York Telephone Co. case, did not spell out how far judges could go in ordering cooperation with federal investigators, but it did say that the authority "is not without limits" and that "unreasonable burdens may not be imposed."

Following are excerpts from the majority and dissenting opinions in the Supreme Court's Dec. 7, 1977, decision authorizing federal judges to order telephone company cooperation with federal investigators to install surveillance devices:

No. 76-835

United States, Petitioner, *v.* New York Telephone Company.	On Writ of Certiorari to the United States Court of Appeals for the Second Circuit.

[December 7, 1977]

MR. JUSTICE WHITE delivered the opinion of the Court.

This case presents the question of whether a United States District Court may properly direct a telephone company to provide federal law enforcement officials the facilities and technical assistance necessary for the implementation of its order authorizing the use of pen registers[1] to investigate offenses which there was probable cause to believe were being committed by means of the telephone.

I

On March 19, 1976, the United States District Court for the Southern District of New York issued an order authorizing agents of the Federal Bureau of Investigation (FBI) to install and use pen registers with respect to two telephones and directing the New York Telephone Company (the Company) to furnish the FBI "all information, facilities and technical assistance" necessary to employ the pen registers unobtrusively. The FBI was ordered to compensate the Company at prevailing rates for any assistance which it furnished.... The order was issued on the basis of an affidavit submitted by an FBI agent which stated that certain individuals were conducting an illegal gambling enterprise at 220 East 14th Street in New York City and that, on the basis of facts set forth therein, there was probable cause to believe that two telephones bearing different numbers were being used at that address in furtherance of the illegal activity.... The District Court found that there was probable cause to conclude that an illegal gambling enterprise using the facilities of interstate commerce was being conducted at the East 14th Street address in violation of Title 18, United States Code, §§ 371 and 1952, and that the two telephones had been, were currently being, and would continue to be used in connection with those offenses. Its order authorized the FBI to operate the pen registers with respect to the two telephones until knowledge of the numbers dialed led to the identity of the associates and confederates of those believed to be conducting the illegal operation or for 20 days, "whichever is earlier."

A pen register is a mechanical device that records the numbers dialed on a telephone by monitoring the electrical impulses caused when the dial on the telephone is released. It does not overhear oral communications and does not indicate whether calls are actually completed.

885

The Company declined to comply fully with the court order. It did inform the FBI of the location of the relevant "appearances," that is, the places where specific telephone lines emerge from the sealed telephone cable. In addition, the Company agreed to identify the relevant "pairs," or the specific pairs of wires that constituted the circuits of the two telephone lines. This information is required to install a pen register. The Company, however, refused to lease lines to the FBI which were needed to install the pen registers in an unobtrusive fashion. Such lines were required by the FBI in order to install the pen registers in inconspicuous locations away from the building containing the telephones. A "leased line" is an unused telephone line which makes an "appearance" in the same terminal box as the telephone line in connection with which it is desired to install a pen register. If the leased line is connected to the subject telephone line, the pen register can then be installed on the leased line at a remote location and be monitored from that point. The Company, instead of providing the leased lines, which it conceded that the court's order required it to do, advised the FBI to string cables from the "subject apartment" to another location where pen registers could be installed. The FBI determined after canvassing the neighborhood of the apartment for four days that there was no location where it could string its own wires and attach the pen registers without alerting the suspects, in which event, of course, the gambling operation would cease to function....

On March 30, 1976, the Company moved in the District Court to vacate that portion of the pen register order directing it to furnish facilities and technical assistance to the FBI in connection with the use of the pen registers on the ground that such a directive could be issued only in connection with a wiretap order conforming to the requirements of Title III of the Omnibus Crime Control and Safe Streets Act of 1968.... (Title III). It contended that neither Fed. Rule Crim. Proc. 41 nor the All Writs Act...provided any basis for such an order.... The District Court ruled that pen registers are not governed by the prescriptions of Title III because they are not devices used to intercept oral communications. It concluded that it had jurisdiction to authorize the installation of the pen registers upon a showing of probable cause and that both the All Writs Act and its inherent powers provided authority for the order directing the Company to assist in the installation of the pen registers.

On April 9, 1976, after the District Court and the Court of Appeals denied the Company's motion to stay the pen register order pending appeal, the Company provided the leased lines.

The Court of Appeals affirmed in part and reversed in part, with one judge dissenting on the ground that the order below should have been affirmed in its entirety.... It agreed with the District Court that pen registers do not fall within the scope of Title III and are not otherwise prohibited or regulated by statute. The Court of Appeals also concluded that district courts have the power, either inherently or as a logical derivative of Fed. Rule Crim. Proc. 41, to authorize pen register surveillance upon an adequate showing of probable cause. The majority held, however, that the

District Court abused its discretion in ordering the Company to assist in the installation and operation of the pen registers. It assumed, *arguendo,* "that a district court has inherent discretionary authority or discretionary power under the All Writs Act to compel technical assistance by the Telephone Company," but concluded that "in the absence of specific and properly limited Congressional action, it was an abuse of discretion for the District Court to order the Telephone Company to furnish technical assistance."... The majority expressed concern that "such an order could establish a most undesirable, if not dangerous and unwise, precedent for the authority of federal courts to impress unwilling aid on private third parties" and that "there is no assurance that the court will always be able to protect [third parties] from excessive or overzealous Government activity or compulsion."...

We granted the United States' petition for certiorari challenging the Court of Appeals' invalidation of the District Court's order against respondent.

II

We first reject respondent's contention, which is renewed here, that the District Court lacked authority to order the Company to provide assistance because the use of pen registers may only be authorized in conformity with the procedures set forth in Title III for securing judicial authority to intercept wire communications. Both the language of the statute and its legislative history establish beyond any doubt that pen registers are not governed by Title III.

Title III is concerned only with orders "authorizing or approving the *interception* of a wire or oral communication...." Congress defined "intercept" to mean "the *aural* acquisition of the *contents* of any wire or oral *communication* through the use of any electronic, mechanical, or other device."... Pen registers do not "intercept" because they do not acquire the "contents" of communications, as that term is defined.... Indeed, a law enforcement official could not even determine from the use of a pen register whether a communication existed. These devices do not hear sound. They disclose only the telephone numbers that have been dialed—a means of establishing communication. Neither the purport of any communication between the caller and the recipient of the call, their identities, nor whether the call was even completed are disclosed by pen registers. Furthermore, pen registers do not accomplish the "aural acquisition" of anything. They decode outgoing telephone numbers by responding to changes in electrical voltage caused by the turning of the telephone dial (or the pressing of buttons on push button telephones) and present the information in a form to be interpreted by sight rather than by hearing.

The legislative history confirms that there was no congressional intent to subject pen registers to the requirements of Title III. The Senate Report explained that the definition of "intercept" was designed to exclude pen registers.... It is clear that Congress did not view pen registers as posting a threat to privacy of the same dimension as the interception of oral communications and did not intend to impose Title III restrictions upon their use.

III

We also agree with the Court of Appeals that the District Court had power to authorize the installation of the pen registers. It is undisputed that the order in this case was predicated upon a proper finding of probable cause, and no claim is made that it was in any way inconsistent with the Fourth Amendment. Fed Rule Crim. Proc. 41 (b) authorizes the issuance of a warrant to:

> "search for and seize any (1) property that constitutes evidence of the commission of a criminal offense; or (2) contraband, the fruits of crime, or things otherwise criminally possessed; or (3) property designed or intended for use or which is or has been used as the means of committing a criminal offense."

This definition is broad enough to encompass a "search" designated to ascertain the use which is being made of a telephone suspected of being employed as a means of facilitating a criminal venture and the "seizure" of evidence which the "search" of the telephone produces. Although Rule 41 (h) defines property "to include documents, books, papers and any other tangible objects," it does not restrict or purport to exhaustively enumerate all the items which may be seized pursuant to Rule 41. Indeed, we recognized in *Katz* v. *United States,...*(1967), which held that telephone conversations were protected by the Fourth Amendment, that Rule 41 is not limited to tangible items but is sufficiently flexible to include within its scope electronic intrusions authorized upon a finding of probable cause.... See also *Osborn* v. *United States...*(1966).

Our conclusion that Rule 41 authorizes the use of pen registers under appropriate circumstances is supported by Fed. Rule Crim. Proc. 57 (b), which provides: "If no procedure is specifically prescribed by rule, the court may proceed in any lawful manner not inconsistent with these rules or with any applicable statute." Although we need not and do not decide whether Rule 57 (b) by itself would authorize the issuance of pen register orders, it reinforces our conclusion that Rule 41 is sufficiently broad to include seizures of intangible items such as dial impulses recorded by pen registers as well as tangible items.

Finally, we could not hold that the District Court lacked any power to authorize the use of pen registers without defying the congressional judgment that the use of pen registers "be permissible. "...Indeed, it would be anomalous to permit the recording of conversations by means of electronic surveillance while prohibiting the far lesser intrusion accomplished by pen registers. Congress intended no such result. We are unwilling to impose it in the absence of some showing that the issuance of such orders would be inconsistent with Rule 41....

IV

The Court of Appeals held that even though the District Court had ample authority to issue the pen register warrant and even assuming the applicability of the All Writs Act, the order compelling the Company to provide technical assistance constituted an abuse of discretion. Since the Court of Appeals conceded that a compelling case existed for requiring the assistance of the Company and did not point to any fact particular to this case which would warrant a finding of abuse of discretion, we interpret its holding as generally barring district courts from ordering any party to assist in the installation or operation of a pen register. It was apparently concerned that sustaining the District Court's order would authorize courts to compel third parties to render assistance without limitation regardless of the burden involved and pose a severe threat to the autonomy of third parties who for whatever reason prefer not to render such assistance. Consequently the Court of Appeals concluded that courts should not embark upon such a course without specific legislative authorization. We agree that the power of federal courts to impose duties upon third parties is not without limits; unreasonable burdens may not be imposed. We conclude, however, that the order issued here against respondent was clearly authorized by the All Writs Act and was consistent with the intent of Congress.

The All Writs Act provides:

> "The Supreme Court and all courts established by Act of Congress may issue all writs necessary or appropriate in aid of their respective jurisdictions and agreeable to the usages and principles of law."...

The assistance of the Company was required here to implement a pen register order which we have held the District Court was empowered to issue by Rule 41. This Court has repeatedly recognized the power of a federal court to issue such commands under the All Writs Act as may be necessary or appropriate to effectuate and prevent the frustration of orders it has previously issued in its exercise of jurisdiction otherwise obtained: "This statute has served since its inclusion, in substance, in the original Judiciary Act as a 'legislatively approved source of procedural instruments designed to achieve the rational ends of law.' " *Harris* v. *Nelson*...(1969), quoting *Price* v. *Johnston*...(1948). Indeed, "[u]nless appropriately confined by Congress, a federal court may avail itself of all auxiliary writs as aids in the performance of its duties, when the use of such historic aids is calculated in its sound judgment to achieve the ends of justice entrusted to it." *Adams* v. *United States ex rel. McCann*...(1942).

The Court has consistently applied the Act flexibly in conformity with these principles. Although § 262 of the Judicial Code, the predecessor to § 1651, did not expressly authorize courts, as does § 1651, to issue writs "appropriate" to the proper exercise of their jurisdiction but only "necessary" writs, *Adams* held that these supplemental powers are not limited to those situations where it is "necessary" to issue the writ or order "in the sense that the court could not otherwise physically discharge its duties.'... In *Price* v. *Johnson*...§ 262 supplied the authority for a United States Court of Appeals to issue an order commanding that a prisoner be brought before the court for the purpose of arguing his own appeal. Similarly...§ 1651 furnished the District Court with authority to order that a federal prisoner be produced in court for purposes of a hearing. *United States* v. *Hayman*...(1952). The question in *Harris* v. *Nelson*...was whether, despite the absence of specific statutory authority, the District Court could issue a discovery order in connection with a habeas corpus proceeding pending before it. Eight Justices agreed that the district courts have power to require discovery when essential to render a habeas corpus proceeding effective. The Court has also held that despite the absence of express statutory authority to do so, the Federal Trade Commission may petition for, and a Court of Appeals may issue, pursuant to § 1651, an order preventing a merger pending hearings before the Commission to avoid impairing or frustrating the Court of Appeals appellate jurisdiction. *Federal Trade Comm'n* v. *Dean Foods Co.*...(1966).

The power conferred by the Act extends, under appropriate circumstances, to persons who though not parties to the original action or engaged in wrong doing are in a position to frustrate the implementation of a court order or the proper administration of justice. *Mississippi Valley Barge Line Co.* v. *United States*...(ED Mo. 1967), aff'd....(1968); *Board of Education* v. *York*...(CA10 1970), cert. denied...(1971), and encompasses even those who have not taken any affirmative action to hinder justice. *United States* v. *McHie*...(ND Ill. 1912); *Field* v. *United States*...(CA2), cert. denied...(1951).

Turning to the facts of this case, we do not think that the Company was a third party so far removed from the underlying controversy that its assistance could not be permissibly compelled. A United States District Court found that there was probable cause to believe that the Company's facilities were being employed to facilitate a criminal enterprise on a continuing basis. For the Company, with this knowledge, to refuse to supply the meager assistance required by the FBI in its efforts to put an end to this venture threatened obstruction of an investigation which would determine whether the Company's facilities were being lawfully used. Moreover, it can hardly be contended that the Company, a highly regulated public utility with a duty to serve the public, had a substantial interest in not providing assistance. Certainly the use of pen registers is by no means offensive to it. The Company concedes that it regularly employs such devices without court order for the purposes of checking billing operations, detecting fraud, and preventing violations of law. It also agreed to supply the FBI with all the information required to install its own pen registers. Nor was the District Court's order in any way burdensome. The order provided that the Company be fully reimbursed at prevailing rates, and compliance with it required minimal effort on the part of the Company and no disruption to its operations.

Finally, we note, as the Court of Appeals recognized, that without the Company's assistance there is no conceivable way in which the surveillance authorized by the District Court could have been successfully accomplished. The FBI, after an exhaustive search, was unable to find a location where it could install its own pen registers without tipping off the targets of the investigation. The provision of a leased line by the Company was essential to the fulfillment of the purpose—to learn the identities of those connected with the gambling operation—for which the pen register order had been issued.

The order compelling the Company to provide assistance was not only consistent with the Act but also with more recent congressional actions.... Congress clearly intended to permit the use of pen registers by federal law enforcement officials. Without the assistance of the Company in circumstances such as those presented here, however, these devices simply cannot be effectively employed. Moreover, Congress provided in a 1970 amendment to Title III that "[a]n order authorizing the interception of a wire or oral communication shall, upon request of the applicant, direct that a communication common carrier...shall furnish the applicant forthwith all information, facilities, and technical assistance necessary to accomplish the interception unobtrusively...." 18 U.S.C. § 2518 (4). In light of this direct command to federal courts to compel, upon request, any assistance necessary to accomplish an electronic interception, it would be remarkable if Congress thought it beyond the power of the federal courts to exercise, where required, a discretionary authority to order telephone companies to assist in the installation and operation of pen registers, which accomplish a far lesser invasion of privacy. We are convinced that to prohibit the order challenged here would frustrate the clear indication by Congress that the pen register is a permissible law enforcement tool by enabling a public utility to thwart a judicial determination that its use is required to apprehend and prosecute successfully those employing the utility's facilities to conduct a criminal venture. The contrary judgment of the Court of Appeals is accordingly reversed.

So Ordered.

MR. JUSTICE STEWART, concurring in part and dissenting in part.

I agree that the use of pen registers is not governed by the requirements of Title III and that the District Court had authority to issue the order authorizing installation of the pen register, and so join Parts I, II, and III of the Court's opinion. However, I agree with MR. JUSTICE STEVENS that the District Court lacked power to order the telephone company to assist the Government in installing the pen register, and thus join Part II of his dissenting opinion.

MR. JUSTICE STEVENS, with whom MR. JUSTICE BRENNAN and MR. JUSTICE MARSHALL join, dissenting in part.

Today's decision appears to present no radical departure from this Court's prior holdings. It builds upon previous intimations that a federal district court's power to issue a search warrant under Fed. Rule Crim. Proc. 41 is a flexible one, not strictly restrained by statutory authorization, and it applies the same flexible analysis to the All Writs Act, 28 U.S.C. § 1651 (a). But for one who thinks of federal courts as courts of limited jurisdiction, the Court's decision is difficult to accept. The principle of limited federal jurisdiction is fundamental; never is it more important than when a federal court purports to authorize and implement the secret invasion of an individual's privacy. Yet that principle was entirely ignored on March 19 and April 2, 1976, when the District Court granted the Government's application for permission to engage in surveillance by means of a pen register, and ordered the respondent to cooperate in the covert operation.

Congress has not given the federal district courts the power either to authorize the use of a pen register, or to require private parties to assist in carrying out such surveillance. Those defects cannot be remedied by a patchwork interpretation of Rule 41 which regards the Rule as applicable as a grant of authority, but inapplicable insofar as it limits the exercise of such authority. Nor can they be corrected by reading the All Writs Act as though it gave federal judges the wide-ranging powers of an ombudsman. The Court's decision may be motivated by a belief that Congress would, if the question were presented to it, authorize both the pen register order and the order directed to the Telephone Company. But the history and consistent interpretation of the federal court's power to issue search warrants conclusively show that, in these areas, the Court's rush to achieve a logical result must await congressional deliberations. From the beginning of our Nation's history, we have sought to prevent the accretion of arbitrary police powers in the federal courts; that accretion is no less dangerous and unprecedented because the first step appears to be only minimally intrusive.

I

Beginning with the Act of July 31, 1789...and concluding with the Omnibus Crime Control and Safe Streets Act of 1968,...Congress has enacted a series of over 35 different statutes granting federal judges the power to issue search warrants of one form or another. These statutes have one characteristic in common: they are specific in their grants of authority and in their inclusion of limitations on either the places to be searched, the objects of the search, or the requirements for the issuance of a warrant. This is not a random coincidence; it is a reflection of a concern deeply imbedded in our revolutionary history for the abuses that attend any broad delegation of power to issue search warrants. In the Colonial period, the oppressive British practice of allowing courts to issue "general warrants" or "writs of assistance" was one of the major catalysts of the struggle for Independence. After Independence, one of the first State Constitutions expressly provided that "no warrant ought to be issued but in cases, and with the formalities, prescribed by the laws." This same principle motivated the adoption of the Fourth Amendment and the contemporaneous, specific legislation limiting judicial authority to issue search warrants.

It is unnecessary to develop this historical and legislative background at any great length, for even the rough contours make it abundantly clear that federal judges were not intended to have any roving commission to issue search warrants. Quite properly, therefore, the Court today avoids the error committed by the Courts of Appeals which have held that a district court has "inherent power" to authorize the installation of a pen register on a private telephone line. Federal courts have no such inherent power.

While the Court's decision eschews the notion of inherent power, its holding that Fed. Rule Crim. Proc. 41 authorized the District Court's pen register order is equally at odds with the 200-year history of search warrants in this country and ignores the plain meaning and legislative history of the very Rule on which it relies. Under the Court's reading of the Rule, the definition of the term "property" in the Rule places no limits on the objects of a proper search and seizure, but is merely illustrative.... The Court treats Rule 41 as though it were a general authorization for district courts to issue any warrants not otherwise prohibited.... This is a startling approach. On its face, the Rule grants no such open-ended authority. Instead, it follows in the steps of the dozen of enactments that preceded it: it limits the nature of the property that may be seized and the circumstances under which a valid warrant may be obtained. The continuing force of these limitations is demonstrated by the congressional actions which comprise the Omnibus Crime Control and Safe Streets Act of 1968.

In Title III of that Act, Congress legislated comprehensively on the subject of wiretapping and electronic surveillance. Specifically, Congress granted federal judges the power to authorize electronic surveillance under certain carefully defined circumstances. As the Court demonstrates in Part II of its opinion (which I join), the installation of pen register devices is not encompassed within that authority. What the majority opinion fails to point out, however, is that in Title IX of that same Act, Congress enacted another, distinct provision extending the power of federal judges to issue search warrants. That statute, which formed the basis of the 1972 Amendment to Rule 41, authorized the issuance of search warrants for an additional class of property, namely, "property that constitutes evidence of a criminal offense in violation of the laws of the United States."... In order to understand this provision, it must be remembered that, prior to 1976, "mere evidence" could not be the subject of a constitutionally valid seizure.... In *Warden* v. *Hayden*...[1967] this Court removed the constitutional objection to mere evidence seizures. Title IX was considered necessary because, after *Warden* v. *Hayden*, there existed a category of property—mere evidence—which could be the subject of a valid seizure incident to an arrest, but which could not be seized pursuant to a warrant. The reason mere evidence could not be seized pursuant to warrant was that, as Congress recognized, Rule 41 did not authorize warrants for evidence. Title IX was enacted to fill this gap in the law.

Two conclusions follow ineluctably from the congressional enactment of Title IX. First, Rule 41 was never intended to be a general authorization to issue any warrant not otherwise prohibited by the Fourth Amendment. If it were, Congress would not have perceived a need to enact Title IX, since constitutional law, as it stood in 1968, did not prohibit the issuance of warrants for evidence.

Second, the enactment of Title IX disproves the theory that the definition of "property" in Rule 41 is only illustrative. This suggestion was first put forward by the Court in *Katz* v. *United States*....[1967]. The issue was not briefed in *Katz*, but the Court, in dicta, indicated that Rule 41 was not confined to tangible property. Whatever the merits of that suggestion in 1967, it has absolutely no force at this time. In 1968 Congress comprehensively dealt with the issue of electronic searches in Title III. In the same Act, it provided authority for expanding the scope of property covered under Rule 41. But the definition of property in the Rule has never changed. Each item listed is tangible, and the final reference to "and any other tangible items" surely must now be read as describing the outer limits of the included category. It strains credulity to suggest that Congress, having carefully circumscribed the use of electronic surveillance in Title III, would then, in Title IX, expand judicial authority to issue warrants for the electronic seizure of "intangibles" without the safeguards of Title III. In fact, the safeguards contained in Rule 41 make it absurd to suppose that its draftsmen thought they were authorizing any form of electronic surveillance. The paragraphs relating to issuance of the warrant, Rule 41 (c), the preparation of an inventory of property in the presence of the person whose property has been taken, Rule 41 (d), and the motion for a return of property, Rule 41 (e), are almost meaningless if read as relating to electronic surveillance of any kind.

To reach its result in this case, the Court has had to overlook the Rule's specific language, its specific safeguards, and its legislative background. This is an extraordinary judicial effort in such a sensitive area, and I can only regard it as most unwise. It may be that a pen register is less intrusive than other forms of electronic surveillance. Congress evidently thought so.... But the Court should not try to leap from that assumption to the conclusion that the District Court's order here is covered by Rule 41. As I view this case, it is immaterial whether or not the attachment of a pen register to a private telephone line is a violation of the Fourth Amendment. If, on the one hand, the individual's privacy interest is not constitutionally protected, judicial intervention is both unnecessary and unauthorized. If, on the other hand, the constitutional protection is applicable, the focus of inquiry should not be whether Congress has prohibited the intrusion, but whether Congress has expressly authorized it, and no such authorization can be drawn from Rule 41. On either hypothesis, the order entered by the District Court on March 19, 1976, authorizing the installation of a pen register, was a nullity. It cannot, therefore, support the further order requiring the New York Telephone Company to aid in the installation of the device.

II

Even if I were to assume that the pen register order in this case was valid, I cannot accept the Court's conclusion that the District Court had the power under the All Writs Act...to require the New York Telephone Company to assist in its installation. This conclusion is unsupported by the history, the language, or previous judicial interpretations of the Act.

The All Writs Act was originally enacted, in part, as § 14 of the Judiciary Act of 1789.... The Act was, and is, necessary because federal courts are courts of limited jurisdiction having only those powers expressly granted by Congress, and the statute provides these courts with the procedural tools—the various historic common-law writs—necessary for them to exercise their limited jurisdiction. The statute does not contain, and has never before been interpreted as containing, the open-ended grant of authority to federal courts that today's decision purports to uncover. Instead, in the language of the statute itself, there are two fundamental limitations on its scope. The *purpose* of any order authorized by the Act must be to aid the court in the exercise of its jurisdiction; and the *means* selected must be analogous to a common-law writ. The Court's opinion ignores both limitations.

The Court starts from the premise that a district court may issue a writ under the Act "to effectuate and prevent the frustration of orders it has previously issued in its exercise of jurisdiction otherwise obtained."... As stated, this premise is neither objectionable nor remarkable and conforms to the principle that the Act was intended to aid the court in the exercise of its jurisdiction. Clearly, if parties were free to ignore a court judgment or order, the court's ability to perform its duties would be undermined. And the court's power to issue an order requiring a party to carry out the terms of the original judgment is well settled.... The courts have also recognized, however, that this power is subject to certain restraints. For instance, the relief granted by the writ may not be "of a different kind" or "on a different principle" than that accorded by the underlying order or judgment....

More significantly, the courts have consistently recognized and applied the limitation that whatever action the court takes must be in aid of *its* duties and *its* jurisdiction. The fact that a party may be better able to effectuate its rights or duties if a writ is issued never has been, and under the language of the statute cannot be, a sufficient basis for issuance of the writ....

Nowhere in the Court's decision or in the decisions of the lower courts is there the slightest indication of why a writ is necessary or appropriate in this case to aid the District Court's jurisdiction. According to the Court, the writ is necessary because the Company's refusal "threatened obstruction of an investigation...." ...Concededly, citizen cooperation is always a desired element in any government investigation, and lack of cooperation may thwart such an investigation, even though it is legitimate and judicially sanctioned. But unless the Court is of the opinion that the District Court's interest in its jurisdiction was coextensive with the Government's interest in a successful investigation, there is simply no basis for concluding that the inability of the Government to achieve the purposes for which it obtained the pen register order in any way detracted from or threatened the District Court's jurisdiction. Plainly, the District Court's jurisdiction does not ride on the Government's shoulders until successful completion of an electronic surveillance.

If the All Writs Act confers authority to order persons to aid the government in the performance of its duties, and is no longer to be confined to orders which must be entered to enable the court to carry out its functions, it provides a sweeping grant of authority entirely without precedent in our Nation's history. Of course, there is precedent for such authority in the common law—the writ of assistance. The use of that writ by the judges appointed by King George was one British practice that the revolution was specifically intended to terminate.... I can understand why the Court today does not seek to support its holding by reference to that writ, but I cannot understand its disregard of the statutory requirement that the writ be "agreeable to the usages and principles of law."

III

The order directed against the Company in this case is not particularly offensive. Indeed, the Company probably welcomes its defeat since it will make a normal profit out of compliance with orders of this kind in the future. Nevertheless, the order is deeply troubling as a portent of the powers that future courts may find lurking in the arcane language of Rule 41 and the All Writs Act.

I would affirm the judgment of the Court of Appeals.

CARTER'S WORLD TRIP: STOPS IN POLAND AND IRAN
December 29-31, 1977

President Carter left Washington, D.C., Dec. 29 on the first leg of a grueling trip that took him to three continents in nine days. He spent the first two nights of the journey in Warsaw, Poland, and the following evening, with his wife, Rosalynn, was the guest of the Shah and Empress Farah of Iran at a New Year's Eve party in Tehran. By the time he returned to the White House Jan. 6, Carter had visited seven countries and had flown 18,500 miles.

The President's itinerary was criticized before the trip as lacking a "theme." But Carter, in remarks before his departure, said that the journey would reflect "both the diversity of the world we live in and our own nation's ability to deal creatively and constructively with that diversity."

In the same vein, Zbigniew Brzezinski, the President's national security adviser and the trip's architect, said that the stops on the journey would reflect the current dispersal of global economic, political and military power among the nations—in contrast to the dual hegemony of the United States and the Soviet Union, the superpowers in the years following World War II.

Brzezinski accompanied Carter on the trip, as did Secretary of State Cyrus R. Vance, about 25 White House and State Department aides and 200 members of the press. The marathon journey took the President from Iran to India and then to Saudi Arabia, Egypt, France and Belgium. A two-hour stop in Egypt was the briefest of the trip and the only one not planned before departure.

The Presidential trip had been scheduled originally for late November, but it had been postponed so that Carter could continue to press for passage of his energy legislation. Indeed, the President had said that he would not leave the country without the legislation in hand. At year's end, however, the legislation was stalled in a deadlocked conference committee and not expected to be passed in any form for several weeks at the earliest. (Energy bill, p. 277)

Poland

Soon after he arrived on Polish soil, Carter held a press conference in which he responded to Polish journalists' questions as well as to those of American reporters. In a diplomatic manner, he pointed out that Poland's record on human rights was less oppressive than that of other Eastern-bloc countries.

The President said, "There is a substantial degree of freedom of the press, exhibited by this conference this afternoon; a substantial degree of freedom of religion, demonstrated by the fact that approximately 90 per cent of the Polish people profess faith in Christ; and an open relationship between Poland and our country and Poland and Western European countries in trade, technology, cultural exchange, student exchange, tourism.

"So I don't think there is any doubt that the will of the Polish people for complete preservation and enhancement of human rights is the same as our own." Carter added that both Poland and the United States sometimes fall short of those goals. "I think...the best thing that we can do at this point is to continue to insist upon a rigid enforcement and interpretation of the Human Rights Section of the Helsinki Agreement. (Historic Documents of 1975, p. 559)

While in Poland, President Carter movingly paid homage to the heroism of Jews of the Warsaw ghetto and to the millions of other Polish victims of the Nazis and of World War II.

Throughout the President's visit in Poland, the attention of the press was somewhat distracted by mistakes made by Carter's interpreter. The errors in translation occurred as the President, on his arrival at Warsaw Airport, was greeted by Edward Gierek, the Polish leader. Carter's freelance interpreter, Steven Seymour, translated the President's comments about the "desires" of the Polish people for the future into the "lusts" of the Poles for the future. And for the President's reference to his departure from Washington, Seymour chose a Polish verb that implied "abandoning" rather than "leaving." However, in a hand-written note that he sent Seymour a few days after his return, Carter said, "Don't let the exaggerated criticisms disturb you. Those who analyzed your translation say that the errors were minor."

Iran and Egypt

Although the President might well have considered the Shah's New Year's Eve gala in Tehran the social highlight of his trip, he found the time during his visit in Iran for substantive business. After a meeting between Carter and the Shah, U.S. officials announced that Iran would accept "full international safeguards" in purchasing nuclear reactors from the United States. Carter also had a brief conference in Tehran with Jordan's King Hussein regarding Middle East peace plans.

In offering a toast at the Shah's New Year's Eve dinner, President Carter called Iran "an island of stability in one of the more troubled areas of the world." He also asserted, "We have no other nation on earth who is closer to us in planning for our mutual military security. We have no other nation with whom we have closer consultations on regional problems that concern us both. And there is no other leader with whom I have a deeper sense of personal gratitude and personal friendship."

Although Carter engaged in substantive discussions with leaders in the other countries on his itinerary, many of the events he participated in were largely ceremonial. Others, according to reporters accompanying him, appeared to have been arranged primarily as "media events" for the television audience in the United States.

On the other hand, a two-hour stop at Aswan, Egypt, Jan. 4 might have been the most important stop on the entire trip. Remarks the President had made before the journey regarding U.S. attitudes toward an independent Palestinian homeland had upset Egyptian President Anwar el-Sadat. To reassure Sadat, Carter agreed to the hasty Aswan conference. The brief visit appeared to have achieved Carter's objectives. (Sadat's Mideast initiative, p. 827)

> *Following are excerpts from President Carter's remarks at the White House prior to his departure Dec. 29, 1977; from his press conference in Warsaw, Poland, Dec. 30, 1977; from the exchange of toasts between President Carter and Edward Gierek, First Secretary of the Polish United Workers' Party, in Warsaw, Dec. 30; and from the exchange of toasts between President Carter and His Imperial Majesty, Mohammad Reza Pahlavi, the Shah of Iran, in Tehran, Iran, Dec. 31.:*

REMARKS OF THE PRESIDENT

THE PRESIDENT: Good morning, everybody.

I depart today on a journey that reflects both the diversity of the world we live in and also our own Nation's ability and desire to deal creatively and constructively with that diversity.

It is a rapidly changing world, a world in which the old ideological labels have less meaning than ever, in which the universal desire for freedom and for a better life is being expressed more strongly, and in more ways than ever before; a world in which political awakening, economic independence and technological progress have created new demands on the foreign policy of our people.

The variety of places that we will visit over the next nine days is symbolic of the breadth and the variety of American interest in this new world.

In France and in Western Europe, we will reaffirm the historic bonds and our common values, and we will explore ways to meet the common problems of the industrial democracies.

In Poland, the ancestral home of millions of Americans, we will nourish the improving relationships between the United States and the peoples of Eastern Europe.

In Iran and in Saudi Arabia, we will discuss key economic relationships and press for a continuation of the dramatic progress that is being made in bringing peace to the Middle East.

In India, which is the largest democracy on earth, we will seek new paths of cooperation and communication between the developing nations of the world and the industrial north.

In all these places, we will be reaffirming our dedication to peace and our support of justice and of human rights.

It is a changing world, a different world, and I believe that it is also a different America whose message we will carry; an America more confident and more united at peace with other nations and also at peace with itself; an America which is ready and able to cooperate wherever possible and to compete when necessary.

After a long period of doubt and turmoil here, we are finding our way back to the values that made us a great nation, and in this new spirit we are eager to work with all countries...in building the kind of world and...world community that serves the needs of all....

We undertake this trip to express our own views clearly and proudly, but also to learn and to understand the opinions and the desires of others. We will try to represent our Nation and our people well, and I will take the goodwill of America everywhere we go. Thank you very much.

THE VICE PRESIDENT [Walter F. Mondale]: Mr. President, we wish you and Mrs. Carter well as you undertake this most important mission on behalf of our Nation. And I know that I speak for everyone here and for the American people when I say you take with you not only our best wishes but our love as well. We know it will be a successful journey, and we eagerly await your return.

CARTER'S NEWS CONFERENCE IN WARSAW

THE PRESIDENT: Good afternoon. Dzien dobry.

It is a great honor for me to be here in Poland to reaffirm and to strengthen the historic and strong ties of friendship and mutual purpose which exist between our two countries. I have had very fruitful discussions with First Secretary Gierek and the other officials of Poland on bilateral questions—on questions involving NATO and the Warsaw Pact countries, matters relating to SALT, mutual and balanced force reductions, and a general commitment to peace in the future.

This morning I had a chance to visit memorials to the brave people of Poland, and particularly of Warsaw. I doubt that there is any nation on earth which has suffered more from the ravages of war. In the Second World War the Nazis killed 800,000 people in Warsaw alone and six million Poles. And I was able to pay homage to their courage and bravery.

I also visited the ghetto monument, a memorial to Polish Jews who stood alone to face the Nazis but who will forever live in the conscience of the world.

This afternoon I would like to answer questions from the reporters assembled here. There were a few who wanted to attend who were not permitted to come. Their questions will be answered by me in writing. And now I would be glad to respond to questions, beginning with Mr. Wojna.

SALT Prospects

Q: Mr. President, Poland and the entire world has attached great importance to the relations between the United States and the Soviet Union. Could you answer what is your assessment of the chance for a prompt conclusion on SALT talks and in other discussions on strategic matters? And how in this respect do you assess the latest pronouncement by Leonid Brezhnev in an interview for the Pravda daily?

A: In the last few months the United States and the Soviet Union have made great progress dealing with a long list of important issues, the most important of which is to control the deployment of strategic nuclear weapons. We hope to conclude the SALT II talks this year, hopefully in the spring.

We have resolved many of the major issues. A few still remain. We have made good progress in recent months. At the same time we have made progress for the first time in establishing principles on which there can be a total prohibition against all tests of nuclear explosives in the future. We have made progress on prohibiting additional military build-up in the Indian Ocean, recently commenced talks to reduce the sale of conventional weapons to other nations in the world. And I will pursue this same subject with President Giscard next week.

In addition, the Soviets and we are making progress in how we can prevent the use in the future of chemical and biological warfare, and we hope that we can reinstigate progress in the mutual and balanced force reductions which have been stalemated in Vienna for a number of years. So I would say that in summary I am very encouraged at the new progress that I have witnessed personally among our negotiators.

When Foreign Minister Gromyko was in Washington recently, in a few hours we resolved many of the difficult issues. Our negotiators are at work on all of those subjects at this present time. There has been no cessation of the effort. And I believe that in 1978 we will see a resolution of many of these issues.

Mr. Cormier?

Possible Visit to Egypt

Q: Mr. President, are you likely to go to Egypt next Wednesday, and if you do, will it be primarily because President Sadat has urged you to go, or for some other purpose, or why?

A: Well, I have a standing invitation from President Sadat to visit Egypt that he extended to me on his trip to Washington. He has re-emphasized it several times since that date. We have had no discussions with President Sadat on that particular visit to Egypt while I am on this trip. We will try to keep our schedule flexible. If it is mutually convenient and desirable, we would certainly consider it, but we have no plans at this time to stop in Egypt next Wednesday or any other time on this trip.

I might say that our own relations with the Arab nations, including, certainly, Egypt, are very good and harmonious. There has been no change in our own position relating to the Middle Eastern talks. And we communicate almost daily with the Egyptian and Israeli leaders. And, as you know, I will be meeting King Hussein in Teheran on our next stop on this trip.

Q: You said often you don't intend and you don't desire to dictate the terms of a Middle East settlement.

A: Yes, this is true.

West Bank and Gaza

Q: Yet President Sadat seems to think that you have pulled the rug out from under him and that you are in fact dictating terms when you are backing an Israeli military presence on the West Bank and Gaza after there would be a settlement.

A: We don't back any Israeli military settlement in the Gaza Strip or on the West Bank. We favor, as you know, a Palestinian homeland or entity there. Our own preference is that this entity be tied into Jordan and not be a separate and independent nation. That is merely an expression of preference which we have relayed on numerous occasions to the Arab leaders, including President Sadat when he was with me in Washington. I have expressed the same opinion to the Israelis, to King Hussein and to President Sadat and also to the Saudi Arabians. We have no intention of attempting to impose settlement. Any agreement which can be reached between Israel and the Arab neighbors would be acceptable to us. We are in a posture of expressing opinions, trying to promote intimate and direct negotiations and communications, expediting the process when it seems to be slow and adding our good offices, whenever requested. But we have no intention or desire to impose a settlement.

Baptists in Poland

THE PRESIDENT: Let me go back to the Polish side.

Q: I will speak Polish. Let me welcome you not only as the President of the United States but as an eminent American Baptist. I am a Baptist myself. I am preoccupied with editing a Baptist magazine in Poland, and I would like to express my gladness that you have been elected to the post of the President of the United States, as a man, as a believer who is not ashamed of it and of his evangelical convictions. This prompts me to wish you and your family the best of the very best in 1978 and also in your activity in strengthening peace the world over.

Now over to our question. We all know that you are a practicing Christian, as every Baptist should be—as every good Baptist should be. And I would like to ask whether your religious convictions help you in executing the job of President of such a big country. Can you quote an example in how the evangelical principles helped you in solving any complicated problem? And the second question: We the Polish Baptists live in an extra Catholic country and on occasions we are discriminated against. As a believer, as a Baptist, can you influence a change of the situation?

A: Well, as you know, the United States believes in religious freedom. And I am very grateful for the degree of religious freedom that also exists in Poland. Dr. Brzezinski, my national security adviser, and my wife, Rosalynn, had a visit with Cardinal Wyszynski this morning and did this as an expression of our appreciation for the degree of freedom to worship in this country.

This is a matter of conscience, as a Baptist and as an American leader. We believe in separation of church and state, that there should be no unwarranted influence on the church or religion by the state and vice versa. My own religious convictions are deep and personal. I seek divine guidance when I make a difficult decision as President and also am supported, of course, by the common purpose which binds Christians together, and a belief in the human dignity of mankind and also in the search for worldwide peace, recognizing, of course, that those who don't share my faith quite often have the same desires and hopes.

My own constant hope is that all nations would give maximum freedom of religion and freedom of expression to their people, and I will do all I can within the bounds of propriety to bring that hope into realization.

Freedom for Poland

Q: Mr. President, during those Presidential debates, in a celebrated exchange, President Ford claimed that Eastern Europe was not under Soviet domination. You replied, "Tell it to the Poles." Now that you are here, is it your view that this domination will continue almost into perpetuity or do you see a day when Poland may be actually free? And if so, how would that come about?

A: Well, this is obviously a decision for the Polish leaders and the Polish people to make. Our nation is committed to the proposition that all countries would be autonomous, they would all be independent, and they would all be free of unwanted interference and entanglement with other nations. The Polish people have been bound very closely to the Soviet Union since the Second World War, and they belong to a Warsaw Pact military alliance which is, of course, different from the NATO relationship to which we belong. My own assessment within the European theater, Eastern European theater, is that here, compared to some other nations, there is a great religious freedom and otherwise, and I think this is a hope that we all share and cherish. I think this has been the origin of the Polish nation more than a thousand years ago and it is a deep commitment of the vast majority of the Polish people, a desire and commitment not to be dominated.

Q: If you don't mind, they are dominated, Mr. President.

A: I think I have commented all I wish on that subject.

Human Rights in Poland

Q: Mr. President, what is the potential for realization of the Helsinki Final Act as an integral entity, especially in view of the Belgrade meeting? And what is your opinion abour Chancellor Schmidt's proposal to repeat in one or another form the meeting on the top level?

A: I think the Helsinki agreement, which calls for cooperation and security in Europe and which has a so-called third basket component and insistence upon maximum enhancement and preservation of human rights, is an agreement that is important to the Poles and also to our country and other signatories of that treaty.

We believe that the Belgrade conference has been productive. This is a question that must be approached on a multinational basis. The treaty terms provide for open and frank criticism of other signatories when standards are not met. There has been a free exchange of opinion between ourselves and the Soviet Union and, indeed, all the nations involved.

We hope that this session will come to a rapid and successful conclusion and that there will be repeated scheduled meetings based upon the Belgrade conference that would be held in the future so that all nations who participated in the Helsinki agreement and all those who didn't become signatories would have a constant reminder before them of the importance of cooperation, mutual security, the sharing of information, the recombination of families, free emigration and the preservation of basic human rights. I hope this will be a continuing process scheduled repeatedly and that this issue of human rights will never be forgotten.

Q: Mr. President, then how satisfied are you that your concept of the preservation of human rights is currently being honored here in Poland?

A: I think that our concept of human rights is preserved in Poland—as I have said—much better than other familiar [sic]. There is a substantial degree of freedom of the press exhibited by this conference this afternoon, a substantial degree of freedom of religion demonstrated by the fact that approximately 90 per cent of the Polish people profess faith in Christ, and an open relationship between Poland and our country and Poland and Western European countries in trade, technology. So I don't think there is any doubt that the will of the Polish people for complete preservation and enhancement of human rights is the same as our own.

Q: What steps, then, do you believe should be taken here in Poland to come closer to reaching your concept?

A: I think Poland shares with us a commitment which is sometimes embarrassing for us and them to have our own faults publicized evocatively at conferences like the one in Belgrade, where there is a free and open discussion and criticism and a singular pointing out of violations of high standards of human rights preservation. We have been criticized at Belgrade, sometimes legitimately, sometimes, I think, mistakenly. The same applies to nations in Eastern Europe and to the Soviet Union.

I think this is the best thing that we can do at this point, is to continue to insist upon a rigid enforcement and interpretation of the human-rights section of the Helsinki agreement.

Cooperation on Energy

Q: The United States is facing an energy crisis which is also an international problem. How can you see the possibilities of solving that crisis, like a multilateral conference, a European conference or bilateral agreements, and are you of the opinion that the cooperation between the United States and Poland in this respect is possible?

A: One of the worst domestic problems that we have is the overconsumption and waste of energy. I have no doubt that every country I visit on this tour will be pressing us on the question of what will the United States do to save energy and not to import too much of very scarce oil, in particular, which is available on the world markets. We are addressing this as a top priority among domestic issues.

Poland is, as you know, self-sufficient in both hard coal and also brown coal, which is increasing in production in Poland itself. We call it lignite in our country. One of the things we can do is on a worldwide basis to try to hold down unnecessary demand for oil and natural gas, therefore providing stable prices. Another is to consume those energy sources which we have most available, in our country and in yours—coal—shift to permanent sources of energy, primarily those derived from solar power and share research and development information and commitments, a subject which I was discussing early today with First Secretary Gierek.

How to burn lignite coal so that it will have minimum effect on the environment and also have maximum heat derivation is a question of importance to you and to us. We are now shifting to the production and consumption of lignite coal in our own country, for instance, and so are you. So I think sharing on an international basis of data and technological advantages and progress in the energy field and conservation of scarce energy sources for all nations would be the two basic things which we could do jointly.

U.S.-Polish Relations

Q: What is involved in the entity of Polish-American cooperation, so far, and what is your opinion as far as this cooperation between Poland and the United States is concerned and how in the light of today's talks can you see the prospects for the development of such cooperation as well as what the United States wants to do to contribute to this development?

A: We already have a good relationship with Poland in cultural exchange, in technological and scientific cooperation, and a rapidly growing level of trade. About four years ago we had total trade with Poland of only about $500 million; in 1978 the level of trade will probably exceed $1 billion.

I have just informed First Secretary Gierek that in addition to the $300 million in commodity-credit grain sales that has been authorized by our own country that we would increase that by $200 million more worth of food and feed grains. Poland has had a devastating and unprecedented four years of crop failure because of adverse weather conditions—three years of drought, the last year of excessive floods. We, on the other hand, have had very good and bountiful harvests, and we want to share our grain with Poland on legal credit terms which have already been established by our Government.

I think another thing that Poland can help with is to improve even further the better relationships that we are working out with the Soviet Union. Poland is a nation that has good communications and cooperation with the nations in Western Europe, with Germany, Belgium, Holland, France and others, and also is an integral part of the Warsaw Pact nations. I think this ease of communication and this natural and historical friendship is a basis on which Poland can provide additional cooperation and communication between ourselves and the Soviet Union. I don't say this to insinuate that we have a lack of communication now, but Poland's good offices can be of great benefit to us.

Divergence of Viewpoints

Q: In your discussions earlier today with First Secretary Gierek and other Polish leaders, did they in your mind express any points on international questions that diverged in tone or substance from the viewpoints generally expressed by the Soviet Union?

A: We discussed a wide range of subjects. I didn't detect any significant differences of opinion between ourselves and the Polish leaders, and we did not go into detail on matters that now are not resolved between ourselves and the Soviets.

For instance, the details of the SALT negotiations and the comprehensive test ban were not discussed by me and Mr. Gierek. So I would say that we found no disharmonies of any significance between ourselves and the Poles or between the Poles and the Soviet Union.

Mr. Gierek did express a concern that there might be a bilateral agreement between Israel and Egypt in the Middle East to the exclusion of the other Arab countries. This is an opinion also held by the Soviet Union. It is an opinion also held by us and by Israel and by Egypt. I pointed out to Mr. Gierek that had the Egyptians and Israelis wanted to seek a solution only for the Sinai region and the Egyptian-Israeli relationship, they could probably already have consummated such an agreement.

But President Sadat and Prime Minister Begin do not want such an agreement. I pointed this out to Mr. Gierek and he was relieved to hear this.

He also was quite concerned about the lack of progress on the mutual and balanced force reductions which have been stalemated in Vienna for years. He pointed out the primary responsibility lay on the shoulders of the United States and the Soviet Union. This is not exactly the case because we consult very closely with our NATO allies before any common opinion or proposition is put forward. I hope to relieve this stalemate shortly. We are consulting closely with the Germans and others in the Western European theater and also with the Soviets on this matter.

He was very pleased that we want to reduce our international sales of conventional weapons. This is a subject on which we have just begun to talk with the Soviet Union, and perhaps Poland is ahead of the Soviet Union in this particular subject. But I hope they would be amenable to that same suggestion.

So the answer is I don't know of any disagreements between the Poles and the Soviets that came out this morning, nor do I know of any significant disagreements that came out between ourselves and the Poles.

Neutron Bomb

Q: Mr. President, the Soviet leader, Leonid Brezhnev, has put forward a suggestion recently that Eastern and Western countries renounce the neutron bomb together. Would you be ready to accept such a proposal?

A: One of the disturbing failures up until this point in nuclear weaponry has been a complete absence of discussions concerning tactical or theater nuclear weapons. The only discussions that have ever been held between ourselves and the Soviets related only to strategic weapons—those that can be fired from one continent to another or from the sea into a continent. I would hope that as a result of the SALT II talks we might agree with the Soviets to start addressing the question of the so-called tactical nuclear weapons, of which the enhanced radiation or neutron bomb would be one. This weapon is much less destabilizing in its effect, if it should be deployed, than, for instance, some of the advanced new Soviet weapons like the SS 20 missile, which is much more destructive than any weapon held by the NATO allies and has a much greater range. So my hope is that in general we can reduce the threat of nuclear destruction in the European area.

There are now several thousand tactical nuclear weapons already deployed on both sides in the European theater, and the whole matter must be addressed in its entirety rather than one weapon at a time. We would not deploy the neutron bomb or neutron shells unless there was an agreement by our NATO allies. That is where the decision will be made. But there are other new weapons including the SS 20 much more threatening to the balance that presently exists.

Reunification of Families

Q: You said that you have agreed to expand the agricultural credits to Poland.

A: Yes.

Q: In talking with us the other day, your advisers have linked that with a human rights concern, namely, that the reunification of families between the Eastern and Western blocs be improved in Poland. Have the Poles agreed to do that? Have they given you any satisfaction that this, too, would be done?

A: One of the first subjects which I discussed with First Secretary Gierek in our private talks today was the land and the United States. In the last four years there have been about 15,000 Poles who have been permitted to emigrate to our country. We still have about 250 families—we call them nuclear families, that is, a father, mother and children who desire to be unified and permission has not yet been obtained.

First Secretary Gierek said that he would give his own personal attention to alleviating this problem. And he directed his Foreign Minister and I directed our Secretary of State to proceed with this discussion during this afternoon. Their assurance was that our concern would be alleviated.

[THE PRESS]: Thank you, Mr. President.

CARTER-GIEREK REMARKS

FIRST SECRETARY GIEREK: Dear. Mr. President, dear Mrs. Carter, ladies and gentlemen:

I wish to express, Mr. President, our satisfaction on your visit to Poland. I rest assured that together with the highest authorities of the Polish Peoples' Republic, it is indeed shared by the entire people of Poland.

We take great pleasure in seeing Mrs. Carter in our midst. We also welcome prominent members of the Party accompanying you on this visit.

In your visit, Mr. President, we see a reaffirmation of the friendly feelings of the American people of Poland and a reflection of the intentions to further expand cooperation between our two countries. Indeed, these feelings and intentions enjoy our full reciprocity as has the expansion of Polish-American cooperation remains [sic.] in keeping with the traditional friendship between our two peoples.

It is in the interest of our two countries. It helps deepen detente and shape up constructive international relations. Rich and noble are the traditions we jointly refer to. Poles were among the first settlers on the American soil. In the American struggle for independence a splendid chapter has been written by Kosciuszko, Pulaski, and other great Polish patriots, for whom the cause of the freedom of their own land was inseparably hinged with that of all peoples.

It can be assumed with all certainty that from the outset and all through the Bicentennial of the United States, which, along with the American people, we mark here with friendly observances, a significant share of the expansion of the American economy and culture has been contributed by Poles.

We are glad that today the overwhelming majority of the multi-millions of masses of Americans of Polish extraction as good United States citizens keep maintaining their sentimental and cultural ties with the lands of their ancestors, that they wish favorable development of cooperation with the Polish Peoples' Republic. The people of Poland are also cognizant of our common struggle in the great anti-Nazi coalition.

Mr. President, I trust that the paramount cause guiding us mutually is the consolidation of peace. The Polish people in particular only too well know both its price and value, for wasn't it so that the City of Warsaw—which we have risen from the ashes—had been doomed to total extinction, for its heroic resistance, for its contribution for the victory of nations over the fascists, our nation paid the price of more than six million human lives, of the loss of over 40 per cent of national wealth.

It paid the price of most cities turned to ruins and thousands of villages reduced to ashes. The memory of those tragic experiences impressed forever in the Polish minds and hearts imposes the loftiest of obligations upon us to do all in our power to insure security and peaceful development.

It is with lasting peace, the joy of which we want to share with all other countries of Europe and the world, that we are linking our aspirations, our plans and expectations, for today and for tomorrow. Hence, it is only natural and understandable, Mr. President, that we view with due attention and support warmly actions which serve that great and supreme cause to all nations.

The key factor of the process of detente we perceive in relations between your country, Mr. President, and the Soviet Union. The dialogue between the two big powers determines the climate, the overall climate of international relations in saving mankind from a nuclear holocaust.

This is why there is a special responsibility for world peace. Hence, our profound satisfaction over the incipient progress in the talks on offensive strategic arms limitations. Hence our hopes, in fact shared by the broadest public opinoion, for a prompt new agreement, as well as for positive results of discussions between the two powers on other important questions.

With its Socialist allies and friends, Poland spares no effort to consolidate the process of detente and make it irreversible, for detente is the only alternative. It indeed represents a great chance of our times. Its proper utilization depends in particular on containing the arms race which weighs heavily upon international relations, wastes economic resources, imposes great threats.

I am sure you are aware, Mr. President, that Poland has always attached special significance to preventing proliferation of nuclear armaments. We have been advancing our own initiatives to this effect, which have enjoyed general recognition.

Today, when the danger of proliferation of those armaments and introduction of new kinds of weapons of mass destruction is greater than ever before, we are bound to appeal for moderation for the containment of the dangerous phenomenon, for the strengthening and extension of the system of treaties to protect against it.

Remembering, as we do, what you, yourself, Mr. President, have been saying in that matter, we trust it will be given the maximum attention. By the same token, we lend our full support to the initiative made by Leonid Brezhnev to conclude an agreement to mutually reduce, renounce the introduction of nuclear weapons.

Poland proceeds from the principle of full and integrated implementation of the decisions and recommendations of the final act of the Helsinki Conference which we treat as the magna carta of peace in Europe. Guided by its principles, we are favorably shaping up our bilateral relations with all state signatories of the final act to take efforts to achieve positive results of the Belgrade meeting.

Progress in the Vienna talks on the reduction of armed forces and armaments in Central Europe would, too, no doubt, serve to strengthen the general sense of security.

There is much to be said, Mr. President, of the climate of international relations. There is need for mutual understanding and trust; only in such circumstances there can be progress in constructive and friendly international cooperation.

Dear Mr. President, we are glad that you share our desire of continuation of the positive processes in Polish-American relations. Our constructive discussions today have confirmed this.

In recent years, important joint statements, agreements and contracts were signed between our two countries. They do provide a good basis for further mutually beneficial cooperation. Our economic relations have dynamically expanded. As you know, we attach special significance to them and wish to continue expanding them. Our scientific and technical exchanges have grown; constantly enriching is our cultural cooperation, as is the growing tourist traffic, more frequent our conduct serving to get our respective nations to know better and bring them closer together.

It gives me satisfaction to expect that your visit will effect a further growth of Polish-American cooperation.

Mr. President, we are sorry you are visiting us for such a short time. We would certainly wish that you could get to know our country better, a country of great progress and, at the same time, still overcoming century-old underdevelopment.

Following the gravest tragedies in its own history, our nation has made a choice which offers it lasting safeguards of independence, sovereignty and security which provides for the best premises for development. These premises compromise its own ever more growing potential present day Poland, its alliance with the Soviet Union and other friends.

Today Poland belongs to the group of countries of the world which are having the greatest development scale as far as production in industry is concerned. And for the last seven years we are maintaining a very high indices of further growth.

There has been a tremendous revival, biological revival, of our people. In the current decade, the age of maturity is being reached by seven million young Polish girls and boys. We insure to all of them education and work. We have created just, democratic socio-political conditions. We are implementing the fullest possible code of socio-economic and political rights.

In maintaining and cultivating all what has been most precious in our national tradition, we are enriching contemporary life of Poles by new profoundly humanistic contents.

Our greatest achievement is the moral and political unity of our people in which we perceive the paramount safeguard for successful implementation of all noble aspirations of Poles and also a dignified place of our country among other states of Europe and the world.

Mr. President, tomorrow you will be leaving Poland, departing for other countries. May I be permitted to express my conviction that the impressions you will be taking with you from the first leg of your trip, and first of all the friendly feelings of the Polish people to the American people and our strivings to peace and cooperation, will stay in your good memory for long.

I wish to propose a toast and ask all those present to join me to drink to you, Mr. President, and Mrs. Carter, to the successes of the great American people, to the further expansion of friendly Polish-American relations. (Applause)

THE PRESIDENT. First Secretary and Mrs. Gierek, distinguished leaders in politics, the military, music, drama, art, poetry, education, science, engineering.

We are very proud to be here in Poland and to have had a chance to meet with and to learn from First Secretary Gierek. We have already become close personal friends. He has taught me things that I can use in my own nation. He has this afternoon discussed with me—and tonight—how he proposes to have a balance of trade in Poland. He sells hare or rabbits to adjacent countries for a lease in hunting preserves, and the rabbits are trained to return to Poland. (Laughter)

When I was running for President of the United States for two years, I met hundreds of thousands of Americans of Polish ancestry. I saw very quickly that they had a deep love for the United States and simultaneously for Poland. They recognize the historical ties which have bound our nations together since the very origins of our country. They have a natural hospitality inherited from their ancestors, and this made us look forward to this trip with great anticipation.

Our country has observed closely the distinguished Poles who have affected world history and our own nation—ancient and modern scientists like Copernicus and Madam Curie, favorite authors like Joseph Conrad; musicians like Artur Rubenstein, who still loves Poland very deeply, and one of the greatest engineers of all time, Admiral Hyman Rickover, who developed the peaceful use of atomic power.

We have much to learn from Poland—how to use coal, and particularly brown coal, efficiently in this day of short energy supplies. We share cultural and scientific and engineering knowledge.

A hundred and twenty thousand Americans each year come back to visit their homeland here, and today I have seen...at your memorials a demonstration of affection for those who suffered so bravely in recent wars.

Georgia's capital city of Atlanta was completely destroyed in war, as was the city of Warsaw. But although we have suffered greatly, no other nation has borne such suffering as Poland. In the World War, 6 million Poles died, 300,000 in Warsaw alone. Poles were the first people to fight the horrors of Nazism and earn the admiration and appreciation of the world. You were the ones who demonstrated a deep commitment to human rights, a belief in the value of human freedom and human life.

You have seen the horrible consequences of racial hatred when the Polish Jews were exterminated by Nazi terrorists. From these terrible experiences, valuable lessons have been learned. There is a tendency for those in the West to distrust those nations in the East. Sometimes perhaps you distrust our motives and our judgment. Sometimes we feel that you might be a danger to us as NATO allies face the Warsaw Pact nations. But I know in more vivid terms than before that nations like your own and like the Soviet Union, which have suffered so deeply, will never commence a war unless there is the most profound provocation or misunderstanding brought about by lack of communication.

We also want peace and would never start a war except by mistake, when we didn't understand the motives and attitudes and desire for peace on the part of our potential adversaries.

I am pleased to know that there is increasing communication, consultation, and cooperation between the Socialist nations and the nations of the West. Although we belong to different military alliances, our hunger for peace is the same. We are working closely with the Soviet leaders to eliminate the constant and horrible threat of atomic destruction. This is an extremely complicated and technical discussion, but good motivations and common purposes can resolve those differences.

I have every expectation that this next year will bring success. We will do our utmost to realize this dream. We want to prevent the development of new and more powerful weapons and also to prevent any test of atomic explosions. We want to prevent nations which do not presently have atomic explosions [sic.] from desiring those capabilities. We want to reduce the sale of conventional weapons to nations around the world. And we want to seek in every possible way closer communications, better trade, closer friendship between our countries.

Poland and your leaders have an ability and experience to look knowledgeably both to the East and to the West, and you can contribute greatly to the mutual efforts of ourselves and the Soviet Union to reach those agreements which we both desire.

The ancient alliance between the United States and Poland in peace and war has given our people good lives. We have helped to establish and to maintain the independence of one another. This sharing of culture, blood kinship and close cooperation in the past can give us a basis for an even better future together.

I hope that at the earliest convenient time we might be permitted to repay the hospitality to your leaders, First Secretary Gierek and others, that you have extended to us on this visit. It is very valuable to have Polish and American friendship combined together to give us what all men and women want—peace throughout the world.

On behalf of the people of the United States, I would like to propose a toast to the indomitable spirit and to the freedom of the Polish people, to your enlightened leaders—particularly First Secretary Gierek and his wife—and to peace throughout the world. (Applause)

EXCHANGE OF TOASTS: IRAN

THE SHAHANSHAH: Mr. President, Mrs. Carter, Excellencies, ladies and gentlemen. It gives the Shahbanou and myself great pleasure to welcome you to our country. This reception is particularly auspicious since it takes place on the eve of 1978, and your presence here represents a New Year's gift for your Iranian friends.

In our country, according to ancient tradition, the visit of the first guest in the new year is an omen for that year. And although the annual new year is celebrated with the advent of spring, nevertheless, since the distinguished guest tonight is such a person of good will and achievements, naturally we consider it as a most excellent omen.

Mr. President, you now have come to a country which has always had unshakable links with your country and your great nation. We are united together by a special relationship made all the closer by a wide community of mutual interests, which we share in our firm determination to contribute to the maintenance of world peace and security in assuring human progress and betterment.

History has been witnessed through the growth and development of an outstanding relationship between two nations motivated by common trust, good will, and respect which has repeatedly withstood the test of time.

Humanitarianism, liberty, good will, constructiveness and creativeness, which are the distinctive qualities of the great American nation, have always been highly regarded by us. Fortunately, our American friends have also perceived this friendship and regarded our people from the very beginning.

The Reverend Mr. Smith, the first American that set foot on the land of Iran in the year 1832 wrote in his assignment report that living among good people like Iranians and serving them was more pleasant for him than anything else, and that he considered the best days of his life those spent in this country.

It gives me pleasure to state that the fruitful cooperation, the social and cultural fields have commenced even prior to the establishment of diplomatic relations.

The first modern school was established in Iran in the year 1836 by American missionaries. The American College in Tehran, which was established 100 years ago, was an outstanding center for education and training of Iranian youth during the whole course of its activities. Our people carry such good memories of its beloved principal, Dr. Samuel Jordan, that one of the highways of Tehran has been named after him.

Now that we are reminiscing on our meritorious American friends, it is perhaps suitable to cherish the memory of Howard Baskerville, a young American who upon completion of his studies at Princeton was for a time a teacher in the Memorial School of Tabriz, and during the constitutional revolution of Iran heroically and bravely lost his life in the fight for freedom.

This feeling towards Iran has always been evidenced in the literary works of your nation. For instance, the poetry of Ralph Waldo Emerson, in glorifying Iran, is one of the most beautiful examples of its kind in the world of literature. The basic and comprehensive work of Arthur P. Pope regarding the art of Iran is the best research work that has ever been prepared. Likewise, the extensive studies of William Jackson regarding the culture and civilization of Iran are among the most valuable research in the history of Iranology.

Numerous universities in the United States have expanded activities in the field of Iranian studies and its language. Also valuable treasures of the culture and art of Iran are preserved in various libraries and museums of your country. Moreover, American archeologists have attained an eminent role in archeological discoveries in art.

In the political field, our nation carries unforgettable memories of the role of America in our crisis and times of stress, from the beginning of the present century.

For instance, we will never forget that in the great political and economic adversity of our country, in the second decade of this century, William Schuster, upon invitation of the Government of Iran, sincerely endeavored to bring in order the finances of Iran. Moreover, following the 1919 agreement, Iran was in danger of losing independence. America raised its voice to the world in support of the sovereignty of Iran, as also in the years after the Second World War America provided us with vital economic and political assistance.

During World War II, I personally had the pleasure of meeting Franklin Roosevelt in our capital. Since then I had the opportunity of welcoming to Iran several Presidents of the United States. I personally have also traveled repeatedly to your great country, and I am glad to say that all these visits have been accompanied with the spirit of friendship and cooperation, which is a distinct quality of our relationship.

An example of this cooperation is the long-term economic exchange agreement between Iran and the United States which was recently signed, and in its scope is the largest agreement ever signed between us and any other country.

Almost 100 years ago the first American Ambassador, Samuel G. W. Benjamin, who had been assigned by President Chester Alan Arthur, came to Iran. In his book, *Persia and the Persians,* he wrote, "Iran today is a weak and unknown country, but certainly this country will step into (inaudible) progress and in the not too distant future will again play an important role in the world."

Now with this prediction coming true, our country has started its role within its potentialities and possibilities. Perhaps it need not be mentioned, but this is a positive and constructive role and in conformity with the principle that your great country has always supported independence, of which you, Mr. President, are the most notable advocate.

From the early days of your election campaign you indicated how much you will attach to high ideals of right and justice, moral belief in human value. These are all qualities that have elevated the American society in such a short period of time to its present high prestige in the world; and a nation like ours with its ancient culture can very well feel to what extent such concepts in moral principles are vital, especially in the world of today which is suffering from some sort of a civilization crisis.

I entertain excellent memories of the fruitful discussions which I had with you in Washington a few weeks ago. The cordial hospitality extended by Mrs. Carter and yourself and the warmth of your attitude and the understanding which you showed in our discussions have deeply touched me. I am glad our discussions were so meaningful, particularly in the case of energy which is one of the most important and vital problems of our era.

We who are among the greatest producers share the same view that the present unrestricted use of oil—which is an expendable and finite resource—is not logical and that this valuable commodity, instead of the present normal daily use, should be utilized mainly in the petrochemical industry. In the meantime, efforts should be exerted to find a substitute in new resources of energy.

Fortunately we enjoy close cooperation with your country in the field of energy which will no doubt be consolidated in the future. We also share the same opinion regarding the establishment of an honorable and durable peace and we sincerely hope that 1978, which begins tomorrow, will be a year of such a peace of which you are the harbinger.

I wish every success to you, Mr. President and Mrs. Carter, who has proved to be such a successful ambassador of good will, motivated, as she is, by high humanitarian ideals in your present role, and hope that this will prove to be a fruitful trip in the interest of the whole world and that of peace, security and welfare for human society.

With this hope I propose a toast, Mr. President, for you and Mrs. Carter's health and happiness; for the further progress and prosperity of the great and noble American people; for the ever-increasing friendship and cooperation between our two countries and for international peace and understanding. (Applause)

THE PRESIDENT: Your Majesties and distinguished leaders of Iran from all walks of life: I would like to say just a few words tonight in appreciation for your hospitality and the delightful evening that we have already experienced with you. Some have asked why we came to Iran so close behind the delightful visit that we received from the Shah and Empress Farah just a month or so ago. After they left our country, I asked my wife, "With whom would like to spend New Year's Eve?" And she said, "Above all others, I think with the Shah and Empress Farah." So we arranged the trip accordingly. (Applause)

These visits and the close cooperation that we share, the intense personal and group negotiations and consultations are very beneficial to both our countries. They are particularly beneficial to me as a new leader of the United States. I might pause parenthetically and say I apologize for taking ten years off your service this afternoon when I said twenty-seven years. It should have been thirty-seven years, and Empress Farah, thank you very much for correcting me on that. The Shah said he felt ten years younger when I did that. (Laughter)

But we do have a close friendship that is very meaningful to all the people in our country. I think it is a good harbinger of things to come, that we could close out this year and begin a new year with those in whom we have such great confidence and with whom we share such great responsibilities for the present and for the future.

As we drove in from the airport this afternoon to the beautiful white palace where we will spend the night, and saw the monument in the distance, I asked the Shah what was the purpose of the beautiful monument. And he told me that it was built several years ago, erected to commemorate the 2500th Anniversary of this great nation. This was a sobering thought to me. We have been very proud in our nation to celebrate our 200th birthday, a couple of years ago. But it illustrates the deep and penetrating consciousness that comes from an ancient heritage and a culture that preceded any that we have ever known in our own lives.

Recently, Empress Farah gave us a beautiful book called *The Bridge of Turquoise*. We get many gifts of that kind from visitors and for a few days I have to admit that we didn't pay enough attention to it. And one night I started to thumb through the pages and I called my wife Rosalynn and I called my daughter Amy, who climbed into my lap and we spent several hours studying very carefully the beautiful history that this book portrays of Persia, of Iran, of its people, of its land, of its heritage and its history, and also of its future. It caused me to be reminded again of the value of ancient friendships and the importance of close ties that bind us as we face difficult problems.

Iran, because of the great leadership of the Shah, is an island of stability in one of the more troubled areas of the world.

This is a great tribute to you, Your Majesty, and to your leadership and to the respect and the admiration and love which your people give to you.

The transformation that has taken place in this nation is indeed remarkable under your leadership. As we sat together this afternoon discussing privately for a few moments what might be done to bring peace to the Middle East, I was profoundly impressed again not only with your wisdom and your judgment and your sensitivity and insight, but also with the close compatibility that we found in addressing this difficult question.

As we visit with leaders who have in their hands the responsibility for making decisions that can bring peace to the Middle East, and ensure a peaceful existence for all of us who live in the world, no matter where our nations might be, it is important that we continue to benefit from your sound judgment and from your good advice.

We also had a chance to discuss another potential troubled area, the Horn of Africa. And here again we live at a great distance from it. But this region which already sees the initiation of hostility and combat needs to be brought under the good influence of you and others who live in this region. And we will be glad to cooperate in any way that we can. We want peace to return. We want Somalia and Ethiopia to be friends again, border disputes to be eased and those of us who do have any influence at all to use their influence for these purposes.

We have also known about the great benefits that we derive in our own nation from the close business relationships that we have with Iran.

As I drove through the beautiful streets of Tehran today with the Shah, we saw literally thousands of Iranian citizens standing beside the street with a friendly attitude, expressing their welcome to me. And I also saw hundreds, perhaps even thousands of American citizens who stood there welcoming their President in a nation which has taken them to heart and made them feel at home. There are about 30,000 Americans here who work in close harmony with the people of Iran, to carve out a better future for you, which also helps to insure, Your Majesty, a better future for ourselves.

We share industrial growth, we share scientific knowledge, and this gives us the stability...which is...valuable to both our countries....

We are also blessed with the largest number of foreign students in our country from your own nation. And I think this ensures, too, that we share the knowledge that is engendered by our great universities, but also that when these young leaders come back to your country for many years in the future, for many generations in the future, our friendship is ensured.

We are very grateful for this and value it very much.

I have tried to become better acquainted with the culture of Iran in the preparation for my visit here. I was particularly impressed with a brief passage from one of Iran's great poets, Saadi. And I would like to read a few words from him. Empress Farah tells me that he lived about 600 years ago.

"Human beings are like parts of a body, created from the same essence. When one part is hurt and in pain, others cannot remain in peace and quiet. If the misery of others leaves you indifferent and with no feeling of sorrow, then you cannot be called a human being."

I asked Empress Farah why this poet was so famous here in Iran, because he had impressed me so greatly, too. And she said because he had the greatest facility for professing profound thoughts in the simplest possible words that the average citizen could understand.

Well, that brief passage shows that there is within the consciousness of human beings a close tie with one's neighbors, one's family, and one's friends, but it also ties us with human beings throughout the world. When one is hurt or suffers, all of us, if we are human beings, are hurt and we suffer.

The cause of human rights is one that also is shared deeply by our people and by the leaders of our two nations.

Our talks have been priceless, our friendship is irreplaceable, and my own gratitude is to the Shah, who in his wisdom and with his experience has been so helpful to me, a new leader.

We have no other nation on earth who is closer to us in planning for our mutual military security. We have no other nation with whom we have closer consultation on regional problems that concern us both. And there is no leader with whom I have a deeper sense of personal gratitude and personal friendship.

On behalf of the people of the United States, I would like to offer a toast at this time to the great leaders of Iran, the Shah and the Shahbanou and to the people of Iran and to the world peace that we hope together we can help to bring. (Applause)

Happy New Year to you.

CUMULATIVE INDEX, 1973-77

CUMULATIVE INDEX, 1973-1977

A

ABM. *See* Anti-Ballistic Missile.
ABORTION
    Ethics of Fetal Research, 544, 549-556 *(1975)*
    National Women's Conference, 865-866 *(1977)*
    Supreme Court on, 101-114 *(1973);* 483 *(1976);* 407-430 *(1977)*
ABRAMS, CREIGHTON W.
    Secret Bombing of Cambodia, 730 *(1973)*
ADULT PERFORMANCE LEVEL STUDY (APL), 691-705 *(1975)*
AEROSOL SPRAYS AND THE ATMOSPHERE, 437-453 *(1975)*
AFL-CIO
    California Farm-Labor Law, 377 *(1975)*
    Committee on Political Education Enemies List, 678 *(1973)*
    Foreign Trade, 380 *(1973)*
    Solzhenitsyn Speech, 481-491 *(1975)*
    Youth Vote Turnout, 36 *(1973)*
AFRICA. *See also* names of countries.
    Amin's Message to Carter, 143 *(1977)*
    Arafat U.N. Speech, 919-937 *(1974)*
    Democratic Party Platform, 593 *(1976)*
    Kissinger at UNCTAD, 299 *(1976)*
    Kissinger on Africa, 287 *(1976)*
    Republican Party Platform, 658 *(1976)*
    Rhodesian Independence Plan, 721 *(1976)*
    Rhodesian Settlement Plan, 583-590 *(1977)*
    Third World Solidarity, 256 *(1974)*
    U.N. Anti-Zionism Resolution, 826-827 *(1975)*
AGED
    Albert News Conference, 40 *(1975)*
    Democratic Party Platform, 565 *(1976)*
    Nixon Re-election Campaign, 603 *(1974)*
    Republican Party Platform, 640 *(1976)*
    State of the Union, 311 *(1973);* 20-21 *(1976)*
AGNEW, SPIRO T.
    FBI Abuses Report, 880-882 *(1975)*
    Nixon on Charges Against, 750 *(1973);* 353 *(1977)*
    Resignation, 827-838, 898, 899 *(1973)*
AGRICULTURE. *See also* Food Supply.
    Boumediene on Third World, 261-262 *(1974)*
    California Farm-Labor Law, 377-399 *(1975)*
    Democratic Party Platform, 577 *(1976)*
    Economic Controls, Phase IV, 708 *(1973)*
    Economic Cooperation and the U.N., 609 *(1975)*
    Ford Foreign Economic Policy, 195-197 *(1975)*
    Ford News Conference, 762 *(1976)*
    Milk Price Supports, 963 *(1973)*
    Phase III, 60-day Price Freeze, 580 *(1973)*
    Republican Party Platform, 623 *(1976)*
    Soviet-U.S. Pact, 608 *(1973)*
    State of the Union, 222 *(1973);* 44 *(1974);* 20 *(1976)*
AID TO FAMILIES WITH DEPENDENT CHILDREN, 304, 310, 311 *(1973)*
AIR FORCE
    B-1 Bomber Decision, 529-533 *(1977)*
    Congressional Budget Report, 184 *(1976)*
    Cost Overruns of Contracts, 194, 202 *(1973)*
    Secret Bombing of Cambodia, 729-735 *(1973)*
AIR POLLUTION. *See* Environment.
AIRCRAFT. *See also* Transportation.
    Anti-hijacking Pact, 265-268 *(1973)*
    SST, Environmental Risks of, 235-244 *(1973)*
ALASKA
    Pipeline, 472, 805, 914, 919 *(1973);*120 *(1974)*
    Project Independence, 912, 914, 917 *(1974)*
ALBERT, CARL (D Okla.)
    Agnew Resignation, 832-834 *(1973)*
    Congress vs. the President, 4, 171 *(1973)*
    Emergency Economic Plans, 32-41 *(1975)*
    Ford as Vice President, 970 *(1973)*
    Ford Economic Summit, 863-866 *(1974)*
    White House Tapes, 697 *(1973);* 674 *(1974)*

C

D

G

I

J

P

954

U

UGANDA. *See also* Africa.
  Amin's Message to Carter, 143-148 *(1977)*
  Entebbe Rescue, 517 *(1976)*
ULASEWICZ, ANTHONY T.
  Senate Watergate Report, 601, 611 *(1974)*
UNEMPLOYMENT. *See* Employment and Unemployment.
UNION OF SOVIET SOCIALIST RE-PUBLICS. *See* Soviet Union.
UNITED FARM WORKERS (UFW)
  California Farm-Labor Law, 377-399 *(1975)*
UNITED KINGDOM. *See* Great Britain.
UNITED NATIONS
  Action on Third World Poverty, 255 *(1974)*; 587 *(1975)*; 299 *(1976)*
  Anti-Zionism Resolution, 825-827 *(1975)*
  Arafat Speech, 919-937 *(1974)*
  Arms Embargo Against South Africa, 823-825 *(1977)*
  Boumediene Speech on Raw Materials, 255-264 *(1974)*
  Carter on Arms Control, 737-744 *(1977)*
  Carter's Human Rights Speech, 189-197 *(1977)*
  Democratic Party Platform, 589 *(1976)*
  Egyptian-Israeli Disengagement, 29-32 *(1974)*
  Egyptian-Israeli Truce Terms, 931-934 *(1973)*
  General Assembly Opening, 833-851 *(1974)*
  Global Economic Cooperation, 587-611 *(1975)*; 425 *(1976)*
  Japan, Permanent Seat, 718, 721, 722 *(1973)*
  Kissinger, Gromyko Speeches, 809-824 *(1973)*
  Kissinger at UNCTAD, 299 *(1976)*
  Kissinger on Middle East, 882-890, 892, 894 *(1973)*
  Moynihan on Democracy, 645-651 *(1975)*
  Nixon-Brezhnev Summit, 591, 593, 603, 605 *(1973)*; 565 *(1974)*
  Nixon View of Mideast Crisis, 898, 900 *(1973)*
  Republican Party Platform, 661 *(1976)*
  Restructuring Proposals, 325-351 *(1975)*
  Scranton on Israeli-occupied Terri-tories, 191 *(1976)*
  South West Africa Statement, 611 *(1976)*
  Soviet-West German Treaties, 558 *(1973)*
  Syrian-Israeli Disengagement, 435-439 *(1974)*
  U.N. Conference on Trade and Develop-ment, 299 *(1976)*

  Vietnam Act, 333 *(1973)*
  Waldheim Message, 753-765 *(1973)*
  War Powers, 929 *(1973)*
  World Conference on Status of Women, 507-522 *(1975)*
  World Food Conference, 939-953 *(1974)*
  World Population Agreement, 777-797 *(1974)*
U.S. COMMISSION ON CIVIL RIGHTS
  Report, 227-234 *(1973)*
U.S. CONFERENCE OF MAYORS. *See* National League of Cities.
U.S. FOREST SERVICE, 21-26 *(1973)*
U.S. PUBLIC HEALTH SERVICE. *See* Public Health Service.
UNITED STEELWORKERS OF AMERI-CA
  Labor Management Pact, 437-444 *(1973)*
URBAN AFFAIRS. *See* Cities.

V

VAN. For Vietnamese names with Van, see the first element; e.g., Pham Van Dong under Pham.
VANCE, CYRUS R.
  Carter on Cabinet Appointments, 877, 887 *(1976)*
  Carter's World Trip, 897 *(1977)*
  Panama Canal Treaties, 592 *(1977)*
  SALT Negotiations, 245-250 *(1977)*
VENEZUELA
  1974 Trade Act Restrictions, 224-233 *(1975)*
VESCO, ROBERT L.
  Nixon Campaign Contribution, 564, 665 *(1973)*; 143 *(1975)*
VETERANS' BENEFITS
  Democratic Party Platform, 566 *(1976)*
  Ford News Conference, 772 *(1974)*
  Nixon News Conference, 151 *(1974)*
  Republican Party Platform, 641 *(1976)*
VETERANS OF FOREIGN WARS
  Carter's Draft Evader Pardon, 96 *(1977)*
  Ford Vietnam Amnesty Plan, 819, 821 *(1974)*
  Nixon on Secret Bombing of Cambodia, 731-735 *(1973)*
VETOES
  War Powers Resolution Override, 923-930 *(1973)*
VICE PRESIDENCY
  Agnew Resignation, 828, 833 *(1973)*
  Dole Nomination Speech, 665 *(1976)*
  Ford on Rockefeller Duties, 770 *(1974)*
  Ford Swearing-in Ceremony, 969-973 *(1973)*
  Mondale Acceptance Speech, 595 *(1976)*
  Rockefeller Nomination, 707 *(1974)*
  Rockefeller Swearing-in, 987-990 *(1974)*

W

XYZ